D0233165

3854

Social Structure
and
Social Process

SOCIAL STRUCTURE

AND

SOCIAL PROCESS

an introductory reader

edited by **PETER ORLEANS**

University of California, Los Angeles

in collaboration with Sonya Orleans

Allyn and Bacon, Inc.

Boston, Mass.

Library of Congress Catalog Card Number: 70-76419

Printed in the United States of America

PREFACE

Today there is little to justify the addition of yet another introductory reader into the field of sociology save perhaps the presentation of a new organization of material ordinarily covered in introductory courses. Therefore, in developing this reader we chose to deal with material that should be emphasized in the introductory course, but usually is not. We decided to stress (1) the role of techniques and strategies in sociological analysis, (2) a distinctive analytical framework through which the diverse subject matter of an introductory survey course could be integrated, and (3) the significance of values in the sociological endeavor.

TECHNIQUES AND STRATEGIES

Consistent with the prevailing philosophy of liberal arts education many introductory sociology courses attempt to provide the undergraduate student with an inventory of the currently established substantive contributions of the discipline. Often, as a result, there is a general lack of concern with the techniques and strategies of sociological analysis. This is reflected in the failure of most collections of introductory readings to include any substantial consideration of the methodology of sociology.

Methodology is often taken for granted in the introductory course, either because it is presumed to be too difficult for the neophyte, or because it is deemed not relevant to an adequate understanding of the material presented. Thus, many collections of introductory readings are restricted to extended essays on a given sociological topic. And, there is a paucity of specific research reports. Methodology is ignored except when it becomes necessary to demonstrate to the student that sociology is more than common-sense—that it is a *science* because it poses distinctive questions and possesses definite procedures for the collection, evaluation, and analysis of data.

One may reasonably ask whether the undergraduate student, exposed, perhaps for the first time, to sociological material can judge it without some understanding of the techniques and strategies of sociological analysis. For this reason we have included a short section (Part II, Chapter 2) dealing with methods. The material was selected to provide the student with a minimal understanding of the wide array of data amenable to sociological analysis, some of the problems involved in different types of sociological research, and some of the techniques and strategies employed in the collection, evaluation, and analysis of data generated by sociologists.

v

ANALYTICAL FRAMEWORK

The material reprinted in Part III has been organized to accentuate four aspects of the social order: dimensions of the social order (Chapter 3), maintenance of the social order (Chapter 4), tensions in the social order (Chapter 5), and changes in the social order (Chapter 6). These concerns form the basic subject matter of sociology. In one way or another this is what the sociologist studies.

It is true that our curriculum still reflects the traditional institutional concerns of the discipline. We teach courses in distinctive substantive areas —the sociology of the family, deviance, stratification, political sociology, ethnic and status groups, and the like. Such a curriculum, however, has come increasingly to reflect the specialized subject matter interests of scholars more than theoretically distinct fields of study.

What relates the various courses in our curriculum, what is common to the study of deviance and to the study of the family, for example, is the fact that at some point the sociologist in each field finds himself dealing with one or more of the four aspects of the social order enumerated previously. What separates us as individual scholars from our colleagues is the specialized area in which we choose to deal with these concerns, not the questions we pose in our research or in the classroom. Whether we are studying the family as an institution or deviance as a form of behavior we are interested ultimately in the relation each bears to one or more of these four aspects of the social order.

Thus, it is in the conviction that sociology as a field of study possesses a logical coherence, if not yet a carefully explicated and unified theory, that we have arranged the readings in Part III into the four specified sections. If sociology is to advance as a field of study we must increasingly make our students aware of the (emergent) continuity of our discipline, even as we individually pursue our preferred fields of study. And we know of no better place to start to do this than in the introductory course, the course in which we attempt to expose the fledgling sociologist to the logic of our form of inquiry.

SIGNIFICANCE OF VALUES

Across the campuses of the country a new generation of students is seeking (often in established, occasionally in unorthodox, ways) to broaden the relevance of the academic experience. These students are disaffected with traditional teaching techniques and appalled by the ivory tower quality of college and university curricula. They are matched by a new generation of sociologists, who after the first blush of innocence which found expression in the social problems approach of the 1930's, followed by a strong positivistic reaction, are increasingly addressing questions relevant to policy in their research and writing.

Sociology today, perhaps more than any of the other social sciences, finds itself under tremendous and increasing pressure to deal with policy matters. The increased availability of research monies alone is significant in this regard. The demands may be premature, and sociology, in the end, may be diverted from the task of developing a coherent analytical science to the resolution of pragmatic problems. Or, with its added resources of expanded personnel and improved technologies for the collection and processing of data, sociology may begin to resolve some of the knotty problems which inevitably confront a discipline whose central focus and concern is the human condition.

In either case it seems that sterile protestations to the effect that if sociology is to be scientific it must be objective, and avoidance of the ethical problems involved in sociological analysis, must eventually give way to a direct confrontation of the significance of values in sociological analysis. There is no better place to begin than with the skeptical undergraduate in the introductory course. It is for this reason that we have included a section (Part IV) in this collection of readings which can serve as a basis for examining the role of values in the sociological enterprise.

Peter Orleans
Sonya Orleans

Contents

Dimensions of the Social Order: Integration

Dimensions of the Social Order: Context

Chapter Four: Maintenance of the Social Order

Maintenance of the Social Order: Socialization

Changes in the Social Order: Organizational Transformation

COMMENTARY

PART IV: SIGNIFICANCE OF VALUES IN SOCIOLOGICAL ANALYSIS

COMMENTARY

Social Structure
and
Social Process

PART I

Preliminaries

COMMENTARY

Robert Nisbet's essay on "Sociology as an Art Form" seems an apt introduction to this collection of readings because it is largely in the spirit of his thesis that the selections have been made. Much time is wasted in the introductory course debating about the scientific status of the discipline of sociology. It is our view that the question, if it is important at all, is best resolved through demonstration rather than disputation. In any event, it is our hope that the reader will beware what Nisbet has referred to as *the idols of the profession*. He should continually question the conventional sociological view of the world. He should guard against the obscurantism fostered by the specialization of knowledge. He should avoid the natural tendency to reify sociological concepts. And he should adopt the perspective of the iconoclast when exposed to routinized systems of sociological thought.

Sociology when it is at its best approximates more an art form than a technology. Nisbet, in our view, is correct in stressing the idea that, at root, sociology is a humanistic endeavor concerned with elements of the human condition, approached as much through intuition as through rational deduction, for the purpose of interpretation rather than problem solving. Our progress as a discipline will depend largely on our ability to recognize that "the creative [scholar] lives in 'the wildness of logic' where reason is the handmaiden and not the master."

Although Leo Schnore's concern in "The Myth of Human Ecology" is to discuss ecology's place within sociology, his commentary provides a description of the four theoretical orientations which inform most sociological research and writing. Accordingly, his concise dissertation provides the reader with a basis for assessing the orientation which underlies any given piece of sociological work.

If sociology is as sociologists do, then Schnore has defined sociology for us in its broadest sense. However, if sociology is limited to but one of the perspectives described by Schnore, then his essay provides us with a basis for contrasting and evaluating the conceptual status of any attempt at sociological

3

analysis. In either case, an examination of "The Myth of Human Ecology" should provide the reader with a basis for understanding the presuppositions which inform each of the articles included in this volume.

1   ROBERT A. NISBET

Sociology as an Art Form

I admit readily that both by temperament and academic background I have always been more interested in the non-uses of our discipline than the uses. I admit further to believing that theories should be tested as much by their reach as their grasp, their importance as their validity, and their elegance as their congruence with such facts as may be at hand. It is my major contention that the science of sociology makes its most significant intellectual advances under the spur of stimuli and through processes that it largely shares with art; that whatever the differences between science and art, it is what they have in common that matters most in discovery and creativeness.

Nothing I say is intended to imply that sociology is not a science. I am quite willing, for present purposes, to put sociology on the same line with physics and biology, applying to each of these the essence of what I say about sociology. Each is indeed a science, but each is also a form of art, and if we forget this we run the risk of losing the science, finding ourselves with a sandheap empiricism or methodological narcissism, each as far from science as art is from billboard advertisements.

My interest in sociology as an art form was stimulated recently by some reflections on ideas that are by common assent among the most distinctive that sociology has contributed to modern thought. Let me mention these: *mass society, alienation, anomie, rationalization, community, disorganization.* I will have more to say about these ideas and their contexts a little later. Here it suffices to note that all of them have had lasting effect upon both the theoretical and empirical character of sociology. And all have exerted notable influence on other fields of thought, scientific and humanistic.

It occurred to me that not one of these ideas is historically the result of the application of what we are today pleased to call scientific method. If there is evidence that any one of these ideas as first set forth in the writings of such men as Tocqueville, Weber, Simmel, and Durkheim, is the result of problem-solving thought, proceeding rigorously and self-consciously from question to hypothesis to verified conclusion, I have been unable to discover it. On the contrary, each of these profound and seminal ideas

Reprinted from *Pacific Sociological Review*, 5:2 (1962), pp. 67–74, by permission of the author and the publisher.

would appear to be the consequence of intellectual processes bearing much more relation to the artist than the scientist, as the latter tends to be conceived by most of us. Apart from processes of intuition, impressionism, iconic imagination (the phrase is Sir Herbert Read's), and even objectification, it seems unlikely that any one of these ideas would have come into being to influence generations of subsequent thought and teaching.

For a few, no doubt, this conclusion, if believed at all, may seem like throwing vile suspicion on trusted ancestors: like a child's discovery that his father is a member of the John Birch Society or his mother a descendant of the Jukes or Kallikaks. It may smack of an anthropologist's gratuitous demonstration to a pentecostal communicant of the totemistic origins of Christianity. But let us withhold further comment on this aspect of our subject, turning instead for a few moments to a more fundamental and inclusive matter—the habit of treating science as though it were substantively and psychologically different from art.

It is a deeply rooted habit, but by no means universal in the history of modern thought. We need go back no further than the Renaissance to discover a time when art and science were universally regarded as but different manifestations of the same form of creative consciousness. We know that Leonardo da Vinci thought of his paintings and his ingenious works in physiology and mechanics as, equally, art and science. The type of thought and even the outcome in each did not seem significantly different from the other. And, three centuries later, Goethe seems to have felt the same way. He did not suppose that one type of thought operated while he was writing *Faust* and another during his remarkable inquiries in geology and botany. In both the Renaissance and Enlightenment a radical distinction between art and science would have been incomprehensible.

When, then, did the change take place that produced self-consciousness in the scientist and the artist, so like that of Adam and Eve after the Fall? Like a few other things that plague us, it was, I think, in the nineteenth century. Beginning with social movements generated by the French Revolution, and closely connected with processes of division of labor introduced by the industrial revolution, we find a growing tendency in the nineteenth century to assume that the artist and scientist work in ways that are alien, even antagonistic to one another. Gilbert and Sullivan were but giving lyric expression to what everyone knew when they wrote that the scientist is "a matter-of-fact young man, an alphabetical, arithmetical, every-day young man" whereas the artist is "a crotchety, cracked young man, an ultra-poetical, super-esthetical, out-of-the-ordinary young man."

In art there had developed, by the end of the nineteenth century, the view that creation works through some inscrutable process called genius or inspiration, never through technique and experimental work. We see this vividly in Romanticism and especially in the *fin de siècle*. Associated with this stereotype was the equally fundamental one that the artist is not concerned with reality or truth, but only beauty—timeless supra-terrestrial beauty. And, forming the context of both of these, was the fateful view of the artist's role in society. Far from admitting any continuity with, or dependence on, society, the Romantic artist emphasized instead the gulf between him and society, seeking in solitary escape the anodyne that his medieval and Renaissance forebears had found in fellowship and social purpose. His rejection of the world that was being created by the industrial revolution was total.

But while art was becoming mythicized in this fashion, science was succumbing to another myth, one of reverse character and of equal influence on the popular mind. This was the myth, not of inspiration, but of method. Here, as in the case of art, we are dealing with something related to the industrial revolution. But, whereas art was generally repelled by the new industrial society, science was virtually absorbed by it. Just as industry began to dominate technology, technology dominated science, making it not what it had been for centuries, primarily a pursuit of the reflective mind, but a profession governed by rules and by criteria of service, all of a piece with law, engineering, and medicine.

The new universities in both Europe and America gave immense impetus to science but, to a very large extent, it was science of the applied type. In the United States the rise of the Land Grant colleges, based in their earliest years on an unrelieved vocationalism, was a major step in the union of science and industry and in the cultivation of the stereotype that science, like industry, is practical, the very opposite of art. The "mechanic arts" became, for several generations, the prime conception of everything scientific, placing their stamp upon the type of science done and respected at large. It was Thomas Edison who became the archetype of the scientist in the United States. A Willard Gibbs was simply overlooked.

Gradually the idea spread that science, unlike art, flows along the same methodical and systematic channels that business or law or medicine does. What is crucial, it was felt, was not free reflection, intuition, and imagination but rigorous adherence to procedure. The machine in the factory was proof that skill could be transferred from man to technology, making human ingenuity an expendable item. Could not method be the analogue of the machine? Several generations of Americans thought that it could, and schools and colleges were filled with students doggedly learning what was thought to be scientific method—not, alas, as an aid to ratiocination but as a substitute for it.

It is little wonder, given the overwhelmingly practical and methodical character of American science that Europeans looked for a long time with scant respect upon American science. It is a safe generalization that had it not been for the European institutes to which Americans in rising number went for advanced work, thus acquiring a truer conception of science, American science would never have burst forth from its shell of useful mediocrity. To be sure there were those of like mind in Europe, especially England; those for whom science was profession, subject to and limited by rules and techniques. But in Europe, where the humanistic tradition was stronger as the result of a much older pre-democratic, pre-industrial past, and where a mind of the stature of Faraday's could reject for himself the title of physicist, preferring that of philosopher, and be understood and honored for it, there was less likelihood of science becoming mired in unrelieved method and technique.

II

The worst result of the nineteenth century separation of art and science is not one of historical interpretation. It is the continuing belief in many classrooms and laboratories that the objectives as well as thought processes are different. At its worst, this view tells us that science alone is concerned with reality; that art's function is simply to titillate the senses in a kind of aimless quest of the decorative and eye-pleasing.

Nothing could be farther from the truth. Any art form that is serious, be it the novel, poem, or painting, is concerned first and foremost with reality. It is interested in throwing light upon reality, and in somehow communicating this light to others. And this, basically, is what science— as contrasted with technology—is concerned with. I venture the judgment that there is more in common between Picasso and Einstein—in objective, in inspiration, and mode of fulfillment—than there is between Picasso and, say, Norman Rockwell or between Einstein and any of the stolid practitioners of what A. N. Whitehead once called "dustbowl empiricism." Both the artist and the scientist are driven by the desire to understand, to interpret, and to communicate their understanding to the rest of the world.

The artist, let it be trumpeted, is *not* interested in decoration, and it is only because Non-Artists have worked as though decoration, fatuous reminiscence, and eye titillation were the highest ends of art that many persons still find themselves accepting or rejecting an artwork largely in terms of whether it is beautiful to the eye. Of course art can be beautiful, but not if it seeks beauty as its chief end. So, let it be remembered, can science be beautiful though no one would suppose that even a mathematician is actuated fundamentally by the goal of beauty.

"The essential nature of art," writes Sir Herbert Read, "will be found neither in the production of objects to satisfy practical needs, nor in the expression of religious or philosophical ideas, but in its capacity to create a synthetic and self-consistent world: a world which is neither the world of practical needs and desires, nor the world of dreams and fantasy, but a world compounded of these contradictions: a convincing representation of the totality of experience: a mode therefore of envisaging the individual's perception of some aspect of universal truth. In all its essential activities art is trying to tell us something: something about the universe, something about nature, about man, or about the artist himself. . . . It is only when we have clearly recognized the function of art as a mode of knowledge parallel to the other modes by which man arrives at an understanding of his environment that we can begin to appreciate its significance in the history of mankind."[1]

The artist's interest in form is the scientist's interest in structure. In each the desire for vision and understanding is dominating. Each works empirically; each strives to communicate what it finds through a pattern or formal structure requiring technique for its mastery. It is worth noting that the word "theory" comes from the same Greek root as the word "theatre." It means, basically, looking fixedly at, contemplation. It is allied with the word imagination—that is, literally, internalizing the outer world to an image that the mind holds tenaciously. Both art and science, in short, depend upon the capacity for detachment and upon the ability to hold back from commitment. The essence of each, wrote Santayana, "is the steady contemplation of things in their order and worth."

In truth, science and art have had a profoundly important cultural relationship for the greater part of the history of man. Eugene Rabinowitch, distinguished chemist and science editor, has recently written some words that might fittingly hang in every hall of learning.

"The evolution of the human mind is a single process, revealed with different intensity, different clarity, and different timing—in its various manifestations—in art, science, philosophy, social and political thought. It is like a fugue, or an oratorio, in which different instruments or voices enter in turn. The voice of the artist is often the first to respond. The artist is the most sensitive individual in society. His feeling for change, his apprehension of new things to come, is likely to be more acute than of the slower-moving, rational, scientific thinker. It is in the artistic production of a period, rather than in its thinking, that one should search for shadows cast in advance by coming events, for prophetic anticipation. I do not mean the forecast of future events, but rather the revelation, in the framework of artistic production, of the mental attitudes which only later will become apparent in other fields of human endeavour. Thus the impending breakdown of the existing order of things, of the generally accepted system of values, should be—and often is—first recognizable in a revolt against the values and canons that had dominated artistic creation; a revolution in art precedes the revolution in society."[2]

Repeatedly, the history of the West has shown these words to be true. Historians of both ancient and modern European culture have emphasized the directive role played by the artist's mind: how philosophical and scientific images of man were preceded by those to be seen first in the drama, the sonnet, and in painting or sculpture. This first became a vivid truth for me several years ago while going through the great Uffizi gallery in Florence. Here it is possible to trace, in hall after hall, standing for age after age, the historically evolving images of man in Western Europe: from the spiritual, almost mystical and transcendent representations of man to be found in the Italian Primitives, through transitional manifestations that are both divine and human in appearance, to the frankly human, self-contained, and overwhelmingly terrestrial men and women of the Renaissance and Baroque. It is a development that plainly precedes the analogous transitions of image in philosophy and science. It was art with its swift, encompassing, and iconic vision that formed the bridge from medieval asceticism and corporatism to modern humanism; from organism to the obsessing problem of man's relation to society and values.

It was indeed in the Renaissance—and what else was the Renaissance but the conception of man and society as works of art?—that the whole modern view came into existence. This is a view that has since been modified in countless ways—now enhanced, now vulgarized; now made tragic, now trivial; sometimes ennobled, sometimes debased—but never really changed after the late fourteenth century in Italy. Whether the objective was the building of a cathedral or a bridge, the planning of a tapestry or a voyage to the Indies, the forming of a guild or the state itself, Renaissance man saw the world around him from the vantage point of the artist-scientist; not as something to worship or to manipulate but to understand and master even as Michelangelo mastered the marble he worked or Marco Polo the route to Cathay.

The problems and answers that form the core of modern culture are the work, not of the Usefuls in society but of the Visionaries, those who are lost in wonder and who, not knowing where they are going, go therefore the farthest. The same impulse to reality and its communication drove Michelangelo and Machiavelli alike—the one to the majestic David, the other to the Renaissance state—each a product of the artist-scientist.

The basic affinity between the artist and the scientist is, as the mathematician Marston Morse has told us, psychological and spiritual. "The first essential bond between mathematics and the arts is found in the fact that discovery in mathematics is not a matter of logic. It is rather the result of mysterious powers which no one understands, and in which the unconscious recognition of beauty must play an important part. Out of an infinity of designs a mathematician chooses one pattern for beauty's sake, and pulls it down to earth, no one knows how. Afterwards the logic of words and of forms sets the pattern right. Only then can one tell someone else. The first pattern remains in the shadows of the mind."[3]

These are important words, burning words. They might hang over the entrance to every methodology seminar as a prophylaxis to pedantry. Too many sociologists have assumed that because scientific thought is by definition rational and logical in expression, its psychological roots must therefore be limited to strictly empirical and logical processes. Only that is scientific—so runs the folklore of scientism—that proceeds from an unambiguous and precisely delimited problem, drawn from statistically aseptic data, to a carefully tailored hypothesis. All else is, by definition, art or philosophy. It is hard to think of a better way to apotheosize the routine and insignificant.

Of course science is concerned with problems, with questions rooted in empirical observation as well as reflection. Like the artist, the scientist is interested in understanding the world around him and in discovering significant relationships. But from the large and incontestable truth that scientific thought is ultimately rooted in a preoccupation with the unknown, in a gnawing desire to reduce the tensions of uncertainty, it does not follow that scientific discovery is wholly, or even largely, the simple consequence of problem-defining and problem-solving thought. Such a conclu-sion has done much to drive sociology into areas of study chosen not because of their intrinsic intellectual importance, but because in them quantitative methodologies can work frictionlessly.

The late Florian Znaniecki foresaw, a generation ago, the trend that things are taking. He was referring to the already manifest influence of methodology courses. "This influence consists in substituting tabulating technique for intellectual methods, and thus eliminating theoretical thinking from the process of scientific research. . . . A condition can be foreseen— indeed, it has almost been reached—when anybody who has learned by heart the various technical rules and formulae of statistics, with no other education whatsoever and no more intelligence than a moron, will be able to draw from a given material all the conclusions which statistical prob-lematization makes possible. . . . The role of creative thinking in science, according to this conception, will be reduced to the function of formulating hypotheses which are to be tested by technical means. But we have seen that the only hypotheses statisticians ever have formulated, and ever can formulate, in view of the unavoidable limitations of their method, are no more than superficial generalizations of common-sense practical reflection. There is little place for creative thought and even less for scientific progress in this kind of problematization."[4]

Despite the candor of many distinguished scientists in telling about their work, and despite what we are on the way to learning about processes of creativity in general, there is still a great deal that we do not know about how scientists arrive at their problems, do the really crucial work on them, and draw their basic insights. But this much is clear. Such problems and ideas, from all that we can presently learn, seem to come as often from the unconscious as the conscious mind; from wide and extraneous reading, or from buried experience, as from the data immedi-ately in view; from the "left handed" processes of feeling and intuition as from the "right handed" imperatives of logic and reason. Therefore, may we not draw this conclusion?: Anything that shrinks the field of experience and imagination, that in any way diminishes the sources of inspiration, that routinizes the workings of the intelligent mind, is to be regarded with suspicion.

III

It is time to return to the ideas in sociology I referred to at the outset of my paper. Let me describe them briefly again, for they are indubitably the most distinctive and illuminating contributions of sociology to the study of culture and society. There is, first, the view of human association as containing endemic processes of disorganization, dysfunction, call them what we will. Second, there is the view of the individual as alienated and anomic. Third, there is the perspective of community—in contrast to rationalistic and contractual forms of relationship—involving the key con-cepts of hierarchy and status. Fourth, we have the great theme of rationali-zation as a process in history and in the whole structure of modern society.

We know where these ideas came from: from the writings of four or five remarkable minds in the late nineteenth century: Tocqueville, Weber, Simmel, Tönnies, and Durkheim. I need not enlarge upon their formulations of the ideas. I am more interested in the processes by which the ideas came into being: that is, the contexts in which the ideas were uttered, the traditions they came out of, and, if it were possible, the mental states behind the ideas. Obviously, we are limited in what we can say positively, but I believe certain points are clear.

There is, first, the manifest discontinuity of these ideas in the history of modern social thought. Not one of them could have been deduced from the propositions of rationalism on human behavior that flourished in the Enlightenment. The true heritage of the Enlightenment is to be found, not in sociology, but in classical economics, individual psychology, and utilitarian political science. What we find in sociology—that is, in its distinctive currents—is a revolt against the rationalist view of man and society.

The second point is this. Not only are the key ideas of sociology unrelated to prior "scientific" ideas; they have their closest affinity with an art movement, Romanticism. In the same way that the Renaissance image of man proceeded from prior currents in art, so I argue, the sociological image arises in the first instance from visions which had their earliest and most far reaching appeal in Romantic art.[5]

Weber has somewhere likened his own concept of rationalization to the poet Schiller's earlier view of the "disenchantment of the world." He was candid and accurate. Tocqueville, Simmel, and Durkheim might well have done likewise. From the first burst of the Romantic spirit in the late eighteenth century—rising to do battle with the classicist-rationalist view —we find luminously revealed two central visions: (1) the estrangement of the individual from a growingly impersonal and disorganized society (and the consequent spiritual inaccessibility of modern institutions—city, factory, mass society); (2) a celebration of status and community— whether rural, religious, or moral—in contrast to the individualistic and contractual society of the *philosophes*.

Third, and most important, even if most elusive, are the psychological affinities between the Romantic artists and the sociologists. It is impossible, as I have already suggested, to entertain seriously the thought that these major ideas were arrived at in a manner comparable to what we think of as scientific methodology. Can you imagine what would have happened had any one of them been subjected, at the moment following its inception, to a rigorous design analysis? Can anyone believe that Weber's vision of rationalization in history, Simmel's vision of metropolis, or Durkheim's vision of *anomie*, came from logico-empirical analysis as this is understood today? Merely to ask the question is to know the answer. Plainly, these men were not working with finite and ordered problems in front of them. They were not problem-solving at all. Each was, with deep intuition, with profound imaginative grasp, reacting to the world around him, even as does the artist, and, also like the artist, objectifying internal and only partly conscious, states of mind.

Consider one example: the view of society and man that underlies Durkheim's great study of suicide. Basically, it is the view of the artist as much as that of the scientist. Background, detail, and characterization blend into something that is iconic in its grasp of an entire social order. How did Durkheim get his controlling idea? We may be sure of one thing: he did not get it, as the stork story of science might have it, from a preliminary examination of the vital registers of Europe, any more than Darwin got the idea of natural selection from his observations during the voyage of the *Beagle*. The idea, the plot, and the conclusion of *Suicide* were well in his mind before he examined the registers. Where, then, did he get the idea? We can only speculate. He might have got it from reading Tocqueville who could certainly have got it from Lamennais who could have got it from Bonald or Chateaubriand. Or, it could have come from personal experience—from a remembered fragment of the Talmud, from an intuition born of personal loneliness and marginality, a scrap of experience in Paris. Who can be sure? But one thing is certain. The creative blend of ideas behind *Suicide*—a blend from which we still draw in our scientific labors—was reached in ways more akin to those of the artist than to those of the data processor, the logician, or the technologist.

It is not different with the ideas and perspectives of Simmel—in many ways the most imaginative and intuitive of all the great sociologists. His treatment of fear, love, conventionality, power, and friendship show the mind of the artist-essayist, and it is no distortion of values to place him with such masters as Montaigne and Bacon. Remove the artist's vision from the treatments of the stranger, the dyad, and the role of secrecy, and you have removed all that gives life. In Simmel there is that wonderful tension between the esthetically concrete and the philosophically general that always lies in greatness. It is the esthetic element in Simmel's work that makes impossible the full absorption of his sociological substance by anonymous, systematic theory. One must go back to Simmel himself for the real insight. As with Darwin and Freud, it will always be possible to derive something of importance from the man directly that cannot be gleaned from impersonal statements in social theory.

This leads to another important fact. Our dependence upon these ideas and their makers is akin to the artist's dependence upon the artists who precede him. In the same way that the novelist will always be able to learn from a study and re-study of Dostoevski or James—to learn a sense of development and form, as well as to draw inspiration from the creative source —so the sociologist can forever learn from a re-reading of such men as Weber and Simmel.

It is this element that separates sociology from some of the physical sciences. There is, after all, a limit to what the young physicist can learn from even a Newton. Having once grasped the fundamental points of the *Principia*, he is not likely to draw very much as a physicist from re-readings (though he could as a historian of science). How different is the relation of the sociologist to a Simmel or Durkheim. Always there will be something to be gained from a direct reading; something that is informative, enlarging, and creative. This is precisely like the contemporary artist's return to the study of medieval architecture, the Elizabethan sonnet, or the paintings of Matisse. This is the essence of the history of art, and why the history of sociology is so different from the history of science.

IV

That such men as Weber, Durkheim, and Simmel fall in the scientific tradition is unquestioned. Their works, for all the deep artistic sensitivity and intuition, no more belong in the history of art than the works of Balzac or Dickens do in the history of social science. The conclusion we draw is not that science and art are without differences. There are real differences, as there are among the arts and among the sciences.[6] No one asks a Picasso to verify one of his visions by repeating the process; and, conversely, we properly give short shrift to ideas in science that no one but the author can find supported by experience. The ideas of Durkheim may, as I have suggested, be dependent upon thought-processes like those of the artist, but none of them would have survived in sociology or become fruitful for others were it not for criteria and modes of communication that differ from those in art.

The conclusion, then, is not that science and art are, or should be, alike. It is the simpler but more fundamental conclusion that in both art and science the same type of creative imagination works. And everything that impedes or frustrates this imagination strikes at the source of the discipline itself. This unhappily is what is happening today in large areas of sociological instruction and research. It is a recurrent phenomenon in philosophy and science.

All too often in the history of thought we find techniques, methods, and doctrines becoming puny earthworks, hiding the view of the Olympian heights. How many mute, inglorious Simmels, how many village Cooleys lie today buried in required sequences of curriculum and in the computer rooms, their talents occupied not by development of ideas and insights but the adaptation of trivial or well worn ideas to the language of the machine or the endless replication of studies that often shouldn't have been done in the first place? Such servitude is justified on the false and appalling ground that the student can thus be taught the "method" of science. One may observe cynically that he sees no Simmels and Durkheims walking the campus today. I venture the statement that there would have been none in their day had certain curricular requirements and terminological fashions been then in existence.

Which leads me to my final observations. I have stressed the art element in sociology not because I think the villain is the machine—any more than it is the machine tender who occasionally walks like a social scientist. The danger, if I may indulge myself in the presidential prerogative of the sermon, is non-technological; it is sociological; it is the systematics and the dogmatics that always threaten to seep into the cellars of intellectual disciplines, thus driving out the art elements. For art's war is with system building, not science. I know of no better way of expressing this than in the form that Francis Bacon chose three centuries ago. That is, in the form of the Idols of the Mind. Let us call them the Idols of the Profession.

There are, first, you will remember, the Idols of the Tribe. These are the inclinations, perspectives, and modes of perception that are common to all; they are unavoidable, but must nevertheless be allowed for. The mere fact that we are sociologists—instead of biologists or economists— means that there are certain endemic, uniting ways of seeing the world around us. They are valuable and unavoidable, but not final.

Second, there are the Idols of the Cave—those that come, not from the character of the profession as a whole, but of that small part of the profession each of us lives in. Here we have the idols of specialization; the human but nevertheless dangerous tendency to reduce the richness and variety of the whole to the specialized perspective and techniques that each of us operates with and that always threaten to become as rigid and fixed as the skills of technicians.

Third, we have the Idols of the Market Place—words, phrases, and neologisms that become substitutes for ideas. Who among us has not learned to his advantage or disadvantage of the hypnotic fascination that is exerted upon foundations, research committees, and certain editors, by phraseology? And who does not know of the ease with which the words conveying the concept become the thing itself—with resulting inability to go beyond the words?

But, the greatest and most formidable of the Idols are those of the Theatre. Here Bacon had reference to systems of thought, systems which become, like bureaucracies, their own reason for being; where original goals have become displaced, leaving only the goals of systematic survival and self-maintenance. It seems to be the mark of all systems that their very degree of initial success leads before long to an almost ritualistic conclusion. We have all laughed at the teacher of classics who saw in the *Antigone* "a veritable treasure house of grammatical peculiarities." And for this teacher's students the classics were indeed killed. But why do we not laugh also at the teacher of sociology who introduces his students not to the rich and endlessly diversified field of social and cultural experience but to dull and potentially alienating analyses of fashionable systems and methodologies. Is not at least part of the attraction today of the natural sciences for the gifted student the assurance that he will be introduced immediately to the materials and problems of science and not to the locutions of systems? Systems so easily become bureaucracies of the spirit, subject to the same pettifogging rules and regulations.

Art abhors systems, and so does all creativity. History is the graveyard of systems, and this is precisely why Simmel and Cooley and Sumner remain fresh and valuable for us today and why few read Spencer or Ward. How often do system-builders produce students who are themselves creative and viable? The system killeth, the insight giveth life. What remains today of nominalism, realism, sensationalism, pragmatism, and all the other systems that once paraded over the landscape of Europe?

Dead, all dead. God lives, Blake wrote, in the details. I amended this to say he lives in the insights, the intuitions, the imaginations of the artist. I cannot better conclude than with one final excerpt from Marston Morse. "The creative scientist lives in 'the wildness of logic' where reason is the handmaiden and not the master. I shun all monuments that are coldly legible. I prefer the world where the images turn their faces in every direction, like the masks of Picasso. It is the hour before the break of day when science turns in the womb, and, waiting, I am sorry that there is between us no sign and no language except by mirrors of necessity. I am grateful for the poets who suspect the twilight zone.

"The more I study the interrelations of the arts the more I am convinced that every man is in part an artist. Certainly as an artist he shapes his own life, and moves and touches other lives. I believe that it is only as an artist that man knows reality. *Reality is what he loves, and if his love is lost it is his sorrow.*"[7]

NOTES

[1] Sir Herbert E. Read, *Art and Society* (London: W. Heinemann, 1937), pp. x–xii.

[2] Eugene Rabinowitch, "Integral Science and Atomized Art," *Bulletin of the Atomic Scientists*, 15 (1959), p. 64. The entire issue is organized around the theme, science and art, and contains a number of highly perceptive pieces by both scientists and artists. Particularly valuable are those by Rabinowitch, Marston Morse, Carl Holty, and Martin Kamen and Beka Doherty.

Some prolonged, if unsystematic, personal questioning of scientists suggests to me that there is a stratification of acceptance of the art element in creative science. Mathematicians and theoretical physicists, currently high in the status system of modern science, are prone to accept immediately the reality of intuitive and non-logical elements in scientific discovery. So, for the most part, are those working in such relatively new and highly creative areas as biophysics and biochemistry. Geologists, today low in the pecking order of science, appear least likely to accept or understand the art element in science, although they have much company in the more established and formalized areas of other disciplines, including biology and physics and chemistry. In the behavioral sciences generally there is a greater insistence upon rigor and logic of method—and preoccupation with method itself—than is true of the physical sciences. There are differences, of course, by field. Thus the educationists are more likely to fluff their scientific feathers than are the anthropologists in whose number unabashed artists have always flourished and who have, on the whole, spent least time on matters of abstract methodology. Similarly, my experience indicates, acceptance of the art element in science seems to follow the curve of personal distinction. I am told that one Nobel laureate, a chemist, dismissing method, describes scientific discovery as "rape followed by seduction."

[3] Marston Morse, "Mathematics and the Arts," *Bulletin of the Atomic Scientists*, *op. cit.*, pp. 56–57. Two recent literary studies have shown, with impressive imagination and learning, how unreason and reason, unconscious and conscious, hunch and hypothesis, have worked together historically. See Wayne Shumaker, *Literature and the Irrational* (Englewood Cliffs, N.J.: Prentice-Hall, 1960), and Ernest Tuveson, *Imagination as a Means of Grace; Locke and the Aesthetics of Romanticism* (Berkeley, Calif.: University of California Press, 1960).

[4] Florian Znaniecki, *The Method of Sociology* (New York: Farrar and Rinehart, 1934), pp. 234–235.

[5] I have discussed this at greater length in an article "Conservatism and Sociology," *American Journal of Sociology*, 134 (1952), pp. 167–175. See also Leon Bramson's interesting discussion in his *The Political Context of Sociology* (Princeton, N.J.: Princeton University Press, 1961), Chap. 1.

⁶ Charles Morris, the philosopher, has suggested that the major difference is this: although both science and art communicate by the use of ideas and representations not completely describable in terms of sense experience, science typically seeks to make its communications capable of identification or verification by the largest number of individuals, whereas art tends to insist that each individual translate the original vision into something peculiarly his own creation.

There are probably also interesting role differences between artists and scientists, though this is, so far as I can discover, a relatively unexplored area of study. Martyl Lansdorf, an artist, and Cyril S. Smyth, a scientist, in a joint article in the *Bulletin of the Atomic Scientists* already cited, say: "In many contacts with humanist and scientific friends we have noticed only one consistent difference of professional attitudes—the scientists are jealous of their ideas; the humanists do not seem to mind if someone appropriates their ideas but are outraged by a plagiarism of form." This is an important insight, but I judge that it has more relevance to painters and sculptors, and possibly poets, than to novelists and playwrights who are certainly as jealous of ideas, and as secretive, as are the scientists. Legal battles over plots are not unknown.

One commonly alleged difference between scientists and artists deserves critical comment. It is an old stereotype of the scientist, sedulously cultivated in many a seminar, that the scientist, simply because he is scientist and not artist, is preconditioned to a willingness, even a desire, to be displaced by the work of students and others. But this stereotype says more about the ideal world of science than it does about actual scientists. The desire for self-preservation is surely as strong among scientists as among artists, and the evidence suggests that in such matters as protection of personal theories, hoarding of data, and secretiveness of intent, there may not be very significant role differences.

Passion for self-preservation may be more functional in scientific thought than is commonly supposed. Marston Morse, in the article referred to above, is of this view so far as mathematics is concerned. He cites the famous feud between Poincaré and his young colleague Lebesque, suggesting the similarity of conflict and outcome to the revolt of Philipp Emanuel Bach against the work of his father, Johann Sebastian. In each case the reactions were dictated by instincts of self-preservation which, as Professor Morse points out, were clearly to the advantage of posterity.

On one point the evidence is clear. Scientists have a far higher sense of priority—though not of competitiveness—than artists. This would seem to follow from the broad differences of context. It is highly unlikely that anything in the history of art resembles what Robert Merton has emphasized in his studies of priority in science or what Frederick Reif has described as prevailing practice among physicists in an article, "The Competitive World of the Pure Scientist," *Science*, 134 (1961), pp. 1957–1962.

⁷ Morse, *op. cit.*, p. 58.

2 LEO F. SCHNORE

The Myth of Human Ecology

I have been motivated to give some thought to the matter of ecology's place in sociology by Kingsley Davis's recent discussion of "The Myth of Functional Analysis." I was struck, for example, by his reference to the

Reprinted from *Sociological Inquiry*, 31:2 (1961), pp. 128–139, by permission of the author and the publisher.

fact that "Characteristics that the functionalists themselves regard as either accidental faults or as totally alien to their point of view . . . critics often regard as the essence of the approach."[1] Davis also observes that "so-called functionalists and professed enemies of functionalism are often *doing* the same kind of analysis."[2] Both of these remarks, of course, could be applied to human ecology and ecologists with some justification, and one could list examples at some length. An ecologist is not inclined to claim that his approach is the only mode of analysis that deserves recognition as distinctively sociological, but if we agree from the start that human ecology does not represent the sum and substance of sociology, where does it fit? How does it articulate with the main body of sociological analysis? In my opinion, the prevailing *"myth"* of human ecology is that ecology is somehow *"marginal"* to sociology.

One finds ecology represented as marginal, for example, in introductory textbooks, as when Arnold Rose states that sociology, as a discipline, "has historically come to include the study of two sets of phenomena which are not logically part of their central subject matter, any more than economics and political science are part of sociology. These two subdisciplines are demography . . . and human ecology."[3] A more extreme version is to be found in Boskoff's assertion that "In seeking a distinctive set of phenomena, orthodox human ecology has not only seceded from modern sociology—it has largely withdrawn from science."[4] But advocates as well as critics are numbered among those who regard ecology as marginal to sociology. Thus we find one of the acknowledged founders of human ecology—Ernest W. Burgess—contending that "human ecology, strictly speaking, falls outside of sociology. . . . Human ecology, logically, is a separate discipline from sociology. Like population studies, it has become attached to sociology because it provides the substructure for the study of social factors in human behavior."[5]

In the following sections, I intend to argue that human ecology—rather than being marginal to sociology—represents one effort to deal with *the central problem of sociological analysis*. Further, I shall argue that the ecologist's efforts appear to be marginal only in the light of certain *tendencies within American sociology*—tendencies which are themselves to be explained in large part by methodological developments. Finally, I shall argue that ecology's real potential lies in its *contributions to a macro- as over against a microsociology*. I shall take up these points in somewhat different order, and then proceed to identify ecology's distinctive attack upon the central problem of sociology.

THE NEED

One key task confronting anyone who advocates a particular approach is the obligation to demonstrate that it has emerged naturally as an extension of prior work. In an essay concerned with Durkheim's "social morphology," I tried to show that ecology has a legitimate *sociological* ancestry, and that it is something more than a simple attempt to "apply" some rudimentary biological concepts to social phenomena; the latter is one of the older and lesser myths of human ecology.[6] A more critical task is to show that the approach one advocates is fruitful, i.e., that it yields distinctive hypotheses for research. This stipulation amounts to saying that one must demonstrate the existence of a genuine *need*. While I do not pretend that there is a great popular clamor on behalf of the ecological perspective, I am convinced that there is a widespread and barely hidden dissatisfaction with certain salient features of contemporary American sociology.

First of all, several writers, including representatives of radically different schools of thought, have commented upon the microsociological— and even psychological—drift of American sociology in recent decades. Some of these writers adopt a neutral stance, expressing no explicit preference for the macroscopic as over against the microscopic approach. Others, however, have expressed varying degrees of dissatisfaction with the current state of the field. Thus Bellah has observed that "Since the generation of Weber and Durkheim macroscopic problems involving comparative and historical research have been somewhat slighted as microscopic research based on new methods and instruments has come to the fore. Not only general sociology, but microsociology itself, would suffer if this imbalance were to go too far."[7]

The technical-methodological basis of this drift toward the microscopic has been noted elsewhere. Perhaps the most sweeping indictment of all is to be found in the charges leveled by James Coleman: "Social theory has, I think, allowed itself to be sidetracked off its main task, which is to develop theories for social systems—whether they be total social systems or systems of behavior in small groups. Our attention is too often drawn away from the system itself to the individuals within it, so that we construct theories to account for some individual's behavior."[8] Coleman agrees that our techniques have led us in the direction of microsociology:

> Two things have happened: the complexity of these [data-gathering] techniques has shifted our focus from substantive problems to the techniques themselves; and secondly, this very move down to the individual level has kept us fascinated there, unable to get back up to the social level. Survey research has continued to be a kind of aggregate psychology, rather than sociology; it has continued to study the opinions of a population sample rather than public opinion, to study buyers rather than the market, to study individuals rather than the community. . . .
>
> The second problem, the psychologizing of sociology through survey research has already shown signs of solution. Techniques are being devised, and studies are being designed and carried out, which pervert the survey into a truly sociological instrument. Structural effects analysis, comparing several social contexts, relational analysis, using sociometric techniques, and more traditional survey methods, using variables like social class and sibling position in the family, or status in an organization, and so on, are beginning to allow the study of sociological problems rather than purely psychological ones. . . .
> Yet in most of these techniques, the individual behavior or attitude is still

the dependent variable, though social structure or norms are the independent variables. The functioning of a social system is seldom analyzed by quantitative techniques—as it has been by qualitative observational studies.[9]

With respect to the difficulties attending the microscopic interpretation of macroscopic problems, C. Wright Mills has presented an equally forceful statement:

> The idea of social structure cannot be built up only from ideas or facts about a specific series of individuals and their reactions to their milieux. Attempts to explain social and historical events on the basis of psychological theories about "the individual" often rest upon the assumption that society is nothing but a great scatter of individuals and that, accordingly, if we know all about these "atoms" we can in some way add up the information and thus know about society. It is not a fruitful assumption.[10]

But enough of appeals to authority. Each of these eminent writers would very probably prescribe different solutions to the same problem. I am not trying to persuade anyone that these anti-microscopic views have suddenly become dominant; far from it, for these are the words of "critics of the existing order." Nor am I advocating an ecological approach as the sole solution—or even the "best" solution—to the problems they have raised. Certainly human ecology is not widely regarded as a strong intellectual force in contemporary American sociology, if one may judge (1) from the fact that only 100 out of 4200 members of our professional association select it as a major interest, and (2) from the extremely limited attention given it in three recent evaluations of the current status and future prospects of the field as a whole. Ecology receives only brief treatment in the chapters devoted to urban sociology in the volumes entitled *Sociology in the United States of America, Review of Sociology: Analysis of a Decade,* and *Sociology Today: Problems and Prospects.*[11] In the last two, in fact, emphasis is placed upon the rash of criticisms of the ecological approach that appeared in the late forties and early fifties. But some of us are persuaded that human ecology—despite its possible defects and imperfections—has a great deal to offer contemporary sociology, and that its signal contribution might be toward a genuine *macrosociology.*

We can start with the proposition that the study of *social organization* is the central focus of the entire sociological enterprise.[12] In Rossi's words, "The proper study of sociology is social organization. On this perspective there is probably the greatest degree of agreement in our discipline."[13] But the logical status of the concept "organization" varies significantly according to its *analytical position* in the frame of reference that is employed. At risk of oversimplification, it can be said that aspects of organization—or, more generally, structural properties of whole populations —appear in two quite separate guises in sociological analysis: as *independent* and as *dependent* variables. Similarly, properties of individual organisms have these dual analytical positions. The logically possible frames of reference are four in number, and we may first of all distinguish two general modes of analysis directed to the explanation of the behavior of the individual organism: *individual* psychology and *social* psychology.

INDIVIDUAL PSYCHOLOGY

"Individual psychology" largely seeks its explanatory variables among properties of individual organisms other than that which is the *explanandum* at the moment. Thus a psychologist setting out to account for variations in learning or perception tends to confine himself to properties of the organism in his search for independent variables. Because sociology is our subject, a universally acceptable definition of individual psychology is not essential to my purposes, but we might pause to consider the following statement by Tolman: "The final dependent variable in which, as a psychologist, I am interested is behavior. It is the behavior of organisms, human and subhuman, which I wish to predict and control." He goes on to identify "the five independent variables of (1) *environmental stimuli*, (2) *psychological drive*, (3) *heredity*, (4) *previous training*, and (5) *maturity*."[14]

The last four of these are clearly properties of individual organisms, but "environmental stimuli" are clearly external to the organism. However, it seems to be commonly accepted as axiomatic that it is only as these stimuli are experienced by the organism that behavioral reactions ensue. Thus there is justification for asserting that individual psychologists tend generally to predict from one property of an individual organism to another, or to another set of behaviors. If this effort is pursued self-consciously and consistently at the individual level of analysis, the result is a kind of biological or physiological inquiry; it seeks a universalistic explanation of a particular psychological process, an account that holds for all men everywhere, without respect to social position, group membership, allegiance to particular norms, etc.

SOCIAL PSYCHOLOGY

As soon as these last-named variables enter the analysis, however, the analyst leaves the domain of individual psychology *per se*—psychology unadorned by qualifying adjectives—and enters the realm of "social psychology."

This view is distinctive in that it seems to represent an attempt to move between two levels of analysis, with certain group properties (e.g., size) serving as independent variables, and certain individual properties (e.g., cognitive processes) taken as dependent variables. Much of the work in "small group" research is of this nature, but this mode of analysis is by no means confined to situations in which face-to-face interaction is possible. (In addition, we shall see that not all small-group research is social psychological in orientation.) The use of "social" explanations of "psychological" processes can also be found in analyses of society in the large, especially within that portion of the literature that focuses upon "cultural" differences in behavior.

In general, it may be said that any effort to explain individual behavior by reference to group membership or position, real or imagined, makes use of a social-psychological hypothesis. Social psychology tends to ignore what is common to all men (this is left to individual psychology) and to ignore what is unique to particular individuals (this is left to the biographer); it deals with what is common to classes of individuals in a particular culture, a particular stratum, a particular role. (This point sometimes leads to needless confusion. Some social psychologists firmly deny that they deal with "individual behavior." What they mean is that they eschew any concern with the actions of particular, named individuals. However, the conduct of classes of individuals or "actors"—or class of individual behavior—is precisely central to their interests.)

Now the treatment of "social organization" is not inevitably the same in all social-psychological inquiries. The explanation ordinarily proceeds by predicting from population to individual properties. An example is Wirth's famous analysis of "urbanism as a way of life," in which variations in population size, density, and heterogeneity are employed in an attempt to account for variations in individual behavior and outlook in the urban setting.[15] In addition to appearing as attributes of populations, however, certain aspects of social organization may be transmuted into individual properties for analytical purposes. Examples of social-psychological analyses strictly confined to the individual level are to be found in most of the work subsumed under "role analysis," almost all of contemporary survey research, and in the analysis of "reference groups." Here the individual's position in the social structure is essentially regarded as a *personal* attribute, analytically speaking, and it is employed to explain his behavior *vis-à-vis* other persons playing complementary roles, or in particular areas of conduct that are amenable to a survey approach, such as voting or fertility. The "reference group" too is an individual attribute, in that it designates an individual's sense of allegiance to or affiliation with a group or category, without respect to actual membership; in some instances, in fact, it refers to little more than a stereotype in the mind of an individual, while in others it specifies a specific position or a broad social category to which he aspires.

Organization has a different meaning in these various inquiries, some- times appearing as the "social environment" which is perceived by the actor, sometimes as a set of normative constraints, sometimes as a con- geries of cultural values. In all of them, however, the common stamp is an effort to explain individual behavior by reference to organizational attributes of populations or to real or imagined positions within the social structure. In summary, we may identify the major mode of social-psy- chological inquiry as a broad-scale research strategy that attempts to predict—if only contextually—from some aspect of social organization to some individual behavior or conduct. Thus Newcomb has specified "the characteristic point of view of social psychology" as follows:

> We may say that social psychology deals with the association of variations in the behavior of one or more individuals with variations in social environ-

ment. . . . Secondly, differences in social environment and the way in which they are experienced are very largely determined by the way in which the individual's society is organized.[16]

PSYCHOLOGICAL SOCIOLOGY

In contrast to "social psychology" is an approach that I prefer to call "psychological sociology." The positions of the adjective and the noun designate the independent and dependent variables respectively. "Psychological sociology" subsumes all efforts to explain properties of populations by reference to the properties of the individuals who—from one perspective—may be said to compose these populations. One of the most succinct expressions of this point of view is to be found in a plea by Swanson, who asks

that we take seriously the dictum of Thomas, Znaniecki, and a host of others that, in theorizing about the causes of *any* behavior, *individual or collective*, we conceive of our independent variables in terms of the environment as experienced by those behaving, and that we assume that their acts are efforts to deal with the world as they perceive it. This has many implications. The only one stressed here is the suggestion that, assuming human biology to be constant for purposes of theory-building, *one may predict variations in the organization of a group* from variations in environmental problems as its members experience them.[17]

Many other examples are to be found in the literature on "culture and personality," at least in that phase of this work which attempts to account for such macroscopic features as forms of political organization in terms of individual experience with child-rearing practices, etc. Particular analyses, of course, are likely to slip into the social-psychological mode of reasoning from time to time. Moreover, certain population attributes appear sometimes as no more than "intervening variables," where individual properties are said to give rise to certain group properties, and the latter—in their turn—are viewed as influencing individual behavior. One of the best-known examples is to be found in Kardiner's discussion of "primary" and "secondary" institutions and their mutual relations to individual behavior.[18]

In any event, most efforts to explain macroscopic social phenomena in terms of "basic personality structure" or "national character" partake of the assumptions identified here as those of psychological sociology. To a strict and doctrinaire Durkheimian, these efforts are almost doomed to defeat, since they patently violate his famous methodological stricture: "The determining cause of a social fact should be sought among the social facts preceding it and not among the states of the individual consciousness."[19] However, to the extent that these efforts are ultimately directed, no matter how circuitously, toward the explanation of individual behavior they may be regarded as entirely legitimate, even from the standpoint of one who insists upon viewing society as a phenomenon *sui generis*.

It is evident here that one's assumptions concerning levels of "emergence" are crucial to the development of his position on these matters. Some writers assume that "only the individual is real," and that social structure is either a kind of convenient fiction or a shorthand designation for summarizing individual behavior in aggregate terms; these "social nominalists" are inclined to the view here labelled "psychological sociology," although they eclectically adopt certain aspects of social-psychological thought as it suits their analytical needs. In contrast, "social realists" assert that social structure represents something other than the simple sum of individual actions, and they are much more likely to confine themselves to social psychology, as defined here, or else to adopt an ecological perspective.[20] They tend to be Durkheimian in orientation, rejecting the easy reductionism that underlies psychological sociology. Needless to say, it is difficult to place individual writers in one or another of these convenient categories; different portions of the work of particular authors, however, can be readily identified in these terms. One might even say that a sure index of an analyst's theoretical sophistication is the extent to which he gives evidence that he is aware of a shift in the direction of his analysis when it does occur.

MACROSOCIOLOGY

The first of the two modes of analysis identified here as "macrosociological" has one feature in common with "psychological sociology" as defined above. Both approaches take organization, or some particular aspect of it, as the *explanandum*. Aside from a common interest in the same type of dependent variable, however, there are few other similarities. This is most clear with respect to human ecology, especially as it has been developed by Amos H. Hawley.[21] For one thing, the ecological mode of analysis remains at one level with respect to the variables it employs; it seeks its independent variables among other "attributes of organized populations," such as their demographic features. (It should be added, of course, that there is nothing to prevent the use of other organizational features in the effort to explain a given facet of organization. Durkheim's use of increasing "dynamic density" and competition to explain mounting structural differentiation is a case in point. In fact, this is the only one of the perspectives discussed so far that conforms strictly to Durkheim's rule regarding the explanation of "social facts.")

There is, however, another macrosociological mode of analysis that can be identified, and it is one that ecologists are inclined to use from time to time. Here organization appears—not as the dependent variable—but as one of the *independent* variables. In point of fact, human ecology represents a broad *type* of analysis, within which more specific types can be identified, with their designation depending upon the nature of the dependent variable. Within the ecological framework, effort can be directed to the explanation of technological, environmental, or demographic features, so that several "ecologies" might be identified. Just as different varieties of individual psychology are designated by subclassification according to the analytical purposes at hand (e.g., the various "psychologies" of perception, learning, memory, etc.) one can similarly identify "population ecology" and "organizational ecology."[22]

Now both of the "macrosociological" approaches I have identified can be applied to populations of any size and degree of complexity; that is why I label them "macrosociological" rather than "ecological." Human ecology is only one of a *variety* of conceivable mascrosociological modes of analysis. In fact, one of the major themes in "small group" research and theory is directed toward the analysis of group properties *per se*. For example, the analysis of the interrelations of group size and patterns of internal communication can be conducted from either of these last two perspectives. In addition, of course, sociometric techniques are adaptable to these modes of inquiry; rather than utilizing sociometric observations to identify individuals (as "stars," "isolates," etc.), one simply characterizes whole networks of interaction according to patterns, and then proceeds to deal with these patterns *as properties of aggregates.*[23]

CONCLUSIONS

The four modes of analysis identified here are broad indeed; they crosscut much of social science. For one thing, a single "discipline" may employ all of them at one point or another. And I have already noted that a particular investigator may use all of them in different parts of his work. Even a single study—particularly a comprehensive effort—may employ these different approaches in rapid succession; an outstanding example is the recent study of *Union Democracy* by Lipset, Trow and Coleman.[24] Community studies are particularly prone to make use of all of these devices at one point or another in the analysis. Perhaps there is danger in undisciplined eclecticism, for the analyst may not be aware that he is shifting perspectives, or moving to another level of analysis. Burgess has sounded a clear warning against this hazard:

> It is possible to inquire how ecological processes work, without the necessity of doing research on the social psychological processes. It is also possible to inquire about the social psychological processes, without doing research on the ecological aspects. These are two different ways of looking at human behavior. . . . While it is true that both approaches can be brought together to produce significant findings on particular problems, their joint use should be conscious and deliberate. Many research workers unwittingly mix the two; as a consequence, they make a mess of their studies.[25]

Despite these reservations, however, a single "subject matter" may be greatly illuminated by the use of all four perspectives. To take an area with which I have some acquaintance—population analysis—valuable examples of each type of inquiry can be readily cited. First, there is a substantial literature dealing with the individual physiology and psychology of reproduction, aging, and death; contributions can be found in disciplines located throughout the full range of biology. Secondly, the social-psychological approach is employed with increasing frequency, particularly by students of migration and fertility. There is even an occasional effort to apply the approach that I have labelled "psychological sociology," for some writers have tried to explain certain aspects of the reorganization and redistribution of metropolitan populations by reference to assumed individual propensities.[26] Lastly, there are numerous instances of the "macrosociological"—and particularly the ecological—modes of analysis. For example, a substantial literature has accumulated in which the organizational consequences of variations in population size are examined; a recent and detailed illustration may be found in the work of Duncan and Reiss.[27] Organizational variables are also frequently utilized as explanatory factors in demographic analysis, as in various efforts to account for variations in population composition in terms of the economic base and functional organization of communities.

In summary, I have attempted to identify four more or less distinctive modes of analysis to be found in social science, one of which is the "macrosociological." I have indicated some of the ways in which I see this mode as different from two other major types of inquiry within sociology, and I have suggested that *"human ecology" might be best regarded as a type of "macrosociology."* Its most distinctive feature can perhaps be seen in its adherence to a single level of analysis, in which properties of whole populations are at issue. Although other approaches also take social organization as an independent or dependent variable, this adherence to a consistent level of analysis makes the perspective of human ecology somewhat unusual in the analytical *armamentarium* of the discipline. At the same time, the central role given to organization—as dependent or independent variable—places ecology clearly within the sphere of activities in which sociologists claim distinctive competence, i.e., the analysis of social organization. If human ecology is "marginal" to socology, what is central?

NOTES

[1] Kingsley Davis, "The Myth of Functional Analysis as a Special Method in Sociology and Anthropology," *American Sociological Review*, 24 (1959), p. 758.

[2] *Ibid.*, p. 771.

[3] Arnold M. Rose, *Sociology: The Study of Human Relations* (New York: Knopf, 1956), p. 366.

[4] Alvin Boskoff, "An Ecological Approach to Rural Society," *Rural Sociology*, 14 (1949), p. 308.

[5] Quoted in Howard W. Odum, *American Sociology* (New York: Longmans, Green & Co., 1951), p. 353.

[6] Leo F. Schnore, "Social Morphology and Human Ecology," *American Journal of Sociology*, 63 (1958), pp. 620–634.

[7] Robert N. Bellah, "Durkheim and History," *American Sociological Review*, 24 (1959), p. 461.

[8] James S. Coleman, "The Future of Sociology," a paper presented at the 36th Annual Institute of the Society for Social Research, University of Chicago, May 23, 1959, p. 10.

[9] *Ibid.*, pp. 19–20.

[10] C. Wright Mills, *The Sociological Imagination* (New York: Oxford University Press, 1959), p. 163.

[11] Hans H. Zetterberg, ed., *Sociology in the United States of America* (Paris: UNESCO, 1956); Joseph B. Gittler, ed., *Review of Sociology: Analysis of a Decade* (New York: Wiley, 1957); Robert K. Merton, Leonard Broom, and Leonard S. Cottrell, eds., *Sociology Today: Problems and Prospects* (New York: Basic Books, 1959).

[12] Jack P. Gibbs and Walter T. Martin, "Toward a Theoretical System of Human Ecology," *Pacific Sociological Review*, 2 (1959), pp. 29–36.

[13] Peter H. Rossi, "Comment," *American Journal of Sociology*, 65 (1959), p. 146.

[14] Edward C. Tolman, "The Intervening Variable," in *Psychological Theory*, Melvin N. Marx, ed. (New York: Macmillan, 1951), pp. 88–89.

[15] Louis Wirth, "Urbanism as a Way of Life," *American Journal of Sociology*, 44 (1938), pp. 1–24.

[16] Theodore Newcomb, *Social Psychology* (New York: Dryden Press, 1950), p. 25.

[17] G. E. Swanson, "A Preliminary Laboratory Study of the Acting Crowd," *American Sociological Review*, 18 (1953), p. 522; italics added.

[18] Abram Kardiner, *The Individual and His Society* (New York: Columbia University Press, 1939).

[19] Emile Durkheim, *The Rules of Sociological Method* (Glencoe, Ill.: The Free Press, 1950), p. 110.

[20] For a recent use of the distinction between realism and nominalism, see Kurt H. Wolff, "The Sociology of Knowledge and Sociological Theory," in *Symposium on Sociological Theory*, Llewellyn Gross, ed. (Evanston, Ill.: Row, Peterson, 1959), pp. 557–602.

[21] Amos H. Hawley, *Human Ecology: A Theory of Community Structure* (New York: Ronald Press, 1950).

[22] Jack P. Gibbs and Walter T. Martin, "Urbanization and Natural Resources: A Study in Organizational Ecology," *American Sociological Review*, 23 (1958), pp. 266–277.

[23] One would hesitate to call such sociometric inquiries "ecological," and to regard small-group interests as "macrosociological," but the fundamental similarity in approach is noteworthy, despite the strain placed on the language. Perhaps "holistic" versus "atomistic" would provide a more clearcut set of alternatives; this possibility was suggested by Professor Duncan in a private communication. With him, I am inclined to reserve the term "human ecology" for efforts to understand the interconnections between variations in population, organization, environment, and technology in the context of such macroscopic *units* as communities, regions, and societies. See Otis Dudley Duncan, "Human Ecology and Population Studies," in *The Study of Population*, Phillip M. Hauser and Otis Dudley Duncan, eds. (Chicago: University of Chicago Press, 1959), pp. 678–716; and Otis Dudley Duncan and Leo F. Schnore, "Cultural, Behavioral, and Ecological Perspectives in the Study of Social Organization," *American Journal of Sociology*, 65 (1959), pp. 132–146.

[24] S. M. Lipset, Martin A. Trow, and James S. Coleman, *Union Democracy* (Glencoe, Ill.: The Free Press, 1957).

[25] Ernest W. Burgess, "The Ecology and Social Psychology of the City," in *Needed Urban and Metropolitan Research*, Donald J. Bogue, ed. (Oxford, Ohio, and Chicago: Scripps Foundation for Research in Population Problems, and Population Research and Training Center, University of Chicago, 1953), p. 80.

[26] Wendell Bell, "Familism and Suburbanization: One Test of the Social Choice Hypothesis," *Rural Sociology*, 21 (1956), pp. 276–283; Sylvia Fleis Fava, "Suburbanism as a Way of Life," *American Sociological Review*, 21 (1956), pp. 34–37.

[27] Otis Dudley Duncan and Albert J. Reiss, Jr., *Social Characteristics of Urban and Rural Communities*, 1950 (New York: Wiley, 1956).

PART II

*Theoretical Constructs
and Research Strategies*

CHAPTER ONE
Critical Concepts
in Sociological Analysis

COMMENTARY

We cherish the conception of ourselves as individuals, different from our neighbors and friends. Indeed, we are individuals, unique and new in the world. Perhaps because each of us lives his life encased, so to speak, in a private world influenced by a distinctive heritage and set of experiences, it is difficult to accept the idea that much of the behavior of men can be understood and explained without reference to individual motives, needs, aspirations, or attitudes. But when one gives it some thought, it is equally difficult to conceive of man apart from other men—apart from the social milieu in which he lives. There are few hermits among us. Thus, to say that man is a social being is to say that his attitudes and behavior are influenced and modified, at least in part, by his social environment and that much of that behavior and those attitudes can be interpreted without reference to the unique individual.

All disciplines seek to simplify and abstract from the complexity of concrete reality. And it is the manner in which this is accomplished, the nature of the abstractions and the assumptions underlying them, which in large measure accounts for the distinctive orientations of different disciplines. In addition, the questions addressed in theory and research serve to delimit disciplinary boundaries, but the questions which can be asked are shaped by the concepts employed and the assumptions (often implicit) which underly them.

Although in some sense the sociologist always deals with the behavior of individuals, he does so by understanding the situation in which the individual is found. Thus, the sociologist seeks to understand and explain those aspects of the behavior and attitudes of individuals which can be attributed to the constraining effects of the external environment and without reference to individual psychology. This is the essence of the Durkheimian dictum that social facts are to be explained with reference to social facts.

In their attempts to understand the intricacies of the structuring of relations among men, the patterning of their behavior, and the etiology and effects of their attitudes, sociologists have formulated a set of critical concepts and have employed these concepts in a distinctive manner. Some of the papers included in this section seek to explicate one or more of these concepts. Others illustrate their application in sociological research and theory.

The papers by Ferenc Merei and Robert Bierstedt deal with the concepts of individual and group. In attempting to formulate a sociology of majorities, Bierstedt examines the concept of the group. He is led to a critical review of the development and use of the concept of group. As a part of this effort he enumerates criteria for distinguishing groups from other collectivities.

In examining the relationship between leader and group, in "Group Leadership and Institutionalization," Merei focuses on an elusive aspect of group membership—the individual is strengthened by his association with others and at the same time he finds himself subservient to the group as a whole. On the basis of his research Merei concludes that the group has a uniqueness which transcends the mere aggregation of its individual members, that the group is more than the sum of its parts.

Dealing with phenomena far removed from the nursery school setting explored by Merei, Earl Raab and Seymour Lipset also address the question of the relation of the individual and the group. They do this in an attempt to understand the etiology and persistence of prejudice and to account for the situational modification of individual attitudes and actions. Raab and Lipset aptly illustrate some of the negative consequences attributable to the coercive effects of the perpetuation of group traditions—in this instance the tradition of prejudice.

Analysis of the structure and functioning of personality usually is thought to be the domain of clinical psychology. However, as Leo Schnore noted in "The Myth of Human Ecology" reprinted above, some sociologists do engage in work which deals with the ways in which society affects personality. Ralph Turner, in his paper "The Problems of Social Dimensions in Personality," suggests how the sociologist might make contributions to the study of personality organization.

In contrast to personality which has as its referent the person or individual, the concept of role implies social relationship. Although sociologists differ as to whether they define role as a set of norms which organize behavior, or as normatively ordered behavior, they agree that what is of concern is the patterning of the behavior of one social actor vis-à-vis other social actors. The work of George Herbert Mead has had a major influence on sociologists concerned with role analysis. In the selection reprinted here he implies that, by taking the role of others in social situations, the person learns what others expect of him and what his obligations are in a given situation. Mead suggests that when the person internalizes the attitudes and values of the social group, his behavior is normatively controlled and the self is fully developed.

Collective social life is possible because of the existence and effects of a normative order. The patterning, regularity, and repetitiveness of human behavior, unlike the instinctual behavior of animals, are due in large measure to the constraints imposed by norms and values. Moreover, the cultural differences characteristic of men located in different social orders result from differences in the prevailing norms and values.

In "Sponsored and Contest Mobility and the School System," Ralph Turner emphasizes the critical role played by the distinctive mobility norms and values in American and English society for the structure of education in each. Milton Yinger, on the other hand, is concerned with the misuse of the concept of subculture. In his article "Subculture and Contraculture," he urges the refinement of the concept of subculture. He proposes the adoption of a new term, *contraculture*, to account for situations in which "the normative system of a group contains . . . a theme of conflict with the values of the total society."

Thus, whereas Turner deals with differences in the norms and values of two societies, Yinger focuses on variations in adherence to norms and values by different segments within a single society.

| Critical Concepts in Sociological Analysis | INDIVIDUAL AND GROUP |

3 Ferenc Merei

Group Leadership and Institutionalization

PRELIMINARIES TO THE EXPERIMENT

The problem we set ourselves concerns the relationship between leader and group. To tackle it, we took the following steps.

Children suitable to form a group were selected. Previous observation showed that from the age of 5 upward, in spontaneously formed groups the sexes as a rule do not mix. Hence, the groups had to be homogeneous as to sex. They had to be homogeneous as to age, too, because, as our observations showed, in spontaneous groupings the age differences seldom exceed two years. Homogeneity was desirable also regarding the

Reprinted from *Human Relations*, 2:1 (1949), pp. 23–39, by permission of Tavistock Publications, Ltd. The material contained in this article appeared in a larger Hungarian publication by the author, and with the author's consent was translated and prepared in its present form by Mrs. David Rappaport for *Human Relations*.

ties between members, e.g., children had to be chosen who had no strong likes or dislikes for one another. Finally, for the most pertinent purpose of our experiment, we tried to select children with an average capacity for leadership and social influence.

To rate the individual on these scores, we made some preliminary observations. We saw the children of two day nurseries for 35 to 40 minutes each day for a period of two weeks. Two people worked simultaneously and afterward unified their notes. The observations were not selective: everything that occurred in the nursery during that period was chronologically and fully recorded. On the basis of these observations we picked out those children whose social qualities were an average for that nursery group and who were *not* leaders. Children were selected in whom the frequency of: (1) "following orders" greatly outnumbered "giving orders"; (2) imitation outnumbered being imitated; (3) participation in group play was an average in number as well as in degree of cooperation; and (4) acts of attacking, crying, telling on each other, were about the average of the group. Furthermore, their ties to one another had to be no more solid or lasting than to other members of the nursery.

The children were formed into a group.   An assembly was considered a group when it developed a relatedness, with permanent rules, habits, traditions, entirely of its own.

The children chosen were put in a separate room. Their field was permanent: the same set of furniture, toys, and tools every day. In this room they spent 30 to 40 minutes each day. Their actions were fully recorded by two observers who later synchronized and combined their notes. The observers were completely passive.

The group thus met until a tendency to "institutionalization" became noticeable, and their habits and traditions appeared to become lasting. Only such habits were considered traditions as were not found in the day nurseries, but had developed during the experimental period. This gave us an objective criterion of the point at which an assembly constituted a group. To form a tradition from three to six meetings were needed.

The children formed traditions such as permanent seating order (who should sit where); permanent division of objects (who plays with what); group ownership of certain objects, ceremonies connected with their use, expressions of belonging together; returning to certain activities; rituals; sequence of games; forming a group jargon out of expressions accidentally uttered, etc.

A leader was placed in the group so formed.   The leader was chosen from the same day nursery. He was a child who the nursery-school teachers —they had spent many days with him—considered to have initiative and directing power, who was older than the members of the group, and who, during the preliminary observation, more often gave than followed orders, more often was imitated than imitating, and more often was the attacker than the attacked.

Thus the leader was chosen because he was older, domineering, imitated, aggressive rather than submissive, and because he had initiative.

After the group had formed fixed traditions we added such a leader. The place, the objects remained the same. Recording went on as before.

What did we expect to learn from the experiment thus set up? Our question was: Do group habits and traditions change with the appearance of a leader? Does the leader introduce new habits, and does the group accept them? Does the group follow the leader, or does it force its traditions upon him? We see the group through its traditions—the objective expressions of the existing relationship. Hence, the vector of forces between the stronger leader and the group of weaker individuals is determined not by *who* gives the orders but by *what* the orders are. The question is not whether they accept leadership, but whether they give up their traditions by accepting what the leader initiates, whether they form new habits, rules, traditions, under his influence.

By carrying out this experiment we hoped to get the answer to our question.

THE EXPERIMENTAL PLAN

The experimental plan used the method of *varying the situation*. Individuals who scored high on leadership were observed in three situations: (1) in a larger group, where the members had no particular relationship with each other and where the leader's influence was felt by the group as a whole; (2) in a more closely knit group of the presocial stage formed through evolving group traditions; and (3) in a group with strong traditions of its own, facing a leader stronger than any one group member.

To record the entire process, we needed an adequate technique. We evolved a system of 76 symbols, each representing one complex act. The five people taking the notes synchronized them at 5-minute intervals.

Further variation was afforded through the objects in the room. By giving as many toys as there were children, we weakened group activity, since each could find something to do. By giving one object only we strengthened group activity, since all had to congregate around it. Setting a concrete task also strengthened the group. If an object familiar only to the leader was given, he was strengthened and the group weakened.

The choice of objects offers further possible variations which we have not sufficiently explored as yet.

We tried out many objects. Finally, the younger children (4 to 7 years) were given a tin toy house and a box of building blocks, the older ones (8 to 11 years) cardboard, picture magazines, scissors, crayons, paste, and paint brushes, and the instruction, "We want to make an exhibition." Of the latter objects there were fewer than there were children in the group, so that some manner of collaboration was required.

Most groups consisted of three children plus the leader, with some groups of four and six as well. The number chosen was determined by previous observations which showed that spontaneously formed groups, up to the age of 7, lasted longer when consisting of three to four children, and, between the ages of 7 and 10, of three to six children. Larger groups easily disintegrated.

We worked with twelve groups. In them we tried out the power of penetration of twenty-six children capable of leadership. The ages of all children ranged from 4 to 11 years. The difference within a group never exceeded two years. In every case but one the leader was older than any group member.

THE CONQUERED CONQUEROR

Let us now see the results of this experiment.

To summarize schematically, the same definite tendencies could be observed in all the experimental units: the group absorbed the leader, forcing its traditions on him. The leader takes over the habits and traditions of children who are younger than himself and who in the day nursery had been his underlings following his guidance. Now he engages in those activities which the group had developed before he entered it. His own undertakings either remain unsuccessful or gain acceptance only in a modified form suiting the traditions of that group.

Examples from our material demonstrate the point.

Table 1 will be understood from the following definitions:

Modeling is one of the most important types of social behavior. When a child's act or behavior is spontaneously imitated by some others, the child, we say, is *modeling*. When a child, even if unintentionally, imitates another—as members of a group do to take over each other's mode of behavior and thereby form common habits—we say that he is *being modeled*. We avoid the word "imitation" because it has a connotation of intention.

The ratio of *modeling* to *be modeled* is a measure of the social penetrating power of a person.

Table 1 shows the ratio *modeling/being modeled* of four children (Nos. 13, 15, 25, 10). In the day nursery all four tended to follow some model,

TABLE 1. MODELING : BEING MODELED

Subject no.	In day nursery	In the experimental situation	
		Without leader	With leader
13	3:4	17:5	10:5
15	1:4	3:8	1:2
25	1:5	1:11	3:4
10	2:8	0:2	0:3
20 (leader)	6:3		5:11

rather than to serve as a model to others. It was for just this behavior that we selected them.

When they became members of a separate group forming its own traditions, a change occurred: one of the four children (No. 13) took on the modeling role, while the others went on being modeled.

It was after this change had taken place that the leader (No. 20) joined the group. In the day nursery he did the modeling: he served as a model six times, but followed another model only three times, making this ratio of social penetration 6:3. (Column 2 "In day nursery" shows an inverse ratio for all the others in this group.)

In the experimental situation—when the leader was confronted with a developed group—his ratio changed: his power of social penetration diminished. Formerly he was *modeling* (6:3), but now he was being *modeled* (5:11)—that is, the others did not take over his mode of action, but he took over the habits developed by the group. In other words, he followed those who in the day nursery had followed him.

In other groups and with other leaders a similar tendency was observed. The ratio *modeling/being modeled* of an extremely influential and willful leader in the day nursery changed from 9:5 to 0:8. For another such child the ratio changed from 6:2 to 1:6.

This portion of our results shows that, in a group possessing traditions, the leader introduced does not become the source of new habits and rules; rather, he will be the one to take over existing group traditions and thus to follow a model. This happens in spite of the fact that in the larger social formation (day nursery) he had served as a model to every member of the group.

Since "forming traditions" was our criterion of social influence, we came to the conclusion that, *confronted by a group having its own traditions, the leader proves weak; this in spite of the fact that when confronting them singly he is stronger than any one member of the group—stronger precisely as to his social penetrating power.*

PLAY OF FORCES

The last paragraph is only a schematic summary of our results. Reality is richer and more varied; what we see in reality is a wide variety of *tendencies*—a pull of the group force facing other pulls in other directions.

What does this mean? Though the group generally assimilates the leader, we find that it does so only on certain conditions and within certain limits. We find that the leading personality, while accepting the traditions and habits of the group, also influences and changes them. Let us then inquire into the modes of this influence, into the conditions which allow the assimilated leader to become that group's leader.

On the twenty-six leaders of the experiment the group force acted in varied ways.

At one extreme is the case where the group entirely assimilated the child who previously showed definite capacity to lead. This occurred in a group that possessed particularly strict traditions, and had well established and meticulously carried out rituals of activity. One such group played with a doll house and two dolls. In the course of three play periods they worked out a ritual of activity of playing around the house and of taking the dolls for a walk. The leader, one and a half years their senior, joining the group at its fourth meeting, tried to introduce something new (fourth and fifth play periods). He suggested a circle game and group singing. He was not followed. When he started singing alone they followed him for a few moments, then returned to their old game. The third time he came (sixth play period), the leader joined in the group's original game. Only for a few moments, here and there, did he start new activities, but he was followed by no one. At the seventh and eighth play periods no sign was left that this child had once (before these same children had developed a group habit) been a leader among them.

At the other extreme is the case of the child who proved to be stronger than the group: he broke its traditions. There was one such case. The leader, a little girl (a year and a half older than the members) completely reorganized the group. She gave orders, she modeled, she decided what to do and how to play. The rules she introduced took the place of those the group had had.

This group's history is important: it was subjected to increasing difficulties, while the leader was given virtual training in leadership. After the group had formed its habits, each day a different leader was introduced. In three days three different leaders tried to foist their initiative upon it and to change its rituals. Against these three leaders the group was able to preserve its customs, rejecting their suggestions, in the face of all the enticing and aggression these leaders tried out on it. However, the struggle exhausted the group and it began to weaken. This weakening showed itself in that the children more often played by themselves, less often played their old organized games, playing instead merely side by side. The traditions were still formally there, but the members of the group tended to observe them singly, by themselves. The group lost much of its coherence.

These are borderline cases. *In the overwhelming majority of our cases the leader was forced to accept the group's traditions—that is, he proved weaker than the group but still managed to play the role of leader.* We observed each leader's ways of doing this.

1. *The Order-giver* The group whose data on "modeling" and "being modeled" were given above had fully developed customs when the leader was introduced. The new boy, older, more experienced, and more of a leader than any member of the group, attempted to take over. He gave orders, made suggestions, bossed everybody. The children carefully avoided him, ignored his orders, and carried on in their traditions.

Soon the leader found himself alone. Suddenly his behavior changed, he joined the group in its activities and quickly learned its rituals. He learned their expressions, their habits, their games. During his second play period with them, he again gave orders. Though keeping within the frame of activities he had just learned from them, and according to their rules, he told the children what to do—that is, he ordered them to do exactly what they would have done anyway. He appropriated the leadership without being able to change the group's traditions. The members accepted this situation by following his orders, since this did not change their habitual activities.

The data on the frequency of group activity shows this. Table 2 contains the proportion of *order-giving* to *order-following*.

TABLE 2.   ORDER-GIVING : ORDER-FOLLOWING

Experimental subject no.	In day nursery	In experimental situation	
		Without leader	With leader
13	3:5	3:6	1:4
15	1:2	8:1	0:2
25	1:4	0:2	2:5
10	2:3	0:3	0:3
20	12:2		11:3

Four members of the group (Nos. 13, 15, 25, 10) were *order-followers* in the day nursery. After they had formed a separate homogeneous group, one of them (No. 15) became an *order-giver*. When group habits were developed and a leader (No. 20) was added, all followed the leader's orders, as in the day nursery. In the group with a tradition, the leader became just as much of an order-giver (11:3) as he was in the day nursery (12:2). Regarding order-giving, then, the leader was stronger than the group (he gave orders—they accepted them). At the same time, however, he was the one to copy the others, he took over their ways (his modeling proportion changed from 6:3 to 5:11).

If a person should observe the group for only a short period of time, for example by the Goodenough 1-minute or 5-minute method, he would see a leader giving orders and a group obeying. A prolonged observation of the group plus its history would, however, soon disclose the inner workings of this *order-giving*: the leader gives such orders as have reference to the group's traditional activities; he expropriates the leadership without changing the group's traditional modes of activity.

The leader is weaker than the group because he takes over its traditions and because his own suggestions do not take root. At the same time he is also stronger because everyone follows his orders.

The gist of the phenomenon lies just in this dichotomy.

The leader is stronger than any one group member. (He gives orders —they obey.) He is weaker than *group traditions* and is forced to accept them. He is stronger than the individual member, weaker than the "plus" which a group is over and above the sum of the individuals in it. He is stronger than the members, weaker than the formation.

In the relationship between group and leader, two factors stand out: (1) the group as a particular order of quality, whose strength is expressed by the change of the leader's modeling proportion (from 6:3 to 5:11); and (2) the members, whose *weakness* is expressed by the constancy (12:2 to 11:3) of the leader's ratio of *order-giving/order-following.*

Thus the curious situation obtains where the order-giver imitates, while the models follow the orders of their imitator.

What appears here is the "group plus"—the unique reality of a group —experimentally verified.

2. *The Proprietor* A second way in which leadership may express itself is ownership: the leader joining the developed group takes possession of all the objects in the room. They continue being used according to group tradition; the games played with them remain the same. The leader joins in these games, but all the objects "belong" to him. Table 3 presents the data on this phenomenon, concerning the group discussed before.

TABLE 3. FREQUENCY OF OBJECT APPROPRIATION
(Borrows or takes away from another child)

	In the experimental situation	
Experimental subject no.	Without leader	With leader
13	21	1
15	9	0
25	7	1
10	3	1
20		12

The frequency of taking possession of objects sharply falls for group members, and rises for the leader.

Into some groups, after traditions had been formed, outstanding leading personalities were placed—leaders obeyed in the day nursery by everyone, virtual dictators to more than thirty children. Let us follow one of them. If a child's behavior displeased him, he beat up that child; he allowed no opposition, and always had to have his way. The group into which he was put consisted of children younger than himself, children who in the day nursery always obeyed him. The result was unexpected: this structured group virtually swallowed him. (His proportion of modeling changed from 9:5 to 0:8.) He followed the group's every activity, accepted its every custom, while his own suggestions were *never* followed.

However, his exceptional personality still asserted itself with the group. The children gave him every object without his asking, and with that acknowledged his authority. The group had two traditional activities: using blocks they built a train, and using chairs they built a bridge. The leader soon learned these constructions and used the objects acquired to build just these. From time to time the group gathered around him, eloquently praising whatever he did. They praised his beautiful creation, his skill, the wonderful things he made (which he had learned from them), as if to placate some dangerous genie. At the same time they followed him in nothing; on the contrary they drew him into their own activities and caused him to accept their habits. Their play remained unchanged; the same game with the same toys. They talked of the toys as they did before—Johnny's blocks, Tom's box—but occasionally they said: "The blocks belong to Andrew" (Andrew was the leader), or: "Tom's box belongs to Andrew." The owners of the objects became their users, while the right of ownership was given over, voluntarily or otherwise, to the new leader.

Observation over only a short period would lead to mistaken conclusions. One might see only that one child has all the toys, while the others surround and admire him. Only prolonged observation would show that those are but scenes of ceremonial offerings with which the children purchase, as it were, the leader's continued trust, with which they protect their traditions.

Again we see that apparently the leader is stronger than *the members* of the group (he appropriates their belongings), but weaker than *the group* because he is forced to accept its customs, traditions, and forms of activity.

3. *The Diplomat* The third way of asserting leadership, as observed in our experimental situation, is quite devious. The cases belonging here are peculiar. The leader, having a greater force of social penetration than the group members, attempts to force upon them a new mode of activity. He fails. However, the leader, for reasons as yet unclear to us—perhaps because of the tense situation—does not get lost in the group, nor take over its habits, as did those leaders who complied in order to rule or in order to take possession of the toys.

This type of leader takes a roundabout course: he accepts the traditions of the group in order to change them.

Into old forms he pours new contents. What takes place here is a veritably dramatic struggle. We had one group with particularly strong traditions and institutionalization. This group rose to the highest level of spontaneous organization of games: to the level of division of roles.

One of the children, who in the day nursery showed no leadership, in this narrower group developed into a leader: games he suggested were followed, and their various parts become traditional with the group. It was at this point that a new leader was added. He tried to suggest new games but was not accepted. Then he joined their traditional game and slowly took over the leadership. The first day there were only two instances in which he led, the second day there were already nine. However, he was the one being modeled, taking over the group's habits. He accepted those habits but introduced minute changes. For example, he joined in the block game traditional with the group, but he demanded that always the red side of a block be on top. He was being modeled, he imitated, but he also introduced changes; then he became the leader of the traditional activities thus changed.

The third time he was with the group he again suggested new activities. One was "hide and seek." (They had a game involving hiding, and this feature attracted the leader.) The group did not accept the suggestion and played instead another traditional game they called "acting with hats."

The leader yielded, joined the "hat game" and instantly began to organize it, in the course of which he made changes so as to combine with it the hide-and-seek game he had suggested. He was *being modeled* to the group, but he also *modeled* the group; he accepted their traditions but changed them.

His roundabout road to leadership is clear here:

1. *He tries to do away with the group traditions and lead it on to new ones.*
2. *He is rejected.*
3. *He accepts the traditions and quickly learns them.*
4. *Within the frame of those traditions he soon assumes leadership, and, though reluctantly, the group follows him because he does a good job.*
5. *He introduces insignificant variations, loosening the tradition.*
6. *He then introduces new elements into the ritual already weakened by variation.*

In this case accepting the traditions is a roundabout way to introducing new ones. This is a very active process in which the leader plays an important role. Only children with exceptional social influence and a great deal of initiative could act this way.

Thus, between the extremes of total assimilation and total conquest, we find three types of behavior. In the experimental situation the leader either (1) is being modeled—but gives orders; or (2) is being modeled —but obtains possession of the toys; or again (3) is being modeled—but he also models the others.

It has to be emphasized that in all these cases the leader must accept the traditions and can give orders only within their framework. The following is a nice example: into a well-developed group of children, 4 to 5 years old, a leader of 6½ with a strong personality was introduced. The group had traditional ways of using the toys. It was exactly determined who would play with what. Each toy, though they might exchange them for a while, traditionally constituted the possession of a certain child.

The leader was unable to change this rule of ownership. Yet he found himself a place in the system. At the beginning of the play period he distributed the objects, giving each child the one that "belonged to him." The children continued to ask the "owners" for the blocks or boxes when they wanted to play with them; they continued to exchange toys as before. Only now the blocks, house, or boxes were distributed by the leader at the beginning of the period. Thus he found himself a role in an order which was there when he first arrived, though unable essentially to change the existing traditions.

THE FORMING OF TRADITION

We have examined the influence of the group on a new leader. We have seen that the group forces its traditions on the leader; and that with varying circumstances the process involves changes while the basic tendency remains the same. We have seen that the capitulating leader still makes his superior personality felt. Even though he accepts the group's traditions, he exerts an influence. Even in the case of total assimilation of the leader we find changes in the group's life which can be ascribed to his influence.

For example, one group always built trains out of blocks. The leader followed this activity. He too built trains, only he put a chimney on his locomotive. The others followed suit.

Another group's traditional game was to climb up and hang on to the top edge of a wardrobe and to swing there. The leader—of the type that gives orders but is being modeled—soon joined the game. Only one child at a time could swing on the wardrobe. On each side stood a chair to climb up on. Shortly after the leader joined the group he introduced a "one-way traffic." Everything went on as before with the exception that the children had to climb up one side and down the other. This innovation added color to the game without changing its structure. Such phenomena occurred often. Almost every leader, just as soon as he met the group, reorganized it, introducing direction and order.

In other cases this coloring lent by the leader pertained rather to the contents, as when a fitting little story was introduced. One group that played with a small house said: "This is the mailman's house—in the evening he comes home—in the morning he leaves." In the game itself there was no mailman. The children put nothing into the house. The mailman was not even symbolically represented. The words were merely additional coloring. On this the leader elaborated: "The mailman brings coal —they put it on wagons and trucks, etc." The others took over these little themes and their activity, though undamaged, became more colorful.

Often the leader would step up the pace of activity. This is another way to impose his will on the group. He would dictate a very fast tempo, driving them. A certain type of leader needed to create this acceleration of pace: a child who is very active, who has many interests, whose attention is divided, and who has a stormy temperament. Such leaders busy themselves with several things at once, join several games at once, and with their "swing" accelerate the group's life.

An interesting influence of the leader is the *widening of the terrain*. The group's accustomed space becomes larger: a group that has worked in one portion of the room will, after the leader appears, expand into the entire room. The way this occurs clearly shows the relationship between a developed group and a new leader.

One group would play around a table in the middle of the room. From time to time they would go to the wardrobe in one corner of the room and try to climb up. Then the new leader appropriated the table, whereupon a migration to the wardrobe took place where they started the game of climbing up. The leader followed them and started organizing that game. Slowly the children shifted back to the table, but the leader was on their trail. The result was a pendulum-like movement between table and wardrobe. Then one child went to a new place and started doing something there. At once the leader extended his pendulum motion to that place. A veritable pilgrimage began. Everywhere the leader was being modeled: he was the one who adjusted to the others' mode of activity.

Another frequent influence of the leader is that he changes the degree of concerted action. The degree of group action is not to be confused with the degree of creative activity of a person. When a presocial formation of four people sit together, one reading a philosophical treatise, the other solving a mathematical problem, the third writing an ode, etc., without having anything in common with each other, the group is of a lower social level than a foursome playing bridge.

During our investigations we observed that in some cases the leader brings a presocial group to a higher degree of concerted action, in other cases to a lower one. If, for example, a group that has merely congregated around a set of toys is organized into one with a division of roles, the group level has been raised. It will be lowered if group activity is reduced to mere side-by-side play. Such raising or lowering of group level depends mostly on the personal qualities of the leader, especially on his capacity to organize. The capacity consists of the bent to remember every custom, to see to it that objects are returned where they belong and that the rituals are observed, even if these were learned from the group. The leader who has this quality raises the group level even if he totally submits to the group's traditions.

THE POWER OF THE GROUP

Our question was: Which is stronger, the group made up of individuals of average social penetration, or the individual of high degree of social penetration but alien to the group?

Our criterion was, not the relationship between the new leader and the individual group members, but that "plus" arising from "groupness" which raises the power of the group above the aggregate strength of its members. This "plus" shows in the habits, customs, rules, and relationships making for institutionalization. Accordingly, the individual is the stronger of the two if he can change those traditions; but the group is the stronger if it assimilates the leader.

Couching our inquiry in these terms lent decisive importance to the ratio *modeling/being modeled.*

Our investigations have shown that the group with a tradition is stronger than the leader (though he is stronger than any one group member).

The play of forces between leader and group resulted in the following graduations:

1. The leader is totally assimilated;
2. The leader is being modeled but gives orders;
3. The leader is being modeled but gains possession of the toys;
4. The leader is being modeled but modifies the traditions;
5. The leader destroys the group's traditions and introduces new ones. It is rare that the leader should become not only the center of the group but also the maker of its rules.

Which of these five situations will obtain depends on:

1. The degree of crystallization of traditions;
2. The extent of collaborative play;
3. The degree of group cohesion (the marginal child included).

These conditions issue from the nature of the group. It is no doubt important what kind of person, what character type the new leader is. It may be that in the child who expropriates the toys in order to set himself up as leader a desire for acquisition asserts itself; it may be that the child who gives orders is driven by narcissism and aggression. However, our investigation did not extend to these motivations.

Even the leader who is forced to accept existing traditions makes his superiority felt: he may lend color to activities, step up the pace, widen the field, or change the group level by influencing cohesion.

In our experiment, individuals of strong social penetrating power seldom became changers of traditions; however, being modeled to the existing traditions, they influenced them.

We were thus able to experience that "plus" which makes the group more than and different from the aggregate of its members: as in cases where the new leader conquered everyone, where each child followed his orders—as long as *what* he ordered was in agreement with the group's traditions.

It is in this peculiar strength of tradition that this group "plus" appears. Its carriers are the individuals constituting the group. By belonging to the group each is "more" and stronger. This became clear when children who in the day nursery were *being modeled* by leaders there, became the models of these leaders in the organized group.

Thus the group "plus" is not some substance hovering above the group; it is the hold their customs and habits have on the members; it is tradition, the carrier of which is the individual, who, in turn, is strengthened by it. Conceivably, the feeling of heightened intensity always evoked by group experience is the experiencing of just this "plus."

Why does the leader accept the group's traditions? Is it because he is weaker than its members, or more suggestible? No. We have seen him in the day nursery, modeling the others. Is it because he is in a new situation where the group members have the advantage of being familiar with the situation? This is contraindicated by the behavior of leaders who give orders quite without inhibition. The dichotomy is clear: the leader is supraordinated since he gives orders; but he is also subordinated since he is being modeled. He has the upper hand *vis-à-vis* the members but has to bow to group tradition.

Thus the reaction of the group to the new leader clearly brings into view the power of the group "plus." It is this "plus" that is stronger than the leader who is stronger than any one group member.

With this we can discard all hypotheses which deny the uniqueness of the group, and which attempt fully to account for the group by assessing its members.

Our experiment refutes the prejudice of metaphysical social psychology that the group, through an evening effect, lowers the level of the individual. We observed exactly the opposite: the strength of the group strengthens its members. Group experience not only pleases, it also strengthens.

4 Robert Bierstedt

The Sociology of Majorities

A casual but not uninterested observer of the current sociological scene could not fail to notice the serious concern within the field for problems of minorities and minority groups. If he pauses to reflect upon this phenomenon the thought may occur to him that nowhere is there a similar or even comparable concern for majorities and majority groups. Systematic treatments of this latter subject are distinguished by their scarcity, and this may seem doubly strange in view of the fact that some of the societies in which sociology has reached its highest development accept as almost axiomatic the political principle of majority rule.

The proposition that majorities have been neglected requires no more than negative evidence. Even those sociologists like Simmel,[1] von Wiese,[2] and MacIver,[3] who have touched upon the subject, have done so largely in a political rather than a sociological context.[4] Without implying that political and sociological concerns are mutually exclusive, it may nevertheless be suggested that the latter might be broader in significance than the former and may present issues which a political emphasis obscures.

Reprinted from *American Sociological Review*, 13:5 (1948), pp. 700–710, by permission of the author and the publisher.

Some of these issues we should expect to see treated in sociography. When we turn to the sociology of groups, however, a subject which has properly been regarded as of central and indeed of pivotal concern,[5] we find an almost infinite number of classifications of types of groups, but no mention of majorities. There are open groups and closed groups, organized groups and unorganized groups, primary groups and secondary groups, "A" groups and "B" groups, in-groups and out-groups, "real" groups and "nominal" groups, horizontal groups and vertical groups, voluntary groups and involuntary groups, large groups and small groups, long-lived groups and short-lived groups, "unibonded" groups and "multibonded" groups, and many others in terms of sociological form, and others still, such as age, sex, ethnic, occupational, economic, educational, class, religious, linguistic, territorial, and so on,[6] in terms of sociological content.[7] In all these classifications the majority-minority distinction is conspicuous by its absence. If not in sociography at least in the general texts on sociology one would expect the majority-minority distinction to have achieved some prominence, particularly in view of the heavy emphasis upon minorities, but again the distinction fails to appear, and there is no discussion of majorities as such. Finally, one would expect to find treatments of majorities in texts on social control, but once again a cursory examination leaves the expectation unfulfilled.[8] Social control is treated almost exclusively in terms of such cultural factors as folkways, mores, institutions, laws, and so on, rather than in terms of such social factors as the influence of majorities. It is almost as if sociologists had unanimously agreed to leave the subject of majorities to the devices of political scientists.

The subject, however, is worth considering for several reasons. The first of these is that number is a necessary category in sociology and that phenomena of many different kinds change not only in degree but also in their nature as they vary in size. Certainly small groups, for example, are different from large groups in other ways than that the former are small, the latter large.[9] In like manner, majorities differ from minorities in other ways than that they are larger, and it is these other ways that it is instructive to analyze. Differences of this kind have an intrinsic sociological interest and, difficult as they may be to discern, comprise an integral part of group theory. In this connection von Wiese has the following comment:

> It is difficult to assign the proper place to the concepts of majority and minority. They are primarily expressions of a purely numerical relation, and they therefore belong among the other colorless terms here discussed [swarm, band, pack, and herd]. The social relationships between majority and minority, however, play an extremely important part in many plurality patterns. . . . The circumstance that these two categories taken in conjunction denote a proportion and not a mere summation makes them sociologically important. Majority and minority are not primarily or unusually plurality patterns, but in certain situations they may become groups, and hence should receive attention for this reason as well.[10]

Secondly, it is apparent that the majority-minority distinction differs in principle from distinctions based upon number and size. As von Wiese says in the passage quoted immediately above, a proportion is different from a summation. Groups of whatever size differ from other groups of the same size when the former are majorities and the latter are not. Furthermore, it is obvious that a majority may be relatively small, a minority relatively large, although not, of course, when they are in opposition in the same context. It is also obvious that majorities may vary considerably in size, in relation to their conjoint minorities, without ceasing to be majorities. In a group of 100, 51 and 99 both constitute majorities. For these reasons the majority-minority distinction is not comprehended by any other formal categories of groups and the distinction is, in fact, unique.

In the third place, majorities and minorities are universal in all societies and in all groups, except those which have an even number of members evenly divided and those which are unanimous. In all complex societies, where integration is imperfect and unanimity nonexistent, majorities and minorities are constant phenomena.

A fourth reason for studying majorities has both theoretical and practical consequences, and the latter outweigh the former. For it has often been observed by writers concerned with oppressed minorities that the problems are essentially not minority problems at all, but majority problems. Writers on the Negro in the United States, for example, and especially Myrdal, have insisted that there is no such thing as a Negro problem, that the problem is actually a "white" problem. In a sense, of course, this is only a manner of speaking, but there can be no doubt that the problem, whether Negro or white, would have a dramatically different impact upon American life if (1) the Negro population were not so large as it is, (2) the Negro population were not so small as it is, (3) the white population comprised not a majority but a dominant minority, (4) the Negro population were the same size but comprised a dominant minority, (5) Northern whites were not a majority and Southern whites not a minority, and so on through many diverse combinations. Whatever the way in which the issue is phrased, it is easy to agree that there is something about majorities which causes and creates minority problems and that a knowledge of the nature and characteristics of the former may contribute to an understanding of the latter. We know, for example, that people become prejudiced not through contact with minority (i.e., oppressed) groups, but through contact with prevailing attitudes toward minority groups.[11] Attitudes "prevail" in a society when they are held by majorities.

Finally, as suggested above, a sociological approach to the subject of majorities may assist in discerning attributes and properties which are not insignificant for the purposes of political science and which tend to be obscured in the latter approach. It may be suggested, for example, that political majorities and what we are unfortunately forced to call societal majorities (i.e., the majority of all people in a society) do not necessarily coincide, either in personnel or in political predilections. Even under conditions of universal suffrage a political majority may represent only a small societal minority. Of even greater significance, however, is the fact that majorities have so often been conceived of in purely political terms that the broader sociological nature of the subject has suffered neglect. Political majorities are only one kind of majority and, even if they are the most important kind, it does not follow that other kinds are unimportant. Nor does it follow that the nature and characteristics of majorities in general can be discerned in an investigation of political majorities or, for that matter, of any particular kind of majority. In other words, as in most cases affecting the relationships between sociology and the other social sciences, certain phenomena appear which have a more generic and universal significance than can be grasped in any inquiry more specialized than the sociological. It is not inconceivable that a general sociological analysis of majorities may illuminate some of the more special political implications of majorities.[12]

These five reasons, among others, support the opinion that the subject merits attention by sociologists. In the present place it is naturally not possible to inquire into all of the problems presented by majorities, but it is at least desirable to indulge in some preliminary observations of a formal and necessarily hypothetical nature.

A preliminary analysis may begin with the recognition that majorities, like other groups, may be large or small (both absolutely and relative to their conjoint minorities), open or closed, primary or secondary, active or inactive, cohesive through one or many bonds, relatively permanent or relatively impermanent, and so on. Indeed, many additional adjectives of this polar kind may be attached to them. These adjectives will not, however, contribute anything substantial to an investigation of their specific characteristics. One aspect of groups, on the other hand, is significant. This is the aspect which determines whether the group, or the majority, is organized or unorganized. There has been a tendency in sociology, not dominant perhaps but nevertheless discernible, to consider organized groups, often called associations, to be of greater significance than unorganized groups. Attention to majorities may help to dispel the opinion that this is always, or even usually, the case. For majorities, in many situations of interest to sociology, are unorganized, and this absence of organization does not diminish their significance.

The distinction between organized and unorganized groups, however, is insufficiently discriminating when applied to majorities. It is doubtful, in fact, if it is wholly satisfactory when applied to groups. A consideration of majorities illustrates that there are four general kinds, as different one from the other as the kinds of groups of which they are a part. In attempting to delineate these kinds one is embarrassed, as so often in sociology, by the paucity of terms with which to label them and by the consequent necessity of utilizing words already burdened with connotations. In spite of this hazard, we may distinguish four kinds of groups as exhibited in

Table 1. These four may be called the statistical, the societal, the social, and the associational. Statistical groups are synonymous with logical classes. They have only an "analytical" existence and are "formed," if one may be permitted the expression, not by people themselves but by people who write about people—in other words by sociologists, statisticians, demographers, and so on. Whether they have members or not is immaterial, and we may accordingly have null groups in sociology in the same sense in which we have null classes in logic. Statistical groups, therefore, have no social organization, they have "members" in a logical but not in a sociological sense; and consciousness of kind, in the absence of a social stimulus to evoke it, is only potential. Similarly, the "members" do not enter into social relations with each other on the basis of the trait in terms of which they constitute a group. They may have one or several traits in common, but they have no interests in common, nor any like interests.[13] Examples of such statistical groups are right-handed persons, red-headed persons, persons fifty years of age, persons who are five feet tall, persons who have had the measles, who have died of tuberculosis, persons who prefer soap operas to Italian operas, and so on.

TABLE 1. CLASSIFICATION OF GROUPS

	Organization	Social relations between members	Consciousness of kind
A. Statistical	No	No	No
B. Societal	No	No	Yes
C. Social	No	Yes	Yes
D. Associational	Yes	Yes	Yes

Societal groups differ from statistical groups in that they do have members and these members are conscious of their kind, of the similarity or identity of traits they all possess. There are no null groups here and the trait itself may be single or multiple. Here appear external signs by means of which the members recognize each other, such as skin color, language, accent, grammar, response to patriotic symbol, appearance, and so on. The members, in short, are or may easily become "visible" to each other. They have like interests but not common interests. They do not, however, in the absence of a social stimulus, enter into social relations with each other. Examples of societal groups are males, females, Negroes, whites, Southerners, New Yorkers, golfers, the blind, college professors and indeed all occupational groups, and so on.

Social contact and communication appear in the third category. The social group differs from the societal group in that its members have social relations with one another and from the statistical group both in this respect and in that consciousness of kind is present. Social relations are the distinguishing additional characteristic. The members may have like but not common interests, common but not like interests (e.g., an assortment of persons on a life-raft after a shipwreck), or both like and common interests. Examples are groups of acquaintances, relatives, cliques, audiences, spectators, crowds, mobs, passengers on board a small ship, and many other unorganized groups discussed in the texts.

When a group has these characteristics and is, in addition, organized, we have the fourth kind of group indicated above, the associational group or, more simply, the association. Examples are a fraternity, a lodge, a club, a team, an orchestra, a committee, and so on. In these groups it is the formal organization which is the prominent characteristic and membership in them in itself confers consciousness of kind and generates social relations in accordance with procedural norms. Here, finally, the members usually have both like and common interests.

Before commenting upon its uses, it is necessary to say that this is not an inclusive classification. Some groups find no place in these categories; for example, groups which involve social relations but no necessary consciousness of kind, and groups comprised not of individuals but of other groups. It should also be recognized that none of these groups is stable, and that in the process of social life they may become transformed into groups in other categories under the impress of events. Red-headed people, a statistical group, would become a societal group with the improbable passage of legislation taxing them, a social group if they entered into social relations on the basis of the color of their hair and attended a meeting, for example, to which only red-headed people were invited, and an associational group if they organized a Red-Headed League for the purpose of resisting the legislation. Finally, the classification is a logical but not a temporal continuum; a statistical group may become an association immediately, without passing through the intervening categories; and the reverse could happen on the occasion of the dissolution of an association.

When we return from this digression on group classification in general to the question of majorities in particular, an interesting reflection emerges. For it immediately appears that all four of these groups, the statistical no less than the associational, have sociological significance when they are majorities. And in many cases it is only because they are majorities that they acquire general social significance in the societies in which they occur. This significance can be illustrated by a number of examples. Consider the significance of the majority first of all when it is a statistical group, where no social relations are involved. A society or group in which the majority of the population were of age fifty and above would be a different kind of a society from one in which the majority were fifty and below. Substitute any age categories and the generalization retains its cogency. Similarly, societies differ when or if right-handed persons or left-handed persons are in the majority, urban-dwellers or rural-dwellers, literates or illiterates, and so on. In other words, statistical groups do have sociological significance when they are majorities. They determine to an extensive degree the general characteristics of a society and of a social group. Statistical majorities always have more than a statistical significance. It is therefore a mistake to limit sociology, as formal sociologists are sometimes inclined to do, to a study of social relationships as such, if that term implies social contact and communication between people. For it is apparent that many phenomena of the highest import for sociology, those responsible for the character of an entire society, are determined by the juxtaposition within it of majorities whose members have never met, who do not know each other, and who may, in fact, be unaware of the individual existence of each other.[14]

Comparable observations are relevant to the role of societal majorities. Men's college communities are different from women's college communities, and the differential status of "faculty wives" in the two situations is striking. Of more importance, however, is the fact that minority group problems, problems involving ethnic and national minorities, appear in societies when consciousness of kind and consciousness of difference characterize majority and minority groups. Tension in such situations, in the absence of compensating factors, is directly proportional to the size of the minority and inversely proportional to the size of the majority. That is, majority-minority tension appears to be least when the majority is large, the minority small, and greatest when the minority threatens, by increase in size, to become the majority. Meanwhile, ethnic minorities are oppressed largely in proportion not to their absolute but their relative size. Conversely, a very small minority, again relatively speaking may suffer the satiric sanction but no specific social disability. This point unfortunately requires more development than can be offered here, but it is noteworthy that it is amenable to empirical research.

The social group also, the group that is unorganized but in which social relations occur, is dependent for its function upon a majority. Whether a group of friends goes to a play or to a musical comedy, to an expensive nightclub or to an inexpensive tavern, drinks coffee or beer on a given occasion, and so on, depends, often unconsciously, upon majority desires. Similarly, in larger groups, a lynching can occur only if it is at least tacitly sanctioned by a majority of those present, and a panic can occur only if a majority of the persons involved in a situation fail to "keep their heads." A clique clearly operates under the influence of the majority of its own members and an elite, although a minority, suffers no discrimination only because it embodies social values of which the majority approves and would like to emulate.

It is in the organized group, the association, in which majorities seem, on the surface, to have the least significance. As social organization introduces a hierarchical structure into a group the significance of numbers, and therefore of majorities, diminishes in proportion. The more highly organized the association the fewer functions belong to the majority. Here majority action is, in fact, constrained and limited by organization, by rules and regulations, and by the creation of authority. It would be an error to assert that the majority exercises any official influence in a tightly organized, hierarchically ordered association like, for example, the Roman Catholic Church, the United States Navy, or the Communist Party, three associations which, whatever their diverse goals, exhibit a remarkable sociological similarity in internal organization and structure.[15] There are many more priests than cardinals, seamen than admirals, and party-workers than members of the Politburo, and it is the latter, not the former, which possess the power. This, of course, is true in varying extent of all associations, even the most "democratic." The power structure is always pyramidal.

But even here majorities play a role. This role appears with the recognition that all associations have two types of organization, a formal organization and an informal organization,[16] and that, while majorities exercise no formal function whatever—except when they constitute a legitimate party[17]—they ofen exercise covert and sometimes even overt informal control in associations. Utilizing only the most extreme and rigid cases for illustration, that is, associations in which majorities would seem to have the least influence, it can be demonstrated that they are not immune from the pressures of majorities. A clear example is afforded by the Navy during the recent war. Not even the highly inflexible rules and regulations of the service, enforced by Regular Navy officers in command positions, were impervious to the pressure of the large majority of Reserve officers who considered some of the niceties of naval etiquette, particularly with respect to salutes, ceremonies, and relations with enlisted men, to be more than a little ridiculous. The exodus of Reserve officers after the war, their declining majority and ultimate minority, contributed increasing conformity to the rules and reduced the discrepancy between the formal and informal organization.[18]

The Roman Catholic Church offers another illustration in a totally different sphere. The long struggle with "modern errors" began in 1543 with the publication of *On the Revolutions of the Celestial Orbs* by Nicolai Copernicus and became intense when Galileo was summoned once in 1616 and five times in 1633 to the bar of the Inquisition. This story is well known. What is not so well known is that a license to print a book espousing the heliocentric hypothesis was refused as late as 1820 and that not until September 11, 1822 was the following decree quietly issued by the Holy Office:

> There is no reason why the present and future Masters of the Sacred Palace should refuse license for printing and publishing works treating of the mobility of the earth and the immobility of the sun, according to the common opinion of modern astronomers.[19]

What scientific evidence was unable to accomplish, majority and "common" opinion finally did, even though several centuries were consumed in the process.[20] One is tempted to say that no association, no matter how rigidly organized, is able to withstand the permanent pressure of a majority and that an organized majority is the most potent social force on earth. There is a certain authority in a majority which no hierarchy can wholly obliterate.

From these instances and others another principle can be induced. It concerns the nature of formal and informal organization in any association and the role of majorities with respect to these two forms of organization. First, however, it is appropriate to clarify the meaning of these terms which have appeared in preceding paragraphs. The formal organization of an association consists of the formally recognized and established statuses of the members in accordance with the rank of the offices and other positions they occupy, together with the rules and regulations which set out the obligations, duties, privileges, and responsibilities of these positions. The status of non-office holding members, their duties and privileges, is also, of course, a part of the formal organization—formal because formally recognized and concurred in as a condition of membership. Social relations between the members are conducted formally in terms of these statuses, in conformity with explicit norms, and in accordance with "extrinsic" and "categoric" evaluations of persons. In the formal organization, statuses have differential prestige in independence of the persons who occupy them.

Since this independence is difficult if not impossible to maintain in the dynamics of associational life, however, an informal organization arises to exist coevally with the formal. The informal organization consists of roles rather than statuses, of patterns of dominance and ascendancy, affection, hostility, or indifference of the members in accordance with their intrinsic and personal evaluations of each other. These role patterns may or may not coincide with or conform to the status hierarchy of the formal organization. In the informal organization social relations occur on the basis of the esteem which the members have for one another in independence of their statuses. In short, in formal organization social relations proceed in terms of the prestige of statuses in accordance with explicit associational norms; in informal organization they proceed in terms of the esteem for persons in accordance with implicit societal (i.e., extra-associational) norms. Prestige attaches to statuses; esteem to persons.[21] The former is a component of formal organization, the latter of informal organization.[22]

Now it is apparent that in some associations there may be a close coincidence between the formal and the informal organization and that this coincidence may be relatively permanent. In such cases the statuses which carry the greatest prestige are occupied by the persons who are held in the highest esteem. On the other hand, an association may exhibit a wide discrepancy between its formal and informal organization. In these cases the prestige continues to attach to the status while esteem is withheld from the person who occupies the status and who thereupon becomes a figurehead. The officers then have the formal authority of their positions but not the informal authority sustained by esteem. Now, whether or not offices are filled by "democratic" vote, it is within the power of the majority to confer actual as well as statutory authority upon the officers or to retain authority residually in the informal organization. Similarly, it is within the power of the majority to determine whether social relations in the association shall proceed only in terms of the formal rules and regulations, which are explicit norms, or in terms of informal norms which may or may not coincide with the former. Here then is the principle to which attention is invited, that the discrepancy between the formal and informal organization of any association will be least when the majority gives full support and sanction to the former and greatest when this support is for any reason or in any particular withheld. That this power of determination is a function of the majority rather than of any aspect of social organization itself is clear from the consideration that it is prior to social organization and determines the form which social organization takes. Finally, it is the support of the majority which sustains the association, the absence of this support which moves it in the direction of change or of ultimate dissolution.

We may now inquire whether some of these observations have a similar relevance in the larger society. Here the problem becomes involved in the more general question of the nature and kinds of social power, especially when we attempt to probe the source of the power which the majority exercises. Unfortunately, the subject of social power is not one which has received a comprehensive analysis in the literature, and to discourse on majorities in terms of power is like pronouncing the words of a language one does not fully understand.[23] MacIver defines it variously as "the capacity in any relationship to command the service or the compliance of others,"[24] and "the capacity to control the behavior of others either directly by fiat or indirectly by the manipulation of available means."[25] Among the sources of power MacIver lists property, status, office (apart from status[26]), special knowledge, managerial and executive function, financial resources, artistic, religious or other eminence, publicity, and so on. It is clear from his discussion that social power, whatever its sources and manifestations, is "responsive to the *mores* of the society."[27] And it is the majority which sustains the mores. Here then we find the authority which lies "beyond the realm of government," the authority which community and society retain, which they may or may not confer upon the state, and which, even when it is wrested from the community, wells up again and restrains the actions of governments. Not even an autocrat can remain unresponsive to the will of a majority.[28]

It would, of course, be highly unrealistic to assert that the power of the majority always manifests itself, or is always successful when it does. Majorities are frequently inert and frequently too have no means of expression. Indeed, it is one of the lessons of history that majorities of one kind or another have long suffered oppression. Nevertheless, it is of sociological significance to note that majorities remain the source of so much residual power, even in these situations, that autocrats and oligarchs bend every effort to prevent them from organizing. It is the power of a majority which gives meaning to the imperial command, "Divide and rule."

We find, thus, in the larger society the same principle which was found in the association. Where there is no organization, the majority determines. In the absence of stratification, likewise, the majority determines. When there is formal organization there is also informal organization, and in the latter the majority plays an important role. Indeed, society itself is an informal organization, the state a formal organization; the laws belong to the formal structure, the mores to the informal. It is the majority which sustains the mores, the minority which initiates changes in them which are then either resisted or finally sanctioned by the majority. In all societies of any complexity there is a discrepancy between the laws and the mores. This discrepancy will be wide or narrow depending upon the position of the majority. Where it is wide it will be found that the majority supports the mores, a minority supports the laws. It is the role that majorities play in societies which gives point to what is one of the most profound and cogent of all sociological principles—"When the mores are adequate, laws are unnecessary, when they are inadequate, laws are useless." The mores are adequate when they are supported by a large majority; they are inadequate when they lack this support. There is a power in the majority which can contravene any law.

It is the majority, in short, which sets the culture pattern and sustains it, which is in fact responsible for whatever pattern or configuration there is in a culture. It is the majority which confers upon folkways, mores, customs, and laws the status of norms and gives them coercive power. It is the majority which guarantees the stability of a society. It is the majority which requires conformity to custom and which penalizes deviation—except in ways which the majority sanctions and approves. It is the majority which is the custodian of the mores and which defends them against innovation. And it is the inertia of majorities, finally, which retards the processes of social change.

Throughout the preceding discussion we have, except for several incidental references, omitted from consideration the question of the size of majorities. Here it is possible to note only one implication of size, one which relates to the general problem of social and cultural integration. Reflection upon majorities enables us to see that cultural integration is a function to the size of the majority which conforms to a single set of patterns, which subscribes to the same myths, and which aspires to attain the same societal goals. When this majority is large, the culture is integrated, no matter how extensively the society is stratified. When it is small the culture lacks integration. When it dissolves into competing minorities all vestiges of integration disappear. A culture is in fact dependent upon the existence in a society of a majority. Without it the society is split into partial and fragmented cultures. Whatever the value of the cultural approach in sociology, when used exclusively it sometimes obscures the *social* factors which create and sustain a society and which determine both its coherence and its cohesion. What, finally, is the ultimate ground for the power which the majority exercises? The answer is so deceptively simple as to discourage ready acceptance. It rests in the elemental fact, a fact so formidable as to seem incontrovertible, that the majority is stronger than the minority or, in Simmel's words, "dass die Vielen mächtiger sind als die Wenigen."[29] It is certainly incontrovertible that two men can force one man to do what they want, and that ten men can do it even more easily. Given the same organization, the larger number can always control the smaller, can command its service, and secure its compliance. This, incidentally, is a social and not a cultural fact.[30]

In summary, we have noted the neglect of majorities in contemporary sociology and have introduced, in a very preliminary fashion, some hypotheses which a sociology of majorities might subject to further investigation. We have observed that the majority-minority distinction is a distinction *sui generis* which requires inclusion in any comprehensive group theory; that majorities play significant roles in both organized and unorganized social groups, and particularly in the informal aspects of the former; that majorities play a similar role in the larger society; that majorities constitute a residual locus of social power; that they sustain the mores; and that they are responsible for whatever cultural integration a society exhibits. Majorities doubtless have in addition multifarious characteristics and functions which we have neglected to mention. But these will suffice to show that the subject merits sustained sociological analysis.

NOTES

[1] "Exkurs über die Überstimmung," in *Soziologie* (Leipzig: Duncker & Humblot, 1908), pp. 186–197.

[2] Leopold von Wiese and Howard Becker, *Systematic Sociology* (New York: Wiley, 1932), pp. 267–268, 431–432, 598.

[3] See *Leviathan and the People* (Baton Rouge: Louisiana State University Press, 1939); *The Web of Government* (New York: Macmillan, 1947); and *The Elements of Social Science* (London: Methuen, 1921), pp. 174–176.

[4] Political treatments of the principle of majority rule embrace almost the entire literature of political philosophy, and particularly the philosophy of democracy. For an excellent discussion, with carefully selected bibliography, see Willmoore Kendall, *John Locke and the Doctrine of Majority Rule* (Urbana: University of Illinois Press, 1941). Kendall suggests that while in one sense no political scientist can avoid the problem of majorities, in another sense it is the " 'dark continent' of modern political theory" (p. 16). See also von Gierke, "Über die Geschichte des Majoritätsprinzipes," *Schmollers Jahrbuch für Gezetsbegung Verwaltung und Volkswirtschaft im Deutschen Reiche*, 39 (1915), pp. 565–587 and Ladislas Konopczynski, "Majority Rules," *Encyclopedia of the Social Sciences*, 10, pp. 55–59.

[5] For a comprehensive summary of this subject see Logan Wilson, "The Sociography of Groups," in *Twentieth Century Sociology*, Gurvitch and Moore, eds. (New York: Philosophical Library, 1945), pp. 139–171. Also, Florian Znaniecki, "Social Organization and Institutions," *Ibid.*, pp. 172–217; Wiese-Becker, *op. cit.*, pp. 488–555; G. A. Lundberg, *Foundations of Sociology* (New York: Macmillan, 1939), pp. 339–

374, and "Some Problems of Group Classification and Measurement," *American Sociological Review*, 5 (1940), pp. 351–360.

[6] For a recent discussion of the problem of group classification see P. A. Sorokin, *Society, Culture, and Personality* (New York: Harper, 1947), pp. 145–255.

[7] In view of the difficulty of finding a *fundamentum divisionis* for a logically rigorous classification of groups, the question arises as to whether a classification can serve any useful purpose, even if an adequate construction could be achieved. Ogburn and Nimkoff, for example, contend with some cogency that all such classifications are of limited usefulness. See *Sociology* (Boston: Houghton Mifflin, 1946), p. 251. In support of this view it may be said that a good deal of so-called formal or structural sociology, whatever its intrinsic merit or logical appeal, has little or nothing to do with sociological theory. Taxonomy is not theory, although the two are often confused. Sociological taxonomy belongs to methodology, sociological theory to sociology itself; taxonomy deals with the logical relations between sociological concepts; sociological theory deals with the spatio-temporal and causal relations between social variables. Logical order is the goal of the former inquiry, scientific truth of the latter; the former issues, ideally, in a modified Tree of Porphyry; the latter in universal propositions. On the other hand, in opposition to the view of Ogburn and Nimkoff, classifications, like nominal definitions, are, if not systematically necessary, at least a desirable propaedeutic to the construction of sociological theories.

[8] On this subject see L. L. Bernard, *Social Control* (New York: Macmillan, 1939); Paul H. Landis, *Social Control* (Philadelphia: Lippincott, 1939); Jerome Doud, *Control in Human Societies* (New York: Appleton-Century, 1936); E. A. Ross, *Social Control* (New York: Macmillan, 1916), (Ross notes, however, that "The prestige of *numbers* gives ascendancy to the crowd," p. 78); and Joseph S. Roucek and Associates, *Social Control* (New York: Van Nostrand, 1947). On the other hand, there is relevant material in William Albig, *Public Opinion* (New York: McGraw-Hill, 1939), although not couched specifically in terms of majorities and minorities. See especially Chapters I, II, and XVI.

[9] On the influence of number and size upon social groups see Simmel, *op. cit.*, pp. 47–133, and Wiese-Becker, *op. cit.*, pp. 498–501.

[10] Wiese-Becker, *op. cit.*, pp. 431–32. These few lines, under the section on "Concepts and Categories: Numerical," are unfortunately all these authors have to say about majorities, with two minor exceptions.

[11] There is a vast literature which can be invoked in support of this point. See, for example, Murphy, Murphy, and Newcomb, *Experimental Social Psychology* (New York: Harper, 1937); Murphy and Likert, *Public Opinion and the Individual* (New York: Russell & Russell, 1938); Theodore M. Newcomb, "The Influence of Attitude Climate upon Some Determinants of Information," *Journal of Abnormal and Social Psychology*, 41 (1946), pp. 291–302; Arnold Rose, *Studies in Reduction of Prejudice* (mimeographed) (Chicago: American Council on Race Relations, 1947); Robin M. Williams, Jr., "The Reduction of Intergroup Tensions," *Bulletin 57*, Social Science Research Council, 1947; and Robert M. MacIver, *The More Perfect Union* (New York: Macmillan), 1948. For psychological studies of the influence of majorities in the formation of opinion see H. E. Burtt and D. R. Falkenburg, Jr., "The Influence of Majority and Expert Opinion on Religious Attitudes," *Journal of Social Psychology*, 14 (1941), pp. 269–278; and C. H. Marple, "The Comparative Suggestibility of Three Age Levels to the Suggestion of Group vs. Expert Opinion," *Journal of Social Psychology*, 4 (1933), pp. 176–186. These last two studies, unfortunately, were made with very small groups and are not conclusive. In short, the experimental evidence on the influence of majorities upon opinion is meager.

[12] Kendall, for example, says that Simmel's "Excursus," cited *infra*, note 1, is "a discussion which no student of the social sciences can read without subsequently paying to it the unusual compliment of wishing that it had been many times as long." *Loc. cit.*, p. 27.

[13] For a distinction between the like and the common see R. M. MacIver, *Society* (New York: Farrar & Rinehart, 1937), pp. 28, 30.

14 It is similarly a mistake to emphasize the role of organized groups in a society at the expense of the unorganized, and especially of those in the latter category which are only statistical groups, i.e., as defined above, groups the sociologist himself constructs in the process of classifying people in various ways. It may be safe to say, incidentally, that the conclusions of demographers have not been integrated into formal sociology and that chapters on population remain somewhat logically separate from those on social structure, even though frequently bound together in the same book.

15 One interesting similarity, among others, is that the distinction between "associational" and "private" statuses of the functionaries tends to disappear and extra-associational statuses have little importance. Such associations differ in this respect from the "corporate groups" delineated by Max Weber which exemplify "rational-legal" authority and in which distinctions between official and private statuses are maintained. On this point see *Max Weber: The Theory of Social and Economic Organization*, edited by Talcott Parsons (New York: Oxford, 1947), pp. 324ff, and especially Parsons' Introductory essay, "The Institutionalization of Authority," pp. 56–77. See also E. T. Hiller on the professions and on the office, *Social Relations and Structures* (New York: Harper, 1947), pp. 544–596.

16 Although E. T. Hiller has not used these concepts, his distinctions between intrinsic and extrinsic valuations of persons and between personal and categoric social relations are directly relevant. See *Ibid.*, pp. 191–213, 631–645. The interrelations between formal and informal organization represent an important junction of formal sociology and social psychology and require, perhaps, more intensive analysis than they have as yet received.

17 In sociological terms a party is a device for recruiting a majority and can, as Max Weber suggests, exist only within an organized group or association (Weber: *Verband*; Parsons: "corporate group"), even though it operates, as do political parties in the United States, without specific constitutional sanction. See Max Weber, *loc. cit.*, p. 407. See also R. M. MacIver, *The Web of Government, op. cit.*, pp. 208–224 and especially p. 213.

18 For an excellent analysis of formal and informal organization in the Navy see Charles H. Page, "Bureaucracy's Other Face," *Social Forces*, 25 (1946), pp. 88–94. For an implicit fictional treatment of the same theme see *Mister Roberts*, by Thomas Heggen (Boston: Houghton Mifflin, 1946).

19 Quoted in Preserved Smith, *A History of Modern Culture* (New York: Holt, 1930), Vol. I, p. 58.

20 Illustrations for the third example, the Communist Party, are more difficult to exhibit because of lack of information. It is possible, however, that increasing anti-semitism in the high councils of the Party in Russia, as reported by Drew Middleton in articles in the *New York Times* in February, 1948, may be concessions to majority opinion even though in direct opposition to both constitutional and doctrinal orthodoxy.

21 The writer is indebted to Professor E. T. Hiller for this distinction between prestige and esteem.

22 It is not altogether clear in what respect it may be appropriate to refer to these informal elements in terms of "structure" or even "organization." In some respects they may be antithetical to organization and in that case the concept "informal organization" becomes an oxymoron. This is particularly true because it is these informal elements which are susceptible to frequent change in contrast to the formal which are, by comparison, relatively stable.

23 R. M. MacIver observes that "There is no reasonably adequate study of the nature of social power," although he himself contributes some highly pertinent remarks. See *The Web of Government, op. cit.*, p. 458, and especially Chapter 5, "The Pyramid of Power," pp. 82–113. E. A. Ross's discussion, while short, is still suggestive. See *Social Control, op. cit.*, pp. 77–88.

24 *Ibid.*, p. 82.

25 *Ibid.*, p. 87.

26 That is, the power which proceeds from the *possession* of status.

27 *Ibid.*, p. 98.

28 In an eloquent passage, MacIver has described this situation as follows: "The authority of government does not create the order over which it presides and does not sustain that order solely by its own fiat or its accredited power. There is authority beyond the authority of government. There is a greater consensus without which the fundamental order of the community would fall apart. This consensus plays a different role under different forms of government. Sometimes it has nothing to do with the processes that make or unmake the princes or potentates who rule the people. Sometimes it has no mode of expression, should the ruler get out of hand and violate the fundamental order he is presumed to protect, save the rare violence of revolution. Sometimes it is alert and sensitive to all that government does and sets its seal of approval or disapproval on the policies that government pursues. But always, whether mainly acquiescent or creatively active, it is the ultimate ground on which the unity and the order of the state repose." *Ibid.*, p. 85.

29 *Loc. cit.*, p. 190.

30 For an expansion of this thesis see John Dollard, "Culture, Society, Impulse, and Socialization," *American Journal of Sociology*, 45 (1939), pp. 53–56.

5   EARL RAAB AND SEYMOUR MARTIN LIPSET

The Prejudiced Society

The problem of prejudice, as it presents itself to society, consists of overt acts which deny equal status or opportunity to people because of their racial, religious or ethnic identity. However, "prejudice" is often used in a specialized sense to describe an individual's state of mind or attitude. There has long been a popular tendency to reify "prejudiced attitude"; to conceive of it as a little mental package tucked away in a corner of the brain, waiting for the proper stimulus to bring it to life. According to this view, if a person has "a prejudiced attitude" against Filipinos, then when a Filipino brushes up against him, or enters the same room he's in, or applies to him for a job, or tries to move next door, this attitude would be triggered and the "prejudiced person" would act accordingly.

The evidence clearly indicates, however, that prejudiced attitudes are very far from being neat little mental packages; and that, at the very least, they do not predetermine prejudiced behavior.

Gordon Allport has partly defined an attitude as a "mental and neural state of readiness."[1] The meaningful reference here is to the fact that an attitude is a "mental and neural" state and not just to the fact that it is a state of readiness. A mechanical jack-in-the-box, crouched on its springs, might be said to have an attitude of readiness. Its attitude is such that it will jump up when the cover is removed. But a human attitude describes

Reprinted from *American Race Relations Today*, edited by Earl Raab (New York: Doubleday Anchor Books, 1962), pp. 29–55, by permission of the Anti-Defamation League of B'nai B'rith.

an internal state that has an independent existence, apart from any resultant behavior. If a child were simulating a jack-in-the-box in a school play, his attitude towards jumping out of the box in which he was crouched might consist of a combination of elements, e.g.: he may be displeased about the physical prospect of jumping out; on the other hand, he may have a strong fear of the derision he will face if he fails to jump. Both of these elements comprise his "attitude about jumping" at a given point. The attitude exists as a real fact even if the show is cancelled and he never does have the opportunity of jumping or not jumping.

Hostility and Stereotype   It is common to think of the prejudiced attitude as consisting of both hostility and an over-generalization or stereotype. It is even common to think of the hostility as flowing from the stereotype. But, in fact, it is possible for an individual to have the stereotype. It is possible to cloak two groups with the same stereotype, and have different feelings about them. Saenger and Flowerman questioned some 450 college students as to their feeling of dislike for a number of human groups. They also asked these students to indicate the characteristics which they believed marked these groups. Presumably their likes or dislikes would be based on the kinds of characteristics which they attributed to these groups. This was not the case. Students who expressed a dislike for Jews ascribed to them characteristics which they also ascribed to other groups for whom they did *not* express a dislike. For example, 31 percent of the students complained that the Jews were mercenary; but 24 percent of them complained that Americans were mercenary and 38 percent that businessmen were mercenary. However, Jews were more often disliked for this quality than were Americans and businessmen.

In a study made by B. M. Kramer, he marked off five "distance zones" from an area in which Negroes were moving and interviewed white residents in each of the zones. Zone 1 was the closest to this area of expanding Negro movement. Zone 5 was the most remote, three miles away. There was a general desire among white residents in all five zones to exclude Negroes from their neighborhoods. Kramer checked the stereotypes held by these white residents about Negroes, e.g., that Negroes were personally unclean or diseased. In Zone 1, where the white residents had the closest contact with the Negroes, only 5 percent offered such stereotypes as reasons for exclusion; as against 25 percent of the residents in Zone 5. However, the intensity of hostility in Zone 1 was higher than in Zone 5; in Zone 1, 64 percent of the residents made spontaneous expressions of hostility, as against only 4 percent in Zone 5. Whatever else may have been involved in the situation, it was clear that hostility and stereotype were not tied to each other.

A negative stereotype may exist without hostility; hostility without a negative stereotype; a combination of both cognitive and emotional elements may exist with varying degrees of intensity and with varying targets. A prejudiced attitude is indeed not a homogeneous mental package.

Prejudiced attitude #1 is different from prejudiced attitude #2, and there is almost an endless variety of possibilities.

Frame of Reference—The Situational Factor   Not only do prejudiced attitudes differ widely from one individual to another, but they tend to differ from one situation to another for any given individual. For an attitude is not a thing, it is a process; it is an interaction. It is an interaction involving not only the person and the object, but all other factors that are present in any situation. A crude illustration: In his own home town, Jones may have the deepest contempt for Smith, who lives up the block. He considers Smith a rough character with bad manners and worse taste, socially unacceptable and intellectually barren. Jones has a *feeling* of distaste when he thinks of Smith, and avoids him conscientiously. It happens that Jones, alone on an unguided world tour, has a transportation breakdown in a primitive village in a backward country. The villagers are unfriendly, unlettered, and unsanitary. Into this unhappy and improbable scene, after a couple of days, rides Smith. Jones may well greet him with a joyful embrace, rather than with distaste. His image of Smith as a boor may be replaced by the image of a man who at least has the good sense to speak English and to wash his hands before eating. Whether or not this feeling and image will carry over in any way when the two men return to their home town is another matter—but the fact remains that a different external situation has evoked a different attitude.

Sherif and Cantril have called this situational factor "frame of reference." They write:

> The term "frame of reference" is simply used to denote the functionally related factors (present and past) which operate at the moment to determine the particular properties of a psychological phenomenon (such as perception, judgment, affectivity).

In psychological literature, the critical importance of the situational factor is supported by experiments on many levels. Wever and Zener had subjects judge the weight of a series of objects as "light" or "heavy." When the series of objects was changed from a light series to a heavy series, the same object that was formerly judged heavy was now perceived as light. McGarvey had her subjects rate the "social prestige" of various occupations and found that the desirability of any given occupation was dependent on the kind of occupational series with which it appeared.

Many research roads lead to the understanding that prejudiced attitudes can be highly situational in character. One evening at a summer camp, 30 young men were tested as to their attitudes towards Japanese-Americans. Following this, they were scheduled to attend a show at a local theatre. Instead, their show-going was canceled, and they were forced to accomplish a series of complicated tasks. The same night, following the tasks, their attitudes towards Japanese-Americans were retested, and were found to be less favorable than they had been earlier in the evening. Nothing had changed in the interim with respect to the young men vis-à-vis Japanese-Americans, but some other factors in the situation had changed.

Deitrich Reitzes examined a situation, in which a group of white people had favorable attitudes towards Negroes at work and in shopping centers, but had unfavorable attitudes towards them living in their residential neighborhood. He traced these inconsistencies to different attitudinal "fields"; that is, each of these situations had different external forces operating to form the interaction of attitude. The unions to which the white people belonged were actively committed to intergroup equality at work. The Chamber of Commerce and business groups in the area involved were actively seeking Negro trade. The neighborhood civic club, however, was actively exclusionist. There were different "collective interests" involved in the different situations. In short, an individual does not typically have "an attitude" toward Negroes; he has many different attitudes depending on the circumstances.

There are a number of different ways in which this "situational" character of prejudice may be described:

A general attitude, about Negroes, for example, does not predetermine specific attitudes about Negroes. In other words, if a person has a general stereotype of Negroes, and a general hostility towards Negroes, this does not automatically mean that he will have an unfavorable attitude towards working in the same factory with Negroes.

One specific attitude towards Negroes, e.g., working with them, may have a quite different texture from another specific attitude, e.g., living next to them.

The same person may have one attitude about working next to Negroes in one situation, and a different attitude about working next to them in another situation.

In sum, a prejudiced attitude may shift from one moment and situation to another.

Disparity Between the Attitude and the Act   The situational nature of prejudice is evident, too, in the mass of evidence concerning the disparity between *expressed* attitudes and behavior.

A Chinese couple traveled twice across the United States, and up and down the Pacific Coast. During the course of this trip, they asked for service in hundreds of hotels, auto camps, tourist homes, and restaurants. They were refused accommodations in only one sleeping place, and in none of the eating places. Six months after their trip, R. T. LaPiere sent a mail questionnaire to each of these places asking if Chinese could be accommodated. Over 90 per cent of the 47 sleeping places and of the 81 eating places that replied said that Chinese would *not* be accommodated.

In a Northeastern suburban community, three young women, two white and one Negro, entered 11 restaurants. They encountered no problems, and received nothing less than exemplary service. Two weeks later a letter was sent to the same restaurants asking for reservations for a similar group. There was no answer to the letters, and great resistance to the follow-up phone calls.

Saenger and Gilbert studied customer reactions to the employment of Negro sales personnel in New York City department stores. One group they interrogated had been observed as customers in stores where there were both Negro and white clerks. Twenty percent of those who had bought from Negro clerks said they would disapprove of the policy of employing Negro clerks in the department stores; 21 percent of those who had bought from white clerks expressed the same attitude. In other words, prejudice towards Negro clerks did not cause customers to avoid them in the stores. Over 40 percent of those who said they would not buy in a store with Negro clerks had actually been observed not only in such a store but at a counter where there was a Negro clerk. One-third of those who said they would never buy from a Negro clerk had been observed buying from a Negro clerk less than an hour before they were interviewed.

The Behavior—Not the Attitude   It is true, of course, that the expression of an attitude may be different from, or at least only a surface part of an attitude. A person who is asked whether he would have any objection to rooming with someone of another racial extraction may honestly say, and honestly believe, that he is free of such prejudiced attitudes. But he may find, to his own shock, that when it comes down to it, he does have internal resistance to such a relationship; or indeed, without realizing it himself, he may find reasons and devices for avoiding such a relationship. Likewise, he may say that he *does* have objections, and when it comes down to it, he may not have these objections, or may not find them operative. His initial response may depend on the circumstances: who asks him and where. His ultimate reaction may also depend on the circumstances. This disparity between attitude as expressed and as it ultimately affects behavior merely reemphasizes the *situational* character of the whole complex of prejudice. And it is the act of prejudice, not the attitude itself, which is the social problem of prejudice as earlier defined.

Andrew Kapos surveyed the attitudes of 30 segregated white gentile fraternities at the University of Michigan in 1953. He found a more intensive feeling of general prejudices against Jews than against Negroes. But he also found more willingness to admit Jews than Negroes to the fraternities, possibly because of the group standards which the fraternity members felt existed in the world around them. The attitudes of almost a thousand Texas manufacturers towards Negroes were tested; and the results were compared with the actual hiring practices of these manufacturers. It was found that the general attitude of a man towards Negroes had little to do with whether or not he employed them. An employer's willingness to hire Negroes was not significantly related to the degree of general hostility he felt or expressed towards Negroes.

In Panama there are places where one side of a street falls in the American Canal Zone, and the other side of the same street falls in Panamanian territory. Biesanz and Smith found that Panamanian Negroes tend to conform to discriminatory practices when they go to the Zone side of the street; while white Americans tend to adjust to nondiscriminatory practices when they go to the Panamanian side.

Whether in the fraternities of Ann Arbor, the factories of Texas, or the streets of Panama, it is not the prejudiced attitude which is itself important to the social problem of prejudice. It is the act of excluding Negroes from the fraternities and from the factories that makes prejudice a problem for society. The attitudes are important to that problem only insofar as they *cause* these acts. It is clear, however, that a prejudiced attitude is not a kind of pushbutton, nor a constant psychic bundle; it is, more accurately, an interaction in any given situation. It is clear that general attitudes of prejudice do not necessarily predetermine prejudiced behavior; it is clear that a specific attitude at one moment does not predetermine the act that will eventuate at another moment. What, then, *is* the relationship between attitudes and behavior?

LEARNING PREJUDICE

Prejudiced behavior typically shapes and alters prejudiced attitudes. The learning of prejudice is affected primarily by the kinds of social situations in which people live.

The fact that attitudes do not necessarily predetermine behavior, does not mean that attitudes and behavior do not typically accompany each other. The human being is not a mechanical jack-in-the-box. We do normally have feelings and conceptions that accompany our behavior. But our feelings and conceptions—our attitudes—do not necessarily *precede* our behavior. The attitude of the boy who is going to jump out of the box in the school play may be altered by the very fact that he is going to jump out of the box; just as his attitude immediately after his act may be shaped by the bare fact that he did jump out.

In brief, behavior typically shapes and alters attitudes. Cantril examined attitude polls on the subject of "lend-lease" assistance to the Allies before the United States was involved in World War II. He found that immediately after Congress actually passed lend-lease legislation, attitudes toward such legislation became more favorable by about 10 percent. The point, according to Cantril, is that public opinion tends to follow accomplished fact.

Stouffer and his associates asked white soldiers: How would you like it if your division had companies which included both Negro and white platoons? Seven percent of those who already were in a company with Negro platoons replied that they disliked the situation; 20 percent of those questioned who were in the same regiment but not in the same company as Negro platoons replied that they would dislike it; 24 percent of those who were in the same division but not the same regiment as Negro platoons replied that they would dislike it; 62 percent of those questioned who were not even in the same division as Negro platoons replied that they would dislike it. The further they were from the accomplished fact, the more they disliked it.

Deutsch and Collins surveyed attitudes of white residents in four different public housing projects in New York. In two, Negro and white families were assigned indiscriminately to the same apartment buildings. In the other two, Negroes were assigned to different buildings within the same project.

In all cases, the assignments were made under an automatic procedure that did not take into account the preference of those assigned. Asked if they would dislike living in the same buildings with Negroes, about three-quarters of the white respondents in the segregated projects said they would, as against only about one-quarter of those already living in the fully integrated units. About 50 percent of those in the integrated projects said they desired to be friendly with their Negro neighbors, as against only about 10 percent in the segregated projects. General attitudes towards Negroes seemed to be affected as well: about 75 percent of those in the integrated units said they respected Negroes in general, as against well below 50 percent of those in the segregated projects.

Attitudes After the Fact   Many research studies show that specific attitudes change after the fact, e.g.: attitudes towards living in the same neighborhood, serving in the same Army company. These studies are evidence that specific attitudes do shape themselves to specific behavior. However these studies do *not* indicate that a shift in one specific attitude towards a minority group will necessarily affect other specific attitudes towards the same group; or that a shift in a specific attitude will always affect the expression of a general attitude as it apparently did in the Deutsch and Collins study.

Harding and Hogrefe studied the attitudes of white employees towards Negro co-workers in department stores. The white employees were divided into three groups according to the nature and extent of their contact with Negroes. Group I included those who had worked in departments where there had been at least one Negro whose job was on an equal or superior plane. Group II included those who had worked in departments where Negroes had been of lower working status than themselves. Those in Group III had never worked in a department with Negroes.

They were all asked: "How would you feel about taking a new job in which there were both Negroes and white people doing the same kind of work as you?" Seventy-three percent of Group I, 61 percent of Group II, and 48 percent of Group III said they would be favorable. But there was no significant difference between the three groups when they were asked, for example, whether they would want to sit next to Negroes on the bus or train. The experience of working with Negroes apparently only produced a more favorable attitude towards Negroes in that specific "fellow-employee" frame of reference.

A further clue may be found in the study of Daniel Wilner and his associates of attitudes of white residents in public housing projects. This three-year study compared two kinds of white tenants: those who lived close to Negroes and those who lived at a relative distance. In neither case was the distance a matter of choice for the white residents who had been assigned to their quarters in these public projects. As in the Deutsch-Collins study, it was discovered that attitudes changed favorably as the distance to the Negroes decreased. Not only was there a significant difference in the specific attitude (i.e., living near Negroes), but again an apparent shift in general attitudes. In one project, for example, where Negroes and whites lived in the same buildings, 53 percent of the respondents said that they generally liked and respected Negroes; in another project where the buildings were all-white and all-Negro, only 36 percent of the respondents said that they generally liked and respected Negroes.

However, the Wilner study went further. Among one group of women who lived close to Negroes, 32 percent who had no personal contact with the Negro neighbors beyond casual greetings, had a high degree of general esteem for Negroes; 45 percent who, in addition, had extended street conversation with their Negro neighbors had a high degree of general esteem for Negroes; and 74 percent who had neighborly associations with Negroes, i.e., behaved like neighbors, had a high degree of esteem generally for Negroes.

Proximity was not a matter of choice but of automatic assignment. The greater the proximity, the more likely was there to be neighborlike activity. A point made by the Wilner study is that the shift in general attitudes came not so much from mere contact or proximity, but from a changed pattern of behavior. The white residents who *acted* like neighbors came most often to *feel* like neighbors on many levels.

I. N. Brophy found a very marked reduction in general anti-Negro prejudice among white merchant seamen who, without the benefit of choice, had worked with Negro sailors. Thirty-three percent of those who had never shipped with Negroes were rated as unprejudiced; 46 percent of those who had shipped with Negroes once; 62 percent who had shipped with Negroes twice; and 82 percent of those who had shipped with Negroes five or more times were rated as unprejudiced. This was in sharp contrast to the Harding and Hogrefe study of the limited shifts in general attitudes for whites who had worked with Negroes in department stores. But these seamen not only worked together very closely, but also lived together 24 hours a day. And neighborly relationships are, of course, more general and encompassing than working relationships.

Behavior Shapes Attitude   In other words, evidence indicates that specific attitudes shape themselves to behavior. People who actually work with Negroes, especially as equals, develop attitudes favorable towards working with Negroes. People who actually are neighbors of Negroes develop attitudes favorable towards being neighbors of Negroes. Evidence also indicates that general attitudes shape themselves to behavior only if that behavior is itself general in nature. People who behave towards Negroes as full equals on every level tend to develop attitudes toward them as full equals on every level.

Thus, the mass of modern evidence runs counter to the "attitudes-first" fallacy, which holds that prejudice is a lurking state of mind that spills over into overt behavior. It might be more accurate to say that the prejudiced state of mind is typically a function of behavior; except for the danger that *this* formula might be over-simplified into a kind of reverse fallacy. Actually, there emerges an understanding that the key to prejudice must be found *outside* the realm of attitude-behavior relationships. The evidence has demonstrated how both attitudes and behavior are affected by the social frame of reference in which they occur.

In an integrated housing situation, attitudes and behavior are different than in a segregated housing situation. In an integrated army situation, attitudes and behavior are different than in a segregated army situation. In a shopping center situation attitudes and behavior towards Negroes are different than in a neighborhood situation. On one side of a Panamanian street, a white man's behavior towards Negroes may be different than on the other side of the street. It is this *situational* factor which is central to both attitude and behavior; which can stand outside any behavior-attitude spiral and avoid the fruitless question: "Which comes first?"

The effect of the situational factor on the social problem of prejudice can be found in the dramatic story of post-war integration in the armed forces. A military installation comprises a kind of community in itself, with its own community practices and patterns. Soldiers, sailors, marines and airmen for the most part live as well as work within the military setting. Traditionally, the armed forces community had followed the racial patterns of the nation's lowest common denominator: the deep South. The assumption was made that only in this way could the armed forces accommodate the young men from the South as well as from other parts of the country who entered the services with deep-set attitudes of prejudice. Segregation was the rule on almost every level. Most military leaders expected it to stay that way indefinitely. In 1948, however, an edict was handed down by administrative order from President Truman's office: all of the armed forces were to be thoroughly and effectively integrated.

In its own inimitable way, the armed forces implemented this edict by a series of direct military orders. Today, there is effective integration throughout all the branches of service. In 1953, in an extensive survey of the effects of the desegregation edict five years after it was issued, Lee Nichols was able to report that Negroes and whites from all parts of the country were not just training and fighting together, but were also eating at the same tables, sleeping in the same quarters, drinking beer together, going to church and the movies together.

Beyond the Call of Duty   A typical illustration of the process has been provided by Brigadier General Frank McConnell who had been assigned, shortly after the integration edict, to command a major training base in South Carolina. Customarily, as the recruits poured in, the Negroes were separated from the whites and established in separate organizations. General McConnell issued an order that the next 55 draftees who arrived would comprise a platoon, regardless of their color, and that this procedure would be followed with all subsequent arrivals. The order was issued verbally and "that," he said, "was the end of segregation in Fort Jackson." There were no interracial incidents then or thereafter.

"I would see recruits, Negro and white, walking down the street, all buddying together," said the General. "The attitude of the Southern soldiers was that this was the Army way; they accepted it the same way they accepted getting booted out of bed at 5:30 in the morning."

This was the Army way. This was the new social situation, the new set of practices which surrounded the white soldier who had been accustomed to quite another way of life. His new community accepted it, he accepted it. There were no incidents of any consequence. Scattered grumbling that was heard when the policy was announced, but before it was implemented, disappeared when integration actually took place. Apprehension had been unwarranted. A Congressional committee reported that "the almost total absence of opposition that had been anticipated in the enlisted men is a contributing factor in the success of this policy. The men were more ready for equality of treatment than the officer corps had realized." Commanders reported that interracial incidents had *lessened* under the policy of integration, as a result of the lessening of tensions.

The servicemen did not necessarily retain these specific attitudes or behavior patterns when they returned to their home towns: The situational factors had shifted back again. In many cases, their *general* attitudes may have altered somewhat, at least temporarily, because of their total-living experiences in integration; and the aspiration levels of the Negro servicemen may also have been raised as a result. But they settled back without difficulty in the segregated patterns of their home communities. More definitively, the practices of the armed forces had a direct impact on certain practices in the nonmilitary community. Negro and white soldiers sat side by side on a city bus in Columbia, South Carolina, where such mingling was actually prohibited by law. Restaurants near military posts decided to admit Negroes along with white soldiers, partly because white and Negro soldiers began to accompany each other in town. In Amarillo, Texas, the USO club was opened to Negro airmen for the first time. Amarillo University began to admit Negroes to its extension classes, George L. P. Weaver, formerly of the CIO, told Lee Nichols that the elimination of segregation in the armed forces opened new job opportunities for Negroes with government contractors; indeed in the integrated military, Negro servicemen were often able to learn vocational skills which they otherwise could have had no opportunity to learn.

At the very least, within the relatively uncomplicated society bounded by the armed forces, the *social problem* of prejudice had been virtually eliminated by the outlawing of prejudiced practices. Equality of opportunity is in effect. The aspirations of the non-whites within the military setting are being met. Interracial "incidents" and tensions have been reduced. This is not really being enforced at bayonet point, but has come to be accepted by servicemen. In terms of attitudes, they have, by and large, responded "beyond the call of duty," in their fraternization with fellow-servicemen of another race. Not only has behavior changed, which is the crux of the social problem, but behavior has patently shaped attitudes.

The Situation or The Personality   Perhaps then the most effective and workable approach to understanding the phenomenon of prejudice is through an investigation of the kinds of *social situations* which give rise to and sustain prejudiced behavior and attitudes. This is a sharply different approach from that which would investigate what kinds of *people* are prone to prejudice.

This is not to underestimate the special validity of an approach to prejudice from the vantage point of personality and personality differences. There are good reasons for making such a psychological approach. Prejudice serves an emotional function for many people. It helps them to shift blame from themselves to others, to rationalize their aggressions, or otherwise provides an outlet for their special emotional needs. Some people with special emotional needs have a special susceptibility to prejudice. In attempting to understand or remedy the particular virulence or persistence of a given individual's prejudice, it is often necessary to understand his psychological history.

One white factory worker got along very well with his co-worker who happened to be Negro. They were friendly, ate their lunches together, worked together harmoniously. Suddenly the white worker began to have severe marital troubles and seemed headed towards a divorce. He began to make slurring references to the Negro's race and they finally had to be separated. Another man, bitter because he was making no progress in his business firm, blamed the "Jews" in top management and became vocally anti-Semitic, although it turned out that there weren't any Jews in the management of the firm. One study of veterans found that those who were generally frustrated and felt that they had been subject to "bad breaks" in the service were more often prejudiced than those who felt they had experienced "good breaks" in the service. There is evidence that many of those who stigmatize the Negro as hypersexual are indeed guilt-ridden by their own sexuality, and are attempting to rid themselves of that guilt by projecting it onto the Negro.

The body of psychological knowledge which throws light on these reactions is extremely helpful in explaining individual differences and in helping to treat individual problems. Since certain emotional needs are universal, in one degree or another, this knowledge even helps to explain the special "attractiveness" that prejudice seems to have for human beings in general.

But it does not explain the specific *social problem* of prejudice with which our society is currently burdened. Presumably the factory worker who was having trouble with his wife would have found *some* scapegoat, even if there were no Negro available. It might have been the thinnest man in the factory, or the fattest, or the one with red hair, or perhaps just the one with whom he was most incompatible. The need to blame other people instead of oneself; irrelevantly to work out on other people one's guilt or aggressiveness or fear is an unhealthy condition in itself. It is a problem in mental health. Those who have this problem are undoubtedly more susceptible to prejudice and to the social aberrations than those who do not have such a problem. But this condition itself does not create the specific social evils attending prejudice as described earlier. It is only when these problems are displaced on groups and help establish a deep-going pattern of denying equal opportunity to specific groups that the social problem of prejudice emerges. In short, the factory worker's psychological reaction does not create the social problem of prejudice, it merely operates within the social framework of a pattern of prejudice which already exists.

Furthermore, the psychological approach, as valuable as it is, does not explain the preponderance of people who engage in prejudiced behavior, but do *not* have special emotional problems. It does not explain the widespread pattern of prejudice. It does not explain why prejudice is more intense in one place and time than in another.

The Lessons of Social Situations   These aspects of the social problem of prejudice are explainable only in terms of our *learning* prejudice much as we learn our other basic patterns of social behavior. But people do not typically learn their social values and social behavior in the same way that they learn the arithmetic table. It is not a matter of formal training or mere intellectual acceptance. A child may "learn" the social precept that it is wrong to steal, but may steal nonetheless. He has effectively learned the social value of honesty only to the extent that he has "internalized" that value; i.e., to the extent that this social value has become a natural and unthinking part of his behavior. It is not that he weighs consequences, but that it would "go against his grain" to steal.

This is not the kind of learning which basically is effected in the classroom, or even at the mother's knee. It is shaped fundamentally not by lecture or exhortation, but, in a kind of "creeping socialization," by the kinds of social situations in which people live, and, especially, in which they grow up.

It then becomes necessary to define more precisely the nature of "social situation" as it applies to prejudice; and to discover the kinds of social situations which give rise to and sustain prejudice.

THE PREJUDICED COMMUNITY

The pattern of community practices *is the fountainhead of prejudice: of prejudiced behavior and of prejudiced attitudes.*

The growing child learns his social behavior primarily by following the modes and models of behavior around him. Indeed, he has little choice. He learns how to behave towards people of other racial and religious groups by seeing how other people behave, and by automatically participating in the behavior patterns which already exist.

Consider the extreme but not atypical case of a community where the Negro population has been traditionally subordinate on every level. The Negro with whom the young child comes into contact is a domestic in his home; or an elevator operator or janitor or a worker in some other menial capacity. The Negroes he knows are not as well educated as the white people he knows, nor as well dressed, nor as well housed. The white people in his community do not socialize with Negroes, nor share the same public accommodations with them. No Negroes sit down at the same dinner table with him or with the people he knows; Negroes are not customers in the restaurants or hotels to which he is taken. Negroes are addressed by their first name, but always address the white people as "Mr." or "Mrs." They do not go to the same school as white children. They sit in separate sections of the bus. They use different rest rooms in the bus stations. If there is a tight fit on the sidewalk, it is the Negro pedestrian who gives way.

These are the social situations, i.e., the overt sets of relationships with which the child is surrounded. He does not have to be *told* that Negroes are "inferior" or what his relationships to them are supposed to be. These are apparent. Even more important, he is part of the white community and necessarily he *behaves* within the framework of these existing relationships. It is not just that his parents use a different rest room than do the Negroes. *He* uses a different rest room than the Negroes. *He* sits in the white section of the bus. *He* behaves towards them as social inferiors, and naturally comes to accept them as social inferiors. It isn't necessary to inculcate in him explicit attitudes about the social inferiority of Negroes. More likely, it is necessary for him to develop attitudes that do not conflict with his behavior.

Negroes conform to the prevailing patterns in such a community not only because they must, but also in part because they have accepted the values of the dominant community, and for the same reasons. They have been part of the same behavior patterns.

This process takes place at an early age. In one nursery school study, when preschool Negro children were given a white and Negro doll to play with, they almost uniformly preferred the white doll.

Schools for Prejudice   There is a tendency to believe that these kinds of prejudicial behavior patterns are to be found preponderantly in the deep

South. It is often startling to those in the northern and western parts of the country to find, by the most casual self-survey, the extent to which their own communities are "schools for prejudice" by dint of similar ongoing situations.

In the North and West, Negroes and whites typically live in different neighborhoods. That these Negro neighborhoods are usually inferior to the white is a fact readily apparent to the young observer. The proportion of substandard housing occupied by Negroes in 1952, according to U. S. Census standards, was six times as great as that occupied by whites. This was a uniform condition around the country. Nor is residential separatism restricted to the racial level. The Anti-Defamation League found, in a 1959 survey, that housing segregation on a religious basis was becoming more prevalent than was thought to be the case. For example, it found that a number of residential communities in the Chicago area were almost completely closed to Jews, and others had "large areas where Jews are barred."

Negroes typically work in lower-status jobs in communities throughout the nation. An index of this comparative status is the fact that the average earnings of the Negro worker is little more than half that of the white worker. This is partly the result of the history of educational and economic disadvantage which is the heritage of the Negro. But it is to a large extent the result of current prejudice. Where surveys have been made of job orders by employers in the North and West, in communities as widely separated as Los Angeles and Chicago, it has been found that at least 75 percent of the job orders for white collar workers specify "white only." At least 25 percent of these job orders specify "Christian only." (In 1959, the State of California took steps to remedy this situation with the passage of a Fair Employment Practices Act.)

It has been estimated that about one-quarter of the Negro school children *outside* the South go to schools that are in fact substantially all-Negro, and about half go to schools where there is only token mixing. This is largely a result of segregated housing patterns.

John P. Dean supervised a study of 248 cities, ranging in population from 10,000 to 500,000, to determine the extent to which American Jews were thoroughly integrated. Three tests were used: admission to Junior League; admission to country clubs and city clubs; admission to exclusive residential areas. In one-third of the cities, Jews are denied admission to all three. In only 20 out of the 248 cities are some Jews accepted in all three, and these 20 are smaller cities. In more than half of the 50 largest cities in the study, Jews are denied admission to all three categories; and in only one are they admitted to all three.

These behavior patterns are not only the substance of prejudice as a social problem; they are also the breeding conditions of prejudice. In a very real sense, prejudiced behavior reproduces itself; carries within it its own seeds of continuity. In the same sense, prejudice is a dramatic example of the "self-fulfilling prophecy." The prejudiced image of a Negro as a constitutionally menial worker is sustained by the prejudiced behavior which in fact freezes him as a menial worker.

The Projection of Prejudice   The learning of prejudice is a natural result of actual participation in patterns of prejudiced behavior; or of first-hand observation of the patterns of prejudiced behavior in the community; but it may also result from *vicarious* participation, or *second-hand* observation of the patterns of prejudiced behavior. A society provides many "cues" for social behavior, e.g.: "white" and "colored" signs above public drinking fountains; or classified ads in the newspapers which read "gentile only"; or house-for-sale signs which read "white only" or "restricted."

In these several ways, then, it is on the level of actual behavior situations that the normal reproduction of prejudice is effected. It is within the framework of these behavior situations that individual differences, except perhaps the most pathological, operate. It is on the base of these behavior situations that the behavior-attitude spiral of prejudice builds. Attitudes and explicit ideologies are most firmly constructed on the foundation of these existing social situations.

Indeed, the attitudes which must develop to accompany human behavior are *implied* in this behavior and it is in this way that such attitudes are primarily learned rather than by direct instruction. By the time a child is told for the first time that "Negroes are inferior," he is already convinced of it. On the other hand, by the time he is told for the first time that "Negroes are *not* inferior" it is already often too late. He will resist the idea. Or, if he is finally intellectually convinced of the fact that Negroes are not inferior, he may evade the consequences. He may find some other reason for behaving towards the Negroes *as though* they were inferior. It is axiomatic in all learning situations that rhetorical exhortations have little chance of success when they are in battle against actual behavior patterns. For example, a child will not tend to be honest because his father tells him to be, if the same father is constantly engaged in dishonest practices himself.

Studies of the development of prejudice in children show that young children who have not yet been involved in prejudiced behavior patterns, may pick up prejudiced talk, but this doesn't affect their unprejudiced behavior. Later, after having become involved in prejudiced behavior patterns, they may pick up democratic language in the schools or elsewhere, but this doesn't affect their prejudiced behavior. By the age of 15, Gordon Allport points out, "considerable skill is shown in imitating the adult pattern."[2]

They are now able to rationalize their prejudiced behavior whenever necessary and resort to the prejudiced ideologies which do not precede but follow prejudiced behavior patterns.

In brief, the pattern of *community practices* serves as the primary source of prejudice in behavior and attitude. This does not mean that we are merely back on the causative merry-go-round, where behavior chases attitude and attitude chases behavior in a dismally unending circle. "Community practices" connotes more than just the sum total of individual behavior at any given time. It means customary collective behavior. It means collective habits which tend to perpetuate themselves with their own momentum, such as the collective habit of smoking tobacco or drinking coffee.

Similarly, prejudiced community practices typically reproduce themselves by force of *custom*. All other things being equal, these practices are passed automatically from one generation to the next. John Dollard, after studying traditional patterns of prejudice in a Southern town, wrote:

> The master defense against accurate social perception . . . is always . . . the tremendous conviction of rightness about any behavior form which exists. What is done is de facto right and is justified by the consideration that it has not been invented by current culture bearers but comes to them through sacred tradition.

The Persistence of Prejudice   The sheer power of custom recreates prejudiced community practices—which in turn, typically, breeds individual practices of prejudice, and, then, individual attitudes of prejudice. As a matter of fact, it is possible for prejudiced custom to persist without building up *any* corresponding attitudes.

For example, it has become commonplace for investigators of prejudiced employment practices to find the following kind of situation:

A personnel officer in a large firm tells a Jewish applicant, in effect, that he is sorry but the firm does not hire Jews as salesmen. A complaint is brought to the head of the firm, who expresses genuine astonishment. "What difference does it make?" he asks. "A good salesman is a good salesman." A visit is then made to the personnel officer who himself expresses genuine astonishment. No Jews had ever been hired by that firm, and he had just assumed that it was policy.

The department stores of a city with a fairly large Negro population had never hired a Negro clerk. As the store owners were approached on this situation, one by one, they indicated that they really had no objection to employing Negroes, and really hadn't given the matter much thought. It just "hasn't been done." One department store departed from the custom and hired Negro clerks; the others followed cheerfully and without incident.

These customary community practices, with or without corresponding attitudes, are the "frame of reference," the *situational* key to the prevention of and altering of the widespread phenomenon of prejudiced behavior and prejudiced attitudes. This pattern of community practices is the basic remedial target, rather than emotional maladjustment, or any given set of prejudiced attitudes. When this pattern of community practice changes—whether by law, direct action or otherwise; whether willingly or reluctantly —the prevailing pattern of community attitudes will be likely to change accordingly. Laws prohibiting the sale of liquor in the United States have dramatically failed to change attitudes about liquor; but these laws have failed to change community practices in the first place. There is impressive indication, however, that in the area of social relationships, and specifically in the area of intergroup relationships, community practices *can* be changed prior to corresponding attitudinal changes, and will then serve to effect such attitudinal changes.

NOTES

[1] Gordon Allport, "Attitudes," in *A Handbook of Social Psychology*, C. Murchison, ed. (Worcester: Clark University Press, 1935), p. 798.

[2] Gordon W. Allport, *The Nature of Prejudice* (Reading, Mass.: Addison-Wesley, 1954), p. 310.

| Critical Concepts in Sociological Analysis | ROLE AND PERSONALITY |

6   RALPH H. TURNER

The Problems of Social Dimensions in Personality

CLOSED AND OPEN SYSTEM MODELS

No one today seriously discounts the impact of culture and society in the formation of personality, nor denies the fruitfulness of a search for differences in modal personality types among cultures and subcultures. There is dispute over the extent and nature of such differences and the character of the causal principles linking personality to society, but the relationship itself has become axiomatic.

Nevertheless, in the study of sociocultural determinants of personality an implicit assumption is frequently made which precludes what might be the sociologist's major contribution to the field. Personality is treated as a psychogenically closed system which society activates but does not structure. Social environment selects from among the predetermined ways in which the organism can function and determines the rate of function. Because societies activate the several dimensions of personality at varying rates, there is considerable range in modal configurations. The differences are nevertheless reducible to varying combinations of rates for the same set of personality variables.

Reprinted from *Pacific Sociological Review*, 4:2 (1961), pp. 57–62, by permission of the author and the publisher.

The closed system model resembles a piece of machinery which is designed to perform a set of tasks and each of which tasks is controlled by specific intake devices. At any given moment an organism can be usefully regarded as such a closed system, capable only of a repertoire of responses and capable of being activated only by stimuli which are suited to its activators. But such sociological and anthropological study of personality assumes that the character of the closed system is independent of culture, especially with respect to the dimensions of functioning, if not of intake. From the early studies in the ecology of mental disorders to recent research in social psychiatry the problem has been defined as discovering a relationship between a sociological variable and a preestablished psychiatric type. Culture-personality studies and research into personality characteristics of social classes and age and sex subcultures have likewise sought a fit between a group dimension and a prevalidated personality classification. The social science investigator typically employs an instrument which has been designed to measure or classify personalities according to some established psychological school of thought.[1] The sociologist, who cannot claim competency in deciding which psychological theories of personality are correct, must nevertheless choose, running the risk that his own work will be rendered irrelevant when the tides of thought in psychology change.

The point of our discussion can best be grasped by considering the accomplishment and limitation of the modal character approach to culture-personality study. Investigations which compare the frequency of given personality configurations in various societies depend upon the assumption that their types or variables are equally valid in each of the societies. Implicitly denied from the start is the assumption that what societies do is to *organize* the complex of behavior in distinctive ways. The personalities of the Zuni looked amazingly uniform to Ruth Benedict, leading her to describe a modal type which probably reflected her experience with variation inside of American culture.[2] The apparent uniformity may have been an artifact of the failure of Zuni society to differentiate personality into the types and along the dimensions most common in Western society. At the same time, Zuni society may have differentiated personality along other dimensions to which the Western observer was not sensitized by his own culture. The modal personality approach then diverts attention from the possibility that culture may create the dimensions along which personality varies, because of its preoccupation with finding one or more dimensions on which societies can be compared.

An instructive example is supplied by Thomas and Znaniecki's discussion of the Philistine, Bohemian, and Creative types of social character.[3] While these types are offered as products of a universal socialization process, the authors comment, "An unavoidable consequence of the now prevalent social organization is that the immense majority of individuals is forced either into Philistinism or Bohemianism." The competition among many rival complexes for the individual's conformity violates the requirements of personal integrity. The individual then either adheres to one scheme hypocritically, or continually passes from one unsatisfactory system to another. Thus Thomas and Znaniecki describe a type of society in which people tend to be differentiated along a Philistine-Bohemian dimension, leaving unstated the implication that in a differently ordered society character structures might be organized along other dimensions. In light of their speculation it might be more fruitful to compare societies in which the Bohemian-Philistine differentiation is marked with those in which there is little consistent differentiation of this kind, than to compare societies according to the degree of Bohemianism and Philistinism.

Confusion about the proper dependence upon ultimately psychological and neuropsychological concepts sometimes derives from failure to distinguish between the study of elementary psychological processes and the organization of personality. The study of personality is distinctive chiefly because its object is the *organization* of behavior in individuals. One could hardly defend a conception of infinite malleability which denies a set of common human psychological processes. But organization at the *person* level—the characteristic orientations of persons toward social objects—cannot be inferred directly from a knowledge of elementary neural properties, and consequently need not be uniform from society to society.

Our object in this paper is to suggest that sociologists can make a useful contribution by testing the assumption which is normally implicit. In order to test the assumption, investigators must formulate hypotheses which proceed from the opposite axiom, and from some conception of the social processes of personality organization. If such hypotheses are consistently refuted, the model of the psychogenically closed system may be followed with greater assurance. If the hypotheses are confirmed, an extensive area of investigation will have been opened up. Beginning with an examination of the criteria by which we identify dimensions and type of personality we shall suggest clues to probable relationships between social structure and the nature of personality organization.

THE BASES FOR PERSONALITY CLASSIFICATION

Treatment of personality always takes its reference from behavior, observed or hypothesized. But personality study looks at behavior in a distinctive fashion which supplies the criteria for useful classifications of personality. First, a personality variable or type refers to some observable *consistency* in behavior. An unrepeated type of action is not in itself made the basis for establishing a dimension or type of personality, and the dimensions we make the basis of personality theory reflect areas in which considerable behavioral consistency has been noted on the part of large segments of the population.

Second, categories of personality incorporate interrelatednesses of behavior. A *constellation* of behaviors is implied, such that if you observe one or two elements of the constellation in an individual you also expect to find the others. A concept such as the authoritarian personality, for example, would be totally without justification except for the assumption that its various elements are predictable from one another.[4]

A third criterion for a category in personality analysis is that it must *differentiate* people.

Fourth, we apply a criterion of *significance* to the behavior whose consistency, interrelatednesses, and interpersonal differentiation are the bases for a personality category. From time to time the Sunday supplements amuse us by noting that we probably are consistent about which sock we put on first, and that this is related to how we get into an automobile, etc. But we do not make such regularities a basis for personality study because the behavior is not of a kind which has much effect on the behavior of other people. We study authoritarianism, introversion, ego-strength, because they denote configurations of behavior which make a difference in interaction with others. Significant behavior is behavior which others notice, consider important, and characteristically respond to by an adjustment in their own behavior.

Fifth, we distinguish between personality and mere conformity to the norms of position. For example, on a ritual occasion two military officers may display equally commanding behavior, but we discount this as concealing true personality differences, and look to their behavior when they are off their ceremonial guard. This criterion is merely an extension of the requirement that personality categories differentiate persons rather than positions, but is worthy of special stress because it leads us to some crucial observations about the social sources of personality organization.

There is a rather simple moral from this list of criteria for categories of personality. The study of personality should be in large part the study of sources and processes of organization of behavior. If we are to search for the dynamics which account for the peculiar structure which personality exhibits, we must look for them in the sources of consistency, interrelatedness of behavior, differentiation among individuals, and significance. If we can locate important causes of consistency in behavior, we shall have discovered some of the dynamic factors accounting for the organization of personality. The same observation applies to the other criteria.

SOCIAL SOURCES OF PERSONALITY ORGANIZATION

Cultural Choice and Personality   The fifth criterion for personality classification is a good starting point for specifying probable relationships. When we discounted ceremonial behavior as an indicator of personality, saying that one soldier was a decisive and commanding sort of person and the other a weak person underneath the surface, we assumed that there were other occasions when such differences would be reflected in behavior. But a society in which there is considerable achieved status may be necessary for such a notion of personality as the *real*, the *underlying tendency*, to emerge. When human behavior is dominated by ascribed status the opportunities for a person to behave in non-ritual circumstances in a way which can be recognized as weakness or strength will be fewer and less important than in American society. The opportunity to undergo systematic learning of a pattern of behavior inconsistent with the ascribed role will be less well developed and a conception of the "real self" or "real personality" hidden behind public behavior is likely to be less salient than it is in our theorizing about personality.

The foregoing observation suggests one determinant of personality organization. Personality dimensions form about areas of choice, where the culture is permissive, either by explicit value or by default. Stated another way, personality dimensions are related to the lines of slack in the social order. Where the culture is entirely compelling and behavior is defined precisely, the possibility for personality dimensions to arise is severely limited.

An example which may be germane to this principle is the importance of the domination-submission theme in the study of personality in the United States and some Western societies. Almost every system for the study of personality devised in the United States has emphasized variations of some sort about the idea of domination among its major variables. In Winch's study of mate selection the "needs" which conform to the complementarity hypothesis are generally those related to a dimension of assertiveness and receptiveness.[5] But the variable of ascendance, dominance, assertiveness, etc. may be less crucial in personality differentiation in other societies. There may be less consistency along this dimension outside of ritual situations, fewer other variables may cluster about it, it may be a less significant variable in interaction. The preoccupation with questions of relative dominance in the family and in marital relations in the American family is likewise exceptional, and arises from the undefined character of dominance. The result is that instead of the individual moving smoothly according to cultural dictate between situations demanding dominance and situations demanding submission in his relations with different categories of people, he learns a predominantly dominant or predominantly submissive orientation which becomes his characteristic stance to such a degree that it impinges upon his ability to perform in situations where the proper dominance is unambiguously defined.[6]

Organization of Socializing Experiences   The first criterion of personality organization which we suggested was consistency of behavior. The most general social and cultural sources of consistency are of two kinds. One of these is exposure to a consistent sequence of socializing experiences, but experiences which are consistently different from those of some other persons. The second is the presence of cultural values which sensitize self and other disproportionately to some facets of behavior. These sources supply further clues to the social correlates of personality differentiation.

Socialization takes place through a succession of many experiences in many relationships. If the result is some personal consistency the explanation must be that threads of consistency run through these experiences.

The parent-child relationship may be as important as we suppose it is chiefly because of its continuity in the life of the individual. The social organization helps to determine which aspects of the socializing relationship between parent and child will be most consistent and which least consistent, which elements of the relationship will be grouped, and what the major alternative groupings will be. The socializing agent's relationship to the socializee is shaped in large part by what responsibilities he performs outside of the socializing relationship and the timing of these activities. Consistencies, then, will be determined by the alternative patterns of extrasocializing tasks and by the alternative systems of combining the tasks with the socialization relationship.

The axes of consistency will also vary according to the concentration or dispersion of socializing responsibility, and the generality or specialization in socializing relationships. Many anthropologists have called attention to the difference in modal personality produced in the extended family relationship as compared with the nuclear system.[7] But a systematic exploration of alternate modes of adaptation by the child to each of the two kinds of family relationship might supply the framework for discovering different axes of personality organization. A family system such as the Trobriand Islanders, which makes a sharp differentiation between the indulgent father and the stern uncle, might be examined from this standpoint.

Major Values and Self-Conception   The idea of a self-conception which brings some order into personality on the basis of self-other relationships is commonplace for sociologists. Sociologists are also aware that it is not only an internal strain for consistency which is at work.[8] Only if the individual's behavior is sufficiently orderly that others can make minimal predictions will the responses of the others be sufficiently predictable to the individual that he can exercise some control over his social environment. Because ability to control others depends upon being sufficiently predictable oneself, the individual early acquires some consistent organized orientations toward social objects. The orderliness in behavior of which we speak is designated by values. The interactive pressures toward consistency are therefore organized according to the major types of value differentiation made in a society. In accordance with the predominant modal personality approach we have excellent studies which attempt to relate dominant value to modal personality, but few to the internal differentiation of personality types in response to specific values.[9]

The range of deviant personality types is relevant here. Margaret Mead in a pioneering study called attention to the absence of the type of homosexuality with which we are acquainted in American society in some of the primitive groups she studied.[10] One notable feature of the berdache appears to be the absence of polarization into active and passive roles among homosexuals to which we are accustomed. Here may be an example of a type of personality differentiation which arises out of one way of valuing and treating homosexuality which does not arise out of another.

Many of our classifications of personality convey implicitly a favorable or unfavorable valuation. This frequently embarrasing observation may not stem from tendencies in the investigator to import his values into the investigation, but from the impact of values upon the formation of consistencies and clusters of behavior during socialization. If socialization serves chiefly to make the individual predictable, if the major basis of predictability is personal consistency, and if the most important axes of predictability are major values, there is good reason to expect useful personality dimensions to be value-loaded.

Major Divisions of Labor   In discussing the two previous facets of social structure we have emphasized the sources of consistency in behavior. We can also uncover clues from the sources of tendencies for behavior to form constellations. The major divisions of labor supply an important basis for linkages of behavior. While the more refined specialties of labor may not appear until adolescence or adulthood, there are some pervasive divisions for which children are prepared early in life. Each such division separates a large variety of behavior into a few sets, creating the expectation with supporting social pressure that an individual will pattern his behavior principally from one of the clusters rather than randomly from all.

A review of correlational studies would undoubtedly reveal that a large proportion of the dimensions and types employed in personality analysis are associated with the sex of the individual. As long as the personality variables are assumed to derive their structure from the psychogenic properties of the organism, interpretation of such relationships is the conventional problem of understanding correlations between two independent variables. But alternatively, such correlations may reveal that social definitions of sex roles have helped to account for the organization of behavior into the clusters which are being employed in the personality analysis. The more pervasive the division of labor between the sexes the wider the range of behaviors which will be associated and the more strongly they will be associated with the sex division.

Thorsten Veblen, in *The Instinct for Workmanship*, develops the theory that the dominant type of occupation in any era created a general outlook on life and approach to the natural and social world.[11] These dominant occupations also probably establish a fundamental set of dimensions which serve as a reference in the organization of personality. Again, the discovery that many personality characteristics bear some correlation with occupation may be partly the discovery of one of the sources of the prevailing differentiations of personality.

Instrumental Consequences of Roles   The other important way in which social organization leads to the grouping of behaviors is through attaching instrumental consequences to the performance of various roles. A highly speculative account of how such linking of characteristics might take place can be suggested, not for its intrinsic merit but as an example of the kinds of possibilities worth exploring. The introversion-extroversion dimension is one which rests empirically upon the clustering several kinds of tendencies. The extravert, for example, prefers sociability to solitude, prefers action to reflection, and is insensitive to minor slights and unfavorable reactions. While Jungian theory interrelates these and other elements on the basis of the psychogenic character of the organism, there is room for alternate hypotheses. The last few centuries in Western civilization have been a period in which traditional social controls have been weakened so that the individual who is moderately insensitive to disapproval from others is a "favored" type. Because of the reward structure, such an individual develops self-confidence and is prepared to act readily and is comfortable in the presence of others. In a society in which sensitivity to others was an asset rather than a liability, the same correlations might be lacking. If American society is swinging, as Riesman proposes, from inner direction to other direction, the interrelationship among these elements should be altered in the process. The change would mean not principally that introversion or extraversion would become less common, but that the clustering of forms of behavior necessary to justify the use of such a concept would be altered.

The object of offering these five points has been to demonstrate that a plausible case can be made for the position that the dimensions along which personality is organized may vary with the society. The five general relationships can serve as a starting point for hypotheses which can be used to test whether the usual axiom or the alternative view best fits actual situations.

RELATIONSHIP BETWEEN SOCIOGENIC AND PSYCHOGENIC

Separation Between Levels At this point account must be taken of criticisms lodged against excessive social determinism by such writers as Inkeles[12] and Wrong.[13] Wrong's criticisms apply largely to an overly simplistic conception of socialization as a process whereby individuals are fitted into a cultural mold, rather than learning to take account of society and culture systematically in their behavior. Inkeles asserts that some psychological theory must be assumed in the sociological study of personality. Both of these criticisms indicate that sociological studies of personality cannot merely ignore the psychogenic system of organization in personality. The presence of two levels of organization means that behavior will never be wholly predictable on the basis of socio-cultural personality variables. We have approached the problem of this paper by searching for the sources of consistency, interrelatedness, and significance in behavior; clearly there are such sources in the nature of the organism as well as in social structure. The knotty problem is therefore the nature of the relationship between the levels of organization, and what account must be taken of each in study of the other.

One approach to this problem is to show that processes at the two levels correspond so as to produce the same set of dimensions. Talcott Parsons' examination of the differentiation of roles during socialization is a monumental effort to establish such a relationship.[14] While such careful logic cannot easily be discounted, the solution seems too easy. It seems improbable that the dynamics of one level should correspond to those at another unless one is merely an extension of the other.

Earlier Ernest Burgess dealt with this problem imaginatively in his distinction between the psychogenically determined "personality type" and the sociogenically determined "social type."[15] While the two levels do not correspond, the effective adoption of a social type depends upon its supplying avenues for expression of the personality type. Thus the psychogenic is causally prior and less flexible, and while it does not determine directly the sociogenic level it sets limits within which sociogenic processes must operate. The problem in Burgess' analysis, however, is that the psychogenic includes too much and the sociogenic too little. The sociogenic is limited to the adoption of culturally identified roles, and the psychogenic includes such obviously social learning as a characteristic reaction to authority and supervision. With a more comprehensive conception of the sociogenic, the Burgess hypothesis remains a highly promising approach to this problem.

Whatever the functioning relationship between the levels of personality, the recognition of intrinsically social dimensions of organization suggests the principle that homogeneity at one level may correspond to heterogeneity at the other. This principle can be most simply illustrated through the generalizing effect of culture. The "favored personality" concept indicates that attitudes which have one dynamic in the individual who serves as model may be emulated by others who lack these dynamics.[16] The parent who has a set of attitudes because of her own unique psychological dynamics may transmit them to her children without the original dynamics. Thus the system of orientations toward social objects may be homogenous but the psychogenic constellations heterogeneous.

An interesting correspondence can be found between Horney's neurotic with his need to be loved and to control and Riesman's other-directed man.[17] The two sets of symptomatic descriptions are largely variations on a common theme. But Horney calls her type neurotic and discovers its dynamics in a reaction to the sense of isolation and powerlessness which arises in consequence of competitiveness. Riesman's type, on the other hand, is assertedly functional to our society and arises through the normal processes of social transmission. It is possible that the two views accurately reflect the situation as it prevailed two decades apart. Perhaps the pattern developed first as Horney specifies, and then became subject to the generalizing impact of culture so that it now may be acquired with or without the dynamics described by Horney. If this were so we could reasonably observe that the socially homogeneous other-directed personality type need not correspond to any strictly psychological type. By this reasoning the discovery of small correlations, such as those in the monumental authoritarian personality studies, need not supply any clue to the determination of a socially important personality type.

Perhaps such observations can help to shed light on the debate over Durkheim's famous assertion that a social fact must always be explained by a social fact.[18] Durkheim's social facts correspond to the organization of behavior at the sociogenic level. The organization of behavior at this level bears a stable relationship only to causes at that level. Relationships to other levels are fortuitous and impermanent, though non-the-less important while they exist. Theory always posits some kind of closed system in which relationships are necessary rather than fortuitous, and theory can consequently be developed only within such a level.[19] But theory and the prediction of actual behavior are different matters. Theory at any one level gives only a partial accounting for behavior. Hence, Durkheim himself was forced to work with broad correlations, on the assumption that relationships at other levels were random with respect to the social level he was studying.

CONCLUSION

The import of the foregoing is not to detract from the many exciting achievements of the standard approaches to personality study. It is rather to call attention to the dilemma of the sociologist who depends for his theory upon the psychologist or the anthropologist, and to urge the fruitfulness of another line of inquiry which has received scant attention.

It is of interest to note that sociology made a vigorous start in the area of culture-personality study in the work of Durkheim, Thomas, and others, but in recent years has largely abdicated to anthropologists and psychologists. Psychologists who had devised the instruments and the concepts for the study of personality, and anthropologists who had refined the techniques for summarizing cultures, monopolized the skills required in the conventional approaches to culture and personality. The sociologist, whose forte lay in elaborating the processes and differentiation within a society, could enter the area only by abandoning his interest in social structure for the anthropologist's interest in culture, or by simplifying his conceptions of social structure in order to note rough associations between the psychologists' categories and broad subcultures. But the problem of how a given society supplies unique patterns of organization for personality, corresponding to the differentiating processes at work within that society, calls for precisely the skills of the analysis of social structure which are nearest to the sociologist's stock in trade.

It is time to rejuvenate the sociological field of study once called "social differentiation." But in rejuvenating it we should add an important dimension. Differentiation is not only the elaboration of social structure: it may also be the source of a major level of organization in individual personality. Because societies differentiate their populations differently, they may also provide different organizing frameworks for personality. The study of more profound relationships between social structure and personality organization may well be the most promising next step after culture-personality. And such traditional sociological types as Thomas' types of immigrants,[20]

Park's marginal man,[21] and Strong's social types of Negroes,[22] need not be disparaged because they have not been translated into a set of psychological variables.

NOTES

[1] Daniel Miller phrases the approach in typical fashion when he suggests that the problem in cross-cultural investigation is to know which of the systems to select from a standard psychological text on personality. Cf. "Personality and Social Interaction," in *Studying Personality Cross-Culturally*, Bert Kaplan, ed. (Evanston, Ill.: Row, Peterson, 1961), p. 271.

[2] *Patterns of Culture* (Boston: Houghton Mifflin), 1934.

[3] Edmund H. Volkart, ed., *Social Behavior and Personality* (New York: Social Science Research Council, 1951), p. 185.

[4] Theodore Adorno, et al., *The Authoritarian Personality* (New York: Harper, 1950), esp. pp. 224–241.

[5] Robert Winch, *Mate Selection* (New York: Harper, 1958).

[6] Margaret Mead has noted a difference of this sort in Samoa. "Such a man does not develop a fixed response to others which is definitely either dominance or submission, leadership or discipleship, authoritarian insistence or meek compliance, exhibitionism or refusal to play any public part; the multiplicity and contrast between his roles prevent any commitment to one personality type from developing." *Cooperation and Competition Among Primitive Peoples* (New York: McGraw-Hill, 1937), p. 296.

[7] Cf. Dorothea Leighton and Clyde Kluckhohn, *Children of the People* (Cambridge: Harvard University Press, 1947), pp. 42–49.

[8] Prescott Lecky, *Self-Consistency: A Theory of Personality* (New York: Island Press, 1951).

[9] Among the interesting exceptions to this observation is Raymond A. Bauer's discussion of two alternate forms of adaptation in "The Psychology of the Soviet Middle Elite: Two Case Histories,'" in *Personality in Nature, Society, and Culture*, Clyde Kluckhohn and Henry A. Murray, eds. (New York: Knopf, 1953), pp. 633–650.

[10] *Sex and Temperament in Three Primitive Societies* (New York: William Morrow & Co., 1934), pp. 290–309.

[11] *The Instinct for Workmanship* (New York: B. W. Huebsch, 1918).

[12] "Personality and Social Structure," in *Sociology Today*, Robert K. Merton, Leonard Broom, and Leonard S. Cottrell, Jr., eds. (New York: Basic Books, 1959), pp. 249–276.

[13] "The Oversocialized Conception of Man in Modern Sociology," *American Sociological Review*, 26 (1961), pp. 183–193.

[14] Talcott Parsons and Robert F. Bales, *Family, Socialization and Interaction Process* (Glencoe, Ill.: The Free Press, 1955), pp. 35–257.

[15] "Discussion," in Clifford R. Shaw, *The Jackroller* (Chicago: University of Chicago Press, 1930), pp. 184–197.

[16] Cf. Don Martindale and Elio Monachesi, *Elements of Sociology* (New York: Harper, 1951), pp. 312–378.

[17] Karen Horney, *The Neurotic Personality of Our Time* (New York: W. W. Norton, 1937); David Riesman, *The Lonely Crowd* (New Haven: Yale University Press, 1950).

[18] Emile Durkheim, *Les Regles de la Methode Sociologique* (Paris: Librairie Felix Alcan, 1927), pp. 120–137.

[19] Cf. Ralph H. Turner, "The Quest for Universals in Sociological Research," *American Sociological Review*, 18 (1953), pp. 604–611.

[20] Robert E. Park and Herbert A. Miller, *Old World Traits Transplanted* (Chicago: Society for Social Research, 1925), pp. 81ff.

[21] Robert E. Park, "Human Migration and the Marginal Man," *American Journal of Sociology*, 33 (1928), pp. 881–893.

[22] Samuel M. Strong, "Social Types in a Minority Group: Formulation of a Method," *American Journal of Sociology*, 48 (1943), pp. 563–573.

7 GEORGE HERBERT MEAD

Play, the Game, and the Generalized Other

We were speaking of the social conditions under which the self arises as an object. In addition to language we found two illustrations, one in play and the other in the game, and I wish to summarize and expand my account on these points. I have spoken of these from the point of view of children. We can, of course, refer also to the attitudes of more primitive people out of which our civilization has arisen. A striking illustration of play as distinct from the game is found in the myths and various of the plays which primitive people carry out, especially in religious pageants. The pure play attitude which we find in the case of little children may not be found here, since the participants are adults, and undoubtedly the relationship of these play processes to that which they interpret is more or less in the minds of even the most primitive people. In the process of interpretation of such rituals, there is an organization of play which perhaps might be compared to that which is taking place in the kindergarten in dealing with the plays of little children, where these are made into a set that will have a definite structure or relationship. At least something of the same sort is found in the play of primitive people. This type of activity belongs, of course, not to the everyday life of the people in their dealing with the objects about them—there we have a more or less definitely developed self-consciousness —but in their attitudes toward the forces about them, the nature upon which they depend; in their attitude toward this nature which is vague and uncertain, there we have a much more primitive response; and that response finds its expression in taking the role of the other, playing at the expression of their gods and their heroes, going through certain rites which are the representation of what these individuals are supposed to be doing. The process is one which develops, to be sure, into a more or less definite technique and is controlled; and yet we can say that it has arisen out of situations similar to those in which little children play at being a parent, at being a teacher—vague personalities that are about them and which affect them and on which they depend. These are personalities which they take, roles they play, and in so far control the development of their own personality. This outcome is just what the kindergarten works toward. It takes the characters of these various vague beings and gets them into such an organized social relationship to each other that they build up the character of the little child.[1] The very introduction of organization from outside supposes a lack of organization at this period in the child's experience. Over against such a situation of the little child and primitive people, we have the game as such.

The fundamental difference between the game and play is that in the latter the child must have the attitude of all the others involved in that game. The attitudes of the other players which the participant assumes organize into a sort of unit, and it is that organization which controls the response of the individual. The illustration used was of a person playing baseball. Each one of his own acts is determined by his assumption of the action of the others who are playing the game. What he does is controlled by his being everyone else on that team, at least in so far as those attitudes affect his own particular response. We get then an "other" which is an organization of the attitudes of those involved in the same process.

The organized community or social group which gives to the individual his unity of self may be called "the generalized other." The attitude of the generalized other is the attitude of the whole community.[2] Thus, for example, in the case of such a social group as a ball team, the team is the generalized other in so far as it enters—as an organized process or social activity—into the experience of any one of the individual members of it.

If the given human individual is to develop a self in the fullest sense, it is not sufficient for him merely to take the attitudes of other human individuals toward himself and toward one another within the human social process, and to bring that social process as a whole into his individual experience merely in these terms: he must also, in the same way that he takes the attitudes of other individuals toward himself and toward one another, take their attitudes toward the various phases or aspects of the common social activity or set of social undertakings in which, as members of an organized society or social group, they are all engaged; and he must then, by generalizing these individual attitudes of that organized society or social group itself, as a whole, act toward different social projects which at any given time it is carrying out, or toward the various larger phases of the general social process which constitutes its life and of which these projects are specific manifestations. This getting of the broad activities of any given social whole or organized society as such within the experiential field of any one of the individuals involved or included in that whole is, in other words, the essential basis and prerequisite of the fullest development of that individual's self: only in so far as he takes the attitudes of the organized social group to which he belongs toward the organized, cooperative social activity or set of such activities in which that group as such is engaged, does he develop a complete self or possess the sort of complete self he has developed. And on the other hand, the complex cooperative processes and activities and institutional functionings of organized human society are also possible only in so far as every individual involved in them or belonging to that society can take the general attitudes of all other such individuals with reference to these processes and activities and institutional functionings, and to the organized social whole of experiential relations and interactions thereby constituted—and can direct his own behavior accordingly.

It is in the form of the generalized other that the social process influences the behavior of the individuals involved in it and carrying it on, i.e., that the community exercises control over the conduct of its individual members; for it is in this form that the social process or community enters as a determining factor into the individual's thinking. In abstract thought the individual takes the attitude of the generalized other[3] toward himself, without reference to its expression in any particular other individuals; and in concrete thought he takes that attitude in so far as it is expressed in the attitudes toward his behavior of those other individuals with whom he is involved in the given social situation or act. But only by taking the attitude of the generalized other toward himself, in one or another of these ways, can he think at all; for only thus can thinking—or the internalized conversation of gestures which constitutes thinking—occur. And only through the taking by individuals of the attitude or attitudes of the generalized other toward themselves is the existence of a universe of discourse, as that system of common or social meanings which thinking presupposes at its context, rendered possible.

The self-conscious human individual, then, takes or assumes the organized social attitudes of the given social group or community (or of some one section thereof) to which he belongs, toward the social problems of various kinds which confront that group or community at any given time, and which arise in connection with the correspondingly different social projects or organized cooperative enterprises in which that group or community as such is engaged; and as an individual participant in these social projects or cooperative enterprises, he governs his own conduct accordingly. In politics, for example, the individual identifies himself with an entire political party and takes the organized attitudes of that entire party toward the rest of the given social community and toward the problems which confront the party within the given social situation; and he consequently reacts or responds in terms of the organized attitudes of the party as a whole. He thus enters into a special set of social relations with all the other individuals who belong to that political party; and in the same way he enters into various other special sets of social relations, with various other classes of individuals respectively, the individuals of each of these classes being the other members of some one of the particular organized subgroups (determined in socially functional terms) of which he himself is a member within the entire given society or social community. In the most highly developed, organized, and complicated human social communities—those evolved by civilized man—these various socially functional classes or subgroups of individuals to which any given individual belongs (and with the other individual members of which he thus enters into a special set of social relations) are of two kinds. Some of them are concrete social classes or subgroups, such as political parties, clubs, corporations, which are all actually functional social units, in terms of which their individual members are directly related to one another. The others are abstract social classes or subgroups, such as the class of debtors and the class of creditors, in terms of which their individual members are related to one another only more or less indirectly, and which only more or less indirectly function as social units, but which afford or represent unlimited possibilities for the widening and ramifying and enriching of the social relations among all the individual members of the given society as an organized and unified whole. The given individual's membership in several of these abstract social classes or subgroups makes possible his entrance into definite social relations (however indirect) with an almost infinite number of other individuals who also belong to or are included within one or another of these abstract social classes or subgroups cutting across functional lines of demarcation which divide different human social communities from one another, and including individual members from several (in some cases from all) such communities. Of these abstract social classes or subgroups of human individuals the one which is most inclusive and extensive is, of course, the one defined by the logical universe of discourse (or system of universally significant symbols) determined by the participation and communicative interaction of individuals; for all such classes or subgroups, it is the one which claims the largest number of individual members, and which enables the largest conceivable number of human individuals to enter into some sort of social relation, however indirect or abstract it may be, with one another—a relation arising from the universal functioning of gestures as significant symbols in the general human social process of communication.

I have pointed out, then, that there are two general stages in the full development of the self. At the first of these stages, the individual's self is constituted simply by an organization of the particular attitudes of other individuals toward himself and toward one another in the specific social acts in which he participates with them. But at the second stage in the full development of the individual's self that self is constituted not only by an organization of these particular individual attitudes, but also by an organization of the social attitudes of the generalized other or the social group as a whole to which he belongs. These social or group attitudes are brought within the individual's field of direct experience, and are included as elements in the structure or constitution of his self, in the same way that the attitudes of particular other individuals are; and the individual arrives at them, or succeeds in taking them, by means of further organizing, and then generalizing, the attitudes of particular other individuals in terms of their organized social bearings and implications. So the self reaches its full development by organizing these individual attitudes of others into the organized social or group attitudes, and by thus becoming an individual reflection of the general systematic pattern of social or group behavior in which it and the others are all involved—a pattern which enters as a whole into the individual's experience in terms of these organized group attitudes which, through the mechanism of his central nervous system, he takes toward himself, just as he takes the individual attitudes of others.

The game has a logic, so that such an organization of the self is rendered possible: there is a definite end to be obtained; the actions of the different individuals are all related to each other with reference to that end so that they do not conflict; one is not in conflict with himself in the attitude of another man on the team. If one has the attitude of the person throwing the ball he can also have the response of catching the ball. The two are interrelated so that they further the purpose of the game itself. They are interrelated in a unitary, organic fashion. There is a definite unity, then, which is introduced into the organization of other selves when we reach such a stage as that of the game, as over against the situation of play where there is a simple succession of one role after another, a situation which is, of course, characteristic of the child's own personality. The child is one thing at one time and another at another, and what he is at one moment does not determine what he is at another. That is both the charm of childhood as well as its inadequacy. You cannot count on the child; you cannot assume that all the things he does are going to determine what he will do at any moment. He is not organized into a whole. The child has no definite character, no definite personality.

The game is then an illustration of the situation out of which an organized personality arises. In so far as the child does take the attitude of the other and allows that attitude of the other to determine the thing he is going to do with reference to a common end, he is becoming an organic member of society. He is taking over the morale of that society and is becoming an essential member of it. He belongs to it in so far as he does allow the attitude of the other that he takes to control his own immediate expression. What is involved here is some sort of an organized process. That which is expressed in terms of the game is, of course, being continually expressed in the social life of the child, but this wider process goes beyond the immediate experience of the child himself. The importance of the game is that it lies entirely inside of the child's own experience, and the importance of our modern type of education is that it is brought as far as possible within this realm. The different attitudes that a child assumes are so organized that they exercise a definite control over his response, as the attitudes in a game control his own immediate response. In the game we get an organized other, a generalized other, which is found in the nature of the child itself, and finds its expression in the immediate experience of the child. And it is that organized activity in the child's own nature controlling the particular response which gives unity, and which builds up his own self.

What goes on in the game goes on in the life of the child all the time. He is continually taking the attitudes of those about him, especially the roles of those who in some sense control him and on whom he depends. He gets the function of the process in an abstract sort of a way at first. It goes over from the play into the game in a real sense. He has to play the game, The morale of the game takes hold of the child more than the larger morale of the whole community. The child passes into the game and the game expresses a social situation in which he can completely enter; its morale may have a greater hold on him than that of the family to which he belongs or the community in which he lives. There are all sorts of social organizations, some of which are fairly lasting, some temporary, into which the child is entering, and he is playing a sort of social game in them. It is a period in which he likes "to belong," and he gets into organizations which come into existence and pass out of existence. He becomes a something which can function in the organized whole, and thus tends to determine himself in his relationship with the group to which he belongs. That process is one which is a striking stage in the development of the child's morale. It constitutes him a self-conscious member of the community to which he belongs.

Such is the process by which a personality arises. I have spoken of this as a process in which a child takes the role of the other, and said that it takes place essentially through the use of language. Language is predominantly based on the vocal gesture by means of which cooperative activities in a community are carried out. Language in its significant sense is that vocal gesture which tends to arouse in the individual the attitude which it arouses in others, and it is this perfecting of the self by the gesture which mediates the social activities that gives rise to the process of taking the role of the other. The latter phrase is a little unfortunate because it suggests an actor's attitude which is actually more sophisticated than that which is involved in our own experience. To this degree it does not correctly describe that which I have in mind. We see the process most definitely in a primitive form in those situations where the child's play takes different roles. Here the very fact that he is ready to pay out money, for instance, arouses the attitude of the person who receives money; the very process is calling out in him the corresponding activities of the other person involved. The individual stimulates himself to the response which he is calling out in the other person, and then acts in some degree in response to that situation. In play the child does definitely act out the role which he himself has aroused in himself. It is that which gives, as I have said, a definite content in the individual which answers to the stimulus that affects him as it affects somebody else. The content of the other that enters into one personality is the response in the individual which his gesture calls out in the other.

We may illustrate our basic concept by a reference to the notion of property. If we say "This is my property, I shall control it," that affirmation calls out a certain set of responses which must be the same in any community in which property exists. It involves an organized attitude with reference to property which is common to all the members of the community. One must have a definite attitude of control of his own property and respect for the property of others. Those attitudes (as organized sets of responses) must be there on the part of all, so that when one says such a thing he calls out in himself the response of the others. He is calling out the response of what I have called a generalized other. That which makes society possible is such common responses, such organized attitudes, with reference to what we term property, the cults of religion, the process of education, and the relations of the family. Of course, the wider the society the more definitely universal these objects must be. In any case there must be a definite set of responses, which we may speak of as abstract, and which can belong to a very large group. Property is in itself a very abstract concept. It is that which the individual himself can control and nobody else can control. The attitude is different from that of a dog toward a bone. A dog will fight any other dog trying to take the bone. The dog is not taking the attitude of the other dog. A man who says "This is my property" is taking an attitude of the other person. The man is appealing to his rights because he is able to take the attitude which everybody else in the group has with reference to property, thus arousing in himself the attitude of others.

What goes to make up the organized self is the organization of the attitudes which are common to the group. A person is a personality because he belongs to a community, because he takes over the institutions of that community into his own conduct. He takes its language as a medium by which he gets his personality, and then through a process of taking the different roles that all the others furnish he comes to get the attitude of the members of the community. Such, in a certain sense, is the structure of a man's personality. There are certain common responses which each individual has toward certain common things, and in so far as those common responses are awakened in the individual when he is affecting other persons he arouses his own self. The structure, then, on which the self is built is this response which is common to all, for one has to be a member of a community to be a self. Such responses are abstract attitudes, but they constitute just what we term a man's character. They give him what we term his principles, the acknowledged attitudes of all members of the community toward what are the values of that community. He is putting himself in the place of the generalized other, which represents the organized responses of all the members of the group. It is that which guides conduct controlled by principles, and a person who has such an organized group of responses is a man whom we say has character, in the moral sense.

It is a structure of attitudes, then, which goes to make up a self, as distinct from a group of habits. We all of us have, for example, certain groups of habits, such as the particular intonations which a person uses in his speech. This is a set of habits of vocal expression which one has but which one does not know about. The sets of habits which we have of that sort mean nothing to us; we do not hear the intonations of our speech that others hear unless we are paying particular attention to them. The habits of emotional expression which belong to our speech are of the same sort. We may know that we have expressed ourselves in a joyous fashion but the detailed process is one which does not come back to our conscious selves. There are whole bundles of such habits which do not enter into a conscious self, but which help to make up what is termed the unconscious self.

After all, what we mean by self-consciousness is an awakening in ourselves of the group of attitudes which we are arousing in others, especially when it is an important set of responses which go to make up the members of the community. It is unfortunate to fuse or mix up consciousness, as we ordinarily use that term, and self-consciousness. Consciousness, as frequently used, simply has reference to the field of experience, but self-consciousness refers to the ability to call out in ourselves a set of definite responses which belong to the others of the group. Consciousness and self-consciousness are not on the same level. A man alone has, fortunately or unfortunately, access, to his own toothache, but that is not what we mean by self-consciousness.

I have so far emphasized what I have called the structures upon which the self is constructed, the framework of the self, as it were. Of course we are not only what is common to all: Each one of the selves is different from everyone else; but there has to be such a common structure as I have sketched in order that we may be members of a community at all. We cannot be ourselves unless we are also members in whom there is a community of attitudes which control the attitudes of all. We cannot have rights unless we have common attitudes. That which we have acquired as self-conscious persons makes us such members of society and gives us selves. Selves can only exist in definite relationships to other selves. No hard-and-fast line can be drawn between our own selves and the selves of others, since our own selves exist and enter as such into our experience only in so far as the selves of others exist and enter as such into our experience also. The individual possesses a self only in relation to the selves of the other members of his social group; and the structure of his self expresses or reflects the general behavior pattern of this social group to which he belongs, just as does the structure of the self of every other individual belonging to this social group.

NOTES

[1] "The Relation of Play to Education," *University of Chicago Record*, 1 (1896–97), pp. 140ff.

[2] It is possible for inanimate objects, no less than for other human organisms, to form parts of the generalized and organized—the completely socialized—other for any given human individual, in so far as he responds to such objects socially or in a social fashion (by means of the mechanism of thought, the internalized conversation of gestures). Any thing—any object or set of objects, whether animate or inanimate, human or animal, or merely physical—toward which he acts, or to which he responds, socially, is an element in what for him is the generalized other; by taking the attitudes of which toward himself he becomes conscious of himself as an object or individual, and thus develops a self or personality. Thus, for example, the cult, in its primitive form, is merely the social embodiment of the relation between the given social group or community and its physical environment—an organized social means, adopted by

the individual members of that group or community, of entering into social relations with that environment, or (in a sense) of carrying on conversations with it; and in this way that environment becomes part of the total generalized other for each of the individual members of the given social group or community.

[3] We have said that the internal conversation of the individual with himself in terms of words or significant gestures—the conversation which constitutes the process or activity of thinking—is carried on by the individual from the standpoint of the "generalized other." And the more abstract that conversation is, the more abstract thinking happens to be, the further removed is the generalized other from any connection with particular individuals. It is especially in abstract thinking, that is to say, that the conversation involved is carried on by the individual with the generalized other, rather than with any particular individuals. Thus it is, for example, that abstract concepts are concepts stated in terms of the attitudes of the entire social group or community; they are stated on the basis of the individual's consciousness of the attitudes of the generalized other toward them, as a result of his taking these attitudes of the generalized other and then responding to them. And thus it is also that abstract propositions are stated in a form which anyone—any other intelligent individual—will accept.

| Critical Concepts in Sociological Analysis | NORMS AND VALUES |

8 Ralph H. Turner

Sponsored and Contest Mobility and the School System

This paper suggests a framework for relating certain differences between American and English systems of education to the prevailing norms of upward mobility in each country. Others have noted the tendency of educational systems to support prevailing schemes of stratification, but this discussion concerns specifically the manner in which the *accepted mode of upward mobility* shapes the school system directly and indirectly through its effects on the values which implement social control.

Two ideal-typical normative patterns of upward mobility are described and their ramifications in the general patterns of stratification and social control are suggested. In addition to showing relationships among a number of differences between American and English schooling, the ideal-types have broader implications than those developed in this paper: they suggest

Reprinted from *American Sociological Review*, 25:6 (1960), pp. 855–867, by permission of the author and the publisher.

a major dimension of stratification which might be profitably incorporated into a variety of studies in social class; and they readily can be applied in further comparisons between other countries.

THE NATURE OF ORGANIZING NORMS

Many investigators have concerned themselves with rates of upward mobility in specific countries or internationally,[1] and with the manner in which school systems facilitate or impede such mobility.[2] But preoccupation with the *extent* of mobility has precluded equal attention to the predominant *modes* of mobility. The central assumption underlying this paper is that within a formally open class system that provides for mass education the organizing folk norm which defines the accepted mode of upward mobility is a crucial factor in shaping the school system, and may be even more crucial than the extent of upward mobility. In England and the United States there appear to be different organizing folk norms, here termed *sponsored mobility* and *contest mobility*, respectively. *Contest* mobility is a system in which elite[3] status is the prize in an open contest and is taken by the aspirants' own efforts. While the "contest" is governed by some rules of fair play, the contestants have wide latitude in the strategies they may employ. Since the "prize" of successful upward mobility is not in the hands of an established elite to give out, the latter cannot determine who shall attain it and who shall not. Under *sponsored* mobility elite recruits are chosen by the established elite or their agents, and elite status is *given* on the basis of some criterion of supposed merit and cannot be *taken* by any amount of effort or strategy. Upward mobility is like entry into a private club where each candidate must be "sponsored" by one or more of the members. Ultimately the members grant or deny upward mobility on the basis of whether they judge the candidate to have those qualities they wish to see in fellow members.

Before elaborating this distinction, it should be noted that these systems of mobility are ideal types designed to clarify observed differences in the predominantly similar English and American systems of stratification and education. But as organizing norms these principles are assumed to be present at least implicitly in people's thinking, guiding their judgments of what is appropriate on many specific matters. Such organizing norms do not correspond perfectly with the objective characteristics of the societies in which they exist, nor are they completely independent of them. From the complex interplay of social and economic conditions and ideologies people in a society develop a highly simplified conception of the way in which events take place. This conception of the "natural" is translated into a norm—the "natural" becomes what "ought" to be—and in turn imposes a strain toward consistency upon relevant aspects of the society. Thus the norm acts back upon the objective conditions to which it refers and has ramifying effects upon directly and indirectly related features of the society.[4]

In brief, the conception of an ideal-typical organizing norm involves the following propositions: (1) The ideal types are not fully exemplified in practice since they are normative systems, and no normative system can be devised so as to cope with all empirical exigencies. (2) Predominant norms usually compete with less ascendant norms engendered by changes and inconsistencies in the underlying social structure. (3) Though not fully explicit, organizing folk norms are reflected in specific value judgments. Those judgments which the relevant people regard as having a convincing ring to them, irrespective of the logic expressed, or which seem to require no extended argumentation may be presumed to reflect the prevailing folk norms. (4) The predominant organizing norms in one segment of society are functionally related to those in other segments.

Two final qualifications concerning the scope of this paper: First, the organizing folk norm of upward mobility affects the school system because one of the latter's functions is the facilitation of mobility. Since this is only one of several social functions of the school, and not the most important function in the societies under examination, only a very partial accounting of the whole set of forces making for similarities and differences in the school systems of the United States and England is possible here. Only those differences which directly or indirectly reflect the performance of the mobility function are noted. Second, the concern of this paper is with the current dynamics of the situation in the two countries rather than with their historical development.

DISTINCTIONS BETWEEN THE TWO NORMS

Contest mobility is like a sporting event in which many compete for a few recognized prizes. The contest is judged to be fair only if all the players compete on an equal footing. Victory must be won solely by one's own efforts. The most satisfactory outcome is not necessarily a victory of the most able, but of the most deserving. The tortoise who defeats the hare is a folk-prototype of the deserving sportsman. Enterprise, initiative, perseverance, and craft are admirable qualities if they allow the person who is initially at a disadvantage to triumph. Even clever manipulation of the rules may be admired if it helps the contestant who is smaller or less muscular or less rapid to win. Applied to mobility, the contest norm means that victory by a person of moderate intelligence accomplished through the use of common sense, craft, enterprise, daring, and successful risk-taking[5] is more appreciated than victory by the most intelligent or the best educated.

Sponsored mobility, in contrast, rejects the pattern of the contest and favors a controlled selection process. In this process the elite or their agents, deemed to be best qualified to judge merit, choose individuals for elite status who have the appropriate qualities. Individuals do not win or seize elite status; mobility is rather a process of sponsored induction into the elite.

Pareto had this sort of mobility in mind when he suggested that a governing class might dispose of persons potentially dangerous to it by admitting them to elite membership, provided that the recruits change character by adopting elite attitudes and interests.[6] Danger to the ruling class would seldom be the major criterion for choice of elite recruits. But Pareto assumed that the established elite would select whom they wished to enter their ranks and would inculcate the attitudes and interests of the established elite in the recruits.

The governing objective of contest mobility is to give elite status to those who earn it, while the goal of sponsored mobility is to make the best use of the talents in society by sorting persons into their proper niches. In different societies the conditions of competitive struggle may reward quite different attributes, and sponsored mobility may select individuals on the basis of such diverse qualities as intelligence or visionary capability, but the difference in principle remains the same.[7]

Under the contest system society at large establishes and interprets the criteria of elite status. If one wishes to have his status recognized he must display certain credentials which identify his class to those about him. The credentials must be highly visible and require no special skill for their assessment, since credentials are presented to the masses. Material possession and mass popularity are altogether appropriate credentials in this respect, and any special skill which produces a tangible product and which can easily be assessed by the untrained will do. The nature of sponsored mobility precludes these procedures, but assigns to credentials instead the function of identifying elite members to one another.[8] Accordingly, the ideal credentials are special skills that require the trained discrimination of the elite for their recognition. In this case, intellectual, literary, or artistic excellencies, which can be appraised only by those trained to appreciate them, are fully suitable credentials. Concentration on such skills lessens the likelihood that an interloper will succeed in claiming the right to elite membership on grounds of the popular evaluation of his competence.

In the sporting event there is special admiration for the slow starter who makes a dramatic finish, and many of the rules are designed to insure that the race should not be declared over until it has run its full course. Contest mobility incorporates this disapproval of premature judgments and of anything that gives special advantage to those who are ahead at any point in the race. Under sponsored mobility, fairly early selection of only the number of persons necessary to fill anticipated vacancies in the elite is desirable. Early selection allows time to prepare the recruits for their elite position. Aptitudes, inherent capacities, and spiritual gifts can be assessed fairly early in life by techniques ranging from divination to the most sophisticated psychological test, and the more naive the subjects at the time of selection the less likely are their talents to be blurred by differential learning or conspiracy to defeat the test. Since elitists take the initiative in training recruits, they are more interested in the latters' capabilities than in what they will do with them on their own, and they are concerned that no one else should first have an opportunity to train the recruits' talents in the wrong direction. Contest mobility tends to delay the final award as long as practicable to permit a fair race; sponsored mobility tends to place the time of recruitment as early in life as practicable to insure control over selection and training.

Systems of sponsored mobility develop most readily in societies with but a single elite or with a recognized elite hierarchy. When multiple elites compete among themselves the mobility process tends to take the contest pattern, since no group is able to command control of recruitment. Sponsored mobility further depends upon a social structure that fosters monopoly of elite credentials. Lack of such monopoly undercuts sponsorship and control of the recruitment process. Monopoly of credentials in turn is typically a product of societies with well entrenched traditional aristocracies employing such credentials as family line and bestowable title which are intrinsically subject to monopoly, or of societies organized on large-scale bureaucratic lines permitting centralized control of upward social movement.

English society has been described as the juxtaposition of two systems of stratification, the urban industrial class system and the surviving aristocratic system. While the sponsored mobility pattern reflects the logic of the latter, our impression is that it pervades popular thinking rather than merely coexisting with the logic of industrial stratification. Patterns imported into an established culture tend to be reshaped, as they are assimilated, into consistency with the established culture. Thus it may be that changes in stratification associated with industrialization have led to alterations in the rates, the specific means, and the rules of mobility, but that these changes have been guided by the but lightly challenged organizing norm of sponsored mobility.

SOCIAL CONTROL AND THE TWO NORMS

Every society must cope with the problem of maintaining loyalty to its social system and does so in part through norms and values, only some of which vary by class position. Norms and values especially prevalent within a given class must direct behavior into channels that support the total system, while those that transcend strata must support the general class differential. The way in which upward mobility takes place determines in part the kinds of norms and values that serve the indicated purposes of social control in each class and throughout the society.

The most conspicuous control problem is that of ensuring loyalty in the disadvantaged classes toward a system in which their members receive less than a proportional share of society's goods. In a system of contest mobility this is accomplished by a combination of futuristic orientation, the norm of ambition, and a general sense of fellowship with the elite. Each individual is encouraged to think of himself as competing for an elite position so that loyalty to the system and conventional attitudes are cultivated in the process of preparation for this possibility. It is essential that this futuristic orientation be kept alive by delaying a sense of final irreparable failure to reach elite status until attitudes are well established. By thinking of himself in the successful future the elite aspirant forms considerable identification with elitists, and evidence that they are merely ordinary human beings like himself helps to reinforce this identification as well as to keep alive the conviction that he himself may someday succeed in like manner. To forestall rebellion among the disadvantaged majority, then, a contest system must avoid absolute points of selection for mobility and immobility and must delay clear recognition of the realities of the situation until the individual is too committed to the system to change radically. A futuristic orientation cannot, of course, be inculcated successfully in all members of lower strata, but sufficient internalization of a norm of ambition tends to leave the unambitious as individual deviants and to forestall the latters' formation of a genuine subcultural group able to offer collective threat to the established system. Where this kind of control system operates rather effectively it is notable that organized or gang deviancy is more likely to take the form of an attack upon the conventional or moral order rather than upon the class system itself. Thus the United States has its "beatniks"[9] who repudiate ambition and most worldly values and its delinquent and criminal gangs who try to evade the limitations imposed by conventional means,[10] but very few active revolutionaries.

These social controls are inappropriate in a system of sponsorship since the elite recruits are chosen from above. The principal threat to the system would lie in the existence of a strong group the members of which sought to *take* elite positions themselves. Control under this system is maintained by training the "masses" to regard themselves as relatively incompetent to manage society, by restricting access to the skills and manners of the elite, and by cultivating belief in the superior competence of the elite. The earlier that selection of the elite recruits is made the sooner others can be taught to accept their inferiority and to make "realistic" rather than phantasy plans. Early selection prevents raising the hopes of large numbers of people who might otherwise become the discontented leaders of a class challenging the sovereignty of the established elite. If it is assumed that the difference in competence between masses and elite is seldom so great as to support the usual differences in the advantages accruing to each,[11] then the differences must be artificially augmented by discouraging acquisition of elite skills by the masses. Thus a sense of mystery about the elite is a common device for supporting in the masses the illusion of a much greater hiatus of competence than in fact exists.

While elitists are unlikely to reject a system that benefits them, they must still be restrained from taking such advantage of their favorable situation as to jeopardize the entire elite. Under the sponsorship system the elite recruits—who are selected early, freed from the strain of competitive struggle, and kept under close supervision—may be thoroughly indoctrinated in elite culture. A norm of paternalism toward inferiors may be inculcated, a heightened sensitivity to the good opinion of fellow elitists and elite recruits may be cultivated, and the appreciation of the more complex forms of aesthetic, literary, intellectual, and sporting activities may be taught. Norms of courtesy and altruism easily can be maintained under sponsorship since elite recruits are not required to compete for their standing and since the elite may deny high standing to those who strive for position by "unseemly" methods. The system of sponsorship provides an almost perfect setting for the development of an elite culture characterized by a sense of responsibility for "inferiors" and for preservation of the "finer things" of life.

Elite control in the contest system is more difficult since there is no controlled induction and apprenticeship. The principal regulation seems to lie in the insecurity of elite position. In a sense there is no "final arrival" because each person may be displaced by newcomers throughout his life. The limited control of high standing from above prevents the clear delimitation of levels in the class system, so that success itself becomes relative: each success, rather than an accomplishment, serves to qualify the participant for competition at the next higher level.[12] The restraints upon the behavior of a person of high standing, therefore, are principally those applicable to a contestant who must not risk the "ganging up" of other contestants, and who must pay some attention to the masses who are frequently in a position to impose penalties upon him. But any special norm of paternalism is hard to establish since there is no dependable procedure for examining the means by which one achieves elite credentials. While mass esteem is an effective brake upon over-exploitation of position, it rewards scrupulously ethical and altruistic behavior much less than evidence of fellow-feeling with the masses themselves.

Under both systems, unscrupulous or disreputable persons may become or remain members of the elite, but for different reasons. In contest mobility, popular tolerance of a little craftiness in the successful newcomer, together with the fact that he does not have to undergo the close scrutiny of the old elite, leaves considerable leeway for unscrupulous success. In sponsored mobility, the unpromising recruit reflects unfavorably on the judgments of his sponsors and threatens the myth of elite omniscience; consequently he may be tolerated and others may "cover up" for his deficiencies in order to protect the unified front of the elite to the outer world.

Certain of the general values and norms of any society reflect emulation of elite values by the masses. Under sponsored mobility, a good deal of the protective attitudes toward and interest in classical subjects percolates to the masses. Under contest mobility, however, there is not the same degree of homogeneity of moral, aesthetic, and intellectual values to be emulated, so that the conspicuous attribute of the elite is its high level of material consumption—emulation itself follows this course. There is neither effective incentive nor punishment for the elitist who fails to interest himself in promoting the arts or literary excellence, or who continues to maintain the vulgar manners and mode of speech of his class origin. The elite has relatively less power and the masses relatively more power to punish or reward a man for his adoption or disregard of any special elite culture. The great importance of accent and of grammatical excellence in the attainment of high status in England as contrasted with the twangs and drawls and grammatical ineptitude among American elites is the most striking example of this difference. In a contest system, the class order does not function to support the *quality* of aesthetic, literary, and intellectual activities; only those well versed in such matters are qualified to distinguish authentic products from cheap imitations. Unless those who claim superiority in these areas are forced to submit their credentials to the elite for evaluation, poor quality is often honored equally with high quality and class prestige does not serve to maintain an effective norm of high quality.

This is not to imply that there are no groups in a "contest" society devoted to the protection and fostering of high standards in art, music, literature, and intellectual pursuits, but that such standards lack the support of the class system which is frequently found when sponsored mobility prevails. In California, the selection by official welcoming committees of a torch singer to entertain a visiting king and queen and "can-can" dancers to entertain Mr. Khrushchev illustrates how American elites can assume that high prestige and popular taste go together.

FORMAL EDUCATION

Returning to the conception of an organizing ideal norm, we assume that to the extent to which one such norm of upward mobility is prevalent in a society there are constant strains to shape the educational system into conformity with that norm. These strains operate in two fashions: directly, by blinding people to alternatives and coloring their judgments of successful and unsuccessful solutions to recurring educational problems; indirectly, through the functional interrelationships between school systems and the class structure, systems of social control, and other features of the social structure which are neglected in this paper.

The most obvious application of the distinction between sponsored and contest mobility norms affords a partial explanation for the different policies of student selection in the English and American secondary schools. Although American high school students follow different courses of study and a few attend specialized schools, a major educational preoccupation has been to avoid any sharp social separation between the superior and inferior students and to keep the channels of movement between courses of study as open as possible. Recent criticisms of the way in which superior students may be thereby held back in their development usually are nevertheless qualified by the insistence that these students must not be withdrawn from the mainstream of student life.[13] Such segregation offends the sense of fairness implicit in the contest norm and also arouses the fear that the elite and future elite will lose their sense of fellowship with the masses. Perhaps the most important point, however, is that schooling is presented as an opportunity, and making use of it depends primarily on the student's own initiative and enterprise.

The English system has undergone a succession of liberalizing changes during this century, but all of them have retained the attempt to sort out early in the educational program the promising from the unpromising so that the former may be segregated and given a special form of training to fit them for higher standing in their adult years. Under the Education Act of 1944, a minority of students has been selected each year by means of a battery of examinations popularly known as "eleven plus," supplemented in varying degrees by grade school records and personal interviews, for admission to grammar schools.[14] The remaining students attend secondary modern or technical schools in which the opportunities to prepare for college or to train for the more prestigeful occupations are minimal. The grammar schools supply what by comparative standards is a high quality of college preparatory education. Of course, such a scheme embodies the logic of sponsorship, with early selection of those destined for middle-class and higher-status occupations, and specialized training to prepare each group for its destined class position. This plan facilitates considerable mobility, and recent research reveals surprisingly little bias against children from manual laboring-class families in the selection for grammar school, when related to measured intelligence.[15] It is altogether possible that adequate comparative study would show a closer correlation of school success with measured intelligence and a lesser correlation between school success and family background in England than in the United States. While selection of superior students for mobility opportunity is probably more efficient under such a system, the obstacles for persons not so selected of "making the grade" on the basis of their own initiative or enterprise are probably correspondingly greater.

That the contrasting effects of the two systems accord with the social control patterns under the two mobility norms is indicated by studies of student ambitions in the United States and in England. Researches in the United States consistently show that the general level of occupational aspiration reported by high school students is quite unrealistic in relation to the actual distribution of job opportunities. Comparative study in England shows much less "phantasy" aspiration, and specifically indicates a reduction in aspirations among students not selected following the "eleven-plus" examination.[16] One of the by-products of the sponsorship system is the fact that at least some students from middle-class families whose parents cannot afford to send them to private schools suffer severe personal adjustment problems when they are assigned to secondary modern schools on the basis of this selection procedure.[17]

This well-known difference between the British sorting at an early age of students into grammar and modern schools and the American comprehensive high school and junior college is the clearest application of the distinction under discussion. But the organizing norms penetrate more deeply into the school systems than is initially apparent. The most telling observation regarding the direct normative operation of these principles would be evidence to support the author's impression that major critics of educational procedures within each country do not usually transcend the logic of their respective mobility norms. Thus the British debate about the best method for getting people sorted according to ability, without proposing that elite station should be open to whosoever can ascend to it. Although fear of "sputnik" in the United States introduced a flurry of suggestions for sponsored mobility schemes, the long-standing concern of school critics has been the failure to motivate students adequately. Preoccupation with motivation appears to be an intellectual application of the folk idea that people should *win* their station in society by personal enterprise.

The functional operation of a strain toward consistency with the organizing norms of upward mobility may be illustrated by several other features of the school systems in the two countries. First, the value placed upon education itself differs under the two norms. Under sponsored mobility, schooling is valued for its cultivation of elite culture, and those forms of schooling directed toward such cultivation are more highly valued than others. Education of the non-elite is difficult to justify clearly and tends to be half-hearted, while maximum educational resources are concentrated on "those who can benefit most from them"—in practice, this means those who can learn the elite culture. The secondary modern schools in England have regularly suffered from less adequate financial provision, a higher student-teacher ratio, fewer well trained teachers, and a general lack of prestige in comparison with the grammar schools.[18]

Under contest mobility in the United States, education is valued as a means of getting ahead, but the contents of education are not highly valued in their own right. Over a century ago Tocqueville commented on the absence of an hereditary class "by which the labors of the intellect are held in honor." He remarked that consequently a "middling standard is fixed in America for human knowledge."[19] And there persists in some measure the suspicion of the educated man as one who may have gotten ahead without really earning his position. In spite of recent criticisms of lax standards in American schools, it is in keeping with the general mobility pattern that a Gallup Poll taken in April, 1958, reports that school principals are much more likely to make such criticisms than parents. While 90 percent of the principals thought that ". . . our schools today demand too little work from the students," only 51 percent of the parents thought so, with 33 percent saying that the work was about right and six percent that schools demanded too much work.[20]

Second, the logic of preparation for a contest prevails in United States schools, and emphasizes keeping everyone in the running until the final stages. In primary and secondary schools the assumption tends to be made that those who are learning satisfactorily need little special attention while the less successful require help to be sure that they remain in the contest and may compete for the final stakes. As recently as December, 1958, a nationwide Gallup Poll gave evidence that this attitude had not been radically altered by the international situation. When asked whether or not teachers should devote extra time to the bright students, 26 percent of the respondents replied "yes" and 67 percent, "no." But the responses changed to 86 percent "yes" and only nine percent "no" when the question was asked concerning "slow students."[21]

In western states the junior college offers many students a "second chance" to qualify for university, and all state universities have some provision for substandard high school students to earn admission.

The university itself is run like the true contest: standards are set competitively, students are forced to pass a series of trials each semester, and only a minority of the entrants achieve the prize of graduation. This pattern contrasts sharply with the English system in which selection is supposed to be relatively complete before entrance to university, and students may be subject to no testing whatsoever for the first year or more of university study. Although university completion rates have not been estimated accurately in either country, some figures are indicative of the contrast. In American institutions of higher learning in 1957–1958, the ratio of bachelor's and first-professional degrees to the number of first-time degree-credit enrollments in the fall four years earlier was reported to be .610 for men and .488 for women.[22] The indicated 39 and 51 percent drop-out rates are probably underestimates because transfers from two-year junior colleges swell the number of degrees without being included in first-time enrollments. In England, a study of the careers of individual students reports that in University College, London, almost 82 percent of entering students between 1948 and 1951 eventually graduated with a degree. A similar study a few years earlier at the University of Liverpool shows a comparative figure of almost 87 percent.[23] Under contest mobility, the object is to train as many as possible in the skills necessary for elite status so as to give everyone a chance to maintain competition at the highest pitch. Under sponsored mobility, the objective is to indoctrinate elite culture in only those presumably who will enter the elite, lest there grow a dangerous number of "angry young men" who have elite skills without elite station.

Third, systems of mobility significantly affect educational content. Induction into elite culture under sponsored mobility is consistent with an emphasis on school *esprit de corps* which is employed to cultivate norms of intra-class loyalty and elite tastes and manners. Similarly, formal schooling built about highly specialized study in fields wholly of intellectual or aesthetic concern and of no "practical" value serves the purpose of elite culture. Under contest mobility in the United States, in spite of frequent faculty endorsement of "liberal education," schooling tends to be evaluated in terms of its practical benefits and to become, beyond the elementary level, chiefly vocational. Education does not so much provide what is good in itself as those skills, especially vocational skills, presumed to be necessary in the competition for the real prizes of life.

These contrasts are reflected in the different national attitudes toward university students who are gainfully employed while in school. More students in the United States than in Britain are employed part-time, and relatively fewer of the American students receive subsidies toward subsistence and living expenses. The most generous programs of state aid in the United States, except those applying to veterans and other special groups, do not normally cover expenses other than tuition and institutional fees. British maintenance grants are designed to cover full living expenses, taking into account parental ability to pay.[24] Under sponsored mobility, gainful employment serves no apprenticeship or testing function, and is thought merely to prevent students from gaining the full benefit of their schooling. L. J. Parry speaks of the general opposition to student employment and asserts that English university authorities almost unanimously hold that ". . . if a person must work for financial reasons, he should never spend more than four weeks on such work during the whole year."[25]

Under contest mobility, success in school work is not viewed as a sufficient test of practical merit, but must be supplemented by a test in the world of practical affairs. Thus in didactic folk tales the professional engineer also proves himself to be a superior mechanic, the business tycoon a skillful behind-the-counter salesman. By "working his way through school" the enterprising student "earns" his education in the fullest sense, keeps in touch with the practical world, and gains an apprenticeship into vocational life. Students are often urged to seek part-time employment, even when there is no financial need, and in some instances schools include paid employment as a requirement for graduation. As one observer describes the typical American view, a student willing to work part-time is a "better bet" than "the equally bright student who receives all of his financial support from others."[26]

Finally, training in "social adjustment" is peculiar to the system of contest mobility. The reason for this emphasis is clear when it is understood that adjustment training presumably prepares students to cope with situations for which there are no rules of intercourse or for which the rules are unknown, but in which the good opinions of others cannot be wholly ignored. Under sponsored mobility, elite recruits are inducted into a homogeneous stratum within which there is consensus regarding the rules, and within which they succeed socially by mastering these rules. Under contest mobility, the elite aspirant must relate himself both to the established elite and to the masses, who follow different rules, and the elite itself is not sufficiently homogeneous to evolve consensual rules of intercourse. Furthermore, in the contest the rules may vary according to the background of the competitor, so that each aspirant must successfully deal with persons playing the game with slightly different rules. Consequently, adjustment training is increasingly considered to be one of the important skills imparted by the school system.[27] That the emphasis on such training has had genuine popular support is indicated by a 1945 *Fortune* poll in which a national sample of adults was asked to select the one or two things that would be very important for a son of theirs to get out of college. Over 87 percent chose "Ability to get along with and understand people"; and this answer was the second most frequently chosen as the *very* most important thing to get out of college.[28] In this respect, British education may provide better preparation for participation in an orderly and controlled world, while American education may prepare students more adequately for a less ordered situation. The reputedly superior ability of "Yankees" to get things done seems to imply such ability.

To this point the discussion has centered on the tax-supported school systems in both countries, but the different place and emphasis of the privately supported secondary schools can also be related to the distinction between sponsored and contest mobility. Since private secondary schools in both countries are principally vehicles for transmitting the marks of high family status, their mobility function is quite tangential. Under contest mobility, the private schools presumably should have little or no mobility function. On the other hand, if there is to be mobility in a sponsored system, the privately controlled school populated largely with the children of elite parents would be the ideal device through which to induct selectees from lower levels into elite status. By means of a scholarship program, promising members of lesser classes could be chosen early for recruitment. The English "public" schools, in fact, have incorporated into their charters provisions to insure that a few boys from lesser classes will enter each year. Getting one's child into a "public" school, or even into one of the less prestigeful private schools, assumes an importance in England relatively unknown in the United States. If the children cannot win scholarships the parents often make extreme financial sacrifices in order to pay the cost of this relatively exclusive education.[29]

How much of a role private secondary schools have played in mobility in either country is difficult to determine. American studies of social mobility usually omit information on private vs. tax-supported secondary school attendance, and English studies showing the advantage of "public" school attendance generally fail to distinguish between the mobile and the nonmobile in this respect. However, during the nineteenth century the English "public" schools were used by *nouveaux riches* members of the manufacturing classes to enable their sons to achieve unqualified elite status.[30] In one sense, the rise of the manufacturing classes through free enterprise introduced a large measure of contest mobility which threatened to destroy the traditional sponsorship system. But by using the "public" schools in this fashion they bowed to the legitimacy of the traditional system—an implicit acknowledgment that upward mobility was not complete without sponsored induction. Denis Brogan speaks of the task of the "public" schools in the nineteenth century as "the job of marrying the old English social order to the new."[31]

With respect to mobility, the parallel between the tax-supported grammar schools and the "public" schools in England is of interest. The former in important respects have been patterned after the latter, adopting their view of mobility but making it a much larger part of their total function. Generally the grammar schools are the vehicle for sponsored mobility throughout the middle ranges of the class system, modelled after the pattern of the "public" schools which remain the agencies for sponsored mobility into the elite.

EFFECTS OF MOBILITY ON PERSONALITY

Brief note may be made of the importance of the distinction between sponsored and contest mobility with relation to the supposed effects of upward mobility on personality development. Not a great deal is yet known about the "mobile personality" nor about the specific features of importance to the personality in the mobility experience.[32] However, today three aspects of this experience are most frequently stressed: first, the stress or tension involved in striving for status higher than that of others under more difficult conditions than they; second, the complication of interpersonal relations introduced by the necessity to abandon lower-level friends in favor of uncertain acceptance into higher-level circles; third, the problem of working out an adequate personal scheme of values in the face of movement between classes marked by somewhat variant or even contradictory value systems.[33] The impact of each of these three mobility problems, it is suggested, differs depending upon whether the pattern is that of the contest or of sponsorship.

Under the sponsorship system, recruits are selected early, segregated from their class peers, grouped with other recruits and with youth from the class to which they are moving, and trained specifically for membership in this class. Since the selection is made early, the mobility experience should be relatively free from the strain that comes with a series of elimination tests and long-extended uncertainty of success. The segregation and the integrated group life of the "public" school or grammar school should help to clarify the mobile person's social ties. (One investigator failed to discover clique formation along lines of social class in a sociometric study of a number of grammar schools.[34]) The problem of a system of values may be largely met when the elite recruit is taken from his parents and peers to be placed in a boarding school, though it may be less well clarified for the grammar school boy who returns each evening to his working-class family. Undoubtedly this latter limitation has something to do with the observed failure of working-class boys to continue through the last years of grammar school and into the universities.[35] In general, then, the factors stressed as affecting personality formation among the upwardly mobile probably are rather specific to the contest system, or to the incompletely functioning sponsorship system.

It is often taken for granted that there is convincing evidence to show that mobility-oriented students in American secondary schools suffer from the tendency for cliques to form along lines predetermined by family background. These tendencies are statistically quite moderate, however, leaving much room for individual exceptions. Furthermore, mobility-oriented students usually have not been studied separately to discover whether or not they are incorporated into higher-level cliques in contrast to the general rule. Nor is it adequately demonstrated that the purported working-class value system, at odds with middle-class values, is as pervasive and constraining throughout the working class as it is conspicuous in many delinquent gangs. The model of contest mobility suggests, then, that there is more serious and continuing strain over the uncertainty of attaining mobility, more explicit and continued preoccupation with the problem of changing friendships, and more contradictory learning to inhibit the acquisition of a value system appropriate to the class of aspiration than under sponsored mobility. But the extent and implications of these differences require fuller understanding of the American class system. A search for personality-forming experiences specific to a sponsorship system, such as the British, has yet to be made.

CONCLUSION: SUGGESTIONS FOR RESEARCH

The foregoing discussion is broadly impressionistic and speculative, reflecting more the general impression of an observer of both countries than a systematic exploration of data. Relevant data of a variety of sorts are cited above, but their use is more illustrative than demonstrative. However, several lines of research are suggested by this tentative analysis. One of these is an exploration of different channels of mobility in both England and the United States in an attempt to discover the extent to which mobility corresponds to the mobility types. Recruitment to the Catholic priesthood, for example, probably strictly follows a sponsorship norm regardless of the dominant contest norm in the United States.

The effect of changes in the major avenues of upward mobility upon the dominant norms requires investigation. The increasing importance of promotion through corporation hierarchies and the declining importance of the enterpreneurial path of upward mobility undoubtedly compromise the ideal pattern of contest mobility. The growing insistence that higher education is a prerequisite to more and more occupations is a similar modification. Yet, there is little evidence of a tendency to follow the logic of sponsorship beyond the bureaucratic selection process. The prospect of a surplus of college-educated persons in relation to jobs requiring college education may tend to restore the contest situation at a higher level, and the further possibility that completion of higher education may be more determined by motivational factors than by capacity suggests that the contest pattern continues within the school.

In England, on the other hand, two developments may weaken the sponsorship system. One is positive response to popular demand to allow more children to secure the grammar school type of training, particularly by including such a program in the secondary modern schools. The other is introduction of the comprehensive secondary school, relatively uncommon at present but a major plank in the labour party's education platform. It remains to be determined whether the comprehensive school in England will take a distinctive form and serve a distinctive function, which preserves the pattern of sponsorship, or will approximate the present American system.

Finally, the assertion that these types of mobility are embedded in genuine folk norms requires specific investigation. Here, a combination of direct study of popular attitudes and content analysis of popular responses to crucial issues would be useful. Perhaps the most significant search would be for evidence showing what courses of action require no special justification or explanation because they are altogether "natural" and "right," and what courses of action, whether approved or not, require special justification and explanation. Such evidence, appropriately used, would show the extent to which the patterns described are genuine folk norms rather than mere by-products of particular structural factors. It would also permit determination of the extent to which acceptance of the folk norms is diffused among the different segments of the populations.

ACKNOWLEDGMENTS

Special indebtedness is expressed to Jean Floud and Hilde Himmelweit for helping to acquaint the author with the English school system.

NOTES

[1] A comprehensive summary of such studies appears in Seymour M. Lipset and Reinhard Bendix, *Social Mobility in Industrial Society* (Berkeley and Los Angeles: University of California Press, 1959).

[2] Cf. C. A. Anderson, "The Social Status of University Students in Relation to Type of Economy: An International Comparison," *Transactions of the Third World Congress of Sociology*, London, 1956, Vol. V, pp. 51–63; J. E. Floud, *Social Class and Educational Opportunity* (London: Heinemann, 1956); W. L. Warner, R. J. Havighurst, and M. B. Loeb, *Who Shall Be Educated?* (New York: Harper, 1944).

[3] Reference is made throughout the paper to "elite" and "masses." The generalizations, however, are intended to apply throughout the stratification continuum to relations between members of a given class and the class or classes above it. Statements about mobility are intended in general to apply to mobility from manual to middle-class levels, lower-middle to upper-middle class, and so on, as well as into the strictly elite groups. The simplified expressions avoid the repeated use of cumbersome and involved statements which might otherwise be required.

[4] The normative element in an organizing norm goes beyond Max Weber's *ideal type*, conveying more of the sense of Durkheim's *collective representation*; cf. Ralph H. Turner, "The Normative Coherence of Folk Concepts," *Research Studies of the State College of Washington*, 25 (1957), pp. 127–136. Charles Wagley has developed a similar concept which he calls "ideal pattern" in his as yet unpublished work on Brazilian kinship. See also Howard Becker, "Constructive Typology in the Social Sciences," *American Sociological Review*, 5 (1940), pp. 40–55.

[5] Geoffrey Gorer remarks on the favorable evaluation of the successful gamble in American culture: "Gambling is also a respected and important component in many business ventures. Conspicuous improvement in a man's financial position is generally attributed to a lucky combination of industry, skill, and gambling, though the successful gambler prefers to refer to his gambling as 'vision.' " *The American People* (New York: Norton, 1948), p. 178.

[6] Vilfredo Pareto, *The Mind and Society* (New York: Harcourt, Brace, 1935), Vol. 4, p. 1796.

7 Many writers have noted that different kinds of societies facilitate the rise of different kinds of personalities, either in the stratification hierarchy or in other ways. Cf. Jessie Bernard, *American Community Behavior* (New York: Dryden, 1949), p. 205. A particularly interesting statement is Martindale's exploration of "favored personality" types in sacred and secular societies. Don Martindale and Elio Monachesi, *Elements of Sociology* (New York: Harper, 1951), pp. 312–378.

8 At one time in the United States a good many owners of expensive British Jaguar automobiles carried large signs on the cars identifying the make. Such a display would have been unthinkable under a sponsored mobility system since the Jaguar owner would not care for the esteem of persons too uninformed to tell a Jaguar from a less prestigious automobile.

9 See, e.g., Lawrence Lipton, *The Holy Barbarians* (New York: Messner), 1959.

10 Cf. Albert K. Cohen, *Delinquent Boys: The Culture of the Gang* (Glencoe, Ill.: The Free Press, 1955).

11 D. V. Glass, ed., *Social Mobility in Britain* (Glencoe, Ill.: The Free Press, 1954), pp. 144–145, reports studies showing only small variations in intelligence between occupational levels.

12 Gorer, *op. cit.*, pp. 172–187.

13 See, e.g., *Los Angeles Times*, May 4, 1959, Part I, p. 24.

14 The nature and operation of the "eleven plus" system are fully reviewed in a report by a committee of the British Psychological Society and in a report of extensive research into the adequacy of selection methods. See P. E. Vernon, ed., *Secondary School Selection: A British Psychological Inquiry* (London: Methuen, 1957); and Alfred Yates and D. A. Pidgeon, *Admission to Grammar Schools* (London: Newnes Educational Publishing Co., 1957).

15 J. E. Floud, A. H. Halsey, and F. M. Martin, *Social Class and Educational Opportunity* (London: Heinemann, 1956).

16 Mary D. Wilson documents the reduction in aspirations characterizing students in British secondary modern schools and notes the contrast with American studies revealing much more "unrealistic" aspirations; see "The Vocational Preferences of Secondary Modern School-children," *British Journal of Educational Psychology*, 23 (1953), pp. 97–113. See also Ralph H. Turner, "The Changing Ideology of Success," *Transactions of the Third World Congress of Sociology, 1956*, London, Vol. V, esp. p. 37.

17 Pointed out by Hilde Himmelweit in private communication.

18 Less adequate financial provision and a higher student-teacher ratio are mentioned as obstacles to parity of secondary modern schools with grammar schools in *The Times Educational Supplement*, February 22, 1957, p. 241. On difficulties in achieving prestige comparable with grammar schools see G. Baron, "Secondary Education in Britain: Some Present-Day Trends," *Teachers College Record*, 57 (1956), pp. 211–221; and O. Banks, *Parity and Prestige in English Secondary Education* (London: Routledge and Kegan Paul, 1955). See also Vernon, *op. cit.*, pp. 19–22.

19 Alexis de Tocqueville, *Democracy in America* (New York: Knopf, 1945), Vol. I, p. 52.

20 An earlier Gallup Poll had disclosed that 62 percent of the parents opposed stiffened college entrance requirements while only 27 percent favored them. Reported in *Time*, April 14, 1958, p. 45.

21 Reported in the *Los Angeles Times*, December 17, 1958, Part I, p. 16.

22 U. S. Department of Health, Education, and Welfare, Office of Education, *Earned Degrees Conferred by Higher Education Institutions, 1957–1958* (Washington, D. C.: Government Printing Office, 1959), p. 3.

23 Nicholas Malleson, "Student Performance at University College, London, 1948–1951," *Universities Quarterly*, 12 (1958), pp. 288–319.

24 See, e.g., C. A. Quattlebaum, *Federal Aid to Students for Higher Education* (Washington, D. C.: Government Printing Office, 1956); and "Grants to Students: University and Training Colleges," *The Times Educational Supplement*, May 6, 1955, p. 446.

[25] "Students' Expenses," *The Times Educational Supplement*, May 6, 1955, p. 447.

[26] R. H. Eckelberry, "College Jobs for College Students," *Journal of Higher Education*, 27 (1956), p. 174.

[27] Adjustment training is not a necessary accompaniment of contest mobility. The shift during the last half century toward the increased importance of social acceptability as an elite credential has brought such training into correspondingly greater prominence.

[28] Reported in *Public Opinion 1935–1946*, Hadley Cantril, ed. (Princeton: Princeton University Press, 1951), p. 186.

[29] For one account of the place of "public" schools in the English educational system see Denis Brogan, *The English People* (New York: Knopf, 1943), pp. 18–56.

[30] A. H. Halsey of Birmingham University has called my attention to the importance of this fact.

[31] *Op. cit.*, pp. 24–25.

[32] Cf. Lipset and Bendix, *op. cit.*, pp. 250ff.

[33] See, e.g., August B. Hollingshead and Frederick C. Redlich, *Social Class and Mental Illness* (New York: Wiley, 1958); W. Lloyd Warner and James C. Abegglen, *Big Business Leaders in America* (New York: Harper, 1955); Warner et al., *Who Shall be Educated?*, *op. cit.*; Peter M. Blau, "Social Mobility and Interpersonal Relations," *American Sociological Review*, 21 (1956), pp. 290–300.

[34] A. N. Oppenheim, "Social Status and Clique Formation among Grammar School Boys," *British Journal of Sociology*, 6 (1955), pp. 228–245. Oppenheim's findings may be compared with A. B. Hollingshead, *Elmtown's Youth* (New York: Wiley, 1949), pp. 204–242. See also Joseph A. Kahl, *The American Class Structure* (New York: Rinehart, 1957), pp. 129–138.

[35] Floud et al., *op. cit.*, pp. 115ff.

9   J. MILTON YINGER

Contraculture and Subculture

In recent years there has been widespread and fruitful employment of the concept of subculture in sociological and anthropological research. The term has been used to focus attention not only on the wide diversity of norms to be found in many societies but on the normative aspects of deviant behavior. The ease with which the term has been adopted, with little study of its exact meaning or its values and its difficulties, is indicative of its utility in emphasizing a sociological point of view in research that has been strongly influenced both by individualistic and moralistic interpretations. To describe the normative qualities of an occupation, to contrast the value systems of social classes, or to emphasize the controlling power of the code of a delinquent gang is to underline a sociological aspect of these phenomena that is often disregarded.

In the early days of sociology and anthropology, a key task was to document the enormous variability of culture from society to society and to explore the significance of the overly simplified but useful idea that "the

Reprinted from *American Sociological Review*, 25:5 (1960), pp. 625–635, by permission of the author and the publisher.

mores can make anything right." In recent years that task has been extended to the study of the enormous variability of culture *within* some societies. It is unfortunate that "subculture," a central concept in this process, has seldom been adequately defined.[1] It has been used as an *ad hoc* concept whenever a writer wished to emphasize the normative aspects of behavior that differed from some general standard. The result has been a blurring of the meaning of the term, confusion with other terms, and a failure frequently to distinguish between two levels of social causation.

THREE USAGES OF SUBCULTURE

Few concepts appear so often in current sociological writing. In the course of twelve months, I have noted over 100 books and articles that make some use, from incidental to elaborate, of the idea of "subculture." The usages vary so widely, however, that the value of the term is severely limited. If chemists had only one word to refer to all colorless liquids and this led them to pay attention to only the two characteristics shared in common, their analysis would be exceedingly primitive. Such an analogy overstates the diversity of ideas covered by "subculture," but the range is very wide. Nevertheless three distinct meanings can be described.

In some anthropological work, subculture refers to certain universal tendencies that seem to occur in all societies. They underlie culture, precede it, and set limits to the range of its variation. Thus Kroeber writes: "Indeed, such more or less recurrent near-regularities of form or process as have to date been formulated for culture are actually subcultural in nature. They are limits set to culture by physical or organic factors."[2] In *The Study of Man*, Linton uses subculture to refer to various pan-human phenomena that seem to occur everywhere. Thus good-natured and tyrannical parents may be found in societies that differ widely in their family patterns.[3] This use shades off into other concepts that are similar but not identical: Edward Sapir's "precultural" and Cooley's "human nature" refer to biological and social influences that underlie all cultures.[4] Since subculture is only rarely used today to refer to this series of ideas, I shall exclude them from further consideration, with the suggestion that the use of Sapir's term "precultural" might well clarify our thinking.

Two other usages of subculture represent a much more serious confusion. The term is often used to point to the normative systems of groups smaller than a society, to give emphasis to the ways these groups differ in such things as language, values, religion, diet, and style of life from the larger society of which they are a part. Perhaps the most common referent in this usage is an ethnic enclave (French Canadians in Maine) or a region (the subculture of the South),[5] but the distinctive norms of much smaller and more temporary groups (even a particular friendship group) may be described as a subculture. Kluckhohn, for example, refers to "the subculture of anthropologists" and Riesman to "subcultures among the faculty."

This second meaning, which itself contains some ambiguities, as we shall see, must be distinguished from a third meaning associated with it when the reference is to norms that arise specifically from a frustrating situation or from conflict between a group and the larger society. Thus the emergent norms of a delinquent gang or the standards of an adolescent peer group have often been designated "subcultural." In addition to a cultural dimension, this third usage introduces a social-psychological dimension, for there is direct reference to the personality factors involved in the development and maintenance of the norms. Specifically, such personality tendencies as frustration, anxiety, feelings of role ambiguity, and resentment are shown to be involved in the creation of the subculture. The mutual influence of personality and culture is not a distinctive characteristic of this type of subculture, of course, for they are everywhere interactive. Thus:

> Tendencies for parents to respond harshly to their children's aggressive behavior, for instance, if common to the members of a society, are to be referred equally to the culture and to the modal personality of the parents. But the result in the developing child is not a foregone conclusion: present knowledge suggests that under specifiable conditions outcomes as different as rigid politeness or touchy latent hostility may follow. These consequences in turn may lead to cultural elaborations that seem superficially remote from the cultural starting point, yet are dynamically linked with it. . . .[6]

As this quotation suggests, culture and personality are always empirically tied together. Yet the nature of the relation is not the same in all cases. The term subculture, when used in the third way described here, raises to a position of prominence one particular kind of dynamic linkage between norms and personality: the creation of a series of inverse or counter values (opposed to those of the surrounding society) in face of serious frustration or conflict. To call attention to the special aspects of this kind of normative system, I suggest the term *contraculture*. Before exploring the relationship between subculture and contraculture, however, the range of meanings given subculture even when it is limited to the second usage requires comment.

SUBCULTURE AND ROLE

The variety of referents for the term subculture is very wide because the normative systems of sub-societies can be differentiated on many grounds. The groups involved may range from a large regional subdivision to a religious sect with only one small congregation. The distinctive norms may involve many aspects of life—religion, language, diet, moral values—or, for example, only a few separate practices among the members of an occupational group. Further distinctions among subcultures might be made on the basis of time (has the subculture persisted through a number of generations?), origin (by migration, absorption by a dominant society, social or physical segregation, occupational specialization, and other sources), and by the mode of relationship to the surrounding culture (from indifference to conflict). Such wide variation in the phenomena covered by a term can be handled by careful specification of the several grounds for subclassification. Confusion has arisen not so much from the scope of the term subculture as from its use as a substitute for "role." Only with great effort is some degree of clarity being achieved in the use of the role concept and the related terms "position" and "role behavior."[7] Were this development retarded by confusion of role with subculture it would be unfortunate. All societies have differentiating roles, but only heterogeneous societies have subcultures. Role is *that part of* a full culture that is assigned, as the appropriate rights and duties, to those occupying a given position.[8] These rights and duties usually interlock into a system with those of persons who occupy other positions. They are known to and accepted by all those who share the culture. Thus the role of a physician is known, at least in vague outline, by most persons in a society and it is seen as part of the total culture. (This is not to prejudge the question of role consensus, for there may be many nonrole aspects of being a physician.) But subculture is not tied in this way into the larger cultural complex: it refers to norms that set a group apart from, not those that integrate a group with, the total society. Subcultural norms, as contrasted with role norms, are unknown to, looked down upon, or thought of as separating forces by the other members of a society. There are doubtless subcultural aspects of being a physician— normative influences affecting his behavior that are not part of his role, not culturally designated rights and duties. But the empirical mixture should not obscure the need for this analytic distinction.

Along with confusion with the role concept, subculture carries many of the ambiguities associated with the parent concept of culture. In much social scientific writing it is not at all clear whether culture refers to norms, that is, to expected or valued behavior, or to behavior that is widely followed and therefore normal in a statistical sense only. This dual referent is particularly likely to be found in the work of anthropologists. Perhaps because their concepts are derived largely from the study of relatively more stable and homogeneous societies, they draw less sharply the distinction between the statistically normal and the normative. Sociologists are more apt to find it necessary to explore the tensions between the social order and culture, to be alert to deviations, and they are therefore more likely to define culture abstractly as a shared normative system. Yet much of the commentary on subculture refers to behavior. In my judgment this identification is unwise. Behavior is the result of the convergence of many forces. One should not assume, when the members of a group behave in similar ways, that cultural norms produce this result. Collective behavior theory and personality theory may also help to account for the similarities.

CONTRACULTURE

Failure to distinguish between role and subculture and vagueness in the concept of culture itself are not the only difficulties in the use of the idea of subculture. Perhaps more serious is the tendency to obscure, under this one term, two levels of explanation, one sociological and the other social-psychological, with a resulting failure to understand the causal forces at work. On few topics can one get wider agreement among sociologists than on the dangers of reductionism. If a psychologist attempts to explain social facts by psychological theories, we throw the book (probably Durkheim) at him; we emphasize the "fallacy of misplaced concreteness." In view of the widespread neglect of sociocultural factors in the explanation of behavior, this is a necessary task. It makes vitally important, however, keen awareness by sociologists that they also deal with an abstract model. Perhaps we can reverse Durkheim's dictum to say: Do not try to explain social psychological facts by sociological theories; or, more adequately, do not try to explain *behavior* (a product of the interaction of sociocultural and personality influences) by a sociological theory alone. Yablonsky has recently reminded us that an excessively sociological theory of gangs can result in our seeing a definite group structure and a clear pattern of norms where in fact there is a "near-group," with an imprecise definition of boundaries and limited agreement on norms.[9] Carelessly used, our concepts can obscure the facts we seek to understand.

To see the cultural element in delinquency or in the domination of an individual by his adolescent group, phenomena that on the surface are noncultural or even "anticultural," was a long step forward in their explanation. But it is also necessary to see the noncultural aspects of some "norms"— phenomena that on the surface seem thoroughly cultural. Our vocabulary needs to be rich enough to help us to deal with these differences. The tendency to use the same term to refer to phenomena that share *some* elements in common, disregarding important differences, is to be content with phyla names when we need also to designate genus and species.

To sharpen our analysis, I suggest the use of the term contraculture wherever the normative system of a group contains, as a primary element, a theme of conflict with the values of the total society, where personality variables are directly involved in the development and maintenance of the group's values, and wherever its norms can be understood only by reference to the relationships of the group to a surrounding dominant culture.[10] None of these criteria definitely separates contraculture from subculture because each is a continuum. Subsocieties fall along a range with respect to each criterion. The values of most subcultures probably conflict in some measure with the larger culture. In a contraculture, however, the conflict element is central; many of the values, indeed, are specifically contradictions of the values of the dominant culture. Similarly, personality variables are involved in the development and maintenance of all cultures and subcultures, but usually the influence of personality is by way of variations around a theme that is part of the culture. In a contraculture, on the other hand, the theme itself expresses the tendencies of the persons who compose it. Finally, the norms of all subcultures are doubtless affected in some degree by the nature of the relationship with the larger culture. A subculture, as a pure type, however, does not require, for its understanding, intensive analysis of interaction with the larger culture; that is, its norms are not, to any significant degree, a product of that interaction. But a contraculture can be understood only by giving full attention to the interaction of the group which is its bearer with the larger society. It is one thing to say that the subculture of the rural, lower-class Negro encourages slow, inefficient work. It is another thing to say, with Charles S. Johnson, that such a norm represents "pseudo-ignorant malingering," a contracultural way of describing the same phenomenon. Johnson stressed the conflict element, the extent to which the norm was a product of interaction of white and Negro. There is certainly value in emphasizing the subcultural source of some of the values of southern Negroes. Against racist views or individual explanations, the sociologist opposes the subcultural: If they strive less, have different sexual mores, or otherwise vary from standards of the dominant society, it is in part because they have been socialized in accordance with different norms. But this is not enough, for their similar behavior may be interpreted in part as a shared response to a frustrating environment.

Empirically, subcultural and contracultural influences may be mixed, of course. Delinquency and adolescent behavior almost certainly manifest both influences. The need, however, is to develop a clean analytic distinction between the two in order to interpret the wide variations in their mixture.

ADOLESCENT SUBCULTURE AND CONTRACULTURE

The utility of the distinction between contraculture and subculture can be tested by applying it to several research problems where the concept of subculture has been widely used. There is an extensive literature that interprets the behavior of adolescents substantially in these terms.[11] In the words of Havighurst and Taba: "Recent studies of adolescents have emphasized the fact that boys and girls in their teens have a culture of their own with moral standards and with moral pressures behind those standards. This culture has been called the 'adolescent peer culture.'"[12] Or Riesman: "All the morality is the group's. Indeed, even the fact that it is a morality is concealed by the confusing notion that the function of the group is to have fun, to play. . . ."[13] A close reading of the literature on adolescent culture reveals at least four different levels of interpretation, often only partially distinguished:

1. There is a cultural level, in which the roles of adolescent boys and girls are described, or the specialties (in Linton's sense) are designated. There is no reason to introduce concepts other than role or specialty to refer to norms that are generally accepted by elders and youths alike as appropriate to youth.

2. On the subcultural level, there are norms that manifest some separate system of values accepted within the adolescent group. These norms are not part of the role of youth. In part they are unknown to the elders; in part they conflict with standards accepted by the elders. They are learned, not by socialization in the total society, but by interaction within the sub-society of youth. Thus interests, games, speech patterns, and aesthetic tastes may be communicated among an age-group with little reference to the larger culture.

3. There are currents of fashion or of other collective behavior that sweep through an adolescent group, strongly influencing the behavior of its members.[14] Although it is difficult to distinguish fashion from culture—many empirical phenomena have aspects of both—it is wise to keep them apart conceptually. This is not always done. The terminology of Riesman is closer to that of fashion than of culture, but the net impression of his analysis is that he is thinking of control by the peer group primarily as a cultural phenomenon.[15] And the sentence following the one quoted above from Havighurst and Taba reads: "Boys and girls, desiring the approval of their age mates, follow the fashions of the peer culture in morals, dress, and speech. . . ." If the peer group influence stems from fashion, then strictly speaking it is not culture. The two differ to some degree in their origins, their functions, and their consequences.[16]

4. Many analyses of the control exercised by a youth group over its members employ the *concept* of contraculture, although the terminology and the assumptions are often those of subculture or culture. There is emphasis on the cross-pressures which young people feel: they want to be adults, yet fear to leave the securities of childhood; they experience contradictory adult treatment—a demand for grownup behavior here, the prevention of it there; ambiguity of self-image leads to efforts to prove oneself a full-fledged adult; there is sexual frustration. The peer group may help one to struggle with these cross-pressures, as described by Parsons: "Perhaps the best single point of reference for characterizing the youth culture lies in its contrast with the dominant pattern of the adult male role. By contrast with emphasis on responsibility in this role, the orientation of the youth culture is more or less specifically irresponsible."[17] This irresponsibility cannot be understood simply as another cultural norm, as part of the "role" of youth, although these are Parsons' terms. It must be studied in the context of strain, of role ambiguity. Some sociologists explain this irresponsibility as merely a manifestation of the youth culture, thus obscuring the personality factors also involved. The description and analysis of an adolescent subculture, to be sure, are an important contribution to the sociology of youth. Many adolescents spend a great deal of time in groups that sustain norms different from those of the adult world; and adults often respond to the behavior that follows these norms in an "ethnocentric" way. To rely on a subcultural explanation alone, however, is to disregard the emergent quality of many of the standards and to minimize the fact that they are often in direct conflict with adult standards (which most adolescents themselves will soon accept).

This sharp conflict of values requires explanation. Parsons states the facts clearly: "Negatively, there is a strong tendency to repudiate interests in adult things, and to feel at least a certain recalcitrance to the pressure of adult expectations and disciplines. . . . Thus the youth culture is not only, as is true of the curricular aspects of formal education, a matter of age status as such but also shows signs of being a product of tensions in the relationship of younger people and adults."[18] At several other points

Parsons develops the "reaction" theme and later uses the concept of "reaction-formation." [19] Should these various phenomena be subsumed under the concept of culture? It is one thing for a society to train its youth to certain ways of behaving. It is quite another for a youth group to develop inverse values in an effort to struggle with role ambiguities and strains. The adolescent may experience both as normative sanctions; but that should scarcely lead the social analyst to disregard their differences. I suggest the term contraculture in order to indicate the normative *and* the conflict aspects of this type of situation.

DELINQUENT CONTRACULTURE

The usefulness of separating subcultural and contracultural influences is seen particularly clearly in the analysis of delinquency and of criminality generally. Perhaps in no other field were there more substantial gains in understanding made possible by the introduction of a sociological point of view to supplement and to correct individualistic and moralistic interpretations. There is little need to review the extensive literature, from *Delinquent Gangs* to *Delinquent Boys*, to establish the importance of the normative element in criminal and delinquent behavior. It is a mistake, however, to try to stretch a useful concept into a total theory. A "complex-adequate" analysis [20] may seem less sharp and definitive than one based on one factor, but it is likely to be far more useful. Cohen's excellent work,[21] although labelled as a study of the culture of the gang, does not overlook the psychogenic sources of delinquency. In fact, his explanation of the origins of the subculture (contraculture) and its functions for the lower class male makes clear that the norms of the gang are not learned, accepted, and taught in the same way that we learn what foods to eat, what clothes to wear, what language to speak. The very existence of the gang is a sign, in part, of blocked ambition. Because tensions set in motion by this blockage cannot be resolved by achievement of dominant values, such values are repressed, their importance denied, countervalues affirmed. The gang member is often ambivalent. Thwarted in his desire to achieve higher status by the criteria of the dominant society, he accepts criteria he can meet; but the reaction-formation in this response is indicated by the content of the delinquent norms—non-utilitarian, malicious, and negativistic, in Cohen's terms. This negative polarity represents the need to repress his own tendencies to accept the dominant cultural standards. This is not to say that the values of the gang cannot be explained partially by cultural analysis, by some extension of the idea that "the mores can make anything right." But I suggest that Cohen's multiple-factor analysis might have been clearer, and less subject to misinterpretation, had he introduced the concept of contraculture alongside the concept of subculture. One reviewer, for example, completely disregards the "negative polarity" theme:

> In an overall summary, cultural delinquency is a phenomenon of culture, society, and sociocultural experience. It is a positive thing: members of the several social classes are socialized, but there is a differential content in

the socialization. Delinquency is not a negative thing; it is not a result of the breakdown of socicty, nor of the failure to curb criminal instincts, nor of the failure of the family, the church, or the school. The same set of concepts, the same social processes, and the same set of logical assumptions account for both delinquency and lawfulness. Since delinquency is of this character, it is unnecessary to invent any pathology to account for it.[22]

This statement neither adequately represents Cohen's thesis nor encourages us to explore a number of important questions: Why do only some of those who are exposed to the delinquent "subculture" learn it?[23] Why do those who follow the subculture often manifest ambivalence and guilt feelings?[24] Why do many of the same patterns of behavior occur in areas and among groups where the presence of the subculture is much less clear (middle-class delinquency)?[25] What is the significance of the fact that the delinquent subculture is not only different from but in part at least a reversal of the values of the dominant culture? The use of a purely subcultural model of analysis discourages or even prevents the raising of these questions and thus precludes adequate answers to them.

Cohen and Short have dealt with several of these issues by suggesting the need for a typology. Specifically for the study of delinquency, they propose five types of subcultures: the parent male (the central pattern described in *Delinquent Boys*), the conflict-oriented, the drug addict, the semi-professional theft, and the middle-class subcultures.[26] Although the criteria of classification are not entirely clear, these categories are primarily descriptive. The concept of contraculture might be added to this list as a type of subculture, if the one distinctive criterion used to designate a subculture is the presence in a subsociety of a normative system that separates it from the total society. Such a procedure does not seem, however, to produce an adequate taxonomy. If the shift is made from description to analysis, or from an interest in the content of norms to their etiology, an important difference emerges between subculture and contraculture: the one set of norms derives from standard socialization in a subsociety; the other stems from conflict and frustration in the experience of those who share many of the values of the whole society but are thwarted in their efforts to achieve those values.

It should be stressed once more that these are analytic concepts, no one of which is adequate to handle the empirical variations of delinquent behavior. Failure to recognize the abstract quality of our conceptual tools leads to unnecessary disagreements. When Miller describes the "Lower Class Culture as a Generating Milieu of Gang Delinquency," for example, he points to an important series of influences that derive from the value system of the lower-class community.[27] In his effort to emphasize this aspect of the etiology of delinquency, however, he tends to overlook the kind of evidence reported by Sykes and Matza, Cohen, Finestone, Yablonsky, the McCords, and others concerning collective behavior and personality variables.[28] Surely the evidence is now rich enough for us to state definitively that delinquency is a multi-variable product. The task ahead is not to prove that it stems largely from cultural or subcultural or contracultural influences, but to spell out the conditions under which these and other factors will be found in various empirical mixtures.[29]

CONTRACTURAL ASPECTS OF CLASS AND OCCUPATION

The same admixture of the concepts of culture, subculture, and contraculture is found in the extensive literature on occupations and classes. Doubtless all three forces are found in many instances, and the research task is to untangle their various influences. It may stretch the meaning of the term too far to speak of the *position* of the "middle-class member," with its culturally designated role specifications; although in relatively stable societies the usage seems appropriate. In such societies, many of the rights and obligations of various status levels are culturally defined. In more mobile class systems, however, subcultural and contracultural norms become important. Our understanding of the American class system has certainly been deepened in the last twenty years by the descriptions of differences, among classes, in value perspectives, time orientations, levels of aspiration, leisure-time styles, and child rearing practices.[30]

The introduction of the concept of subculture has helped to avoid class derived biases in the interpretation of the wide variations in these phenomena. In class analysis as in the study of deviations, however, there may be some overcompensation in the effort to eliminate the distortions of a middle-class and often rural perspective.[31] There is evidence to suggest that differences between classes are based less upon different values and norms than the subcultural approach suggests. The "innovations" of lower-class members, to use Merton's term, are not simply subcultural acts defined as innovative by middle-class persons. They are in part responses to a frustrating situation. They are efforts to deal with the disjunction of means and ends. When the disjunction is reduced, the variations in value and behavior are reduced. Thus Rosen found, "surprisingly," that Negroes in the Northeast made higher scores on an "achievement value" test than his description of Negro "culture" led him to expect. This may indicate that the low achievement response is less the result of a subcultural norm than a protest against a difficult situation. If the situation improves, the achievement value changes.[32] Stephenson's discovery that occupational plans of lower-class youth are considerably below those of higher-class youth, but that their aspirations are only slightly lower, bears on this same point. His data suggest that the classes differ not only in norms, but also in opportunity.[33] Differences in behavior, therefore, are only partly a result of subcultural contrasts. The lower educational aspirations of lower-class members are also found to be in part situationally induced, not simply normatively induced. When the situation changes, values and behavior change, as Mulligan found in his study of the response of the sons of blue-collar workers to the educational opportunities of the GI Bill, and as

Wilson reports in his investigation of the aspirations of lower-class boys attending higher-class schools and upper-class boys attending lower-class schools.[34]

In short, our thinking about differences in behavior among social classes will be sharpened if we distinguish among those differences that derive from role influences, those based on subcultural variations, and those that express contracultural responses to deprivation. The proportions will vary from society to society; the research task is to specify the conditions under which various distributions occur. One would expect, to propose one hypothesis, to find more contracultural norms among lower-class members of an open society than in a similar group in a closed society.

The interpretation of differential behavior among the members of various occupational categories can also be strengthened by the distinctions made above. Here the contrast between role and subculture is especially useful. The role of a teacher consists of the rights and duties that *integrate* him into a system of expected and established relationships with others. The teaching subculture, on the other hand, insofar as it exists, *separates* teachers from the cultural world of others. It is either unknown to others or, if known, a source of disagreement and perhaps of conflict with others. There are also contracultural aspects of some occupational styles of life. In interpreting the differences between the values of jazz musicians and "squares," for example, Becker writes: "their rejection of commercialism in music and squares in social life was part of the casting aside of the total American culture by men who could enjoy privileged status but who were unable to achieve a satisfactory personal adjustment within it."[35] Their style of life, in other words, can be understood only by supplementing the cultural and subcultural dimensions with the conflict theme. Cameron develops the same point. Although he makes no use of the term subculture, he describes the differentiating norms of the dance-band group, presumably a result of the "esoteric" aspects of their art, the differences in their time schedule, and the like. But he also describes the *contra* aspects of some of the norms, and suggests that they derive from the fact that early recruitment ties the jazz musician to the adolescence problem.[36]

CONCLUSION

Poorly defined terms plague research in many areas, particularly in the specification of relationships between sociological and social psychological levels of analysis. Thus "anomie" is still used to refer both to a social structural fact and to a personality fact, although this confusion is gradually being reduced. "Role" may refer, alternately, to rights and duties prescribed for the occupants of a position or to individual performance of that position. And subculture, I have suggested, is used to designate both the traditional norms of a subsociety and the emergent norms of a group caught in a frustrating and conflict-laden situation. This paper indicates that there are differences in the origin, function, and perpetuation of traditional and emergent norms, and suggests that the use of the concept contraculture for the latter might improve sociological analysis. Hypotheses to guide the study of subculture can most profitably be derived from a general theory of culture. As an illustration, it may be hypothesized that a subculture will appear, in the first instance, as a result of mobility or an extension of communication that brings groups of different cultural background into membership in the same society, followed by physical or social isolation or both that prevents full assimilation.

Hypotheses concerning contracultures, on the other hand, can best be derived from social psychological theory—from the study of collective behavior, the frustration-aggression thesis, or the theory of group formation. One might hypothesize, for example, that under conditions of deprivation and frustration of major values (in a context where the deprivation is obvious because of extensive communication with the dominant group), and where value confusion and weak social controls obtain, contracultural norms will appear. One would expect to find, according to these propositions, many subcultural values among southern rural Negroes. Among first and second generation urban Negroes, however, one would expect an increase in contracultural norms. Both groups are deprived, but in the urban situation there is more "value leakage" from the dominant group, more value confusion, and weakened social controls.[37]

The subculture of the sociologist requires sophistication about the full range of human behavior. This desideratum has led to the proposition that the vast diversity of norms believed in and acted upon by the members of a modern society is not a sign of value confusion and breakdown but rather an indication that urban life brings into one system of interaction persons drawn from many cultural worlds. One unanticipated consequence of the sociological subculture may be that we exaggerate the normative insulation and solidarity of these various worlds. An important empirical question concerns the extent and results of their interaction.

NOTES

[1] There are a few formal definitions. For example: "The term 'subculture' refers in this paper to 'cultural variants displayed by certain segments of the population.' Subcultures are distinguished not by one or two isolated traits—they constitute relatively cohesive cultural systems. They are worlds within the larger world of our national culture." (Mirra Komarovsky and S. S. Sargent, "Research into Subcultural Influences upon Personality," in *Culture and Personality*, S. S. Sargent and M. W. Smith, eds. [New York: The Viking Fund, 1949], p. 143.) These authors then refer to class, race, occupation, residence, and region. After referring to subgroup values and language, Kimball Young and Raymond W. Mack state: "Such shared learned behaviors which are common to a specific group or category are called *subcultures*." (*Sociology and Social Life* [New York: American Book, 1959], p. 49.) They refer then to ethnic, occupational, and regional variations. Blaine Mercer writes: "A society contains numerous subgroups, each with its own characteristic ways of thinking and acting. These cultures within a culture are called *subcultures*." (*The Study of Society* [New York: Harcourt-Brace, 1958], p. 34.) Thereafter he discusses Whyte's *Street-*

corner Society. Although these definitions are helpful, they fail to make several distinctions which are developed below.

[2] A. L. Kroeber, "The Concept of Culture in Science," *Journal of General Education,* 3 (1949), p. 187. See also Clyde Kluckhohn's reference to this idea in "Culture and Behavior," in *Handbook of Social Psychology,* Gardner Lindzey, ed. (Reading, Mass.: Addison-Wesley, 1954), Vol. 2, p. 954; and A. L. Kroeber in "Problems of Process: Results," in *An Appraisal of Anthropology Today,* Sol Tax *et al.,* eds. (Chicago: University of Chicago Press, 1953), p. 119.

[3] Ralph Linton, *The Study of Man* (New York: Appleton-Century, 1936), p. 486. See also his *The Cultural Background of Personality* (New York: Appleton-Century-Crofts, 1945), pp. 148–151. Elsewhere in *The Study of Man,* Linton uses subculture in a different sense, similar to the second usage described below.

[4] Edward Sapir, "Personality," in *Encyclopedia of the Social Sciences* (New York: Macmillan, 1931), Vol. 12, p. 86; Charles H. Cooley, *Human Nature and the Social Order,* rev. ed. (New York: Scribner, 1922).

[5] See, e.g., John K. Morland, *Millways of Kent* (Chapel Hill: University of North Carolina Press, 1958); Julian Steward, *The People of Puerto Rico* (Champaign: University of Illinois Press, 1956); Charles Wagley and Marvin Harris, "A Typology of Latin American Subcultures," *American Anthropologist,* 57 (1955), pp. 428–451; Evon Z. Vogt, "American Subcultural *Continua* as Exemplified by the Mormons and Texans," *American Anthropologist,* 57 (1955), pp. 1163–1172; Murray Straus, "Subcultural Variations in Ceylonese Mental Ability: A Study in National Character," *Journal of Social Psychology,* 39 (1954), pp. 129–141; Joel B. Montague and Edgar G. Epps, "Attitudes Toward Social Mobility as Revealed by Samples of Negro and White Boys," *Pacific Sociological Review,* 1 (1958), pp. 81–84; Hylan Lewis, *Blackways of Kent* (Chapel Hill: University of North Carolina Press, 1955); Robin M. Williams, Jr., *American Society* (New York: Knopf, 1951), Chap. 10; T. S. Langner, "A Test of Intergroup Prejudice Which Takes Account of Individual and Group Differences in Values," *Journal of Abnormal and Social Psychology,* 48 (1953), pp. 548–554.

[6] Brewster Smith, "Anthropology and Psychology," in *For a Science of Social Man,* John Gillin, ed. (New York: Macmillan, 1954), p. 61. See also Talcott Parsons and Edward A. Shils, eds., *Toward A General Theory of Action* (Cambridge: Harvard University Press, 1951), esp. the monograph by the editors; and Ralph Linton's preface to Abram Kardiner, *The Psychological Frontiers of Society* (New York: Columbia University Press, 1945).

[7] See, e.g., Neal Gross, Ward S. Mason, and A. W. McEachern, *Explorations in Role Analysis* (New York: Wiley, 1958); F. L. Bates, "Position, Role, and Status: A Reformulation of Concepts," *Social Forces,* 34 (1956), pp. 313–321; Robert K. Merton, "The Role-Set: Problems in Sociological Theory," *British Journal of Sociology,* 8 (1957), pp. 106–120; S. F. Nadel, *The Theory of Social Structure* (Glencoe, Ill.: The Free Press, 1957); Theodore R. Sarbin, "Role Theory," in *Handbook of Social Psychology, op. cit.,* Vol. 1, Chap. 6.

[8] It is possible, of course, for a subculture to specify roles within its own system.

[9] Lewis Yablonsky, "The Delinquent Gang as a Near-Group," *Social Problems,* 7 (1959), pp. 108–117.

[10] By the noun in "contraculture" I seek to call attention to the normative aspects of the phenomena under study and by the qualifying prefix to call attention to the conflict aspects. Similar terms are occasionally found in the literature, but they are either defined only by their use in context or are used differently from the meaning assigned to contraculture in this paper. Harold D. Lasswell uses the term "countermores" to refer to "culture patterns which appeal mainly to the id . . . ." (*World Politics and Personal Insecurity* (New York: McGraw-Hill, 1935), p. 64). He then designates "revolutionists, prostitutes, prisoners, obscene and subversive talk"—which scarcely suggest a clear analytic category. In *World Revolutionary Propaganda* (New York: Knopf, 1939), Lasswell and Dorothy Blumenstock discuss the use of inverse

values as a revolutionary propaganda weapon and comment on the presumed vulnerability of deprived persons to the countermores stressed in this propaganda. In *Power and Society* (New Haven: Yale University Press, 1950), p. 49, Lasswell uses the term somewhat differently: "*Countermores* are culture traits symbolized by the group as deviations from the mores, and yet are expected to occur." A certain amount of bribery, for example, is "normal" "and must be included by the candid observer as part of culture."

At various points, Talcott Parsons more nearly approaches the meaning of the concept contraculture as used here, although more by implication than by direct definition, and without distinguishing it from the concept of subculture. Referring to the ideological aspects of a subculture, he writes: "In such cases of an open break with the value-system and ideology of the wider society we may speak of a 'counter-ideology.' " (*The Social System* [Glencoe, Ill.: The Free Press, 1951], p. 355.) And later: "If, however, the culture of the deviant group, like that of the delinquent gang, remains a 'counter-culture' it is difficult to find the bridges by which it can acquire influence over wider circles" (p. 522). It is not clear from these uses how counter-ideology and counter-culture are to be defined; but the important place Parsons gives to the element of ambivalence in his use of the concept subculture suggests that he has in mind something similar to our concept of contraculture in his use of these various terms. (See *ibid.*, p. 286.)

[11] See Talcott Parsons, *Essays in Sociological Theory Pure and Applied* (Glencoe, Ill.: The Free Press, 1949), Chap. 5; Howard Becker, *German Youth: Bond or Free* (New York: Oxford, 1946); S. N. Eisenstadt, *From Generation to Generation. Age Groups and the Social Structure* (Glencoe, Ill.: The Free Press, 1956); David Riesman *et al., The Lonely Crowd* (New Haven: Yale University Press, 1950); R. J. Havighurst and Hilda Taba, *Adolescent Character and Personality* (New York: Wiley, 1949); Kingsley Davis, "The Sociology of Parent-Youth Conflict," *American Sociological Review*, 5 (1940), pp. 523–534; Ralph Linton, "Age and Sex Categories," *American Sociological Review*, 7 (1942), pp. 589–603; Joseph R. Gusfield, "The Problem of Generations in an Organizational Structure," *Social Forces*, 35 (1957), pp. 323–330. For some contradictory evidence see W. A. Westley and Frederick Elkin, "The Protective Environment and Adolescent Socialization," *Social Forces*, 35 (1957), pp. 243–249; and Elkin and Westley, "The Myth of Adolescent Culture," *American Sociological Review*, 20 (1955), pp. 680–684.

[12] *Op. cit.*, p. 35.

[13] *Op. cit.*, p. 72.

[14] See Harold Finestone, "Cats, Kicks, and Color," *Social Problems*, 5 (1957), pp. 3–13. Here the "cat" among some Negroes is seen as "the personal counterpart of an expressive social movement."

[15] See Riesman, *op. cit.*, esp. Chap. 3, "A Jury of Their Peers."

[16] The desirability of keeping distinct the analytic concepts of culture and collective behavior, including fashion, cannot be elaborated here. See Herbert Blumer, "Collective Behavior," in *Principles of Sociology*, A. M. Lee, ed. (New York: Barnes and Nobel, 1951); Ralph H. Turner and Lewis M. Killian, *Collective Behavior* (Englewood Cliffs, N. J.: Prentice-Hall, 1957); Edward Sapir, "Fashion," *Encyclopedia of the Social Sciences* (New York: Macmillan, 1931), Vol. 6, pp. 139–144; Georg Simmel, "Fashion," *American Journal of Sociology*, 62 (1957), pp. 541–558.

[17] Parsons, *op. cit., Essays . . .* , p. 92.

[18] *Ibid.*, pp. 92–93.

[19] See *ibid.*, pp. 101–102, 189–190, 342–345, 355.

[20] See Robin M. Williams, Jr., "Continuity and Change in Sociological Study," *American Sociological Review*, 23 (1958), pp. 619–633.

[21] Albert K. Cohen, *Delinquent Boys* (Glencoe, Ill.: The Free Press, 1955).

[22] Frank Hartung, in a review of *Delinquent Boys, American Sociological Review*, 20 (1955), p. 752.

[23] See Solomon Kobrin, "The Conflict of Values in Delinquency Areas," *American*

Sociological Review, 16 (1951), pp. 653–661; Alex Inkeles, "Personality and Social Structure," in *Sociology Today*, Robert K. Merton *et al.*, eds. (New York: Basic Books, 1959), p. 254.

[24] See Gresham M. Sykes and David Matza, "Techniques of Neutralization: A Theory of Delinquency," *American Sociological Review*, 22 (1957), pp. 664–670.

[25] John I. Kitsuse and David C. Dietrick, "*Delinquent Boys:* A Critique," *American Sociological Review*, 24 (1959), pp. 208–215.

[26] See Albert Cohen and James Short, "Research in Delinquent Subcultures," *The Journal of Social Issues*, 14:3 (1958), pp. 20–37.

[27] Walter B. Miller, "Lower Class Culture as a Generating Milieu of Gang Delinquency," *The Journal of Social Issues*, 14:3 (1958), pp. 5–19.

[28] In addition to the studies of Sykes and Matza, Cohen, Finestone, and Yablonsky cited above, see William McCord and Joan McCord, *Origins of Crime. A New Evaluation of the Cambridge-Somerville Youth Study* (New York: Columbia University Press, 1959).

[29] In a recent manuscript, Sykes and Matza suggest that delinquent behavior can profitably be studied as an exaggerated expression of certain "subterranean values" of the dominant society (the search for excitement, the use of "pull" to get by without too much work, and aggression). This idea deserves careful study. The main research task is to discover the conditions which promote selective and exaggerated attention to these values at the cost of neglect of the more prominent "public" values. It seems likely that this task will lead to the incorporation of the "subterranean values" thesis into the larger complex of theories of delinquency. The thesis raises a question of terminology in connection with the present paper: At what point does exaggerated emphasis on a value become a counter-value by virtue of the exaggeration? *Some* cultural support can be found in a complex society for many patterns of behavior that are not fully valued. A society may accept or even applaud a pattern that is used to a limited degree while condemning its extravagant use. And the meaning of the pattern in the life of the individual when found in culturally approved degree differs from what it is when the pattern becomes a dominant theme. To discover why some subterranean values are raised into a style of life, therefore, requires more than cultural analysis. (See Gresham M. Sykes and David Matza, "Juvenile Delinquency and Subterranean Values," unpublished manuscript, 1960.)

[30] Of the many studies in this area, see Charles McArthur, "Personality Differences Between Middle and Upper Classes," *Journal of Abnormal and Social Psychology*, 50 (1955), pp. 247–254; Melvin L. Kohn, "Social Class and Parental Values," *American Journal of Sociology*, 64 (1959), pp. 337–351; A. B. Hollingshead and Frederick C. Redlich, *Social Class and Mental Illness* (New York: Wiley, 1958); Clyde R. White, "Social Class Differences in the Uses of Leisure," *American Journal of Sociology*, 61 (1955), pp. 145–151; John A. Clausen and Melvin L. Kohn, "The Ecological Approach in Social Psychiatry," *American Journal of Sociology*, 60 (1954), pp. 140–151; A. B. Hollingshead, *Elmtown's Youth* (New York: Wiley, 1949); Louis Schneider and Sverre Lysgaard, "The Deferred Gratification Pattern: A Preliminary Study," *American Sociological Review*, 18 (1953), pp. 142–149; Urie Bronfenbrenner, "Socialization and Social Class Through Time and Space," in *Readings in Social Psychology*, Eleanor E. Maccoby *et al.*, ed. (New York: Holt, 1958), pp. 400–425.

[31] C. Wright Mills, "The Professional Ideology of Social Pathologists," *American Journal of Sociology*, 49 (1943), pp. 165–180.

[32] Bernard C. Rosen, "Race, Ethnicity, and the Achievement Syndrome," *American Sociological Review*, 24 (1959), pp. 47–60. It is highly important, in aspiration studies, to compare, not absolute levels, but the extent of aspiration above the existing level of individuals or their families. A low absolute target for lower-class members may require a larger *reach* than a higher target for middle-class persons. See Leonard Reissman, "Levels of Aspiration and Social Class," *American Sociological Review*, 18 (1953), pp. 233–242.

[33] Richard M. Stephenson, "Mobility Orientation and Stratification of 1,000 Ninth Graders," *American Sociological Review*, 22 (1957), pp. 204–212.

[34] Raymond A. Mulligan, "Socio-Economic Background and College Enrollment," *American Sociological Review*, 16 (1951), pp. 188–196; Alan B. Wilson, "Residential Segregation of Social Classes and Aspirations of High School Boys," *American Sociological Review*, 24 (1959), pp. 836–845.

[35] Howard S. Becker, "The Professional Dance Musician and His Audience," *American Journal of Sociology*, 57 (1951), pp. 136–144.

[36] W. B. Cameron, "Sociological Notes on the Jam Session," *Social Forces*, 33 (1954), pp. 177–182.

[37] There are numerous alternative ways in which the protest against deprivation can be expressed. Delinquency and drug addiction often have a contracultural aspect; but somewhat less clearly, political and religious movements among disprivileged groups may also invert the values of the influential but inaccessible dominant group. Thus the concept of contraculture may help us to understand, for example, the Garveyite movement, the Ras Tafari cult, and some aspects of the value schemes of lower-class sects. (See, e.g., Liston Pope, *Millhands and Preachers* (New Haven: Yale University Press, 1942); and George E. Simpson, "The Ras Tafari Movement in Jamaica: A Study of Race and Class Conflict," *Social Forces*, 34 (1955), pp. 167–170.)

CHAPTER TWO

Methods and Techniques
of Sociological Analysis

COMMENTARY

Survey analysis, a method particularly applicable to the study and process of many aspects of the structure of complex societies, has long been considered the *deus ex machina* of the sociological enterprise. The seven papers included in this section emphasize the fact that a wide array of techniques and tools is available to the research sociologist, and that the appropriateness of any particular research procedure depends ultimately upon the nature of the analytical problem and the type of data to be obtained.*

The experimental method is the method *par excellence* of science, for it is in the experiment that the researcher can control extraneous variables in testing his hypotheses. Donald Campbell outlines factors which act to confound data, and discusses the adequacy of various research designs in controlling them.

Many sociological problems do not lend themselves to laboratory investigation. Campbell suggests one design, the "post-test only" design, which can be employed in field experimentation as well as in laboratory studies. William Evan and Morris Zelditch's paper "A Laboratory Experiment on Bureaucratic Authority," included in Chapter Three, illustrates the "post-test only" design in a laboratory study.

It may be virtually impossible for the researcher of many sociological problems to be able to control the causal variable in his hypothesis. A value of Campbell's article for the student of sociology is in making him aware of the kinds of factors which may confound research, thereby enabling him to evaluate a piece of research and to design, creatively, ways of ruling out rival explanations to account for the results obtained.

James Davis' paper "Great Books and Small Groups: An Informal History of a National Survey" provides a rather forthright discussion of the strategies

---

* Conspicuous by their absence are discussions of such procedures as content analysis, simulation, ethnomethodology, modeling, sociometry, and demographic techniques, to mention but a few. The interested reader is referred to the suggested readings for discussions of these methods and techniques.

126

of survey research. In his description of NORC Survey No. 408 Davis calls attention to, and examines, some of the exigencies of client commissioned research. He makes evident the nature of the difficulties entailed in the execution of academic research—research oriented to knowledge for its own sake—supported by pragmatically oriented donors who seek specific solutions to definite problems. The conflict between pure and applied research and a concern about the relevance of the particular instance for more universal phenomena can no longer be considered epiphenomena. As sociologists are increasingly called upon to engage in policy relevant research these considerations, perceptively discussed by Davis, take on an unavoidable cogency.

A second consideration illuminated by Davis' discussion is the interrelationship of empirical research and sociological theory. What is perhaps most important about this aspect of the discussion is Davis' stress on how constraints in the research setting, and the intellectual biography and predelictions of the researcher, intervene to shape study design and analytical strategy.

Finally, it is worth noting and emphasizing that, in part, Davis' conclusions echo the sentiments expressed by Robert Nisbet in his essay on "Sociology as an Art Form" found in Part I of this text. Davis characterizes survey research as "an art very much like architecture, in which it is possible to show disciplined creativity by producing elegant structures while working with raw materials characterized by limited engineering properties and for clients with definite goals and finite budgets."

While survey analysis is, perhaps, the most widely used technique for gathering data, there are other methods which are fruitful for sociological analysis. Participant observation is one such method. In their article "Participant Observation and Interviewing: A Comparison," Howard Becker and Blanche Geer describe participant observation and its particular advantages, and contrast it with the interview. In making this comparison they point out some of the weaknesses of the interview technique. Martin Trow's critique of the Becker and Geer paper correctly points out, we think, that Becker and Geer went "overboard" in their praise of participant observation and criticism of the interview. He states that one research tool is not better than another, but that it is more or less appropriate to a particular research problem. Trow underlines what is basic to this section of the text, that a variety of techniques is available to the sociologist for data collection.

Oscar Grusky's article "Managerial Succession and Organizational Effectiveness" illustrates how the research sociologist can make creative use of available archival data. Census statistics, compiled by government agencies, provide a more obvious example of archival data. But Grusky's work calls attention to the existence and availability of useful material in unlikely sources. A recent volume by Eugene Webb, et al., *Unobtrusive Measures: Nonreactive Research in the Social Sciences,* cited in the list of additional readings, suggests additional sources of such material and discusses some of the advantages which may accrue from their use.

As was indicated above, the gist of Campbell's paper on experimental design is that it is incumbent upon the researcher to rule out alternative explanations which might account for his findings. William Gamson and Norman Scotch, in their commentary "Scapegoating in Baseball," on Grusky's study, suggest how Grusky's finding might be accounted for by plausible rival interpretations. They develop an analysis whereby three alternative hypotheses, each of which could account for Grusky's finding, can be subjected to empirical test.

| Methods and Techniques of Sociological Analysis | EXPERIMENTAL DESIGN |

10 DONALD T. CAMPBELL

Factors Relevant to the Validity of Experiments in Social Settings

What do we seek to control in experimental designs? What extraneous variables which would otherwise confound our interpretation of the experiment do we wish to rule out? The present paper attempts a specification of the major categories of such extraneous variables and employs these categories in evaluating the validity of standard designs for experimentation in the social sciences.

Validity will be evaluated in terms of two major criteria. First, and as a basic minimum, is what can be called *internal validity*: did in fact the experimental stimulus make some significant difference in this specific instance? The second criterion is that of *external validity, representativeness,* or *generalizability*: to what populations, settings, and variables can this effect be generalized? Both criteria are obviously important although it turns out that they are to some extent incompatible, in that the controls required for internal validity often tend to jeopardize representativeness.

Reprinted from *Psychological Bulletin,* 54:4 (1957), pp. 297–312, by permission of the author and the publisher. Copyright © 1957 by the American Psychological Association, Inc.

The extraneous variables affecting internal validity will be introduced in the process of analyzing three pre-experimental designs. In the subsequent evaluation of the applicability of three true experimental designs, factors leading to external invalidity will be introduced. The effects of these extraneous variables will be considered at two levels: as simple or main effects, they occur independently of or in addition to the effects of the experimental variable; as interactions, the effects appear in conjunction with the experimental variable. The main effects typically turn out to be relevant to internal validity, the interaction effects to external validity or representativeness.

The following designation for experimental designs will be used: X will represent the exposure of a group to the experimental variable or event, the effects of which are to be measured; O will refer to the process of observation or measurement, which can include watching what people do, listening, recording, interviewing, administering tests, counting lever depressions, etc. The Xs and Os in a given row are applied to the same specific persons. The left to right dimension indicates temporal order. Parallel rows represent equivalent samples of persons unless otherwise specified. The designs will be numbered and named for cross-reference purposes.

THREE PRE-EXPERIMENTAL DESIGNS AND THEIR CONFOUNDED EXTRANEOUS VARIABLES

The One-Shot Case Study As Stouffer[1] has pointed out, much social science research still uses Design 1, in which a single individual or group is studied in detail only once, and in which the observations are attributed to exposure to some prior situation.

$$X \quad O \qquad \text{1. One-Shot Case Study}$$

This design does not merit the title of experiment, and is introduced only to provide a reference point. The very minimum of useful scientific information involves at least one formal comparison and therefore at least two careful observations.[2]

The One-Group Pretest-Posttest Design This design does provide for one formal comparison of two observations, and is still widely used.

$$O_1 \quad X \quad O_2 \qquad \text{2. One-Group Pretest-Posttest Design}$$

However, in it there are four or five categories of extraneous variables left uncontrolled which thus become rival explanations of any difference between O_1 and O_2, confounded with the possible effect of X.

The first of these is the main effect of *history*. During the time span between O_1 and O_2 many events have occurred in addition to X, and the results might be attributed to these. Thus in Collier's[3] experiment, while his respondents[4] were reading Nazi propaganda materials, France fell, and the obtained attitude changes seemed more likely a result of this event than of the propaganda.[5] By history is meant the specific event series other than X, i.e., the extra-experimental uncontrolled stimuli. Relevant to this variable is the concept of experimental isolation, the employment of experimental settings in which all extraneous stimuli are eliminated. The approximation of such control in much physical and biological research has permitted the satisfactory employment of Design 2. But in social psychology and the other social sciences, if history is confounded with X the results are generally uninterpretable.

The second class of variables confounded with X in Design 2 is here designated as *maturation*. This covers those effects which are systematic with the passage of time, and not, like history, a function of the specific events involved. Thus between O_1 and O_2 the respondents may have grown older, hungrier, tireder, etc., and these may have produced the difference between O_1 and O_2, independently of X. While in the typical brief experiment in the psychology laboratory, maturation is unlikely to be a source of change, it has been a problem in research in child development and can be so in extended experiments in social psychology and education. In the form of "spontaneous remission" and the general processes of healing it becomes an important variable to control in medical research, psychotherapy, and social remediation.

There is a third source of variance that could explain the difference between O_1 and O_2 without a recourse to the effect of X. This is the effect of *testing* itself. It is often true that persons taking a test for the second time make scores systematically different from those taking the test for the first time. This is indeed the case for intelligence tests, where a second mean may be expected to run as much as five IQ points higher than the first one. This possibility makes important a distinction between *reactive* measures and *nonreactive* measures. A reactive measure is one which modifies the phenomenon under study, which changes the very thing that one is trying to measure. In general, any measurement procedure which makes the subject self-conscious or aware of the fact of the experiment can be suspected of being a reactive measurement. Whenever the measurement process is *not* a part of the normal environment it is probably reactive. Whenever measurement exercises the process under study, it is almost certainly reactive. Measurement of a person's height is relatively nonreactive. However, measurement of weight, introduced into an experimental design involving adult American women, would turn out to be reactive in that the process of measuring would stimulate weight reduction. A photograph of a crowd taken in secret from a second story window would be nonreactive, but a news photograph of the same scene might very well be reactive, in that the presence of the photographer would modify the behavior of people seeing themselves being photographed. In a factory, production records introduced for the purpose of an experiment would be reactive, but if such records were a regular part of the operating environment they would be nonreactive. An English anthropologist may be nonreactive as a participant-observer at an English wedding, but might be a highly reactive measuring instrument at a Dobu nuptials. Some measures are so extremely reactive that their use in a pretest-posttest design is not usually considered. In this class would be tests involving surprise, deception, rapid adaptation, or stress. Evidence is amply present that tests of learning and memory are highly reactive.[6] In the field of opinion and attitude research our well-developed interview and attitude test techniques must be rated as reactive, as shown, for example, by Crespi's evidence.[7]

Even within the personality and attitude test domain, it may be found that tests differ in the degree to which they are reactive. For some purposes, tests involving voluntary self-description may turn out to be more reactive (especially at the interaction level to be discussed below) than are devices which focus the respondent upon describing the external world, or give him less latitude in describing himself.[8] It seems likely that, apart from considerations of validity, the Rorschach test is less reactive than the TAT or MMPI. Where the reactive nature of the testing process results from the focusing of attention on the experimental variable, it may be reduced by imbedding the relevant content in a comprehensive array of topics, as has regularly been done in Hovland's attitude change studies.[9] It seems likely that with attention to the problem, observational and measurement techniques can be developed which are much less reactive than those now in use.

Instrument decay provides a fourth uncontrolled source of variance which could produce an O_1-O_2 difference that might be mistaken for the effect of X. This variable can be exemplified by the fatiguing of a spring scales, or the condensation of water vapor in a cloud chamber. For psychology and the social sciences it becomes a particularly acute problem when human beings are used as a part of the measuring apparatus, as judges, observers, raters, coders, etc. Thus O_1 and O_2 may differ because the raters have become more experienced, more fatigued, have acquired a different adaptation level, or have learned about the purpose of the experiment, etc. However infelicitously, this term will be used to typify those problems introduced when shifts in measurement conditions are confounded with the effect of X, including such crudities as having a different observer at O_1 and O_2, or using a different interviewer or coder. Where the use of different interviewers, observers, or experimenters is unavoidable, but where they are used in large numbers, a sampling equivalence of interviewers is required, with the revelant N being the N of interviewers, not interviewees, except as refined through cluster sampling considerations.[10]

A possible fifth extraneous factor deserves mention. This is statistical *regression*. When, in Design 2, the group under investigation has been selected for its extremity on O_1, O_1-O_2 shifts toward the mean will occur which are due to random imperfections of the measuring instrument or random instability within the population, as reflected in the test-retest reliability. In general, regression operates like maturation in that the effects increase systematically with the O_1-O_2 time interval. McNemar has demonstrated the profound mistakes in interpretation which failure to control this factor can introduce in remedial research.[11]

The Static Group Comparison   The third pre-experimental design is the Static Group Comparison.

$$\frac{X \; O_1}{O_2} \qquad \text{3. The Static Group Comparison}$$

In this design, there is a comparison of a group which has experienced X with a group which has not, for the purpose of establishing the effect of X. In contrast with Design 6, there is in this design no means of certifying that the groups were equivalent at some prior time. (The absence of sampling equivalence of groups is symbolized by the row of dashes.) This design has its most typical occurrence in the social sciences, and both its prevalence and its weakness have been well indicated by Stouffer.[12] It will be recognized as one form of the correlational study. It is introduced here to complete the list of confounding factors. If the Os differ, this difference could have come about through biased *selection* or recruitment of the persons making up the groups; i.e., they might have differed anyway without the effect of X. Frequently, exposure to X (e.g., some mass communication) has been voluntary and the two groups have an inevitable systematic difference on the factors determining the choice involved, a difference which no amount of matching can remove.

A second variable confounded with the effect of X in this design can be called experimental *mortality*. Even if the groups were equivalent at some prior time, O_1 and O_2 may differ now not because individual members have changed, but because a biased subset of members have dropped out. This is a typical problem in making inferences from comparisons of the attitudes of college freshmen and college seniors, for example.

TRUE EXPERIMENTAL DESIGNS

The Pretest-Posttest Control Group Design   One or another of the above considerations led psychologists between 1900 and 1925 to expand Design 2 by the addition of a control group, resulting in Design 4.[13]

$$\begin{array}{cc} O_1 & X & O_2 \\ O_3 & & O_4 \end{array} \qquad \text{4. Pretest-Posttest Control Group Design}$$

Because this design so neatly controls for the main effects of history, maturation, testing, instrument decay, regression, selection, and mortality, these separate sources of variance are not usually made explicit. It seems well to state briefly the relationship of the design to each of these confounding factors, with particular attention to the application of the design in social settings.

If the differences between O_1 and O_2 were due to intervening historical events, then they should also show up in the O_3–O_4 comparison. Note, however, several complications in achieving this control. If respondents are run in groups, and if there is only one experimental session and one control session, then there is no control over the unique internal histories of the groups. The O_1–O_2 difference, even if not appearing in O_3–O_4, may be due to a chance distracting factor appearing in one or the other group. Such a design, while controlling for the shared history or event series, still confounds X with the unique session history. Second, the design implies a simultaneity of O_1 with O_3 and O_2 with O_4 which is usually impossible. If one were to try to achieve simultaneity by using two experimenters, one working with the experimental respondents, the other with the controls, this would confound experimenter differences with X (introducing one type of instrument decay). These considerations make it usually imperative that, for a true experiment, the experimental and control groups be tested and exposed individually or in small subgroups, and that sessions of both types be temporally and spatially intermixed.

As to the other factors: if maturation or testing contributed an $O_1–O_2$ difference, this should appear equally in the $O_3–O_4$ comparison, and these variables are thus controlled for their main effects. To make sure the design controls for instrument decay, the same individual or small-session approximation to simultaneity needed for history is required. The occasional practice of running the experimental group and control group at different times is thus ruled out on this ground as well as that of history. Otherwise the observers may have become more experienced, more hurried, more careless, the maze more redolent with irrelevant cues, the lever-tension and friction diminished, etc. Only when groups are effectively simultaneous do these factors affect experimental and control groups alike. Where more than one experimenter or observer is used, counterbalancing experimenter, time, and group is recommended. The balanced Latin square is frequently useful for this purpose.[14]

While regression is controlled in the design as a whole, frequently secondary analyses of effects are made for extreme pretest scorers in the experimental group. To provide a control for effects of regression, a parallel analysis of extremes should also be made for the control group.

Selection is of course handled by the sampling equivalence ensured through the randomization employed in assigning persons to groups, perhaps supplemented by, but not supplanted by, matching procedures. Where the experimental and control groups do not have this sort of equivalence, one has a compromise design rather than a true experiment. Furthermore, the $O_1–O_3$ comparison provides a check on possible sampling differences.

The design also makes possible the examination of experimental mortality, which becomes a real problem for experiments extended over weeks or months. If the experimental and control groups do not differ in the number of lost cases nor in their pretest scores, the experiment can be judged internally valid on this point, although mortality reduces the generalizability of effects to the original population from which the groups were selected.

For these reasons, the Pretest-Posttest Control Group Design has been the ideal in the social sciences for some thirty years. Recently, however, a serious and avoidable imperfection in it has been noted, perhaps first by Schanck and Goodman.[15] Solomon has expressed the point as an *inter-*

action effect of testing.[16] In the terminology of analysis of variance, the effects of history, maturation, and testing, as described so far, are all *main* effects, manifesting themselves in mean differences independently of the presence of other variables. They are effects that could be added on to other effects, including the effect of the experimental variable. In contrast, interaction effects represent a joint effect, specific to the concomitance of two or more conditions, and may occur even when no main effects are present. Applied to the testing variable, the interaction effect might involve not a shift due solely or directly to the measurement process, but rather a sensitization of respondents to the experimental variable so that when X was preceded by O there would be a change, whereas both X and O would be without effect if occurring alone. In terms of the two types of validity, Design 4 is internally valid, offering an adequate basis for generalization to other sampling-equivalent *pretested* groups. But it has a serious and systematic weakness in representativeness in that it offers, strictly speaking, no basis for generalization to the *unpretested* population. And it is usually the *unpretested* larger universe from which these samples were taken to which one wants to generalize.

A concrete example will help make this clearer. In the NORC study of a United Nations information campaign,[17] two equivalent samples, of a thousand each, were drawn from the city's population. One of these samples was interviewed, following which the city of Cincinnati was subjected to an intensive publicity campaign using all the mass media of communication. This included special features in the newspapers and on the radio, bus cards, public lectures, etc. At the end of two months, the second sample of 1,000 was interviewed and the results compared with the first 1,000. There were no differences between the two groups except that the second group was somewhat more pessimistic about the likelihood of Russia's cooperating for world peace, a result which was attributed to history rather than to the publicity campaign. The second sample was no better informed about the United Nations nor had it noticed in particular the publicity campaign which had been going on. In connection with a program of research on panels and the reinterview problem, Paul Lazarsfeld and the Bureau of Applied Social Research arranged to have the initial sample reinterviewed at the same time as the second sample was interviewed, after the publicity campaign. This reinterviewed group showed significant attitude changes, a high degree of awareness of the campaign and important increases in information. The inference in this case is unmistakably that the initial interview had sensitized the persons interviewed to the topic of the United Nations, had raised in them a focus of awareness which made the subsequent publicity campaign effective for them but for them only. This study and other studies clearly document the possibility of interaction effects which seriously limit our capacity to generalize from the pretested experimental group to the unpretested general population. Hovland[18] reports a general finding which is of the opposite nature but is, nonetheless, an indication of an interactive effect. In his Army studies the initial pretest served to reduce the effects of the experimental variable, presumably by creating a commitment to a given position. Crespi's[19] findings support this expectation. Solomon[20] reports two studies with school children in which a spelling pretest reduced the effects of a training period. But whatever the direction of the effect, this flaw in the Pretest-Posttest Control Group Design is serious for the purposes of the social scientist.

The Solomon Four-Group Design   It is Solomon's[21] suggestion to control this problem by adding to the traditional two-group experiment two unpretested groups as indicated in Design 5.

$$O_1 \ X \ O_2$$
$$O_3 \quad O_4$$
$$\quad X \ O_5 \qquad \text{5. Solomon Four-Group Design}$$
$$O_6$$

This Solomon Four-Group Design enables one both to control and measure both the main and interaction effects of testing and the main effects of a composite of maturation and history. It has become the new ideal design for social scientists. A word needs to be said about the appropriate statistical analysis. In Design 4, an efficient single test embodying the four measurements is achieved through computing for each individual a pretest-posttest difference score which is then used for comparing by t test the experimental and control groups. Extension of this mode of analysis to the Solomon Four-Group Design introduces an inelegant awkwardness to the otherwise elegant procedure. It involves assuming as a pretest score for the unpretested groups the mean value of the pretest from the first two groups. This restricts the effective degrees of freedom, violates assumptions of independence, and leaves one without a legitimate base for testing the significance of main effects and interaction. An alternative analysis is available which avoids the assumed pretest scores. Note that the four posttests form a simple two-by-two analysis of variance design:

	No X	X
Pretested	O_4	O_2
Unpretested	O_6	O_5

The column means represent the main effect of X, the row means the main effect of pretesting, and the interaction term the interaction of pretesting and X. (By use of a t test the combined main effects of maturation and history can be tested through comparing O_6 with O_1 and O_3.)

The Posttest-Only Control Group Design   While the statistical procedures of analysis of variance introduced by Fisher[22] are dominant in psychology and the other social sciences today, it is little noted in our discussions of experimental arrangements that Fisher's typical agricultural experiment involves no pretest: equivalent plots of ground receive different experimental treatments and the subsequent yields are measured.[23] Applied to a social experiment as in testing the influence of a motion picture upon attitudes, two randomly assigned audiences would be selected, one exposed to the movie, and the attitudes of each measured subsequently for the first time.

$$\begin{array}{ccc} A & X & O_1 \\ A & & O_2 \end{array}$$ 6. Posttest-Only Control Group Design

In this design the symbol A had been added, to indicate that at a specific time prior to X the groups were made equivalent by a random sampling *assignment*. A is the point of selection, the point of allocation of individuals to groups. It is the existence of this process that distinguishes Design 6 from Design 3, the Static Group Comparison. Design 6 is not a static cross-sectional comparison, but instead truly involves control and observation extended in time. The sampling procedures employed assure us that at time A the groups were equal, even if not measured. A provides a point of prior equality just as does the pretest. A point A is, of course, involved in all true experiments, and should perhaps be indicated in Designs 4 and 5. It is essential that A be regarded as a specific point in time, for groups change as a function of time since A, through experimental mortality. Thus in a public opinion survey situation employing probability sampling from lists of residents, the longer the time since A, the more the sample underrepresents the transient segments of society, the newer dwelling units, etc. When experimental groups are being drawn from a self-selected extreme population, such as applicants for psychotherapy, time since A introduces maturation (spontaneous remission) and regression factors. In Design 6 these effects would be confounded with the effect of X of the As as well as the Os were not contemporaneous for experimental and control groups.

Like Design 4, this design controls for the effects of maturation and history through the practical simultaneity of both the As and the Os. In superiority over Design 4, no main or interaction effects of pretesting are involved. It is this feature that recommends it in particular. While it controls for the main and interaction effects of pretesting as well as does Design 5, the Solomon Four-Group Design, it does not measure these effects, nor the main effect of history-maturation. It can be noted that Design 6 can be considered as the two unpretested "control" groups from the Solomon Design, and that Solomon's two traditional pretested groups have in this sense the sole purpose of measuring the effects of pretesting and history-maturation, a purpose irrelevant to the main aim of studying the effect of X.[24] However, under normal conditions of not quite perfect sampling control, the four-group design provides in addition greater assurance against mistakenly attributing to X effects which are not due it, inasmuch as the effect of X is documented in three different fashions (O_1 vs. O_2, O_2 vs. O_4, and O_5 vs. O_6). But, short of the four-group design, Design

6 is often to be preferred to Design 4, and is a fully valid experimental design.

Design 6 has indeed been used in the social sciences, perhaps first of all in the classic experiment by Gosnell, *Getting Out the Vote*.[25] Schanck and Goodman, Hovland and others[26] have also employed it. But, in spite of its manifest advantages of simplicity and control, it is far from being a popular design in social research and indeed is usually relegated to an inferior position in discussions of experimental designs if mentioned at all.[27] Why is this the case?

In the first place, it is often confused with Design 3. Even where Ss have been carefully assigned to experimental and control groups, one is apt to have an uneasiness about the design because one "doesn't know what the subjects were like before." This objection must be rejected, as our standard tests of significance are designed precisely to evaluate the likelihood of differences occurring by chance in such sample selection. It is true, however, that this design is particularly vulnerable to selection bias and where random assignment is not possible it remains suspect. Where naturally aggregated units, such as classes, are employed intact, these should be used in large numbers and assigned at random to the experimental and control conditions; cluster sampling statistics[28] should be used to determine the error term. If but one or two intact classrooms are available for each experimental treatment, Design 4 should certainly be used in preference.

A second objection to Design 6, in comparison with Design 4, is that it often has less precision. The difference scores of Design 4 are less variable than the posttest scores of Design 6 if there is a pretest-posttest correlation above .50,[29] and hence for test-retest correlations above that level a smaller mean difference would be statistically significant for Design 4 than for Design 6, for a constant number of cases. This advantage to Design 4 may often be more than dissipated by the costs and loss in experimental efficiency resulting from the requirement of two testing sessions, over and above the considerations of representativeness.

Design 4 has a particular advantage over Design 6 if experimental mortality is high. In Design 4, one can examine the pretest scores of lost cases in both experimental and control groups and check on their comparability. In the absence of this in Design 6, the possibility is opened for a mean difference resulting from differential mortality rather than from individual change, if there is a substantial loss of cases.

A final objection comes from those who wish to study the relationship of pretest attitudes to kind and amount of change. This is a valid objection, and where this is the interest, Design 4 or 5 should be used, with parallel analysis of experimental and control groups. Another common type of individual difference study involves classifying persons in terms of amount of change and finding associated characteristics such as sex, age, education, etc. While unavailable in this form in Design 6, essentially the same correlational information can be obtained by subdividing both experimental and control groups in terms of the associated characteristics, and examining the experimental-control difference for such subtypes.

For Design 6, the Posttest-Only Control Group Design, there is a class of social settings in which it is optimally feasible, settings which should be more used than they now are. Whenever the social contact represented by X is made to single individuals or to small groups, and where the response to that stimulus can be identified in terms of individuals or type of X, Design 6 can be applied. Direct mail and door-to-door contacts represent such settings. The alternation of several appeals from door-to-door in a fund-raising campaign can be organized as a true experiment without increasing the cost of the solicitation. Experimental variation of persuasive materials in a direct-mail sales campaign can provide a better experimental laboratory for the study of mass communication and persuasion than is available in any university. The well-established, if little-used, split-run technique in comparing alternative magazine ads is a true experiment of this type, usually limited to coupon returns rather than sales because of the problem of identifying response with stimulus type.[30] The split-ballot technique[31] long used in public opinion polls to compare different question wordings or question sequences provides an excellent example which can obviously be extended to other topics.[32] By and large these laboratories have not yet been used to study social science theories, but they are directly relevant to hypotheses about social persuasion.

Multiple X Designs   In presenting the above designs, X has been opposed to No-X, as is traditional in discussions of experimental design in psychology. But while this may be a legitimate description of the stimulus-isolated physical science laboratory, it can only be a convenient shorthand in the social sciences, for any No-X period will not be empty of potentially change-inducing stimuli. The experience of the control group might better be categorized as another type of X, a control experience, an X_C instead of No-X. It is also typical of advance in science that we are soon no longer interested in the qualitative fact of effect or no-effect, but want to specify degree of effect for varying degrees of X. These considerations lead into designs in which multiple groups are used, each with a different X_1, X_2, X_3, X_n, or in multiple factorial design, as X_{1a}, X_{1b}, X_{2a}, X_{2b}, etc. Applied to Designs 4 and 6, this introduces one additional group for each additional X. Applied to 5, The Solomon Four-Group Design, two additional groups (one pretested, one not, both receiving X_n) would be added for each variant on X.

In many experiments, X_1, X_2, X_3, and X_n are all given to the same group, differing groups receiving the Xs in different orders. Where the problem under study centers around the effects of order or combination, such counterbalanced multiple X arrangements are, of course, essential. Studies of transfer in learning are a case in point.[33] But where one wishes to generalize to the effect of each X as occurring in isolation, such designs are not recommended because of the sizable interactions among Xs, as repeatedly demonstrated in learning studies under such labels as proactive inhibition and learning sets. The use of counterbalanced sets of multiple Xs to achieve experimental equation, where natural groups not randomly assembled have to be used, will be discussed in a subsequent paper on compromise designs.

Testing for Effects Extended in Time   The researches of Hovland and his associates[34] have indicated repeatedly that the longer range effects of persuasive Xs may be qualitatively as well as quantitatively different from immediate effects. These results emphasize the importance of designing experiments to measure the effect of X at extended periods of time. As the misleading early research on reminiscence and on the consolidation of the memory trace indicate,[35] repeated measurement of the same persons cannot be trusted to do this if a reactive measurement process is involved. Thus, for Designs 4 and 6, two separate groups must be added for each posttest period. The additional control group cannot be omitted, or the effects of intervening history, maturation, instrument decay, regression, and mortality are confounded with the delayed effects of X. To follow fully the logic of Design 5, four additional groups are required for each posttest period.

True Experiments in Which O *is Not under* E's *Control*   It seems well to call the attention of the social scientist to one class of true experiments which are possible without the full experimental control over both the "when" and "to whom" of both X and O. As far as this analysis has been able to go, no such true experiments are possible without the ability to control X, to withhold it from carefully randomly selected respondents while presenting it to others. But control over O does not seem so indispensable. Consider the following design.

$$
\begin{array}{ll}
A \; X \; O_1 & \\
A \quad\;\; O_2 & \text{6. Posttest Only Design, where } O \text{ cannot} \\
\quad\;\; (O) & \quad\text{be withheld from any respondent} \\
\quad\;\; (O) & \\
\quad\;\; (O) &
\end{array}
$$

The parenthetical Os are inserted to indicate that the studied groups, experimental and control, have been selected from a larger universe all of which will get O anyway. An election provides such an O, and using "whether voted" rather than "how voted," this was Gosnell's design.[36] Equated groups were selected at time A, and the experimental group subjected to persuasive materials designed to get out the vote. Using precincts rather than persons as the basic sampling unit, similar studies can be made on the content of the voting.[37] Essential to this design is the ability to create specified randomly equated groups, the ability to expose one of these groups to X while withholding it (or providing X_2) from the other group, and the ability to identify the performance of each individual or unit in the subsequent O. Since such measures are natural parts of the environment to which one wishes to generalize, they are not reactive, and Design 4, the Pretest-Posttest Control Group Design, is feasible if O has a predictable periodicity to it. With the precinct as a unit, this was the design of Hartmann's classic study of emotional vs. rational appeals in a public election.[38] Note that 5, the Solomon Four-Group Design, is not available, as it requires the ability to withhold O experimentally, as well as X.

FURTHER PROBLEMS OF REPRESENTATIVENESS

The interaction effect of testing, affecting the external validity or representativeness of the experiment, was treated extensively in the previous section, inasmuch as it was involved in the comparison of alternative designs. The present section deals with the effects upon representativeness of other variables which, while equally serious, can apply to any of the experimental designs.

The Interaction Effects of Selection Even though the true experiments control selection and mortality for internal validity purposes, these factors have, in addition, an important bearing on representativeness. There is always the possibility that the obtained effects are specific to the experimental population and do not hold true for the populations to which one wants to generalize. Defining the universe of reference in advance and selecting the experimental and control groups from this at random would guarantee representativeness if it were ever achieved in practice. But inevitably not all those so designated are actually eligible for selection by any contact procedure. Our best survey sampling techniques, for example, can designate for potential contact only those available through residences. And, even of those so designated, up to 90 percent are not contactable for an interview in their own homes even with five callbacks.[39] It seems legitimate to assume that the more effort and time required of the respondent, the larger the loss through nonavailability and noncooperation. If one were to try to assemble experimental groups away from their own homes it seems reasonable to estimate a 50 percent selection loss. If, still trying to extrapolate to the general public, one further limits oneself to docile preassembled groups, as in schools, military units, studio audiences, etc., the proportion of the universe systematically excluded through the sampling process must approach 90 percent or more. Many of the selection factors involved are indubitably highly systematic. Under these extreme selection losses, it seems reasonable to suspect that the experimental groups might show reactions not characteristic of the general population. This point seems worth stressing lest we unwarrantedly assume that the selection loss for experiments is comparable to that found for survey interviews in the home at the respondent's convenience. Furthermore, it seems plausible that the greater the cooperation required, the more the respondent has to deviate from the normal course of daily events, the greater will be the possibility of nonrepresentative reactions. By and large, Design 6 might be expected to require less cooperation than Design 4 or 5, especially in the natural individual contact setting. The interactive effects of experimental mortality are of similar nature. Note that, on these grounds, the longer the experiment is extended in time the more respondents are lost and the less representative are the groups of the original universe.

Reactive Arrangements   In any of the experimental designs, the respondents can become aware that they are participating in an experiment, and this awareness can have an interactive effect, in creating reactions to X which would not occur had X been encountered without this "I'm a guinea pig" attitude. Lazarsfeld, Kerr, and Rosenthal and Frank, all have provided valuable discussions of this problem.[40] Such effects limit generalizations to respondents having this awareness, and preclude generalization to the population encountering X with nonexperimental attitudes. The direction of the effect may be one of negativism, such as an unwillingness to admit to any persuasion or change. This would be comparable to the absence of any immediate effect from discredited communicators, as found by Hovland.[41] The result is probably more often a cooperative responsiveness, in which the respondent accepts the experimenter's expectations and provides pseudoconfirmation. Particularly is this positive response likely when the respondents are self-selected seekers after the cure that X may offer. The Hawthorne studies,[42] illustrate such sympathetic changes due to awareness of experimentation rather than to the specific nature of X. In some settings it is possible to disguise the experimental purpose by providing plausible façades in which X appears as an incidental part of the background.[43] We can also make more extensive use of experiments taking place in the intact social situation, in which the respondent is not aware of the experimentation at all.

The discussion of the effects of selection on representativeness has argued against employing intact natural preassembled groups, but the issue of conspicuousness of arrangements argues for such use. The machinery of breaking up natural groups such as departments, squads, and classrooms into randomly assigned experimental and control groups is a source of reaction which can often be avoided by the use of preassembled groups, particularly in educational settings. Of course, as has been indicated, this requires the use of large numbers of such groups under both experimental and control conditions.

The problem of reactive arrangements is distributed over all features of the experiment which can draw the attention of the respondent to the fact of experimentation and its purposes. The conspicuous or reactive pretest is particularly vulnerable, inasmuch as it signals the topics and purposes of the experimenter. For communications of obviously persuasive aim, the experimenter's topical intent is signaled by the X itself, if the communication does not seem a part of the natural environment. Even for the posttest-only groups, the occurrence of the posttest may create a reactive effect. The respondent may say to himself, "Aha, now I see why we got that movie." This consideration justifies the practice of disguising the connection between O and X even for Design 6, as through having different experimental personnel involved, using different façades, separating the settings and times, and embedding the X-relevant content of O among a disguising variety of other topics.[44]

Generalizing to Other X*s* After the internal validity of an experiment has been established, after a dependable effect of X upon O has been found, the next step is to establish the limits and relevant dimensions of generalization not only in terms of populations and settings but also in terms of categories and aspects of X. The actual X in any one experiment is a specific combination of stimuli, all confounded for interpretative purposes, and only some relevant to the experimenter's intent and theory. Subsequent experimentation should be designed to purify X, to discover that aspect of the original conglomerate X which is responsible for the effect. As Brunswik[45] has emphasized, the representative sampling of Xs is as relevant a problem in linking experiment to theory as is the sampling of respondents. To define a category of Xs along some dimension, and then to sample Xs for experimental purposes from the full range of stimuli meeting the specification while other aspects of each specific stimulus complex are varied, serves to untie or unconfound the defined dimension from specific others, lending assurance of theoretical relevance.

In a sense, the placebo problem can be understood in these terms. The experiment without the placebo has clearly demonstrated that some aspect of the total X stimulus complex has had an effect; the placebo experiment serves to break up the complex X into the suggestive connotation of pill-taking and the specific pharmacological properties of the drug—separating two aspects of the X previously confounded. Subsequent studies may discover with similar logic which chemical fragment of the complex natural herb is most essential. Still more clearly, the sham operation illustrates the process of X purification, ruling out general effects of surgical shock so that the specific effects of loss of glandular or neural tissue may be isolated. As these parallels suggest, once recurrent unwanted aspects of complex Xs have been discovered for a given field, control groups especially designed to eliminate these effects can be regularly employed.

Generalizing to Other O*s* In parallel form, the scientist in practice uses a complex measurement procedure which needs to be refined in subsequent experimentation. Again, this is best done by employing multiple Os all having in common the theoretically relevant attribute but varying widely in their irrelevant specificities. For Os this process can be introduced into the initial experiment by employing multiple measures. A major practical reason for not doing so is that it is so frequently a frustrating experience, lending hesitancy, indecision, and a feeling of failure to studies that would have been interpreted with confidence had but a single response measure been employed.

Transition Experiments The two previous paragraphs have argued against the *exact* replication of experimental apparatus and measurement procedures on the grounds that this continues the confounding of theory-relevant aspects of X and O with specific artifacts of unknown influence. On the other hand, the confusion in our literature generated by the heterogeneity of results from studies all on what is nominally the "same" problem but varying in implementation, is leading some to call for exact replication of initial procedures in subsequent research on a topic. Certainly no science can emerge without dependably repeatable experiments. A suggested resolution is the *transition experiment*, in which the need for varying the theory-independent aspects of X and O is met in the form of a multiple X, multiple O design, one segment of which is an "exact" replication of the original experiment, exact at least in those major features which are normally reported in experimental writings.

Internal vs. External Validity If one is in a situation where either internal validity or representativeness must be sacrificed, which should it be? The answer is clear. Internal validity is the prior and indispensable consideration. The optimal design is, of course, one having both internal and external validity. Insofar as such settings are available, they should be exploited, without embarrassment from the apparent opportunistic warping of the content of studies by the availability of laboratory techniques. In this sense, a science is as opportunistic as a bacteria culture and grows only where growth is possible. One basic necessity for such growth is the machinery for selecting among alternative hypotheses, no matter how limited those hypotheses may have to be.

SUMMARY

In analyzing the extraneous variables which experimental designs for social settings seek to control, seven categories have been distinguished: history, maturation, testing, instrument decay, regression, selection, and mortality. In general, the simple or main effects of these variables jeopardize the internal validity of the experiment and are adequately controlled in standard experimental designs. The interactive effects of these variables and of experimental arrangements affect the external validity or generalizability of experimental results. Standard experimental designs vary in their susceptibility to these interactive effects. Stress is also placed upon the differences among measuring instruments and arrangements in the extent to which they create unwanted interactions. The value for social science purposes of the Posttest-Only Control Group Design is emphasized.

ACKNOWLEDGMENTS

A dittoed version of this paper was privately distributed in 1953 under the title "Designs for Social Science Experiments." The author has had the opportunity to benefit from the careful reading and suggestions of L. S. Burwen, J. W. Cotton, C. P. Duncan, D. W. Fiske, C. I. Hovland, L. V. Jones, E. S. Marks, D. C. Pelz, and B. J. Underwood, among others, and wishes to express his appreciation. They have not had the opportunity of seeing the paper in its present form, and bear no responsibility for it. The author also wishes to thank S. A. Stouffer and B. J. Underwood for their public encouragement.

NOTES

[1] S. A. Stouffer, "Some Observations on Study Design," *American Journal of Sociology*, 55 (1949–1950), pp. 355–361.

[2] E. G. Boring, "The Nature and History of Experimental Control," *American Journal of Psychology*, 67 (1954), pp. 573–589.

[3] R. M. Collier, "The Effect of Propaganda upon Attitude Following a Critical Examination of the Propaganda Itself," *Journal of Social Psychology*, 20 (1944), pp. 3–17.

[4] In line with the central focus on social psychology and the social sciences, the term *respondent* is employed in place of the terms *subject, patient,* or *client.*

[5] Collier actually used a more adequate design than this, an approximation to Design 4.

[6] B. J. Underwood, "Interference and Forgetting," *Psychology Review*, 64 (1957), pp. 49–60. B. J. Underwood, *Psychological Research* (New York: Appleton-Century-Croft, 1957).

[7] L. P. Crespi, "The Interview Effect in Polling," *Public Opinion Quarterly*, 12 (1948), pp. 99–111.

[8] D. T. Campbell, "The Indirect Assessment of Social Attitudes," *Psychology Bulletin*, 47 (1950), pp. 15–38.

[9] C. I. Hovland, I. L. Janis, and H. H. Kelley, *Communication and Persuasion* (New Haven: Yale University Press, 1953).

[10] L. Kish, "Selection of the Sample," in *Research Methods in the Behavioral Sciences*, L. Festinger and D. Katz, eds. (New York: Dryden Press, 1953), pp. 175–239.

[11] Q. McNemar, "A Critical Examination of the University of Iowa Studies of Environmental Influences upon the IQ," *Psychology Bulletin*, 37 (1940), pp. 63–92.

[12] Stouffer, *op. cit.*

[13] Boring, *op cit.* R. W. Solomon, "An Extension of Control Group Design," *Psychology Bulletin*, 46 (1949), pp. 137–150.

[14] B. R. Bugelski, "A Note on Grant's Discussion of the Latin Square Principle in the Design and Analysis of Psychological Experiments," *Psychology Bulletin*, 46 (1949), pp. 49–50.

[15] R. L. Schanck and C. Goodman, "Reactions to Propaganda on Both Sides of a Controversial Issue," *Public Opinion Quarterly*, 3 (1939), pp. 107–112.

[16] Solomon, *op. cit.*

[17] S. A. Star and H. M. Hughes, "Report on an Educational Campaign: The Cincinnati Plan for the United Nations," *American Journal of Sociology*, 50 (1949–1950), p. 389.

[18] C. I. Hovland, A. A. Lumsdaine, and F. D. Sheffield, *Experiments on Mass Communication* (Princeton, N.J.: Princeton University Press, 1949).

[19] Collier, *op. cit.*

[20] Solomon, *op. cit.*

[21] *Ibid.*

[22] R. A. Fisher, *The Design of Experiments* (Edinburgh: Oliver & Boyd, 1935).

[23] This is not to imply that the pretest is totally absent from Fisher's designs. He suggests the use of previous year's yields, etc., in convariance analysis. He notes, however, "With annual agricultural crops, knowledge of yields of the experimental area in a previous year under uniform treatment has not been found sufficiently to increase the precision to warrant the adoption of such uniformity trials as a preliminary to projected experiments," Fisher, *op. cit.*, p. 176.

[24] S. L. Payne, "The Ideal Model for Controlled Experiments," *Public Opinion Quarterly*, 15 (1951), pp. 557–562.

[25] H. F. Gosnell, *Getting Out the Vote: An Experiment in the Stimulation of Voting* (Chicago: University of Chicago Press, 1927).

[26] Schanck and Goodman, *op. cit.*; Hovland, Lumsdaine, and Sheffield, *op. cit.*; A. D. Annis and N. C. Meier, "The Induction of Opinion Through Suggestion by Means of Planted Content," *Journal of Social Psychology*, 5 (1934), pp. 65–81; A. Greenberg, "Matched Samples," *Journal of Marketing*, 18 (1953–1954), pp. 241–245; S. C. Menefee, "An Experimental Study of Strike Propaganda," *Social Forces*, 16 (1938), pp. 574–582; J. A. Parrish and D. T. Campbell, "Measuring Propaganda Effects with Direct and Indirect Attitude Tests," *Journal of Abnormal and Social Psychology*, 48 (1953), pp. 3–9; R. E. Rankin and D. T. Campbell, "Galvanic Skin Response to Negro and White Experimenters," *Journal of Abnormal and Social Psychology*, 51 (1955), pp. 30–33.

[27] Hovland, Lumsdaine, and Sheffield, *op. cit.*; M. Jahoda, M. Deutsch, and S. W. Cook, *Research Methods in Social Relations* (New York: Dryden Press, 1951); W. A. Kerr, "Experiments on the Effect of Music on Factory Production," *Applied Psychology Monograph*, No. 5, 1945.

[28] Kish, *op. cit.*

[29] Hovland, Lumsdaine, and Sheffield, *op. cit.*, p. 323.

[30] D. B. Lucas and S. H. Britt, *Advertising Psychology and Research* (New York: McGraw-Hill, 1950).

[31] H. Cantril, *Gauging Public Opinion* (Princeton, N.J.: Princeton University Press, 1944).

[32] Greenberg, *op. cit.*

[33] B. J. Underwood, *Experimental Psychology* (New York: Appleton-Century-Crofts, 1949).

[34] Hovland, Janis, and Kelley, *op. cit.*; Hovland, Lumsdaine, and Sheffield, *op. cit.*

[35] B. J. Underwood, *Psychological Research* (New York: Appleton-Century-Crofts, 1957).

[36] Gosnell, *op. cit.*

[37] D. T. Campbell, "On the Possibility of Experimenting with the 'Bandwagon' Effect," *International Journal of Opinion Attitude Research*, 5 (1951), pp. 251–260.

[38] G. W. Hartmann, "A Field Experiment on the Comparative Effectiveness of 'Emotional' and 'Rational' Political Leaflets in Determining Election Results," *Journal of Abnormal and Social Psychology*, 31 (1936), pp. 99–114.

[39] Williams, R. "Probability Sampling in the Field: A Case History," *Public Opinion Quarterly*, 14 (1950), pp. 316–330.

[40] P. F. Lazarsfeld, "Training Guide on the Controlled Experiment in Social Research," dittoed, Columbia University, Bureau of Applied Social Research, 1948; Kerr, *op. cit.*; D. Rosenthal and J. O. Frank, "Psychotherapy and the Placebo Effect," *Psychology Bulletin*, 53 (1956), pp. 294–302.

[41] Hovland, Janis, and Kelley, *op. cit.*

[42] E. Mayo, *The Human Problems of an Industrial Civilization* (New York: Macmillan, 1933).

43 L. Postman and J. S. Bruner, "Perception Under Stress," *Psychology Review*, 55 (1948), pp. 314–322; Rankin, *op. cit.*; Schanck, *op. cit.*

44 For purposes of completeness, the interaction of X with history and maturation should be mentioned. Both affect the generalizability of results. The interaction effect of history represents the possible specificity of results to a given historical moment, a possibility which increases as problems are more societal, less biological. The interaction of maturation and X would be represented in the specificity of effects to certain maturational levels, fatigue states, etc.

45 E. G. Brunswik, *Perception and the Representative Design of Psychological Experiments* (Berkeley: University of California Press, 1956).

| Methods and Techniques of Sociological Analysis | SURVEY RESEARCH |

11   JAMES A. DAVIS

Great Books and Small Groups: An Informal History of a National Survey

This is, within the narrow limits imposed by perceptual defense and criminal libel, my recollection of how National Opinion Research Center Survey No. 408, the Great Books study, proceeded from its inception in the summer of 1957 to the publication of a book in 1961. Although I tend to view the chronicle as the struggle of a brave study director against time, money, clients, winter weather, Texas Great Books groups, and NORC's business staff, these events may better be viewed as a reasonably typical case study of how modern social research proceeds in a large nonprofit research organization.

This bring us to the subject of money. I think it may be stated as a matter of indisputable fact that there is no money available in the contemporary United States for unrestricted support of large-scale social research. On occasion, a professor whose work is fashionable or whose years of loyal back-scratching on professional committees is deemed worthy of a reward will receive the munificent unrestricted sum of $1,000 or $2,000, most of which he passes on to subsidize graduate students, but private donors prefer to see their names on university dormitories; the association of sociology and socialism is graven in the minds of congress-

Reprinted from *Sociologists at Work*, edited by Phillip E. Hammond, pp. 212–234, by permission of the author and the publisher. Copyright © 1964 by Basic Books, Inc.

men; and foundations have (let us face it) retreated from social research. No one is going to give NORC or similar private institutions the wherewithal to pursue their own research interests at $50,000 per interest. The citizens of Michigan do subsidize the Survey Research Center, and its senior staff members have sabbaticals and swimming pools and who knows what else; but the private, nonprofit research center is in there hustling in the market place along with Ford, General Dynamics, and Joe's Drugstore.

Thus is born "the client," typically a large foundation or a government agency with a particular research question which it feels is worth the exorbitant costs and personal frustrations involved in commissioning research. And with the birth of the client comes the eternal triangle of client, organization, and study director. It is the operation of this triangle which is the key process in the poignant histories of surveys.

Let me begin, however, with a few kind words for clients. As a matter of fact, the client for this study, a foundation executive in one of the many progeny spawned by the Ford Foundation, is a fine guy, and at least prior to his reading of this document, I consider him my friend. But, as we know from introductory sociology, personalities and roles are two different matters. Rolewise, to be a client is somewhat like being a sugar daddy responsible to a board of directors. It is an extraordinarily expensive business, the satisfactions are occasional and fleeting, there is the distinct impression that one is being ruthlessly exploited, and all of this has to be justified at the annual meeting.

At the same time, those in the humanistic studies who are so enraged at the funds they see flowing into social research might momentarily consider how it would be to receive an enormous commission, most of which disappeared into $25 checks to unknown ladies in New Jersey and a mysterious maw called "overhead," and to have the Medici Fund tell you that you could paint anything you liked as long as it matched the rug in their private audience room.

All of this would work out cozily, as it does in business, were it not for the motivations of study directors. There are, I would guess, no more than a hundred people in the country today leading the lives of noisy desperation characteristic of study directors, but they fall into two types. Historically, relatively few study directors in market research and in nonprofit organizations came from graduate study in sociology or social psychology, a Ph.D. in sociology being no more necessary for competence in this area than a degree in electrical engineering. Among NORC's senior study directors, for instance, are non-Ph.D.'s trained in history, anthropology, and undergraduate liberal arts. Into this occupation, however, like locusts, have come the Ph.D.'s. They tend to be ambitious, steely-nerved young men who have worked out the implication of the following propositions: (1) academic success is contingent on research publication, regardless of the topic; (2) young men seldom get research grants on their own; (3) people come to research centers and give them the wherewithal to do large-scale studies.

While the two types of study directors appear indistinguishable to the naked eye, they vary considerably in their view of research and of their jobs. The "old-line" staff tend to identify with the research organization and to gain their rewards from pride in craftsmanship and budgetmanship, reputed client satisfaction, and the feeling that they have contributed to the success of the organization. The new men, however, while often willing to deliver a thorough and honest piece of work for the sponsor, find their major satisfactions in milking the research for journal articles or publications to throw into the potlatch of academia, whence cometh their eventual reward: a research professorship.

I am, in truth, accentuating differences that are far from the polar, for most people in research work find their major rewards from intellectual challenge (as well as salaries superior to teaching), and "applied" research is generally more challenging intellectually. That is what I said: applied work is usually more challenging—because there are more definite standards of accomplishment. In social-science theoretical work, the feeling that it "sounds right" or has the requisite polysyllabic mumbo jumbo is the typical yardstick; in "pure" empirical research, if *any* significant correlations can be wrung out, the material is generally publishable; but in applied research, there are rather precise questions at issue and the failure to answer them is painfully apparent. In addition, applied research in government agencies, the larger commercial firms, and centers like NORC is characterized by superior probability sampling, larger samples, better interviewing, more careful control of coding and tabulations, and informal monitoring of the work by colleagues who are specialists in the same area. One wonders why the Ph.D.'s have continual intellectual dissatisfaction in their jobs.

The root of the problem, I think, lies in the difference between generality and specificity. Clients commission research because they are interested in something specific: who has health insurance, whether enough people are training for careers in biochemistry, how much scholarship money is available to graduate students, to what extent people near airports are bothered by jet noise, and so on. Sociology is, however, the enemy of the specific. Even though the facts of social life in modern America are less well documented than the facts of marine life at the bottom of the ocean, the academic sociologist (the ultimate judge, employer, or journal editor whom our young Ph.D. wants to impress) has a phobia against research which "merely" describes. This is "nose-counting," "dust-bowl empiricism," "trivia," and so forth and is not part of the grand scheme for building the science of sociology. That the history of natural science is in the reverse order—theories having been developed to explain facts, rather than facts gathered to ornament theories—weighs little against the pressure of intellectual tradition. Therefore, the academically oriented study director is faced with a dilemma. If he completes his research in such a fashion as to satisfy the sponsors, it will lack academic glamour. If, on the other hand, he completes a piece suitable for academic publication, it will probably tell the sponsor nothing about the questions which led to the research.

If one has attained sufficient eminence, one proceeds to conduct the study as one pleases, considering the client lucky to have his problem studied by an important person, even if in the process the client's problem disappears. For younger people and the struggling research organization, this is a dangerous tactic, and the natural strategy is to attempt both tasks: a specific descriptive report "for the client" and a high-brow article or monograph for the study director's self-aggrandizement. Thus, as well as a description of who gets scholarships comes a test of the theory of relative deprivation among graduate students; along with the descriptive materials on whether poor boys go on to college comes a paper on status crystallization and career choice; along with the statistics on what doctors prescribe brand-X drugs comes a paper on sociometric aspects of innovation; and so on.

It must be made clear to the reader, however, that these theoretical forays have little or no connection with the specific research questions. As currently developed, sociological and social-psychological theories are almost useless in predicting a dependent variable, either because they are stated so abstractly and vaguely that it is impossible to translate them into research operations or, if stated in usable terms, they are often wrong or account for only a negligible portion of the variance when compared with the "trivial" things such as age, sex, education, and marital status. I, personally, hold great hopes for the theories now being developed under the general rubric of "dissonance" and for much of George Homans' work, and I have to admit that a little exposure to theory suggests some interesting intellectual problems for research; but my reluctant conclusion is that in 90 percent (plus or minus 20 percent) of the research work, "theory" is dragged in only as a status symbol or to improve the eventual merchandising of the results.

Considered, then, as roles, social research is typically conducted by (1) a study director, who may be willing to do what he is paid for, but is more interested in wresting an academic article from the remains, (2) a sponsor, who stokes the fires with money and hopes vaguely that the evasive, fast-talking young man will complete within his lifetime a report bearing vaguely on the topic, and (3) a research organization, beset with financial woes and firmly aware of the fact that the study director (who gets no profits when a study makes money and pays no refund when he runs it into the red) is capable of spending the organization into the poorhouse without shedding a tear and in the process alienating the client beyond the point at which he can be persuaded to pony up the deficit.

Let us now see how these three archetypal characters proceeded to produce NORC Survey 408.

I did not have much to do with the Great Books study until it was about six weeks old. During the early summer of 1957, I was away from

Chicago doing field work in Ohio for a community study directed by Peter Rossi. Why? Because I had been hired by NORC in the summer of 1957 to direct a study of physicians, which never took place. In order to keep me busy, I had been sent into darkest Ohio as gunbearer for Mr. Rossi, who was stalking community leaders there.

The infant Great Books study had been ushered into the world by Clyde Hart, NORC's director at that time, and the staff at the Fund for Adult Education, my role being that of pediatrician rather than obstetrician.

Had I been in Chicago for every moment of the initial negotiations, I would probably have little more to add to this chronicle than I can from my observation post in a commercial hotel in "Mediana," Ohio. Indeed, the exact origins of this survey, as for many, are a mystery. My hearsay version goes as follows.

The Fund for Adult Education, a subsidiary of the Ford Foundation, had since 1951 been supporting diverse activities in the area of adult education by grants to ongoing study-discussion programs, continuing educational centers, educational-television experiments, and so on. The fund was oriented to action, not research, and had commissioned little or no professional research prior to the Great Books study.

I am told that it came to pass that from within the parent Ford Foundation came word that the time had arrived for the Fund for Adult Education to render an accounting of its stewardship and that the conventional medium for such an accounting was "research." The Fund for Adult Education, not unexpectedly, proceeded to commission a number of studies, of which Great Books was one.

Now, if the Fund for Adult Education was bemused to find itself bankrolling a statistical survey, the object of the inquiry—the Great Books Foundation—was flabbergasted. The foundation, an independent, non-profit corporation with headquarters in Chicago (which has no connection with Great Books of the Western World, a commercial publishing venture), coordinates the national program of Great Books, using a small professional staff and a large number of volunteers. As intellectual types, the personnel of Great Books stand somewhere to the right of Jacques Barzun and Arthur Schlesinger, Jr., in their opinion of sociological surveys; but it is amazing how persuasive a large foundation with a history of generosity can be, so eventually the foundation was persuaded to cooperate. I think it would be fair to say that, while the foundation did provide the requisite liaison to complete the study, its stance was of one about to be photographed with a midget on his lap at a congressional hearing.

At this point, the following parties are involved: NORC, a research organization fully aware that evaluation studies usually make the client look bad; the Fund for Adult Education, an action organization already persuaded of the merits of Greak Books, but hopeful of gaining concrete evidence of these merits; and the Great Books Foundation, already persuaded of the merits of its program, but quite doubtful that surveys can measure them.

Here ensued a number of conferences in Chicago and New York, during which the basic framework of the study was established. The only firm agreement prior to that time had been that the study was to be concerned with participants rather than the operations of the foundation and that we were interested in "the effects" of participation in Great Books.

For those of you who have not had the opportunity to read *Great Books and Small Groups*, the Great Books program in 1957 was roughly as follows. In 1957–1958, it consisted of some 1,960 discussion groups dispersed through the United States, with some additional groups in Canada and overseas. Each group meets every other week from September to June, and at each meeting the members discuss a specific selection which they have read before the meeting (e.g., Milton, *Areopagitica*; Tolstoy, *The Death of Ivan Ilyich*; Rousseau, *The Social Contract*). The readings are organized into blocks of one year each and, in theory, should be read in sequence. The groups vary in size (from around five to around thirty-five, with an average of eleven in our sample); in sponsorship (most are affiliated with public libraries, but a number are sponsored by churches, business firms, and individuals); and in leadership (some have a single leader, most have two leaders, a few rotate the leadership each meeting). The leaders are not formally trained teachers, but a number have had brief training courses conducted by the foundation. The members do not pay any tuition or get any certificate for completing the program. In fact, no one can complete the program, as additional years of reading are always available. Members are encouraged to buy the inexpensive readings from the foundation but are not required to do so.

It was this program which was to be evaluated, to the end of discovering whether the effects on the participants were such as to justify the continuation or expansion of Fund for Adult Education support. As a separate operation, the Fund for Adult Education commissioned a management-consultant firm to assess the organization of the foundation, market potential for Great Books, and similar internal affairs.

The design of such research falls naturally into two parts, which can be thought of as sampling, in the sense of deciding which people are to be studied and in what numbers; and questionnaire construction, in the sense of deciding what measures to use on the sampled respondents.

Of the two, sampling presented the fewest problems. It so happened that this is one social-science situation for which there is a clear-cut textbook sample design. According to the course I teach in research methods, one should collect a large number of people, arrange for a random subgroup to participate in Great Books, prevent the remainder from participating in the program and measure both groups on the dependent variables before and after the experiment. (Technically, if you have done it perfectly, you do not need to measure both groups before.) It also so happened that, as usual, the textbook design was out of the question. Such an experimental study would be "possible," although there would be an enormous number of difficulties—making sure that the controls do not get

Great Books or equivalent experience, establishing community programs which mask the mechanics of the sample design, and so forth. The major obstacle turned out to be time. We began active work on the study in the late summer of 1957 and had to deliver a report by fall 1958. It would have been plainly impractical (as well as quite expensive) to get a field experiment organized in two months before the 1957–1958 Great Books year got under way and results of a spring-1958 follow-up assessed by fall 1958. In addition, we all agreed that if the program's effects were as expected, some of them might not show up until after several years of exposure to the program.

It was this idea of long-term effects which enabled us to find a compromise design. If it is correct that, unlike indoctrination movies or television debates, the effects of Great Books require a long, long time for their appearance, then beginning participants should make a reasonably good "control group," particularly if the field work could be hurried so that first-year members were reached before they had attended more than one or two meetings. Because, in addition, both beginning and advanced-year members are equally self-selected, this design even has the advantage over a control group of nonmembers in that the latter would necessarily be suspected of less motivation or interest in joining Great Books.

The great problem with this design—and a problem which remained one of the main issues of the research—is that, as compared with a true experiment, the design left open the possibility that advanced-year members differ systematically from beginners, and it would be their other differences which produced any differences in the dependent variables. For example, almost necessarily, advanced-year members are older than beginners, and if age were related to the dependent variables, spurious differences would emerge. While this problem would give nightmares to an experimental purist, by and large it did not bother me too much. I knew that we were going to have sufficient cases so that by cross-tabulations we could control for any differences in gross variables such as age, sex, education, occupation, and so forth. A major pitfall, however, was the problem of retention. Nobody really knew the dropout rates in Great Books, but from all that is known of volunteer organizations, they had to be high. Furthermore, it made plain common sense that retention in the program would be correlated with the dependent variables, for people who were not getting the "effects," whatever they may be, would be prime candidates for dropping out, as in any educational institution. Even worse, there was no way of controlling for dropouts in a sample limited to current members, since we would have to introduce as statistical controls events that had not happened yet. The best we could do was to introduce some questions about intention to continue and use these for controls in comparing beginning and advanced members.

Looking back now, I wonder why we let it go at that. We could have interviewed some ex-members without too much difficulty, but I do not remember that this was seriously raised as a possibility. Perhaps at that time I already had the germ of the idea of a second study to determine actual dropouts; perhaps I did not. At any rate, I am glad now we let it go; for without the continuing problem of attrition, the study would have begun and ended as another evaluation project.

The net result of all of this was a decision to sample from existing discussion groups, stratified to oversample the advanced-year groups wherein lay the pay dirt, if any. At this point, another vital, but not deliberate, decision was made. The Great Books Foundation has no individual membership rolls but merely a rather loose file of group registrations. Given the lack of coercive structure for the program, a number of groups exist without the official blessing of the foundation; and at least in 1957, rather than groups' petitioning Great Books for the right to exist, functionaries of the foundation continually scanned press clippings to find their groups, which were then sent registration materials. If a file of individuals had existed, I do not know whether we would have used it; but having no choice, we sampled groups—a very important decision, as it turned out.

The final crucial decision was an economic one. Because of the money to be saved, we decided to raise the case base by asking entire groups to fill out a self-administered questionnaire at their meeting, gambling that the members would be literate and thus capable of filling out a questionnaire and hopefully sophisticated enough to cooperate with a research project. We also had the naïve hope that the foundation would put a little heat on the groups to increase cooperation.

In sum, while from an abstract point of view we should have had a sample of individuals both in and out of the Great Books program, because of a series of unwitting decisions based on practical exigencies we ended up with a sample of discussion groups within the program. We began with the Great Books, but the Small Groups got into the study by default.

While limitations of time and budget usually provide enough restrictions so that sample designs for national surveys amount to choosing among a number of restricted possibilities, when it comes to writing a questionnaire, the sky is the limit; or rather, one's guess as to how lengthy a document the respondents will complete without rebellion is the only boundary. Within this area—and it is amazing how much respondents will actually do for you if approached correctly—we had all of Western culture from which to pick items. It is precisely the major advantage and the major problem of surveys that an enormous amount of information can be collected, the marginal increment in cost for an additional item being very small when compared with the fixed costs of sampling and contacting respondents. At the same time, *the* intellectual challenge in survey analysis is in ordering and synthesizing the diverse information—in this schedule ranging from father's occupation to the respondent's opinion as to whether the course of history is capricious, purposive, or mechanistic. (In case you are curious, 25 percent thought it capricious, 48 percent thought it purposive, 13 percent thought it mechanistic, and 13 percent were "no answer.")

A certain amount of disagreement arose among the parties: the Fund for Adult Education backing two horses, the Great Books Foundation a third, and the study director a dark fourth horse. The first horse was "community participation," a matter of considerable interest to the Fund for Adult Education, which was convinced that participation in Great Books should and maybe even did lead people to become more active in community affairs. The general idea was that after reading, say, the Greek philosophers on the nature of the good society, the Great Books members would be impelled to remodel Toledo, Ohio, and Minneapolis, Minnesota. The idea met with polite skepticism on the part of Great Books and me.

The Great Books Foundation maintained, and with some justice, I think, that their program did not have any purposes at all, at least in the sense of the sort of thing that can be listed and translated into surveys. With the naïveté of a young man who had read all the texts on evaluation research, I kept hounding the foundation to list—1, 2, 3—the purposes of their program so that they might at least be tried on charges of their own devising. In the face of such pressures for oversimplification, all the foundation staff could come up with was the denial that participants were expected to become more active, passive, liberal, conservative, or anything that directional. Rather, they were expected to become more sophisticated, more critical in their thinking, broader in their approach, and so on, whether or not they chose to favor the left, right, center, or to refrain from community life. In this the participants in the actual survey agreed, the bulk opting for the response, "The Great Books provide an intellectual understanding (of specific social and community problems), but few or no keys to plans for action," as opposed to "Great Books provide both an understanding of the problems and a key to plans of action" or "Great Books are not applicable to specific social and community problems." While the foundation opposed the community-participation stress on the basis of intellectual ideology, I was against it on the practical grounds that I doubted we would get any effects. To begin with, I thought that Great Books members were typically fugitives from community life, rather than involved. I was dead wrong, but more on that later. In addition, from all that I knew of the literature, I was sure that class, sex, political preference, for example, played such an important part in community participation that exposure to a reading discussion program could not make much difference. I was perfectly willing to let the facts speak, but I was not going out of my way to disappoint somebody who had given me $40,000 to do research.

At this point, the inevitable answer occurred: to stress both purely intellectual and also community-participation materials. However, this led to a knotty problem of measurement. In assessing community and political involvement, we felt we were on safe grounds, for there is rich experience in survey measurement of such phenomena, and the content is heavily behavioral and hence fairly easy to translate into questions. In the measurement of such things as "critical thinking," "tolerance of ambiguity," "intellectual sophistication," that way madness lies. I was toying with pulling out existing tests of critical thinking and similar measures, and the Great Books Foundation had in desperation proposed that the respondents be given essay examinations which the foundation staff would evaluate, when the Fund for Adult Education split into two spokesmen, with the entrance of the late Carl Hovland, then a consultant to the fund. Hovland, as a psychologist, was highly concerned about the details of testing: whether the tests could be given under standard conditions, timed, collusion prevented, motivation maintained, and so forth. The answer, of course, is that they could not, or at least could not to the satisfaction of a testing specialist. Hovland felt that we might get away with it but that the resuls could never be sold to a really hostile critic who was oriented to psychological measurement.

The compromise decision actually became a sellout of the Great Books Foundation's position, for on the basis of Hovland's technical doubts, critical thinking and open-mindedness essentially disappeared, except in the form of some very simple attitude and opinion items in which, for example, the respondents were asked to name "any particular authors or schools which you once disliked, but now find more acceptable." Rather, we began to search for some sugar-coated test-oid materials to get at more superficial things. We actually found two good ones, a set of cartoon items (e.g., a gentleman in a nightshirt nailing a paper on a door, to denote Martin Luther posting his theses; a child in diapers composing at the piano, to denote the young Mozart, etc.), which had originally appeared in *Life* magazine, and a marvelous poetry test developed in the early 1920's by M. R. Trabue and Allan Abbott. Trabue and Abbott presented the original version of a well-known poem, along with versions systematically deformed in aesthetic content, and the respondent was asked to pick the one liked best. We never did find a complete set of the poetry-test items, even by long-distance calls to Prof. Trabue, by then a sprightly emeritus, but we got enough to go into print. In addition, we packed in voluminous materials on reading quality and musical taste and picked a number of items on philosophical points from the work of Charles Morris.

Note what was happening here. What should have been a series of technical measures of cognitive functioning became a set of crude information measures along with considerable materials on aesthetics and ideologies. Part of the shift can be explained by Hovland's technical qualms, part by the inability of the Great Books Foundation to come up with neat objectives for which nice tests exist, but a good proportion came from the wily maneuvers of the study director.

What was I up to? Viewed from the perspective of getting some academic yardage out of the study, Great Books appeared to have three possibilities, of which I picked the wrong one. The first possibility would have been to conduct an evaluation study of such methodological luster that it would attract attention despite the offbeat character of the sample and the stigma of "Adult Education." I knew in my bones that because of the design limitation and the fuzziness of the measures, this one could not make it. Now, get me right. I felt all along that we could deliver useful and valid information to the client on the effects of Great Books (and I think we did), but I doubted that we could get out a study which would be cited as technically outstanding or particularly convincing to a *resistant* reader. This meant that while for report purposes the materials had to yield an evaluation study, for academic purposes I had to find an analytical theme such that the whole sample could be treated as a single group and differences in exposure to Great Books (our analogue of experimental and control groups) ignored.

Looking back now, I think there were actually two possibilities. It turned out that Great Books members are phenomenally active and involved in local community affairs and that we had the makings of a detailed study of community involvement among young, educated, middle-class Americans. Actually, Vickie Beal, who was on the staff, managed to get a good Ph.D. thesis on this theme, but for some reason I did not pick that tack. The third possibility was a detailed analysis of the members' intellectual lives, their tastes, ideologies, philosophical positions, and so forth. I had done a Ph.D. thesis on taste and status symbols, and I have always been fascinated by the writings of Russell Lynes, David Riesman, Eric Larrabee, etc. In the back of my mind, I envisioned the development—from data, mind you—of typologies of kinds of intellectual stances and styles within the Great Books members.

My own proclivities here were reinforced by a marvelous but misleading field experience. Because of the timing of the program, there was no way to see a Great Books group in action before the questionnaire was completed. (My record is still perfect. I have never actually seen a Great Books discussion, despite several years of almost full-time work on this project.) However, in the summer of 1957 Great Books was running a summer program at Aspen, Colorado, which I arranged to visit. While my strongest memory is of the magnificent train ride through the Rockies—a revelation to a midwestern boy—professionally I came away with two hunches. The first was that Great Books tends to attract a social type which can perhaps be described as "isolated intellectuals." It seemed to me that at Aspen a large number of the people I met were extraordinarily well read, very serious, and given to the construction of homemade philosophical systems, without being hooked into the orbit of academic intellectuals or professional creative artists. I do not mean they were screwballs, but they did seem to be the sort of people whose opinions on whether the course of history was purposive might be interesting. Apparently the people who attended that summer conference were quite unrepresentative of the Great Books membership, for the actual survey showed the Great Books participants to be a pretty clean-cut group of PTA joiners and *Time* readers, not much given to the construction of homemade philosophical systems.

I came away with one other impression which did have a pay-off, although indirect. While I have never seen a legal, in-season Great Books discussion, I did watch a number of the sessions in Aspen and tried to make some guesses about the group dynamics beneath the surface of the discussions. It seemed to me that what was going on was a sort of political process in which people would advance ideas, allies would rally to them, and enemies would muster forces against them and that the course of the discussions was heavily influenced by latent attractions and antagonisms among the participants. Mulling this over later in Chicago, I decided to insert some sociometric questions to see whether a member's isolation or acceptance by others in the discussion group affected his reactions to the program. In the back of my mind was the idea that perhaps the discussions worked best when there were fairly "even sides" in the ideological and interpersonal teams. However, the Great Books Foundation vetoed these questions on the grounds that it might produce complaints if members were asked to name their friends and enemies.

The key items in the final study—a series of questions about functional roles in the groups—were actually devised as a substitute. The items asked each members to rate himself and others in the group in terms of such roles as "joking and kidding," "making tactful comments," "providing 'fuel' for the discussion," and others. The logical structure of the items was suggested by the work of Freed Bales. I have never had a course in small groups, but Bales's influence is very strong at Harvard, where I did my graduate work, and a sort of Balesian, functional approach to roles and group dynamics, absorbed by osmosis during graduate-school days, was the only one I knew.

This is the intellectual history of the questionnaire, a lengthy document bearing the stamp of the Fund for Adult Education's interest in community participation, some vestigial traces of the foundation's interest in "critical thinking," a lot of my own penchant for materials on aesthetics and ideologies, and a good bit of information on functional roles, inserted as a substitute for the excised sociometric items.

Were I to recount in detail the field work, coding, key-punching, and card-cleaning which took up the next ten months, this essay would become a book about a book. Let me merely say that with the superb help of Grace Lieberman, Mary Booth, Ursula Gebhard, Joe Zelan, and a charming group of Antioch College cooperators we came into the possession of schedules from over 90 percent of the sampled groups and coded the data from the 1,909 individual respondents onto some dozen decks of IBM cards.

I am also going to gloss over the first report, a bulky, 256-page, single-spaced mimeographed document completed in August 1958. It consisted of (1) a description of the Great Books participants, (2) analyses of the members' reported effects of participation in the program, (3) comparisons between beginning and advanced members in terms of dependent variables, and (4) data on role structures and social correlates of role performance. Vickie Beal, who had joined the project staff in the spring of 1958, analyzed the materials on community participation; Ursula Gebhard had done most of the role analysis, and I did the rest.

Because the report was done under great pressure, the entire analysis and writing being concentrated in a period of about three months, the document was overly long and underly organized. In essence, however, we showed (1) strong differences in knowledge between beginners and advanced-year members, (2) slight differences in attitudes, consistent with the idea of increased tolerance or open-mindedness, and (3) few differences in behavior. Taken together, I feel that the material pretty well showed that exposure to Great Books does add to the intellectual depth and perspective of the members but does not produce striking or consistent effects on behavior, which is, after all, just what the results should be if the program does what its organizers think it does. We also found that, rather than being socially marginal, the Great Books members were highly educated, highly involved in their communities, and *less* upwardly mobile than comparable college graduates. While this may be a comfort to the friends of Great Books, it "did in" my plans for analyzing their intellectual lives. If the members had turned out to have a considerable proportion of homely philosophers, upwardly mobile people, or members of strange cults, the results might have been quite "marketable" because academic sociologists gobble up materials on strange cults and deviant people; but since the participants turned out to be quite typical suburban types, without being statistically representative of suburban types, it would be hard to justify detailed analysis of their tastes and ideologies.

The Fund for Adult Education received the report and must have been clairvoyant, for they gave Great Books a large-scale grant about a month before they saw the results, such being the crucial role that social research plays in decision-making in modern America.

The project was far from over in fall 1958. During the preceding winter and spring, while coding and key-punching were going on, I had been brooding about the dropout problem and came up with an idea. It occurred to me that if we could collect data in 1958 to determine which of our respondents had actually dropped out of the program during the year, we could subtract them from the tables and make comparisons only among members who were "destined" to continue. Table 1 illustrates the idea.

TABLE 1.   PERCENT HIGH ON DEPENDENT VARIABLE

1957 status	1958 status		
	Dropped	Continued	Total
Advanced Year	$45_{(200)}$	$70_{(300)}$	$60_{(500)}$
Beginning Year	$10_{(200)}$	$60_{(300)}$	$40_{(500)}$

In this hypothetical example, 60 percent of the advanced members are high on the item, in contrast to 40 percent of the beginners. This would suggest that exposure to Great Books has a positive effect. However, it is seen that the item is strongly associated with retention, and when the beginners who continued are compared with advanced-year members, there is no difference, each group having a percentage of 60. Thus, the original difference can be explained because of selective attrition. Such a design, of course, could not catch spurious differences due to "historical trends," such as a decrease over the years in the proportion of new members possessing the trait in question, but it looked as if it would help a lot in solving the problems raised by dropouts. In addition, the data-collection problems were minimal, as no new sample had to be drawn and no information collected beyond continuation status.

In the summer of 1958, we proposed such a project to the Fund for Adult Education, and although they had not yet seen any pay-off from the initial grant, they were kind enough to support a follow-up that year. Ursula Gebhard superintended this operation, as by then I was working on another study, a survey of the financial problems of arts and science graduate students.

Because the follow-up data were simple, we were able by February 1959 to submit an edited version of the original report with dropout controls introduced into the key tabulations. (By the way, they did not greatly change the results, but I felt much more confident with these materials to support our findings.) This report, *A Study of Participants in the Great Books Program*, was printed and distributed by the Fund for Adult Education, and although it has never received any attention outside of those immediately concerned with Great Books and not much among those who are concerned, I think it is a reasonably good nonexperimental evaluation study.

Enough budget money remained to support the substantive analysis of factors associated with retention in Great Books. Thus, *Great Books and Small Groups* has its operational origins in the evaluation study completed in February 1958, but its intellectual roots lie elsewhere—a substantive root reaching to Harvard University and a methodological one to Columbia.

Substantively, the major idea in the new study came from viewing the data, not as "why some people quit Great Books," but as "why some small-scale social systems lose the commitment of their members." The research problem is clearly structural-functional and comes simply because that was how I was indoctrinated at Harvard. My courses with Talcott Parsons and my informal contacts with the students working with Freed Bales had steeped me in the tradition of viewing social behavior as functional or dysfunctional for a given social system. In particular, I had been much impressed with an article, "The Functional Prerequisites of a Society" by Aberle, Cohen, Davis, Levy, and Sutton (*Ethics*, 9 [1950], pp. 100–111). I was not actually so much impressed with the content, which is highly speculative, as with the marvelous euphony of the names, and I remember that Parsons once mentioned in class that the paper had been done while the authors were graduate students at Harvard. It had never occurred to me that graduate students could make actual contributions to sociology, and the knowledge that Aberle, Cohen, Davis, Levy, and Sutton had made them served to buck up my spirits in many dark hours in Cambridge.

George Homans was involved, too. While I was at Harvard, I had few contacts with him, and my strong attraction to Homansian theory has come in the last few years. In rereading *The Human Group* while preparing a lecture, I came across his astringent remark, "If we turn to history for help, it is astonishing how few societies have failed to survive . . . [but] small groups are breaking up every day. . . ." Thus was born the idea of studying the functional prerequisites for the survival of small groups. To be absolutely candid, there is also a less cerebral aspect to all this. My own work and interests diverge considerably from that of my graduate-student friends and the intellectual climate of the Harvard department, and I think in the back of my mind was the hope that such a study would show "them" that I was not a naïve empiricist but was capable of wrestling with the high-brow problems of sociological theory with a big T.

The methodological contribution of the book comes from a statistical technique for "contextual analysis" which Joe Spaeth, Carolyn Huson, and I worked out during 1958 and 1959. Joe was a senior assistant in the Graduate Student Finances study, and Carolyn was the research assistant on the Great Books continuation, Vickie Beal and Ursula Gebhard having moved on to Grinnell College and San Francisco, respectively. The statistical technique is farily complicated, and I am going to have to assume that the reader is familiar with it, as a detailed explanation runs to ten or twelve pages. In essence, the contribution lies not in the idea, which can be traced to Paul Lazarsfeld and Patricia Kendall at Columbia University, but in spelling out in a mathematical form the logical possibilities which can occur. What is new here is the idea that there are specific "kinds" of "structural effects."

The "influential" in the flow of influence here is Peter Blau, a Columbia Ph.D., now of the department of sociology at Chicago. As of 1959, I was quite unaware of "contextual analysis," although some had rubbed off on me from Jim Coleman when he was in Chicago, and I had read but not fully appreciated Lazarsfeld and Kendall's discussion in their classic article, "Problems of Survey Analysis." However, the longer I was around Chicago, the more I heard my graduate assistants talking about "structural effects," as discussed by Peter Blau in his courses. One day, Joe Spaeth came back from a Blau lecture and started talking about structural effects. I remember asking Joe what they really were. He tried to explain them to me in Blau's formulation, but I did not understand it. When I do not understand something statistical, I try to work it out with dummy data, and I remember sitting around with Joe, trying various examples in order to pinpoint the idea. The result was that it occurred to both of us that there were probably several kinds of structural effects, and we instantly got the idea of trying to systematize them.

The trick lay in how to systematize them. I have never had any mathematics training beyond college algebra, and I try, without much success, to teach myself by reading on my own. At that time, I was reading E. F. Beach's *Economic Models*, so linear and nonlinear functions were on my mind. It was only a short step from there to seeing that when the contextual attribute is expressed as a proportion, its variation could be treated as quantitative and the contextual effect could be described as a mathematical function.

There were two different versions. In the first, the contextual effects were treated as deviations from a regression line. This version was sent off to *Sociometry*, which was quite unenthusiastic, one reader saying that structural effects were very important but we did not really understand them, the other reader saying that although we probably understood structural effects, they were not worth analyzing.

Although Joe and I were quite discouraged by this, we picked up the idea every so often and in spring of 1959 came up with the version which finally appeared in print. Carolyn Huson did most of the work on the section regarding tests of significance, so the final paper was authored by Davis, Spaeth, and Huson. An interesting case of independent invention soon turned up. At the fall 1959 meetings of the American Sociological Association, I read the paper and learned that two study directors at the Bureau of Applied Social Research at Columbia, David Caplowitz and Wagner Thielens, Jr., had worked out a similar scheme, which, however, they had dropped to work on something else. Apparently it was an idea which would come to light inevitably, once the problem was seen. I was convinced that this version would "sell," so I sent it off to *The American Sociological Review*, which accepted it and printed it without unseemly hate in April 1961.

The rest was just hard work. During the spring and summer of 1959, the statistical technique was applied to the data on dropouts from the fall-1958 follow-up. Carolyn Huson analyzed the materials on group leadership and its effects; Herbert Hamilton, an advanced graduate student, came on the project and analyzed the individual level differences; and Ursula Gebhard's scholarly master's thesis on correlates of role performance was reworked in my "breezy" prose as background for the materials on the relationship between role structure and retention. It was immediately clear that the strongest effect in the data was that membership retention increased considerably in groups where a high percentage of the members had some role (i.e., were named by people in their group as active in some phase of the discussion), but it did not make much difference what the role was. The functional theories which suggest that role content is important did not pan out at all, but they had led us to find the important variable; and, for that matter, my idea of balance of power never paid off either.

The work was complex and tricky. The actual data never quite fitted any of the theoretical models, and the tabulations for partial relationships when the same characteristic has to be held constant twice (at the group level and at the individual level) were nasty; but, once it became clear that role systems were the key to the whole thing, the parts fell into place, and a final report was completed in November 1959.

The report was submitted to The University of Chicago Press, which turned it down because they said it did not have any sales potential, and to The Free Press, which also said that it would not sell but agreed to print it, apparently just for the fun of it. During the 1959–1960 academic year, I was tied up with the final report of the Graduate Student Finances study (a story which would make quite a chronicle itself, but which chronicle could not be sent through the United States mails), so I reorganized and rewrote the report in the summer of 1960, delivering the manuscript to Jeremiah Kaplan of The Free Press and a waiting world in the fall of 1960. The Free Press was delivered of the completed volume in the fall of 1961, a little over four years after my visit to Aspen.

Were I to draw morals from this history, they would be these.

First, I think the chronicle of *Great Books and Small Groups* illustrates the tremendous importance of technical methodological developments in the substantive development of social science. It is commonly believed that research technology is a mere servant of substantive or theoretical interests. Actually, research technology makes a direct contribution to the content of the field in the same way that the invention of the microscope or radiotelescope shaped the content of physical science, or perhaps more exactly in the same way that Whorfians claim language shapes our thinking. We can ask of the data only questions that can be translated into specific research operations, and until such translations exist, the research questions remain purely ruminative. Thus, the existence of a national research center makes it both possible and inevitable that comparative studies of groups will take place. Thus, the statistics of correlation and partial correlation give meaning to the vague concepts of "cause," "intervening factors," "spurious relationships," and such, and thus, the development of techniques for contextual analysis focuses our attention on "social climates." The history of content in social science is the history of fad, fashion, and momentary preoccupations, but the history of research methods is one of cumulative developments which have enabled us to ask increasingly precise and sophisticated questions about human behavior. In this sense, I believe progress in social science is mostly in the ability to ask questions, not in the ability to foresee the answers.

Second, I think that this chronicle illustrates the ways in which survey analysis is much akin to artistic creation. There are so many questions which might be asked, so many correlations which can be run, so many ways in which the findings can be organized, and so few rules or precedents for making these choices that a thousand different studies could come out of the same data. Beyond his technical responsibility for guaranteeing accuracy and honest statistical calculations, the real job of the study director is to select and integrate. Of all the findings, only some should be selected for presentation, but which ones? Is this particular finding so unimportant that it should be left out as confusing to the reader, or so important that it must be reported even though it will make the results appear terribly complicated? Should we emphasize the smashing difference which is, however, "obvious," or should we give play to the puzzling surprise, even though it produces only a small difference? The 101 (an IBM machine used for cross tabulations) takes independent variables in batches of four; and having listed the seven obvious columns for cross tabulations, which "unobvious" one do you choose as a gamble for the eighth? How much attention shall we give to the client's areas of success and how much to his areas of failure? How much of the data shall we present in the report: so much that no one will read it, or so little that the reader cannot check our conclusions against the evidence? In multivariate analyses, one can produce a large range in percentages either by dividing a very few variables into fine categories (e.g., cutting income by thousands of dollars versus dividing it at the median) or by taking a larger number of items and dichotomizing them. Which is preferable? Statistics books will not help you, for the answers must come from the study director's experience and his intellectual taste, his ability to simplify but not gloss over, to be cautious without pettifoggery, to synthesize without distorting the facts, to interpret but not project his prejudices on the data. These, I submit, are ultimately aesthetic decisions, and the process of making these decisions is much like aesthetic creation.

But all this should not be construed as support for the fallacious idea that "you can prove anything with statistics." Short of deliberate falsification, statistical data are remarkably resistant, as anyone who has desperately tried to save a pet hypothesis knows. It is almost impossible for two competent study directors to arrive at *contradictory* conclusions from the same data, but it is almost inevitable that they will differ considerably in their emphases, organization, and selection.

Thus, if survey analysis is an art, it is not an art like sculpture or painting, in which one can make almost anything out of the raw materials. Rather, it is an art very much like architecture, in which it is possible to show disciplined creativity by producing elegant structures while working with raw materials characterized by limited engineering properties and for clients with definite goals and finite budgets.

Balance between discipline and creativity is very difficult in social science. By and large, the fashionable people in sociology are "action painters" who dribble their thoughts on the canvas of the journals, unrestrained by systematic evidence, while at the opposite pole there are hordes of "engineers" who grind out academic development housing according to the mechanical formulas of elementary statistics texts. It is not easy to steer between these courses, and I am not claiming that I did so in this study, but my opinion is that the fun lies in trying to do so.

There is a lot of misery in surveys, most of the time and money going into monotonous clerical and statistical routines, with interruptions only for squabbles with the client, budget crises, petty machinations for a place in the academic sun, and social case work with neurotic graduate students. And nobody ever reads the final report. Those few moments, however, when a new set of tables comes up from the machine room and questions begin to be answered, when relationships actually hold under controls; when the pile of tables on the desk suddenly meshes to yield a coherent chapter; when in a flash you see a neat test for an interpretation; when you realize you have found out something about something important that nobody ever knew before—these are the moments that justify research.

Methods and Techniques of Sociological Analysis | OBSERVATION

12 HOWARD S. BECKER and BLANCHE GEER

Participant Observation and Interviewing: A Comparison

The most complete form of the sociological datum, after all, is the form in which the participant observer gathers it: An observation of some social event, the events which precede and follow it, and explanations of its meaning by participants and spectators, before, during, and after its occurrence. Such a datum gives us more information about the event under study than data gathered by any other sociological method. Participant observation can thus provide us with a yardstick against which to measure the completeness of data gathered in other ways, a model which can serve to let us know what orders of information escape us when we use other methods.[1]

By participant observation we mean that method in which the observer participates in the daily life of the people under study, either openly in the role of researcher or covertly in some disguised role, observing things that happen, listening to what is said, and questioning people, over some length of time.[2] We want, in this paper, to compare the results of such

Reprinted from *Human Organization*, 16:1 (1957), pp. 28–35, by permission of the authors and the publisher. Copyright © 1957 by The Society for Applied Anthropology.

intensive field work with what might be regarded as the first step in the other direction along this continuum: the detailed and conversational interview (often referred to as the unstructured or undirected interview).[3] In this kind of interview, the interviewer explores many facets of his interviewee's concerns, treating subjects as they come up in conversation, pursuing interesting leads, allowing his imagination and ingenuity full rein as he tries to develop new hypothesis and test them in the course of the interview.

In the course of our current participant observation among medical students,[4] we have thought a good deal about the kinds of things we were discovering which might ordinarily be missed or misunderstood in such an interview. We have no intention of denigrating the interview or even such less precise modes of data gathering as the questionnaire, for there can always be good reasons of practicality, economy, or research design for their use. We simply wish to make explicit the difference in data gathered by one or the other method and to suggest the differing uses to which they can legitimately be put. In general, the shortcomings we attribute to the interview exist when it is used as a source of information about events that have occurred elsewhere and are described to us by informants. Our criticisms are not relevant when analysis is restricted to interpretation of the interviewee's conduct *during the interview*, in which case the researcher has in fact observed the behavior he is talking about.[5]

The differences we consider between the two methods involve two interacting factors: the kinds of words and acts of the people under study that the researcher has access to, and the kind of sensitivity to problems and data produced in him. Our comparison may prove useful by suggestive areas in which interviewing (the more widely used method at present and likely to continue so) can improve its accuracy by taking account of suggestions made from the perspective of the participant observer. We begin by considering some concrete problems: learning the native language, or the problem of the degree to which the interviewer really understands what is said to him; matters interviewees are unable or unwilling to talk about; and getting information on matters people see through distorting lenses. We then consider some more general differences between the two methods.

LEARNING THE NATIVE LANGUAGE

Any social group, to the extent that it is a distinctive unit, will have to some degree a culture differing from that of other groups, a somewhat different set of common understandings around which action is organized, and these differences will find expression in a language whose nuances are peculiar to that group and fully understood only by its members. Members of churches speak differently from members of informal tavern groups; more importantly, members of any particular church or tavern group have cultures, and languages in which they are expressed, which differ somewhat from those of other groups of the same general type. So, although we speak one language and share in many ways in one culture, we cannot assume that we understand precisely what another person, speaking as a member of such a group, means by any particular word. In interviewing members of groups other than our own, then, we are in somewhat the same position as the anthropologist who must learn a primitive language,[6] with the important difference that, as Icheiser has put it, we often do not understand that we do not understand and are thus likely to make errors in interpreting what is said to us. In the case of gross misunderstandings the give and take of conversation may quickly reveal our mistakes, so that the interviewee can correct us; this presumably is one of the chief mechanisms through which the anthropologist acquires a new tongue. But in speaking American English with an interviewee who is, after all, much like us, we may mistakenly assume that we have understood him and the error be small enough that it will not disrupt communication to the point where a correction will be in order.

The interview provides little opportunity of rectifying errors of this kind where they go unrecognized. In contrast, participant observation provides a situation in which the meanings of words can be learned with great precision through study of their use in context, exploration through continuous interviewing of their implications and nuances, and the use of them oneself under the scrutiny of capable speakers of the language. Beyond simply clarifying matters so that the reseacher may understand better what people say to each other and to him, such a linguistic exercise may provide research hypotheses of great usefulness. The way in which one of us learned the meaning of the word "crock," as medical students use it, illustrates these points.

I first heard the work "crock" applied to a patient shortly after I began my field work. The patient in question, a fat, middle-aged woman, complained bitterly of pains in a number of widely separated locations. When I asked the student who had so described her what the word meant, he said that it was used to refer to any patient who had psychosomatic complaints. I asked if that meant that Mr. X _____, a young man on the ward whose stomach ulcer had been discussed by a staff physician as typically psychosomatic, was a crock. The student said that that would not be correct usage, but was not able to say why.

Over a period of several weeks, through discussion of many cases seen during morning rounds with the students, I finally arrived at an understanding of the term, realizing that it referred to a patient who complained of many symptoms but had no discoverable organic pathology. I had noticed from the beginning that the term was used in a derogatory way and had also been inquiring into this, asking students why they disliked having crocks assigned to them for examination and diagnosis. At first students denied the derogatory connotations, but repeated observations of their disgust with such assignments soon made such denials unrealistic. Several students eventually explained their dislike in ways of which the following example is typical: "The true crock is a person who you do a great big workup for and who has all of these vague symptoms, and *you really can't find anything the matter with them."*

Further discussion made it clear that the students regarded patients primarily as objects from which they could learn those aspects of clinical medicine not easily acquired from textbooks and lectures; the crock took a great deal of their time, of which they felt they had little enough, and did not exhibit any interesting disease state from which something might be learned, so that the time invested was wasted. This discovery in turn suggested that I might profitably investigate the general perspective toward medical school which led to such a basis for judgment of patients, and also suggested hypotheses regarding the value system of the hospital hierarchy at whose bottom the student stood.

At the risk of being repetitious, let us point out in this example both the errors avoided and the advantages gained because of the use of participant observation. The term might never have been used by students in an ordinary interview; if it had, the interviewer might easily have assumed that the scatological term from which it in fact is descended provided a complete definition. Because the observer saw students on their daily rounds and heard them discussing everyday problems, he heard the word and was able to pursue it until he arrived at a meaningful definition. Moreover, the knowledge so gained led to further and more general discoveries about the group under study.

This is not to say that all of these things might not be discovered by a program of skillful interviewing, for this might well be possible. But we do suggest that an interviewer may misunderstand common English words when interviewees use them in some more or less esoteric way and not know that he is misunderstanding them, because there will be little chance to check his understanding against either further examples of their use in conversation or instances of the object to which they are applied. This leaves him open to errors of misinterpretation and errors of failing to see connections between items of information he has available, and may prevent him from seeing and exploring important research leads. In dealing with interview data, then, experience with participant observation indicates that both care and imagination must be used in making sure of meanings, for the cultural esoterica of a group may hide behind ordinary language used in special ways.

MATTERS INTERVIEWEES ARE UNABLE OR UNWILLING TO TALK ABOUT

Frequently, people do not tell an interviewer all the things he might want to know. This may be because they do not want to, feeling that to speak of some particular subject would be impolitic, impolite, or insensitive, because they do not think to and because the interviewer does not have enough information to inquire into the matter, or because they are not able to. The first case—the problem of "resistance"—is well known and a considerable lore has developed about how to cope with it.[7] It is more difficult to deal with the last two possibilities for the interviewee is not likely to reveal, or the interviewer to become aware, that significant omissions are being made. Many events occur in the life of a social group and the experience of an individual so regularly and uninterruptedly, or so quietly and unnoticed, that people are hardly aware of them, and do not think to comment on them to an interviewer; or they may never have become aware of them at all and be unable to answer even direct questions. Other events may be so unfamiliar that people find it difficult to put into words their vague feelings about what has happened. If an interviewee, for any of these reasons, cannot or will not discuss a certain topic, the researcher will find gaps in his information on matters about which he wants to know and will perhaps fail to become aware of other problems and areas of interest that such discussion might have opened up for him.

This is much less likely to happen when the researcher spends much time with the people he studies as they go about their daily activities, for he can see the very things which might not be reported in an interview. Further, should he desire to question people about matters they cannot or prefer not to talk about, he is able to point to specific incidents which either force them to face the issue (in the case of resistance) or make clear what he means (in the case of unfamiliarity). Finally, he can become aware of the full meaning of such hints as are given on subjects people are unwilling to speak openly about and of such inarticulate statements as people are able to make about subjects they cannot clearly formulate, because he frequently knows of these things through his observation and can connect his knowledge with these half-communications.

Researchers working with interview materials, while they are often conscious of these problems, cannot cope with them so well. If they are to deal with matters of this kind it must be by inference. They can only make an educated guess about the things which go unspoken in the interview; it may be a very good guess, but it must be a guess. They can employ various tactics to explore for material they feel is there but unspoken, but even when these are fruitful they do not create sensitivity to those problems of which even the interviewer is not aware. The following example indicates how participant observation aids the researcher in getting material, and making the most of the little he gets, on topics lying within this range of restricted communication.

A few months after the beginning of school, I went to dinner at one of the freshman medical fraternities. It was the night non-resident members came, married ones with their wives. An unmarried student who lived in the house looked around at the visitors and said to me, "We are so much in transition. I have never been in this situation before of meeting fellows and their wives."

This was just the sort of thing we were looking for—change in student relationships arising from group interaction—but I failed in every attempt to make the student describe the "transition" more clearly.

From previous observation, though, I knew there were differences (other than marriage) between the non-residents and their hosts. The former had all been elected to the fraternity recently, after house officers had gotten to know them through working together (usually on the same cadaver in anatomy lab). They were older than the average original member; instead of coming directly from college, several had had jobs or Army experience before medical school. As a group they were somewhat lower in social position.

These points indicated that the fraternity was bringing together in relative intimacy students different from each other in background and experience. They suggested a search for other instances in which dissimilar groups of students were joining forces, and pointed to a need for hypotheses as to what was behind this process of drawing together on the part of the freshman and its significance for their medical education.

An interviewer, hearing this statement about "transition," would know that the interviewee felt himself in the midst of some kind of change but might not be able to discover anything further about the nature of that change. The participant observer cannot find out, any more than the interviewer can, what the student had in mind, presumably because the student had nothing more in mind than this vague feeling of change. (Interviewees are not sociologists and we ought not to assume that their fumbling statements are attempts, crippled by their lack of technical vocabulary, to express what a sociologist might put in more formal analytic terms.) But he can search for those things in the interviewee's situation which might lead to such a feeling of transition.

While the participant observer can make immediate use of such vague statements as clues to an objective situation, the interviewer is often bothered by the question of whether an interviewee is not simply referring to quite private experiences. As a result, the interviewer will place less reliance on whatever inferences about the facts of the situation he makes, and is less likely to be sure enough of his ground to use them as a basis for further hypotheses. Immediate observation of the scene itself and data from previous observation enable the participant observer to make direct use of whatever hints the informant supplies.

THINGS PEOPLE SEE THROUGH DISTORTING LENSES

In many of the social relationships we observe, the parties to the relation will have differing ideas as to what ought to go on in it, and frequently as to what does in fact go on in it. These differences in perception will naturally affect what they report in an interview. A man in a subordinate position in an organization in which subordinates believe that their superiors are "out to get them" will interpret many incidents in this light though the incidents themselves may not seem, either to the other party in the interaction or to the observer, to indicate such malevolence. Any such mythology will distort people's view of events to such a degree that they will report as fact things which have not occurred, but which seem to them to have occurred. Students, for example, frequently invent sets of rules to govern their relations with teachers, and, although the teacher may never have heard of such rules, regard the teachers as malicious when they "disobey" them. The point is that things may be reported in an interview through such a distorting lens, and the interviewer may have no way of knowing what is fact and what is distortion of this kind; participant observation makes it possible to check such points. The following is a particularly clear example.

> Much of the daily teaching was done, and practical work of medical students supervised, in a particular department of the hospital, by the house residents. A great deal of animosity had grown up between the particular group of students I was with at the time and these residents, the students believing that the residents would, for various malicious reasons, subordinate them and embarrass them at every opportunity. Before I joined the group, several of the students told me that the residents were "mean," "nasty," "bitchy," and so on, and had backed these characterizations up with evidence of particular actions.
>
> After I began participating daily with the students on this service, a number of incidents made it clear that the situation was not quite like this. Finally, the matter came completely into the open. I was present when one of the residents suggested a technique that might have prevented a minor relapse in a patient assigned to one of the students; he made it clear that he did not think the relapse in any way the student's fault, but rather that he was simply passing on what he felt to be a good tip. Shortly afterward, this student reported to several other students that the resident had "chewed him out" for failing to use this technique: "What the hell business has he got chewing me out about that for? No one ever told me I was supposed to do it that way." I interrupted to say, "He didn't really chew you out. I thought he was pretty decent about it." Another student said, "Any time they say anything at all to us I consider it a chewing out. Any time they say anything about how we did things, they are chewing us out, no matter how God damn nice they are about it."

In short, participant observation makes it possible to check description against fact and, noting discrepancies, become aware of systematic distortions made by the person under study; such distortions are less likely to be discovered by interviewing alone. This point, let us repeat, is only relevant when the interview is used as a source of information about situations and events the researcher himself has not seen. It is not relevant when it is the person's behavior in the interview itself that is under analysis.

INFERENCE, PROCESS, AND CONTEXT

We have seen, in the previous sections of this paper, some of the ways in which even very good interviews may go astray, at least from the perspective of the field observer. We turn now to a consideration of the more general areas of difference between the two methods, suggesting basic ways in which the gathering and handling of data in each differ.

Since we tend to talk in our analyses about much the same order of thing whether we work from interviews or from participant-observational materials, and to draw conclusions about social relations and the interaction that goes on within them whether we have actually seen these things or only been told about them, it should be clear that in working with interviews we must necessarily infer a great many things we could have observed had we only been in a position to do so. The kinds of errors we have discussed above are primarily errors of inference, errors which arise from the necessity of making assumptions about the relation of interview statements to actual events which may or may not be true; for what we have solid observable evidence on in the first case we have only secondhand reports and indices of in the second, and the gap must be bridged by inference. We must assume, when faced with an account or transcription of an interview, that we understand the meaning of the everyday words used, that the interviewee is able to talk about the things we are interested in, and that his account will be more or less accurate. The examples detailed above suggest that these assumptions do not always hold and that the process of inference involved in interpreting interviews should always be made explicit and checked, where possible, against what can be discovered through observation. Where, as is often the case, this is not possible, conclusions should be limited to those matters the data directly describe.

Let us be quite specific, and return to the earlier example of resident-student hostility. In describing this relationship from interviews with the students alone we might have assumed their description to be accurate and made the inference that the residents were in fact "mean." Observation proved that this inference would have been incorrect, but this does not destroy the analytic usefulness of the original statements made to the field-worker in an informal interview. It does shift the area in which we can make deductions from this datum, however, for we can see that such statements, while incorrect factually, are perfectly good statements of the perspective from which these students interpreted the events in which they were involved. We could not know without observation whether their descriptions were true or false; with the aid of observation we know that the facts of the matter are sometimes quite different, and that the students' perspective is strong enough to override such variant facts. But from the interview alone we could know, not what actually happened in such cases, but what the students thought happened and how they felt about it, and this is the kind of inference we should make. We add to the accuracy of our data when we substitute observable fact for inference. More important, we open the way for the discovery of new hypotheses for the fact we observe may not be the fact we expected to observe. When this happens we face a new problem requiring new hypothetical explanations which can then be further tested in the field.

Substitution of an inference about something for an observation of that thing occurs most frequently in discussions of social process and change, an area in which the advantages of observation over an extended period of time are particularly great. Much sociological writing is concerned, openly or otherwise, with problems of process: The analysis of shifts in group structure, individual self-conception and similar matters. But studies of such phenomena in natural social contexts are typically based on data that tell only part of the story. The analysis may be made from a person's retrospective account, in a single interview, of changes that have taken place; or, more rarely, it is based on a series of interviews, the differences between successive interviews providing the bench marks of change. In either case, many crucial steps in the process and important mechanisms of change must be arrived at through inferences which can be no more than educated guesses.

The difficulties in analyzing change and process on the basis of interview material are particularly important because it is precisely in discussing changes in themselves and their surroundings that interviewees are least likely or able to give an accurate account of events. Changes in the social environment and in the self inevitably produce transformations of perspective, and it is characteristic of such transformations that the person finds it difficult or impossible to remember his former actions, outlook, or feelings. Reinterpreting things from his new perspective, he cannot give an accurate account of the past, for the concepts in which he thinks about it have changed and with them his perceptions and memories.[8] Similarly, a person in the midst of such change may find it difficult to describe what is happening, for he has not developed a perspective or concepts which would allow him to think and talk about these things coherently; the earlier discussion of changes in medical school fraternity life is a case in point.

Participant observation does not have so many difficulties of this sort. One can observe actual changes in behavior over a period of time and note the events which precede and follow them. Similarly, one can carry on a conversation running over weeks and months with the people he is studying and thus become aware of shifts in perspective as they occur. In short, attention can be focused both on what has happened and on what the person says about what has happened. Some inference as to actual steps in the process or mechanisms involved is still required, but the amount of inference necessary is considerably reduced. Again, accuracy is increased and the possibility of new discoveries being made is likewise increased, as the observer becomes aware of more phenomena requiring explanation.

The participant observer is both more aware of these problems of inference and more equipped to deal with them because he operates, when gathering data, in a social context rich in cues and information of all kinds. Because he sees and hears the people he studies in many situations of the kind that normally occur for them, rather than just in an isolated and formal interview, he builds an evergrowing fund of impressions, many of them at the subliminal level, which give him an extensive base for the interpretation and analytic use of any particular datum. This wealth of information and impression sensitizes him to subtleties which might pass unnoticed in an interview and forces him to raise continually new and different questions, which he brings to and tries to answer in succeeding observations.

The biggest difference in the two methods, then, may be not so much that participant observation provides the opportunity for avoiding the errors we have discussed, but that it does this by providing a rich experiential context which causes him to become aware of incongruous or unexplained facts, makes him sensitive to their possible implications and connections with other observed facts, and thus pushes him continually to revise and adapt his theoretical orientation and specific problems in the direction of greater relevance to the phenomena under study. Though this kind of context and its attendant benefits cannot be reproduced in interviewing (and the same degree of sensitivity and sense of problem produced in the interviewer), interviewers can profit from an awareness of those limitations of their method suggested by this comparison and perhaps improve their batting average by taking account of them.[9]

NOTES

[1] We wish to thank R. Richard Wohl and Thomas S. McPartland for their critical reading of an earlier version of this paper.

[2] Cf. Florence R. Kluckhohn, "The Participant Observer Technique in Small Communities," *American Journal of Sociology*, 45 (1940), pp. 331–43; Arthur Vidich, "Participant Observation and the Collection and Interpretation of Data," *ibid.*, 60 (1955), pp. 354–60; William Foote Whyte, "Observational Field-Work Methods," in *Research Methods in the Social Sciences*, Marie Jahoda, Morton Deutsch, and Stuart W. Cook, eds. (New York: Dryden Press, 1951), Vol. II, pp. 393–514, and *Street Corner Society*, enlarged ed. (Chicago: University of Chicago Press, 1955), pp. 279–358.

[3] Two provisos are in order. In the first place, we assume in our comparison that the hypothetical interviewer and participant observer we discuss are equally skilled and sensitive. We assume further that both began their research with equally well formulated problems, so that they are indeed looking for equivalent kinds of data.

[4] This study was sponsored by Community Studies, Inc., of Kansas City, Mo., and was carried out at the University of Kansas Medical Center, to whose dean and staff we are indebted for their wholehearted cooperation. Professor Everett C. Hughes of the University of Chicago was director of the project.

[5] For discussion of this point see Thomas S. McPartland, *Formal Education and the Process of Professionalization: A Study of Student Nurses* (Kansas City, Mo.: Community Studies, Inc., 1957), pp. 2–3.

[6] See the discussion in Bronislaw Malinowski, *Magic, Science, and Religion and Other Essays* (Glencoe, Ill.: The Free Press, 1948), pp. 232–8.

[7] See, for example, Arnold M. Rose, "A Research Note on Interviewing," *American Journal of Sociology*, 51 (1945), pp. 143–4; and Howard S. Becker, "A Note on Interviewing Tactics," *Human Organization*, 12:4 (1954), pp. 31–2.

[8] Anselm L. Strauss, "The Development and Transformation of Monetary Meanings in the Child," *American Sociological Review*, 17 (1952), pp. 275–86, and *An Essay on Identity* (unpublished manuscript), *passim*.

[9] We are aware that participant observation raises as many technical problems as it solves. (See, for instance, the discussions in Morris S. Schwartz and Charlotte Green Schwartz, "Problems in Participant Observation," *American Journal of Sociology*, 60 (1955), pp. 343–53, and in Vidich, *op. cit.*) We feel, however, that there is considerable value in using the strong points of one method to illuminate the shortcomings of another.

Discussion

I

MARTIN TROW: Insofar as the paper by Becker and Geer says: "Participant observation is a very useful way of collecting data, and here are some illustrations to show how useful we found it in one study," I can take no issue with them. On the contrary, I profited from their discussion of the method and their illustrations of its use.

But, unfortunately, Becker and Geer say a good deal more than that. In their first paragraph they assert that participant observation, by virtue of its intrinsic qualities, "gives us more information about the event under study than data gathered by any other sociological method." And since this is true, "it provides us with a yardstick against which to measure the completeness of data gathered in other ways. . . ."

It is with this assertion, that a given method of collecting data—*any* method—has an inherent superiority over others by virtue of its special qualities and divorced from the nature of the problem studied, that I take sharp issue. The alternative view, and I would have thought this the view most widely accepted by social scientists, is that different kinds of information about man and society are gathered most fully and economically in different ways, and that the problem under investigation properly dictates the methods of investigation. If this is so, then we certainly can use other methods of investigation as "yardsticks" against which to measure the adequacy of participant observation for the collection of certain kinds of data. And my impression is that most of the problems social scientists are studying seem to call for data gathered in other ways than through participant observation. Moreover, most of the problems investigated call for data collected in several different ways, whether in fact they are or not. This view seems to me implied in the commonly used metaphor of the social scientist's "kit of tools" to which he turns to find the methods and techniques most useful to the problem at hand. Becker and Geer's argument sounds to me very much like a doctor arguing that the scalpel is a better instrument than the forceps—and since this is so we must measure the forceps' cutting power against that of the scalpel.

Much of the paper by Becker and Geer is devoted to measuring "the interview" against the yardstick of "participant observation." To make the "contest" between interviewing and participant observation a fair one, the authors make the proviso (footnote 3) that they are employed by men who are equally competent, and who start with equally well formulated problems, "so that they are indeed looking for equivalent kinds of data." I would assume, on the contrary, that interviewing and participant observation would rarely produce "equivalent" kinds of data, and should not be asked to, but rather produce rather different kinds of data designed to answer quite different kinds of questions about the same general phenomenon. Here again we have Becker and Geer's view of the forceps as a rather poor kind of cutting instrument.

But if I respectfully decline to enter debate on the question of whether the scalpel is a better instrument than the forceps (unless it is rather closely specified "for what")—nevertheless, it may be useful to consider some of the assumptions about the nature of social research out of which such an unreal question can emerge.

II

The first thing that struck me on reading this paper is its oddly parochial view of the range and variety of sociological problems. To state flatly that participant observation "gives us more information about the event under study than . . . any other sociological method" is to assume that all "events" are directly apprehensible by participant observers. But what are some of the "events" that sociologists study? Is a national political campaign such an "event"? Is a long-range shift in interracial attitudes an "event"? Is an important change in medical education and its aggregate of consequences an "event"? Are variations in suicide rates in different social groups and categories an "event"? If we exclude these phenomena from the definition of the term "event" then we exclude most of sociology. If we define "event" broadly enough to include the greater part of what sociologists study, then we find that most of our problems require for their investigation data of kinds that cannot be supplied by the participant observer alone.

But the answer of the participant observation enthusiast, if I read Becker and Geer correctly, would be "that is all very true, but very sad. Many students do require the gathering of data in all kinds of defective and suspect ways, but the closer they approximate to participant observation, and the more frequently they check their findings against those of participant observation, the better." To deal with this, let us for the moment drop the whole question of scalpel *versus* forceps, and consider one or two specific research studies, and the ways their data bear on their questions. This may allow us at least to raise what I feel is a far more fruitful set of questions: What kinds of problems are best studied through what kinds of methods; what kinds of insights and understandings seem to arise out of the analysis of different kinds of data; how can the various methods at our disposal complement one another? I can hardly attempt to contribute to the systematic discussion of these questions in a short "rebuttal" paper, but we can perhaps at least restate the questions in connection with some illustrative evidence.

The central problem of a recent study of the organization and internal politics of a trade union[1] was to explain the development, and especially the persistence, of a two party system within the union's political structure. To this end the research team examined a variety of documents, conducted various kinds of unstructured, focused, and highly structured interviews, examined voting records, and also engaged in participant observation.

Among the problems that we confronted was that of assessing the degree of legitimacy imputed to the party system by various groups and social categories within the union. This, I maintain, we could not have done at all adequately through participant observation. Let us leave aside the question, clearly not within the grasp of the participant observer, of whether the several hundred union officers and "leaders" were more or less inclined to think the party system a good thing in its own right as compared with the ten thousand men in a local or the one hundred thousand men in the international union we were studying. More to the point is the fact that the workings of the party system inhibited direct expressions of hostility to the system. In the ordinary give and take of conversation in the shop, party meeting, club meeting, informal gatherings after hours, such expressions were not likely to be expressed; they violated strongly held norms, and called down various kinds of punishments. It was only when we interviewed leaders individually and intensively that we could get some sense of the reservations that they held about the party system, how widely and strongly those reservations were held, and thus could make some assessment of those sentiments as a potentially disruptive force in the party system. It is true, as Becker and Geer point out, that men will do and say things in their customary activities and relationships that point to factors which might be wholly missed in the course of an interview—and where these things come to the attention of a participant observer he gains insights thereby. But the converse is also true, though perhaps not as widely recognized: Ordinary social life may well inhibit the casual expression of sentiments which are actually or potentially important elements in the explanation of the social phenomena under study. And participant observation is a relatively weak instrument for gathering data on sentiments, behaviors, relationships which are normatively proscribed by the group under observation.

I might note in passing that we gained useful insights into some of the mechanisms operating to sustain this union's political system through our observations at union meetings, party meetings, and during ordinary working days (and nights) spent in the shops. But these insights only took on full meaning in light of much other knowledge about that organization and its social and political structure that had been gained in other ways.

A recent study in the sociology of medicine—the field from which Becker and Geer draw their own illustrations—emphasizes the need for the widest variety of research methods in attacks on comprehensive problems.[2] The index to the volume in which the first reports of this study are published list, under the heading "Methods of social research," the following sources of information used: diaries; documentary records; intensive interviews; observation; panel techniques; questionnaires; sociometry. Most of the papers in this volume deal with problems that could not have been studied solely through direct observation. One paper, for example, deals with the question of the processes by which medical students select their profession.[3] The author finds, among other things, that the occupation of the student's father was an important element in how and when he made that decision. Becker and Geer argue that the interview is not a good source of information "about events that have occurred elsewhere and are described to us by informants." But surely certain important facts about a man's early life experience—and these include what his father did for a living—can be reported quite accurately to an interviewer or on a questionnaire, and give the analyst invaluable data for the analysis of the forces and processes involved in the choice of a profession or occupation. But the bearing of one's father's occupation, or of one's religion, on attitudes and behaviors may never emerge in the ordinary course of events which the participant observer apprehends. Moreover, it is just not true, as Becker and Geer suggest, that the interview is a reliable source of information only regarding the interviewer's conduct *during the interview.* The amount of information people can tell us, quite simply and reliably, about their past experience is very great; and it is only in light of that information, I would maintain, that we can frequently understand their behaviors in the "here and now" that the participant observer is so close to.[4]

True, if we imagine that interviews can deal with past events only through questions of the sort: "Now, why did you choose medicine as a career?" then we may indeed worry about the distortions in reporting information retrospectively. But this effort to make the respondent do the analysis for the sociologist is not the only, and almost certainly not the best, way to assess the bearing of prior events on past or current decisions.

III

We all profit, as I have from this paper, when social scientists broaden our knowledge of the special strengths of the methods which they have found useful and in the use of which they have acquired expertise. The danger lies in the kind of exclusive preoccupation with one method that leads to a systematic neglect of the potentialities, even the essential characteristics, of another. Becker and Geer seem to display this neglect when they contrast participant observation with "the interview." But with some exceptions, the data gathered by the interviewer are not usually embodied in "the interview" taken one at a time, but in the series of interviews through which a body of comparable data has been gathered. It is all of the comparable interviews, with their analysis, that must be compared with participant observation, and not the interviews taken one at a time. The charge is frequently made, and Becker and Geer repeat it, that the interview (and especially the highly structured survey interview) is a very "crude" instrument for collecting data—its artificiality and directedness ensure that much of the "richness" of social life as it is lived passes through its meshes. I would argue that there is more than one way to gain knowledge of the richness, the subtlety and infinite variety, of social life, and that sufficiently sensitive and intensive analysis of "crude" survey data is one such way. Durkheim, whose data in his study of suicide was even "cruder" and further removed from the "rich experiential context" than that of the survey analyst, nevertheless adds much to our understanding of some of the most subtle and complex aspects of social life. How much a social scientist can add to our understanding of society, I submit, is more a product of the way he defines his problem, the questions he brings to his data, and the adequacy of his data to answer his questions and suggest new ones, than it is of how "close," in a physical sense, he gets to the social life he is studying. And this, I think, is as true for social scientists who gather most of their data through participant observation, as for those who use that method to supplement others, and for those who use it not at all.

It is no disparagement of the legitimate uses of participant observation to suggest that some of the uncritical enthusiasm and unwarranted claims for it show what seems to be a certain romantic fascination with the "subtlety and richness" of social life, and especially with "cultural esoterica," the ways very special to a given group. But it seems to me profoundly mistaken to search for the special essence of a method of data collection, and appraise it in terms of its ability to directly reflect this "subtlety and richness." As social scientists, our business is with describing and explaining social phenomena; our judgment of the usefulness of data is properly made against the criterion; how much does this help us understand the phenomenon we are studying? It may well be that participant observation is more successful than any other method in gathering data on the "cultural esoterica" of a group. But this is not a good in itself; the question remains, is this information useful, and importantly useful, for our purposes? And that of course will depend on our purposes. The correlative question is equally important: could the matters which these esoteric cultural items point to—the matters we are *really* interested in—have been learned in other, and perhaps more economical, ways? I suspect that very often they can. But at the very least the question should be raised more often than it is.

The argument the authors make for the superiority of participant observation comes finally to an expression of a preference for what can be observed "directly" over what we must make inferences about. But the authors' strong commitment to observation leads them, I believe, to an unnecessarily dim, and basically incorrect, view of the process of inference in social science. All interpretations of data, however collected—through observations, interviews, or whatever—involve inferences regarding their meaning and significance. We confuse ourselves if we believe that the people whose behavior we are concerned with, whether we observe them or interview them, can themselves provide an adequate explanation of their own behavior. That is our job, and the participant observer makes inferences from the data he collects just as the survey analyst makes inferences from the data collected for him. The data gathered by participant observers are still data, despite the perhaps misleading circumstance that the participant observer usually both gathers and interprets the data himself, and to a large degree simultaneously.[5] But the data he collects are not a substitute for the interpretive inference. We all forget that at our peril.

The fact that social scientists are constantly making inferences from their data does not especially disturb me, as it does Becker and Geer. Our progress in social science will come not through an effort to get "closer" to the source of data, and thus try to minimize or do away with the process of inference by dissolving it back into data collection and somehow apprehending reality directly. That simply isn't possible. Our progress will come as we are increasingly able to develop systems of theoretically related propositions—propositions which are "checked" at more and more points against data collected through a variety of means. The inferences that we make from data, and the theory from which they derive and to which they contribute, may indeed be nothing more than "educated guesses"—but that is the nature of scientific theory. Our aim is to make them increasingly highly educated guesses. We cannot evade that fate, which is the fate of science, through reliance on a wrongly conceived participant observation which apprehends social reality "directly."

IV

Every cobbler thinks leather is the only thing. Most social scientists, including the present writer, have their favorite research methods with which they are familiar and have some skill in using. And I suspect we mostly choose to investigate problems that seem vulnerable to attack through these methods. But we should at least try to be less parochial than cobblers. Let us be done with the arguments of "participant observation" vs. interviewing—as we have largely dispensed with the arguments for psychology vs. sociology—and get on with the business of attacking our problems with the widest array of conceptual and methodological tools that we possess and they demand. This does not preclude discussion and debate regarding the relative usefulness of different methods for the study of specific problems or types of problems. But that is very different from the assertion of the general and inherent superiority of one method over another on the basis of some intrinsic qualities it presumably possesses.

NOTES

[1] S. M. Lipset, M. A. Trow, and J. C. Coleman, *Union Democracy* (Glencoe, Ill.: The Free Press, 1956).

[2] R. K. Merton, George Reader, and P. L. Kendall, eds., *The Student-Physician* (Cambridge: Harvard University Press, 1957). See especially George Reader, "The Cornell Comprehensive Care and Teaching Program," section on "Methods," pp. 94–101.

[3] Natalie Rogoff, "The Decision to Study Medicine," in Merton, Reader, and Kendall, eds., *op. cit.*, pp. 109–131.

[4] This suggests, more generally, that participant observation *by itself* is most nearly satisfactory in studies of small, isolated, relatively homogeneous populations, such as primitive tribes, where variations in the character of early life experience, and the

effects of those variations on present sentiments and behaviors, are not so great. Where variations in experience outside the arena being observed are great, we must, for most problems, turn to other methods of data collection to learn about them.

[5] This involves special strengths and hazards, a matter which has been discussed extensively elsewhere, and also in the paper by Becker and Geer and their references.

Methods and Techniques | ARCHIVAL DATA
of Sociological Analysis

13   Oscar Grusky

Managerial Succession and Organizational Effectiveness

The major purpose of this study was to test two related hypotheses: (1) that rates of administrative succession and degree of organizational effectiveness are negatively correlated, and (2) that a change in the rate of administrative succession is negatively correlated with a change in organizational effectiveness.[1] The hypotheses are deliberately stated so as not to attribute causality solely to either succession or effectiveness. We assumed that the variables induce reciprocal effects. High rates of succession should produce declining organizational effectiveness, and low effectiveness should encourage high rates of administrative succession.

To obtain anything resembling an adequate field test of these hypotheses required a substantial number of formal organizations that, ideally, were identical in official goals, size, and authority structure. If the objectives of the organizations were not similar, then obviously it would not be feasible to compare their relative effectiveness, since this concept refers to the extent to which an organization is able to move toward the accomplishment of its official aims. We know that for business organizations and certain public agencies, and perhaps for other kinds as well, rates of succession are positively related to organizational size.[2] Therefore, we sought a sample of organizations of similar size.

There is some evidence, although it is highly limited, that organizations with different types of authority structures respond in very different ways to personnel changes at top levels in the hierarchy.[3] Hence, organizations with similar types of structures of authority were desirable.

Reprinted from *American Journal of Sociology*, 69:1 (1963), pp. 21–31, and 70:1 (1964), pp. 69–76, by permission of the authors and the publisher.

In addition, a relatively "clean" field test of the hypotheses demanded reliable and valid measures of rates of administrative succession and organizational effectiveness. Since the sixteen organizations selected for study, professional baseball teams, met all the relatively stringent requirements described, a second objective of this research was to illustrate some of the potentialities of sports organizations as objects of sociological investigation.

METHODS AND FINDINGS

All data for this study were gathered by means of secondary analysis of published documents.[4] Baseball teams and, in fact, most professional sports clubs offer the research advantages of public records of team personnel and team performance. This fact, as we shall see, also has important implications for the behavior of the organization.

Two time periods, 1921–41 and 1951–58, were selected for study. It was deemed wise to skip the World War II and immediate post-World War II periods.

The structure of baseball organizations is such that ultimate responsibility for the performance of the team is almost always fixed on one position, that of field manager. At the same time, official authority is generally concentrated in this position. Therefore, it was clear that personnel changes among field managers rather than club presidents, general managers, or team captains were central to the study. The number of managerial changes for each time period or the average length of managerial tenure constituted the rate of succession for each team.

The measure of organizational effectiveness was team standing, based on the number of games won and lost at the completion of the season. This might be considered analogous in some respects to productivity in industrial organizations. Georgopoulos and Tannenbaum's study of thirty-two similar suborganizations or stations demonstrated significant correlations between their various measures of organizational effectiveness: expert assessment of station effectiveness, productivity, intragroup strain, and flexibility.[5] It would certainly be safe to say that, among baseball experts, team standing is the most widely accepted criterion of effectiveness. Financial profit is also an important criterion. It would appear that the profitability of a baseball club is highly related to its team standing. Consistent with this assumption, we found a strong positive correlation between team standing and yearly attendance.[6]

Table 1 presents the basic data of the study. The data for Periods I and II taken separately or together strongly supported the hypothesized negative correlation between rates of managerial succession and organizational effectiveness. The correlations were considerably greater in the second time period, 1951–58, than in the earlier one. Rates of succession and team standing correlated −.40 in the first period and −.60 in the second. One team that contributed to the lower correlation in the earlier period was the Philadelphia Athletics. Despite the fact that the team consistently finished in the second division between 1921 and 1941, no managerial successions took place during this period. Undoubtedly, manager Connie Mack's owner-ship of the club assisted his long tenure. The Athletics experienced fre-quent managerial succession during 1951–58 with the departure of Mack from the scene.

In contrast, the Yankees, as Table 1 suggests, contributed to the magni-tude of the correlation in both time periods. Not only were they highly effective, but they also experienced few managerial changes.

TABLE 1.   MEASURES OF SUCCESSION AND EFFECTIVENESS FOR SIXTEEN PROFESSIONAL BASEBALL ORGANIZATIONS OVER TWO TIME PERIODS*

Team	No. of Successions			Average Team Standing†		
	Period I	Period II	Periods I and II	Period I	Period II	Periods I and II
	(1)	(2)	(3)	(4)	(5)	(6)
Phillies	7	3	10	7.2	4.8	6.5
Giants	1	1	2	2.7	3.4	2.9
Cardinals	10	4	14	3.0	3.8	3.2
Braves	7	3	10	6.3	6.9	5.3
Pirates	6	3	9	3.2	6.9	4.2
Cubs	8	3	11	3.5	6.2	4.4
Dodgers	4	1	5	4.9	2.2	4.2
Reds	7	3	10	4.9	4.9	4.9
Athletics	0	4	4	4.8	6.6	5.3
Nats	6	3	9	4.2	6.8	4.9
Yankees	2	0	2	1.8	1.2	1.6
White Sox	8	2	10	5.6	2.9	4.9
Red Sox	8	2	10	6.0	3.9	5.4
Indians	6	1	7	3.9	2.6	3.6
Browns (Orioles) ..	9	5	14	5.6	6.8	5.9
Tigers	4	4	8	3.9	5.4	4.3

* Period I, 1921–41; Period II, 1951–58. Rank-order correlations (Kendall's tau) and one-tail p values are: cols. (1) and (4), $-.40(p < .02)$; cols. (2) and (5), $-.60(p < .001)$; and cols. (3) and (6), $-.43(p < .001)$.
† A numerically high team standing meant low effectiveness.

The second hypothesis was tested by examining the relationship between changes from Period I to Period II in the average length of time a manager retained his position with a team and changes in the team's standing. That is, we wanted to see if teams that kept their managers for shorter periods (experienced more succession) in Period II than they had in Period I were less effective in the later period and vice versa. In fact, the average tenure for managers declined in Period II for all but two clubs. As Table 2 demon-strates, our hypothesis was again strongly supported.[7] All eight teams that increased considerably their rate of managerial succession over that of the earlier period experienced a decline in average team standing. Moreover, the two clubs that decreased their rate of succession increased their effec-tiveness. However, it was evident that those teams that had experienced

TABLE 2. Relationship between Change in Average Length of Managerial Tenure and Average Team Standing from Period I to Period II for Fifteen Professional Baseball Teams*

	Change in Average Team Standing	
Change in Average Managerial Tenure	Increased Effectiveness	Decreased Effectiveness
Tenure longer	2	0
Tenure about same†	4	1
Tenure much shorter	0	8

* $P = .0014$ by Fisher's Exact Test if the categories "Longer tenure" and "Tenure about same" are combined. One team (Reds) that did not change its average team standing was excluded.
† Defined as a decrease of 0.3 year or less.

frequent and infrequent succession in the original period needed to be analyzed separately. Therefore, we controlled for average length of managerial tenure in Period I (a control for average team standing in Period I also would have been desirable, but we did not have a sufficient number of cases). The hypothesis was supported when the relationship was examined separately for teams that were below and above the median with respect to rates of succession in the first period (Table 3). Moreover, it should be noted that the single deviant case in Table 3 (the St. Louis Cardinals) was the team with the *lowest managerial tenure of any team in Period I*. This low rate remained about the same in Period II, although team effectiveness declined somewhat. We might speculate that perhaps (1) the very slight alteration of the club's policy of frequent succession was not above the threshold necessary to raise the organization's effectiveness, and/or (2) the slight decrease in the club's effectiveness did not encourage the owners to alter their policy of frequent succession.

The findings of this study may be compared with a recent laboratory investigation by Trow.[8] Using Leavitt's Common-Symbol problem and the five-position chain organizational network, Trow found no significant linear relationship between mean rate of succession and long-run organizational performance. He did find that the mean performance of the twelve teams with the lowest replacement rates was significantly superior to the mean performance of the twelve teams with the highest rates of succession. Trow discovered that *variability* in the rate of succession was a more important factor in team performance, noting that "whatever the average rate of succession, an increase in the rate, i.e., a temporal clustering of succession, tends to bring about a decrease in the level of organization performance." In addition, he found that ability of the successor was a major factor in organizational performance. Thus, despite considerable differences between the techniques of secondary analysis and contrived experimentation, the findings of the two studies appear to be consistent at least with respect to the second hypothesis.

TABLE 3. RELATIONSHIP BETWEEN CHANGE IN AVERAGE LENGTH OF MANA-
GERIAL TENURE AND AVERAGE TEAM STANDING FROM PERIOD I TO PERIOD II
FOR FIFTEEN PROFESSIONAL BASEBALL TEAMS, CONTROLLING FOR AVERAGE
LENGTH OF MANAGERIAL TENURE IN PERIOD I*

Change in Average Managerial Tenure	Change in Average Team Standing		
	Increased Effectiveness	Decreased Effectiveness	One-Tail p Level†
A. Short tenure in Period I (below median):			
Tenure longer or about same‡	3	1	
			.11
Tenure much shorter	0	3	
B. Long tenure in Period I (above median):			
Tenure longer or about same	3	0	
			.018
Tenure much shorter	0	5	

* One team (Reds) that did not change its average team standing was excluded.
† By Fisher's Exact Test.
‡ "About same" was defined as a decrease of 0.3 year or less.

SUCCESSION AND EFFECTIVENESS

It is apparent that theoretical explanations for the findings of this study
may be pursued from two opposite directions; it may be assumed that either
effectiveness or succession functions as the primary independent variable.
Our data demonstrate only the existence of an association, not its cause.
Logic or common knowledge will not permit us to decide the issue. However, there is no intrinsic reason why a particular variable, such as rate of
succession, could not be *both* a cause and an effect of effectiveness. This
may very well be so in this instance.

A common-sense explanation for our results might suggest that effectiveness alone is the cause. The manager is fired because the team performs
badly. Not only is the simplicity of this explanation appealing, but the
negative correlation between succession and effectiveness is fully consistent
with it. However, if taken by itself, this approach possesses all the deficiencies properly attributed to orientations that rest only on common knowledge: they typically do not stimulate careful empirical test; they typically
do not suggest additional propositions which might be worthy of examination; they typically do not fit in systematically to a comprehensive body of
generalizations in the field of interest. Naturally, we prefer explanations
that can meet these and other criteria described by Nagel somewhat more
adequately.[9]

If we assume that effectiveness and succession influence each other by
contributing to managerial role strain, it is possible to formulate an alterna-

tive explanation for the major findings, one that ties in with a growing body of theory and research. It was this assumption that originally provoked this study. Succession, because it represents a universal organizational process, and effectiveness, because all formal organizations tend to strive toward the attainment of their official objectives, are strategic concepts for studying organizations within a comparative framework. Numerous studies conducted in the laboratory as well as in the field suggest that these variables produce reciprocal effects. For example, both Gouldner's and Guest's field research as well as Trow's experiment indicate that succession influences organizational effectiveness.[10] On the other hand, Hamblin's laboratory study suggests that the ineffectiveness of the group contributes to high rates of succession among the leaders. When the leader could not solve a crisis problem confronting the group, he was replaced.[11] Accordingly, the relationship between rates of succession and organizational effectiveness was analyzed within the context of a conceptual scheme that focused on their interrelationships with a number of other variables: managerial (or executive) role strain, expectation of replacement, style of supervision, subgroup stability, morale, clientele support, degree of discrepancy between managerial authority and responsibility, and availability of objective assessment of organizational performance.

Figure 1 presents the proposed network of interrelations of the variables. The arrows indicate the direction of influence. Key propositions discussed

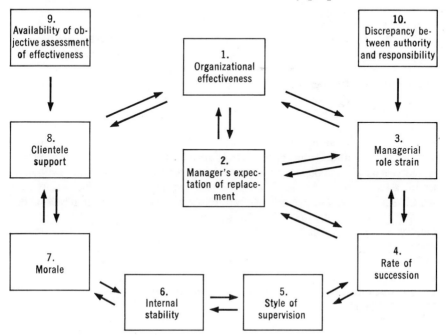

Figure 1. Organizational factors in team performance.

below are followed by a numerical reference to the relevant variables. Of course, no attempt was made to exhaust the logical possibilities in the formation of propositions.

The magnitude of managerial role strain is a general factor conditioning the nature of the relationship between succession and effectiveness.[12] By role strain is meant the extent to which role performance produces stress for the occupant of a position that cannot be fully relieved by institutionally legitimated means. Hence, this concept refers to the amount of tension with which a person is confronted as a result of occupying a particular office in an organization. The sources of strain will vary, of course, with the nature of the organizational setting, rank of the position, experience of the person, and so on. In general, organizational effectiveness should be inversely related to strength of managerial role strain (1 and 3); high levels of effectiveness (of the manager's unit) should be associated with low managerial strain and low levels of effectiveness correlated with high managerial strain. Perhaps, however, some optimum level of managerial strain is associated with maximum organizational effectiveness. At the same time, again assuming all else equal, the magnitude of managerial role strain should be positively correlated with rates of succession (3 and 4). Low strain defines a position as desirable. If the strain is too high, the manager searches for opportunities elsewhere, or redefines previous opportunities as attractive and eventually leaves the organization. Once again a simple monotonic relationship may be an oversimplification; too little strain may indicate a lack of "challenge" to the manager and thereby also stimulate turnover.

If rates of succession in a position have been high, and expectation of replacement arises, this, in turn, should contribute to managerial role strain. All else being equal, the stronger the expectation of replacement, the greater the role strain (2 and 3). Organizational effectiveness should be inversely related to strength of expectation of replacement; if the organization is performing well, the manager would not normally expect to be replaced (1 and 2). Strength of managerial role strain should also be related to style of supervision. All else being equal, the greater the role strain, the greater the likelihood that supervision will be close (3 and 5).[13] There are numerous studies relating closeness of supervision, morale, and organizational effectiveness (1 and 7; 1 and 5).[14] Judging from Guest's study, we would expect that the greater the rate of succession in an organization, the greater would be the tendency to supervise closely (4 and 5). There is evidence suggesting that closeness of supervision is associated with degree of internal organizational stability (5 and 6).[15]

Two special sources of strain seemed pertinent to the analysis of the managerial role in baseball organizations: (1) the discrepancy between official responsibility and authority (we assumed that, in general, the greater this discrepancy, the greater the role strain [3 and 10]) and (2) the availability of objective assessment of managerial and team performance to the organization's clientele and higher levels of authority. We would expect that when objective assessment is available, the negative correlation between effectiveness and managerial role strain should be higher than when such objective assessment is not available (*8* and *9*). The first attribute concerns primarily the nature of the internal structure of baseball organizations, the second the relationship between the organization and its interested public.

Many of the role strains of the field manager emerge from the fact that he alone is acknowledged to be officially responsible for team performance. Therefore, it is defined as illegitimate for him to delegate ultimate responsibility for results either upward to the "Front Office" or downward to the coaches and individual players. At the same time, however, he depends, particularly over the long run, upon the front office for assistance by providing a strong farm system and advantageous trades, and, at all times, upon the quality of performance of the lower-level members of the hierarchy, the players. If they perform well, his position is secure; if they do not, it is in jeopardy.

However, although other managerial positions, such as those in business, often carry responsibility for results, what distinguishes the baseball manager is the fact that not only is he acknowledged to be responsible, but his superiors have objective data with which they can readily evaluate his performance. Unlike the typical business executive, for whom few clear standards of performance tend to exist, the baseball manager is exposed continually to seemingly unassailable comparative measures of effectiveness.[16] Moreover, the effects of many of the manager's daily decisions are a matter of public record. This means that every managerial decision that turns out to be an unfortunate one for the team, such as substituting in a key situation a mediocre left-hand hitting pinch batter for the team's star right-hand hitting slugger, is immediately "second-guessed" by the players, coaches, the front office, and the fans. The manager is constantly open to criticism, public and private.

The relationship between the field manager and his subordinates, upon whom he depends so heavily, is also influenced by the availability of public and objective measures of performance. Outstanding performance on the part of individual players insures their remaining with the club, and, importantly, the evaluation of this performance rests *not* with managerial subjective judgment as it does frequently in business firms, but instead is based largely on relatively objective standards of performance. Hence, the player in many respects is independent of managerial control. Where the ballplayer tends to resemble the traditional entrepreneur, the manager resembles the bureaucrat.[17] But the manager is a bureaucrat stripped of many vital bureaucratic controls. For example, the typical manager in a bureaucracy possesses power because he can limit the access of his subordinates to higher positions. However, the average ballplayer does not anticipate upward mobility in the ordinary sense within the structure of the professional baseball organization. In his case, upward career mobility applies primarily to the income and popularity rank systems; the players' major sources of reward are external to managerial control.

To a certain extent each manager develops his own inimitable way of handling players. After a while, the players feel comfortable with this style, and the younger ones in particular may feel that no successor can quite measure up to the standard (Willie Mays's reported fondness for Leo Durocher is a case in point). A managerial change inevitably upsets old patterns of behavior. New organizational policies, a different style of leadership, perhaps new players, and the addition of new coaches produce changes of great magnitude in the internal structure of the team. Members are forced to adapt not only to the successor's new ways of doing things but also to the new informal coalitions that inevitably develop. The recruitment of the successor from the present staff or from outside the organization may be an important factor affecting the degree of instability created by succession.[18] Moreover, a high rate of managerial succession on a team tends to generate expectations, especially during a losing streak, that the current manager's job is in danger. This may encourage dissatisfied players to challenge the manager's authority and increase even more the felt discrepancy between his responsibility and authority. The result is greater managerial role strain.

In addition to the internal sources of tension, constant pressure on both the manager and the ordinary team members emanates from the organization's clientele. Unlike many other kinds of organizations, professional baseball teams must deal with a clientele that is both highly committed and highly informed. The strong emotional identification of the fan with "his" professional baseball or football club is often a part of the resident's identification with his local community. In some locales, such as Los Angeles, comprised of a large number of suburban subcommunities, it probably represents one of the more important integrative symbols. In the Green Bay area, the Green Bay Packers football team is referred to as a "regional religion."

Not only are the clientele strongly committed but in addition, as we suggested, they can readily and continually evaluate the effectiveness of the team since performance criteria are public knowledge.[19] In other types of organizations, the clientele cannot evaluate the effectiveness of the system with comparable precision. Consumers of an industrial corporation's products, for example, typically possess neither the propensity nor the knowledge to compare objectively the quality of the products they purchase or the "efficiency" of the corporation's employees. Accordingly, public relations and advertising men are probably able to manipulate the image of the corporation and its products much more effectively than can professional baseball teams.[20] Not even the best advertising men could have undone the damage to the Philadelphia Phillies' game attendance between 1934 and 1941 when they finished in last or next to last place every year.

Clientele support is critical because of its close relationship to morale and team effectiveness (8 and 7; 8 and 1); it is important in two ways. First, attendance is ostensibly highly related to profitability, and a drop in profitability produces strong pressures for managerial change. Second, high rates of attendance, by raising team morale, may contribute to team effectiveness as well as being affected by it. Our data revealed a strong correlation between effectiveness based on team standing and ranked yearly attendance. The zero-order correlations, by Kendall's tau, were as follows: for Period I, $T = .60$, $p < .0007$; for Period II, $T = .44$, $p < .009$; for Periods I and II combined, $T = .58$, $p < .001$. These data, of course, do not allow us to separate cause and effect. Mosteller's statistical study of the effects of playing "at home" and "away" upon winning World Series games found no significant differences in performance under the two conditions.[21] However, as he pointed out, outcomes of regular season games might still be influenced by this factor. He noted: (1) Baseball teams are often tailored to the home park because half the games are played there. Perhaps league champions are more skilful hitters and therefore less limited by the dimensions of a particular park. (2) Fatigue from excessive traveling may disadvantage the away team to a greater extent during the regular season than during the World Series. Still another possibility is that clientele support is less critical for team performance during World Series competition than during the day-in-day-out play of the regular season. The extensive publicity and assured popular interest in the World Series generates sufficient enthusiasm on the part of the player whether he is playing at home or away. We suspect that the home crowd can exercise considerable influence on player performance during a regular season game. Under these conditions, enthusiastic support from the crowd may stimulate the player to "put out" more in the same way that a responsive audience can help produce scintillating dramatic performances on the stage. The ineffective team is less likely to receive this added inducement to perform well.

To summarize briefly: Our orientation focused on a set of ten variables. Analysis of the situation of the ineffective team may be used illustratively. If a team is ineffective, clientele support and profitability decline. Accordingly, strong external pressures for managerial change are set in motion and, concomitantly, the magnitude of managerial role strain increases. A managerial change may be viewed in some quarters as attractive in that it can function to demonstrate publicly that the owners are taking concrete action to remedy an undesirable situation.[22] The public nature of team performance and the close identification of community pride with team behavior combine to establish a strong basis for clientele control over the functioning of the team. These external influences tend to increase the felt discrepancy between managerial responsibility and actual authority. Since the rewards of popularity are controlled externally, individual rather than team performance may be encouraged. Similarly, the availability of objective performance standards decreases managerial control and thereby contributes to role strain. The greater the managerial role strain, the higher the rates of succession. Moreover, the higher the rates of succession, the stronger the expectations of replacement when team performance declines. Frequent managerial change can produce important dysfunctional consequences within the team by affecting style of supervision and disturbing the informal network of interpersonal relationships. New policies and new personnel create the necessity for restructuring primary relationships. The resulting low primary-group stability produces low morale and may thereby contribute to team ineffectiveness. Declining clientele support may encourage a greater decline in team morale and performance. The consequent continued drop in profitability induces pressures for further managerial changes. Such changes, in turn, produce additional disruptive effects on the organization, and the vicious circle continues.

Our findings demonstrating a negative correlation between rates of succession and effectiveness and a positive correlation between clientele support and effectiveness constitute only two connections of the chain depicted in Figure 1. The methodological weaknesses of studies such as the present one, based wholly on official documents, should not be underestimated. Clearly, such inquiries are not adequate substitutes for well-designed field and laboratory investigations. Systematic research examining, for example, the nature of the relationship between morale and effectiveness in baseball teams (morale and productivity studies of industrial organizations have produced contradictory findings[23]), morale and strength of clientele support, and managerial role strain and team effectiveness, would be highly desirable.

Herbert A. Simon has pointed out that the problem of organizational effectiveness is essentially an empirical one. He observes: "What is needed is empirical research and experimentation to determine the relative desirability of alternative administrative arrangements."[24] In addition, he emphasized two canons of research design: "First, it is necessary that the objectives of the administrative organization under study be defined in concrete terms so that results, expressed in terms of these objectives, may be accurately measured. Second, it is necessary that sufficient experimental control be exercised."[25] As an approximation to these principles, this study, by means of secondary analysis of published documents, has, in effect, compared the performance of professional baseball teams operating under contrasting administrative arrangements, the conditions of frequent and relatively infrequent managerial succession.

ACKNOWLEDGMENTS

A number of people have contributed to this study. I am grateful to Judith Kairath for doing the coding and to John Vincent and Jerry King for computational work. The Helms Athletic Foundation was most gracious in permitting use of its library and records. I am also indebted to the members of the Department of Sociology, University of California, Davis, for their numerous helpful comments when an earlier version of this paper was presented at a seminar. Professors Mayer Zald, Charles R. Wright, and Fritz J. Roethlisberger and an anonymous reviewer gave much constructive advice. This is an expanded version of a paper read at the annual meetings of the American Sociological Association in Washington, D.C., 1962.

NOTES

[1] This hypothesis was discussed in my "Administrative Succession in Formal Organizations," *Social Forces*, 39 (1960), pp. 105–15.

[2] See my "Corporate Size, Bureaucratization, and Managerial Succession," *American Journal of Sociology*, 67 (1961), pp. 261–69, and L. Kriesberg, "Careers, Organization Size, and Succession," *American Journal of Sociology*, 68 (1962), pp. 355–59. For a comprehensive discussion of other variables related to size see T. Caplow, "Organizational Size," *Administrative Science Quarterly*, 2 (1957), pp. 484–505.

[3] D. M. Sills, *The Volunteers* (Glencoe, Ill.: The Free Press, 1957); W. A. Lunden, "The Tenure and Turnover of State Prison Wardens," *American Journal of Corrections*, 19 (1957), pp. 14–15; and A. Etzioni, "Authority Structure and Organizational Effectiveness," *Administrative Science Quarterly*, 4 (1959), pp. 43–67.

[4] H. Hurkin and S. C. Thompson, *The Official Encyclopedia of Baseball*, 2d rev. ed. (New York: A. S. Barnes & Co., 1959); H. Johnson, *Who's Who in Baseball* (New York: Buston Publishing Co., 1953); F. Menke, *The Encyclopedia of Sports*, 2d rev. ed. (New York: A. S. Barnes & Co., 1960); *1958 Baseball Guide and Record Book* (St. Louis, Mo.: Sporting News, 1958); T. Spink and Son, *Baseball Register*, compiled by T. Spink and P. Rickart (St. Louis, Mo.: Sporting News, 1940–41, 1951–58).

[5] B. S. Georgopoulos and A. S. Tannenbaum, "A Study of Organizational Effectiveness," *American Sociological Review*, 22 (1957), pp. 534–40.

[6] Profitability, attendance, and effectiveness are related in part because prolonged increases in profits tend to yield increases in organizational control over the market for new talent and therefore tend to produce a more effective farm system. Interpretation of the correlation between team standing and attendance should be approached cautiously. Attendance may also be a function of variables such as the total population of the metropolitan area, its particular age and sex distribution, and, of course, the number of professional baseball teams in the community.

[7] We realize some of the interpretative limitations of utilizing team averages as measures of succession. A study comparing the "effectiveness" and length of tenure of the successor and his managerial predecessor is in progress. In this investigation the object of study is the manager and not the team. Some limitations in our measure of effectiveness also should be noted. Team standing may not reflect perfectly the ability of the team, just as fielding and batting averages are not ideal measures of individual performance. E.g., a team may improve over the course of a season and because of a poor start finish only second, although it is the best team by other standards. And the bias of the official scorer has a lot to do with the players' fielding and batting averages.

[8] D. B. Trow, "Membership Succession and Team Performance," *Human Relations*, 13 (1960), pp. 259–68. An immediate problem in making such a contrast is the critical difference in the objects of study. Trow applies his findings to "self-organizing" groups and points out several limitations of the experimental situation relevant to generalizing the findings. Formal organizations typically possess properties that laboratory organizations such as Trow's do not possess, such as: a formal system of authority, at least three levels of authority, and planned task differentiation. Moreover, when laboratory investigations have attempted to manipulate some of these differentiating variables, important results have been indicated. Hence, H. H. Kelley found that the existence of a hierarchy influenced communication ("Communication in Experimentally Created Hierarchies," *Human Relations*, 4 (1951), pp. 39–56, and I. D. Steiner and W. I. Field found that the assignment of roles to persons in laboratory groups affected persons' perceptions of and reactions to one another ("Role Assignment and Interpersonal Influence," *Journal of Abnormal and Social Psychology*, 60 (1960), pp. 239–45). Of course, there are outstanding examples of experimental studies that have attempted to establish structures which legitimately could be called formal organizations. See, e.g., W. M. Evan and M. Zelditch, Jr.,

"A Laboratory Study on Bureaucratic Authority," *American Sociological Review*, 26 (1961), pp. 883–93.

⁹ Ernest Nagel in a recent book provides an excellent discussion of the elements of the scientific and common sense approaches. He observed that "the sciences seek to discover and to formulate in general terms the conditions under which events of various sorts occur, the corresponding happenings. This goal can be achieved only by distinguishing or isolating certain properties in the subject matter studied and by ascertaining the repeatable patterns of dependence in which these properties stand to one another. In consequence, when the inquiry is successful, propositions that hitherto appeared to be quite unrelated are exhibited as linked to each other in determinate ways by virtue of their place in a system of explanation" (*The Structure of Science* [New York: Harcourt, Brace & World, 1961], p. 4).

¹⁰ A. Gouldner, *Patterns of Industrial Bureaucracy* (Glencoe, Ill.: The Free Press, 1954); R. H. Guest, *Organizational Change* (Homewood, Ill.: Dorsey Press, 1962); and Trow, *op. cit.* See also W. F. Whyte, "The Social Structure of the Restaurant Industry," *American Journal of Sociology*, 54 (1949), pp. 302–10; C. R. Christiansen, *Management Succession in Small and Growing Enterprises* (Boston: Graduate School of Business Administration, Harvard University, 1953); E. Dale, "Du Pont: Pioneer in Systematic Management," *Administrative Science Quarterly*, 2 (1957), pp. 26–30; O. Grusky, "Role Conflict in Organization: A Study of Prison Camp Officials," *Administrative Science Quarterly*, 3 (1959), pp. 463–67; and R. H. McCleery, *Policy Change in Prison Management* (East Lansing: Michigan State University, 1957), pp. 10–27.

¹¹ R. L. Hamblin, "Leadership and Crisis," *Sociometry*, 21 (1958), pp. 322–35.

¹² Position or office refers to a category that is located in the formal social structure of an organization. In a formal organization the category is defined in terms of its relationship with other positions that in turn are organized around the official objectives of the system. By role is meant a "set of evaluative standards applied to an incumbent of a particular position" (see N. Gross, W. S. Mason, and A. W. McEachern, *Explorations in Role Analysis* [New York: Wiley, 1958], p. 60). Role strain is viewed in the present study as a more inclusive concept than role conflict. The latter is limited to situations of strain produced by incompatible expectations. W. J. Goode defines role strain as "the felt difficulty in fulfilling role obligations." Our definition differs in that it does not require a perfect association between perceived and objective role strain ("A Theory of Role Strain," *American Sociological Review*, 24 [1960], pp. 483–96).

¹³ Guest, *op. cit.*, Chap. 3.

¹⁴ Many of these studies are discussed in P. Blau and W. R. Scott, *Formal Organizations* (San Francisco: Chandler Publishing Co., 1962), pp. 140–64.

¹⁵ Gouldner, *op. cit.*, and R. O. Carlson, *Executive Succession and Organizational Change* (Chicago: Midwest Administrative Center, University of Chicago, 1962).

¹⁶ See F. X. Sutton, S. E. Harris, C. Kaysen, and J. Tobin, *The American Business Creed* (New York: Schocken Books, 1962), pp. 336–38. In this study the authors point out how the *lack* of clear standards of performance can contribute to role strain. It should be pointed out that the skill of the baseball manager also is greatly affected by subjective judgments. As Sutton *et al.* point out, it often matters not that the effectiveness of the organization was in fact unrelated or only slightly related to the behavior of the manager. It is typically assumed in business, in baseball, and elsewhere, that a strong correlation exists between organizational effectiveness and the performance and ability of the manager in charge.

¹⁷ Sports columnist Frank Finch of the *Los Angeles Times* (April 1, 1962) reported the difficult problem of control confronting Coach Pete Reiser of the Dodgers. Although Reiser is referred to as Howard's "father-confessor," it appears that the player refused to alter his batting stance to fit the coach's demands. "I'd like to have the authority to tell Frank to hit the way I say or else not play," the exasperated Reiser is quoted as saying, "but in baseball you just don't order people to do anything in a certain way." Of course, the fact that Howard in 1961 hit fifteen home

runs and batted .296 contributed to his independence. Howard's reported point of view in this dispute parallels the individualistic spirit of the traditional entrepreneur: "I appreciate advice, and I accept it if it will help me, but Frank Howard, and nobody else, is going to help Frank Howard hit the ball on the button. When you step into the batter's box you're on your own. . . . This is a game made up of individuals." It would be a gross exaggeration to assert that Howard's attitude is universally found among ballplayers. Obviously, co-operation is common, perhaps especially among infielders who tend not to have high batting averages. Their skills are more likely to lie with the kinds of plays that require smooth coordination and not with the bat. For this and other related reasons, we hypothesized in another study that infielders and catchers would be more likely than outfielders and pitchers to become managers.

[18] See Carlson, *op. cit.*

[19] Manager Freddie Hutchinson of the Cincinnati Reds once rather grimly described baseball as "the only sport in the world where everybody thinks he is an expert." No wonder several managers feel, as does Hutchinson, that fans are much too preoccupied with baseball statistics: "Now every club has to have a statistician, ours included. The statistician gives his figures to the newsmen and the broadcasters and now he's got everybody conscious of them."

[20] I am indebted to Professor R. J. Murphy for this observation.

[21] F. Mosteller, "The World Series Competition," *Journal of the American Statistical Association*, 47 (1942), pp. 355–80.

[22] Although officially the manager may be held responsible for a team's poor showing, the fact that managers frequently are hired later by other clubs would suggest that their alleged ineptness is partly a screen. It is not easy for the front office to resist public pressures even if they might feel that the decision to replace the manager is unwise. The case of Mike Higgins and the Boston Red Sox is instructive, for it is one where the owner really did not want to fire the manager but did so anyway. Yawkey, the owner, and Higgins, the manager, were the best of friends. Yet a few years back when the Red Sox were doing very poorly, Yawkey gave in to public criticism and replaced Higgins. However, he kept Higgins on in the rather vague position of "troubleshooter." When the team still did poorly under Billy Jurges, Higgins was rehired. A new manager at least provides the fans with some hope for the coming season. Professor Gerard Brandmeyer kindly provided this example.

[23] E.g., R. L. Kahn and N. C. Morse, "The Relationship of Productivity to Morale," *Journal of Social Issues*, VII, No. 3 (1951), 8–17; D. Katz, N. Maccoby, and N. C. Morse, *Productivity, Supervision and Morale in an Office Situation* (Ann Arbor, Mich.: Institute of Social Research, 1950); D. Katz, N. Maccoby, and L. G. Floor, *Productivity, Satisfaction and Morale among Railroad Workers* (Ann Arbor, Mich.: Institute of Social Research, 1951); and N. C. Morse, *Satisfactions in the White-Collar Job* (Ann Arbor, Mich.: Institute for Social Research, 1953); H. Wilensky's paper in C. Arensberg *et al.* (eds.) *Research in Industrial Human Relations: A Critical Appraisal* (New York: Harper & Bros., 1957), pp. 25–50.

[24] *Administrative Behavior*, 2d ed. (New York: Macmillan, 1958), p. 42.

[25] *Ibid.*

Discussion

(Scapegoating in Baseball)

WILLIAM A. GAMSON AND NORMAN A. SCOTCH: Oscar Grusky's "Managerial Succession and Organizational Effectiveness" makes use of an ingenious source of data for comparative organizational analysis. By picking major league baseball clubs for his focus, he has available to him twenty organizations which are identical in goals and in a wide variety of other structural characteristics. There is considerable potentiality here, but unfortunately Grusky's analysis offers us no more than the fact that those clubs which have done the worst over the years have changed their field managers most frequently.

For this rather obvious correlation Grusky suggests two possible explanations. He quickly disposes of the common-sense explanation of one-way causality: the manager is fired because the team performs poorly. Despite the fact that this explanation is consistent with the data he presents, he charges it with, among other things, the failure "to stimulate careful empirical test."

Such a charge is doubly puzzling. First of all, it is not at all clear why this particular explanation offers any less of a clear empirical test than the alternative offered. Second, one looks in vain for the careful empirical tests that Grusky's more complicated explanation has produced. At the very least, one might have expected the specification of how one might get data that would allow a choice. Faced with two explanations that apparently handle the available data equally well, we prefer the simpler one. Grusky's invocation of Ernest Nagel notwithstanding.

However, we wish to suggest that the common-sense explanation, Grusky's explanation, and a third one which we will suggest each has different implications and can be tested with little difficulty. A small amount of data toward such a test is offered below. As a prior step, we present the three explanations of the succession-effectiveness relationship and the different predictions which they make.

THREE EXPLANATIONS

1. *The Common-Sense One-Way Causality Theory*   This explanation fully accepts the fact that the field manager of a baseball team is a major influence on a team's performance. When the team is doing poorly, he is rightfully held responsible. Consequently, he is fired and replaced with an alternative manager who, it is hoped, will do better. A new manager typically will raise the performance of a team, since he can benefit by avoiding the errors that his predecessor made.

There is no reason, by this theory, to expect any diminution in a team's performance after a new manager has been hired. Instead, deteriorating performance leads to managerial succession which in turn leads to *increased* effectiveness of performance. A team which is fortunate enough to have acquired a good manager will perform effectively over a prolonged period and will have few managerial changes. A team that is not so fortunate in its choice of managers will have poorer performance and a high frequency of managerial succession.

2. *The Grusky Two-Way Causality Theory*   Grusky also assumes that the field manager is a major influence on a team's performance. However, the relationship between effectiveness and succession, he argues, is recipro-

cal rather than one way. It is certainly true that a team performing badly will frequently cause the manager to be fired. However, such managerial changes tend to have a number of interrelated and undesirable consequences. To quote Grusky:

> A managerial change inevitably upsets old patterns of behavior. New organizational policies . . . produce changes of great magnitude in the internal structure of the team. Members are forced to adapt not only to the successor's new way of doing things but also to the new informal coalitions that inevitably develop.
>
> Frequent managerial change can produce important dysfunctional consequences within the team by affecting style of supervision and disturbing the informal network of interpersonal relationships. . . . The resulting low primary group stability produces low morale and may thereby contribute to team ineffectiveness. Declining clientele support may encourage a greater decline in team morale and performance. The consequent continued drop in profitability induces pressures for further managerial changes. Such changes in turn produce additional disruptive effects on the organization and the vicious circle continues.

Clearly, a managerial change by the Grusky theory should produce a further deterioration in performance by an already faltering team.

3. *The Ritual Scapegoating No-Way Causality Theory* Unlike the above theories, this one assumes that the effect of the field manager on team performance is relatively unimportant.[1] In the long run, the policies of the general manager and other front-office personnel are far more important. While judicious trades are helpful (here the field manager may be consulted but does not have the main responsibility), the production of talent through a well-organized scouting and farm system is the most important long-run determinant. The field manager, who is concerned with day-to-day tactical decisions, has minimal responsibility for such management functions.

In the short run, the supply of available baseball talent is the most important determinant of performance, that is, the players themselves. The manipulation of this talent by the field manager will make very little difference. The New York Yankees, while Casey Stengel was the manager, won ten pennants in twelve years. Is this the measure of Stengel's skill or do the New York Mets, who are winning no pennants, more accurately reflect it? We suggest that the Yankees would have done as well and the Mets would have (or more accurately, could have) done no worse.

Two qualifications are worth making before one dismisses the field-manager role out of hand. First of all, a truly talented manager such as Gene Mauch of the Phillies may make a long-term contribution through his skilful development of the potentialities of young players. This may not be reflected in immediate change in team performance.

A second qualification acknowledges some over-all effect by field managers but assumes that the *variance* in skill between those who become field managers is so small that managerial skill may be considered a constant. It is worth noting, in this respect, that few "new" managers make their appearance when managerial shifts are made. Instead, there is a pool of *former* managers, frequently employed as coaches by various teams, who are usually called upon when changes are to be made. Most of these coaches were fired from their positions as managers, presumably because they failed to produce winning teams. Such recruiting practices strongly suggest the interchangeability of managers and the improbability of explaining variance in team performance by anything the field manager does.

If the field manager makes little difference, how does one account for the high correlation which Grusky reports between team performance and rate of managerial succession? The answer is quite simple: The firing of the field manager is a classic example of ritual scapegoating. It is a convenient, anxiety-reducing act which the participants in the ceremony regard as a way of improving performance, even though (as some participants may themselves admit in less stressful moments) real improvement can come only through long-range organizational decisions.

Those involved have a strong stake in maintaining the myth of managerial responsibility. If the field manager himself denies responsibility for the team's failures, then his claim for responsibility when the team is successful is weakened. As for the front office and the players, it is a happy excuse for what is really their own responsibility. Finally, as Grusky notes, the fans of a poorly performing team can be appeased and their hopes of future success rekindled by this simple ritual act.

Note that if we were simply to compare the performance of the team after the manager's dismissal with the performance before we would surely find some immediate improvement. Such a result is an artifact of the conditions that produce the ritual, namely, a slump in performance. If we compared average rainfall in the month preceding and the month following the performance of the Hopi rain dance, we would find more rain in the period after. The dance is not performed unless there is a drought, so such a comparison would be misleading. Nevertheless, this "slump-ending" effect may help to account for the tenacity of belief in the effectiveness of the ritual.

Our prediction would be that if the slump-ending effect is controlled, there will be no difference in performance under the old manager and the new manager. However, teams which perform poorly over a prolonged period will have more frequent occasion to resort to the act of ritual scapegoating; hence the correlation between team effectiveness and rate of succession among field managers.

A TEST OF THE THEORIES

Managerial successions take place at particular moments in time. Those that occur in the middle of the season are particularly appropriate for analysis for two reasons: (1) mid-season changes tend to maximize disruptive effects and thus should produce a fairer test for Grusky's theory;

and (2) there is less opportunity for influences other than the field manager's influence to operate. In the gap between one season and the next, trades, the aging and retirement of present players, and the development of players from the farm system may serve to alter the available talent with which the new manager has to work.

If we compare the performance of a team during one season in a period prior to a managerial change and in the period following the change, then we get a different prediction from each of the above theories. (1) By common sense, we should expect an increase in team effectiveness. (2) By Grusky, we should expect a decrease in team effectiveness due to the disruption of succession. (3) By the scapegoat theory, we should expect no change (after controlling for the slump-ending effect).

We shall present data on twenty-two mid-season managerial changes from 1954 to 1961.[2] Team won-lost record was recorded at four points in time: (1) as of approximately two weeks before dismissal; (2) as of the day of dismissal; (3) as of approximately two weeks after dismissal; and (4) as of the end of the season (Table 1).

TABLE 1. TEAM PERFORMANCE AFTER CHANGING MANAGER, 1954–61

Comparison	Improvement	Deterioration	N
Two weeks prior versus time of dismissal	4	18	22
Time of dismissal versus two weeks later	15	7	22
Two weeks prior to dismissal versus two weeks after dismissal	1	17	18*
Two weeks before dismissal versus post-dismissal record	13	9	22
Two weeks before dismissal versus record from two weeks after dismissal until end of season . .	12	10	22

* This comparison refers only to those eighteen teams whose performance was declining at the time of dismissal.

There are a number of comparisons of interest. First of all, it is quite clear that dismissals take place in periods of declining performance. Only four of the twenty-two teams had a higher percentage at the time of dismissal than in the previous time period. There is some indication of immediate improvement, as fifteen of the twenty-two teams show better performance in the next two weeks. In only one case, however, does a slumping team recover under the new manager to a point where the team's won-lost percentage is higher two weeks after dismissal than it was two weeks before. Such data seem to document the existence of a slump-ending effect but are equally consistent with all of the theories.

The most relevant test of the theories is the comparison between won-lost record up to two weeks prior to the dismissal of the old manager and won-lost record for the remainder of the season under the new manager.

Thus, the two weeks preceding the dismissal of the manager are removed from the performance record to control the slump effect.

In thirteen of the twenty-two cases, the team performs better under the new manager than it had under the old manager up to two weeks prior to his dismissal. This is unfortunately not a very definitive result for choosing between the common-sense and the scapegoating prediction, but it clearly goes against the Grusky prediction. If managerial succession disrupts the primary group relations of ball players, it apparently does not lead to any visible deterioration of performance.

Perhaps there is some slight improvement which can be attributed to the ritual itself. The new manager may have no effect through anything he does, but the players' belief in the efficacy of the ritual boosts their morale and brings about a short-run improvement. To test this, we can compare performance up until two weeks before dismissal with performance for the remainder of the season starting two weeks after dismissal. In this comparison, both the periods immediately preceding and immediately following are controlled. Here there is even less evidence of effect: in twelve cases, the team does better under the new manager, in ten cases it does worse.

CONCLUSION

The modest amount of data presented here warrants no firm conclusion. However, Grusky's cavalier dismissal of the simple common-sense explanation seems unwarranted. We do not know if it is as "scientific" as Grusky's more elaborate theory, but it proves the better predictor here. However, it still remains to be established that the field manager has any effect on team performance. Until it is, we prefer the scapegoating explanation of the correlation between effectiveness and rate of managerial succession.

NOTES

[1] Grusky suggests this possibility on p. 193, n. 22, but he does not pursue its implications.

[2] We are indebted to Andréa Modigliani for compiling the data reported here.

Reply

OSCAR GRUSKY: Professors Gamson and Scotch present data on twenty-two mid-season managerial changes from 1954 to 1961. All of their comparisons required team won-lost record as of "approximately" two weeks before or after the manager's dismissal. In our replication of their study we found twenty-three cases that qualified when we defined two weeks to mean exactly fourteen days.[1] We excluded two cases, the 1954 White Sox and the 1958 Cardinals, where a full fourteen days did not follow the dismissal of the manager. In each case the new manager took over eleven days before the season ended. If approximately two weeks were to be defined so as to include these two, the case total would have been twenty-five. We also found evidence of a number of other mid-season managerial changes of considerable relevance to the analysis of the effects of managerial succession.[2]

Gamson and Scotch have indicated that in their opinion the critical test of the three theories is the won-lost record up to two weeks prior to the old manager's dismissal compared with the new manager's won-lost record for the remainder of the season.[3] This comparison allows a two-week control for the slump effect. Table 1 presents a comparison of the Gamson-Scotch study and our replication. In fourteen of twenty-three cases the team shows an improvement. These data and the last comparison in Table 1 seem to me to be most supportive of the common-sense theory and inconsistent with the other two explanations.

TABLE 1.   REPLICATION OF GAMSON-SCOTCH STUDY OF TEAM PERFORMANCE
AFTER CHANGING MANAGER, 1954–61

Two Weeks before Dismissal versus Post-dismissal Record	Gamson-Scotch	Replication		
		"In-side"	"Out-side"	Total
Improvement	13	7	7	14
Deterioration	9	2	7	9
Total	22	9	14	23

However, the theory described in my study did not claim that succession would be equally disruptive under all conditions. In selecting mid-season changes Gamson and Scotch asserted that "mid-season changes tend to maximize disruptive effects and thus produce a fairer test for Grusky's theory." Actually, quite the opposite was the case with the data they presented. As a number of studies have shown, an important factor affecting degree of disruption is whether or not the successor is recruited from within the present staff or from outside the organization.[4] Inside successors tend to be less disruptive than outside successors, and mid-season successions in baseball frequently tend to involve inside replacements. In fact, nine of the twenty-three managerial replacements were so close as to have had daily contact with the playing personnel.[5] Eight coaches and one player who became managers of their own teams were designated "inside" successors, and the remaining fourteen were designated "outsiders."

The Gamson-Scotch theory would suggest that since the manager has essentially no effect on team performance it really does not matter whether or not the successor is an insider or an outsider. The common-sense theory presented also did not take this factor into consideration. (It could be argued that inside managers are aware of the predecessor's errors and hence more likely to avoid repeating them.) On the other hand, our theory predicts that inside successions should be less disruptive than outside successions.[6] Let us consider the comparison considered most important by

Gamson and Scotch. We find, as shown in Table 1, that the team improved in seven of nine cases involving an inside succession, and deteriorated in seven of fourteen outside successions. These data suggest (1) that type of succession does appear to make a difference, contrary to the Gamson and Scotch theory, (2) that inside succession is associated with team improvement relative to two weeks before dismissal, and (3) that outside succession is associated with no deterioration in team performance, contrary to our theory.[7]

Although it is certain that some control for the low effectiveness of the team prior to succession is essential, one might question whether or not a two-week control for the slump effect is adequate. It seems unfair to the predecessor to take as a measure of the team's performance under his leadership the won-lost record for the season up until two weeks before he is replaced. The limitations of this technique can be illustrated by the case of the 1959 Cleveland Indians, an instance that qualified for inclusion in the Gamson-Scotch study. On May 2, after losing two of sixteen games played, the manager was fired. Two weeks prior to that date the team had played only six games and lost them all. Now if one inherits a ball club that has a team percentage of .125 there is almost no direction to go but up. And if one compares the Indians' performance two weeks before the dismissal of the manager with the post-dismissal record (Gamson and Scotch call this the critical test of the theories), then the new manager needed to win only a single game for the remainder of the season in order to show improvement. For this reason we thought that another and perhaps fairer test of the theories would be to compare team performance under the old manager in the year previous to his succession with the record of the new manager. (In sixteen of the nineteen cases that qualified, the manager was with the club for the entire year. In the other three cases he was with the club for most of the year, and the won-lost record while he was with the club was used.) Two comparisons were made. The first was identical to the Gamson-Scotch critical test except that it used the predecessor's performance as manager in the previous year as base. The second allowed the successor a two-week period of grace to get used to his new job and may therefore be more appropriate. These comparisons ask the question: Did the team perform better under the new manager than it had in the previous year (with essentially the same player material) under his predecessor? As shown in Table 2, the first comparison reveals that improvement in team performance takes place in about the same number of cases as does deterioration. This supports the Gamson-Scotch argument until one examines the difference between inside and outside successors. Seven of nine teams showing improvement involved replacements by inside managers and eight of eight of those showing deterioration involved replacements by outside managers. Even more compelling evidence for our theory was revealed by the second comparison which gives the players a two-week period to adapt to the new manager and the new man the same amount of time to learn the requirements of his new position before evaluating his performance. We

TABLE 2. TEAM PERFORMANCE AFTER CHANGING MANAGER, USING
OLD MANAGER'S PREVIOUS YEAR'S RECORD AS BASE, 1954–61

Comparison	Improvement			About same*			Deterioration			Total
	"In-side"	"Out-side"	Total	"In-side"	"Out-side"	Total	"In-side"	"Out-side"	Total	
Old manager's previous year's record vs. new manager's record	7	2	9	1	1	2	0	8	8	19†
Old manager's previous year's record vs. new manager's record from two weeks after dismissal to end of season	5	1	6	2	0	2	1	10	11	19

* Defined as a difference of .005 or less.
† In four cases the old manager was not with the same club the previous year.

find that deterioration in team performance takes place in almost twice as many cases as does improvement. In only six of nineteen cases did the team do better under the new manager than it had in the previous year under his predecessor. Clearly, this goes against the Gamson-Scotch and the common-sense explanation. Again, the most pronounced findings of the entire study were revealed when inside and outside successors were compared. Five of six managers who showed improvement were inside successors and ten of eleven of those whose teams deteriorated were outsiders. These data support our theory.

Despite this evidence there is merit in the explanation in cultural terms offered by Gamson and Scotch which stresses the myth of managerial responsibility. Their theory and the methods they have devised for testing it are highly provocative. However, it is one thing to assert that such a myth of managerial effectiveness exists and that the manager's reputation is tied closely to the fate of the system which he may not always clearly affect, and quite another matter to claim, as Gamson and Scotch do, that the manager's behavior can have *no* influence at all on organizational effectiveness except in the long run. Such a position unwarrantedly de-emphasizes the potential importance of social organizational factors for effectiveness and, in so doing, fails to explain the findings of numerous studies which reveal an opposite set of conclusions.[8]

NOTES

[1] I have learned through sad experience that it is highly desirable to have two coders independently code and tabulate data of this kind. This was accomplished by Daniel Willick and Don Baker, whose help I greatly appreciate. Their results were compared, and disagreements were rechecked and resolved. The sources were the sports sections of the *Los Angeles Times* and the yearly *Baseball Guide and Record*

Book, compiled by J. G. Taylor Spink in collaboration with Paul A. Rickart *et al.* (St. Louis: Sporting News Publishing Co.). The use of the facilities of the Helms Athletic Foundation is gratefully acknowledged. I am also grateful to Lindsey Churchill for his advice on the manuscript.

² The definition of what constitutes a managerial succession was not without problems in the study. Actually, more than twenty-five successions turned up in the replication. In 1959 the Cleveland Indians fired their manager on September 22 only to rehire him the next day. The manager of the 1960 Phillies quit on April 12, after only one game of the season. The manager of the 1961 Minnesota Twins was relieved temporarily by a coach. He returned as manager only to be dismissed ten days later. We used the date on which he was actually fired and not the date he was temporarily relieved. Also, the 1960 Red Sox had an interim manager, a coach, for five days before a new manager took over, and the 1959 Red Sox had an interim manager, also a coach, for only a few hours. There may very well have been other cases of interim managers that we missed. These cases involving interim managers and the Minnesota Twins' case point up the inadequacies of taking the won-lost record two weeks before dismissal as an index. Anticipation of replacement may and probably does occur before this. Perhaps it would be more advisable to select as base a month before dismissal or, as we decided for Table 2, the preceding season.

³ The replication revealed numerous other errors. Our findings for the other four comparisons were as follows:

Comparison	Improve- ment	Deterio- ration	Total
Two weeks prior vs. time of dismissal	4	19	23
Time of dismissal vs. two weeks later	16	7	23
Two weeks prior to dismissal vs. two weeks after dismissal	6	13	19
Two weeks before dismissal vs. two-week post-dismissal record	15	8	23

⁴ See, e.g., A. Gouldner, *Patterns of Industrial Bureaucracy* (Glencoe, Ill.: The Free Press, 1954), and R. O. Carlson, *Executive Succession and Organizational Change* (Chicago: Midwest Administrative Center, University of Chicago, 1962).

⁵ As indicated in an earlier study, inside-outside is often a relative matter. The nine inside managers were distinguished because they seemed to have the closest association with the players. Many of the remaining fourteen had considerable though less extensive contact. Three were farm club managers for the same team; four were in the team's front office; one was a broadcaster of the team's games; two were coaches on different clubs; and two were managers of other clubs. Only two were not associated with baseball at the time they were hired.

⁶ The "our" is not merely editorial. Gouldner, for example, made the same prediction ten years ago (*op. cit.*, p. 72).

⁷ There are some problems with the Gamson-Scotch data that may be noted here: (1) The timing of the managerial succession can have a significant impact on the Gamson-Scotch measure of team performance. A single victory or loss affects the over-all won-lost record greatly at the start of the baseball season and considerably less at the end of the season. To evaluate team performance properly requires some control for this statistical artifact. Seven of the cases that qualified for inclusion in the Gamson-Scotch study would be markedly affected by this factor. Four successions took place at the start of the season, in April and May, and three occurred near the end, that is, in mid-August or later. (2) The use of won-lost record also has some limitations. For example, a minute percentage difference may produce a classification of team performance as improvement or deterioration. It may very well be that team standing is a more useful measure as this index takes into account the relative performance of the team.

[8] See esp. R. Likert, *New Patterns of Management* (New York: McGraw-Hill, 1961), and P. Blau and W. R. Scott, *Formal Organizations* (San Francisco: Chandler Publishing Co., 1962). The problem of assessing the relative importance of the manager's contribution to team performance is an important one. Daniel Willick, a research assistant, has devised a rough but ingenious measure for this purpose. He compares each team's final yearly standing with its rank on three "abilities" measures: team batting, team fielding, and pitchers' earned-run averages. He then assumes that teams which are ranked about the same on all four indexes are being managed at a level consistent with their skills. Those teams which have a higher team standing than their rank on the other indexes are considered to be well managed and those with a much lower team standing than rank on the "abilities" indexes are considered poorly managed.

PART III

Aspects of Social Structure
and Social Process

CHAPTER THREE
Dimensions of the Social Order

Dimensions
of the Social Order | DIFFERENTIATION

COMMENTARY

From the pecking order of chickens to the Indian caste system, all societies, human as well as subhuman, are differentiated. By differentiation is meant the division of people according to socially relevant criteria. Biological characteristics such as age, sex, and, in many respects most critically, race, are one basis of differentiation. The social order is differentiated also by the tasks that men perform. This is known as the division of labor. While the division of labor separates men into theoretically equivalent social positions, the stratification system orders men into hierarchies of power and prestige. It is this aspect of differentiation—the ordering of men into systems of differential power and esteem—that is dealt with in this section.

Max Weber, in his classic essay "Class, Status and Party," distinguishes three bases of stratification, or access to power: economic, social, and political. It is Weber's contention that classes, status groups, and parties differ not only in the bases of their formation, but in their structures as well. He discusses the conditions which transform class interests into class actions and those that transform status groups into castes.

John Goldthorpe, in a provocative article, reviews and criticizes the thesis which states that industrial societies tend to have similar social structures. He discusses data which are not in accord with some of the major hypotheses which stem from this thesis. Goldthorpe questions the assumption that the economic system is more fundamental or critical than the political system. Regardless of whether one agrees with the specifics of his analysis of Soviet society, his fundamental point concerning the relevance of differing values and ideologies to, and the role of purposive action in, shaping the social order bear consideration.

207

Most sociologists base their investigations of stratification on the objective existence of differences in the positions of men in society. By contrast, in his essay "The Sociology of Poverty," Lewis Coser suggests it is the social definition of poverty that is the critical datum for sociological analysis. According to Coser it is not the fact that a man may be economically deprived that is at issue—what is important is whether he is defined by society as "poor." He discusses some of the consequences resulting from assignment to the social category of the poor.

The last article in this section concerns ethnic differentiation. In their paper "The Negro as an Immigrant Group: Recent Trends in Racial and Ethnic Segregation," Karl Taeuber and Alma Taeuber report the results of a study designed to determine whether Negroes are becoming less segregated as their socio-economic status improves. Their analysis of census data indicates that Negroes, unlike other ethnic migrants to large cities, are not becoming less segregated. Their data indicate that the most recent migrants to the city, although more economically deprived than Negroes, are less segregated than Negroes. Their study suggests that race, rather than such factors as income or education, is the primary impetus for the residential segregation of Negroes.

14 MAX WEBER

Class, Status, and Party

ECONOMICALLY DETERMINED POWER AND THE SOCIAL ORDER

Law exists when there is a probability that an order will be upheld by a specific staff of men who will use physical or psychical compulsion with the intention of obtaining conformity with the order, or of inflicting sanctions for infringement of it.[1] The structure of every legal order directly influences the distribution of power, economic or otherwise, within its respective community. This is true of all legal orders and not only that of the state. In general, we understand by "power" the chance of a man or of a number of men to realize their own will in a communal action even against the resistance of others who are participating in the action.

"Economically conditioned" power is not, of course, identical with "power" as such. On the contrary, the emergence of economic power may be the consequence of power existing on other grounds. Man does not

Reprinted from *From Max Weber: Essays in Sociology*, translated and edited by H. H. Gerth and C. Wright Mills, pp. 180–195, by permission of Oxford University Press, Inc. Copyright © 1946 by Oxford University Press, Inc.

strive for power only in order to enrich himself economically. Power, including economic power, may be valued for its own sake. Very frequently the striving for power is also conditioned by the social "honor" it entails. Not all power, however, entails social honor: The typical American Boss, as well as the typical big speculator, deliberately relinquishes social honor. Quite generally, "mere economic" power, and especially "naked" money power, is by no means a recognized basis of social honor. Nor is power the only basis of social honor. Indeed, social honor, or prestige, may even be the basis of political or economic power, and very frequently has been. Power, as well as honor, may be guaranteed by the legal order, but, at least normally, it is not their primary source. The legal order is rather an additional factor that enhances the chance to hold power or honor; but it cannot always secure them.

The way in which social honor is distributed in a community between typical groups participating in this distribution we may call the "social order." The social order and the economic order are, of course, similarly related to the "legal order." However, the social and the economic order are not identical. The economic order is for us merely the way in which economic goods and services are distributed and used. The social order is of course conditioned by the economic order to a high degree, and in its turn reacts upon it.

Now: "classes," "status groups," and "parties" are phenomena of the distribution of power within a community.

DETERMINATION OF CLASS-SITUATION BY MARKET-SITUATION

In our terminology, "classes" are not communities; they merely represent possible, and frequent, bases for communal action. We may speak of a class when (1) a number of people have in common a specific causal component of their life chances, in so far as (2) this component is represented exclusively by economic interests in the possession of goods and opportunities for income, and (3) is represented under the conditions of the commodity or labor markets. [These points refer to "class situation," which we may express more briefly as the typical chance for a supply of goods, external living conditions, and personal life experiences, in so far as this chance is determined by the amount and kind of power, or lack of such, to dispose of goods or skills for the sake of income in a given economic order. The term "class" refers to any group of people that is found in the same class situation.]

It is the most elemental economic fact that the way in which the disposition over material property is distributed among a plurality of people, meeting competitively in the market for the purpose of exchange, in itself creates specific life chances. According to the law of marginal utility this mode of distribution excludes the nonowners from competing for highly valued goods; it favors the owners and, in fact, gives to them a monopoly to acquire such goods. Other things being equal, this mode of distribution monopolizes the opportunities for profitable deals for all those who, provided with goods, do not necessarily have to exchange them. It increases, at least generally, their power in price wars with those who, being propertyless, have nothing to offer but their services in native form or goods in a form constituted through their own labor, and who above all are compelled to get rid of these products in order barely to subsist. This mode of distribution gives to the propertied a monopoly on the possibility of transferring property from the sphere of use as a "fortune," to the sphere of "capital goods"; that is, it gives them the entrepreneurial function and all chances to share directly or indirectly in returns on capital. All this holds true within the area in which pure market conditions prevail. "Property" and "lack of property" are, therefore, the basic categories of all class situations. It does not matter whether these two categories become effective in price wars or in competitive struggles.

Within these categories, however, class situations are further differentiated: on the one hand, according to the kind of property that is usable for returns; and, on the other hand, according to the kind of services that can be offered in the market. Ownership of domestic buildings; productive establishments; warehouses; stores; agriculturally usable land, large and small holdings—quantitative differences with possibly qualitative consequences—; ownership of mines; cattle; men (slaves); disposition over mobile instruments of production, or capital goods of all sorts, especially money or objects that can be exchanged for money easily and at any time; disposition over products of one's own labor or of others' labor differing according to their various distances from consumability; disposition over transferable monopolies of any kind—all these distinctions differentiate the class situations of the propertied just as does the "meaning" which they can and do give to the utilization of property, especially to property which has money equivalence. Accordingly, the propertied, for instance, may belong to the class of rentiers or to the class of entrepreneurs.

Those who have no property but who offer services are differentiated just as much according to their kinds of services as according to the way in which they make use of these services, in a continuous or discontinuous relation to a recipient. But always this is the generic connotation of the concept of class: that the kind of chance in the *market* is the decisive moment which presents a common condition for the individual's fate. "Class situation" is, in this sense, ultimately "market situation." The effect of naked possession *per se*, which among cattle breeders gives the non-owning slave or serf into the power of the cattle owner, is only a forerunner of real class formation. However, in the cattle loan and in the naked severity of the law of debts in such communities, for the first time mere "possession" as such emerges as decisive for the fate of the individual. This is very much in contrast to the agricultural communities based on labor. The creditor-debtor relation becomes the basis of class situations only in those cities where a "credit market," however primitive, with rates of interest increasing according to the extent of dearth and a factual monopolization of credits, is developed by a plutocracy. Therewith class struggles begin. Those men whose fate is not determined by the chance of using goods or services for themselves on the market, e.g., slaves, are not, however, a "class" in the technical sense of the term. They are, rather, a "status group."

COMMUNAL ACTION FLOWING FROM CLASS INTEREST

According to our terminology, the factor that creates class is unambiguously economic interest, and indeed, only those interests involved in the existence of the market. Nevertheless, the concept of "class-interest" is an ambiguous one: even as an empirical concept it is ambiguous as soon as one understands by it something other than the factual direction of interests following with a certain probability from the class situation for a certain average of those people subjected to the class situation. The class situation and other circumstances remaining the same, the direction in which the individual worker, for instance, is likely to pursue his interests may vary widely, according to whether he is constitutionally qualified for the task at hand to a high, to an average, or to a low degree. In the same way, the direction of interests may vary according to whether or not a *communal* action of a larger or smaller portion of those commonly affected by the "class situation," or even an association among them, e.g., a trade union, has grown out of the class situation from which the individual may or may not expect promising results. [Communal action refers to that action which is oriented to the feeling of the actors that they belong together. Societal action, on the other hand, is oriented to a rationally motivated adjustment of interests.] The rise of societal or even of communal action from a common class situation is by no means a universal phenomenon.

The class situation may be restricted in its effects to the generation of essentially *similar* reactions, that is to say, within our terminology, of "mass actions." However, it may not have even this result. Furthermore, often merely an amorphous communal action emerges. For example, the "murmuring" of the workers known in ancient oriental ethics: the moral disapproval of the work-master's conduct, which in its practical significance was probably equivalent to an increasingly typical phenomenon of precisely the latest industrial development, namely, the "slow down" (the deliberate limiting of work effort) of laborers by virtue of tacit agreement. The degree in which "communal action" and possibly "societal action" emerges from the mass actions of the members of a class is linked to general cultural conditions, especially to those of an intellectual sort. It is also linked to the extent of the contrasts that have already evolved, and is especially linked to the *transparency* of the connections between the causes and the consequences of the class situation. For however different life chances may be, this fact in itself, according to all experience, by no means gives birth to class action (communal action by the members of a class). The fact of being conditioned and the results of the class situation must be distinctly recognizable. For only then the contrast of life chances can be felt not as an absolutely given fact to be accepted, but as a resultant from either (1) the given distribution of property, or (2) the structure of the concrete economic order. It is only then that people may react against the class structure not only through acts of an intermittent and irrational protest, but in the form of rational association. There have been class situations of the first category (1), of a specifically naked and transparent sort, in the urban centers of Antiquity and during the Middle Ages; especially then, when great fortunes were accumulated by factually monopolized trading in industrial products of these localities or in foodstuffs. Furthermore, under certain circumstances, in the rural economy of the most diverse periods, when agriculture was increasingly exploited in a profit-making manner. The most important historical example of the second category (2) is the class situation of the modern proletariat.

TYPES OF CLASS STRUGGLE.

Thus every class may be the carrier of any one of the possibly innumerable forms of class action, but this is not necessarily so. In any case, a class does not in itself constitute a community. To treat "class" conceptually as having the same value as "community" leads to distortion. That men in the same class situation regularly react in mass actions to such tangible situations as economic ones in the direction of those interests that are most adequate to their average number is an important and after all simple fact for the understanding of historical events. Above all, this fact must not lead to that kind of pseudoscientific operation with the concepts of class and class interests so frequently found these days, and which has found its most classic expression in the statement of a talented author, that the individual may be in error concerning his interests but that the class is infallible about its interests. Yet, if classes as such are not communities, nevertheless class situations emerge only on the basis of communalization. The communal action that brings forth class situations, however, is not basically action between members of the identical class; it is an action between members of different classes. Communal actions that directly determine the class situation of the worker and the entrepreneur are: the labor market, the commodities market, and the capitalistic enterprise. But, in its turn, the existence of a capitalistic enterprise presupposes that a very specific communal action exists and that it is specifically structured to protect the possession of goods *per se*, and especially the power of individuals to dispose, in principle freely, over the means of production. The existence of a capitalistic enterprise is preconditioned by a specific kind of legal order. Each kind of class situation, and above all when it rests upon the power of property *per se*, will become most clearly efficacious when all other determinants of reciprocal relations are, as far as possible, eliminated in their significance. It is in this way that the utilization of the power of property in the market obtains its most sovereign importance.

Now "status groups" hinder the strict carrying through of the sheer market principle. In the present context they are of interest to us only from this one point of view. Before we briefly consider them, note that not much of a general nature can be said about the more specific kinds of antagonism between classes (in our meaning of the term). The great shift, which has been going on continuously in the past, and up to our times, may be summarized, although at the cost of some precision: the struggle in which class situations are effective has progressively shifted from consumption credit toward, first, competitive struggles in the commodity market and, then, toward price wars on the labor market. The class struggles of antiquity—to the extent that they were genuine class struggles and not struggles between status groups—were initially carried on by indebted peasants, and perhaps also by artisans threatened by debt bondage and struggling against urban creditors. For debt bondage is the normal result of the differentiation of wealth in commercial cities, especially in seaport cities. A similar situation has existed among cattle breeders. Debt relationships as such produced class action up to the time of Cataline. Along with this, and with an increase in provision of grain for the city by transporting it from the outside, the struggle over the means of sustenance emerged. It centered in the first place around the provision of bread and the determination of the price of bread. It lasted throughout antiquity and the entire Middle Ages. The propertyless as such flocked together against those who actually and supposedly were interested in the dearth of bread. This fight spread until it involved all those commodities essential to the way of life and to handicraft production. There were only incipient discussions of wage disputes in antiquity and in the Middle Ages. But they have been slowly increasing up into modern times. In the earlier periods they were completely secondary to slave rebellions as well as to fights in the commodity market.

The propertyless of antiquity and of the Middle Ages protested against monopolies, preemption, forestalling, and the withholding of goods from the market in order to raise prices. Today the central issue is the determination of the price of labor.

This transition is represented by the fight for access to the market and for the determination of the price of products. Such fights went on between merchants and workers in the putting-out system of domestic handicraft during the transition to modern times. Since it is quite a general phenomenon we must mention here that the class antagonisms that are conditioned through the market situation are usually most bitter between those who actually and directly participate as opponents in price wars. It is not the rentier, the share-holder, and the banker who suffer the ill will of the worker, but almost exclusively the manufacturer and the business executives who are the direct opponents of workers in price wars. This is so in spite of the fact that it is precisely the cash boxes of the rentier, the shareholder, and the banker into which the more or less "unearned" gains flow, rather than into the pockets of the manufacturers or of the business executives. This simple state of affairs has very frequently been decisive for the role the class situation has played in the formation of political parties. For example, it has made possible the varieties of patriarchal socialism and the frequent attempts—formerly, at least—of threatened status groups to form alliances with the proletariat against the bourgeoisie.

STATUS HONOR

In contrast to classes, *status groups* are normally communities. They are, however, often of an amorphous kind. In contrast to the purely economically determined "class situation," we wish to designate as "status situation" every typical component of the life fate of men that is determined by a specific, positive or negative, social estimation of *honor*. This honor may be connected with any quality shared by a plurality, and, of course, it can be knit to a class situation: class distinctions are linked in the most varied ways and with status distinctions. Property as such is not always recognized as a status qualification, but in the long run it is, and with extraordinary regularity. In the subsistence economy of the organized neighborhood, very often the richest man is simply the chieftain. However, this often means only an honorific preference. For example, in the so-called pure modern democracy, that is, one devoid of any expressly ordered status privileges for individuals, it may be that only the families coming under approximately the same tax class dance with one another. This example is reported of certain smaller Swiss cities. But status honor need not necessarily be linked with a class situation. On the contrary, it normally stands in sharp opposition to the pretensions of sheer property.

Both propertied and propertyless people can belong to the same status group, and frequently they do with very tangible consequences. This "equality" of social esteem may, however, in the long run become quite precarious. The equality of status among the American "gentlemen," for instance, is expressed by the fact that outside the subordination determined by the different functions of business, it would be considered strictly repugnant—wherever the old tradition still prevails—if even the richest "chief," while playing billiards or cards in his club in the evening, would not treat his "clerk" as in every sense fully his equal in birthright. It would be repugnant if the American chief would bestow upon his clerk the condescending benevolence marking a distinction of position, which the German chief can never dissever from his attitude. This is one of the most important reasons why in America the German "clubby-ness" has never been able to attain the attraction that the American clubs have.

GUARANTEES OF STATUS STRATIFICATION

In content, status honor is normally expressed by the fact that above all else a specific *style of life* can be expected from all those who wish to belong to the circle. Linked with this expectation are restrictions on social intercourse (that is, intercourse which is not subservient to economic or any other of business's "functional" purposes). These restrictions may confine normal marriages to within the status circle and may lead to complete endogamous closure. As soon as there is not a mere individual and socially irrelevant imitation of another style of life, but an agreed-upon communal action of this closing character, the status development is under way.

In its characteristic form, stratification by status groups on the basis of conventional styles of life evolves at the present time in the United States out of the traditional democracy. For example, only the resident of a certain street ("the street") is considered as belonging to society, is qualified for social intercourse, and is visited and invited. Above all, this differentiation evolves in such a way as to make for strict submission to the fashion that is dominant at a given time in society. This submission to fashion also exists among men in America to a degree unknown in Germany. Such submission is considered to be an indication of the fact that a given man *pretends* to qualify as a gentleman. This submission decides, at least *prima facie*, that he will be treated as such. And this recognition becomes just as important for his employment chances in swank establishments, and above all, for social intercourse and marriage with "esteemed" families, as the qualification for dueling among Germans in the Kaiser's day. As for the rest: certain families resident for a long time, and, of course, correspondingly wealthy, e.g., "F. F. V.," i.e., First Families of Virginia," or the actual or alleged descendants of the Indian Princess Pocahontas, of the Pilgrim fathers, or of the Knickerbockers, the members of almost inaccessible sects and all sorts of circles setting themselves apart by means of any other characteristics and badges . . . all these elements usurp status honor. The development of status is essentially a question of stratification resting upon usurpation. Such usurpation is the normal origin of almost all status honor. But the road from this purely conventional situation to legal privilege, positive or negative, is easily traveled as soon as a certain stratification of the social order has in fact been "lived in" and has achieved stability by virtue of a stable distribution of economic power.

ETHNIC SEGREGATION AND CASTE

Where the consequences have been realized to their full extent, the status group evolves into a closed "caste." Status distinctions are then guaranteed not merely by conventions and laws, but also by *rituals*. This occurs in such a way that every physical contact with a member of any caste that is considered to be "lower" by the members of a "higher" caste is considered as making for a ritualistic impurity and to be a stigma which must be expiated by a religious act. Individual castes develop quite distinct cults and gods.

In general, however, the status structure reaches such extreme consequences only where there are underlying differences which are held to be "ethnic." The caste is, indeed, the normal form in which ethnic communities usually live side by side in a "societalized" manner. These ethnic communities believe in blood relationship and exclude exogamous marriage and social intercourse. Such a caste situation is part of the phenomenon of "pariah" peoples and is found all over the world. These people form communities, acquire specific occupational traditions of handicrafts or of other arts, and cultivate a belief in their ethnic community. They live in a diaspora strictly segregated from all personal intercourse, except that of an unavoidable sort, and their situation is legally precarious. Yet, by virtue of their economic indispensability, they are tolerated, indeed, frequently privileged, and they live in interspersed political communities. The Jews are the most impressive historical example.

A status segregation grown into a caste differs in its structure from a mere ethnic segregation: the caste structure transforms the horizontal and unconnected coexistences of ethnically segregated groups into a vertical social system of super- and subordination. Correctly formulated: a comprehensive societalization integrates the ethnically divided communities into specific political and communal action. In their consequences they differ precisely in this way: ethnic coexistences condition a mutual repulsion and disdain but allow each ethnic community to consider its own honor as the highest one; the caste structure brings about a social subordination and an acknowledgment of "more honor" in favor of the privileged caste and status groups. This is due to the fact that in the caste structure ethnic distinctions as such have become "functional" distinctions within the political societalization (warriors, priests, artisans that are politically important for war and for building, and so on). But even pariah people who are most despised are usually apt to continue cultivating in some manner that which is equally peculiar to ethnic and to status communities: the belief in their own specific honor. This is the case with the Jews.

Only with the negatively privileged status groups does the "sense of dignity" take a specific deviation. A sense of dignity is the precipitation in individuals of social honor and of conventional demands which a positively privileged status group raises for the deportment of its members. The sense of dignity that characterizes positively privileged status groups is naturally related to their "being" which does not transcend itself, that is, it is to their "beauty and excellence" ($\kappa\alpha\lambda o$-$\kappa\dot{\alpha}\gamma\alpha\theta\iota\alpha$). Their kingdom is "of this world." They live for the present and by exploiting their great past. The sense of dignity of the negatively privileged strata naturally refers to a future lying beyond the present, whether it is of this life or of another. In other words, it must be nurtured by the belief in a providential mission and by a belief in a specific honor before God. The "chosen people's" dignity is nurtured by a belief either that in the beyond "the last will be the first," or that in this life a Messiah will appear to bring forth into the light of the world which has cast them out the hidden honor of the pariah people. This simple state of affairs, and not the resentment which is so strongly emphasized in Nietzsche's much admired construction in the *Genealogy of Morals*, is the source of the religiosity cultivated by pariah status groups. In passing, we may note that resentment may be accurately applied only to a limited extent; for one of Nietzsche's main examples, Buddhism, it is not at all applicable.

Incidentally, the development of status groups from ethnic segregations is by no means the normal phenomenon. On the contrary, since objective racial differences are by no means basic to every subjective sentiment of an ethnic community, the ultimately racial foundation of status structure is rightly and absolutely a question of the concrete individual case. Very frequently a status group is instrumental in the production of a thorough-bred anthropological type. Certainly a status group is to a high degree effective in producing extreme types, for they select personally qualified individuals (e.g., the Knighthood selects those who are fit for warfare, physically and psychically). But selection is far from being the only, or the predominant, way in which status groups are formed: Political membership or class situation has at all times been at least as frequently decisive. And today the class situation is by far the predominant factor, for of course the possibility of a style of life expected for members of a status group is usually conditioned economically.

STATUS PRIVILEGES

For all practical purposes, stratification by status goes hand in hand with a monopolization of ideal and material goods or opportunities, in a manner we have come to know as typical. Besides the specific status honor, which always rests upon distance and exclusiveness, we find all sorts of material monopolies. Such honorific preferences may consist of the privilege of wearing special costumes, of eating special dishes taboo to others, of carrying arms—which is most obvious in its consequences—the right to pursue certain nonprofessional dilettante artistic practices, e.g., to play certain musical instruments. Of course, material monopolies provide the most effective motives for the exclusiveness of a status group; although, in themselves, they are rarely sufficient, almost always they come into play to some extent. Within a status circle there is the question of intermarriage: the interest of the families in the monopolization of potential bridegrooms is at least of equal importance and is parallel to the interest in the monopolization of daughters. The daughters of the circle must be provided for. With an increased inclosure of the status group, the conventional preferential opportunities for special employment grow into a legal monopoly of special offices for the members. Certain goods become objects for monopolization by status groups. In the typical fashion these include "entailed estates" and frequently also the possessions of serfs or bondsmen and, finally, special trades. This monopolization occurs positively when the status group is exclusively entitled to own and to manage them; and negatively when, in order to maintain its specific way of life, the status group must *not* own and manage them.

The decisive role of a "style of life" in status honor means that status groups are the specific bearers of all "conventions." In whatever way it may be manifest, all "stylization" of life either originates in status groups or is at least conserved by them. Even if the principles of status conventions differ greatly, they reveal certain typical traits, especially among those strata which are most privileged. Quite generally, among privileged status groups there is a status disqualification that operates against the performance of common physical labor. This disqualification is now "setting in" in America against the old tradition of esteem for labor. Very frequently every rational economic pursuit, and especially entrepreneurial activity, is looked upon as a disqualification of status. Artistic and literary activity is also considered as degrading work as soon as it is exploited for income, or at least when it is connected with hard physical exertion. An example is the sculptor working like a mason in his dusty smock as over against the painter in his salonlike studio and those forms of musical practice that are acceptable to the status group.

The frequent disqualification of the gainfully employed as such is a direct result of the principle of status stratification peculiar to the social order, and of course, of this principle's opposition to a distribution of power which is regulated exclusively through the market. These two factors operate along with various individual ones, which will be touched upon below.

We have seen above that the market and its processes "knows no personal distinctions": "functional" interests dominate it. It knows nothing of "honor." The status order means precisely the reverse, viz.: stratification in terms of honor and of styles of life peculiar to status groups as such. If mere economic acquisition and naked economic power still bearing the stigma of its extrastatus origin could bestow upon anyone who has won it the same honor as those who are interested in status by virtue of style of life claim for themselves, the status order would be threatened at its very root. This is the more so as, given equality of status honor, property per se represents an addition even if it is not overtly acknowledged to be such. Yet if such economic acquisition and power gave the agent any honor at all, his wealth would result in his attaining more honor than those who successfully claim honor by virtue of style of life. Therefore all groups having interests in the status order react with special sharpness precisely against the pretensions of purely economic acquisition. In most cases they react the more vigorously the more they feel themselves threatened. Calderon's respectful treatment of the peasant, for instance, as opposed to Shakespeare's simultaneous and ostensible disdain of the *canaille* illustrates the different way in which a firmly structured status order reacts as compared with a status order that has become economically precarious. This is an example of a state of affairs that recurs everywhere. Precisely because of the rigorous reactions against the claims of property per se, the "parvenu" is never accepted, personally and without reservation, by the privileged status groups, no matter how completely his style of life has been adjusted to theirs. They will only accept his descendants who have been educated in the conventions of their status group and who have never besmirched its honor by their own economic labor.

As to the general *effect* of the status order, only one consequence can be stated, but it is a very important one: the hindrance of the free development of the market occurs first for those goods which status groups directly withheld from free exchange by monopolization. This monopolization may be effected either legally or conventionally. For example, in many Hellenic cities during the epoch of status groups, and also originally in Rome, the inherited estate (as is shown by the old formula for indiction against spend-thrifts) was monopolized just as were the estates of knights, peasants, priests, and especially the clientele of the craft and merchant guilds. The market is restricted, and the power of naked property *per se*, which gives its stamp to class formation, is pushed into the background. The results of this process can be most varied. Of course, they do not necessarily weaken the contrasts in the economic situation. Frequently they strengthen these contrasts, and in any case, where stratification by status permeates a community as strongly as was the case in all political communities of antiquity and of the Middle Ages, one can never speak of a genuinely free market competition as we understand it today. There are wider effects than this direct exclusion of special goods from the market. From the contrariety between the status order and the purely economic order mentioned above, it follows that in most instances the notion of honor peculiar to status absolutely abhors that which is essential to the market: higgling. Honor abhors higgling among peers and occasionally it taboos higgling for the members of a status group in general. Therefore, everywhere some status groups, and usually the most influential, consider almost any kind of overt participation in economic acquisition as absolutely stigmatizing.

With some oversimplification, one might thus say that classes are stratified according to their relations to the production and acquisition of goods; whereas status groups are stratified according to the principles of their *consumption* of goods as represented by special styles of life.

An occupational group is also a status group. For normally, it successfully claims social honor only by virtue of the special style of life which may be determined by it. The differences between classes and status groups frequently overlap. It is precisely those status communities most strictly segregated in terms of honor (*viz.* the Indian castes) who today show, although within very rigid limits, a relatively high degree of indifference to pecuniary income. However, the Brahmins seek such income in many different ways.

As to the general economic conditions making for the predominance of stratification by status, only very little can be said. When the bases of the acquisition and distribution of goods are relatively stable, stratification by status is favored. Every technological repercussion and economic transformation threatens stratification by status and pushes the class situation into the foreground. Epochs and countries in which the naked class situation is of predominant significance are regularly the periods of technical and economic transformations. And every slowing down of the shifting of economic stratifications leads, in due course, to the growth of status structures and makes for a resuscitation of the important role of social honor.

PARTIES

Whereas the genuine place of classes is within the economic order, the place of status groups is within the social order, that is, within the sphere of the distribution of "honor." From within these spheres, classes and status groups influence one another and they influence the legal order and are in turn influenced by it. But "parties" live in a house of "power."

Their action is oriented toward the acquisition of social power, that is to say, toward influencing a communal action no matter what its content may be. In principle, parties may exist in a social club as well as in a state. As over against the actions of classes and status groups, for which this is not necessarily the case, the communal actions of parties always mean a societalization. For party actions are always directed toward a goal which is striven for in planned manner. This goal may be a cause (the party may aim at realizing a program for ideal or material purposes), or the goal may be personal (sinecures, power, and from these, honor for the leader and the followers of the party). Usually the party action aims at all these simultaneously. Parties are, therefore, only possible within communities that are societalized, that is, which have some rational order and a staff of persons available who are ready to enforce it. For parties aim precisely at influencing this staff, and if possible, to recruit it from party followers.

In any individual case, parties may represent interests determined through class situation or status situation, and they may recruit their following respectively from one or the other. But they need be neither purely class nor purely status parties. In most cases they are partly class parties and partly status parties, but sometimes they are neither. They may represent ephemeral or enduring structures. Their means of attaining power may be quite varied, ranging from naked violence of any sort to canvassing for votes with coarse or subtle means: money, social influence, the force of speech, suggestion, clumsy hoax, and so on to the rougher or more artful tactics of obstruction in parliamentary bodies.

The sociological structure of parties differs in a basic way according to the kind of communal action which they struggle to influence. Parties also differ according to whether or not the community is stratified by status or by classes. Above all else, they vary according to the structure of domination within the community. For their leaders normally deal with the conquest of a community. They are, in the general concept which is maintained here, not only products of specially modern forms of domination. We shall also designate as parties the ancient and medieval parties, despite the fact that their structure differs basically from the structure of modern parties. By virtue of these structural differences of domination it is impossible to say anything about the structure of parties without discussing the structural forms of social domination *per se*. Parties, which are always structures struggling for domination, are very frequently organized in a very strict authoritarian fashion. . .

Concerning classes, status groups, and parties, it must be said in general that they necessarily presuppose a comprehensive societalization, and especially a political framework of communal action, within which they operate. This does not mean that parties would be confined by the frontiers of any individual political community. On the contrary, at all times it has been the order of the day that the societalization (even when it aims at the use of military force in common) reaches beyond the frontiers of politics. This has been the case in the solidarity of interests among the Oligarchs and among the democrats in Hellas, among the Guelfs and among Ghibellines in the Middle Ages, and within the Calvinist party during the period of religious struggles. It has been the case up to the solidarity of the landlords (international congress of agrarian landlords), and has continued among princes (holy alliance, Karlsbad decrees), socialist workers, conservatives (the longing of Prussian conservatives for Russian intervention in 1850). But their aim is not necessarily the establishment of new international political, i.e., territorial, dominion. In the main they aim to influence the existing dominion.[2]

NOTES

[1] *Wirtschaft und Gesellschaft*, Part III, Chap. 4, pp. 631–40. The first sentence in paragraph one and the several definitions in this chapter which are in brackets do not appear in the original text. They have been taken from other contexts of *Wirtschaft und Gesellschaft*.

[2] The posthumously published text breaks off here. An incomplete sketch of types of "warrior estates" is omitted.

15 JOHN H. GOLDTHORPE

Social Stratification in Industrial Society

For a decade or so now, a growing interest has been apparent, chiefly among American sociologists, in the pattern of long-term social change within relatively mature industrial societies. This interest appears to derive from two main sources.

In the first place, it can be seen as resulting from broadly based studies of the sociology of industrialization, concentrating originally on the underdeveloped or developing countries of the world. For example, work conducted as part of the Inter-University Study of Labour Problems in Economic Development led up to the theoretical statement on the "logic" of industrialism attempted by Clark Kerr and his associates in their book, *Industrialism and Industrial Man*.[1] Secondly, this interest has undoubtedly been stimulated by the revival in comparative studies of social structure and social processes in economically advanced countries. Important here, for example, has been the work of Professor Lipset and a number of other

Reprinted from *The Development of Industrial Society*, edited by Paul Halmos (*The Sociological Review*, Monograph No. 8, 1964), pp. 97–122 by permission of the publisher.

members of the Berkeley campus of the University of California; and even more so, perhaps, studies which have chiefly involved comparisons between Western and Communist societies, such as those produced in connection with the Harvard Project on the Soviet Social System by Professor Inkeles and his colleagues.[2]

However, it is notable that in spite of possibly different origins, current American interpretations of the development of industrial societies often reveal marked similarities. Basically, it may be said, they tend to be alike in stressing the standardizing effects upon social structures of the exigencies of modern technology and of an advanced economy. These factors which make for uniformity in industrial societies are seen as largely overriding other factors which may make for possible diversity, such as different national cultures or different political systems. Thus, the overall pattern of development which is suggested is one in which, once countries enter into the advanced stages of industrialization, they tend to become increasingly comparable in their major institutional arrangements and in their social systems generally. In brief, a *convergent* pattern of development is hypothesized.

Kerr and his associates have been the most explicit in this connection— and also in the matter of specifying the type of society on which the process of convergence is focussed. In their conception, "the road ahead" for all advanced societies leads in the direction of what they call "pluralistic" industrialism. By this they mean a form of industrial society in which the distribution of power is neither "atomistic" nor "monistic," nor yet radically disputed by warring classes; but rather a social order in which an "omnipresent State" regulates competition and conflict between a multiplicity of interest groups on the basis of an accepted "web of rules," and at the same time provides the means through which a degree of democratic control can be exercised over the working of the economy and over other key social processes such as the provision of welfare and public services, education and so on.[3] Other theorists have usually been a good deal more guarded than this in their formulations; but it would nonetheless be fair to say that, in the main, they have adopted views which have been broadly consistent with the Kerr thesis. In general, the "logic" of industrialism has been regarded as powerfully encouraging, even if not compelling, the emergence of a new type of society from out of former "class" and "mass" societies alike.[4]

Clearly, then, a central theme in the interpretations in question concerns the development in advanced societies of systems of social stratification. And it is perhaps indicative of the importance of this theme that it has on several occasions been singled out for special discussion. In this paper[5] my main purpose will be to consider this particular aspect of current theories of industrialism and, further, to raise certain doubts and objections which seem to me to be of a serious kind and to have negative implications for these theories *in toto*. But at the outset I should say that I in no way intend to criticize the *kind* of sociological endeavour which is here represented. On the contrary, we are, I believe, much indebted to the authors of these theories for showing us a way to escape from the cramped quarters of trivialized empiricism without falling victim to highly speculative building with "empty boxes."

The arguments concerning the development of social stratification which form a core element in American interpretations of industrialism can be usefully stated under three main heads: differentiation, consistency and mobility.[6] To begin with, I would like to consider these three sets of arguments in turn.

DIFFERENTIATION

In regard to differentiation, the major proposition that is put forward is that, in the course of industrial advance, there is a decrease in the degree of differentiation in all stratification subsystems or orders. In other words, to follow Inkeles' formulation: "a process of relative homogenization takes place, reducing the gap or range separating the top and bottom of the scale"—in income and wealth, in status formal and informal, and in political powers.[7] As a result of this process, a marked increase occurs within each stratification order in the proportion of the total population falling into the middle ranges of the distribution. The "shape" of the stratification hierarchy thus ceases to be pyramidal and approximates, rather, to that of a pentagon or even of a diamond.

This trend is related to the "logic" of industrialism in several different ways. But, primarily, the connection is seen as being through the changing division of labour. An advancing technology and economy continually repattern the occupational structure, and in ways which progressively increase the number of higher level occupational roles; that is to say, roles requiring relatively high standards of education and training and at the same time commanding relatively high economic rewards and social status. Thus, the middle of the stratification hierarchy becomes considerably expanded.

So far as Western societies are concerned, a further factor in this homogenizing process is also recognized in the growing intervention of the state in economic affairs; particularly in governmental policies which lead to the redistribution and control of economic power. For example, it is observed that policies of progressive taxation and of social welfare in various ways modify for the benefit of the less privileged the division of income and balance of social advantage which would have resulted from the free operation of market mechanisms. However, in this case great stress is placed on the close relationship that exists between this expansion in the regulatory functions of government and the direct requirements of the industrialization process. The state, it is argued, *must* be the key regulatory organization in any advanced society: the complexity of its technology and economy demand this. At minimum, the state must be responsible for the general rate of economic progress, and thus ultimately, for the overall allocation of resources between uses and individuals, for the quality of the national labour force, for the economic and social security of individuals and so on.[8]

In other words, even where greater social equality results directly from the purposive action of governments, the tendency is to see behind this action not a particular complex of sociopolitical beliefs, values or interests but rather the inherent compulsions of "industrialism" itself.[9] For example, on the subject of the development of education and its consequences, Kerr and his associates write as follows:

> Education is intended to reduce the scarcity of skilled persons and this after a time reduces the wage and salary differentials they receive; it also pulls people out of the least skilled and most disagreeable occupations and raises wage levels there. *It conduces to a new equality which has nothing to do with ideology. . . .*[10]

Furthermore, one should note, a similar viewpoint is taken in arguing that greater equality in political power—in the form of a pluralistic system—will tend to emerge in societies which now have totalitarian (or autocratic) regimes. In the first place, it is held, the production technolology of an industrial society is such that any regime must become increasingly interested in the consent of the mass of the labour force; for the efficient use of this technology requires responsible initiative and freely given cooperation on the part of those who operate it. Secondly, the growing complexity of technical problems arising in the process of government itself necessitates the greater involvement in decision-making of experts and professionals, and in this way the latter come to acquire some independent authority. Thus, a monolithic structure gives way to one in which there are a number of "strategic" elites and of different foci of power. In brief, industrialism is regarded as being ultimately inimical to any form of monistic political order.[11]

CONSISTENCY

In this respect, the central argument is that as societies become increasingly industrial, there is a growing tendency within the stratification system towards what Inkeles terms "equilibration"; that is, a tendency for the relative position of an individual or group in any one stratification order to be the same as, or similar to, their position in other orders.[12] In traditional societies, it is observed, inconsistencies in the stratification system may have been contrary to the prevailing ideology but were nonetheless frequent because of the rigidity of the levels within the different subsystems and the relatively low degree of interaction between them. For example, a merchant might become extremely wealthy yet be debarred from "noble" status; in fact, legally, he could be of peasant status and might be treated as such in certain circumstances in spite of his wealth. In industrial societies, by contrast, there are far fewer difficulties in the way of "adjustments" which serve to bring the position of individuals and groups more or less into line from one stratification order to another. Moreover, there is also a shift away from the relative diversity of the bases of stratification which is characteristic of traditional society. With industrialism, the occupational structure takes on overwhelming primacy in this respect. The occupational rôle of the individual is in general in close correlation with most other of his attributes which are relevant to his position in the stratification hierarchy as a whole: his economic situation, his educational level, his prestige in the local community and so on.[13]

In the same way as the trend towards greater equality, the trend towards greater consistency in stratification systems is also treated as an integral part of the industrialization process and as being directly linked to technological and economic advance. In industrial society, it is argued, the distribution of both economic rewards and prestige must come into a close relationship with occupational performance since this type of society in fact presupposes an overriding emphasis upon achievement, as opposed to ascription, as the basis of social position—and specifically upon achievement in the sphere of production. At the same time, though, as a result of technological progress, occupational achievement becomes increasingly dependent upon education, and in this way closer ties are formed between economic standing on the one hand and life-styles and subculture on the other. The ignorant and vulgar tycoon and the poor scholar are seen alike as figures of declining importance. In other words, the argument is that inevitably in modern societies, the various determinants of an individual's placing in the overall stratification hierarchy come to form a tight nexus; and that in this nexus occupation can be regarded as the central element— providing as it does the main link between the "objective" and "subjective" aspects of social inequality.

Implicit, then, in this interpretation is the view that in industrial societies stratification systems tend to become relatively highly integrated, in the sense that specifically class differences (i.e., those stemming from inequalities in the economic order) are generally paralleled by status differences (i.e., those based on inequalities in social evaluation); and, thus, that changes in the pattern of the former will automatically result in changes in the pattern of the latter. For example, Kerr and his associates see the growth of "middle incomes" as making for a "middle class society"; that is, a society in which middle class values are widely accepted, both among manual workers and elite groups, and in which the bulk of the population share in "middle class" status.[14]

MOBILITY

In regard to mobility, the central proposition that is made is one which complements the previous arguments concerning differentiation and consistency. It is that once societies have reached a certain level of industrialization, their overall rates of social mobility tend to become relatively high—higher that is, than is typical in preindustrial or traditional societies. The increasing number of intermediate positions in the stratification hierarchy widens the opportunity for movement upward from the lower levels, while the emphasis upon occupational achievement rather than on the ascription of social positions means that intergenerationally the talented will tend to rise at the expense of those whose talent is unequal to their birth. In this respect, the educational system is seen as the crucial allocative mechanism, sieving ability and matching capacity to the demands and responsibilities of occupational roles.[15]

In other words, then, industrial society is regarded as being essentially "open" and "meritocratic." And once more, one should note, the interpretation derives from a conception of the structural and functional imperatives of this type of social order. The high level of mobility is taken as an inevitable consequence of the technologically and economically determined division of labour and of the necessary pressure within a highly dynamic form of society for the increasingly efficient use of talent. To quote again from the authors of *Industrialism and Industrial Man*:

> The industrial society is an open community encouraging occupational and geographic mobility and social mobility. In this sense industrialism *must* be flexible and competitive; it is against tradition and status based upon family, class, religion, race or caste.[16]

In this approach, thus, there is little room for consideration of institutional variations or of value differences between industrial societies which might be associated with *differing* patterns of mobility. It is taken that the overall similarities in this respect are, or at any rate are certainly becoming, the feature of major significance.

These, then, in a necessarily abbreviated form, are the main arguments concerning the development of stratification systems which figure, with varying degrees of refinement or crudity, in current American theories of industrialism. I would now like to turn to what I have to say by way of criticism of these arguments and, to begin with, I would like to comment on each of the three themes on which I based the foregoing exposition. My main purpose here will be to indicate that the views which I have outlined are not always in entire accord with empirical data, and in this connection I shall refer primarily to the industrial societies of the West. Subsequently, however, I shall offer certain more basic, theoretical criticisms which are suggested by a consideration of social stratification in modern Communist society.

On the question of reduced differentiation—or greater equality—in stratification systems, my remarks at this stage will be largely confined to the economic order. This is because it is chiefly in this regard that we have data which will permit, at least in principle, some test of the arguments involved; that is, data on the distributions of income and wealth.[17]

At the outset it may be said that, although the evidence is often very patchy, a broad trend towards greater economic equality *does* seem to be discernible in the case of all those societies which have so far progressed from a traditional to an industrial form. Myths of "golden ages" of economic equality in pre-industrial times are now little heeded, and, as a rough generalization, it would, I think, be widely accepted that the poorer the society, the greater the "skew" one may expect in its distributions of income and wealth alike.[18] With this view I would not wish to quarrel—provided that it is taken merely as a formula summing up historical experience, and as one which is subject to exceptions. But there are no grounds at all, in my view, for regarding the regularity in question as manifesting the operation of some process inherent in industrialism—of some general economic law—which will necessarily persist in the future and ensure a continuing egalitarian trend. Rather, the possibility must be left quite open that where such a trend exists, it may at some point be checked—and at a point, moreover, at which considerable economic *in*equality remains. In fact, in my assessment, the relevant data suggest that such a check may already be occurring in some of the more advanced societies of the West; or, at any rate, I would say that on present evidence *this* conclusion is indicated as much as any other.

For the distributions of income and wealth alike, it is true that figures exist to show a movement towards greater equality in most western industrial societies over the years for which adequate time-series are available; that is, from the late interwar or early postwar period onwards.[19] However, it is now becoming increasingly clear that these figures, which are largely based on tax returns, are not always to be taken at their face value. And, in general, their defects appear to be such that they tend on balance to underestimate the income and wealth which accrue to the economically more favoured groups and in this and other ways to give a somewhat exaggerated idea of the degree of "levelling" that has taken place. In fact, for some western societies at least, there are now grounds for believing that during the last twenty years or so, overall economic inequality has in reality declined only very little, if at all. And particularly so far as wealth is concerned, it is likely that such changes as have occurred have been virtually negligible in their implications for social stratification.[20] Such conclusions have been suggested for the United Kingdom, for example, in Professor Titmuss' recent study, *Income Distribution and Social Change*. It must, of course, be admitted that the whole matter remains a highly controversial one,[21] and it is not possible here to enter into all its complexities. But what is, I think, justified by the evidence, and what is certainly most relevant to my general argument, is Titmuss' contention that "we should be much more hesitant in suggesting that any equalising forces at work in Britain since 1938 can be promoted to the status of a 'natural law' and projected into the future. . . . There are other forces, deeply rooted in the social structure and fed by many complex institutional factors inherent in large-scale economies, operating in reverse directions."[22]

A similar point of view is maintained, with reference to the United States, in Gabriel Kolko's somewhat neglected book, *Wealth and Power in America*. This study involves not only a critique of previous findings on the distribution of income and wealth in the USA but also a positive reappraisal of the situation. This is particularly important in regard to income. Kolko supplements material from official sources with generally more reliable survey data, and on this basis suggests that over as long a period as 1910 to 1959 there has been no significant *general* trend in the USA towards greater income equality.[23]

Kolko's study prompts one to note the often overlooked point that simply because there may be some levelling of incomes going on in *certain ranges* of the total income distribution, this does not necessarily mean that *overall* equality is increasing; for in other ranges inegalitarian trends may simultaneously be operating. For example, there may be a tendency towards greater equality in that the number of middle-range incomes is growing; but at the same time the position of the lower income groups, relative to the upper and middle groups alike, may be worsening.

In fact, it seems more than possible that a pattern of change of this kind is now going on in the United States. This is indicated by a good deal of recent investigation, apart from that of Kolko, and particularly by the growing volume of work on the extent of poverty. Gunnar Myrdal, for example, has argued in his book, *Challenge to Affluence*, that while many Americans in the intermediate social strata may well be benefiting from a levelling upwards of living standards, at the base of the stratification hierarchy there is increasing inequality, manifested in the emergence of an "underclass" of unemployed and unemployable persons and families. In other words, the middle ranks of the income distribution may be swelling, but the gap between the bottom and the higher levels is, if anything, tending to widen.[24]

Moreover, what is also significant in Myrdal's study for present purposes is the way in which he brings out the *political* aspects of the problem. Myrdal observes that structural unemployment, resulting from technological innovation in industry, is a basic, and increasingly serious, cause of poverty in America, whereas, in a country like Sweden, in which technological advance is also proceeding rapidly, full employment has been steadily maintained. Again, he notes the relative failure of the United States, compared with most western European countries, to stabilize aggregate demand in its economy on a high and rising level.[25] The explanation of these differences, Myrdal then argues, while not of course entirely political, must nonetheless be regarded as being significantly so. In particular, he stresses the inadequate achievement of government in America in long-range economic planning, in redistributional reforms, and in the provision of public services and advanced social welfare schemes. And the sources of this governmental inadequacy he traces back to certain basic American sociopolitical dispositions and also to a relative lack of "democratic balance" in the institutional infrastructure of the American policy. On the one hand, Myrdal claims, there is among the powerful business community and within government itself a reluctance to take the long view and to envisage more central direction and control of the economy; also "a serious and irrational bias against public investment and consumption." On the other hand, among the lower strata of American society there is an unusual degree of political apathy and passivity which is most clearly seen in the general failure of the poorer sections of the population to organize themselves effectively and to press for the fundamental social reforms that would be in their interest. In this way an imbalance in organized power is brought about within the "plural society" which makes the need for initiative on the part of government all the more pressing—at the same time as it seems to paralyse this.[26]

If, then, Myrdal's analysis has any general validity—and it has yet, I think, to be seriously disputed—it follows that we should look somewhat doubtfully on arguments about a new equality which "has nothing to do with ideology" but which is the direct outcome of technological and economic advance. Such new equality there may be for some. But for those at the base of stratification hierarchies at least—how "equal" they are likely to become seems to have a good deal to do with ideology, or at any rate with purposive social action, or lack of this, stemming from specific social values and political creeds as well as from interests.[27] And differences between some industrial societies in these respects may well be giving rise to divergent, rather than convergent, patterns of change in their stratification systems.

On the second set of arguments—those concerning growing consistency between different stratification orders—I shall have relatively little to say for the good reason that there is little empirical data which directly bears on the crucial issue here; that is, the issue of whether there really is a *continuing* increase in the degree of integration of the stratification systems of *advanced* societies. About the long-term historical trend, one would not wish to argue; but again it is a question of whether such a trend is a reliable guide to the present and the future.

My main comment is that such evidence as does appear relevant to this issue indicates that in some industrial societies, at least, on-going economic progress is resulting in stratification systems becoming, if anything, somewhat *less* well integrated in certain respects. This evidence refers to what has become known as the "new working class." It suggests that the appreciable gains in income and in general living standards recently achieved by certain sections of the manual labour force have not for the most part been accompanied by changes in their life-styles of such a kind that their *status* position has been enhanced commensurately with their *economic* position. In other words, there is evidence of cultural and, in particular, of "social" barriers still widely existing between "working class" and "middle class" even in cases where immediate material differences have now disappeared.[28] Thus it seems that, contrary to the expectations of Kerr and his associates, "middle incomes" have not resulted, as yet at least, in the generalization of "middle class" ways of life or of "middle class" status.

Moreover, there are grounds for believing that notable discrepancies in stratification will persist in industrial societies. As Kerr himself recognizes, there will still exist in the foreseeable future in such societies a division between "managers" and "managed"—between those who are in some way associated with the exercise of authority in productive and administrative organizations and those who are not. And this division, one would suggest, will remain associated with differences in prestige, as well as in power, while at the same time managers and managed overlap to some extent in terms of living standards. One would agree that in an economically advanced society a broad stratum of workers, performing skilled or, one would add, particularly arduous or irksome jobs, are likely to earn middle-range incomes. But there are no grounds for automatically assuming that they will thereby become socially accepted and assimilated into even the lower levels of what Renner has usefully termed the "service class."[29] After all, it must be recognized that groups which have some serious basis for claiming superior status generally take advantage of this. And further, it should be borne in mind that, increasingly, the members of this "service class" will be selected through their educational attainments rather than being recruited from the rank and file. Thus, if anything, they are likely to become more set apart from the latter in terms of culture and life-styles than they are at present.

In sum, one might suggest that the "increasing consistency" argument is flawed because it fails to take into account first, that occupational roles with similar economic rewards may in some instances be quite differently related to the exercise of authority; and secondly, that relatively high income may serve as recompense for work of otherwise high "disutility" to the operative as well as for work involving expertise and responsibility.

Lastly, then, we come to the matter of social mobility. In this case, the first question which arises is that of whether it is in fact valid to regard industrial societies as having regularly higher rates of mobility than pre-industrial societies. Several writers, one should note, have recently argued that this view should not be too readily taken and have produced evidence to suggest that certain pre-industrial societies were far less rigidly stratified than seems generally to have been supposed.[30] Nevertheless, I would not wish to argue here against the more orthodox view, except to make the point that an increased rate of *inter*generational mobility in advanced societies is likely to be associated with some limitation of *intra*generational or "career" mobility. To the extent that education becomes a key determinant of occupational achievement, the chances of "getting ahead" for those who start in a lowly position are inevitably diminished. This fact is most clearly demonstrated in recent studies of the recruitment of industrial managers. These show that as the educational standards of managers have risen, the likelihood of shop floor workers being promoted above supervisory level has been reduced.[31] Furthermore, in an advanced society, increasingly dominated by large scale organizations, the possibilities for the "little man" of starting up a successful business of his own also tend to be more limited than they were at an earlier phase in the industrialization process. Thus, for that large proportion of the population at least, with rank-and-file jobs and "ordinary" educational qualifications, industrial society appears to be growing significantly *less* "open" than it once was.

However, other, and perhaps more basic, issues arise from the arguments concerning mobility which I earlier outlined; in particular issues relating to the determinants of mobility patterns and rates. What are the grounds, one might ask, for believing that in advanced societies the crucial factor here is the occupational distribution, and thus that from one such society to another social mobility will tend to be much the same? Support for this view can be found in the well-known Lipset and Zetterberg study which led, in fact, to the conclusion that Western industrial societies have broadly similar rates of intergenerational mobility, and which produced no evidence to suggest that factors other than the "standardizing" one of the occupational structure were of major significance.[32] Their data, the authors claim, give no backing for the idea that differences in social ideologies, religious beliefs or other aspects of national cultures exercise a decisive influence on mobility. But it has to be noted that, as Lipset and Zetterberg themselves make quite clear, their findings in this respect refer only to "mass" mobility; that is, simply to movements across the manual-nonmanual line. And indeed they point out that the investigation of some aspects of "élite" mobility—for example, the recruitment of higher civil servants—has indicated some important national variations.[33]

Moreover, we have more recently the outstanding study of comparative social mobility made by Professor S. M. Miller.[34] This covers a still greater amount of data than Lipset and Zetterberg's work and demonstrates fairly conclusively that when *range* as well as frequency of mobility is taken into consideration, industrial societies do reveal quite sizeable differences in their mobility patterns. Such differences tend to be most evident in the case of long-range mobility. This is generally low—another reason for querying just how "open" and "meritocratic" industrial societies have so far become—but certain countries, the USA and USSR, for example, appear to have attained quite significantly higher rates of "élite" mobility than do others, such as many in western Europe. Further, though, Miller shows that countries with low long-range mobility may still have relatively high short-range mobility—as, for instance, does Great Britain: there is no correlation between rates of mobility of differing distance. Thus, industrial societies have quite various "mobility profiles"; the overall similarity indicated by the study of "mass" mobility turns out to be somewhat spurious.

On this basis, then, Miller is able to argue very strongly that patterns of social mobility in advanced societies cannot be understood *simply* in terms of occupational structure[35]—or, one would add, in terms of any "inherent" features of industrialism. Their diversity precludes this. It appears necessary, rather, to consider also the effects on mobility of other, and more variable, aspects of social structure—educational institutions, for example, and their articulation with the stratification hierarchy itself—

and further, possibly, *pace* Lipset and Zetterberg, the part played by cultural values.[36] As Miller points out, what is perhaps most surprising about his data is the *lack* of convergence in mobility patterns that is indicated between societies at broadly comparable levels of economic development. The "logic" of industrialism, it appears, is often confused by "extraneous" factors.

These, then, are some of the objections that may be made on empirical grounds to the hypotheses concerning changes in stratification systems which I previously outlined. Accepting the arguments in question on their own terms, as it were, it is possible to indicate a number of points at which they do not appear to fit well with the findings of empirical research in western industrial societies or, at least, at which they remain unproven. However, in conclusion of this paper, I would like to make a more basic objection which relates to the theoretical position underlying these arguments. Specifically, I would like to question the idea that the stratification systems of all industrial societies are *ipso facto* of the same generic type, and thus that they may in principle be expected to follow convergent or parallel lines of development. Against this view, I would like to suggest that social stratification in the advanced societies of the Communist world —or at any rate in the USSR and its closer satellites—is *not* of the same generic type as in the West and that, because of this, the hypotheses earlier discussed cannot in this case really apply.

Soviet society is, of course, stratified; and, furthermore, it is true that in spite of the absence of private property in production, it appears to be stratified on an often similar pattern to the capitalist or post-capitalist societies of the West. For example, to a large degree there is apparent similarity in the connections between occupational role, economic rewards and social prestige, in the part played by education in determining occupational level, in the operation of an informal status system, and so on. But, I would argue, this similarity is only of a phenotypical kind: genotypically, stratification in Soviet society is significantly different from stratification in the West.

Primarily, it may be said, this difference derives from the simple fact that in Soviet society the economy operates within a "monistic," or totalitarian, political order and is, in principle at least, totally planned, whereas in advanced Western societies political power is significantly less concentrated and the economy is planned in a far less centralized and detailed way. From this it results that in the West economic, and specifically market forces act as the crucial stratifying agency within society. They are, one could say, the major source of social inequality. And consequently, the *class* situation of individuals and groups, understood in terms of their economic power and resources, tends to be the most important single determinant of their general life-chances. This is why we can usefully speak of Western industrial society as being "class" stratified. However, in the case of Soviet society, market forces cannot be held to play a comparable role in the stratification process. These forces operate, of course, and differences in economic power and resources between individuals and groups have, as in the West, far-reaching social and human consequences. But, one would argue, to a significantly greater extent than in the West, stratification in Soviet society is subjected to *political* regulation; market forces are not permitted to have the primacy or the degree of autonomy in this respect that they have even in a "managed" capitalist society. Undoubtedly, the functional requirements of the economy exert pressures upon the system of stratification, and these pressures may in some cases prove to be imperative. But the nature of the political order means that far more than with Western democracy, the pattern of social inequality can be shaped through the purposive action of the ruling party, and still more so, of course, the "life-fates" of particular persons.[37]

For example, during the years of Stalin's rule, economic inequality in the USSR generally increased. Numerous writers have in fact commented upon the progressive abandonment over this period of the egalitarian aspects of Marxist-Leninist ideology and of post-revolutionary attempts to operate egalitarian economic and social policies.[38] From the early 1930's differential rewards in relation to skill, effort and responsibility were introduced into industry and administration, and thus from this point the range of wages and salaries tended to widen. Further, changes in the 1940's in the income tax and inheritance laws were conducive to greater inequalities in incomes and personal wealth alike. Then again, high ranking officials and other favoured persons appear to have received increasingly important non-monetary rewards in the form of cars, apartments, villas, free holidays and so on. By the end of the war decade, these developments had led to a degree of inequality in Soviet society which, in the view of many commentators, was greater than that which was generally to be found in the industrial societies of the West.[39] However, in more recent years it has become clear that contrary to most expectations, this inegalitarian trend in the USSR has been checked and, moreover, that in certain respects at least it has even been reversed. Minimum wages in industry have been increased several times since the late 1950's and the incomes of the *kolkhozy* have for the most part risen quite considerably. This latter development has had the effect of closing somewhat the income gap between industrial and agricultural workers and has also been associated with a reduction in differentials in the earnings of the *kolkhoz* peasants themselves. At the same time, there is evidence of limitations being placed on the more excessive salaries of higher officials and of more stringent measures being taken against the abuse of privileges. Finally, tax changes in the past few years have tended to favour the poorer against the richer groups, and various kinds of welfare provision have been substantially improved. In these ways, then, economic differences between the manual and nonmanual categories overall have almost certainly been reduced to some extent, as well as differences within these categories.[40]

Now these changes can, of course, be rightly regarded as being in some degree economically conditioned. Clearly, for instance, the increased differentiation in wages and salaries in the Stalin era must in part be understood in terms of the exigencies and consequences of rapid industrialization. But, I would argue, there can be little question that at the same time these changes were the outcome of political decisions—of choices made between realistic alternatives—and, furthermore, that frequently they were brought about with political as well as with specifically economic ends in view. Stalin, it is true, wanted rapid industrialization: but he had the further political objective that this process should be carried through under his own absolute control. Thus, this entailed not only depriving a large section of the population of material returns from their labour in order to achieve maximum expansion of industrial capacity, but also the building-up of a group of exceptionally favoured administrators and managers who would be highly motivated to retain their enviable positions through loyalty to Stalin and through high level performance. To this latter end, in fact, appropriate status as well as economic inequalities were also developed. For example, during and after the war years, formal titles, uniforms and insignia of rank were introduced into various branches of industry and the governmental bureaucracy. Moreover, the wide social distance which was in this way created between the top and bottom of the stratification hierarchy had the manifest function of insulating the "élite" from the masses and from their needs and wishes. And thus, as Professor Feldmesser has pointed out, those in high positions were helped to learn "that success was to be had by winning the favour not of those below them but of those above them, which was exactly what Stalin wanted them to learn."[41]

Similarly, the more recent moves towards reducing inequalities have again fairly evident political aims, even though, in some cases, they may also have been economically required.[42] On the one hand, it seems clear that the present Soviet leadership is working towards a future Communist society which will be characterized by a high level of social welfare, and indeed eventually by private affluence, while still remaining under the undisputed dominance of the Party. In other words, the creation of the "good life" for all appears destined to become one of the regime's most important sources of legitimacy. In fact, as Professor Shapiro has noted, the 1961 Programme of the CPSU makes this more or less explicit. The Programme, he writes,

> enunciates squarely the concrete fact that party rule has come to stay. It calls upon the Soviet citizen to recognize and accept this fact, and to abandon the illusion that in this respect, things are going to change. In return, it promises him great material benefits and prosperity.[43]

On the other hand, the security of the regime also requires that the bureaucratic and managerial "élite" does not become so well established as to gain some measure of independence from the Party chiefs. Thus, Khrushchev has been concerned to show the members of this group that they remain the creatures of the Party and that their privileges are not permanent but still rest upon their obedience and service to the Party. Those whom Djilas has referred to as the "new class" in Communist society[44] cannot in fact be allowed by the Party leadership to become a class—in the sense of a collectivity which is capable of maintaining its position in society (and that of its children) through its own social power, and which possesses some degree of group consciousness and cohesion. For the emergence of such a class would constitute a serious threat to the Party's totalitarian rule, different only in degree from the threat that would be posed by the emergence of an independent trade union, professional body or political organization. It is awareness of this danger, one would suggest, which chiefly lies behind the recent attacks—verbal as well as material—which have been made upon higher officialdom and the top industrial personnel. For apart from the curtailment of economic rewards in some cases, it is interesting to note that the quasi-military status distinctions of the war decade have now been largely abolished and that the Party has actually encouraged rank and file employees in industry and agriculture to expose inadequacy and inefficiency on the part of their superiors.[45] Furthermore, there has been some weeding out of superfluous posts, and demotions appear to have become much more common.[46] Finally, though, it is probably Khrushchev's educational reforms which have been of greatest significance. These were carried through at a time when pressure on the institutions of secondary and higher education was reaching a peak; yet they were designed to make access to these institutions less dependent than previously upon economic resources and the new rules for competitive entry which were introduced seem, if anything, to shift the balance of "social" advantage away from the children of the "élite" and towards candidates from worker or peasant families. As Feldmesser notes, if a "new class"—a "state bourgeoisie"—were in fact in existence in the USSR, then exactly the reverse of this might have been expected; that is, a move to make access to these scarce facilities *more*, rather than less, dependent upon the ability to pay.[47]

It is then not too much to say that in Soviet society hierarchical differentiation is an instrument of the regime. To a significant degree stratification is *organized* in order to suit the political needs of the regime; and, as these needs change, so too may the particular structure of inequality. In other words, the Soviet system of stratification is characterized by an important element of "deliberateness," and it is this which basically distinguishes it from the Western system, in spite of the many apparent similarities. In the industrial societies of the West, one could say, the action of the state sets limits to the extent of social inequalities which derive basically from the operation of a market economy: in Soviet society the pattern of inequality also results in part from "market" forces, but in this case these are subordinated to political control up to the limits set by the requirements of the industrial system.[48] For this reason, one may conclude, Soviet society is not, in the same way as Western society, *class* stratified. As Raymond Aron has observed, class stratification and a monistic political system are to be regarded as incompatibles.[49]

If, then, the foregoing analysis is accepted, it follows that the arguments I earlier outlined on the development of stratification systems can have no general validity. Their underlying rationale, in terms of the exigencies of an advanced industrial technology and economy, is destroyed. The experience of Soviet society can be taken as indicating that the structural and functional imperatives of an industrial order are not so stringent as to prevent quite wide variations in patterns of social stratification, nor to prohibit the systematic manipulation of social inequalities by a regime commanding modern administrative resources and under no constraints from an organized opposition or the rule of law.

The crucial point, in fact, at which the rationale breaks down is in the supposition that industrialism and totalitarianism cannot "in the long run" coexist; that is, in the idea that with industrial advance a progressive diffusion of political power must of necessity occur. Were this idea valid, then it would become difficult to maintain the claim that differences between the stratification systems of the Western and Communist worlds are of a generic kind. However, it may be said that no serious grounds exist for believing that within Soviet society any such diffusion of power is taking place, or at least, not so far as the key decision-making processes are concerned.[50] The regime may be compelled to give more consideration to the effect of its decisions on popular morale and to rely increasingly on the expertise of scientists, technicians and professionals of various kinds; it may also find it desirable to decentralize administration and to encourage a high degree of participation in the conduct of public affairs at a local level. But the important point is that all these things can be done, and in recent years *have* been done, without the Party leadership in any way yielding up its position of ultimate authority and control. Indeed, it is far more arguable that since the end of the period of "collective" rule, the power of the Party leadership has become still more absolute and unrivalled. This situation, one would suggest, has been brought about as a result of Khrushchev's success in reducing the power and independence, relative to the Party machine, of the other major bureaucratic structures within Soviet society—those of the political police, of the military and of government and industry. In some cases, it might be noted, the changes involved here can be seen as aspects of "destalinization"—for example, the mitigation of the terror or the dissolution of a large part of the central state apparatus. Yet at the same time these changes have had the effect of accentuating still further the totalitarian nature of Party rule. As Bialer points out:

> The party bureaucracy is at present the only remaining apparatus which is centralized in its organization, which operates at all levels of the society, and which "specializes" in every sphere of societal activity. In its functions of communicating, controlling and to an ever greater degree directly organizing the tasks set forth by the leadership, it influences the operation of the

other bureaucratic apparatuses, but is not in turn subject to any outside interference. It is subordinate only to the top leadership and to its own hierarchical line of authority.[51]

It is, I think, significant that Inkeles himself sees the weakest spot in the entire thesis of "declining differentiation" as being in the application of this to the "realm of power" within Communist society. He acknowledges the distinct possibility that here his model of stratification change may have to be revised and the prediction of increased homogenization restricted to realms other than that of power.[52] Moreover, Inkeles has elsewhere stated quite explicitly that

. . . there is no necessary, or even compelling, force in the modern industrial social order which clearly makes it incompatible with totalitarianism.

and again that

. . . the modern industrial order appears to be compatible with either democratic or totalitarian political and social forms.[53]

What one would wish to stress, then, is that if such views as these are sound (as I believe they are), it becomes difficult to see how one can formulate *any* general and comprehensive propositions concerning stratification change as part of a "logic" of industrial development. For the essential assumption involved in such propositions—that of some necessary "primacy" of the economic system over the political—is no longer a reliable one. It has to be recognized, rather, that stratification systems are not to be understood as mere "reflections" of a certain level of technology and industrial organization but are shaped by a range of other factors, important among which may be that of purposive political action; and further, that the importance of this latter factor in societies in which political power is highly concentrated is such as to create a distinctive type of stratification which is difficult even to discuss in terms of concepts developed in a Western, capitalist context.[54]

To end with, it might be observed that the arguments pursued in the latter part of this paper have negative implications not only for the model of stratification change with which I have been specifically concerned, but also for the kind of general theory of industrialism with which this model may be associated. The rejection of the particular hypotheses on stratification on the grounds that have been suggested obviously entails a rejection too of the idea of the convergent development of advanced societies focussed on "pluralistic industrialism," and equally of the key notion of a rigorous "logic" of industrialism which is the engine of such development.

At least as expressed in the somewhat brash manner of Kerr and his colleagues, these ideas would seem to amount to little more than what might be called an evolutionary para-Marxism; and, as such, one would say, they share certain major flaws with the developmental theories of Marx and of the social evolutionists alike. In the first place, there is the exaggeration of the degree of determinism which is exercised upon social structures by "material" exigencies, and, concomitantly with this, the underestimation of the extent to which a social order may be shaped through purposive action within the limits of such exigencies. Secondly, and relatedly, there is the further underestimation of the diversity of values and ideologies which may underlie purposive action; and thus, from these two things together, there results the tendency to envisage a future in which the complex patterns of past development will become increasingly orderly and aligned—the tendency, in fact, to think in terms of "*the* road ahead" rather than in terms of a variety of roads.[55] And then finally, and perhaps most culpably, there is the ethnocentric bias; that failure of the imagination which leads the sociologist to accept his own form of society, or rather some idealized version of this, as the goal towards which all humanity is moving.

NOTES

[1] Clark Kerr, J. T. Dunlop, F. H. Harbison, and C. A. Myers (*Industrialism and Industrial Man*, 1960).

[2] See, e.g., Raymond A. Bauer, Alex Inkeles, and Clyde Kluckhohn, *How the Soviet System Works* (1956); Inkeles and Bauer, *The Soviet Citizen* (1959).

[3] *Op. cit.*, Chaps. 1, 2, and 10 especially.

[4] The issue on which, of course, there has been greatest doubt and discussion is that of whether totalitarian regimes will *inevitably* become less "monistic" with continuing industrial advance. As emerges later in this paper, Inkeles appears somewhat uncertain on this point. Another leading American theorist of industrialism, W. E. Moore, has expressly rejected the idea that industrialization necessarily engenders increased political participation and more representative government. See his section, "Industrialisation and Social Change" in *Industrialisation and Society*, B. F. Hoselitz and W. E. Moore, eds. (1963), pp. 357–359 especially. Nevertheless, the greater part of this section is written in terms of the social exigencies of an industrial technology and economy.

[5] I am indebted to my friend M. Alfred Willener for his criticisms of an earlier draft of this paper and also to colleagues in the Faculty of Economics and Politics of the University of Cambridge who have discussed many specific points with me.

[6] The following exposition is derived chiefly from Kerr *et al., op. cit.*; Inkeles, "Social Stratification in the Modernization of Russia" in *The Transformation of Russian Society*, Cyril E. Black, ed. (1960); and Moore, *loc. cit.*, pp. 318–322, 353–359 especially. It is, however, important to note the very marked differences in tone and style between these contributions. Kerr and his colleagues are most dogmatic and "prophetic," but also the most diffuse in their arguments; Inkeles, on the other hand, is the most explicit yet is clearly writing, as he says, "not to settle a point but to open a discussion"; while Moore, aiming at the summing-up of a body of research data, puts forward by far the most cautious and qualified statements.

[7] *Loc. cit.*, p. 341. Cf. Kerr *et al.*, pp. 286–294. Moore (p. 354) claims that during early industrialization "differences in social origin, education and power of managers and workers are likely to be widest" and the following paragraph appears to support the "relative homogenization" thesis. It is not clear, however, how far Moore is prepared to regard the trend towards reduced differentiation as one which has so far continued progressively with industrial advance.

[8] Cf. Kerr *et al.*, pp. 31, 40–41, 273–274, 290–292; Moore, pp. 357–359.

[9] For a discussion of the strengths and weaknesses of attempts to apply this approach to the explanation of the development of social policy in 19th century England, see John H. Goldthorpe, "Le Développment de la Politique Sociale en Angleterre de 1800 à 1914," *Sociologie du Travail*, No. 2 (1963). (English version in *Transactions of the Vth World Congress of Sociology*, Vol. IV [1964].)

[10] *Op. cit.*, p. 286 (my italics). The theme of "the end of ideology"—in the West at least—runs strongly throughout *Industrialism and Industrial Man.* Moore, by contrast, is sufficiently detached and sophisticated to recognize "the ideology of a pluralistic society."

[11] Cf. Kerr *et al.*, pp. 274–276, 288–290; Inkeles, p. 346. As earlier noted, Moore diverges here. He notes (p. 359) the empirical probability of increased political participation as societies become industrial, but argues that so far there is no evidence of a *necessary* incompatibility between industrialism and totalitarianism.

[12] Inkeles' "equilibration" (following E. Benoit-Smullyan, "Status Types and Status Interrelations," *Am. Soc. Rev.*, 9 [1944]) thus largely corresponds to what Lenski and Landecker have referred to as "crystallization" and Adams and Homans as "congruence." See Gerhard E. Lenski, "Status Crystallization: a Non-Vertical Dimension of Social Status," *Am. Soc. Rev.*, 19 (1954); Werner S. Landecker, "Class Crystallization and Class Consciousness," *Am. Soc. Rev.*, 28 (1963); Stuart Adams, "Social Climate and Productivity in Small Military Groups," *Am. Soc. Rev.*, 19 (1954); G. C. Homans, "Status Congruence," in *Sentiments and Activities* (1962). Moore refers simply to "consistency" or "coalescence."

[13] Cf. Kerr *et al.*, pp. 272–273, 284, 292–293; Inkeles, pp. 341–342; Moore, pp. 356–357.

[14] *Op. cit.*, pp. 272–273, 286.

[15] Cf. Kerr *et al.*, pp. 35–37; Moore, pp. 319–321, 343–344. Inkeles does not include the factor of increased mobility as a separate element in his model of the "modernization" of stratification systems. It is, however, incorporated in his discussion of both decreasing differentiation and growing consistency. E.g., in modern societies, "Movement from one to another position on the scale . . . will not be sharply proscribed. Fluidity will characterize the [Stratification] system as a whole. . . ." *Loc. cit.*, p. 341.

[16] P. 35 (my italics).

[17] It should be acknowledged, however, that for the West, at least, there is clear evidence on one other important point; that is, on the reduction, indeed virtual elimination, of *formal* inequalities of status. This has been the concomitant of the growth of "citizenship" through which all members of national communities have been granted equal civil, political and social rights. Cf. T. H. Marshall, "Citizenship and Social Class," in *Sociology at the Crossroads* (1963).

[18] Cf. United Nations, *Preliminary Report on the World Social Situation* (1952), pp. 132–134; and *Report on the World Social Situation* (1961), pp. 58–61.

[19] See, e.g., United Nations, *Economic Survey of Europe in 1956, 1957*, Chap. VII; R. M. Solow, "Income Inequality since the War" in *Postwar Economic Trends in the United States*, Ralph E. Freeman, ed. (1960). Studies relating specifically to Great Britain are H. F. Lydall, "The Long-term Trend in the Size Distribution of Income," *Journ. Royal Stat. Soc.*, 122, Part I (1959), and H. F. Lydall and D. C. Tipping, "The Distribution of Personal Wealth in Britain," *Oxford Inst. Stat. Bull.*, 23 (1961).

[20] Chiefly, this is because much levelling which appears to have gone on at the top of the distribution has in fact taken place simply *within* families—particularly between parents and children and generally as a means of avoiding taxation. E.g., Lydall and Tipping (*op. cit.*), note the "growing tendency for owners of large properties to distribute their assets amongst the members of their families well in advance of death." (p. 85). However, it is, of course, the family, not the individual, that must be regarded as the basic unit of stratification.

[21] See, e.g., the critical review of Titmuss' book by A. R. Prest, and Titmuss' reply, in *British Tax Review*, March-April 1963.

[22] *Income Distribution and Social Change*, 1962, p. 198. In this connection it should also be remembered that certain major developments which have made for greater equality in incomes in the recent past are of a non-repeatable kind—notably, the ending of large scale unemployment and the considerable expansion in the number of working class wives in gainful employment.

[23] *Wealth and Power in America*, 1962, Ch. 1. The data in question refer to pre-tax incomes, but Kolko is prepared to argue (Ch. 2) that "Taxation has not mitigated the fundamentally unequal distribution of income. . . ."

[24] *Challenge to Affluence* (1963), Chap. 3. The data assembled by the Conference on Economic Progress, *Poverty and Deprivation in the United States*, 1962, suggest that there was real improvement in the income position of low-income groups during World War II but that since then the economy has not greatly enhanced the living standards of the low-income population. In regard to the distribution of wealth, Robert J. Lampman, *The Share of Top Wealth-Holders in National Wealth* (1962) has produced data to show that the share of personal sector wealth held by the wealthiest 1% of adults in the USA has steadily increased from 1949 to 1956.

[25] *Op. cit.*, pp. 13–15, 27–30.

[26] *Ibid.*, Chs. 4, 6 and 7. A basically similar view is presented in Michael Harrington, *The Other America*, 1962. On the organizational, and thus political, weakness of the poor, see pp. 13–17; on the past failure and present responsibility of the Federal Government, pp. 163–170. Cf. also Stephen W. Rousseas and James Farganis, "American Politics and the End of Ideology," *Brit. Journ. Soc.*, 14:4 (1963).

[27] Cf. Harrington's emphasis on the fact that "If there is to be a way out (of poverty) it will come from human action, from political change, not from automatic processes," (p. 162). Similarly, Raymond Aron has observed that the present problem of poverty in the USA is not that of the "pauperization" envisaged by Marx but that "Il n'en existe pas moins et il rappele opportunément, à ceux qui seraient enclins à oublier, que la croissance économique ou les progrès techniques ne sont pas des recettes miraculeuses de paix sociale ou de relations authentiquement humaines"; and further that ". . . ni la croissance économique livrée à elle-même, ni le progrès technique, emporté par son dynamisme, ne garantissent un ordre juste ni, moins encore, des conditions de vie conformes aux aspirations d'une humanité qui a transformé le monde plus qu'elle ne c'est transformée elle-même." *La Lutte des Classes* (1964), pp. 15–16.

[28] See, e.g., for Great Britain, John H. Goldthorpe and David Lockwood, "Affluence and the British Class Structure," *Soc. Rev.*, 11:2 (1963); for the USA, Bennet Berger, *Working Class Suburb: A Study of Auto Workers in Suburbia* (1960); for France, A. Andrieux and J. Lignon, *L'Ouvrier D'Aujourd'hui* (1960). In all these contributions a common emphasis is that on the growing *disparity* between the situation of the manual worker as *producer* and *consumer*.

[29] Karl Renner, *Wandlungen der modernen Gesellschaft; zwei Abhandlungen über die Probleme der Nachkriegzeit* (1953).

[30] See, e.g., for China, Robert M. Marsh, *The Mandarins: The Circulation of Elites in China, 1600–1900* (1961), and "Values, Demand and Social Mobility," *Am. Soc. Rev.*, 28 (1963), also, Ping-ti Ho, *The Ladder of Success in Imperial China: Aspects of Social Mobility, 1368–1911* (1963).

[31] For Great Britain see Acton Society Trust, *Management Succession* (1965), and R. V. Clements, *Managers: A Study of Their Careers in Industry* (1958). For the USA see W. Lloyd Warner and James C. Abegglen, *Occupational Mobility in American Business and Industry* (1955).

[32] See S. M. Lipset and Hans L. Zetterberg, "A Theory of Social Mobility," *Transactions of the Third World Congress of Sociology*, Vol. III (1956), pp. 155–177, and Chap. II, "Social Mobility in Industrial Society," in *Social Mobility in Industrial Society*, S. M. Lipset and R. Bendix, eds. (1959).

[33] *Ibid.*, pp. 38–42.

[34] S. M. Miller, "Comparative Social Mobility," *Current Sociology*, 9:1 (1960).

[35] *Ibid.*, pp. 22–23, 57–58.

[36] As an example of the kind of study which would seem particularly relevant and valuable, see Ralph H. Turner, "Modes of Social Ascent through Education: Sponsored and Contest Mobility," in *Education, Economy and Society*, A. H. Halsey, Jean Floud and C. Arnold Anderson, eds. (1961). This paper is concerned with the rela-

tion between differences in the American and English educational systems and differences in the prevailing norms in the two societies pertaining to upward mobility. More specifically, the aim is to investigate how the *accepted mode* of upward mobility shapes the pattern of educational institutions.

[37] Also relevant here, of course, is a further distinctive feature of a totalitarian political system—the absence of the "rule of law."

[38] Probably the best analysis in this respect is that provided by Barrington Moore Jnr., *Soviet Politics—the Dilemma of Power* (1950).

[39] See e.g., Alex Inkeles, "Social Stratification and Mobility in the Soviet Union: 1940–1950," *Am. Soc. Rev.*, 15 (1950). This paper contains an excellent factual account of the ways through which both economic and status inequality was increased during the Stalin era.

[40] For a general discussion of these changes see Robert A. Feldmesser, "Towards the Classless Society?" Cf. also Alec Nove, "Is the Soviet Union a Welfare State?", i: *Soviet Society*, Alex Inkeles and Kent Geiger, eds. (1961).

[41] *Op. cit.*, p. 579. This political subordination of members of the "élite," concomitant with their economic and status elevation, is the reason for using inverted commas. As Feldmesser notes, the "élite" created by Stalin is surely distinctive by virtue of its general lack of autonomy.

[42] As, e.g., in the case of the increase in peasant incomes which was essential if genuine incentives to improve production were to be offered in agriculture. Cf. Seweryn Bialer, "But Some are More Equal than Others," *Problems of Communism*, 9:2 (1960).

[43] Leonard Shapiro, "From Utopia towards Realism," in *The USSR and the Future: An Analysis of the New Program of the CPSU*, Shapiro, ed. (1963). See also in this volume Erik Boettcher, "Soviet Social Policy in Theory and Practice." The text of the Programme itself is printed as an Appendix; note, in particular, Part Two, Sections II, III, V and VII.

[44] Milovan Djilas, *The New Class*, 1957.

[45] Feldmesser, *op. cit.*, pp. 573–575.

[46] Bialer, *op. cit.*, pp. 576–578.

[47] *Op. cit.*, pp. 576–578.

[48] This assessment is consistent with the more general interpretations of the Soviet social system advanced by writers such as Brzezinski and Daniel Bell, in some opposition to the interpretation of Inkeles and his associates. "The important thing is that those in charge of Soviet society have assumed that economic and social development in all its aspects can be purposefully steered by man in the direction of an ideal solution. This produces consequences that are not only economic but also political, quite different from those induced by other equally technologically advanced economic systems where, to a large extent, economic life is self-directive and ultimate goals, such as plenty and progress, are purposely vague." Zbigniew K. Brzezinski, *Ideology and Power in Soviet Politics* (1962), p. 31. "The Harvard group . . . shrinks from seeking to specify the motor forces in the social system as they have conceived it. . . . Is it not quite clear, really, that the Soviet system is characterized, essentially, by the centralized control of political power, that it is a *command* system, with few institutional checks. . . . In a society like Russia, where institutional and behaviour patterns are not autonomous, a 'social system' has no meaning unless it can be defined within the context of politics." Daniel Bell, "Ten Theories in Search of Reality: The Prediction of Soviet Behaviour," in *The End of Ideology* (1961), pp. 340–341.

[49] See his "Social Structure and the Ruling Class," *Brit. Journ. Soc.*, 1 (1950).

[50] For recent discussion of the issue of the compatibility of industrialism and totalitarianism from both empirical and theoretical points of view, see Brzezinski, *op. cit.*, Chaps. I and III, and R. Aron, ed., *World Technology and Human Destiny* (1963).

[51] *Op. cit.*, pp. 48–49. In addition to Bialer's paper, see also on the strengthening of Party rule under Krushchev, Brzezinski, *op. cit.*, Chap. III, and Edward Crankshaw, *Krushchev's Russia* (1957), pp. 69, 76–79. Crankshaw shows how this process

is in no way inconsistent with the widening of opportunities for popular participation in administrative work at a local level via the "public organizations." See pp. 94–98.

[52] "Social Stratification in the Modernization of Russia," *loc. cit.*, pp. 345–347.

[53] Inkeles and Bauer, *op. cit.*, p. 390.

[54] As Feldmesser has indicated, the argument that Soviet society is not "class" stratified in the manner of Western industrial societies can also be supported from the "subjective" point of view. See his paper, "Social Classes and the Political Structure," in Black, ed., *op. cit.*, pp. 235–252. The available evidence suggests that Soviet citizens exhibit a relatively low level of class consciousness in the sense that their class situation is not of fundamental importance in patterning their dominant modes of thought and action. Members of different social strata in Soviet society seem more alike in their social ideologies and attitudes than their counterparts in the West, while the feature of the social structure which is most strongly reflected in their social consciousness at all levels is that of the division between "Party people" and "non-Party people." On this latter point see Inkeles and Bauer, *op. cit.*, Chap. XIII.

[55] More radically, it may be objected that, if a long-run view is to be taken, the very concept of "industrial society" will eventually cease to be useful. As the Spanish social scientist, Luis Diez del Corral, has pointed out, the concept remains of some significance while societies exist in which highest priority is assigned to industrial and economic values generally. During this phase, "this secularization and concentration of values helps explain the lessening of ideological conflicts. . . ." But, Del Corral goes on, "This *élan* will only be temporary, and this standardization, this secularization of values which results in economic growth will one day enable all values to flower, all constraints to be forgotten, unless it ends in the apocalyptic destruction of mankind. These two possibilities underline both the grandeur and the misery of our destiny." See R. Aron, ed., *op. cit.*, p. 68.

16 LEWIS A. COSER

The Sociology of Poverty

Discussions of the extent of poverty in a given society usually have been dogged by definitional problems. One man's poverty is another's wealth; minimal standards in a developed industrial society may be viewed as Utopian goals in an underdeveloped one. What may be felt to constitute unendurable deprivation in a society where underprivileged compare their lot with that of others more favorably placed in regard to the distribution of income and wealth, may be accepted as legitimate in societies where no such comparisons are socially available or culturally sanctioned.

One may argue that a poor man is one whose economic means are not commensurate with the economic ends he seeks; yet this does not stand up under scrutiny. In societies that exhibit a strain toward anomy, a disjunction between the ends that are striven for and the means available for attaining them, boundless appetites forever create new dissatisfactions at every level reached. This seems to be typical not only of the deprived but

Reprinted from *Social Problems*, 13:2 (1965), pp. 140–148, by permission of the author and the publisher.

of very large strata of the population. The economies of such societies are geared precisely to the creation of ever new needs.

Rather than taking as a point of departure the condition or felt condition of those presumed to be poor, this paper will attempt to provide a different perspective. Following Simmel's lead, poverty will be dealt with as a social category that emerges through societal definition.[1] Just as in Durkheim's view crime can best be defined as consisting in acts having "the external characteristic that they evoke from society the particular reaction called punishment," [2] so I shall argue here that the poor are men who have been so defined by society and have evoked particular reactions from it. From this perspective, the poor have not always been with us. In Oriental societies, for example, deprivation was not socially visible and not within the focus of social awareness. The modern observer might have discerned there a great prevalence of want and misery, yet the members of the society themselves did not perceive poverty and were unaware of its prevalence. In such societies, the condition of those who were deprived did not seem to touch the sensibilities of the upper strata; and it is, after all, they who determine the conscience and consciousness of the society. The deprived, insofar as they were recognized at all, were simply put into the same category as, say, the victims of disease or natural disaster. They did not exist phenomenologically as a separate category.

Historically, the poor emerge when society elects to recognize poverty as a special status and assigns specific persons to that category. The fact that some people may privately consider themselves poor is sociologically irrelevant. What *is* sociologically relevant is poverty as a socially recognized condition, as a social status. We are concerned with poverty as a property of the social structure.

In medieval society, the poor had the function of affording the rich the opportunity for socially prescribed "good deeds." In the Catholic injunction to give alms the concern was not essentially with the physical condition of the poor but primarily with the moral condition of the rich. The giver rather than the recipient tended to be the moral center of attention. The good works of the Christian man were considered a major avenue to salvation. Giving alms hence was meant to increase the chances of the giver in the next world and not primarily to improve the chances of the poor in this. The poor were not considered in their own right but mainly as a means toward the other-worldly ends of the rich. This peculiar function of the poor was, however, of some consequence for the society for it helped to unify the Christian community.

The medieval status of the poor was very different from that assigned to the poor in Puritan England. Here they were given the social position of the "eternally damned"—confirming to the righteous the fitness of their survival. To the Puritan conscience, the poor, having no calling, were not considered a part of the society. Writes William Perkins, a leading 16th century Puritan preacher, "Rogues, beggars, vagabonds . . . commonly are of no civil society or corporation, nor of any particular Church: and are as rotten legges, and armes, that droppe from the body . . . to wander up and downe from yeare to yeare to this ende, to seek and procure bodily maintenance, is no calling, but the life of a beast." He specifies in another passage: ". . . wandering beggars and rogues, that passe from place to place, beeing under no certain Magistracie or Ministrie, nor joyning themselves to any set societie in Church, or Commonwealth, are plagues and banes of both, and are to bee taken as main ennemies of this ordinance of God."[3] The poor are here defined as not belonging to the body of society and hence not subject to the bonds of solidarity which bind all its members. The poor, like Indian untouchables, are assigned a status which marks their exclusion from the social order.

In modern societies the deprived are assigned to the core category of the poor only when they receive assistance. It might be objected that the category of the economically deprived is presently much larger than that of the assisted poor. Whereas the latter englobes around 8 million persons in contemporary America, between 40 and 50 million fall into the former category. However, the point is precisely that the current widespread discussion of the problems of poverty can be seen in large part as an effort to broaden the core category of the poor by insisting that millions not heretofore included deserve societal assistance. If I understand Michael Harrington and his co-thinkers aright, they argue in effect that a redefinition of the problem of poverty is required so that the very large number of deprived who have so far not received assistance can be included among the poor receiving societal help of one kind or another.

It is not a person's lack of economic means that makes him belong to the core category of the poor. As long as a man continues to be defined primarily in terms of his occupational status, he is not so classified. Doctors, farmers, or plumbers who have suffered financial reverses or strains are still typically called doctors, farmers, or plumbers. "The acceptance of assistance," argues Georg Simmel, "removes the man who has received it from the precondition of the previous status; it symbolized his formal declassification."[4] From that point on his private trouble becomes a public issue. In individual psychological terms the sequence of events leads from the experience of deprivation to a quest for assistance; the matter is reversed however in sociological perspective: those who receive assistance are defined as being poor. Hence, poverty cannot be understood sociologically in terms of low income or deprivation but rather in terms of the social response to such deprivations.

The modern poor are a stratum that is recruited from heterogeneous origins, and individual members of this stratum have a great number of differing attributes. They come to belong to the common category of the poor by virtue of an essentially passive trait, namely that society reacts to them in a particular manner. The poor come to be viewed and classified not in terms of criteria ordinarily used in social categorization, that is, not by virtue of what they do, but by virtue of what is done to them. To quote Simmel again: "Poverty hence presents a unique sociological constellation: a number of individuals occupy a specific organic position within the social whole through purely personal fate; but it is not personal destiny or personal conditions which determine the position but rather the fact that others—individuals, associations, or social totalities—attempt to correct this state of affairs. Hence it is not personal need which makes for poverty; rather, the sociological category of poverty emerges only when those who suffer from want are receiving assistance."[5]

Though the poor are recognized as having a special status in modern societies, it is still a status that is marked only by negative attributes, that is, by what the status-holder does *not* have. This distinguishes him from any other status-holder in that it does not carry with it the expectation of a social contribution. This lack of expectation of a social contribution by the poor is symbolized by their lack of social visibility. Those who are assigned to the status of the poor offend the moral sensibilities of other members of the society who, unwittingly, or wittingly, keep them out of their sight. What is at issue here is not only physical segregation into special areas and districts that right-minded citizens would not normally care to visit and that are typically not shown to tourists, but also a kind of moral invisibility. The Gradgrinds and Bounderbys of Victorian England held views of the poor that were not very far removed from those of their Puritan ancestors. They consequently repressed awareness of the facts of deprivation. Only the persistent agitation of a host of reformers finally led to the horrified discovery by proper Victorian gentlemen that Britain was in fact split into "two nations." This accounts for the fact that, though general well being and standards of living clearly increased in England during the nineteenth century, perceived deprivation increased throughout the century as human misery gained at least some visibility.

Lest it be believed that we deal here only with the more remote past it may be well to remind us of a very similar trend in the recent history of the United States. John K. Galbraith remarked upon this a few years ago when he wrote: "In the United States, the survival of poverty is remarkable. We ignore it because we share with all societies at all times the capacity for not seeing what we do not wish to see. Anciently this has enabled the nobleman to enjoy his dinner while remaining oblivious to the beggars around his door. In our own day it enables us to travel in comfort throughout South Chicago and the South."[6] At the present moment, when poverty is suddenly receiving frontline attention among politicians, scholars and the mass media, it is difficult to remember that only recently it seemed hardly visible at all. Five years ago the editors of *Fortune* magazine published a volume, *America in the Sixties*,[7] in which they attempted to forecast the major social and economic trends of the next decade. They concluded that soon deprivation would no longer be with us at all. They announced with self-congratulatory flourish that "only" 3,600,000 families have incomes under $2,000 and that if a family makes over $2,000 it cannot be considered deprived at all. Two years later Michael Harrington's *The Other America*,[8] followed by a spate of other books and articles, suddenly helped to picture deprivation as the central domestic issue in the United States and led to the emergence of a new social definition of poverty. The deprived in America now were seen as constituting about 25 percent of the population all of whom deserved assistance. The number of objectively deprived is not likely to have changed appreciably between the complacent fifties and the self-critical sixties, but the extent of perceived deprivation changed drastically. As a consequence, what appeared as a peripheral problem only a few years ago suddenly assumes considerable national salience.

[I should like to point out here that it will not do to argue that the statistics indicating the extent of deprivation were available all along. In the first place it is not the availability of statistics but their use which is of social significance. Furthermore, it can be argued that a society bothers to keep accurate statistics mainly of those phenomena it deems worthy of attention. Some extreme cases from totalitarian societies come readily to mind. As Everett Hughes has reminded us in his examination of German Statistical Yearbooks, in the Nazi and pre-Nazi period, "From earlier work with German official statistics, I was practically certain that the pre-Nazi German had a religion, but not a race. The statistical German was the opposite of the statistical American, who had a race but no religion. . . . Race in the pre-Nazi Yearbooks was a characteristic of stallions."[9] But all Yearbooks under the Nazi regime contained, among others, a category "Racial Classification of People who Married in X Year." A characteristic which was hitherto officially unnoticed was suddenly made visible through statistics. Or, to give another example, "In Lebanon there has not been a census since 1932 for fear that taking one would reveal such changes in the religious composition of the population as to make the marvelously intricate political arrangements designed to balance sectarian interests unviable."[10] Finally, in the 1941 Indian census there were 25 million tribal peoples, but in 1951, after independence was attained, the number had shrunk through what has been called "genocide by definition" to 1.7 million.[11]

No such drastic surgery was, of course, performed on American statistics. Yet one cannot help but be struck by the fact that, to give one example, the number of underprivileged will vary greatly depending on where you fix the income line. Thus the aforementioned *Fortune* study defined deprivation as a family income under $2,000 and concluded that there were only 3,600,000 poor families. Robert Lampman used the $2,500 cutoff for an urban family of four and on this basis came to the conclusion that 19 percent of the American population, 32,000,000 people, were underprivileged. In the same period, the AFL-CIO, using a slightly higher definition of what constituted low income, found that 41,500,000 Americans—24 percent of the total population—has substandard incomes. After all these studies were published, the Bureau of Labor Statistics issued a report containing newly calculated budgets for urban families of four which showed that previous calculations had underestimated minimal budgetary requirements. Harrington concludes on the basis of these new figures that the deprived number more nearly 50,000,000.[12]]

Enough has been said to indicate the extent to which objective misery and perceived deprivation may diverge. We can now return to the initial statement that, in modern societies, persons are assigned a position in the status category of the poor when they receive assistance. Receipt of such assistance is predicated upon the society's willingness to assume a measure of responsibility for the poor and upon its recognition of the fact that they are effectively a part of the community. But what are the terms upon which such assistance is granted and what are the consequences for the recipient?

Here I would like to contend that the very granting of relief, the very assignment of the person to the category of the poor, is forthcoming only at the price of a degradation of the person who is so assigned.

To receive assistance means to be stigmatized and to be removed from the ordinary run of men. It is a status degradation through which, in Harold Garfinkel's words, "the public identity of an actor is transformed into something looked on as lower in the local schemes of social types."[13] In this perspective, the societal view of a person becomes significant in so far as it alters his face. Once a person is assigned to the status of the poor his role is changed, just as the career of the mental patient is changed by the very fact that he is defined as a mental patient.[14] Let me give a few illustrative instances of what is at issue here.

Members of nearly all status groups in society can make use of a variety of legitimate mechanisms to shield their behavior from observability by others; society recognizes a right to privacy, that is, the right to conceal parts of his role behavior from public observation. But this right is denied to the poor. At least in principle, facets of his behavior which ordinarily are not public are in this case under public control and are open to scrutiny by social workers or other investigators. In order to be socially recognized as poor a person is obligated to make his private life open to public inspection.[15] The protective veil which is available to other members of society is explicitly denied to him.

Whereas other recipients of social services may upon occasion be visited at home by investigators, most of their contact with the agency is likely to be in the agency rather than in their private homes. Generally, in modern society, the exercise of authority—except within the family—is separated from the home. With regard to the poor on relief, however, this is not the case. Here their home is the place in which most contacts with the agency investigators are likely to take place. They are typically being investigated *in situ* and hence have much less of a chance to conceal their private affairs from the superordinate observers. Such an invasion of home territory, because it prevents the usual stage management for the visit of outsiders, is necessarily experienced as humiliating and degrading.

When money is allocated to members of any other status groups in society, they have the freedom to dispose of it in almost any way they see fit. Here again, the treatment of the poor differs sharply. When monies are allocated to them, they do not have free disposition over their use. They must account to the donors for their expenses and the donors decide whether the money is spent "wisely" or "foolishly." That is, the poor are treated in this respect much like children who have to account to parents for the wise use of their pocket money; the poor are infantilized through such procedures.

As the above examples make clear, in the very process of being helped and assisted, the poor are assigned to a special career that impairs their previous identity and becomes a stigma which marks their intercourse with others. Social workers, welfare investigators, welfare administrators and local volunteer workers seek out the poor in order to help them, and yet, paradoxically, they are the very agents of their degradation. Subjective intentions and institutional consequences diverge here. The help rendered may be given from the purest and most benevolent of motives, yet the very fact of being helped degrades.

Assistance can be given either by voluntary workers or by professionals. The former pattern prevailed till roughly World War I, the latter has come to predominate in our days. Such professionalization of assistance has had two divergent sets of consequences for the recipient. To be cared for by a professional who is paid for his work means that the recipient need not be grateful to him, he doesn't have to say thank you. In fact he can hate the person giving assistance and even display some of his antagonism without losing the institutionally provided aid. Professionalization removes the personal element in the relationship and marks it as an impersonal transaction thereby freeing the recipient both from personal embarrassment and from personal obligation. When the poor is, so to speak, "promoted" to a case he may be spared certain personal humiliations. Yet this is not the whole story. The very manner of bureaucratic procedure used in dealing with a person on relief is different from that employed with respect to, say, an unemployed person. Receipt of unemployment insurance is seen as an unquestioned right which has been earned. Control by the donor agency over the recipient is minimal. Here it stands in contrast to control over the person on relief where control is a precondition for relief. Hence the professional in an agency dealing with the unemployed has little power over persons he serves, but the welfare investigator or the case worker has a great deal of power over the assisted poor. This power was considerably increased, it may be remarked in passing, when the giving of assistance shifted from so-called categorical assistance to granting case workers leeway to vary assistance according to the specific needs of the client. This change of policy was instituted for humanitarian and benevolent reasons, to be sure. But it stands to reason that it has greatly increased the discretionary power of the case worker over the client.

Prescribed impersonality has still other effects on the relationship between professionalized welfare workers and the recipients of aid. As long as volunteers or other non-professionals were the main dispensers of charity, condescension was likely to mark the relationship between donors and recipients of aid, but it was also likely to be characterized by a fairly high level of spontaneity. The relationship was so defined as to make a *reciprocal* flow of affect and emotion between the two actors possible, even if it did not always, or usually, occur. But professionalization by definition prevents the flow of affect. This is not due to happenstance but to the institutionalization of a structurally asymmetrical type of relationship. Those who render assistance have a job to do; the recipient is a case. As in every type of bureaucratic procedure, the impersonal aspects of the case must of need take precedence over distracting personal considerations. In fact, case workers or investigators would be incapacitated in the exercise of their tasks were they to indulge in "over-rapport," that is, in an undue consideration of the personal needs of the client. Excessive sympathy would impair role performance. The welfare worker, moreover, is not supposed to deserve esteem for his accomplishments from the recipient of aid but rather from professional peers and superiors. The client who is defined as "poor" has little if any possibility of controlling his behavior. Hence there exist built-in insulating mechanisms which insure that professional concern with the poor does not corrupt the professional into considering the poor as anything but an object of care and a recipient of aid. In this way the status discrepancy between them is continuously reaffirmed. This is accentuated, moreover, in those cases where welfare workers are of lower middle class origin and feel that close association with clients might endanger the respectable status they have but recently achieved.

The professionals and the poor do in fact belong to two basically different worlds. In Alexander Solzhenitsyn's fine novel about Russian concentration camps, *One Day in the Life of Ivan Denisovich*,[16] occurs an episode in which the hero attempts to get some medical relief from the man in charge of the infirmary but is turned away with indifference. He thereupon reflects, "How can you expect a man who's warm to understand a man who's cold." This beautifully captures the gist of what I have been trying to say. As long as social workers and the poor belong to the opposite worlds of those who are warm and those who are cold, their relationship is necessarily an asymmetrical one. As in other aspects of case work, those in need address those who can relieve some of their wants as supplicants, and the asymmetry is not only one of feelings and attitudes, it is also an asymmetry of power. This is an extreme case of unilateral dependence. Peter Blau's formulation is helpful here: "By supplying services in demand to others, a person establishes power over them. If he regularly renders needed services they cannot readily obtain elsewhere, others become dependent on and obligated to him for these services, and unless they can furnish other benefits to him that produce interdependence by making him equally dependent on them, their unilateral dependence obligates them to comply with his requests lest he ceases to continue to meet their needs." [17]

Blau stresses here that unilateral dependence comes into being when the receiver of benefits is not in a position to reciprocate with benefits that he can in turn bestow upon the donor. This, I believe, touches upon the crux of the matter. The poor, when receiving assistance, are assigned a low and degraded status by virtue of a determination that they cannot themselves contribute to society. Their inability to contribute in turn degrades them to the condition of unilateral receivers. Built into the system of relief is not only the definition of their being noncontributors, but the expectation that they are not even potential contributors. In an instrumentally oriented society, those who cannot give but only receive and who are not expected to give at a future time are naturally assigned the lowest status. They cannot engage in activities that establish interdependence and this is why they cannot be given social recognition. Poverty, therefore, can never be eliminated unless the poor are enabled to give as well as to receive. They can be fully integrated into the social fabric only if they are offered the opportunity to give.

In order to be able to serve, they must first be able to function at optimum capacity. Devices such as a guaranteed minimum income for every citizen, assuring him freedom from pressing want, may very well be a precondition for the abolition of dependency. But it is a precondition only. It needs to be considered not as an end in itself but only as a means which permits the poor to be free from anxiety while they train themselves for the rendering of such services to the community as will make them interdependent with others.

I showed earlier how the core category of the poor arises only when they come to be defined as recipients of assistance. We now see that correlatively the poor will be with us as long as we provide assistance so that the problem of poverty can be solved only through the abolition of a unilateral relationship of dependence.

This is not the place to spell out in detail concrete measures which will "solve" the problem of poverty. I know of no such global solutions at the present moment. But I wish to indicate at least the direction in which, I believe, such solutions are to be looked for. I am impressed, for example, by the number of recent experiments, from Mobilization for Youth to Alcoholics Anonymous, in which "some people who do not seem to benefit from *receiving* help often profit indirectly when they are *giving* help."[18] A number of such projects have of late used a variety of nonprofessionals recruited largely among the poor. The New York State Division for Youth and several other agencies for example employ former youthful offenders in interviewing and related tasks. Howard University's Community Apprentice Program trains delinquent youth to be recreation, child welfare, and research aides. Mobilization for Youth employs indigenous leaders as case aides, homework helpers, and the like. These jobs offer employment opportunities for the underprivileged and hence serve directly to reduce poverty by transforming dependent welfare cases into homemakers, and former delinquents into researchers.[19] This indigenous nonprofessional, as Frank Riessman and Robert Reiff have written, "is a peer of the client and can more readily identify with him. He possesses no special body of knowledge which makes him an expert and can feel, therefore, that in reversed circumstances the client could do the same job just as easily. In the place of subtle patronage or *noblesse oblige* concepts, he is likely to feel that 'there but for the grace of God go I.' To the indigenous nonprofessional, 'helping others' is a reciprocal process. . . ." [20] These are only a few and still very feeble beginnings, but I believe that they point in the right direction. The task is to create valued status positions for those who were formerly passive recipients of assistance. Such valuable status positions can only be those in which they are required and enabled to make a social contribution and become active partners in a joint undertaking of mutual aid. This can be done through helping others with whom but recently they shared similar problems or through working in large-scale projects similar to a domestic Peace Corps or a replica of the New Deal's Civilian Conservation Corps. Yet another case in which the poor may themselves contribute to the abolition of the status they occupy arises when they cease "acting poor," i.e., when they reject the role behavior which is required by the status. When the poor begin to react actively, when they refuse to continue to be passive recipients of aid, they undermine the very status that they occupy. This is why rent strikes, demonstrations, and other political activities by the poor should be seen as avenues of activization which tend to lead to a restructuring of their relationships in the community.

Simmel observes that though the notion of assistance necessarily implies taking from the rich and giving to the poor, it nevertheless was never aimed at an equalization of their positions in society. As distinct from socialist endeavors, it does not even have the tendency to reduce the differences between rich and poor but rather accepts and bolsters them.[21] Or, as T. H. Marshall once put it, "The common purpose of statutory and voluntary effort was to abate the nuisance of poverty without disturbing the pattern of inequality of which poverty was the most obvious unpleasant consequence."[22] This is why what I have suggested diverges sharply from most previous policies. It aims not at alleviating poverty but at abolishing it, through the elimination of the despised status of the receiver of assistance. It is, to be sure, a Utopian proposal. But, as Max Weber, that supreme realist, has argued, "Certainly all political experience confirms the truth— that man would not have attained the possible unless time and again he had reached out for the impossible."[23]

NOTES

[1] Georg Simmel, *Soziologie* (Leipzig: Duncker und Humblot, 1908), pp. 454–493. I have relied very heavily on Simmel's hitherto untranslated essay, "Der Arme," in the above volume. In fact, much of what I say in the first part of this paper is little more than a restatement of some of Simmel's seminal ideas.

[2] Emile Durkheim, *The Rules of Sociological Method* (Glencoe, Ill.: The Free Press, 1950), p. 35.

[3] Quoted in Christopher Hill, *Puritanism and Revolution* (New York: Schocken Books, 1964), pp. 227–228.

[4] Simmel, *op. cit.*, p. 489.

[5] *Ibid.*, p. 493.

[6] John K. Galbraith, *The Affluent Society* (Boston: Houghton Mifflin, 1959), p. 333.

[7] The Editors of Fortune, *America in the Sixties* (New York: Harper Torchbooks, 1960), p. 102. Note the following additional comment: "Only about a million domestic servants, marginal farm operators, and farm laborers and their families still look truly poor." *Ibid.*, p. 102.

[8] Michael Harrington, *The Other America* (Baltimore: Penguin Books), 1963.

[9] Everett C. Hughes, *Men and Their Work* (Glencoe, Ill.: The Free Press, 1958), pp. 146, 150.

[10] Clifford Geertz, "The Integrative Revolution," in *Old Societies and New States*, Geertz, ed. (Glencoe, Ill.: The Free Press, 1963), p. 126.

[11] *Ibid.*

[12] Harrington, *op. cit.*, pp. 192–194.

[13] Harold Garfinkel, "Conditions of Successful Degradation Ceremonies," *American Journal of Sociology*, 61 (1956), p. 420.

[14] Cf. Erving Goffman, *Asylums* (New York: Doubleday Anchor Books, 1961), *passim*.

[15] On the notion of observability cf. Robert K. Merton, *Social Theory and Social Structure* (Glencoe, Ill.: The Free Press, 1957), pp. 374–375, and Rose Laub Coser, "Insulation from Observability and Types of Social Conformity," *American Sociological Review*, 26, pp. 28–39.

[16] Alexander Solzhenitsyn, *One Day in the Life of Ivan Denisovich* (New York: E. P. Dutton, 1963).

[17] Peter Blau, *Exchange and Power in Social Life* (New York: Wiley, 1964), p. 118.

[18] Robert Reiff and Frank Riessman, *The Indigenous Nonprofessional* (New York: National Institute of Labor Education, Mental Health Program), mimeo, p. 11.

[19] *Ibid.*, p. 6.

[20] *Ibid.*, p. 12.

[21] Simmel, *op. cit.*, p. 459.

[22] T. H. Marshall, *Class Citizenship and Social Development* (New York: Doubleday, Anchor Books, 1965), p. 105.

[23] Gerth and Mills, eds., *From Max Weber* (New York: Oxford University Press, 1948), p. 128.

17 KARL E. TAEUBER and ALMA F. TAEUBER

The Negro as an Immigrant Group: Recent Trends in Racial and Ethnic Segregation in Chicago

During the last half of the nineteenth century and the early decades of the twentieth, millions of immigrants from Europe entered the United States.[1] Many of these immigrants settled initially in ethnic colonies in large northern cities and found jobs as unskilled laborers in burgeoning mass-production industries. With the onset of World War I in Europe, and with the

Reprinted from *American Journal of Sociology*, 69:4 (1964), pp. 374–382, by permission of the authors and the publisher.

passage of restrictive legislation in the United States in the early 1920's, the period of massive overseas migration came to an end. At the same time, however, there developed a large-scale migration of Negroes from the South to the same large northern industrial cities. Like the immigrants from abroad, the Negro migrants to northern cities filled the lowest occupational niches and rapidly developed highly segregated patterns of residence within the central cities.

In view of many obvious similarities between the Negro migrants and the various immigrant groups preceding them, it has been suggested that northern urban Negroes are but the latest of the immigrant groups, undergoing much the same processes of adaptation to city life and of assimilation into the general social structure as the European groups preceding them.[2] The persistence of Negroes as a residentially segregated and underprivileged group at the lowest levels of socioeconomic status, however, is frequently interpreted in terms of distinctive aspects of the Negro experience, particularly their historical position in American society.[3]

The question of whether or not a northern urban Negro population can fruitfully be viewed as an immigrant population, comparable to European immigrant populations of earlier decades with respect to the nature and speed of assimilation, will be explored on the basis of data permitting analysis of recent trends in racial and ethnic segregation in Chicago.

The processes by which various immigrant groups have been absorbed into American society are complex and have been studied from a variety of viewpoints. Unfortunately there is no sociological consensus on a definition of assimilation and there is nothing approaching a definitive study of the processes of assimilation for any one immigrant group. It is beyond the scope of our task here to attempt to provide such a definition. We feel that a distinctively sociological approach to the topic must view assimilation as a process of dispersion of members of the group throughout the social structure. Cultural and psychological processes, we feel, should not be incorporated into a sociological definition, although their relationship to institutional dispersion should, of course, be retained as one focus of research on assimilation.

For our purposes, it will suffice to have a working definition of the process of assimilation considerably less sophisticated than that required for a general sociological theory. Accepting the view that both immigrant groups and Negro migrants originally settled in segregated patterns in central areas of cities and ranked very low in terms of socioeconomic measures, assimilation then consisted in large part of a process of social and economic advancement on the part of the original members of the group and their descendants, along with a decreasing residential concentration in ethnic colonies. Our concern with diminishing residential segregation as a necessary concomitant of the assimilation process derives from Myrdal's discussion of the "mechanical" importance of residential segregation in facilitating other forms of segregation and discrimination, and Hawley's discussion of the impact of spatial patterns on race relations.[4] Our concern with socioeconomic advance reflects the initially low status of the groups with which we are concerned, whereas a more general treatment would need to reckon with the unusually high status of some immigrant stocks, as well as with other aspects of social status and institutional dispersion than those for which we have data.

The data in Table 1 illustrate for selected immigrant groups the patterns of socioeconomic advance and residential dispersion from highly segregated ethnic colonies. For each of the larger ethnic groups, data for 1950 show the average standing on three measures of socioeconomic status, standardized for age, of the first generation (the foreign-born white, FBW) and the second generation (native white of foreign or mixed parentage, NWFMP). The nationality groups are split into "old," "new," and "newer" groups in an extension of the traditional system. On the average, comparing within the first or within the second generation, the "old" immigrant groups are the best off on these measures, the "new" groups are intermediate, and the "newer" groups are the worst off. It cannot be determined from these data to what extent the old immigrants are better off by virtue of their longer average length of residence in the United States, or to what extent they may have been better off at their time of immigration than the newer immigrants were at the time of their move.

Comparisons between the first and second generations might appear to be a more direct means for assessing the extent of socioeconomic advance, particularly since the emphasis in the literature on assimilation is on intergenerational processes rather than simply on processes of upward mobility through time in the status of the original immigrants. Comparisons of corresponding status measures for the first and second generations in Table 1 reveal, in general, the expected pattern of intergenerational advance. Data such as these, however, do not refer directly to a specific set of immigrant parents and their native-born children and must be interpreted with great caution.[5] For instance, it would be unwarranted on the basis of these data to assume that descendants of German immigrants are not as well off as their parents in terms of education. It is more credible that recent immigrants from Germany, under our immigration laws, include a large proportion of persons of high socioeconomic status.

Measures of the changing residential patterns of the immigrant groups are given in columns 7–9 of Table 1. The measure, an index of residential segregation between the total foreign stock (FBW + NWFMP) of each nationality and the total native whites of native parentage (NWNP), assumes a value of 100 for maximum residential segregation and a value of 0 if the residential distributions are identical.[6] The indexes were computed from the distribution of each group among the seventy-five community areas of the city of Chicago for 1930 (the last previous census year that included information on the total foreign stock) and 1960. The degree of residential segregation from the native population is highest for the "newer" immigrants and lowest for the "old" immigrants. Between 1930 and 1960, most of the ethnic groups became less segregated from the native

Table 1. Selected Characteristics (Age-Standardized) of Foreign-
Born and Native Ethnic Populations in 1950, and Indexes of Resi-
dential Segregation of Selected Groups of Foreign Stock from
Native Whites of Native Parentage, 1930 and 1960, Chicago*

Country of origin	Percent high school graduates (males age 25 and over)		Percent with income above $3,000 (persons with income)		Percent with white-collar jobs (employed males)		Index of residential segregation (compared with NWNP)		
	FBW	NWFMP	FBW	NWFMP	FBW	NWFMP	1930	1960	Change
"Old" immi- grant groups: England and									
Wales ...	45	50	53	58	49	51	11	18	+ 7
Ireland	24	47	47	56	22	47	23	31	+ 8
Norway	31	47	54	57	24	51	44	37	− 7
Sweden	25	48	59	60	23	51	26	30	+ 4
Germany ...	37	34	53	55	34	42	22	19	− 3
"New" immi- grant groups:									
Austria	29	40	54	57	33	44	30	16	−14
Czecho- slovakia ..	25	33	44	54	22	36	59	37	−22
Italy	15	27	47	53	24	37	52	32	−20
Poland	18	25	42	49	25	30	63	38	−25
U.S.S.R. ...	35	60	60	69	59	74	51	44	− 7
"Newer" immi- grant groups:									
Mexico	14	16	38	29	8	13	71	54	−17
Puerto Rico†	13	29	16	37	22	36	†	67	†

* Data for 1930 and 1950 refer to foreign white stock (foreign-born plus native of
foreign or mixed parentage); data for 1960 refer to total foreign stock. Abbreviations
used are FBW for foreign-born white, NWFMP for native white of foreign or mixed
parentage, and NWNP for native white of native parentage. The three socioeconomic
characteristics refer to the Standard Metropolitan Area population, while the segregation indexes are based on community areas within the city. Age-standardization was
by the direct method, using age groups 25–44 and 45 and over, with the Standard
Metropolitan Area age composition as a standard.
    † Socioeconomic characteristics for Puerto Rican population refer to total United
States; Puerto Rican population by community areas for Chicago available for 1960
only.
    Source: Characteristics from U.S. Bureau of the Census, *U.S. Census of Population:
1950*, Vol. IV, *Special Reports*, Pt. 3, Chap. A, "Nativity and Parentage," and Chap.
D, "Puerto Ricans in Continental United States." Distributions of population by com-
munity areas for 1930 and 1960 from data on file at Chicago Community Inventory,
University of Chicago.

population. Only for England, Ireland, and Sweden did the indexes fail to decline, and these were already at relatively low levels.[7]

This general approach to the measurement or assimilation of immigrant groups has been pursued for a number of cities and longer time periods by Lieberson. He found a remarkably persistent and consistent association through time between residential desegregation of an ethnic group and increasing socioeconomic similarity to native whites, and cross-sectionally between the position of each group as compared to others on measures of residential segregation and its relative levels on status measures.[8]

The index of residential segregation between Negroes and NWNP for 1930 was 84, and for 1960, 82. These values are higher than any of those for specific immigrant stocks. Furthermore, each of the immigrant stocks was highly segregated from Negroes in 1930 and 1960. There is relatively little intermixture of Negro residences with those of any group of whites. Even the "newer" immigrant groups, the Puerto Ricans and Mexicans, are not joining or replacing Negroes in established Negro areas but are moving into separate ethnic colonies of their own at the periphery of Negro areas. Negroes clearly occupy a distinctive position as the most residentially segregated of the principal migrant groups. The separation of Negroes from all groups of whites is sharper than any of the patterns of residential segregation between ethnic groups or between socioeconomic groups within the white population.[9] Apparently this pattern has developed during the last few decades. Lieberson has demonstrated that, although prior to the great Negro migrations of World War I there were instances of immigrant stocks being more segregated from native whites than were Negroes, since 1920 there has been a general tendency for Negro residential segregation to be highest.[10]

Data pertaining specifically to the comparison between whites and non-whites (97 percent of Chicago's nonwhites are Negroes) on measures of socioeconomic status and of residential segregation are presented in Table 2. For each of four measures reflecting socioeconomic status, there was improvement in the status of the nonwhite population between 1940 and 1960. (For whites, improving status would be more clearly evident if the data referred to the entire metropolitan area rather than just the city of Chicago.) The indexes of residential segregation between whites and Ne-groes, in the top panel of the table, show minor fluctuations around an extremely high level and give no indication of the decline anticipated on the basis of the socioeconomic advancement of the Negro population. That this is not an atypical finding is indicated by reference to other data show-ing a long term historical trend toward increasing residential segregation between whites and nonwhites. Increasing racial residential segregation was evident in most large cities of the United States between 1940 and 1950, while during the 1950's, southern cities continued to increase in segre-gation and northern cities generally registered modest declines.[11]

In broad perspective, the historical trend toward improving socioeco-nomic status of immigrant groups has gone hand in hand with decreasing

Table 2. Selected Socioeconomic Characteristics (Unstandardized) of Whites and Nonwhites, Chicago, 1940, 1950, and 1960

Characteristic	Nonwhite	White
Residential segregation index, whites vs. Negroes:*		
1930	85	
1940	85	
1950	79	
1960	83	
Percent high school graduates, age 25+:		
1940	16	25
1950	25	37
1960	29	37
Percent white collar, male:		
1940	17	40
1950	17	41
1960	21	40
Percent home-owners:		
1940	7	26
1950	12	33
1960	16	39
Percent multiple-person households with 1.01 or more persons per room:		
1940	41	17
1950	46	14
1960	34	10

* These values differ slightly from those cited in the text for Negroes as compared to native whites of native parentage.

Source: Data for 1940 from the 1940 Census Tract Bulletin for Chicago; for 1950 from Philip M. Hauser and Evelyn M. Kitagawa, eds., *Local Community Fact Book for Chicago, 1950* (Chicago: Chicago Community Inventory, 1953); and for 1960 from the 1960 Census Tract Bulletin for Chicago.

residential segregation. In contrast, Negro residential segregation from whites has increased steadily over past decades until it has reached universally high levels in cities throughout the United States, despite advances in the socioeconomic status of Negroes.

We have been unable to locate any data permitting a comparison between Negroes long resident in Chicago, or born and raised in the North, and Negroes with lesser periods of residence in the city. Thus we are not able to make even the crude intergenerational comparisons for Negroes that are possible for the immigrant groups. The only analysis of this type possible with census data is a comparison between recent migrants and the rest of the population, and the only published data are residential distributions, with no socioeconomic characteristics. For 1960, with the seventy-five community areas of Chicago as units, the index of residential segregation between nonwhites resident in the metropolitan area five years or more and native whites of native parents is 80.5. Comparing nonwhites with less than five years' residence in the metropolitan area and NWNP, the index was 81.0. Comparing the recent in-migrants with the nonwhites who were resident in the metropolitan area five years or more, the index was 13. Thus the recent nonwhite in-migrants are distributed differently from the rest of the nonwhite population, but each group is highly segregated from the native whites. Unfortunately, these results cannot be readily interpreted in terms of the general assimilation and dispersion processes under consideration. Possibly there are trends toward socioeconomic advancement and residential dispersion on the part of "second generation" Negroes in Chicago that are confounded in the data for the total Negro population.

Decreasing residential concentration of immigrant groups occurred despite the efforts of many nationality organizations to maintain the ethnic colonies.[12] Few Negro organizations have been as explicitly segregationist. In some immigrant groups, many members were dispersing from the ethnic colonies even while large-scale immigration of that group was still under way. For every immigrant group, diminishing residential segregation has been evident since the cessation of large-scale immigration. For Negroes, however, residential segregation has increased since the first period of large-scale in-migration to northern cities, and this increase in residential segregation continued during the late 1920's and 1930's when the volume of migration was at a low level. These observations tend to discredit the argument that a major barrier to residential dispersion of the Negro population of Chicago is its continuing rapid increase. However, the size of the Negro population and the magnitude of its annual increase are larger than for any single ethnic group in the past, and comparisons with smaller groups are not completely convincing. That rapid increase of Negro population does not necessarily lead to increasing residential segregation was demonstrated directly in the intercity comparative study previously cited. There was no definite relationship between increase in Negro population and increase in the value of the segregation index. Indeed, during the 1950–60 decade, there appeared to be a slight relationship in the opposite direction.[13]

More significant in accounting for the divergent trends in residential segregation may be the different urban contexts in which the immigrant and Negro populations found themselves. Comparing the residential locations of Italian-born and Polish-born in Chicago in 1899 and in 1920, Wallace observed:

> it can be seen that the areas of greatest dispersion, low proportion, and presumably of "second" settlement for many immigrants were those which were not settled at all in 1899.
>
> The implication of this fact is that the so-called "assimilation" process was not reflected by the geographic dispersion of the immigrant populations into "cosmopolitan American areas." The dispersal was more directly related to an increase in housing alternatives as the city grew at the periphery.[14]

By the time the Negro concentrations were forming near the central areas of Chicago, the city was built up and the urbanized area extended well beyond the present boundaries. Residential alternatives at a price Negroes could afford and located sufficiently close in to permit inexpensive commuting were no longer available.

It has been suggested that considerable time is required for Negroes to make the transition from a "primitive folk culture" to "urbanism as a way of life."[15] Several types of data indicate that large and increasing proportions of the Negro urban population are city-born and raised. For instance, there is a rapidly decreasing color differential in the percentage of the Chicago population born in the state of Illinois. In 1960, 44 percent of the native-born, nonwhite residents of Chicago were born in Illinois, as contrasted to 66 percent of the white population.[16] National estimates for 1958 showed that of all males aged 45–64 living in metropolitan places of 500,000 or more population, 65 percent of the nonwhites, as compared to 77 percent of the whites, had lived in this size city for twenty years or longer.[17] Estimates of the components of growth of the nonwhite population of Chicago indicate that between 1950 and 1960 natural increase was as important as net in-migration, and that natural increase will in the future account for rapidly increasing proportions of the growth of the nonwhite population.[18]

Unfortunately there is inadequate knowledge of the specific length of time under specified conditions for the required cultural transformation to occur. Wallace's observations indicate a significant degree of dispersal over time among first-generation immigrants. Such processes are more often conceived as primarily intergenerational. That many of the "first generation" Negro migrants to northern cities have lived there for twenty years or more and that in the younger adult ages there are sizable numbers of "second generation" urban Negroes suggest that there has been ample time for any necessary adjustment to urban living, at least for large proportions of the Negro population. It is also clear that if northern Negroes remain inadequately educated for urban living and fail to participate fully in the urban economy, the "primitive folk culture" of the South can less and less be assigned responsibility, and northern cities will be suffering from the neglect of their own human resources.

The "visibility" of Negroes due to skin color and other features which make the large majority of second-, third-, and later-generation descendants readily identifiable as Negroes is often cited as a basic factor in accounting for the distinctive position of Negroes in our society. It is exceedingly difficult to assess the significance of visibility. There is no other group that is strictly comparable to Negroes regarding every factor except visibility. It is not completely irrelevant, however, to note that nonwhite skin color, by itself, is not an insurmountable handicap in our society. The socioeconomic status of the Japanese population of Chicago in 1950 substantially exceeded that of the Negro population; and their residential segregation from whites, although high, was considerably lower than that between Negroes and whites.[19] Unfortunately there are no trend data available on the characteristics of the Japanese in Chicago. A more appropriate Japanese population for comparison, however, is the much larger one in the San Francisco area. A recent study there affirmed that "ethnic colonies of Japanese are gone or rapidly going" and documented their rapid socioeconomic advance.[20]

In the traditional immigrant pattern, the more recent immigrants displaced the older groups at the bottom socioeconomic levels. How do the Negroes compare with the other "newer" immigrant groups, the Mexicans and the Puerto Ricans? The limited data now available suggest that the Negroes may soon be left alone at the bottom of the social and economic scale. We have already noted (from data in Table 1) that the "newer" groups were, in 1950, of very low status compared to the other immigrant groups, and that their residential segregation from the native whites of native percentage was the highest of all the immigrant groups. For 1960, data on distribution within Chicago of persons born in Puerto Rico are available separately from data on those persons born in the United States of Puerto Rican parentage. Thus it is possible to compute indexes of residential segregation for first- and second-generation Puerto Ricans. For Chicago in 1960, these index values were 68.4 for the first generation and 64.9 for the second generation, indicating that residential dispersion has already begun for the Puerto Ricans. This difference actually understates the amount of dispersion, since the second generation consists in large proportion of children still living with their first-generation parents.

Selected socioeconomic measures for the Puerto Rican and the nonwhite populations of Chicago in 1960 are shown in Table 3. On every measure, the Puerto Rican population is less well off—it is less educated, has lower income, is more crowded, is less likely to own homes, is less well housed, and lives in older buildings. Yet the index of residential segregation (computed with respect to NWNP) for Puerto Ricans is 67 as compared with 82 for Negroes.

TABLE 3. SELECTED SOCIOECONOMIC CHARACTERISTICS (UNSTANDARDIZED) OF PUERTO RICANS AND NONWHITES, CHICAGO, 1960

Characteristic	Nonwhite	Puerto Rican
Residential segregation vs. whites	83	67
Percent high school graduates, total	29	11
Median family income	$4,742	$4,161
Percent families earning < $3,000	28	27
Percent families earning > $10,000	9	4
Percent home-owners	16	6
Percent substandard dwellings	26	33
Percent 1.01 or more persons per room	34	52
Percent housing units built since 1940	12	6
Median gross rent	$88	$79
Median number of rooms	3.9	3.7
Median number of persons	3.0	4.0

Source: Data are from the 1960 Census Tract Bulletin for Chicago.

Up to now we have been making comparisons between Negroes and immigrant groups, demonstrating that residential dispersion has not accompanied socioeconomic advance by Negroes in the way that it did for immigrant groups. Economic status and expenditure for housing, however, are clearly correlated, and there is also a correlation between economic status and residential segregation. By virtue of variations in the type, age, and quality of housing, and in the patterns of residential choice by persons of varying socioeconomic status, the subareas of a city are differentiated in terms of the average status of their residents. Since Negroes are of much lower average status than whites, they would be expected to be disproportionately represented in low-status residential areas. In fact, an extreme position regarding the relationships between patterns of socioeconomic residential segregation and racial residential segregation would attribute all of the latter to the former. Such a position is sometimes offered as a counterargument to charges of racial discrimination against the real estate business. To the extent that this position is correct, it might be expected that future economic advances on the part of the Negro population should be translated into decreased residential segregation.

The task of partialing out a component of racial segregation due to economic factors involves some difficult methodological problems, and no method is entirely satisfactory.[21] Our approach utilizes indirect standardization of available census data. Let us delineate the status of a residential area in terms of, say, the income distribution of its residents. Specifically, consider for each community area of Chicago the number of families with incomes below $1,000, from $1,000–1,999, from $2,000–2,999, and so forth. For the city as a whole in 1960, 44 percent of all families with an income below $1,000 were nonwhite, as were 44 percent of families with incomes from $1,000–1,999, and 40 percent of families with incomes from $2,000–2,999. For each community area, we can apply these city-wide percentages to the observed income distribution to obtain the number of nonwhite families expected if income alone determined the residential locations of whites and nonwhites.

By the method of indirect standardization just outlined, we obtain an expected number of nonwhite and white families for each of the seventy-five community areas. We can then compute an index of residential segregation between expected numbers of nonwhite and white families. This index can be regarded as the amount of racial residential segregation attributable to patterns of residential differentiation of income groups. For 1950, the index of residential segregation between the numbers of whites and nonwhites expected on the basis of income was 11, as compared with the actual segregation index of 79. As a rough measure, then, we can attribute 11/79, or 14 percent, of the observed racial residential segregation in Chicago in 1950 to income differentials between whites and nonwhites. For 1960, the corresponding values are 10 for the expected index, 83 for the observed index, and 12 percent for the racial segregation attributable to income differentials.

In a recent study of the relationships between housing consumption and income, Reid has demonstrated many pitfalls in the uncritical use of income distributions in the analysis of housing patterns.[22] We have therefore repeated the above analyses, using distributions by major occupational groups and distributions by educational attainment. For 1960, the index of residential segregation computed from the numbers of whites and nonwhites expected on the basis of patterns of occupational differentiation is 9, and that expected on the basis of patterns of educational differentiation is 3. The results using income distributions are thus supported by the results from other measures of socioeconomic status, and the conclusion seems clear that patterns of socioeconomic differentiation of residential areas can account for only a small proportion of observed racial residential segregation.

Reid demonstrated that differences between whites and nonwhites in observed patterns of housing consumption are largely attributable to income differentials between whites and nonwhites. Our analysis suggests that residential segregation cannot be attributed to these differentials. Apparently the economic structure of the housing market for whites is similar to that for nonwhites, even though nonwhites are excluded from a large share of the housing supply for which their economic circumstances would allow them to compete.

The judicious conclusion from our review of a variety of pieces of data is that we simply do not yet know enough about immigrant assimilation processes and any corresponding processes among Negro migrants to northern cities to be able to compare the two. We believe that this very lack of knowledge makes questionable any attempt to reason from presumed patterns of assimilation among immigrants in the past to current racial problems in northern cities. Furthermore, such evidence as we could compile indicates that it is more likely to be misleading than instructive to make such comparisons.

Our definition of assimilation as involving socioeconomic advancement and residential dispersion is simple, and greater differences between groups would appear were a more complex definition adopted. Restriction of portions of the analysis to the city of Chicago had little effect on the measures for nonwhites, but probably led to an understatement of the degree of assimilation of the immigrant stocks insofar as higher-status members of these groups have moved to the suburbs. The segregation indexes probably overstate somewhat the residential isolation of small groups, such as particular immigrant stocks, as compared with large groups such as total native whites of native parents. Taking account of any of these limitations in our data would tend to increase the differences between Negroes and immigrant groups. Even so, our data showed that second-generation persons from several countries are of higher socioeconomic status than the total native whites of native parentage. Relatively few Negroes in Chicago have white-collar jobs or incomes above the median level for whites, and yet there are large numbers of adult Negroes who were born in the city.

Basic differences between the Negroes and the immigrant groups seems to us implicit in the failure of residential desegregation to occur for Negroes while it has continued for the immigrant groups.

In view of the fundamental impact of residential segregation on extra-legal segregation of schools, hospitals, parks, stores, and numerous other facilities, the failure of residential dispersion to occur strikes us as an especially serious social problem. Socioeconomic advance and residential dispersion occurred simultaneously for the various immigrant groups. It is apparent that the continued residential segregation of the Negro population is an impediment to the continued "assimilation" of Negroes into full and equal participation in the economy and the society at large.

NOTES

[1] Paper No. 15 in the series, "Comparative Urban Research," was issued from the Population Research and Training Center, University of Chicago, under a grant from the Ford Foundation. A preliminary version of this paper was read at the 1962 annual meetings of the American Statistical Association. We appreciate the reactions of Stanley Lieberson, Judah Matras, and Margaret G. Reid to that version.

[2] Philip M. Hauser, "On the Impact of Urbanism on Social Organization, Human Nature and the Political Order," *Confluence*, 7 (1958), p. 65. Elsewhere Hauser has expressed a more cautious view, emphasizing the lack of definitive knowledge; see his *Population Perspectives* (New Brunswick, N.J.: Rutgers University Press, 1960), p. 129.

[3] D. J. Bogue, "Chicago's Growing Population Problem," *Commerce*, 59 (1962), p. 31.

[4] Gunnar Myrdal, *An American Dilemma* (New York: Harper & Bros., 1944), Vol. I, p. 618; Amos H. Hawley, "Dispersion versus Segregation: Apropos of a Solution of Race Problems," *Papers of the Michigan Academy of Science, Arts, and Letters*, 30 (1944), pp. 667–74.

[5] For an enumeration of some of the difficulties see C. A. Price and J. Zubrzycki, "The Use of Inter-marriage Statistics as an Index of Assimilation," *Population Studies*, 16 (1962), pp. 58–69.

[6] The index of residential segregation is an index of dissimilarity between the residential distributions of each group. For further discussion see Otis Dudley Duncan and Beverly Duncan, "A Methodological Analysis of Segregation Indexes," *American Sociological Review*, 20 (1955), pp. 210–17.

[7] For a more detailed discussion of these patterns, using data for 1930 and 1950 see Otis Dudley Duncan and Stanley Lieberson, "Ethnic Segregation and Assimilation," *American Journal of Sociology*, 64 (1959), pp. 364–74.

[8] Stanley Lieberson, *Ethnic Patterns in American Cities* (Glencoe, Ill.: The Free Press, 1963).

[9] For a discussion of class residential segregation in Chicago see Otis Dudley Duncan and Beverly Duncan, "Residential Distribution and Occupational Stratification," *American Journal of Sociology*, 60 (1955), pp. 493–503.

[10] Lieberson, *op. cit.*, pp. 120–32.

[11] Karl E. Taeuber, "Negro Residential Segregation, 1940–1960: Changing Trends in the Large Cities of the United States" (paper read at the Annual Meetings of the American Sociological Association, 1962).

[12] David A. Wallace, "Residential Concentration of Negroes in Chicago" (unpublished Ph.D. dissertation, Harvard University, 1953).

[13] Taeuber, *op. cit.*

[14] Wallace, *op. cit.*, p. 205.

[15] Philip M. Hauser, "The Challenge of Metropolitan Growth," *Urban Land*, 17 (1958), p. 5.

[16] Data from U.S. Bureau of the Census, *U.S. Census of Population, 1960: General Social and Economic Characteristics, Illinois.* Final Report PC(1)-15C, Tables 72 and 77.

[17] Karl E. Taeuber, "Duration-of-Residence Analysis of Internal Migration in the United States," *Milbank Memorial Fund Quarterly*, 39 (1961), Table 3.

[18] D. J. Bogue and D. P. Dandekar, *Population Trends and Prospects for the Chicago-Northwestern Indiana Consolidated Metropolitan Area: 1960 to 1990* (Chicago: Population Research and Training Center, University of Chicago, 1962).

[19] Although the maximum value of the residential segregation index is less than 100 for ethnic groups of small size, this is not sufficient to vitiate the Negro-Japanese comparison.

[20] Harry H. L. Kitano, "Housing of Japanese-Americans in the San Francisco Bay Area," in *Studies in Housing and Minority Groups*, Nathan Glazer and Davis McEntire, eds. (Berkeley: University of California Press, 1960), p. 184.

[21] A general discussion of this problem can be found in the section on explanation of areal variation in Otis Dudley Duncan, Ray P. Cuzzort, and Beverly Duncan, *Statistical Geography* (Glencoe, Ill.: The Free Press, 1961).

[22] Margaret G. Reid, *Housing and Income* (Chicago: University of Chicago Press, 1962).

| Dimensions of the Social Order | INTEGRATION |

COMMENTARY

As members of a social grouping are allocated to different roles and statuses, so too are they integrated into a functioning whole characterized by lines of authority and networks of communication. In highly organized groups the lines of authority and pattern of communication are highly structured. Such groups, commonly thought of as bureaucracies, exist to carry out defined tasks. Although patterns of influence and lines of communication exist in informal social groupings, they are less structured and the group may function around more diffuse tasks.

Richard McCleery's insightful analysis of the social organization of a prison community shows that the pattern of communication and the structure of authority are interdependent. It indicates that lines of communication can function to sustain a particular type of authority structure and that a change in the nature of the communication network can, in turn, influence the system of power. This study clearly points out the critical nature of lines of communication for the integration of a group.

The paper by William Evan and Morris Zelditch describes a laboratory experiment dealing with some of the components of Max Weber's theory of bureaucracy. It is an interesting example of how sociological variables can be manipulated creatively in the laboratory so as to give the experimenter control over "treatment" variables and yet avoid the artificiality characteristic of many laboratory experiments. In this experiment Evan and Zelditch deal with such variables as authority based on knowledge, authority deriving from formal position, and the attribution of legitimacy.

Marvin Sussman and Lee Burchinal, in their paper on the contemporary American family, contrast the conception of the isolated nuclear family with what they term the "modified extended family." Their discussion suggests that the network of kin relationships, within which the nuclear family is located, functions to sustain the family and integrate it into the larger industrial society.

18 RICHARD MCCLEERY

Communication Patterns as Bases of Systems of Authority and Power

The direct application of coercive force has been regarded as the most primitive and fundamental basis of power in interpersonal relations, and a substantial amount of political theory and governmental practice in the past has developed on that basis. In a stable social system, however, a pattern of communication appears in close association with the power structure; and an "authoritative allocation of values" in that society becomes a matter of the creation and circulation of definitions rather than a matter of the application of force. While abstract political theory may find the ultimate basis of authority in force, empirical research often finds interaction equated with influence, and the process by which definitions are given equated with power.[1]

If we assume that communication patterns serve as a functional equivalent of force in sustaining the power structure of a stable society, three propositions would seem to follow: (1) A change in the formal power structure should be reflected in the society's patterns of communication and contact. (2) Change in the patterns of communication, however instituted, should react on the system of formal power and authority. (3) Failure of the communication patterns to correspond to the requirements of a given system of authority should result in disorder and anarchy.

Reprinted from *Theoretical Studies in Social Organization of the Prison* (New York: Social Science Research Council, 1960), Pamphlet 15 and *Policy Change in Prison Management* (East Lansing: Government Research Bureau, Michigan State University, 1957), by permission of the author and the publisher.

The prison, as a distinctive system of power, provides a setting in which to examine these hypotheses. Although a prison should not be considered uncritically as a society in microcosm, the comparative isolation of its social processes from the impact of external variables provides an unusually favorable opportunity for systematic analysis. The vast majority of interaction patterns in its society begin and end within the walls. Power relations may be observed under extreme conditions, and the identification of formal and informal processes is simplified by sharp distinctions between a ruling class and a subject class in the prison community.

The present report is based on material collected in a study of prison management in transition, which compared the processes of inmate society under authoritarian and more liberal penal administrations.[2] The institution that provided the bulk of this material—a small general prison in Hawaii, which housed approximately 400 felons in conditions of medium to maximum security—was studied at the beginning and end of a decade of change from repressive authoritarian control to relatively liberal governing procedures and a philosophy of rehabilitation. This report focuses on the communication patterns that seemed to constitute the bases of these two different systems of power in the institution. Prior to 1946, its administrative policies adhered with little variation to a punitive tradition already outdated in many American prisons. Changes (which provide the independent variable of this analysis) were introduced after 1946, when a new warden was appointed following the death of his predecessor in office. These changes, which flowed from a different approach to administration by the new warden, may be thought of as an almost fortuitous addition to the closed system of the prison, in that they did not represent an administrative shake-up or mandate for reform. Throughout the period of the study the prison was relatively free from political embroilment and public pressures.

In broad outline, the following discussion considers the administrative and social characteristics of the old authoritarian prison, the changes introduced and their administrative and social consequences, and the processes of reconstruction that ensued in the official and inmate societies.

THE AUTHORITARIAN PRISON

The political character of the prison's power system before 1946 can best be shown by analogy with the authoritarian state.[3] The system was totalitarian in that all the basic processes necessary to sustain life within the walls were subject to detailed official regulation. The prison was organized so that a monopoly of discretion and control was retained by the executive. All issues were resolved in the interests of an abstract "state," which was separate from the will and welfare of the subjects. The only orientation that officials gave to new inmates was the assertion that no "rights" but only "privileges" attached to their status. The foundations of stability were laid in the operational values of order, discipline, and the unqualified backing of the official class.

Examples of the exercise of power within the prison system, the organization of the official hierarchy, and the structure of inmate society indicate that each of these elements was conditioned by patterns of communication characteristic of the traditional prison.

Exercise of Power   The procedures of governing may be illustrated in respect to policy decisions, processes of control, and ordinary operations. In principle, the widest policy discretion was centralized in the warden's office. In practice, policy was static and quite at odds with the few available declarations of principles and aims. The locus of decision was beyond the range at which the interests of inmates could be communicated and was not reached by records reflecting their needs. Control over policy followed control over the information on which it was based. The prevailing policy of using inmate labor only in menial tasks of no apparent value to the inmate and little value to the government contradicted formal declarations of institutional policy but illustrated a principle of wide application in this social system: *Decisions reflect the interests that are communicated most effectively on the administrative level at which decisions are made.* The institutional autocrat is not responsible to his subordinates, but he is no less responsive than any other executive to those who define the premises of his discretion.

In the authoritarian prison the exercise of power based essentially on force seemed to be the foundation of social control. But this power was perhaps least effective when it took the form of punitive sanctions imposed on individuals. A high degree of discipline was maintained with the minimum of direct sanctions. Vitally important in social control were procedures of regimentation—frequent counts and assemblies—which imposed a psychology of domination by placing the subject in a posture of silence, respect, and awe. Recognition of distinctions in rank was imposed in all contacts between inmates and officials by the requirement of a salute and special forms of address.

More punitive forms of control rested on summary procedure and a few rules as broad in their application as the officers' judgment of insubordination. Control, rather than "justice" in the familiar sense, was the object. Hence, there was no place for a body of principles or "constitutional" rights to restrain disciplinary procedure. Secret accusation was the rule, and the accused had no notice, hearing, counsel, or appeal. The resulting atmosphere of "terror," produced as much by this secrecy as by the actual use of informers, was a basic element in official control and, as will be shown, a major source of values and social structure of the inmate community. Uncertainty, even more than exemplary punishment, is a keystone of "terror" as a technique of government, and it was a major factor in control in the traditional prison.

The distinguishing characteristic of ordinary operations in the traditional prison was the absence of alternatives for behavior permitted or provided for the subjects. Rewards went only for conformity to prescribed behavior, and initiative was as suspect to the static inmate society as to the officials. This ritual conformity is another characteristic of autocracy. However, a complex system of organization and communication that emerged in the inmate society could not be suppressed by the most stringent "silent system," but only controlled. Contacts with the outside world were subject to rigid official supervision. The close censorship of all outside contacts was as characteristic of the authoritarian prison as it is of the authoritarian state. The subordinate officers as well as inmates were forbidden to communicate any institutional affairs to outsiders. Silence was enforced wherever the inmates congregated, and interactions of lesser officials and inmates were closely restricted. The senior custodial officers were fully aware of the security implications of their censorship of outside contacts.

Organization and Communication   That formal organization is modified by the location and control of communication channels was well illustrated in the authoritarian prison, whose general policy had long recognized industry and reform as goals along with custodial control. Other ends were actually subverted to custody, as the following analysis shows. Control over communication produced effects normally associated with direct exercise of executive power, i.e., it established the hierarchy of organization as actually perceived by the inmates, selectively emphasized certain values, inculcated attitudes, adapted the functions of some units to the service of others, and maintained discipline within the staff.

As already noted, the absence of an effective industrial program was in part a result of the locus of decision making; but the role of the industrial supervisors was institutionalized in relation to the custodial force. The center for all communication was the captain's office, as required by custodial accounting for the movement of inmates. All counts, time books, orders, requests, and reports passed through the custodial hierarchy. With all orders and assignments thus channeled and controlled, the perceived status of work supervisors was below that of the guards, from whom in effect the supervisors took their orders.

The institutional pressures and requirements that dominated the office where communication centered dictated its content and its use, namely, for the constant reassertion of custodial values in all aspects of institutional life. Record items on costs, production, or the needs of inmates might be ignored. Custodial control of communications and the interactional patterns thus established tended to impose custodial attitudes, values, and behavior throughout the industrial program, negating its formal institutional position and purposes.

Work supervisors had little contact with their formal superior, the superintendent of industry, but daily contact with the guards. The supervisors' ability to communicate their day-to-day operational needs thus depended on their relations with the guards. Such contact normally involves effective communication only to the extent that attitudes, values, and definitions are shared. Perhaps as a result of this contact, supervisors as a rule came to think, act, and dress like the guards. The supervisors justified labor in terms of disciplinary rather than productive or training values, maintained sharp class distinctions on the job, and repressed the rare examples of initiative on the part of inmate employees. Accepting the definition of labor and the status of the supervisor implicit in this situation, inmates opposed the industrial program and contributed the bare minimum of effort that would be tolerated. Supervisors in turn borrowed custodial rationalizations and blamed failures of production on the malice and incompetence of the inmates. The resulting institutionally shared belief in the limited possibilities of prison industry further reduced its role. On the basis of the only information available it was asserted that inmates could only work at simple tasks under close supervision.

Professional services, such as psychological testing, were performed occasionally in the authoritarian institution. Referrals to and reports from these services were passed through custodial channels, which emphasized security considerations and neglected all else. Inmates believed, with some justification, that these services were subordinated to custody and in general regarded the professional with a contempt inconsistent with his formal status or the intent of his work.[4] That contempt, in turn, reduced the actual function of professional services to insignificance.

Thus, control of communications permitted the custodial force to adapt the efforts of other institutional units to the support of its own functions and status. All orders and reports were mechanically routed through the captain's office, it censored mail, and passed on requests by inmates for interviews with other officials. These functions implied additional discretionary control and command of information. Although the custodial force enjoyed an actual power to negate or compromise other institutional functions that held equal formal work, this power as perceived by the subjects and their deference to the custodial force were greater than its actual influence on formal policy would seem to justify. The dominance of the custodial position in the prison suggests that any social system in which security involves censorship will tend to assume the characteristics of a "police state." The "police state" must be distinguished here from the classic model of the authoritarian autocracy in that it is the police agency or palace guard that ultimately rules. The delegation of a monopoly of control over communication has far different and greater implications of dictatorial power in a society than has the simple delegation of a monopoly over the instruments of force.

The custodial hierarchy, in which the central power structure was thus institutionally lodged, was a disciplined and uniformed force modeled on military organization. Promotion by seniority was the basic route of advancement from guard through sergeant, watch officer, and senior captain, and to positions such as admissions officer, recreation officer, and mess steward. Within that structure it was necessary to resolve the problems of authoritarian control—the extreme restraint of discretion on the part of subordinates and the unqualified support of the officials in their relations with the inmates.

The principle of "backing up" the subordinate would seem to maximize discretionary authority throughout an organization, but in the authoritarian prison any tendency in this direction was controlled by the absence of two-way communication within the hierarchy. All communication flowed upward, leaving each superior better informed than his subordinate and limiting the information on which discretion could be based at lower levels. Since formal definitions alone are not sufficient to enforce discipline and establish the legitimacy of the superior in a strict hierarchy, the patterns of communication in the authoritarian prison served to make the official hierarchy an intellectual elite and to legitimize the assumption that the superior was correct on any issue. He was always better informed. Captains of the yard perpetuated, with some success, a myth of their omniscience as a means of control.

The techniques of influencing decisions in the prison involved withholding information as well as injecting it into communication channels. However, subordinate officers were hesitant about stopping reports or denying requests where there was any possibility of being reversed. Each superior reinforced his position in the hierarchy with a wider range of movement and wider access to personal contacts than that enjoyed by his subordinates. Status in both the official and the inmate communities was closely related to freedom of movement, although both communities considered power to command others the fundamental basis of prestige. The power to influence was directly proportionate to a person's position in the network of communication channels.

The situation described appears to place the senior captain in a power position superior to that of the warden. As seen from the vantage point of the prison yard, or measured by the relative stability of tenure in the two positions, that would seem to be true. The warden "made" all policy decisions and his deputy countersigned disciplinary orders, but these actions were taken on the basis of the records submitted by the captain's office. This controlled internal policy. The actual superiority of the warden's position appeared in respect to external policy. All correspondence to and from the institution crossed the warden's desk, giving him the broadest perspective and hence the widest discretion in external affairs. Within the institution, however, the power to make definitions and decisions followed control of the information on which these had to be based.

So far, we have seen that the formal power structure of the traditional prison was supported by measures of communications control similar to those associated with authoritarian government, and that the custodial force used its control over communications to assert its dominance over other institutional purposes and to support its own disciplined hierarchy. Through this structure the institution performed its function, as defined by the guards, of "waking them, working them, and locking them up again." In order to understand how a few aging and ill-educated custodians, as few as 8 men to a night watch, could control 400 bitter and frustrated felons in custody, some comment on the inmate social system is necessary.

Inmate Society   Two apparent contradictions in the inmate community in the authoritarian prison—the emergence of a strict hierarchy of power among inmates presumed to be powerless, and the dominant patterns of conformity found in just those prisons whose repressive regimes would seem most likely to provoke rebellion—are resolved in the light of the direct consequences that the informational environment of inmate society has for its social process and structure.

Inmates demanded and officials asserted as a premise of prison life that all inmates must be treated equally. However, the basic interpersonal relationship among inmates was actually that of dominance and subordination, and the highest value was placed on the exercise of coercive power.[5] This goal of control over men may have been uncritically borrowed by inmates from officials, for there were striking parallels between the values of the inmate and official societies. The pursuit of power, however, was more than simply an end in itself.[6] Having power meant gaining freedom from the pressures and exploitations operating within the inmate social system.

A general goal of inmates was to achieve independence from official pressures and sanctions. To achieve this freedom from interference, inmate society enforced conformity by sanctions more severe than those used by officials. Defying formal premises of equality, contradicting official discriminations against recidivists, lacking familiar symbols of class in position or possessions, inmate society developed a power hierarchy as sharply defined and immobile as that of the administration. The survival of that inmate hierarchy and the process by which it was sustained depended on a basic rule of the inmate code: *Never talk to a screw.*

The absence of published regulations and the lack of a formal orientation program, the secrecy and the arbitrariness associated with the enforcement of discipline, the shocking unfamiliarity of the prison situation, and the demands that regimentation imposed, all combined to make the newly admittted inmate completely dependent on the experienced prisoner.[7] In a unique sense, his knowledge was power. He could share on his own conditions his knowledge of the limits of official tolerance and the means by which sanctions could be avoided, which could make life tolerable for the new man. The conditions of his inclusion in the inmate community were acceptance of a subordinate role in the community and adoption of its attitudes and values. Its values began with rejection of contact with officials and culminated in rejection of allegiance to society as a whole.

At the bottom of the social scale were the *fish* (men who had just been caught) and those homosexuals whose role symbolized abject submission. Authoritarian society in the prison, as elsewhere, regarded the weak with a contempt not unmixed with hatred and fear. The lower classes consisted of inmates suspected of illicit conversation with officials, those who held com-

promising jobs with the administration, men whose strong ties to the outside world and hopes of freedom made them disinclined to resist official
pressure, and those few who openly rejected inmate values. The prison
community protected itself from betrayal by ostracizing such men from
communication and the benefits of membership. At the same time, it regarded isolates as fair game for abuse, domination, or exploitation. The
inmates classified and segregated the men who seemed least attached to
criminal values in a manner difficult for official classification to match. By
constant emphasis on the idea of the *rat*, and the use of isolation as a sanction, inmate society retained its maximal valuation of power and still restricted the most obvious recourse to power—the appeal to official sanctions
by individuals in their own interest.

Against this background it is possible to interpret the inmates' demand
for equality of treatment. This was not a demand upon the administration,
but an assertion among inmates that power obtained by contacts outside
their community had no legitimacy there. Inmates did talk to the *screws*
and obtain the currency of inmates—candy and cigarettes—through outside contacts; but a man's status in the inmate community depended on
his role there and his conformity to its norms. The principle of equality
meant that each inmate started even at the bottom of the social scale,
subordinate to those who shared the knowledge of experience. The denial
of validity to outside contacts protected the inmate culture from criticism
and assured the stability of the social system.

Courage, the ability to take punishment without complaint, and conformity to group norms were the means by which a new inmate gradually
gained acceptance into a protective primary group. In the authoritarian
prison the prevailing hostility and fear of betrayal normally prevented
coalitions of these groups for rational action. The senior inmates who had
proved their "rightness" to several primary groups over a period of years
or previous confinements held a distinct advantage. Their wider range of
communication contacts enabled them to influence transfers, to manipulate
the system by which goods were exchanged or stolen, and to circulate
warnings of official action. Their ability to predict where force would fall,
and to give or withhold warning, was a vital source of power and freedom
from sanctions in a society that valued these above all else.

Leadership in the inmate society involved the ability to explain, predict,
or control to some degree a situation in which others were uncertain and
helpless. Other inmates gained protection and security by attaching themselves to the leaders and rendering them the petty tributes that conveyed
status. This type of dominance depended on access to informal communications, whereas in a society in which information is a free good, leadership
normally depends on the functions that one performs in meeting the needs
and problems of the group, i.e., on ability to manipulate an objective situation. The problems of the prison society were not those of food, shelter,
or management but of uncertainty and ego threat in an environment of
arbitrary power. Hence, leadership there meant having contacts with the

"grapevine" and with official sources. Whether the leaders actually manipulated power or simply manipulated belief, they were expected to mediate between the official forces and their own followers, and were given license to talk with officials that was never extended to men of unproven dependability.

The "squad-room lawyer" or "water-fountain lawyer" is a familiar figure in many modern organizational settings. This role was elevated to one of leadership in the prison situation by certain of its characteristics that are remarkably similar to those of a primitive society, confronted by a hostile and mysterious universe. Lacking any understanding of the forces that moved their world, prisoners, like primitives, invented a class of devils, evil spirits, or *rats* to explain the appearance of arbitrary forces. Accepting a "devil theory" to account for such forces, inmate society, like its primitive counterpart, was easily dominated by a "priesthood" skilled in manipulating its concepts. This leadership provided satisfying explanations and a sense of security, never corroded by a natural or official explanation of the facts. The "myths" of inmate society attributed a certain dignity and freedom to the inmate class while holding officials in contempt.

The experienced old *con*, with his connection in the captain's office, his stolen key to the supply room, and his ready stock of satisfying interpretations, performed important adjustive functions which were suitably rewarded by inmate society. However, the atmosphere of condemnation and the sense of guilt imposed by the prison itself provided still another basis of dominance: the inmate who had no fear of official penalties was always able to dominate those whose obvious longing for freedom made them avoid trouble at all costs. In order to protect themselves against such fearless individuals, all inmates were under compulsion to act tough and pretend that they were not afraid of losing their accumulated good time. Up to a point, the valued ability to be tough, to take punishment without breaking, and to *do your own time* simply reaffirmed official aims and was a central part of the process by which inmate society adjusted to prison life.

In a period of disorganization or challenge to inmate values, however, the assertion of "moral independence" and contempt for the official system had a special, self-justifying aspect, which raised the inmate whose rebellion was uncurbed even by the most violent official sanctions to the status of a Promethean *hero*.[8] The utter disregard of consequences, expressed by attacks on officials or repeated attempts to escape, assumed the stature of moral courage, which was enhanced by the disproportionate weight of the punishment involved. The function performed for inmate society by the *hero* is suggested by the extent to which normally aggressive inmates conspired to smuggle food, candy, cigarettes, and even better clothing into the punishment cell, and the efforts made to enlist him into various primary groups on his release.[9]

Under stable conditions, inmate culture reasserted the custodial values. Its emphasis on conformity, on doing one's own time without breaking or complaint, on never talking to a *screw*, and on avoiding any activity that would *bring on the heat* was ideally suited to custodial control. Inmate culture stressed the goals of adjustment within the walls and the rejection of outside contacts, supported a rigid hierarchy with the strictest social controls, reduced new arrivals to subordination, and resolved its own social problems with sanctions more severe than those available to the guards. As shown by later developments in the prison, control of a disorganized body of inmates was beyond the skill of the custodial force. Control of a rigid social structure in which the vast majority of definitions and sanctions were informally imposed was much simpler. The custodial goals of peace, order, and adjustment dictated an alliance between senior guards and inmate leaders in the interests of stability and minimized the role of the *hero*.

In some respects the inmates ran the authoritarian prison. Those whose leadership rested on ability to predict and control power gained a voice in the assignment of men to jobs and quarters. The evasion of rules and pilfering of supplies that supported the position of the leaders were tolerated by officials; and their power to tolerate misbehavior conditionally is critical to any understanding of their role. "Surprise" searches were made known in advance to key inmates who dispensed warnings as a form of patronage.

Integrating relations between officials and inmate leaders were normally conducted in a responsible way and often by top officials and high-status inmates who shared a sincere contempt for *rats*. The exchanges were not motivated by a desire to employ sanctions against individuals or to gain an immediate private advantage, but to maintain peaceful and orderly conditions in which each senior group enjoyed its superior position. Each group held power in its own sphere by virtue of its ability to predict events, and each was able to extend its power by communication. These intergroup contacts gave warning of danger, and their collapse threatened the entire social system of the prison. While the authoritarian system might be accused of tolerating abuse, corruption, exploitation, and inequality, these were permitted in the interests of security and submission—the values most firmly institutionalized in the system.

THE LIBERAL REVOLUTION

The period of transition in the prison studied can be divided into three somewhat overlapping phases. The first extended from the death of the warden in August 1946 to the end of 1950. During this period a liberal group emerged in the prison staff, gained formal authority, and revolutionized formal institutional policy. From 1950 through 1953 this liberal group engaged in a contest with the custodial force for control over operating procedures and, in effect, for control over the prison population. This contest, in which control was nearly lost altogether, ended in the defeat of the "old guard." The period from 1954 to the present has been one of reconstruction, adjustment of conflict, and (in official language) "tightening up the organization."

The seeds of institutional revolution were contained in the appointment of five new staff members without previous penal experience, who would not or could not adjust to the traditional processes by which custody had become fixed as the basic institutional goal. The extent to which these new men injected into the prison behavior patterns drawn from the free community, as much as their explicitly democratic policy statement which was adopted later, categorizes the change as a liberal or democratic revolution. The character of this congenial staff group and of the changes they introduced may be indicated by examples of their impact on the institution— specifically of the effects of new patterns of interpersonal contact on general policy decisions, disciplinary procedures and control, industrial policy and operations, and the authoritarian traditions that had determined the nature of contacts between staff and inmates in the past.

Changing Patterns of Interpersonal Contact   First, the appointment of a new and inexperienced warden altered the environment of decision making and its consequences. In his view, his task was to create an open situation from which informed decisions would emerge, rather than to make these decisions himself. Except for a personal belief in frankness and fair play, he arrived with no commitment to change policy or personnel; but his easy personal accessibility and "open door" management techniques in themselves had radical implications for policy. These practices greatly enlarged the range of interests and information that bore on policy decisions.

The automatic endorsement of the punishment orders prepared by custodial officers came to an end in 1947 with the resignation of the old deputy warden. The new deputy refused to sign these orders without a hearing and the presentation of evidence. This requirement of "due process" in the imposition of sanctions tended to introduce "justice" rather than control as the object of disciplinary procedures and, also, to narrow the range of custodial discretion at a critical point. It eliminated some of the information (general considerations of security) that had controlled past decisions and introduced into the decision-making process certain new evidence and the bearers of it. The establishment of these new semijudicial procedures was reflected almost immediately in a lessened atmosphere of "terror" in the prison but also in an increase in disorder and disciplinary violations.

The traditional design of a prison industrial program, the assignment of inmates to simple tasks under close supervision, was rejected by a new industrial superintendent, appointed in 1948. That design was replaced with plans for a craft-shop type of enterprise in which major responsibilities for production were delegated to inmates under light and cooperative supervision. A breakdown of authoritarian relationships and sharp class distinctions soon appeared within the work program and later posed a challenge to authoritarian traditions within the prison proper.

A less tangible element—an informality in interpersonal relations—was added by a new director of education, who introduced social practices from his background as a boy's camp official. He acted out in the prison his faith in the basic goodness of men. To his seat on the newly formed disciplinary committee he brought a presumption of the innocence of the accused which no amount of judicial due process alone can impose.

A fifth man, who joined the staff as a part-time consultant and rose to the post of superintendent, introduced leadership techniques and group discussion procedures from his own background in adult education. Believing in the importance of written principles, he wove the scattered liberal ideas that gained a foothold in the institution into a "Policy and Philosophy Manual," which came to have "constitutional" standing.

The appointment of these men did not in itself represent a mandate to alter the formal power structure or policy of the prison, although the appointments of course were policy choices in their own right and exercises of power in respect to the system. For the purposes of this analysis, the complex variable introduced into the system consisted of new patterns of interpersonal contact and communication. These new patterns violated the traditional set of relationships by which authority and the power structure of the institution had been maintained. The following sections trace the way in which these new patterns affected formal policy and the structure of authority in both the official and inmate communities. The relationship between a pattern of communication and power may be seen in these unanticipated consequences of change.

Reformulation of Policy   Few substantial changes were made in the first 18 months of the new warden's tenure. At the time of his appointment he had been warned of corruption in the custodial ranks. His efforts to investigate this illustrate the custodial control over policy by monopoly of communication contacts and the nature of relations between guards and inmates in the traditional prison. After a year of fruitless efforts to gain information through the custodial hierarchy, the warden employed an outside investigator. This inquiry resulted in the dismissal of several employees for blatant and continued violations of the rules concerning trading with the inmates. Because of the long toleration of such practices and their place in the informal system of control, and particularly because of the fact that in some cases information had been acquired from inmates, the guards felt a sharp sense of injustice and resentment.

The disciplined traditions of the custodial force and its attitudes toward authority, however, blocked its use of the new warden's "open door." Those who took advantage of access were the new employees who had little awareness of the traditional chain of command, except as a device by which their functions were frustrated. (Other, noncustodial employees in the past had resigned in the face of such frustration.) The new men by-passed traditional channels and organized an informal policy caucus around the warden. Thus their concerns—industry, education, and treatment—gained a direct hearing which they had not previously enjoyed.

At that point the technique of controlling decisions by limiting the records on which they were based reacted against the custodial force. The new group was able to introduce a wider range of pertinent considerations for policy making than had reached the warden in the past. Access to the decision-making process by officials charged with treatment responsibilities constituted a virtual representation of the interests and welfare of the inmates. This access also kept free from custodial restriction a wider scope of treatment and industrial activities than had previously been the case. The addition of training classes and production shops to the prison program brought the new officials into direct and less formal contact with inmates.

The liberal group established itself as an advisory body and produced a chart of the organization of the prison. In contradiction of the actualities of custodial domination, this chart placed the new functions on a level coordinate with custody. This was a critical redefinition of roles, if not of powers, within the institution. Discarding its advisory capacity, the next step of the liberal group was to formalize, with the warden's consent, its position as a policy-making agency for internal affairs. This policy committee was dominated by an alliance between treatment and production officials, skillfully led by the director of treatment. The custodial force, numerically the largest group of employees, had only minority representation on the committee; and other officials who had risen through the custodial ranks to high position in the old, informal power structure were excluded.

There had been no formal statement of purpose in the traditional prison between the establishing statute and the descriptive, "wake 'em, work 'em . . ." slogan of the guards. An authoritarian system resolves issues by appeal to the superior official rather than to principle and so is necessarily weak in ideology. Furthermore, authoritarian discipline is subverted by the publication of principles to which appeals from individuals can be made. A "Policy and Philosophy Manual" nevertheless was the next project of the liberal group. This Manual asserted "rehabilitation through treatment and constructive industry" to be the primary purpose of the institution, and stated that "the democratic approach to management is the soundest." It included as commitments:

> The delegation to lower management levels of all possible responsibility and authority commensurate with sound management.
> A practice of constant consultation, dissemination of information, and discussion of problems up and down the management chain.

These principles struck at the heart of authoritarian hierarchy and control. Custodial officers were members of the council that produced the Manual, and there is no indication of any effective resistance to its publication. Unable to communicate effectively in the new forum of decision, suspicious and on the defensive, the custodial force retreated to its base of control over actual operations, procedures, and communications in the prison yard. Armed with their formalized principles, the liberal group moved to contest that area. The warden himself defended the establishment of an elected inmate council on the ground that men could not be *prepared* for return to the free community while their every action was dictatorially governed. The reaction of the guards, not transmitted to the policy level, was that prisoners could not be *prevented* from returning to the free community by democratic means.

From one point of view it would seem that the revolution in the prison had been accomplished by 1950. The liberal group had gained status and influence, drafted a "constitution," and seized control of the policy-making process thus created. In terms of the operating procedures of the institution, however, the revolution had scarcely begun. As long as the work supervisors reported to the custodial force, their programs operated on essentially traditional lines. The policy committee wrote new regulations, but the guards continued to enforce the old. At this point—one not uncommon in the administration of penal or other public institutions—the reformulation of general policy had little visible impact on actual procedures, but it had set the stage for conflict over operational definitions.

Procedural Revolution   Consistent with the new policy that all those affected by a decision should have an understanding of the issues and a voice in their determination, discussion meetings were started in several sections of the organization. Led by the treatment director, these discussions were most effective in the new and more complex units of the industrial program, where they enabled the supervisors' interests to be advanced outside the custodial hierarchy and stimulated revision of the rules: the time-honored salute and other elements of regimentation that had hindered productive work were abandoned. Within the custodial force the discussion meetings had almost no noticeable impact. The inmate council, established at the beginning of 1951, was given the right to debate any issue and to make proposals for decision by the staff policy committee. The council, with an adviser from the treatment unit, set up working committees on such areas as food, hobby and craft work, education, recreation, and public relations. Significantly, it called itself "the voice of the inmates."

Developments which followed began to challenge the realities of custodial control in one area after another. In the past, punishment, job assignment, good-time allowance, promotion, and every type of petty privilege had been administered by the custodial force with particular concern for control. When that administration had been, in effect, delegated to senior inmates, it served the interests of control no less in reinforcing the stability of the inmate social system than in applying sanctions to individuals. The use of seniority and the appearance of adjustment within the walls as bases for the distribution of privilege had reinforced the dominance of conservative and *con-wise* old prisoners. The basic tactic of the liberals was to alter the method and, hence, the dominant motive in decisions on privilege and punishment. The treatment office moved into decisions in this area, urging that privilege should be "meaningful" and that incentives should be concentrated behind the "goals of the institution." In defense of treatment personnel, it must be said that they had little conception of the extent or manner in which all operations had been concentrated behind the goals of security and custody. They had no understanding of the "economy of scarcity" that prevailed in the inmate community and the extent to which a small privilege extended to the "wrong" inmate could disturb the social order.[10] Their focus on the individual rather than the system—a focus permitted by their lack of custodial responsibilities—was a basic element in their conflict with the authoritarian tradition.

Participation in the expanding range of activities sponsored by the treatment unit became the basis of a record. For adequate performance of the more complex processes of production it was necessary for supervisors to reward their more effective workmen. The records of each inmate's work behavior were sent directly to the treatment office and were considered relevant to daily operating decisions; the decisions responded to the interests that were communicated most effectively. For example, "time off for good behavior" became a committee decision on commutation in which six factors, only one of which was conduct, were given equal weight; and the interest in teaching trades became the ground for moving the administration of transfers from the custodial force to the treatment office.

In successive areas, extending finally to recreation and entertainment, the treatment office first asserted an informed interest and then assumed the management of the function. When the custodial force was stripped of everything but its guns as a basis of control, the rise of disorder indicated that such a basis is weak indeed. The range of discretionary power held by an agency of the institution is no wider than, but tends to be as wide as, its store of information on which discretion is based.

SOCIAL IMPACT OF CHANGE

The old prison, like most institutions of its type, was highly resistant to formal declarations of policy change. Only as new policy was translated into patterns of daily contact and communication did it produce significant consequences in the prison as a social system. However, the consequences went far beyond the intentions of policy or any of the participants. The extent to which altered patterns of interaction undermined traditional values and authority in the prison, the way in which this provoked a revolt by the "old guard" custodial employees, and the ensuing social disorganization in the inmate community are traced in this section.

Challenge to Authority   As noted earlier, much of the social control of the old prison rested on the structure and informal sanctions of inmate society. These were the controls first challenged by new channels of communication. A change of major significance was that of publishing a detailed statement of policy and rules. This substituted something of a "rule of law" for the rule of discretionary authority. The publication of policy, prohibitions, and defined limits on penalties gave each inmate equal access to that information and avoided differentiations of influence based on the variable ability of "cell-block lawyers" to predict the consequences of an act.

Another important change was the establishment of the inmate council. This provision for legitimate group discussion subverted that clique of experienced inmates who, by monopolizing the limited channels of contact, previously had supplied definitions for the entire group. In addition, the council provided a means of recognition for the men most able to work effectively with or for the administration. Both the council and the publication of policy destroyed the definitional role of the custodial force in the traditional system.

The doctrine of individualized treatment was realized to only a limited degree in actual programs, but it called for new contacts and fuller hearings for the expressions of inmates. Regular consultation and counseling with inmates made some members of the treatment staff advocates of inmate needs in the policy discussions of the administration. Changes in the industrial policy of the prison permitted new social relationships in the workshops and gave some inmates new channels of influence and representation through their supervisors. Officials whose most frequent personal contacts were with inmates became a source of criticisms of the administration that circulated in inmate society.

While these changes took place elsewhere in the prison, the custodial force retained its previous hierarchical structure of communications. This limited system of contact within the institution sustained the traditional custodial attitudes free from challenge or criticism, but at the same time frequently left watch officers less well-informed than the inmates they guarded and so removed the legitimate basis of the authority of the guards. For the relative decline of status that inevitably followed, they tended to blame the treatment unit and its programs. The over-all consequence of the policy change that provided equal access to information and influence was to flatten the status pyramid of prison society and to narrow the gaps in social distance between the hierarchical levels of authority. At the same time the seeds of conflict were planted in both official and inmate societies.

Revolt of the "Old Guard" Each of the developments described served to undermine the status and authority of the guards and the control they had exercised over the inmates. In spite of public beliefs to the contrary, the theme of the old inmate culture had been adjustment and not rebellion. The rise of a new orientation, which followed the concentration of incentives behind treatment, threatened to cause a crisis in the prison community.

The custodial force resisted the changes to the best of its ability. In its view the new officials violated the chain of command and the prerogatives of rank at every turn. The failure of treatment officials to maintain the distinctions of rank with inmates threatened the psychology of domination.

Policy discussions with the inmate council, plus the new disciplinary procedures, broke down control based on secrecy and fear. Through the council the inmates achieved more direct representation in policy decisions than the guards themselves enjoyed. The freedom of movement given by treatment officials to some inmates, in connection with new activities, confounded custodial accounting for movement and disorganized the status system of the yard. Finally, the guards thought, with reason, that they knew more about inmate behavior in the authoritarian prison than did treatment officials. Guards were in a favorable position to see the inmates exploiting new activities in pursuit of traditional institutional values of dominance and power.

The limited communication to subordinates, which had supported the authoritarian hierarchy among both guards and inmates, had been supplemented by a "grapevine" of horizontal communication, which had supported the functions of each level of the hierarchy with self-justifying rationalizations. The price of acceptance into the peer group at any level had been acceptance of the legitimacy of these concepts and justifications. This informal indoctrination had been a central part of the process of social control. The guards, who had no idea of an authority of function as opposed to that of rank, regarded the powers of treatment officials as improperly assumed and irresponsibly used. As the liberal revolution redistributed power and status in the institution, it challenged the moral order of the guards' universe and provoked an organized and effective revolt—based on a righteous conviction that the liberal program was a compromise with criminals and sin.

The tactics of the custodial counterattack are pertinent to this analysis. Literal enforcement of old rules against communication and movement halted the follow-up activities of the council and clubs sponsored by treatment units. Inmates who "got out of their place" by participation in these activities were harassed and placed on report. Guards manipulated traditional inmate values against such men by classing them as *politicians* and suggesting that they cooperated only to *beat their time.* In spite of the increasing number of privileges that could be manipulated through the treatment office, the influence of its inmate employees was neutralized in the yard. Conservative inmates withdrew from the new activities, leaving them to be exploited by others in ways that challenged even the faith of the liberal officials.

By 1953, these custodial tactics had raised serious questions about the new treatment programs. Violence and escape had increased to a point that demanded new emphasis on custody, swinging the once liberal deputy warden to the support of the guards. The older officers predicted the treatment activities would fail and, to fulfill their predictions, exploited their contacts with senior inmates. One element of the custodial force, the "old guard," was not content simply to defeat the liberal program, but set out to regain control over prison policy. Lacking the former means of control through internal communication, the "old guard," in alliance with men who had been discharged earlier and groups in the community, challenged the new policy through a legislative investigation. The guards supplied the information on which the critical inquiry was based.[11]

The position of the guards, which had merit from the standpoint of control and strong prospects of success in the conflict within the prison, was flatly rejected in the more democratic forum of the legislature. The conflict was settled by a formal endorsement of the liberal position.

Certain influential persons who had supported the traditional position retired, and others accepted the new role of custody with the best spirit they could muster. The prison changed in character from a military dictatorship to an institution in which armed force was subordinate to the objective of rehabilitative treatment. Certain personnel changes made voluntarily indicate the extent of the shift in power. The senior captain asked for a reduction to the rank of sergeant after 15 years in grade and was replaced by a captain who had been the first to borrow treatment-unit techniques. The deputy warden resigned the following year and was replaced, in a position enlarged and reclassified as superintendent, by the director of treatment. Some guards continued to believe that all control over the inmates was lost; but a decline in escape, violence, and disorder indicated, and the inmate community recognized, that control had passed to the treatment officials.

A cynical interpretation of this transfer of control might be that the liberal group had waged a deliberate and insightful campaign to undercut custodial authority. There is, however, no evidence in support of that assumption. The implementation of new goals simply required a major expansion of communication of information, plus the policy of open discussion with inmates. None of the participants fully recognized the extent to which open communication has anarchic consequences for an authoritarian power structure. None of the liberals, at least, realized the extent to which control was institutionalized in the social structure of the inmate community.

Social Disorganization of the Inmate Community   A shift in communication patterns and their control produced a drastic shift of power within a highly formalized official structure. A parallel transition can be traced more clearly in the inmate community because no formal legitimacy attached to the power structure that existed there under the traditional regime. As noted earlier, inmate society in the old prison was static and stratified. While it was composed of many primary groups in minimal contact, these shared a common code and turned to a small circle of senior men for information, policy, and the arbitration of disputes. These old *cons*, in turn, supported their role as "elders" by means of certain tolerated contacts with the guards. As new developments undercut the defined roles of the guards and the old *cons*, other distinct elements emerged in the community. These included a group of first offenders oriented toward treatment and one of aggressive young toughs who rejected all guidance.

The first period of policy transition (1946–50) was marked by little disturbance in the social system of the yard. The investigation that removed certain guards and crippled commerce between guards and inmates brought no direct sanctions against the dominant inmate clique. While some operations by which inmate leadership was asserted were denied, no alternative routes to power appeared. The old leaders were able to monopolize new privileges and claim "credit for the sunshine." Their control of discretion in the orientation of new inmates kept the conservative group in power. Low custodial morale and revision of disciplinary procedures were followed by increases in escapes and disorder, but these had returned to normal levels by 1949.

In the meantime, new activities and relationships in the treatment and production units created new communities of interest in the inmate body with functional leadership of their own. Especially where cooperative supervision by officials was involved, the concept of the *rat* in the old culture and its sanctions against contact with officials had collapsed. Old inmate leaders rejected opportunities for information and contact on work crews when accepting new relationships with officers and inmates was involved. They entered into a more overt alliance with custodial officers and attempted to sustain status by traditional means in the yard. During the early period the impact of new work situations was isolated from the power and social processes of the yard, but in 1951 the inmate council opened avenues to recognition for men previously subordinated in inmate society.

The old inmate hierarchy, like the custodial force, was never able to participate effectively in group discussions and decision making. In spite of a conservative majority on the first council, a clique of comparatively inexperienced inmates seized the initiative in drafting its constitution and bylaws. In the opinion of new officials, the council was a substantial privilege for the inmates, giving them some measure of control as well as a voice in their affairs. But to their old leaders it was a small boon in comparison with the monopoly they had once enjoyed. The council's operation during its first months provoked widespread inmate resistance and opposition, ending with the resignations of several old leaders. However, that move came too late to discredit the council as a new route to influence in the prison.

By the middle of 1951, the monolithic structure of inmate society had developed broad cracks. The marginally criminal first offenders, the lowest caste in the old prison, had found a focus of interest and organization in the treatment unit and the council. As official frankness, publication of rules, and a formal orientation program made new inmates independent of indoctrination by the old, another group of tough young reform-school graduates declared their independence from the old leadership and embarked on a radical course of exploitation and trouble making. In the following year neither the traditional "code" nor the old leadership com-manded the respect that would permit them to define roles or adjust conflicts in the community. In the absence of controlling definitions, dis-putes were increasingly submitted to arbitration by force, and the status of the physically powerful and aggressive men rose.

Factions in the yard corresponded to those that split the administration in 1953. Conservative leaders allied with the old guard to neutralize the influence of inmates associated with the treatment program. However, the mounting disciplinary reports for that year did not reflect a direct conflict between the two elements. It was the young toughs, who were not attached to either official orientation, who were out of control. The failure of con-stantly increased security measures to reduce disorder during that period of social disorganization indicates the importance of informal social con-trols, even in a society governed mainly by force and fear.

In this vacuum of accepted values and definitions which had aided adjustment in the past, younger men tended to follow *heroes* who dramati-cally demonstrated ideals of toughness and rebellion. Men made desperate by long sentences had once been absorbed into the ordered structure of inmate society. Status had been geared to adjustment in the prison, and it was bad form even to ask about another man's "case." But now, desperate men were urged by their youthful followers to live up to their newspaper reputations through sensational escapes and Promethean resistance. These disorders contributed to the setting in which the revolt of the old guard occurred. At one point a mass outbreak was avoided by posting machine guns on the roof and transferring leaders of the younger group to another prison. Inmate society approached a condition of anarchy in which physical force was the only recognized authority.

RECONSTRUCTION

Just as violence and disorder followed the collapse of the customary patterns of communication, the reestablishment of new processes of defini-tion fostered a return toward stability. Disciplinary records serve as an index of this readjustment, along with the evidence of increasing voluntary participation in treatment activities.

Even at the height of the crisis, press reports of the legislative hearings at which penal policy was debated seem to have had a stabilizing effect on the inmate community. Certain policy issues, which had seemed at first to be part of a simple administrative contest for power, were defined for the inmates as matters of principle. One of the old leaders submitted testimony in favor of the "old guard's" position, but two of the major *heroes* of the inmate community made a declaration in support of the new administra-tion. After the defeat of the custodial position, the warden met with the inmates in a series of discussion sessions which are credited with major importance in restoring order. These meetings gave the inmates the expla-nations of the situation so necessary to a sense of security, which no inmate group was able to supply in the period of factionalism. The frequency of escapes and violence immediately decreased, and there was a concomitant decline in the status of the young toughs in the community.

With the defeat of the "old guard," the effort to isolate the influence of men oriented toward treatment ceased, and a new social order began to emerge in the prison yard. The change in the administration was more than a palace revolution, however, and the social structure of the yard reflects certain qualitative differences in the present prison government. The idea of the *rat*, with its implications for all social control and structure of the inmate society, is almost forgotten; and all inmates except those who are barred by their own attitude have access to the officials. This in itself signifies a wider redistribution of influence and is protection against much of the exploitation that once characterized inmate society. Voluntary educational programs enlist over half of the inmates and sustain an atmosphere in which a majority are willing to accept definitions expressed by officials.

An uncensored newspaper, edited by inmates and published in the treatment office, supplements the warden's meetings as a means of presenting definitions and interpretations to the inmates. A coalition of liberal inmates and experienced conservatives has challenged both the reactionary old *cons* and the young toughs for control of the inmate council. Inmates manipulate the privileges available with a minimum of partisanship and so as to enlarge opportunities for first offenders. The social mobility of newly admitted inmates is greatly increased, and their orientation is a joint project of the administration and the council. Men with talent are recruited into an expanding number of voluntary treatment activities, and participation in these contributes toward the achievement of status in the yard. Accepting the social patterns developed in the industrial area, the society of the yard now recognizes means by which position may be achieved. The status once ascribed to experience and "connections" has declined. The sum of these changes can be sensed in an atmosphere less charged with fear and hatred and somewhat softened by cooperation and respect.

CONCLUSIONS

Interpretation of this study starts with reference to familiar, common-sense impressions of prison officers. No analysis can afford to ignore these impressions, for if research is to make a contribution to correctional practice, common sense must be reformulated into more comprehensive generalizations. The product then may prove to be relevant to a wider range of social situations.

Many prison officials show a growing skepticism toward further individualization of treatment and more relaxed conditions of confinement. The extension of privileges, which seems to be involved in the requirements for a treatment program, is thought to incite disorder and to increase inmate demands. The administrative principle that all change involves an element of risk—a principle that seems to control many administrations—must be endorsed on the basis of this study. At the same time it supports the claim that the dangers of change can be minimized or predicted by analysis of the power implications of the communication system.

The present study has emphasized that social control in inmate society, as in any other, rests largely on informal bases. Even in the most regimented authoritarian prison, or especially there, the bulk of all definitions, demands, and compulsions affecting an inmate's behavior comes from his fellows. From the reformer's standpoint, these pressures are corrupting simply because they are controlling. However, they are not anarchic or subversive of the administration. They require each inmate to do his own time, enforce adjustment within prison society, and gain covert support from custodial officers. Removal of these pressures may well be anarchic.

Presumably anything that subverts the processes by which definitions, demands, and compulsions are transmitted is a source of disorder; and any individualization of contact or easing of communications in the authoritarian prison will challenge the special position of those in its social system who have formulated and transmitted demands. To those who benefit from a redistribution of access to influence, the change will be a privilege. Those whose power position is adversely affected will take the lead in demanding new privileges as symbols of their old status. This is true in both the official and inmate societies; and the first group caught in the conflicts of institutional change is the custodial force. If a breakdown of authority is to be avoided, any change must be accompanied by heavy emphasis on informing and training the guards or on reinforcing the legitimacy of their status by other means.

Where change challenges the informal power structure of inmate society —and that is often a direct objective of new officials—the administration must assume the function, previously performed by inmate leaders, of defining the situation to the inmate body. If officials wish to support the status of certain inmates, this may be done by giving them an advantage in the ability to predict events, but it should be recognized that the advantage may be used to gain power over others. And it must be recognized that any endeavor to maintain both an authoritarian system and conditions of equality among inmates involves inherent contradictions. The authoritarian system seems to require censorship and control over communications for its own support and to insure that those who make the decisions are, in fact, best informed to do so. The processes by which the formal hierarchy is sustained create the conditions for a parallel hierarchy in the inmate community. Exploitive and authoritarian inmate leaders may be segregated, but their role is filled by others because it is necessary in the situation.

To minimize the disruptive effects of new programs, it may be enough to insist that they employ only established lines of formal or informal authority. However, new programs involve the exercise of some delegated discretion and generate needs and demands for information on which this can be based. A professional class, distinguished by knowledge and skill rather than by specific tasks, is under special compulsion to alter the channels through which information and definitions flow. In an authoritarian system this necessarily creates conflicts of status, which cannot be resolved by administrative fiat alone. Where orientation toward treatment is to be tolerated, a deliberate restructuring of communication channels, with awareness of its consequences for both formal and informal power structures, seems to be required.

The course of events in both official and inmate societies in the prison studied seems to confirm the hypotheses advanced for examination. The establishment of a treatment unit in the prison was reflected in its patterns of communication and interpersonal contact. New communication patterns in turn influenced the traditional systems of policy, authority, and power in the institution. Finally, during the transitional period in which communication patterns did not correspond to the power structure and failed to support it, authority reached its lowest point. Hence, the pattern of communications in a social system may be considered a functional equivalent of power and a necessary supplement to force in the maintenance of a stable system of authority.

ACKNOWLEDGMENT

This article was based on material collected in research for my doctoral dissertation, "Power, Communications and the Social Order: A Study of Prison Government," University of North Carolina, 1956.

NOTES

[1] For a review of the approach that identifies power structure in terms of patterns of contact, participation, and the communication of influence see Robert E. Agger, "Power Attributions in the Local Community: Theoretical and Research Considerations," *Social Forces*, 34 (1956), p. 322–331. For more general theoretical considerations see Harold D. Lasswell and Abraham Kaplan, *Power and Society* (New Haven: Yale University Press, 1950). For development of the concept of authoritative allocation of values, see David Easton, *The Political System* (New York: Knopf, 1953).

[2] For condensed materials on the dynamic elements in modern penal administration see *The Annals*, 293 (May 1954), an issue edited by Thorsten Sellin.

[3] The prison has been treated as a research model for authoritarian society by Norman A. Polansky, "The Prison as an Autocracy," *Journal of Criminal Law and Criminology*, 33 (1942), pp. 16–22.

[4] The formal status of the professional on the prison staff is above that of the custodial officer in pay, position on an organizational chart, and freedom from the time clock. The striking contrast between these symbols and the perceived or effective status of the professional poses the problem analyzed here. Harvey Powelson and Reinhard Bendix discuss the conflict with custodial forces and the attitudes of inmates that negate the work of the professional, in "Psychiatry in Prison," *Psychiatry*, 14 (1951), pp. 73–86.

[5] The apparent contradiction between the rigid hierarchy of power in inmate society and its constant demand for equality of treatment of individuals has been noted by Lloyd W. McCorkle and Richard Korn, "Resocialization Within Walls," *The Annals*, 293 (1954), p. 89ff.

[6] Erich Fromm writes in his study of authoritarian culture, "In any society the spirit of the whole culture is determined by the spirit of those groups that are most powerful in that society."—*Escape From Freedom* (New York: Rinehart, 1941),

pp. 112f. A reformulation of this proposition in behavioral terms permits its application to prison communities. The effective pursuit of certain mediate goals by the ruling class in the prison community imposes patterns of organization and social process on the subjects; these patterns in turn determine the dominant goals and values that can emerge in inmate society.

⁷ The complex processes by which the new inmate becomes oriented or "prisonized" in the unfamiliar setting are outlined by Donald Clemmer, "Observations on Imprisonment as a Source of Criminality," *Journal of Criminal Law and Criminology*, 41 (1950), pp. 311–319.

⁸ The elements of a "hero-making situation" are discussed by Orrin E. Klapp, "The Creation of Popular Heroes," *American Journal of Sociology*, 54 (1948), pp. 135–141.

⁹ The significance of the constant exchange of luxury items and forbidden delicacies in the prison society has been subject to conflicting interpretations. The amount of this exchange led Norman S. Hayner and Ellis Ash to state, "The organization of this community is primarily an economic arrangement devoted to obtaining goods and services denied by the administration."—"The Prisoner Community as a Social Group," *American Sociological Review*, 4 (1939), p. 369. Others, however, are concerned that the prison society has no basic economic functions requisite to its survival. Sykes treats the prison as an example of a predatory society and interprets its economic functions in terms of a theory of conspicuous consumption declaring status. See his "Men, Merchants, and Toughs: A Study of Reactions to Imprisonment," *Social Problems*, 4 (1956), pp. 130–138. The present study suggests that the display of goods and privileges among inmates serves to symbolize status that must be gained by other means. The symbols declare an ability to manipulate or resist power; and the inmate body betrays a compulsion to supply these symbols to men undergoing punishment, although their only function is to resist power bravely.

¹⁰ Chapter 4 infra discusses the general problem of administering individualized treatment to a population that views "special treatment" as "special privilege." See pp. 100ff.

¹¹ A direct parallel to this development, noted by Lloyd Ohlin and Donald Cressey, suggests that a tendency of administrative units, when cut off from customary lines of influence, to establish power contacts outside the agency may be advanced as an administrative principle.

19 WILLIAM M. EVAN AND MORRIS ZELDITCH, JR.

A Laboratory Experiment on Bureaucratic Authority

A significant recent trend in organization theory is the separation of the dimensions in Weber's construct of bureaucracy. Udy, for example, has recently obtained illuminating results from a cross-cultural analysis of production organizations in which "bureaucratic" properties, such as hierarchy and the existence of an administrative staff, are shown to be independent of "rational" properties of formal organization, such as limited objectives and segmental participation.¹ Similarly, Gouldner has made an

Reprinted from *American Sociological Review*, 26:6 (1961), pp. 883–893, by permission of the authors and the publisher.

effort to separate "rational" from "legal" components of bureaucratic authority in defining the "representative" and the "punishment-centered" types of bureaucracy.[2] In this paper we report a laboratory experiment intended to contribute to this trend in organization theory.

THE PROBLEM

The *rational* component of bureaucratic authority refers to the use of technical knowledge in the allocation of means to the efficient attainment of ends. "Bureaucratic administration," says Weber, means "the exercise of control on the basis of knowledge. This is the feature of it which makes it specifically rational."[3] The *legal* component of authority relates to the normative order which regulates relations among incumbents of a graded system of offices. To ensure impersonal and impartial administration, authority is vested in the office and not in the office-holder. The claims to legitimacy of such an authority system are based on a belief in the validity of the normative order and in the right of the office-holder to issue commands. Thus, Weber's "rational-legal" system of bureaucratic authority may be interpreted as having two dimensions, "the authority of knowledge" and "the authority of office."[4]

As a consequence of his ideal-type method, Weber treated these dimensions as perfectly correlated; bureaucratic authority rests on office, but offices[5] are filled solely on grounds of merit. Parsons was perhaps the first to point out that the two dimensions of authority are conceptually, and even empirically, independent.[6] If they are dichotomized and conceived to be independent, four types can be identified. Each type can be illustrated by an empirical case:

Type 1. The ideal type: the qualified official.
Type 2. Knowledge without office: the staff specialist in industrial organizations.
Type 3. Office without knowledge: the "lay" administrator in professional organizations.
Type 4. Neither office nor knowledge: the "job holder."

Type 2 has received a considerable amount of attention, and its strains are well known.[7] Conflict would probably be very much greater if organizations did not develop structural arrangements to accommodate to this strain. Barnard, for example, thought that knowledge without office could not command obedience; but it could exercise influence through institutionalized advisory relations.[8] Thus the staff-line arrangement may be an accommodation which actually reduces the degree of disruption inherent in having members in an organization who have knowledge without office.

Type 3, although perhaps not as well understood, is also very common. In hospitals, for example, authority is frequently in the hands of persons with either equal or less knowledge than those over whom it is exercised. The accommodation may be very similar to that known for Type 2. Goss reports that the staff in a large teaching and research hospital distinguishes between problems of administration and problems of a technical nature. With respect to the former, superiors may give commands and they will be obeyed; with respect to the latter they may give only advice.[9]

In the experiment reported here the problem of office without knowledge is investigated in an artificial professional bureaucracy which is not permitted the accommodations observed in natural situations. The knowledge differential between supervisors and subordinates is varied, office remaining constant. The effects predicted are probably consistent with Weber's analysis and also with Barnard's.[10] The effects examined are: (1) the performance of subordinates; (2) the beliefs of subordinates regarding the legitimacy of their superior's authority; (3) the conformity of subordinates to the rules of the organization and to the commands of their superiors. The first two dependent variables are explicitly considered by Weber; the third is implicitly recognized as an organizational problem. We expect all three variables to be negatively affected by office without knowledge, and we expect legitimacy—the willingness of subordinates to accept the authority of their superiors as valid—to play the role of an intervening variable. We also hypothesize that subordinates will discriminate among the commands of their superiors, considering some of these actions to be primarily *administrative* and others to be primarily *technical*. The negative effects of office without knowledge should be confined to the latter.

DESIGN OF THE EXPERIMENT

In designing this experiment we attempted to simulate some features of an actual organization. Although we used college students as subjects, we did not recruit them in their role as students or as experimental subjects. Instead, we "hired" 45 students as part-time employees, at the rate of $1.25 an hour, to code the face sheet of a questionnaire supposedly distributed nationally by a fictitious survey organization called *National Social Surveys, Inc.* The knowledge differential between superordinate and subordinate was manipulated by varying the responses of coding supervisors to questions asked by the subjects. To make sure that some questions were asked, a set of "traps" was created; that is, subjects were given a code book that did not provide the solution to certain coding problems. Coders were told that in such cases the decision was the responsibility of the coding supervisor whom they never saw but with whom they could communicate by telephone. Communication with supervisors was mediated by telephone for two reasons: (1) to simulate one of the features of an organization which distinguish it from a small group;[11] and (2) to avoid contaminating the experimental variable of knowledge differential with other variables such as the supervisor's personality or his other statuses, for example, ethnic, religious, racial, etc.

An effort was made to reduce the number of calls that concerned matters other than the trap questions in order to have a uniform administration of the experimental stimulus. A pretest indicated how to avoid many such calls, but they were not entirely eliminated. Coding supervisors were given a standard set of responses to each trap, varying for each treatment, and a general set of instructions for dealing with other calls, which also varied with each treatment.

The sequence of the experiment may be divided into three time periods which we may label t_0, t_1, and t_2. In t_0 three coders at a time were instructed by one of the experimenters, identified as the project director, in both the practice of coding and in the rules of the organization. The introductory statement describing the organization emphasized the professional and non-profit nature of the organization, and the importance of avoiding DK's and NA's. It read, in part, as follows:

National Social Surveys, Inc. is a nonprofit research organization sponsored by several universities. It is dedicated to the discovery of scientific knowledge about human behavior, principally through the use of sample surveys. To realize this objective, it takes great pains to recruit personnel who will conduct research of the highest caliber. All personnel of the organization, whether directors of projects, coding supervisors, or coders, are expected to perform their work in accordance with traditional scientific standards of objectivity, accuracy, and integrity. Imagination as well as meticulousness are requirements of scientific research.

As a coder for National Social Surveys, you perform operations which are of critical importance for the conduct of a research project. Errors in coding diminish the validity of the data which have been collected with great care and at a great cost. To avoid errors, *please read the following coding and operating instructions carefully.*

The experimenter also stressed calling the supervisor if difficulty was encountered. This instruction period, in which each subject also practiced coding, took about one-half hour. At the end, the subject was given a code book, a statement of the organization's rules, a batch of questionnaires to code, code sheets, and time sheets on which to keep a record of his work.

The three subjects were then taken to separate rooms. It was explained that efficiency was greater if each coder worked independently. We did this to eliminate the effects of group interaction among subjects. However, in each room there was an observer to record spontaneous comments and nonverbal behavior of the subjects. The observer, if he was asked, said he was working on a different project and knew nothing about the project on which the subjects were working. His behavior was unobtrusive and he was not recognized as an observer.

In t_1 all subjects were exposed to technically competent supervisors for about 45 minutes. The supervisors were confederates of the experimenters. This period had several functions: it permitted the coder to establish a standard of comparison where otherwise he might not be able to discriminate incompetent responses; it increased the homogeneity of the subjects by giving them at least some common prior experience with the organization; and finally, in order to reduce heterogeneity due to differences in intelligence and personality differences such as degree of authoritarianism, which we were unable to measure before allocation of treatments to subjects, we wanted repeated measurements on the same individuals.

The beginning of t_2 was signalled when the supervisor called the coder, announced that he had to leave, and assigned him to another supervisor on another extension. The supervisors were then rotated among subjects to control for variations in the personalities of the confederates. At the same time, a messenger brought a new batch of questionnaires to ensure that all subjects started t_2 with the same task. The allocation of both confederates and treatments was random, yielding a randomized complete blocks design in which the confederates in the role of second supervisor are the blocks.

The independent variable was translated into three experimental treatments: exposure to a superior-knowledge supervisor, to an equal-knowledge supervisor, and to an inferior-knowledge supervisor. In the superior-knowledge treatment the coding supervisor exhibited special resources and special knowledge of his job; he invariably replied to the coder's questions with a rational and occasionally a technical justification for his decision. In the equal-knowledge treatment the coding supervisor exhibited about as much knowledge as the coder himself had by that time: the supervisor sometimes indicated this by asking the coder what he thought and by arriving at a decision with the aid of the code book, thus evidencing no resources superior to those of the coder. In the inferior-knowledge treatment the supervisor always said he was uncertain and advised the coder to code the problematic item "no answer."[12]

In addition to their responses to trap-items, which constitute technical orders, the supervisors in each period gave certain administrative orders, common to all treatments, concerning the signing of code sheets and the keeping of time sheets.

After the 45 minutes of t_2 elapsed, coders were visited by interviewers who identified themselves as representatives of a management research organization studying *National Social Surveys, Inc.* The interviewer asked questions designed to obtain evaluations of the supervisors, perceptions of incorrect decisions, the grounds for obeying such decisions, and beliefs regarding the right of the supervisors to hold their jobs and their right to expect obedience. The interviewer then explained the experiment to the subject. All but three of the subjects responded to the explanation in good humor. These three, and others who were really in need of a part-time job and were disappointed to learn that it was an experiment, were placed on actual coding jobs on other projects. In designing the experiment, we were mindful of the ethical problems involved and took precautions to minimize the chances of any harmful effects on the subjects.

The experiment was completed in three days during the Easter vacation in order to reduce contamination from interaction of students. Subjects were instructed not to talk about the experiment until they returned to school.

RESULTS

Validation of the Independent Variable   Despite some success during the pretest, we were concerned that the independent variable might not be induced. The equal-knowledge treatment appeared particularly difficult to discriminate from the inferior-knowledge treatment, and it was not clear how much effect the personality of the supervisor would have on heterogeneity within treatment. To validate the independent variable we used several items of information: how the coders evaluated the t_2 supervisors compared to the t_1 supervisors on a 10-point scale of technical competence; how they evaluated themselves compared to both their supervisors on the same scale; how many of their supervisors' decisions they perceived as wrong; and how they spontaneously reacted during the trial as recorded by the observers.

On all four indicators the inferior and superior levels of knowledge were clearly differentiated (see Table 1). The equal level of knowledge, however, does not fall halfway between the inferior and superior levels. On three of the four indicators it is differentiated from the inferior and superior levels sufficiently to consider it a separate treatment, but it is consistently closer to the inferior level of knowledge than to the superior level. Nor can the equal-knowledge treatment be accurately thought of as "equal"; subjects in this treatment see themselves as 1.5 points *more* competent than their second supervisors.

Despite these difficulties with the equal level of knowledge, all treatment differences, with the exception of spontaneous gestures and comments, are

TABLE 1.   VALIDATION OF THE INDEPENDENT VARIABLE

Indicator	Treatment: second supervisor's level of knowledge*			Mood-Brown Analysis of variance [13]		
	Inferior	Equal	Superior	Treatment χ^2	df	P
Wrong decisions perceived: Increase in number ...	2.0	1.6	−0.3	16.88	2	<.01
Evaluation of 1st and 2nd supervisors: Mean difference	5.0	3.3	0.2	22.13	2	<.01
Evaluation of self and 2nd supervisor: mean difference	2.7	1.5	−3.2	20.06	2	<.01
Spontaneous negative comments: Increase in number ...	10	8	3	3.72†	2	.10<P<.20

* Block means, block χ^2, and the χ^2 for interaction are not shown. No block or interaction effects were significant.

† Significance computed by a straightforward χ^2 rather than by Mood-Brown analysis of variance.

statistically significant. This indicates that the treatments differentiated among subjects. No block differences are significant, indicating that supervisors played their roles well enough to eliminate effects of their own personalities. And no interaction effects are significant, indicating that supervisors played all roles equally well so that no particular supervisor combined with any particular knowledge-level had some effect not predictable from the main effects of the experiment.

Performance   We expected that performance would be differentiated by treatment; we found that it was not. We used two measures of performance. First, we measured the coder's rate of speed. The amount of time actually spent coding, after subtracting the time spent on telephone calls to the supervisors, was divided by the number of questionnaires completed for each time period. We then subtracted the rate in t_2 from the rate in t_1, yielding a measure of the increasing rate of speed of the coder between the two periods. There was no difference by either treatment or block. Second, we measured the percent of "nontrap" items that were coded incorrectly in the two coding periods, subtracting the rate in the first period from the rate in the second period. This yields a measure of increasing error from t_1 to t_2. Here also there were no treatment or block differences.

We were, of course, surprised by the lack of performance results, despite the fact that a number of experiments with organizational variables find equally little result in the area of performance.[14] We first checked our randomization, thinking that more intelligent subjects might have been assigned to the inferior-knowledge treatment, counteracting the treatment effects. But the tendency, although not statistically significant, is actually for them to be in the superior-knowledge treatment. We then thought that the nature of the task was such that more intelligent subjects would be more adversely affected by its routine character than the less intelligent subjects. But the correlation of ability—indicated by verbal and mathematical scores on the College Entrance Board Examination—with the distribution of performance differences is almost exactly zero.

Other possibilities suggest themselves. First, there simply may not have been enough time for performance effects to show themselves. Second, performance of such a routine task, with such limited variation in its time-and-motion aspects, may have been an insensitive indicator of treatment effects. Third, it is quite possible that the negative findings are real. The market situation of the "employees" of this particular "organization" may have led them to perform as well as possible, independently of their reactions to their supervisors. They were interested in short-run job opportunities, did not have quickly-marketable skills in other labor markets, and possibly regarded their initial performance as a "test" on which subsequent employment was contingent. The result might have been like that described by Goode and Fowler, who found that productivity in a feeder plant which employed primarily handicapped, non-unionized workers was independent of morale. Workers could be easily fired, found it difficult to get other jobs, and consequently produced at a high level of efficiency despite low morale.[15]

Conformity to Technical Rules and Commands   The most important technical rule of the organization concerned telephoning the supervisor when a coding problem was encountered. We had expected that subjects in the inferior- and equal-knowledge treatments would be more likely to violate this rule than those in the superior treatment. There was, in fact, a tendency in all three groups to telephone the supervisor less in t_2 than in t_1. But, while the drop-off rate in the inferior treatment is more rapid than the drop-off rate in the superior treatment, the treatments are not significantly different in this respect (see Table 2). Otherwise, our expectations concerning technical rules and orders were generally confirmed.

Our most marked result in the area of non-conformity was in the "trap-error" rates. By a "trap-error" we mean coding errors on trap-items only. The three treatments differ significantly in the number of trap-errors made, i.e., in the number of acts of non-conformity (see Table 2). This effect appears to be due to three distinct factors. First, there is some tendency for subjects in the inferior treatment to telephone less often, and thus to discover the correct response less often, even though this tendency is not statistically significant. Those who guess at the code and do not telephone very often guess incorrectly. Second, there is some tendency for subjects actually to disobey the instructions of their supervisor in the inferior treatment and to guess at an answer rather than code it NA. We will call this overt or active disobedience. Third, and most important, there is a distinct tendency to passive or covert disobedience; many subjects, told to code a

TABLE 2.   CONFORMITY: MEAN DECREASE IN "TRAP" CALLS,* MEAN INCREASE IN ERROR,† AND MEAN INCREASE IN DISOBEDIENCE ‡

| Conformity | Treatment: second supervisor's level of knowledge § | | | Mood-Brown analysis of variance | | |
	Infe-rior	Equal	Supe-rior	Treat-ment χ^2	df	P
Mean decrease in "trap" calls..	−.26	−.21	−.15	5.69	6	$.30 < P < .50$
Mean increase in "trap" error..	2.50	1.36	1.53	10.81	2	$P < .01$
Mean increase in disobedience	1.25	0.57	0.00	8.31	2	$.01 < P < .02$

* Decrease in trap calls is measured by subtracting the percent of items on which the coder telephones the supervisor in the second coding period from the percent on which he telephones in the first coding period. The base of the percentage is the number of trap-items on which it was *possible* for the coder to telephone; the base was adjusted for individuals who did not complete a sufficient number of questionnaires to code all trap-items.

† Non-conformity is measured here by subtracting the number of trap-errors in the first coding period from the number in the second.

‡ If, on a given trap-item, a subject telephoned his supervisor, was instructed how to code an item, but then made an error of any kind in coding that item, the error was defined as disobedience to the supervisor's instructions. The number of acts of disobedience in the first period was subtracted from the number in the second.

§ To save space, block means, block χ^2 and interaction χ^2 are omitted. No block or interaction effects were significant.

response NA, manage to code NA incorrectly or fail to code the item at all.[16] Covert disobedience accounts for most of the disobedience that occurs. There are, in all treatments combined, 59 acts of disobedience—that is, instances in which the subject telephones his supervisor, is instructed by the supervisor, and then makes a trap-error. Only 27 percent of these instances are overt acts of disobedience; i.e., instances in which the error is due to the subjects apparently attempting to violate directly the supervisor's instruction. Covert and overt nonconformity combined differ significantly by treatment (see Table 2).

Conformity to Administrative Rules and Commands   Concerning administrative rules and commands, we had expected that there would be no differences in conformity by treatment. By and large this expectation was borne out. In the coding-instruction period subjects were told to sign their full names on each code sheet after completion of each questionnaire. In the middle of t_2 the second supervisor changed this rule, prescribing initials in the place of full signatures. Subjects were also directed by the coding-instructor (who was identified as the project director, it will be recalled) to record the time, on time sheets, after every 10 completed questionnaires. The second-period supervisor changed this rule to every five minutes. A third administrative rule remained constant throughout; this was an instruction to draw a line through errors and re-code correctly on the same code sheet, never erasing or destroying code sheets.

With respect to two of these indicators, the results are clear-cut; with respect to the third, the results are in the same direction but the data are unreliable. There are no treatment differences in conformity to the signature order; nor is erasing of errors on code sheets differentiated by treatment. The time sheet data are inconclusive because the recording by both subjects and observers was sufficiently unclear that reliable coding of the results was not possible.

These negative results, as in the case of the performance results, may be due to the brief time of the trials rather than to the true absence of treatment effects.

Legitimacy of Technical Commands   The process of legitimation is complex and as yet little understood. We had intended to avoid the difficult question of how it operates by measuring only its end-product, legitimacy of the supervisor's authority—that is, belief in the obligation to obey his commands. But regardless of what subjects thought of their supervisors, in post-session interviews virtually no one questioned the supervisor's right to expect obedience to his commands even where subjects said they thought the decisions embodied in these commands were wrong.

This result made conclusive analysis of the process intervening between treatments and effects almost impossible. First, since no attempt had been made before the experiment to conceptualize the legitimation process, very few indicators of it were available for analysis. Those that were available were in some respects contaminated. Second, because components of the legitimation process had not been intentionally manipulated, a complete set of replicates for all appropriate contrasts could not be obtained with the available results. Third, the hypotheses which would guide such an analysis were in danger of being both result-guided and *ad hoc*.

Yet some of the post-session interview responses did yield clues to the operation of this process, and we made an effort to trace the intervening process as far as the data permitted. To guard against result-guided, *ad hoc* interpretation, new hypotheses were grounded as far as possible in the original conceptualization of the experiment.

At least three components of the process of legitimation are probably at work in the experiment. One is the subject's judgment that the supervisor has authority of office. While we have no indicator of this judgment, there were no differences in this variable incorporated into treatments and there should be no effects due to it. A second component is the subject's judgment that the supervisor has authority of knowledge. This is indicated by a post-session question in which subjects were asked, for each supervisor, if the supervisor had a right to his job. A third component is the subject's conception of the basis on which legitimacy should be accorded in this particular type of organization. This would include, for example, their views regarding the relative importance of knowledge vs. office as a basis of legitimacy. This is indicated by the reasons subjects gave for their feeling an obligation to obey.

As one would expect, feelings about the supervisor's right to his job were sharply differentiated by treatment (see Table 3). Quite unexpectedly, the basis on which legitimacy was granted also differed by treatment. Responses to interviewer probes into the obligation to obey were classified as: (1) *bureaucratic*, if subjects stressed legal obligations of their status ("I was hired to obey," or "It's his job to give orders") or bureaucratic principles of organization ("Organizations must have hierarchies"); (2) *professional*, if subjects stressed expertise of the supervisor ("The supervisor knows

TABLE 3.   CHANGES IN CONCEPTIONS OF LEGITIMACY: SUBJECTS' JUDGMENT OF
RIGHT TO JOB OF FIRST AND SECOND SUPERVISORS

Subjects' judgment of right to job		Treatment: second supervisor's level of knowledge			
of 1st sup.	of 2nd sup.	Inferior	Equal	Superior	Total
		(N=16)	(N=14)	(N=15)	(N=45)
Yes	Yes	13%	36%	67%	38%
Yes	Qual. Yes, No	81%	43%	7%	44%
Qual. Yes, No	Qual. Yes, No	..	..	13%	13%
Any NA		6%	21%	13%	13%
	Total	100%	100%	100%	99%

$\chi^2 = 15.53$; df $= 2$; P $< .001$.
χ^2 was computed after removing rows 3 and 4.
Qual. Yes = Qualified Yes.

more about it") or the scientific goals of the survey ("uniform categories and consistent decisions ensure valid results"); and (3) *mixed* responses, if subjects mentioned both. The instructions during coder-training had clearly stressed the professional goal of the organization. But the treatments shifted the basis on which subjects accorded legitimacy from "professional" to "bureaucratic" grounds (see Table 4). Only 2 percent of those who obeyed the first supervisor on "bureaucratic" grounds changed in response to the second supervisor, but there was a marked shift of those who obeyed the first supervisor on "professional" grounds if they were subjected to the inferior- or equal-knowledge treatment.

TABLE 4. CHANGES IN CONCEPTIONS OF LEGITIMACY: SUBJECTS' GROUNDS FOR BELIEF IN LEGITIMACY OF FIRST AND SECOND SUPERVISORS

Subjects' grounds for legitimation		Treatment: second supervisor's level of knowledge			
of 1st sup.	of 2nd sup.	Inferior	Equal	Superior	Total
		(N=16)	(N=14)	(N=15)	(N=45)
P, M	P,M	12%	..	47%	20%
P, M	Bur.	38%	36%	7%	27%
Bur.	P, M	..	..	7%	2%
Bur.	Bur.	38%	36%	12%	29%
Any NA		12%	28%	27%	22%
	Total	100%	100%	100%	100%

$\chi^2 = 14.80$; df $= 4$; $.01 < P < .001$.
χ^2 was computed after removing rows 3 and 5.
P = Professional, Bur. = Bureaucratic, M = Mixed.

The way in which these two components of the legitimation process interacted is difficult to discern in the experiment because shifts in "right to office" responses were associated with shifts in "basis of legitimacy" responses. The two were completely independent in the initial period of the experiment ($\phi = .06$, $\chi^2 = 0.17$, $.50 < P < .70$), but in t_2 there was a marked increase in their association ($\phi = .44$, $\chi^2 = 4.63$, $.02 < P < .05$). This association was brought about by two kinds of shifts: (1) subjects who gave "bureaucratic" responses in t_1 and felt the first supervisor had a right to his job were likely to remain "bureaucratic" and feel the second supervisor did *not* have a right to his job if they received the inferior- or equal-knowledge treatment; (2) subjects who gave "professional" or "mixed" responses in t_1 and felt the supervisor had a right to his job were likely to change both responses if they received the inferior- or equal-knowledge treatment.

That "right to job" responses did act as an intervening variable in the experiment is evident from their relation to conformity. Shifts on this item from "yes" in t_1 to "qualified yes" or "no" in t_2 were significantly related to increases in disobedience. This effect was independent of any effects due to shifts in the "basis of legitimacy." Among those who did not shift the basis on which they granted legitimacy, subjects who shifted "right to job" response, compared with subjects who did not, had a significantly higher increase in disobedience (H = 3.88; .02<P<.05).[17] There were very few subjects who shifted the basis on which they granted legitimacy and at the same time remained constant in "right to job" response. It is therefore impossible to say how this variable would operate independently. But it is possible to examine its interaction effects. Our conjecture was that shifts in basis of according legitimacy would dampen the effects of shifts in "right to job," since authority of office would replace authority of knowledge as the more important criterion for granting legitimacy. There was no difference, however, between those who shifted on both variables and those who shifted only "right to job" responses (H = 0).

Legitimacy of Administrative Rules and Commands The post-session interview probed into beliefs regarding legitimacy of administrative rules and commands as well as into beliefs regarding legitimacy of technical commands. As we had anticipated, there was no difference in beliefs regarding legitimacy of administrative rules and commands by treatment. Almost all subjects felt obliged to obey a supervisor's decisions about administrative matters, just as they had about technical matters. Unlike the case of technical commands, however, the grounds for legitimacy also were not differentiated by treatment. Subjects generally advanced "bureaucratic" rather than "professional" justifications for obeying administrative rules and commands.

SUMMARY AND CONCLUSION

The purpose of the present experiment is to separate the *rational* and *legal* components of Weber's theory of bureaucratic authority, and to vary the dimension of authority of knowledge while holding authority of office constant. Hypotheses concerning the effects of variations in authority of knowledge on performance, conformity, and legitimacy are suggested by Weber's theory.

In order to separate systematically the two dimensions under controlled conditions, and also to observe systematically instances in which officials without knowledge gave technical as well as administrative commands, a small part of a fictitious research organization was simulated. Three statuses in this organization were activated: a project director, a status occupied by one of the experimenters who appeared only during a training session; a coding supervisor, a status occupied by confederates of the experimenters; and a coder, a status occupied by naive subjects, hired at $1.25 an hour for what they thought were real jobs. The main operative unit of the organization was the supervisor-coder relationship. Other parts of the organization were simulated by occasional inputs to this unit, and beliefs about the organization were manipulated by information given in the instruction period. The organization was "professional" in its goals, but clearly the subjects were not themselves professionals nor oriented to careers in this organization, despite efforts to induce a professional attitude in the instruction period. Various extraneous sources of variation were eliminated by (1) a before-after design, to remove effects of individual differences in subjects; and (2) extreme simplification of the organizational context— e.g., communication by telephone only, elimination of interaction between subordinates—to eliminate contaminating organizational processes.

The independent variable was manipulated by varying supervisors' responses to requests for decisions made by subjects who were faced with "traps" in the coding process. "Traps" were built into the task by presenting coding situations for which no solutions were provided in instructions in the code book.

We hypothesized that (1) if an official held office without commensurate knowledge, subjects would not accord legitimacy to the official's authority; (2) that this erosion of the supervisor's authority would have negative effects both on the subordinates' performance and on their conformity to technical rules and commands; (3) but that conformity to administrative rules and commands would not be affected by treatment differences.

The following results were actually obtained:

1. The treatments did not differentiate performance measures.
2. Marked treatment differences appeared in rates of conformity to technical commands, particularly in "covert" nonconformity.
3. Treatment differences in rates of conformity were accounted for in part by shifts in the belief that the supervisor had a right to occupy his office.
4. The treatments induced subjects to change the grounds appropriate to defining legitimate authority in such an organization. Subjects in inferior- and equal-knowledge treatments were likely to shift from *"professional"* to *"bureaucratic"* bases of legitimacy.
5. Almost all subjects, regardless of treatment, felt obligated to obey commands of their supervisor, even though for different reasons.
6. No treatment effects were observed in either conformity to, or in beliefs regarding legitimacy of, administrative rules and commands.

As for the significance of the experiment: many important questions are suggested simply by observing that both office without knowledge and knowledge without office empirically occur. For example, what are the consequences of these combinations of office and knowledge for different kinds of organizations? Under what conditions does one occur rather than the other? What are the possible variations in the structural arrangements through which organizations accommodate to discrepant combinations of office and knowledge? These questions presuppose that discrepant combinations of office and knowledge will pose a "problem" in the absence of certain kinds of socially-structured accommodations. In general, our experiment seems to confirm this proposition, which suggests that the questions based on it are meaningful and are likely to provide fruitful lines of inquiry.

Organizational experiments,[18] such as the one presented here, obviously need not be confined to authority problems, critical as these are for any organization. They can also revolve around problems of division of labor, types of rewards, reward differentials, or any of a large number of other organizational variables. It seems to us likely that if experimental sociologists succeed in designing theoretically significant simulations of organizational structures and organizational processes, they will considerably accelerate progress in a field already developing rapidly.

ACKNOWLEDGMENTS

We wish to acknowledge our indebtedness to the Council for Research in the Social Sciences of Columbia University for a grant which defrayed part of the cost of the experiment. We are also immensely grateful to the following graduate students at Columbia University whose enthusiasm and competence made this experiment possible: Sanci Cohen Michael, project assistant; Koya Azumi, Joan Dulchin, Theodore Ernst, Jerald Hage, Paul Lehrman, John Lofland, John Michael, Jane Mullins, Elaine Rosenbaum, and Robert Smith. We also wish to thank Morton Deutsch and Stanley Udy, Jr., for especially helpful comments on the manuscript. For a discussion of the methodological aspects of this experiment see Morris Zeldich, Jr. and William M. Evan, "Simulated Bureaucracies: A Methodological Analysis," in *Simulation of Social Systems*, Harold Guetzkow, ed. (Englewood Cliffs, N. J.: Prentice-Hall, 1962).

NOTES

¹ Stanley H. Udy, Jr., " 'Bureaucracy' and 'Rationality' in Weber's Organization Theory: An Empirical Study," *American Sociological Review*, 24 (1959), pp. 791–795.

² Alvin W. Gouldner, *Patterns of Industrial Bureaucracy* (Glencoe, Ill.: The Free Press, 1954), pp. 19–24; see also "Organizational Analysis," in *Sociology Today*, Robert K. Merton, Leonard Broom, and Leonard S. Cottrell, Jr., eds. (New York: Basic Books, 1959), pp. 402–403, 413–417.

³ A. M. Henderson and Talcott Parsons, eds., *Max Weber: The Theory of Social and Economic Organization* (New York: Oxford University Press, 1947), p. 339.

⁴ Authority of office also entails a body of experience and knowledge of a nontechnical character which is distinguishable from authority of knowledge. Administrative knowledge, as it may be called, includes not only "official secrets" but access to information about rules and policy decisions which is generally confined to certain categories of statuses in an organization.

⁵ "Office" is used as an abbreviation of "authority of office" and "an office" is used for a status in an organization which has authority of office. Note that some statuses in an organization do not have office, hence the term is not synonymous with "status."

⁶ Henderson and Parsons, *op. cit.*, "Introduction" by Talcott Parsons, pp. 58–60, fn 4.

⁷ Cf. Melville Dalton, "Conflicts between Staff and Line Managerial Officers," *American Sociological Review*, 15 (1950), pp. 342–351.

⁸ Chester I. Barnard, *The Functions of the Executive* (Cambridge, Mass.: Harvard University Press, 1938), pp. 174–175.

⁹ Mary E. W. Goss, "Physicians in Bureaucracy: A Case Study of Professional Pressures on Organizational Roles," (Unpublished Doctoral Dissertation, Columbia University, 1959). See also William M. Evan, "Some Consequences of a Discrepant Authority Relationship," *Proceedings and Summaries of the 23rd Annual Meeting, New York State Psychological Association*, (May, 1960), pp. 32–34.

¹⁰ See Barnard, *op. cit.*, and "Functions and Pathology of Status Systems in Formal Organizations," in *Industry and Society*, W. F. Whyte, ed. (New York: McGraw-Hill, 1946).

¹¹ Cf. Harold Guetzkow and Anne E. Bowes, "The Development of Organizations in a Laboratory," *Management Science*, 3 (1957), pp. 380–381.

[12] We intended to have 15 subjects in each treatment; the actual distribution of subjects is 15 in the superior-knowledge treatment, 14 in the equal-knowledge treatment, and 16 in the inferior-knowledge treatment.

[13] Almost all of the distributions in this experiment are markedly platykurtic, which led us to use nonparametric methods throughout. Kurtosis affects particularly the power of the parametric test. See, for example, A. B. L. Srivastava, "The Effect of Nonnormality on the Power of the Analysis of Variance Test," *Biometrika*, 46 (1959), pp. 114–122. The Mood-Brown two-way analysis of variance, based on median tests, was used for the following reasons: (1) for cell sizes greater than two it is distribution-free; (2) it is not disturbed by unequal cell sizes; (3) the more familiar Friedman two-way analysis of variance by ranks demands too great a cost in degrees of freedom; and (4) the interpretation of interaction effects in the Friedman test is disturbed by more than one observation per cell. See G. W. Brown and A. M. Mood, "On Median Tests for Linear Hypotheses," in *Second Berkeley Symposium on Mathematical Statistics and Probability*, J. Neyman, ed. (Berkeley: University of California Press, 1951); A. M. Mood, *Introduction to the Theory of Statistics* (New York: McGraw-Hill, 1950), pp. 402–406; and M. W. Tate and R. C. Clellands, *Nonparametric and Short-cut Statistics* (Danville, Ill.: Interstate Printers and Publishers, 1957), pp. 115–129.

[14] Guetzkow and Bowes, *op. cit.*, p. 393; see also Harold Guetzkow and William R. Dill, "Factors in the Organizational Development of Task-Oriented Groups," *Sociometry*, 20 (1957), p. 179.

[15] William J. Goode and Irving Fowler, "Incentive Factors in a Low Morale Plant," *American Sociological Review*, 14 (1949), pp. 619–624.

[16] This is rather difficult to detect after the fact, but not impossible. For example, in one trap-item occupational skill-level and prestige are to be coded for an occupation that does not appear listed in the code book. The inferior-knowledge supervisor instructs the coder to code it DK, which is a 9 in column 4 and an X in column 5. Many subjects in this treatment make the error of coding either 9 only or X only, or code $9XX$, there being a vacant space in column 6. These are called errors but they are hardly direct acts of disobedience.

[17] Where only one-way analysis of variance was required, the Kruskal-Wallis H-test was used. See W. H. Kruskal and W. A. Wallis, "The Use of Ranks in One-criterion Variance Analysis," *Journal of American Statistical Association*, 47 (1952), pp. 583–621; and the very convenient description in S. Siegel, *Nonparametric Statistics for the Behavioral Sciences* (New York: McGraw-Hill, 1956), pp. 184–193.

[18] For examples of noteworthy organizational experiments see Donald F. Clark and Russell L. Ackoff, "A Report on Some Organizational Experiments," *Operations Research*, 7 (1959), pp. 279–293; C. West Churchman and Philburn Ratoosh, "Innovation in Group Behavior," *Management Science Nucleus*, Working Paper No. 10 (January, 1960), dittoed.

20   MARVIN B. SUSSMAN AND LEE BURCHINAL

Kin Family Network: Unheralded Structure in Current Conceptualizations of Family Functioning

Most Americans reject the notion that receiving aid from their kin is a good thing. The proper ideological stance is that the individual and his

Reprinted from *Marriage and Family Living*, 24:3 (1962), pp. 231–240, by permission of the authors and the publisher.

family should fend for themselves. The family in this instance is nuclear in structure and consists of husband and wife and children. Further investigation would probably reveal that most of these rejectors are receiving or have received financial and other types of aid from their kin long after the time they were supposed to be on their own. After marriage many are involved within a network of mutual assistance with kin, especially with parents. Moreover, one would find that independence of the nuclear family of procreation is being maintained. Where independence is threatened, it is probably due to other causes. The rejection of the idea of receiving aid from kin and actually being helped by them is another case of discrepancy between belief and practice.

Discrepancies between belief and practice of "ideal" and "real" behavior are common in our society. In family sociology the reason is "academic cultural lag"; the lag between apparently antiquated family theory and empirical reality. The theory stresses the social isolation and social mobility of the nuclear family while findings from empirical studies reveal an existing and functioning extended kin family system closely integrated within a network of relationships and mutual assistance along bilateral kinship lines and encompassing several generations.[1]

The major purpose of this paper is to reduce the lag between family theory and research in so far as it concerns the functioning of the American kin family network and its matrix of help and service among kin members. The procedure is to review relevant theory and conclusions derived from research on kin family networks completed by sociologists and anthropologists. Appropriate modifications of existing theory which posits the notion of the isolated nuclear family are then suggested.[2]

NUCLEAR FAMILY THEORY

Durkheim, Simmel, Toennies, and Mannheim have stressed that the family in urban society is a relatively isolated unit. Social differentiation in complex societies requires of its members a readiness to move, to move to where there are needs for workers and where there are opportunities for better jobs.

American social theorists such as Linton,[3] Wirth,[4] and Parsons,[5] support this position. Parsons suggests that the isolated nuclear family system consisting of husband and wife and offspring living independent from their families of orientation is ideally suited to the demands of occupational and geographical mobility which are inherent in modern industrial society. Major obligations, interactions and nurturance behavior occur within the nuclear family. While bonds exist between the nuclear family and other consanguineous relatives and affinals of the kin group, these lack significance for the maintenance of the individual conjugal family.

Family sociologists generally accept the isolated nuclear theory as promulgated above. They report the changes in the structure and functions of the American family system which have occurred as the system has adapted to the demands of a developing industrial society. There is general agreement that the basic functions reserved for the family are procreation, status placement, biological and emotional maintenance and socialization.[6] However, these functions are generally analyzed in the context of the "isolated" nuclear family. The functions of intergenerational and bilateral kin family networks regarding the processes of biological and emotional maintenance or socialization are given little attention by theorists or analysts. The conclusion reached is that demands associated with occupational and geographical mobility have brought about a family pattern in urban areas consisting of relatively isolated nuclear family units which operate without much support from the kinship system.

The textbooks are written by family sociologists. Few among them, either texts on the sociology of the family or those written for marriage and family preparation courses, give theoretical or empirical treatment to the maintenance of the family system by the mutual assistance activities of the kin group. Among the texts examined, only one considers in any detail financial arrangements among kin members.[7] One result of the review of basic family and preparation for marriage texts regarding current knowledge of the functioning of the kin network and its matrix of help and service is that the theory of the isolated nuclear family prevails.

DISCUSSION OF THE THEORETICAL ARGUMENT

The lack of research until the 1950's and the almost complete omission of the topic, kin family network and its matrix of help and services, in family texts are closely related. If the generalized description of the American family system as atomistic and nuclear were valid, there would be very little exchange of financial help or services within the kin family network. Parental support of married children or exchange of services and other forms of help among kin members would be comparatively rare and hence, unimportant.[8] Research would be unnecessary and discussion of the subject, except in crisis situations, could be safely omitted from textbook discussions. However, accepting this theory as essentially valid without considerable empirical substantiation has contributed to errors in descriptions of kin family networks and aid patterns among families. A new empiricism emerging in the late 1940's questioned the persistence of the isolated nuclear family notion and presented evidence to support the viability of kin family network in industrial society.

The ideal description of the isolated nuclear character of the American family system cannot be applied equally to all segments of American society. Regional, racial, ethnic, and rural and urban, as well as socioeconomic status differences in modified extended relations and family continuity patterns are known to exist. Family continuity and inheritance patterns of families in several social strata have been described.[9] Among upper class families direct, substantial and continuous financial support flows from the parents, uncles, aunts, and grandparents to the children both before and after marriage (see Table 1). Only by receiving substantial kin support can the young high-status groom and his bride begin and sustain their family life at the financial and social level which is shared by their parents,

TABLE 1. FUNCTIONAL ANALYSIS OF PARENTAL AID TO MARRIED CHILDREN

Familial Variables Affecting Economic Support

1. Family Values
   a. Neo-familism
   b. Individualism vs. Organizationism
   c. Developmental values (Permissiveness)
2. Position of family in the Social Structure
   a. Social class
   b. Residential location
   c. Occupation (Bureaucratic-Entrepreneurial)
   d. Status aspiration
   e. Ethnic group membership
3. Family Economic Position
   a. Wealth relative to class
   b. Security against retirement & catastrophe
   c. Perception of own economic position as relatively risk-free
4. Family Structure
   a. Number of children
   b. Degree of family integration
   c. Patterns of role differentiation
   d. Ordinal position of children
5. Relation to Married Child
   a. Son or daughter
   b. Parent-child harmony
   c. Parental approval of marriage
   d. Age at marriage

Types of Parent-Child Economic Support

1. Goods
   a. Furnishings at wedding and at later periods during marriage
   b. Hospitality gifts
   c. Use of parent's equipment; automobiles, rent-free house, summer cottage, appliances
   d. Food gifts
   e. Transfer of property
2. Money
   a. Given at wedding, childbirth, holidays, and anniversaries
   b. Education
   c. Low interest of interest free loans
   d. Endowments
   e. Subsidized visits and vacations
3. Services
   a. Emergency and crises: care of family members
   b. Babysitting
   c. Boarding of grandchildren
   d. Shopping
   e. Recreation
   f. Home decorating
   g. Garden and yard work
   h. Home construction

Intervening Variables

1. Amount of Aid
2. Expectation for aid & regularity
3. Stage in family cycle
4. Disguise of aid
5. Parental expectations
6. H. or W's parents
7. Parental approval of marriage
8. Emotional attachment to parents
9. Geographical distance
10. Family status
11. Married child's image of in-law
12. Generalized Attitudes

Consequence For Family Patterns

H-W relations: friction, power, harmony
1. Intergenerational integration
2. Parental power
   a. Occup. choice
   b. Mobility
   c. Mate-choice
3. Higher fertility
4. Support for aged parents
5. Lower divorce (teen marriages)

Consequence For Individual Personality

1. Dependency
2. Striving & achievement motivation
3. Anxiety & security
4. Freedom to concentrate on arts, politics, family life

General Societal Consequences

1. Reduction or implementation of geographical and occup. mobility
2. Population growth
3. Economic & occup. striving
4. Cultural development
5. Individualistic vs. other directed values

Societal Supports and Constraints on Parental Aid

1. Economic & technological
   a. Productivity and affluence
   b. Inflation
   c. Tax system
2. Group structure
   a. Bureaucratization
   b. Professionalization
   c. Suburbanization
3. Demographic structure
   a. Lengthened education
   b. Early age at marriage
   c. Early child bearing
   d. Lengthened life span
4. Values (as in box at left)

other relatives and their friends. This support frequently includes obtaining a position for the husband in his or his in-law family's economic enterprise.

Members of lower class kin groups generally have few financial resources with which to assist married children. Among certain European ethnic groups some effort is made to assist the young couple at marriage; the notion of a dowry still persists. Generally, however, there is little knowledge, tradition or tangible forms of assistance transmitted to children which directly aids children in establishing or enhancing their socioeconomic status.[10] Kin support in this class most frequently takes the form of providing services and sharing what financial resources are available at the time of crises or of exchanging nonmonetary forms of aid. Marginal financial resources and the impact of unemployment hit all kin members alike.[11]

The description of the isolated, nuclear American family system, if valid, is most suited to the white, urban, middle class segment of American society.[12] Presumably, the leisure time of the members of these families is absorbed in the activities of secondary, special interest social groups. Since urban, lower-class family members participate less than middle class family members in voluntary organizations, it is believed that social activities of adult lower class family members are restricted to informal visiting patterns. Visiting with relatives would be a significant proportion of all of their social relations. However, prevailing sociological theory suggests that the disparities between an extended kin family system and the requirements of a mobile labor force and intergenerational family discontinuities generated by social mobility should be reflected in the lack of continuity among lower class families as well as among middle class families.

The degree to which urban lower or middle class families function as relatively isolated from their extended kin family systems is critical for all subsequent discussions of the question of kinship network and its matrix of help and service. Unless there is a reasonably frequent occurrence of primary group interaction among kin members, very likely there will be an insignificant help pattern.

The emphasis on the atomistic character of urban families has contributed to incorrect assumptions concerning interaction within the kinship matrix. It has led family sociologists to incorrectly assume that assistance among kin members was comparatively rarely sought or offered. A reconsideration of these assumptions is necessary. The bases of reconsideration are logical constructs and empirical realities set forth in the following data.

FAMILY NETWORKS AND MUTUAL AID: CONCEPTUALIZATION AND RESEARCH

A theory is here considered to be composed of logically interrelated propositions which explain phenomena. Concepts are elements of a theory, defining what is to be observed. Concepts by themselves cannot be construed as a theory. They require integration into a logical scheme to become a theory.

The existence of a modified extended family with its intricate network of mutual aid in lieu of the isolated nuclear family notion is probably more of a conceptualization than a theory. However, it approaches the state of being a theory since it is not an isolated concept but is integrated with other propositions concerned with the maintenance over time of the family and other social systems of the society.

Family networks and their patterns of mutual aid are organized into a structure identified as a "modified extended family" adapted to contemporary urban and industrial society.[13] This structure is composed of nuclear families bound together by affectional ties and by choice. Geographical propinquity, involvement of the family in the occupational placement and advancement of its members, direct intervention into the process of achieving social status by members of nuclear family units, and a rigid hierarchical authority structure are unrequired and largely absent. The modified extended family functions indirectly rather than directly to facilitate the achievement and mobility drives of component families and individual members. Its tasks complement those of other social systems. By achieving integration with other social systems, concerned with the general goals of maintenance and accomplishment of these systems, the extended family network cannot be considered as an isolated or idiosyncratic concept. Its elements require organization as logically interrelated propositions and whereupon it should emerge as a theory replacing the prevalent one of the isolated nuclear family.

Our concepts die hard and one way to speed their demise is to examine the evidence supporting the new ones. Evidence and measurement are difficult terms to define. When do you have evidence and when have you achieved a measurement? The reader will have to judge. The approach here is to examine the writings and research emerging from several disciplines. In some cases the work is focused on testing hypotheses or describing relationships relevant to the new conceptualization. In others, the discussions and findings emerge incidentally to the major purpose of the study. These are cases of serendipity. They occur more frequently than one would expect and add to the uncertainty of the notion of the isolated nuclear family.

One assumption of the isolated nuclear family conceptualization is that the small nuclear family came into existence in Western Europe and the United States as a consequence of the urban-industrial revolution. Furthermore its small size is ideally suited for meeting requirements of an industrial society for a mobile workforce. The effect of the urban-industrial revolution is to produce a small sized family unit to replace the large rural one. This assumption can be challenged. A study of different societies reveals that industrialization and urbanization can occur with or without the small nuclear family.[14]

If household size reflects in any way the structure and characteristics of the joint extended family in India, then little change has occurred in this system during the period of industrialization in India from 1911 to 1951.[15]

The uprooting of the rural family, the weakening of family ties, and the reshaping of the rural family form into a nuclear type as a consequence of the industrial revolution are disclaimed for one Swiss town in a recent investigation. On the contrary many fringe rural families were stabilized and further strengthened in their kin ties from earning supplementary income in nearby factories. Able-bodied members obtained work nearby and no longer had to leave the family unit in search of work. Families which moved closer to their place of employment were accommodated in row houses; these units facilitated the living together of large family groups.[16] These findings question the impact of industrialization upon the structure and functioning of the pre-industrial family.

It is difficult to determine if the conditions of living during the transition from a rural to an industrial society ended the dominance of the classical extended family and replaced it with a modified kin form, or if it was replaced by the nuclear one. The question is whether the modified extended family has existed since industrialization occurred; is it a recent phenomenon or an emergent urban familism, a departure from the traditional nuclear form; or is it nonexistent? The evidence to support either of these positions is inconclusive. It remains, however, that the family network described variously as "an emergent urban familism" or "modified extended family" exists and functions in the modern community.

The family network and its functions of mutual aid has implications for the functioning of other social systems. With the growth of large metropolitan areas and concomitant occupational specialization, there is less need for the individual to leave the village, town, city or suburb of the urban complex in order to find work according to his training. Large urban areas supply all kinds of specialized educational and occupational training. The individual can remain in the midst of his kin group, work at his speciality and be the recipient of the advantages or disadvantages preferred by the kin family network. If individuals are intricately involved within a kin family network, will they be influenced by kin leaders and be less amenable to influence by outsiders; will they seek basic gratifications in kin relationships in lieu of the work place or the neighborhood; will they modify drastically current patterns of spending leisure time thus affecting current leisure forms and social systems?[17]

Empirical evidence from studies by investigators in a variety of disciplines substantiate the notion that the extended kin family carries on multitudinous activities that have implications for the functioning of other social systems of the society. The major activities linking the network are mutual aid and social activities among kin related families. Significant data have been accumulated on the mutual aid network between parents and their married child's family in a number of separate and independent investigations [18,19,20] (see Table 2). The conclusions are:

1. Help patterns take many forms, including the exchange of services, gifts, advice and financial assistance. Financial aid patterns may be direct as in the case of the young married couples Burchinal interviewed; or indirect and subtle, such as the wide range of help patterns observed by Sussman, Sharp and Axelrod.

2. Such help patterns are probably more widespread in the middle and working class families and are more integral a feature of family relation-

TABLE 2. DIRECTION OF SERVICE NETWORK OF RESPONDENT'S FAMILY
AND RELATED KIN BY MAJOR FORMS OF HELP

Major forms of help and service	Direction of service network				
	Between respondent's family and related kin Percent*	From respondents to parents Percent*	From respondents to siblings Percent*	From parents to respondents Percent*	From siblings to respondents Percent*
Any form of help ...	93.3	56.3	47.6	79.6	44.8
Help during illness ..	76.0	47.0	42.0	46.4	39.0
Financial aid	53.0	14.6	10.3	46.8	6.4
Care of children	46.8	4.0	29.5	20.5	10.8
Advice (personal and business)	31.0	2.0	3.0	26.5	4.5
Valuable gifts	22.0	3.4	2.3	17.6	3.4

* Totals do not add up to 100 percent because many families received more than one form of help or service.
Source: Marvin B. Sussman, "The Isolated Nuclear Family: Fact or Fiction," Social Problems 6 (1959), p. 338.

ships than has been appreciated by students of family behavior. Very few families included in available studies reported neither giving nor receiving aid from relatives. However, these relationships until recently have not been the subject of extensive research.

3. The exchange of aid among families flows in several directions, from parents to children and vice versa, among siblings, and less frequently, from more distant relatives. However, financial assistance generally appears to flow from parents to children.

4. While there may be a difference in the absolute amount of financial aid received by families of middle and working class status, there are insignificant differences in the proportion of families in these two strata who report receiving, giving or exchanging economic assistance in some form.

5. Financial aid is received most commonly during the early years of married life. Parents are probably more likely to support financially "approved" than "disapproved" ones, such as elopements, interfaith and interracial marriages. Support can be disguised in the form of substantial sums of money or valuable gifts given at the time of marriage, at the time of the birth of children, and continuing gifts at Christmas, anniversaries or birthdays. High rates of parental support are probably associated with marriages of children while they are still in a dependency status; those among high school or college students are examples.

6. Research data are inadequate for assessing the effects of parental aid on family continuity and the marital relations of the couple receiving aid.

Few studies report associations between the form and amount of aid given with the parents' motivations for providing aid. Additional studies on these points are necessary before the implications of aid to married children can be better known.[21]

Social activities are principal functions of the kin family network. The major forms are interfamily visitation, participation together in recreational activities, and ceremonial behavior significant to family unity. Major research findings are:

1. Disintegration of the extended family in urban areas because of lack of contact is unsupported and often the contrary situation is found. The difficulty in developing satisfactory primary relationships outside of the family in urban areas makes the extended family *more important* to the individual.[22]

2. Extended family get-togethers and joint recreational activities with kin dominate the leisure time pursuits of urban working class members.[23]

3. Kinship visiting is a primary activity of urban dwelling and outranks visitation patterns found for friends, neighbors, or co-workers.[24,25,26,27,28]

4. Among urban middle classes there is an almost universal desire to have interaction with extended kin, but distance among independent nuclear related units is a limiting factor.[29]

5. The family network extends between generational ties of conjugal units. Some structures are identified as sibling bonds,[30] "occasional kin groups"[31] family circles and cousin clubs.[32] These structures perform important recreational, ceremonial, mutual aid, and often economic functions.

Services performed regularly throughout the year or on occasions are additional functions of the family network. The findings from empirical studies are:

1. Shopping, escorting, care of children, advice giving and counselling, cooperating with social agencies on counselling and welfare problems of family members, are types of day-to-day activities performed by members of the kin network.[33,34]

2. Services to old persons such as physical care, providing shelter, escorting, shopping, performing household tasks, sharing of leisure time, etc. are expected and practiced roles of children and other kin members. These acts of filial and kin responsibility are performed voluntarily without law or compulsion.[35,36,37,38,39,40,41,42]

3. Families or individual members on the move are serviced by units of the family network. Services range from supplying motel-type accommodations for vacationing kin passing through town, to scouting for homes and jobs for kin, and in providing supportive functions during the period of in-migration and transition from rural to the urban pattern of living.[43,44,45,46,47]

4. Services on occasions would include those performed at weddings or during periods of crisis, death, accident, disaster, and personal trouble of family members. A sense of moral obligation to give service or acknowledgement of one's kin appropriate to the occasion is found among kin

members. The turning to kin when in trouble before using other agencies established for such purposes is the mode rather than the exception.[48,49,50,51]

5. General supportive behavior from members of the kin family network facilitate achievement and maintenance of family and community status.[52] Supportive behavior of kin appears to be instrumental in affecting fertility rates among component family members.[53]

A convergence of many of these findings occurs in the work of Eugene Litwak. In an extensive study of a middle class population Litwak tests several hypotheses on the functional properties of the isolated nuclear family for an industrial society: (a) occupational mobility is antithetical to extended family relations; (b) extended family relations are impossible because of geographical mobility. His findings summarized briefly are: (1) The extended kin family as a structure exists in modern urban society at least among middle class families. (2) Extended family relations are possible in urban industrial society. (3) Geographical propinquity is an unnecessary condition for these relationships. (4) Occupational mobility is unhindered by the activities of the extended family, such activities as advice, financial assistance, temporary housing, and the like provide aid during such movement, and (5) The classical extended family of rural society or its ethnic counterpart are unsuited for modern society, the isolated nuclear family is not the most functional type, the most functional being a modified extended kin family.[54]

CONCLUSIONS

There exists an American kin family system with complicated matrices of aid and service activities which link together the component units into a functioning network. The network identified by Litwak as extended family relations is composed of nuclear units related by blood and affinal ties. Relations extend along generational lines and bilaterally where structures take the form of sibling bonds and ambilineages, i.e., the family circle or cousin club.

As a consequence of limited historical work and particularistic developments in theory and research in sociology there is uncertainty concerning the impact of industrialization upon the structure and function of the preindustrial family. Was the extended classical type found in rural society replaced by a nuclear one, or did it evolve into the modified kin form described in this paper? It is suggested that the notion of the isolated nuclear family stems from theories and research on immigrant groups coming into the city to work during the period of urbanization in Western society.[55] Anomie in family behavior resulted from individual and institutional failure to make appropriate adjustments required by this migration. The coldness and indifference of the workplace and the city as a steel and concrete bastion contributed to a feeling of aloneness and isolation. The basic concern of the in-migrant was survival in an unknown man-made jungle. Survival was related to dependence upon small family units. These could make quicker and more complete adjustments to the new ways of urban life. The ethos of a competitive and expanding industrial society supported the flexibility of movement now possible by an atomistic unit. Every man is for himself, every man should be unencumbered by ties that will hinder his economic or social progress, and every man should seize opportunities to better himself. One assumption of this position is that early urban man had little time for concern or activity with kinsmen. A more logical assumption is that isolation, a depressive workplace, and uncertainty produced greater reliance upon kin. Once new immigrants became established in the city they served as informants, innkeepers, and providers for later kin arrivals.[56] Once these followers arrived the kin family network then functioned most effectively to protect and acculturate their members into urban ways.

Major activities of this network are that members give to each other financial aid and goods of value, and a wide range of services at specific times and under certain conditions. The aid and service provided within the network supplement rather than displace the basic activities of nuclear family units. Kinship behavior assists more than negates the achievement of status and occupational advance of component families and their members.

The main flow of financial aid is along generational lines, from parents to young married children and from middle-aged parents to aged parents. Such aid is not restricted to emergencies, but may be given at various occasions such as support for education, to start a family, at time of marriage, to begin a career, and the like.

The network is used among middle class families as a principal source of aid and service when member families or individuals are in personal difficulty, in times of disaster and crisis, and on ceremonial occasions. There are some indications that established working class families are following the same pattern. Some situations cannot be handled by the nuclear unit alone, e.g., destruction of the family home by a tornado; while other situations involve more than one nuclear family or individual member, e.g., the death of an aging parent. In such situations there are mutual expectations of going to the aid of kin. Aid is sought from the most immediate kin chiefly along sibling or generational lines. Then it is followed by help from more distant kin.

In many instances everyday or weekly activities link together the members of the kin family network. Joint participation in leisure time activities are possible because of reduction of the work week. Visiting among kin is facilitated by high speed highways and other conveyances of a modern transportation system. Constant communication among kin members is possible by the widespread adoption on all class levels of the telephone as a household necessity.[57, 58]

The feasibility of the kin network in modern society is due to the existence of modern communication and transportation systems which facilitate interaction among members; a bureaucratic industrial structure suited to modern society which removes the responsibility for job placement from the network will still permit the network to concentrate on activities intended to aid the social and economic achievement of network members;[59, 60] and expansion of metropolitan areas in which individuals can obtain educational, occupational and status objectives without leaving their kin area. Kin members can live some distance from each other within the metropolitan area and still have relationships within the network. Nuclear units function autonomously. Decisions on what and when to act are responsibilities of the nuclear family. Influence may be exerted by the kin group upon the nuclear units so that the latter may make the "right" decision. However, the kin group seldom directs the decision or action of the nuclear family in a given situation. Immunity from such control is guaranteed by legal and cultural norms which reaffirm the right and accountability of the nuclear family in such situations. The role of the family kin network is supportive rather than coercive in its relationship with the nuclear family.

Understanding of the family as a functioning social system interrelated with other social systems in society is possible *only by rejection of the isolated nuclear family concept*. Accepting the isolated nuclear family as the most functional type today has led to erroneous conclusions concerning the goals and functions of these other social systems. In social service fields, for instance, institutions establish goals and programs concerned with caring for individuals and families who are unable to fend for themselves. Institutions assume that the family unit is a small and isolated unit easily injured and upset by the many problems it faces in contemporary society. The therapeutic approach is to treat the individual or at best the members of the nuclear family. The kin network is overlooked. Often nuclear families respond hesitantly to the overtures of these institutions; the nuclear unit prefers to find solutions to its problems within the family kin network. When such solutions are impossible then the specialized service institution may be used. How the operations of the kin family network effect the functioning of other social systems is yet to be established. Their positive or negative effects are unknown. Some beginning research on this problem is now underway.[61]

ACKNOWLEDGMENTS

This article was originally published as Journal Paper No. J-4197 of the Iowa Agricultural and Home Economics Experiment Station, Ames, Iowa, Project No. 1370.

NOTES

[1] The authors adopt Eugene Litwak's interpretation of the modified extended family. It is one that "does not require geographical propinquity, occupational nepotism, or integration, and there are no strict authority relations, but equalitarian ones." See "Geographical Mobility and Extended Family Cohesion," *American Sociological Review*, 25 (1960), p. 385. The components of the system are neolocal nuclear families in a bilateral or generational relationship. This system is referred to as the "Kin Family Network."

[2] The implications of parental support to the married child's family for the functioning of the American Family System is discussed in another paper. The major

question is whether parental aid effects the independence of the married child's family. "Parental Aid to Married Children: Implications for Family Functioning," *Marriage and Family Living* (November, 1962).

³ Ralph Linton, "The Natural History of the Family," in *The Family: Its Function and Destiny*, Ruth N. Anshen, ed. (New York: Harper & Row, 1959), pp. 45–46.

⁴ Louis Wirth, "Urbanism As a Way of Life," *American Journal of Sociology*, 44 (1938), pp. 1–24.

⁵ All by the same author, see Talcott Parsons, "The Kinship System of the Contemporary United States," *American Anthropologist*, 45 (1943), pp. 22–38; "Revised Analytical Approach to the Theory of Social Stratification," in *Class, Status, and Power*, R. Bendix and S. M. Lipset, eds. (Glencoe, Ill.: The Free Press, 1953), p. 166ff.; "The Social Structures of the Family," in Ruth Anshen, *op. cit.*, p. 263ff.; Parsons and Robert F. Bales, *Family, Socialization and Process* (Glencoe, Ill.: The Free Press, 1955), pp. 3–33.

⁶ Cf. Robert F. Winch, *The Modern Family* (New York: Holt, 1952), and William J. Goode, "The Sociology of the Family," in *Sociology Today*, Robert K. Merton, Leonard Broom, and Leonard S. Cottrell, Jr., eds. (New York: Basic Books, 1959), pp. 178–96.

⁷ Evelyn M. Duvall, *Family Development* (Chicago: Lippincott, 1957), pp. 129–33, 206–10.

⁸ See Reuben Hill, *Families Under Stress* (New York: Harper, 1949).

⁹ W. Lloyd Warner and Paul S. Lunt, *The Social Life in a Modern Community* (New Haven, Conn.: Yale University Press, 1941). See also Cavan, *The American Family, op. cit.*, pp. 119–87, for a review of other studies of social status differentials in family behavior.

¹⁰ R. E. L. Faris, "Interactions of Generations and Family Stability," *American Sociological Review*, 12 (1947), pp. 159–64.

¹¹ Ruth S. Cavan, "Unemployment-Crisis of the Common Man," *Marriage and Family Living*, 21 (1959), pp. 139–46.

¹² Someone has facetiously suggested the samples of white, urban, middle-class Protestant respondents be labeled as WUMP samples. If family sociologists continue to draw samples principally from this segment of our social structure or wish to limit generalizations to this segment, there would be more than a facetious basis for arguing for the merit of the convenient shorthand expression represented by WUMP.

¹³ Litwak, *op. cit.*, p. 355. See also by the same author, "Occupational Mobility and Extended Family Cohesion," *American Sociological Review*, 25 (1960), p. 10.

¹⁴ Sidney M. Greenfield, "Industrialization and the Family in Sociological Theory," *American Journal of Sociology*, 67 (1961), pp. 312–22.

¹⁵ Henry Orenstein, "The Recent History of the Extended Family in India," *Social Problems*, 8 (1961), pp. 341–50.

¹⁶ Rudolph Braun, *Industrialisierung Volksleben* (Erbenback-Zierrich: Reutsch, 1960).

¹⁷ A. O. Haller raises interesting questions on the significance of an emerging urban familism. See "The Urban Family," *American Journal of Sociology*, 66 (1961), pp. 621–22.

¹⁸ Marvin B. Sussman, "The Help Pattern in the Middle Class Family," *American Sociological Review*, 18 (1953), pp. 22–28. For related analyses by the same author see, "Parental Participation in Mate Selection and Its Effect Upon Family Continuity," *Social Forces*, 32 (1953), pp. 76–81; "Family Continuity: Selective Factors Which Affect Relationships Between Families at Generational Levels," *Marriage and Family Living*, 16 (1954), pp. 112–20; "Activity Patterns of Post Parental Couples and Their Relationship to Family Continuity," *Marriage and Family Living*, 27 (1955), pp. 338–41; "The Isolated Nuclear Family: Fact or Fiction," *Social Problems*, 6 (1959), pp. 333–40; "Intergenerational Family Relationships and Social Role Changes in Middle Age," *Journal of Gerontology*, 15 (1960), pp. 71–75.

[19] Harry Sharp and Morris Axelrod, "Mutual Aid Among Relatives in an Urban Population," in *Principals of Sociology,* Ronald Freedman and associates, eds. (New York: Holt, 1956), pp. 433–39.

[20] Lee G. Burchinal, "Comparisons of Factors Related to Adjustment in Pregnancy-Provoked and Non-Pregnancy-Provoked Youthful Marriages," *Midwest Sociologist,* 21 (1959), pp. 92–96; also by the same author, "How Successful Are School-Age Marriages?" *Iowa Farm Science,* 13 (1959), pp. 7–10.

[21] Further analyses on the implications of parental aid to married children are found in a paper, "Parental Aid to Married Children: Implications for Family Functioning," *Marriage and Family Living* (November, 1962).

[22] William H. Key, "Rural-Urban Differences and the Family," *Sociological Quarterly,* 2 (1961), pp. 49–56.

[23] F. Dotson, "Patterns of Voluntary Association Among Urban Working Class Families," *American Sociological Review,* 16 (1951), pp. 689–93.

[24] Morris Axelrod, "Urban Structure and Social Participation," *American Sociological Review,* 21 (1956), pp. 13–18.

[25] Scott Greer, "Urbanism Reconsidered," *American Sociological Review,* 21 (1956), pp. 22–25.

[26] Wendell Bell and M. D. Boat, "Urban Neighborhoods and Informal Social Relations," *American Journal of Sociology,* 43 (1957), pp. 381–98.

[27] Marvin B. Sussman and R. Clyde White, *Hough: A Study of Social Life and Change* (Cleveland: Western Reserve University Press, 1959).

[28] Paul J. Reiss, "The Extended Kinship System of the Urban Middle Class" (Unpublished Ph.D. Dissertation, Harvard University, 1959).

[29] E. Franklin Frazier, "The Impact of Urban Civilization Upon Negro Family Life," in *Cities and Society,* rev. ed., P. K. Hatt and H. S. Reiss, Jr., eds. (Glencoe, Ill.: The Free Press, 1957), pp. 495–96.

[30] Elaine Cumming and David M. Schneider, "Sibling Solidarity: A Property of American Kinship," *American Anthropologist,* 63 (1961), pp. 498–507.

[31] Millicent Ayoub, "American Child and his Relatives: Kindred in Southwest Ohio," project supported by the Public Health Service, 1961, Dr. Ayoub is continuing her studies under the subtitle, "The Nature of Sibling Bond." She examines the solidarity or lack of it between siblings in four focal subsystems and at different stages of the life cycle.

[32] William E. Mitchell, "Descent Groups Among New York City Jews," *The Jewish Journal of Sociology,* 3 (1961), pp. 121–28; "Lineality and Laterability in Urban Jewish Ambilineages," read at the 60th Annual Meeting of the American Anthropological Association in Philadelphia, Pa., November 16, 1961; and William E. Mitchell and Hope J. Leichter, "Urban Ambilineages and Social Mobility," unpublished paper based on research from the project, "Studies in Family Interaction" sponsored jointly by the Jewish Family Service of New York City and the Russell Sage Foundation.

[33] Sussman, *op. cit.,* "The Help Pattern in the Middle Class Family."

[34] Hope J. Leichter, "Kinship and Casework," paper read at the meetings of the Groves Conference, Chapel Hill, N.C., 1959; "Life Cycle Changes and Temporal Sequence in a Bilateral Kinship System," read at the annual meetings of the American Anthropological Association, 1958; Washington, D.C. "Normative Intervention in an Urban Bilateral Kinship System," paper read at the meetings of the American Anthropological Association, 1959.

[35] John Kosa, Leo D. Rachiele, and Cyril O. Schommer, S. J., "Sharing the Home with Relatives," *Marriage and Family Living,* 22 (1960), pp. 129–31.

[36] Alvin L. Schorr, *Filial Responsibility in a Modern American Family* (Washington, D.C.: Social Security Administration, U.S. Department of Health, Education and Welfare, 1960), pp. 11–18.

[37] Peter Townsend, *The Family Life of Older People: An Inquiry in East London* (London: Routledge and Kegan Paul, 1957).

[38] Michael Young and Peter Willmott, *Kinship and Family in East London* (Glencoe, Ill.: The Free Press, 1957).

[39] Elizabeth Bott, *Family and Social Network* (London: Tavistock Publications, Ltd., 1957).

[40] See *Adjustment in Retirement*, by Gordon F. Streib and Wayne E. Thompson, *Journal of Social Issues*, 14 (1958). Streib and Thompson have done the most creative thinking and analysis of data on these points. Streib's paper "Family Patterns in Retirement," pp. 46–60 in this issue is most pertinent.

[41] Ethel Shanas, "Older People and Their Families," paper given at the meetings of the American Sociological Association, September, 1961. A more complete report is in *Family Relationships of Older People*, Health Information Foundation, 1961.

[42] The best treatment of uses of leisure during the later years of life is found in Robert W. Kleemeier, ed., *Aging and Leisure* (New York: Oxford University Press, 1961). See particularly the chapters by Wilensky, Streib, and Thompson.

[43] M. B. Sussman and R. C. White, *op. cit., Hough: A Study of Social Life and Change*.

[44] C. Wright Mills, Clarence Senior and Rose K. Goldsen, *Puerto Rican Journey* (New York: Harper & Row, 1950), pp. 51–55.

[45] James S. Brown, Harry K. Schwarzweller, and Joseph J. Mangalam, "Kentucky Mountain Migration and the Stem Family: An American Variation on a Theme by LePlay," paper given at the meetings of the American Sociological Association, September 1, 1961.

[46] Peter H. Rossi, *Why Families Move* (Glencoe, Ill.: The Free Press, 1955), pp. 37–38.

[47] Earl L. Koos, *Families in Trouble* (New York: Columbia University Press, 1946).

[48] Sussman, *op. cit.*, "Family Continuity: Selective Factors Which Affect Relationships Between Families at Generational Levels."

[49] Seymour S. Bellin, *Family and Kinship in Later Years*, N.Y. State Dept. of Mental Hygiene, Mental Health Research Unit Publication, 1960.

[50] Sharp and Axelrod, *op. cit., Mutual Aid Among Relatives*.

[51] Enrico L. Wuarantelli, "A Note on the Protective Function of the Family in Disasters," *Marriage and Family Living*, 22 (1960), pp. 263–64.

[52] Bernard Barber, "Family Status, Local-Community Status, and Social Stratification: Three Types of Social Ranking," *Pacific Sociological Review*, 4 (1961), pp. 3–10. In this paper Barber challenges the current conceptualization of social class for designating an individual's position, and power within a community. He differentiates social class position, family status and local-community statuses into three types of social ranking. Each one has its own structure and functions; each allocates position, power and prestige; and each has its own range of variation. The family kin network and support received from it determines family status. President Kennedy's family and its extended family relations illustrates the point of this thesis.

[53] David Goldberg, "Some Recent Developments in Fertility Research," Reprint No. 7, *Demographic and Economic Change in Developed Countries*, Princeton University Press, 1960. Recent fertility research has focused upon the relationship of family organization to differential fertility since variations in family planning and family size cannot be explained by differences in socioeconomic status. One variable of family organization is the family kin network. Goldberg observes, "—and incidentally one which may ultimately prove fruitful in cross-cultural studies, is a consideration of the relative benevolence of the environment in defraying the economic and social costs of having children. Here it is hypothesized that the greater the amount of help available from one's community or kinship system the weaker the desire to prevent or postpone pregnancy." *Ibid.*, p. 9.

[54] Eugene Litwak, "The Use of Extended Family Groups in the Achievement of Social Goals: Some Policy Implications," *Social Problems*, 7 (1959–60), pp. 177–87;

op. cit., "Occupational Mobility and Extended Family Cohesion"; *op. cit.,* "Geographical Mobility and Family Cohesion."

[55] Key, *op. cit.,* "Rural-Urban Differences and the Family," p. 56; Sussman, *op. cit.,* "The Isolated Nuclear Family: Fact or Fiction," p. 340.

[56] Key discusses this point in his paper "Rural-Urban Differences and the Family," *op. cit.* From studies on immigration to the United States and geographical movement of families within the country one concludes that family members perform invasion or scout roles and then attract other kin into their communities and neighborhoods.

[57] Several empirical studies have been made on the extensity of kin family network functions in metropolitan areas. Robert W. Habenstein and Alan D. Coult conducted one in Kansas City on "The Functions of Extended Kinship in an Urban Milieu." "The purpose of this research is to discover, describe, and analyse the social correlates and functions of extended kinship in representative samples of blue collar and white collar socioeconomic classes in Kansas City." Research proposal, July 1, 1961, p. 1.

[58] A second study was undertaken by Marvin B. Sussman and Sherwood B. Slater in Cleveland, Ohio. "The objectives of the Cleveland Study are to investigate the working and middle-class families; to compare the kinship networks of 'illness' and 'non-illness' families; to estimate the normative form of kinship networks for social class and family life cycle stages to variations in normative patterns." Research plan, September 27, 1961, p. 1.

[59] One investigation conducted by John Bennett is concerned with the variations in business operations due to kinship behavior. Business organization practice according to current theory operates with bureaucratic, universalistic, and impartial norms. Bennett investigated the compatibility and conflict between these bureaucratic norms and those which characterize the kinship network, particularistic behavior for idiosyncratic situations. "Kinship in American Business Organization," meetings of the Central States Anthropological Society, May, 1961.

[60] William Mitchell, "Lineality and Laterality in Urban Jewish Ambilineages," *op. cit.,* finds some integration of kinship and business activity. There is a tendency to "throw business to kin members."

[61] Hope J. Leichter, *op. cit.,* see fn 34.

| Dimensions of the Social Order | CONTEXT |

COMMENTARY

Basic organizational processes have been examined under the topics of differentiation and integration presented above. The articles reprinted here deal with the role played by the social milieu in shaping the attitudes and behavior of individuals. The significance of the social milieu is illustrated in an evaluation of behavioral differences indicated by aggregate statistics and in an examination of the individual in an organizational environment.

In his paper on "Structural Effects," Peter Blau attempts to assess the impact of the social milieu, apart from that of individual characteristics, in accounting for the patterning of behavior and attitudes. He illustrates several types of structural effects and notes that both individual and aggregate data are required for an assessment of the importance of the social context.

Albert Reiss, Jr. and Albert Rhodes, in "The Distribution of Juvenile Delinquency in the Social Class Structure," examine variations in rates of delinquent behavior by age, I.Q., and ascribed social status. Their essentially statistical notion of delinquency life chances, and their concepts of underrepresentation and overrepresentation of delinquents in various milieux, provide a further illustration of the independent effect of the social context on the patterning of individual behavior and attitudes.

21   PETER M. BLAU

Structural Effects

Two basic types of social fact can be distinguished: the common values and norms embodied in a culture or subculture; and the networks of social relations in which processes of social interaction become organized and through which social positions of individuals and subgroups become differentiated.[1] Kroeber and Parsons have recently reemphasized the importance of this analytical distinction.[2] Many theoretical concepts illustrate the distinction: Weber's Protestant ethic and Sumner's mores exemplify social values and norms, while Marx's investigation of the class structure and Simmel's study of coalitions in triads deal with networks of social relationships.

These concepts refer to attributes of social collectivities, not to those of individuals, but they have counterparts that do refer to characteristics of individuals. Individuals can be described in terms of their orientations and dispositions, just as groups or entire societies can be described in terms of the prevailing social values and norms; and individuals can be distinguished on the basis of their social status, just as communities can be distinguished on the basis of the status distribution in them.[3] These parallels tend to conceal the fundamental difference between the implications of group structure and those of the individual's own characteristics for his conduct. Even socially acquired or socially defined attributes of individuals are clearly distinct in their effects from attributes of social structures.

Reprinted from *American Sociological Review*, 25:2 (1960), pp. 178–193, by permission of the author and the publisher.

Systematic social research has often been criticized for distorting, if not entirely ignoring, crucial characteristics of social structure.[4] Interviewing surveys have provided much information about the influences of attitudes of individuals and their social status on human behavior, but they have contributed little to our knowledge of the structural constraints exerted by common values and status distributions in groups or communities, because sampling procedures tend to make isolated individuals the focus of the analysis. And while ecological studies have examined social units, with a few exceptions,[5] they have not separated the consequences of social conditions from those of the individual's own characteristics for his behavior, because ecological data do not furnish information about individuals except in the aggregate. But the systematic analysis of structural constraints requires, as Merton and Kitt have pointed out, the simultaneous use of indices of social structure and of individual behavior.[6] This paper suggests and illustrates a method for isolating the effects of social structure.[7]

SOCIAL VALUES AND NORMS

Social values and norms are common orientations toward social conduct that prevail in a society or group. Social values govern the choice of objectives that are experienced as worth striving for, and social norms differentiate between proper and improper conduct.

Since social values and norms are shared, internalized orientations, the most plausible procedure for ascertaining them in empirical research would seem to be to determine, first, what values the members of a number of communities hold and, then, which ones of these are shared by members of any given community. For example, one could administer the F-Scale to a sample of the American population[8] and divide communities on the basis of whether authoritarian values are more or less prevalent. Let us assume that such a study finds that the relative prevalence of authoritarian values in a community is associated with a high degree of discrimination against minorities. (We shall also assume that other relevant conditions have been controlled and that we have evidence that authoritarianism is the antecedent variable and discrimination the dependent one.) Two conclusions could be drawn from this finding: first, if a community has an authoritarian subculture, discriminatory practices will prevail in it; second, if an individual has an authoritarian personality, he will tend to discriminate against minorities.

There is a fundamental difference between these two interpretations: the former implies that social processes external to individual personalities are responsible for the differences in discrimination; the latter that internal psychological processes are responsible. To be sure, the prevalence of authoritarian dispositions in some communities and not in others may well be largely due to differences in their social structures. What the determinants of prevailing values are, however, has no direct bearing on what their consequences are or on how these consequences are effected. These are the issues under consideration here. The individual's orientation undoubtedly influences his behavior; the question is whether the prevalence of social values in a community also exerts social constraints upon patterns of conduct that are independent of the influences exerted by the internalized orientations.

The sociologist assumes that this is the case. But how can one demonstrate that social values and norms exert *external* constraints upon the acting and thinking of individuals if they only exist in the minds of individuals? Durkheim, who is concerned with various aspects of this problem in most of his writings, suggests a specific answer in *Suicide*. After admitting, notwithstanding his social realism, that "social consciousness" exists only in individual minds, he states that the social force it exerts, nevertheless, is *"external to each average individual taken singly."*[9]

The common values and norms in a group have two distinct kinds of effect upon the conduct of its members. Ego's conduct is influenced by his own normative orientation for fear of his conscience, and ego's conduct is also influenced by alters' normative orientation for fear of social sanctions. In other words, people conform to prevailing norms partly because they would feel guilty if they did not and partly because they gain social approval and avoid disapproval by doing so. This conception is somewhat oversimplified. It ignores, for example, the fact that the strength of ego's normative orientation itself is in part due to the reinforcement it receives from the social sanctions of alters. Despite its oversimplification, however, this analytical distinction makes it possible to demonstrate empirically the external constraints exerted by social values and norms by differentiating them from the influences of the internalized orientations of individuals.

The structural effects of a social value can be isolated by showing that the association between its prevalence in a community or group and certain patterns of conduct is independent of whether an individual holds this value or not. To return to our illustration: if we should find that, regardless of whether or not an individual has an authoritarian disposition, he is more apt to discriminate against minorities if he lives in a community where authoritarian values prevail than if he lives in one where they do not, we would have evidence that this social value exerts external constraints upon the tendency to discriminate—structural effects that are independent of the internalized value orientation of individuals.

DIRECT EFFECTS

To illustrate the method of analysis suggested above and the distinguishable types of structural effects, data from a pilot study of a public assistance agency will be used.[10] The clients who came to the agency as applicants for general public assistance constituted the poorest stratum in a large American city. The primary job of the caseworker was to determine whether new applicants are eligible for public assistance and to check recurrently whether old recipients continue to be eligible. This involved visiting the clients in their homes and a considerable amount of paper work in the office. Many workers tried to provide some casework service as well, although their ability to do so was limited by their heavy work loads—the average number of cases per worker was over 120—and by their lack of training—the majority of workers had only a college degree and no professional training in social work.

Caseworkers were organized into units of five or six under a supervisor. After a period of observation in the agency, the members of twelve supervisory units were interviewed. The analysis presented below is based on these interview responses of 60 caseworkers who were members of twelve work groups. Not quite half of these workers were women; one-third of them were Negroes; and one-third had been with the agency less than one year, which indicates the high rate of turnover of personnel characteristic of public assistance agencies.

When caseworkers were asked whether the amount of public assistance should be increased, remain the name, or be decreased, one-half stated unequivocally that it should be increased; the majority of the rest felt that an increase is needed only for certain special cases, for example, clients who must pay high rent; and a few thought that no increase is necessary. Nobody suggested that the amount should be decreased. The number of correlations between this item and other measures of orientation to clients is larger than that of any other, which suggests that it is indicative of a fairly basic aspect of orientation to clients.

Does the prevalence of pro-client values in a group affect the performance of duties of its members independently of the individual's own attitude to clients? The description by workers of what they did when visiting clients provides a measure of their orientation in the performance of duties. It indicates that some largely confined their work to checking on eligibility, whereas others were also concerned with furnishing casework service. To isolate the structural effects of pro-client values, groups are divided on the basis of whether or not a majority of group members favors raising the assistance budget for all clients, and within each type of group, individuals are divided into those that favor an increase in assistance for all clients and those that do not. The first item in Table 1 shows that individuals with pro-client attitudes were more often service-oriented in their work than others (compare adjacent columns). It also shows, and this is the pertinent finding, that regardless of their own attitudes, members of groups in which pro-client values prevailed were more apt to be oriented toward casework service than members of groups with other values (compare alternate columns). Of the pro-client individuals, 60 percent in pro-client groups and 44 percent in other groups were service-oriented; of the other workers, 44 percent in pro-client groups and 27 percent in other groups were service-oriented.

Although the differences in the proportion of service-oriented workers associated with contrasting group values are not large, they are just as large as those associated with contrasting individual attitudes. (The combination of group value and individual attitude made a considerable dif-

TABLE 1.   EFFECTS OF VALUE ORIENTATION TOWARD CLIENTS

	Group's prevailing value orientation toward clients			
	Positive		Not positive	
	Individual's orientation		Individual's orientation	
	Positive	Not positive	Positive	Not positive
1. Orientation to work				
Checking eligibility	30%	56%	56%	55%
Intermediate	10	0	0	18
Casework service	60	44	44	27
Total	100	100	100	100
2. Visits to recipients *				
Forty or less per month	59	50	44	31
Over 40 per month	41	50	56	69
Total	100	100	100	100
3. Delegating responsibility to clients				
Unwilling to delegate	45	22	67	50
Willing to delegate	55	78	33	50
Total	100	100	100	100
4. Involvement with work				
High (worry much)	75	44	89	68
Low (worry little)	25	56	11	32
Total	100	100	100	100
Number of cases	20	9	9	22

* This information is taken from performance records; since insufficient information was available for the newer workers the totals for this item in the four columns, reading from left to right are: 17, 6, 9, 13.

ference for orientation toward work: only about one-quarter of the workers who neither had pro-client attitudes nor were in groups where pro-client values prevailed were service-oriented, compared to three-fifths of those with pro-client attitudes most of whose co-workers shared these pro-client values.) Moreover, other measures of performance reveal the same pattern of relationships with group values. For example, making relatively few field visits generally implied the provision of more intensive services. Individuals with pro-client attitudes tended to make slightly fewer visits to recipients than other workers, and whatever the individual's attitudes were, he was more prone to make fewer visits if he was a member of a group in which pro-client values prevailed than of a group with different values (see Table 1, #2). Although all these relationships are small, their consistency makes it unlikely that they are entirely due to chance.[11]

These findings suggest that the social values that prevail in a work group do exert external constraints upon the thinking and acting of its members. If pro-client values prevail in a group, merely checking on the eligibility of clients meets with social disapproval while providing casework services gains a worker approval and respect. But this is not the case if pro-client values do not prevail; indeed, the opposite may be the case. In other words, the pro-client values of the members of a group motivate them not only to furnish more intensive service to their own clients but also to express social approval of colleagues who are service-oriented and social disapproval of those who are not. In response to those sanctioning patterns, individuals tend to modify their approach to clients.

The conclusion that pro-client group values have structural effects on the performance of duties rests on the assumptions that the relationships observed are not spurious and that pro-client values are the independent variable in these relationships. Differences in supervision might constitute a correlated bias that accounts for the relationships, but examination of the data reveals that this is not the case. Of course, this does not exclude the possibility of other influential correlated biases, and neither can the possibility be excluded that pro-client values are actually consequence rather than antecedent in these relationships. But this is a limitation of cross-sectional studies, not on the method of isolating structural effects. Given more adequate data than those used here for illustrative purposes, this method makes it possible to demonstrate structural effects as firmly as the effects of a characteristic of individuals can be demonstrated.

INVERSE EFFECTS

The structural effects of the prevailing values in a group are not necessarily parallel to the effects of the individual's value orientation. In some respects pro-client group values and the individual's own pro-client attitudes have opposite implications for his conduct.

In this agency, clients received money to buy clothing when needed; the caseworker and his supervisor exercised considerable discretion in establishing this need. In some other public assistance agencies, recipients receive a regular clothing allowance, which they spend at their own discretion. Respondents were asked whether they would favor giving such a regular allowance to clients. This change would save the caseworker some tedious and time-consuming work, but would also deprive him of discretionary power over clients and their welfare.

Individuals with pro-client attitudes were *less* willing than others to delegate this responsibility to clients, but the prevalence of pro-client values in a group *increased* the willingness to delegate it (see Table 1, #3)— from one-third to 55 percent for pro-client workers, and from one-half to 78 percent for others. Pro-client values had the same kind of inverse structural effect on the extent to which workers worried about their cases after working hours: individuals with pro-client attitudes worried *more* than others, but the members of groups in which pro-client values prevailed worried *less* than the members of other groups (see Table 1, #4).

The fact that an individual is favorably disposed toward clients would be expected to increase his concern for their welfare and the gratification he receives from helping them, and thus to make him eager to exercise responsibilities that permit him to furnish more help to them and that make them grateful to him. If most members of a group share pro-client values, their common interest in the welfare of clients will induce them to develop at least implicit normative standards that promote the interest of clients. They are likely to react with social disapproval toward a colleague whose involvement leads him to lose his temper when talking to a client or toward one who uses his discretion not to help clients more but to withhold help from them or to hold a club over their heads. Discussion of such experiences by pro-client members of a group may lead to an agreement that the interest of clients is best served by encouraging detachment and the delegation of responsibilities to them. Or these group members may adopt explicit professional standards of social work, according to which a worker should remain detached toward his clients and foster their independence by letting them make their own decisions. The members of groups where pro-client standards do not prevail are less apt to adopt professional casework standards.

Such inverse structural effects of social values call attention to the importance of social norms. Since the emotional reaction to pro-client dispositions is greater involvement and an unwillingness to delegate responsibility, whereas the welfare of clients is best served by detachment and delegation of responsibility, the workers most interested in the welfare of clients are psychologically least able to provide effective service to them. But the prevalence of positive values in a group promotes the development of casework standards, which curb the psychological consequences of pro-client feelings that impede effective service. Professional training in social work probably leads to the internalization of these casework standards, but the untrained workers in this agency had not fully internalized them; if they had, no inverse structural effects would have been observed.

CONTINGENCY EFFECTS

The influence of the prevalence of social values in a group may be more indirect than in the examples discussed above. Instead of having an effect on a third variable that is independent of the individual's value orientation, it may determine whether the individual's value orientation and a third variable are related or how they are related. In technical terms, the group values and the individual's orientation may have an interaction effect on a third variable. Conceptually, this implies that the relationship between the individual's orientation and another variable is contingent on the prevalence of this value orientation in his group.

All assistance budgets made out by caseworkers were reviewed by an audit section. Caseworkers tended to accuse auditors of being too rigid about eligibility procedures and too little concerned with the welfare of clients, and conflicts with them were frequent. In groups most of whose members were service-oriented, the individual's orientation had no bearing upon his conflicts with auditors; seven out of every ten workers, whatever their orientation, reported such conflicts. In groups where an eligibility orientation prevailed, however, the individual's orientation made a pronounced difference; all five of the service-oriented workers reported conflicts with auditors, in contrast to less than half of the 24 workers oriented toward eligibility (see Table 2). It seems that the chances of conflict with auditors decline only if neither the individual's own orientation nor that of the other members in his group demand that he place serving the interests of clients above strict conformity with eligibility procedures.

TABLE 2. EFFECTS OF ORIENTATION TOWARD WORK

	Group's prevailing orientation			
	Casework service		Checking eligibility	
	Individual's orientation		Individual's orientation	
	Service	Eligibility	Service	Eligibility
Reported conflicts with auditors				
None	29%	30%	0%	54%
Some	71	70	100	46
Total	100	100	100	100
Number of cases	21	10	5	24

The extreme case of contingency effect is the one where the relationship between the individual's orientation and another factor becomes reversed, dependent on the prevalence of the orientation in the group. The extent of involvement with the work had such contingency effects. Respondents were asked how often they worry about their work after working hours, which is the measure of involvement used; then they were asked to exemplify what they worry about. The illustrations of the majority reveal worries about clients: "If they'd have enough to eat over the weekend," "Problems the people have—I hope that a deserted family can manage— I remember the expressions on their faces." But some workers worried about their own performance: "If you mean their personal problems, then the answer is, no; but I worry about the record which is open to the supervisor's checking."

If involvement—that is, extensive worrying—prevailed in a group, there was an inverse relationship between the individual's involvement and whether he worried about clients rather than his own performance, but if involvement did not prevail in a group, these two factors were directly related. The implications of this interaction effect can be clearly seen when percentages are computed horizontally (for each half-row) instead of vertically, as in Table 3, #1. If all the members within any given group were alike in their involvement, 100 percent of those in groups with much involvement would be highly involved, but none of those in groups with little involvement. In other words, the two central columns (marked by

TABLE 3. PATTERNS OF DEVIANCY IN RESPECT TO INVOLVEMENT WITH WORK

	Group's dominant climate							
	Much involvement				Little involvement			
	Individual's involvement				Individual's involvement			
	High	Low*	Total	N†	High	Low*	Total	N†
1. Source of worries								
Client's welfare ..	47%	53%	100%	19	54%	46%	100%	13
Own performance	89	11	100	9	14	86	100	7
Not asked‡				3				9
2. Status in work group								
Integrated	50	50	100	18	50	50	100	16
Not integrated ..	62	38	100	13	0	100	100	13
3. Self-confidence								
High	50	50	100	8	50	50	100	10
Low	57	43	100	23	16	84	100	19

* These two columns represent the deviants—the lows in much-involved groups and the highs in little-involved groups.

† The number of cases on which the percentages, computed horizontally for each half-row, are based.

‡ Respondents who said they never worried, and thus are classified among those with low involvement, could not be asked what they worried about; they are, therefore, not considered in this comparison.

a single asterisk) of the table represent the deviants—the lows in groups with much involvement and the highs in groups with little involvement. It is evident that workers mostly concerned with their clients' welfare were deviants in disproportionate numbers in both kinds of groups. They were *more* apt than workers primarily concerned with their own performance to be involved in groups where involvement was rare, but they were *less* apt than the others to be involved in groups where involvement was common.[12] Indeed, they apparently were not at all influenced by the prevailing group climate; whether they were in groups where the majority was involved or in groups where the majority was not, about half of these client-identified workers were highly involved. In contrast to only two of the 16 workers who were concerned about their performance, 17 of the 32 who were concerned with their clients' welfare deviated from the group climate. This suggests that identification with clients is a source of strength which makes a worker somewhat independent of peer group pressures.

This finding has a general methodological implication. Whenever the distribution of value orientations in a group and the individual's value orientation show such an interaction effect on a third variable, the latter differentiates members who tend to deviate from the standards of their own group from those who tend to conform to them, regardless of what these standards are. For this pattern of findings inevitably indicates that the X's have orientation Y *more* often than the non-X's in groups where this orientation is rare but *less* often than the non-X's in groups where it is common, which means that the X's tend to be the deviants whatever the prevailing orientation of the group.

Several studies have investigated the relationship between an individual's social integration among peers or his informal status and his conformity or resistance to group pressure.[13] An important problem is whether social integration increases, or decreases, resistance to group pressure independent of the kind of pressure involved. The procedure outlined above facilitates the study of the relationship between social position and response to *opposite* kinds of group pressure.

Individuals who were integrated in their work group were more prone than those who were not to deviate from the prevailing group climate in respect to involvement. (Whether a worker was called by his first name by some of the other members of this group, as reported by the others, is the measure of social integration used.) In groups where the majority was involved with their work, integrated workers were slightly less likely to be involved than others, but in groups where the majority was not involved, integrated workers were more likely to be involved than others (see Table 3, #2). In other words, whether much or little involvement characterized the group climate, the integrated workers were more apt than the rest to deviate from it. Their resistance to group pressure is indicated by the fact that their involvement was quite independent of the group climate; the proportion of integrated workers who were involved in their work was the same in groups with much involvement as in groups with little involvement. One-half of the 34 integrated workers deviated from the prevailing group climate, as contrasted with only one-fifth of the 26 unintegrated workers.

This finding seems to be typical. If other measures of orientation toward work and clients are substituted for involvement, and if other aspects of informal status are used instead of integration, one also finds superior status among peers associated with the tendency to deviate from the prevailing orientation in a group regardless of the particular content of this orientation.[14] Since it is improbable that deviation creates more liking and respect than conformity, the opposite direction of influence is the plausible inference. The acceptance and respect of his colleagues provides a worker with social support. His consequent feelings of security apparently permit him to resist group pressures and depart from group norms more readily than can the worker whose insecure position provides strong incentives to improve his standing and to court social approval through strict conformity. This interpretation implies that self-confident workers are more prone to deviate from the prevailing group pattern than those lacking in self-confidence. Indeed, this seems to have been the case (see Table 3, #3).[15]

SOCIAL COHESION

An important aspect of the network of social relations in a group is the strength of the bonds that unite its members—the group's social cohesion.

One possible procedure for measuring group cohesion is to ascertain how strongly each member is identified with the group and compute some average. The objection that such an index is purely phenomenological and does not pertain to the group structure could be met by isolating the structural effects of group identification, using the method suggested in this paper.

Another measure of group cohesion, which Festinger and his colleagues have made popular, is based on ingroup sociometric choices, for example, the proportion of friendship choices made by the members of a group.[16] The conception of cohesion underlying this measure has been criticized by Gross and Martin because it emphasizes "individual perceptions and minimizes the importance of the relational bonds between and among group members."[17] Sociometric measures, however, are indicative of relational bonds, since they are based on reports of choices made by one individual and received by another. Moreover, the alternative the authors propose is not likely to bring us closer to a structural definition of cohesion. They suggest that it should be measured by subjecting groups to disruptive forces of varying degrees and observing when they "begin to distintegrate."[18] But the sign of beginning distintegration would undoubtedly be that some members quit the group, or that some stop attending meetings, and an index based on such signs of disintegration relies as much on the strength of the group ties of individual members as does Festinger's sociometric index.[19]

Nevertheless, Gross and Martin's criticism should not be summarily dismissed. It draws attention to the important distinction between group structure and interpersonal relations. To be sure, interpersonal relationships (and relationships between subgroups, if they exist) are the very core of group structure. But atomizing group structure into its component interpersonal relations is as little justified as reducing groups to the individual personalities who compose them. Group structure refers to the distribution or network of social relationships, which may have a significance that is quite distinct from that of the social relationships in which specific individuals are involved. Thus, it cannot be assumed that the influence of the network of cohesive bonds in a group is the same as that of the interpersonal bonds of individual group members. The method of isolating structural effects makes it possible to distinguish between these two kinds of influence—those exerted by the prevalence of cohesive ties in a group and those exerted by the integrative ties of the individual members.

EFFECTS OF SOCIAL COHESION

Group cohesion is operationally defined in terms of ingroup sociometric choices. Respondents were asked to name the five persons in the agency with whom they were most friendly. The median proportion of ingroup choices is used to divide groups into cohesive and non-cohesive ones. Within each type of group, individuals are divided on the basis of whether or not they received ingroup choices. (An alternative procedure would have been to divide individuals by the ingroup choices they *made*. But if we accept the notion that cohesion is related to group attractiveness, and wish to hold constant the aspect of the individual's interpersonal relations that is most parallel, received choices, which indicate attractiveness, are preferable to choices made.)

Cohesion in these work groups had structural effects on the approach of caseworkers to clients, that is, effects that were independent of the individual's interpersonal bonds in the group. Respondents were asked, "What are the things clients do that are particularly trying?" The answers of some reveal behavior of clients they considered a personal affront—"Demands get under my skin, or a client's trying to tell me my job," "If they cheat on me it makes me awfully mad"—whereas those of others refer to behavior that is improper or harmful to the client and his family—". . . they were winos, constantly drunk and beating each other up," ". . . she hadn't even gotten her children the routine inoculations." Thus, some workers reacted in personal terms and objected to behavior of clients when they felt offended, while others reacted in accordance with generally accepted rules of conduct and objected to behavior of clients not primarily because it was discourteous to them but because it was morally wrong.[20]

The members of cohesive groups were less apt to take personal affront at the behavior of clients than those of less cohesive groups, and this difference persists if the individual's sociometric position is held constant (see Table 4, #1). Only about one-third of the former, in contrast to over two-thirds of the latter reacted in personal terms. The prevalence of supportive ties in cohesive groups is a source of emotional strength for their members. The absence of extensive ego support in less cohesive groups throws their members upon other social resources for this support, such as their relations with clients. If an individual defines an interpersonal relationship as a potential source of ego support, he is apt to react in personal terms, feeling insulted or more or less appreciated, but if he does not, it is easier for him to take the view of an outsider and judge the behavior of others in accordance with impersonal criteria. Apparently, it is the general extensive support of group cohesion rather than the specific intensive support of the individual's own interpersonal ties that promotes an impersonal approach in social interaction with clients. Only group cohesion was associated with this approach; the individual's sociometric position was not.

Performance, too, was influenced by social cohesion. Data taken from production records show that the members of cohesive groups, whether or not they personally received sociometric choices, tended to make more field visits than those of other groups (see Table 4, #2). Since numerous field visits indicate both that much work has been accomplished and, probably, that less intensive service has been furnished, one may deduce from the finding either that cohesion fosters the fulfillment of tasks or that it

TABLE 4. EFFECTS OF GROUP COHESION

	Group cohesion			
	High		Low	
	Individual's attractiveness		Individual's attractiveness	
	High	Low	High	Low
1. Reaction to clients *				
Personal	38%	34%	70%	80%
Impersonal	62	66	30	20
Total	100	100	100	100
2. Total field visits †				
Sixty or less per month	60	67	77	82
Over 60 per month	40	33	23	18
Total	100	100	100	100
3. High respect for own supervisor				
Present	76	58	50	41
Absent	24	42	50	59
Total	100	100	100	100
4. Orientation to work				
Checking eligibility	29	59	50	53
Intermediate	18	8	7	6
Casework service	53	33	43	41
Total	100	100	100	100
Number of cases	17	12	14	17

* Since some clients were not asked this question, the column totals for this item, reading from left to right, are: 13, 6, 10, 15.

† This information is taken from performance records; insufficient information for newer workers reduces the column totals for this item to: 15, 6, 13, 11. The total number of visits rather than only visits with recipients are used here, where concern is with productivity.

lessens concern with the provision of much service to clients. Two factors, however, make the first inference the more probable: cohesion is not inversely related to a service orientation, as the second interpretation implies; and a number of other studies suggests that cohesion promotes high productivity.[21]

When asked to choose the best supervisors in the organization, members of cohesive groups were more prone to name their own supervisor than members of less cohesive groups (see Table 4, #3). Independent of this relationship, individuals who received sociometric choices from the ingroup were also somewhat more likely to name their own supervisor than others. Perhaps the fact that a supervisor commands the respect of his workers increases the chances that cohesive ties will develop among them. But it is also possible that the absence of strong ingroup bonds produces strains and tensions which find expression in more critical attitudes toward the supervisor.

A contingency effect is illustrated by the implications of ingroup choices for the caseworker's orientation to his work; that is, group cohesion and its individual counterpart had an interaction effect upon whether a worker was oriented primarily toward checking eligibility or toward casework service. In groups with low cohesion, whether or not an individual received ingroup choices did not influence his orientation, but in groups with high cohesion, individuals who received choices from their peers were less apt than others to confine themselves to checking on the eligibility of clients (see Table 4, #4). Social support from prevailing cohesive bonds and from specific interpersonal bonds both seem to be necessary to reduce the chances that workers will confine their work to rigid enforcement of eligibility procedures. The group and the individual measure of ingroup choices also had interaction effects on other indications of strict adherence to established procedures, such as ritualistic punctuality and opposition to change in the rules defining responsibilities.

EFFECTS OF COMMUNICATION STRUCTURE

Instrumental as well as socio-emotional patterns of social interaction form into networks of social relationships which characterize group structures. The pattern of friendly associations among workers is one aspect of the social structure of the work group, the pattern of communication assumed by their consultations and discussions of problems is another. The two are not unrelated, but neither are they identical.

The procedure used to define the communication structure is a familiar one. Respondents were asked with which colleagues they usually discuss their problems; they were free to name any number of colleagues, either members of their own group or outsiders. On the basis of the ingroup choices, groups are divided into those with relatively dense and those with sparse internal communication networks, and within each type of group, individuals are divided according to whether or not they were named as regular consultants by two or more colleagues.

In several instances, the structural effects of this consultation network were quite similar to those of social cohesion. Both aspects of group structure, for example, had closely parallel consequences for the respect workers accorded to their supervisor. In other cases, however, their impact was different. Thus, the consultation structure did not influence a worker's reaction to the behavior of clients in personal or impersonal terms. In still other respects, the degree of reciprocity in the consultations of a group rather than their frequency had effects that paralleled those of cohesion. For instance, reciprocity in consultation, like cohesion, was associated with high productivity (many field visits). Further research with a larger number of groups is needed to derive generalizations about the different implications of various aspects of group structure.

The density of the group's communication network had an interesting double effect on attitudes toward clients, as indicated by attitudes toward increasing the amount of assistance. Negative attitudes were more common in groups where consultation was frequent than in those where it was rare (see Table 5). Whether a worker was regularly consulted or not, he was three times as likely to oppose any increase in the assistance allowance if he was a member of a group in which consultation was prevalent than one in which it was rare. This does not mean, however, that the individual's social status—how often he was consulted—was entirely unrelated to his attitude toward clients. But whether or not these two factors were related was contingent on the group structure. In groups whose members consulted little the attitude of consultants toward increasing public assistance did not differ from that of others, but in groups whose members consulted much consultants were more likely to advocate an increase than nonconsultants. Hence, the group's communication network had two effects on the attitudes toward clients: first, frequent communication fostered more negative attitudes; and second, such communication partly determined whether or not the individual's position in the communication network influenced his attitudes toward clients. Furthermore, while the frequency of consultation in a group was associated with *negative* attitudes toward clients, the fact that an individual member of a group where consultation prevailed was often consulted was associated with *positive* attitudes.[22]

To interpret this finding, it is necessary to examine briefly the strained relations between caseworkers and clients in this agency. There were many reasons for conflict. Most clients were in dire need and had strong incentive to conceal any slim resources they might have had or otherwise to try to increase the amount of assistance they would get even if this required some dishonesty. Caseworkers, many of whom came to the agency directly from college with idealistic views about helping people, tended to experience what Everett Hughes has called a "reality shock" when they encountered clients who, instead of appreciating their help, lied to them and broke their promises, and whose values were so different from their

TABLE 5.   EFFECTS OF COMMUNICATION NETWORK

	Extent of communication in group			
	Much consultation		Little consultation	
	Individual's position		Individual's position	
	Consultant	Not	Consultant	Not
Attitudes to clients				
Negative	25%	36%	8%	9%
Qualified	17	36	42	36
Positive	58	28	50	55
Total	100	100	100	100
Number of cases	12	14	12	22

own. Even when a worker tried to help clients he sometimes found that they blamed him for limitations the agency's procedure imposed on him. Caseworkers protected themselves against such frustrating experiences by developing and publicly flaunting a hardened attitude toward clients. Their discussions among themselves were dominated by aggressive remarks and jokes about clients. Many workers were undoubtedly much more favorably disposed toward recipients than their statements to colleagues indicated. Even those who clearly had positive attitudes toward clients seemed to feel compelled to present a hardened front by making aggressive remarks about them when talking to colleagues. This pattern of relieving tension appears to be typical of work groups whose members experience conflicts with clients.[23] Most members of this agency did not have a callous attitude toward clients, but expressing anti-client sentiments was the prevailing norm.

The enforcement of social norms requires an effective network of communication in a group. Hence, a group with a strong communication network will be more effective in enforcing the prevailing anti-client norms than one with a weak network. To be sure, the anti-client norms in this organization were not so severe as to include opposition to any increase in the assistance allowance; after all, only a minority of respondents expressed such opposition. However, the more effective the enforcement of general anti-client norms in a group, the greater the chances that some of its members will take an extreme position—one more extreme than that called for by the norms—and this is what the finding shows. Informal status in a group, as data presented earlier suggest, is inversely associated with conformity to the normative orientation toward clients. In groups with communication networks that permit effective enforcement of anti-client norms, nonconsultants, whose low status makes them subject to the full impact of group pressures, therefore have more negative attitudes toward clients than consultants, whose high status removes them somewhat from group control. But in groups where consultation is rare, the status of consultant has less significance, and since, moreover, the prevailing anti-client norms are not effectively enforced in these groups, whether or not an individual is regularly consulted does not influence his attitudes toward clients. These considerations also explain the seeming paradox: the fact that there is much consultation in a group and the fact that a member of such a group is much consulted have opposite consequences for attitudes toward clients. An effective network of communication increases the group's power to enforce prevailing anti-client norms, but the superior status of consultant reduces the individual's conformity to these group norms.

CONCLUSIONS: TYPES OF STRUCTURAL EFFECTS AND THEIR STUDY

Robinson has criticized research based on ecological correlations for implicitly assuming that these indicate relationships between the characteristics of individuals, and he has demonstrated that an ecological correlation between, say, the proportion of Negroes and the proportion of illiterates in an area does not prove that more Negroes than whites are illiterate.[24] Menzel has pointed out, however, that ecological studies may well be concerned with relationships between aspects of social structures without making any assumptions about relationships between attributes of individuals.[25] But Robinson's strictures apply also to Menzel's sociological conception. If the psychologically oriented investigator assumes that ecological correlations *are* due to correlations between traits of individuals, the sociologically oriented analyst assumes that they *are not*, and neither assumption is warranted. A correlation between divorce rates and suicide rates, for example, might be sociologically interpreted to indicate that anomie in the marital institutions of a society, operationally defined by a high divorce rate, increases suicide rates. This theory clearly implies that the ecological correlation is *not* entirely due to the fact that divorced persons are more apt to commit suicide than married ones; for if it were, a much simpler explanation would suffice. To demonstrate that it is anomie, as measured by divorce rates, rather than the psychological state or personality of the divorced individual that is responsible for high suicide rates, it is necessary to show that married as well as divorced persons have higher suicide rates in countries where divorce is frequent than in those where it is rare. This, of course, is precisely how Durkheim tested his theory of anomic suicide.[26]

Durkheim, then, some sixty years ago, illustrated the method of isolating structural effects. The essential principle is that the relationship between the distribution of a given characteristic in various collectivities and an effect criterion is ascertained, while this characteristic is held constant for individuals. This procedure differentiates the effects of social structures upon patterns of action from the influences exerted by the characteristics of the acting individuals or their interpersonal relationships. If a structural effect is observed, it invariably constitutes evidence that social processes originating outside the individual personality are responsible for the differences in the dependent variable, since the influences of psychological processes have been controlled in the analysis. The futile arguments of whether or not a certain concept or empirical measure is *really* a social factor can be dismissed if this method of analysis is employed, since its results demonstrate whether social forces or psychological ones produce given effects regardless of the empirical index used to define the independent variable. Take such an individualistic characteristic as intelligence. If it were found that the average IQ scores in fraternities are associated with the scholastic records of their members when the individual's score is held constant, there could be no doubt, provided other relevant conditions are controlled, that the level of intelligence in a fraternity influences performance on examinations through *social* processes (although, of course, the finding would not show whether these processes involve social stimulation of learning or collaboration on examinations).

A tentative typology of structural effects can be derived by classifying them along two dimensions. The first distinguishes between the consequences of the common values or shared norms of a collectivity and those of its networks of social relationships or distribution of social positions. Second, either of these two basic aspects of the social structure can have direct effects, inverse effects, and contingency effects. (Still another type is that where the variance of a characteristic in a group, rather than its frequency, exerts an influence upon social conduct. But such an association between the variance and an effect criterion usually indicates the impact of a social force even when the characteristic is not held constant for individuals,[27] and therefore this type, which generally requires no special method of analysis, is not discussed in this paper.)

These two dimensions differentiate six types of structural effects:

1. *Direct structural effects of common values* indicate that the individual's conduct is influenced not only by the motivating force of his own value orientation but also by the social pressure resulting from the shared values of the other members of the group. In a public assistance agency, for example, a worker's positive orientation toward clients seemed to increase his tendency to provide casework services, and quite independently of the individual's orientation, the prevalence of a positive orientation in a group also made it more likely that casework services were provided.

2. *Inverse structural effects of common values* suggest that group values give rise to normative constraints that counteract the individual's psychological reaction to his own value orientation. Thus, the individual's positive attitude to clients tended to *increase* his involvement with his work and his unwillingness to delegate responsibility to recipients, but the prevalence of positive attitudes in a group tended to *decrease* involvement and unwillingness to delegate responsibility.

3. *Contingency effects of common values* are those in which the distribution of a value in a group influences the correlation between the individual's value orientation and a third variable. In the extreme case, the prevalence of the value in a group determines whether this correlation is positive or negative, and this pattern of findings identifies the deviants. It shows that individuals with a certain characteristic in terms of the third variable are more prone than others to resist group pressures and deviate from group norms regardless of the specific content of these norms. Whether most members of a group were much involved with their work or only little involved, those with an integrated status among peers, for instance, were more apt than others to deviate from the prevailing group climate, and so were workers identified with clients.

4. *Direct structural effects of relational networks* abstract the supportive or constraining force exerted by the social *organization* of the relationships between individuals and subgroups in a collectivity from the influences of each member's interpersonal relationships or social status. This is illustrated by the findings that group cohesiveness, defined by the extent

of ingroup ties, apparently promoted a more impersonal approach to clients and high productivity, and that these effects were independent of the ingroup ties particular individuals had established.

5. *Inverse structural effects of relational networks* are indicative of the fact that the status distribution or network of social relations in a collectivity has an impact which is the very opposite of that of the individual's social status or his social relationships. A perfect case is the well-known finding reported by Stouffer that a soldier's rank was *directly* associated with favorable attitudes toward the army's promotion system, but the proportion of high-ranking enlisted men in a military unit was *inversely* associated with favorable attitudes.[28] A more complex instance of this type has been observed in the public assistance agency: in work groups where consultation was frequent, *negative* attitudes toward clients were more prevalent than in other groups, but individuals who were often consulted had more *positive* attitudes than those who were not; however, this difference between individuals existed only in groups where consultation was common and not in those where it was rare.

6. *Contingency effects of relational networks* are those in which the association between the individual's social position or relations and another factor depends on the distribution of social positions or relations in the collectivity. This pattern of findings demonstrates that individuals whose social status differs from that of the majority in their group, regardless of the nature of this difference, also tend to have different characteristics in another respect. Contingency effects of status variables identify the implications of minority status as such, just as contingency effects of normative variables identify the correlates of deviancy as such. For example, Zena S. Blau finds that the proportion of widowed in an age-sex category determined the influence widowhood had on the friendships of older people. Among men in their sixties, only a small minority of whom were widowed, the widowed had much less extensive friendships than the married; but among women over seventy, three-quarters of whom were widowed, the widows had slightly more extensive friendships than the married women. Older people whose marital status places them in a minority position among age-sex peers seem to have less chance to maintain friendship ties than others.[29]

This list of effects of social structures is tentative and incomplete. Further refinements are needed, for example, with respect to differences in the nature of the dependent variable, and with respect to the distinction between large societies and small groups. Omitted from the enumeration are influences of those aspects of social structures that are not manifestations of frequency distributions, such as the form of government in a community, because in these cases there are no corresponding individual characteristics to be held constant. However, even if the empirical measure of social structure is not based on a frequency distribution but the theoretical conception implies one, corresponding characteristics of individuals should be controlled. Thus, if we are concerned with the differential impact on social conduct of democratic and authoritarian cultures, rather than with that of political institutions, and use the form of government in a country merely as an inexpensive and indirect index of its culture, we implicitly refer to differences in prevailing value orientations and should control the individual's value orientation in order to distinguish the external constraints of culture patterns from the influences of internalized values.

The method of isolating structural effects presented above underestimates the social constraints of structural differences, since the prevalence of certain shared values or social relationships in some collectivities and not in others, which is taken as given, is also often due to social forces, specifically, processes of socialization. It cannot be simply assumed, however, that any observed group pattern is the result of socialization. Other processes, such as differential selection, might be responsible. Moreover, whatever its plausibility, the claim that the common values of communities are social in origin and the product of processes of socialization is a hypothesis that requires empirical confirmation, and testing this hypothesis involves the use of procedures essentially similar to those discussed in this paper. To demonstrate its validity requires evidence that individuals who do not have a certain orientation but live in communities where this orientation prevails are more apt to develop such an orientation over time than those in other communities. Thus, Lazarsfeld and Thielens use this procedure to show that members of conservative university faculties are more apt to become increasingly conservative as they grow older than members of less conservative faculties.[30] In diachronic as well as synchronic investigations where social structures are defined, explicitly or implicitly, in terms of frequency distributions, structural effects on patterns of conduct must be analytically separated from the influences of the individuals' own characteristics or interpersonal relations.

NOTES

[1] See, e.g., Rubin M. Williams, Jr., *American Society* (New York: Knopf, 1951), pp. 443–448.

[2] A. L. Kroeber and Talcott Parsons, "The Concepts of Culture and of Social System," *American Sociological Review*, 23 (1958), pp. 582–583.

[3] The relationships between measures of individual attributes and of group attributes are discussed by Patricia L. Kendall and Paul F. Lazarsfeld, "Problems of Survey Analysis," in *Continuities in Social Research*, Robert K. Merton and Paul F. Lazarsfeld, eds. (Glencoe, Ill.: The Free Press, 1950), pp. 187–196.

[4] See, e.g., Herbert Blumer, "Public Opinion and Public Opinion Polling," *American Sociological Review*, 13 (1948), pp. 542–549.

[5] For example: Robert E. L. Faris and H. Warren Dunham, *Mental Disorders in Urban Areas* (Chicago: University of Chicago Press, 1939).

[6] Robert K. Merton and Alice S. Kitt, "Contributions to the Theory of Reference Group Behavior," in Merton and Lazarsfeld, *op. cit.*, pp. 82–83; see also pp. 70–81. Cf. Samuel A. Stouffer *et al.*, *The American Soldier* (Princeton: Princeton University Press, 1949), Vol. II, pp. 242–272, for a notable exception to the tendency of ignoring effects of social structure in survey research.

[7] I have briefly discussed this method in "Formal Organization," *American Journal of Sociology*, 63 (1957), pp. 63–65. Structural effects are a special type of the "contextual propositions" discussed by Paul F. Lazarsfeld in "Problems in Methodology,"

in *Sociology Today*, Robert K. Merton *et al.*, eds. (New York: Basic Books, 1959), pp. 69–73.

[8] T. W. Adorno *et al.*, *The Authoritarian Personality* (New York: Harper & Row, 1950).

[9] Emile Durkheim, *Suicide* (Glencoe, Ill.: The Free Press, 1951), p. 316 (italics in original); see also pp. 309–320 for what may be Durkheim's most perceptive discussion of the problem.

[10] Philip M. Marcus was of great help in the collection and analysis of these data. I am also indebted to the Social Science Research Committee of the University of Chicago, which provided the funds for this study.

[11] Structural effects cannot be expected to account for most of the variance in dependent variables, but since there are a mere 60 cases divided into four unequal columns, only large differences would be statistically significant. It was necessary, therefore, to include in the illustrations findings that are not significant at the .05 level. (But it should be noted that each type of structural effect was observed repeatedly.) Since the respondents are not a representative sample, the applicability of tests of significance is questionable in any case. For a recent criticism of the indiscriminate use of statistical tests of significance, see Hanan C. Selvin, "A Critique of Tests of Significance in Survey Research," *American Sociological Review*, 22 (1957), pp. 519–527.

[12] Contrary to what this finding seems to imply, differences in supervisory practices were not associated with amount of worrying.

[13] See, e.g., George C. Homans, *The Human Group* (New York: Harcourt, Brace, 1950), pp. 140–144; and Harold H. Kelley and M. M. Shapiro, "An Experiment on Conformity to Group Norms," *American Sociological Review*, 19 (1954), pp. 667–677.

[14] But informal status was differently related to orientation to the supervisor. For a discussion of the implications of these and similar findings, see my paper, "Patterns of Deviation in Work Groups," *Sociometry*.

[15] The measure used is the respondent's confidence in his ability to work without supervision. Several indices of informal status, such as popularity, were directly related to self-confidence, but the index of integration used here was not.

[16] Leon Festinger *et al.*, *Social Pressures in Informal Groups* (New York: Harper & Row, 1950).

[17] Neal Gross and William E. Martin, "On Group Cohesiveness," *American Journal of Sociology*, 57 (1952), p. 554.

[18] *Loc. cit.*

[19] See also Lazarsfeld's discussion of this controversy, *op. cit.*, pp. 55–59.

[20] This distinction is related to Parsons' distinction between particularism and universalism.

[21] A pioneering study, of course, is F. J. Roethlisberger and William J. Dickson, *Management and the Worker* (Cambridge: Harvard University Press, 1951), pp. 1–186. For a more recent study, see Daniel Katz and Robert L. Kahn, "Some Recent Findings in Human Relations Research in Industry," in *Readings in Social Psychology*, Guy E. Swanson *et al.*, eds. (New York: Holt, 1952), pp. 650–665. Neither these investigations nor the findings reported here can exclude the alternative interpretation that low productivity impedes cohesion.

[22] An earlier study makes the parallel finding that a competitive work group was less productive than a cooperative one, but in the former group competitive individuals were more productive than others; see Peter M. Blau, *The Dynamics of Bureaucracy* (Chicago: University of Chicago Press, 1955), pp. 49–67.

[23] For another illustration of this pattern, see *ibid.*, pp. 82–96.

[24] W. S. Robinson, "Ecological Correlations and the Behavior of Individuals," *American Sociological Review*, 15 (1950), pp. 351–357.

[25] Herbert Menzel, "Comment on Robinson's 'Ecological Correlations and the Behavior of Individuals,'" *American Sociological Review*, 15 (1950), p. 674.

[26] Durkheim, *op. cit.*, pp. 259–276. The hypothesis is confirmed only for men; Durkheim advanced another though related interpretation to account for the suicide rates of women.

[27] Only if the distribution of the characteristic is not normal is there a need to control it for individuals when ascertaining the structural effects of its variance.

[28] Stouffer *et al.*, *op. cit.*, Vol. I, pp. 250–254.

[29] Zena S. Blau, "Structural Constraints on Friendships in Old Age."

[30] Paul F. Lazarsfeld and Wagner Thielens, Jr., *The Academic Mind* (Glencoe, Ill.: The Free Press, 1958), pp. 247–250.

22   ALBERT J. REISS, JR. AND ALBERT LEWIS RHODES

The Distribution of Juvenile Delinquency in the Social Class Structure

A number of theories of deviating behavior and juvenile delinquency posit social class variation in rates of delinquency, particularly gang delinquency, such that the lowest social stratum has the highest delinquency rate.[1] The validity of this postulate is questioned by some who maintain that middle and high status persons have a much higher rate of delinquency than is shown in a statistical test of the hypothesis.[2] These critics demonstrate that the data of law enforcement or judicial agencies give biased estimates of a true rate of delinquency in the population. They suggest that the delinquency life chances are equal for all socioeconomic status groups. The apparently higher rate of the low socioeconomic status group is due solely to the fact that agencies of social control are more likely to classify them as delinquents.[3] This paper is an attempt to shed some light on this disagreement by providing evidence on variation in white male delinquency rates among the social classes of the Nashville, Tennessee Standard Metropolitan Area.

THE STUDY

Nine thousand two hundred thirty-eight white boys, 12 years old and over, and registered in one of the public, private or parochial junior or senior high schools of Davidson County, Tennessee during the 1957 school year comprise the base population. Any boy who at some time since his twelfth birthday was referred to the Davidson County Juvenile Court and was adjudged a delinquent by either court referees or the presiding judge is classified as a delinquent in Tables 1–5 of this paper. The time span covered, therefore, during which any boy might have been adjudged a delinquent is the period 1950–58. Information is lacking to calculate an age-specific delinquency rate for all boys in the county, since the in-school population does not include all boys of a given age group and many acts

Reprinted and abridged from *American Sociological Review*, 26:5 (1961), pp. 720–732 by permission of the authors and the publisher.

of delinquency never are known to a juvenile court. Neither of these differences is sufficient to obviate the kind of analysis undertaken in this paper, as previous analysis of these data demonstrates.[4]

No attempt, therefore, is made to estimate the absolute rate of delinquency by social classes, since it is demonstrated that social classes are categoric risk groups for selection into a juvenile court population. Although it is shown that the low status boy is more likely to be apprehended by juvenile authorities, more likely to be held for juvenile court procedures, more likely to have his delinquent act made a matter of court record, and more likely to have an official rather than an unofficial court record, the evidence also supports the contention that there is a greater prevalence of delinquency in the lower class.[5] The focus in this paper is on the more precise description of patterned variation in delinquency rates by social class categories and structures.

Limiting the population of boys to those still in school does not bias our conclusions about differentials in delinquency rates among social categories, but it does not permit us to estimate precisely the magnitude of these differences. The rate of delinquency is higher for out-of-school than for in-school boys since out-of-school boys are on the average older, of lower IQ and social status than are in-school boys. Below it is shown that the rate of delinquency is higher for older boys, lower status boys, and dropouts. The rate for out-of-school boys and hence the rate for all adolescent boys must be higher than the observed rate for in-school boys alone. Confidence in the observed differences presented in this paper is therefore justified since the inclusion of the out-of-school groups would increase the magnitude of the observed differences.

A cross-section sample of boys age 12 to 16 was also selected, since almost all boys in the county from this age group are still in school. Self reports of delinquent acts were secured from each of these boys by means of a personal interview. A boy from this sample was classified as a delinquent person if, on the basis of these self-reports, his acts would have classified him as a delinquent person by juvenile court criteria of delinquency or, if he had been classified as a delinquent person by the court. This cross section sample provides the data for the final section of the paper.

Three status groups were defined in terms of the occupation of the head of the household.

Low Status   All laborers, including farm laborers, operatives and kindred workers, service workers (except protective service workers), and peddlers and door-to-door salesmen.

Middle Status   All craftsmen, foremen and kindred workers, clerical and kindred workers, protective service workers, managers and proprietors of small business, sales workers of wholesale and retail stores, and technicians allied to the professional services.

High Status All managers, officials, and proprietors, and professional, and semiprofessional workers not included in the middle status category, and sales workers in finance, insurance, and real estate.

The number of status positions was restricted to three in order to increase the sampling reliability of within-status group comparisons. In some tables, data are reported for only two status positions to increase the number of cases within subgroups created by the detailed breakdown of other variables cross-classified with status. The dichotomous class of *white collar status* includes all "high status" and "middle status" subjects *except* craftsmen, foremen, and kindred workers and protective service workers while *blue collar status* includes these exceptions plus all "low status" subjects.

Delinquency rates of residential areas were calculated for the in-school population of an area. These delinquency rates are based on the combined total of official and unofficial cases known to the juvenile court.

The social status structure of residential areas in the United States varies considerably. Some are quite homogeneous in class status while others tend to be more representative of the class structure of American society. Residential areas, therefore, vary considerably in opportunities for cross-class contacts, institutional access to legitimate and illegitimate means, and so on. These differences in the status structure of residential areas may mean, in turn, that the effects of a class status position are not uniform from one residential status structure to another. The pressures for conformity on a lower class boy, for example, may be greater in a middle than in a lower class residential area. The independent effects of ascribed social status position and of social status structures on delinquency rates were therefore investigated.

The operational definition of the social status structure of a residential area is the distribution derived from aggregating the data for the ascribed status position of pupils in schools. Seven types of social status context were defined in this way. More than one school is included within each of the contexts.

1. *Upper and Upper Middle Status Context:* Approximately 60 percent of all students have fathers classified as old or new professionals, managers, officials and proprietors, and 90 percent are from white collar origins; (6 schools).
2. *Balanced Upper and Lower Middle Status Context:* Approximately 90 percent are from white collar origins with roughly an equal balance between top and bottom white collar occupations; (6 schools).
3. *Crosscuts Social Status Structure: Overrepresentation at Top Context:* Crosscut criterion,[6] plus 15 percent more than expected in the top two occupation groups of the six major white-collar occupation groups; (7 schools).
4. *Crosscuts Social Status Structure: Overrepresentation at Center Context:* Crosscut criterion, plus 15 percent more than expected in the two "center" occupation groups of the six major white-collar occupation categories; (4 schools).

5. *Representative of All Schools Context:* Within two percent of the distribution for all schools; (4 schools).
6. *Crosscuts Social Status Structure: Overrepresentation at Bottom Context:* Crosscut criterion, plus 15 percent more than expected in the bottom two of the four major blue-collar occupation groups; (7 schools).
7. *Lower Social Status Context:* Approximately 75 percent are in blue-collar occupations with 50 percent in the lowest of the four major blue-collar occupation groups; (5 schools).

VARIATION IN DELINQUENCY RATES BY AGE, IQ, AND ASCRIBED SOCIAL STATUS

There is considerable variation in the rate of court recorded delinquency by age. For the in-school population of white boys, only 2.3 percent of all boys age 10 to 13 were known to the court as delinquent while eight percent of all boys age 16 and over were known as delinquents. The relationship with age is somewhat more striking when ascribed social status is also considered. The age relationship persists within each ascribed status category but it varies from a low of 0.6 percent for all high status boys, age 10 to 13, to a high of 10.1 percent of all low status boys, age 16 and over. Inasmuch as the school dropout rate is highest for the low status boys age 16 and over and lowest among the high status boys age 10 to 13, the

TABLE 1. RATE OF DELINQUENCY PER 100 WHITE SCHOOL BOYS BY IQ AND OCCUPATIONAL STATUS OF FATHER

Occupational status of father and type of delinquent offense	IQ							
	Low		Middle		High		Total*	
	Number	Rate per 100	Number	Rate per 100	Number	Rate per 100	Number	Rate per 100
White collar	280	(8.2)	1,263	(6.8)	1,115	(4.6)	3,302	(6.2)
J.C.† serious ...	10	3.6	15	1.2	5	0.4	42	1.3
J.C. petty	8	2.8	25	2.0	15	1.4	67	2.0
Subtotal	(18)	(6.4)	(40)	(3.2)	(20)	(1.8)	(109)	(3.3)
J.C. truant	1	0.4	1	0.1	..	0.0	4	0.1
J.C. traffic	4	1.4	44	3.5	31	2.8	93	2.8
No J.C. record ..	257	0.0	1,178	0.0	1,064	0.0	3,096	0.0
Blue collar	926	(10.9)	2,091	(9.4)	672	(5.2)	4,661	(8.8)
J.C. serious	42	4.5	47	2.2	111	1.7	124	2.7
J.C. petty	48	5.2	85	4.1	115	2.2	174	3.7
Subtotal	(90)	(9.7)	(132)	(6.3)	(26)	(3.9)	(298)	(6.4)
J.C. truant	10	1.2	11	0.6	2	0.3	33	0.7
J.C. traffic	..	..	53	2.5	7	1.0	81	1.7
No J.C. record ..	826	0.0	1,895	0.0	637	0.0	4,249	0.0

* Includes all cases for which IQ information was not obtained.
† J.C. = Juvenile Court.

inclusion of boys who left school would increase subgroup differences in the delinquency rates of low and high status boys.

Table 1 provides information on the rate of delinquency for types of offenders[7] in ascribed social status and IQ subgroups. The probability of being classified a serious, petty or truancy offender is greater for the blue-collar than white-collar boys. The relationship holds within each IQ subgroup. But, the probability of being classified a traffic-only violator is greater for white-collar than blue-collar boys and this relationship is also independent of IQ. White-collar boys are more likely to use an automobile regularly than are blue-collar boys and they therefore have a greater opportunity to commit traffic-only offenses. This is not, however, the main reason for their higher incidence of traffic-only offenses. The principal reason for the difference lies in the fact that among blue-collar boys, traffic offenses are more likely to be included among other, more serious offenses. The white-collar boy, therefore, lacking the serious offenses, is more likely to be charged with traffic-only offenses.

There is also a substantial relationship between IQ and rate of delinquency which is independent of ascribed social status. High IQ adolescents have the lowest rate of delinquency within each of the major ascribed status subgroups in Table 1. This variation in the rate of delinquency for IQ and ascribed social status subgroups in Table 1 holds for the serious, petty and truancy offender subgroups but not for traffic-only cases. The low IQ boys subgroup has the lowest rate of traffic-only cases; the middle IQ subgroup has the highest rate.

VARIATION IN DELINQUENCY RATES BY SOCIAL STATUS STRUCTURES AND RESIDENTIAL RATES OF DELINQUENCY

Sociological theories which maintain that delinquency is primarily a lower class phenomenon differ in their explanatory use of the social class concept. The cultural transmission-differential association theorists view delinquency as behavior which is learned from other delinquents in residential areas where there is an established delinquent culture and organization. Although they usually describe the residential areas supporting a delinquent culture as "lower class," "slum" or "disorganized" areas, it can be inferred from their theory that delinquency rates should be high for *all* social class groups resident in high delinquency areas of a city.[8] Albert K. Cohen defines the social class variable as generating a delinquent gang subculture. His "status frustration" hypothesis holds that subcultural delinquency is a reaction-formation against a middle-class organized status dilemma in which the lower-class boy suffers status frustrations in competition with middle status boys. The delinquent subculture provides a solution to these problems when boys who are similarly frustrated interact together, by conferring status on the frustrated boys.[9] Following Cohen's reasoning, one would deduce that: (1) lower status boys, regardless of their residential location, should generate subcultural delinquency (and perhaps the highest rate of all delinquency as well) if they interact and,

(2) that the rate of subcultural delinquency among low status boys who interact should be higher in areas and schools where they are in direct competition with middle status ones (the competition is presumably more intense) and the lowest in the monolithic low-status area. A test of these hypotheses and the deductions from them is made below.

The effects of social class status stem from two principle sources so far as the adolescent in our society is concerned. One source is the status of his family in the larger society, e.g., whether he is middle or lower class, regardless of where he resides. This is sometimes referred to as his mass society status position. The other major effect of status is the status structure of the school and residential community. It may be one thing to be a low status boy in a primarily low status school or community and quite another to be one in a school which crosscuts the class structure or in one of a primarily high status composition. The first status component is referred to as his *ascribed social status* since his status position is that of the family status in the social structure. The second component is referred to as the *social status structure* of the school (and usually therefore of the residential community in American cities). The purpose of our investigation is to learn whether both of these components independently affect the rate of delinquency consistent with deductions from the Cohen and differential association theories and, in turn, whether the effect of the rate of delinquency of an area is independent of both status components in delinquency.

Variation in delinquency rates for the ascribed social status position of boys and the social status structure of schools is described in Table 2. Delinquency rates, in general, vary inversely with the prestige component of the social status structure of the school (except for the Crosscut: Center schools) and by the ascribed social status of the boy. The range of variation of ascribed social status is less (3.9 percent) than that for variation in status structures of schools (12.4 percent), suggesting that the status structure of the school exercises a greater effect on delinquent behavior than does ascribed social status.[10]

The effect of the occupational status structure of the school on ascribed status position is to alter, for an adolescent in any ascribed status group, the life-chances of becoming a delinquent. The occupational structure of the school "virtually eliminates" the *risk* of being a delinquent of court record for low status boys in schools with a predominantly high status student body and substantially increases the *risk* of a low status boy in a predominantly low status school. The average rate of court recorded delinquency is 9.6 for all low status boys, but in the two top status structures it is zero, while in the lowest one it is over 16 percent. The effect of the status structure is somewhat less for middle status boys and least marked for high status boys. If all traffic offenses are eliminated, however, the results are as striking for the middle and low status boys and somewhat more clearcut for high status ones. The effect of the social structure of a residential community on the rate of delinquency is virtually to double

TABLE 2. RATE OF DELINQUENCY PER 100 WHITE SCHOOL BOYS CALCULATED SEPARATELY FOR ALL OFFENSES * AND ALL OFFENSES WITH TRAFFIC OFFENSES EXCLUDED, BY OCCUPATIONAL STATUS OF FATHER AND STATUS STRUCTURE OF THE SCHOOL

| | Occupational status of father | | | | | | | | | | | |
| | High | | | Middle | | | Low | | | Total † | | |
Status structure of the school	Sub-total	All of-fenses	Excl. traffic	Sub-total	All of-fenses	Excl. traffic	Sub-total	All of-fenses	Excl. traffic	Num-ber	All of-fenses	Excl. traffic
Upper & upper middle	292	3.8	0.7	109	2.8	0.0	6	0.0	0.0	434	3.2	0.5
Balanced middle	389	6.2	2.6	310	5.8	2.0	35	0.0	0.0	749	5.6	2.2
Crosscut: top	567	6.5	3.9	1,039	5.9	3.7	372	5.9	4.4	2,119	6.1	3.8
Crosscut: center	117	9.4	6.3	446	10.1	6.0	217	9.6	5.8	797	9.7	5.8
Representative of all	160	2.5	1.9	446	6.3	5.3	294	8.5	6.9	965	6.2	5.2
Crosscut: bottom	237	5.5	3.4	1,026	9.4	7.5	914	9.2	8.4	2,267	8.7	7.3
Lower	52	7.7	6.0	423	15.4	13.5	353	16.4	14.5	847	15.6	13.8
Total	1,814	5.7	3.0	3,799	8.3	5.7	2,191	9.6	7.6	9,238	7.8	5.6

* Includes all official and unofficial court cases of delinquency other than minor traffic offenses (violation of registration and driver's license laws).

† The number of cases for which information on father's occupation is not reported can be obtained by subtraction from the total column of each school prestige status context.

the rate for any status group in the lowest status context and to bring it to its lowest point (approaching zero) in the highest status context.

Despite the effect which the social structure of the school has on the delinquency *rate* of boys, it nevertheless is true that the majority of delinquents at the high and low status levels come from those schools where the class stratification "favors" their status level. Examining Table 3, we

TABLE 3. PERCENTAGE OF JUVENILE COURT DELINQUENTS AND OF NONDELINQUENTS AT EACH ASCRIBED STATUS LEVEL FROM EACH TYPE OF STATUS STRUCTURE

Status structure of the school	Occupational status of father							
	High		Middle		Low		Total	
	J.C.*	Not J.C.	J.C.	Not J.C.	J.C.	Not J.C.	J.C.	Not J.C.
Upper & upper middle ..	10.6	16.4	0.9	3.0	0.0	0.3	2.1	5.6
Balanced middle	23.1	21.3	5.7	8.4	0.0	1.8	6.4	9.4
Crosscut: top	35.6	31.1	19.3	28.1	10.5	17.7	20.0	26.4
Crosscut: center	10.6	6.2	14.2	11.5	10.0	9.9	11.8	9.6
Crosscut: representative of all	3.8	9.1	8.9	12.0	11.9	13.6	9.2	12.0
Crosscut: bottom	12.5	13.1	30.4	26.7	40.0	41.8	30.3	27.5
Lower	3.8	2.8	20.6	10.3	27.6	14.9	20.2	9.5
Total percent	100.0	100.0	100.0	100.0	100.0	100.0	100.0	100.0
Number	114	1,807	366	3,893	253	2,393	759	8,479

* J.C. = Juvenile Court.

can see that 70 percent of all high status delinquents are residents of the top three contexts while 68 percent of all lower status delinquents are drawn from the lower two status contexts. The pattern of residential segregation in American cities, of course, exerts this effect on the proportionate distribution of delinquents by social structure.

At each status level delinquents are *over*represented in some stratification context relative to their representation in that context. Thus, twice as many of the delinquents, as of all boys, are drawn from the low ascribed social status position in the lower status structure context. Correlatively, lower class delinquents are *under*represented in the top stratification contexts. There are, in fact, proportionally fewer delinquents of all status levels in the upper status contexts than would be expected from their status context distribution. The delinquency life-chances of a boy in any ascribed status position also varies with the delinquency rate of the residential area, as examination of Table 4 shows. In both the low and high rate delinquency areas, the probability that a boy will be delinquent varies inversely with his status position. This means that in low and in high delinquency areas, the low status boy has the greatest chance of becoming delinquent, although,

TABLE 4. RATE OF DELINQUENCY * PER 100 WHITE SCHOOL BOYS BY OCCUPATIONAL STATUS OF FATHER AND DELINQUENCY RATE OF RESIDUAL AREAS

Delinquency rate of residential area	Occupational status of father									Total †		
	High			Middle			Low					
	Delin-quents	Sub-total	Rate per 100	Delin-quents	Sub-total	Rate per 100	Delin-quents	Sub-total	Rate per 100	Delin-quents	Number	Rate per 100
0.0– 1.9	0	298	0.0	3	354	.8	2	213	.9	6	898	.7
2.0– 3.9	3	184	1.6	14	461	3.0	11	313	3.5	28	999	2.8
4.0– 5.9	10	382	2.6	43	1,075	4.0	47	776	6.1	106	2,358	4.5
6.0– 7.9	12	182	6.6	10	103	9.7	5	80	6.3	28	399	7.0
8.0– 9.9	37	481	7.7	54	726	7.4	30	290	10.3	124	1,564	7.9
10.0–11.9	14	114	12.3	44	424	10.4	30	271	11.1	94	874	10.8
12.0–13.9	15	130	11.5	42	322	13.0	10	103	9.7	69	566	12.2
14.0–15.9	2	34	5.9	25	184	13.6	20	138	14.5	49	374	13.1
16.0–17.9	11	80	13.8	49	308	15.9	40	237	16.9	101	635	15.9
18.0 & over	3	37	8.1	52	299	17.4	43	222	19.4	101	566	17.8
Total	107	1,922	5.6	336	4,258	7.9	238	2,644	9.0	707	9,238	7.7

* Includes all official and unofficial court cases of delinquency other than minor traffic offenses (violation of registration and driver's license laws).

† The number of cases for which information on father's occupation is not reported can be obtained by subtraction from the total column of each school prestige status context.

to be sure, his chances are only one in a hundred in the low delinquency area, while they are one in five in the high delinquency areas. The relationship is less clear for the areas with "average" rates of delinquency where the probability of being a delinquent is almost as great for high as low status boys.

The joint effects of the delinquency rate of an area and its social status structure on the delinquency rate of ascribed status positions must be

TABLE 5. RATE OF DELINQUENCY PER 100 WHITE SCHOOL BOYS BY DELINQUENCY RATE OF RESIDENTIAL AREA, PRESTIGE STATUS CONTEXT OF SCHOOL AND OCCUPATIONAL STATUS OF FATHER *

School prestige status context & occupational status of father	Delinquency rate of residential area										Total
	0.0 to 1.9	2.0 to 3.9	4.0 to 5.9	6.0 to 7.9	8.0 to 9.9	10.0 to 11.9	12.0 to 13.9	14.0 to 15.9	16.0 to 17.9	18.0 and over	
Upper & upper middle											
High	0.0	..	..	6.8	..	..	..	..	..	..	3.8
Middle	0.0	..	..	8.1	..	..	..	..	..	..	2.8
Low	0.0	..	..	0.0	..	..	..	..	..	..	0.0
Balanced middle											
High	0.0	..	..	8.2	..	..	..	..	..	..	6.2
Middle	0.0	..	..	8.8	..	..	..	..	..	..	5.8
Low	0.0	..	..	0.0	..	..	..	..	..	..	0.0
Crosscut: top											
High	0.0	1.6	3.0	..	10.0	13.4	10.6	..	..	..	6.5
Middle	0.0	2.3	3.7	..	5.8	9.1	13.0	..	..	..	5.9
Low	0.0	2.2	4.9	..	8.3	11.9	9.4	..	..	..	5.9
Crosscut: center											
High	0.0	..	2.0	..	..	..	13.9	..	20.0	..	9.4
Middle	0.0	..	4.8	..	..	..	13.1	..	13.7	..	10.1
Low	0.0	..	3.6	..	..	..	9.9	..	19.6	..	9.7
Crosscut: representative of all											
High	0.0	..	2.5	..	3.6	..	..	5.0	..	..	2.5
Middle	2.7	..	3.6	..	7.8	..	..	16.7	..	..	6.3
Low	0.0	..	8.8	..	15.2	..	..	15.2	..	..	8.5
Crosscut: bottom											
High	0.0	2.9	0.0	..	4.2	9.4	..	..	10.9	..	5.5
Middle	1.6	4.7	6.3	..	7.2	11.3	..	..	17.3	..	9.4
Low	2.5	3.2	3.5	..	10.9	10.8	..	..	16.0	..	9.2
Lower											
High	0.0	..	..	..	..	..	..	7.1	..	8.1	7.7
Middle	0.0	..	..	..	..	..	..	11.6	..	17.4	15.4
Low	0.0	..	..	..	..	..	..	14.3	..	19.4	16.4

* Based on 9,238 cases of white boys.

investigated to clarify the effect of these variables on the delinquency life-chances of a boy. Table 5 provides such a distribution. Within each ascribed status group, the delinquency rate usually rises with the delinquency rate of the area regardless of the social status composition of the area. Using a sign test, the probability is less than .01 that the observed differences in rates for ascribed status groups in Table 5 would occur by chance. In every status stratification context, the chances that a high, middle or low status boy will be a delinquent are greater if he resides in a high than in a low delinquency rate area. Both the occupational stratification of the area and the delinquency rate of residential areas, then, are independent sources of variation in the rate of delinquency for ascribed social status groups.

IMPLICATIONS FOR DELINQUENCY THEORY

At this point we have several empirical findings that may be related to the major theories of delinquency causation. First, it is clear that there is no simple relationship between ascribed social status and delinquency. Both the status structure of an area and the extent to which delinquency occurs as a cultural tradition affect the delinquency life-chances of a boy at each ascribed status level. While the life-chances of low ascribed status boys becoming delinquent are greater than those of high status ones, a low status boy in a predominantly high status area with a low rate of de-linquency has almost no chance of being classified a juvenile court delin-quent. In this latter situation, the delinquency life-chances of a high status boy are greater than for low status boys.[11]

Likewise, there does not seem to be much evidence that the lower class boy is more likely to be delinquent the more he is subjected to pressure from middle-class norms. The more the lower class boy is in a minority in the school and residential community,[12] the less likely is he to become delinquent.[13] What seems more apparent is that the largest proportion of delinquents for any status group comes from the more homogenous status areas for that group and that the delinquency life-chances of all status groups tend to be greatest in the lower status area and in the high delin-quency rate areas.

Examination of the data in Tables 4 and 5 lends some support to Miller's thesis that delinquency (violative behavior) is normative in lower class culture while conformity (nonviolative behavior) is normative in middle class culture. Yet a number of facts in these tables do not support Miller's position as he has formulated it.[14] The more important of these are: (1) delinquency does not appear to be normative in all lower class areas if the rate is taken as an indicator of a norm; (2) substantial numbers of delinquents come from residential areas where the majority of residents are from other than the lower class; (3) high status boys in the three top status contexts have somewhat higher delinquency rates than middle or low status boys. It is possible for Miller to rationalize these exceptions with his more general formulation. He holds that lower class culture is seldom found in its pure form in most residential areas. Consequently, the rate in a residential area is not a simple function of class culture, but of both the relative prevalence of the classes in an area and the extent to which the class culture of each is diffused to the other.

The third major conclusion which seems warranted at this point is that the factors related to where a family of a given ascribed status will live are important in predicting the delinquency life-chances of a boy of any ascribed status. The evidence seems to be consistent with what we already know but have not generally incorporated in our theory—that lower class status is not a necessary and sufficient set of conditions in the etiology of any type of delinquency. Rather, we know there are some lower class areas of large American cities that consistently produce a high volume of all delinquency and most of the systematically organized career delinquency, while other lower class areas, particularly rural ones, do not. The theoretical problem is: *why should delinquency be so widespread in some lower class areas, and not in others?* Cloward and Ohlin suggest that variation in the availability of both legitimate and illegitimate opportunity structures is crucial in determining the delinquency orientation of lower class boys in status dilemmas.[15] There probably are other community conditions as well which account for these differences.

ACKNOWLEDGMENT

This research was performed pursuant to a contract with the United States Office of Education, Department of Health, Education, and Welfare.

NOTES

[1] William Kvaraceus, "Juvenile Delinquency and Social Class," *Journal of Educational Sociology*, 18 (1944), pp. 51–54; Robert K. Merton, *Social Theory and Social Structure* (Glencoe, Ill.: The Free Press, 1957), pp. 144–145; Albert K. Cohen, *Delinquent Boys* (Glencoe, Ill.: The Free Press, 1955), pp. 36–44; Walter Miller, "Lower Class Culture as a Generating Milieu of Gang Delinquency," *Journal of Social Issues*, 14:3 (1958), pp. 5–19.

[2] Austin Porterfield, *Youth in Trouble* (Fort Worth: Leo Potishman Foundation, 1946); James S. Wallenstein and C. J. Wyle, "Our Law Abiding Law Breakers," *National Probation* (March-April, 1947), pp. 107–112; F. Ivan Nye, James F. Short, and V. J. Olson, "Socioeconomic Status and Delinquent Behavior," in *Family Relationships and Delinquent Behavior* (New York: Wiley, 1958), pp. 23–33.

[3] Walter Reckless maintains, for example, that delinquency rates designate *categoric risks* in the population of being reported to a juvenile court. See Walter C. Reckless, *The Crime Problem* (New York: Appleton-Century-Crofts, 1950), p. 194.

[4] Albert J. Reiss, Jr. and Albert Lewis Rhodes, "A Sociopsychological Study of Conforming and Deviating Behavior Among Adolescents," U.S. Office of Education Cooperative Research Project 507, 1959, Chap. VIII.

[5] *Ibid.*, Chap. VIII.

[6] The "Crosscut" social status structure criterion is defined as follows: The occupational distribution of each occupation group is within five percent of the distribution for all schools. There are 10 major occupation groups: old and new professions; proprietors; managers and officials; quasi-professions; clerical and kindred workers; sales workers; craftsmen, foremen and kindred workers; protective service workers;

operatives and kindred workers; laborers and service workers, except protective service.

[7] The major types of offenders are defined and rank ordered as to their "seriousness" as follows:

Serious offenses include assault with a weapon, armed robbery, grand larceny, including larceny of an auto, and burglary; *Petty offenses* including petit larceny, receiving and concealing stolen property, assault, malicious destruction of property, malicious mischief, and loitering, drinking, trespassing, curfew, and breach of peace violations, including disorderly conduct; All runaway and truancy cases for which a petition for a court hearing was entered are called the *truancy offenses*. Drag racing, speeding, reckless driving, and violation of registration and driver's license laws are called *traffic offenses*. Many delinquents of course are brought to court and charged with an offense in more than one of the four offense types. An adolescent who was charged with an offense in more than one of the four types was classified within only one of these four types. The offender was placed in that offense type rated as the "more serious" type of offense, thus the category of truant offenders, for example, does not include all truancy petition cases.

[8] This seems to be a valid inference from the Shaw-McKay and Sutherland positions, although it is never quite explicitly formulated in this way.

[9] Albert K. Cohen, *Delinquent Boys, op. cit.*, Chap. V.

[10] It should be kept in mind, however, that the defined range of variation is restricted to only three classes for ascribed social status but seven classes of social status structures; some ascribed social status variation probably is lost with fewer classes.

[11] To some it will seem obvious that low-status boys in high-status areas are not "representative" of low-status boys. The theories do not specify what "lower class criteria" are to be utilized in identifying low-status boys who are "delinquency prone." If class selectivity operates by residential areas, then perhaps no area has a "representative" lower class.

[12] Sociometric data are available for only a cross-section of boys. These data show however, that lower class boys in middle class areas interact together in that they are most likely to choose, and to have reciprocated the choices of, lower class boys.

[13] Some readers may have discerned that the delinquency rate of Crosscut: center schools is higher than might be expected, given its status composition. The higher rate here is altogether accounted for by two schools. One of these schools is the vocational high school which tends to selectively recruit boys who are "in trouble" in some other school. The other school serves a very large territorial area made up of relatively homogeneous class areas so that the social structure of each junior high school which "feeds" this high school falls either "above" or "below" the structure of the senior high context.

[14] Walter F. Miller, *op. cit.*

[15] Richard A. Cloward and Lloyd E. Ohlin, *Delinquency and Opportunity: A Theory of Delinquent Gangs* (Glencoe, Ill.: The Free Press, 1960).

```
┌─────────────────────────────────────────────┐
│  CHAPTER FOUR                                 │
│  Maintenance of the Social Order              │
└─────────────────────────────────────────────┘
```

Maintenance of the Social Order	SOCIALIZATION

COMMENTARY

Socialization is the process by which the individual is instructed in the ways of society. By means of socialization, values and norms, perspectives and life styles, are learned by the newcomer to a group be he infant, immigrant, army recruit, or religious convert. Although the most dramatic instance of socialization concerns the child, the individual undergoes new socialization experiences each time he moves into a community, changes jobs, joins a club, or is conscripted into an organization. The agents of socialization vary during the life span of the individual as well as with the situations about which he is learning.

The paper by Eleanor Maccoby discusses some important aspects of the behavior of parents in child training. She reviews research and theory dealing with types of discipline and the nature of the parent-child relationship.

Joshua Fishman's paper "Childhood Indoctrination for Minority-Group Membership" deals with the school as an agent of socialization. His concern is with the role of the parochial school in socializing the student to the values of his particular subculture.

Finally, the research reported by Harold Wilensky and Hugh Edwards focuses on the question of whether socialization before or after entrance into a new occupational stratum is critical in determining the class ideology of the downwardly mobile worker.

23 Eleanor E. Maccoby

The Choice of Variables in the Study of Socialization

Perhaps the greatest change that has occurred in the field of child develop-ment in the past 15 years has been the increasing emphasis on socialization. The change may be traced by comparing the more traditional textbooks with recent ones. The scholarly child psychology text by Munn, for exam-ple, does not bring up the topic of parent-child interaction until the 16th chapter, and here devotes only eight pages to a topic called "environmental influences and personality," a heading under which he presents all that the book has to say on "mothering," on Freudian theory of development stages, on ordinal position—in fact, on socialization in general.[1] Contrast this with a book such as Watson's, in which more than half the book is devoted to a discussion of socialization theory and a detailed consideration of the im-pressive amounts of research that have recently been done on the subject.[2]

The same increasing emphasis on socialization may be seen in the child-development journals. And, of course, the widespread research interest in this topic has led to the development of several research instruments for the measurement of parental attitudes and behavior. There are the Fels scales, developed during the 40's, for the rating of parent behavior;[3] the parent interview schedule developed by Sears and his associates at Harvard and Stanford,[4] the parent attitude scales developed by Shoben at U.S.C.,[5] and the widely used Parent Attitude Research Instrument scales developed at the National Institutes of Health by Schaeffer and Bell,[6] to mention only a few. Each investigator, when he sat down to make a first draft of his rating scale or interview schedule or attitude scale items, had to ask himself the question: What shall I measure? What are the important variables in parental behavior that ought to make a difference in the development of the child? The process of selecting and defining variables is, of course, the very heart of theory-making. There are as many possible variables as there are ideas about what causes what in human development. I cannot attempt here to give any sort of roster of variables; the task would be too great and might not prove very useful. I simply want to point out some of the major classes of variables that have been used and give a little of the history of the reasons why we have chosen to measure these things and not others and perhaps point to a few ways in which we could clarify the meaning of the dimension we are using.

Let us start with the traditional child psychologist, with his interests in motor development, emotional development, intelligence, concept forma-

Reprinted from *Sociometry*, 24:4 (1961), pp. 357–371, by permission of the author and the publisher.

tion, and personality development, all grounded in traditional principles of learning and maturation. He may look upon the current work in socialization with a jaundiced eye and inquire what the excitement is all about. He may feel that he has actually been studying socialization for years without calling it by this name. He might put his question this way: If it is true that socialization is the process of transmitting culture from one generation to another, and that the child acquires the modes of behavior prescribed by his culture through the process of learning, then how is the study of socialization any different from the study of learning itself? One might reply that in socialization studies, we study not only the child as learner but the parent as teacher. But a skeptic might still wonder how much difference this actually makes. For example, laboratory studies of learning have demonstrated that behavior which is followed by reward will be strengthened, and its probability of recurrence will be increased. Now, if a student of socialization does a study of dependency, and discovers that parents who reward their children for dependency have more dependent children, has he really found out anything that we didn't know already?

In my opinion, it *is* valuable to carry out at the human level studies which attempt to employ the standard variables that have grown out of laboratory study on learning, where most of the work has been done on sub-human species. But, in the process of applying such variables to socialization studies, the variables almost perforce undergo certain modifications and elaborations, with the result that translating traditional behavior theory variables into the socialization setting sometimes results in the addition of something new, and the possibility of getting new kinds of principles.

Let me give an example. Suppose we wanted to study the effects of a particular schedule of reward. What do we mean by reward? The traditional approach to reward has been to produce a physiological drive, such as hunger or thirst, through deprivation; and then to reinforce the desired behavior by presenting a drive-relevant reinforcing stimulus. But even in fairly young children, a rapid development of complex motivation occurs, and this changes the nature of the reinforcements to which children will be responsive. B. F. Skinner encountered this fact when he was developing his teaching machines. The early models were devised so as to emit little pieces of chocolate candy whenever a child made the correct response. But it was soon evident that a child progressed through a series of arithmetic or spelling problems just as readily without the candy; in fact, the giving of candy sometimes disrupted the learning process. Skinner, therefore, abandoned the candy rewards, and the current models of his machine rely upon no other reward than the child's interest in doing his work correctly— buttressed, no doubt, by a certain amount of pressure from the teacher and parents. This incident illustrates a major question about the definition of variables: what happens to the variable "amount of reward" when it is translated into situations of teacher-child, or parent-child, interaction? In modern societies, children's physiological drives are regularly and quite fully satisfied and are seldom used as a basis for training. That is, most parents do not let the child get hungry, thirsty, wet, or overtired, and then make the satisfaction of these needs conditional on good behavior. Rather, the rewards used are money, a trip to the zoo, being allowed to stay up for a special TV program, etc. A gift of candy for some children becomes symbolic of affection instead of vice versa. Very commonly, behavior is reinforced simply through the giving of approval, affection, or attention. So the concept "reward," when it refers to the rewards which parents use in socializing their children is not directly comparable to the concept as it was originally developed in studies of animal learning. Of course, it is not really a new idea to point out that different kinds of organisms are capable of being rewarded by different kinds of things. It is clear enough that there are as many kinds of rewards as there are distinguishable motives, and that both motives and rewards vary between species and within species. But the new idea that has been added in socialization studies is that there may be distinguishable *classes* of rewards which may have different effects. The primary distinction made in studies so far has been between material reward and praise. Material reward covers all instances of giving the child some object or privilege that he wants, conditional upon good behavior. Praise depends to some degree upon the previous establishment of a relationship between the socializing agent and the child, such that the approval of this particular adult is something the child wants. That is, the effectiveness of praise ought to depend upon the identity of the person doing the praising and upon this person's being someone the child loves, fears, or must depend upon for the satisfaction of needs.

The same kind of differentiation of a variable has occurred with respect to punishment. Students of the socialization process have been working under the assumption that not all kinds of aversive events following a child's act will have the same effect. The distinction most commonly made is that between physical punishment and so-called love-oriented discipline, or withdrawal of love. There are other categories of punishment, too, such as withdrawal of privileges and ridicule, which are less interesting than the first two because there are fewer hypotheses about their probable effects. Let us concentrate for a moment on the distinction between physical punishment and withdrawal of love. Physical punishment is easy enough to define, although in rating its frequency and severity, the researcher is always troubled about the problem of how to weigh slaps and shakings in relation to formal spankings. More tricky by far is the matter of defining withdrawal of love. Sears and his associates[7] have defined it as any act or statement on the part of the parent that threatens the affectional bond between the parent and child. This would include the mother's turning her back on the child, refusing to speak to him or smile at him or be in the same room with him, saying she doesn't like him when he does disapproved things, etc. The system of classification of techniques of discipline presented by Beverly Allinsmith in her chapter in Miller and Swanson's book, *Inner Conflict and Defense*,[8] similarly emphasizes the distinction between "psychological" and "corporal" punishment, but defines psychological discipline somewhat differently. This classification for Allinsmith includes manipulating the child by shaming the child, appealing to his pride or guilt, and expressing disappointment over his misdeeds. But there is another dimension considered in the rating: namely, the amount of emotional control the mother displays in administering her discipline. Thus, if a mother shouts angrily at the child, "I hate you for doing that," Allinsmith would *not* classify this as psychological discipline, while Sears *et al.* would. But the mother who says calmly and perhaps coldly, "Now, dear, you know I don't like little boys who do that," would be classified as using psychological discipline in both systems. The difference in these two classification systems stems in part from two different views of the nature of the process which gives psychological discipline its effect. Sears *et al.* view it as a technique which arouses the child's anxiety over whether he is loved and approved of, and thereby elicits efforts on the child's part to regain his parents' approval by conforming, apologizing, or making amends. Allinsmith, on the other hand, emphasizes two things: (1) the *modeling* function of discipline, pointing out that a mother who loses her temper at the same time she is trying to teach the child to control his, will have a child who will do as the mother *does* rather than as she *says*; and (2) the target the child chooses for the aggressive impulses aroused in him as a consequence of punishment. The reasoning here is that the openly angry mother becomes a more legitimate target for the child's counter-aggression. The distinction between the two definitions of the dimension is further brought out when we consider the kinds of findings reported in the studies using them: Sears *et al.* found that withdrawal of love was associated with high development of conscience, physical punishment with low; Allinsmith found that psychological discipline, as she defined it, was associated with *indirect* fantasy expressions of aggression in the children they studied, corporal punishment with *direct* expression of aggression. All this illustrates the fact that fairly subtle differences in the definition of a dimension can affect the nature of child behavior that can be predicted from it. But more importantly, both these studies illustrate the fact that when we attempted to take over the variable "punishment" from the learning laboratories, we found it necessary to subdivide and differentiate the variable and gained predictive power by doing so.

I have been attempting to cite ways in which I think that socialization studies have improved upon some of the standard variables employed in laboratory studies. There are instances, alas, in which we have not taken note of the differences which exist between the laboratory and the standard socialization settings, and thus have failed to identify and make use of some potentially promising variables. For example, in laboratory studies, we can take it for granted that the experimenter is there during training sessions, administering either reinforcements or aversive stimuli in some orderly relationship to the subject's responses. In the parent-child relationship, the parent is by no means always functioning as a trainer, and parents differ greatly in the degree to which they do so. Some parents keep track quite continuously of what the child is doing, and engage in a constant flow of interaction, both verbal and non-verbal, with the child. Other parents, for a substantial portion of the time they are with their children, are bored, busy, withdrawn, intoxicated, watching television, or subject to some other state or activity which precludes their responding to the child unless he becomes very insistent. In such a household the children are, of course, in a very different learning situation than children growing up with more wholly attentive parents. I think the sheer amount of interaction may in some cases be a more important variable for predicting characteristics of the child than the nature of the interaction that does occur. Let me give an example. In a study Dr. Lucy Rau and I are now doing at Stanford, we have selected groups of children who show discrepancies in their intellectual abilities. That is, we have one group of children who are good at verbal tasks but poor at number, another group who are good at spatial tasks but poor at verbal, etc. One of our students, Mrs. Bing, has interviewed the mothers of the children, and has also conducted some observation sessions in which the mother presents achievement tasks to the child while the observer records the kind and amount of the mother's involvement with the child's work. Mrs. Bing has found that it is the *amount*, rather than the *kind*, of mother-child interaction that best predicts what the child's pattern of intellectual skills will be. That is, the mothers of the highly verbal children use more praise, but also more criticism, than do the mothers of equally bright children whose area of special skill is non-verbal. Their total level of interaction with the child is greater, and this interaction includes the administration of what we would regard as aversive stimuli as well as reinforcements. The variable "amount of interaction" emerged in our factor analysis of the scales in the *Patterns of Child Rearing* study—we titled this variable "responsible child-rearing orientation" for lack of a better name, but we never made much use of the variable because it did not fit in with the thoretical formulation of our study.[7] But I suspect that for any future work in which we are trying to predict such things as the child's cognitive maturity level or his achievement motivation, we may find that this variable is a better predictor than the less global variables (such as amount of praise) that we have been relying on up till now.

So far, I have been discussing the process of translating variables from laboratory studies of learning to the socialization setting, and have pointed out that we have been successful in employing such variables as reward and punishment, but that in the process of using these variables, we have found useful ways of subdividing them. Let us consider the theoretical meaning of the elaborations of these variables that have occurred.

When we make the distinction between material reward and praise, and the distinction between love-oriented punishment and punishment that depends for its effect upon producing direct physical pain, we are really taking note of the fact that the effect of discipline, and in fact the very nature of the discipline that is possible to use with a child, depends upon the history of the relationship that has been developed between the child and the person who is training him. And here is a new class of variables that socialization studies have added to the list of variables derived from classical studies of learning. In laboratory studies of learning, it has not been found necessary (at least until very recently) to ask whether the experimental subject loved or hated the machine that was emitting pellets of food and drops of water, or whether the characteristics of the machine or person presenting the rewards made any difference in the effectiveness of the reinforcement. Socialization studies, on the other hand, have found the identity of the socializing agent, and certain of his personality characteristics, to be important.

The emphasis on the importance of the relationship between trainer and learner came, of course, out of psychodynamic theories of personality development. Learning theory and psychoanalytic theory differ, I think, with respect to what they believe the basic nature of the socialization process is. This is an oversimplification, but I believe it would be reasonably accurate to say that a learning theorist would regard socialization as a learning process in which certain actions of the child's are selected out by virtue of reinforcement, others tried and dropped because they are in some way punished or non-reinforced. The parents have a primary role in administering the rewards and punishments for the child's actions, although they do not necessarily do this deliberately and consciously as a teaching effort. And, of course, there are other sources of reward and punishment than the parents' reactions which will help to determine what behavior the child retains.

The psychoanalytic approach, on the other hand, would emphasize not the detailed learning of specific actions on the basis of their outcome, but the providing of conditions which will motivate the child to take on spontaneously the socialized behavior the parent wants him to have. The terms introjection, internalization, learning through role-playing, and identification have been used in this connection; they all refer to the child's tendency to copy, to take on as his own, the behavior, attitudes, and values of the significant people in his life, even when the socializing agents have not said "that's a good boy" or given him a piece of candy for performing these acts or holding these values. I will not go into the controversy concerning which so much has been written as to whether the child is more likely to identify with the person who is powerful and feared or with the person who is loved; nor will I discuss the several thoughtful efforts by personality theorists to reconcile the two points of view. The only important point for our consideration here is that the psychoanalytic view of socialization has led to an exploration of such variables as the warmth or hostility of the socializing agent toward the child.

There can be no doubt that measures of the warmth of the parent-child relationship have turned out to be enormously useful in socialization studies, in a number of ways. In some studies, warmth has been found to have a direct relationship to some dependent variable. For example, McCord and McCord have found that warmth in fathers was associated with low crime rate in sons.[9] In other studies, warmth has turned out to be a useful cross-cutting variable which interacts with other variables in such a way that other variables only begin to show their effects when the sample is first subdivided into groups differing in parental warmth. For example, in the *Patterns of Child Rearing* study, Sears *et al.* found that withdrawal of love is associated with rapid development of conscience, but only if this technique is employed by a warm mother; also that punishment for toilet accidents disrupts the toilet-training process, but that the greatest disruption occurs if punishment is administered by a cold mother.

Warmth also occupies a central role in socialization studies in its relationship to other measures of child-training variables. There have been, to my knowledge, three factor analyses carried out on sets of socialization variables. One of these was on the Fels parent behavior rating scales,[10] one on the PARI,[11] and one on the dimensions employed by Sears *et al.* in the *Patterns* study. In the latter two, warmth emerged as a fairly clear factor. In the first, there were two factors, one called "concern for the child" and the other called "parent-child harmony," which taken together are probably close to what is meant by warmth in the other two studies. It is clear, then, that both in terms of its predictive value for the child's behavior and its central place among the other interrelated child-training variables, warmth is a variable to be taken seriously. Why is it so important? I have already pointed out why the psychodynamic theorists believe it to be so—because of its role in producing identification. But the laboratory learning theorists can acknowledge its importance for another very simple reason. Before a parent can socialize a child, he must have established a relationship with the child such that the child will stay in the vicinity of the parent and orient himself toward the parent. A warm parent keeps the child responsive to his directions by providing an atmosphere in which the child has continuous expectations that good things will happen to him if he stays near his parent and responds to his parent's wishes. Fear of punishment can also make the child attentive to the parent, of course, but it establishes as well the conflicting motivation to escape out of reach of the punisher.

I'm sure I needn't belabor any further the notion that warmth is an important variable. But to say this is not enough. We still are faced with considerable difficulty in definition. It has been the experience of a number of people working with child-training data that they find themselves able to make reliable distinctions between mothers they call warm and mothers they call cold, and they find it possible to train others to make similar distinctions, but find it difficult indeed to define exactly what cues they are using to make the rating.

I suspect one source of difficulty is that the behavior we look for as indicating warmth varies with the age of the child the mother is dealing with. When the child is an infant, we are likely to label a mother as warm if she gives a good deal of the contact comfort that Harlow[12] has described. As the child grows older, the part played by the giving of contact comfort in the total constellation of warmth undoubtedly declines. When a child is ten, a mother seldom expresses her warm feelings for him by holding him on her lap. Rather, they are more likely to be expressed by the mother showing interest in the child and what he is doing, by helping unconditionally when help is needed, by being cordial and relaxed. Now warmth as expressed this way is not the same thing as giving contact comfort, and it is not to be expected that the same individuals would necessarily be good at both. Those of you who have read Brody's fascinating, detailed descriptions of mothers' behavior toward their infants will perhaps have noted that the mothers who gave effective contact comfort, in the sense of holding the child comfortably and close, stroking it occasionally, imparting some rocking motion, handling it skillfully and gently in the process of caring for the child—the women who could do all these things well were not necessarily the same women who expressed delight and pride in their children, who noticed their little accomplishments, or who looked upon their infants as individuals.[13] We should therefore not be surprised if there are low correlations between a mother's warmth toward her infant and her warmth toward the same child when it is older. If a primary ingredient of warmth is being able to gratify the child's needs unconditionally, and if the child's needs change from the infantile needs for being fed and being given contact comfort to the more mature needs for various kinds of ego support, then it is necessary for a mother to change considerably as her child changes, in order to be warm towards him at all ages. Some mothers make this change more easily than others. It is true that Schaeffer and Bayley, in their longitudinal study of a group of mothers, did find a substantial degree of continuity in the degree of warmth displayed by a given mother toward a given child as the child grew older.[14] There were undoubtedly individual differences in the ways warmth was manifested, and in the appropriateness of a mother's particular style of warmth-giving to the needs of her child at each developmental stage.

From the standpoint of making use of the variable in research, it appears that we should recognize that measuring the mother's current warmth at the time the child is, say, in nursery school or in the primary grades may not be an especially good index of how warm she was to the child as an infant. Furthermore, her warmth in infancy might predict quite different characteristics of the child than her warmth in middle childhood. If there is any relation at all between nurturance to an infant and its later personality traits, infant nurturance ought to relate only to those aspects of personality that presumably have their foundation in infancy—such as Erikson's dimension of trust,[15] or various aspects of orality. Achievement motivation, on the other hand, if it is related to the mother's warmth at all, ought to be related to measures of this variable taken when the child is older. A finding of Bronfenbrenner's seems to support this point about the importance of warmth-giving being appropriate to the developmental level of the child.[16] He was studying high-school-aged children and employed several variables relating to the kind and amount of affectionate interchange between these adolescents and their parents. He measured the parents' affection-giving (in the sense of direct demonstrativeness), use of affective rewards, nurturance, and affiliative companionship. Among these variables, it was only the last one, affiliative companionship, that correlated with the child's current level of responsibility taking. We can speculate that this particular aspect of warmth is the one that fits in much better with an adolescent's needs than either giving him kisses or peanut butter sandwiches. All this means that warmth has to be defined in terms of parental responsiveness to the changing needs of the child.

I have referred to socialization variables that came originally from laboratory studies of learning, and that have been adapted for use in studying the socialization process. I have also referred to variables that originated in psychodynamic thinking. There is a set of variables that is difficult to classify in terms of these two theoretical systems; I am referring to the dimension "permissiveness vs. restrictiveness," which emerged in our factor analysis of the *Patterns* variables, and to the related dimension of "control vs. laissez-faire" which has come out of the factor analysis of the PARI scales. The theoretical status of these variables is confusing because they relate to both psychoanalytic and learning theory, but the predictions from the two theories as to the probable effects of "permissiveness" or "control" are sometimes quite different. To cite a familiar example, there is the issue of what ought to be the effects of permissive treatment of the infant's sucking responses. The question is complex, but a simplified version of the opposing positions would be this: the learning theorist would argue that if an infant is permitted extensive sucking, his sucking habit will be strengthened, and he will be more likely to suck his thumb, pencils, etc., at a later age. The psychodynamic theorist would argue that permitting extensive infantile sucking satisfies oral needs and reduces the likelihood of excessive oral behavior at a later age. The same kind of difference of opinion can be found concerning whether permissive treatment of a child's aggressive or dependent responses should increase or decrease those responses. Now, of course, the fact that different theories produce different predictions concerning the effects of a variable is no reason for abandoning the variable. On the contrary, it is cause for rejoicing, and we should by all means continue to use the variable so that we can get data which will bear upon the validity of the theories. The trouble is that when we arrive at the point of trying to get agreement on the interpretation of findings, it sometimes turns out that the two schools of thought did not mean the same thing by "permissiveness." If a study shows that the more permissive parents are toward their children's aggression the more aggressive the children become, the psychodynamic theorist may say, "Well, by permissiveness I didn't mean *license*; the child must have limits set for him but he must also be allowed to express his feelings." If, on the other hand, a study shows that children heavily punished for aggression are more aggressive on the playground, or prefer aggressive TV programs, the learning theorist may say, "Well, of course, if the parents' methods of stopping aggression are such as to provide additional instigation to aggression, then their non-permissiveness won't eliminate the behavior." We begin to see that there are some hidden meanings in such a term as "permissiveness" and that we are dealing with several dimensions. Continuing with the example of aggression, we can see that permissiveness for aggression could mean the following things:

1. The mother holds the attitude that aggression is an acceptable, even desirable, form of behavior.
2. The mother does not like aggressive behavior and expects to limit it in her children, but feels that it is natural and inevitable at certain ages and so does not react strongly when her young child displays anger. A related definition of permissiveness would be pacing the demands for self-control placed upon the child to correspond with his developmental level.
3. The mother is not especially interested in the child or is otherwise occupied, and does not act to stop or prevent his aggression because she does not notice what he is doing.
4. The mother does not act early in a sequence of her child's aggressive behavior, but waits till the behavior has become fairly intense.

And at the other end of the scale, the effect of *non*permissiveness ought to depend upon how the nonpermitting is done—whether by punishment, by reinforcing alternative behavior, by environmental control that removes the instigations to undesired behavior, or some other means. The basic point I wish to emphasize is that I believe "permissiveness" is not a unitary variable, and that we need to work more directly with its components.

So far I have discussed several classes of variables: the ones translated as directly as possible from laboratory studies of learning (e.g., amount and kind of reward and punishment), and variables such as warmth and permissiveness of the socializing agent, which have their origins more in psycho-dynamic theories. There is another class of variables which has been emerging as more and more important, namely the "social structure" variables. These variables have their origin largely in sociological thinking. I do not have time to give them more than the most cursory attention, but I do not believe they can be omitted if we are to do any sort of justice to the scope of significant variables employed in current socialization studies. One has only to list a few findings which have come out of the investigation of social structure factors to see how essential it has become to take them into account. Here is a brief sampling of such findings:

1. With adolescents, parents are most strict with children who are of the same sex as the dominant parent.[17]
2. A mother's use of strongly dominant child-rearing techniques (called "unqualified power assertion" in this study) is related to her husband's F score (authoritarian personality score), but not to her own.[18]
3. A mother's behavior toward her children is more closely related to her husband's education than her own, and her behavior is more closely related to her husband's education than is *his* behavior to his own education. Thus it appears that it is the family's social status, as indicated by the husband's education, that influences the mother's socialization practices.[19]
4. Sons are more intrapunitive if their mothers are primarily responsible for discipline than they are if their fathers are the primary disciplinarians.[20]

5. Aspects of social organization such as whether residence is patrilocal, matrilocal, or neolocal, and whether marriage is polygamous or monogamous, determine such aspects of culture as the length of the postpartum sex taboo, the duration of exclusive mother-child sleeping arrangements, and the amount of authority the father has over the child; these factors in turn influence such socialization practices as the age of weaning, the severity of the socialization pressures which are directed toward breaking up the child's dependency upon the mother, and the existence and nature of puberty rites at adolescence. These socialization practices then in their turn influence certain aspects of personality, including certain culturally established defense systems.[21]

6. When offered a choice between a small piece of candy now vs. a large one later, children from father-present homes can postpone gratification more easily than children from father-absent homes.[22]

These findings all represent efforts to put socialization practices into a cultural or social-structural context. In each case, socialization practices are regarded as a link in a several-step chain, and consideration is given to the factors which determine the socialization practices themselves, as well as to the effects these practices in their turn have upon the child. It is clear that the way parents treat their children will be a function of their relationship to each other (especially of the distribution of authority between them), of the place the family has in the status system of the society in which the family resides, of the society's kinship system, etc. Of course, not every student of socialization need concern himself with all the steps in the complex sequence; he may, and often does, select a set of socialization practices and relate them to the child's behavior without going back to the conditions which led to these practices. But he needs to be aware of the degree to which socialization practices are embedded in a cultural context, and even needs to be alert to the possibility that the "same" socialization practice may have different effects when it is part of different cultural settings. So far, few studies have been planned or analyzed with this possibility in mind, but it might be worth some empirical examination.

It is time to make explicit an assumption that has been implicit so far about the constancy of personality from one situation to another and from one time to another. When we select aspects of parental behavior to study, and try to relate these to measured characteristics of the child, we usually measure what we believe to be reasonably pervasive, reasonably enduring "traits" of the parent and child. Orville Brim[23] in a recent paper, has leveled a direct attack at the notion of trait constancy. He has asserted that there is no such thing as a "warm" person, nor an "aggressive" person, nor a "dependent" person, but that behavior is specific to roles. This would mean that the same individual may be aggressive with his subordinates and dependent toward his boss; that a child may be emotionally expressive with his same-sexed age mates, but not with his teachers or his parents. The question of exactly how general personality traits are, is, of course, a matter that personality theorists have struggled with for many years. But our view of this matter will have some bearing upon our selection and definition of socialization variables. For if a child's behavior is going to be entirely specific to roles, then there is no point in trying to predict any generalized traits in the child; rather, we should be looking for those aspects of the socialization situation that will determine what behavior will be adopted by the child in each different role relationship in which he will find himself. If we wanted to find what socialization practices were associated with the child's becoming dominant or submissive, for example, we would have to study how his dominant behavior had been reacted to when he was playing with same-sexed siblings, and study this separately from the socialization of the same behavior when he was playing with opposite-sexed siblings. Only thus could we predict, according to Brim, how dominant he would be with other boys in the classroom; and we would have to make a separate prediction of his dominance with girls in the classroom. We have already been following Brim's advice, in essence, when we do studies in which we test how the child's behavior varies with the role characteristics of the person with whom he is interacting. A good example is Gewirtz' and Baer's study on the interaction between the sex of the experimenter and the effects of interrupted nurturance.[24] But to follow Brim's point further, we would have to investigate the ways in which the child's behavior toward specific categories of "others" was conditioned by differential socialization in these role relationships.

I do not believe that either socialization or the child's reaction tendencies are as role-specific as Brim claims; but obviously role differentiation does occur, and he is quite right in calling our attention to the fact that, for some variables at least, we should be studying socialization separately within roles. Actually, role is only one aspect of situational variability; we have known ever since the days of Hartshorne and May that trait behavior like "honesty" is situation-specific.[25] They found, for example, that the child who will cheat on the playground is not necessarily the same child who will cheat in the classroom, and that cheating is a function of the specific task presented to the child. This means that, in studying the effects of socialization, we either have to abandon efforts to predict characteristics like "honesty" and attempt to study only those characteristics of the child that are at least somewhat constant across situations, or we have to choose socialization variables that are themselves much more situation-specific, and make much more detailed predictions. An example of the utility of making socialization variables more specific to the situations they are intended to predict is provided in a study by Levy,[26] in which it was found that a child's adjustment to a hospital experience was *not* a function of the parents having trained the child generally to meet many different kinds of stress situations; rather, the child's response to hospitalization was predicted only from the amount of training the parent gave in advance for the meeting of this *particular* stress situation.

The same sort of situation prevails with respect to trait constancy over time. In their recent article on dependency, Kagan and Moss were able to present repeated measurements of dependency in the same group of individuals—measurements which began at the age of three and continued into the late twenties. The most notable feature of their findings was the absence of continuity in this trait.[27] The children who were dependent at age three and four were not the same individuals who emerged as dependent in adulthood. There was simply no continuity at all for boys, while there was some, but not a great deal, for girls. Let us consider Kagan's findings from the standpoint of efforts to study the socialization practices that are related to dependency. The first and obvious point is that we cannot expect to find any characteristic of the parent's behavior that will correlate with dependency in the young child and also correlate with dependency when the child is an adolescent or adult. This is not to say that the only correlations we can hope for are those between socialization practices and child characteristics measured at the same point in time. It is of course most likely that we shall be able to find aspects of a parent's current behavior that correlate with characteristics his child is displaying at the same time. But it is also possible that we could find aspects of the parent's current behavior whose effects will not show up until later. That is, perhaps there were things the parents of Kagan's sample of children were doing when these children were three and four that had some bearing upon how dependent the children became at the age of ten or eleven. But it is clear enough that whatever these delayed-action variables are, they could hardly be the same variables as the ones which determined how dependent the children were at age three, since it was not the same children who were displaying large amounts of dependency behavior at the two ages.

I have pointed to the way in which different theoretical systems, and different social-science disciplines, have converged to define and elaborate some of the variables which have been used in studies of socialization. In some cases this convergence has produced useful new knowledge; in others it has produced confusion over the meaning of variables. More importantly, it has produced a startling range of findings which have not yet been integrated into a theory of socialization. This is a major task that remains to be done.

NOTES

[1] N. L. Munn, *The Evolution and Growth of Human Behavior* (Boston: Houghton Mifflin, 1955).

[2] R. I. Watson, *Psychology of the Child* (New York: Wiley, 1959).

[3] A. L. Baldwin, J. Kalhorn, and F. H. Breese, "The Appraisal of Parent Behavior," *Psychological Monographs*, 63:4 (1949).

[4] R. R. Sears, E. E. Maccoby, and H. Levin, *Patterns of Child Hearing* (Evanston, Ill.: Row-Peterson, 1957).

[5] E. J. Shoben, "The Assessment of Parental Attitudes in Relation to Child Adjustment," *Genetic Psychology Monographs*, 39 (1949).

[6] E. S. Schaeffer and R. Q. Bell, "Development of a Parental Attitude Research Instrument," *Child Development*, 29 (1958), pp. 339–361.

[7] Sears, *op. cit.*

[8] B. Allinsmith, "Directness with Which Anger Is Expressed," in *Inner Conflict and Defense*, D. R. Miller and G. E. Swanson, eds. (New York: Holt-Dryden, 1960).

[9] W. McCord and J. McCord, *The Origins of Crime* (New York: Columbia University Press, 1959).

[10] M. Roff, "A Factorial Study of the Fels Parent Behavioral Scales," *Child Development*, 20 (1949), pp. 29–45.

[11] M. Zuckerman, B. Barrett-Ribback, I. Monashkin, and J. Norton, "Normative Data and Factor Analysis on the Parental Attitude Research Instrument," *Journal of Consulting Psychology*, 22 (1958), pp. 165–171.

[12] H. F. Harlow, "On the Nature of Love," *American Psychologist*, 13 (1958), pp. 673–685.

[13] S. Brody, *Patterns of Mothering* (New York: International Universities Press, 1957).

[14] E. S. Schaeffer and N. Bayley, "Consistency of Maternal Behavior from Infancy to Pre-Adolescence," *Journal of Abnormal and Social Psychology*, 61 (1960), pp. 1–6.

[15] E. H. Erikson, *Childhood and Society* (New York: Norton, 1950).

[16] U. Bronfenbrenner, "Some Familial Antecedents of Responsibility and Leadership in Adolescents," Cornell University, 1959 (dittoed paper).

[17] M. L. Papanek, "Family Structure and Child-Training Practices," Ph.D. dissertation, Radcliffe College, 1954 (unpublished).

[18] M. L. Hoffman, "Power Assertion by Parents and Its Impact on the Child," *Child Development*, 31 (1960), pp. 129–144.

[19] Bronfenbrenner, *op. cit.*

[20] A. F. Henry, "Family Role Structure and Self-Blame," *Social Forces*, 35 (1956), pp. 34–38.

[21] J. W. M. Whiting, "Sin, Sorcery and the Superego," in *Nebraska Symposium on Motivation*, M. R. Jones, ed. (Lincoln, Neb.: University of Nebraska Press, 1959); J. W. M. Whiting, E. H. Chasdi, H. F. Antonovsky, and B. C. Ayres, "The Learning of Values," in *The Peoples of Rimrock: A Comparative Study of Values Systems*, F. Kluckhohn and E. Vogt, eds. (in press); J. W. M. Whiting, R. Kluckhohn, and A. Anthony, "The Function of Male Initiation Rites at Puberty," in *Readings in Social Psychology*, E. E. Maccoby, T. M. Newcomb, and E. L. Hartley, eds. (New York: Holt, 1958).

[22] W. Mischel, "Preference for Delayed Reinforcement: An Experimental Study of Cultural Observation," *Journal of Abnormal and Social Psychology*, 56 (1958), pp. 57–61.

[23] O. G. Brim, "Personality Development as Role Learning," in *Personality Development in Children*, I. Iscoe and H. Stevenson, eds. (Austin, Tex.: University of Texas Press, 1960).

[24] J. L. Gewirtz, and D. M. Baer, "Does Brief Social 'Deprivation' Enhance the Effectiveness of a Social Reinforcer ('Approval')?," *American Psychologist*, 11 (1956), pp. 428–429.

[25] H. Hartshorne and M. A. May, *Studies in Deceit* (New York: Macmillan, 1928).

[26] E. Levy, "Children's Behavior Under Stress and Its Relation to Training by Parents to Respond to Stress Situation," *Child Development*, 30 (1959), pp. 307–324.

[27] J. Kagan and H. A. Moss, "The Stability of Passive and Dependent Behavior from Childhood through Adulthood," *Child Development*, 31 (1960), pp. 577–591.

24 Joshua A. Fishman

Childhood Indoctrination for Minority-Group Membership

This paper deals with the minority-group child and the schools specifically set up for his education within the group. It attempts to examine the effects

Reprinted from *Daedalus*, Journal of the American Academy of Arts and Sciences, 90:2 (1961), pp. 329–349, by permission of the publisher.

of such formal education on the attitudes and behavior of the child toward the values, customs, and individuals of the larger society. It also inquires into the effects of the school on his view of himself as an American and as a member of a specific ethnic group. It attempts to assess the extent to which the school contributes to his self-definition and his aspirations as a member of his own group, as well as of American society as a whole.

The school in America operates within a complex cultural environment. There exists an "American" society, in no way dependent on Jews or Catholics, Poles or Italians, Negroes or Orientals. The core of that society is white, Protestant, middle class, and it attracts all other particles to it. This is the culture into which immigrants are assimilated, and it forms the one accepted set of standards, expectations, and aspirations, whether they pertain to clothing, household furnishings, personal beauty, entertainment, or child-rearing.

Yet this does not mean that there is a single core group. Certainly, the white, Protestant, middle-class Americans cannot be said to share a single clear-cut set of cultural patterns. There are important rural-urban, North-South-West, Episcopalian-Lutheran-Baptist, and other differences. Psychologically, however, the term "core culture" still makes sense, particularly when it is used from the point of view of any given minority. It is no more difficult to speak of American than of French or Russian national characteristics. The American cultural constellation is not a fixed one, but it is certainly there as a structural, dynamic, meaningful whole.

The present discussion deals with only one theater of activity, the life of the minority-group child, and with only one instrument, his school. There are infinitely more complex and diversified social processes that affect both school and child, but it is nevertheless useful to concentrate on a specific set of problems and to build on a single set of assumptions. The assumptions posit a compelling American core culture, toward which the minority-group child has ambivalent feelings. He is attracted to it, surrenders willingly to it, desires to participate fully in it. The imperfect congruence between his aspiration and the possibility of his being absorbed generates ambivalence whenever he is rejected. Nevertheless, the minority-group child is ever ready to swallow his pride and try once more. This core culture, therefore, establishes the direction and intensity of America's impact on the minority-group child and on his feelings of belonging. We are here attempting to examine the effects that schools established by minority groups have upon these attitudes.

It will be useful to say something about the concepts of retentionism, separatism, integrationism, and biculturism that figure in the discussion that follows. By "retentionism," I mean the attempts by the minority group, either through the school or by any other means, to retain unique values and behavior, either in an altered or adapted form, or under the maximal self-determining conditions which a given minority group has attained.

By "separatism," I mean a tendency not to interact with the American core. Separatism is exclusive; it posits the superiority of the in-group, and the inferiority or undesirability (often in moral or ethical terms) of the core group. Separatism is a matter of degree, however, and the above definition merely indicates its extreme forms.

By "integrationism," I mean a tendency to maximal interaction with the American core. Integrationism posits the preferability of the "core" group to that of the minority in-group. Integrationism looks toward the incorporation of the member of the minority group in the "core." Although integrationism is regarded by its opponents as a euphemism for "a will to disappear," it is not necessarily that. When it is weak, it may not even mean a denial of separatism, since the two may co-exist within the same individual or group.

By "biculturism," I mean an orientation toward a maximally creative and positive involvement in the value-behavior complex of both the minority and the core. Biculturism involves selection from both systems and a synthesis of the elements selected. Biculturism results from the interaction of two healthy cultural systems within a single individual or group, with neither system dominating the other. It also represents a nonextreme and unfinished solution, one that must be worked out, bit by bit, over time. It is not an immediately available system which provides ready-made solutions to all present and future problems, as do the extremes of separatism or of integrationism.

These remarks will be limited to only three of the American minority groups, the Negroes, the Catholics, and the Jews. These are the groups on which most psychological and sociological research has been concentrated; studies of their schools extend over more than three decades. Furthermore, these are the largest minority groups, and their success in the bicultural rearing of their children, therefore, will strikingly affect the course of other, smaller minorities. What is more, since they constitute a quarter or more of the American population, their experiences are of great importance for the entire structure of life in the United States. Finally, these three groups differ radically as to their relation to the core, their internal organization, and their retentionist interests and activities. It will be useful to note whether these differences affect the retentionist outcomes of stimuli derived from school experiences. If not, it is possible that all American minority groups display strong psychological and social similarities in relation to the core.

The problems of Negroes in the United States are in many ways markedly dissimilar from those of other American minority groups. Instead of the removable stain of immigrant status, they carry the indelible stain of pejorative pigmentation. Their former bondage sets them apart from even the most disadvantaged white-skinned minorities, while their liberation has left a still sensitive scar in American social, political, and economic life. They constitute the only American minority with whom memories of white fratricide and of interracial homicide are alike associated. Severe sexual taboos and dislocations in status surround their acceptance into white, Protestant, middle-class society. Their deliverance is still a long way off.

Negro secular schools, staffed and supported by the Negro community specifically to foster a positive biculturism, do exist at all rungs of the educational ladder.* Negro religious schools may also aid the same purpose. Unfortunately, there have been few studies of children or young people attending either type of schools.

The only parochial setting in which Negro children have been fairly intensively studied is the segregated public school. This school differs from those of other minority groups, first because it is neither maintained, directed, nor, indeed, positively regarded by the community it serves, and second, because its curriculum and standards are limited by the very community which imposes inferior status on the Negro. As a result, the segregated public school has often functioned under conditions inverse to those governing other minority-group schools: both the direct and the indirect stimuli for keeping segregated schools come from the outside, not the inside.

Nevertheless, the similarities in striving among America's minority-group children are such that findings based on the segregated Negro schools do not differ significantly from those based on the voluntarily segregated institutions sponsored by other groups. One may ask about segregated Negro education some of the questions we ask about Catholic and Jewish schools. To what extent do they succeed in bolstering pride and security in one's group? To what extent do they succeed in communicating to their students the accomplishments of Negro culture in this country and elsewhere? To what extent do their students develop positive self-feelings and identifications with being Negro, as well as the ability to interact positively with white society without denying the values and achievements of their own group?

An early series of studies and more recent ones as well[1] have consistently pointed toward the high premium placed on light pigmentation by Negro nursery-school children attending both voluntarily and involuntarily segregated, semisegregated, and mixed schools. All Negro children, from the lightest to the darkest, tend to report their own pigmentation as lighter than it actually is, and light-skinned Negro children still frequently identify themselves as white at ages when darker Negro children have accepted the actuality, though not the desirability, of their negroid features. Light-skinned nursery-age children are preferred as friends, are oftener assigned desirable characteristics, and report fewer difficulties later in connection with being Negro when they are aged ten to twelve. The Northern Negro

* Even more than in the case of other American minority groups, it is important to spell out the values of American Negro societies, with respect to both their congruences and conflicts with the American core values. There are a few studies which indicate that upper-, middle- and lower-class Negroes and whites have very similar values and child-rearing practices. On the other hand, the variants in Christian tenets, the folksongs and tales, the group values related to recent servitude, the ties with African groups now achieving or approaching nationhood, the "typical" views of self and of life that are related to being Negro—all these are known only intuitively, and are suggested here as elements in a specifically American-Negro cultural milieu.

child permits himself white self-ascriptions more frequently and until a later age than the Southern Negro child.

These attitudes and preferences certainly do not spring from stimuli originating in the school. The Negro child derives them from adult Negro values, and the latter, in turn, are derived from the core society and the core values, toward which the values of the American Negro are oriented. These values are not bicultural, and they permeate the Negro child's attitudes to himself and others.

A number of studies over a long span of years have reported that the attitudes of Negro children (attending segregated and semisegregated schools) toward white children are more favorable than the attitudes of the white children toward them.[2] This preference has been found to increase with the age of the Negro children. Negro children have also been found to be critical or nonaccepting of other Negroes in some of the areas mentioned by white children, for example, in their mechanical and intellectual ability.[3] Several investigators have concluded from such data that American children reflect the social attitudes of the society of which they seek to be a part, regardless of the race, color, or creed of the particular group of which they are members.[4] Differences are only in degree, not in kind. The fact that the attitude of segregated Negro high-school students toward Negroes was, before the Supreme Court decision of 1954, more positive than was previously reported[5] may have wide-reaching implications if it can be related to other social processes in both the Negro and the white communities. One related factor was the recorded improvement in white children's attitudes to Negroes in the same communities. The upheaval and dislocation after the Supreme Court decision may have negated the mutually facilitating process that was possibly in operation.

Two other studies of great theoretical interest compare Negro children attending schools of various degrees and types of segregation. Both are more than a decade old, so that further investigation would be needed to make sure that their conclusions still obtain. A comparison of attitudinal adjustment toward Negroes and whites on the part of Negro students in mixed and segregated high schools in Ohio[6] found that the least significant difference between these two groups of students was in their attitudes toward "other" pupils (these were predominantly white in the mixed schools), although even specific attitudes to Negroes were not reliably different. A highly provocative study compared the attitudes of children living in all-Negro communities in Oklahoma with those of Negro children residing in various biracial communities of the South and North.[7] The investigator concluded that an individual growing up in an all-Negro society would have virtually the same attitudes toward whites as would any other American Negro. On the other hand, the individuals reared in the all-Negro communities were found to have much more favorable attitudes toward Negroes. This last finding recalls a much earlier one pointing to certain general benefits to personality accruing to children who attended segregated rather than mixed schools in Cincinnati.[8] Actually, the balance of benefits as between the two types of schools was precarious. The segregated group showed more social participation but less versatility in play, a greater tendency toward self-criticism, but also a greater interest in skilled professions, and, therefore, perhaps less inclination to leave school and try to get a job.

This research overwhelmingly supports the conclusion that the attitudes of American Negro children educated in segregated schools to their own group and to others, including the dominant white group, their vocational aspirations, their concepts of right and wrong, their hobbies and interests, to an overwhelming extent are influenced by the attitudes and behavior of significant core groups and by the attitude-forming media which the core society controls. Similar findings for Negro children attending nonsegregated schools are also plentiful. Although new conditions are now appearing, their general effect will probably make Negro children even more responsive and more exposed to the standards, strivings, and values of the core society. If this is really true for the Negro child (whose social distance from the core, to begin with, is greatest and is "legally" reinforced) and for the segregated school (at which attendance is enforced by external authorities), then the implications for children in other minority-group schools are unmistakable.

The American Catholic minority is quite different. Its schools, unlike those of the Negroes, are directly maintained by strong forces arising from within, rather than as a result of exclusion from without. Attendance is mandatory rather than merely desirable—although a large area of "extenuating circumstances" is recognized as excusing nonattendance. Unlike the case of the Negro minority, the issue of self-directed separation versus greater integration in the American community is a live one among Catholics, with both alternatives actively competing. Unlike the Jewish community, there are no structurally safeguarded gradational subdivisions within the Catholic religious leadership that correspond to alternative retentivistic philosophies. Like the Jewish minority, American Catholics come from a variety of European backgrounds. Two important factors in the development of American Catholic institutions, however, have been the numerical superiority and the superior status of Catholics of Irish derivation. Certain uniquely Irish-Catholic experiences in the "old country," as well as specifically Irish experiences on their arriving in America after the potato famines, have all left a stamp on the course of Catholicism in the United States.

Though they are the largest and best organized religious-cultural group in this country, Catholics have influenced American values and institutions far less than their thirty-odd million might have led one to predict. This is probably attributable to two opposing forces: the engulfing appeal of American secular life, on the one hand, and the tenacious in-breeding of Catholic energies through a huge network of educational, social, cultural, and economic institutions paralleling those of the core society, on the other. Although non-Catholic Americans have pointed to the separatist-retentionist power of this latter complex of forces (not to mention some people's dread that Catholics might dominate American life), Catholic leaders have even oftener recognized the constantly debilitating influence on Catholics of the dominant forces in American society as a whole. Recent changes in Catholic voting behavior, the rising rate of Catholics' marrying non-Catholics, the extremely high rate of their attendance at non-Catholic institutions of secondary and higher education—these are facts not to be overlooked in discussing the success of Catholic retentionist efforts in contemporary America.

A large-scale, thorough study of boys attending Catholic high schools[9] revealed the preponderant influence of the home and neighborhood over church and school in establishing interests and attitudes. Nearly half the two thousand boys studied in twenty schools throughout the country declared that their schools had not influenced their vocational choices, and fully two-thirds considered that their teachers did not understand their problems. Only 12 percent named the priest as their source of intimate counsel, while 56 percent believed that their parish provided insufficient social meetings for boys and girls. An athlete ranked first as their ideal or hero, while Jesus took third place. As to the aspirations they expressed, money ranked first, material possessions for pleasure ranked second, and eternal happiness and salvation third. Heading the list of their personal problems was the question of purity and sex. One-third reported they were unaware of what was sinful. Their primary sources of information on sex were companions (half of the boys), secular books (39 percent), secular magazines (32 percent), priests (26 percent) and "the street" (23 percent). A study of girls, while it revealed slightly less of a departure from the values of school and church, also showed a noticeably questioning attitude toward restrictions in reading, movies, and drinking.[10]

The ability of the Catholic parochial school to further retentionism may be measured in terms of religious understanding, belief, and practice, and of leisure-time and vocational interests. With respect to religion, Catholic educators have reported many findings that demonstrate the difficulties of their task. A series of interesting studies shows the lack of success as late as the eighth, ninth, and tenth grades in training children to recognize the central position of the Mass in Catholic worship: almost two-thirds of over a thousand parochial-school eighth-grade children investigated gave unsatisfactory replies.[11] By far the largest number of parochial-school children leave the Catholic school system after the eighth grade to attend public high, vocational, and technical schools. Those remaining in the ninth and tenth grades are a much more select group, at least as far as parental and home factors are concerned. Even so, studies of children in these two grades revealed that the gain in understanding and attitudes concerning the Mass was small, in spite of one or two years of difference in maturity and in instruction.[12] Even graduates of twelve- and sixteen-year programs of Catholic-sponsored study are described as retaining merely "a string of dogmas and moral precepts, threats and promises, customs and rites, tasks and duties [which are regarded as] imposed on unfortunate Catholics whilst the non-Catholic gets off free."[13]

A series of studies of the topics Catholic high-school boys remember in connection with retreats consistently points to purity and sex as of major interest, as compared with a negligible interest in God, ultimate ends, prayer, grace, and the sacraments. Reading interests during periods of retreat show a similar trend. Although in one study students attending Catholic schools were found to be more spiritually motivated in forgoing their own immediate satisfactions for the benefit of others, they did not differ at all from comparable students attending public schools in their readiness for such self-sacrifice.[14]

The familiar pattern of accepting direction from elsewhere than the school is also observed in leisure activities and vocational goals. The reading interests of Catholic high school boys, for instance, are concentrated almost exclusively on sports, adventure and mystery stories. Indifference to Catholic publications of any kind is general.[15] Interest in religious vocations, as reported by a variety of investigators, or the influence of religion on any vocational choice is slight and steadily decreases as the children grow older.[16]

In intergroup relations, the successful inculcation of school-derived and school-supported views also seems negligible. Thus the attitudes to Negroes on the part of white, Catholic, parochial-school children in the South have been found to be negative; they showed no improvement with an increased length of school attendance, and differed not at all from those of Catholic children attending public schools. The phenomenon cannot be ascribed to the Negro's overwhelming non-Catholicism, since Catholic parochial-school children in the Southwest are even more intensely anti-Mexican (and the Mexicans are Catholic) than the students in the South are anti-Negro. Anti-Jewish sentiments among parochial-school children have also been chronicled. Thus it seems that the child arrives at the Catholic parochial school with already established attitudes and needs in relation to his total American environment, and that the school itself is not strong enough to change these attitudes, even when it regards change as desirable. A similar conclusion concerning the impact of Catholicism on the political, social, and economic attitudes of adult Catholics appears from the nationwide Catholic public-opinion surveys conducted by the Catholic University of America.

Perhaps the extent of intermarriage is the best criterion of the ability of the Catholic parochial school to regulate its students' integration with the general American community. Although even in the absence of intermarriage it may well prove impossible to maintain a dynamic minority-group community, it certainly seems improbable that such a community can be maintained if the group cannot control attitudes to intermarriage. The many studies (with only one to the contrary) which have disclosed that attendance at parochial school does not appreciably affect the Catholic child's attitudes toward intermarriage[17] must be taken as evidence that the retentionist effectiveness of the Catholic school, when face to face with the "indulgent" American Protestantism and nonviolent secularism of the twentieth century, is far less than obtained during earlier periods, when Catholics suffered actual persecution.

The tireless efforts of Catholic leaders to employ parochial education to transmit the deep philosophical and religious differences which separate Catholicism from American Protestantism and from secularism have been most consistently embarrassed by the strivings of Catholic parents, young people, and children. Although the educators protest that it is "surely not enough" for parochial schools "to boast that their graduates are fine Americans [since] this is not the divine standard by which they shall be judged,"[18] they nevertheless suspect that they have often been forced to trade their "splendid educational heritage for a 'mess of North Central Association pottage.' "[19]

The Jewish school of whatever type can be no more effective in creative retentionism than the Catholic school. In fact, Jewish education, serving a numerically smaller and far less organized and unified group, functioning most frequently on a supplementary basis (on weekday afternoons or Sunday only), and concentrating on the short time span of late childhood and early adolescence, faces many problems unknown to Catholic education. In many ways the Jewish minority epitomizes values and trends found in the core, and it is the most urbanized group in a society tending to increasing urbanization. Its tradition of universal intellectual and higher-order conceptual interests dovetails with the core's increasing devaluation of manual drudgery. Its traditional educational emphasis brings it into contact with the very best of American and worldwide cultural and technical proficiency at a time when the core society itself is entering on a frenzied pursuit of higher and technical education. The shedding of Jewish traditional ways and beliefs has therefore been hastened in a period of unparalleled American pragmatism, secularism, and permissiveness in the personal, social, and economic spheres. Under such circumstances, the current which the Jewish retentivist school must battle is strong indeed.

There have been surprisingly few studies of the effects of Jewish schooling of any kind upon concurrent or later interaction with the "America-American-Americans" complex. In most Jewish educational circles there is a strong disinclination for objective studies of "outcomes"; such calculation is nontraditional, and in addition there is probably an unconscious recognition that the better the calculation, the less pleasant the truths revealed. Estimates of outcomes involving Americanism are doubly taboo. At one ideological extreme there is a hypersensitivity to the idea that perhaps anything less than a "perfect adjustment" to the American environment is obtained, particularly in view of the fact that something quite different from an adjustment to "American success" is desired in the first place. At the other extreme is a similar fear born of the realization that the biculturative efforts of the school cannot really compensate for the rebuffs the child receives from the core society.

In a group such as this, that needs at least eleven distinct types of schools, all for the purpose of indoctrinating its young for membership in a minority group, in accord with varying philosophies, one might expect somewhat differing results for retentionism. On the whole, however, a fragmented Jewish education can no more point to any signs of successful biculturistic retentionism than can a seemingly uniform Catholic education. In fact, the results are strikingly similar for both groups, even if, regrettably, we must rely on studies conducted over many years, with many disparate instruments.

A series of studies spanning twenty-five years by the only investigator to have done more than superficial work provides us with interesting and consistent results.[20] With respect to attitudes toward and knowledge of Jews and Jewishness, L. Lehrer has consistently found that there are only insignificant differences between children receiving a formal Jewish education and those without such an education, or among children differentiated as to the specific type of Jewish education received. Some minor differences in sex and age do approach significance, but their consistency from one study to another is low. It seems justifiable to conclude that the highly differentiated organization-ideological sponsorship of Jewish education corresponds neither to dynamic differences in the parental societies from which Jewish school children come, nor, most emphatically, to the different milieus of Jewish children. Lehrer concludes that "no matter how divergent the various circles of the Jewish people in America, no difference is noticeable among their children in the . . . character of their national belonging. Apparently, the Jewish environment is so constructed that every circle leads to the same psychological state in early childhood."[21] Yet another quotation from Lehrer's work suggests a conclusion which seems as relevant today as it was over a decade ago, and as applicable to children attending non-Jewish minority-group schools as to those attending Jewish schools:[22]

> In a community where Jewishness is restricted to an existence primarily on an ideological intellectual plane and is insufficiently enriched by the natural forces that exist in a full way of life . . . a child who is detached from our social functioning will sense in us primarily our weak and discriminated status, a status from which it is imperative that he escape. This will lead him to seek proximity to others, to search for protection by identifying with those objectively stronger, not knowing that this mode of adjustment also opens the way for tragic disappointments and conflicts.

That the Jewish schools, therefore, wield insufficient forces for "attaching" the vast majority of children from "unattached" homes to Jewish social functioning is an undeniable fact.

Other studies point to the mild effect of Jewish education in establishing unique behavior or values. That such education does not appreciably affect traits of character and personality is shown by at least two early studies.[23] A comparatively recent one concludes that in choosing friends Jewish boys' behavior toward one another does not reflect the degrees or kinds of Jewish education their parents have selected for them.[24] A highly regarded recent investigation states that Jewish boys in attending synagogue and neighborhood centers strive for increasingly broader, "in common," non-Jewish friendships and activities as they grow older and as their socio-economic level rises.[25] This is also the finding of a companion study of both boys and girls in another city.[26] Some insignificant correlations between childhood Jewish education and early adult Jewish activities have also been reported.[27] A study comparing Zionist and non-Zionist college students reports that both groups failed to mention Jewish education (a background variable on which they differed significantly and in the expected direction) among the facts they believed had affected their current attitudes toward the Jewish group.[28]

Two studies point to interesting successes in retentionism. In one, the students of Yiddish secular schools who had obtained the highest scores on a scale reflecting the degree to which they heard and used the Yiddish language also defined themselves as Jews (not employing the "American" option) more frequently than did children with lower scores on this scale. These children, however, did not differ from the others with respect to leisure activities,[29] the number of intimate friends they claimed, or the public-school marks they achieved. They did differ significantly from the others in the frequency with which they expressed interest in Yiddish for its general cultural and group-survival values, rather than for family, secretive, or general educational values. The investigator concluded that the high scores on his bilingual scale were concomitants of specific in-group identifications, but that they had no concomitants in the child's general activities and interests beyond the control of the in-group. In the absence of reliable data concerning either the measure of bilingualism or its concomitants, as well as in the absence of any following study of the longitudinal permanence of the findings, this claim—although it may be valid —seems somewhat premature. Assuming its validity, we cannot but be impressed by its separatist connotations, as opposed to a biculturism that is truly open in both directions.

The same author also recently reported a large-scale study of the negative stereotypes concerning American values, practices, and persons subscribed to by students attending eleven separate ideological structural types of Jewish schools.[30] Except for one type of school, no significant difference in their readiness to accept these negative stereotypes was noted between students attending different types of Jewish schools, whether the children were classified only by types of school or were further classified by age, length of attendance at the Jewish school, parental occupation, parental birthplace, or parental education. The one consistent exception involved the students of Orthodox all-day schools. These students showed a significantly greater willingness to accept such negative stereotypes. However, when these students were grouped by age, from eight to thirteen, their acceptance of negative stereotypes lessened steadily, with the result that by the time they were thirteen there was no longer any important difference between these students and all the others. Within the Orthodox all-day school, an analysis by years of study (holding age constant) also suggested a decreasing acceptance of negative stereotypes concerning American values, practices, and persons. The author concluded that American-Jewish children, regardless of the specific type of minority-group indoctrination they receive, seek acceptance by and participation in the American core society. For many Orthodox all-day school students, coming as they do from separatist homes and adult milieus, the school functions as a major agency for Americanization, acquainting them with American pastimes, cultural values, and societal opportunities. Again, the conclusions are probably exaggerated; but, if we grant their validity, the only retentionist successes to which they point are heavily tinged with exclusiveness and separatism at the direct expense of biculturism.

A few additional studies may be mentioned. A recent study compared the attitudes toward non-Jews on the part of Jewish children attending a "traditional" all-day school with those of other Jewish children (equated for age, sex, and parental socio-economic status) attending public schools. This study substantiates the hypothesis advanced by an earlier investigation, that no significant differences would appear.[31] The two samples of pupils were also compared with respect to their in-group attitudes. No clear differences emerged between the two groups of children, so dissimilar in their Jewish experiences. Dissatisfaction with being Jewish was about equally prevalent. Although differently rationalized and verbalized, the dissatisfactions in both samples derived from the individual and social restrictions and from the penalties perceived as being the concomitants of Jewishness. In addition, both groups regarded the positive features of Jewishness in much the same manner; they overrated the importance of Chanukkah, for example, and underrated other features of Jewish tradition. This compensatory mechanism for feelings of inferiority because of the colorful pageantry of Christmas is a significant index of the source of values and aspirations for both groups. Just as "parochial" as opposed to "public" education for Jewish children does not seem to be the "controlling variable . . . in the etiology of positive and negative out-group feelings in young children," neither does it seem to be such a variable in ambivalent feelings toward membership in the Jewish group.

Yet another recent study, with somewhat different primary interests, considered not only the ideological affiliation but also the generational position among Jewish children.[32] Its findings agree with those of the studies previously reported. Jewish boys from the first to the third generation show an ascending "inner maladjustment" on a projective scale for measuring personality. Socioeconomic status and the ideological affiliation of the school or synagogue attended seem to have little effect on these or subsequent scores. Scores on a structured measure of "social maladjustment" show an opposite trend, with the third-generation boys scoring best, and the first generation, worst. In connection with this last measurement, the author believes that boys born abroad, whose parents are not fully Americanized, may either feel somewhat insecure in their overt relationships with American society, or they may not as yet be endeavoring to adopt American norms of social adjustment. The third-generation boys, however, seek to appear as fully Americanized, as socially indistinguishable from the core group, as possible. In connection with the first measurements cited above, the author believes that the higher the degree of acculturation without acceptance by the dominant group, the greater the probability of "inner maladjustment" and marginal feeling. The generational trends were as clear among boys attending Orthodox schools of various structural types as among boys attending schools of other ideological and structural combinations.

Finally, it is appropriate to mention a study of those who continue their Jewish education past the normally terminal, elementary level.[33] These young people, attending Jewish supplementary high schools and teachers' seminaries in various cities, were asked to describe any crises they had experienced which had almost brought them to the verge of quitting. The respondents with the most intensely Jewish home environment most frequently named crises involving the attractions or demands of the surrounding, non-Jewish, cultural sphere. Subjects from less intensely Jewish homes, and, therefore, probably in no such conflict about the attractive features of the general American environment, usually attributed their crises to dissatisfaction with the Jewish school itself.

Many people are concerned about the marginal man, and in truth he represents a conspicuous problem in the participation of Jewish and other minority-group children in American core society, whether or not these children attend a minority-group school. The school is generally too weak to produce enduring conflicts or enduring retentionism. The reason for a marginal relation lies in the core society and its "look me over but don't touch me" invitation to the minority-group child. A vigorous biculturism could abolish this marginal relation, as could a vigorous separatism. The minority-group school, however, is too debilitated and timid for either of these ventures. It is certainly in no position to undertake the more difficult and the more initially disruptive of the two, a genuine biculturism.

This does not mean that the minority-group school accomplishes nothing, however. It exists in order to maintain certain minority values, which wage a losing conflict with core values; but this is only one level at which the effectiveness of minority-group schools can be evaluated. There is undoubtedly a second level, that of social relations, and here the school serves to maintain intragroup relations among minority-group children. It is one of the institutions of the minority-group community that preserves a relative amount of solidarity and intragroup feeling from childhood through marriage, and as such it affects choices in friendship, political opinions, levels of aspiration, and biases. The relation between school and neighborhood should perhaps be studied more carefully. The most effective minority-group school may prove to be one located in the more highly organized or more culturally intensive of the minority-group communities.

The foregoing studies are sadly insufficient as a research program for answering many significant questions about the minority-group child.

Spread over a quarter of a century or more, they suffer from shortcomings in their design and in their statistical analysis; they reveal a bewildering proliferation of methods and lack the refinements of controls and independent checks—above all, they lack the interdisciplinary focus and enrichment that differentiate true research programs from fragmentary short-term excursions.

Nevertheless, these studies do serve as straws in the wind, and our confidence in them is bolstered by the consistent trend they show. The minority-group school is patently unable to rechannel the major strivings and the behavior of the child in relation to the "America-American-Americans" complex. Not only is the child's response to American values, goals, and opportunities beyond regulation or substantial modification by the school, but also this response is well established even before the child attends school. With these values, goals, and opportunities beckoning to the minority-group child as attractively (if not more so) as to the child with a core background, the ethical, ethnological, and logical arguments for biculturism run against insurmountable difficulties from an entirely different realm. Dynamic biculturism may exist in certain parts of the globe, but not in any setting like America's constellation of socio-psychological and politicoeconomic realities. These realities make it simpler for American minorities to maintain a "separatist" existence than a bicultural balance. A two-front campaign is beyond their logistic resources; a one-front campaign is frequently beyond their emotional and material longings, for it entails excluding one's self from the American dream.

The weakness of retentionism is perceived even by minority-group leaders. Thus, the basic needs of children and adolescents are chiefly met by activities and programs that have little if any in-group distinctiveness. These programs imply that, if the leadership must painlessly work toward its long-range retentionist goals, it must provide art, recreation, counseling, comradeship, medals, and newspaper publicity. The less central and less distinctive goals are played up because these, not the retentionistic goals, are of natural and immediate interest.

Retentionism as inculcated by the schools, therefore, has often had little to show for its pains other than an ability to retreat according to plan. The few reported instances of the successful inculcation by the schools of minority attitudes and behavior are striking indeed. Their common denominator is some type of ethnic exclusivism, rather than pluralism or a broadly conceived biculturism. Furthermore, a longitudinal study of them has unfortunately been entirely neglected. After all, our ultimate interest is not merely in the consequences of indoctrinating children, but in the mature adult, and at present we have very little from which to extrapolate the successes in retentionism beyond the meager studies of children reviewed above. A few investigations, however, do indicate a substantial consistency between childhood and adult patterns, and in these cases the findings and their implications confirm the conclusion that the schools have only a slight retentionist effect.

If, as it appears, the attitudes and responses of minority-group individuals to American core society do not originate mainly in the school, then we may turn briefly to the following factors, some of which, at least theoretically, may better determine such responses—indeed, may determine the nature of the minority-group school itself.

The Compatibility of Values and Behavior   To what degree are the "modal" traits of personality, the "typical" values, goals, and customs of the minority group compatible with those of the core society? This question must be reexamined periodically, since such compatibility as may exist is itself a function of other variables mentioned below. Retentionism is probably facilitated when a minority and a core society, from the beginning, do not share similar values in terms of material success, attitudes toward centralized governmental intervention, political democracy, and characteristics such as aggressiveness, independence, and experimentalism. Ultimately, it may be more difficult for retentionism to operate successfully in areas where the values are maximally dissimilar or discrepant.

Participationism and Separatism   Does the minority group reach out toward participation in the core society, or does it so structure its life that separatism is the conscious or preferred outcome? The minority-group school can probably function best against a separatist background. In fact, even the core school may find that under optimally separatist conditions it must accommodate the views of the minority. Participationism as well as separatism undoubtedly exist to some degree within any minority group. Their extent and influence must be mapped, and the effectiveness of the school studied in that light.

Change vs. No Change   Intimately related to the two considerations above is the attitude to changes in its own values on the part of the minority group. It would be misleading to claim that each group merely desires to maintain its own way of life. Societies vary tremendously in their attitudes toward change. The direction of change must also be considered, since the school that is subject to emphases on revitalization or nativism may receive from the society at large impulses different from those that operate when retentionism alone is at issue.

Vitality and Exclusiveness   Minority groups differ in the degree to which they try to provide their members with structured activities in diverse areas of life. They also differ in the degree to which they succeed in attracting and holding interest in such activities. When the school is the only agent for retentionism, its effectiveness will be the less, and correspondingly, when it is a part of the whole constellation of adult and child activities in all spheres (recreational, cultural, social, religious, and economic), it is the greater.

Generational Cleavage   To some extent this is a variable related to time. The cleavages in language, customs, values, and goals are probably least either soon after or long after the first exposure of the minority group to the American core society. This curvilinear relation affects the school, and the attitude of an in-group society to such a cleavage must therefore be ascertained before the effectiveness of the school can be gauged. When I. L. Child (1943) posited his rebellious, in-group, and apathetic types,[34] he was speaking of a society in the throes of a generational cleavage. Now that our minorities, to the third and fourth generation, have been exposed to American life, this typology may have less meaning. If it still has value, the proportions in each of his three types may show marked changes and thus may produce side effects with which the school must cope.

Contributions from Abroad   A minority society which is continually receiving blood transfusions from abroad may be able to maintain schools exhibiting greater retentionism than one to which no new blood arrives. The new blood may consist either of ordinary immigrants or teachers, leaders, writers, or others coming from the "old country" to settle in or visit the "colonies" here. Books, music, periodicals, and financial subventions may also stiffen retentionism. Thus, communication with the old country, cultural envoys from the old country, even campaigns to help the old country—all may serve to strengthen emotional and behavioral bonds, just as the school does. On the other hand, if the old country has disappeared, the effect on the school can be shattering.

The Status of the Old Country   The disappearance of the old country from the political or cultural map is the extreme instance of dislocation in origins. Wars, political and social changes, economic transformations, or any factors that make the home country different from what it was when the minority group lived there, will affect retentionism. Tensions between the home country and the United States, the appearance of new elites, extensive reforms in language—these are all disruptive factors which must affect the minority-group school here.

The "New Country"   The American mass media, not only in communications, but also in education, recreation, consumption, and production, are a potent force in reducing the distinctiveness of any segment of our population. Even if the democratic and self-determining values of the core group do affect the minorities, such values may be powerless against a uniformity that grows by mutual consent.

Demographic Factors   The importance of numerical factors is self-evident, particularly if the group settles in highly urbanized surroundings and places a premium on participation. Since the minority-group school often serves a limited area and may therefore have a small enrollment, such further demographic factors as sex ratio, age distribution, population density, and the presence and status of other minority groups must be considered.

It would not be putting it too strongly to say that these factors (and any other larger societal factors) determine either the bicultural or retentionist success of the minority-group school. They interact, of course, and, in different groups at any time or in the same group at different times, they account for the variations in ascertaining school outcomes. If the school is to be a success, some need must be felt for the survival of the minority group. There must be some soil from which it can get nourishment— economic necessity, the social protection of the individual, religious convictions, or national pride. There must be some sociogenic or biogenic purposes it helps to serve better than do other groups in our complex society, in which multiple reference groups are so common. The school itself must build on these foundations, with greater or less success. It cannot normally be expected to provide those foundations.

In most sizable American minority groups, the trend of the variables mentioned above does not encourage the successful pursuit of creative bicultural retentionism. On the other hand, the American core society, even in the distant future, cannot be expected to assimilate physically the American Negro, Jewish, or Catholic societies. A triple or quadruple (or higher multiple) melting pot is here to stay. This represents the final problem— or tragedy—of the large American minority groups. Both psychologically and socially, the minorities are destined for a state of suspended animation. Having surrendered their own creative cultural props in the pursuit of the American ideal, they are left with the dilemma that the creators of the dream have themselves lost faith in it, and the dream itself cannot then be realized.

NOTES

[1] K. B. and M. K. Clark, "The Racial Identification of Negro Pre-School Children," *Journal of Experimental Education*, 8 (1939), pp. 161–163; "The Development of Consciousness of Self in Negro Pre-School Children," *Journal of Social Psychology*, 10 (1939), pp. 591–599; "Skin Color as a Factor in Racial Identification," *ibid.*, 11 (1940), pp. 159–169; R. M. Goff, *Problems and Emotional Difficulties of Negro Children* (New York: Teachers College, 1949); D. Senter and F. Hawley, "The Grammar School [and] Native New Mexicans," *Social Forces*, 24 (1946), pp. 398–407.

[2] E. Helgerson, "Race and Facial Expression in Choice of Playmate," *Journal of Negro Education*, 12 (1943), pp. 617–622; D. H. Russel and L. V. Robertson, "Minority Groups in a Junior High School," *School Review*, 55 (1947), pp. 205–213.

[3] T. E. Davis, "Negro College and Grade School Students," *Journal of Negro Education*, 5 (1937), pp. 525–533.

[4] S. Gray, "The Wishes of Negro School Children," *Journal of Genetic Psychology*, 64 (1944), pp. 225–227; W. L. Murray, "Social Sensitivity of Some Negro High School Pupils," *Journal of Negro Education*, 14 (1945), pp. 149–152.

[5] G. D. Mayo and J. R. A. Kinzer, " 'Racial' Attitudes of White and Negro Students, 1940, 1948," *Journal of Psychology*, 29 (1950), pp. 397–405; Q. F. Schenk and A. K. Romney, "Differential Distance Attitudes among Adolescents," *Sociology and Social Research*, 35 (1950), pp. 38–45.

⁶ R. W. Pugh, "Negro Students in Mixed and Separate High Schools," *Journal of Negro Education*, 12 (1943), pp. 607–616.

⁷ M. C. Hill, "Race Attitudes in the All-Negro Community in Oklahoma," *Phylon*, 7 (1946), pp. 260–268.

⁸ I. B. Prosser, "Negro Children in Mixed and Segregated Schools," *Journal of Negro Education*, 3 (1934), pp. 269–273.

⁹ V. H. Fleege, *Self-Revelation of the Adolescent Boy* (Milwaukee: Bruce, 1945).

¹⁰ M. A. Dowd, "Changes in Moral Reasoning through the High School Years," *Studies in Psychology and Psychiatry*, 7:2 (1948).

¹¹ M. Brendan (Leger), "Mistaken Conceptions of Catholic School Children regarding the Mass," *Catholic Education Review*, 46 (1948), pp. 267–274.

¹² M. B. Fannon, "Tenth Grade Students' Understanding of the Mass," *Catholic Educational Review*, 53 (1955), p. 188; M. C. McGowan, "Understanding of the Mass among Ninth-Grade Negro Boys and Girls," *Catholic Educational Review*, 53 (1955), p. 187.

¹³ Paul M. Baier, "Supernatural Life," *Catholic Educational Review*, 56 (1956), pp. 319–327; R. Morris, "The Institutionalizing of Religion," *American Catholic Sociological Review*, 17 (1956), pp. 98–108.

¹⁴ M. S. Walz, "High School Students' Attitude to Self-Sacrifice," *Catholic Educational Review*, 48 (1950), pp. 401–402.

¹⁵ E. F. Donahue, "Reading Interests of Catholic Boys," *Catholic Educational Review*, 45 (1947), pp. 525–533.

¹⁶ M. A. Ketterer, "Motives of Catholic High School Boys in Choosing Occupations," *Catholic Educational Review*, 47 (1949), p. 401; G. W. Holdbrook, "Attitudes of High School Girls toward Religious Life," *ibid.*, 46 (1948), p. 238; M. B. Luther, "Vocational Motivation of Adolescents," *ibid.*, 48 (1950), pp. 400–401.

¹⁷ H. F. Hoover, "Attitudes of High School Students toward Mixed Marriages," *Catholic Educational Review*, 47 (1949), p. 400; 48 (1950), p. 475; E. A. Leyden, "High School Pupils of Catholic and Mixed Marriage Families," *ibid.*, 48 (1950), pp. 185–186; E. J. Vollmer, "Attitudes of Boarding and Day Students toward Mixed Marriage," *ibid.*, 47 (1942), p. 116; K. J. Watters, "High School Students' Attitudes toward Mixed Marriages," *ibid.*, 47 (1949), p. 115.

¹⁸ "Catholic Education and the 'American Way.' " *America*, 91 (1954), p. 535.

¹⁹ B. J. Sheil, "The Subtleties of Secularism," National Catholic Education Association *Bulletin*, 44 (1948), pp. 6–12.

²⁰ L. Lehrer, "The Psychology of the Jewish Child in America," *Yivo Annual of Jewish Social Science*, 1 (1946), pp. 195–216; "American-Jewish Children," *Tsukunft*, 40 (1935), pp. 513–518; "Teachers and Schools under Various Conditions," *Yivo Bleter* (Bulletin), 9 (1936), pp. 76–106; "Children in Wartime," *Jewish Review*, 1 (1943), pp. 31–50; "The Role of Jewish Symbols," *Yivo Annual of Jewish Social Science*, 6 (1951), pp. 37–72.

²¹ *Yivo Annual Jewish Social Science*, 1 (1946), pp. 195–216.

²² *Yivo Bulletin*, 9 (1936), pp. 76–106.

²³ A. N. Franzblau, *Religious Beliefs and Character among Jewish Adolescents* (New York: Teachers College, 1934); M. L. Lurie and M. Weinreich, eds., "Jewish Social Research," *Yivo Annual Jewish Social Science*, 4 (1949), pp. 147–312.

²⁴ M. Rosenbaum, "Indoctrination for Minority Group Membership," *Microfilm Abstracts*, 9 (1949), pp. 168–170.

²⁵ I. Chein and J. I. Hurwitz, *The Reaction of Jewish Boys to Being Jewish* (New York: National Jewish Welfare Board, 1950). Mimeo.

²⁶ M. Radke, *Group Belonging of Jewish Children* (New York: American Jewish Congress, n.d. [1951?]). Mimeo.

²⁷ S. M. Blumfield, "Elementary Jewish Education and Interests," *Jewish Education*, 9 (1937), pp. 143–147.

²⁸ M. Radke, *The Meaning of Minority Membership to Jewish College Students* (New York: American Jewish Congress, n.d. [1951?]). Mimeo.

[29] J. A. Fishman, "Bilingualism in a Yiddish School," *Journal of Social Psychology*, 36 (1952), pp. 155–165.

[30] J. A. Fishman, "Negative Stereotypes Concerning Americans," *Genetic Psychology Monographs*, 51 (1955), pp. 107–182.

[31] D. A. Golovensky, "Ingroup and Outgroup Attitudes of Young People," Ph.D. dissertation, New York University, 1954.

[32] V. Sanua, "Personality Adjustment among Different Generations," Ph.D. dissertation, University of Michigan, 1956.

[33] A. Eisenberg and S. Warkow, "Continuity of Higher Hebrew Study," *Jewish Education*, 26 (1956), pp. 42–50.

[34] I. L. Child, *Italian or American? The Second Generation in Conflict* (New Haven, Conn.: Yale University Press, 1943).

25 HAROLD L. WILENSKY AND HUGH EDWARDS

The Skidder: Ideological Adjustments of Downward Mobile Workers

This is a secondary analysis of data from a study of two large factories in a small Midwestern city.[1] It seeks to demonstrate that in a period of prosperity (1) downward occupational mobility ("skidding") has a conservative impact on values and beliefs regarding the stratification order among urban workers; but (2) the strength of the relationship between mobility and ideology varies with age, type of mobility, and aspirations (situs vs. stratum). Alternative explanations of the skidder's conservatism are tested. In the manner of Sombart's *Why Is There No Socialism in the United States?*[2] the analysis underscores one cultural constraint on political extremism—the optimism of even those who have suffered status deprivation about their chances to recoup losses.

THEORY AND HYPOTHESES

Since Durkheim called attention to the possible disruptive consequences of social mobility for person and society,[3] students of stratification have seen the mobile person as deviant from his status peers. Whether moving up or down, he tends to lack firm ties to either the groups he has left behind or those into which he is moving. This is reflected in the findings of the few systematic studies which contrast the patterns of behavior and belief of mobile and nonmobile persons. The differences show up in prejudice,[4] politics,[5] union membership and activity,[6] the control of family size,[7] marital adjustment,[8] mental disorder, social isolation, nervousness, and preoccupation with health,[9] tendencies to suicide, homicide, and other crime.[10]

Investigators agree on the political effects of downward social mobility. Workers with white collar fathers are more conservative than those with

Reprinted from *American Sociological Review*, 24:2 (1959), pp. 215–231, by permission of the authors and the publisher.

blue-collar fathers. In the United States, Centers found that, of the 50 urban skidders in his national sample, 40 percent were "conservative" (anti-New Deal liberal) as compared with 25 percent of 236 nonskidders.[11] Lipset and Gordon indicate that mobile individuals in their Oakland, California sample are less likely than others to belong to or to report themselves as active in trade unions.[12] Three election studies give the same picture: intergenerational skidders are more likely to support the Republican candidate than two-generation workers, though the differences are not great.[13] In Europe, too, the two available studies report the skidder as less prone to leftist politics than his nonmobile brethren. In an investigation in Germany, 64 percent of 357 workers whose fathers were manual workers supported the Social Democratic party, compared to 52 percent of the 58 workers with nonmanual fathers.[14] In Finland, two-generation workers have been more likely to vote Communist than workers of middle class origin—a difference of 20 percent.[15]

Speculations about the reasons for the ideological conservatism of the downward mobile worker are varied. The main arguments fall into two categories:

1. *Resistance to failure in a society which emphasizes success values and the belief in an open class system.* Skidders resist the status implications of downward mobility by denying failure and striving to succeed.[16]

2. *Early, retrospective, anticipatory, or later socialization.* (a) *Early*: Skidders have earlier absorbed inappropriate attitudes from a "middle class environment" or "white collar occupational culture."[17] (b) *Retrospective*: Skidders reject full participation in the working class and retrospectively come to value what they have lost—they adopt attitudes and practices of the middle class.[18] (c) *Anticipatory*: Skidders aspire and expect to return to their former status and so, in anticipation, take on the values of a middle class reference category.[19] (d) *Acculturation, or later socialization*: Skidders lack firm integration with any social class, communicate little with other people, and receive little social support from them. "In the absence of extensive communication, [the mobile individual] cannot fully assimilate the style of life of the members of his new social class, with the result that his beliefs and practices are intermediate between theirs and those of the members of his class of origin."[20] Non-mobile workers, on the other hand, in frequent contact and communication with others like themselves and free from counteracting cross-class influences, acquire and maintain working class patterns of behavior and thought.[21] Differences between skidders and nonskidders, then, are a function of time for acculturation.

All of these explanations imply differences in class ideology between mobile and non-mobile workers: the skidder, more than the nonskidder, should adhere to the success ideology, cherish high occupational ambition, and be optimistic about the chance for himself and his children to return to white collar status. In short, he should be more "middle class" in what he believes, wants, and expects. The present study affords further test of this general hypothesis. (Hypothesis I in "Findings" below.)

The specific explanations—resistance to failure, class socialization—have further implications, however, which remain unexplored in the stratification literature. To tackle these, we must make certain distinctions between types of mobility, aspirations, and age.

One explanation of ideological conservatism among skidders pictures them as denying failure at the same time that they strive to regain what they have lost. For several reasons, this adherence to the tradition of opportunity should apply more to young intergenerational skidders than to young worklife skidders; more to older worklife skidders than to older intergenerational skidders; and more to older worklife skidders than to young worklife skidders (Hypothesis II, in "Findings" below). First, the real worklife skidders are the *older* factory *workers* who were white collar employees before entering the plant; unlike the youngsters, their occupational history is long enough to make worklife skidding meaningful in failure-success terms. Moreover, skidders under 40 or 50, like those under 30, in fact have a good chance to regain lost status.[22] Finally, where lie the coercive comparisons that men make in evaluating their class situation? If the skidder adheres to the success ideology and has an occupational history, he is more likely to compare himself with his own white collar past than with his father's—and to find a spur to his ambition in the process. Contrast the youngster. In some cases the young white collar worker may have deliberately *chosen* the better starting wage of the workbench as a temporary expedient. Gripped for the moment by a young adult subculture with its call for cars, trips, tailormade suits, expensive outings with the girl friend or wife,[23] he shows up in our samples as a worklife skidder—but he feels little sense of failure and no need to resist its status implications. For the majority who have *not* chosen the downward path, worklife skidding should again count for little: the youngster has scanty labor market experience, and is fresh from the controls of a middle class family; the important comparison for him is the one in which he comes out second best to his father. As he grows older, however, the intergenerational skidder is moved to adapt to working class values and beliefs: the success ideology holds that what he is has nothing to do with his father's status; less and less will he remind himself or be asked by his peers, "What did your father do?" In sum, when we deal with the ideological conservatism of downward mobile workers, intergenerational mobility should count more for very young workers, while worklife mobility should have its most solid impact upon older workers (Hypothesis II below).

What about the explanations of ideological conservatism that point to class socialization—early, retrospective, anticipatory, or later? What do they imply for the differential effect of types of mobility on age categories? If socialization is early or retrospective, the implications follow our previous argument: as workers grow older and family values and beliefs are screened through labor market experience, worklife comparisons become salient and intergenerational comparisons fade into the background (as, indeed, they should in accordance with the success ideology). As our intergenerational skidder moves into his thirties and forties, if he remains in the working class, he adapts to working class culture and by the time we interview him as a downward mobile worker, the effect of mobility has been attenuated.

On the other hand, if the anticipatory socialization and later socialization arguments are valid, our predictions would be wrong: the skidder who wants and expects to move out and up can adopt the appropriate values, beliefs, and life style whatever his age, whatever the type of mobility. No differences would show up (contrary to Hypothesis II). And the worklife skidder who has spent ten or twenty years in the working class, according to this view, should surely learn working class ideology more thoroughly than the youngster fresh from a white collar job—which means that the differences between older worklife skidders and nonskidders (due to common later socialization) should be *less* than the differences between younger skidders and nonskidders (contrary to Hypothesis II 6).

Finally, in addition to making these distinctions between age and types of mobility, we must ask: In what system is the deprivation felt or the aspiration held? We cannot lump together the worker whose ambitions are limited to the next step on the shop ladder, a skilled worker's or foreman's job, and the worker whose gaze is directed toward higher rungs on quite different ladders—independent proprietorship or further training for a semi-professional career (see Hypothesis III).[24]

The specific hypotheses and indicators derived from these considerations are elaborated with the findings below.

COMPANY, SETTING, AND METHODS OF STUDY

Data were derived from questionnaires using mainly fixed-alternative questions filled out anonymously under direction of the investigators by 2,499 nonsupervisory employees—virtually all of the manual workers in the "Rockwell Company." Our index of mobility is movement from white collar to manual occupations.[25] "Manual" applies to jobs coded as skilled, semiskilled, unskilled (including service other than protective), and mining; the "white collar" categories are professional and semiprofessional, office work, sales work, managers, officials, self-employed businessmen or artisans, and protective service.[26] A worker reporting that his father was a white collar man when he was growing up is classified as an intergenerational skidder. A worker who himself entered the factory from a white collar job is classified as a worklife skidder.[27] All others are nonskidders. On ideology, we used twelve items which seemed to us most unequivocally to reveal attitudes toward social class and job opportunities in the workplace.[28] We label all workers under 30, "young," all those 30 and over, "older."

To permit tests of our hypotheses we eliminated the following categories: (1) Female workers, whose status is not derived mainly from employment. (2) Male workers whose fathers were farmers when they were growing up, or who had themselves worked on farms before entering the factory. While most shifts from farm to factory in the course of early industrialization are moves from low rural to low urban position (nonskidder), the situation is probably more ambiguous for the midwest sample under consideration. (3) Workers who were students or had no occupation prior to entering the Rockwell Company. (4) All workers who failed to specify either their father's occupation or their own prior to employment at Rockwell. The study sample thus consists of male, urban, manual workers who had jobs elsewhere before entering this company—495 in all.

In the fall of 1951 these men were working in two separate plants, one new, one old, containing foundries, machine shops, and assembly units; most jobs were semiskilled. The setting is a one-industry city of about 15,000 population, surrounded by farmland and located 35 miles from a metropolitan area. The Rockwell Company, an established, family enterprise, manufacturing home appliances, is the largest single employer in the city, employing about 4,000 people. In a tight labor market it competes for labor with the metropolis.

The union local is presently an affiliate of the UAW-AFL-CIO. Rockwell was originally organized by the United Electrical Workers in 1938, after a long, bitter strike. In 1951, after the UE was expelled from the CIO for Communist domination, the local joined the UAW. A brief strike was called shortly thereafter—only a few months before data were collected. These events may have served to make ideological responses more readily available and to highlight contrasts between variously situated workers.

Rockwell's manual workers are quite stable. Most of them live in the city in which the plant is located and plan to remain at Rockwell "as long as I can work here." They are predominantly male (80 percent), married (74 percent), with at least one dependent (78 percent). The median age for all manual workers is 35 and for the study sample, 30. (Only one in eight of the sample is older than 50.) A third have at least five years seniority; the comparable figure for the study sample is 39 percent. Four in ten Rockwell workers grew up on a farm, three in ten in a small town; while those in the study sample are very much more urbanized.

This small city, ex-farm boy milieu should minimize class-conscious responses and hence reduce the differences between the mobile and nonmobile. Moreover, a quasicompany town like this one may afford more cross-class communication than, say Detroit, where more diversified work environments yield less basis for conversation between the classes, and where more homogeneous working class neighborhoods foster greater sharing of intraclass grievances. If recent events favor our general thesis, the social setting of the Rockwell Company works against it.

By our definitions, 19 percent of the 495 men were intergenerational skidders, and 20 percent were worklife skidders. There is reason to believe that in this respect our sample typifies national mobility patterns.[29]

Since we predicted the relationships discussed above, we used chi square as a one-tailed test; percentage differences serve as a measure of the strength of relationships. Our argument rests not only upon the size but also upon the consistency of predicted differences within a homogeneous sample exposed to a common working class culture in the same workplace and community.

FINDINGS

The data, presented in detail in Table 1, generally confirm our hypotheses. Of 48 possible comparisons of skidders and nonskidders called for by Hypotheses I and II (holding age and mobility type constant and counting aspiration for foremanship as middle class aspiration) only five comparisons show percentage differences in the unexpected direction (items 4, 6, 9, and 11 for the young intergenerational category and item 5 for the young worklife category). The net average difference in the predicted direction is 11 percent.[30] The main findings are the following:

I. *Skidders are more conservative in their values and beliefs regarding the stratification order than nonskidders.* This appears for all attitudes toward social class and mobility. A larger proportion of workers who have moved downward reject identification with the working class (items 1 and 5); believe in an open class system and in ability as the proper basis for promotion (items 4 and 10); aspire to middle class position for themselves, attach importance to promotion opportunity, and say they would accept the job of foreman if offered (items 2, 9, and 12); anticipate leaving the factory soon (item 6); and expect their children to achieve middle class position (item 3). In general, the men who have lost status adhere more firmly to the free mobility ideology than those who have not.

Results which are statistically insignificant or contradictory can be explained with reference to our hypotheses about types of mobility, age differences, and, to some extent, by the distinction between situs and stratum aspirations.

II. *The ideological conservatism of skidders can be explained almost entirely by the presence of, first, older worklife skidders and, second, young intergenerational skidders.* The following comparisons demonstrate the point:

1. *Older worklife skidders* (column 7) vs. *nonskidders* (column 8). For all five items on social class there are significant differences in the predicted direction—a net average difference of 27 percent. All seven items on inplant mobility conform in direction to our hypotheses, six of them significantly. The net average difference in predicted direction for all items is 21 percent.

2. *Older intergenerational skidders* (column 5) vs. *nonskidders* (column 6). The weaker impact of intergenerational comparisons for older workers is seen in the fact that the differences here are significant only on class identification and aspiration (items 1 and 2) and the foremanship items (11 and 12). The net average difference in predicted direction for social class items is 11 percent, for all items 9 percent.[31]

3. *Young intergenerational skidders* (column 1) *vs. nonskidders* (column 2). Significant differences appear in four of five social class items (item 4, belief in open class system, shows a 7 percent reversal). Differences are in the predicted direction in four of seven workplace items (7, 8, 10, 11), none of them significant. The net average difference in predicted direction for social class items is 17 percent, for all items 7 percent.

4. *Young worklife skidders* (column 3) *vs. nonskidders* (column 4). Significant differences emerge on only two of five social class items (1 and 3), and one of seven workplace items (12, accept foremanship). Relationships tend to be weak. The net average difference for social class items is seven percent, the same as for all items. The impact of worklife skidding thus seems much greater for older men while intergenerational skidding is a bit more important for the young. This is not a product of our definition of "older," since drawing the line at 40 instead of 30 yields the same results.

Item 1 provides a striking example of how even these rough controls for type of mobility and age sharpen the contrasts between mobile and nonmobile workers. Centers found for a national sample that 34 percent of intergenerational downward mobile workers identified with the middle or upper class as compared with 19 percent of the nonskidders,[32] figures nearly identical with our distribution for young worklife and older intergenerational categories. But in our sample the differences double when the crucial skidder-nonskidder comparisons are made—young intergenerational (54 *vs.* 19 percent) and older worklife (49 *vs.* 16 percent).

5. *Young intergenerational* (column 1) *vs. older intergenerational skidders* (column 5). If the early and retrospective socialization arguments are correct, this analysis should show decreasing ideological conservatism with age as the coercive effect of comparisons with father wears off and adaptation to working class culture begins. Significant differences in this direction appear for four of five class items (all but item 4) and for two of seven workplace items (6, 7). There is almost no difference for items 8, 10 and 12. But two significant reversals appear: 19 percent more of the older skidders stressed the importance of a chance for foremanship and 16 percent more of them believe in an open class system. The net average difference in predicted direction for social class items is 14 percent, for all items 8 percent.

6. *Older worklife skidders* (column 7) *vs. young worklife skidders* (column 3). The explanation in terms of denial of failure predicts more ideological conservatism in the older category; on this score all five class items come out in the right direction, one significantly. The workplace items show an inconsistent picture. The net average difference in predicted direction for social class is 12 percent, and for all items 4 percent. In contrast, the later socialization hypothesis holds that the worklife skidder will in time become acculturated to the working class and will be less conservative than the young man who just took off the white collar; but all of the relevant comparisons tend to contradict this view. Older worklife skidders are clearly more "middle class" in what they believe, want, and expect than

Table 1. Distribution of Responses in Percent by Age and Type of Mobility Experience

Item number	Question	Mobility experience								Significance level		Percent difference in predicted direction
		Young workers, under 30				Older workers, 30 & over				Comparison by cols.	P <	
		(1) Intergeneration skidders N=24	(2) IG non-skidders N=193	(3) Worklife skidders N=52	(4) WL non-skidders N=165	(5) IG skidders N=66	(6) IG non-skidders N=212	(7) Worklife skidders N=45	(8) WL non-skidders N=233			
Social Class												
1 Class identification	"If you were asked to use one of these four names for your social class, which would you say you belonged in?"									(1) vs. (2)	.01	35
	Middle or upper class	54	19	33	19	33	18	49	16	(3) vs. (4)	.05	14
	Working class	46	81	65	81	67	81	49	83	(5) vs. (6)	.01	15
	Lower class	—	—	2	—	—	1	2	1	(7) vs. (8)	.01	33
	No answer									(1) vs. (5)	.05	21
										(3) vs. (7)	n.s.	16
2 Class aspiration	"Which social class would you *like* to belong in?									(1) vs. (2)	.05	19
	Middle or upper class	79	60	63	62	59	44	78	42	(3) vs. (4)	n.s.	1
	Working class	21	35	29	35	39	53	22	55	(5) vs. (6)	.05	15
	Lower class	—	5	8	3	2	2	—	3	(7) vs. (8)	.01	36
	No answer									(1) vs. (5)	.05	20
										(3) vs. (7)	n.s.	15
3 Expectations for children	"If you have children, which social class do you think they will belong in when they have families of their own?"									(1) vs. (2)	.05	23
	Middle or upper class	71	48	65	46	50	47	71	43	(3) vs. (4)	.01	19
	Working class	16	36	17	39	38	41	18	45	(5) vs. (6)	n.s.	3
	Lower class	13	16	17	15	12	12	11	12	(7) vs. (8)	.01	28
	No answer									(1) vs. (5)	.05	21
										(3) vs. (7)	n.s.	6

Table 1. Distribution of Responses in Percent by Age and Type of Mobility Experience (Cont'd)

| | | Mobility experience | | | | | | | | Significance level | | Percent difference in predicted direction |
| | | Young workers, under 30 | | | | Older workers, 30 & over | | | | | | |
Item number	Question	(1) Intergeneration skidders N=24	(2) IG non-skidders N=193	(3) Worklife skidders N=52	(4) WL non-skidders N=165	(5) IG skidders N=66	(6) IG non-skidders N=212	(7) Worklife skidders N=45	(8) WL non-skidders N=233	Comparison by cols.	$P <$	
4 Belief in open class system	"Suppose a person belongs to one class and wants to belong in a different social class. If he has ability and works hard, what do you think his chances are for moving from one social class to another?"									(1) vs. (2)	n.s.	− 7
										(3) vs. (4)	n.s.	0
										(5) vs. (6)	n.s.	12
										(7) vs. (8)	.01	21
										(1) vs. (5)	.05	−16
										(3) vs. (7)	.05	18
	Good or very good	63	70	69	69	79	67	87	66			
	Fair or not too good	38	26	25	28	20	27	11	28			
	No answer	—	4	6	3	2	6	2	6			
5 Support of class conscious unionism	"Suppose there is a section of the country where very few workers are unionized. A drive is started to try to unionize the companies there. Union workers all over the country are asked to give some money to help support the drive. Some union people think they should give money;									(1) vs. (2)	.05	17
										(3) vs. (4)	n.s.	− 3
										(5) vs. (6)	n.s.	9
										(7) vs. (8)	.01	19
										(1) vs. (5)	.05	24
										(3) vs. (7)	n.s.	2

TABLE 1. DISTRIBUTION OF RESPONSES IN PERCENT BY AGE AND TYPE OF MOBILITY EXPERIENCE (*Cont'd*)

Item number	Question	Mobility experience								Significance level		Percent difference in predicted direction
		Young workers, under 30				Older workers, 30 & over				Comparison by cols.	P <	
		(1) Intergeneration skidders N=24	(2) IG non-skidders N=193	(3) Worklife skidders N=52	(4) WL non-skidders N=165	(5) IG skidders N=66	(6) IG non-skidders N=212	(7) Worklife skidders N=45	(8) WL non-skidders N=233			
	others think they shouldn't. How do you think you would feel about this?"											
	Think would give	25	42	42	39	49	58	40	59			
	Don't think would give or unsure	75	55	58	58	52	39	60	39			
	No answer	—	3	—	3	—	3	—	3			
Workplace 6 *Commitment to factory	"About how long do you expect to be working at Rockwell?"									(1) vs. (2)	n.s.	−10
	As long as can	63	53	46	57	77	77	67	79	(3) vs. (4)	n.s.	11
	A lesser time	38	44	50	41	18	20	29	18	(5) vs. (6)	n.s.	0
	No answer	—	3	4	2	5	3	4	3	(7) vs. (8)	.05	12
										(1) vs. (5)	.05	14
										(3) vs. (7)	.05	−21
7 *Interest in other job in plant	"Is there any other job in the plant you would rather have than the one you now have?"									(1) vs. (2)	n.s.	5
	Yes	25	30	29	30	46	48	36	50	(3) vs. (4)	n.s.	1
	No	75	69	71	69	54	43	62	43	(5) vs. (6)	n.s.	2
	No answer	—	1	—	1	—	9	2	8	(7) vs. (8)	.05	14
										(1) vs. (5)	.05	21
										(3) vs. (7)	n.s.	− 7
8 *Interest in higher wages	"How important is it to you to be able to make higher wages on a job?"									(1) vs. (2)	n.s.	12
	Very important	21	33	27	33	18	21	9	23	(3) vs. (4)	n.s.	6
	Not too important	79	67	73	67	82	77	91	76	(5) vs. (6)	n.s.	3
	No answer	—	—	—	—	—	1	—	1	(7) vs. (8)	.05	14
										(1) vs. (5)	n.s.	− 3
										(3) vs. (7)	.05	18

TABLE 1. DISTRIBUTION OF RESPONSES IN PERCENT BY AGE AND TYPE OF MOBILITY EXPERIENCE (Cont'd)

Item number	Question	Mobility experience								Significance level		Percent difference in predicted direction
		Young workers, under 30				Older workers, 30 & over						
		(1) Intergeneration skidders N=24	(2) IG non-skidders N=193	(3) Worklife skidders N=52	(4) WL non-skidders N=165	(5) IG skidders N=66	(6) IG non-skidders N=212	(7) Worklife skidders N=45	(8) WL non-skidders N=233	Comparison by cols.	P <	
9 Interest in promotion	"Different people want different things out of their jobs. What are the things you yourself feel are *most important* in a job?"									(1) vs. (2)	n.s.	−14
										(3) vs. (4)	n.s.	9
										(5) vs. (6)	n.s.	5
										(7) vs. (8)	.01	32
										(1) vs. (5)	n.s.	11
										(3) vs. (7)	n.s.	−7
	Promotion important	50	64	69	60	39	34	62	30			
	Promotion not important (ranks 6-10)	50	35	29	39	52	59	36	61			
	No answer	—	1	2	1	9	8	2	9			
10 Ability as criterion for promotion	"How much do you think seniority and ability *should* count in *promotion to a higher job grade or transfer to a better job?*"									(1) vs. (2)	n.s.	2
										(3) vs. (4)	n.s.	−7
										(5) vs. (6)	n.s.	4
										(7) vs. (8)	.01	18
										(1) vs. (5)	n.s.	3
										(3) vs. (7)	n.s.	5
	Seniority as important or more important than ability	67	68	64	69	70	72	58	74			
	Ability more important than seniority	33	31	37	30	30	26	42	24			
	No answer	—	1	—	1	—	2	—	2			

TABLE 1. DISTRIBUTION OF RESPONSES IN PERCENT BY AGE AND TYPE OF MOBILITY EXPERIENCE (Cont'd)

Item number	Question	Mobility experience								Significance level		Percent difference in predicted direction
		Young workers, under 30				Older workers, 30 & over				Comparison by cols.	P <	
		(1) Intergeneration skidders N=24	(2) IG non-skidders N=193	(3) Worklife skidders N=52	(4) WL non-skidders N=165	(5) IG skidders N=66	(6) IG non-skidders N=212	(7) Worklife skidders N=45	(8) WL non-skidders N=233			
11 *Importance of chance to become foreman	"How important is it to you to have a good chance of becoming a foreman?"											
	Important	25	35	39	33	44	26	40	30	(1) vs. (2)	n.s.	−10
	Not important	75	64	61	66	56	67	58	65	(3) vs. (4)	n.s.	6
	No answer	—	1	—	1	—	8	2	5	(5) vs. (6)	.01	18
										(7) vs. (8)	n.s.	10
										(1) vs. (5)	.05	−19
										(3) vs. (7)	n.s.	1
12 *Would accept foreman's job	"If you were offered the job of foreman, would you take it?"											
	Yes	50	44	56	41	53	36	60	36	(1) vs. (2)	n.s.	6
	No	42	51	38	54	42	57	38	57	(3) vs. (4)	.05	15
	No answer	8	5	6	6	5	7	2	7	(5) vs. (6)	.01	17
										(7) vs. (8)	.01	24
										(1) vs. (5)	n.s.	−3
										(3) vs. (7)	n.s.	4

* Counted as indicators of situs aspiration, Hypothesis III. Because of the ambiguity of the foreman's position, results are reported in the text both ways. In the table items 11 and 12 are counted as class aspiration (Hypotheses I and II).

comparable nonskidders, and on the most directly relevant measures (1, 2, 3, 4, 10) they adhere more to the free mobility ideology than do the young worklife skidders. Finally, for all 12 items the size of predicted differences between older worklife skidders and nonskidders is greater than the size of differences which appear between young worklife skidders and nonskidders.

III. *Skidders, because of their adherence to the success ideology, are more interested in escape from the factory than movement within it; modest aspirations and expectations for in-plant mobility and bolder aspirations and expectations for out-plant mobility tend to be mutually exclusive.* Using the concept of "situs"—a group of occupations whose status system may be considered a unit[33]—we hypothesized that workers who show little interest in interclass mobility may still aspire to better themselves within the status system of the factory, and that workers who adopt the mobility stance of the middle class (for example, our skidders) are not likely to be interested in intrasitus movement. The two types of movement, we reasoned, call for incompatible kinds of behavior. Class mobility requires more detachment from the moral order of the plant and the working class subculture; situs mobility requires, or at least is compatible with, commitment to both (even the foreman must in some degree adhere to working class values and beliefs, as well as those workplace norms which cut across status levels). Accordingly, for the workplace items available, we predicted that our skidders would show more interest in getting out of the factory but less interest in current wages or some other job in the plant; more interest in promotions generally and ability as the criterion, but less interest in foremanship. Table 1 shows this reasoning to be correct for everything but the foreman's job. It accents further the salience of older worklife skidders as a source of ideological conservatism among workers.

Older worklife skidders were significantly less committed to Rockwell, less interested in workplace mobility (as indicated by the importance attached to high wages and the desire for another job in the plant). At the same time they rated "good chance for promotion" high in their evaluation of a job more often and displayed more opposition to seniority as a promotion criterion. Contrary to our predictions, however, the skidders showed more desire for and willingness to accept a foreman's job. The foremanship issue also provides the only significant reversal for our point that intergenerational mobility should count for *less* than worklife mobility for older workers (see item 11) and *more* for young workers (see item 12).[34] The celebrated ambiguity of the foreman's position in the status system and the ambivalence of workers toward this "master and victim of double talk" may account for the ambiguity of our results whenever the foreman was mentioned.

A more direct test of Hypothesis III— relating situs aspiration (items 6, 7, 8, 11, 12) to class identification and aspiration (items 1 and 2)— shows that while the two are not mutually exclusive, there is no relation between them. Low and high class aspiration are equally compatible with strong situs aspiration. But cross-class identifiers (those who say they are working class but want to be middle class) tend to reject situs aspiration. At best the data give Hypothesis III as stated only weak support. Better measures of types of aspiration would be desirable.

In summary, then, analysis of 495 Rockwell workers with urban background and previous occupational history shows that skidding has a conservative impact on values and beliefs regarding the stratification order. More precisely, those experiences which precede and accompany downward occupational mobility play a part in making the skidder more conservative than workers in his class of destination. (We lack comparisons with norms of class of origin—baseline data from which to measure changes in ideology.) The relationship between mobility and ideology was affected in the expected direction by age, type of mobility (intergenerational vs. worklife), and to a lesser extent by type of mobility aspirations (situs vs. stratum). The strongest and most consistent relationships prevail among older worklife skidders, whether the age split is made at 30 or 40.

The anomalous conservatism of the status-deprived can be understood with reference to early or retrospective socialization leading to denial of failure and individual striving. Like a man falling from a skyscraper, our skidder reaches not in the direction of his fall, but back up the structure. The values and beliefs of the middle class family or the white collar workgroup retain their force despite later status loss.

These explanations are borne out more than the later socialization hypothesis, which, contrary to our results, implies that older worklife skidders should be less conservative than young ones. There may be a general tendency, evident in these and other data, for most workers to give up hope of getting ahead as they approach the age of 40 and become embedded in the working class, but older skidders in Rockwell plainly resist this tendency.

Finally, our data provide no support for the anticipatory socialization argument. This is given further emphasis in a study of upward-moving workers—an ingenious natural experiment in the same company—in which Lieberman found that workers who become foremen or stewards do not adopt attitudes that "fit" the position until *after* the move.[35]

SOME IMPLICATIONS

Why so little anticipatory socialization—either for our mobility-oriented skidders or for Lieberman's mobility-oriented future foremen and stewards? An explanation is suggested by the following features of the organizational context: (1) industrial conflict is not severe enough and positions most readily available to mobile men—foreman, steward, or similar jobs out of the plant—are not authoritative enough to demand recruitment on the basis of "loyalty" criteria; (2) positions so strongly instituted, with relatively clear (if inconsistent) behavior directives, do not require prior attitudes that "fit" the positions; (3) anticipatory socialization is functional only where mobility channels are wide open, while promotion possibilities at Rockwell are quite limited.[36]

Why so little acculturation? The findings on the conservatism of skidders must also be put in a larger social context. We deal here with the impact of regular patterns of urban occupational mobility at a time of sustained prosperity in a country at a high level of economic development. Structural and cultural conditions which might dispose our skidders to more radical political adjustments—for example, rejection of the stratification order— include: (1) the insecurities of early industrialization, with its painful transformations from peasant to proletarian, rural to urban, alien to citizen;[37] (2) economic slump in an advanced society accompanied by a widespread sense of declining opportunity;[38] (3) a structure of opportunity similar to that confronting Rockwell workers but cultural values which put less emphasis on an open class system and the urgency of success; (4) a society in which the working class has not moved up, relatively, in income, style of life, and sources of prestige other than occupation (a radical response would then be more available to the skidder).

Rockwell data remind us of promising leads for stratification research:

1. *The need to take account of types of mobility and aspirations in studies of the social and psychological consequences of mobility.* Few such studies have used work history as a variable; our analysis shows worklife mobility to be much more influential than intergenerational mobility in shaping the adult perspectives of all but very young workers and older educated workers. Still fewer studies have distinguished the status system of workplace from that of community and society. Our data here are equivocal. In fact, they contain a suggestion contrary to Hypothesis III but one consistent with two hypotheses in the literature of psychology and sociology: aspiration levels in different contexts are interdependent,[39] and status achievement in one system exerts a strain toward achievement in other systems.[40] Those who aim to move up aim at all rank systems possible; the worker who wishes to leave the factory for some other occupational ladder or who has in the past achieved a white collar position also wants to be foreman if that will yield a similar result by other criteria of status (income, style of life).

2. *The gains and costs of mobility and the need to consider descent as well as ascent.* Even where data have been collected on mobility patterns, the stratification literature attends more to the consequences of upward than downward mobility—a reflection, perhaps, of the relatively low rate of skidding in American society during the boom period when the research was under way.[41] Moreover, the more systematic studies following Durkheim's lead have emphasized the consequences of rapid ascent for the *person*—disruption of primary relations is the main theme.[42] The impact of mobility upon larger *social structures* has received less systematic attention, although many writers have speculated imaginatively about possible social consequences of mobility. Rockwell data are indirectly relevant to

one such speculation. Does a high rate of rapid social mobility produce a social category which powerfully reinforces the cult of optimism and gratitude, thereby deadening social criticism?[43] Or does it, on the contrary, develop a cadre of creative men of independent mind, released from traditional norms, ready to provide some needed novelty and flexibility?[44] The more skilled segments of the mobile population—the professional, scientist, artist—are under scrutiny here; but it is possible that those who have not made out so well nevertheless love the system. Indeed, our data picture the skidder as optimistic-grateful rather than creative-independent. In so far as lively debate about the social order is vital for the maintenance of a democratic society, this represents a loss. On the other hand, it seems likely that the presence of our skidders in the working class, with their adherence to the free mobility ideology, constrains tendencies toward political extremism among two-generation workers, who, sharing the same grievances and perspectives, if unexposed to deviant views of skidders would be more susceptible to totalitarian solutions.

In short, our skidders, along with other workers who escape from working class culture psychologically or actually, function to reduce working class solidarity and social criticism from below—and thereby slow down the push toward equality. But if the declassé were not optimistic-grateful, they might combine with normally apathetic workers to form the vanguard of extremist political movements. What American society loses in equality, it may gain in the maintenance of freedom.

Whatever its consequences, and whether we applaud or condemn them, we surely cannot ignore the fact of downward mobility. The Organization Man on the make, who has gained the center of the stage, represents a tiny fraction of the population. The skidder, as we have defined him, represents perhaps a fifth of the working class of urban background, almost a tenth of all urbanites in the labor force—in time of recession, more.

NOTES

[1] Field work was conducted by the Survey Research Center of the University of Michigan in the Fall of 1951. The original study used a long questionnaire administered to all nonsupervisory personnel on company time. It was directed by Gerald M. Mahoney, Gerald Gurin, and Seymour Lieberman. We are grateful to Angus Campbell, Director of the Center, for access to the data, and to Jacob J. Feldman and Gerhard E. Lenski for many helpful suggestions.

[2] Werner Sombart, *Warum gibt esin den Vereingten staaten keinen Sozialismus?* (Tübingen: J. C. B. Mohr (Paul Siebeck), 1906).

[3] Emile Durkheim, *Suicide* (Glencoe, Ill.: The Free Press, 1951), pp. 242–254.

[4] B. Bettelheim and M. Janowitz, *The Dynamics of Prejudice* (New York: Harper & Row, 1950); J. Greenblum and L. I. Pearlin, "Vertical Mobility and Prejudice: A Socio-Psychological Analysis," in *Class, Status and Power*, R. Bendix and S. M. Lipset, eds. (Glencoe, Ill.: The Free Press, 1953), pp. 480–491.

[5] See, e.g., E. E. Maccoby, "Youth and Political Change," *Public Opinion Quarterly*, 18 (1954), pp. 23–39; and E. Havemann and P. S. West, *They Went to College* (New York: Harcourt, Brace, 1952), pp. 117–120.

[6] S. M. Lipset and J. Gordon, "Mobility and Trade Union Membership," in Lipset and Bendix, op. cit., pp. 491–500.

[7] R. Riemer and C. V. Kiser, "Economic Tension and Social Mobility in Relation to Fertility Planning and Size of Planned Family,'" in Social and Psychological Factors Affecting Fertility, P. K. Whelpton and C. V. Kiser, eds., Vol. IV (New York: Milbank Memorial Fund, 1954), pp. 1005–1068.

[8] J. Roth and R. F. Peck, "Class and Social Mobility Factors Related to Marital Adjustment," American Sociological Review, 16 (1951), pp. 478–487.

[9] A. B. Hollingshead, R. Ellis, and E. Kirby, "Social Mobility and Mental Illness," American Sociological Review, 19 (1954), pp. 577–584; E. Ellis, "Social Psychological Correlates of Upward Social Mobility Among Unmarried Women," American Sociological Review, 17 (1952), pp. 558–563; E. Litwak, "Conflicting Values and Decision Making," Ph.D. dissertation, Columbia University, 1956 (unpublished).

[10] Inferences from A. F. Henry and J. F. Short, Suicide and Homicide (Glencoe, Ill.: The Free Press, 1955); and L. N. Robins and P. O'Neal, "Mortality, Mobility, and Crime: Problem Children Thirty Years Later," American Sociological Review, 23 (1958), pp. 162–171.

[11] R. Centers, The Psychology of Social Classes (Princeton: Princeton University Press, 1949), p. 180. Cf. Maccoby's finding that downward mobile persons conformed or overconformed to middle class norms of Republican voting and affiliation (op. cit., pp. 34–35).

[12] Op. cit. Cf. A. S. Tannenbaum and R. L. Kahn, Participation in Union Locals (Evanston, Ill.: Row Peterson, 1958), pp. 142–148.

[13] Differences range from 8 to 21 percent. Of 283 union auto workers in Detroit, 40 percent of those from white collar families voted for Eisenhower in 1952, as compared with 29 percent of the sons of farmers, 26 percent of the sons of skilled workers, and 19 percent of the sons of other manual workers. A. Kornhauser, H. L. Sheppard and A. J. Mayer, When Labor Votes (New York: University Books, 1956), p. 43. The 1952 Survey Research Center data on 156 urban manual workers show that 46 percent of the skidders and 38 percent of the nonskidders favored the Republicans. The comparable difference is 18 percent for the 1948 election. Based on tabulations by S. M. Lipset and H. L. Zetterberg in "A Theory of Social Mobility," Transactions of the Third World Congress of Sociology, Vol. III (London: International Sociological Association, 1956), p. 174.

[14] Based on a 1953 study by the UNESCO Institute of Social Science in Cologne, Germany, reported in Ibid.

[15] Ibid., p. 174.

[16] Compare the conclusions of a study of class variations in defense mechanisms. The mechanism of denial in fantasy, a product of harsh, external child-rearing practices (e.g., beatings), is concentrated among children of working class parents (indexed by occupation and income). D. R. Miller and G. E. Swanson, Inner Conflict and Defense (New York: Holt), Chap. 8, 9 (in press). One reason is that denial of reality is disfunctional for the maintenance and enhancement of social position, and middle class children are handled in ways that assure status continuity. According to this psychological hypothesis, when the man who has learned to favor the mechanism of denial fails and suffers status anxiety, he substitutes in fantasy a picture of success or of a system in which he is sure to rise. Some of our intergenerational skidders may have slipped not only because of bad breaks but because they were taught the "wrong" defense mechanisms; worklife skidders with working class parents are simply using the typical mechanism of the class (which handicapped them in their attempt to breach the class barrier).

[17] Lipset and Gordon, op. cit., pp. 492ff.

[18] Ibid., p. 496. "Retrospective" seems to imply "early" socialization; it may be distinguished on the assumption that the early experience did not fully penetrate but nevertheless the person is moved to conform to norms which by distasteful comparison he now realizes are prestigeful.

[19] *Ibid.*, pp. 493, 496.

[20] P. M. Blau, "Social Mobility and Interpersonal Relations," *American Sociological Review*, 21 (1956), p. 292. Cf. H. H. Hyman, "The Value Systems of Different Classes," in Lipset and Bendix, *op. cit.*, p. 441.

[21] Lipset and Gordon, *op. cit.*, p. 493; Blau, *op. cit.*, p. 291. At the logical extreme, we would find complete ecological segregation permitting communication only with those of identical occupation and social class. The militancy of miners, seamen longshoremen, etc. throughout the Free West has often been explained in terms of this social isolation hypothesis. C. Kerr and A. Siegel, "The Interindustry Propensity to Strike—An International Comparison," in *Industrial Conflict*, A. Kornhauser *et al.*, eds. (New York: McGraw-Hill, 1954), pp. 189–212.

[22] While ". . . there is relatively little permanent crossing between manual and nonmanual occupations . . . the temporary crossings occur more frequently downward than upward . . . from 40 to 80 percent of [the nonmanual workers in the Oakland, Calif., sample of men over 30] have at one time or another worked in the manual occupations." S. M. Lipset and R. Bendix, "Social Mobility and Occupational Career Patterns II," in Lipset and Bendix, *op. cit.*, pp. 455–456. Consistent with the Oakland findings are synthetic working life patterns constructed from data on urban workers from the Six City Study. A. J. Jaffe and R. O. Carleton, *Occupational Mobility in the United States 1930–1960* (New York: King's Crown Press, 1954), pp. 51–59. These studies tell us that worklife skidders in the second or third decade of their careers can still strive with justified optimism.

[23] Cf. D. Riesman and W. Bloomberg, "Work and Leisure: Fusion or Polarity?," in *Research in Industrial Human Relations*, C. Arensberg *et al.*, eds. (New York: Harper & Row, 1957), pp. 75–78.

[24] See Ely Chinoy's sensitive discussion of the differences between workers whose ambitions are factory-bound and those who talk about escape. *Automobile Workers and the American Dream* (New York: Random House, 1955), pp. 47–95.

[25] The case for using this move as the best single index of social mobility is stated elsewhere. See, e.g., J. A. Kahl, *The American Class Structure* (New York: Rinehart, 1957), p. 46; Hans Speier, "The Worker Turning Bourgeois," in his *Social Order and the Risks of War* (New York: Stewart, 1952), p. 65. Among the well-known limits of this index is the fact that many of the jobs classified as white collar—especially "proprietor," "clerk," and "salesman"—carry only slightly more prestige than the jobs called "manual." For our purposes, this may not be so severe a limit: a status difference seen as real but small often pains more poignantly than a large one. As Lipset and Gordon (*op. cit.*, pp. 703–704) suggest, status panic may be inversely related to the decline in status.

[26] "Protective service" includes eight respondents and 22 fathers. Of the alternative assumptions about working class perspectives, it seemed that the move from fireman, policeman, regular army, etc. to factory worker was downward.

[27] The question: "If you had a job before you came to Rockwell, what kind of work did you spend most time at?"

[28] "Face validity" was the criterion for acceptance or rejection of items. For example, of the two possible indicators of "class conscious unionism," we rejected "Suppose you went to work in a company where the union was very weak and could not get anything for the workers. Do you think you would join anyway?" A class conscious worker who had experienced weak unionism or worse might well answer "no."

[29] In the three national samples available, between one-sixth and one-fourth of the manual workers had nonmanual fathers. We eliminated females and farmer sons and fathers, made minor adjustments, and retabulated to achieve some comparability with Rockwell. Of 288 manual worker sons in Centers' study (July, 1945, quota sample), 18 percent reported white collar fathers (large business owners and managers; professional, small business owners and managers, and white collar). This is the only sample that excludes Negroes. Richard Centers, "Occupational Mobility of Urban Occupational Strata," *American Sociological Review*, 13 (1948), p. 198. Of 256 sons

in manual or farm labor occupations in the 1952 Survey Research Center election study (area-probability sample) 24 percent had nonmanual fathers. Based on tabulation by Lipset and Zetterberg, *op. cit.*, p. 165. Kahl's adaptation of census-classified NORC data (spring, 1947, quota sample) eliminates service worker sons and counts the few service worker fathers with the unskilled. The further elimination of farm sons and fathers and "Don't Know's," yields 314 manual worker sons, of whom 24 percent were skidders. "Jobs and Occupations: A Popular Evaluation," *Opinion News*, 9 (September 1, 1947), p. 12; and Joseph A. Kahl, *The American Class Structure* (New York: Rinehart, 1957), p. 260.

The size of our sample did not permit statistical analysis of categories combining mobility types (men who have experienced *both* intergenerational and worklife mobility). Only about one in four of our intergenerational skidders is also a worklife skidder. Tables comparing these two-time skidders with nonskidders, however, suggest a consistently additive effect on social class items for the two types of mobility within age categories.

30 Applying hypothesis III, in which we count a desire to be a foreman as situs aspiration, less applicable to class ideology, the number of errors is 12 in 48; the average difference in the predicted direction is eight percent.

31 Our skidders, whatever their age, tend to have more education (e.g., some college for 22 percent of intergenerational and 27 percent of worklife skidders in contrast with 8 and 6 percent for comparable nonskidders). Therefore we tried to control for education, as an ideological force intervening between early socialization and labor market experience. Although the small N in some age-mobility categories limits the analysis, these tables suggest the following hypotheses: (1) education has very little effect on the relationship between worklife skidding and ideology; (2) a high school education or more strengthens the long-run impact of intergenerational skidding (older intergenerational skidders are more conservative than nonskidders); (3) little education slightly reduces the intergenerational effect for youngsters.

32 *Op. cit.*, p. 180.

33 P. K. Hatt suggests the following situses: manual work, business, political, professional, recreation and aesthetics, service, agriculture, military. "Occupation and Social Stratification," *American Journal of Sociology*, 55 (1950), p. 539.

34 Answers to the question, "Would you take the job of foreman," consistently contradict our expectations: older skidders, especially worklife skidders, are more willing to accept foremanship than nonskidders, as are young worklife skidders. There is some indication that many of the disinterested young intergenerational skidders (75 percent say the chance to become a foreman is not important) will end up as enthusiastic management men (only 42 percent say they would not accept the job). See also footnote 35 below.

35 Twenty-three Rockwell workers who became company foremen and 35 who were elected union stewards between the administration of questionnaires in the fall of 1951 and December, 1952, plus matched control groups were re-studied in December. Comparisons of the initial characteristics of workers who later moved up with the rest of Rockwell's workers measured anticipatory socialization; before-and-after comparisons of those who changed roles with control groups measured socialization in role. Lieberman found that workers who moved to foremanship were *not* initially pro-management (indicated by attitudes toward Rockwell, the union, the incentive and seniority systems); workers who became stewards were *not* initially pro-union. If anything, they were both somewhat antimanagement and antiunion—that is, until they got their new jobs, whereupon the unseemly sentiments were quickly cast off. This study also found that foremen and stewards both tend to come from those elements of the rank and file who are more capable (educated, skilled, have read the contract), stable (integrated in community), dissident (active griper), younger (nine in ten were 20 to 40 years old), and mobility-oriented. Many of our skidders would fit. Seymour Lieberman, "The Relationship Between Attitudes and Roles," unpublished Ph.D. dissertation, University of Michigan, 1954.

[36] Cf. R. K. Merton and A. S. Kitt, "Contributions to the Theory of Reference Group Behavior," in *Studies in the Scope and Method of "The American Soldier*," R. K. Merton and P. F. Lazarsfeld, eds. (Glencoe, Ill.: The Free Press, 1950), pp. 86ff.

[37] W. E. Moore, *Industrialization and Labor* (Ithaca: Cornell University Press, 1951). Cf. H. L. Wilensky and C. N. Lebeaux, *Industrial Society and Social Welfare* (New York: Russell Sage Foundation, 1958), Chaps. 3–5.

[38] We have been unable to locate directly relevant data. However, several students at the University of Michigan have been engaged in field explorations of the impact of unemployment. Among especially deprived segments of the population antisystem responses are common. For instance, J. C. Leggett, D. P. Street, and R. O. Richards have analyzed 121 interviews with three groups of Negroes who were hard hit by the recession of 1957–58. Fifty displaced Negroes in a study directed by H. L. Sheppard and L. A. Ferman of an auto plant shutdown were asked, "If a bad depression were to happen again what do you think would happen?" The modal responses were: (1) *Collective violence*—predicts revolution, rioting, etc., *28 percent* (". . . we would have a revolution and knock out a few of these capitalists who dog it and hog it;" "I don't see much hope for the country. These youngsters aren't going to take what we took in the last depression. They will tear up the country;" etc.). (2) *Individual acts of violence*—assault, killing, etc., *18 percent* ("We won't have no country. There'll be fighting, stealing, starving. No one will have no chance. Not even the rich man," etc.). These were high seniority semiskilled workers who had achieved a foothold in Detroit industry and partial home ownership. Almost identical distribution of response—about half projecting violence—was found in two other Negro samples, one in a close-knit Negro neighborhood with radical leadership and younger population, half of which was unemployed ($N = 32$), the other in a neighborhood chosen for comparable deprivation but the absence of political organization ($N = 39$). Most of these 121 Negroes had experienced considerable recent unemployment or the threat of it by virtue of low seniority position; the data suggest that the most deprived are most prone to "violent" verbal responses. That depression makes a radical perspective more available to skidders and nonskidders alike is, of course, illustrated by some of the sociology of the 'thirties. See, e.g., A. W. Jones, *Life, Liberty and Property* (New York: Lippincott, 1941). Since all industrial societies are subject to economic instability, bringing with it variations in the incidence of status deprivation, it would seem wise to relate variations in the rates and effects of skidding to the business cycle.

[39] Kurt Lewin et al., "Levels of Aspiration," in *Personality and the Behavior Disorders*, J. McV. Hunt, ed. (New York: Ronald, 1944), Vol. I, pp. 333–378. G. H. Fenchel, J. H. Monderer, and E. L. Hartley, "Subjective States and the Equilibration Hypothesis," *Journal of Abnormal and Social Psychology*, 46 (1951), pp. 476–479.

[40] The status consistency hypothesis is stated in a different context by G. C. Homans in "Status Among Clerical Workers," *Human Organization*, 12 (1953), pp. 5–10. Cf. G. Lenski, "Status Crystallization: A Non-Vertical Dimension of Social Status," *American Sociological Review*, 19 (1954), pp. 405–413.

[41] The "sociological" novels and TV shows about mobility are almost exclusively preoccupied with the psychological strains of successful businessmen and professionals. Apparently even the "humanists" who make a business of expropriating then attacking social science for its ideological or methodological conservatism have seen richer material in the point of no return than in the death of a salesman.

[42] See two careful reviews of this literature: P. M. Blau, *op. cit.*; M. Janowitz, "Some Consequences of Social Mobility in the United States," *Transactions of the Third World Congress of Sociology*, Vol. III (London: International Sociological Association, 1956), pp. 191–201.

[43] M. M. Tumin, "Some Unapplauded Consequences of Social Mobility in a Mass Society," *Social Forces*, 36 (1957), p. 35.

[44] Janowitz, *op. cit.*, p. 195. See also the several discussions of the "marginal man."

| Maintenance of the Social Order | SOCIAL CONTROL |

COMMENTARY

Maintenance of the social order depends as much upon social control involving externally imposed constraints as it does upon the socialization of the individual to the values and norms of the group. The articles selected for inclusion under this topic deal with some of the conditions of social control.

In writing on the "Relation of the Individual to the State," Emile Durkheim was principally concerned with how individual freedom and autonomy could be secured in the context of the individual's involvement in small groupings as well as in relation to the larger collectivity, the state, formed to assure individual assent to the rudimentary requirements of social life. It is in this essay, drawn from his larger work *Professional Ethics and Civic Morals*, that Durkheim outlines the nature of the problem of social control and enunciates his notion of *the triangular relation* of individual, state, and society.

In the companion article, "Institutions of Privacy in the Determination of Police Administrative Practice," Arthur Stinchcombe gives contemporary relevance to much of the thesis developed by Durkheim. Stinchcombe distinguishes between public and private spheres of activity, he describes differences in the types of behavior requiring control in each realm, and he discusses the implications of these differences for variations in police practices from one type of situation to the other.

Everett Wilson, in "Mobility and the Maverick," focuses on the difficult problems of social control created by the conditions of excessive mobility so characteristic of the modern urban industrial society. Thus, with the essay by Wilson we come full circle. It is through his examination of why the migrant is a maverick, and through his consideration of how he is subjected to effective social control, that he deals with the problem of individual autonomy in relation to group coercion that was so critical to Durkheim.

26 EMILE DURKHEIM

Relation of the State and the Individual

There is no doubt, in the case of very many societies, what was the true nature of the aims pursued by the State. To keep on expanding its power and to add lustre to its fame—this was the sole or main object of public activity. Individual interests and needs did not come into the reckoning. The ingrained religious character of the political system of societies makes us appreciate this indifference of the State for what concerns the individual. The destiny of a State was closely bound up with the fate of the gods worshipped at its altars. If a State suffered reverses, then the prestige of its gods declined in the same measure—and vice versa. Public religion and civic morals were fused: they were but different aspects of the same reality. To bring glory to the City was the same as enhancing the glory of the gods of the City: it worked both ways. Now, the phenomena in the religious sphere can be recognized because they are wholly unlike those of the human order. They belong to a world apart. The individual *qua* individual is part of the profane world, whilst the gods are the very nucleus of the religious world, and between these two worlds there is a gulf. The gods are, in their substance, different from men: they have other ideas, other needs and an existence with no likeness to that of men. Anyone who holds that the aims of the political system were religious and the religious aims political, might as well say that there was a cleavage between the aims of the State and the ends pursued by individuals on their own. How then came it that the individual could thus occupy himself with the pursuit of aims which were to such a degree foreign to his own private concerns? The answer is this: his private concerns were relatively unimportant to him and his personality and everything that hung on it had but slight moral weight. His personal views, his private beliefs and all his diverse aspirations as an individual seemed insignificant factors. What was prized by all, were the beliefs held in common, the collective aspirations, the popular traditions and the symbols that were an expression of them. That being so, it was gladly and without any demur that the individual yielded to the instrument by which the aims of no immediate concern to himself were secured. Absorbed, as he was, into the mass of society, he meekly gave way to its pressures and subordinated his own lot to the destinies of collective existence without any sense of sacrifice. This is because his particular fate had in his own eyes nothing of the meaning and high significance that we nowadays attribute to it. If we are right in that estimate,

Reprinted from *Professional Ethics and Civic Morals* by Emile Durkheim, translated by Cornelia Brookfield, pp. 55–64, by permission of Routlege & Kegan Paul Ltd. Copyright © 1958 by Routledge & Kegan Paul Ltd.

it was in the nature of things that it should be so; societies could only exist at that time by virtue of this subservience.

But the further one travels in history, the more one is aware of the process of change. In the early stage, the individual personality is lost in the depths of the social mass and then later, by its own effort, breaks away. From being limited and of small regard, the scope of the individual life expands and becomes the exalted object of moral respect. The individual comes to acquire ever wider rights over his own person and over the possessions to which he has title; he also comes to form ideas about the world that seem to him most fitting and to develop his essential qualities without hindrance. War fetters his activity, diminishes his stature and so becomes the supreme evil. Because it inflicts undeserved suffering on him, he sees in it more and more the supreme form of moral offence. In the light of this, it is utterly inconsistent to require from him the same subordination as before. One cannot make of him a god, a god above all others, and at the same time an instrument in the hands of the gods. One cannot make of him the paramount end and reduce him to the role of means. If he be the moral reality, then it is he who must serve as the polestar for public as well as private conduct. It should be the part of the State to try to bring his innate qualities to the light. Shall we find some people saying that the cult of the individual is a superstition of which we ought to rid ourselves? That would be to go against all the lessons of history: for as we read on, we find the human person tending to gain in dignity. There is no rule more soundly established. For any attempt to base social institutions on the opposite principle is not feasible and could be convincing only for a moment: we cannot force things to be other than they are. We cannot undo the individual having become what he is—an autonomous centre of activity, an impressive system of personal forces whose energy can no more be destroyed than that of the cosmic forces. It would be just as impossible to transform our physical atmosphere, in the midst of which we breathe and have our being.

Do we not arrive here at a contradiction that cannot be resolved? On the one hand we establish that the State goes on developing more and more: on the other, that the rights of the individual, held to be actively opposed to those of the State, have a parallel development. The government organ takes on an ever greater scale, because its function goes on growing in importance and because its aims, that are in line with its own activity, increase in number; yet we deny that it can pursue aims other than those that concern the individual. Now, these aims are by definition held to belong to individual activity. If, as we suppose, the rights of the individual are inherent, the State does not have to intervene to establish them, that is, they do not depend on the State. But then, if they do not, and are outside its competence, how can the cadre of this competence go on expanding, in face of the fact that it must less and less take in things alien to the individual?

The only way of getting over the difficulty is to dispute the postulate that the rights of the individual are inherent, and to admit that the institution of these rights is in fact precisely the task of the State. Then, certainly, all can be explained. We can understand that the functions of the State may expand, without any diminishing of the individual. We can see too that the individual may develop without causing any decline of the State, since he would be in some respects the product himself of the State, and since the activity of the State would in its nature be liberating to him. Now, what emerges, on the evidence of the facts, is that history gives sound authority for this relation of cause and effect as between the progress of moral individualism and the advance of the State. Except for the abnormal cases we shall discuss later, the stronger the State, the more the individual is respected. We know that the Athenian State was far less tightly constructed than Rome, and it is clear that the Roman State, again, more especially the City State, was built on very simple lines, compared with the great centralized States of our own day. Progress in concentration of government in the Roman City took a different course from that in any of the Greek Cities, and the unit of the State had a different emphasis. This point we settled last year. One outstanding fact makes us aware of this difference: in Rome, the direction of religious practices was in the hands of the State. In Athens, it was dispersed amongst the many sacerdotal colleges. Nothing is to be found in Athens corresponding to the Roman Consul, in whose hands all governmental power was concentrated. The administration in Athens was distributed amongst an unco-ordinated crowd of various officials. Each of the group elements that made up the society—clans, *phratries* and tribes—had preserved an autonomy far greater than in Rome, where they were very soon absorbed in the social mass. In this respect, the distance that stretches between the modern European States and the Greek or Italian States is obvious. Now, individualism had a different development in Rome as compared with Athens. In Rome, the lively sense of the respect due to the person was expressed, first, in recognized terms affirming the dignity of the Roman citizen and, secondly, in the liberties which were its distinguishing juridical features.

This is one of the points on which Ihering has helped to throw a sharp light. We are in the same case in respect of freedom of thought. But remarkable as Roman individualism may be, it is slight enough compared to that which developed within Christian societies. The Christian form of religion is an inward one: it consists of inward faith rather than outward observances, for a deeply held faith eludes any external constraint. In Athens, intellectual development—scientific and philosophical—was far greater than in Rome. Now, it is held that science and philosophy and collective thinking develop in the same way as individualism. True, they very often accompany it, but that is not inevitably so. In India, Brahmanism and Buddhism have a very learned and very subtle metaphysic: the Buddhist religion rests on a whole theory of the world. The sciences were developed to a high degree in the temples of Egypt. We know, however, that in the case of both India and Egypt, there was an almost complete absence of individualism. It is this fact more than any other that goes to prove the pantheistic nature of these metaphysics and religions: they attempted to give the pantheism a kind of rational and charted formula. Clearly, a pantheistic faith is not possible where individuals have a lively sense of their individuality.

Again, letters and philosophy were widely pursued in the medieval monasteries. That was because intensity of speculation, in the individual as in the society, is in fact in inverse ratio to practical activity. When we find activity in the practical field falling below the normal in any one section of society, for some reason or other, then the intellectual forces will develop all the more and flow into the space thus left open to them. So it was with the priests and monks, especially in the contemplative religions. From another angle, we know too that for the Athenian, the matter of practical life was reduced to something insignificant. He lived a life of leisured pursuits. In such a setting there comes a remarkable flowering of science and philosophy. Once they flower, they may, to be sure, inspire an individualist movement, but we cannot say they derive from it. It is possible, of course, that speculation, opening out in this way, may not have this result and that it remains in its essence conservative. In that case it is taken up with making a theory of the state of things as they exist or perhaps with a commentary on it. Such, in the main, is the nature of sacerdotal speculation: and even Greek speculation as a whole had this same tendency over a long period. The political and moral theories of Plato and Aristotle hardly do more than reflect in their systems the political structure of Sparta and Athens respectively.

Finally, one last reason that prevents our measuring the degree of individualism in a country by the development reached in the faculties of speculative thought. This is, that individualism is not a theory: it lies in the region of practice, not in that of speculation. For it to be true individualism, it must make its mark on morals and social institutions. There are times, too, when it dissipates itself entirely, as it were, in speculative dreaming instead of getting through to reality and initiating that whole collection of customs and institutions that would be adequate to its needs. It is then we see systems come into view that reveal social ideals looking to a more highly developed individualism. That, however, remains a mere desideratum, since the conditions needed to make it a reality are lacking. Is this not rather the case with our own French individualism? It was expressed theoretically in the Declaration of the Rights of Man, although in exaggerated form; it is, however, far from having any deep roots in the country. The proof of this is seen in the extreme ease with which we have accepted an authoritarian regime several times in the course of this century—regimes which in reality rest on principles that are a long way from individualism. The old habits persist more than we think, more than we should like, in spite of the letter of our moral code. The reason is, that in order to set up an individualistic moral code, it is not enough to assert it or to translate it into fine systems. Society, rather, must be so ordered that this set-up is made feasible and durable. Otherwise, it remains in a vague doctrinaire state.

History seems indeed to prove that the State was not created to prevent the individual from being disturbed in the exercise of his natural rights: no, this was not its role alone—rather, it is the State that creates and organizes and makes a reality of these rights. And indeed, man is man only because he lives in society. Take away from man all that has a social origin and nothing is left but an animal on a par with other animals. It is society that has raised him to this level above physical nature: it has achieved this result because association, by grouping the individual psychic forces, intensifies them. It carried them to a degree of energy and productive capacity immeasurably greater than any they could achieve if they remained isolated one from the other. Thus, a psychic life of a new kind breaks away which is richer by far and more varied than one played out in the single individual alone. Further, the life thus freed pervades the individual who shares in it and so transforms him. Whilst society thus feeds and enriches the individual nature, it tends, on the other hand, at the same time inevitably to subject that nature to itself and for the same reason. It is precisely because the group is a moral force greater to this extent than that of its parts, that it tends of necessity to subordinate these to itself. The parts are unable *not* to fall under its domination. Here there is a law of moral mechanics at work, which is just as inevitable as the laws of physical mechanics. Any group which exercises authority over its members by coercion strives to model them after its own pattern, to impose on them its ways of thinking and acting and to prevent any dissent.

Every society is despotic, at least if nothing from without supervenes to restrain its despotism. Still, I would not say that there is anything artificial in this despotism: it is natural because it is necessary, and also because, in certain conditions, societies cannot endure without it. Nor do I mean that there is anything intolerable about it: on the contrary, the individual does not feel it any more than we feel the atmosphere that weighs on our shoulders. From the moment the individual has been raised in this way by the collectivity, he will naturally desire what it desires and accept without difficulty the state of subjection to which he finds himself reduced. If he is to be conscious of this and to resist it, individualist aspirations must find an outlet, and that they cannot do in these conditions.

But for it to be otherwise, we may say, would it not be enough for the society to be on a fairly large scale? There is no doubt that when it is small—when it surrounds every individual on all sides and at every moment—it does not allow of his evolving in freedom. If it be always present and always in action, it leaves no room to his initiative. But it is no longer in the same case when it has reached wide enough dimensions. When it is made up of a vast number of individuals, a society can exercise over each a supervision only as close and as vigilant and effective as when the surveillance is concentrated on a small number. A man is far more free in the midst of a throng than in a small coterie. Hence it follows that individual diversities can then more easily have play, that collective tyranny declines and that individualism establishes itself in fact, and that, with time, the fact becomes a right. Things can, however, only have this course on one condition: that is, that inside this society, there must be no forming of any secondary groups that enjoy enough autonomy to allow of each becoming in a way a small society within the greater. For then, each of these would behave towards its members as if it stood alone and everything would go on as if the full-scale society did not exist. Each group, tightly enclosing the individuals of which it was made up, would hinder their development; the collective mind would impose itself on conditions applying to the individual. A society made up of adjoining clans or of towns or villages independent in greater or lesser degree, or of a number of professional groups, each one autonomous in relation to the others, would have the effect of being almost as repressive of any individuality as if it were made up of a single clan or town or association. The formation of secondary groups of this kind is bound to occur, for in a great society there are always particular local or professional interests which tend naturally to bring together those people with whom they are concerned. There we have the very stuff of associations of a special kind, of guilds, of coteries of every variety; and if there is nothing to offset or neutralize their activity, each of them will tend to swallow up its members. In any case, just to take the domestic society: we know its capacity to assimilate when left to itself. We see how it keeps within its orbit all those who go to make it up and are under its immediate domination. (At any rate, if secondary groups of this sort are not formed, at least a collective force will establish itself at the head of the society to govern it. And if this collective force itself stands alone, if it has only individuals to deal with, the same law of mechanics will make those individuals fall under its domination).

In order to prevent this happening, and to provide a certain range for individual development, it is not enough for a society to be on a big scale; the individual must be able to move with some degree of freedom over a wide field of action. He must not be curbed and monopolised by the secondary groups, and these groups must not be able to get a mastery over their members and mould them at will. There must therefore exist above these local, domestic—in a word, secondary—authorities, some overall authority which makes the law for them all: it must remind each of them that it is but a part and not the whole and that it should not keep for itself what rightly belongs to the whole. The only means of averting this collective particularism and all it involves for the individual, is to have a special agency with the duty of representing the overall collectivity, its rights and its interests, vis-à-vis these individual collectivities.

These rights and these interests merge with those of the individual. Let us see why and how the main function of the State is to liberate the individual personalities. It is solely because, in holding its constituent societies in check, it prevents them from exerting the repressive influences over the individual that they would otherwise exert. So there is nothing inherently tyrannical about State intervention in the different fields of collective life; on the contrary, it has the object and the effect of alleviating tyrannies that do exist. It will be argued, might not the State in turn become despotic? Undoubtedly, provided there were nothing to counter that trend. In that case, as the sole existing collective force, it produces the effects that any collective force not neutralized by any counter-force of the same kind would have on individuals. The State itself then becomes a leveller and repressive. And its repressiveness becomes even harder to endure than that of small groups, because it is more artificial. The State, in our large-scale societies, is so removed from individual interests that it cannot take into account the special or local and other conditions in which they exist. Therefore when it does attempt to regulate them, it succeeds only at the cost of doing violence to them and distorting them. It is, too, not sufficiently in touch with individuals in the mass to be able to mould them inwardly, so that they readily accept its pressure on them. The individual eludes the State to some extent—the State can only be effective in the context of a large-scale society—and individual diversity may not come to light. Hence, all kinds of resistance and distressing conflicts arise. The small groups do not have this drawback. They are close enough to the things that provide their *raison d'être* to be able to adapt their actions exactly and they surround the individuals closely enough to shape them in their own image. The inference to be drawn from this comment, however, is simply that if that collective force, the State, is to be the liberator of the individual, it has itself need of some counter-balance; it must be restrained by other collective forces, that is, by those secondary groups we shall discuss later on. . . . It is not a good thing for the groups to stand alone, nevertheless they have to exist. And it is out of this conflict of social forces that individual liberties are born. Here again we see the significance of these groups. Their usefulness is not merely to regulate and govern the interests they are meant to serve. They have a wider purpose; they form one of the conditions essential to the emancipation of the individual.

It remains a fact that the State is not of its own volition antagonistic to the individual. It is only through the State that individualism is possible, although it cannot be the means of making it a reality, except in certain precise conditions. We might say that in the State we have the prime mover. It is the State that has rescued the child from patriarchal domination and from family tyranny; it is the State that has freed the citizen from feudal groups and later from communal groups; it is the State that has liberated the craftsman and his master from guild tyranny. It may take too violent a course, but the action becomes vitiated only when it is merely destructive. And that is what justifies the increasing scope of its functions. This concept of the State is, then, an individualistic one, but it does not limit the State to the administration of an entirely prohibitive justice. And in this concept there is recognition of the right and duty of the State to play the widest possible part in all that touches collective life, without however having a *mystique*.* For the purpose assigned to the State in this concept is comprehensible to individuals, just as they understand the links between the State and themselves. They may cooperate in this, fully realizing what they are about and the ultimate aim of their actions, because it is a matter that concerns themselves. They may even find themselves in opposition to that aim and thus even become instruments of the State, for it is towards making them a reality that the action of the State tends. And yet they are not (as held by the individualistic utilitarians or the school of Kant) wholes that are self-sufficing and that the State should merely respect, since it is through the State, and the State alone, that they have a moral existence.

* N.B. "without becoming, as it were, a mystic concept of State."

27 ARTHUR L. STINCHCOMBE

Institutions of Privacy in the Determination of Police Administrative Practice

Legal institutions in general depend on rare events, such as arrests or civil court cases, to structure the field in which frequent events take place. This makes the operation of legal institutions very difficult to study, except when fairly comparable types of frequent events operate in strikingly different legally structured fields. The institutions of liberty generally, and of legally protected privacy in particular, have the characteristic that rare events, such as a case being thrown out of court because the law of search and seizure has been violated, structure the field in which the everyday activity of police is carried out. The many types of crimes that police deal with are very differently situated with respect to the legal institutions of privacy, as we shall try to demonstrate in the first part of this paper.

Certain statistics on the arrest and conviction rates for different types of crimes as well as pieces of common knowledge can be used to explore the different characteristics of police administrative practice in these different legally structured fields. We will then try to show that police administrative practice with respect to different types of crime varies strikingly and systematically with the relation of the crimes to the legal institutions of privacy. This paper then tries to conduct an empirical study of that kind of "structural effect" on which the regulatory power of the law depends, namely, an effect on the behavior of many of an action by the courts that specifically applies only to the action of a few.

Reprinted from *American Journal of Sociology*, 69:2 (1963), pp. 150–160, by permission of the author and the publisher.

The order of presentation will be as follows: first I shall outline some well-known characteristics of the legal institutions by which "private places" are defined, and the effects of the growth of large cities on the social structure of "public places." Then I shall outline the relation of certain types of crime to these legal institutions and show how the location of crimes with respect to private and public places affects the organized activities of the police in handling these crimes. Since the police "organization" is made up of organized activities with respect to crime, this is really an indirect approach to studying the effect of social structure on organizational structure. To show this more clearly, in the final part of the section I shall summarize the way that the socially determined activities of police for particular types of crime are organized into police subsections with different characteristics.

LEGAL RELATIONS OF POLICE POWER TO PRIVACY

Most of our daily life is lived in a number of small, bounded social systems, such as families, schools, factories, clubs, etc., that have their own norms, goals, and facilities. The maintenance of the boundaries of these systems is necessary to their free and autonomous development. If agents of the state or strange private citizens could enter these systems arbitrarily and interfere with interaction within them, they cannot develop freely.

The central practical boundaries are such mundane things as walls, doors, window shades, and locks. But in modern society few of these are made to withstand a concerted effort by a group of men to breach them (in contrast to feudal societies, for example). Yet these fragile doors and windows effectively prevent police or private citizens from interfering with our sleep, our classrooms, our toolbenches, or our bars, at least most of the time. This is because a door is a legal entity of great importance: legitimate concerted social efforts to break down a door may only take place on legally defined occasions. These occasions are defined in the law of arrest[1] and the law of search and seizure,[2] and therefore, derivatively, in the criminal law.

The legal defense of doors and walls and windows means that small social systems which have legal possession of a place can maintain *continuous, discretionary* control over who crosses their boundaries. And this discretion may be enforced against agents of the state unless they have legal cause to penetrate the system or are invited in. Whenever such continuous discretionary control is maintained, the law speaks of "private places." The legal existence of "private places," then, is the main source of the capacity of small social systems to maintain their boundaries and determine their own interaction without interference from the outside. The distinctive feature of a modern *liberal* state is that it uses the monopoly of violence (which all modern industrial states have) to guarantee the boundaries of small, autonomous social systems.

The central importance in our society of the private places created in this way is indicated by two facts. First, in Maryland, a state not much less free than others, a man entirely without access to private places is legally unfree:

> Every person, not insane, who wanders about in this state and lodges in market houses, market places, or in other public buildings [note that some of these "public buildings" are "private property"] or in barns, outhouses, barracks, or in the open air, without having any lawful occupation in the city, town, or county in which he may so wander, and without having any visible means of support, shall be deemed to be a tramp, and to be guilty of a misdemeanor, and shall be subject to imprisonment, at the discretion of the Court or Justice of the Peace hearing the charge, for a period of not less than thirty days nor more than one year. This section not to apply to Allegany County.[3]

That is, if a man is not a member of some organization or family or other group that has control over a "private place" (which may, of course, be "public property," as for instance a county hospital), then he has to *satisfy a policeman* that his occupation in the area is lawful, and has to make visible his means of support (except in Allegany County). Access to private places is itself sufficient evidence that a man has a legitimate relation to the social structure; without that evidence, special evidence of legitimate occupation has to be provided. "Occupation" here means any legitimate activity, not specifically a job.

The second fact indicating the importance of the legal definition of private places is that unless continuous discretionary control of access to a piece of property is maintained (creating a "private place"), police may freely enter and supervise interaction and arrest without a warrant:

> An officer in uniform or in citizen's clothes, may enter any public house, if open, as other people enter, for the purpose of detecting or suppressing crime, and having peaceably entered, may arrest for any offense committed in his presence. [Apparently a common law rule, as cases are cited for authority rather than statutes.][4]

A man's affairs are never, then, legally free of police supervision except within private places. Police may not legally, of course, forbid actions in public places that are not prohibited by law. But there is a fundamental difference between conducting the affairs of a small social system in such a manner that no crimes committed shall *come to the attention* of the police, and conducting them so that a physically present policeman will approve. In the first case, the problem is to prevent complaints, perhaps by agreement; in the second, the problem is to satisfy the police, rather than other members of the system, that all is as it should be. Few of us ever see a policeman in those places where we spend most of our time; a "tramp" sees one wherever he goes, and the policeman has the discretionary power to "run him in."

DISTRIBUTION OF PRIVATE PLACES AND URBAN-RURAL POLICE PRACTICE

The concentration of the population into cities concentrates intensively used "public places" within a small geographical area, thus greatly reducing the amount of "public" area per person and making professional control of public places much more economical. At the same time the size and anonymity of the city decrease the chance of small social systems to control the behavior of their members in public. In a small village, activity in public places easily comes to the attention of the family, the priest, the employer, and the peers of the offender. Further, in large cities there are much stronger norms about "deliberately not noticing" the behavior of other people. This means that in cities, much more behavior is *only* inquired into by the police.

That is, in cities it is economically possible to patrol public places, and at the same time it is functionally necessary. City police can therefore depend much more on their own presence and information for the detection of crime (especially certain types of crime) than can a rural police force. To a large degree (except for the patrol of main highways) rural police depend on complaints from people who are injured or know of a crime rather than on their own patrol.

Besides leading to different structural conditions of police practice, intensively used public places pose new problems. The most important are, of course, traffic jams and accidents. But also, extensive traffic creates opportunities for the use of public places for private profit in ways that create a "nuisance." Soliciting for prostitution, begging, street vending, speech-making, all become profitable uses of public places when the traffic gets heavy enough. The control of these "nuisances" is easily done without access to private places, along with other patrol duties.

The increasing predominance of patrol of public places means that policemen act much more on their own initiative. Much or all of the evidence that justifies arrest will be collected by the policeman on the spot. The arrest often need not involve any invasion at all of private places. Consequently these arrests are much more likely than are those in rural areas to be arrests without a warrant, and therefore without prior check by the judiciary, or to be a direct summons to appear in court (as in traffic cases).

ARRESTS INVOLVING ENTRY INTO PRIVATE PLACES

Private autonomy alone cannot guarantee liberty in the sense in which we understand it today. Feudal manors or plantations in the ante bellum South were much more autonomous and free of state interference than modern factories and business places. But this private autonomy did not create liberty in the modern sense because the police power was privately appropriated and consequently not exercised according to "due process of law." The practical implication of this is that besides *not* entering small systems *except* on legally defined occasions, *entering* them *on* those occasions is a duty of the police in liberal societies. A primary function of the criminal law is the limitation of coercion within small social systems.

But once the small systems are entered by the state, "due process of law" means mainly a set of procedures which guarantee that the autonomy of individuals and small social systems will be restored as quickly as possible if a crime has not in fact been committed. And it means that the process of investigating and legally establishing the existence of a crime shall not so far damage the small social system that they cannot function after they have been found innocent.

Due process thus involves a grading of coercion applied by the police, into arrest and the seizure of evidence, coerced appearance in court, and coerced paying of the penalty of crime. Each of these grades of coercion changes the legal status of the presumed offender. Each of these changes of the legal condition of the presumed offender must be justified by evidence of a probability that a crime has been committed and probability that the defendant committed the crime. The probabilities increase with the increase in severity of coercion. The probability required to justify arrest (by a police officer at least) is not as high as that required to coerce an appearance in court (a "prima facie case"). To justify conviction the commission of a crime must be established "beyond reasonable doubt." We now have sufficient background to discuss the structural location of different types of crime with respect to the institutions of privacy and the effect of this structural distribution on police practice.

THE EFFECT OF THE SOCIAL LOCATION OF DIFFERENT CRIMES ON POLICE PRACTICE

It is immediately evident that different types of crime will be distributed differently with respect to the institutions of privacy. For instance, wife-beating rarely goes on in public places. Soliciting for prostitution requires some systematic contact with an anonymous public through a pimping apparatus. Except for call girls and prostitutes in well-known houses, this requires soliciting (often by the woman herself) in some public places. But prostitution takes place in private places. Burglary consists in the invasion of the private place of another, generally in secret, which results in a complaint against an unknown person. The person's identity has to be established by the police. Murder generally takes place within small social systems, behind doors. Riots takes place in street and other public places.

Of course these variations in the social location of crimes imply differences in police practice. Information relevant to each stage of the criminal process comes to the police in different ways, different degrees and kinds of coercion have to be applied for different purposes, different things have to be proved with the evidence. There are differences in the number and types of private places that have to be penetrated, and in the amount of preparation of the case previous to this penetration. The kinds of people who commit different types of crime have different stability of social ties, which makes due process work differently.[5] We may distinguish the following types of crime.

Coercion in Private Life   The application of force or other coercion in private life is either controlled and adjusted within the small social system (as when a wife puts up with a beating), or it is not. When it is not, the crimes are, generally speaking, "crimes of passion." Probably the legally defined crimes with the highest proportion originating in this way are incest and murder,[6] but some unknown proportion of other crimes against persons (rape, aggravated assault) originate the same way.

Such crimes generally either result in complaint to the police or in such heinous crimes that access to private places is hardly a difficulty, at least for investigation. Because the people who participate in small social systems are highly visible once the system is penetrated, and because often the complainant knows perfectly well who coerced whom, arrests are fairly easy to make. Crimes against persons generally have a high proportion of "crimes known to the police" that are "cleared by arrest" (see Table 1).

TABLE 1. Proportion of Crimes Known to the Police "Cleared by Arrest," and Proportion of Those Charged Who Are Convicted, for Various Crimes *

Crime	Percentage cleared by arrest	Percentage convicted
Crimes indicating coercion in private life:		
Murder, including non-negligent manslaughter ..	92.7	59.4
Forcible rape	73.6	43.0
Aggravated assault	64.7	43.9
Crimes indicating coercion in public places:		
Robbery	42.5	64.8
Crimes indicating invasion of private places of another:		
Burglary	30.7	71.4
Larceny (over $50)	20.9	72.6
Auto theft	26.2	67.5
Crimes indicating individual public disorder:		
Vagrancy	N.a.	77.5
Drunkenness	N.a.	86.5
Disorderly conduct	N.a.	69.7

* Computed from Federal Bureau of Investigation, *Uniform Crime Reports—1959* (Washington, D.C.: Government Printing Office, 1960), Tables 12 and 14.

But the same conditions that produce easy arrests create another characteristic of enforcement against these crimes, namely, that arrests quite often do not result in conviction. Legal responsibility of the assailant must be established. His intentions are not immediately obvious from the nature of the act (as they are, for example, in burglary). The kind of passionate conflicts that lead to murders rarely make the motives of the crime absolutely clear. In the highly intensive interaction between the presumed offender and the victim the crime may have been provoked, for example, by requiring self-defense, or by consent before the presumed rape of a woman.

In addition, conviction before a jury generally requires that the defendant be judged not only legally but also morally responsible for the crime. In spite of the legal tradition, rape of a prostitute or murder of a really oppressive husband, seems to be a lesser crime. Evidence of moral responsibility is much harder to produce in crimes of passion. Finally, complaint to the police is something of a betrayal of those to whom we have close personal ties. Once the complaint is made, and the immediate danger and anger past, the personal ties or embarrassment of the complainant quite often reassert themselves, and the main source of evidence refuses to testify further.

The processing of the presumed offender then typically takes the following form: the arrest may be made on a warrant after preliminary investigation, but fairly often the offender is still at the scene and is arrested without a warrant; after the arrest supporting evidence must be collected by skilled investigation, both questioning and examination of physical clues; this is generally challenged very carefully and fully in court. A fairly general administrative pattern then is for uniformed patrol police to be called first; they come and take control of the scene and of the relevant evidence, and perhaps make arrests. Then the work passes to the detective force, which tries to establish the case (and generally takes credit for the conviction or blame for the poor case).

Crimes against persons in public places tend to depart from this pattern in several respects. In the first place, the officer is much more likely to happen on the scene, so that his own information is sufficient to justify arrest. Second, the assailant is generally unknown and not intimately tied to the victim. Consequently the location of the assailant may be more of a problem. In the case of strange assailants, however, the establishment of legal and moral responsibility is easier if they are located, and there is less motivation for the complainant to drop the case. The only crime for which statistics are given that uniformly falls in this category is robbery. As expected, the proportion cleared by arrest is somewhat smaller (42.5 percent) and the proportion of charges leading to conviction considerably higher (64.8 percent). ("Robbery" refers to taking things from persons, generally strangers, by violence or threat of violence.)

Crimes against persons, then, normally takes place within the boundaries of morally dense small social systems. They come to the attention of the police typically through complaint, and arrests are usually easy to make. But conviction is very problematic, and requires detailed investigation of high skill.

Illegitimate businesses and "dangerous" organizations   Illegitimate businesses, such as prostitution, the illegal narcotics trade, and gambling in most of the United States, use the institutions of privacy to cloak activities that the society chooses to suppress. "Dangerous" organizations such as revolutionary or conspiratorial political parties stand in approximately the same relation to the institutions of privacy. These types of crime do not have "victims" in the same sense as do theft or murder. Instead the "victim" is an active participant in the system, either as a customer or party member. Consequently complaints do not come from within the system to the same degree that they do with crimes against persons. On the other hand, illegitimate businesses do not generally (directly) create disorder in public places. This means that patrol alone does not produce evidence justifying arrest or conviction. And although revolutionary political organizations must produce speech in public places, the speech is generally tempered enough (or if not tempered, ineffective enough) not to threaten the peace.

These conditions set the stage for the characteristic police practices in this field: "undercover" work, harassment, and regulation of the (relatively epiphenomenal) public aspects of the business. The prevalence of "undercover" work follows directly from the nature of the offense: the fact that it does not produce complaints, and that it takes place behind the barriers that protect privacy. Secret police activity is more prevalent *in societies* where the government routinely invades and distorts the functioning of small social systems; it is more prevalent *within* liberal societies when the suppression of illegitimate business or "dangerous" organizations is demanded by law and police policy.

By harassment I mean periodic or continuous enforcement of laws not normally enforced against the general public against people in illegitimate businesses or "dangerous" organizations. For instance, street soliciting of various kinds may be held to be a nuisance, but this is more likely to be enforced against prostitutes than against the Salvation Army, and the quality of evidence required to arrest prostitutes may be negligible.[7] Or a license required for "street vendors" may be required of the salesman of radical newspapers, though no other news vendors have been required to have licenses.

Harassment is easy to carry out because the participants are quite often infamous, without many friends who will appear in public in their defense, and personally demoralized, without a conviction of their own innocence. This is, of course, more true of people who run illegitimate businesses than of those who belong to "dangerous" organizations. The pattern of harassment produces a degree of discretionary power over illegitimate business by police. This discretion may be privately appropriated by the officer or by a political machine and used to "tax" illegitimate business.

The third pattern of law enforcement activity often produced by illegitimate business or "dangerous" organizations is tight regulation of public manifestations. In Baltimore, for example, the set of bars in which solicitation for prostitution goes on is concentrated in a relatively small area, and during the evening hours this area is very heavily patrolled. This prevents street soliciting and obnoxious forms of "barking" of the strip shows (prevalent, at least several years ago, in San Francisco), prevents the bars from serving minors, keeps bars closed after hours, and generally maintains public decorum without substantially disturbing the business. The same pattern is found in many large cities in the area set aside for "lunatic fringe" speakers. Heavy patrol helps prevent speakers being attacked, prevents potential riots from getting very far, prevents audiences from interrupting traffic, and so forth.

The general problem presented to police by illegitimate business or "dangerous" organizations, then, is that "crimes" do not become "known to the police."[8] When they do become known, conviction is generally relatively easy for the demoralized employees of illegitimate businesses, and for "dangerous" organizations depends on the public temper and the mood of the Supreme Court. In liberal societies, activity by secret police posing as customers of illegitimate businesses or as members of "dangerous" organizations tends to be concentrated in this field. The barriers of privacy require that the police get permission to enter where the "crime" is being carried on, and they have difficulty getting that permission if they are openly policemen. Harassment and corruption are both latent consequences of the legal suppression of systems that function behind barriers of privacy.

Invasion of Private Places by Criminals Burglary, much larceny, and trespass involve the invasion of the private place of another without permission, generally in secret. These crimes present distinctive enforcement problems because they very often result in complaint to the police, yet the secrecy of the act makes it difficult to locate offenders. Relatively few of the "crimes known to the police" are "cleared by arrest." The proportion is lower than that of crimes against persons, either in public (robbery) or in private (see Table 1).

Unless they are caught in the act (which is the main way complaints of trespass originate), the offenders can generally be caught only by physical evidence (e.g., possession of contraband), by informers, or by confession. Confession quite generally happens only when the offender is arrested on some other charge or illegally arrested "on suspicion," and some informing takes place under the same conditions.

If enough evidence has been collected to connect a particular person with the crime to justify arrest, there is generally enough evidence to justify conviction. Contraband does not change its testimony out of love or pity. The act itself communicates its intention much better than does, say, the act of killing someone. The establishment of legal and moral responsibility is therfore not so difficult, and more arrests result in convictions.

These are crimes, then, where both arrest and preparation of evidence are generally the job of specialized investigative police. These police must be highly trained in scientific analysis of physical evidence, must have contacts in the underworld for information, and may find a period of questioning arrested people "under pressure" very useful. Although relatively few arrests are made, generally on the basis of carefully collected evidence and therefore on a warrant, a large share of these result in conviction. These are the crimes, and not the murders that figure so heavily in detective stories, which produce the ideal typical pattern of "detective" activity. A latent consequent of this type of crime is the "third degree."

Disorder and Nuisance in Public Places   The regulation of public places is the central responsibility of patrol police. We may distinguish three main types of public disorder: individual, collective, and structural. Perhaps the ideal type of individual disorder is "drunk and disorderly." By "collective disorder" I refer primarily to riot, parades that get out of hand, and other types of collective behavior, though in unusual circumstances private military groups may create collective disorder. By "structural disorder" I refer especially to the modern phenomenon of the traffic jam. No crowd or individual "wills" a traffic jam.

1. Individual disorder in public places consists mainly of doing things that would be entirely legitimate if done in private, such as getting too drunk to stand up, or sleeping on park benches. Other individual disorder, such as soliciting for prostitution, or begging, may be illegal even if done in private, but is in fact relatively safe there.

This means first of all that there is a good deal of difference in the "commission" of these "crimes" according to the degree of access people have to private places. Homeless men are obviously more likely to commit the crime of vagrancy, which is the crime of being a homeless man. And if they get drunk, homeless men are more likely to have to sleep it off in the street. Since there is a rough correlation between social class and access to private places (particularly *enough* private places to cover most of one's social life), individual public disorder is related to social class even if the behavior of all classes is the same.

The fact that the "commission" of individual disorder is an index of the lack of connection to small social systems results in a main characteristic of these offenders, that they have not the will, the money, the friends, or the reputation to make good use of their legal right to defend themselves. For will depends on social support of intimates; money for defense often comes from the collective resources (or credit) of a small system; friends are products of intimate interaction; and reputation is generally dependent on a guaranty of good behavior by a small system. Those whose ties to small systems are weak are at a disadvantage in all these ways. Hearings before a police court magistrate in these cases are generally purely formalities; it is assumed by all concerned, including the defendant, that the presumed offender is guilty. The only question that remains to be decided is how much *noblesse oblige* the magistrate should show. As Table 1 shows, the conviction rates for these crimes are quite high, and this is not the result of the sterling qualities of the evidence.

The information on which arrest is based is generally collected entirely by the patrolman, and he has a relatively wide degree of discretion about whether behavior constitutes "disorder." Arrests are almost entirely without a warrant. The fact that police information rather than complaint starts the proceedings means that there are no "crimes known to the police" that have not been solved. The FBI has the good sense not to try to report how many people were drunk or disorderly on the streets of the nation during the year. Investigative police are hardly ever involved.

In summary, the substitution of police for small bounded social systems in the government of the streets produces discretionary power in the hands of the police, particularly over population groups that are unlikely to defend themselves vigorously and effectively in court. The arrest is rarely justified to a judicial officer before it takes place, nor afterward except by the word of the policeman. When convictions do not follow on arrest, it is generally due to *noblesse oblige* rather than to defense by the presumed offender.

2. Collective public disturbances are quite often the immediate stimulus to the formation of quasi-military uniform police forces. The London Metropolitan Police were partly an answer to the impending Chartist agitation; many state police forces in the United States were originally designed as a more controllable and delicately adjusted mechanism than the National Guard for dealing with industrial disturbances. Since police forces are almost always in a minority in a riot, their military organization is essential in this field.

Collective public disturbances by their nature involve questions of political legitimacy, the channels of political expression, the nature and role of the military, and other very complex topics. These are beyond the scope of this paper. Briefly, however, police are appropriate tools only for temporary control of acting crowds and are rarely competent to defeat an organized military effort by a social movement (unless they have much more military organization than American police do, as the Spanish *Guardia Civil*), and rarely have much to do with the basically political process of channeling the discontent that results in riot. Their competence does extend to expressive crowds that get out of hand, but, as the reams of material on the collective disturbances surrounding the House Un-American Activities Committee hearings in San Francisco in the Spring of 1960 show, the ultimate questions are not police questions.

3. Structural disorder in public places, as opposed to collective disorder, arises from the disorderly effects of individual "innocent" actions. A traffic jam, or a smog problem, is at most attributable to "negligence" of individuals, that is, to *their* not taking account of the structural effects of their actions. More often, the traffic jam could not have been avoided by people as individuals, even if they tried. Traffic control then consists in the regulation of otherwise innocent action that would have unfortunate consequences if not regulated.

Since the "offenses" do not offend the moral sensibilities of the population, being convicted is not much of a defamation. There are few reasons to protest innocence except to avoid the penalty, but the penalty for "minor" infractions cannot be very great. Though generally preserved in fiction, the whole adversary procedure is generally dispensed with, and all the complicated changes of status of due process are done away with. Patrolmen have factual discretionary power to levy penalties for traffic infractions. The police here play the peculiar role of administrators of the anonymous masses, rather than the role of detectors and punishers of crime.

DETERMINATION OF DIVISION OF LABOR
IN POLICE PRACTICE

We may briefly group these socially determined activities into the functional divisions they normally have in police departments:

1. Traffic patrol and other patrol of structural disorder, which enforce regulations not involving moral turpitude of those who break the law. Typically due process of law is irrelevant to the processing of offenders, arrests are uncommon, and when made are made without a warrant. Enforcement does not involve the invasion of private places.

2. Street patrol (including radio cars), especially in downtown areas, to control individual offenses in public places and to be quickly available in cases of coercion within small social systems. The offenses generally involve some degree of moral disapproval, but the friendlessness and lack of resources of the defendants largely eliminates due process of law. Information is obtained primarily by the patrolman's observation, on which both arrest and conviction are based. Arrests are generally without a warrant.

3. Investigative work, generally involving complaint from a small social system, which has to be turned into acceptable evidence of crime. The crimes may be against people within these small systems, in which case arrest is easy (often done by patrolmen) but conviction difficult. Or it may involve the invasion of private places by criminals, in which case arrest is difficult but conviction easy. Most arrests made on warrants and focus on due process derive from this area. But these kinds of offenses create pressures toward the "third degree," toward illegal search and seizure. It is police activity in this area that makes the police force a heroic and newsworthy enterprise, rather than merely a technical device for administering the streets of a city. And much police ideology about "hardened criminals" derives from work in this area. Many of the differences between federal police and local police, generally attributed to the federal agents' greater competence or the greater control by federal courts (e.g., the fact that federal police generally arrest on a warrant), are attributable instead to their work being almost entirely investigative.

4. Undercover work, in which fraud is used to get inside social systems otherwise protected by the institutions of privacy. Subversion and illegitimate business are the main offenses dealt with.

5. Quasimilitary action, in which the problem is to apply coercion to control the public riot of some social movement. There quite often are few arrests. Perhaps most of the military trappings of police departments derive from their historical origin in the control of rioting.

CONCLUSIONS

The argument of this paper is that differences in police practice with respect to different types of crimes are closely related to the social location of these types of crime vis-à-vis the institutions of privacy. We would be on more solid ground if direct classifications of crimes of one type (such as murder) were made by social location, rather than depending on the known correlation of murder with private places. Then we could determine whether murders that took place between mutually anonymous people showed a systematically different administrative pattern than murders among kin, eliminating the possibility that other features of murder explain the differences in administration noted. Or people arrested for a crime could be systematically classified by the solidity of their connection to small social structures, to see how much of the variation in the operation of due process of law in criminal matters really derives from differences in the strength of the social ties of the offender.

Second, the indexes of differences between administrative practices for different types of crime used here are extraordinarily crude. While this may convince us that there must have been a strong difference in reality to create a difference in such crude measures, and hence indicate that further research is worthwhile, many of the more interesting hypothesized relations cannot be tested by these data. For instance, the proportion of witnesses changing their testimony or refusing to testify further for different types of crime (either the crude types we have used here, or refined social-location types as suggested above) could be computed, to see whether this indeed explains any of the variation between the conviction rates of murder and burglary. Likewise, the proportion of times the complainant named a suspected offender, the length of time between complaint and arrest, the official status of the officer making an arrest, the proportions of arrests where a warrant was previously obtained, the number of entries into private places by police officers in the course of enforcement, and so on, could be precisely computed.

From knowledge of the characteristic social location of different types of crime, we can make predictions about the structural changes that are likely to take place in a subsection of a police department when a new crime is added to its responsibility. If the crime has a fundamentally different social location than the crimes that have traditionally been the responsibility of the subsection, then we would predict that new specialized roles will be developed in the subsection to deal with the new crime. On the other hand, if the new crime is fundamentally similar in social location to the crimes previously dealt with, responsibility for it will probably be added to the role obligations of old roles. For instance, if the control of the narcotics trade (an illegitimate business) is newly added to a police subsection which has previously dealt with burglary, murder, and other crimes of a different kind, we would predict that narcotics law enforcement will quite quickly become the responsibility of specially designated officers. If a newly serious narcotics problem is made the responsibility of a police subsection that already handles illegitimate businesses, such as a vice squad, we would expect much less pressure toward specialization. Any actual study would have to take account of other forces that help determine the degree of specialization, such as the size of police departments. Both the establishment of such a phenomenon, and an exploration of the dynamics of role differentiation under these circumstances, would increase our knowledge of the causes of the division of labor in organizations.

As for the general problem of studying the causal relations between rare events and frequent events, which is in some ways the foundation of the problem of studying authority, we have less to say. It is commonly alleged in police circles that Supreme Court cases on admissible evidence (e.g., whether evidence will be admitted that is collected in an "unreasonably long" period between arrest and appearance before a magistrate) will have a large effect on the efficiency of police practice. I am less hopeful. It seems that with our present research technology, the connection between such rare events and the frequent events on which we can collect statistics must remain a qualitative step in the research process. The definition of private and public places in the law and its application to the situations in which different types of crime are committed is an example of such a qualitative step in this paper. Presumably there is a long chain of events on a large scale, structuring rewards and constraints in police practice, and structuring criminal behavior of different types with respect to the norms established and continually enforced in a few court cases. This chain of events should, in theory, be amenable to study. But it is often a matter of historical time and of rather subtle readjustments of other rare events (such as promotions of policemen) to the new situation, so that in practice such studies are extremely difficult to carry out. It seems to me that if sociology is to enter in a systematic way into the empirical study of the sociology of law, the technique of combining qualitative judgments of which norms apply to which behavior, with statistical study of that behavior, is going to need substantial development. I hope that the strong relations among variables derived in this qualitative way, found in Table 1, help to provide motivation for more attention to this problem.

NOTES

[1] A good summary of the law of arrest is R. M. Perkins, "The Law of Arrest," *Iowa Law Review*, 24 (1940), pp. 201–89.

[2] See E. W. Machen, Jr., *The Law of Search and Seizure* (Chapel Hill: University of North Carolina Press, 1950).

[3] H. E. Flack, ed., *The Annotated Code . . . of Maryland, 1951*, Art. 27, Sec. 666.

[4] *Instructions . . . and Digest of the Statutes, Ordinances and Decisions* (Baltimore: Baltimore Police Department, 1939), p. 13.

[5] A statistical reflection of this could be obtained by computing the proportion of appeals to higher courts of convictions for those types of crime that indicate weak connection to the social structure, such as vagrancy, and comparing this with the rate of appeals for other types of crimes with approximately the same penalties.

[6] For instance, in a study in Denmark, 57.0 percent of murder victims were relatives, 30.8 percent acquaintances (ranging from "close" to "met the day before"),

and only 12.2 percent strangers (see K. Svalastoga, "Homicide and Social Contact in Denmark," *American Journal of Sociology*, 62 [1956], pp. 37–41.

⁷ For the situation in London, see Anonymous, *Women of the Streets* (London: British Social Biology Council, Secker and Warburg, 1955), pp. 18–23.

⁸ Statistics on "crimes known to the police" are not given for these offenses in the *Uniform Crime Reports*, probably for the reasons given above.

28   Everett K. Wilson

Mobility and the Maverick

Congressman Walter went recently to Camp Kilmer for a first-hand check on the maverick migrants from Hungary. Maverick is the word for the mobile—unbranded cattle, calves of unknown maternity. Are they our kind of people? "These are men and women of the same character and integrity as their and our ancestors who, generation upon generation, have come to America to find peace and work, to build for themselves new homes in freedom." So said the President in commenting on the Refugee Relief Act of 1953. Or do they carry the hidden virus of Communism, as Congressman Walter suspects; and as, *mirabile dictu*, Scott McLeod denies?

The alien has always posed problems. Sometimes they seem insuperable; or so formidable as to outweigh any advantages accruing from immigration. The American Indians, apparently, had little confidence in their ability to assimilate the newcomers from Europe. Nor did the "native" Americans who resisted successive waves of migrants, shifting their animus from one ethnic group to another. (A fine study of this resistance is found in Barbara Solomon's recent book, *Ancestors and Immigrants*.)

Resistance to the migrant is neither new nor distinctively American. Wop or dago, Mick or cross-back, kike or sheeny, Okie, Arkie and briar-hopper all have their parallels among peoples elsewhere. Consider "White Australia" or more precisely, as Warren Thompson suggests, "British Australia." On the view and treatment of Indians in Durban, South Africa: or Burmese reaction to the Chinese (the "Jews of the Orient"). Such resistance has a venerable history: the Greek view of the barbarian, the English settlement acts of the 1600's aimed at restricting mobility; and the supercilious rejection of western overtures by the Chinese in the nineteenth century.

The intriguing question is: Why? Why, Ralph Linton asks, does the American, reading "the news of the day, imprinted in characters invented by the ancient semites by a process invented in Germany upon a material invented in China . . . thank a Hebrew God in an Indo-European language that he is a one hundred percent (decimal system invented by the Greeks)

Reprinted from *The Antioch Review*, 17:1 (1957), pp. 60–71, by permission of the author and the publisher.

American (from Americus Vespucci, Italian geographer)?" Why is the migrant viewed as a maverick? But before attacking this question, let's get a fix on our position—or some conception of our fix. What are the dimensions of migratory movement?

For despite the common opposition to the migrant, these movers are a hardy and persistent breed. Some moving slowly, peacefully and generally into uninhabited territory have dispersed through time from Alaska to Tierra del Fuego. Invasion, conquest and colonization have prompted major movements—Mongols and Manchurians, the treks of Boers and Bantus, the peopling of the Mediterranean rim and the Atlantic seaboard. Forced migration drove the Huguenots from France, the Mormons westward, the Nazi victims across the globe. Immigration and internal migration are the contemporary movements with which we're most familiar— peaceful movements, yet not without that pathos possessing "the sad heart of Ruth when, sick for home, she stood amid the alien corn." (This is the mood, if not the message, of Harriet Arnow's bitter tale, *The Dollmaker*.)

Yet still they move, with courage and pertinacity. It seems to us a matter for wonder, if not for irritation, that one of our nationals should wish to live elsewhere. In the great cosmic scheme of things, the chances were at least 180 to 1 against our being native white Christian citizens of the United States. But having beaten the odds, it seems quixotic if not perverse that one should wish to change his citizenship. Yet a fair proportion of European nationals would like to do so had they a choice in the matter. In 1948 the Netherlands Institute of Public Opinion made a study of the number of people in several European countries who would like to emigrate, had they a choice. The percentage were as follows:

England	42 %
Netherlands	32.5
Italy	29
Norway	28
France	25
Denmark	24
Sweden	13

While such responses undoubtedly reflect the worries associated with the current situation at the time of inquiry, a series of studies from 1946 to 1951 reveals a remarkably stable figure representing the percent of Netherlands nationals who would like to emigrate. It has been quite consistently about one-fourth of the population. The Netherlands is an "emigration-minded country."

But many others are so minded, as some scattered illustrations will suggest. Net emigration from Europe between 1946 and 1952 amounted to about 450,000 persons per year. In 1940, about one out of every twenty Japanese lived beyond the islands. Large numbers of overseas Chinese (who formerly participated actively in Chinese government, despite their distance from home) lived in southeast Asia. Fairly large colonies of Indians have settled in Burma, South Africa, Thailand and elsewhere.

Israel is the dramatic example from the receiving end. (If there was little resistance to the migrant here, it was for the obvious reason that Israel is made up of rejected wanderers.) In 1951 the population was 1.4 million. Between 1919 and 1951 Israel had admitted 1.1 million immigrants, a figure representing about 80 percent of the 1951 population. At the end of 1951, new immigrants were 43 percent of the total population of Israel.

In the course of our own immigration history—say 1820 to the present—about 40 million persons have come to the United States; just over a million of them between 1941 and 1950. On the last day of last year the Refugee Relief Act expired under which visas were to have been granted to 209,000 of the 2½ million refugees in Western Europe. Under current executive action we anticipate something on the order of 21,500 immigrants from Hungary.

Readers of [The Antioch Review] will be familiar with the general pattern of internal movements in the United States: the rural-urban migration; the movement from the South and Southeast to the North, East and West; the massive movement of Negroes to northern industrial areas. This movement has probably been promoted in part by military service which, like college and university attendance, often seems to operate as a way-station along the line between farm and factory. Thirty-five percent of our Korean war veterans were classified, before military service, as "employed in agriculture." In June, 1953, only 5 percent were in this classification. Similarly, in the thirteen North Central states between 1940 and 1950, "net migration added 199,532 persons to the urban population while it removed 850,957 persons from the rural population." And for the country as a whole between 1940 and 1950, the decline in rural-farm population due to migration was 8.6 millions. This was a loss of about 31 percent. It occurred during a period when our population increased by about 19 millions.

Examples of movement could be provided indefinitely. We live in a world of flux, a time of transition; and mobility is a continuing and dramatic symbol of the times. Equally persistent is resistance to the mover. Even in the case of Israel, welcoming a polyglot crew of migrants in enormous numbers, there is a tendency among the Sabara to look with derision upon these nouveaux arrivés. This is the problem: why the almost invariable suspicion, derogation of the mover?

The conventional explanations, as we hear the issue debated in this country, are not very convincing. It is asserted that people who move are the rootless incompetents, unable to make good where their conationals succeed. (So, it has been argued, the courageous and worthy Hungarians did not flee; but remained to resist the Communist threat to their country.)

This is countered with the contention that the movers are the adventurous, the daring, those with imagination and initiative. Lacking any measures of these vices and virtues, and with evidence for each side ready at hand, such talk is largely fruitless.

The position once taken by organized labor in the United States is a familiar attempt to explain opposition to migrants. They take jobs, threaten the standard of living of the native American. Warren Thompson has proposed a kind of Gresham's law of population. "Where peoples having different levels of living, based on somewhat similar processes of making a living [technologies], come into competition on the land, it always seems to work out that those willing to work the hardest, live on the least, and raise the largest families, supplant those whose level of living demands more leisure, more consumption goods, and smaller families." But in the United States, at any rate, it has not been a matter of contact between people with similar technologies. Industrial productivity in this country has always surpassed that of our immigrant sources. (Today, with about 6 percent of the world's population, we turn out nearly half the world's industrial product.) And this productive efficiency made possible the absorption of immigrants whose standard of living, however it differed initially from ours, soon reflected the same aspirations. The record of immigration and unemployment since 1890 shows that the two vary inversely: immigration is high when unemployment is low, and conversely. So also President Truman's Commission on Immigration and Naturalization found a striking positive relationship between the percent of foreign born in various regions of the country, and per capita income. Immigrants have been of some economic advantage in filling the ranks of unskilled labor (and perhaps boosting native labor into higher paid occupations). They have contributed to the skilled labor (e.g., barbers, stone masons). Occasionally they have set up industries employing native labor. Yet despite the tenets of free enterprise which might suggest a free flow of labor in a competitive world market, we have been more disposed to place tariffs on labor than on commodities.

The antipathy for the alien has been "explained" in terms of their queer ways, their criminal proclivities, and their subversive propensities. To this the response is made that such queernesses provide a rich cultural diversity; that first generation immigrants have lower rather than higher crime rates; and that the Americanism of the newcomer, a citizen by choice, is likely to approach chauvinism in its ardor.

And so the interminable argument runs. Whether or not any of these "explanations" is in some measure correct, whether correct as a matter of fact or correct as people distort the fact, they seem to be singularly unenlightening. Let me propose another explanation for the general and recurrent view of the migrant as maverick, the alien as a threat.

I anticipate the conclusion by summarizing the argument. This can be put in the form of five propositions. An ordered articulation of human activities is necessary to sustain the values cherished by any human community. To maintain a given social order, appropriate conduct must be rewarded and deviant conduct punished. The effectiveness of such sanctions is a function of frequency and intimacy of human intercourse. The migrant, by definition, is one with whom we have neither frequent nor intimate contact: and thus he escapes the complex of sanctions which guarantees appropriate conduct. His behavior, unpredictable and beyond control, is a threat to those ordered human relationships which reflect and sustain the central values of the group.

The basic proposition postulates order as the *sine qua non* of the human group. To extrapolate from experimental work with hamsters is always dangerous. But it seems certain that when given stimuli cannot be interpreted as leading to predictable outcome, a state can be induced in the experimental animal comparable to a human psychosis. When one synapse doesn't know what the other is up to, the universe falls apart. Take a more homely example. If to the banal greeting "How are you?" we respond literally with a detailed account of our state of health, we may well jeopardize a beautiful friendship. The importance of guaranteeing ordered relationships has been recognized in every enduring human group. It is not, as the currently fashionable excoriation of conformity would suggest, an American invention of recent vintage. The organization man, like the poor, we have always with us. And however much we may reconsider individualism, there are limits beyond which no group can tolerate behavior eccentric to its norms. The procedures of recruitment, indoctrination and separation are tacit recognitions of this basic requirement of order in every human association. Robert MacIver has put it this way:

> Without law there is no order, and without order men are lost, not knowing where they go, not knowing what they do. A system of ordered relationships is a primary condition of human life at every level. More than anything else it is what society means. Even an outlaw group, a pirate ship, a robber gang, a band of brigands, has its own code of law, without which it could not exist.

But we should not overemphasize law as the principal sanction sustaining ordered human relationships. It is not law which urges the concert-goer to rise in his place when the orchestra strikes up the first notes of the national anthem. That the sanction is none the weaker we readily recognize as we conjure up the repercussions for the man who remains—or tries to—with posterior fixed to seat. But it would be gratuitous to belabor the point—the subtle, perhaps insidious, ways in which sanctions are applied to reinforce a given order and limit defections: the indoctrination of the relatively impotent child, the pressures of rumor and gossip, the embarrassment we feel at our gaucheries (essentially behavior inappropriate to the situation and thus unpredicted), the ultimate sanctions of ostracism and death. The point is simply this: that order which is the elementary requirement for human life is not automatically given. From Moses and Darius to Emily Post, this order depends upon the presence of effective sanctions, systematically applied.

Now we come to the heart of the matter, the notion that the migrant escapes or avoids those sanctions which maintain the order. There is an element of hit-and-run about the mobile person. Perhaps the figure of the cop in futile pursuit of the fugitive is appropriate. It is easier to sin in flight than standing still—not merely to get away with it, but to overcome the inhibitions of an internalized code. One is more inclined to heave his banana peel out the car window while moving, rapidly, through a distant countryside than in one's own neighborhood. From the time of Sherman's triumphal depredations to the pillaging of troops in World War II we see mobile armies emancipated from the restrictions of a stationary existence. Perhaps it is true that in such instances a vindictive spirit was linked to retributive justice (although I doubt this was so with the average G.I.). But the case is not so different from that of the ordinary transient who has inflicted injury upon those who are unable to retaliate.

Another example comes to mind. Somewhat less than a year after the establishment of a certain military post, rates of illegitimacy in a neighboring town rose sharply. While the ladies might have expected and the authorities might have anticipated such an outcome, the impact on a relatively small community was sudden, sharp and demanded prompt remedy. Now common sense might indicate the simple and obvious solution: placing the town "off limits." But since there is no record of any rule which cannot be circumvented by a determined enlisted man in the pursuit of happiness, this solution was ineffective. An altogether different proposal was finally accepted. A fair number of girls were recruited to fill clerical positions at the post. Rates of illegitimacy levelled off; and presently declined. To put it coyly, this does not mean that happiness declined. It may mean—and this is my argument—that the influence of subtle sanctions growing out of frequent and intimate contact, transformed exploitive into more responsible—i.e., conforming—behavior. Inter-sex mobility was reduced, intimacy and frequency of contact increased, informal sanctions were effectively if unwittingly applied, and illegitimacy declined.

So much for the first point: a moving target is hard to hit. The second is this: a distant one is hard to hit, too. The details are blurred, the vital spots obscured. It is only when we know a person quite well, his petty prides, his overweening weakness, the values he professes but fails to practice, that we are able to thrust home with telling effect. It is accidental if the stranger rubs us raw. But it is far from accidental with his intimates who can point unerringly to each man's Achilles' heel. Mobility dulls the weapons of control, the effectiveness of sanctions. Ignorance of the other means we do not know how best to wound. Nor, for that matter, how we may best induce, persuade, cajole, reward. The case is quite otherwise with those we know intimately and deal with frequently.

Thus in a basic sense the central characteristics of community provide the mechanisms of constraint. Insofar as we can communicate with others, insofar as we share things in common, self and other merge. This psychic permeability is the essence of community. If the other's conduct is understandable, it is because and to the extent that it reflects our own experiences, capacities, and inclinations. So to fail to meet others' expectations of us is to fail to meet our own requirements of ourselves. To understand that others do expect thus-and-so is to see such expectations from a point of view which is in some measure ours. (Upon this circumstance rests the only chance of resolving differences.) Hence deviation becomes uncomfortable directly to ourselves. This is the recrimination of conscience.

But neither retaliation nor self-recrimination can be effective sanctions for the person who moves. Retaliation doesn't work if the migrant outdistances the cops. But more significantly, the internal controls of self-recrimination are ineffective if there is no community of values to which all subscribe.

I've been suggesting that the migrant is a deviant. But the social and psychological aspects of mobility become clearer if we reverse the proposition: the deviant is a migrant. The deviant is precisely the person whose conduct does not reflect commitment to the group's canons of propriety and rectitude. In this sense he belongs elsewhere. Indeed, this is exactly the way offended natives respond: "Why don't they go back where they belong?" Thus it is altogether possible to be firmly rooted in space, yet emphatically mobile. Who is more mobile than the actor travelling from role to role, emancipated from philistine prescriptions? And who more derogated in respectable society than this same bohemian?

Especially in our present-day world the rootless and the mobile are such role-to-role travellers. It is reflected in multiple group memberships which reduce frequency and intimacy of contact. To continue our figure, you can't hit more than one differently located target at a time. (And if you don't know where the others are located, you'll never even draw a bead on them.) Let us contrast two patterns of group membership as representing the mobile and the rooted. There is the person who is bound to the *same* others by familiar, religious, recreational, economic, political ties. Thus he is linked repeatedly to the same person, but in differing contexts. His circle of interaction is limited. His relationships are repetitive. This is the situation we may see in some small communities: every citizen a Pooh-bah—a variety of hats, but under each a quite familiar face. This is the provincial, the immobile, the rooted. We may find it in isolated population pockets, especially where low literacy and simple technology reinforce physical isolation. (But it should be emphasized that such immobility is not necessarily related to physical isolation. For mobility, if it is as I've suggested a social and psychological fact, is to be understood in social and psychological terms. Physical movement *may*, then, be a condition; but never the core element in understanding mobility. Thus the physically fixed schoolboy may be more mobile than the hobo. Physical isolation, given our means of communication, need not restrict intercourse or limit contact.) Such a pattern of repetitive relationships may be found in a utopian group, a self-acknowledged circle of arbiters of taste—any tight little knot of the elect, as well as in the physically isolated group of rustics. The relevant point here is that under these conditions the vulnerability of each to sanctions applied by others is mightily increased. To offend in situation A invites retaliation not only *in situ*, but in B, C, D, and E.

Contrast this situation with that in which a member of five groups associates in each with altogether different people. Thus he is united with any other by just a single bond. This brings us closer, I think, to the real meaning of mobility. The single-bonded person is liberated from exclusive allegiance to any one of his relationships. He has multiple exposures. Clearly all of his relationships will not be of equal significance to him; or of equal significance in controlling his conduct. But the point is that the intensity of the relationship, especially its coercive character, is greatly diminished in the case of the single-bonded relationship. In the former case, Jones' relationship to Smith is quintupled if both belong to the same five organizations. In the latter case, Jones has a specific relationship with Smith in *one* of the five groups; and with a *different other* in each of the remaining four. In this lies a significant aspect of mobility.

Thus reducing the number of situations in which two persons deal with one another limits the points at which conformity-inducing sanctions can be applied. But beyond this, it involves typically a more fragmentary relationship. For two people unknown to each other outside a given situation, the single-bonded relationship is likely to imply well-defined and limited roles beyond which there are neither rights nor obligations. And so again, the narrow specificity of such a relationship reduces the leverage which can be applied to the role-hopping transient.

This restriction of frequency and intimacy of contact characteristic of the single-bonded relationships in our intricately differentiated society leads to another feature promoting rejection of the mobile. The view of another which is partial and rigid we call a stereotype. From the rich diversity of attributes which makes a man, it seizes upon one, or a few, and identifies the part as the whole. Just as a distant physical object must be incompletely and incorrectly described, so a distant social object is subject to partial and erroneous stereotypes. Indeed the social distance entailed by mobility tends to transmute a social object into a physical object. This not only means that the alien, the migrant is viewed incorrectly; but that he is often seen as intransigent, scarcely assimilable. And so it is supposed that those sanctions promoting order in the community must necessarily prove ineffective.

One final suggestion as to the source of the migrant's intractability—a reason for the peculiar difficulty in bringing him into line. It is hard to apply sanctions effectively to a person of unequal status while retaining him as a member of the group. Note, first of all, that the migrant is generally *not* of equal status with members of the group he joins. The newcomer is always at a disadvantage. He is in a way a suppliant, subordinate, lesser in knowledge, in power and prestige. He may resign himself to the necessities of an unfamiliar situation; but full assimilation as a member of the new group requires more than grudging accommodation. He must accept within himself the goals and means of new associates. But because of his subordinate position, commandment rather than persuasion is the way of gaining conformity. Persuasion—much the more coercive—is the way of peers; commandment is the way of governors.

Sanctions, then, can be more effectively applied between persons of equal status. It is true that the person of higher status may level sanctions against his inferior. But the heaviest sanction, e.g. the discharge of an employee, breaks the relationship altogether. Thus the more powerful person completely loses control over the other. A threat to his power also lies in the inferior's choice of resignation or, in business and industry, the possibility of mitigating the penalty through reparations exacted under some pretext from management by the union; or through retaliatory techniques like feather-bedding or soldiering on the job. Furthermore, in the mass society, the imposition of sanctions is likely to be by remote control and exceedingly impersonal. Hence rather than being an effective sanction, a penalty may be regarded like rain on the day of a picnic—as an act of God.

But under conditions of equal status contact, those sanctions which impose conformity can be effectively applied. Where one is no "better" than the other it is likely to be because the other is dealt with as a person, judged not in terms of technical efficiency but in terms of motives or intent, kindnesses or helpfulness. The effective sanctions are approval and dislike. This implies repeated contacts, conceivably in a broad range of situations. And thus again, at many points in time, in many situations, and with respect to many aspects of his personality, one is vulnerable to the sanctions which may be applied by others.

But such frequency and intimacy of contact among peers is precisely what the migrant lacks. Hence the effective sanctions levelled by one's peers are lacking.

These vagrant notions, then, amount to this. Mobility is by its nature fundamentally disruptive. Barring complete cultural identity, the natures of both host and migrant are such that sanctions inducing appropriate behavior are fairly ineffective. The migrant is a maverick. The social-psychological meaning of ancestry lies in the predictability of conduct. The social-psychological meaning of "acceptable" lies in the control of conduct. The migrant is unacceptable not because his behavior is queer; but because his host is impotent. Almost paradoxically, the migrant is the stronger; his host the weaker. The latter lacks the leverage of peer influence. The stereotyping of a distant social object makes for error; and a conviction (self-fulfilling?) of the migrant's resistance to assimilation. A moving target as he is, the migrant avoids that effective coercion applied to those whose relationships with others are repetitive.

This is the sense in which the migrant is a maverick. I do not mean to suggest that this is bad. There are times when the heat generated by friction is a useful by-product. Mobility may create problems; but this is what begets thought and emotion and sets us seeking for solutions. If problem-solving is the highest task of Homo Sapiens, this is not such a bad outcome.

CHAPTER FIVE
Tensions in the Social Order

Tensions in the Social Order	CONFLICT

COMMENTARY

By focusing attention on how the social order is maintained sociologists have often ignored the fact that there are constant stresses and strains within society which challenge the *status quo*. Men act in ways which challenge the norms and institutions of society. Their behavior may be interpreted by others as deviant or undesirable. They may enter into associations with one another to confront and modify things as they are.

Ralf Dahrendorf, in the chapter on "Conflict Groups, Group Conflicts, and Social Change" drawn from his larger work *Class and Class Conflict in Industrial Society*, considers one of the critical sources of tension in the social order. He examines conflict as it contributes to the integration of social systems and as it promotes social change. Dahrendorf distinguishes between the intensity and violence aspects of conflict and discusses some of the factors which account for the variability of each. Specifically, he examines these aspects of conflict as they relate to differences in the structure of cleavage within society. It is at this point that he distinguishes between the conditions of pluralism and superimposition discussed by Joseph Gusfield in his article "Mass Society and Extremist Politics" in Reading 34 of this text, and examined empirically by William Gamson in his research on "Rancorous Conflict in Community Politics." In his consideration of the factors of structural conduciveness, strain, and integration, Gamson is looking at the same phenomenon from a different perspective.

29 RALF DAHRENDORF

Conflict Groups, Group Conflicts, and Social Change

THE "FUNCTIONS" OF SOCIAL CONFLICT

Classes, understood as conflict groups arising out of the authority structure of imperatively coordinated associations, are in conflict. What are—so we must ask if we want to understand the lawfulness of this phenomenon—the social consequences, intended or unintended, of such conflicts? The discussion of this question involves, almost inevitably, certain value judgments. I think that R. Dubin is right in summarizing at least one prominent attitude toward the functions of social conflict as follows: "From the standpoint of the social order, conflict is viewed from two positions: (*a*) it may be destructive of social stability and therefore 'bad' because stability is good; (*b*) it may be evidence of the breakdown of social control and therefore symptomatic of an underlying instability in the social order. Both positions express a value preference for social stability."[1] I would also agree with Dubin's own position: "Conflict may be labeled dysfunctional or symptomatic of an improperly integrated society. The empirical existence of conflict, however, is not challenged by the stability argument. . . . The fact of the matter is that group conflict cannot be wished out of existence. It is a reality with which social theorists must deal in constructing their general models of social behaviour."[2] But I think that in two respects Dubin might have been rather less cautious. First, I should not hesitate, on the level of value judgments, to express a strong preference for the concept of societies that recognizes conflict as an essential feature of their structure and process. Secondly, and quite apart from value judgments, a strong case can be made for group conflict having consequences which, if not "functional," are utterly necessary for the social process. This case rests on the distinction between the two faces of society—a distinction which underlies our discussions throughout this study. It is perhaps the ultimate proof of the necessity of distinguishing these two faces that conflict itself, the crucial category in terms of the coercion model, has two faces, i.e., that of contributing to the integration of social "systems" and that of making for change.

Both these consequences have been admirably expressed by L. Coser. (Although, to my mind, Coser is rather too preoccupied with what he himself tends to call the "positive" or "integrative functions" of conflict.) On the one hand, Coser states in the unmistakable terminology of the integra-

Abridged from *Class and Class Conflict in Industrial Society* by Ralf Dahrendorf, pp. 206–223, with the permission of the publishers, Stanford University Press, Copyright © 1959 by the Board of Trustees of the Leland Stanford Junior University.

tion theory of society (for which see my italics): "Conflict may serve to remove dissociating elements in a relationship and to *reestablish* unity. Insofar as conflict is the resolution of tension between antagonists it has *stabilizing functions* and becomes an *integrating component* of the relationship. However, not all conflicts are *positively functional* for the relationship. . . . Loosely structured groups, and open societies, by allowing conflicts, institute safeguards against the type of conflict which would *endanger basic consensus* and thereby *minimize the danger of divergences* touching core values. The interdependence of antagonistic groups and the crisscrossing within such societies of conflicts, which *serve to 'sew the social system together'* by cancelling each other out, thus *prevent disintegration* along one primary line of cleavage."[3] On the other hand, Coser follows Sorel in postulating "the idea that conflict . . . prevents the ossification of the social system by exerting pressure for innovation and creativity" and states: "This conception seems to be more generally applicable than to class struggle alone. Conflict within and between groups in a society can prevent accommodations and habitual relations from progressively impoverishing creativity. The clash of values and interests, the tension between what is and what some groups feel ought to be, the conflict between vested interests and new strata and groups demanding their share of power, wealth and status, have been productive of vitality."[4]

Conflict may, indeed, from a Utopian point of view, be conceived as one of the patterns contributing to the maintenance of the *status quo*. To be sure, this holds only for regulated conflicts, some of the conditions of which we shall try to explore presently. Coser's analysis of Simmel[5] has convincingly demonstrated that there is no need to abandon the integration theory of society simply because the phenomenon of conflict "cannot be wished away" but is a fact of observation. In this sense, conflict joins role allocations, socialization, and mobility as one of the "tolerable" processes which foster rather than endanger the stability of social systems. There seems little doubt, however, that from this point of view we can barely begin to understand the phenomenon of group conflicts. Were it only for its "positive functions," for which Coser found so many telling synonyms, class conflict would continue to be rather a nuisance which the sociologist would prefer to dispense with since it may, after all, "endanger basic consensus." So far as the present study is concerned, "continuing group conflict" will be regarded as "an important way of giving direction to social change."[6] Societies are essentially historical creatures, and, because they are, they require the motive force of conflict—or, conversely, because there is conflict, there is historical change and development. The dialectics of conflict and history provide the ultimate reason of our interest in this phenomenon and at the same time signify the consequences of social conflict with which we are concerned.

Dubin's observation that conflict is a stubborn fact of social life is undoubtedly justified. Earlier, we have made the assertion explicit that social conflict is ubiquitous; in fact, this is one of the premises of our analysis.

Possibly, this premise permits even further generalization. There has been in recent years some amount of interdisciplinary research on problems of conflict. In specific features the results of these interdisciplinary efforts remain as yet tentative; but one conclusion has been brought out by them with impressive clarity: it appears that not only in social life, but wherever there is life, there is conflict.[7] May we perhaps go so far as to say that conflict is a condition necessary for life to be possible at all? I would suggest, in any case, that all that is creativity, innovation, and development in the life of the individual, his group, and his society is due, to no small extent, to the operation of conflicts between group and group, individual and individual, emotion and emotion within one individual. This fundamental fact alone seems to me to justify the value judgment that conflict is essentially "good" and "desirable."

If I here assume social conflict, and the particular type of group conflict with which we are concerned in the present study, to be ubiquitous, I want this statement to be understood more rigidly than is usual. At an earlier point I have intimated what I mean by rigidity in this sense. One or two remarks in addition to these earlier hints seem in order. In summarizing earlier research, Mack and Snyder state with some justice that by most authors "competition is not regarded as conflict or a form of conflict."[8] The alleged difference between the two is identified differently by different authors. T. H. Marshall emphasizes common interests, rather than divergent interests, as characteristic of states of competition or conflict.[9] For Mack and Snyder, "competition involves striving for scarce objects . . . according to established rules which strictly limit what the competitors can do to each other in the course of striving; the chief objective is the scarce object, not the injury or destruction of an opponent per se."[10] It seems to me, however, that it is not accidental if Mack and Snyder state a little later that "conflict arises from 'position scarcity' and 'resource scarcity,' " and that therefore "conflict relations always involve attempts to gain control of scarce resources and positions."[11] Despite terminological traditions, I can see no reason why a conceptual distinction between competition and conflict should be necessary or, indeed, desirable.[12] Like competition, conflict involves a striving for scarce resources. From the point of view of linguistic usage, it is perfectly proper to say that conflicting interest groups compete for power. As far as the "established rules" of competition are concerned, they emphasize but one type of conflict, namely, regulated conflict. In the present study, the notion of conflict is intended to include relations such as have been described by many other authors as competitive.

Another distinction almost general in the literature is that between changes "within" and changes "of" or conflicts "within" and conflicts "about" the system. Many authors have been at pains to define these differences. Coser, e.g., proposes "to talk of a change *of* system when all major structural relations, its basic institutions and its prevailing value system have been drastically altered," but admits that "in concrete historical reality, no clear-cut distinctions exist."[13] Marshall distinguishes more specifically "conflict that arises out of the division of labor, conflict, that is to say, over the terms on which cooperation is to take place, as illustrated by a wage dispute between employer and employed," from "conflict over the system itself upon which the allocation of functions and the distribution of benefits are based."[14] Thinking in terms of inclusive epochs like "feudalism" and "capitalism" as well as in terms of the existence of political parties that propose to change "the whole system" can probably explain the widespread feeling that a distinction between "changes within" and "changes of" is necessary. But apart from these, it is surely no coincidence that it was Parsons who emphasized that "it is necessary to distinguish clearly between the processes *within* the system and processes of change *of* the system." This very distinction betrays traces of the integration approach to social analysis. If conflict and change are assumed to be ubiquitous, there is no relevant difference between "changes within" and "changes of," because the "system" is no longer the frame of reference. It may be useful to distinguish more or less intense or violent conflicts and major and minor changes, but these are gradations to be accounted for in terms of intervening variables of an empirical nature. In the present study, no assumption is implied as to the type of change or conflict effected by the antagonism of conflict groups. Wage disputes as well as political conflicts "over the system itself" will be regarded as manifestations of class conflict, i.e., of clashes of interest arising out of and concerned with the distribution of authority in associations.

As with the theory of class formation, the real problems of the theory of class conflict consist in the identification of the empirical variables delimiting the range of variability of forms and types. Change and conflict are equally universal in society. But in historical reality we always encounter particular changes and specific conflicts, and these, even in the more limited sphere of class conflict, present a varied picture of manifold types and forms. Assuming the ubiquity of conflict and change, we have to try to discover some of the factors that influence its concrete shapes.

INTENSITY AND VIOLENCE: THE VARIABILITY OF CLASS CONFLICT

The substance of the theory of class action, or class conflict, can be summarized in one statement: conflict groups in the sense of this study, once they have organized themselves, engage in conflicts that effect structure changes. The theory of class action presupposes the complete formation of conflict groups and specifies their interrelations. However, this tautological statement is evidently not all that can be said about group conflicts, nor is it all that one would expect a theory of group conflict to provide. Beyond a basic assumption of this kind, a theory of class conflict has to identify and systematically interrelate those variables that can be shown to influence patterns of intergroup conflict. In the present chapter several such variables will be discussed in some detail, their selection being guided by the significance they suggest for the course and outcome of class conflict. Before we embark upon this discussion, however, there is one preliminary question that has to be settled. The statement that class conflicts are empirically variable is sufficiently vague to be almost meaningless. What is it—we must ask—about class conflicts that is variable and therefore subject to the influence of factors to be identified? In this question, the categories of intensity and violence are essential. In some connection or other, the terms "intensity" and "violence" can be found present in any discussion of conflict. Here is one example. Mack and Snyder, in their summary of earlier research, on the one hand derive the proposition "a high degree of intimacy between the parties, as contrasted with a high degree of functional interdependence, will *intensify* conflict,"[15] while, on the other hand, they suggest "the more integrated into the society are the parties to conflict, the less likely will conflict be *violent*." The distinction between the two concepts is not perhaps entirely clear from these statements, and, indeed, many authors use them almost synonymously. Yet there is an important difference between them, as Simmel knew when he said: "It is almost inevitable that an element of commonness injects itself into . . . enmity once the stage of open *violence* yields to another relationship, even though this new relation may contain a completely undiminished sum of *animosity* between the two parties."[17] That conflict is variable means that its intensity and violence are variable; but the two may vary independently and are, therefore, distinct aspects of any conflict situation.[18]

The category of intensity refers to the energy expenditure and degree of involvement of conflicting parties. A particular conflict may be said to be of high intensity if the cost of victory or defeat is high for the parties concerned. The more importance the individual participants of a conflict attach to its issues and substance, the more intense is this conflict. For class conflict a continuum might be constructed ranging, e.g., from a conflict within a chess club which involves but a small segment of the individual personalities concerned to the overriding class conflict, in Marx's analyses, in which individuals are engaged with almost their entire personalities. In operational terms, the cost aspect is here crucial. Members of a group that strives to upset the authority structure of a chess club stand to lose less in case of defeat than members of a trade union who endeavor to change the authority structure of the enterprise (or their own social conditions by way of this authority structure).[19] The cost of defeat, and with it the intensity of conflict, differs in these cases.

By contrast to its intensity, the violence of conflict relates rather to its manifestations than to its causes; it is a matter of the weapons that are chosen by conflict groups to express their hostilities. Again, a continuum can be constructed ranging from peaceful discussions to militant struggles such as strikes and civil wars. Whether or not class conflict expresses itself in militant clashes of interest is in principle independent of the intensity of involvement of the parties. The scale of degree of violence, including discussion and debate, contest and competition, struggle and war, displays its own patterns and regularities.[20] Violent class struggles, or class wars, are but one point on this scale.

While violence and intensity of conflict vary independently, several of the factors shortly to be discussed affect both. This fact can be illustrated with reference to one factor which has been mentioned already and which need not therefore be discussed again at any length. I have mentioned in the preceding chapter that the conditions of organization of interest groups continue to affect group conflict even after the complete formation of conflict groups. They are, in this sense, a factor which, among others, accounts for variations of intensity and violence. With respect to the intensity of class conflict, the political conditions of organization appear especially relevant. It may be suggested that, for the individuals concerned, involvement in conflicts decreases as the legitimacy of conflicts and, by implication, their issues become recognized. However, in the ensemble of factors affecting intensity of conflict, the specific weight of the conditions of organization is probably not very great. By contrast, it is considerable among the variables involved in determining the violence of conflict manifestations. As soon as conflict groups have been permitted and been able to organize themselves, the most uncontrollably violent form of conflict, that of guerrilla warfare, is excluded. Moreover, the very fact of organization presupposes some degree of recognition which in turn makes the most violent forms of conflict unnecessary and, therefore, unlikely. This is not to say, of course, that conflict between organized groups cannot be highly intense and violent. The conditions of organization are but one, and not the most important, factor among many. Of these I have selected four which seem to me of particular importance and which will be dealt with separately in the following sections of this chapter.

PLURALISM VS. SUPERIMPOSITION: CONTEXTS AND TYPES OF CONFLICT

One of the crucial elements of the theory of group conflict consists in the strict relation of conflicts to particular associations. Any given conflict can be explained only in terms of the association in which it arose and, conversely, any given association can be analyzed in terms of the conflicts to which it gives rise. In theory, this approach would suggest that inclusive societies present the picture of a multitude of competing conflicts and conflict groups. The two-class model applies not to total societies but only to specific associations within societies (including, of course, the inclusive association of the state, i.e., the whole society in its political aspect). If, in a given society, there are fifty associations, we should expect to find a hundred classes, or conflict groups in the sense of the present study. Apart from these, there may be an undetermined number of conflict groups and conflicts arising from antagonisms other than those based on the authority structure of associations. In fact, of course, this extreme scattering of conflicts and conflict groups is rarely the case. Empirical evidence shows that different conflicts may be, and often are, superimposed in given historical societies, so that the multitude of possible conflict fronts is reduced to a few dominant conflicts. I suggest that this phenomenon has considerable bearing on the degree of intensity and violence of empirical conflicts.

The pluralism-superimposition scale which might thus be constructed has two distinct dimensions. One of these relates to the separation or combination of conflicts of the class type in different associations. Let us restrict ourselves, for purposes of illustration, to the three associations of the state, industry, and the church in countries in which one church dominates the sphere of religious institutions. It is conceivable that the ruling and the subjected groups of each of these associations are largely separate aggregations. The dignitaries of the church may be mere citizens of the state and may have no industrial property or authority. Similarly, the citizens of the state may be church dignitaries or industrial managers. This is the kind of situation here described as pluralistic. Within each of the three associations there are (class) conflicts, but, as between these, there is dissociation rather than congruence. Evidently, complete dissociation and pluralism are, in the case mentioned, empirically rather unlikely. It is more probable that the workers of industry are at the same time mere members of the church and mere citizens of the state. One might expect that the dignitaries of the church are in some ways connected with the rulers of the state and possibly even with the owners or managers of industry. If this is the case, (class) conflicts of different associations appear superimposed; i.e., the opponents of one association meet again—with different titles, perhaps, but in identical relations—in another association. In this case, the personnel of the conflict groups of different associations is the same.

Such congruence may also occur with conflict groups of different types. Again, a realistic example may serve to illustrate the point. We might suppose that in a given country there are three dominant types of social conflict: conflict of the class type, conflict between town and country, and conflict between Protestants and Catholics. It is of course conceivable that these lines of conflict cut across each other in a random fashion, so that, e.g., there are as many Protestants among the ruling groups of the state as there are Catholics and as many townspeople in either denomination as there are country people. However, here, too, we might suspect that dissociation and pluralism are empirically rather unlikely to occur. One would not be surprised to find that most Protestants live in towns and most Catholics in the country, or that only one of the denominations commands the instruments of political control. If this is so, we are again faced with a phenomenon of superimposition in the sense of the same people meeting in different contexts but in identical relations of conflict.

With respect to the violence of manifestations of conflict, the pluralism-superimposition scale is not likely to be a factor of great significance. While there is a possible (negative) correlation between the degree of pluralism and the violence of conflicts in a given society, there is little reason to believe that dissociation of types and contexts of conflict makes industrial strikes, for example, impossible. Only in the inclusive association of the state would there seem to be a probability of pluralism reducing and superimposition increasing the violence of interest clashes.

At the same time, this scale is of the utmost importance for variations in the intensity of class conflict. The proposition seems plausible that there is a close positive correlation between the degree of superimposition of conflicts and their intensity. When conflict groups encounter each other in several associations and in several clashes, the energies expended in all of them will be combined and one overriding conflict of interests will emerge. The situation with which Marx dealt is a case in point. If incumbents of subjected positions in industry are also subjected in all other associations; if they are, moreover, identical with conflict groups other than those determined by authority relations, a "division of society into two large hostile classes" may indeed result—a situation, that is, in which one inclusive conflict dominates the picture of the total society. If, on the other hand, the inevitable pluralism of associations is accompanied by a pluralism of fronts of conflict, none of these is likely to develop the intensity of class conflicts of the Marxian type. There is in this case, for every member of the subjected class of one association, the promise of gratification in another association. Every particular conflict remains confined to the individual in one of his many roles and absorbs only that part of the individual's personality that went into this role.[21] The empirical analysis of pluralism and superimposition of contexts and types of conflict is one of the important problems suggested by the theory of social classes and class conflicts.

PLURALISM VS. SUPERIMPOSITION: AUTHORITY AND THE DISTRIBUTION OF REWARDS AND FACILITIES

In connection with the concept of class situation, we have briefly (and, for the most part, critically) considered the relation between class structure and social stratification at several points in the preceding chapters. It is not my intention to repeat here what has been said before. Rather, I propose to summarize and extend these earlier discussions with particular emphasis on the problems of intensity and violence of class conflicts. It is evident that in the context of a theory of group conflict of the type under discussion, "class situation" is an unnecessary concept. It means no more than what we have described as the authority position of aggregates in association. The condition of a quasi-group in terms of the distribution of authority signifies the "situation" that underlies class conflict. However, the traditional concept of class situation includes a number of elements which, while irrelevant for the formation of social classes, affect their patterns of conflict in ways to be defined. Property, economic status, and social status are no determinants of class, but they do belong to the factors influencing the empirical course of clashes of interest between conflict groups.

As with contexts and types of conflict, the problem of rewards and facilities can be seen in terms of a contrast between divergence and parallelism, or pluralism and superimposition. Thus, property can, but need not, be associated with the exercise of authority. It is conceivable that those who occupy positions of domination in industry do not own industrial property—and, indeed, that those in positions of subjection do own such property. The separation of ownership and control, and certain systems of the distribution of shares to industrial workers, are cases in point. While neither of these structural arrangements eliminates the causes of (industrial) conflict, they have an impact on its intensity and violence. Once again, a certain parallelism between authority and property ownership may seem more probable, but it is not necessary.

The same holds for the economic status of persons in different authority positions. By economic status I shall here understand status in terms of strictly occupational rewards such as income, job security, and general social security as it accrues from occupational position. It is both possible and reasonably probable that those in positions of domination enjoy a somewhat higher economic status, and that these two attributes of social position are in this sense superimposed. But numerous illustrations could also be given for divergences between the two. In the early labor unions, and for many shop stewards and local union secretaries today, authority involves a comparative loss of income and security. In the Roman Catholic Church, authority is supposed, in theory if not in practice, to be accompanied by low economic status. In totalitarian countries, political authority usually conveys high incomes but also a high degree of insecurity which lowers the economic status of dominant groups. Such divergences of authority position and economic status make for a plurality of noncongruent scales of position in a society, which constitutes one of the critical facts of class analysis.

Divergences of position are even more evident if we contrast authority positions with people's social status in the sense of the prestige attached to their position by themselves and by others in relevant universes of ranking. The prestige of power is a highly precarious quantity in all societies. Unless all existing studies are wrong in their findings, there would in fact seem to be, for persons in the upper ranges of the status scale, an inverse relation between the authority and the prestige. The judge (United States), the doctor (Britain), and the university professor (Germany) enjoy a markedly higher prestige than the cabinet minister or the large-scale entrepreneur.[22] Probably, the theory of class conflict with its assumption of opposing role interests would account for this phenomenon. On the other hand, there are and have been associations in which the division of authority and the scale of prestige followed identical lines. In the industrial enterprise, this would still seem to be the case in most countries (and with the possible exception of scientifically trained staff members). Thus, we also find here an empirically variable relation that is likely to affect the course of class conflict.

All examples chosen in the preceding paragraphs serve to illustrate the phenomenon of relative deprivation, i.e., the situation in which those subjected to authority are at the same time relatively worse placed in terms of socioeconomic status. However, in nineteenth-century Europe, and in some countries even today, we encounter what by contrast may be called an absolute deprivation of groups of people in socioeconomic terms. If the social condition of industrial workers, who are as such excluded from authority, falls below a physiological subsistence minimum or "poverty line," the effects of such deprivation are likely to be different in kind from those of relative deprivation. I would suggest that in this case, and in this case only, the superimposition of scales of status and the distribution of authority is likely to increase the violence of class conflict. This is a subtle and complex relation. So far as we know, oppression and deprivation may reach a point at which militant conflict motivation gives way to apathy and lethargy. Short of this point, however, there is reason to believe that absolute deprivation coupled with exclusion from authority makes for greater violence in conflict relations.

Relative deprivation, on the other hand, tends to affect the intensity of conflict rather than its violence. If incumbents of positions of subjection enjoy the countervailing gratification of a relatively high socioeconomic status, they are unlikely to invest as much energy in class conflicts arising out of the authority structure of associations as they would if they were deprived of both authority and socioeconomic status. Dominant groups are correspondingly not so likely to be as involved in the defense of their authority unless their high socioeconomic status is simultaneously involved. In terms of the intensity of conflict, pluralism would again seem to make for a decrease, and superimposition or congruence for an increase:[23] the lower the correlation is between authority position and other aspects of socioeconomic status, the less intense are class conflicts likely to be, and vice versa.

MOBILITY VERSUS IMMOBILITY:
THE "CLASSLESS" SOCIETY

Since Marx, the idea of a "classless society" has remained an often-used category in sociological literature. By "Marxist" scholars it is applied to a number of existing societies as an allegedly valid category of description. But among "non-Marxist" social scientists, too, the concept of classless society is occasionally used for describing empirical states of society. Thus S. Landshut[24] has tried to demonstrate the classlessness of present-day Western industrial societies. In a rather more definite sense, a number of sociologists have employed the concept of a classless society to describe more limited phenomena, such as the agricultural cooperatives of Israel. J. Ben-David, for example, speaks on this basis of a "collectivist," "classless" stage of the social development of Israel.[25] We have now assembled the materials for examining the sense and nonsense of the sociological category of a classless society. This examination will reveal an additional factor affecting the intensity and violence of class conflict.

On the basis of the assumptions and models introduced in this study, the concept of classless society can mean either of two things. First, it may be intended to describe societies in which there are no structures of authority that give rise to the formation of conflict groups and group conflicts. A society is classless if it is "powerless," i.e., if there is no authority exercised in it at all, or if such authority is distributed equally among all citizens. But in this sense the category of classless society is sociologically meaningless. It may be possible to conceive of a society in which all differences of *income* and *prestige* are leveled and which is therefore "stratumless," but it is hardly possible to imagine a society in which there is no differentiation of roles in terms of legitimate *power*. Permanent anarchism is socially Utopian. Any society, and, indeed, any social organization, requires some differentiation into positions of domination and positions of subjection. No matter what the formal nature of the authority mechanism, it is a functional imperative of social organizations. Since classes can be explained in terms of the differential distribution of authority, there is no sociological substance in the assumption of a classless society devoid of differentiated authority structures.

However, the idea of a classless society may be understood in a second sense. It is possible to conceive of a society whose structure contains positions equipped with different authority rights but which does not enable any group of persons to occupy these positions regularly and exclusively. The same might hold in imperatively coordinated associations other than the state, e.g., in industry. Associations may be governed by the principle of an alternating chairmanship, according to which the incumbency of positions of domination may or may not be patterned. The collective settlements (*kibbutzim*) of Israel seem to provide a case in point. At least originally it was stipulated that every member in turn was to occupy the positions of leadership for relatively short periods of time.[26] In view of examples of this kind, it seems plausible to argue that where there is no group which is capable of monopolizing the positions of authority, it is virtually impossible for coherent conflict groups to emerge, and the society or association in question is therefore classless. To be sure, this is a kind of classlessness rather different from that of the Utopian anarchy; still, it cannot be denied that it makes sense of speak of classlessness in this case alone. We might say that societies and associations governed by a permanently "alternating chairmanship" are classless so far as social mobility is concerned, for it is not the structure of positions but the fluctuation of personnel that in this case prevents the formation of classes and conflict between them. The example of classlessness by fluctuation provides a welcome opportunity to try to settle the intricate problem of the relationship of social mobility to class conflict.

Here, as elsewhere, the concept of social mobility is too general to be useful. Different types of mobility have to be distinguished, and their relation to class conflict examined separately. For purposes of this analysis, it seems sufficient to distinguish between intergeneration mobility—i.e., fluctuations that from the individual's point of view occur at the beginning of his occupational (or even educational) career—and intrageneration mobility, i.e., fluctuations during the occupational life of the individual. Either of these, if present to any considerable extent, of course characterizes societies in which class membership is not an inescapable and inherited fate. We shall presently have to return to this other extreme of the mobility scale which, according to our theory, suggests a very high intensity of class conflict.

Intergeneration mobility seems fully compatible with class formation and class conflict. If a man's position in the authority structure of an association remains the same throughout his membership in this association, it appears likely that he belongs to a quasi-group as well as to an interest group growing out of this, even if his son or his father belongs to a different class. Schumpeter's comparison of classes with "a hotel or an autobus" which "are always occupied, but always by different people," is here pertinent.[27] Where the personnel of classes changes between generations only, there is a sufficient degree of stability to permit the formation of conflicting interest groups. Janowitz's finding that intergeneration mobility has no detrimental consequences for the coherence of secondary groupings may be regarded as an empirical confirmation of this thesis.

The case of societies in which there is a high degree of intrageneration mobility is rather more difficult. To begin with, further distinctions are here required. Not all types of intrageneration mobility affect class formation and class conflict. At least potentially, classes are large groupings which may display, from the point of view of social stratification, considerable differentiation within themselves. Mobility within classes, however, is entirely irrelevant for our context. Thus, upward and downward movements between skilled, semiskilled, and unskilled industrial occupations do not affect the stability of the conflict group of industrial workers. Moreover, single upward or downward moves by individuals, even if they involve a change of class allegiance, do not appear destructive of classes. It is only the institutionalized principle of an alternating chairmanship that may give rise to a state of quasiclasslessness. If the individual can change his class belongingness at will, or is even forced to do so regularly; if, e.g., the worker can become an entrepreneur merely if he wants to; or if every member of the community has to be mayor at least once—then we encounter a type and a degree of intrageneration mobility that makes class formation and class conflict impossible. In this case, class belongingness becomes an accidental or merely temporary occurrence. Although there still is a quasi-group structure of authority roles, the continuous exchange of their incumbents makes impossible the organization of interest groups defending or attacking the legitimacy of authority structures: there is no class conflict, and there are no classes in the strict sense.

As a mobile society (of the intrageneration variety), the classless society is thus a sociological category of realistic significance. However, one qualification to this conclusion is necessary. There is something to be said for an empirical generalization which Mosca calls the "law of inertia": "All political forces have the property which in physics is called inertia, i.e., a tendency to stay in a given state."[28] Ben-David has specified this "law" with respect to Israel. For him, classlessness in the indicated sense characterizes "revolutionary periods" of social development rather than lasting types of social order.[29] Usually, these periods last but a few years. Then, that "articulation of the power structure" and "functional differentiation" sets in which Ben-David demonstrates for the social structure of the professions in Israel.[30] Although the rulers of totalitarian states like to operate with an "ideology of perpetual national emergency," as demonstrated impressively by Bendix,[31] for which the well-known theory of the "permanent revolution" is an example, it is plausible that the indicated state of quasiclasslessness is never more than a combination of transitory processes of radical change (which soon gives way to a minimum of stability) and of monopolization of power that makes possible the formation of classes and conflict between them. Classlessness by (intrageneration) mobility is, in sociological analysis, a limiting case that always tends toward its own abolition and that may therefore be ignored. There is no reason to assume that a stable society can operate on the principle of the continuous patterned exchange of the personnel of authority positions.[32]

While social mobility, apart from its limiting case of permanent exchange between the classes within generations, cannot thus be said to present an obstacle to the formation of classes and the existence of class conflict, there can be little doubt that it affects the intensity of class conflict. From the point of view of mobility two distinct types of classes may be disinguished. With respect to dominant conflict groups, Mosca calls one of these the "aristocratic class" bent on the "maintenance of authority for the descendants of those who possess it at a given point of time," and distinguishes it from the "democratic class" characterized by the "tendency to rejuvenate the ruling class by upward mobility of persons from the ruled class."[33] G. D. H. Cole confines the term "class" to the first of these types and refers to the second as "elite."[34] In analogy to those terms of Max Weber's frequently used in connection with social mobility I would recommend speaking here of "closed" and "open" classes. Where allocation to authority positions is based on ascriptive criteria, we find closed classes. By contrast, open classes are recruited anew in every generation. These types are nevertheless but two points on a scale of numerous gradations. From caste-like rigidity to quasiclasslessness there is a continuum of types of social classes determined by degrees of inter- and intrageneration social mobility. It seems plausible that this continuum also defines a scale of conflict intensity. There is an inverse relation between the degree of openness of classes and the intensity of class conflict. The more upward and downward mobility there is in a society, the less comprehensive and fundamental are class conflicts likely to be.[35] As mobility increases, group solidarity is increasingly replaced by competition between individuals, and the energies invested by individuals in class conflict decrease.

It is easy to see that the correlations between conflict intensity and empirical variables suggested in the preceding sections of this chapter all involve a psychological factor as well. The intensity of conflicts is a function of the involvement of individuals. Earlier I have suggested that this involvement is likely to be greater if the individual participates in specific conflicts with several of his roles than if he participates only with one. With respect to mobility, our proposition might be reformulated in psychological terms also. If the individual sees for his son, or even for himself, the chance of rising into the dominant or falling into the subjected class, he is not as likely to engage his whole personality in class conflicts as he is when class position is of a more permanent nature. While in general these psychological assumptions are probably safe to make, it has to be recognized that from the individual's point of view nonstructural factors may also influence his involvement in group conflict. Without doubt there are psychological constellations that make one individual more "quarrelsome" than another. I would suggest that individual variations of this kind are of but minor significance for the overall intensity of class conflict; at the same time, their presence must not be overlooked in a comprehensive analysis.

NOTES

[1] "Approaches to the Study of Social Conflict: A Colloquium," *Conflict Resolution*, 1 (1957), p. 183. Hereafter referred to as "Approaches . . ."

[2] *Ibid.*, p. 184.

[3] L. A. Coser, *The Functions of Social Conflict* (Glencoe, Ill.: The Free Press, 1956), p. 80.

[4] L. A. Coser, "Social Conflict and Social Change," *British Journal of Sociology*, 7 (1957), pp. 197, 198.

[5] Coser, *The Functions of Social Conflict, op. cit.*

[6] "Approaches . . . ," p. 194.

[7] This and numerous other statements in the present chapter are based on discussions with and publications of psychologists, anthropologists, lawyers, and social psychologists at the Center for Advanced Study in the Behavioral Sciences, Stanford, California. John Bowlby, M.D., and Professor Frank Newman, LL.D., have been particularly helpful in making suggestions. In support of the statement in the text I might also refer, however, to the symposium published in *Conflict Resolution* ("Approaches . . .") which includes contributions by economists, sociologists, social psychologists, anthropologists, and psychologists, and strongly supports my point.

[8] "Approaches . . . ," p. 217.

[9] T. H. Marshall, "The Nature of Class Conflict," in *Class Conflict and Social Stratification* (London: n.p., 1938), p. 99. See also Reinhard Bendix and S. M. Lipset, eds., *Class, Status and Power: A Reader in Social Stratification* (Glencoe, Ill.: The Free Press, 1953) and T. H. Marshall, *Citizenship and Social Class* (Cambridge: n.p., 1950).

[10] "Approaches . . . ," p. 217.

[11] *Ibid.*, pp. 218–219.

[12] At least, no such reason has been put forward. It might be argued, of course, that the concept of competition employed in economic theory is rather different from that defined by Marshall or Mack and Snyder, and does not carry any conflict connotation. I am not entirely sure that this argument is justified, but for purposes of the present analysis competition in a technical economic sense will be excluded.

[13] Coser, "Social Conflict and Social Change," *op. cit.*, p. 202.

[14] T. H. Marshall, "The Nature of Class Conflict," *op. cit.*, p. 99.

[15] "Approaches . . . ," p. 225.

[16] *Ibid.*, p. 227.

[17] Coser, *The Functions of Social Conflict, op. cit.*, p. 121.

[18] All italics in the quotations of this paragraph are mine.

[19] I have as yet not given a systematic exposition of the patterns of change effected by class conflict; the formulation in the text may therefore give rise to misunderstandings. These will, I hope, be cleared up in the section on "class conflict and structure change" later in this chapter.

[20] In terms of the distinction thus introduced, we are now able to reformulate the contrast between the conception of conflict here assumed and that of several other authors. The latter tend to confine the term "conflict" to one point on the scale of degree of violence, namely, highly violent clashes. In the present study, however, conflict is conceived as including the whole scale, i.e., any clash of interest independent of the violence of its expressions.

[21] This type of analysis seems to me to provide one of the answers to the question why there is no socialism in the United States. Throughout her history, the pluralism of associations and conflicts has made inclusive conflict groups held together by quasi-religious ideologies unnecessary. There has been no single group that enjoyed universal privilege or suffered universal alienation.

[22] For relevant data, cf. the studies by the National Opinion Research Center (National Opinion Research Center, "Jobs and Occupations: A Popular Evaluation," in *Class, Status and Power: A Reader in Social Stratification*, Reinhard Bendix and S. M. Lipset, eds. [Glencoe, Ill.: The Free Press, 1953]), Glass (D. V. Glass, ed., *Social Mobility in Britain* [New York: Humanities Press, 1954]), and Bolte (K. M. Bolte, *Sozialer Aufstieg und Abstieg. Eine Untersuchung über Berufsprestige und Berufsmobilität* [Stuttgart: n.p., 1959]).

[23] This proposition must be opposed to the assumption of integration theorists that the congruence of different scales of social position is a requisite of stable, integrated societies (cf. Parsons in *Class, Status and Power: A Reader in Social Stratification*, Bendix and Lipset, eds., *op. cit.*). The exact opposite seems true, even from the point of view of integration theory. I cannot help feeling that this is one of the points at which integration theorists display—unwillingly, to be sure—almost totalitarian convictions.

[24] Siegfried Landshut, "Die Gegenwart im Lichte der Marxschen Lehre," in *Hamburger Jahrbuch für Wirtschafts- und Gesellschaftspolitik*, H.-D. Ortlieb, ed., Vol. I (Tübingen: n.p., 1956).

[25] Joseph Ben-David, "The Rise of a Salaried Professional Class in Israel," in *Transactions of the Third World Congress of Sociology*, Vol. III, London, 1956.

[26] The same principle (of "annuity") may also be found in other organizations, such as in German universities where the administrative and scholastic head (*Rektor*) changes every year, and every full professor must (or may) expect to be elected in his time.

[27] J. A. Schumpeter, "Die sozialen Klassen im ethnisch homogenen Milieu" (1927), in *Aufsätze zur Soziologie* (Tübingen: 1953), p. 171.

[28] Gaetano Mosca, *Die herrschende klasse* (Bern: n.p., 1950), p. 61.

[29] Joseph Ben-David, "The Rise of a Salaried Professional Class in Israel," in *Transactions of the Third World Congress of Sociology*, Vol. III, London, 1956, p. 303.

30 *Ibid.*, p. 309.

31 Reinhard Bendix, *Work and Authority in Industry: Ideologies of Management in the Course of Industrialization* (New York: Harper & Row, 1956), p. 443.

32 There is possibly some connection between the size of associations and the feasibility of the principle of alternating chairmanship: the larger the association, the smaller the probability that complete openness of the authority positions will be maintained for longer periods of time. It may be noted, here, that even in the Soviet Union purges have become more difficult technically today than they were in 1935.

33 Gaetano Mosca, *Die herrschende klasse* (Bern: n.p., 1950), p. 322.

34 G. D. H. Cole, *Studies in Class Structure* (New York: Humanities Press, 1955).

35 From this point of view, the limiting case of quasiclasslessness becomes part of the intensity scale; it is distinguished in this sense not by the absence of classes, but by an intensity of conflict amounting to zero. In view of our assumption that class conflicts are universal, this seems the most plausible formulation of the case.

30 William A. Gamson

Rancorous Conflict in Community Politics

Community issues differ in many respects. Some involve vitriolic exchanges of threats and denunciations while others run their course through routine hearings and are resolved before unfilled council chambers. The same issue—for example, fluoridation—may run its course in undramatic fashion in one town, but prove to be the trigger for an explosive confrontation in another town with seemingly similar characteristics. This paper addresses itself to the structural differences between those communities in which such outbursts occur and those in which they do not.

In particular, two ways of carrying on conflict in the local community are contrasted. In *conventional conflicts*, established means of political expression are used to influence the outcome of issues. Opponents regard each other as mistaken or as pursuing different but legitimate goals, but not as the representatives of evil forces. Such tactics as threats of punishment, personal vilification, and deliberate, conscious deceptions are not involved. In contrast to conventional conflicts, *rancorous conflicts* are characterized by the belief that norms about the waging of political conflict in American communities have been violated. In such conflicts, actions occur which produce a shared belief that tactics used to influence the outcome are "dirty," "underhanded," "vicious" and so forth.

Some communities are much more prone than others to rancorous conflicts. The differences between rancorous and conventional communities can be organized under three general headings: structural conduciveness, structural strain, and structural integration.[1] *Conduciveness* refers to the extent to which structural characteristics in the community permit or encourage rancorous conflicts. *Strain* refers to the extent to which structural

Reprinted from *American Sociological Review*, 31:1 (1966), pp. 71–80, by permission of the author and the publisher.

characteristics generate discontent or dissatisfaction among the community members. *Integration* refers to the extent to which structural characteristics prevent or inhibit rancorous conflict. Although integration is just the other side of conduciveness, each refers to different structural elements. In other words, we do not consider the absence of integration as an element of conduciveness or the presence of integration as the absence of conduciveness.

The three categories of determinant are highly related to each other. High conduciveness will not produce rancorous conflict if unaccompanied by strain nor if, although accompanied by strain, structural integration is great. High strain will not produce rancorous conflict unless the social structure is conducive to conflict and structural integration is inadequate. The absence of structural integration will not produce rancorous conflict if there is little strain or conduciveness. In other words, we should expect rancorous conflicts *to occur most frequently in those communities characterized by high conduciveness, high strain, and low integration.*

Structural Conduciveness   Such highly general categories as conduciveness, strain, and integration need specification if they are to be measured. With respect to conduciveness, we will focus on two aspects of community social structure: the degree to which it encourages widespread citizen participation and the degree to which it offers highly visible targets for the expression of rancor.

Participative Political Structure   *The more the political structure permits or encourages widespread citizen participation, the greater is the conduciveness to rancorous conflict.* Since it is typically argued that such conflict is encouraged by the *closing* of channels of legitimate political expression, this hypothesis needs defense. The argument for the proposition may take a weak or a strong form. In the weak form, a distinction is made between the intensity and the frequency of rancorous conflict. In high participation communities, it is argued, the political system offers not only an instrumental channel but an expressive one as well. Mild discontent which might otherwise find no outlet or a nonpolitical one is encouraged to find political expression. In finding frequent release in this fashion, such discontent does not build up an explosive potential. Although rancorous conflicts may occur less frequently in communities with a nonparticipative political structure, they have more intensity when they do occur.

The stronger form of the argument is a denial of the counter-proposition that the blocking of channels of political expression encourages rancorous conflict. This argument challenges the assumption that there is a reservoir of discontent which will either find controlled outlet in legitimate political expression or will accumulate until the dam bursts. Instead, it is assumed that the relief or exacerbation of discontent depends on the nature of the resultant decisions made and not on the catharsis which comes from political expression. If the political system allows for high political participation but does not deal successfully with the sources of dissatisfaction, then rancorous conflicts are *more* likely to occur because strain is combined with high conduciveness. Only when political participation is combined with the influence which can alleviate the source of discontent do rancorous conflicts become less likely. This argument does not imply that high citizen participation is necessarily conducive to rancorous conflict (and hence is bad), but merely that participation does not automatically remove strain.

Given the truth of this proposition, then it is false that such actions as civil rights demonstrations must lessen the probability of other less orderly expressions. As long as the underlying sources of strain are not dealt with, such participation simply increases structural conduciveness and thus makes other expressions more likely. Of course, if the action also helps to remove the strain, for example, by aiding the passage of remedial legislation, then the *net* effect may be to reduce the probability of other less orderly expressions.

A study of fluoridation by Crain, Katz, and Rosenthal contains some suggestive results concerning this hypothesis.[2] They find that the participative nature of the political structure affects both the degree of controversy about fluoridation and the likelihood of its adoption. "Governments which do not place 'obstacles' such as political parties between the citizen and the decision-makers experience the pattern of a large number of referenda and high controversy [as well as high rejection]." Fluoridation is at least more likely to provoke strong controversy where participative political structures provide conduciveness.[3]

Solidary Groups   The greater the clarity of solidary groups within a social structure, the greater is the conduciveness to rancorous conflict. Communities differ in the extent to which they contain subgroups with: (1) feelings of membership or identification with a group or collectivity; (2) feelings of common interest with respect to political decisions; (3) a common style of life, norms, and values; (4) a high rate of interaction among themselves. The degree of solidarity of a subgroup is its magnitude on the above characteristics; the clarity of solidary group structure is the extent to which there exist community subgroups of high solidarity.

Clearly identifiable solidary groups are conducive to rancorous conflict because they provide readily identifiable targets for hostility. Such subdivisions of the community do not in themselves signify cleavage. Nevertheless, any clear-cut basis of differentiation among the citizens of a town may provide a structural basis for the development of intergroup hostility if there also exist strains and low integration among solidary groups.

Structural Strain   Any part of the social structure may produce strains which are relevant for rancorous conflict in the community. Many strains originate outside of the community but have ramifications for the social and political life of the town. There are undoubtedly strains deriving from fear of nuclear war, increasing bureaucratization, depersonalization, commer-

cialism, manipulation, and so forth. Such strains may make their own contributions to rancorous conflicts in the community,[4] but they are felt by all
communities, rancorous as well as conventional. Therefore, we must turn
to strains which can differentiate our communities in order to explain why
some are prone to rancorous conflict and others are not.

There are many possibilities. Although the specification of such strains
requires detailed knowledge of the particular communities in question, it
seems likely that they are connected with change. The change might
include, for example, rapid economic growth or decline, heavy in-migration
or out-migration, or shifts in the distribution of power in the community.
For two reasons I have chosen to focus on strains emanating from a shift
in political control: (1) the existence or nonexistence of a shift in control
sharply differentiates the communities studied here; (2) a shift in political
control is likely to be a reflection of other strains as well as a creator of
strains in its own right.

*Shifts in political control are a source of structural strain which con-
tribute to rancorous conflict.* I have in mind here something broader than
the circulation of elites. In particular, two kinds of shift will be considered.
They have in common the existence of a relatively homogeneous group
whose leaders find that they face competition in areas of decision-making
where they did not before, or that they are competing less successfully than
before. In one type of community, there are clear solidary groups with one
gaining or losing political power relative to others. In a second type of
community, a homogeneous native population has been, or threatens to be,
supplanted by a large, heterogeneous, and politically active group of
newcomers.

Structural Integration   Strain and conduciveness deal with those characteristics of social structure that promote or encourage rancorous conflict.
We now turn our attention to those features which tend to control or inhibit
such expressions. Basically, we expect rancorous and conventional communities to differ in the extent to which potential antagonists are bound
together. In particular, we examine the connections which exist between
those with different opinions on community issues. Are proponents and
opponents bound by associational ties, by friendship, or by shared backgrounds? If they are not, then we should expect a given amount of strain
and conduciveness to be more likely to produce rancorous conflict. We will
consider three kinds of ties here.

Organizational Ties   *The greater the degree of common organizational
membership among proponents and opponents, the greater the resistance
to rancorous conflict.* If the organizational life of a community puts potential antagonists together in a variety of meetings over a variety of issues,
they are likely to find occasions for agreement, to develop bonds of friendship, a sense of joint accomplishment, and other integrative ties. When a

disagreement occurs, it should be less likely to produce the kind of break in a relationship which rancorous conflict represents.

Interpersonal Ties   The greater the degree of friendship among proponents and opponents, the greater the resistance to rancorous conflict. If potential antagonists know each other well socially, such friendship bonds should help to provide that degree of trust and belief in good faith which inhibit rancorous conflicts.

Shared Background   The more proponents and opponents tend to be of different length of residence, nationality background, education, and religion, the less the resistance to rancorous conflict. These four bases of differentiation were chosen because they seemed particularly likely to be correlated with partisan divisions in the set of New England communities we studied. Since these are the bases of differentiation that presumably underlie solidary groups, this hypothesis might appear to be simply another statement of the earlier one on structural conduciveness. We argued above that the existence of clear sub-groups was conducive to rancorous conflict but that they did not, in themselves, signify cleavage. It is possible to have solidary groups which cross-cut issues, thus giving proponents and opponents an important common group membership. It is also possible to find the opposite—that proponents and opponents have different background characteristics but lack any feeling of membership or identification with distinct community sub-groups. Even where clear solidary groups are not present, the absence of these integrative bonds should make such communities more vulnerable to rancorous conflict. Finally, it is possible to have full fledged cleavages in which clearly defined solidary groups exist and do correspond to divisions on issues. This condition combines conduciveness with lack of integration; when strain is added, we should particularly expect rancorous conflict.

STUDY DESIGN

The data to be presented here are drawn from a study of fifty-four issues in eighteen New England communities. The towns ranged in size from 2,000 to 100,000, with a median of approximately 10,000. Seven of the communities were essentially suburbs of Boston, three were resort towns, and the remaining eight were more or less independent cities with some industrial base of their own. All but two of the communities were in Maine or Massachusetts.

Material on these communities was gathered through interviews with 426 informants, an average of twenty-four per town, supplemented by information from a variety of documents. Interviewing was done by teams of three or four individuals who stayed in each community for several days. Three issues were studied in each town, one of which, fluoridation, was common to all eighteen. The presence of a decision on fluoridation was, in fact, the basis of selection of these communities; the eighteen comprise all those New England communities which made a fluoridation decision during an eighteen-month period of data collection.

Before any interviewing began, each town was investigated through such sources as the local newspaper, formal statistical data from the state and federal censuses, city planning reports, annual town reports, and various state manuals. The persons interviewed fell into two categories: active partisans on both sides of each of the three issues; and people named by these "issue leaders" as influential in the community, i.e., as "reputational leaders."

Identifying Rancorous Conflicts   Respondents were not asked directly about the fairness or legitimacy of the tactics used to influence the outcome of the three issues studied in their town. They were asked what those in favor did and what those against did to promote their side, in addition to a number of more specific questions about activities designed to influence the outcome. To identify rancorous conflict, we must rely on charges made spontaneously about the illegitimacy of tactics used. Despite the absence of direct efforts to elicit such statements and the reluctance of some informants to discuss such matters with outsiders, there were 161 different charges of illegitimate tactics made by the 426 people interviewed.

We coded various kinds of charges. They had in common the belief on the part of the informant that individuals or groups in the community deliberately and with full consciousness used improper means in an attempt to influence the outcome of a community decision. In a few cases, the objectionable tactics were not specified, but the campaign as a whole was described as dirty, vicious or underhanded. More specific charges concerned the use of threats, efforts to degrade or humiliate, attempts to punish people in ways like depriving them of their jobs, lying, and deliberate efforts to play on prejudice or irrational fears.[5]

In some communities, as many as half of the informants made such charges on at least one issue, while in others there was no more than a single charge. Even though some of the charges were doubtful, the existence of charges by independent informants will be taken as sufficient evidence in itself of the collective phenomenon of rancorous conflict. In other words, we simply require assurance that the belief in illegitimate tactics is a *shared* and not an idiosyncratic one; the veracity of a charge of dirty politics is generally a matter of interpretation in any event.

Those communities in which such charges are prevalent will be called *rancorous*; those in which they are rare will be called *conventional*. The following criterion divides the eighteen towns into two groups of nine: all towns in which at least two individuals make charges of illegitimate tactics on at least two different issues are rancorous; the remainder are conventional. In the nine rancorous towns so defined, an average of ten informants per town make such charges and in none of them do fewer than six different individuals make charges. In the nine conventional towns, an average of three informants per town make such charges and in only one of them[6] do more than four individuals make a charge.

Selection of Issues   Since we are classifying towns as a whole by what happens on as few as two issues, the question of how each issue was selected is important. The two issues studied in addition to fluoridation were chosen because of their local salience. To the extent that controversy, and especially hostile controversy, made issues salient to informants, it is highly unlikely that unchosen issues would produce as many charges of illegitimate tactics as chosen ones. Among the rancorous towns, there may have been other rancorous conflicts in addition to the ones studied, but this would not alter the classification of the town as rancorous or conventional.

Both "issue leaders" and "reputational leaders" were asked to name the most important issues that had arisen in their town in the previous five years and they named, on the average, between three and four issues. Clearly, there are many competing criteria of importance.[7] Degree of controversy, amount of money involved, and number of people affected are a few of those that might be invoked. Some issues may qualify on more than one criterion. Issues which involve a lot of money are likely to affect many people and in different ways, and thus provoke controversy.

Perhaps this latter fact accounts for the relatively high degree of consensus which one gets in answer to a question on important issues. Of the 54 issues studied, 26 were mentioned by a majority of the respondents in the town.[8] Furthermore, there was a good deal of convergence on the issue mentioned first or singled out as most important. In eleven of the eighteen towns, a majority mentioned a particular issue first or as most important, and in all but one of these the issue was included in the 54 studied.[9] Eighteen of the issues concern fluoridation, eleven concern schools, eleven are issues over the development of some new community facility or service, eight are zoning issues, and the other six are an assortment which includes changes in the form of government and urban renewal.

INDEPENDENT VARIABLES

Participation Political Structure.   This variable refers to the *formal* political structure of the community. Indices of a participative structure include formal provision for frequent referenda, direct primaries, and other occasions for direct citizen participation in decision-making.

New England communities are peculiar in political structure. An extremely large number of decisions are made by the electorate rather than by representative bodies. In some instances, state laws make referenda mandatory. For example, fluoridation can only be adopted through this form of decision in Maine and Massachusetts. Only 12 of the 54 issues studied were decided by representative decision-making bodies. However, since eleven of the communities studied had a town meeting form of government but seven did not, they can be differentiated on this basis. Nevertheless those designated here as "non-participative" would hardly warrant this description if we considered a national sample of communities.

Solidary Groups The identification of solidary groups, when they play a prominent role in the political life of a town, is not difficult. They become such a salient part of the social landscape that their existence is explicitly or implicitly recognized in almost any detailed description of the town. Statements referring to any distinct sub-group in the community were identified in the interviews, and specifically those which attributed some common outlook to the groups mentioned. Questions on community changes, on the characteristics of newcomers, and on religious and ethnic groupings provided the major stimuli for such comments although they appeared spontaneously in many other parts of the interview. The following quotations from respondents in different towns are illustrative:

> There is a terrific growth of population, an influx of largely Jewish Democratic voters, which is changing the complexion of the city.
> [The newer group] tends to be younger, more liberal and not Protestant.
> [One] thing is the influx of people from the larger towns who want to say that they live in a small town, but have big city ideas.
> We have an extremely active Franco-American population. . . . never could see eye to eye with the rest of the town. . . . they are a very closely knit clannish group—church, political interests hold them together. They regard themselves as a minority group.

Communities were classified as having clearly defined solidary groups if 50 percent or more of the respondents in the town mentioned some specific group or set of groups. Nine of the eighteen towns have clearly defined solidary groups by this criterion. Seven of these nine have ethnic groupings while the other two have separate geographical enclaves which are not ethnically distinct. There is an element of arbitrariness in the ethnic label for those seven towns, since members of some of these solidary groups not only have the same ethnic origin but also live in a particular section of town, hold predominantly working class jobs, have the same religion, speak a common second language other than English, go to separate schools, and share a similar political ethos. The ethnic label is shorthand for a large number of similarities.

Shifts in Political Control Respondents were asked a number of questions on political agreement and disagreement among groups and leaders in the town. At the end of this series, they were asked, "You've given me a description of the way the town is now. Has the town been like this throughout the last ten or fifteen years?" and, if they dissented, "What was it like before?" Only certain kinds of answer were coded as indicating shifts in political control. If the respondent said, "A younger, more vigorous group has taken over in the last few years," this was *not* coded as a shift unless some characteristic in addition to age was mentioned. Typical examples of the sort that *were* coded as representing a shift include:

Before the [X] plant opened this was pretty much a country town. Now the newcomers have pretty much taken over and introduced a lot of changes. It used to be that the French were all concentrated in Ward 5 and they had one man on the Council. Now they have Ward 5 and 4 and a good part of 3. They could even elect a mayor now if they tried and that would have been simply inconceivable 15 years ago.

If at least five respondents *explicitly* mentioned such shifts, the community was characterized as undergoing shifts in political control. Four of the nine communities with solidary groups can be so characterized and three of those without solidary groups have recently undergone the radical transformation from a small, homogeneous, independent town to a much more heterogeneous, suburban town.

Organizational Ties   Respondents in each community were asked which "men's or women's clubs and organizations are most active in community affairs?" The eight most frequently mentioned organizations were coded and membership in these organizations was ascertained for all respondents. Our measure of organizational ties centers on the extent to which a single major organization provides a common focus for people active in political affairs. Here, we measure the ratio of the largest number of respondent-memberships in any single organization to the total number of respondents in the town.

Interpersonal Ties   Respondents were asked to name active partisans on each side of each of the issues. They were also asked to indicate how well they knew each of the individuals named, using a scale with four degrees of acquaintanceship—from "an intimate friend" at one end, to "someone I have no contact with" at the other end. To form an overall measure of proponent-opponent[10] friendship ties this information was used in the following way: only those friendship ratings for people named on the side which the particular respondent opposed were counted and these ratings were averaged for all respondents.

Shared Background   This measure focuses on four variables—length of residence, nationality background, education and religion. On each dimension, we ask to what extent the maximum possible correlation between issue position and the variable in question was achieved. The scores on the four dimensions are summed to form a coefficient of cleavage which expresses the total amount of cleavage on a given issue.

More specifically, each of the four variables is dichotomized as follows: (1) length of residence is split at the median for a town; (2) nationality background is divided into the most frequent and all others; (3) education is divided into college and non-college; (4) religion is divided into the most frequent and all others. Respondents' positions on each variable are compared, in turn, with positions on the issues, each separate combination of variable and issue forming a separate two-by-two table. The marginals of this table are used to calculate expected frequencies and maximum possible frequencies. The difference between the maximum possible and the expected frequency forms the denominator for the coefficient; the difference between the expected and the actual frequency constitutes the numerator.[11]

It is important to point out that whenever a town is homogeneous on a particular dimension, this dimension makes no contribution to the coefficient of cleavage. Thus, if every respondent in a particular town were Protestant, the denominator of the above coefficient would be zero for religion, and this dimension would simply be excluded. This means that the coefficient of cleavage tends, if anything, to overrate the degree of cleavage in homogeneous towns by giving them no credit for dimensions on which *all* proponents and opponents share a common characteristic. Put another way, a low coefficient of cleavage indicates not homogeneity, but high *cross-cutting* between these dimensions and issue position. Eight of the eighteen communities have at least one issue on which the coefficient of cleavage is 0.5 or higher.

RESULTS

As Table 1 indicates, shifts in political control are clearly related to rancorous conflict in this particular set of New England communities. Only

TABLE 1. RANCOROUS CONFLICT AND POLITICAL INSTABILITY

	Rancorous	Conventional
Undergoing political change	6	1
Politically stable	3	8
N	9	9

P < .05 (Fisher's Exact Test).

one of the nine conventional towns is undergoing political change while two-thirds of the rancorous towns are undergoing such change. Are these rancorous towns also higher on our measures of conduciveness and lower on integration than the conventional towns?

There is a limit to how far one can examine interrelationships among variables with only eighteen communities. Nevertheless, some attempt at this is necessary even at the risk of breaking these eighteen cases down into meaninglessly small cells. Eighteen may be a small number, but it is a great deal larger than the case study or comparison of two or three communities which is typical of the literature on community politics.

There is little overall relationship between the measures of conduciveness used here—participative political structure and presence of clear solidary groups—and the presence of rancorous conflict. As Table 2 indicates, communities without town meetings are about as likely to have rancorous

TABLE 2. RANCOROUS CONFLICT AND STRUCTURAL CONDUCIVENESS

	Rancorous	Conventional
Has town meeting form of government	6	5
Does not have town meeting form of government..	3	4
N	9	9
Solidary groups present	4	5
Solidary groups absent	5	4
N	9	9

conflicts as those with them. Solidary groups are present about as often in rancorous as in conventional ones. These results are not, in themselves, negative evidence since we would not expect higher conduciveness alone (without evidence of strain) to produce differences between the two kinds of community. However, there is little suggestion in these data that, for those seven towns with political instability, the presence of town meetings or solidary groups increases the likelihood of rancorous conflict. It is true that four out of five politically unstable communities which have town meetings are rancorous, but then both of the unstable towns without town meetings are rancorous also. Three out of four of the unstable towns with solidary groups are rancorous but all three of the unstable towns without such groups are rancorous. Put another way, the one exception among the seven politically unstable communities is *not* lower on our measures of conduciveness; it has both solidary groups and town meetings to accompany its political strain but still it is not rancorous. For the measures used here the evidence on the conduciveness hypotheses must be considered inconclusive at best.

There is no overall relationship between rancorous conflict and the extent to which some organization provides a central focus for those involved in community affairs. However, if we focus specifically on the seven politically unstable towns, there is some indication that this variable does have an effect. Using as our measure the ratio of the largest number of respondent memberships in any single organization to the total number of respondents in a town, we find that the six politically unstable rancorous communities have an average ratio of 0.32 as against 0.41 for the eleven towns without political strain ($p < 0.05$); the one conventional town among the politically unstable has a ratio of 0.45, well above average on this measure of integration.

The average degree of acquaintance among opponents is substantially lower in rancorous than in conventional towns—2.89 vs. 2.39 ($p < 0.05$, using a one tailed test).[12] Among the politically unstable towns, the relationship is even stronger; the average is 2.97 for the six rancorous towns and the score is 1.50 for the conventional town, ranking it first among the set of 18 in friendship among opponents.

The Coefficient of Cleavage, our last measure of integration or lack of integration, shows similar results. As Table 3 indicates, six of eight towns which have at least one issue with a high degree of cleavage between proponents and opponents are rancorous. Five of the six politically unstable and rancorous towns have such sharp differences between proponents and opponents but only three of the other twelve.

TABLE 3. RANCOROUS AND CLEAVAGE

	Rancorous	Conventional
All towns		
CC of .5 or higher on at least one issue *	6	2
CC of less than .5 on all issues	3	7
N	9	9
Politically unstable towns		
CC of .5 or higher	5	0
CC of less than .5	1	1
Politically stable towns		
CC of .5 or higher	1	2
CC of less than .5	2	6
N	9	9

* (Or, 50 percent or less cross-cutting on at least one issue.) CC stands for Coefficient of Cleavage.

Summary In the towns studied here there were four exceptions to the relationship between political instability and the appearance of rancorous conflict. One of these, a town which is politically changing but is not rancorous, scores high on all our measures of integration. But there are also three towns without the kind of political strain measured here which are rancorous. One of these three is the only town among the eighteen which is experiencing severe economic strain. Seven years earlier, a major mill closed and the unemployment rate remained quite high. Numerous stores were empty on Main Street and many of those who were able to leave had already done so. The two other exceptions are not so easily explained. Not only are they not undergoing any political or other obvious strain but they score high on our measures of integration as well. One can, of course, always find some sort of strain in any town but in the absence of special evidence to suggest such strains, rancorous conflict in these two communities must be regarded as unexplained by the hypotheses presented here.

There are two final variables which while they play no role in the hypotheses, might well be affecting the results. The first of these—the type of community—has no relationship to rancorous conflict for this set of towns; four of the nine rancorous communities and four of the nine conventional ones are independent towns rather than suburbs or resorts. Size of town, the second control variable, also has no overall relationship to rancorous conflict; five of the nine largest and four of the nine smallest towns are rancorous. Nevertheless it turns out that all of the exceptions fall among those with population under 5000. As Table 4 indicates, there is a perfect relationship between political instability and rancorous conflict for communities over 5000.

DISCUSSION

It is important to specify some content for such general classes of variable as structural strain, conduciveness, and integration. I have tried to do this here by explaining rancorous conflict in terms of the strain which political change provides or reflects, the conduciveness which a participative structure and solidary groups provide, and the integrative ties which a common organizational focus, friendships, and common bonds of nationality, religion, education and length of residence provide.

TABLE 4. RANCOROUS CONFLICT AND POLITICAL INSTABILITY
CONTROLLED FOR SIZE OF TOWN

	Rancorous	Conventional
Town over 5000		
Undergoing political change	6	0
Politically stable	0	5
Towns under 5000		
Undergoing political change	0	1
Politically stable	3	3
N	9	9

Rancorous conflict is similar in many respects to what Smelser has called "the hostile outburst."[13] But there are some differences worth noting. Connotatively, the term "hostile outburst" conjures up images of such dramatic and violent events as the Los Angeles riots. In the small communities studied here, even the most rancorous issue did not produce so much as a black eye. At best, we find a little public vilification and an occasional mild threat. However, even in a large community, it is easy to underrate the humiliation caused by apparently minor attacks. There was a day when men fought duels over insults no worse than many included here as manifestations of rancorous conflict.

A more important difference between the hostile outburst and the phenomenon described here resides in the relationship of rancorous conflict to collective behavior. Collective behavior is the mobilization of noninstitutionalized action on the basis of a generalized belief which redefines social action.[14] In Smelser's formulation, a critical element of the belief involved in collective behavior is its "short-circuiting" of the necessary steps between the highly generalized component of action on which the belief focuses and the specific operative solutions which are expected to follow from collective action. For example, the belief that the removal of encroachments of the federal government will ameliorate a variety of specific frustrations illustrates this sort of compression from generalized belief to operative solution. The hostile outburst in particular, involves "not only a redefinition of generalized forces in an ambiguous situation but also an identification and modification of persons thought to be agencies of these forces. The modification is to be effected by destroying, injuring, removing, or restricting a person or class of persons considered responsible for the evils at hand."[15]

By defining rancorous conflict in terms of beliefs about the means of influence used rather than the nature of the target of the generalized belief, we may include some episodes which would not be considered collective behavior as defined above. Specifically, it is not a criterion for inclusion that the target of the rancor be regarded as *symbolic* of some more generalized evil. Scapegoating need not be involved. In the issues studied here, it is frequently but not necessarily the case that the targets of rancor are regarded as symbolic of larger forces. Political opponents may be seen as agents or dupes of intricate conspiracies aimed at removing precious freedoms, or as tools of a giant "power grab." But they may also be seen as themselves, the ultimate perpetrators of some mischief. Nor is it assumed that these perceptions are inaccurate or oversimplified; the charges made may be true, the targets of hostility may be guilty.

This paper has a purpose more general than understanding modes of community conflict. Both the specific variables used and the general strategy of analysis are relevant to a wide variety of political expression. The politics of fluoridation is not so far removed from battles over open-occupancy housing or school Bible readings. The present explanation of rancorous conflict in small communities is not very different in kind from the explanation we would use in contrasting countries with or without revolutionary movements. Of course, the content of such general classes of variable as structural conduciveness, strain, and integration may vary in different social-organizational settings. However, if one can establish that a participative political structure promotes conduciveness to rancorous conflict in one setting, it becomes a more plausible hypothesis for other settings. For example, this may explain why apparent improvements or efforts to remove strains may be accompanied by increases in rancorous conflict. Such changes may have their initial or most radical effects on conduciveness or on sources of structural integration or control and only secondary effects on the removal of sources of discontent. The study of such limited phenomena as rancorous conflicts in communities may teach us something more general about social movements and social change.

Because of the negative connotations of a term like "rancorous conflict," some final observations about the towns studied here are worth making. Many of the conventional communities are rather dull and stagnant, while some of the rancorous ones are among the most vital. Some of the conventional towns not only have an absence of rancorous conflict but a general absence of change; the rancorous towns have the strains that accompany change but some of them also have the advantages of stimulation and growth. The absence of rancorous conflict is no necessary sign of an "ideal" community.

NOTES

[1] I draw here on Neil J. Smelser, *Theory of Collective Behavior* (Glencoe, Ill.: The Free Press, 1963). He organizes his discussion of the determinants of collective behavior under six categories. Three of them are covered here with slight differences in terminology and formulation. The other three—the growth and spread of a generalized belief, precipitating factors, and mobilization of participants for action—are not included because our objective is to understand the structural differences between communities rather than the outbreak of a given episode at a particular time in a community. The discussion which follows also draws heavily on James S. Coleman, *Community Conflict* (Glencoe, Ill.: The Free Press, 1957).

[2] Robert L. Crain, *Elihu Katz*, and Donald B. Rosenthal, *The Fluoridation Decision: Community Structure and Innovation* (Indianapolis: Bobbs-Merrill, 1967).

[3] The volatile nature of California politics may be due (among other things) to the structural conduciveness stemming from a long tradition of initiative and referendum.

[4] A good deal of recent work on such strains has used the rubric of "alienation." See, e.g., John E. Horton and Wayne E. Thompson, "Powerlessness and Political Negativism: A Study of Defeated Local Referendums," *American Journal of Sociology*, 68 (1962), pp. 485–493; Kenneth Keniston, "Alienation and the Decline of Utopia," *American Scholar*, 29 (1960), pp. 161–200; and William A. Gamson, "The Fluoridation Dialogue: Is it an Ideological Conflict?" *Public Opinion Quarterly*, 25 (1961), pp. 526–537.

[5] In coding charges of unfair tactics, five specific categories were used but no distinction is made in this paper among different types of charge. Intercoder agreement on the existence of charges was above 80 percent.

[6] The fluoridation issue, incidentally, produced two or more charges in 12 of 18 towns. All but one of the rancorous towns had a rancorous fluoridation issue. In one town, however, fluoridation was the only issue studied which did not produce charges. Charges over fluoridation, of course, were never sufficient to have a town classified as rancorous since at least two such issues were required; four of the conventional towns did have a single rancorous fluoridation issue.

[7] A number of authors have addressed themselves to the problems involved in selecting issues to study. See, for e.g., Nelson Polsby, *Community Power and Political Theory* (New Haven, Conn.: Yale University Press, 1963), pp. 95–97; and Linton C. Freeman *et al.*, *Local Community Leadership* (Syracuse: Syracuse University Press, 1960), pp. 7–8.

[8] Issues were selected for study through examination of community newspapers and some informal checking with newspaper editors and city clerks. It was possible to miss issues on whose importance there was considerable consensus since this could not be discovered until the interviews were completed. Thus, five issues named by a majority of respondents were *not* studied. Three of these were in rancorous towns and their inclusion would, thus, not affect the classification of the town. In one conventional town, none of the three issues studied produced as many as two charges; thus, the inclusion of the missed issue would not be sufficient to change the classification of the town even if it did produce charges. The other conventional town *could* have been shifted into the rancorous column by the inclusion of the missed issue, but there is no indication from examining the few sparse comments about this issue that it would have.

[9] What consensus exists is not an artifact of the use of active partisans as respondents. A comparison of self-rated actives and inactives shows almost no differences in their mention of issues or ratings of community concern about issues. On 23 of the 26 issues mentioned by a majority of all respondents, a majority of inactive informants named the issue as well. On seven of these issues, there is actually a higher proportion of mentions among inactive respondents.

[10] The terms *proponent* and *opponent* are used to include both active and inactive supporters of a position, i.e., we include those who have expressed an opinion about the issue even if they have not made any attempt at influencing the outcome.

[11] For example, if there are 10 Protestants and 10 Catholics among 12 proponents and 8 opponents on fluoridation, we would expect by chance to get six Protestant proponents. However, we could get as many as 10 or a few as 2. Thus, the denominator of the coefficient of cleavage (CC) would be: 10 (Maximum frequency) -6 (Expected frequency) $=4$. If there were actually nine Protestant proponents, the numerator of the CC would be: 9 (Actual frequency) -6 (Expected frequency) $=3$, and the CC would be $\frac{3}{4} = 0.75$. The direction of relationship has no significance here. To avoid artificial results due to discontinuity and to simplify calculation, the expected frequencies were always rounded to the nearest integer.

[12] A lower score indicates closer friendship.

[13] Smelser, *op. cit.*

[14] This is a paraphrase of Smelser, *op. cit.*, pp. 67–73. The brief discussion of relevant portions which is necessary here does not do full justice to Smelser's highly complex and interconnected discussion of collective behavior.

[15] *Ibid.*, p. 101.

Tensions | DEVIANCE
in the Social Order

COMMENTARY

There are three factors which account for behavioral variations which society at large, or some segments of society, define as deviant. First, socialization is never perfect. The child does not grow up to be an exact replica of his parents. The life histories of any two individuals are never identical. Moreover, in a heterogeneous society people engage in a variety of different associations and are members of different subgroups. The behaviors of persons in one group may conflict with the values of members of other groups. And finally, because society is stratified, opportunities to attain the values of society are not equally distributed among all of the subgroups in society.

John Kitsuse addresses the phenomenon of deviance by asking how it is that the behaviors of individuals come to be called deviant by others, and how the members of society react to a person defined by them as deviant.

Richard Cloward poses a different question. In his paper "Illegitimate Behavior, Anomie and Deviant Behavior," he asks under what conditions people wittingly engage in deviant or illegitimate acts. He suggests that access to legitimate and illegitimate means for attaining goals is critical.

31   JOHN I. KITSUSE

Societal Reaction to Deviant Behavior: Problems of Theory and Method

Sociological theory and research in the area traditionally known as "social pathology" have been concerned primarily with the classification and analysis of *deviant forms of behavior* and relatively little attention has been given to societal reactions to deviance.[1] In a recent paper, Merton has noted this lack of a "systematic *classification* of the responses of the conventional or conforming members of a group to deviant behavior."[2] Similarly, Cohen has observed that "a sociology of deviant behavior-conformity will have to devise ways of conceptualizing responses to deviant behavior from the standpoint of their relevance to the production or extinction of deviant behavior."[3] In this paper, I shall discuss some of the theoretical and methodological issues posed by the problem of societal reactions to deviant behavior and report on a preliminary attempt to formulate a research design which specifically takes them into account.

I propose to shift the focus of theory and research from the forms of deviant behavior to the *processes by which persons come to be defined as deviant by others*. Such a shift requires that the sociologist view as problematic what he generally assumes as given—namely, that certain forms of behavior are *per se* deviant and are so defined by the "conventional or conforming members of a group." This assumption is frequently called into question on empirical grounds when the societal reaction to behaviors defined as deviant by the sociologist is non-existent, indifferent, or at most mildly disapproving. For example, in his discussion of "ritualism" as a form of deviant behavior, Merton states that it is not that such behavior is treated by others as deviant which identifies it as deviant "since the overt behavior is institutionally permitted, though not culturally prescribed."[4] Rather, the behavior is deviant because it "clearly represents a departure from the cultural model in which men are obliged to move onward and upward in the social hierarchy."[5] The discrepancy between the theoretically hypothesized and empirically observable societal reaction is also noted by Lemert: "It is fairly easy to think of situations in which serious offenses against laws commanding public respect have only a mild penalty or have gone entirely

Reprinted from *Social Problems*, 9:3 (1962), pp. 247–257, by permission of the author and the publisher.

unpunished. Conversely, cases are easily discovered in which a somewhat minor violation of legal rules has provoked surprisingly stringent penalties."[6]

Clearly, the forms of behavior *per se* do not activate the processes of societal reaction which sociologically differentiate deviants from nondeviants. Thus, a central problem for theory and research in the sociology of deviance may be stated as follows: What are the behaviors which are defined by members of the group, community, or society as deviant, and how do those definitions organize and activate the societal reactions by which persons come to be differentiated and treated as deviants? In formulating the problem in this way, the point of view of those who interpret and define behavior as deviant must explicitly be incorporated into a sociological definition of deviance. Accordingly, deviance may be conceived as a process by which the members of a group, community, or society (1) interpret behavior as deviant, (2) define persons who so behave as a certain kind of deviant, and (3) accord them the treatment considered appropriate to such deviants. In the following pages, this conception of deviance and societal reaction will be applied to the processes by which persons come to be defined and treated as homosexuals.

SOCIETAL REACTIONS TO "HOMOSEXUAL BEHAVIOR"

As a form of deviant behavior, homosexuality presents a strategically important theoretical and empirical problem for the study of deviance. In the sociological and anthropological literature[7] homosexual behavior and the societal reactions to it are conceptualized within the framework of ascribed sex statuses and the socialization of individuals to those statuses. The ascription of sex statuses is presumed to provide a complex of culturally prescribed roles and behaviors which individuals are expected to learn and perform. Homosexual roles and behaviors are conceived to be "inappropriate" to the individual's ascribed sex status, and thus theoretically they are defined as deviant.

With reference to American society, Allison Davis states: "Sex-typing of behavior and privileges is even more rigid and lasting in our society than is age-typing. Indeed, sexual status and color-caste status are the only life-long forms of rank. In our society, one can escape them in approved fashion only by death. Whereas sexual mobility is somewhat less rare today than formerly, sex-inappropriate behavior, social or physical, is still one of the most severely punished infractions of our social code."[8] In Lemert's terminology, norms concerning sex-appropriate behavior have a high degree of "compulsiveness" and social disapproval of violations is stringent and effective.[9] Homosexuals themselves appear to share this conception of the societal reaction to their behavior, activities, and subculture.[10]

Such a view of homosexuality would lead one to hypothesize that "sex appropriate" (and conversely "sex-inappropriate") behaviors are unambiguously prescribed, deviations from those prescriptions are invariably interpreted as immoral, and the reactions of the conventional and conforming members of the society to such deviations are uniformly severe and effective. The evidence which apparently supports this hypothesis is not difficult to find, particularly with reference to the definition and treatment of male homosexuals. Individuals who are publicly identified as homosexuals are frequently denied the social, economic, and legal rights of "normal" males. Socially they may be treated as objects of amusement, ridicule, scorn, and often fear; economically they may be summarily dismissed from employment; legally they are frequently subject to interrogation and harassment by police.

In citing such evidence, however, it is important to note that the societal reaction to and the differentiation of homosexuals from the "normal" population is a consequence of the fact that the former are "known" to be homosexuals by some individuals, groups or agencies. Thus, within the framework of the present formulation of homosexuality as a form of deviant behavior, the processes by which individuals come to be "known" and treated as sexually deviant will be viewed as problematic and a problem for empirical investigation. I shall not be concerned here with the so-called "latent homosexual" unless he is so defined by others and differentially treated as a consequence of that definition. Nor will I be concerned with the variety of "internal" conflicts which may form the "clinical" picture of the homosexual except insofar as such conflicts are manifested in behavior leading others to conceive of him as a homosexual. In short, I shall proceed on the principle that it is only when individuals are defined and identified by others as homosexuals and accorded the treatment considered "appropriate" for individuals so defined that a homosexual "population" is produced for sociological investigation.[11] With reference to homosexuality, then, the empirical questions are: What forms of behavior do persons in the social system consider to be "sex-inappropriate," how do they interpret such behaviors, and what are the consequences of those interpretations for their reactions to individuals who are perceived to manifest such behaviors?

In a preliminary attempt to investigate these questions, an interview schedule was constructed[12] and administered to approximately seven hundred individuals, most of whom were college undergraduates. The sample was neither random nor representative of any specified population, and the generalizability of the interview materials is limited except insofar as they are relevant to the previously noted hypothesis that homosexual behavior is uniformly defined, interpreted, and negatively sanctioned. The interview materials will therefore be used for the purpose of illustrating the theory and method of the present conception of deviance and societal reaction.

The objectives of the interview were threefold: It attempted to document (1) the behavior forms which are interpreted as deviant, (2) the processes by which persons who manifest such behaviors are defined and (3) treated as deviant. Thus, in the construction of the interview schedule, what the interviewees considered to be "deviant" behavior, the interpretations of such behavior, and the actions of subjects toward those perceived as deviant were addressed as empirical questions. Labels such as alcoholic, illiterate, illegitimate child, and ex-convict were assumed to be categories employed by persons in everyday life to classify deviants, but the behavioral forms by which they identify individuals as deviants were treated as problematic "Sexual deviant" was one of ten categories of deviants about which subjects were questioned in the interview. Among the more than seven hundred subjects interviewed, seventy-five stated they had "known" a homosexual and responded to questions concerning their experiences with such individuals. The data presented below are drawn from the protocols of interviews with this group of subjects.

The interview proceeded as follows:

The subject was asked "Have you ever known anyone who was a sexual deviant?" If he questioned the meaning of "deviant," the subject was asked to consider the question using his own meaning of "sexual deviant."

When the subject stated he had known a sexual deviant—a homosexual in this case—as he defined the term, he was asked to think about the most recent incident involving him in an encounter with such a person. He was then asked "When was the first time you noticed (found out) that this person was a homosexual?" followed by "What was the situation? What did you notice about him? How did he behave?" This line of questioning was focused on the interaction between the subject and the alleged deviant to obtain a detailed description of the situation which led the subject to define the person as homosexual. The subject's description of the person's behavior was systematically probed to clarify the terms of his description, particularly those which were interpretive rather than descriptive.

EVIDENCE OF HOMOSEXUALITY

Responses to the question "When was the first time you noticed (found out) that this person was homosexual?" and the related probes suggest that an individual's sexual "normality" may be called into question with reference to two broad categories of evidence. (a) *Indirect evidence* in the form of a rumor, an acquaintance's experience with the individual in question subsequently communicated to the subject, or general reputational information concerning the individual's behavior, associates, and sexual predelictions may be the occasion for suspecting him to be "different." Many subjects reported that they first "found out" or "knew" that the individuals in question were homosexuals through the reports of others or by "reputation." Such information was generally accepted by the subjects without independent verification. Indeed, the information provided a new perspective for their retrospective as well as prospective observations and interpretations of the individuals' behaviors. An example of how hearsay organizes observation and interpretation is the following statement by a 35-year-old male (a draftsman):

I: Then this lieutenant was a homosexual?
S: Yes.
I: How did you find out about it?

S: The guy he approached told me. After that, I watched him. Our company was small and we had a bar for both enlisted men and officers. He would come in and try to be friendly with one or two of the guys.

I: Weren't the other officers friendly?

S: Sure, they would come in for an occasional drink; some of them had been with the company for three years and they would sometimes slap you on the back, but he tried to get over friendly.

I: What do you mean "over friendly"?

S: He had only been there a week. He would try to push himself on a couple of guys—he spent more time with the enlisted personnel than is expected from an officer.

(b) *Direct observation* by the subject of the individual's behavior may be the basis for calling the latter's sexual "normality" into question. The descriptions of behavior which subjects took to be indicative of homosexuality varied widely and were often vague. Most frequently the behaviors cited were those *"which everyone knows"* are indications of homosexuality. For example, a 20-year-old male subject reports an encounter with a stranger at a bar:

I: What happened during your conversation?

S: He asked me if I went to college and I said I did. Then he asked me what I was studying. When I told him psychology he appeared very interested.

I: What do you mean "interested"?

S: Well, you know queers really go for this psychology stuff.

I: Then what happened?

S: Ah, let's see. I'm not exactly sure, but somehow we got into an argument about psychology and to prove my point I told him to pick an area of study. Well, he appeared to be very pensive and after a great thought he said, "Okay, let's take homosexuality."

I: What did you make of that?

S: Well, by now I figured the guy was queer so I got the hell outta there.

The responses of other subjects suggest that an individual is particularly suspect when he is observed to behave in a manner which deviates from the *behaviors-held-in-common* among members of the group to which he belongs. For example, a behavior which is presumed to be held-in-common among sailors in the U.S. Navy is intense and active sexual activity. When a sailor does not affirm, at least verbally, his interest in such activity, his competence as a "male" may be called into question. A 22-year-old engineer, recently discharged from the Navy, responds to the "how did you first know" question as follows:

All of a sudden you just get suspicious of something. I began to wonder about him. He didn't go in for leave activities that most sailors go for. You know, girls and high times. He just never was interested and when you have been out at sea for a month or two, you're interested. That just wasn't Navy, and he was a career man.

Although the responses of our subjects indicate there are many behavioral gestures which "everyone knows" are indicators of homosexuality in males, there are relatively few such gestures that lead persons to suspect females of homosexuality. Following is an excerpt from a 21-year-old college co-ed whose remarks illustrate this lack of definite indicators *prior* to her labeling of an acquaintance as a homosexual:

I: When was the first time you noticed she was a deviant?
S: I didn't notice it. I thought she had a masculine appearance when I first saw her anyway.
I: What do you mean?
S: Oh, her haircut, her heavy eyebrows. She had a rather husky build.
I: Exactly when did you think she had a masculine appearance?
S: It was long after [the first meeting] that I found out that she was "one."
I: How do you define it?
S: Well, a lesbian. I don't know too much about them. It was _____ who told me about her.
I: Did you notice anything else about her [at the first meeting]?
S: No, because you really don't know unless you're looking for those things.

Unlike "effeminate" appearance and gestures in males, "masculine" appearance in females is apparently less likely to be immediately linked to the suspicion or imputation of homosexuality. The statements of the subject quoted above indicate that although "masculine appearance" is an important element in her conception of a lesbian, its significance did not become apparent to her until a third person told her the girl was homosexual. The remarks of other subjects in our sample who state they have "known" female homosexuals reveal a similar ambiguity in their interpretations of what they describe as indicators of sexual deviance.

A third form of evidence by direct observation is behaviors which the subjects interpreted to be *overt sexual propositions*. Descriptions of such propositions ranged from what the subjects considered to be unmistakable evidence of the person's sexual deviance to ambiguous gestures which they did not attempt to question in the situation. The following is an excerpt from an interview with a 24-year-old male school teacher who recounts an experience in a Korean Army barrack:

I: What questions did he [the alleged homosexual] ask?
S: "How long have you been in Korea?" I told him. "What do you think of these Korean girls?" which I answered, "Not too much because they are dirty." I thought he was probably homesick and wanted someone to talk to. I do not remember what he said then until he said, "How much do you have?" I answered him by saying, "I don't know, about average I guess." Then he said, "Can I feel it just once?" To this I responded with, "Get the hell out of here," and I gave him a shove when he reached for me as he asked the question.

In a number of interviews, the subjects' statements indicate that they interpreted the sequence of the alleged deviants' behavior as progressively inappropriate or peculiar in the course of their interaction with them. The link between such behavior and their judgment that a sexual proposition was being made was frequently established by the subjects' growing realization of its deviant character. A 21-year-old male subject recalls the follow-

ing experience involving his high school tennis coach who had invited him
to dinner:

S: Anyway, when I got there he served dinner, and as I think back on it—
I didn't notice it at the time—but I remember that he did act sort of
effeminate. Finally he got up to change a record and picked up some of
my English themes. Then he brought them over and sat down beside me.
He began to explain some of my mistakes in my themes, and in the meantime he slipped his arms around me.

I: Would you say that this was done in a friendly manner or with an intent
of hugging you or something?

S: Well, no, it was just a friendly gesture of putting his arm around my
shoulder. At that time, I didn't think anything of it, but as he continued
to explain my mistakes, he started to rub my back. Then he asked me if
I wanted a back rub. So I said, "No! I don't need one." At this time, I
began thinking something was funny anyway. So I said that I had to
go. . . .

THE IMPUTATION OF HOMOSEXUALITY

When a detailed description of the subject's evidence concerning the
alleged homosexual was obtained, he was asked, "What did you make of
that?" to elicit information about how he interpreted the person's observed
or reported behavior. This line of questioning yielded data on the inferential
process by which the subject linked his information about the individual
to the deviant category "homosexual."

A general pattern revealed by the subjects' responses to this section of
the interview schedule is that when an individual's sexual "normality" is
called into question, by whatever form of evidence, the imputation of homosexuality is documented by *retrospective interpretations* of the deviant's
behavior, a process by which the subject re-interprets the individual's past
behavior in the light of the new information concerning his sexual deviance.
This process is particularly evident in cases where the prior relationship
between the subject and the alleged homosexual was more than a chance
encounter or casual acquaintanceship. The subjects indicate that they reviewed their past interactions with the individuals in question, searching
for subtle cues and nuances of behavior which might give further evidence
of the alleged deviance. This retrospective reading generally provided the
subjects with just such evidence to support the conclusion that "this is what
was going on all the time."

Some of the subjects who were interviewed were themselves aware of
their retrospective interpretations in defining individuals as sexually deviant.
For example, a 23-year-old female graduate student states:

I: Will you tell me more about the situation?

S: Well, their relationship was a continuous one, although I think that it
is a friendship now as I don't see them together as I used to; I don't think
it is still homosexual. When I see them together, they don't seem to be
displaying the affection openly as they did when I first realized the situation.

I: How do you mean "openly"?
S: Well, they would hold each other's hand in public places.
I: And what did you make of this?
S: Well, I really don't know, because I like to hold people's hands, too! I guess I actually didn't see this as directly connected with the situation. What I mean is that, if I hadn't seen that other incident [she had observed the two girls in bed together] I probably wouldn't have thought of it [i.e., hand-holding] very much. . . . Well, actually, there were a few things that I questioned later on that I hadn't thought really very much about. . . . I can remember her being quite affectionate towards me several times when we were in our room together, iike putting her arm around my shoulder. Or I remember one time specifically when she asked me for a kiss. I was shocked at the time, but I laughed it off jokingly.

THE INTERACTIONAL CONTEXTS OF SOCIETAL REACTIONS

When the description of the alleged deviant's behavior and the subject's interpretations of that behavior were recorded, the subject was asked "What did you do then?" This question was directed toward documenting societal reactions to deviant behavior. Forms of behavior *per se* do not differentiate deviants from non-deviants; it is the responses of the conventional and conforming members of the society who identify and interpret behavior as deviant which sociologically transform persons into deviants. Thus, in the formulation of deviance proposed here, if the subject observes an individual's behavior and defines it as deviant but does not accord him differential treatment as a consequence of that definition, the individual is not sociologically deviant.

The reactions of the subjects to individuals they defined as homosexuals ranged from immediate withdrawal from the scene of interaction and avoidance of further encounters with the alleged deviants to the maintenance of the prior relationship virtually unaltered by the imputation of deviance. The following responses to the question "What did you do then?" illustrate the variation in sanctions directed toward persons defined as homosexuals.

Explicit Disapproval and Immediate Withdrawal The most negatively toned and clearly articulated reaction reported by our subjects is that of the previously quoted Korean War veteran. It is interesting to note that extreme physical punishment as a reaction to persons defined as homosexuals, a reaction which is commonly verbalized by "normal" males as proper treatment of "queers," is not reported by any of the subjects. When physical force is used, it is invariably in response to the deviant's direct physical overtures, and even then it is relatively mild, e.g., "I gave him a shove when he reached for me."

Explicit Disapproval and Subsequent Withdrawal In the following excerpt, a 20-year-old male college student describes an encounter with a man whom he met in a coffee shop. In the course of their conversation, the man admitted his homosexuality to the subject. The two left the coffee shop and walked together to the subway station.

I: What happened then?

S: We got to the subway whereupon he suggested that he hail a cab and take me up to Times Square—a distance of almost 40 blocks.

I: Did you agree, and what did you think?

S: Yes, I thought he was just being very nice and I had no qualms about getting in a cab with a homosexual since I was quite sure I could protect myself against any advances in a cab.

I: What happened then?

S: When we had ridden a little distance, he put his hand on my knee, and I promptly removed it saying that it just wasn't right and that I wanted nothing of it. However, after a while, he put his hand back. This time I didn't take it away for a while because I was interested in what he would do. It was the funniest thing—he rubbed and caressed my knee the same way in which I would have done this to a girl. This time I took his hand and hit him across the chest with it, telling him to "cut it out." Finally, we got to Times Square, and I got out.

This example and that provided by the Korean War veteran's reaction to behavior interpreted as overt sexual propositions suggest the possibility that responses to persons suspected of homosexuality or defined as homosexuals on the basis of more indirect evidence of appearance, "confessions," hearsay, reputation, or association will vary within an even wider range of applied sanctions. Indeed, the statements of subjects concerning their responses to persons alleged to be deviant on such evidence indicate that the modal reaction is disapproval, implicitly rather than explicitly communicated, and a restriction of interaction through partial withdrawal and avoidance. It should be noted further that although the subject's silent withdrawal from an established relationship with an alleged deviant may represent a stronger disapproval than an explicitly communicated, physically enforced sanction against a stranger, moral indignation or revulsion is not necessarily communicated to the deviant. The subject's prior relationship with the alleged deviant and the demands of propriety in subsequent interactions with him qualify the form and intensity of the sanctions which are applied. Thus, when the organization of the subject's day-to-day activities "forces" him into interaction with the deviant, expressions of disapproval are frequently constrained and diffused by the rules of deference and demeanor.[13] The following excerpts provide illustrations:

Implicit Disapproval and Partial Withdrawal A 20-year-old co-ed's reaction to a girl she concluded was a homosexual was expressed as follows:

"Well, I didn't want to be alone with X [the homosexual] because the four of us had two connecting rooms and I was in the room with X. As much as I liked the girl and felt sorry for her, I knew she could really wring me through the wringer. So the rest decided that I should tell her that if she and Y wanted to be homos, to do it somewhere else and not in the room."

No Disapproval and Relationship Sustained The "live and let live" response to homosexuals, which is implied in the preceding reaction, was not uncommon among the subjects. Some subjects not only affirmed the right of the homosexual to "live his own life" but also reported that their knowledge of the deviance has had little or no effect upon their subsequent relationships with the deviants. In this regard, the mildest reaction, so mild that it might be considered no reaction at all, was that of a 19-year-old male college student:

I: What was your reaction to him?

S: My reactions to him have always been friendly because he seems like a very friendly person. Uh, and he has a very nice sense of humor and I've never been repelled by anything he's said. For one thing, I think he's tremendously interesting because he seems to have such a wide range for background. . . .

I: When was the last time you saw this person?

S: Last night. . . . I was sitting in a restaurant and he walked in with some friends . . . he just stopped in and said hello, and was his usual friendly self.

I: What in particular happened after that?

S: Actually, nothing. He sat down with his friends and we exchanged a few words about the records that were playing on the juke box. But nothing, actually. . . .

The theoretical significance of these data for the conception of deviance and societal reaction presented here is not that the subjects' information is of dubious accuracy or questionable relevance as evidence of homosexuality. Nor is it that the subjects interpretations of them are unreasonable, unjustifiable, or spurious. They suggest rather that the conceptions of persons in everyday life concerning "sex-appropriate" or "sex-inappropriate" behavior may lead them to interpret a variety of behavioral forms as indications of the same deviation, and the "same" behavioral forms as indications of a variety of deviant as well as "normal" behavior. An individual's sexual "normality" may be made problematic by the interpretations and re-interpretations of his behavior by others, and the interpretive process may be activated by a wide range of situational behaviors which lend new significance to the individual's past and present behavior. His behavior with respect to speech, interests, dress, dating, or relations with other males are not *per se* significant in the deviant-defining process. The data suggest that the critical feature of the deviant-defining process is not the behavior of individuals who are defined as deviant, but rather the interpretations others make of their behaviors, whatever those behaviors may be.

With specific reference to homosexuality as a form of deviant behavior, the interview materials suggest that while reactions toward persons defined as homosexuals tend to be negatively toned, they are far from homogeneous as to the forms or intensity of the sanctions invoked and applied. Indeed, reactions which may appear to the sociological observer or to the deviant himself as negative sanctions, such as withdrawal or avoidance, may be expressions of embarrassment, a reluctance to share the burden of the deviant's problems, fear of the deviant, etc., as well as moral indignation or revulsion. In none of the interviews does the subject react with extreme violence, explicitly define or directly accuse the deviant of being a "queer," "fairy," or other terms of opprobrium, nor did any of them initiate legal actions against the deviant. In view of the extreme negative sanctions against homosexuality which are posited on theoretical grounds, the generally mild reactions of our subjects are striking.

The relative absence of extreme and overtly expressed negative sanctions against homosexuals among our subjects may, of course, reflect the higher than average educational level of the sample. A sample of subjects less biased toward the highly educated, middle-class segment of the population than was interviewed in this preliminary study may be expected to reflect a more definite pattern with reference to such negative reactions. We must, therefore, be cautious in generalizing the range of reactions among our subjects to the general population. It is equally important to note, however, that these data do indicate that reactions to homosexuals in American society are not *societal* in the sense of being uniform within a narrow range; rather, they are significantly conditioned by subcultural as well as situational factors. Thus, not only are the processes by which persons come to be defined as homosexuals contingent upon the interpretations of their behavior by others, but also the sanctions imposed and the treatment they are accorded as a consequence of that definition vary widely among conventional members of various subcultural groups.

The larger implications of these data are that a sociological theory of deviance must explicitly take into account the variety and range of conceptions held by persons, groups, and agencies within the society concerning any form of behavior. The increasing differentiation of groups, institutions, and subcultures in modern society generates a continually changing range of alternatives and tolerance for the expression of sexual as well as other forms of behavior. Consequently, it is difficult if not impossible to theoretically derive a set of *specific behavioral prescriptions* which will in fact be normatively supported, uniformly practiced, and socially enforced by more than a segment of the total population. Under such conditions, it is not the fact that individuals engage in behaviors which diverge from some theoretically posited "institutionalized expectations" or even that such behaviors are defined as deviant by the conventional and conforming members of the society which is of primary significance for the study of deviance. A sociological theory of deviance must focus specifically upon the interactions which not only define behaviors as deviant but also organize and activate the application of sanctions by individuals, groups, or agencies. For in modern society, the socially significant differentiation of deviants from the non-deviant population is increasingly contingent upon circumstances of situation, place, social and personal biography, and the bureaucratically organized activities of agencies of control.[14]

ACKNOWLEDGMENTS

I have profited from the critical comments and suggestions of Herbert R. Barringer, Aaron V. Cicourel, Sheldon L. Messinger, and H. Jay Shaffer. Troy S. Duster's valuable assistance in the analysis of the data is gratefully acknowledged.

NOTES

[1] A notable exception is the work of Edwin M. Lemert who systematically incorporates the concept of societal reaction in his theory of sociopathic behavior. See *Social Pathology* (New York: McGraw-Hill, 1951).

[2] Robert K. Merton, "Social Conformity, Deviation, and Opportunity-Structures: A Comment on the Contributions of Dubin and Cloward," *American Sociological Review*, 24 (1959), pp. 177–189.

[3] Albert K. Cohen, "The Study of Social Disorganization and Deviant Behavior," in *Sociology Today*, R. Merton, L. Broom, and L. Cottrell, eds. (New York: Basic Books, 1959), pp. 465–466.

[4] Robert K. Merton, *Social Theory and Social Structure*, rev. ed. (Glencoe, Ill.: The Free Press, 1957), p. 150.

[5] *Ibid.*, p. 150.

[6] *Op. cit.*, p. 55.

[7] For examples, see Talcott Parsons and Robert F. Bales, *Family Socialization and Interaction Process* (Glencoe, Ill.: The Free Press, 1955), pp. 103–105; Ruth Benedict, "Continuities and Discontinuities in Cultural Conditioning," *Psychiatry*, 1 (1938), pp. 161–167; Abram Kardiner and Associates, *Psychological Frontiers of Society* (New York: Columbia University Press, 1945), pp. 57, 88, etc.; Clifford Kirkpatrick, *The Family* (New York: Ronald Press, 1955), pp. 57–58; Margaret Mead, *Sex and Temperament* (New York: William Morrow, 1955).

[8] Allison Davis, "American Status Systems and the Socialization of the Child," *American Sociological Review*, 6 (1941), p. 350.

[9] *Op. cit.*, Chap. 4.

[10] Evelyn Hooker, "Sequences in Homosexual Identification," read at the meetings of the American Sociological Association, 1960; Donald Webster Cory, *The Homosexual in America* (New York: Greenburg, 1951), esp. Part I.

[11] This principle has been suggested by Harold Garfinkel. See "Some Sociological Concepts and Methods for Psychiatrists," *Psychiatric Research Reports*, 6 (1956), pp. 181–195.

[12] The interview schedule and methods were conceived and constructed in consultation with Aaron V. Cicourel.

[13] Erving Goffman, "The Nature of Deference and Demeanor," American Anthropologist, 58 (1956), pp. 473–502.

[14] For a discussion of such contingencies, see Edwin M. Lemert, *op. cit.*, Chapter 4, and Erving Goffman, "The Moral Career of the Mental Patient," *Psychiatry*, 22 (1959), pp. 123–142.

32 RICHARD A. CLOWARD

Illegitimate Means, Anomie, and Deviant Behavior

This paper[1] represents an attempt to consolidate two major sociological traditions of thought about the problem of deviant behavior. The first, exemplified by the work of Emile Durkheim and Robert K. Merton, may be called the anomie tradition.[2] The second, illustrated principally by the studies of Clifford R. Shaw, Henry D. McKay, and Edwin H. Sutherland,

Reprinted from *American Sociological Review*, 24:2 (1959), pp. 164–176, by permission of the author and the publisher.

may be called the "cultural transmission" and "differential association" tradition.[3] Despite some reciprocal borrowing of ideas, these intellectual traditions developed more or less independently. By seeking to consolidate them, a more adequate theory of deviant behavior may be constructed.

DIFFERENTIALS IN AVAILABILITY OF LEGITIMATE MEANS: THE THEORY OF ANOMIE

The theory of anomie has undergone two major phases of development. Durkheim first used the concept to explain deviant behavior. He focussed on the way in which various social conditions lead to "overweening ambition," and how, in turn, unlimited aspirations ultimately produce a breakdown in regulatory norms. Robert K. Merton has systematized and extended the theory, directing attention to patterns of disjunction between culturally prescribed goals and socially organized access to them by *legitimate* means. In this paper, a third phase is outlined. An additional variable is incorporated in the developing scheme of anomie, namely, the concept of *differentials in access to success-goals by illegitimate means.*[4]

Phase I: Unlimited Aspirations and the Breakdown of Regulatory Norms
In Durkheim's work, a basic distinction is made between "physical needs" and "moral needs." The importance of this distinction was heightened for Durkheim because he viewed physical needs as being regulated automatically by features of man's organic structure. Nothing in the organic structure, however, is capable of regulating social desires; as Durkheim put it, man's "capacity for feeling is in itself an insatiable and bottomless abyss."[5] If man is to function without "friction," "the passions must first be limited. . . . But since the individual has no way of limiting them, this must be done by some force exterior to him." Durkheim viewed the collective order as the external regulating force which defined and ordered the goals to which men should orient their behavior. If the collective order is disrupted or disturbed, however, men's aspirations may then rise, exceeding all possibilities of fulfillment. Under these conditions, "deregulation or anomy" ensues: "At the very moment when traditional rules have lost their authority, the richer prize offered these appetites stimulates them and makes them more exigent and impatient of control. The state of de-regulation or anomy is thus further heightened by passions being less disciplined precisely when they need more disciplining." Finally, pressures toward deviant behavior were said to develop when man's aspirations no longer matched the possibilities of fulfillment.

Durkheim therefore turned to the question of *when* the regulatory functions of the collective order break down. Several such states were identified, including sudden depression, sudden prosperity, and rapid technological change. His object was to show how, under these conditions, men are led to aspire to goals extremely difficult if not impossible to attain. As Durkheim saw it, sudden depression results in deviant behavior because "something like a declassification occurs which suddenly casts certain individuals into a lower state than their previous one. Then they must reduce their requirements, restrain their needs, learn greater self-control. . . . But society cannot adjust them instantaneously to this new life and teach them to practice the increased self-repression to which they are unaccustomed. So they are not adjusted to the condition forced on them, and its very prospect is intolerable; hence the suffering which detaches them from a reduced existence even before they have made trial of it." Prosperity, according to Durkheim, could have much the same effect as depression, particularly if upward changes in economic conditions are abrupt. The very abruptness of these changes presumably heightens aspirations beyond possibility of fulfillment, and this too puts a strain on the regulatory apparatus of the society.

According to Durkheim, "the sphere of trade and industry . . . is actually in a chronic state [of anomie]." Rapid technological developments and the existence of vast, unexploited markets excite the imagination with the seemingly limitless possibilities for the accumulation of wealth. As Durkheim said of the producer of goods, "now that he may assume to have almost the entire world as his customer, how could passions accept their former confinement in the face of such limitless prospects"? Continuing, Durkheim states that 'such is the source of excitement predominating in this part of society. . . . Here the state of crisis and anomie [are] constant and, so to speak, normal. From top to bottom of the ladder, greed is aroused without knowing where to find ultimate foothold. Nothing can calm it, since its goal is far beyond all it can attain."

In developing the theory, Durkheim characterized goals in the industrial society, and specified the way in which unlimited aspirations are induced. He spoke of "dispositions . . . so inbred that society has grown to accept them and is accustomed to think them normal," and he portrayed these "inbred dispositions": "It is everlastingly repeated that it is man's nature to be eternally dissatisfied, constantly to advance, without relief or rest, toward an indefinite goal. The longing for infinity is daily represented as a mark of moral distinction. . . ." And it was precisely these pressures to strive for "infinite" or "receding" goals, in Durkheim's view, that generate a breakdown in regulatory norms, for "when there is no other aim but to outstrip constantly the point arrived at, how painful to be thrown back!"

Phase II: Disjunction Between Cultural Goals and Socially Structured Opportunity Durkheim's description of the emergence of "overweening ambition" and the subsequent breakdown of regulatory norms constitutes one of the links between his work and the later development of the theory by Robert K. Merton. In his classic essay, "Social Structure and Anomie," Merton suggests that goals and norms may vary independently of each other, and that this sometimes leads to malintegrated states. In his view, two polar types of disjunction may occur: "There may develop a very heavy, at times a virtually ‑exclusive, stress upon the value of particular goals, involving comparatively little concern with the institutional prescribed means of striving toward these goals. . . . This constitutes one type of malintegrated culture."[6] On the other hand, "A second polar type is found where activities originally conceived as instrumental are transmuted into self-contained practices, lacking further objectives. . . . Sheer conformity becomes a central value." Merton notes that "between these extreme types are societies which maintain a rough balance between emphases upon cultural goals and institutionalized practices, and these constitute the integrated and relatively stable, though changing societies."

Having identified patterns of disjunction between goals and norms, Merton is enabled to define anomie more precisely: "Anomie [may be] conceived as a breakdown in the cultural structure, occurring particularly when there is an acute disjunction between cultural norms and goals and the socially structured capacities of members of the group to act in accord with them."

Of the two kinds of malintegrated societies, Merton is primarily interested in the one in which "there is an exceptionally strong emphasis upon specific goals without a corresponding emphasis upon institutional procedures." He states that attenuation between goals and norms, leading to anomie or "normlessness," comes about because men in such societies internalize an emphasis on common success-goals under conditions of varying access to them. The essence of this hypothesis is captured in the following excerpt: "It is only when a system of cultural values extols, virtually above all else, certain *common* success-goals for the population at large while the social structure rigorously restricts or completely closes access to approved modes of reaching these goals *for a considerable part of the same population*, that deviant behavior ensues on a large scale." The focus, in short, is on the way in which the social structure puts a strain upon the cultural structure. Here one may point to diverse structural differentials in access to culturally approved goals by legitimate means, for example, differentials of age, sex, ethnic status, and social class. Pressures for anomie or normlessness vary from one social position to another, depending on the nature of these differentials.

In summary, Merton extends the theory of anomie in two principal ways. He explicitly identifies types of anomic or malintegrated societies by focussing upon the relationship between cultural goals and norms. And, by directing attention to patterned differentials in the access to success-goals by legitimate means, he shows how the social structure exerts a strain upon the cultural structure, leading in turn to anomie or normlessness.

Phase III: The Concept of Illegitimate Means   Once processes generating differentials in pressures are identified, there is then the question of how these pressures are resolved, or how men respond to them. In this connection, Merton enumerates five basic categories of behavior or role adaptations which are likely to emerge: conformity, innovation, ritualism, retreatism, and rebellion. These adaptations differ depending on the individual's acceptance or rejection of cultural goals, and depending on his adherence to or violation of institutional norms. Furthermore, Merton sees the distribution of these adaptations principally as the consequence of two variables: the relative extent of pressure, and values, particularly "internalized prohibitions," governing the use of various illegitimate means.

It is a familiar sociological idea that values serve to order the choices of deviant (as well as conforming) adaptations which develop under conditions of stress. Comparative studies of ethnic groups, for example, have shown that some tend to engage in distinctive forms of deviance; thus Jews exhibit low rates of alcoholism and alcoholic psychoses.[7] Various investigators have suggested that the emphasis on rationality, fear of expressing aggression, and other alleged components of the "Jewish" value system constrain modes of deviance which involve "loss of control" over behavior.[8] In contrast, the Irish show a much higher rate of alcoholic deviance because, it has been argued, their cultural emphasis on masculinity encourages the excessive use of alcohol under conditions of strain.[9]

Merton suggests that differing rates of ritualistic and innovating behavior in the middle and lower classes result from differential emphases in socialization. The "rule-oriented" accent in middle-class socialization presumably disposes persons to handle stress by engaging in ritualistic rather than innovating behavior. The lower-class person, contrastingly, having internalized less stringent norms, can violate conventions with less guilt and anxiety.[10] Values, in other words, exercise a canalizing influence, limiting the choice of deviant adaptations for persons variously distributed throughout the social system.

Apart from both socially patterned pressures, which give rise to deviance, and from values, which determine choices of adaptations, a further variable should be taken into account: namely, *differentials in availability of illegitimate means.* For example, the notion that innovating behavior may result from unfulfilled aspirations and imperfect socialization with respect to conventional norms implies that illegitimate means are freely available— as if the individual, having decided that "you can't make it legitimately," then simply turns to illegitimate means which are readily at hand whatever his position in the social structure. However, these means may not be available. As noted above, the anomie theory assumes that conventional means are differentially distributed, that some individuals, because of their social position, enjoy certain advantages which are denied to others. Note, for example, variations in the degree to which members of various classes are fully exposed to and thus acquire the values, education, and skills which facilitate upward mobility. It should not be startling, therefore, to find similar variations in the availability of illegitimate means.

Several sociologists have alluded to such variations without explicitly incorporating this variable in a theory of deviant behavior. Sutherland, for example, writes that "an inclination to steal is not a sufficient explanation of the genesis of the professional thief."[11] Moreover, "the person must be appreciated by the professional thieves. He must be appraised as having an adequate equipment of wits, front, talking-ability, honesty, reliability, nerve and determination." In short, "a person can be a professional thief only if he is recognized and received as such by other professional thieves." But recognition is not freely accorded: "Selection and tutelage are the two necessary elements in the process of acquiring recognition as a professional thief. . . . A person cannot acquire recognition as a professional thief until he has had tutelage in professional theft, *and tutelage is given only to a few persons selected from the total population.*" Furthermore, the aspirant is judged by high standards of performance, for only "a very small percentage of those who start on this process ever reach the stage of professional theft." The burden of these remarks—dealing with the processes of selection, induction, and assumption of full status in the criminal group—is that motivations or pressures toward deviance do not fully account for deviant behavior. The "self-made" thief—lacking knowledge of the ways of securing immunity from prosecution and similar techniques of defense—"would quickly land in prison." Sutherland is in effect pointing to differentials in access to the role of professional thief. Although the criteria of selection are not altogether clear from his analysis, definite evaluative standards do appear to exist; depending on their content, certain categories of individuals would be placed at a disadvantage and others would be favored.

The availability of illegitimate means, then, is controlled by various criteria in the same manner that has long been ascribed to conventional means. Both systems of opportunity are (1) limited, rather than infinitely available, and (2) differentially available depending on the location of persons in the social structure.

When we employ the term "means," whether legitimate or illegitimate, at least two things are implied: first, that there are appropriate learning environments for the acquisition of the values and skills associated with the performance of a particular role; and second, that the individual has opportunities to discharge the role once he has been prepared. The term subsumes, therefore, both *learning structures* and *opportunity structures.*

A case in point is recruitment and preparation for careers in the rackets. There are fertile criminal learning environments for the young in neighborhoods where the rackets flourish as stable, indigenous institutions. Because these environments afford integration of offenders of different ages, the young are exposed to "differential associations" which facilitate the acquisition of criminal values and skills. Yet preparation for the role may not insure that the individual will ever discharge it. For one thing, more youngsters may be recruited into these patterns of differential association than can possibly be absorbed, following their "training," by the adult criminal structure. There may be a surplus of contenders for these elite positions, leading in turn to the necessity for criteria and mechanisms of selection. Hence a certain proportion of those who aspire may not be permitted to engage in the behavior for which they have been prepared.

This illustration is similar in every respect, save for the route followed, to the case of those who seek careers in the sphere of legitimate business.

Here, again, is the initial problem of securing access to appropriate learning environments, such as colleges and post-graduate school of business. Having acquired the values and skills needed for a business career, graduates then face the problem of whether or not they can successfully discharge the roles for which they have been prepared. Formal training itself is not sufficient for occupational success, for many forces intervene to determine who shall succeed and fail in the competitive world of business and industry—as throughout the entire conventional occupational structure.

This distinction between learning structures and opportunity structures was suggested some years ago by Sutherland. In 1944, he circulated an unpublished paper which briefly discusses the proposition that "criminal behavior is partially a function of opportunities to commit specific classes of crimes, such as embezzlement, bank burglary, or illicit heterosexual intercourse."[12] He did not, however, take up the problem of differentials in opportunity as a concept to be systematically incorporated in a theory of deviant behavior. Instead, he held that "opportunity" is a necessary but not sufficient explanation of the commission of criminal acts, "since some persons who have opportunities to embezzle, become intoxicated, engage in illicit heterosexual intercourse or to commit other crimes do not do so." He also noted that the differential association theory did not constitute a full explanation of criminal activity, for, notwithstanding differential association, "it is axiomatic that persons who commit a specific crime must have the opportunity to commit that crime." He therefore concluded that "while opportunity may be partially a function of association with criminal patterns and of the specialized techniques thus acquired, *it is not determined entirely in that manner*, and consequently differential association is not the sufficient cause of criminal behavior." (emphasis not in original)

In Sutherland's statements, two meanings are attributed to the term "opportunity." As suggested above, it may be useful to separate these for analytical purposes. In the first sense, Sutherland appears to be saying that opportunity consists in part of learning structures. The principal components of his theory of differential association are that "criminal behavior is learned," and, furthermore, that "criminal behavior is learned in interaction with other persons in a process of communication." But he also uses the term to describe situations conducive to carrying out criminal roles. Thus, for Sutherland, the commission of a criminal act would seem to depend upon the existence of two conditions: differential associations favoring the acquisition of criminal values and skills, and conditions encouraging participation in criminal activity.

This distinction heightens the importance of identifying and questioning the common assumption that illegitimate means are freely available. We can now ask (1) whether there are socially structured differentials in access to illegitimate learning environments, and (2) whether there are differentials limiting the fulfillment of illegitimate roles. If differentials exist and can be identified, we may then inquire about their consequences for the behavior of persons in different parts of the social structure. Before pursuing this question, however, we turn to a fuller discussion of the theoretical tradition established by Shaw, McKay, and Sutherland.

DIFFERENTIALS IN AVAILABILITY OF ILLEGITIMATE MEANS: THE SUBCULTURE TRADITION

The concept of differentials in availability of illegitimate means is implicit in one of the major streams of American criminological theory. In this tradition, attention is focussed on the processes by which persons are recruited into criminal learning environments and ultimately inducted into criminal roles. The problems here are to account for the acquisition of criminal roles and to describe the social organization of criminal activities. When the theoretical propositions contained in this tradition are reanalyzed, it becomes clear that one underlying conception is that of variations in access to success-goals by illegitimate means. Furthermore, this implicit concept may be shown to be one of the bases upon which the tradition was constructed.

In their studies of the ecology of deviant behavior in the urban environment, Shaw and McKay found that delinquency and crime tended to be confined to delimited areas and, furthermore, that such behavior persisted despite demographic changes in these areas. Hence they came to speak of "criminal tradition," of the "cultural transmission" of criminal values.[13] As a result of their observations of slum life, they concluded that *particular importance must be assigned to the integration of different age-levels of offenders*. Thus:

> Stealing in the neighborhood was a common practice among the children and approved by the parents. Whenever the boys got together they talked about robbing and made more plans for stealing. I hardly knew any boys who did not go robbing. The little fellows went in for petty stealing, breaking into freight cars, and stealing junk. The older guys did big jobs like stick-up, burglary, and stealing autos. The little fellows admired the "big shots" and longed for the day when they could get into the big racket. Fellows who had "done time" were the big shots and looked up to and gave the little fellow tips on how to get by and pull off big jobs.[14]

In other words, access to criminal roles depends upon stable associations with others from whom the necessary values and skills may be learned. Shaw and McKay were describing deviant learning structures—that is, alternative routes by which people seek access to the goals which society holds to be worthwhile. They might also have pointed out that, in areas where such learning structures are unavailable, it is probably difficult for many individuals to secure access to stable criminal careers, even though motivated to do so.[15]

The concept of illegitimate means and the socially structured conditions of access to them were not explicitly recognized in the work of Shaw and McKay because, probably, they were disposed to view slum areas as "disorganized." Although they consistently referred to illegitimate activities as being organized, they nevertheless often depicted high-rate delinquency areas as disorganized because the values transmitted were criminal rather than conventional. Hence their work includes statements which we now perceive to be internally inconsistent, such as the following:

> This community situation [in which Sidney was reared] was not only disorganized and thus ineffective as a unit of control, but it was characterized by a high rate of juvenile delinquency and adult crime, not to mention the widespread political corruption which had long existed in the area. Various forms of stealing and many organized delinquent and criminal gangs were prevalent in the area. These groups exercised a powerful influence and tended to create a community spirit which not only tolerated but actually fostered delinquent and criminal practices.[16]

Sutherland was among the first to perceive that the concept of social disorganization tended to obscure the stable patterns of interaction among carriers of criminal values. Like Shaw and McKay, he had been influenced by the observation that lower-class areas were organized in terms of both conventional and criminal values, but he was also impressed that these alternative value systems were supported by patterned systems of social relations. He expressly recognized that crime, far from being a random, unorganized activity, was typically an intricate and stable system of human arrangements. He therefore rejected the concept of "social disorganization" and substituted the concept of "differential group organization."

> The third concept, social disorganization, was borrowed from Shaw and McKay. I had used it but had not been satisfied with it because the organization of the delinquent group, which is often very complex, is social disorganization only from an ethical or some other particularistic point of view. At the suggestion of Albert K. Cohen, this concept has been changed to differential group organization, with organization for criminal activities on one side and organization against criminal activites on the other.[17]

Having freed observation of the urban slum from conventional evaluations, Sutherland was able to focus more clearly on the way in which its social structure constitutes a "learning environment" for the acquisition of deviant values and skills. In the development of the theory of "differential association" and "differential group organization," he came close to stating explicitly the concept of differentials in access to illegitimate means. But Sutherland was essentially interested in learning processes, and thus he did not ask how such access varies in different parts of the social structure, nor did he inquire about the consequences for behavior of variations in the accessibility of these means.[18]

William F. Whyte, in his classic study of an urban slum, advanced the empirical description of the structure and organization of illegitimate means a step beyond that of Sutherland. Like Sutherland, Whyte rejected the earlier view of the slum as disorganized:

> It is customary for the sociologist to study the slum district in terms of "social disorganization" and to neglect to see that an area such as Cornerville has

a complex and well-established organization of its own. . . . I found that in every group there was a hierarchical structure of social relations binding the individuals to one another and that the groups were also related hierarchically to one another. Where the group was formally organized into a political club, this was immediately apparent, but for informal groups it was no less true.[19]

Whyte's contribution to our understanding of the organization of illegitimate means in the slum consists primarily in showing that individuals who participate in stable illicit enterprise do not constitute a separate or isolated segment of the community. Rather, these persons are closely integrated with the occupants of conventional roles. In describing the relationship between racketeers and politicians, for example, he notes that "the rackets and political organizations extend from the bottom to the top of Cornerville society, mesh with one another, and integrate a large part of the life of the district. They provide a general framework for the understanding of the actions of both 'little guys' and 'big shots.' "[20] Whyte's view of the slum differs somewhat from that conveyed by the term "differential group organization." He does not emphasize the idea that the slum is composed of two different systems, conventional and deviant, but rather the way in which the occupants of these various roles are integrated in a single, stable structure which organizes and patterns the life of the community.

The description of the organization of illegitimate means in slums is further developed by Solomon Kobrin in his article, "The Conflict of Values in Delinquency Areas."[21] Kobrin suggests that urban slum areas vary in the degree to which the carriers of deviant and conventional values are integrated with one another. Hence he points the way to the development of a "typology of delinquency areas based on variations in the relationship between these two systems," depicting the "polar types" on such a continuum. The first type resembles the integrated areas described in preceding paragraphs. Here, claims Kobrin, there is not merely structural integration between carriers of the two value systems, but reciprocal participation by each in the value system of the other. Thus:

> Leaders of [illegal] enterprises frequently maintain membership in such conventional institutions of their local communities as churches, fraternal and mutual benefit societies and political parties. . . . Within this framework the influence of each of the two value systems is reciprocal, the leaders of illegal enterprise participating in the primary orientation of the conventional elements in the population, and the latter, through their participation in a local power structure sustained in large part by illicit activity, participating perforce in the alternate, criminal value system.

Kobrin also notes that in some urban slums there is a tendency for the relationships between carriers of deviant and conventional values to break down. Such areas constitute the second polar type. Because of disorganizing forces such as "drastic change in the class, ethnic, or racial characteristics of its population." Kobrin suggests that "the bearers of the conventional culture and its value system are without the customary institutional machinery and therefore in effect partially demobilized with reference to the diffusion of their value system." At the same time, the criminal "value system remains implicit" since this type of area is "characterized principally by the absence of systematic and organized adult activity in violation of the law, despite the fact that many adults in these areas commit violations." Since both value systems remain implicit, the possibilities for effective integration are precluded.

The importance of these observations may be seen if we ask how accessibility of illegal means varies with the relative integration of conventional and criminal values from one type of area to another. In this connection, Kobrin points out that the "integrated" area apparently constitutes a "training ground" for the acquisition of criminal values and skills.

> The stable position of illicit enterprise in the adult society of the community is reflected in the character of delinquent conduct on the part of children. While delinquency in all high rate areas is intrinsically disorderly in that it is unrelated to official programs for the education of the young, in the [integrated community] boys may more or less realistically recognize the potentialities for personal progress in local society through access to delinquency. In a general way, therefore, delinquent activity in these areas constitutes a training ground for the acquisition of skill in the use of violence, concealment of offense, evasion of detection and arrest, and the purchase of immunity from punishment. Those who come to excel in these respects are frequently noted and valued by adult leaders in the rackets who are confronted, as are the leaders of all income-producing enterprises, with problems of the recruitment of competent personnel.

With respect to the contrasting or "unintegrated area," Kobrin makes no mention of the extent to which learning structures and opportunities for criminal careers are available. Yet his portrayal of such areas as lacking in the articulation of either conventional or criminal values suggests that the appropriate learning structures—principally the integration of offenders of different age levels—are not available. Furthermore, his depiction of adult violative activity as "unorganized" suggests that the illegal opportunity structure is severely limited. Even if youngsters were able to secure adequate preparation for criminal roles, the problem would appear to be that the social structure of such neighborhoods provides few opportunities for stable, criminal careers. For Kobrin's analysis—as well as those of Whyte and others before him—leads to the conclusion that illegal opportunity structures tend to emerge in lower-class areas only when stable patterns of accommodation and integration arise between the carriers of conventional and deviant values. Where these values remain unorganized and implicit, or where their carriers are in open conflict, opportunities for stable criminal role performance are more or less limited.[22]

Other factors may be cited which affect access to criminal roles. For example, there is a good deal of anecdotal evidence which reveals that access to the upper echelons of organized racketeering is controlled, at least in part, by ethnicity. Some ethnic groups are found disproportionately in the upper ranks and others disproportionately in the lower. From an historical perspective, as Bell has shown, this realm has been successively dominated by Irish, East-European Jews, and more recently, by Italians.[23]

Various other ethnic groups have been virtually excluded or at least relegated to lower-echelon positions. Despite the fact that many rackets (especially "policy") have flourished in predominantly Negro neighborhoods, there have been but one or two Negroes who have been known to rise to the top in syndicated crime. As in the conventional world, Negroes are relegated to the more menial tasks. Moreover, access to elite positions in the rackets may be governed in part by kinship criteria, for various accounts of the blood relations among top racketeers indicate that nepotism is the general rule.[24] It has also been noted that kinship criteria sometimes govern access to stable criminal roles, as in the case of the pickpocket.[25] And there are, of course, deep-rooted sex differentials in access to illegal means. Although women are often employed in criminal vocations—for example, thievery, confidence games, and extortion—and must be employed in others—such as prostitution—nevertheless females are excluded from many criminal activities.[26]

Of the various criteria governing access to illegitimate means, class differentials may be among the most important. The differentials noted in the preceding paragraph—age, sex, ethnicity, kinship, and the like—all pertain to criminal activity historically associated with the lower class. Most middle- or upper-class persons—even when interested in following "lower-class" criminal careers—would no doubt have difficulty in fulfilling this ambition because of inappropriate preparation. The prerequisite attitudes and skills are more easily acquired if the individual is a member of the lower class; most middle- and upper-class persons could not easily unlearn their own class culture in order to learn a new one. By the same token, access to many "white collar" criminal roles is closed to lower-class persons. Some occupations afford abundant opportunities to engage in illegitimate activity; others offer virtually none. The businessman, for example, not only has at his disposal the means to do so, but, as some studies have shown, he is under persistent pressure to employ illegitimate means, if only to maintain a competitive advantage in the market place. But for those in many other occupations, white collar modes of criminal activity are simply not an alternative.[27]

SOME IMPLICATIONS OF A CONSOLIDATED APPROACH TO DEVIANT BEHAVIOR

It is now possible to consolidate the two sociological traditions described above. Our analysis makes it clear that these traditions are oriented to different aspects of the same problem: differentials in access to opportunity. One tradition focusses on legitimate opportunity, the other on illegitimate. By incorporating the concept of differentials in access to *illegitimate* means, the theory of anomie may be extended to include seemingly unrelated studies and theories of deviant behavior which form a part of the literature of American criminology. In this final section, we try to show how a consolidated approach might advance the understanding of both rates and types of deviant conduct. The discussion centers on the conditions of access to *both* systems of means, legitimate and illegitimate.

The Distribution of Criminal Behavior One problem which has plagued the criminologist is the absence of adequate data on social differentials in criminal activity. Many have held that the highest crime rates are to be found in the lower social strata. Others have suggested that rates in the middle and upper classes may be much higher than is ordinarily thought. The question of the social distribution of crime remains problematic.

In the absence of adequate data, the theorist has sometimes attacked this problem by assessing the extent of pressures toward normative departures in various parts of the social structure. For example, Merton remarks that his "primary aim is to discover how some social structures exert a definite pressure upon certain persons in the society to engage in nonconforming rather than conforming conduct."[28] Having identified structural features which might be expected to generate deviance, Merton suggests the presence of a correlation between "pressures toward deviation" and "rate of deviance."

> But whatever the differential rates of deviant behavior in the several social strata, and we know from many sources that the official crime statistics uniformly showing higher rates in the lower strata are far from complete or reliable, *it appears from our analysis that the greater pressures toward deviation are exerted upon the lower strata.* . . . Of those located in the lower reaches of the social structure, the culture makes incompatible demands. On the one hand they are asked to orient their behavior toward the prospect of large wealth . . . and on the other, they are largely denied effective opportunities to do so institutionally. *The consequence of this structural inconsistency is a high rate of deviant behavior.*[29]

Because of the paucity and unreliability of existing criminal statistics, there is as yet no way of knowing whether or not Merton's hypothesis is correct. Until comparative studies of crime rates are available the hypothesized correlation cannot be tested.

From a theoretical perspective, however, questions may be raised about this correlation. Would we expect, to raise the principal query, the correlation to be fixed or to vary depending on the distribution of access to illegitimate means? The three possibilities are (1) that access is distributed uniformly throughout the class structure, (2) that access varies inversely with class position, and (3) that access varies directly with class position. Specification of these possibilities permits a more precise statement of the conditions under which crime rates would be expected to vary.

If access to illegitimate means is *uniformly distributed* throughout the class structure, then the proposed correlation would probably hold—higher rates of innovating behavior would be expected in the lower class than elsewhere. Lower-class persons apparently experience greater pressures toward deviance and are less restrained by internalized prohibitions from employing illegitimate means. Assuming uniform access to such means, it would therefore be reasonable to predict higher rates of innovating behavior in the lower social strata.

If access to illegitimate means varies *inversely* with class position, then the correlation would not only hold, but might even be strengthened. For pressures toward deviance, including socialization that does not altogether discourage the use of illegitimate means, would coincide with the availability of such means.

Finally, if access varies *directly* with class position, comparative rates of illegitimate activity become difficult to forecast. The higher the class position, the less the pressure to employ illegitimate means; furthermore, internalized prohibitions are apparently more effective in higher positions. If, at the same time, opportunities to use illegitimate methods are more abundant, then these factors would be in opposition. Until the precise effects of these several variables can be more adequately measured, rates cannot be safely forecast.

The concept of differentials in availability of illegitimate means may also help to clarify questions about varying crime rates among ethnic, age, religious, and sex groups, and other social divisions. This concept, then, can be systematically employed in the effort to further our understanding of the distribution of illegitimate behavior in the social structure.

Modes of Adaptation: The Case of Retreatism   By taking into account the conditions of access to legitimate *and* illegitimate means, we can further specify the circumstances under which various modes of deviant behavior arise. This may be illustrated by the case of retreatism.[30]

As defined by Merton, retreatist adaptations include such categories of behavior as alcoholism, drug addiction, and psychotic withdrawal. These adaptations entail "escape" from the frustrations of unfulfilled aspirations by withdrawal from conventional social relationships. The processes leading to retreatism are described by Merton as follows: "[Retreatism] arises from continued failure to near the goal by legitimate measures and from an inability to use the illegitimate route because of internalized prohibitions, *this process occurring while the supreme value of the success-goal has not yet been renounced.* The conflict is resolved by abandoning *both* precipitating elements, the goals and means. The escape is complete, the conflict is eliminated and the individual is asocialized."[31]

In this view, a crucial element encouraging retreatism is internalized constraint concerning the use of illegitimate means. But this element need not be present. Merton apparently assumed that such prohibitions are essential because, in their absence, the logic of his scheme would compel him to predict that innovating behavior would result. But the assumption that the individual uninhibited in the use of illegitimate means becomes an innovator presupposes that successful innovation is only a matter of motivation. Once the concept of differentials in access to illegitimate means is introduced, however, it becomes clear that retreatism is possible even in the absence of internalized prohibitions. For we may now ask how individuals respond when they fail in the use of *both* legitimate and illegitimate means. If illegitimate means are unavailable, if efforts at innovation fail, then retreatist adaptations may still be the consequence, and the "escape" mechanisms chosen by the defeated individual may perhaps be all the more deviant because of his "double failure."

This does not mean that retreatist adaptations cannot arise precisely as Merton suggests: namely, that the conversion from conformity to retreatism takes place in one step, without intervening adaptations. But this is only one route to retreatism. The conversion may at times entail intervening stages and intervening adaptations, particularly of an innovating type. This possibility helps to account for the fact that certain categories of individuals cited as retreatists—for example, hobos—often show extensive histories of arrests and convictions for various illegal acts. It also helps to explain retreatist adaptations among individuals who have not necessarily internalized strong restraints on the use of illegitimate means. In short, retreatist adaptations may arise with considerable frequency among those who are failures in both worlds, conventional and illegitimate alike.[32]

Future research on retreatist behavior might well examine the interval between conformity and retreatism. To what extent does the individual entertain the possibility of resorting to illegitimate means, and to what extent does he actually seek to mobilize such means? If the individual turns to innovating devices, the question of whether or not he becomes a retreatist may then depend upon the relative accessibility of illegitimate means. For although the frustrated conformist seeks a solution to status discontent by adopting such methods, there is the further problem of whether or not he possesses appropriate skills and has opportunities for their use. We suggest therefore that data be gathered on preliminary responses to status discontent—and on the individual's perceptions of the efficacy of employing illegitimate means, the content of his skills, and the objective situation of illegitimate opportunity available to him.

Respecification of the processes leading to retreatism may also help to resolve difficulties entailed in ascertaining rates of retreatism in different parts of the social structure. Although Merton does not indicate explicitly where this adaptation might be expected to arise, he specifies some of the social conditions which encourage high rates of retreatism. Thus the latter is apt to mark the behavior of downwardly mobile persons, who experience a sudden breakdown in established social relations, and such individuals as the retired, who have lost major social roles.[33]

The long-standing difficulties in forecasting differential rates of retreatism may perhaps be attributed to the assumption that retreatists have fully internalized values prohibiting the use of illegitimate means. That this prohibition especially characterizes socialization in the middle and upper classes probably calls for the prediction that retreatism occurs primarily in those classes—and that the hobohemias, "drug cultures," and the ranks of the alcoholics are populated primarily by individuals from the upper reaches of society. It would appear from various accounts of hobohemia and skid row, however, that many of these persons are the products of slum life, and, furthermore, that their behavior is not necessarily controlled by values which preclude resort to illegitimate means. But once it is recognized that retreatism may arise in response to limitations on both systems of means, the difficulty of locating this adaptation is lessened, if not resolved. Thus retreatist behavior may vary with the particular process by which it is generated. The process described by Merton may be somewhat more characteristic of higher positions in the social structure where rule-oriented socialization is typical, while in the lower strata retreatism may tend more often to be the consequence of unsuccessful attempts at innovation.

SUMMARY

This paper attempts to identify and to define the concept of differential opportunity structures. It has been suggested that this concept helps to extend the developing theory of social structure and anomie. Furthermore, by linking propositions regarding the accessibility of *both* legitimate and illegitimate opportunity structures, a basis is provided for consolidating various major traditions of sociological thought on nonconformity. The concept of differential systems of opportunity and of variations in access to them, it is hoped, will suggest new possibilities for research on the relationship between social structure and deviant behavior.

NOTES

[1] This paper is based on research conducted in a penal setting. For a more detailed statement see Richard A. Cloward, *Social Control and Anomie: A Study of a Prison Community* (Glencoe, Ill.: The Free Press).

[2] See especially Emile Durkheim, *Suicide*, translated by J. A. Spaulding and George Simpson (Glencoe, Ill.: The Free Press, 1951); and Robert K. Merton, *Social Theory and Social Structure* (Glencoe, Ill.: The Free Press, 1957), Chaps. 4 and 5.

[3] See especially the following: Clifford R. Shaw, *The Jack-Roller* (Chicago: University of Chicago Press, 1930); Clifford R. Shaw, *The Natural History of a Delinquent Career* (Chicago: University of Chicago Press, 1931); Clifford R. Shaw et al., *Delinquency Areas* (Chicago: University of Chicago Press, 1940); Clifford R. Shaw and Henry D. McKay, *Juvenile Delinquency and Urban Areas* (Chicago: University of Chicago Press, 1942); Edwin H. Sutherland, ed., *The Professional Thief* (Chicago: University of Chicago Press, 1937); Edwin H. Sutherland, *Principles of Criminology*, 4th ed. (Philadelphia: Lippincott, 1947); Edwin H. Sutherland, *White Collar Crime* (New York: Dryden, 1949).

[4] "Illegitimate means" are those proscribed by the mores. The concept therefore includes "illegal means" as a special case but is not coterminous with illegal behavior, which refers only to the violation of legal norms. In several parts of this paper, I refer to particular forms of deviant behavior which entail violation of the law and there use the more restricted term, "illegal means." But the more general concept of illegitimate means is needed to cover the wider gamut of deviant behavior and to relate the theories under review here to the evolving theory of "legitimacy" in sociology.

[5] All of the excerpts in this section are from Durkheim, *op. cit.*, pp. 247–257.

[6] For this excerpt and those which follow immediately see Merton, *op. cit.*, pp. 131–194.

[7] See, e.g., Seldon D. Bacon, "Social Settings Conducive to Alcoholism—A Sociological Approach to a Medical Problem," *Journal of the American Medical Association*, 16 (1957), pp. 177–181; Robert F. Bales, "Cultural Differences in Rates of Alcoholism," *Quarterly Journal of Studies on Alcohol*, 16 (1946), pp. 480–499; Jerome H. Skolnick, "A Study of the Relation of Ethnic Background to Arrests for Inebriety," *Quarterly Journal of Studies on Alcohol*, 15 (1954), pp. 451–474.

[8] See Isidor T. Thorner, "Ascetic Protestantism and Alcoholism," *Psychiatry*, 16 (1953), pp. 167–176; and Nathan Glazer, "Why Jews Stay Sober," *Commentary*, 13 (1952), pp. 181–186.

[9] See Bales, *op. cit.*

[10] Merton, *op. cit.*, p. 151.

11 For this excerpt and those which follow immediately, see Sutherland, *The Professional Thief, op. cit.,* pp. 211–213.

12 For this excerpt and those which follow immediately see Albert Cohen, Alfred Lindesmith, and Karl Schuessler, editors, *The Sutherland Papers* (Bloomington: Indiana University Press, 1956), pp. 31–35.

13 See especially *Delinquency Areas,* Chap. 16.

14 Shaw, *The Jack-Roller,* p. 54.

15 We are referring here, and throughout the paper, to stable criminal roles to which persons may orient themselves on a career basis, as in the case of racketeers, professional thieves, and the like. The point is that access to stable roles depends in the first instance upon the availability of learning structures. As Frank Tannenbaum says, "it must be insisted on that unless there were older criminals in the neighborhood who provided a moral judgement in favor of the delinquent and to whom the delinquents could look for commendation, the careers of the younger ones could not develop at all." *Crime and the Community* (Boston: Ginn, 1938), p. 60.

16 Shaw, *The Natural History of a Delinquent Career, op. cit.,* p. 229.

17 Cohen, Lindesmith, and Schuessler, *op. cit.,* p. 21.

18 It is interesting to note that the concept of differentials in access to *legitimate* means did not attain explicit recognition in Sutherland's work, nor in the work of many others in the "subculture" tradition. This attests to the independent development of the two traditions being discussed. Thus the ninth proposition in the differential association theory is stated as follows:

> (9) *Though criminal behavior is an expression of general needs and values, it is not explained by those general needs and values since noncriminal behavior is an expression of the same needs and values.* Thieves generally steal in order to secure money, but likewise honest laborers work in order to secure money. The attempts by many scholars to explain criminal behavior by general drives and values, such as the happiness principle, striving for social status, the money motive, or frustration, have been and must continue to be futile since they explain lawful behavior as completely as they explain criminal behavior.

Of course, it is perfectly true that "striving for status," the "money motive" and similar modes of socially approved goal-oriented behavior do not as such account for both deviant and conformist behavior. But if goal-oriented behavior occurs under conditions of socially structured obstacles to fulfillment by legitimate means, the resulting pressures might then lead to deviance. In other words, Sutherland appears to assume that the distribution of access to success-goals by legitimate means is uniform rather than variable, irrespective of location in the social structure. See his *Principles of Criminology,* 4th ed., pp. 7–8.

19 William F. Whyte, *Street Corner Society,* original ed., 1943 (Chicago: University of Chicago Press, 1955), p. viii.

20 *Ibid.,* p. xviii.

21 *American Sociological Review,* 16 (1951), pp. 657–658, which includes the excerpts which follow immediately.

22 The excellent work by Albert K. Cohen has been omitted from this discussion because it is dealt with in a second article, "Types of Delinquent Subcultures," prepared jointly with Lloyd E. Ohlin (mimeographed, December, 1958, New York School of Social Work, Columbia University). It may be noted that although Cohen does not explicitly affirm continuity with either the Durkheim-Merton or the Shaw-McKay-Sutherland traditions, we believe that he clearly belongs in the former. He does not deal with what appears to be the essence of the Shaw-McKay-Sutherland tradition, namely, the crucial social functions performed by the integration of offenders of differing age-levels and the integration of adult carriers of criminal and conventional values. Rather, he is concerned primarily with the way in which discrepancies between status aspirations and possibilities for achievement generate pressures for delinquent behavior. The latter notion is a central feature in the anomie tradition.

23 Daniel Bell, "Crime as an American Way of Life," *The Antioch Review* (summer, 1953), pp. 131–154.

[24] For a discussion of kinship relationships among top racketeers see Stanley Frank, "The Rap Gangsters Fear Most," *The Saturday Evening Post* (August 9, 1958), p. 26ff. This article is based on a review of the files of the United States Immigration and Naturalization Service.

[25] See David W. Maurer, *Whiz Mob: A Correlation of the Technical Argot of Pickpockets with Their Behavior Pattern*, Publication of the American Dialect Society, No. 24, 1955.

[26] For a discussion of racial, nationality, and sex differentials governing access to a stable criminal role, see *ibid.*, Chap. 6.

[27] Training in conventional, specialized occupational skills is often a prerequisite for the commission of white collar crimes, since the individual must have these skills in hand before he can secure a position entailing "trust." As Cressey says, "it may be observed that persons trained to carry on the routine duties of a position of trust have at the same time been trained in whatever skills are necessary for the violation of that position, and the technical skill necessary to trust violation is simply the technical skill necessary to holding the position in the first place." (Donald R. Cressey, *Other People's Money* [Glencoe, Ill.: The Free Press, 1953], pp. 81–82.) Thus skills required in certain crimes need not be learned in association with criminals; they can be acquired through conventional learning.

[28] Merton, *op. cit.*, p. 132.

[29] *Ibid.*, pp. 144–145.

[30] Retreatist behavior is but one of many types of deviant adaptations which might be re-analyzed in terms of this consolidated theoretical approach. In subsequent papers, being prepared jointly with Lloyd E. Ohlin, other cases of deviant behavior— e.g., collective disturbances in prisons and subcultural adaptations among juvenile delinquents—will be examined. In this connection, see fn. 22.

[31] Merton, *op. cit.*, pp. 153–154.

[32] The processes of "double failure" being specified here may be of value in re-analyzing the correlation between alcoholism and petty crime. Investigation of the *careers* of petty criminals who are alcoholic may reveal that after being actively oriented toward stable criminal careers they then lost out in the competitive struggle. See, e.g., Irwin Deutscher, "The Petty Offender: A Sociological Alien," *The Journal of Criminal Law, Criminology and Police Science*, 44 (1954), pp. 592–595; Albert D. Ullman *et al.*, "Some Social Characteristics of Misdemeanants," *The Journal of Criminal Law, Criminology and Police Science*, 48 (1957), pp. 44–53.

[33] Merton, *op. cit.*, pp. 188–189.

Tensions in the Social Order	EXTREMISM

COMMENTARY

Extremist tendencies, most obvious in their political form, reflect conditions of conflict which transcend tolerable bounds and therefore represent a threat to the social order. According to one widely held view, restated recently by John Bunzel in his study of *Anti-Politics in America*, extremism derives from the

intolerance of ambiguity—its source being a moral certitude which is fundamentally incompatible with the normal political process. Just such a contention
is examined by Martin Trow in his attempt to ferret out the sources of political
support for the late Senator Joseph McCarthy. On the basis of his research
Trow concludes that dissatisfaction with the political, economic and social order,
rather than intolerance *per se* is productive of extremist tendencies.

Joseph Gusfield, in essential agreement with Trow on the existence of structural sources of extremism, examines the weakness of theories of mass politics
in accounting for the etiology of extremism. It is the thesis of his "Mass Society
and Extremist Politics" that the mass society, contrary to the common sense
expecation, may actually facilitate a tolerable degree of political conflict, and
that isolation from mass culture may encourage and reinforce local sources of
extremist politics.

33 Martin Trow

Small Businessmen, Political Tolerance, and Support for McCarthy

In the past few years social scientists have responded to the threat symbolized by but by no means confined to Joseph McCarthy and have made
efforts to explain the variety of illiberal and repressive movements that flourished during much of the first decade following World War II. Such social
scientists as Parsons, Reisman, Shils, Hofstadter, and Lipset have written
books or essays on the men, sentiments, and movements that came to be
known as the "radical right."[1] These writings, and especially the essays that
were collected in the volume *The New American Right*,[2] show an impressively high measure of agreement on the nature of the social forces underlying such diverse popular movements as McCarthyism, the movement for
the Bricker amendment, and the many organized actions against "subversion" in schools, libraries, the mass media, and elsewhere. In addition to the
generally high measure of agreement (or at least convergence) in these
essays, they are also, taken together, both highly persuasive and based on
almost no empirical evidence at all, at least so far as their efforts to explain
the popular support of these movements are concerned.

The essayists in *The New American Right* treated McCarthyism as one
manifestation of the new "radical right," largely assumed its close connection with political intolerance, and discussed the nature and sources of
both as part of their interpretation of the larger phenomenon. And they
saw the rise of this "radical right" as largely a consequence (or manifesta-

Reprinted from *American Journal of Sociology*, 64:3 (1958), pp. 270–281, by permission of the author and the publisher.

tion) of the increasing importance during the postwar years of "status politics"—the projection of people's status anxieties and frustrations onto the political arena—and the correlative decline in the relative importance of class or "interest" politics. Moreover, say the writers, the "status politics" which underlies the rise of the "radical right" tends to flourish in prosperous times, as "interest politics" is associated with depression and economic discontent. And the essayists deal with the "radical right's" mass support chiefly by speculating on the likely locations in our society of pockets of acute status anxieties or concerns.[3] They do this job so thoroughly that they have left little room for surprise regarding the social composition of McCarthy's popular support. The essays show, and quite persuasively, how and why McCarthy got disproportionate support almost everywhere: among old Americans and among new Americans; among the upwardly mobile, the downwardly mobile, and the low status nonmobile; among Catholics, Yankee Protestants, and rural fundamentalists; among workers, small businessmen, the new middle class, and the "new rich," etc. This kind of analysis, which explains every possible or supposed appearance of the phenomenon, is, of course, in part a function of the paucity of data on the issue. But, while such an analysis precludes surprises, it also explains a good deal too much. Unless we can account for the actual distribution of support for a given issue or for a leader or spokesman of this political tendency, without finessing the crucial questions of "more or less," then our analysis loses much of its power and cogency.

A study done in Bennington, Vermont, during 1954 provided data for an intensive analysis of some of the social and social-psychological characteristics of McCarthy supporters in the general population.[4] And though the movement and its leader are no longer part of the American political scene, the Bennington study indicates that the social forces that made for support of McCarthy did not die with his power or his person but remain available to other illiberal and repressive men and movements of the radical right. If that is so, then the study of McCarthy's popular support not merely is of interest to the antiquarian but may shed light on one aspect of the continuing vulnerability of a mass democratic society to radical, right-wing movements.

The study, part of which is reported in this paper,[5] aimed to investigate the social characteristics of McCarthy's supporters in its sample and on this basis make some inferences regarding the social sources of his popular support.[6] At the same time we were able to look into correlates of "political tolerance,"[7] explore the nature and sources of McCarthy's support and "political tolerance" separately and simultaneously, and, by contrast and comparison, throw into bold relief the similarities and differences in the forces underlying these two different sets of sentiments.[8]

McCARTHY'S SUPPORT AND POLITICAL TOLERANCE

The widespread assumption that support for McCarthy was almost always associated with political intolerance seems to gain empirical support when we observe that support for McCarthy and political intolerance were both strongly related to the amount of formal education completed. There is nothing very startling about this: we hardly need an extensive study to know that McCarthy gained much of his popular support from poorly educated, lower-class people who are, as many studies tell us, also least likely to be tolerant of unpopular political minorities and views.

But the matter becomes not quite so routine when we examine the relationship between support for McCarthy and political tolerance holding formal education constant. When we do this, the relationship between intolerance and support for McCarthy almost or wholly disappears (Table 1). On every educational level McCarthy's supporters were about as likely as his opponents to have been tolerant toward the exercise of free speech by political dissidents. In other words, while support of McCarthy and political intolerance were both related to formal education, they were very little related to each other.

TABLE 1.   Support for McCarthy by Political Tolerance,
Holding Formal Education Constant
(Percent)

Education	Grade school		Some high school		High school graduate		Some college and more	
Political tolerance....	High	Low	High	Low	High	Low	High	Low
Favor McCarthy's methods	51	63	44	44	43	45	23	18
N	(54)	(94)	(55)	(68)	(113)	(62)	(197)	(33)

The implications of this finding are many. In its simplest terms it means that, whatever the character and content of the *public* fight between McCarthy and his more prominent opponents, the sources of his support and popularity in the population at large appear to have had little relation to how strongly people support the principles of free speech.

The division over McCarthy in the population at large, at least in Bennington, was not a division between the supporters of and encroachers upon civil liberties. To see it that way is to overlook the very genuine elements of "radicalism"—of anticonservatism—in the McCarthy appeal. On the one hand, many of those who disapproved of McCarthy and his methods did so not out of any particular concern for the preservation of civil liberties or freedom of speech for unpopular minorities but rather out of a feeling that what is done to suppress "subversion" be done in conservative ways through regular legislative or judicial or administrative procedures. But these men, as their responses to our questions show, were often no more concerned with the preservation of freedom of speech than McCarthy himself and much less so than many of his followers. For many of these latter, the majority of them lower class, with little formal schooling, McCarthy's appeal was not that of a man *repressing* free speech but of a man *exercising* it, in what appeared to be bold and fearless ways. Moreover, much of his boldness, violence, and aggression was directed precisely against the conservative authorities and institutions—the "big shots," the "stuffed shirts," the "bureaucrats"—against whom many of his supporters felt anger and resentment. The men who opposed McCarthy, by and large, were solid, better educated, middle-class citizens who identified with the authorities and institutions which were McCarthy's chief targets of attack by the summer of 1954. Many an executive or engineer who watched McCarthy alternately patronize and bully Army Secretary Stevens felt, and not without reason, that he himself and men like him were also under attack.

Our finding that McCarthy's support and political intolerance were not strongly related to each other does not rest solely or even primarily on the one tabulation which shows that the apparent relationship disappears when the education is held constant. That finding did indeed stimulate further inquiry in that same direction, but, as evidence accumulated, it became apparent in many other ways that the social forces underlying McCarthy's popular support were simply not the same as those making for political intolerance. And, like most empirical findings, this one posed a question: If support for McCarthy were not simply an expression of political intolerance, what were its social sources, and how did they differ from the social sources of political intolerance?

Before proceeding to report one part of our investigation into that question, it may be useful to summarize briefly some of its more general findings. It précis, we found that political tolerance is a norm or cluster of norms, very strongly related to cultural sophistication, or "cosmopolitanism," and thus to the level of formal education achieved—*and to very little else.* By contrast, popular support for McCarthy can best be understood as the channeling of certain dissatisfactions with aspects of the social, economic, and political orders. There are two elements present in that formulation: the presence of considerable discontent and dissatisfaction and the ways and directions in which those dissatisfactions are channeled. We found the highest levels of support for McCarthy in social classes and categories which, on one hand, show considerable hostility toward important elements in the social structure and, on the other hand, do not have their hostilities and discontents channeled into and through existing political and economic institutions. By contrast, neither the *level* of discontent nor the *channeling* of discontent appeared to have appreciable bearing on the levels of political tolerance characteristic of these same classes and social categories.

McCARTHY'S SUPPORT, POLITICAL TOLERANCE, AND OCCUPATION

Part of the evidence on which these general propositions are based bears on the relation of economic class and occupation to the sentiments in question. When we divide our sample into the two broad categories of "manual" and "non-manual" workers, the latter including both salaried and self-employed white-collar people, we find little or no difference between them in their support of McCarthy, holding formal education constant. Even when we divide the "non-manual" category into "lower-" and "upper-middle-class" categories, on the basis of income, we still find no appreciable differences in attitudes toward McCarthy within educational categories. But when we distinguish *within* the middle class between salaried and self-employed men, we found marked differences in their respective levels of support for McCarthy (Table 2).

TABLE 2.   SUPPORT FOR McCARTHY BY OCCUPATIONAL GROUP,
            HOLDING FORMAL EDUCATION CONSTANT
                        (Percent)

Education... Occupation..	Less than 4 years of high school			High school graduate			Some college and more		
	Man.*	Sal.*	S.B.*	Man.	Sal.	S.B.	Man.	Sal.	S.B.
Favor McCarthy's methods...	53	38	65	49	36	58	32	22	32
N.........	(188)	(53)	(52)	(59)	(78)	(38)	(35)	(124)	(44)

* Occupation: "Man.": manual workers; "Sal.": salaried employees, including lower and upper white collar, salaried professionals, and executives; "S.B.": small businessmen, including merchants and other small proprietors. Free professionals, farmers, unemployed, and retired people are excluded.

In every educational category the small businessmen showed a distinctly higher proportion of McCarthy supporters than did the salaried men of similar education, and, among those who had not been to college, the small businessmen were even more pro-McCarthy than the manual workers. And the differences were substantial. For example, among the men who did not finish high school, two-thirds of the small businessmen supported McCarthy, as compared with only half the workers who did and only a little more than a third of the salaried employees who did. Among the men who had been to college the differences by occupational group are smaller but still substantial: where one in three of these better-educated small businessmen supported McCarthy, only a little over one in five of the salaried employees with this education did.

There are a number of possible interpretations of this finding, some of which were investigated and rejected in light of the Bennington data.[9] The interpretation that gained strongest support from the data can be summarized in the hypothesis that small businessmen in our society disproportionately tend to develop a generalized hostility toward a complex of symbols and processes bound up with industrial capitalism: the steady growth and concentration of government, labor organizations, and business enterprises; the correlative trend toward greater rationalization of production and distribution; and the men, institutions, and ideas that symbolize these secular trends of modern society. These trends and their symbols were, we believe, McCarthy's most persuasive targets.[10] Quite apart from the questions of Communists in government, and blunders or worse in foreign policy, the congruence between McCarthy's attacks on and small businessmen's hostility to the dominant characteristics and tendencies of modern society account, we believe, for much of the disproportionate support McCarthy gained from small businessmen.[11]

This hypothesis can be explored further by looking at the connections between support for McCarthy and attitudes toward the most characteristic economic institutions of our society, that is, large corporations and trade unions. A simple but serviceable typology emerges from responses to questions asking how the respondent feels about big companies and trade unions and permits us to distinguish empirically four important and easily recognizeable patterns of orientations toward the dominant economic institutions in the population at large.[12] The group which expressed approval of labor unions but suspicion of the power of big companies, (I), is closest to the familiar "labor-liberals," who in this country gave their support to the labor-oriented, administrative liberalism of the New Deal and its descendants. The pro-big business, antiunion group, (IV), resemble the equally familiar "right-wing conservatives." The orientation I have called "modern conservatism," (III), is held by people who are reconciled to the continued existence both of big companies and of trade unions; this is the dominant political orientation of both major parties today.

To the student of right-wing radicalism the most interesting of these four orientations is that which expresses hostility toward both big business and trade unions (II). At the risk of some distortion, I have called this orientation "nineteenth-century liberalism." In the middle of the twentieth century the important thing about this orientation is not its intellectual content but rather its emotional tone, its diffused anger, and its generalized suspicion toward modern tendencies of all kinds. Among our respondents, this nineteenth-century liberalism appears both as a wistful nostalgia for a golden age of small farmers and businessmen and also as an expression of a strong resentment and hatred toward a world which makes no sense in terms of older ideas and which is conducted in apparent violation of old truths and values of economic and political life.[13]

If we look at the distribution of McCarthy support among the holders of these four political orientations (and we did this separately for better- and less-well-educated men), we find that there were scarcely any differences among holders of three of the four orientations in their proportions of McCarthy supporters (Table 3).

But among the poorly educated, as among the better educated, the nineteenth-century liberals gave McCarthy distinctly higher proportions of support than any of the other three orientations we examined. Among the men who had less than four years of high school, the difference between the nineteenth-century liberals and all the others in the proportions supporting McCarthy is the difference between two-thirds and a half. Among

Table 3. McCarthy's Support by Domestic Political Orientations, among Better- and Less-Well-Educated Men
(Percent)

Education........ DPO *	Less than 4 years of high school				4 years of high school and more			
	I	II	III	IV	I	II	III	IV
Favor McCarthy's methods........	44	67	51	51	32	50	29	32
N..............	(90)	(84)	(53)	(43)	(101)	(58)	(137)	(97)

* DPO Type I: Labor-liberal (pro-union; anti-big business)
II: Nineteenth-century liberal (anti-union; anti-big business)
III: Moderate conservative (pro-union; pro-big business)
IV: Right-wing conservative (anti-union; pro-big business)

the better educated, the difference is between a half as compared with a third of all others who gave McCarthy their support.

There are two findings here which are perhaps of equal interest to the student of right-wing radicalism. The first—that there was little difference in the support McCarthy gained among labor-liberals, moderate conservatives, and the right-wing conservatives—contradicts the widespread liberal assumption that McCarthy got much of his mass support from the traditional right-wing conservatives.[14] The other finding, with which we are chiefly concerned here, is that men holding the nineteenth-century liberal orientation toward big business and trade unions showed a markedly greater vulnerability to McCarthy's appeal. These men, as I have noted, are often angrily confused and deeply resentful of a world that continually offends their deepest values. But as important is the fact that this particular well of resentment and indignation has no effective and institutionalized channels of expression. Right-wing conservatives have substantial power in the business community and the Republican party; labor-liberals are a strong force in the trade unions, some big-city machines, and are well represented in the Democratic party; and the moderate conservatives have everything else. It is precisely the political orientation which has no institutionalized place on the political scene, little representation or leadership in the major parties, which sought that voice and place through McCarthy. And he expressed for them their fear and mistrust of bigness and of the slick and subversive ideas that come out of the cities and the big institutions to erode old ways and faiths.

It should come as no surprise to find that the small businessmen in our sample were distinctly more likely than manual workers or salaried employees to hold nineteenth-century liberal views regarding trade unions and large corporations (Table 4). Where small businessmen comprised only one-fifth of the men in these occupational categories in our sample, they contributed a third of the nineteenth-century liberals. Moreover, the small businessmen who *held* these views gave McCarthy a very high measure of support.[15] The very highest proportion of McCarthy supporters among

TABLE 4. DOMESTIC POLITICAL ORIENTATIONS BY OCCUPATIONAL GROUP,
FOR BETTER- AND LESS-WELL-EDUCATED MEN
(Percent)

Education .... Occupation	Less than 4 years of high school			4 years of high school and more		
	Man.*	Sal.*	S.B.*	Man.	Sal.	S.B.
DPO †						
Group I	42	27	19	48	20	21
Group II	29	25	41	12	12	18
Group III	18	25	19	25	40	36
Group IV	11	23	21	15	28	25
Total	100	100	100	100	100	100
N	(180)	(52)	(52)	(87)	(191)	(80)

*See note to Table 2.
†DPO:
Group I: Labor-liberals
Group II: Nineteenth-century liberals
Group III: Moderate conservatives
Group IV: Right-wing conservatives

these categories was found among the poorly educated small businessmen holding these nineteenth-century liberal attitudes; almost three out of four of these men were McCarthy supporters. Here is evidence that a generalized fear of the dominant currents and institutions of modern society was an important source of McCarthy's mass appeal, not *only* among small businessmen, but perhaps especially among a group like small businessmen whose economic and status security is continually threatened by those currents and institutions.

One can hardly consider the connection between economic class and right-wing radicalism in America without thinking of the analysis of the Nazi party's mass support before Hitler took power, an analysis developed by such men as Erich Fromm, Sigmund Neumann, Karl Mannheim, Emil Lederer, and Alfred Meusal.[16] The comparison suggests itself despite, or perhaps even because of, the very great differences in the historical backgrounds and in the social, political, and economic contexts of right-wing radical movements in Europe and the United States. All the observers of naziism are agreed that lower-middle-class tradesmen, shopkeepers, and artisans gave the Nazis a disproportionately large measure of their support before the Nazis took power. And they did so, these observers agree, because of their deep-seated fear of radical proletarianism, on one hand, and of the rapid rationalization of production and distribution—that is to say, the large corporation and the department store—on the other. (These fears involved their concern with *both* material and status security.) To the small German proprietor, Hitler promised to crush radical proletarianism and control big business.

Nothing could seem further from the social scene that these writers were speaking of—societies undergoing almost continuous crisis, experiencing intense class conflicts and increasingly wide desperation and despair —than the general climate in a relatively prosperous, small New England town in 1954. The chief characteristic of Bennington's social and political climate was an absence of intense class conflict or conflict of any kind; rather there was a very considerable amount of tolerance, good humor, and the appearance of widespread optimism about the future. Similarly, nothing could seem more inappropriate to the political orientations of Benningtonians than the apocalyptic analysis applied to pre-Hitler Europe. What is perhaps surprising is that in this climate of optimism, good humor, and low-temperature politics, small businessmen in Bennington were apparently responding to the pressures of industrial capitalism in ways not wholly unlike their beleaguered cousins in the Middle Europe of twenty-five years ago, though at much lower levels of intensity.[17]

McCARTHY'S SUPPORT AND SALARIED EMPLOYEES

But this comparison of the social sources of Hitler's popular support with McCarthy's shows one very striking anomaly. Students of naziism usually speak of the disproportionate support the Nazis got from the German lower middle class, in which they lump small tradesmen, artisans, and businessmen, together with lower white-collar salaried employees. The evidence would seem to justify their approach: Hans Gerth's study of the membership of the Nazi party in 1933 shows that both small proprietors and salaried employees were disproportionately represented in the membership of the Nazi party and to about the same degree, both groups supplying about twice the proportion of Nazi party members as compared with their representation in the population at large.[18] And the students of naziism explain Hitler's support among the salaried white-collar workers in much the same way they explain the support the Nazis got from the small proprietors: largely in terms of their status anxieties—anxieties arising especially out of the discrepancy between their precarious and deteriorating economic positions and their status claims and aspirations.[19]

By contrast, in Bennington the salaried employees not only were not as pro-McCarthy as the small businessmen but were strikingly low in the support they gave him, as indicated above. This was true not only of the better-educated managers, executives, technicians, and salaried professionals who might be expected to identify with McCarthy's high-status targets. It was also true of the less-well-educated and low-income white-collar men. Less than 30 percent of the very large group of salaried employees gave McCarthy their approval and support, as compared with over half of all the small businessmen and merchants.

How can we account for the fact that, while the analysis of the anxieties and politics of small businessmen in pre-Hitler Germany is not irrelevant to our understanding of the political orientations of small businessmen in

Bennington in 1954, the behaviors of the salaried employees in the two situations were almost diametrically opposite? The answer seems to lie in the general orientation of the two classes to modern industrial society. Salaried employees, whether in Germany or the United States, or in the new countries of the Near and Far East,[20] are in general *not* alienated from the dominant trends and institutions of modern society; these trends and developments of concentration, specialization, rationalization, and bureaucratization have created the class of salaried employees and are its natural habitat. But, while accepting the general shape and direction of modern society, the salaried employees in Europe responded violently to short-run crises in capitalist society—to inflation, depression, mass unemployment, and their consequent insecurities of livelihood and social status. In this light it is not surprising that the general orientation of white-collar people in a booming and expanding economy such as the United States has had since World War II should be moderate, conservative, and generally complacent about the political economy and its direction. And this because of, not despite, the fact that the tendencies toward concentration and centralization are great and swift-moving. In pre-Hitler Germany the same classes turned to Hitler in great numbers as the large organizations which structured their lives and careers proved increasingly incapable of providing the material and status security they demanded. Their response was not against large organization but against the collapse of bureaucratic society and toward a man and a party which promised to revive and extend it.[21]

By contrast, small businessmen react not so much to short-run crises in the economy as to its long-range tendencies and direction of development —against the society itself rather than merely to failures of its economy. The tendencies which small businessmen fear—of concentration and centralization—proceed without interruption in depression, war, and prosperity and irrespective of the party in power;[22] thus they are *always* disaffected, though probably the acute pinch they feel in depressions makes their anxieties and angers sharper and more pointed. In this light, the small businessmen in prosperous Bennnigton of 1954 were not so fundamentally different in their response to the social and economic pressures of modern society from the equivalent strata in pre-Hitler Germany, or from their opposite members in the France of the Poujade.

OCCUPATION AND POLITICAL TOLERANCE

It remains to be said, and with some emphasis, that the disproportionate support small businessmen gave to McCarthy is *not* evidence that they constitute a pool of repressive and illiberal sentiments of all kinds. On the contrary, we can see that, despite their vulnerability to a right-wing demagogue like McCarthy, small businessmen are no more politically intolerant than are salaried employees or manual workers of similar education (Table 5). Here again we find that occupation and economic class, and all the varied discontents that flow from membership in different class

Table 5. Political Tolerance by Occupational Group,
Holding Education Constant
(Percent)

Education... Occupation..	Less than 4 years of high school			High school graduate			Some college and more		
	Man.*	Sal.*	S.B.*	Man.	Sal.	S.B.	Man.	Sal.	S.B.
High political tolerance..	36	44	50	60	68	71	81	88	86
N.........	(181)	(52)	(46)	(55)	(78)	(35)	(36)	(120)	(43)

* See Table 2.

and occupational groups, seem to have little bearing on political tolerance, certainly as compared with the bearing of formal education and cultural sophistication. By contrast with support of McCarthy, tolerance of dissidence appears to be almost wholly a function of the degree to which men have learned and internalized the rules of the democratic political game: in the United States this, in turn, is closely related to general political awareness and sophistication, acquired in part through formal education and through exposure to the serious political media which support those norms, rather than through economic or occupational experience.[23] Where political tolerance for the most part is a norm held and enforced in the sub-cultures of sophisticated men, most of whom have been to college, popular support for McCarthy, by contrast, seemed to have been largely the channeled expression of various kinds of socially engendered discontents.[24]

THE "RADICAL RIGHT" AND POPULAR SENTIMENTS

Our findings clearly indicate that students of public opinion on political issues might well be wary of such concepts as the "radical right" and its "pseudo-conservative" members, with all the assumptions regarding a coherent if latent structure of attitudes in the general population that those terms imply. Supporters of the "radical right" have been seen not only as having supported McCarthy but also as hostile to the New Deal, organized labor, the graduated income tax, and the United Nations, as authoritarian in character, intolerant of political non-conformists, and prejudiced against racial and religious groups. Whatever may be said or learned regarding the leaders and activists of right-wing radical movements, it is not likely that these characteristics and sentiments will be found in close association in the population at large. In this respect "radical rightism" may be like "liberalism," whose articulate representatives are usually civil libertarians, internationalists, in favor of organized labor and social welfare programs, whereas in the population at large these supposed components of "liberalism" do not tend to be found together.[25]

The relationship of public opinion to the political process is devious, indirect, and complicated. If it is misleading and dangerous to deduce the structure of political power and its behavior from the distribution of political attitudes in the population at large, as political scientists warn, it is equally erroneous to deduce the nature and distribution of public opinion from the forces and ideologies that clash on high. But the distributions of sentiments on public issues and about public leaders *can* be sensitive indicators to deep-running forces in society—social forces that have heavy political consequences, though *not* necessarily through the public opinions that reveal them. If this is so, then there is a potentially rich source of new knowledge for political sociology in the secondary analysis of existing survey research data.

NOTES

[1] Talcott Parsons, "McCarthyism and American Social Tension: A Sociologist's View," *Yale Review*, 44 (1954), pp. 226–45; David Riesman and Nathan Glazer, "The Intellectuals and the Discontented Classes," *Partisan Review*, 22 (1955), pp. 47–72; Edward A. Shils, *The Torment of Secrecy* (Glencoe, Ill.: The Free Press, 1955); Richard Hofstadter, "The Pseudo-Conservative Revolt," *American Scholar*, 24 (1954), pp. 9–27; S. M. Lipset, "The Radical Right: A Problem for American Democracy," *British Journal of Sociology*, 6 (1955), pp. 176–209.

[2] Daniel Bell, ed., *The New American Right* (New York: Criterion Books, 1955).

[3] In the absence of data, these writers also attempted to *deduce* the character and composition of McCarthy's popular following from their analyses of the movement's economic and historical context and from the ideology of the movement's more prominent spokesmen. But the mass support for a movement and the grounds on which that support is granted may differ very greatly from what we would expect on the basis of an analysis of the public pronouncements of prominent men.

[4] This study of McCarthy's support was part of a larger study of political orientations and formal and informal communications carried out under the over-all direction of Dr. Robert D. Leigh and supported by a grant from Columbia University. The data reported in this paper were gathered through one- to two-hour structured interviews with men living in the Bennington area. Nearly eight hundred such interviews were conducted in the area during the spring and summer of 1954, during and just after the McCarthy-Army hearings, when McCarthy was at or near the peak of his popularity and power. A national survey done in August of that year found a third of its sample giving McCarthy their support (see Charles H. Stember, "Antidemocratic Attitudes in America: A Review of Public Opinion Research" [Publication of the Bureau of Applied Social Research (New York: Columbia University, 1954), p. 52] [mimeographed]). In Bennington over half of the men we interviewed approved of McCarthy's activities, while some 40 percent approved of his methods of investigation—that aspect of his activities which had come under sharpest criticism. Incidentally, interest in and knowledge about McCarthy were very high during the period in which these interviews were collected. In Bennington, fewer than .5 percent of the respondents answered "Don't know" to any of the questions about McCarthy.

[5] For fuller information on this study and its methods of investigation see Martin A. Trow, "Right-Wing Radicalism and Political Intolerance: A Study of Support for McCarthy in a New England Town," Ph.D. dissertation, Columbia University, 1957 (unpublished).

[6] Information on attitudes toward McCarthy was gathered through three questions in the interview: questions bearing on his activities, his methods of investigation, and the value of his investigating committee. Although these three questions could have been combined in a scale of "support for McCarthy," the decision was made to use the single question, "Just speaking of Senator McCarthy's *methods* of investigation, how do you feel about them? Do you strongly favor them, mildly favor them, mildly oppose them, or strongly oppose them?" In most of the tabulations those who favored

his methods, whether strongly or mildly, were compared with those who opposed them. For the reasons this item alone was used see Trow, *op. cit.*, pp. 12–15.

[7] The measure of "political tolerance" was an index based on the three questions: "In peacetime, do you think the Socialist party should be allowed to publish newspapers in this country?" "Do you think newspapers should be allowed to criticize our form of government?" Do you think members of the Communist party in this country should be allowed to speak on the radio?"

While these three specific attitudes were highly related to one another, there was, as we might expect, least support for the right of members of the Communist party to speak on the radio and most support for the rights of newspapers to criticize our form of government. But, on further examination, it appeared that these three questions tapped a common, more basic sentiment regarding the rights of people and groups hostile to our political and economic system to make their criticisms known through the media of public communication. Political tolerance involves, at a minimum, a willingness to grant to others the right to propagate their political views. The willingness to grant this right to unpopular political minorities is the sentiment common to these three items and is the sentiment we are calling "political tolerance."

The index was constructed by assigning a score of 2 to "Yes" responses, 1 to "Yes, qualified," and 0 to "No." In these tabulations the index was dichotomized, with those having a total score of 3 or more comprising the "High" group.

Identically worded questions have been included in a number of national surveys conducted by the National Opinion Research Center in recent years and provide comparisons with the Bennington sample. For further discussion of this measure see Trow, *op. cit.*, pp. 16–17.

[8] This investigation explored the relations between support for McCarthy and political tolerance and economic class, occupation, religious identification, union membership and identification, political party preference, and attitudes toward various national and foreign policy issues. The bearing of formal education on McCarthy's support and political tolerance was analyzed separately; since it was so highly related to both these sentiments, it was controlled in the analysis of all the other relationships.

[9] For example, it has been suggested that small businessmen, as a result of their economic experience and interests, tend to hold extremely conservative economic views and that these views led them into the radical right and support of McCarthy. A somewhat different hypothesis suggests that small businessmen identify with, and tend to take over what they believe to be, the values of big business, which are also the values of the radical right. Neither of these hypotheses is supported by the Bennington data.

[10] For an analysis of McCarthy's ideology and rhetoric see Bell, ed., *op. cit.*, especially the essays by Bell, Parsons, Viereck, and Lipset.

[11] The free professionals, chiefly doctors and lawyers, not shown in this table, were markedly low in their support of McCarthy; only one in five gave him his support. These professions, as Parsons has noted, have developed relatively well-institutionalized ways of dealing with rapid social change, so that "the dynamic process of which they are agents is not so disturbing to them" (Talcott Parsons, *Essays in Sociological Theory Pure and Applied* [Glencoe, Ill.: The Free Press, 1949], p. 267). Nor do they experience the insecurities flowing from the progressive rationalization of economic life that the small businessmen do. They are, in this respect, more like the salaried employees, especially the managers, technicians, and salaried professionals.

[12] The two questions were: "Do you agree or disagree that: The way they are run now, labor unions do this country more harm than good," and "Big companies control too much of American business."

	Big companies control too much of American business	
	Agree	Disagree
The way they are run now, labor unions do this country more harm than good — Disagree	I	III
Agree	II	IV

[13] Much has been said about this perspective, and its illiberal tendencies, most recently by Shils (*op. cit.*, pp. 98–104) and Richard Hofstadter, *The Age of Reform* (New York: Knopf, 1955), pp. 3–22, 60–93, and *passim*, in connection with populism. See also C. W. Mills, *White Collar* (New York: Oxford University Press, 1951), pp. 34–59, and John H. Bunzel, "The General Ideology of American Small Business," *Political Science Quarterly*, 70 (1955), pp. 87–102.

[14] Further investigation of holders of very conservative economic attitudes supports this finding.

[15] Even those small businessmen who held other orientations gave McCarthy more support than did workers and salaried employees with the same orientations. Looked at from another perspective, nineteenth-century liberals among workers and salaried men gave McCarthy more support than did men in similar occupations holding different orientations toward big business and trade unions. Occupation and these politicoeconomic orientations worked independently and cumulatively in their bearing on McCarthy's support.

In this study we are primarily concerned with the relationships and forces underlying McCarthy's popular support. But our findings that support for McCarthy was not highly related to political intolerance and that McCarthy gained disproportionate support from small businessmen should not obscure the fact that *most* of McCarthy's supporters were (1) intolerant and (2) manual workers. Our findings and the latter observations, of course, do not contradict one another.

[16] On the social character and political orientations of the lower middle class in Germany as shaped by their insecure and continually deteriorating social and economic positions before the rise of Hitler see Erich Fromm, *Escape from Freedom* (New York: Farrar & Rinehart, 1941), pp. 211–16; Sigmund Neumann, *Permanent Revolution* (New York: Harper & Row, 1942), p. 28; Karl Mannheim, *Man and Society in an Age of Reconstruction* (New York: Harcourt, Brace & World, 1940), p. 102, *passim*; Emil Lederer, *The State of the Masses* (New York: Norton, 1940), pp. 51–53; and Alfred Meusal, "Middle Class," *Encyclopedia of the Social Sciences* (1933), X, pp. 407–15.

[17] This is not to identify McCarthy with Hitler, or American right-wing movements with naziism or fascism, though this is not the place to discuss the very great differences between these movements. Nor is it meant simply to equate the role of small businessmen in the mass support for those movements. Their differing historical developments and the different political situations and structures within which these movements developed heavily conditioned their actual political *consequences*. Our concern here is not with the manifold factors that affect the translation of political sentiments into action (i.e., with their consequences) but rather with the nature of those sentiments and with their location and sources in the social structure. And here, the evidence suggests, there are certain important parallels in the two situations.

[18] Hans Gerth, "The Nazi Party: Its Leadership and Composition," *American Journal of Sociology*, 45 (1940), pp. 517–41, esp. Table 1.

[19] See, e.g., Sigmund Neumann, "Germany: Changing Patterns and Lasting Problems," in *Modern Political Parties*, Neumann, ed. (Chicago: University of Chicago Press, 1956), pp. 36–37. See also Lederer, *op. cit.*, and Hans Speier, "The Salaried Employee in Modern Society," in his *Social Order and the Risks of War* (New York: George W. Stewart, 1952), pp. 68–85.

[20] Asoka Mehta has pointed out that in the "underdeveloped areas" of Asia the Communists make their first and chief appeal not to the peasants or industrial workers but to the emerging strata of salaried employees, who respond in large numbers precisely to the promise of rapid industrialization and bureaucratization under Communist direction and to the opportunities that will be thus opened up to them (Asoka Mehta, "Can Asia Industrialize Democratically," *Dissent*, 1 [1955], pp. 152–70). See also Morris Watnick, "The Appeal of Communism to the Peoples of Underdeveloped Areas," in *Class, Status, and Power*, Bendix and Lipset, eds. (Glencoe, Ill.: The Free Press, 1953), pp. 651–62.

[21] One study whose findings support this interpretation reports a relationship between the proportion of unemployed among white-collar workers in German cities and the Nazi vote (S. Pratt, "The Social Basis of Nazism and Communism in Urban Germany," M.A. thesis, Michigan State College, 1948, [unpublished]).

[22] See, e.g., Kurt Mayer, "Small Business as a Social Institution," *Social Research*, 14 (1947), pp. 332–49.

Lipset and Bendix, in two articles in the *American Journal of Sociology* (January and March, 1952), point to the very high turnover of small business in this country. Using Department of Commerce figures, they observe that "even during the postwar boom of 1945–48 almost 30 percent of the businesses in the United States were discontinued," the bulk of these, of course, being small businesses (S.M. Lipset and R. Bendix, "Social Mobility and Occupational Career Patterns. II. Social Mobility," *American Journal of Sociology*, 57 [1952], p. 500). Translated into occupational career patterns, the high rate of business turnover reflects itself in the fact that nearly 20 percent of their sample of Oakland, California, men who were not then proprietors had at one time owned their own businesses. And they present further data showing that many businessmen who fail fall back into the ranks of manual labor. It is probable that an awareness of these dangers constitutes a continuing threat to many small proprietors.

Rush Welter finds similar high rates of turnover among the predominantly small- and medium-sized manufacturing firms that have established themselves in Bennington (Rush Welter, "Bennington, Vermont: An Economic History" [Bennington College, 1956] [mimeographed]). Welter has no comparable data on non-manufacturing concerns, specifically the roughly 150 retail stores in the town. But these, in Bennington as elsewhere, are hard pressed by chain stores and the big mail-order houses. All in all, small proprietors earn their livelihood under conditions of considerable economic insecurity and respond to these conditions in some of the ways we have been describing in this essay.

[23] The free professionals, whom we noted were very low in their support for McCarthy, were no more politically tolerant than other men who had been to college.

[24] The kind of discontent we have been dealing with in this essay takes the form of a fearful and suspicious hostility toward the main defining features of modern society. Another kind, not discussed in this essay, is a simpler, more direct envious resentment of the status order and of high-status individuals and groups.

A closer study of politically relevant discontents and their social sources also involves a study of the forces that *channel* them—that determine who become the targets and who the spokesmen for the hostilities of a given group. To identify the nature and social location of discontent is not in itself sufficient to identify its targets, for it cannot be assumed that the conditions which channel social hostilities are necessarily identical with the conditions that generate them. On this see Trow, *op. cit.*, pp. 203–15.

[25] See W. A. Kerr, "Untangling the Liberalism-Conservatism Continuum," *Journal of Social Psychology*, 35 (1952), pp. 111–25; G. H. Smith, "Liberalism and Level of Information," *Journal of Education Psychology*, 39 (1948), pp. 68–81; William McPhee, *Bibliography and Critique of Quantitative Research on Syndromes, Clusters and Factors in Social Attitudes* (New York: Bureau of Applied Social Research, Columbia University, 1954); and Robert J. Williams, "Attitude Dimensions in Public Opinion Questionnaire Material," Ph.D. dissertation, Columbia University, 1953 (unpublished).

These studies report a number of distinct dimensions of "liberalism," some of which are independent, others inversely related in the general population. Our own findings, in parallel fashion, suggest at least two distinct dimensions of "radical rightism," one a general intolerance of minority groups, political, racial, and otherwise; the other a more directly *political* "radical rightism," a propensity to support movements and leaders of the McCarthy-Poujade type. These dimensions, on at least our preliminary findings, seem to be unrelated, or only slightly related, to each other in the general population.

34 Joseph R. Gusfield

Mass Society and Extremist Politics

A dominant stream of thought in current political sociology explains many contemporary antidemocratic movements as products of a distinctive social organization—Mass Society. Writers who utilize this approach have maintained that modern, Western societies increasingly show characteristics of mass organization which sharply differ from the features of such societies in the nineteenth and earlier centuries. Mass societies, in this view, demonstrate a form of politics in which traditional sociological concepts, such as class or culture, are not relevant to an understanding of the sources, genesis, or careers of extremist, antidemocratic political movements. Mass politics is the form of political action unique to mass societies. As modern democratic societies become mass societies, we may then anticipate that political crises are likely to generate extremist, antidemocratic responses. Leading advocates of this theory of "mass politics," in whole or part, are Hannah Arendt, Erich Fromm, Karl Mannheim, William Kornhauser, Robert Nisbet, and Philip Selznick.[1] This paper is a critical analysis of this approach and a reformulation of some of the relations between mass societies and political action.

There are two major contentions in this paper. The first is a criticism of the assumptions about democratic politics underlying the theory of mass politics. The second is a reformulated theory of the relation between mass society and political extremism in contemporary, democratic societies.

It is our first contention that implicit in the theory of mass politics is an idealized conception of the pluralistic social and political system held necessary for the maintenance of democratic institutions. This conception is idealized in that it fails to give adequate weight to barriers which conflicts of interest offer to political harmony and compromise under any political structure.

Our second contention is that the elements of mass societies viewed with alarm by mass politics theorists in actuality contain positive connotations for the maintenance of democratic political institutions. Mass communications, bureaucratic institutions, and equalitarianism have implications which strengthen pluralistic political structures. Extremist politics may be expected in modern societies as a response of those adversely affected by the changes towards a mass society and most insulated from mass institutions. Contrary to the theory of mass politics, traditional concepts of political sociology *are* adequate to the analysis of extremism.

Reprinted from *American Sociological Review*, 27:1 (1962), pp. 19–30, by permission of the author and the publisher.

It must be made clear that our major interest in this paper is in the explanation of antidemocratic movements as they develop within historically democratic societies. This excludes consideration of authoritarian regimes in traditional societies or the development of antidemocratic movements in developing economies under the impact of intensive social and economic change.[2] Our interest is confined to those writers who explain such modern extremist movements as Fascism, Communism, or McCarthyism by reference to characteristics of mass society. These represent one variant of mass society theory, but an influential one.[3]

MASS SOCIETY AND THE THEORY OF MASS POLITICS

Mass Society analysts view modern social systems as significantly different from nonindustrial and earlier societies. Whatever the differences among individual writers, there is a common core of description in the term "mass society" which suggests the attenuation of primary and local associations and groups. Impersonal, bureaucratized relationships in large-scale organizations have replaced the informal systems of loyalty in small groups and local affiliations. Equalitarian conditions and ideologies have weakened systems of political and social authority characteristic of stratified communities. Technological innovations have made possible a high degree of standardization, both of products and ideas. The elongation of the chain of organizational command has enhanced the possibilities of oligarchic control as local groups are less viable, hence less resistant to control. The emphasis is upon the breakdown of immediate relationships and differentiations so that the population is now more homogeneous but also less sharply identified and affiliated with distinctive social groups. It is in this sense that the theorist of mass society views the traditional categories of sociological analysis—family, class, community, ethnic identity, etc.— as having lost significance in mass societies. The mass is masslike: shapeless, structureless, undifferentiated. Mass politics trace the implications of this loss of differentiation for the bonds of loyalty to democratic political institutions.

Exponents of mass politics viewpoints have described modern Western, industrial societies as ones in which persons lack attachment to primary and secondary associations. "The chief characteristic of the mass-man," Hannah Arendt has written, "is not brutality and backwardness, but his isolation and lack of normal social relationships."[4] Political extremism, manifested in antidemocratic movements, is seen as a result of the *structural* and *psychological* consequences for political loyalty or disattachment to democratic procedures and aims.

Supporters of this view hold that structural characteristics of bureaucratization and equality undermine the functions of secondary and primary associations in inculcating values and in transmitting political norms. In mass society, such theories maintain, secondary associations of school, church, community or union, operate in a large-scale fashion. Rank-and-file identification with the organizational elite is diminished as the member's associational life is peripheral and tangential. The high mobility rates and standardized life styles destroy economic class as an important source of motivation and interest in political events. Institutions functioning under conditions of mass society do not touch the character and the personal values of those exposed to them. Being solely instrumental means, the major associations and institutions of the society cannot act as agencies through which values are inculcated. Because of this, the political elites of the society cannot mediate political decisions to the acceptance of the rank-and-file. Such political "untouchables" are described by Selznick when he writes, "He has lost the meaning provided by the articulated social structure to which he belonged."[5]

In previous centuries the lack of integration of rank-and-file members of the society into political institutions was a matter of little political consequence. Mass societies, however, are politically equalitarian. The development of large aggregates of persons unattached to democratic political structures and norms is significant because such groups are capable of spontaneous development unguided by the norms of democratic society. The diminished role of intermediate structures—both institutions and specific political associations—leaves the person unattached and capable of being reunited into a new group. "A strong intermediate structure consists of stable and independent groups which represent diverse and frequently conflicting interests."[6] In mass society, however, the representative nature of these groups (classes, ethnic groups, regions, etc.) is undermined. Both because participation is peripheral and because political elites are limited in authority, mass societies are less able to control the values and political aspirations of citizens.

To the structural disintegration of society there is added the personal disorganization of the individual. The psychological consequences of mass society are described in terms of the feeling of detachment. The key word here is alienation, "a mode of experience in which the person experiences himself as an alien."[7] Whether the emphasis of the writer is on estrangement from work, the normlessness of contemporary culture or the powerless feeling of the individual in large-scale organizations, mass conditions are described as producing feelings of *malaise* and insecurity.

The alienation of the individual in modern societies is the psychological statement of detachment. It describes a condition in which the person is not involved in or committed to primary or secondary groups. It adds to this the description of the person as someone with positive, unfulfilled needs for identity, affection, and assurance.

In both its structural and psychological elements the theory of mass politics states that political alienation—the disattachment of the person from political institutions—is a function of the distintegrating influences of mass society on the ties of sentiment and loyalty to specific groups which characterized the social structure of democracies in an earlier historical period. Without attachment to primary or to intermediate structures, the individual has no bond to national political institutions which commands his loyalty to its political norms.

PLURALISTIC AND EXTREMIST POLITICS

In the emphasis on a transition from an earlier historical period to a modern, mass society the theories here considered have suggested that political democracy functioned relatively unimpeded under non-mass conditions. It is imperative then that we examine the type of political structure from which mass politics is seen as differing. Political extremism is so defined in contradistinction to pluralistic politics. The mass theorist sees pluralistic politics as impaired under current social conditions. As a corollary pluralistic structure is implicitly posited as an essential condition for democratic politics.

The theory of a balance of power among a plurality of groups has been the dominant analytical tool of American political scientists.[8] Its classic defense has been presented in Hamilton and Madison's *The Federalist Papers*. The theory presupposes a society of many and diverse social groups. The political institutions force each group to moderate and compromise their interests in the interplay of party, secondary association, and locality. In the pluralist conception of the citizen, each person is integrated into politics in his capacity as member of some segment of the society— worker or manager, city or country dweller, Southerner or Northerner, immigrant or native, white or black. The units of politics are thus organized groups built upon the sentiments and interests of persons in their affiliations with specific primary associations which occupy positions and perform specific functions within the major institutions.

Pluralistic politics involves certain "rules of the game" by which political conflict is carried on. These "rules of the game," part of the definition of politics as an institution, are adhered to by the participants. Chief among tenets of democratic politics is acceptance of opposing forces into the political process on the same terms as those binding on one's own group. This acceptance supplies the necessity for political compromise and conciliation. If all groups possess some political power and are admitted into the political process, bargaining and negotiation are the chief modes of political conflict. Violence is ruled out as a possible way of solving social or economic conflicts.

It is essential to this process that each group be willing to accept the total or partial defeat of its aims and accept the total or partial achievement of the aims of its opponents. Compromise includes the ability to settle for less than full victory. This "realistic" orientation is achieved in an atmosphere governed by rational calculation of interests. It is most negated when objectives have become correlated with considerations of honor and when compromise, negotiation, and defeat are suffused with connotations of dishonor.

Political extremism occurs when movements advocate violation of the democratic, pluralist "rules of the game." Shils suggests a distinction between pluralistic and ideological politics which emphasizes the disattachment of the extremist from self-limiting and rationally calculative aspects of pluralism:

> Extremism consists in going to an extreme in zealous attachment to a particular value, e.g., private property, ethnic homogeneity, or status equality. . . . The extremist must be deeply alienated from the complex of rules which keep the strivings for various values in restraint and balance. An extremist group is an alienated group. . . . Its hostility is incompatible with that freedom from intense emotion which pluralistic politics needs for its prosperity. . . . The focus of the extremist's attention on one or a few completely fulfilled values and his impatience with compromise when a plurality of values, never internally consistent, have to be reconciled with each other makes the extremist feel that he is worlds apart from the compromising moderates.[9]

This distinction between pluralist and extremist politics differs, as others have pointed out,[10] from traditional distinctions between Right and Left, Conservative, Liberal and Radical, and reform and revolution. It is a distinction between styles and not between contents. It is in this sense that extremism is alienated from the institutions of democratic politics. It denies the legitimacy of democratic political institutions as devices for mediating conflict. Extremist style refuses to accept the possible or probable outcomes of whole or partial defeat. Total victory is too important in the hierarchy of values to permit of compromise.

In several ways, then, the extremist breaks with the normative patterns of pluralist political behavior:

(1) *He attempts to close the political process to opposing forces:* Politics is held to be the legitimate area of conflict for some, but not for all groups. Both Fascism and Communism have made this a cornerstone of the political structure as well as a tenet of their movements.

(2) *He attempts to carry on social and economic conflicts outside of political institutions:* The confinement of conflict to politics marks a cardinal principle of democratic politics. Violence, intimidation and fraud are excluded as means of achieving group ends.

(3) *He impairs the culture of democratic discussion:* An emphasis is placed on the value of uniform opinions and behavior. The criteria of rational calculation of interests is replaced by intensive appeals to sentiment and symbolism. This strain in McCarthyism captured the attention of those concerned with extremism in politics. It is only in this sense that membership and participation in extremist movements seems authoritarian. The extremist style has little appreciation of dissent and schism in the total society.

The extremist movement is marked by the low degree of commitment to the values of procedure in democratic institutions. Pluralist norms enforce tolerance, barter, and the inclusion of opponents as joint members of the same social system. Extremist resentment against democratic politics is not that of indifference but that of intensive conviction. It is the thoroughly moralistic attitude which marks the extremist and distinguishes him from the slightly cynical pluralist.

As we have sketched it so far, political extremism is found in one or both forms: an increased attachment to a single, over-riding value or a weakened attachment to the norms of pluralist politics. In either case, the extremist is alienated from the *existing* democratic order.[11]

The theorists of mass politics visualize extremist movements as consequences of weakened attachments to political institutions and persons resulting from the breakdown in functioning of primary and secondary associations in mass societies. Without a sense of affiliation to specific interest groups, the citizen has no way to develop a frame of reference for political events. Intermediate secondary associations cannot touch him sufficiently to act as forces limiting intensity of opposition and resentment of rival political claims. Political figures become distrusted and democratic institutions no longer legitimate sources of social control. In Kornhauser's words:

> . . . intermediate groups help to protect elites by functioning as channels through which popular participation in the larger society (especially in the national elites) may be directed and restrained.[12]

The mass theorist goes a step further and suggests that such detachment from democratic political institutions leaves the individual susceptible to political participation in extremist channels. The socially alienated individual is not only politically alienated; he is also more likely to become the extremist activist than is the member of a structured interest group. He is no longer limited in his attack on rivals by the controls of a structured pluralistic society. His resentments against opposing groups and against the existing institutions themselves need not be confined to the calculative, instrumental style of democratic politics. The mass man is a passionate supporter of ideology.

Lack of control mechanisms regulating the political attitudes and behavior of mass citizenry furthers the extremist character of participation in politics. It enables the person to project destructive impulses into the political arena. Mannheim, for example, maintained that in traditional societies collective impulses and wishes are absorbed by smaller groups and directed toward group aims. The social distintegration of modern society, he felt, set such impulses free to seek integration around some new object, often a symbol or a leader.[13]

The attenuation of local and primary associations and mediating secondary interest groups and associations, is, in the theory of mass politics, the source of the extremism frequent in contemporary mass societies. As a system of analysis this view finds that traditional concepts of class and status aims are limited ways of characterizing political movements. As a philosophy of politics, the theory adds up to a defense of the virtues of a pluralistic political system. The transition from a pluralistic society to a mass society is implicitly and explicitly bemoaned. For this reason, the analysis of pluralist assumptions is central to our discussion.

PLURALISTIC SOURCES OF POLITICAL EXTREMISM

The theory of mass politics assumes that a pluralistic social structure diminishes the possibilities that political action will take extremist directions. Conflicts and demands for change will occur but will be moderated by adherence to the style of democratic institutions. An analysis of this assumption, however, shows that extremism both *can* and often *does* occur within pluralistic structures. There are at least four situations in which pluralism either invites or fails to forestall behavior outside the range of democratic norms for the mediation of conflicts:

(1) *Disenfranchised Classes*   Change often brings new groups into formation or increases the demands of old ones. In any case, at any given time, some groups are excluded from the political process. Often it is not in the interest of some or most of the included groups to accept new political forces. Excluded groups must either function outside of the political "game" or force their way into it. The militancy of the American Negro in the South today is of this nature. Compromise and legality are not relevant political alternatives unless a group is within the political structures in the first place.

(2) *Doomed and Defeated Classes*   The theory of democratic politics has never developed a satisfactory answer to the problem: When is compromise to be rejected? When is political defeat not an acceptable alternative to violence and other breaks with pluralist procedure? The facts of the American Civil War and of the Algerian crisis in contemporary France illustrate the thesis that well-structured groups, with channels of representation in parliamentary bodies, are far from willing to accept defeat of important aims through parliamentary procedures. Robert Dahl sees this as a serious impediment in democratic theory. Referring to the election of Abraham Lincoln in 1860, Dahl writes:

> Thus any election interpreted as a clear-cut victory for one side was almost certain to be so intolerable to the other that it would refuse to accept the outcome. . . . Where each side is large and regards the victory of the other as a fundamental threat to some very highly ranked values, it is reasonable to expect serious difficulties in the continued operation of a (pluralistic) system.[14]

This is apt to be the case under conditions of social or economic change which gravely threaten a previous position of power and supremacy. To such "doomed classes,"[15] the future looks far less inviting than the past. A radical reorganization of society might be a solution to their problem, but such a reorganization against politically ascendent forces is precisely what the moderating elements in the structure of political balance operate against. Recent discussions of the plight of the "old middle classes" in American life have stressed the indignation of these groups at their loss of power and status.[16] It is not a failure to "belong" that lies at the source of their alienation and possible "right-wing radicalism." Their response is touched off by the contents of the social changes to which they react.

(3) *Public Opinion and the Imbalance of Competing Interests* The theory of democratic politics as a balance between competing interests often ignores the important role played by the neutral, noncompeting elements in the political process. A great many groups without specific interests in a particular issue nevertheless have power to effect governmental decisions. Such decisions are made with a concern for the general climate of opinion toward an issue. Whether the "public" is friendly or hostile is an important element in an interest group's decision to pursue its aims within or without the political process. As Murray Edelman has pointed out, labor will pursue its goals through economic processes (strikes, bargaining, etc.) when the political climate is hostile.[17] Recourse to nonpolitical means is not ruled out by the existence of pluralistic machinery.

(4) *Development of Periodic Crisis* Mass politics theory generally recognizes economic and military crisis as an essential "trigger" to extremist movements. Because pluralistic politics is oriented toward compromises between groups, it is less open to long run considerations. This is especially the case in issues of foreign policy. Unless there is some consensual basis other than group interest, elites must "sell" policy in terms communicable to specific classes and interests. Even assuming a diffusion of power in the form of what Riesman calls "veto groups,"[18] a hiatus develops between long-run perspectives of governmental leaders and the short-run perspectives of intermediate associations and their constituencies. The result is often a stalemate and an immobilism which enables problems to develop into major crises. One instance of this is contained in LaPalombara's analysis of French and Italian politics in the post-war years.[19] He explains greater cohesion and agreement within the Italian moderate parties than among the French as a consequence of differences in the power of the Communist Party in each of the countries. Italian moderates were forced into agreement by fear.

> While there has not been any serious fear in France that PCF could come peacefully to power, this reassuring assessment has been denied the democratic party leaders in Italy. . . . They have not been able to permit themselves the capricious inaction in which the French Center Party Leaders have indulged over the last decade.[20]

Inability of political elites to deal with crisis is itself one strong source of mass alienation from a political institution. Third parties have fared better at the polls in the United States during periods of economic depression than during periods of prosperity.[21] As Lipset has pointed out, there is a direct correlation between levels of economic well-being and the existence of democratic political systems.[22] Prosperous countries may avoid problems which threaten political stability in less affluent nations.

In each of these four situations, extremist politics is developed and conducted by well-structured groups, representing discrete and organized parts of the social structure, acting to secure goals related to group needs. While such groups are alienated from the existing political institutions they are not socially disintegrated or unrelated to the society and its political system. They function within a pluralist framework in which their values receive short shrift. Failure to recognize that pluralist assumptions cannot alone sustain political institutions is at the root of the implicit ideology of the theorist of mass politics.

THE PLURALIST IDEOLOGY

The sanguine view of political balance at the base of mass politics theory reveals a repetition of the ideological bias of nineteenth century liberalism —the assumption that there is a natural harmony of interests which sustains the social and political system. Occurrences of sharp conflict are therefore indicative of disruptions in the *form* of social arrangements. There is nothing in the *content* of interests and beliefs which makes compromise improbable. Mannheim reflects this ideology in a passage in *Man and Society* in which he suggests that experience in trade unions and in other associations trains participants for planning on a societal basis: "He is gradually realizing that by resigning partial advantages he helps to save the social and economic system and thereby also his own interests."[23]

The belief that participation in the primary and secondary associations of the society will moderate conflict arises from this ideological commitment to pluralist politics. It leads the mass politics theorist to identify political defeat with social alienation, to view extremist movements as actions of disattached persons, unrelated to specific social bases or pursuing interests of a discrete social base. Because of this tendency, the mass politics approach has felt traditional political analysis to be deficient.

It is *not* true that attachment to intermediate structures insures attachment to the larger national institutions and structures. As a society undergoes change, it is likely that specific groups will be adversely affected by economic or social change. Similarly, some groups may develop new aspirations and objectives. In both cases they may come to feel that the existent political order is insufficient to command their allegiance. A shifting balance of forces is, however, not the same phenomenon as the breakup of an associational structure, the shattering of a class, or the decline of primary group support. It is even reasonable to maintain that an external threat to a group promotes its sense of solidarity and aids in the development of group identity and organization.[24] Attachment to intermediate structures may indeed promote a shared sense of alienation of the group from the total political order. The more informal organization the group possesses the more likely is it that politically extremist sentiments can be communicated and legitimated. In playing the game of politics, it is not only important whether or not one is permitted to play, but also whether one is winning or not. This problem is not solved by the degree of access which the group has to political association.

The point can be made through an analysis of a frequently used study of McCarthyist attitudes, which mass politics theorists have used as support for their position. Trow's study of Bennington, Vermont found a disproportionate amount of support for Senator McCarthy among small businessmen, especially those holding the nineteenth century liberal hostility to both big business and labor unions.[25] In explaining his findings, Trow maintains that not only are small businessmen "resentful of a world that continually offends their deepest values" but equally important is the fact that they have little voice or representation in political institutions, such as the major parties. Granting the rather dubious assumption that small business has little place in the current constellation of political and ideological forces in the United States, the picture of disaffection portrayed in Trow's study is a classic picture of a well-organized economic group losing out in the process of social and economic change. This type of disaffection is readily analyzed in terms of class and status conflict. If mass movements are not to be understood in traditional forms of political analysis, they must be shown to be unrelated to analysis in terms of group interests and discrete social bases. This would involve more than the traditional view that social change produces disaffection among groups adversely exposed to it.

The assumption of a natural harmony of interests gives rise to another failing of the mass politics approach. This is the lack of concern for the development of consensus around the norms of democratic politics. If it is assumed that representation of interests assures harmony, then the problem of achieving moral sentiments supportive of the political institution becomes meaningless. However, such moral sentiments *are* essential; otherwise, the source of moderate politics, of commitment to the political process *per se* is missing. When the values at stake are intensely held and the constellation of political forces is adverse to a group, there is nothing in pluralistic theory which suggests a source of loyalty to moderateness. Oscar Gass has expressed this in excellent fashion:

> I know that Democracy is a technique for reaching agreement, but it in turn rests upon a measure of agreement. It is, of course, formally true that, if only you agree on the technique of getting decisions, you don't have to agree on the outcome. But that is merely like saying that people can ride on the same bus even if they wish to get off at different places. The places must not be *too* different—or else they have to set a value on riding beyond that of getting to their destinations.[26]

A pluralistic system can be maintained only if the conflict of interest groups is balanced to some extent by cohesive elements in the cultural and social system which moderate the intensity of conflicts and which provide loyalties to maintenance of a defined area in which politics is conducted under pluralistic rules.[27] The ideology of pluralism has become a defense of moderateness, and an attack on political activism. Yet pluralist structure enhances activist sentiments.

MASS CULTURE AND POLITICAL COHESION

Contrary to mass politics theory, conditions of mass societies are not necessarily detrimental to sentiments supporting pluralistic politics. In fact the opposite appears to be the case. Certain conditions of modern, mass societies function to increase cohesion and consensus around norms of pluralistic politics.

Mass politics approaches have emphasized bureaucratization, equalitarianism, and technological integration as forces weakening past mediating structures. It must also be pointed out that the same forces operate to incorporate persons into a larger national culture and social system. While mediating structures and local units may be weakened, direct attachment to the total society is enhanced. In Shils' phrase, "The new society is a mass society precisely in the sense that the mass of the population has become incorporated into *society*."[28]

Conditions of mass society develop a homogeneous set of cultural experiences for members. Technological forces have led to an economy and a means of communication which can absorb all the citizens in common. As this has occurred, the autonomy of the local community has given way to a national politics, a national economy and a national culture. In an era of high mass consumption, the equalization of incomes and the style-setting influence of a national market have promoted a more homogeneous standard of living. In the use of commodities and of leisure, as well as in high rates of social mobility, class lines are becoming blurred. In this society, major social institutions operate in similar fashion upon all communities and within most classes. School, church, medicine, family and politics are increasingly open to the influence and control of centrally-trained professionals and their organizations. The consequences of such homogenizing forces are the development of a national mass culture and a national society. In this society, common sentiments increasingly cut across the social segments of class, region, and other sub-cultural units. In this sense mass society is a new social system.

These features of mass society, of course, are recognized in the theories considered above. Where we differ, however, is in stressing these as positive agencies of social integration, rather than only as devices which weaken earlier units of social life. The theories of mass politics suggest only one possible relationship between mass societies and political extremism. In the remainder of this paper we wish to suggest another relationship, one in which the trend toward mass society provides opportunities for strengthening the attachments of the individuals to institutions which accept diversity and support political balance. The conditions of mass society, we suggest, mitigate against political extremism because they operate against the isolation of differentiated sub-cultures from which strong ideological attachments can develop. At the same time, they provide conditions which promote acceptance of innovations.

(1) *They provide sources of direct attachment to supralocal institutions.* It has become something of an axiom in electoral behavior studies that interest and participation is at its highest in national rather than local elections. In a mass society, the individual is oriented toward a national culture and stratification system. Mass culture is carried through national systems of communications and education which may be, and often are, in conflict with local groups. Lack of attachment to local agencies, kinship units, and secondary associations by no means implies a lack of attachment to standards, tastes and values of the mass culture. The same is true in respect to political participation. As the range of areas affected by local decisions grows smaller, the orientation of the individual to national political units grows more significant. Studies of cosmopolitan and local types indicate that the individual may be marginal within his local environment but very much committed to structures of occupational, educational and political organization at levels above that of the local community.[29]

(2) *Mass culture enhances the possibilities of substantive consensus.* We have argued above that although cultural and class diversity provides a resistant force against oligarchic controls, it may also develop intensive attachments to particular aims which prevent the compromise and toleration presupposed by political pluralism. Indeed, pluralistic politics is hard to reconcile with intensity of conviction and a moralistic approach to politics. Insofar as mass societies create homogeneous experience for a population, there is an increased possibility of consensus on substantive issues. Will Herberg's[30] thesis of a growing uniformity in American religions is a case in point. Similarity of education, consumer products, income and communications is also associated with similarity in morals and, to some extent, interests. The issues open to political conflict are then limited and less apt to arouse intense opposition. While this may mean a diminution in ideological commitments and controversy, it is hardly the same thing as production of extremist activism. Indeed, those who are critical of contemporary American society for its presumed conformist tendencies are often dismayed at the disappearance of activism, utopian thought and radical attitudes, all of which are also forms of extremism, alienation and discontent.

(3) *Mass culture can, and often does, shore up the support for consensus on procedural norms of pluralistic politics.* Because they include multiple sub-cultures, mass institutions are open to the influence of numerous social segments in ways in which local and class institutions are not. Further, mass culture is more apt to be influenced by norms of cosmopolitan and nationalized groups than local and sub-cultural units. Within American society today, the norms of pluralist styles in politics find more response at the national than at the local levels. Efforts to censor artistic

and educational experiments and dissent are more frequent at the local than at the national levels of education and communications. The development of a mass educational system, with a high degree of equalitarian recruitment, has been a distinctive aid to the acceptance of civil liberties sentiment.[31]

(4) *Mass culture diminishes the intensity of social conflicts by evening out the impact of major social and cultural changes.* Major social changes are frequently disruptive and focus on dimensions which involve clashes between attackers and defenders of tradition. This is particularly true in areas of cultural conflict—religion, morality or race relations are examples. The appearance of mass communications and educational agencies diminishes the degree to which the population is differentially exposed to a new set of norms. This is seen in the current desegregation crisis in the South. Opposition to a national culture of race relations is found most intensively among those most localistic, least educated, least urban, least exposed to mass media, and least integrated into the national economy.[32] Mass media, the extension of education and professionalization tend to equate the rates at which different classes and regions are exposed to changing standards.

(5) *Mass society increases the linkages between groups and minimizes the possibilities of "superimposition."* The concept of a pluralistic social system often fails to differentiate between two types of segmentation.[33] In one, which we will call "linked pluralism," there are multiple groups but membership in one often cuts across membership in others. A situation of linked pluralism, for example, would be one in which many Catholics are lower-class and many are middle-class while Protestants are similarly represented in each class. Both Catholics and Protestants are "linked" as members of the same social class. "Superimposed" segmentation occurs when membership in one group also implies membership in another. If most Catholics were lower-class and most Protestants were middle-class, then class and religion would be superimposed. It is fairly evident that intense social conflicts are maximized under conditions of superimposition and minimized under conditions of linked pluralism. In the example used, superimposition would mean that religious conflicts tended to be class conflicts as well.

The conditions of mass society tend to increase linked forms of pluralism and to minimize superimposed forms of pluralism. Perhaps the most salient aspect of this is a result of equalitarianism and mobility. When groups are not frozen by rigid stratification into a specific occupational and class position, such social categories as religion, race, residence, and community play less of a role as devices isolating one part of society from another.

It follows from this analysis that there are two major ways in which extremist movements may develop within the framework of contemporary mass societies. In one case, we are dealing with the general problem of reactions to social and economic change already discussed above in reference to "doomed classes" and to groups previously excluded from the political process. The transition from pluralistic structure to mass society is most keenly felt as loss and deprivation by those whose social and economic position is threatened by the development of bureaucratic organization, equalitarian social structure and mass culture. The attention given to the status loss and economic hardship of the "old middle classes" as the society becomes more consumption-oriented, more organizationally structured and more technically professionalized provides one strand of evidence in what Lipset has called the "extremism of the Center."[34] Riesman has expressed the same idea of reaction to change in characterological terms in saying:

> . . . his own life experience is often disappointing; he is deprived of a feeling of competence and place. Even this would not be so bad if the world made sense, if he could apply to what goes on his internalized standards of judgment, but as it is, neither his character nor his work is rewarded. In that situation he tends to turn both on himself . . . and on the world.[35]

The other case exists when groups are isolated from the major institutions and cultural streams of mass society. Localized groups are less open to the impact of the mass agencies. The less educated, the lowest income levels, the least protected minorities, the most fundamentalist in religion are least oriented to the rhythm of modernity with which so much of mass influence is carried. In this case, it is those least "caught up" in the historical currents of transition that are most likely to be immune from the moderating influences of mass culture. To cite such groups as products *of* mass society is misleading.

Carried to a logical extreme, the mass society becomes a political community in which bland tolerance and uniform ideas are the rule. Carried to its logical extreme, pluralistic societies are likely to generate either disintegrating conflict or stalemate. It is fruitless, however, to push typologies to their logical extremes. An empirical sociology must be concerned with the interaction between mass and pluralistic conditions. Elements of one model interact with elements of the other, sometimes as figure, sometimes as ground. De Tocqueville pointed out that one of the characteristics of American political institutions was the moderation of popular government by a leaven of aristocratic rule. He viewed the Supreme Court power of review as one such instance of balance.[36]

Mass conditions are thus likely to present many features which are not only consistent with a pluralistic theory of politics but even enhance such features. Rather than providing a source of extremist movements they are just as likely to mitigate the development of opposition and to increase the degree of toleration for dissent. Whether variety and controversy are likely to develop under the dominance of mass conditions is another question. However, those who seek to understand the conditions of stable, democratic institutions are mistaken in dispensing with traditional concepts and in emphasizing mass society as a demonic villain.

NOTES

[1] The following relevant writings embody the theory of mass politics: Hannah Arendt, *The Origins of Totalitarianism* (New York: Harcourt, Brace & World, 1954); Erich Fromm, *Escape From Freedom* (New York: Rinehart, 1945); Karl Mannheim, *Man and Society in an Age of Reconstruction* (London: Routledge & Kegan Paul, 1940); William Kornhauser, *The Politics of Mass Society* (Glencoe, Ill.: The Free Press, 1959); Robert Nisbet, *The Quest for Community* (New York: Oxford University Press, 1953); Philip Selznick, *The Organizational Weapon* (New York: McGraw-Hill, 1952).

[2] See the discussion of the political effects of social and economic change in Western and non-Western societies in Kornhauser, *op. cit.*, Chaps. 7, 8.

[3] We have confined our analysis here to theorists who find mass societies an explanatory tool in analyzing the rise of contemporary anti-democratic movements. Other writers have also described modern society as mass-like and have evaluated it in negative terms. This latter group, however, has not viewed political extremism as a likely consequence of mass conditions. Writers such as David Riesman, in *The Lonely Crowd*, and C. Wright Mills, in *The Power Elite*, have emphasized developing trends toward conformity and passivity rather than toward militance and activism. Still another stream in mass society writings is represented by E. A. Shils. He agrees that modern society is, by reason of mass conditions, best described as qualitatively different from earlier Western societies. This stream of writings, however, denies the disorganizing and overconforming consequences stressed by the other views. See the positive acceptance of mass society in Edward A. Shils, "Mass Society and Its Culture," *Daedalus*, 89 (1960), pp. 288–314.

[4] Hannah Arendt, *op. cit.*, p. 310.

[5] Philip Selznick, *op. cit.*, p. 283.

[6] William Kornhauser, *op. cit.*, p. 78.

[7] Erich Fromm, *The Sane Society* (New York: Rinehart, 1955), p. 120.

[8] The best descriptions of this process in contemporary political science are probably David Truman, *The Governmental Process* (New York: Knopf, 1951), and V. O. Key, *Parties, Politics and Pressure Groups* (New York: Crowley, 1947).

[9] Edward A. Shils, *The Torment of Secrecy* (Glencoe, Ill.: The Free Press, 1955), p. 231. In similar vein, Nathan Leites introduces his study of French politics by a statement exempting the Communists and the "extreme right" from his discussion. He reasons that their style in politics is distinctly different from the "national" groups of the Center. In the period of post-war politics which he studied, "the extremes entered but little in 'the game' so that the patterns of political calculation used in parliament had little reference to their behavior." Nathan Leites, *On the Game of Politics in France* (Stanford, Calif.: Stanford University Press, 1959), p. 1.

[10] Milton Rokeach, *The Open and Closed Mind* (New York: Basic Books, 1960), Chap. 3; Edward A. Shils, "Authoritarianism—Right and Left," in *Studies in the Scope and Method of 'The Authoritarian Personality,'* R. Christie and M. Jahoda, eds. (Glencoe, Ill.: The Free Press, 1954).

[11] It should be emphasized that the degree of commitment of democratic populations to its political institutions is a relative matter. Many studies of attitudes toward civil liberties show a great gap between the acceptance of civil liberties among a minority of educated and participating citizens and the rank and file, especially among the lower-income and lesser educated. In this case, political extremism represents less an alienation *from* political institutions than it does the advent of increased political democracy. For studies of civil liberties see Samuel Stouffer, *Communism, Conformity and Civil Liberties* (Garden City, N. Y.: Doubleday, 1955); Seymour Lipset, "Democracy and Working-Class Authoritarianism," in *Political Man* (Garden City, N. Y.: Doubleday, 1960), pp. 97–130, and Raymond Mack, "Do We Really Believe in the Bill of Rights?", *Social Problems*, 3 (1956), pp. 264–269.

[12] Kornhauser, *op. cit.*, p. 77.

[13] Mannheim, *op. cit.*, p. 62.

[14] Robert Dahl, *A Preface to Democratic Theory* (Chicago: University of Chicago Press, 1956), pp. 97–98.

[15] The term is used by Franz Neumann in "Notes on the Theory of Dictatorship," in *The Democratic and the Authoritarian State* (Glencoe, Ill.: The Free Press, 1957), p. 251.

[16] See the articles by Richard Hofstadter and by Seymour Lipset in *The New American Right*, Daniel Bell, ed. (New York: Criterion Books, 1955). For a fuller treatment of this theme see Seymour M. Lipset, "Social Stratification and Right-Wing Extremism," *British Journal of Sociology*, 10 (1959), pp. 1–32.

[17] Murray Edelman, "Government's Balance of Power in Labor-Management Relations," *Labor Law Journal*, 2 (1951), pp. 31–35. This point is also discussed in C. Wright Mills, *The Power Elite* (New York: Oxford University Press, 1957), pp. 246–248.

[18] David Riesman, *The Lonely Crowd* (New Haven, Conn.: Yale University Press, 1950), pp. 242–255.

[19] Joseph LaPalombara, "Political Party Systems and Crisis Government: French and Italian Contrasts," *Midwest Journal of Political Science*, 11 (1958), pp. 117–139.

[20] *Ibid.*, p. 133.

[21] Murray and Susan Stedman, *Discontent at the Polls* (New York: Columbia University Press, 1950), Chap. 8.

[22] Seymour M. Lipset, "Economic Development and Democracy," in *Political Man, op. cit.*, pp. 45–76.

[23] Mannheim, *op. cit.*, p. 70. For discussions of the assumption of a natural harmony of interests see the analysis of sociological thought in C. Wright Mills, *op. cit.*, Chap 11; Werner Stark, "Christian Thought in Social Theory" in *Social Theory and Christian Thought* (London: Routledge & Kegan Paul, 1959); Ralf Dahrendorf, *Class and Class Conflict in Industrial Society* (Stanford, Calif.: Stanford University Press, 1958).

[24] See the discussions of this factor in the history of labor movements in Sidney and Beatrice Webb, *History of Trade Unionism* (New York: Longmans, Green & Co., 1920), Chap. 1, and in Selig Perlman, *Theory of the Labor Movement* (New York: Augustus M. Kelly, 1928), Chap. 5.

[25] Martin Trow, "Small Business, Political Tolerance, and Support for McCarthy," *American Journal of Sociology*, 64 (1958), pp. 270–281.

[26] Oscar Gass, "Socialism and Democracy," *Commentary*, 29 (1960), p. 574.

[27] For an especially illuminating statement of this view see Adolf Lowe, *The Price of Liberty*, Day-to-Day Pamphlets, No. 36 (London: Hogarth Press, 1937). Also see Edward A. Shils and M. Young, "The Meaning of the Coronation," *Sociological Review*, series 1 (1953), pp. 63–81. Political consensus as a focus of sociological study is a central theme in Seymour M. Lipset, "Political Sociology," in *Sociology Today*, Robert K. Merton, Leonard Broom, and Leonard S. Cottrell, Jr., eds. (New York: Basic Books, 1959).

[28] Edward A. Shils, "Mass Society and Its Culture," *op. cit.*, p. 288.

[29] Robert K. Merton, "Patterns of Influence" in *Communications Research, 1948–49*, Paul Lazersfeld and Frank Stanton, eds. (New York: Harper and Row, 1949), pp. 180–219; Alvin W. Gouldner, "Cosmopolitans and Locals," *Administrative Science Quarterly*, 2 (1957 and 1958), pp. 281–306, 444–480.

[30] Will Herberg, *Protestant, Catholic, Jew* (New York: Doubleday Anchor Books, 1955).

[31] Studies of tolerance and authoritarianism have repeatedly shown a direct relation between amount of education and tolerance for political diversity. See Trow, *op. cit.*, and the summarization of many studies in Seymour Lipset, "Working-Class Authoritarianism," *Political Man, op. cit.*

[32] Melvin Tumin, *Desegregation* (Princeton: Princeton University Press, 1958).

[33] This distinction and the terms "pluralistic" and "superimposed" are used in Ralf Dahrendorf, *op. cit.*, pp. 213–218.

[34] Lipset, *Political Man, op. cit.*, pp. 131–134, 173–176.

[35] Riesman, *op. cit.*, also see Joseph Gusfield, "Social Structure and Moral Reform," *American Journal of Sociology*, 61 (1955), pp. 221–232.

[36] Alexis de Tocqueville, *Democracy in America* (New York and London: Oxford University Press, 1947), pp. 493–499.

Changes in the Social Order	SOCIETAL TRANSFORMATION

COMMENTARY

Changes in the social order are reflected in trends associated with the structural transformation of total societies. In "The Demographic Transition in the Netherlands," William Petersen attempts to relate the broad theory of the demographic transition to the specific population history of one country. Through an examination of the three basic demographic processes of fertility, mortality, and migration as they apply to different segments of the Dutch population through time, Petersen is able to interpret overall population trends. In this manner he succeeds in maintaining that "delicate balance between the specific facts of the historian and the generalizing function of the sociologist" so necessary to an understanding of "the relation between population growth and modernization."

In the next selection Eric Lampard, a historian, pursues the problem of creating a research procedure which lends itself to the development of generalizations about the urbanization of society. His paper, "Urbanization and Social Change: On Broadening the Scope and Relevance of Urban History," heavily influenced by a demographic perspective, has specific relevance for the development of a comparative sociology which deals with urbanization as a critical type of societal transformation.

Norman Ryder's article "The Cohort as a Concept in the Study of Social Change" supplements Lampard's discussion of the interrelationship of *life sequences* and changes in the everyday patterning of *life routines*. By employing a basic demographic concept, that of the cohort, Ryder brings sociological insight to the analysis of several dimensions of societal transformation.

In "The Female Labor Force in Metropolitan Areas: An International Comparison," Andrew Collver and Eleanor Langlois assess a single significant structural aspect of total societies—the involvement of women in the labor force. Through their analysis they are able to relate a change in the structure of production to the urban-industrial development of total societies.

35 WILLIAM PETERSEN

The Demographic Transition in the Netherlands

Offhand one might suppose that demography ought to be one of the happiest meeting-grounds of sociologists and historians. Studying the population of any society is typically begun with a social analysis—comparing the fertility, say, of one class with that of another. And in this case such an analysis is much less likely to be static than is usual in other branches of sociology, for both the flow of life from one generation to the next and the succession of censuses suggest, and sometimes demand, a historical framework. Actually, however, demography has not benefited from very much interpenetration of the two disciplines. Most of the historians seriously concerned with population have concentrated on the period before the advent of reliable statistics, and their demographic expertise has not ordinarily been at a high level. And sociologists have usually been content with that roughest and most simplistic of models, the theory of the demographic transition, the bare bones of which have all too seldom been rounded out with historical detail.

This at least was the situation until rather recently. But the last decade or so has seen a relatively large number of excellent studies, which in sum may eventually revise our ideas of population trends in the early modern period. Perhaps the most important change being made in the conception of the demographic transition is in the refinement of the original thesis that it applies equally well to all countries undergoing modernization. It has by now become obvious that there are more differences than similarities in the population development of, say, nineteenth century England and twentieth century India. Several writers have suggested that among Western cultures, overseas countries like the United States and the British dominions, whose empty lands were filled in large part by immigration, constitute a special subclass. Even population growth in so homogeneous a culture area as Western Europe has differed significantly from one country to another, and in order to obtain a true picture of its demographic

Reprinted from *American Sociological Review*, 25:3 (1960), pp. 334–346, by permission of the author and the publisher.

past it will be necessary to undertake many more national or even local historical studies and at some future time to synthesize them into a more complex, but more accurate, overall model.

In this paper I wish to bring to the attention of their English-speaking colleagues some of the interesting and important work that Dutch sociologists and historians have been doing in population analysis, and to suggest a few of the general theoretical implications of their findings. That the population history of the Netherlands is anomalous is of course well known, but some of its specific features seem also to be variations on Western themes. If the relation between population growth and modernization is to be better understood, we must learn how to maintain a delicate balance between the specific facts of the historian and the generalizing function of the sociologist.

POPULATION GROWTH

In the theory of the demographic transition, one postulate is that the population growth was wholly a natural increase; and before we apply this theory to any specific historical case we must ask whether the net migration actually was insignificant. This was the case in the Netherlands during the nineteenth and twentieth centuries, to the extent that one can tell from the inadequate statistics.[1] But what of earlier centuries? When the Republic of the United Netherlands was established in the sixteenth century, it became a haven for refugees from Catholic Europe, first of all Calvinists from the reconquered Spanish Netherlands (now Belgium) and Jews from Spain itself, later French Protestants and East European Jews. No accurate record was kept of this immigration,[2] nor of the emigration that partly balanced it. That the Spanish Jews and Huguenots had a great impact on Dutch commerce and industry is not a good clue to their numbers, particularly when these are to be taken as a percentage of the national population rather than of the relatively few towns where the immigrants mainly settled. Whether the zero net migration that the model demands was true of the Netherlands is not known, but it is reasonable to assume that it was.

Estimating internal migration is no less difficult, and the problem cannot be wholly bypassed. The best of the early data refer principally to the urban population, and in order to use them for our purpose we must try to distinguish between the natural increase of the towns and the net migration to them. During the three centuries or so preceding the first national census, the towns' population increased greatly,[3] but certain of the data suggest that this was the consequence mainly of large in-migration.[4]

Sometimes it is possible to check this impression by relating the population growth of the towns to that of the countryside by the use of provincial censuses. In the case of Holland Province, for example, we can compare the urban and rural sectors in 1622[5] and in 1795, as shown in Table 1.[6] The increase of 16 percent over 175 years means an average of less than 0.1 percent per year, but this figure can be accepted only with

TABLE 1. POPULATION OF HOLLAND PROVINCE, 1622 AND 1795

	Towns	Countryside	Total
1622	397,882	269,698	667,580
1795	518,561	258,005	776,566
percent increase	+30	−5	+16

three reservations: (1) If we substitute for the two actual census counts the larger figures including underenumeration as estimated by Van Dillen, the increase would be by 25 rather than 16 percent. (2) The calculation of the trend between the two censuses by simple subtraction blurs the fact that the growth curve for both towns and countryside rose during the seventeeth and early eighteenth century and fell off sharply from about 1750. (3) Neither the towns nor especially the rural regions of Holland Province were typical of the Netherlands as a whole.

This last point is worth expanding. In their generalizing function, sociologists tend to structure any analysis of town and country in the early modern period into a fairly rigid functional division between agricultural and nonagricultural localities, and thus between *Gemeinschaft* and *Gesellschaft*. The historical example of Holland Province suggests that in any particular case this can be a gross oversimplification. Its rural economy, according to De Vooys, included the following quite heterogeneous and sometimes dynamic elements: (1) *Agriculture.* In some areas this sector of the economy and the population based on it were relatively static. But in the so-called Westland—the strip along the coast south from The Hague, which to this day is the center of commercial horticulture—the intensification of agriculture afforded a base for population increase during the seventeenth and eighteenth centuries. (2) *Peat-cutting.* With the depletion of peat bogs in South Holland, peat-workers were replaced by a smaller number of agriculturists, resulting in a population loss in this region. (3) *"Suburban" commerce and handicrafts*, particularly in the environs of Amsterdam and Rotterdam. Here the population fluctuated together with that of the cities. (4) *Fishermen and marine workers* living in both coastal and inland villages north of the IJ River. The virtual disappearance of their means of subsistence resulted in a considerable out-migration and decline in population in the second half of the eighteenth century.

That the urban population of Holland Province increased by 30 percent over the designated period while the rural population fell off by five percent was undoubtedly due in large part to migration, both between these sectors and from other provinces to Holland's cities. But in view of the atypical features of Holland Province, it is well to check this conclusion with data from Overijssel, a generally agricultural province with some early industry. In Table 2 the population growth of this province is shown separately for the three largest towns and, below, for the smaller towns and the countryside of the three socioeconomic areas of Salland, Twente, and Vollenhove.[7] Note that before the nineteenth century the rate of increase

TABLE 2.   REGIONAL POPULATION INCREASE IN OVERIJSSEL, 1675–1849

	Percent increase in population			
	1675–1723	1723–1764	1748–1795	1795–1849
Overijssel	37.6	35.9	9.5	60.4
Three largest towns				
(Zwolle, Deventer, Kampen)..	20.7	15.8	3.1	65.8
Other towns in				
Salland	44.1	36.6	12.4	24.3
Twente	33.4	74.9	7.0	58.2
Vollenhove	37.5	4.0	13.4	60.3
Countryside of				
Salland	31.1	34.9	17.1	69.0
Twente	72.5	58.1	8.4	42.0
Vollenhove	41.6	24.6	9.7	75.7

in the three large towns was well below the average for the whole province, and that by and large the growth curves of the small towns and the countryside tended to move together. These figures suggest that rural-urban migration was not so important a factor in urban growth as in Holland Province, and perhaps Overijssel was more representative of the country as a whole. It may be indicative that for the period since 1795, the growth curves of this province and of the Netherlands are almost identical.[8]

According to the estimate of Slicher van Bath, the population of Overijssel at the specified dates was as follows:

1475—	52,660	Earliest estimate possible; not reliable.
1675—	70,678	Earliest fairly reliable estimate.
1795—	134,104	First national census.
1840—	197,694	First reliable national census.
1957—	748,337	A recent estimate from population registers.

This steady and increasingly rapid growth does not include short-term fluctuations. A more detailed analysis[9] permits the population increase from 1675 to 1930 to be divided into four periods, with the average annual rates of growth as follows:

75 years (1675–1748)—0.75 to 1.0 percent.
60 years (1748–1811)—zero to 0.5 percent.
80 years (1811–1889)—almost 1.0 percent.
40 years (1889–1930)—1.3 rising to 1.7 percent.

Do these data take us back to the hypothetical Stage I of the demographic transition? The so-called static population characteristic of this stage typically fluctuates around a horizontal mean, and it would seem that this cycle is to be seen in Overijssel between 1675 and 1811. The average growth during this period, however, was not zero; this suggests that these 136 years constitute rather a transition from Stage I to Stage II. If the upswing from 1675 to 1748 was faster than that of an ordinary Stage I cycle, as may well have been the case, this was presumably because the premodern prosperity was enhanced by the new factors that eventually would effect a steady increase in numbers. In the second half of the 18th century, a time of economic depression, the population growth slowed down and for the leanest thirty years was not much more than zero. Here again we can reasonably hypothesize that the figures reflect two overlapping curves—a decrease in population that would have resulted from a Stage I depression, cancelled by Stage II factors favoring population increase.

It seems reasonable, lacking precise data, to apply this scheme to the population history of the whole country. According to one estimate—or better, guess—the number of inhabitants of the present area of the Netherlands in 1540 was 882,400.[10] To specify this figure to the nearest hundred is certainly unwarranted, but it may well be correct to the nearest hundred thousand. From the middle of the sixteenth to the middle of the eighteenth century, then, the population probably grew from less than a million to something over two million, and during the second half of the eighteenth century it probably remained nearly static. The growth since the date of the first national census, as shown in Table 3, falls within Stage II of the demographic transition, and even within the early phase of this stage, before the long-run growth rate has begun to decline. From 1795 to 1870 the annual increase averaged about 0.75 percent, and since 1870 it has been around 1.25 percent. In the Netherlands, there is not only no indi-

TABLE 3. POPULATION GROWTH IN THE NETHERLANDS, 1795–1958

Year*	Population (–000)	Percent average annual increase during preceding period
1795	2,097	—
1829	2,613	0.72
1839	2,861	0.91
1849	3,057	0.67
1859	3,309	0.80
1869	3,580	0.79
1879	4,013	1.14
1889	4,511	1.18
1899	5,104	1.24
1909	5,858	1.39
1920	6,865	1.45
1930	7,935	1.46
1940	8,923	1.18
1950	10,200	1.35
1958	11,278	1.25

* As of December 31 of the designated year, except for 1849 (November 19) and 1869 (December 1). Figures from 1795 to 1930 are from the census; thereafter from the population registers.

cation of the "incipient decline" in population characteristic of Stage III but hardly any sign of an incipient deceleration of the present rapid rate of growth.

That the population increase characteristic of modern times began in the 17th century or earlier is in accord with the usual macroscopic estimates. Both Willcox and Carr-Saunders took 1650 as their starting date and posited a subsequent continuous growth both of the world's population and, more specifically, of Europe's.[11] In a historical analysis of one particular country's population, however, the probability that the increase in numbers began so early requires reexamination of the usual thesis that its cause was wholly, or almost wholly, the decline in mortality.

MORTALITY

One can trace the course of Holland's mortality by fairly reliable statistics only since the middle of the nineteenth century. Attempts have been made to devise estimates from burial records of earlier centuries, but the data are so poor that they cannot yield even satisfactory local rates. In a recent article, De Haas has compiled from a number of contemporary sources the expectation of life at various ages from 1825 to date.[12] In Amsterdam, expectation of life at birth rose slowly from about 35 years in 1825 to about 38 years in 1845. For the whole of the country, this index was about 38 years in 1845 and only 40 years in 1875; but from that date on the rise has been much faster and, apart from World War II, without interruption.

As Table 4 shows, the remarkable decline in the Dutch death rate over the past century has been, more precisely, only since around 1880.[13]

TABLE 4.   CRUDE DEATH RATES IN THE NETHERLANDS, 1850–1957

	Decennial average	Range of annual rates from low to high	
		National	Provincial
1850–59	25.5	22.3–31.0	17.7–40.4
1860–69	24.9	22.9–28.7	17.7–39.8
1870–79	24.4	22.2–28.4	18.0–39.0
1880–89	21.3	19.7–23.6	16.5–26.4
1890–99	18.7	16.9–21.0	13.8–18.9
1900–09	15.6	13.7–17.9	12.6–16.6
1910–19	13.5	12.3–17.5	11.2–20.0
1920–29	10.6	9.6–12.3	8.9–14.8
1930–39	8.8	8.4– 9.6	6.8–11.0
1940–49	9.9	8.1–15.3	7.0–17.6
1950–57	7.55	7.3– 7.8	6.6– 9.0[a]

[a] This is the range of what might be termed the normal death rate. In the new province of the Northeast Polder, with an almost total absence of elderly people, the death rate was only 1.7 in 1951. In Zeeland in 1953, after the main dikes broke and several of the large islands were flooded, the death rate rose to 11.4.

The 30 years preceding that date saw little change, either in the decennial averages or in the extremes of the considerable variation from year to year and from one province to another. The same trend can be noted in infant and child mortality, which in this period constituted a large fraction of the general death rate.[14] The reasons for the decline from the relatively high plateau on which the death rate rested in the middle of the last century are, of course, no mystery. Both specific cures for various diseases and highly significant improvements in the environment began to be developed with accelerating speed in the last decades of the nineteenth century. That is to say, the application of the most efficient means of death control effected not a transition from a static to a growing population, but the quickening of the rate of growth from 0.75 to 1.25 percent per year that, as we have noted, also took place in the 1870's.

Was the considerable population growth before the introduction of modern medicine and public health also the consequence, either wholly or mainly, of a prior decline in mortality? And, if so, how can we account for this fall in the death rate? While it is not possible to answer these questions directly from mortality statistics, at least plausible hypotheses can be suggested from known institutional changes and their probable effect on the death rate.

The conclusions that McKeown and Brown reached in their important paper on mortality in eighteenth century England are relevant also to other European countries of that period.[15] They divided the possible causes of a reduction in mortality into three broad classes, as follows:

1. Specific preventive or curative therapy. In the Netherlands as in England, most treatments of the various important causes of death can be discounted for the period earlier than the middle of the nineteenth century. It is a moot question whether fever hospitals, for example, helped restrict contagion by the semi-quarantine they imposed or raised the death rate by the fact that virtually all persons who entered them would be infected.[16] So long as bleeding was the first treatment for illness, the contribution that physicians made to their patients' health was minimal; so long as something like half of surgical patients died of infection, it can be questioned whether surgeons saved more patients than they killed. "It might safely be said," McKeown and Brown conclude, "that specific medical treatment had no useful effects at all, were it not for some doubt about the results of the use of mercury in syphilis, iron in anaemia, cinchona in malaria, and inoculation against smallpox."

2. A change in the balance between the virulence of the infective organism and the resistance of the host. In specific instances—for example, the transformation of scarlet fever from a frequently fatal disease to a relatively trivial complaint—this was probably the decisive factor. The general effect of such changes on the long-term trend in the death rate, however, was probably slight.

3. Improvements in the environment. By the partial elimination of the other two classes, this would seem to be the major cause of any impor-

tant decline in mortality before about 1850. It is difficult to analyze these improvements, not only because data of all kinds are less numerous and less accurate before that date, and because the relation between environmental changes and presumably consequent declines in mortality are typically vague, but because it is hardly possible to speak of "improvements" in Dutch living conditions during the century from 1750 to 1850.

It was during this period, a hundred years of almost unrelieved economic depression, that the first systematic studies were made relating mortality in the Netherlands to the environment. As early as 1770, the Academy of Sciences was sufficiently interested in this relation to offer a prize for the best answer to the question, "What human diseases derive from this country's physical conditions?" and the competition stimulated a larger number of persons to statistical research.[17] They and their counterparts in other countries laid a necessary base for the rapid advances in understanding during the past century.

There is very little in these early statistical studies to suggest a rise in the standard of living. Take the matter of food supply, one of the more important environmental influences on mortality. The Netherlands of the seventeenth century was ahead of the rest of Western Europe in its agricultural techniques. In the eighteenth century, thus, the first stimulus to the transformation of the English countryside—improved drainage and fertilizers, new crops, better breeding of farm animals—was an imitation of Holland. There can be little doubt that in both seventeenth century Holland and eighteenth century England the better and more varied diet of the populace resulted in better health. But for the latter decades of the 18th century and the first half of the 19th, the Dutch data recount mostly inadequacy, often misery. In the 1840's, when the potato blight spreading across Europe invaded the Dutch fields, the endemic deficiency developed into a near-famine. "Food consumption, at least in the cities, was just as low as in Ireland."[18]

The variation in infant mortality can also be explained in part by diet. In some regions and among the upper classes generally, babies were breast-fed. But where mothers had to work, they fed their infants on bread soaked in water with a bit of milk or even gin. When the babies cried, they were given a piece of rag in which a piece of chewed bread with sugar had been tied. "This murderous thing," as De Vooys terms it, went by a variety of local names, but everywhere it was more infectious than nutritious.

Living conditions of the poor, particularly in the cities, were deplorable. Often a family of eight shared one bed. Almost one-tenth of the population of Amsterdam lived in damp cellars. According to various urban samples, infant mortality ranged from one-third to one-half. The correlation between size of township and the rate of infant mortality was positive until the 1880's; with the more rapid improvement of urban health facilities the correlation was reversed during the following twenty years.[19]

One reason for the high rates of urban mortality, both infant and general, is that many Dutch cities are in Holland Province, most of which is below sea level. This fact was certainly relevant to their state of health before the full development of modern engineering. The average death rates for 1841–1860 ranged from above 32 per thousand population in the low-lying townships of Holland Province and Zeeland, to below 22 per thousand in the high-lying townships in the East. The segregation of sewage from drinking water was especially difficult in the western provinces, and there were recurrent outbreaks of cholera until the 1860's. What was termed "swamp fever" (*moeraskoorts*) was actually a group of diseases, which each year ran through a seasonal cycle—influenza and malaria in the spring; in June and July diarrhea among infants, often linked to typhus or bacterial dysentery, whose incidence increased in the fall; and at the end of the year the various respiratory diseases. The drinking water in Zeeland was particularly poisonous: on one occasion in the 1780's, of 1,040 Swiss troops stationed in Sluis, only 12 or 13 could stand on their feet after just one month.[20]

In short, there is good circumstantial, though not decisive statistical, evidence to support the thesis that, at least for some social classes and regions, the death rate rose from the average of, say, 1650–1750 to that of 1750–1850. So long as public-health measures were relatively primitive, the congestion of the cities increased the danger of contagion; and under such circumstances the growth of cities would tend to increase mortality. There was probably also a decline in the living standards and especially the diet of the mass of the people. Extant accounts of seventeenth century food habits are concerned principally with the well stocked tables of the bourgeoisie, but in this relatively prosperous period even the poor probably ate better than their more numerous counterparts in the 1820's and 1830's, certainly better than in the 1840's.

If there was any decline in general mortality, then, it was probably quite small. Was it great enough to account for the increase in population— taking only the period measured by national censuses—from roughly 2.1 million in 1795 to almost 3.1 million in 1850? Or is there not a *prima facie* case here for the probability that fertility rose?

FERTILITY

In the conventional model of the demographic transition, it is assumed that Stages I and II were characterized by a more or less constant fertility at close to the physiological maximum. The population growth during Stage II—the consequence thus, wholly or almost wholly, of the fall in mortality—pushed parents to adopt the small-family system, which was based on a new rationalist attitude toward conception and the various contraceptive means invented or popularized during the nineteenth century.

While this model has a certain rough validity, there is little evidence on the face of it to support some of the details. Reproduction up to the physiological maximum is not the typical practice among either primitive peoples or preindustrial civilizations. Conscious family limitation did not have to wait for mechanical and chemical contraceptives; it can be effected by coitus interruptus, abortion, or infanticide—methods as old as human history.[21] The average size of the family, moreover, depends not merely on the parents' will but on the variety of cultural, religious, and magical norms governing the age at marriage, the proportion of adults that marry, the remarriage of widows, the frequency of marital intercourse, and the like.

The conscious regulation of family size in late medieval and early modern Europe was in part accomplished by coitus interruptus, in part by abortion and infanticide.[22] A more significant check to fertility, however, had been gradually inculcated: the principle that a man might not marry until his living was assured.[23] In some cases, this norm was spelled out in detailed regulations of particular institutions. In other cases, it was strong enough to govern family formation without being specified in written laws. The principal check to unlimited procreation in the Dutch countryside of several centuries ago, the joint household, is a good example of the second type.

In the Netherlands as in all Germanic countries, the sib remained an important legal body until the late Middle Ages.[24] And in many parts of the Dutch countryside, the extended family functions still today as a meaningful social organization. Until rather recently a discussion of it could have been based on nothing more than the impressionist writings of folklorists, plus a few incidental jottings by social scientists; but since the war the three-generation household has suddenly become a "social problem," to be studied by social workers, churches, and government agencies. This new interest has culminated in Kooy's excellent sociological analysis,[25] based in part on a questionnaire survey of the Achterhoek (literally, "back corner"), an agrarian region in the province of Gelderland. But this study is also relevant to other areas where a strong organization of the extended family still persists, and to a historical analysis of the Dutch countryside as a whole.

In its typical form, the joint household can be described as follows.[26] One of the sons (or where there are no sons, one of the daughters) is designated as the sole heir to the family farm, either explicitly in a legal document or implicitly by the tradition that all accept. When he marries, his bride comes to live under his parents' roof. In principle, the heir's brothers and sisters leave the farm; in practice, they often remain, unmarried uncles and aunts with a status between that of family members and servants. Variation in the present-day expression of this tradition is illustrated in Table 5.[27] The normal household consists of two families of successive generations (lines 1 and 2, plus some other families, probably, in which both grandparents had died). Attached to this nucleus, however, there may be an unmarried sibling of the heir or his wife (line 3), or a more distant relative (line 5), or servant or farm-worker, also unmarried (line 6). Note how seldom the property is shared by two families of the same generation (line 4). The restriction that this system imposes on fertility is patent. The main desideratum, that from generation to gen-

TABLE 5. PERCENTAGE DISTRIBUTION IN PATTERNS OF JOINT RESIDENCE
IN TWO REGIONS OF THE ACHTERHOEK

	Graafschap	Lijmers
1. Two families of successive generations	49.9	38.6
2. Family with one grandparent	27.5	27.0
3. Family with an unmarried uncle or aunt	8.6	18.2
4. Two families of the same generation	0.1	0.4
5. Family with a more distant relative	4.2	7.4
6. All other patterns	9.7	8.4
	100.0	100.0
	(3,918)	(740)

eration the farm remain undivided in the same family, is safeguarded, but to this principle is sacrificed the normal family life of a considerable proportion of the adult population.

Because of their frustration, this pattern has been inherently unstable under modern conditions. Whenever a change in circumstances makes it possible, the unmarried hangers-on of these joint households rush to set up their own homes and establish their own families. Thus, several times in Holland's recent history there has been an explosive rise in the fertility of certain areas or certain social classes:

1. The extension of arable land by reclamation has had the paradoxical effect of aggravating population pressure. For the settlers on the polders being built out of the former Zuider Zee are mostly younger sons of farmers, many of whom in their prior status would have been unable to marry. And in the new settlements, in part because of the preponderance of young adults, the birth rate has on occasion been more than 70 per thousand population![28]

2. During the last quarter of the 19th century artificial fertilizers were introduced in the sandy regions of the East and South, and the greatly improved productivity of the soil made it possible to divide up family farms into viable units of smaller acreage. For two or three generations, it was possible in this way for a much larger proportion of young adults to marry and procreate. And today these regions generally have the highest fertility rates in the country, for it has been difficult both to reestablish the traditional pattern of family limitation by the nonmarriage of some adults, and to overcome the opposition of the various churches to family limitation by the use of contraceptives.[29]

3. The joint household and the limitation on human fertility that it implies disappeared earlier where agriculture was based on the naturally more fertile clay soil. This process has been analyzed in detail by Hofstee, particularly for the Oldambt, a region in northeast Groningen. Until the eighteenth century, the farm laborers there lived almost as members of the farmer's family, sleeping in the same house, eating at the same table, working together during the day, talking over common interests in the

evening. From about 1775 on, this patriarchal relation began to disappear, to be supplanted eventually by a sharp class differentiation. The well-to-do landowners underwent an *embourgeoisement* that transformed them from traditional peasants into modern farmers. Even earlier than in the cities, they adopted a small-family system by which the relation between the land and the number of landowners was kept almost constant. The farm workers, converted into a landless proletariat, were released from the institutional and moral inhibitions to procreation implicit in the old system. In the century following 1775, their number in the province of Groningen increased four times.[30]

4. If the fertility of agricultural workers increased when they became a *rural* proletariat, should this not have taken place also when they moved to the town and were there released from the same checks to procreation? That urban fertility in the Netherlands was higher than that in the countryside until about 75 years ago has long been an established fact, but its implications have seldom been explored until a recent paper by Hofstee.[31] In order to supplement the existent compilations of township data, Hofstee compiled from provincial and township archives his own breakdown for 1850–1880, and thus obtained a valuable new base for analyzing fertility during this transitional period. Average birth rates for 1851–1855 showed a regional patterning almost precisely the opposite of that to be seen today. The highest birth rates at that time—35 per thousand or more—were in the agricultural provinces with a clay soil (Zeeland, Friesland, and Groningen) and the country's urban center (North and South Holland). Birth rates in specific cities varied somewhat, but in general they were close to the level of the surrounding countryside. This differentiation is not due, as one might suspect, to a difference in age structure; it holds also when the fertility is compared by other measures.

At one time the three-generation household was standard in the Dutch countryside, and something like it seems to have existed also in the cities.[32] In both cases, the principal check to fertility was by the relatively high proportion of the population that remained single. It is reasonable to suppose that the same forces that prevented the marriage of some tended to postpone that of the others. However, the secular trend in the median age at marriage cannot be realistically discussed in statistical terms, for the following reasons:

1. Data are completely lacking for the earlier period.[33]

2. As is well known, in societies where the postponement of marriage constitutes an important method of family limitation, the age generally rises and falls according to economic conditions.[34] Given the poor statistics, it is therefore still more difficult to discern a possible long-term trend underlying these fluctuations.

3. In any case, the trend in the median age at marriage of the whole population, if it were possible to establish it for the early modern period, would not reveal the changes presumably taking place in several of the social classes.

Even so, although the point cannot be statistically documented, it is reasonable to assume that the same institutional changes that permitted a larger number to marry also tended to reduce the age at marriage.[35]

With respect to fertility, a more important consequence of the break-down of the moral and institutional norms inherent in the joint household was the probable rise in illegitimacy. Like all Germanic countries, the Netherlands has inherited a tradition of "window wooing."[36] By this folk norm, premarital intercourse is usual, and marriage does not take place until the bride is pregnant. According to a government survey made just before World War II, the percentage of forced marriages in the Nether-lands ranged from just over 13 in large towns to 16 in villages.[37] In a number of areas, generally quite fundamentalist in religion, the custom is still more prevalent.[38] It is something of a misnomer, however, to call these "forced marriages," a term that suggests a more or less random liaison. With respect to both the timing and the mate chosen, these are usually planned, or at least half-planned, conceptions; and so long as the village's social control is unbroken, marriage follows them almost inevi-tably. Yet this is a system that all but invites dalliance once the control is released—and in the nineteenth century the urban illegitimacy rates were generally high.[39]

CONCLUSIONS

In the theory of the demographic transition, the population growth of an area undergoing modernization is divided into three stages: (1) a more or less static population at high levels of fertility and mortality; (2) a period of constant fertility and falling mortality, with a consequent rapid increase in population; (3) a more or less static population at more efficient levels of birth and death control. It is generally believed that the population of the Western world has increased continuously from 1650 on, at the latest. The decline in mortality that is used in the model to explain this growth cannot be documented for anything like so long a period. In the Netherlands, as generally in the Western world, the most dramatic rise in life expectation dates from the last quarter of the nineteenth century, and for the prior several hundred years the presumed fall in mortality can neither be proved from the statistics nor even— for a substantial portion of this period—plausibly related to institutional changes.

The unlikelihood of a decline in mortality is increased when we exam-ine more closely the other half of the balance—the assumption that fer-tility remained more or less constant at a high level until it began to fall with the advent of the modern small-family system. It is strange that this thesis has not been challenged more often. It is not even in accord with the established statistical record of the nineteenth century. Because of the accident that the high point in the British birth rate coincided with the Bradlaugh-Besant trial, most demographers know that in that country there had been an upward trend prior to that date. But something of the same pattern can be seen in the course of the fertility of most other West European countries. The French pattern of a steady decline in natality since the beginning of reliable records, which has often been taken as the model with which to analyze the fertility of the Western world, seems rather to be an exception.[40]

For the early modern period a statistical analysis must be based on data poor enough to make it suspect, but the hypothesis that there was a rise in fertility is strongly reinforced by what we know of the institutional changes that accompanied modernization. The Middle Ages bequeathed to the present-day Western world a social system with built-in guards against excessive procreation. Whatever their form, these were expressions of the principle that a man might not marry and beget offspring until he had established an appropriate place for himself which would enable him to carry out his family responsibilities. Perhaps the most precise form of this type of institutional check was contained in the regulations of the English guilds, which prohibited marriage during a long apprenticeship and made it difficult for a period thereafter.[41] In the Netherlands (apparently as in most other Continental countries), the control by the guilds was less rigid, but there too one function of the apprenticeship system was to prescribe, or at least to facilitate, this norm of responsible parenthood.

At any time prior to the most recent past, however, the vast majority of all populations lived in the country, and for a long-term analysis the rural institutions governing fertility demand the most attention. In the Netherlands this institution was the joint household.[42] In principle, in each generation only one person on each farm married and had children. The household also furnished a function and a home, however, for the unmarried. Whether as uncles or aunts to the farm-owner's children, or as more distant relatives, or as servants and farm-workers, these had a place as meaningful parts of an economic and social unit. The limitation to fertility in the joint household was efficient but it was dependent on the maintenance of the institutional forms. As the joint household began to disintegrate, in part because in modern times the nuclear family has been more strongly emphasized, or because the unmarried hangers-on found an opportunity to escape from what they began to perceive as sexual and social frustration, it was inevitable that fertility should rise. And this rise can be demonstrated in a number of particular instances.

Generalizing from the Dutch case, we can posit the following hypothesis in place of the present theory concerning fertility trends in a Western country undergoing modernization.[43] In the *traditional family* typical of the preindustrial period, the postponement of marriage, plus the nonmarriage of a portion of the population, constituted an onerous but efficient means of holding fertility in check. In the *proletarian family*, typical of the mass of either rural or urban workers released from the prior institutional and normative restrictions, there was no effective bar either to early marriage or to procreation. Indeed, social control was often barely strong enough to compel marriage once a child had been conceived. In the *rational family* type, which arose first among the middle classes during the nineteenth century and then gradually spread to the rest of society, a sense of parental responsibility reappeared, and with it a limitation of family size. The average age at marriage rose again, and later the same end was achieved with less privation by the use of contraceptives. Thus, in order to trace the changes in the fertility of any country, we would need statistical data on completed family size *by social class* from the seventeenth century at latest. By this time the disintegration of institutional checks to fertility, the development of new means of death control, and the resultant increase in population were all under way. These data will never become available. But such statistical records as we do have, at least in the Dutch case, support the thesis that the population growth characteristic of the modern West must be explained as the consequence of both a rise in fertility and fall in mortality.

ACKNOWLEDGMENTS

The research for this study was done in Holland under a grant from the National Science Foundation. An earlier version was read by G. A. Kooy, E. W. Hofstee, T. van den Brink, F. Kool, and John T. Krause. I am most grateful for their criticisms.

NOTES

[1] See William Petersen, *Planned Migration: The Social Determinants of the Dutch-Canadian Movement* (Berkeley: University of California Press, 1955), Chap. 3.

[2] For example, Amsterdam maintained a "dénombrement de tous les Protestants réfugiés" from 1681 to 1684, but discontinued it just before the revocation of the Edict of Nantes and the consequent much larger migration. During these three to four years, almost 2,000 persons were listed. See the discussion in J. G. van Dillen, "Omvang en samenstelling van de bevolking van Amsterdam in de 17e en 18e eeuw," *Bijdragen en Mededelingen der Dialecten-Commissie van de Koninklijke Nederlandse Akademie van Wetenschappen te Amsterdam*, XIV, *Bevolking en taal van Amsterdam in het verleden* (Amsterdam: Noord-Hollandsche Utigevers Maatschappij, 1954), pp. 1–24. During the eighteenth century, many of the Sephardic (so-called "Portuguese") Jews left Holland, and were replaced by Ashkenazi Jews from Germany and Lithuania; see Ernst Baasch, *Holländische Wirtschaftsgeschichte* (Jena: Gustav Fischer, 1927), pp. 251–252.

[3] Around 1500, which is almost as far back as the first records will take us, the largest city, Utrecht, had fewer than 20,000 inhabitants. Five or six others—in order of size, Leiden, Delft, Haarlem, Amsterdam, Gouda, and Dordrecht—had more than 10,000 each, and a half dozen others something under this figure. About 1550, Amsterdam and Utrecht each had about 35,000, four other cities about 20,000, eight others between 12,000 and 15,000. Shortly after 1600, Amsterdam had over 100,000 and was the largest city in the Low Countries, Leiden and Haarlem were almost half as large, three other towns had more than 20,000 each, four others more than 15,000. In the late seventeenth and eighteenth centuries, the urban growth was slower, and in some regions there was even a considerable decline from about 1750 on. See Roger Mols, *Introduction à la démographie historique des villes d'Europe du XIVe au XVIIIe siècle* (Gembloux: Duculot, 1954–1955), 2, pp. 520–523; Leonie van Nierop, *De bevolkingsbeweging der Nederlandsche stad* (Amsterdam: Binger, 1905); W. S.

Unger, "De oudste Nederlandsche bevolkings-statistiek," *Economist,* 62 (1913), pp. 745–764; Van Nierop, "De aanvang der Nederlandsche demographie," *Economisch-Historisch Jaarboek,* 5 (1919), pp. 192–208.

[4] Of the men inscribed in Amsterdam's marriage registers, for instance, 51 percent were born outside the city during the first quarter of the eighteenth century, 55 percent in 1750, 60 percent in 1791 (*ibid.*). These very high proportions cannot be taken, however, as in-migration rates. The migrants were undoubtedly mostly young adults and thus disproportionately represented among bridegrooms, and whatever out-migration from the city took place usually escaped being recorded. In any case, Amsterdam was not typical of Dutch cities, nor is it today. See also Van Nierop, "Het zielental van Amsterdam in het midden van de achttiende eeuw," *Amstelodamum,* 38 (1951), pp. 151–154, where data of the same type are used to argue that the city's natural increase during the 18th century was nil, so that both the growth and the later decline were the consequence of migration.

[5] The census of 1622 was taken to prepare for the levy of a special head tax, and earlier analysts have for this reason rejected it out of hand. But Van Dillen, who has made the most detailed study of this count, believes that the underenumeration typical of fiscal censuses was less serious than in most others, because in this case the administration was exceptionally efficient. The province was divided into 23 localities, each under a special commissioner who directed the precinct officials in the towns and the sheriffs in the countryside, and both of these latter groups were required to take a special oath of office. Moreover, even at this early date, the tax was a progressive one, adjusted to both the payer's income and the size of his family. See J. G. van Dillen, "Summiere staat van de in 1622 in de Provincie Holland gehouden volkstelling," *Economisch-Historisch Jaarboek,* 21 (1940), pp. 167–189.

[6] A. C. de Vooys, "De bevolkingsspreiding op het Hollandse platteland in 1622 en 1795," *Tijdschrift van het Koninklijk Nederlandsch Aardrijkskundig Genootschap,* 70 (1953), pp. 316–330.

[7] B. H. Slicher van Bath, *Een samenleving onder spanning: Geschiedenis van het platteland in Overijssel* (Assen: Van Gorcum, 1957), pp. 70–71. The overlap of 16 years between columns 2 and 3 is intentional: it is not possible to fix precisely the date when the retardation in population growth began. The early population figures in this work are based on the plausible manipulation of a wide variety of local statistics. While the methodology is an interesting topic in itself, to discuss it here would take us too far afield.

[8] See the graph in *ibid.,* p. 81.

[9] *Ibid.,* p. 56.

[10] J. C. Ramaer, "De middelpunten van bewoning in Nederland voorbeen en thans," *Tijdschrift van het Koninklijk Nederlandsch Aardrijkskundig Genootschap,* 38 (1921), pp. 1–38, 174–214. The estimate was based on counts of the number of *dwellings* in various towns and in the whole of Holland Province, but more than half of the total constitutes the unmeasured rural sector of the other provinces.

[11] Both sets of figures are given in United Nations, *The Determinants and Consequences of Population Trends,* New York, 1953, p. 11.

[12] H. K. de Haas, "De bevolkingsgrooten gedurende de laatste eeuw," *Nederlandsch Tijdschrift voor Geneeskunde,* 94 (1950), pp. 1972–1977. For the period 1825–1845, the calculation is based on Lobatto's study of the population of Amsterdam, which undoubtedly differed somewhat from the rest of the country in its mortality.

[13] The figures are calculated from the convenient compilation in A. Polman, *Ontwikkeling en huidige stand van de sterfte in Nederland en België* (The Hague: Vereniging voor Demografie, 1951).

[14] Infant mortality fluctuated around an almost constant mean from 1840 to 1880, and the age-specific rates for children and adolescents began to fall only in the 1870s. For a good discussion illustrated by a striking graph see J. H. de Haas, "Van strijd tegen sterfte naar strijd voor gezondheid," *Wetenschap en Samenleving,* 13 (1959), pp. 59–63.

[15] Thomas McKeown and R. G. Brown, "Medical Evidence Related to English Population Changes in the Eighteenth Century," *Population Studies*, 9 (1955), pp. 119–141.

[16] Indeed, the hospital that Herman Boerhave (1668–1738) established in Leiden set a new standard for cleanliness and care of patients, but however important it was as a training center, the fact that it had fewer than two dozen beds tells how little effect it can have had on the conquest of the mortality of that time.

[17] See Van Nierop, "De aanvang," *op. cit.* An interesting commentary on these works is given in two articles by A. C. de Vooys: "De opkomst van de medische geografie in Nederland," *Geografisch Tijdschrift*, 4 (1951), pp. 1–8; "Een regionale statistiek uit het begin der 19e eeuw," *ibid.*, 1 (1948), pp. 110–114.

[18] I. J. Brugmans, *De arbeidende klasse in Nederland in de 19e eeuw (1813–1879)* (The Hague: Nijhoff, 1925), p. 155. See also A. C. de Vooys, "De sterfte in Nederland in het midden der 19e eeuw: Een demogeografische studie," *Tijdschrift van het Koninklijk Nederlandsch Aardrijkskundig Genootschap*, 68 (1951), pp. 233–271; P. Geyl, *Geschiedenis van de Nederlandse stam (1751–1798)* (Amsterdam: Wereld-Bibliotheek, 1959), 3, pp. 59–61 and *passim*.

[19] Centraal Bureau voor de Statistiek, *Sterfte van kinderen beneden het jaar in elke gemeente van Nederland*, The Hague, 1910.

[20] Callenfels, as cited in De Vooys, "De sterfte in Nederland," *op. cit.*

[21] Compare A. M. Carr-Saunders, *The Population Problem: A Study in Human Evolution* (Oxford: Clarendon Press, 1922). The thesis of this interesting work, that the conscious restriction of fertility is characteristic of all cultures, is documented in a long bibliographical appendix in which references to ethnological works are classified under R (prolonged restriction of intercourse), A (abortion), and I (infanticide).

[22] The opposition of the Catholic Church to these latter practices was vehement and specific enough to suggest that they were common. Five means of controlling family size were specifically forbidden—inducing sterility by drugs or incantations, aborting the fetus by violent exercise, killing the infant at birth, refusing to nurse one's child, and accidentally sleeping on it. See J. C. Russell, *British Medieval Population* (Albuquerque: University of New Mexico Press, 1948), p. 160. As late as the 17th century, when Vincent de Paul established the charitable order associated with his name, one impetus to his act was to furnish foundling hospitals as a functional substitute for the continuing high rate of infanticide.

[23] This process in England is suggested by the etymology of the two words, *husband* and *anlepiman*. The word *husband* derives from two words meaning "house" and "dwell," and its original meaning (still preserved in *husbandman* and *husbandry*) was a householder, a man who had a home. The Middle English word for a single man was *anlepiman* ("only man"). These two terms, one referring to property and the other to marital status, gradually became associated as opposites, *anlepiman* coming to mean a man who had no living and therefore could not marry, and *husband* a man who was able to care for a family and therefore could get (or, eventually, was) married. See George F. Homans, *English Villagers of the Thirteenth Century* (Cambridge: Harvard University Press, 1941), Chap. 10.

[24] See, e.g., G. A. Kooy, *Het veranderned gezin in Nederland: Een sociaal-historische studie* (Leerdam: Ter Haar & Schuijt, 1957), Chap. 3 and esp. p. 41.

[25] G. A. Kooy, *De oude samenleving op het nieuwe platteland: Een studie over de familie-huishouding in de agrarische Achterhoek* (Assen: Van Gorcum, 1959).

[26] *Ibid.*, pp. 35–36.

[27] Calculated from Table VI, *ibid.*, p. 33. This pattern was influenced in this case by a severe housing shortage, the consequence in part of war damage.

[28] This situation is discussed at greater length in Petersen, *op. cit.*, pp. 103–108. See also Sjoerd Groenman, "L'asséchement du Zuidergée et le problème de la population aux Pays Bas," *Population*, 7 (1952), pp. 661–674; "Zuiderzee gronden en sanering van de kleine boerenbedrijven," *Landbouwkundig Tijdschrift*, 64 (1952), pp. 5–14.

[29] This relation between soil type and human fertility patterns has been analyzed by E. W. Hofstee in "De landbouw en de migratie," *Economisch-Statistische Berichten*, 35 (1950), pp. 1024–1026; "De functie van de internationale migratie," *Tijdschrift voor Economische en Sociale Geografie*, 15 (1949), pp. 10–22.

[30] See E. W. Hofstee, *Het Oldambt: Een sociografie* (Groningen: Wolters, 1937), pp. 193–235. Of the several articles in which the theme of this work is analyzed more intensively, the most recent is "De ontwikkeling van de huwelijksvruchtbaarheid in het Oldambt in de periode 1880–1950," in *De wereld der mensen*, J. Brummelkamp *et al.*, eds. (Groningen: Wolters, 1955), pp. 295–353. This is a report of the marital fertility of the total sample of first marriages in three townships of the Oldambt, with a detailed analysis of differentiation by social class and religion. Among the well-to-do farmers, the completed fertility fell from below four children in the last decades of the nineteenth century to about 2.5 in marriages contracted around 1910, and it has remained at approximately this level. Among agricultural workers, completed family size began at approximately six children around 1880, then fell with varying speeds according to the religious denomination. Among the small local businessmen, the trend in family size has been less clearly defined, but in general this group stands intermediate between farmers and agricultural workers.

[31] E. W. Hofstee, "Regionale verscheidenheid in de ontwikkeling van het aantal geboorten in Nederland in de 2e helft van de 19e eeuw," Koninklijke Nederlandse Akademie van Wetenschappen, *Akademie-dagen*, 7 (1954), pp. 59–106. A typical instance of a certain blindness usual in earlier analyses can be seen in a paper by the highly competent demographer and former director of the Central Bureau of Statistics, H. W. Methorst. In an article published in 1913 he compared the trend in birth rates in townships with more than and fewer than 20,000 inhabitants—a rough but sufficiently accurate differentiation between "urban" and "rural." According to his data, the urban birth rate was higher until 1890, the two were almost identical at the end of the 1890s, and only in the twentieth century was the urban birth rate lower. Yet his analysis is limited to a discussion of the very latest trend. See H. W. Methorst, "Nederlandsche bevolkingsstatistiek," *Economist*, 62 (1913), pp. 126–154, 250–259, 367–400.

[32] So long as apprenticeship entailed living in the master craftsman's home-workshop, which was passed on from father to one son, the similarities with the system in the countryside were clear, though the number of persons affected was of course smaller. Some of the heterogeneity supposedly typical of urban life can be discerned in Dutch cities, but until well into the modern period the guilds—or at least the style of economic organization that they represented—remained one important factor. They were in decline in the eighteenth century, but toward its end there were still 51 trade and craft guilds in Amsterdam, for example. Guilds were formally abolished during the French occupation, but remnants of the system persisted into the nineteenth century. See Cornelius Wiskerke, *De afschaffing der gilden in Nederland* (Amsterdam: Paris, 1938); A. J. M. Brouwer Ancher, *De gilden* (The Hague: Loman & Funke, 1895).

[33] The degree to which this is the case can be illustrated by an article by van Nierop that, with painstaking effort, has winnowed every bit of information from the marriage records in Amsterdam for the last decades of the sixteenth century. As is generally the case until national compilations of civil records began in the middle of the last century, direct data on age at marriage were scarce and deficient in the Amsterdam records, and a number of complicating factors made it difficult even to estimate the trend. See Leonie van Nierop, "De bruidegoms van Amsterdam van 1578 tot 1601," *Tijdschrift voor Geschiedenis*, 48 (1933), pp. 337–359; 49 (1934), pp. 136–160; 52 (1937), pp. 144–162.

[34] This was true of the Netherlands until about 1870, although apparently less so than of some other countries. See J. H. van Zanten and T. van den Brink, *Population Phenomena in Amsterdam in Comparison with Other Big Towns*, Statistical Communication No. 103a (Amsterdam: Municipal Bureau of Statistics, 1939), pp. 4–39.

[35] In contrast to rural Ireland, there is apparently no impetus to the early marriage of the heir. In Ireland the young man takes over the management of the farm when he gets married, but in the Netherlands one of the frequent sources of friction noted in recent publications is that, on the contrary, even responsible family men are still given no voice in running the property. In some areas—for example, the bulb-growing region in Holland Province—fathers try to keep all their sons single as long as possible, paying them small wages for long hours of work. See, e.g., I. Gadourek, *A Dutch Community: Social and Cultural Structure and Process in a Bulb-Growing Region in the Netherlands*, Netherlands Institute of Preventive Medicine, Publication XXX (Leiden: Stenfert Kroese, 1956), pp. 173–174. The effect of this practice on fertility is ambivalent, however, for while marriage is postponed, each horticulturist has an economic incentive to have many sons, which reinforces his traditional, often Catholic, morality.

[36] This is the literal translation of "venster vrijen," one of the terms by which the custom is designated in Dutch. Most books on the family written in English pass lightly over this important element of the West European cultural tradition. The best general account is by a Swede: K. R. V. Wikman, *Die Einleitung der Ehe: Eine vergleichend ethno-soziologische Untersuchung über die Vorstufe der Ehe in den Sitten das schwedischen Volkstums*, Acta Academiae Aboensis, Humaniora XI.1 (Abo: Abo Akademi, 1937).

[37] Kooy, *Het veranderend gezin . . ., op. cit.*, p. 146.

[38] In the village of Staphorst, for example, of the 87 first births in 1937–1938, 34 were within seven months of the marriage ceremony. In the 1920s, a number of ministers cooperated in a determined effort to stamp out the practice and fulminated from their pulpits against the young people who spent Saturday night in sin and then came to church on Sunday morning. Finally they succeeded—but only in having the traditional night for "window wooing" changed to Friday. See Sjoerd Groenman, *Staphorst: Sociografie van een gesloten gemeenschap* (Meppel: Stenvert, 1948[?]), pp. 96, 153ff.

[39] In Amsterdam, for example, almost one out of every five births was illegitimate for the period 1811–1824, the earliest for which this information is available, and the percentage remained high until the last quarter of the century. See "Statistiek der bevolking van Amsterdam tot 1921," *Mededeelingen van het Bureau van Statistiek der Gemeente Amsterdam*, 67 (1923).

[40] See, e.g., Gerhard Mackenroth, *Bevölkerungslehre: Theorie, Soziologie und Statistik der Bevölkerung* (Berlin: Springer, 1953), pp. 122–134. This section is divided into two parts, the first on the general development of fertility in Northwest and Central Europe, the second on the reasons for the exceptional development in France.

[41] "Apprenticeship in its fully grown Elizabethan form requires that those learning any trade then practiced in England should serve an apprenticeship for seven years or until he was twenty-four years of age, with the possible exception of agriculture in which it was sufficient that he should attain the age of twenty-one if the parties had been unable to agree on twenty-four. It is clear that these provisions were looked upon quite as much as a check on the exuberance of youth as essential for the technical education of the country." G. Talbot Griffith, *Population Problems of the Age of Malthus* (Cambridge: Cambridge University Press, 1926), p. 112.

[42] In their excellent analysis of the interrelation among social structure, family type, and fertility, Davis and Blake argue, on the contrary, that a joint household favors high fertility. This is indeed the case in classical China and India, the examples they use to illustrate their thesis. In such a household, marriage and procreation are feasible as soon as they are physiologically possible, for the supervision of household affairs does not depend on the social maturity of each individual couple. See Kingsley Davis and Judith Blake, "Social Structure and Fertility: An Analytical Framework," *Economic Development and Cultural Change*, 4 (1956), pp. 211–235. Krause is presently analyzing the relation between the joint household and fertility in eighteenth century England.

43 The following discussion derives largely from Hofstee, "Regionale verscheiden-heid," *op. cit.* Hofstee acknowledges a debt to Mackenroth (*op. cit.*, p. 474), who in turn notes that a germ of the hypothesis is to be found in Malthus.

36 ERIC E. LAMPARD

Urbanization and Social Change: On Broadening the Scope and Relevance of Urban History

There is a prevalent dissatisfaction with the writing of urban history: some confusion as to its scope, some doubt about its relevance. The present conference, therefore, is addressed to a crucial point. At a time when urbanization is proceeding rapidly throughout the world, "knowledge of man's past experience with urban life . . . is severely limited." This is notably true for the industrial period since the eighteenth century. To be sure, there is a large literature of histories of individual cities and of case studies of particular aspects of urban life "but owing to the fragmentary nature of this work such studies have provided little cumulative knowledge of urbanization."[1] Dissatisfaction with the existing literature is not so much with things done as with things left undone. Appropriate boundaries for urban history today are perhaps more difficult to define than those of the city itself. The present paper discusses the need to broaden the scope of writings in urban history and then outlines an approach to the study of recent urbanization in the context of social change.

For the most part urban history remains a branch of local history.[2] It is actively pursued for its own sake and assumes a wider relevance only when a city is itself important by virtue of its size or of the outstanding events and personalities associated with it. National capitals are obvious examples. Alternatively, local case histories sometimes serve as a corrective to sweeping interpretations of "mainstream" history or to generalizations from sources that have no particular local identification. A large number of deviant cases, however, does not of itself provide any intellectually sound framework against which to construct new interpretations. The distinguished social historian Asa Briggs suggests that historians are in fact "more confused in purpose than most other specialists who have turned to urban studies." Reserving judgment about whether the historian is more confused than, say, the urban sociologist or the city planner, it is true nevertheless that the biographer of a city often does not know "whether he is fitting local history into a stock national framework or whether he is helping to construct a new scaffolding."[3]

Reprinted from *The Historian and the City*, edited by Oscar Handlin and John Burchard, pp. 225–247, by permission of the author and The M.I.T. Press. Copyright © 1963 by The M.I.T. Press.

Even when the more adventurous scholar attempts a comparative history of two or three places having some experience in common, his frame of reference is usually commercial competition, reaction to outside events, or political reform and only rarely comprises the social movements that create cities or give a generic character to the urban life of a period. The principal concern with city and society in modern times has come from outside the self-imposed confines of urban history. It originates in a derivative kind of social history that is largely an offshoot of writing in economic or intellectual history; its attention has been focused on the *problems* rather than the *processes* of social change.

The emphasis of this social historian was very much upon the history of social policy from the standpoint of reform: on organized efforts to revive and rehabilitate the physical and human debris battered by industrial urbanization and economic change. The change created problems which required solutions. Recognition of this need gave rise to reformist ideas and movements through which the new urban-industrial society accommodated the transition from a rural-agrarian society. Amelioration, when and if it came, was usually attributed to the more active intervention of public authorities stimulated by purposeful interest groups. For the social-economic historian the key to the study of change was the conflict of interests; for the social-intellectual historian, it was the conflict of ideas. But neither focused directly on social organization or the structure of social institutions and, as a consequence, they gave only scant attention to relationships of individuals to their families, communities, and larger groupings except the state. The relation between the burgeoning city populations and a larger society was conceived in terms of the impact of the urban-industrial upon a relatively stable rural-agrarian order, leading to a dissolution of the latter after a prolonged and inequitable conflict between opposing ways of life.[4]

Studies of urban impact first gave the modern city a place in historical writings commensurate with its importance in society. Their authors succeeded, where more parochial-minded city historians had failed, in making the growth of nineteenth- and twentieth-century cities a central focus in the history of social thought and policy. Cities were thereafter treated both as distinctive molds of thought and behavior and as the loci of special urban problems. Urban impact historians investigated a narrow range of effects on the assumption that their causes were well understood.

The first social historians, therefore, dealt almost exclusively with the city problem. In Germany, Great Britain, and the United States, materials collected in public inquiries and community surveys by early social scientists (mostly philanthropic and practical investigators) became the primary source. Evidence gathered initially for political campaigning or legislative prescription was thus adapted, together with local newspapers, pamphlets, social manifestos, and descriptive statistics, to furnish the substantive history of urban-industrial life: city problems were virtually the stuff of social history as they were of social science. With such materials, historians were able to throw fresh light on political movements and changes in social thought. Insofar as they dealt with real people in actual places, their work had both charm and credibility. They avoided the unattractive and, in their opinion, unnecessary resort to sociological categories which served only to complicate the obvious. Eschewing the jargon, historians nevertheless adopted many of the same lines of inquiry, asked broadly similar questions of the same types of data, and came up with much the same results as their counterparts in sociology.[5] The sociologists meanwhile came to regard the study of social history as a useful antiquarian pursuit which might occasionally provide background to the purposeful investigations of more methodical scientists. Not surprisingly, many of the early sociologists and social historians were themselves reformers and sometimes avowed partisans of a political cause: *Kathedersozialisten*, Fabians, and Progressives. People who had lived through such transformations and studied their outcome were understandably involved. Of itself this was no disbarment but it riveted attention on problems to the neglect of larger processes. Since most of the critics of this writing were *"Kathederliberalen,"* the first social history was very much present politics.

Bias in the data was compounded by the weighting of reformist thought. The fixation with problems—public health, housing, nutrition, poverty, vice, and their corrupt consort, public apathy—led social thinkers to identify the pathological with the generic character of urban life. Judgment on the new society was often the expression of reformist animus in terms of rustic imagery or a lost corporate world. Disgust with urban conditions joined with an ingrained romanticism or a hope for reconstruction to nourish the conviction that cities were costly deviants from some natural, more verdant, order of community life. By implication rather than inquiry, the country remained a place for natural, personal, and hence "normal" relationships. As if its municipal deficiencies were not enough, the city milieu was said to isolate the individual and decompose all the corporative affiliations of work and family that had hitherto sustained him. Hence, if urban environment were the culprit, housing standards should be imposed and neighborhoods countrified. Insofar as density was the real villain, population should be progressively dispersed to garden cities where optimal conditions would obtain.[6] More radical reformers found industrial capitalism at the root of the "social question." Passage to the city had involved not only a loss of innocence but of humanity itself. Cities were but giant factories and their streets assembly lines for mass-producing labor. That cities generated more varied opportunities for a growing population which might compensate for its congestion and strain or that their meanest streets were also avenues to social and cultural improvement was for a long time overlooked; the redeeming features were discounted, virtues disallowed. It was as if to consider the apologists' claims would disarm the critic. But that critics had also appeared in the countryside and proclaimed against similar rural woes seems to have been ignored in most writings on the city.[7]

So often the familiarity which the contemporary historian feels for his subject breeds not contempt but oblivion. In the inter-World War years the urban-industrial society became so much a part of the established order that scholars took it for granted. The urban impact had been absorbed. If isolated pockets of rural intransigence might be found fighting an ideological rearguard action against the twentieth century, conflict of that sort was no longer a very convincing framework for the analysis of social change. Society went on changing but the city ceased to provide a central focus outside of urban sociology. Social history degenerated into the study of everyday things, a popular genre of lighter nonfiction. Even as professional urban history (local history) was finally coming into its own, the city was dropped from accounts of contemporary events and reappeared only in the aftermath of World War II as a vantage point for viewing the rise of suburbia and its impact on the central city's core.

By the 1950's the memories of older citizens as well as the extended chronicle of reform achievement bore witness to an amelioration of the grosser features of city life. Amenities and services had become diffused among the more accessible rural communities and the urban way of life was no longer encompassed by city or even metropolitan bounds. To be sure, new problems had emerged with the automobile, affluence, and the unplanned flight to suburbia, but these were mostly of an administrative or technical nature—highways, public transportation, pollution, schools, recreation, and urban renewal. But without relaxing the community's dependence on the central city's core, the withdrawal of comfortable residents and profitable business had accelerated neighborhood decay and drastically reduced the local tax base relative to the mounting urgency of *metropolitan problems*.[8] While the city's work force often increased, the number of its inhabitants fell off; their composition reflected a rising share of the aged, the minorities, the impoverished. Otherwise, urban affairs had become questions of service and efficiency: the unit cost of public facilities, priorities in social overhead and, the only unavoidable political issue, who was to pay? Of old-style problems only the endless task of housing the city's poor (complicated as much in some areas by racial tensions as by low incomes) still called for the creative passion of the reformer to supplement the competencies of the planner.

Although measurable socioeconomic differences between town and country have been reduced, the older compartmentalization of society has been reinforced and sharpened by psychological interest. Improved facilities and manifold opportunities notwithstanding, the urban way of life is still characterized by social disorganization and personal breakdown. Many of the alleged symptoms—from mental illness to delinquency—are shared with residents of suburbia, however, and are no longer considered peculiar to the newcomer or the *nouveau arrivé*. Originally, deviant behavior was ascribed to the competitive striving for place and preferment in the capitalist vortex, then simply attributed to the generic impersonality of the city which precluded genuine personal relations. Most recently, it has been linked *via* Freudian metaphors to the intrinsic instability of secularized urban and suburban family life.[9] For many, the receding countryside still remains, inferentially at least, a distinctive folkish place, the natural mold of closer, more satisfying contacts.

No known form of organized community available to today's citizens appears in itself to secrete the long sought elixir that combines material well being with psychic balm. There is evidently much room for improvement in the city-region, if only a limited interest on the part of its citizens. There is even greater need for renovating the concepts and tools of those practicing community therapy. So many of the early prescriptions of political scientists—from "home rule" and city managers to the American Progressive's trinity: initiative, referendum, and recall—have proven weak or vain things. Most of the established sociological maxims concerning reformed environments and redeemed people have become otiose, if not discredited. Once received, notions of town planners have not only been refuted (on paper) by later planners but have been rejected or, worse, ignored by the very people they were intended to save.

Yet without the reformer's long struggle to civilize human life in the industrial society, we would know even less about modern urban development than we do now. Reform has always been a major stock in trade of local and social historians. The business of urban history is not now to belittle what it once commemorated and confirmed. Merely to reverse the bias and shift the weights the other way would not broaden the historical study of the city in society.

The task confronting urban historians, therefore, goes beyond revisionism. Reform ideas and achievements constitute only a part, possibly a minor part, of the amelioration. They scarcely touch the nature of underlying movements in society that have transformed both town and country. The analytical framework of urban-rural conflict is but one political timber in a potentially much larger scaffolding. While acknowledging the contribution of impact studies, it is well to remember their shortcomings as social history: compartmentalization of society on the basis of question-begging criteria, the recourse to political metaphors in default of sociological categories, the neglect of the process of urbanization.[10]

If professional urban historians, local historians for the most part, are to be exempted from many of these strictures it is testimony to their industry rather than their imagination. A myopic view of the general is not corrected by holding a mirror glass to the particular. Much of what is reflected lacks precision or pertinence. Though city histories and local cases supply a more rounded picture of urban life in particular contexts, they do not furnish the needed framework for understanding social change. Not enough is known of urbanization and urbanism in general to enable the microscopic case worker to determine what is unique or otherwise in his cherished specimen: he cannot tell us why one Athens, one Florence, one Vienna, or New York. Variance in the data cannot be defined, let alone appraised, until it is examined in relation to a framework of analysis. Microscopic work in local history, though monumental in detail, rarely furnishes its facts in forms that are amenable to macroscopic treatment. Urban history, therefore, lacks not only general frameworks but consistent and comparable data relevant to them.

Such are the general grounds for dissatisfaction with the scope and relevance of much writing in urban history. If many practical and professional studies of cities remain, as Asa Briggs contends, "imperfectly grounded in more general urban studies" and if, as this paper maintains, most administrators, architects, welfare workers, and planners have not fully grasped the nature of changes they attempt to order, reasons are not hard to find.[11] Social historians and others concerned with the long run have not begun to examine the social processes that create cities. There are no studies of modern urbanization and urbanism nor, until recently, very pertinent studies of particular aspects and cases.[12] Bureaucrats and "problem solving" social scientists have been working, for the most part, with concepts and tools inherited from the last great period of creative thinking about cities—the years before World War I.

Historians have failed to order the recent urban past in either a comprehensive or relevant way and have, in fact, often confused matters by a ritual insistence that they only study "particulars." Although there are limits to which any one discipline could or should treat urban developments in their entirety, it is time surely to frame a broader approach to urban history, one that elucidates concrete local situations in the *same* terms that are used to treat more generalized transformations in society. Individual cities, for example, can be treated as particular *accommodations* to a many-sided societal process: urbanization. Interest lies in so reformulating the generalities of urbanization that they can serve as principles for organizing and evaluating the range of materials found in the diverse, but rarely unique, experiences of particular towns. The scope of historical urban studies should thus be broadened and more systematic efforts made to relate the configurations of individual communities to on-going changes that have been reshaping society.

At stake in a broader view of urban history is the possibility of making the societal process of urbanization central to the study of social change. Efforts should be made to conceptualize urbanization in ways that actually *represent* social change. For this purpose urbanization may be regarded as a process of population concentration that results in an increase in the number and size of cities (points of concentration) and social change as an incremental or arhythmic alteration in the routines and sequences of everyday life in human communities. The method will be to explore possible interrelationships between the phenomenon of population concentration and certain apparent trends in social organization, structure, and behavior.[13]

Historians are accustomed to speak of continuity and change in human affairs and, in ordinary discourse, the implication is often given that change and alteration are wholly circumstantial, if not chance, events. But continuity may be viewed as the periodic or regular recurrence of routines and sequences in the affairs of households and communities, and change as their cumulative or net outcome. Throughout history much of everyday life has been patterned according to repeated or periodic sequences: familiar daily, weekly, monthly, annual, and other recurrent cycles, such as the passing of the seasons and, in case of life histories, the passage of the years. Recurring cycles are, nevertheless, subject to alteration and eventually to trend—otherwise, barring chance, there would be only continuity and never change.

Consider some of the implications of this view for a description of social change. Work and rest in European culture, for example, having usually been instituted in a diurnal routine with some regular interruption on the Sabbath and the further likelihood of seasonal variation. Labor and leisure have alternated in some conventional division of hours of day and night until something occurs to increase or decrease the span of one in relation to the other. Many such occasions come to mind: the introduction of artificial illumination, restrictive legislation, a shift in residence or job. But the alternating routines may also be affected by the unfolding of a given person's life cycle as when he becomes too old to maintain the schedule or type of work of his prime. The regular experience of major life sequences follows the same broad recapitulation through the patterns of childhood and maturity to those of old age and beyond *via* sequential rites of passage. Alterations in this basic progression are effected through the rephasing of sequences either by social or natural modification. Categories such as the length of apprenticeship or age of retirement may be redefined. The achievement of new legal or social "class" status by marriage or acquisition of property, for instance, may have the same effect. Improved diet or hygiene represents joint modification by society and nature and has its effect, for example, in an increased average life expectancy.

Such routines and sequences in the lives of individuals and groups are repeated or recapitulated as the case may be within a customary interval but both are subject to alteration and to trend. Sooner or later routines and sequences are recognizably changed in a determinate direction that appears irreversible. The daily round changes with age or by social qualification. Men growing up learn trades, later they may change them, and eventually work part-time and retire. Women work too but expect to marry and spend much of their time in raising children. With greater or lesser involvement of the community, the family fits the children in turn for their life's career. The unfolding of *life sequences* changes the everyday patterning of *life routines* for each individual and there is a striking modality observable in people of the same broad chronological age. Gradually, the enmeshing sequences of parents' and children's lives alter each other's routines and thereby the routines and structure of the family group. Over the years, the organization of the family is affected by the changing structure of its internal relations. Finally, the changing patterns of domestic routine and family structure will measurably affect the patterning and structure of routine activities in the community that are more or less age-specific—from school attendance and job entry to the establishment of new households and propagation of the next generation.

Differences in routines and sequences between generations are particularly revealing of social change brought about by divergence from the routined ways of parents. Migration, shift of occupation, change of status and social mobility create the interstices through which change takes form in the patterning of people's lives. Organization and structure of both family and community activities are affected in the same way. Departure from the ways of parents may be viewed not only as the alteration of routines by age and social modification in the life-span of a single younger generation but also as variation in a trend of alteration over a longer sequence of intergenerational change. If such nonrecurrent movements in a population can be identified and separated from the recurrent ones, then trends of social change may be identifiable. These in turn may be analyzed into their various strands or components whose interaction and *net* alteration is registered in the trend. Thus a partially quantified expression may be given to an essentially qualitative social change.

All this, to be sure, may seem to be a matter of statistical manipulation and outside the sphere of the historian's interest. But it is a principal contention of this paper that social historians must begin to explore the underlying movements in community structure and organization that go much deeper than the epiphenomenal patterns of politics or the ferment of ideas. An autonomous social history ought to begin with a study of population: its changing composition and distribution in time and space.[14]

Economic history has already faced this necessity in its own development and, as a consequence, the discipline has been made over during the last twenty or thirty years. Little or nothing has been lost in the course of this evolution and a great deal has been gained. If the decomposition of trends into component movements can be accomplished in the analysis of such complex phenomena as the business cycle and capital formation or such demographic changes as social mobility, then some historians must begin to think in these sorts of terms even though requisite data may not yet be at hand. One obvious area in which this new kind of social history would be pertinent is the comparative study of economic growth.

Were the requisite data at hand, there is no reason why they might not be expressed in terms of the distributional change from rural to urban residence; that is be given a spatial referent. Here then is the unmistakable relevance of urbanization to the study of social change. If sufficient data were recovered or reconstructed, the urbanization of population could be correlated with structural characteristics of an economic or social kind, their associations analyzed, and clothed in all the rich detail of historicity.

Historians are as likely to discover these kinds of data for single places over short periods of time (registration records are a good example) as other social scientists are to find adequate coverage for their purposes in national and state enumerations.[15] The point is that, if the same sets of terms are used, similar techniques of analysis may be applied to both micro- and macroscopic situations and there is every reason to believe that the little world will illumine the large.

No doubt the resulting structures of urbanization and associated activity will present an array of diverse developments having significant features in common. Each urban situation will be measurably distinctive but its distinction is a matter of degree, not of kind. It will represent not so much the exception to a rule as a deviation within a trend (or general movement in the population) that needs understanding in historical-contextual terms.[16] Urbanization is the societal process that creates cities but each city is an accommodation of the general movement to a particular set of demographic, institutional, technological, and environmental circumstances— including the contingencies of events and personalities. Insofar as this approach is designed to measure variation it puts people and places back into history. The population is no longer an anonymous crowd dragged on to a stage to celebrate the doings of great men or news of great events. Everyday mundane life led in anonymity in nameless places contributes in its time to the great alterations of history.

What is at stake in this broadened view of urban history is the possibility of examining one of the most comprehensive, profound, and unprecedented manifestations of social change: *the urbanization of society.* Urbanization of society is a particular phenomenon of the last century and a half but, to grasp the nature and magnitude of the changes involved, it is necessary to draw a much longer perspective in order to bring the connection between urbanization and social change into bolder relief. Over the four or more centuries since 1500 it may be possible to discern which of a given set of factors at any time has prevailed in shaping an alteration in the character of the modern city. Was it, for example, the centralizing polity of the nation state, the pricing calculus of the rational capital-using business system, the enormous increase in calorific energy unleashed by the application of fuel-burning machines to production and communication, or the population explosion of the countryside that was decisive, in Oscar Handlin's terms, in shaping the reorganization of the city's space, the reconstruction of its social order, and the adjustment of its citizens?[17]

No single approach is likely to provide a satisfactory explanation of this many-faceted phenomenon. But in the course of this longer inquiry it will be possible to develop three salients from which to advance on the modern city: the demographic, the structural, and the behavioral. The first deals with the growth and distribution of population in space; the second pertains to the organization of communities and society; the third has reference to the conduct of individuals. Although structural and behavioral characteristics provide essential clues to the nature and direction of social change, the demographic approach appears to offer at once the least ambiguity and the most promise from the standpoint of observation and measurement. As Schumpeter remarked: "We need statistics not only for explaining things, but in order to know precisely what there is to be explained."[18]

Human populations have been forming into cities of one kind or another for almost seven millennia but at no point before the eighteenth century did urban centers themselves contain more than a small fraction of the total. For much of that time, moreover, recognizable urban settlements were confined to a few widely separated parts along the rim of southern Asia. Cities, leagues of cities, urban civilizations may later have flourished elsewhere but never an urbanized society.[19] Great cities, to be sure, with populations that at times reached several hundred thousands had appeared in remote antiquity; one fairly late example, Seleucia on the Tigris, probably exceeded 500,000 inhabitants during the third century B.C. Around 1300 A.D., at the peak of the medieval flowering, there were probably only five cities in all Christendom with more than 100,000 residents. London may have exceeded half a million in the third quarter of the seventeenth century and Paris may have during the next century but, in Europe and probably the world they remained comparative freaks.

As recently as 1800 only about three percent of the world's estimated population of 906 millions resided in some 750 local centers of more than 5,000 inhabitants; more than half of this urban population was to be found in forty-five great cities (of 100,000 or more inhabitants) more than half of which again were located outside Europe. Asia had almost sixty percent of this great city population and Edo (Tokyo) may well have been the largest single agglomeration in all human history up to that time.[20] At the close of the eighteenth century only in Britain and the Netherlands did the proportions of total populations resident in towns and cities much exceed ten percent. There was no urbanized society—having from a third to half its people in cities—anywhere in the world.

Between 1800 and 1950 world population increased nearly 165 percent but world urban population resident in cities of 5,000 and over had risen by 2,535 percent. This striking disparity of rates provides a rough quantitative expression of the phenomenon of urbanization. By 1950 the number of cities with more than 5,000 inhabitants had risen to 27,600 and they now contained almost thirty percent of the estimated 2.4 billion world population. At this date the number of great cities, 100,000 and over, was 875 and forty-nine giant agglomerations surpassed the million mark. A larger proportion of the greatly increased world population resided in *Millionenstädte* in 1950 than in 1800 had dwelt in all cities of 5000 and over. In 1950 Australasia, the Americas, and Europe contained the largest relative concentrations of great city dwellers in that order but the growth of such cities was already proceeding at a much faster rate in Asia and Africa than in any other of the major continental regions.

Since about 1800 the world has witnessed a growth in the number and size of cities with repercussions and ramifications which mark that turning point as one of the crucial disjunctions of human history. Whatever conditions of natural and social environment had hitherto checked the growth and redistribution of population had suddenly been relaxed. The appearance of urbanized societies, with well over half their populations resident in cities, represents the most far-reaching social change since the "urban revolution" of Neolithic times.

The most obvious structural movement associated with this unprecedented demographic change was the industrial revolution. Prior to the acceleration of city growth in the later eighteenth century, it is doubtful if urbanization had ever affected more than three percent of world population or more than ten to fifteen percent on a restricted regional or local basis. We know, nevertheless, that profound social transformations had occurred in Europe and elsewhere without benefit of sustained urbanization. A shift of four or five percentage points in levels of urbanization in the later Roman world or the high middle ages of Europe probably sufficed to mark important turning points in the unfolding of Western civilization. Such a transformation took place in the market city of northern Italy when "the market and public square became one thing." Merchants superseded landowners as the acknowledged fathers of self-governing mercantile communities.[21] Men of commerce acquired, not only wealth and influence, but status and dignity. Clearly, deep-seated changes take place wholly disproportionately to the numbers of people actually moving in and out of cities even on a local basis.

A general decline in population after the fourteenth century marked a disintegration of society that did not much abate before the sixteenth century. Activities in the market place were significantly depressed and cities surrendered a large part of their civic autonomy and their populations. The prolonged declension was relieved only by a gradual process of personal emancipation and the cultural flowering of the Renaissance which consolidated certain intellectual foundations of the ensuing era of geographical and scientific discovery epitomized in the new technologies: gunpowder, mining, printing, and navigation. But not before political allegiance, economic interest, and moral authority had been redefined in a viable unit of social organization and expressed in terms of novel legal rights of property and contract were energies and resources effectively channeled to a common end, to the structuring of a new social order. Centralization of political, economic, and religious initiative in the princely nation state had, for the moment at least, the special virtue of linking technological novelty to commercial operations in more systematic efforts to improve production. Mercantilist polity contributed initially to national wealth and power but, outside the colonial areas (notably the Americas), the crowded ports and ostentatious capitals, it did not foster a growth of cities. The most that can be said quantitatively before the eighteenth century is that variations in rates of urbanization locally rather than levels generally provide suggestive clues to underlying currents of change.[22]

If the historian looks only for conspicuous changes in rates and levels of urbanization before 1700 he will overlook important structural movements in society that were scarcely reflected in the city. He must study developments in the country as well as the town and divorce between the two, even for analytical purposes, may lead to serious misunderstanding of urbanization itself. Raising of market crops, for instance, led to a more rational pattern of land use in accessible country districts: a conscious effort not only to maintain the fertility of the soil but to increase its productivity. Rising capital-output ratios rendered old routines inherited from communal land management irrational in the sense that social (as well as technical) limits on output represented a lowering of potential returns on fixed investment. Since mining and many branches of pre-industrial manufacture were also country or village pursuits, their reorganization along capital-intensive lines away from restrictive craft traditions likewise did not affect the internal order of the city nor disrupt the daily circulation of its people. Credit, information, and initiative might be channeled through the centers but reorganization of production in farm, mine, and mill went on mostly in the outlying places. City dwellers provided more of the specialized commercial and administrative services needed to integrate a slowly evolving territorial division of labor.[23] By the seventeenth century there was nothing generically "urban" in the adaptation of a profit-seeking capital-intensive regimen nor in the rational evaluation of people and places in terms of their relative income-earning capacities. Few of these functional relations between town and country or among the cities were altogether without medieval precedent; the range and intensity of later developments marked them off from their predecessors. These were portentous indicators of transformations outside the city's limits that would shortly become concentrated and intensified within its own constricted space.

Thus preindustrial division of labor, centralization, and hierarchical organization were institutional means to implement a larger comity. They were not so much results of social change as its immanent forms: the modes by which it unfolded. Around 1700 small cities performed broadly similar central place functions (trade, civil and ecclesiastical governance, defence, some manufacture) with regional variations across wide areas of territory. Country districts were largely self-sustaining for the bulk of production and service needs. Work, work places, and the working day were scarcely articulated from the domestic routines of everyday life and living. Provincial manners combined with local building materials to give an outwardly variegated texture to a broadly similar social fabric. Large cities, including political capitals, provided only the more specialized services of interregional or international significance; they were the emporia for provincial staples and exotic specialties. Transport and communications factors sufficed, among other things, to mitigate the sense of interdependence for the vast majority. Low rates of urbanization but high levels locally were a consequence of centripetal organization and the intensive utilization of special sites. The industrial revolution was nourished in countrysides such as these and not before the large-scale application of fuel-burning machines to production and communication in the nineteenth century did industrial-urban disciplines impose any wholesale rationalization on population or space.[24] The rationalizing centripetal movements of industrialism, however, were immanent in the social order that had emerged before the perfection of the steam engine. Industrial urbanization did not destroy an old order; it fulfilled the new one.

There is no need to rehearse the marvel of technological unfolding from water wheels and steam engines through turbines to electric generators and internal combustion engines. Each would in turn have its peculiar influence on the morphology of city growth.[25] Both the accelerated pace and the altered form of urbanization after 1800 were determined by the newer technological component of industrialism that imposed an exacting regime of technical efficiency based on the relative work performance and operational requirements of machines. But, insofar as the trend of change was the *net* outcome of variations in existing routines and sequences, the technological component was made effective through the institutional component of the price system.[26] Relative technical possibilities expressed through the more comprehensive and value-laden calculus of bookkeeping reinforced the movement of population and economic activity (other than agriculture) out of the countryside and into the town.

The same exalted conventions, however, did not enter the full cost of a firm's business decisions to the community. "External" as well as "internal" economies, for example, accrued to the firm but not the diseconomies created by the firm's own operations.[27] Some of the latter no doubt fell on other firms and were duly accounted as items of "internal" cost; others were transferred to the household which was now separated institutionally and spatially from place of work. But the balance, and probably the largest part, of "external" diseconomies was carried by the community in the form of "city problems." Political adjustments in the form of regulation and taxation later moderated some of the more dysfunctional aspects of industrialism. Thanks to an increasingly flexible and productive technology, the price system operated *via* rising average levels of personal income to relax the older centripetal pressures somewhat. Built-up areas are now flung out across the countryside without visible unity or identity; city problems are dissolved into metropolitan problems: nobody's or everybody's concern.

Thus the social system of pricing, giving expression to whatever cultural and psychological principles are operative in human scientific creativity,[28] accounts in part for the particular demographic phenomenon of the urbanized society and its characteristic structural order of activities differentiated in space and time. The most evident mutation of this principle of social selection was an artifact which creates wealth, the industrial city. Linked externally to a functionally specialized countryside and to other differentiated urban centers, the industrial city was reorganized and reshaped along institutional lines into spatially segregated areas of residence (households) and work (firms), with sharply differentiated time for labor and domesticity and with necessary interchanges of population from productive to consumptive roles at conventional, albeit temporally specific, points in daily and weekly schedules.

Evolution of this kind of city out of earlier prototypes was variously affected at times by national polity, capitalist business, fuel-burning technology, and not least by the sheer increase in population itself. When death rates declined without a sufficiently rapid change in family structure and size, population boomed. The nation state centralized the polity, renovated property and contractual relations, reduced the autonomy of local institutions, and the strength of traditional ties: it emancipated the individual. The community was even more closely affected by the flowering of rational capital-using business guided along profit-making lines by market competition and conventional accounting technique: it represented people, places, and things as factors of production substitutable in almost infinitely variable proportions to the point of diminishing returns. The technological variable governed the rate, level, and direction of the urbanization trend subject only to modulation in the event of politically serious dysfunction: technology reinforced and magnified the tendencies of political economy. The remaining variable is population itself. In some respects it is independent of the others but in many ways responsive to them, to the level of urbanization and the spatial-structural organization of family and community life.

This last point touches the least tractable of all: the effect of urbanization on human behavior. Urbanization has concentrated unprecedented numbers of human beings into cities of different size and density and, as a consequence, their daily routines and sequences have become radically changed through progressive differentiation. During any day, a person is obliged to play out many specialized roles in his family, at work, on the journey between, and in the community at large. In great cities these roles are often functionally, institutionally, spatially, and temporally specific. Over any life sequence the specificity of roles is modulated with age or change of socioeconomic status. Over generations both periodic routines and sequences become radically changed. Clearly urbanization must have affected human behavior in myriad ways. The fall in the birth rate, for example, and the trend toward smaller family in most urbanizing countries was not only a profound demographic and structural phenomenon, it mirrored a radical alteration in family behavior. Similarly, insofar as rural-to-urban migration brought rising socioeconomic status to many families or their offspring, social mobility may have further modified behavior. Such changes, however, can be apprehended in the same way as demographic and structural alterations; they are often obverse and reverse sides of the same thing.

Nevertheless, it is said that urbanization "is more than a shifting of people from country to city and from landbound work to urban types of work. . . . Urbanization involves basic changes in thinking and behavior of people and changes in their social values." The reference, of course, is to the individual person. If he should display certain patterns of behavior —urban ways of thinking and urban values—he may be said to be urbanized. Indeed, if he exhibits such traits, he need not necessarily "leave his rural work or habitat."[29] Some city dwellers, on the other hand, do not yet manifest these traits. Such an approach has the great advantage of not restricting urbanism to the city milieu and seems to be in accord with many obvious facts of contemporary life. Yet it raises again the same difficult questions of definition and measurement that have plagued urban sociology and social history from the beginning. This kind of behavioralism is especially vulnerable when hypothetical urban traits have obvious counterparts in nonurban communities or are even more obviously related to a particular historic situation that may once have existed, for instance, in Berlin or Chicago. Finally, most of the behavioral studies have so far focused on urban pathology without ever establishing a very clear notion of what constitutes normal behavior in a normal community; hopefully, they never will. But if urbanization does produce notably higher rates of personal breakdown they may well be the consequence of adjustments people have been required to make in the routines and sequences of everyday life. This is especially true of newcomers in which case might not the symptoms be better treated as aspects of migration than of urbanization *per se*? Thus, some of the slum and near-slum neighborhoods in which immigrants to the United States experienced the trauma of their Americanization have apparently developed a richness of ethnic tradition and local cohesion that is personally and socially more therapeutic than the sanitary Superblock. Critics of urban renewal programs deny the need for bulldozer surgery on precisely these grounds.[30] One wonders whether this kind of phenomenon is not more responsive to forms and styles of literature and the arts than to any of the categories and techniques of social science.

From another standpoint, human beings and their communities are highly adaptable. The community is the social institution for human adaptation. Perhaps the predicament of both town and country dwellers in urbanizing societies is that adjustments are required at too great a pace in too many directions, most of which seem irresistible and irreversible. There are simply too many choices to be made and few generally accepted rules, other than those of the price system, to apply. Surely these are among the profoundest dilemmas of modern "Western" man—not simply the distinctive traits of urban thought or values.

In the light of serious shortcomings in the concept, urban, and of the broad connotation we have given to the term social change it is difficult to resist a conclusion that many of the problems and attributes commonly identified with the city or urbanization represent no more than a concentration of the effects of changes which are otherwise dispersed and less visible. Not only are such problems as housing and public health intensified in a city milieu, they are more conspicuous there and the contrast with urban wealth and well-being made more reprehensible. Urbanization concentrated age-old problems of poverty and ignorance and, in great cities, aggravated conditions that were as endemic to civilization as the city itself: congestion and artificiality. In the city they are displayed for all who care to look. It is not surprising that the city becomes a locus for discontent that is by no means generic to urbanism itself.

The high visibility of social changes in the city is a consequence, not of population concentration and spatial segregation alone, but of narrow and near-sighted vision as well. What an observer sees in the city can be established only by relating the focus of his interest to a larger framework of understanding; the proportions of what are seen are determined by the observer's stance and perspective. The casual observer may see nothing of note; a reformer what his predilections allow him to see; an expert sees what he is trained to see. This is the fundamental reason why the practical student of urban affairs needs a filter for penetrating beneath the surface problems to the deep seated processes that create cities and transform them before his eyes.

The broadened perspectives on urbanization and social change sketched in this paper form no more than a partial framework of explanation. They need careful application to both micro- and macrohistorical contexts before they can yield a fuller sense of satisfied understanding. Doubtless, there are many other processes at work in recent history on which very different perspectives would be more revealing. But, in view of the importance of the modern city in society and its rapid spread throughout the world, more effort should be made to interpret social change in terms of urbanization as a process of society. The particular view of social change and the suggestions regarding demographic, structural, and behavioral approaches advanced in this paper are put forward not for acceptance, but hopefully for use.

NOTES

[1] Harvard Summer School Conference on "The City and History," Statement of Purpose, July 24–28, 1961.

[2] Recent surveys of literature in urban history are, e.g., W. H. Chaloner, "Writings on British Urban History, 1934–1957, Covering the Period 1700 to the Present," *Vierteljahrschrift für Sozial- und Wirtschaftsgeschichte*, 45 (März, 1958), pp. 76–87; Erich Keyser, "Neue Veröffentlichungen über deutsche Städtegeschichte, V," *Blätter für deutsche Landesgeschichte*, 95 (1959), pp. 290–329, and previous numbers; Blake McKelvey, "American Urban History Today," American Historical Review, 55 (1952), pp. 919–929.

[3] Asa Briggs, "The Study of Cities," *Confluence*, 7 (1958), pp. 107–114.

[4] Eric E. Lampard, "American Historians and the Study of Urbanization," *American Historical Review*, 67 (1961), pp. 49–61.

[5] Elizabeth Pfeil, *Grossstadtforschung* (Bremen, 1950) is a useful summary of the early German literature on the sociology and social history of cities. On international

aspects of social theorizing and reform thinking see Don Martindale, "Prefatory Remarks: The Theory of the City," in *The City*, Max Weber (tr., Glencoe, Ill., 1958), pp. 9–62, also Arthur Mann, "British Social Thought and American Reformers of the Progressive Era," *Mississippi Valley Historical Review*, 42 (1956), pp. 672–692. See also M. D. Hirsch, "Reflections on Urban History and Urban Reform, 1865–1915," in *Essays in American Historiography*, Donald Sheehan and H. C. Syrett, eds. (New York, 1960), pp. 109–137.

6 William Ashworth, *The Genesis of Modern British Town Planning* (London, 1954), pp. 118–146, 167–190; more generally Lewis Mumford, *The City in History* (New York, 1961), pp. 482–524, and Pierre Lavedan, *Histoire de l'Urbanisme* (3 vols., Paris, 1926, 1941, 1952), es. Vol. 3.

7 E. E. Lampard, *loc. cit.*, pp. 57–59; E. deS. Brunner, *Growth of a Science: A Half-Century of Rural Sociological Research in the United States* (New York, 1957).

8 A review of developing metropolitan problems in the United States is given in Lloyd Rodwin, ed., *The Future Metropolis* (New York, 1961). Up-to-date studies of the planner's art are: Kevin Lynch, *The Image of the City* (Cambridge, Mass., 1960) and Gordon Cullen, *Townscape* (London, 1962).

9 E.g., Georg Simmel, "Die Grossstadt und das Geistesleben," in *Die Grossstadt*, Th. Petermann, ed. (*Jahrbuch der Gehe-Stiftung*, IX, Dresden, 1903), pp. 187–208; Louis Wirth, "Urbanism as a Way of Life," *American Journal of Sociology*, 44 (1938), pp. 1–24; M. A. McCloskey, "Urbanization," in *Dilemmas of Youth in America Today*, R. M. MacIver, ed. (New York, 1961).

10 Lampard, *loc. cit.*, pp. 54–57; A. J. Reiss, Jr., "An Analysis of Urban Phenomena," *The Metropolis in Modern Life*, in R. M. Fisher, ed. (Garden City, N. Y., 1955), pp. 41–49. See also the later views of Louis Wirth, *Community Life and Social Policy* (Chicago, 1956), pp. 173–174.

11 Briggs, *loc. cit.*, pp. 108–111. Briggs emphasizes the importance of visual and subjective elements in urban studies to supplement the social science approach. He recommends the anthologies of Bayrd Still on New York and Bessie L. Pierce on Chicago. See also Anselm Strauss, *Images of the American City* (Glencoe, Ill., 1961).

12 The only general work on urbanization in English is the comparative study by Adna F. Weber, *The Growth of Cities in the Nineteenth Century* (New York, 1899). Paul Meuriot, *Des agglomérations urbaines dans l'Europe contemporaine* (Paris, 1897). An essay in the classic tradition of French demography "Urban Agglomerations and the Social Evolution of Countries" was contributed by Louis Chevalier to R. M. Fisher, ed., *Metropolis in Modern Life*.

13 In what follows the author wishes to acknowledge his indebtedness to the work of Otis Dudley Duncan, Leo F. Schnore, and Norman G. Ryder: especially O. D. Duncan, "From Social System to Ecosystem," *Sociological Inquiry*, 31 (1961), pp. 140–149; Leo F. Schnore, "Social Mobility in Demographic Perspective," *American Sociological Review*, 26 (1961), pp. 407–423, and other unpublished papers by Duncan and by Ryder, especially the latter's analysis of "age cohorts."

14 Useful introductions to population study are Maurice Halbwachs, *Population and Society: Introduction to Social Morphology* (tr., Glencoe, Ill., 1960) and Philip M. Hauser, *Population Perspectives* (New Brunswick, N. J., 1961).

15 E.G., Domenico Sella, "La popolazione di Milano nei secoli XVI e XVII," *Storia di Milano*, 12 (Milano: Fondazione Treccani, 1959); J. D. Chambers, "Population Change in a Provincial Town: Nottingham 1700–1800," in *Studies in the Industrial Revolution*, L. S. Pressnell, ed. (London, 1960), pp. 97–124. Also perceptive commentary by Bayrd Still in "Local History Contributions and Techniques in the Study of Two Colonial Cities," *Bulletin of the American Association for State and Local History*, 2 (1959), pp. 245–250. For community "problems" aggravated by demographic crises before the industrial revolution see Pierre Goubert, *Beauvais et le Beauvaisis de 1600 à 1730* (2 vols., Paris, 1960).

16 An analogous view of deviations in the study of economic "backwardness" is given by Alexander Gerschenkron, "Reflections on the Concept of 'Prerequisites' of

Modern Industrialization," *L'industria: rivista di economia politica*, No. 2 (1957), pp. 357–372.

[17] Oscar Handlin, "The Modern City as a Field of Historical Study," in *The Historian and the City*, Oscar Handlin and John Burchard, eds. (Cambridge, Mass., 1963).

[18] J. A. Schumpeter, *History of Economic Analysis* (New York, 1954), p. 14. A much fuller treatment of these issues of conceptualization and method is given in E. E. Lampard and L. F. Schnore, "Urbanization Problems," *Research Needs for Development Assistance Programs* (Washington, D. C.: Brookings Institution, processed, 1961), LS 6–14.

[19] For a review of urbanization in the ancient Near East see Carl H. Kraeling and R. M. Adams, *City Invincible: A Symposium on Urbanization and Cultural Development in the Ancient Near East* (Chicago, 1960).

[20] Kingsley Davis and Hilda H. Golden, "Urbanization and the Development of Pre-Industrial Areas," *Economic Development and Cultural Change*, 3 (1954), pp. 6–26; P. M. Hauser, ed., *Urbanization in Asia and the Far East* (Calcutta: UNESCO, Tensions and Technology Series, 1958), pp. 55–63. W. W. Lockwood, *The Economic Development of Japan* (Princeton, N. J., 1954), p. 4, and Irene B. Taeuber, "Urbanization and Population Change in the Development of Modern Japan," *Economic Development and Cultural Change*, 9 (1960), suppl., 4.

[21] Robert S. Lopez, "The Crossroads within the Wall," in *The Historian and the City*, Handlin and Burchard, eds., *op. cit.*

[22] Heinz Stoob, "Kartographische Möglichkeiten zur Darstellung der Stadtenstehung in Mitteleuropa, besonders zwischen 1450 und 1800," *Historische Raumforschung, 1, Forschungs-und Sitzungsberichte der Akademie für Raumforschung und Landesplamung*, 6 (Bremen, 1956), pp. 21–76, for alternative ways of representing urbanization. Roger Mols, *Introduction à la démographie historique des villes d'Europe du XIVe au XVIIIe siècle* (3 vols., Louvain, 1955) is an excellent guide to demographic problems and materials before the nineteenth century. On town settlement in the New World: Richard M. Morse, "Some Characteristics of Latin American Urban History," *American Historical Review*, 67 (1962), pp. 317–338.

[23] For this term "integration" in relation to "effective space": John Friedman, "L'influence de l'intégration du système social sur le développement économique," *Diogène*, 33 (1961), pp. 80–104; id., "Cities in Social Transformation," *Comparative Studies in Society and History*, 4 (1961), pp. 86–103. For the profound insight of a contemporary: Giovanni Botero, *A Treatise Concerning the Causes of the Magnificence and Greatness of Cities* written in the late sixteenth century and translated into English, London, 1606.

[24] E. E. Lampard, "History of Cities in the Economically Advanced Areas," *Economic Development and Cultural Change*, 3 (January 1955), pp. 86–102, proposes that, since functional specialization leads to areal differentiation, the degree of interaction among activities distributed in space may be taken as a significant index of the relative maturity of regional urban structures. Thus, during the industrial revolution in England, cotton, wool, and iron districts became more sharply differentiated, each proceeding within its own cycle of technical and organizational development. For comparisons with regional urban structures in France: *ibid.*, pp. 110–115. Also, S. G. Checkland, "English Provincial Cities," *Economic History Review*, n.s. 6 (1953), pp. 200, and F. J. Fisher, "The Sixteenth and Seventeenth Centuries," *Economica*, n.s. 24 (1960), pp. 2–18.

[25] W. F. Cottrell, "The City in the Age of Atoms and Automation," in *The City in Mid-Century*, H. W. Dunham, ed. (Detroit, 1957) for a perceptive analysis of relations between modes of energy conversion and the forms of cities.

[26] E. E. Lampard, "The Price System and Economic Change," *Journal of Economic History*, 20 (December 1960), pp. 617–637, for the social and ecological embededness of market pricing institutions.

[27] Shigeto Tsuro, "The Role of the City in Technological Innovation and Economic Development," in *The Historian and the City*, Handlin and Burchard, eds., *op. cit.*

[28] William N. Parker, "Economic Development in Historical Perspective," *Economic Development and Cultural Change*, 10 (1961), pp. 1–7. Also, A. P. Usher, *A History of Mechanical Inventions* (paperback ed., Boston, 1959), pp. 1–10, and Chaps. 2 and 3.

[29] Nels Anderson, *The Urban Community* (New York, 1959), p. 5.

[30] Jane Jacobs, *The Death and Life of Great American Cities* (New York, 1961).

37 Norman B. Ryder

The Cohort as a Concept in the Study of Social Change

SOCIAL CHANGE AND DEMOGRAPHIC METABOLISM

This essay presents a demographic approach to the study of social change. The particular meaning here given to change is structural transformation rather than the network of actions and interactions predicated in the routine operation of the institutional structure. Discussion is restricted to the variations in social organization that are reflected in measurements on individuals, summarized in aggregate distributions of performances and characteristics. Changes in an individual throughout his life are distinguishable from changes in the population of which he is a component. The biological ineluctability of the individual life cycle carries no necessary implication for transformation of the population. Every society has pretensions to an immortality beyond the reach of its members. The lives and deaths of individuals are, from the societal standpoint, a massive process of personnel replacement, which may be called "demographic metabolism." This essay is concerned with interdependencies between social change and population process, including in the latter both demographic metabolism and the life cycles of individuals considered in the aggregate.

Society is a functioning collectivity of organic components. It persists as if independent of its membership, continually receiving raw material by fertility and discharging depleted resources by mortality. To survive, it must meet the challenge to persistence implicit in this continual change of membership, and especially the incessant "invasion of barbarians." Every individual arrives on the social scene literally without sociopsychological configuration. As a requisite for effective performance, the society seeks and promotes a minimal degree of stability and predictability, and frequently succeeds. The agencies of socialization and social control are designed to give the new member a shape appropriate to the societal design.

Perhaps stability is a more likely institutional goal than innovation because it is simpler and safer, at least in the short run, but any fixed set

Reprinted from *American Sociological Review*, 30:6 (1965), pp. 834–861, by permission of the author and the publisher.

of solutions to problems posed by a threatening environment becomes a liability whenever such problems change. The capacity for societal transformation has an indispensable ally in the process of demographic metabolism. Mortality and fertility make flexibility possible just as they make stability problematic. The continual emergence of new participants in the social process and the continual withdrawal of their predecessors compensate the society for limited individual flexibility. For every species the inevitability of death impels the development of reproduction and thus variation and evolution; the same holds for societies. The society whose members were immortal would resemble a stagnant pond.[1] Of course death is no more an unmixed blessing to the society than it is an unmixed curse to the individual. Metabolism may make change likely, or at least possible, but it does not guarantee that the change will be beneficial. As a minimum, mortality permits perennial reappraisal of institutionalized formulae.

The aggregate by which the society counterbalances attrition is the birth cohort, those persons born in the same time interval and aging together. Each new cohort makes fresh contact with the contemporary social heritage and carries the impress of the encounter through life. This confrontation has been called the intersection of the innovative and the conservative forces in history.[2] The members of any cohort are entitled to participate in only one slice of life—their unique location in the stream of history. Because it embodies a temporally specific version of the heritage, each cohort is differentiated from all others, despite the minimization of variability by symbolically perpetuated institutions and by hierarchically graduated structures of authority.

To assert that the cause of social change is demographic replacement would be tantamount to explaining a variable by a constant, yet each fresh cohort is a possible intermediary in the transformation process, a vehicle for introducing new postures. The new cohorts provide the opportunity for social change to occur. They do not cause change; they permit it. If change does occur, it differentiates cohorts from one another, and the comparison of their careers becomes a way to study change. The minimal basis for expecting interdependency between intercohort differentiation and social change is that change has variant import for persons of unlike age, and that the consequences of change persist in the subsequent behavior of these individuals and thus of their cohorts.

For the most part, the literature on the cohort approach is divisible into two almost antipodal categories. On the one hand, the cohort concept, under the label "generation," has long been used by historians of the arts—in rebellion against the Procrustean frame of chronological sections favored by conventional historians—as well as by political journalists and other humanistic interpreters of the passing scene.[3] The other field of application has been the work of demographers, particularly the recent redirection of the study of fertility time series away from the period-by-period format toward an appraisal of temporal variations from cohort to cohort.[4] Although written by a demographer, the present essay is concerned not with the many contributions to technical demography which utilize the cohort concept, but rather with the sociological arguments underlying it, and the conceptualization of social change it suggests.

THE COHORT FROM A MACROANALYTIC STANDPOINT

A cohort may be defined as the aggregate of individuals (within some population definition) who experienced the same event within the same time interval. In almost all cohort research to date the defining event has been birth, but this is only a special case of the more general approach. Cohort data are ordinarily assembled sequentially from observations of the time of occurrence of the behavior being studied, and the interval since occurrence of the cohort-defining event. For the birth cohort this interval is age. If t is the time of occurrence and a is the age at that time, then the observations for age a, time t, apply (approximately) to the cohort born in year $t-a$, as do observations for age a-1, time t-1, and so forth.

The cohort record is not merely a summation of a set of individual histories. Each cohort has a distinctive composition and character reflecting the circumstances of its unique origination and history. The lifetime data for one cohort may be analyzed and compared with those for other cohorts by all the procedures developed for a population in temporal cross-section. The movement of the cohort, within the politico-spatial boundaries defining the society, is a flow of person-years from time of birth to the death of the last survivor. This differs from a synthetic cross-section because time and age change *pari passu* for any cohort. A cohort has an age distribution of its person-years of exposure, provided by its successive sizes age by age. The age distribution varies from cohort to cohort because of mortality and migration. Thus a cohort experiences demographic transformation in ways that have no meaning at the individual level of analysis, because its composition is modified not only by status changes of the components, but also by selective changes of membership.

The most evident manifestation of intercohort differences is variation, and particularly abrupt fluctuation, in cohort size, attributable to changes in the number of births from year to year or, less commonly, from brief heavy migration or mortality the impact of which is limited to a narrow age span. A cohort's size relative to the sizes of its neighbors is a persistent and compelling feature of its lifetime environment. As the new cohort reaches each major juncture in the life cycle, the society has the problem of assimilating it. Any extraordinary size deviation is likely to leave an imprint on the cohort as well as on the society. In the United States today the cohorts entering adulthood are much larger than their predecessors. In consequence, they were raised in crowded housing, crammed together in schools, and are now threatening to be a glut on the labor market. Perhaps they will have to delay marriage, because of too few jobs or homes, and have fewer children. It is not entirely coincidental that the American cohorts whose fertility levels appear to be the highest in this century were those with the smallest numbers.

Size is only one characteristic by which the cohort aggregate is differentiated from its temporal neighbors. Many statistical facets of cohort composition, broadly influential as independent variables, differ at age zero from one cohort to the next, and remain approximately unchanged throughout the cohort's history. Consider the various inherited items like race, mother tongue and birthplace. The cohort is not homogeneous in such characteristics, but the distribution of its heterogeneity tends to be fixed throughout its life in a shape which may differ from those of preceding and succeeding cohorts. Other birth and childhood characteristics are differentiating: for example, family structure by age, sex and generation determines the relative frequency of only children, younger and older children of like or unlike sex, and younger or older parents. Intercohort variability in these characteristics may derive from fertility, mortality or migration, to the extent that these are selective for the characteristic concerned and variable through time. Differential migration is the most striking influence in the short run, but differential natural replacement is generally more important in the long run.

Cohort differentiation is not confined to characteristics fixed at birth. Other status changes tend to be highly localized by age, relatively universal in occurrence, and influential in the rest of life.[5] Age is not only a general rubric for the consequences, rewards and penalties of experience; it is an important basis for role allocation in every society.[6] Age ascription is the cross-sectional counterpart of cohort differentiation. Similarities of experience within and differentiation of experience between age groups are observable in every culture. Similar functioning is imposed by society on those sharing an age at a particular time. Any legislation that is age-specific, either *de jure*, or, by virtue of its content, *de facto*, differentiates cohorts. Such norms give a distinctive age pattern to the life cycle of each cohort. If age-specific norms, or the context within which they are being applied, change through time, cohort experiences will be differentiated.

Thus marriage has a high probability of occurring within a narrow age span and is responsive to the exigencies of the moment. The members of a cohort are influenced in the age at which they marry, the persons they choose to marry and even their eventual likelihood of marriage by the particular set of circumstances prevailing at the time they reach marriage age. The outcome is not so individualistic as the romantic love ethos might suggest. The state of the marriage market is an aggregate phenomenon: the probability of marriage depends not only on an individual's personal characteristics, but also on the comparative characteristics of all others of the same sex, and also on the availability of those of the opposite sex who meet the approximate criteria of nubility. Underlying this is the propitiousness of the period for marriage, the relevance of which for cohort delineation depends directly on the age variance of marriage for the cohort. The same is true of any major event in personal history which is concentrated by age.

The time of completing education is also highly age-specific in its location and influential both in personal futures and in societal change. The intimate relation of education to social change is properly emphasized in programs of social and economic development. It is "the modern world's cutting edge." Changes through time in the proportions completing various stages of education are familiar trends in modern life which provide an indelible differentiation of cohort character and behavior.[7] The differentiation encompasses not only mere duration but also the quality of teaching, the nature of instructional materials and the content of the curriculum.[8]

The consequences of distinctive educational preparation prevail in the cohort's occupational flow-chart. The experience of the cohort with employment and labor force status begins with the character of the employment market at its time of entry.[9] The cohort is distinctively marked by the career stage it occupies when prosperity or depression, and peace or war, impinge on it. The occupational structure of the cohort is not crystallized upon entry into the labor force, but the configuration imposed on individual economic histories has a high sequential dependence through time.[10] One explanation advanced for the baby boom is that the cohorts responsible had an unprecedented educational advantage when they sought their first jobs.[11] Projections of labor force participation rates for women have been successfully designed on a cohort basis, because of the observed continuity of differences between cohorts.[12]

The attractive simplicity of birth cohort membership as signified by age cannot conceal the ways in which this identification is cross-cut and attenuated by differentiation with respect to education, occupation, marital status, parity status, and so forth. Every birth cohort is heterogeneous. To some extent all cohorts respond to any given period-specific stimulus. Rarely are changes so localized in either age or time that their burden falls exclusively on the shoulders of one cohort. Intercohort analysis is profitably supplemented with cross-classification by relevant compositional variables.[13] The meaning of sharing a common historical location is modified and adumbrated by these other identifying characteristics.[14] Different subsets of the cohort have different time patterns of development. Youth of manual and nonmanual origins differ in length of educational preparation and age at marriage. The various members of a cohort follow differently paced occupational lines. This may be especially true of intellectual histories. The differing tempi of careers in literature, music and mathematics yield different productivity modes by age, and therefore responsiveness to different historical circumstances, despite membership in the same birth cohort.[15]

As a minimum, the cohort is a structural category with the same kind of analytic utility as a variable like social class.[16] Such structural categories have explanatory power because they are surrogate indices for the common experiences of many persons in each category. Conceptually the cohort resembles most closely the ethnic group: membership is determined at birth, and often has considerable capacity to explain variance, but need not imply that the category is an organized group.

Two research suggestions may be advanced. In the first place, age should be so interpreted in every statistical table as to exploit its dual significance— as a point in the cohort life cycle and as a temporal location. Age is customarily used in statistical analyses merely in the former role, if not as a cross-sectional nuisance to be controlled by procedures like standardization. This implicitly static orientation ignores an important source of variation and inhibits the progress of temporal analysis. In the second place, age-cum-cohort should be used not only as a cross-classification to explain the internal variations of other groups, but as a group-defining variable in its own right, in terms of which distributions by other variables may be compared through time. In this way, research results may be compared in cumulated fashion, linking the outputs of the various studies using the same cohort identifications, just as has been done with other quasigroup categorizations. Each such study can enhance the significance of others for the same cohort. Comparison of such composite cohort biographies would yield the most direct and efficient measurement of the consequences of social change.

The proposed orientation to temporal differentiation of cohorts emphasizes the context prevailing at the time members of the cohort experience critical transitions. The approach can be generalized beyond the birth cohort to cohorts identified by common time of occurrence of any significant and enduring event in life history. Cohorts may be defined in terms of the year in which they completed their schooling, the year they married, the year in which they migrated to the city, or the year in which they entered the labor force full-time.[17] Each of these events is important in identifying the kinds of situation to which persons respond differently, and establishing a status to which future experiences are oriented. The research implication of this viewpoint is that more effort should be devoted to collecting items of dated information, to identify not only statuses but times of entry into them. Birth date serves as a surrogate for cohort identification by date of occurrence of other relevant events. It is a satisfactory approximation to the extent that variance in the age at which the event in question occurs is small. Thus the cohort approach may be generalized to consider any class of event in terms of the experience of successive cohorts defined by time of initial exposure to the risk of occurrence of that event.

The strategic focus for research on social change is the context under which each cohort is launched on its own path. The prototype is the cohort of persons entering the labor force each year. The annual meeting of prospective employers and employees produces an occupational distribution which manifests and foretells social change. The process requires macroanalysis because the possibility of an individual finding a particular job, or of an employer securing a needed talent, is a function of the entire set of comparative characteristics of all participants in the market. The educational system has prepared the new labor force entrants for this confrontation. Although the stimulus for innovation is most likely to come from the employers, the feasibility of new directions depends in part on how well they have been anticipated by the educational system. Indeed the conditions determining labor supply go all the way back to the composition of the relevant cohorts at birth. The implicit link between reproduction in one year, and characteristics of the labor market some two decades later, is an important channel for transmission of disturbances through time.

Out of the confrontation of the cohort of any year and the societal structures into which it seeks entry, a shape is forged which influences the directions in which the structures will change. More generally, the proximate indication of direction of change is the movement of personnel from one status to another, as the result of quasimarket activity in one or another role sphere. The market metaphor extends into the consideration of differential rewards, and thus of changing role evaluations, cognate with the Davis-Moore theory of social differentiation.[18] The importance for social change of the kind of selectivity exercised in forming the cohort is largely obscured in this essay by exclusive attention to the birth cohort, which is more random in composition than any other cohort type. The study of the formation of cohorts defined in terms of specific role markets promises to provide a focused view of the processes that transform the different parts of the social system.

THE IMPACT OF HISTORICAL CHANGE ON COHORTS

The preceding section emphasized several stages in the cohort life cycle at which major transitions occur, and proposed that the temporal context of these transitions would differentiate cohorts. The same point can be made from the opposite direction, by observing types of major change, and the extent to which participation in them is age-specific and therefore cohort-differentiating. All those alive at the same time are contemporaries but they respond and contribute to social history in different ways unless they are also coevals. In particular, the potential for change is concentrated in the cohorts of young adults who are old enough to participate directly in the movements impelled by change, but not old enough to have become committed to an occupation, a residence, a family of procreation or a way of life. Furthermore the fact of change facilitates their development of other orientations than those of their parents and their community.

The most dramatic instance is war. Participation in war is limited in age, and the extent of war is limited in time. The Great War weakened a whole cohort in Europe to the extent that normal succession of personnel in roles, including positions of power, was disturbed. Sometimes the old retained power too long; sometimes the young seized power too soon.[19] The most obvious effect of war is the mortality and morbidity of the participants, but war transforms non-combatants as well. Several novels have utilized the theme of the peculiar poignancy of those who were old enough to comprehend the war but not old enough to participate in it.[20] The intellectual development of Mannheim, who brought the cohort concept into sociology, can be partly explained by the historical location of his cohort.[21] Teenagers in France can now meet easily with German youth groups because they are free of war memories.[22] German youths moving into the labor force are reported to be repudiating the labor discipline of their elders, whom they identify with the Nazi era.[23] The cohort consequences of war extend into the intellectual realm. Following the decimation of some French cohorts in the Great War, a split developed between those following the traditional path in mathematics, and those concerned with creating a new vocabulary. The latter produced the bible of modern mathematics, the Elements of Bourbaki.[24]

Anyone reading the newspapers of the past decade needs no reminder of the prominence of uncommitted cohorts in the task forces of nationalistic or revolutionary political movements. The persons most active in the Protestant Reformation and in the Revolutions of England, France and America were youthful.[25] The contemporary "Children's Crusade" is too recent to have been investigated carefully, but there are some suggestive analyses of the position of youth in revolutionary change.[26] In his discussion of China, Levy places primary emphasis on the role of the "ch'ing-nien" in societal transformation:[27] this term for young adults has been retained by the aging leaders of the Communist movement.[28] Eisenstadt has documented the experience of youth movements in Israel and in prewar Germany. Both of these were rebellions against elders and their ideas, viewing youth alone as pure enough to accomplish the task of re-creating society.[29] Perhaps the affiliation of youth with the revolutionary phase of a charismatic movement is linked with the appeal for them of techniques of violence.[30] Young people who are students, or unemployed, in the big cities of developing nations, are likely to be available for demonstrations and have large places in which to congregate.

A popular but unsupportable argument is that the emergence of a new cohort somehow guarantees progress.[31] The entry of fresh cohorts into the political stream represents a potentiality for change, but without specification of its content or direction. The prominent role played by youth in the totalitarian movements of this century has been widely noted.[32] A new cohort provides a market for radical ideas and a source of followers, and they are more likely than their elders to criticize the existing order.[33] Replacement of much older by much younger leaders, as Eisenhower by Kennedy, may have a profound symbolic impact. The direction of change may be to the left or to the right, toward democracy or toward totalitarianism, but whatever the trend, it is most manifest in youth.

Whether new cohorts are more or less crucial to the implementation of a revolution, they are clearly differentiated by its occurrence.[34] The case of the Soviet Union is well documented.[35] Stalin created a generation of modern technicians to supplant the old Bolsheviks, because the latter's skills in the dialectic and in conspiratorial politics did not suit the age of machine tools and modern armies. Now the decision system is passing into the hands of cohorts brought up under socialism.[36] Journalists have recently begun to draw the line between those brought up under Stalin and those whose impressionable years coincided with de-Stalinization.[37] Although these latest cohorts are not yet in positions of political power, they are beginning to have some influence, particularly through cultural activities.

The adaptive transformation of revolutionary movements has frequently been discussed from a structuralist standpoint.[38] The audacity and independence required to overthrow a regime are not the skills requisite for administering a stable government in the sequel. The lions and the foxes must change places. If this comparatively static model is reconsidered in processual terms, it is clear that cohort differentiation will result. Rostow has suggested naming the process the "Buddenbrooks dynamics."[39] If change occurs, those who are brought up in the new world will differ from those who initiated the change. In consequence, more change will occur, but interest is transferred from wrecking a hated system to the task of constructive continuity. Gradually death claims both winners and losers of the old struggle. Support for the new system becomes broad and stable. Thus the cohort succession serves as cause and effect in the phases of revolutionary transformation.

An experiential chasm between cohorts also occurs when immigration or colonization produces an intersection of two cultures. The European immigrant arriving in the New World identified himself with an ethnic group resembling the culture in which he was raised. His children went to American schools, chose American playmates, and often escaped from the subculture.[40] The parents' inadequacy as a basis for orientation toward the new society reinforced the children's resort to peer groups. Similarly, the impact of western culture on primitive peoples is likely to yield disruption of family life, changing mutual evaluation of the generations, and ideological identification of youth with resistance. Kwame Nkrumah recently remarked on the appearance in Ghana of a new cohort without firsthand knowledge of colonial rule and without the habit of obsequiousness to the European.[41]

Traumatic episodes like war and revolution may become the foci of crystallization of the mentality of a cohort. The dramatic impact may mark indelibly the "naïve eyes and virgin senses" of the cohort in the vanguard and change them into an entelechy with an explicit mission, a virtual community of thought and action. Yet such vivid experiences are unnecessary to the argument. Cohorts can also be pulled apart gradually by the slow grind of evolutionary change. The nucleus and epitome of social change, as determinant and consequence, is the city. Urbanization is the outstanding manifestation of the world transformation of the past few centuries. Cities have been populated largely by the continual infusion of new cohorts. Rural-urban migration is highly selective of younger persons; changes requiring population transfer will be undertaken only by the more flexible and less burdened members of the society.[42] The young move away from the community that would envelop them in the traditional mold and into a new way of life. America may be less tradition-bound than Europe because fewer young couples establish homes in the same place as their parents.

The principal motor of contemporary social change is technological innovation. It pervades the other substructures of society and forces them into accommodation. The modern society institutionalizes this innovation and accepts it as self-justifying. To the child of such a society, technological change makes the past irrelevant. Its impact on the population is highly differential by age, and is felt most by those who are about to make their lifelong choices. Technological evolution is accomplished less by retraining older cohorts than by recruiting the new one, and the age of an industry tends to be correlated with the age of its workers. Accessions to the labor force flow most strongly into the new and growing industries; separations from the labor force are predominantly out of declining industries.[43] The distinctive age composition of the industrial structure is nowhere more evident than in the rapid industrialization of a previously traditional economy. In effect, it is accomplished not so much by educating the population as a whole as by introducing each new cohort in turn to the modern way of life. In traditional society, age is a valid surrogate for relevant experience, but when the industrial revolution occurs, age comes to signify historical location and degree of disfranchisement by change, rather than the due prerogatives of seniority.

INDIVIDUAL DEVELOPMENT AND THE FAMILY

Implicit in the foregoing account of the interdependency of social change and cohort differentiation is the assumption that an individual's history is highly stable or at least continuous. If a person's future were molded irrevocably by his earliest experiences, there would be a strong case for assembling data for aggregates of individuals on a cohort-by-cohort basis. The model dominating the literature on human development presents life as a movement from amorphous plasticity through mature competence toward terminal rigidity.[44] The preparatory phase, during which individuals are susceptible to influence, is distinguished from the participatory phase, during which their predetermined destiny is unfolded. The central sociopsychological postulate in the spirit of Freud is that the core of personality is laid down at the beginning of life; what may look like changes later are merely minor variants on the established theme. The popularity of this assertion is as indubitable as its irrefutability. Discussion in this vein confuses ineluctable species characteristics and culturally variable designs, and fails to cope with the phenomenon of societal change.

In the conventional development model, the very young organism is presented as fluid, polymorphous, multipotential and perverse, susceptible to suggestion and rudimentary of will. Each interaction between organism and environment modifies the shape the organism takes into the next encounter. The earlier a situation imposes itself, the more likely it is to add an enduring element, partly because early learning is general enough to escape outright contradiction in subsequent particular experience. Gradually capacities are shaped and strengthened by use, with increasing self-regulation and independence of fluctuations. New experience is assimilated on the stratum of first impressions in a way that preserves self-consistency. The self-perception of persistence is ratified by others' recognition.

Thus the organism acquires an adult's efficiency at the price of a child's versatility. New ideas compete on unequal terms with old ones, because the latter have a place in the structure and have been used to direct behavior. Systematization and ritualization of response frees energy for higher-level integration. When a new situation accords with previous experience learning may be rapid, but not when it competes with established responses. The products of earlier education become debris that chokes off later growth. In due course the adult organism rigidifies and deteriorates into senility.

Any model of individual development which postulates early crystallization is embarrassing to the person explaining rapid social change. If personality is viewed as a quasihereditary phenomenon, the possibilities of change are reduced, following the biological analogy, to evolution through natural selection—a very slow process—and to mutation. Hagen finds himself in this box in his attempt to construct a theory of social change concordant with his belief that persons cannot move in later life from psychological stances established in childhood.[45] Hagen's mutation-like proposal is that parents who encounter status frustration cannot change themselves, but their children may perceive the source of parental anxiety and avoid it by retreating. Their children, in turn, by a similar unconscious perception, may become innovators. The tempo of transformation is thus constrained to a generational rhythm.

The complexity of this construction is a direct consequence of two articles of faith: that social change cannot occur without personality change, and that personality change cannot occur once childhood is past. The present writer would propose that the social system rather than the personality system belongs at the center of any model of societal transformation. In this view personality is considered a by-product, at the individual level, of socialization procedures designed to achieve various objectives at the societal level. Socialization is a process of committing an individual to a term of service in a group, by progressively confining his behavioral potentialities within an acceptable range and by preparing him for the types of role he will be expected to play.[46] Far from being monopolized by the parents, socialization is a continuous process throughout life, shared in by every group of which a person may become a member. Even if the family-fostered self were immune to modification, the society could still retain the necessary degrees of freedom by altering the criteria for selection, from among different personality types, to fill the various roles.

Important to the present argument are two propositions: first, that social change implies a transformation of the relative contributions to socialization made by the various possible agencies of socialization; second, that this transformation identifies the cohort as a social reality, reflecting and implementing the social change to which it owes its existence. The principal socialization agency in every society is the family. It is an omnipresent authoritarian component of the child's environment, a primary group satisfying virtually the entire range of needs and furnishing the context within which the concept of self relative to others first arises. Family socialization is adequate to the extent that the structure of relationships portrayed and utilized in family life resembles that of the society into which the young adult must move. When a society breaks out of a static familistic mold, the family no longer suffices for the tasks of socialization.

Most writing about what is here called a cohort employs instead the term "generation," signifying all those within a broad (characteristically unspecified) age span during a particular epoch, and implicitly those with common characteristics because of common experiences. It is also used in synchronic structural analysis concerning relations between persons of markedly differing age, such as institutionalized deference.[47] For the sake of conceptual clarity, "generation" should be used solely in its original and unambiguous meaning as the temporal unit of kinship structure, and the first two ideas should be signified by the terms "cohort" and "relative age status" respectively. "Generation" may be a fitting general temporal referent in societies where the dominant mode of the role allocation is ascription on the basis of kinship. In such a context cohort identity is often trivial because the bulk of temporal variation coincides with the life cycle, as reproduced in annual cross-section. But societies undergoing cultural revolution must generally break the grip of the family in the individual. In so doing they diminish the social significance of "generation," in both its kinship and relative age connotations, and produce the kind of social milieu in which the cohort is the most appropriate unit of temporal analysis.

A prominent theme in discussions of modern society is intergenerational conflict. Although some of this is probably intrinsic to the family life cycle, current analyses emphasize the exacerbation of the tendency by social change, through intercohort differentiation.[48] As an Arab proverb has it, "Men resemble the times more than they do their fathers." Role differentiation that gives the old power over the young is justified when age is correlated strongly and positively with control of cultural content, but the correlation may even become negative during rapid social change because age differences in one direction signify cohort differences in the opposite direction.[49]

Many writers have used the succession of cohorts as the foundation for theories of sociocultural dynamics.[50] This approach has been aptly labelled "generationism," because the writers mistakenly transfer from the generation to the cohort a set of inappropriate associations. Some generationists maintain that there is a periodicity to sociocultural change caused by the biological fact of the succession of generations at thirty-year (father-son) intervals.[51] There is no such periodicity. Other generationists develop a conflict theory of change, pitched on the opposition between the younger and the older "generations" in society, as in the family. But a society reproduces itself continuously. The age gap between father and son disappears in the population at large, through the comprehensive overlapping of life cycles. The fact that social change produces intercohort differentiation and thus contributes to inter-generational conflict cannot justify a theory that social change is produced by that conflict. Generationists have leaped from inaccurate demographic observation to inaccurate social conclusion without supplying any intervening causality. All these works suggest arithmetical mysticism, and the worst of them, as Troeltsch said, are *"reine Kabbala."*

CHANGING AGENCIES OF CHILD SOCIALIZATION

With the advent of modern society, changes in the agencies of socialization establish a context favorable to the identification of cohorts. The individual mobility and achievement-based status required of a modern occupational structure seem much more harmonious with the conjugal family than with the traditional web of kinship obligations.[52] Revolutionary regimes may adopt specific policies to reduce the importance of the family as an agency of socialization and as a bulwark of the old stratification system. Consider, for example, the Soviet emphasis on early education of the child away from home, the Chinese attempt to shift the locus of authority away from the older generation, and the Israeli use of the kibbutz to communalize child care and restrict parent-child interaction to the affectional realm. Such attempts to place collective identification above family solidarity may not have been completely successful[53] but they are consistent with reorientations throughout the modernizing world. The potentially perpetual consanguineal unit is being supplanted by a conjugal family with a limited lifetime, and the institutional scope of family affairs is narrowing.

In particular, the reallocation of responsibility for child socialization away from the family and toward the school on the formal level and the peer group on the informal level gives analytic form to the cohort, just as specific historical changes give it analytic content. Parental capacity to prepare the child for his adult roles depends on the simplicity and stability of life. In a society of specialization and change parents are inadequate models for children and the specialized agency of formal education must be created. The school develops a commitment to the implementation of societal values, teaches the skills needed to perform adult tasks, and contributes to manpower allocation. As the content of education evolves, it differentiates the knowledge of parent and child, and equips successive cohorts with a progressively enlarged culture. To the extent that school instruction differs from what is learned at home, it provokes independent thought. The radical potentiality of education is clearest in the university, which has the function of discovering as well as transmitting knowledge.

By substituting teachers for parents, society symbolizes the difference in historical location between child and parent, and attenuates the bonds between them. Education expands in a modern society to encompass almost all members of each cohort and for a progressively longer age span, not only up into early adulthood but also down into the "formative" period cherished by personality theorists. The long time during which individuals are embedded in the lock-step age-hierarchized school system gives the cohort an ample opportunity to identify itself as a historical entity. The school is a cohort creator.

Socialization in every society is the function not only of institutionalized authorities but also of coevals. An increase in such "self-socialization" is to be expected during social change, because this makes the experiences of the peer group (the cohort) unique, and develops similarities within and differences between cohorts. One of Riesman's themes in *The Lonely Crowd* is the replacement of the inner-directed type, whose standards are his parents', by the other-directed type, whose standards are his contemporaries'.[54] The congruence with the present position is obvious.

The peer group is a subset of one's cohort. It consists of people of the same age with whom one has attitude-forming relationships, or, to use an old-fashioned but etymologically apt term, one's cronies.[55] It is oriented to its members' needs and interests rather than to the pursuit of goals defined by external authority. Perhaps when a collectivity rather than an individual is being socialized, it develops a sense of cohort solidarity and alters the outcome of socialization. Although providing non-adult approval, it need not be deviant, and may even give strong support to the conventional moral code.[56]

Peer groups are functional in modern society.[57] If the principles regulating family life harmonize with those of other institutional spheres, an individual can attain full membership in the society through behavior learned in the family. But modern society is regulated by criteria which contradict those appropriate to kinship. For the individual this poses the problem of transition from one universe of discourse to the other; for the society it poses the problem of developing bases of extra-familial solidarity. The solution is the peer group, which has the primary group characteristics of the family and the achievement orientation of the society.

It is tempting to treat the peer group phenomenon as signaling the creation of a sense of solidarity if not reality as a social group, and thus derive support for the view that a cohort is more than a mere category in statistical tables. Solidarity is encouraged by idealized self-definitions in reaction to ill-specified rights and responsibilities of the status, by sharing anxieties concerning imminent and hazardous transitions, and by explicit associations that encourage the development of attitudes unsanctioned by family or community. The age (and cohort) variance of membership in voluntary associations is smaller in youth than later, because small age differences mean more during development. The mass media aim specifically labelled appeals at these ages. Vocabularies specific to the age and time are invented to serve as communications channels and boundary-maintaining mechanisms.

In an epoch of change, each person is dominated by his birth date. He derives his philosophy from his historical world, the subculture of his cohort. The community of date equips each cohort with its own expanse of time, its own style and its own truth. The ideas, sentiments and values of members of the same cohort converge; their actions became quasi-organized. As social change creates divergence in the experience of successive cohorts, it may transform them from locations into actualities.[58] It is possible for most of a society's youth to develop an ideological direction (though probably under adult leadership) but the burden of proof is on those who insist that the cohort acquires the organized characteristics of some kind of temporal community. This may be a fruitful hypothesis in the study of small groups of coevals in artistic or political movements but it scarcely applies to more than a small minority of the cohort in a mass society. Commonality is likely but not community.[59]

Age-homogeneous groupings of children and adolescents are common to all societies. Mostly they remain undeveloped because kinship groups form the basic units of task performance. In some cases the cohort—known to anthropologists as an "age grade"—may function continuously throughout life. In the Hamitic culture of East Africa, for example, the age grade is a system of compulsory association enduring from puberty on, with permanent privileges and obligations. The system cuts across family lines, gives the individual interests in tribal concerns, and may be used for governmental or religious functions.[60] This is very different from the history of a modern adolescent peer group. The features that make it attractive to its members are liabilities for its persistence.[61] The peer group has fluid boundaries, with individual members drifting into and out of association. Its numbers are ordinarily small and its functions vague and diffuse. It may provide recruits for radical movements, but it is just as likely to veer toward frivolity or criminality. Its dilemma is that it is terminated by the arrival of adulthood. The peer group has little time to develop effective strength. It faces the common difficulties of any group composed mostly of transients. The members are dispersed by the growth of heterosexual interests, by the formation of families of procreation, and by movement into the labor force and out of the conveniently age-homogeneous arrangements of school.

The peer-group phenomenon provides insufficient support for a cohort approach to social change but it does exemplify the tendency toward cohort identification within the time structure of a changing population. The peer group is a symptom of the strain imposed on modern youth by its location at the fulcrum of change. The schedule of development includes a psychosocial moratorium between preparation and participation.[62]

This is when the youth first gets a chance to temper with reality the rigid precepts implanted in childhood. Lessons too sophisticated for children can now be learned. There are many answers for the questions of the age, from various and often contradictory sources. The imprecision of youth's role definition encourages receptivity to new ideas. Movement out of the equilibrated orientation provided by family and school and into a cognitively unstructured realm leaves them doubtful and uncertain but sometimes creative.[63] The new cohort of young adults lives in a phase of the life cycle when dramatic transitions are occurring in rapid succession. Perhaps the pace of personal change increases sensitivity to the possibilities of social change.

SOURCES OF INDIVIDUAL STABILITY IN ADULT LIFE

The cohort approach to social analysis derives strong support from the continuity of individual life, from a time-specific and thus historically located initiation. A person's past affects his present, and his present affects his future. Persistence is enhanced by the tendency to structure inputs, so that each will disturb as little as possible the previous cognitive, normative or even esthetic design, and, in the extreme, to reject dissonant items. Although individuals differ in the ingenuity with which they may retain disparate elements or achieve reformulation, the feasibility of extensive transformation is obviously quite limited. Individuals seek coherence, and manifest continuity to the extent that they achieve it. An individual's life is an organic entity, and the successive events that constitute it are not random but patterned.

The initial contribution to the design of a lifetime is made at conception, when the individual is provided not only with a fixed genetic constitution but also, under ordinary circumstances, with the two parents to whom society will assign responsibility for his early socialization. Furthermore, every society seizes upon the circumstances of birth as modes of allocating status, limiting the degrees of freedom for the person's path through life. Virtually every subsequent occurrence will depend on the societal plan for utilizing characteristics present at birth: sex, race, kinship, birthplace and so forth. Perhaps the most important influence of status ascription on the future of an individual in a modern society is its effect on access to different amounts and kinds of formal education.

Beyond the age of noncommitment, the new adult begins a process of involvement in the various spheres of life, in which his actions and those of others progressively reduce the degrees of freedom left to him in the societal scheme.[64] Facing various decisions among alternative roles open to him, an individual generally makes choices somewhat congruent with his value-orientations—unless he is to be credited with pure perversity. Within each role, once allocated, he forms a growing commitment to a line of activity. Each contract between group and individual contains a relatively determinate description of role requirements, and the contract is strengthened by stabilized interactions between the individual and occupants of interdependent roles. The temporal commitment is perhaps most relevant to the present argument. Thus a company's interest is served by bureaucratic arrangements, such as pensions and seniority rules, which penalize movement out of the system. On the job, the older employee becomes adjusted to his work, gravitating toward tasks that are congenial to him, and learning enough about them to exploit their advantages and minimize their liabilities. His psychological stake in his niche includes a modification of aspirations in consonance with his true abilities and the demands of the system for them. It should be clear that though this example is occupational, similar principles operate in every group of which a person becomes a member.

The apparent rigidity of an older worker in the face of a demand to adapt to a new procedure may flow simply from the circumstance that something valuable is being taken away from him.[65] The difficulties of learning new skills are more formidable for one who has acquired and utilized traditional work practices.[66] Career continuity is bolstered by investing time and money in a particular kind of vocational preparation. Continuous obsolescence of the individual is a feature of contemporary industrial society. It is to be expected that the old hands will resist innovation; otherwise they may be displaced before they are ready to retire. Resistance may be successful for a while, because the oldest workers are most likely to occupy positions of authority. The term "vested interests" suggests capitalistic profits threatened by change, but it applies equally to the skilled worker standing guard over his way of doing things. Perhaps this is especially true for higher levels of technical skill, where workers are less interchangeable, and the individual and the industry commensurately less flexible.[67]

Around his job, the individual establishes a network of spatial arrangements linking places where he lives, shops, plays and visits. An older man with a family feels obliged to remain in a situation from which a younger unencumbered person would readily move. The assumption of the parental role makes a person an agent of the society as a teacher of its new members, and the private attitude to which a man once felt himself entitled as a youth must now be subordinated to the more conventional public postures expected of the father.[68] "Nothing makes a younger generation settle down faster than a still younger generation showing up." Children are powerful instruments in making conformists of parents. They terminate definitively the brief period of "horizontal" freedom between the vertical structure of the family of orientation and the vertical structure of the family of procreation.

In a modern society, most adult roles are located in hierarchized structures. Factories, churches, labor unions and political parties distribute income, prestige and power along an approximately age-graded continuum. Memberships in such structures decrease the probability of individual transformation. In the majority of occupations a steadily upward progression of status occurs throughout most of the age span. Seniority can be viewed as commitment to particular modes of solving particular problems. The personnel of organizations tend to fall into Old Guard and Young Turk positions, emulating generations within a family. Young men must wait a long time for positions of power and responsibility, and may never arrive if they display ideas and attitudes deviating from those of their seniors.[69] Conformity to such vertical structures, and acceptance of the rewards and duties, defined by superiors, implies resistance to change. To advance in a particular economic order requires support of that order. Success reinforces the way in which success has been achieved; failure is resisted from whatever position of accrued power has been attained. Social change creates continuing conflict between the rewards of seniority and the penalties of membership in older cohorts.

Students of political affiliation have been concerned with the ages at which people's experiences have most influence on their political behavior.[70] The hypothesis that youth acquire a structure of political attitudes from parents and peers, which persists unless disturbed by dissonant events, seems to be contradicted by the conservatism of older voters. Some of the tendency for older Americans to vote Republican may be explained by theories of aging, and by association with preferred statuses accompanying age, but a residual remains to be explained by intercohort differentiation.[71] Perhaps the stereotype of the older person as a dogmatic conservative fits a person whose education dates back to a time when attitudes now regarded as conservative were more common. Yet persistence and continuity in the political as in the occupational sphere seem to grow with commitment to adult affairs, as exposure to alternatives is reduced, and penalties of change increase.[72]

As life takes on a steadier tempo, routinization predominates. Routines are barriers to change because they limit confrontation with the unexpected and the disturbing. Older people learn to exercise greater control over a narrower environment, and avoid risks of venturing into unstructured situations. The feasibility of personal transformation is probably limited more by restricted membership than by physiological aging. A persistent research problem is the difficulty of distinguishing between characteristics which are indeed intrinsic to aging, and those which merely appear to be so because of the cohort contribution to the age vector in times of change. Social change ordinarily touches older persons less closely. They lead a more restricted social life, they read less, they attend fewer movies, and their friends, books and movies are more carefully chosen to conform to their biases. Their residences and their friendships become more stable. The longer a person persists in an established mode of conduct, the less likely its comprehensive redefinition, especially if he invests it with normative content. Aging involves disengagement and withdrawal, a restriction on the quantity and intensity of interaction with others, and an approach toward self-centered and idiosyncratic behavior. Consistency through time is achieved by developing a vested interest in forms to which past behavior has again and again been oriented. To change the basic conceptions by which one has learned to assess the propriety of situations would be to make a caricature of one's life.

In later years, the cohort identity is blurred. Age becomes progressively less precise as an index of a person's social characteristics. Individuals experience what Cain calls asynchronization—they possess different "ages" in the various institutional spheres.[73] People vary physiologically, and also in the extent to which they continue to learn. Adjacent cohorts tend to permeate one another as the pattern of life chances works itself out. Definitions of age become predominantly social rather than biological categories; they change with time, and with the groups one joins and leaves. The intrinsic aging process may be variously accelerated or retarded by many different institutional arrangements.

The research recommendation implicit in the preceding discussion of the sources of continuity in individual lives is longitudinal analysis. The category includes case histories, repeated interviews with the same respondents (of which panel studies are a special case), analyses of diaries and dated letters, and, on a larger scale, continuous work histories or morbidity histories, for insurance purposes.[74] The *raison d'être* of the longitudinal approach is the organization of personal data in temporal sequence, to determine the causal potentiality of otherwise isolated acts. This procedure has dominated behavioral inquiry, particularly under psychoanalytic influence, has become standard operating procedure in social psychology, and has been described as "the perfect type of sociological material."[75]

The data produced by such inquiries are disjunctive with most statistical analyses of aggregates in two ways. First, the intensive detail of longitudinal analyses proliferates hypotheses but ordinarily lacks that broad evidential basis requisite to generalized verification which is a principal virtue of census tabulations, for instance. In this sense life histories and statistical analyses are complementary approaches.[76] But their potential complementarity is prejudiced by the second disjuncture—between the time axes of the two procedures. The life history has been called the long-section and the statistical the cross-section view of culture. The typical emphasis of the latter on simultaneity between corresponding events from different lives implies over-valuation of the existing situation—"the sociological error par excellence."[77] Aggregate analysis destroys individual sequences, and diverts attention from process. By implying that the past is irrelevant, cross-sectional analysis inhibits dynamic inquiry and fosters the illusion of immutable structure.[78]

This outcome can be avoided by using the cohort approach. The cohort record, as macro-biography, is the aggregate analogue of the individual life history. It provides the necessary temporal isomorphism for linking small-scale intensive longitudinal analyses with extensive surveys of the society at a point of time. It has the time dimension of the former and the comforting statistical reliability of the latter. In a similar vein, Ortega has rejected both the collectivist and the individualist interpretations of historical reality, in favor of an orientation based on the cohort—"the dynamic compromise between mass and individual—the most important conception in history."[79]

SOURCES OF FLEXIBILITY: INDIVIDUAL AND GROUP

The predominant theme of literature on socialization and development is early crystallization. Perhaps this is because students of child development are most concerned with the personality, the control of primary drives, and the internalization of general value orientations, and not with the learning of specific norms and skills to be demanded of the adult. Clearly childhood socialization cannot prepare a person for all the roles of his later years. Indeed, parents effectively inhibit many types of learning by selectively sheltering their children from and exposing them to the world outside the home. Many types of economic, political and social participation are effectively limited to later life, e.g., the problem of support for older parents is not ordinarily encountered by the "child" until he approaches middle age. Socialization continues throughout the whole of life. Specific socialization occurs every time a person occupies a role in a new group, for every group has and is an agency for socialization and social control.[80] Although the codes of new groups the individual joins are often limited in content, they may tend to contradict the general precepts of earlier training. That there is considerable flexibility is evident from the experience of social and cultural mobility. For all the resistance of the culturally conditioned personality, individuals do move between cultures, subcultures and classes.

Socialization need not mean rigidification. Normative postures are often acquired imperfectly, incompletely and tentatively. Perhaps it is simpler to indoctrinate entrants with a set of immutable recipes for action in prescribed situations, but room is almost always left for interpretation. The situations to be encountered cannot all be anticipated, and the appropriate prescriptions for them may require improvisation. Experience can strain the sacred formula to the point of forcing reconstruction. The intellectual convenience of the assumption that development ceases once adulthood is attained must be sacrificed in the face of the annoying complexity of reality.[81] Behavior can be modified by increasing rewards for innovation, expanding tolerance of some kinds of deviation, and softening penalties for movement. Indoctrination can be designed to encourage experimentation rather than unreflective obedience, and place primary emphasis on adherence to broad principles. Of particular importance are institutionalized procedures that provide legitimate modes of modification, such as debate in political negotiation and disciplined doubt in scientific inquiry. Such procedures impose a burden of doubt and strain on individual participants, but do leave room for social change through individual change.

Although the difficulty of teaching an old dog new tricks may be inherent, it is also possible that this is a myth given approximate reality by training programs based on it. The feasibility of adult change is probably contingent in large part on the character of early training, and on the opportunities provided for retraining. Perhaps older workers are less adaptable because the earlier cohorts of which they are members received a limited general education. Potential obsolescence may in the future be reduced by more general training, so that people will still be able to acquire in their later years the new capacities and skills needed for continuing employment. It is not outside the bounds of speculation to look toward the day when accelerating change will make economic an extension of education throughout the entire life span, as a continual adjunct to the work week, or as a routine sabbatical renovation.

Yet the flexibility of the social system and its components need not rely on the imperfect tentativeness of socialization procedures, nor on the prospects of retraining the individual. Every group has some control over its own demographic metabolism, and over the content of socialization. The society achieves pattern and direction partly through general selection mechanisms. Change can be mediated through modifications of role allocation as well as through flexible socialization. The system of role allocation can be manipulated to achieve stability and continuity for the group and for the individual, and permit the continuing transformation required by a dynamic society.

Like individuals, organizations (including the total society) have characteristics that influence their degrees of freedom with respect to change. In particular, the different system levels vary in the feasibility of transformation by substituting rather than by modifying components. In biology, the capacity for change is greater at the organismic than at the cellular level. The life of a cell is short relative to that of its encompassing organism. In turn, the organism must die but the species persists and changes, through reproduction and selection. Each higher level has greater modifiability through time, based on the feasibility of metabolism of lower-level components. The analogy of society and organism was always somewhat unfortunate, for reasons unnecessary to rehearse, and also because it may have obscured the more fruitful analogy between society and species. The society is a looser and less sharply defined system than the organism because its constituents possess the possibility of independent mobility in space. In turn, the society is a more flexible system than the species, because it has greater possibility of independent mobility in time. It can control not only the physical replacement of members, like the species, but also the replacement of norms through cultural transmission. In a sense, the society has two types of membership: biological, consisting of human organisms, and cultural, consisting of social norms. The replacement of each is of course interdependent with the replacement of the other.

Now the processes of normative replacement and personnel replacement occur at all levels of social organization. The study of the demographic metabolism of specific groups is a relatively uncharted area of great importance to the student of social change. The individual differs from the organization because he is attached to a mortal body, and lacks the capacity for freedom with respect to time which is within the grasp of the organization. Organizations, like individuals, may acquire structural rigidities, but they can modify their course by replacing individuals as well as by transforming them, through their hiring and firing policies. The scope of possibilities for transforming the character and direction of an organization obviously includes succession in crucial leadership roles and the changing criteria for advancement as different talents become more or less valued.[82]

Indeed, in some respects the subsystems of a society may be even more flexible in this regard than the society itself. They have more scope for applying conditions for remaining and more ways of recruiting new individuals. Enfranchisement and disfranchisement are much more discriminating in their selectivity than natural processes.[83] A society does have some control over the character of its membership, to the extent that differential fertility and mortality are subject to social arrangement, and to the extent that the population is changed by migration, but it is at least common for a society to accept a contractual obligation to all those born within its boundaries (an obligation it has in a sense inherited from its predecessor, the family). But it is perhaps most meaningful from the standpoint of the transmutability of the total society to consider the extent to which its components are groups and organizations rather than individuals. Organizations persist if and because they are successful. New organizations are continually born and old ones die. The replacement of individuals within an organization is paralleled by the replacement of organizations within a society. Once again the opportunities for research are abundant.

CONCLUSION

The case for the cohort as a temporal unit in the analysis of social change rests on a set of primitive notions: persons of age a in time t are those who were age a-1 in time t-1; transformations of the social world modify people of different ages in different ways; the effects of these transformations are persistent. In this way a cohort meaning is implanted in the age-time specification. Two broad orientations for theory and research flow from this position: first, the study of intra-cohort temporal development throughout the life cycle; second, the study of comparative cohort careers, i.e., intercohort temporal differentiation in the various parameters that may be used to characterize these aggregate histories.

The purpose of this essay is to direct the attention of sociologists toward the study of time series of parameters for successive cohorts of various types, in contradistinction to conventional period-by-period analyses. There has been a considerable growth of cohort research in recent years, but the predominant emphasis is still on comparative cross-sectional inquiry. Admittedly the new approach shares the vices as well as the virtues of all studies with an extended time dimension. It is cumbersome, inefficient and laborious; data collection is very time-consuming; and the implicit incomparability accumulates as the group changes its composition (and as the data collectors change their definitions).[84] Yet such difficulties are not so much those of the method itself as meaningful reflections of the research investment necessary to study a long-lived species experiencing structural transformation.

Measurement techniques should be designed to provide data that correspond with the theoretical formulations of the phenomena under examination. In the present essay, the purpose has been to present a frame of reference within which theories can be constructed and empirical inquiry prosecuted. Considering the modest results so far achieved in dynamic analysis, sociologists would be well-advised to exploit the congruence of social change and cohort differentiation.

NOTES

[1] Lemuel Gulliver reported that the Luggnaggians solved the problem with their Struldbruggs by desocializing them at 80. Comte hypothesized that progress is maximized by a length of life neither too ephemeral nor too protracted. Harriet Martineau, *The Positive Philosophy of Auguste Comte* (London: Trübner, n.d.), Vol. II, pp. 152–153.

[2] Robert M. MacIver, *The Challenge of the Passing Years* (New York: Pocket Books, 1963), pp. 110–111.

[3] Julius Petersen, *Die Literarischen Generationen* (Berlin: Junker and Dunnhaupt, 1930); Henri Peyre, *Les Générations Littéraires* (Paris: Bowin, 1948); Yves Renouard, "La notion de génération en histoire," *Revue Historique*, 209 (1935), pp. 1–23. The outstanding sociological contribution is: Karl Mannheim, "The Problem of Generations," in *Essays on the Sociology of Knowledge* (New York: Oxford University Press, 1952), pp. 276–322.

[4] Norman B. Ryder, "La mesure des variations de la fécondité au cours du temps," *Population*, 11 (1956), pp. 29–46.

[5] Bernice L. Neugarten, J. W. Moore, and J. C. Lowe, "Age Norms, Age Constraints and Adult Socialization," *American Journal of Sociology*, 70 (1965), pp. 710–717.

[6] Marion J. Levy, Jr., *The Structure of Society* (Princeton: Princeton University Press, 1952), p. 307.

[7] Talcott Parsons, "The School Class as a Social System: Some of its Functions in American Society," *Harvard Educational Review*, 20 (1959), pp. 297–318.

[8] Nelson N. Foote, "Anachronism and Synchronism in Sociology," *Sociometry*, 21 (1958), pp. 17–29.

[9] Bracker noted that the graduates of American universities of the class of 1929 were united by the distinction of being educated for prosperity and then vaulted into depression. Milton Bracker, "There's No Class Like The Class of '29," *New York Times Magazine*, May 23, 1954, p. 14ff.

[10] Abram J. Jaffe and Robert O. Carleton, *Occupational Mobility in the United States 1930–1960* (New York: Columbia University Press, 1954).

[11] Richard A. Easterlin, "The American Baby Boom in Historical Perspective," *American Economic Review*, 51 (1961), pp. 869–911.

[12] John D. Durand, *The Labor Force in the United States, 1890–1960* (New York: Social Science Research Council, 1948).

[13] William M. Evan, "Cohort Analysis of Survey Data: A Procedure for Studying Long-term Opinion Change," *Public Opinion Quarterly*, 23 (1959), pp. 63–72.

[14] Michel Ralea, "Le problème des générations et la jeunesse d'aujourd'hui," Rencontres Internationales de Genève, *La vie et le temps* (Neuchâtel: Baconnière, 1962), pp. 59–73.

[15] Bennett M. Berger, "How Long is a Generation?" *British Journal of Sociology*, 11 (1960), pp. 557–568.

[16] Seymour Martin Lipset, Paul G. Lazarsfeld, Allen H. Barton, and Juan Linz, "The Psychology of Voting: An Analysis of Political Behavior," in *Handbook of Social Psychology*, Gardner Lindzey, ed. (Reading, Mass.: Addison-Wesley, 1954), II, pp. 1124–1175.

[17] As an exotic example, Hyman Enzer has recently completed a study of the cohort of all 118 American authors whose first novels came out in 1958. See David Dempsey, "First Novelists, Last Words," *Saturday Review*, October 12, 1963, p. 34.

[18] Kingsley Davis and Wilbert E. Moore, "Some Principles of Stratification," *American Sociological Review*, 10 (1945), pp. 242–247.

[19] An extensive bibliography is given in Sigmund Neumann, *Permanent Revolution* (New York: Harper & Row, 1942).

[20] Ernst Gläser, *Jahrgang 1902* (Berlin: Gustav Kiepenheuer, 1928); Vera Brittain, *Born 1925* (London: Macmillan, 1949); Richard Hughes, *The Fox in the Attic* (New York: Signet, 1963).

[21] John Kecscemeti, the preface to Mannheim, *op. cit.* In turn, Mannheim ascribes growing interest in the cohort problem to political discontinuities in the late nineteenth century.

[22] A movie opened in Paris in 1963, called: "Hitler? Never Heard of Him."

[23] Wagner has discussed the significance for the German labor movement of the absorption of cohorts who grew up under National Socialism. Helmut R. Wagner, "A New Generation of German Labor," *Social Research*, 23 (1956), pp. 151–170.

[24] Luciénne Félix, *The Modern Aspect of Mathematics* (New York: Science Editions, 1961).

[25] Pitirim A. Sorokin, *Society, Culture and Personality* (New York: Harper & Row, 1947), p. 193.

[26] E.g., *U. S. News and World Report*, June 6, 1960; *Look*, January 3, 1961. These accounts are more impressive for the frequency than for the detail of instances reported. Somewhat more helpful is Hanson Baldwin, "Turkey's New Soldiers," *New York Times*, June 5, 1960.

[27] Marion J. Levy, Jr., *The Family Revolution in Modern China* (Cambridge, Mass.: Harvard University Press, 1949), p. 297ff.

[28] Irene Taeuber has advocated a research program for China based on the fact that the Communists have now been in power 15 years; change is imminent as these new cohorts are ushered in. Irene B. Taeuber, "China's Population: An Approach to Research," *Social Science Research Council Items*, 18 (1964), pp. 13–19.

[29] Samuel N. Eisenstadt, *From Generation to Generation* (Glencoe, Ill.: The Free Press, 1956), pp. 98ff. Many accounts of the Negro civil rights movement in the United States have contained the assertion that Negro youth provide the initiative for protest, in impatience with the gradualism of their elders.

[30] Hans H. Gerth, "The Nazi Party: Its Leadership and Composition," *American Journal of Sociology*, 45 (1940), pp. 530–571. Rintala has suggested that people who undergo disruptive historical experiences during their formative years may be unusually vulnerable to totalitarian appeals. M. Rintala, "The Problem of Generations in Finnish Communism," *American Slavic and East European Review*, 17 (1958), pp. 190–202.

[31] Mentré reports approvingly Comte's opinion to this effect: François Mentré, *Les Générations Sociales* (Paris: Editions Bossard, 1920); Mannheim reports disapprovingly Cournot's like opinion, *op. cit.*, "The Problem of Generations," p. 297.

[32] Rudolf Heberle, *Social Movements* (New York: Appleton-Century-Crofts, 1951), Chap. 6.

33 This may not be so if youth is directly affected by the change, as with school desegregation. Cf. H. H. Hyman and P. B. Sheatsley, "Attitudes toward Desegregation," *Scientific American*, 211 (1964), pp. 16–23.

34 Robert P. Hinshaw, "The Relationship of Information and Opinion to Age," Ph.D. dissertation, Princeton University, 1944, p. 69.

35 Raymond A. Bauer, Alex Inkeles, and Clyde Kluckhohn, *How the Soviet System Works* (New York: Vintage Books, 1960).

36 Cf. Walt W. Rostow, *The Stages of Economic Growth* (New York: Cambridge University Press, 1960), pp. 134–135.

37 Priscilla Johnson, "The New Men of the Soviet Sixties," *Reporter*, 28 (May 9, 1963), pp. 16–21.

38 Talcott Parsons, *The Social System* (Glencoe, Ill.: The Free Press, 1951), p. 507.

39 *Op. cit.*

40 Will Herberg, *Protestant, Catholic, Jew*, rev. ed., New York: Doubleday, 1960), pp. 28–31.

41 Mannoni has provided an absorbing account of the structural complexities in a population containing two generations of colonists and two generations of natives. Dominique O. Mannoni, *Prospero and Caliban* (London: Methuen, 1956).

42 Donald J. Bogue, "Techniques and Hypotheses for the Study of Differential Migration: Some Notes from an Experiment with U. S. Data," *International Population Conference*, New York, 1961, Vol. I, pp. 405–412.

43 Amos H. Hawley, *Human Ecology* (New York: Ronald, 1950), p. 25; Frederick Le Gros Clark and Agnes Dunne, *Ageing in Industry* (London: Nuffield Foundation, 1955). On December 1, 1963, a federal arbitration board authorized American railroads to eliminate most of their firemen, by attrition.

44 The principal sources for this discussion are: Irvin L. Child, "Socialization," in *Handbook of Social Psychology*, Gardner Lindzey, ed. (Reading, Mass.: Addison-Wesley, 1954), II, pp. 655–692; John E. Anderson, "Dynamics of Development: System in Process," in *The Concept of Development*, Dale B. Harris, ed. (Minneapolis: University of Minnesota Press, 1957), pp. 25–46; Alan T. Welford, *Ageing and Human Skill* (New York: Oxford University Press, 1958); James E. Birren, "Principles of Research on Aging," in *Handbook of Aging and the Individual*, James E. Birren, ed. (Chicago: University of Chicago Press, 1959), pp. 3–42.

45 Everett E. Hagen, *On The Theory of Social Change* (Homewood, Ill.: The Dorsey Press, 1962).

46 William H. Sewell, "Some Recent Developments in Socialization Theory and Research," *Annals*, 349 (1963), pp. 163–181.

47 Leonard D. Cain, Jr., "Life Course and Social Structure," in *Handbook of Modern Sociology*, Robert E. L. Faris, ed. (Chicago: Rand McNally, 1964), pp. 272–309.

48 Kingsley Davis, "The Sociology of Parent-Youth Conflict," *American Sociological Review*, 5 (1940), pp. 523–535; Frederick Elkin and William A. Westley, "The Myth of Adolescent Culture," *American Sociological Review*, 20 (1955), pp. 680–684.

49 This is a familiar literary theme, as in Turgenev's *Fathers and Sons*.

50 For reviews of the literature see: Mentré, *op. cit.*; Pitirim A. Sorokin, *Social and Cultural Dynamics* (New York: American Book Co., 1941), Vol. IV, pp. 504ff.; Renouard, *op. cit.*

51 The Spanish philosopher, Ortega y Gasset, and his disciple, Julian Marias, assert that modern history is punctuated by 15-year caesurae, beginning with 1626, the year Descartes turned 30. (*Vide* Renouard, *op. cit.*)

52 William J. Goode, *World Revolution and Family Patterns* (Glencoe, Ill.: The Free Press, 1962), Chap. 1.

53 Yonina Talmon-Garber, "Social Structure and Family Size," *Human Relations*, 12 (1959), pp. 121–146.

[54] David Riesman, Reuel Denney and Nathan Glazer, *The Lonely Crowd* (New Haven, Conn.: Yale University Press, 1950).

[55] Jesse Pitts, "The Family and Peer Groups," in *A Modern Introduction to the Family*, Norman W. Bell and Ezra F. Vogel, eds. (Glencoe, Ill.: The Free Press, 1960), pp. 266–286.

[56] Albert J. Reiss, Jr., "Sex Offenses; The Marginal Status of the Adolescent," *Law and Contemporary Problems* (1960), pp. 309–333.

[57] Eisenstadt, *op. cit.*, and "Archetypal Patterns of Youth," in *Youth: Change and Challenge*, Erik H. Erikson, ed. (New York: Basic Books, 1963), pp. 24–42.

[58] Mannheim, *op. cit.*

[59] "Belonging to a generation is one of the lowest forms of solidarity," Harold Rosenberg, *The Tradition of the New* (New York: Horizon Press, 1959), pp. 241–258. In Rosenberg's opinion, generation identifications are concocted by journalists out of trivial or ephemeral data.

[60] Jack H. Driberg, "Age Grades," *Encyclopaedia Britannica* (1958), Vol. I, pp. 344–345.

[61] Cf. David Matza, "Position and Behavior Patterns of Youth," in Faris, *op. cit.*, pp. 191–216.

[62] Erik H. Erikson, *Childhood and Society* (New York: Norton, 1950), and "Youth: Fidelity and Diversity," in *Youth: Change and Challenge*, Erik H. Erikson, ed. (New York: Basic Books, 1963), pp. 1–23.

[63] Kurt Lewin, "Field Theory and Experiment in Social Psychology: Concepts and Methods," *American Journal of Sociology*, 44 (1939), pp. 868–896.

[64] The principal source of this discussion is Howard S. Becker, "Notes on the Concept of Commitment," *American Journal of Sociology*, 66 (1960), pp. 32–40.

[65] Arnold S. Tannenbaum, "Adaptability of Older Workers to Technological Change," *Institute for Social Research Newsletter*, October, 1961.

[66] Margaret Mead, *Cultural Patterns and Technical Change*, Paris, UNESCO, 1953. This may also hold for the domestic technology of contraception. See Reuben Hill, J. Mayone Stycos, and Kurt W. Back, *The Family and Population Control* (Chapel Hill: University of North Carolina Press, 1959).

[67] Wilbert E. Moore, *Industrial Relations and the Social Order* (New York: Macmillan, 1946), p. 60.

[68] Sidney L. Pressey and Raymond G. Kuhlen, *Psychological Development Through the Life Span* (New York: Harper & Row, 1957), p. 494ff.

[69] Berger, *op. cit.*

[70] For summaries of the literature, see Lipset *et al.*, *op. cit.*, and Herbert Hyman, *Political Socialization* (Glencoe, Ill.: The Free Press, 1959).

[71] Joseph Crittenden, "Aging and Party Affiliation," *Public Opinion Quarterly*, 26 (1962), pp. 648–657.

[72] Hinshaw, *op. cit.*, p. 67.

[73] Cain, *op. cit.*

[74] For a summary of the technical problems, see Nathan Goldfarb, *An Introduction to Longitudinal Statistical Analysis* (Glencoe, Ill.: The Free Press, 1960).

[75] Herbert Blumer, *Critiques of Research in the Social Sciences I: An Appraisal of Thomas and Znaniecki's "The Polish Peasant in Europe and America"* (New York: Social Science Research Council, Bulletin 44, 1939), pp. 129–130; William I. Thomas and Florian Znaniecki, *The Polish Peasant in Europe and America, Vol. III, Life Record of an Immigrant* (Boston: Gorham, 1919), p. 6.

[76] Edmund H. Volkart, *Social Behavior and Personality* (New York: Social Science Research Council, 1951), p. 24.

[77] John Dollard, *Criteria for the Life History* (New Haven, Conn.: Yale University Press, 1935).

[78] Evan, *op. cit.*

[79] Jose Ortega y Gasset, *The Modern Theme* (New York: Norton, 1933), pp. 13–15.

[80] Orville G. Brim, Jr., "Socialization through the Life Cycle," *Social Science Research Council Items*, 18 (March, 1964), pp. 1–5.

[81] Anselm L. Strauss, *Mirrors and Masks* (Glencoe, Ill.: The Free Press, 1959).

[82] Joseph R. Gusfield, "The Problem of Generations in an Organizational Structure," *Social Forces*, 35 (1957), pp. 323–330.

[83] Georg Simmel, "The Persistence of Social Groups," in *Sociological Theory*, Edgar F. Borgatta and Henry J. Meyer, eds. (New York: Knopf, 1956), pp. 334–358.

[84] William Kessen, Research Design in the Study of Developmental Problems," in *Handbook of Research Methods in Child Development*, Paul H. Mussen, ed. (New York: Wiley, 1960), pp. 36–70.

38   Andrew Collver and Eleanor Langlois

The Female Labor Force in Metropolitan Areas: An International Comparison

The loss of womanpower in conspicuous leisure activities, unproductive household tasks, or various forms of "disguised unemployment," which can be seen in every society, is nowhere more evident than in the cities of underdeveloped countries. In urban areas of Egypt, Iran, and Pakistan, for example, less than 15 percent of all women aged 15–64 are in the labor force. In many cities of Latin America and the Caribbean, to be sure, over 30 percent of all working-age women are in the labor force, but from one-third to half of those who work are employed in domestic service. If more effective use is to be made of the potential womanpower in urban areas, it will be necessary both to increase women's work-participation rates and to channel their labor into genuinely productive tasks. The general trends of development of a modern women's labor force, some effects of this development, and some sources of resistance to it are considered in this paper.

The employment of women is particularly important in the underdeveloped areas today, not only because of its positive contribution to economic production, but also because of its negative effect on human fertility. In fact, the latter may well prove to be the more significant consequence. Most areas attempting to speed up economic development have a surplus of labor. Capital and technical skills are needed more than unskilled labor if growth is to take place. Where the struggle for economic development has become a race between capital accumulation and population growth, high fertility is a major obstacle to the improvement of per capita income. If the recruitment of women into the labor force will help to induce a decline in fertility by changing the character of family and reproductive behavior, it is worthy of high priority in development strategy.

Reprinted from *Economic Development and Cultural Change*, 10:4 (1962), pp. 367–385, by permission of the authors and the publisher.

The plausible notion that women's work participation increases with economic development needs to be modified somewhat. Some countries remain backward despite high work participation of women; others achieve a high level of productivity with relatively little female participation. In the course of economic advancement, especially in countries where there is already a high participation rate, the decline of employment in the subsistence sector may be faster than the growth of employment in the modern sector, so that the total participation rate falls. In the long run the economy benefits primarily from the upgrading of women's work in the modern sector. Thus, the more accurate impression is that the participation of women in *certain kinds of paid work outside the home* increases with economic development.

Two questions arise in the consideration of women's work participation at different levels of economic development. The first pertains to whether changes in the underdeveloped nations are in the direction of bringing their female labor force up to standards set by the more developed economies. The second question is whether even the advanced economies of today actually achieve an optimum employment of their womanpower potential. If they do not, then they provide at best an intermediate goal for developing countries. Once the participation rate of women in the Western European countries has been reached, and assuming a similar industrial composition at that time, there may remain a great deal of room for improvement. Some light on these and other questions will appear from the following analysis of women's work-participation rates and the composition of the female labor force in the metropolitan populations of 38 countries.

PROCEDURE

Our study covers 38 countries selected primarily on the basis of availability of comparable data for their metropolitan areas.[1] The distribution of these countries is as follows: 16 are in Middle and South America, 7 in Africa and Asia, 3 in North America (including Hawaii), 2 in Oceania, and 10 in Western and Southern Europe.[2] Unfortunately, the U.S.S.R., the whole of Eastern Europe, and most of Africa and Asia are omitted because they do not provide data that fit our requirements. The countries selected, then, comprise neither the total universe of countries nor a representative sample of that universe. However, since the aim is primarily analytical rather than descriptive, we assume that the selected countries do provide some basis for conclusions regarding the relations of the female labor force to economic development.

A second methodological problem involved assigning each country to a level of economic development. This was done by devising an index of economic development, which gives equal weight to two indicators: per capita energy consumption, and the percent of the male labor force employed in non-agricultural pursuits. The development score is simply the sum of the two indicators after both have been expressed in terms of a 10-point scale. According to this measure, the Class I countries occupy the upper half of the scale of development, Class II the third quarter, and Class III the lowest quarter of the scale. Countries are listed in descending order of their development scores in Tables 1 and 7.[3]

The unit of analysis used in this study is the *metropolitan population*, defined as the aggregate population of all metropolitan areas within a country. With minor exceptions, the metropolitan areas are as delimited by International Urban Research (now International Population and Urban Research) in 1959.[4] Modifications of this definition were sometimes necessary,[5] but were not sufficiently great in number or scope to alter significantly the characteristics of the metropolitan population. Labor force characteristics were computed for the aggregate metropolitan population, so that the contribution of each metropolitan area is proportionate to its population size.

Two measures of labor force activity were used in the analysis. The first of these, the *work-participation rate*, was designed to estimate the extent to which the adult population is included in the labor force. Defined as the ratio of the labor force to the population aged 15–64, the work-participation rate provides an approximation rather than a direct measure of participation. In using it, we assumed that workers under the age of 15 or over the age of 64 form only a small fraction of the labor force, so that variations in their numbers would have a negligible effect on the size of the labor force. Although the participation rate may be slightly overestimated because of the inclusion of an unknown number of younger and older workers in the labor force, the exaggeration is not great enough to invalidate the measure. This is particularly true of the urban labor force, in which there is relatively little opportunity for child labor or for employment of the aged.

The second measure is the *industrial composition* of the labor force. Although a cross-classification of industry and occupation would have yielded data more suitable for our purposes by showing the *kind* of work done, it was necessary to rely exclusively on industrial statistics in order to maintain a high standard of comparability without further restricting the size of the sample. We therefore used industry statistics which had been collected and organized so as to conform to the major groups of the UN's International Standard Industrial Classification[6]—namely, agriculture, forestry, hunting and fishing (listed as agriculture in our study); mining and quarrying; manufacturing; construction-utilities (combined for our purposes, although listed separately as "construction" and "electricity, gas, water, and sanitary services" by the ISIC); commerce; transport, storage, and communication (listed as transport-communication in our study); services; and activities not adequately described. Agriculture and "activities not adequately described" were excluded from the base in computing the industrial composition of the male, female, and total labor force.[7]

WOMEN'S WORK-PARTICIPATION RATES

Women's work-participation rates, in contrast to the male rates, manifest a remarkably high variability. In virtually every society, adult males are expected to participate in the labor force unless they are in school, disabled, or independently wealthy. Although some variation occurs in the accepted ages of entering or leaving the work force, male participation thus shows a high degree of regularity between countries. The mean male participation rate for the 38 metropolitan populations is 93 with a standard deviation of 4.9. All countries except Puerto Rico fall within a range of 85 to 104.[8] In contrast, the female participation rate ranges from 3 to 73, with a mean of 34 and a standard deviation of 13.4. Evidently women's participation in work is highly dependent on factors that vary greatly from one country to another.

Women's participation in the labor force is patterned by both the organization of the economy and the prevailing family system. Traditionally—and this is hardly less true in modern industrial societies—a married woman's first responsibility has been to her home and family. Her key roles have been, and remain, those of wife, mother, and homemaker; and even when she is not yet married, her expectation of assuming these roles exercises an influence on the character and extent of her economic activities. The extent to which women are free to contribute to economic production, therefore, depends in large part upon the compatibility of their economic and family roles.

Some of the changes associated with economic progress actually make it difficult for women to work. In the traditional agrarian and handicraft economy, where the family is commonly the unit of economic production, both single and married women can often combine work with their other household responsibilities. But where work is separated from the home, as is typical of the modern forms of economic organization, there are physical as well as social inconveniences involved in leaving the home and small children to go to a separate place of work.

Since the trend of economic development is toward large-scale economic units, it appears that changes must be made in the family structure if women are to work for wages. In fact, such modifications as postponement of marriage, lowered fertility, and a general simplification of family structure and duties are typical of countries undergoing industrialization.

It will be seen that women's work-participation rates cannot be explained by level of economic development alone, but that the historic relationships between family and the economy must also be taken into account. Whether women's participation in the metropolitan labor forces rises or falls with economic progress will depend on the level of participation at the start and on the speed with which adjustments are made between the family and work.

Participation in All Industries   As shown in Table 2, the mean female work-participation rate in the top economic class is 39, only 8 percentage points above the rate of 31 for Class III countries. Although at first glance there may seem to be something in this difference, a comparison of countries within each of the three economic classes gives cause to reject the notion that over-all participation rates increase with economic development (see Table 1). The dispersion of rates in Class III from 3 to 73 is so great that the mean of 31 is virtually meaningless. In Europe, the Class I countries clearly have the highest participation rates, but in the Western Hemisphere and Oceania the relation is in the opposite direction. In Latin America and the Caribbean, several Class II and III countries have higher participation rates than the U.S., Canada, Australia, and New Zealand. None of the latter have work-participation rates over 40, while the rates for British Guiana, the British Lesser Antilles, Chile, Jamaica, El Salvador, Haiti, and Paraguay are all above this figure. Finally, it should be noted that although the U.S., Canada, and New Zealand are the most advanced countries, their participation rates are lower than those of most western European countries.

It appears, then, that one cannot state without qualifications that women's work participation expands with economic development.[9] Since economic development brings with it both a *decline* of certain occupations and industries characteristic of underdeveloped economies and an *increase* of industries and occupations characteristic of industrial society, its relation to over-all participation rates is indeterminate. Two opposite trends of participation are discernible, and the sum of the two may be either negative or positive, depending upon the unique circumstances.

Participation in Private Domestic Service   The declining type of employment is well illustrated by private domestic service,[10] which reacts to the process of modernization in the following ways. In the first place, the introduction of wage work (e.g., factory labor) offers attractive competition to domestic work. The pay is generally higher and the hours shorter. (Probably a preference is established for payment in cash instead of in kind.) Then, too, industrialization generally increases the quantity and variety of consumers' goods and special services. One consequence of this is that a number of products and services for the supply of which a household formerly retained domestics, it now purchases on the market. This applies to foods, laundry, etc. A further consequence is that labor-saving devices appear on the market, appealing to those who can no longer afford domestic servants, and encouraging more households to dispense with (at least full-time) help. The result, as we see in most of the Class I countries, is a movement out of private domestic service and into other industries.

In Table 2, the effect of separating out participation in private domestic service can be seen. The mean participation of women in work other than domestic service is twice as high in Class I countries as it is in Class III. And whereas the mean rate of participation in domestic service is only 3 in Class I, it is 11 in Class II.

Not only are the total differences in participation between development classes widened by the exclusion of domestics. What is even more significant is that the high participation rates of Class II and III countries in the Western Hemisphere are all reduced to a level equal to or below that

TABLE 1. WOMEN'S WORK-PARTICIPATION RATES IN METROPOLITAN POPULATIONS

Countries by development class *	Date	Metropolitan population † (thousands)	Work-participation rate ‡		
			All industries	Private domestic service	Excluding private domestic service
Class I					
United States	1950	83,071	37	3	34
Canada	1951	5,769	34	2 §	32 §
U.K.: England and Wales.	1951	32,375	43	2	41
Belgium	1947	3,189	32	3	28
Australia	1954	5,313	34	— ‖	—
Norway	1950	901	42	—	—
Hawaii	1950	353	37	2	35
New Zealand	1951	807	35	—	—
Switzerland	1950	1,632	44	7	36
France	1954	13,332	48	5	43
Class II					
Malta	1948	278	14	3	11
Argentina	1947	4,724	32	7	25
Japan	1955	35,804	41	2	39
Union of South Africa ...	1946	2,900	42	19	24
British Lesser Antilles	1946	277	50	15	34
Chile	1952	1,739	40	—	—
Italy	1951	12,462	28	4 §	24 §
Venezuela	1950	1,321	31	13	18
Cuba	1953	1,740	24	—	—
Puerto Rico	1950	680	28	8	20
Portugal	1950	1,758	34	—	—
British Guiana	1946	94	43	14	30
Spain	1950	7,161	24	—	—
Greece	1951	1,642	26	5	22
Class III					
Panama	1950	193	38	—	—
Egypt	1947	3,363	12	7	5
Jamaica	1953	289	54	—	—
Singapore	1947	941	19	7	12
Colombia	1951	1,685	35	16	19
Brazil	1950	9,234	29	10	19
Paraguay	1950	207	41	14	27
India	1951	26,324	14	2	12
El Salvador	1950	162	46	18	27
Dominican Republic	1950	239	26	11	14
Pakistan	1951	3,727	3	—	—
Nicaragua	1950	114	29	12	17
Haiti	1950	186	73	—	—
Iran #	1956	3,150	10	—	—

Source: National censuses for the dates indicated. See fn. 10.

* For definition of economic development classes see text p. 565 and footnote 3.

† The metropolitan population is the total population living in a country's metropolitan areas. See footnote 4 for a definition of metropolitan area as used here, and footnote 5 for a note on necessary modifications of these units.

‡ Participation rate is the ratio of the number of people in the labor force to the number of people aged 15–64. Note that the units of analysis are not the individual metropolitan areas, but the metropolitan population for each country.

§ Estimate.

‖ Not available.

Due to lack of data, the rank of Iran among the Class III countries could not be determined.

TABLE 2. WOMEN'S MEAN WORK-PARTICIPATION RATES OF METROPOLITAN POPULATION BY TYPE OF WORK AND (NATIONAL) ECONOMIC DEVELOPMENT CLASS

	26 countries *				38 countries	
				Exclud-ing		
			Private	private		
	No. of	All	do-	do-	No. of	All
Development	coun-	indus-	mestic	mestic	coun-	indus-
class	tries	tries	service	service	tries	tries
Class I	(7)	39	3	36	(10)	39
Class II	(10)	34	9	25	(14)	33
Class III	(8)	28	11	17	(14)	31
Total	(26)	33	8	25	(38)	33

Source: Table 1.

* The 26 countries are those for which separate work-participation rates for private domestic service could be obtained; the means for these 26 countries plus the other 12 countries in our study are shown under 38 countries.

of the U.S. Economic development now appears to be clearly associated with increasing participation in non-domestic work in the Western Hemisphere, as well as in Europe, Asia, and Africa.

Social Contexts of Participation   Among the 38 metropolitan populations, four general patterns of women's work-participation are suggested by the statistics presented in Table 1—one type which occurs primarily in the economically advanced countries, and three which are more characteristic of the underdeveloped countries. Although differences among the four are often attributed to "culture," we shall here attempt to interpret them specifically as examples of different forms of adjustment between family and economic organization.

In the metropolitan populations of the first type, the highly developed industrial countries, there is a restricted range of variation in women's work-participation rates. High wages, the desire for a high standard of living, and diminished household responsibilities act together to attract a relatively large share of the potential labor force (the female working-age population) into the market. But at the same time, the persisting notions that woman's place is in the home, and that the economy can spare women from paid productive labor, both act in counter fashion and tend to put an upper limit on participation rates. In some of these countries temporary postponement of marriage keeps many young women in the labor force, while in others—the United States, for example—marriage and employment are not deemed incompatible until the married couple has children.

The second type, a predominantly Latin American pattern, is one in which temporary postponement of marriage for some sectors of society is permitted, providing an interval for wage work. Commonly, young girls, often in-migrants from rural areas, are employed in private homes as domestics. Participation rates show a considerable variation among these metropolitan populations, but nondomestic employment is generally low. In Colombia, for instance, although the women's work-participation rate is 35, the rate for nondomestic participation is only 19. Similar proportions hold for Brazil, Nicaragua, and the Dominican Republic.

The third type, found mainly in the Caribbean, is characterized by weakness and instability in the family system, high illegitimacy rates, and the need for many women to be self-sufficient at numerous intervals throughout their lives. Here too there is a considerable variation in work-participation rates, but due to economic necessity participation is higher than in the other groups. Often employment is less dominated by domestic service, but instead, as we shall see in a later section, is concentrated in commerce—an industry allowing easy entry without capital investment or formal commitment to work. Thus we see in Table 1 that domestic service accounts for only about one-third of the very high participation rates of both El Salvador and the British Lesser Antilles.

The last of the four types may be characterized as an "early marriage and female seclusion" pattern, typified by the Muslim populations of the Middle East, and probably by those of other parts of south Asia. The prohibition of public activity on the part of women is allied with early marriage and exclusive attention to husband and children. Thus we find that in the metropolitan population of Egypt nearly three-fourths of all women between the ages of 20 and 24 are married, and the labor force participation rate is only 12, of which nearly half is accounted for by domestic service. The three Muslim countries in our list—Egypt, Iran, and Pakistan—have a mean female work-participation rate of only 8, whereas the other Class III countries have a mean rate of 37. Also, the lowest rate among the others is found in India, which still has many Muslims and has been influenced by Muslim attitudes toward women.

INDUSTRIAL COMPOSITION

In the study of the relation of work participation to economic development, it soon became apparent that the participation rate is heavily influenced by one type of employment, namely, domestic service. We now turn to the question of how the distribution of women workers among domestic service and other industries is affected by economic development. Since the female labor force composition is determined to a great extent by the economy as a whole, we shall begin by placing it in the context of the total labor force.

Labor Force Composition and Economic Development   Because of the important role of industrialization in economic development, we might expect a much greater portion of the labor force of both sexes to be employed in manufacturing in the metropolitan populations of the most advanced countries than in those of the underdeveloped areas. Actually, there is surprisingly little difference in industrial composition between the development classes, and the differences among broad geographic areas within each class are as great as the differences between classes (see Table 3). The mean percent of the total metropolitan labor force in manufacturing

TABLE 3.   Mean Percent of Metropolitan Non-Agricultural Labor Force in Major Industries by Economic Development Class and Geographic Groupings

Economic development class	No. of countries	Male labor force			Female labor force			Total		
		M	C	S	M	C	S	M	C	S
Europe										
Class I	5	40	16	17	34	22	40	38	18	25
Class II	5	32	17	27	33	11	53	32	15	33
Class III	0									
Total	10	36	17	22	33	17	46	35	17	29
Western Hemiphere and Oceania										
Class I	5	32	20	24	27	26	43	30	21	29
Class II	7	27	21	26	26	12	60	26	19	37
Class III	9	29	17	29	22	16	60	27	18	40
Total	21	29	19	27	25	17	56	27	19	36
Africa and Asia										
Class I	0									
Class II	2	27	18	21	23	20	53	26	18	30
Class III	5	26	24	33	17	11	68	26	23	36
Total	7	26	22	29	18	14	64	26	21	34
All Countries										
Class I	10	36	18	21	30	24	41	34	20	27
Class II	14	29	19	26	28	13	56	28	20	35
Class III	14	28	20	30	20	14	63	26	19	38
Total	38	30	19	26	25	16	55	29	19	34

M—manufacturing; C—commence; S—services.

in five relatively backward countries of Europe is 32 percent, whereas the mean for the five most productive European countries is 38 percent. In the Western Hemisphere and Oceania, the difference is similar but even narrower. The five Class I countries here have a mean of 30 percent of their total metropolitan labor force in manufacturing, while the mean for seven Class II countries is 26 percent, and that for nine Class III countries is 27 percent. Two further facts from the table serve to point up the indeterminacy of the relation of economic development to the industrial composition of the labor force in metropolitan populations: the first is that the percent of workers in manufacturing in Class II countries of Europe is higher than that of Class I countries of the Western Hemisphere and Oceania; and secondly, there is virtually no difference between Classes II and III in manufacturing emphasis.

A host of factors evidently interact to determine the distribution of workers of both sexes among the industry categories considered here. Economic development, at least as we measure it, is evidently not one of the major determinants, at least in the metropolitan labor force, where the shift out of agriculture is not a factor.

Economic progress is not achieved merely by shifting workers out of services and commerce into manufacturing, but by raising the productivity of workers *in all sectors*. The increase of productivity is gained by increasing the scale and efficiency of organization, improving the technical competence of workers, and supplying each worker with a larger amount of capital equipment. All sectors of the economy are subject to improvements of this nature. Manufacturing has no monopoly on either low or high productivity. Transportation can be converted from riksha to railroad, communications from runner to radio, and commerce from bazaar to discount department store. In each case, the effect is the same: a higher rate of production per worker. (The process is usually accompanied by technological unemployment in every sector of the economy, and by the displacement of small-scale operations and handicrafts.) A tremendous volume of manufactured goods can be produced by the modern industrial metropolis with only a moderately higher proportion of manufacturing workers than are found in a backward pre-industrial city.

The tenuousness of the association between economic development and the percent of the labor force in manufacturing can be seen in a comparison of the most highly developed countries in our study. Although the Class I countries of the Western Hemisphere and Oceania have a higher level of per capita production than the most advanced countries of Europe, they have a smaller proportion of the labor force employed in manufacturing.

Briefly stated, the concentration of workers in a given industry depends on the demand for the product and the productivity of labor. One explanation for these differences, then, is the demand for manufactured goods as export products. The economies of many highly developed European countries are dependent on exports of manufactured goods to pay for imports of food and raw materials, while with the exception of the U.S., all Class I countries of the Western Hemisphere and Oceania are heavy importers of manufactured goods.

Part of the explanation may also lie in the high per capita energy consumption of the U.S. and Canada as compared with European countries. The low proportion in manufacturing in the U.S. in 1950 is indicative of a high level of capital and technology in manufacturing as compared with other sectors of the economy. It should also be noted that the western European countries suffered heavy losses of capital during World War II, so that labor-intensive methods became necessary in manufacturing.[11]

Finally, it may be that in Europe certain functions such as advertising, accounting, design, sales, and distribution are integrated with manufacturing firms, whereas in the U.S. many of these functions are performed by specialized firms not classified under manufacturing. With data on occupation, it would be possible to specify more accurately the differences in organization between Europe and America.

Comparison of Male and Female Labor Force Composition The comparison of male and female labor force composition in Table 3 suggests that the percent of workers of each sex in manufacturing increases moderately with economic development. The percent of males in commerce remains constant or declines slightly, while the percent of females in commerce increases substantially. The differences in the percent of women in services are the most striking: the more highly developed countries clearly have a smaller percent of their female labor force in services. As will be shown, this difference can be explained by the reduction of employment in private domestic service. In summary, economic development is apparently accompanied by increasing proportions of all workers in manufacturing, a fall in the proportions of workers of each sex in services, and a replacement of male workers in commerce by females. The decline in the proportion of females in services is the most extreme change, because of the large share of private domestic service in the female labor force of the typical underdeveloped economy. Thus we see that economic developments has a differential impact on male and female labor force composition.

This differential is brought out even more clearly in Table 4, showing the correlation of the proportion of male workers in each major industry with the percent of female workers in the same industry. The correlation coefficient here may be looked upon as an index of sex discrimination in an industry. In all three development classes, the high positive correlations indicate that specialization in manufacturing involves both the female and the male labor force indiscriminately. The same is true of commerce and services in Class I. In Class II, there is a moderate amount of discrimination of the sexes in commerce, and in the lowest class the discrimination is unmistakable. In this group, we found several countries in which commerce is a woman's domain and a number of others where women are excluded. On the whole, this index shows that economic development brings an increasing integration of women into all sectors of the economy.

TABLE 4.   CORRELATION OF THE PROPORTION OF MALE WORKERS IN EACH
MAJOR INDUSTRY WITH THE PROPORTION OF FEMALE WORKERS
IN THE SAME INDUSTRY, IN METROPOLITAN POPULATIONS
BY LEVEL OF ECONOMIC DEVELOPMENT

Development class	No. of countries	Manu-facturing	Commerce	Services
Class I	10	+.88	+.64	+.87
Class II	14	+.79	−.16	+.43
Class III	14	+.73	−.45	+.31
Total	38	+.76	−.28	+.61

Source: National censuses for the dates indicated in Table 1.

Female Labor Force Composition   As noted previously, the Class I countries contrast with those of Class III, in that they have a much smaller proportion of the female labor force in services, and slightly larger proportions in the other major industries. In Table 5 the industry composition of the female labor force is shown in greater detail for 26 countries. Here can also be seen an expansion of female employment in construction-utilities and transport-communication.

Seeing that the proportion in all industries except services increases at higher levels of development, there is reason to suspect that nondomestic employment in services, if separated from employment in private domestic service, would behave similarly. Table 6, a summarization of the figures for 26 countries in Table 7, shows that this is in fact the case.

Since it is now clear that in the process of development, employment in private domestic service diminishes with respect to that in other sectors of the female labor force, the question arises—do all sectors gain proportionately from this move out of services? One way of looking at this question is to consider what would be the industrial composition of the female labor force if employment in domestic services were excluded at all levels of development. This in effect approximates a situation in which all women thus employed now found jobs in other sectors of the economy. Part B of Table 5 shows the distribution of women workers in industries other than private domestic service. In contrast to part A, the distribution shown in part B is strikingly similar for all three development classes. Regardless of the level of development, women nondomestic workers in metropolitan populations are distributed roughly in the ratio of 36 percent in manufacturing, 1 percent in construction-utilities, 23 percent in commerce, 3 percent in transport-communication, 12 and 37 percent in services.

Table 5. Mean Industrial Composition of the Female Non-Agricultural Labor Force of Metropolitan Populations, by Level of Economic Development (26 Countries Only) *

Development class	No. of countries	Manufacturing	Construction–Utilities	Commerce	Communication	Services	Total
A. *Including private domestic service*							
Class I	7	30	1.3	23	3.3	43	100
Class II	10	29	0.8	14	1.6	55	100
Class III	9	21	1.1	14	1.6	62	100
Total	26	26	1.0	17	2.0	54	100
B. *Excluding private domestic service*							
Class I	7	33	1.1	25	3.7	37	100
Class II	10	39	1.0	20	2.2	36	100
Class III	9	35	1.7	25	2.4	36	100
Total	26	36	1.3	23	2.7	37	100

* Data on private domestic service were not available for the remaining twelve countries.

Now that it appears that all sectors gain proportionately from the movement of women workers out of domestic service, another question arises—does this gain affect all sectors equally at each stage of development? This problem is more difficult to deal with statistically, but some possibilities are suggested by our data. In Table 3 we saw that for our 38 countries, while there was a considerable difference in the proportion in services from each class to the next, in the case of manufacturing the major difference occurs between Classes III and II and in commerce between Classes II and I. It seems at least plausible to suggest that in the earlier stages of development more women leaving services enter manufacturing

Table 6. Summary: Mean Percent of Female Nonagricultural Labor Force in Services

	All services	Private domestic	Excluding private domestic
Class I	43	9	33
Class II	55	28	27
Class III	62	41	21

TABLE 7. INDUSTRIAL COMPOSITION OF THE FEMALE NONAGRICULTURAL LABOR FORCE OF METROPOLITAN POPULATIONS, BY LEVEL OF ECONOMIC DEVELOPMENT

Economic development class	Date	M	C/U	Cm.	T/C	Total	PD	Excl. PD
Class I								
United States	1950	27%	1%	25%	4%	43%	9%	34%
Canada	1951	27	1	27	5	40	5	35
U.K.: England and Wales	1951	42	1	19	3	35	5	30
Belgium	1947	36	1	26	2	35	10	24
Australia	1954	33	1	28	3	35	—	—
Norway	1950	28	1	23	5	42	—	—
Hawaii	1950	13	2	24	3	59	7	52
New Zealand	1951	33	1	24	4	38	—	—
Switzerland	1950	30	1	21	2	46	17	29
France	1954	34	2	20	4	40	10	30
Class II								
Malta	1948	18	0	17	1	64	21	43
Argentina	1947	43	1	11	1	44	24	20
Japan	1955	31	2	27	3	37	6	32
Union of South Africa	1946	14	0	14	2	69	49	20
British Lesser Antilles	1946	24	1	19	1	55	34	21
Chile	1952	30	0	11	1	57	—	—
Italy	1951	43	1	13	2	41	15	26
Venezuela	1950	20	1	8	1	69	46	22
Cuba	1953	17	1	9	2	71	—	—
Puerto Rico	1950	27	1	10	2	61	30	30
Portugal	1950	34	0	9	2	54	—	—
British Guiana	1946	23	0	15	1	61	33	28
Spain	1950	27	1	9	2	61	—	—
Greece	1951	42	1	9	2	46	20	26
Class III								
Panama	1950	12	1	15	1	71	—	—
Egypt	1947	8	1	15	1	75	61	15
Jamaica	1953	23	1	20	1	55	—	—
Singapore	1947	17	2	16	4	61	40	21
Colombia	1951	23	1	10	1	65	49	16
Brazil	1950	24	0	7	2	66	35	32
Paraguay	1950	25	0	18	1	56	35	21
India	1951	26	6	12	2	51	18	33
El Savador	1950	21	0	21	1	57	41	16
Dominican Republic .	1950	18	0	11	1	70	51	19
Pakistan	1951	11	0	9	1	79	—	—
Nicaragua	1950	26	0	17	1	56	41	15
Haiti	1950	27	0	29	0	44	—	—
Iran	1956	22	0	2	1	75	—	—

M—manufacturing; C/U—construction-utilities; Cm.—commerce; T/C—transport-communications; PD—private domestic.

than enter commerce, while in the later stages of development the reverse is true. This makes sense when we consider that in the most advanced countries, many women are employed by the wide variety of commercial and financial corporations which exist on a large scale only in highly developed economies. The statistics in part B of Table 5, showing a higher proportion in manufacturing in Class II than in either Class I or III, and a lower proportion in commerce in Class II, may tend to confirm this.

As was the case for the total labor force, some differences in female labor force composition are associated with geographic regions. For instance, we see in Table 3 that manufacturing is higher for Europe than for the Western Hemisphere, while the reverse is true of commerce and services. Although relative emphasis on manufacturing and commerce differs between the countries of Europe and those of the Western Hemisphere and Oceania, it appears that the relationships between the Class I and II countries in each of the two regions is much the same. Both regions have similar proportions in manufacturing in both classes, and both regions show a decided increase in the proportion in commerce from Class II to I.

Unfortunately, it is difficult to discuss development class differences within the countries in Asia and Africa. There are fewer countries of this geographical grouping in our study, and all but two are in Class III—the two are Japan and the Union of South Africa, strikingly dissimilar in many respects. The Class III countries of this group include three Muslim countries, with over 75 percent of their female workers in services.

Individual metropolitan populations differ widely from the typical patterns within both the development classes and geographic regions, as can be seen in Table 7; such variations result from the organization of specific economies and perhaps from differences in the cultural definition of the roles of women. For instance, even within the manufacturing sector, some countries specialize in industries in which women workers are preferred, such as textiles and food processing, while for others the sector is generally devoted to heavy industry employing men. Other countries have unique traditions regarding women's occupations, as in India, for example, where women are employed in mining, rock quarrying, and road construction—tasks that in most other countries are considered strictly men's work. In other cases, men seem to have a monopoly of commerce, so that less than 10 percent of working women are engaged in this sector.

WOMEN'S WORK PARTICIPATION AND FERTILITY

In the introductory remarks, we suggested that the recruitment of women into work outside the home can be a deterrent to fertility. There are a number of methodological problems involved in any effort to establish conclusive evidence on this point. Detailed information on many individuals is needed for this, and surveys or even panel studies may be necessary to discover the nature of the interconnections between fertility and the employment of women. It is not enough to know that working women have fewer children than those who are not in the labor force. Obviously, a process of selection could be operating to remove the most fertile women from the labor force. The detailed consideration of these questions is not possible here. We can only indicate an overall inverse association of fertility with the rate of women's participation in nondomestic work.

The association of work participation with fertility as measured by the adjusted child-woman ratio[13] is depicted graphically in Figure 1. The black dots indicate participation in nondomestic work only; a circle represents participation including domestic service. Separate domestic service data

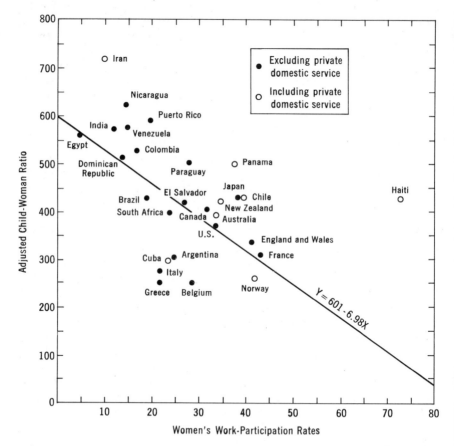

Sources: For adjusted child-woman ratio see footnote 15. For women's work-participation rates see Table 1. Regression line computed for Y = adjusted child-woman ratio, X = women's work-participation rates excluding private domestic service. N = 20.

Figure 1. Women's Work-Participation Rates and Adjusted Child-Woman Ratio for Metropolitan Populations

could not be found for eight of the countries shown. The removal of domestics would lower the participation rates of Iran, Panama, Chile, and Haiti to points nearer the regression line. Judging from other countries in development Class I, the removal of domestic servants from the figures for New Zealand, Australia, and Norway would leave them virtually unchanged. Cuba, however, would fall still farther out of line.

With the exception of a cluster of countries with low fertility and average participation rates, the array in Figure 1 forms a fairly high correlation. Three of the deviants are in Europe, where the child-woman ratios are generally low, regardless of women's work-participation rates. The other two, Argentina and Cuba, have lower child-woman ratios than one would expect on the basis of either their level of economic development or their participation rates. These two metropolitan populations are dominated by Havana and Buenos Aires, and thus the deviations may be explicable by characteristics peculiar to these two metropolitan areas. On the whole, the data do show that fertility is negatively associated with the rate of women's participation in work other than domestic service. The Pearsonian correlation for the 20 countries with domestics excluded is —.60, and the regression equation indicates that the number of children per thousand women declines by 7 for each 1 percent increase in the work-participation rate. This of course provides no basis for causal inference, though we may hazard some thoughts as to the process at work.

Although there are differences in patterns of development, almost inevitably, when development does take place, new opportunities for women to work arise. A number of changes in the family system follow. In general, the family roles of women become less burdensome. Although their first commitment is still to the work of the household, they are increasingly accepted in secondary roles in the industrial labor force. As economic functions are transferred from the home to commercial establishments, the family is simplified and reduced in size. The family's dependence on cash income makes it desirable for the mother to work for wages rather than spend her entire time in housework. High fertility becomes extremely costly under these conditions, since the cost of children comes to be measured not only in the amount of expenditure for their housing, food, clothing, and education, but also in the amount of time the mother loses from work. Gradually, the small family becomes accepted as the norm, and the nuclear family system replaces the extended family. The industrial revolution thus sets off both a family revolution and a demographic revolution. These in turn help to sustain economic growth, by freeing women for participation in the modern labor force, and by diminishing the pressure of population on resources and capital.

CONCLUSIONS

We have attempted to elucidate, in this paper, some of the significant issues for economic development that arise from a study of the participation of women in the metropolitan labor forces of both developed and underdeveloped countries. We have seen that some seemingly obvious relationships between such participation and the level of economic development do not hold up under scrutiny, and we have suggested tentative alternative interpretations that seem to be demanded by the data. Other issues and implications exist, but these are either tenuous, or not of a kind that the data can either validate or invalidate.

It is all too common to assess the benefits to be derived from increases in the size and productivity of the female labor force only in terms of the increase in national product which is expected to result. As we have seen, possibly the indirect effects upon fertility of such changes are of equal importance, at least in some countries. But there are other indirect effects, with mixed costs and benefits. Thus, in the underdeveloped economies high women's (metropolitan) work-participation rates tend to be associated with an unbalanced, highly female sex ratio, suggesting that employment opportunities have to some degree motivated women to migrate to the cities. Such in-migration increases the absolute size of the metropolitan labor force; but more significantly, it draws off a portion of the rural population and contributes to an increased rate of urbanization.

Although a high rate of participation of women in the labor force does not in itself assure economic progress, we have seen that a moderately high rate, from 34 to 45, is typical of the metropolitan populations of the most highly developed countries. This is not to be taken as implying that an upper limit has been reached. It may be that a higher participation rate is desirable in advanced nations today, as they face situations demanding the utilization of their total resources. Moreover, it should not be assumed that in the underdeveloped countries a lower rate of participation necessarily stems only from cultural prohibitions or social resistance to women's work. This may be true in some Islamic nations, but there are other cases where a potential women's labor force awaits jobs to fill.

ACKNOWLEDGMENTS

The help of others at the International Population and Urban Research Center at Berkeley is gratefully acknowledged. The unpublished industry data used throughout the paper were assembled by Richard L. Forstall while a member of the staff; editorial assistance was given by Roy Turner; and the initial idea of the work and subsequent research suggestions were provided by Kingsley Davis.

NOTES

[1] The present study is part of a larger investigation. A later paper deals with individual metropolitan areas rather than with the total metropolitan populations of countries.

[2] Statistics were taken from the most recent available census providing the necessary data; political units have been maintained as they were at that date. As a result, the United States and Hawaii are included separately, as are Jamaica and the British Lesser Antilles, both of which are now within the Caribbean Federation.

[3] Classification of the countries on the basis of these two indicators resulted in the following class limits:

	Per capita energy consumption *	Percent of male labor force in non-agriculture	Delevelopment scores (on a 10-point scale)
Class I	2.13–7.96	69–94	5.5–10.0
Class II	0.26–1.87	47–70	2.5– 5.1
Class III	0.02–0.30	13–41	0.0– 2.1

* Measures in coal equivalents (metric tons).

Note that whereas the discussion that follows deals with metropolitan populations, the economic development grouping is based upon the characteristics of nations.

[4] Metropolitan area, as the term is here used, is "An area with 100,000 or more inhabitants, containing at least one city (or continuous urban area) with 50,000 or more inhabitants and those administrative divisions contiguous to the city (or to the continuous urban area) which meet certain requirements as to metropolitan character." For discussion of these requirements see International Urban Research, *The World's Metropolitan Areas* (Berkeley: University of California Press, 1959), pp. 25–31.

[5] Modifications were made either because population data not available at the time of the original delimitations later indicated the addition of some new areas or revisions in the units comprising others; or because difficulties in obtaining industry data for units comprising the metropolitan area made it necessary to use a somewhat larger or smaller area.

[6] UN Statistical Office, *International Standard Industrial Classification of All Economic Activities*, Statistical Papers, Series M, No. 4, Rev. 1 (New York, 1958). This classification had been prepared for the specific purpose of increasing international comparability of economic statistics and was approved in 1948 by the UN with the recommendation that all member governments make use of it either by adopting it as a national standard or by rearranging their statistical data in accordance with it.

[7] It was necessary to include agriculture and "activities not adequately described" in computations of the participation rate, since there was no way of excluding such persons from the working age population (the base of the fraction). This seems to raise no problems except in the case of Haiti, where the women's work-participation rate is extraordinarily high. In computing the industrial composition of the labor force, it was thought preferable to exclude such categories from the base in order to focus on the major industry groups most significant in a discussion of metropolitan populations.

[8] Participation rates of over 100 occasionally occur when the metropolitan population's labor force is greater than its 15–64 population; in other words, when some members of the labor force are less than 15 years of age or 65 years or over.

[9] The prevalent impression that many more women work in the modern industrial city than in the cities of economically underdeveloped areas perhaps has its basis in the higher *visibility* of women's occupations in the modern city. Where a large proportion of women are employed in household industries and private domestic service, their work is not clearly distinguishable from the roles of wife, mother, and homemaker. As the number of women in the more public jobs increases, one easily draws the conclusion that women's work participation is increasing.

[10] In collecting and organizing data on private domestic service, a category often not clearly defined by national censuses, the standardization procedures used for the rest of the data were of necessity less faithfully followed, but it is expected that departures from the ISIC form are minor and will not significantly affect the relationships we have suggested.

[11] In his classic discussion of the industry composition of the labor force, Colin Clark recognized that variations in energy supplies, the scale of manufacturing

establishments, and the newness of plant and equipment can modify the general tendency for the ratio of secondary to tertiary workers to decline in the most highly developed countries. *The Conditions of Economic Progress*, 3rd ed. (London: Macmillan, 1957), Chap. IX, pp. 490–520.

[12] Only in the case of transport-communication does some difference between development classes remain; but this is small, as Table 5 shows.

[13] Ratio of children 0–4 to women 15–49, adjusted for estimated underenumeration of children. See Richard B. Gamble, M.A. Thesis, University of California, Berkeley, 1961.

Changes | ORGANIZATIONAL
in the Social Order | TRANSFORMATION

COMMENTARY

The articles in the preceding section referred to macrosociological analyses of various aspects of societal transformation. They involved historical and comparative studies informed by a demographic perspective. By contrast the works of Philip Selznick, Sheldon Messinger, and Harry Scoble reprinted here refer to organizational change as it occurs within society.

Selznick's pioneering study of the Tennessee Valley Authority, *TVA and the Grassroots*, stands as one of the most sophisticated sociological attempts to deal with the analysis of social change. It is in the final chapter of the report of that study, "Guiding Principles and Interpretation: A Summary," that he explicates the idea of unanticipated consequences in organized action and discusses the concept of cooptation so important to an understanding of the sociological dimensions of change.

If Selznick emphasizes the *impact* of organizational innovation, Messinger, in his case study of the Townsend Movement, is concerned with organizational *response*—the staying power of organizations—in the face of the unexpected consequences of externally imposed changes.

The concluding paper to this section deals with what is undoubtedly the most significant social movement in American history, one which is attempting to secure the social, economic, and political rights of black Americans. In "Negro Politics: The Quest for Power," Harry Scoble discusses the barriers set up by the existing power structure, as well as difficulties within the movement itself, which must be overcome if political power is to be realized by the Negro.

39 PHILIP SELZNICK

Guiding Principles and Interpretation:
A Summary

The entire science considered as a body of formulae having coherent relations
to one another is just a system of possible predicates—that is, of possible
standpoints or methods to be employed in qualifying some particular experience whose nature or meaning is unclear to us.[1]
                                                          —JOHN DEWEY

It is believed that the interpretation set forth in the preceding chapters
provides a substantially correct picture of a significant aspect of the TVA's
grass-roots policy at work. Far from remote, or divorced from what is
considered pertinent by informed participants, the analysis reflects what
is obvious to those who "know the score" in TVA.[2] Of course, this exposition is more explicit and systematic, and the relevant implications are more
fully drawn out, but in main outline it can come as no surprise to leading
officials of the Authority. This is not to suggest that there are no errors of
detail, perhaps even of important detail. The nature of this kind of research
precludes any full assurance on that. While much of the material is derived
from documentary (though largely unpublished) sources, much is also
based upon interviews with members of the organization and with those
nonmembers who were in a position to be informed. Care was taken to
rely upon only those who had an intimate, as opposed to hearsay, acquaintance with the events and personalities involved. Those who are familiar
with the shadowland of maneuver in large organizations will appreciate
the difficulties, and the extent to which ultimate reliability depends upon
the ability of the investigator to make the necessary discriminations. They
will also recognize the need for insight and imagination if the significance
of behavior, as it responds to structural constraints, is to be grasped. All
this involves considerable risk.

If the use of personal interviews, gossip channels, working papers,[3] and
participation[4] opens the way for error, it remains, however, the only way
in which this type of sociological research can be carried on. A careful
investigator can minimize error by such means as checking verbal statements against the documentary record, appraising the consistency of information supplied to him, and avoiding reliance on any single source. On
the other hand, he will not restrict his data to that which is publicly
acknowledged.

Reprinted from *TVA and the Grassroots* by Philip Selznick, pp. 249–266, by permission of the author and Harper & Row, Publishers, Inc.

The possibilities of factual error, however great, are probably less important as hazard than the theoretical orientation of the study. To be sure, an empirical analysis of a particular organization, of its doctrine, of a phase of policy in action, of its interaction with other structures, was our objective. But in order to trace the dynamics of these events, it has been necessary to attempt a reconstruction, which is to say, a theory, of the conditions and forces which appear to have shaped the behavior of key participants.

Theoretical inquiry, when it is centered upon a particular historical structure or event, is always hazardous. This is due to the continuous tension between concern for a full grasp and interpretation of the materials under investigation as history, and special concern for the induction of abstract and general relations. Abstractions deal harshly with "the facts," choosing such emphases and highlighting such characteristics as may seem factitious, or at least distorted, to those who have a stake in an historically well-rounded apprehension of the events themselves. This is especially true in the analysis of individual personalities or social institutions, for these demand to be treated as wholes, with reference to their own central motives and purposes, rather than as occasions for the development of theoretical systems. This general, and perhaps inescapable, source of misunderstanding being admitted, let us review the concepts which have been used to order the materials of our inquiry.

SOCIOLOGICAL DIRECTIVES

This volume has been subtitled "A Study in the Sociology of Formal Organization." This means that the inquiry which it reports was shaped by sociological directives, more especially by a frame of reference for the theory of organization.[5] These directives are operationally relevant without, however, functioning as surrogates for inductive theory itself. That is, while they provide criteria of significance, they do not tell us what is significant; while they provide tools for discrimination, they do not demand any special conclusions about the materials under investigation.[6] The fundamental elements of this frame of reference are these:

1. All formal organizations are molded by forces tangential to their rationally ordered structures and stated goals. Every formal organization—trade union, political party, army, corporation, etc.—attempts to mobilize human and technical resources as means for the achievement of its ends. However, the individuals within the system tend to resist being treated as means. They interact as wholes, bringing to bear their own special problems and purposes; moreover, the organization is imbedded in an institutional matrix and is therefore subject to pressures upon it from its environment, to which some general adjustment must be made. As a result, the organization may be significantly viewed as an adaptive social structure, facing problems which arise simply because it exists as an organization in an institutional environment, independently of the special (economic, military, political) goals which called it into being.

2. It follows that there will develop an informal structure within the organization which will reflect the spontaneous efforts of individuals and subgroups to control the conditions of their existence. There will also develop informal lines of communication and control to and from other organizations within the environment. It is to these informal relations and structures that the attention of the sociologist will be primarily directed. He will look upon the formal structure, e.g., the official chain of command, as the special environment within and in relation to which the informal structure is built. He will search out the evolution of formal relations out of the informal ones.[7]

3. The informal structure will be at once indispensable to and consequential for the formal system of delegation and control itself. Wherever command over the responses of individuals is desired, some approach in terms of the spontaneous organization of loyalty and interest will be necessary. In practice this means that the informal structure will be useful to the leadership and effective as a means of communication and persuasion. At the same time, it can be anticipated that some price will be paid in the shape of a distribution of power or adjustment of policy.

4. Adaptive social structures are to be analyzed in structural-functional terms.[8] This means that contemporary and variable behavior is related to a presumptively stable system of needs[9] and mechanisms. Every such structure has a set of basic needs and develops systematic means of self-defense. Observable organizational behavior is deemed explained within this frame of reference when it may be interpreted (and the interpretation confirmed) as a response to specified needs. Where significant, the adaptation is dynamic in the sense that the utilization of self-defensive mechanisms results in structural transformations of the organization itself. The needs in question are organizational, not individual, and include: the security of the organization as a whole in relation to social forces in its environment; the stability of the lines of authority and communication; the stability of informal relations within the organization; the continuity of policy and of the sources of its determination; a homogeneity of outlook with respect to the meaning and role of the organization.

5. Analysis is directed to the internal relevance of organizational behavior. The execution of policy is viewed in terms of its effect upon the organization itself and its relations with others. This will tend to make the analysis inadequate as a report of program achievement, since that will be deëmphasized in the interests of the purely organizational consequences of choice among alternatives in discretionary action.

6. Attention being focused on the structural conditions which influence behavior, we are directed to emphasize constraints, the limitation of alternatives imposed by the system upon its participants. This will tend to give pessimistic overtones to the analysis, since such factors as good will and intelligence will be deëmphasized.

7. As a consequence of the central status of constraint, tensions and dilemmas will be highlighted. Perhaps the most general source of tension

and paradox in this context may be expressed as the recalcitrance of the tools of action. Social action is always mediated by human structures, which generate new centers of need and power and interpose themselves between the actor and his goal. Commitments to others are indispensable in action: at the same time, the process of commitment results in tensions which have always to be overcome.

These principles define a frame of reference, a set of guiding ideas which at once justify and explain the kind of selection which the sociologist will make in approaching organizational data. As we review some of the key concepts utilized in this study, the operational relevance of this frame of reference will be apparent.

UNANTICIPATED CONSEQUENCES IN
ORGANIZED ACTION

The foregoing review of leading ideas directs our attention to the meaning of events. This leads us away from the problem of origins.[10] For the meaning of an act may be spelled out in its consequences, and these are not the same as the factors which called it into being. The meaning of any given administrative policy will thus require an excursion into the realm of its effects. These effects ramify widely, and those we select for study may not always seem relevant to the formal goals in terms of which the policy was established. Hence the search for meanings may seem to go rather far afield, from the viewpoint of those concerned only with the formal program. Any given event, such as the establishment of a large army cantonment, may have a multitude of effects in different directions: upon the economy of the area, upon the morals of its inhabitants, upon the pace of life, and so on. The free-lance theorist may seek out the significance of the event in almost any set of consequences. But in accordance with the principle stated above, we may distinguish the random search for meanings —which can be, at one extreme, an aesthetic interest—from the inquiry of the organizational analyst. The latter likewise selects consequences, but his frame of reference constrains his view: it is his task to trace such consequences as redound upon the organization in question; that is, such effects as have an internal relevance. Thus, only those consequences of the establishment of the army cantonment in a given area which result in adjustments of policy or structure in the administration of the cantonment will be relevant.

There is an obvious and familiar sense in which consequences are related to action: the articulation of means and ends demands that we weigh the consequences of alternative courses of action. Here consequences are anticipated. But it is a primary function of sociological inquiry to uncover systematically the sources of unanticipated consequence in purposive action.[11] This follows from the initial proposition in our frame of reference: "All formal organizations are molded by forces tangential to their rationally ordered structures and stated goals" (p. 614, above). Hence the notion of unanticipated consequence is a key analytical tool: where unintended effects occur, there is a presumption, though no assurance,[12] that socio-logically identifiable forces are at work.

There are two logically fundamental sources of unanticipated conse-quence in social action, that is, two conditions which define the inherent predisposition for unanticipated consequences to occur:

1. *The limiting function of the end-in-view.*—A logically important but sociologically insignificant source of unanticipated consequence exists be-cause the aim of action limits the perception of its ramified consequences.[13] This is legitimate and necessary, for not all consequences are relevant to the aim. But here there arises a persistent dilemma. This very necessity to "keep your eye on the ball"—which demands the construction of a rational system explicitly relating means and ends—will restrain the actor from taking account of those consequences which indirectly shape the means and ends of policy. Because of the necessarily abstract and selective character of the formal criteria of judgment, there will always be a minimum residue of unanticipated consequence.[14]

2. *Commitment as a basic mechanism in the generation of unanticipated consequences.*—The sociologically significant source of unanticipated con-sequences inherent in the organizational process may be summed up in the concept of "commitment." This term has been used throughout this study to focus attention upon the structural conditions which shape organiza-tional behavior. This is in line with the sociological directive, stated above, that constraints imposed by the system will be emphasized. A commitment in social action is an enforced line of action; it refers to decision dictated by the force of circumstance with the result that the free or scientific adjust-ment of means and ends is effectively limited. The commitment may be to goals, as where the existence of an organization in relation to a client public depends on the fulfillment of certain objectives;[15] or, less obviously, to means, derived from the recalcitrant nature of the tools at hand. The commitments generated by the use of self-activating and recalcitrant tools are expressed in the proliferation of unintended consequences.[16]

The types of commitment in organizational behavior identify the condi-tions under which a high frequency of unanticipated consequences may be expected to occur:

a. *Commitments enforced by uniquely organizational imperatives.*—An organizational system, whatever the need or intent which called it into being, generates imperatives derived from the need to maintain the system. We say that once having taken the organizational road we are com-mitted to action which will fulfill the requirements of order, discipline, unity, defense, and consent. These imperatives may demand measures of adaptation unforeseen by the initiators of the action, and may, indeed, result in a deflection of their original goals. Thus the tendency to work toward organizational unity will commit the organization as a whole to a policy originally relevant to only a part of the program. This becomes especially true where a unifying doctrine is given definite content by one subgroup: in order to preserve its special interpretation the subgroup presses for the extension of that interpretation to the entire organization so that the special content may be institutionalized.[17]

b. *Commitments enforced by the social character of the personnel.*— The human tools of action come to an organization shaped in special but systematic ways. Levels of aspiration and training, social ideals, class interest—these and similar factors will have molded the character of the personnel. This will make staff members resistant to demands which are inconsistent with their accustomed views and habits; the freedom of choice of the employer will be restricted, and he will find it necessary in some measure to conform to the received views and habits of the personnel. Thus, in recruiting, failure to take into account initial commitments induced by special social origins will create a situation favorable to the generation of unanticipated consequences. The TVA's agricultural leadership brought with it ideological and organizational commitments which influenced over-all policy. This was a basically uncontrolled element in the organization. It is noteworthy that where the character of any organization is self-consciously controlled, recruitment is rigidly qualified by the criterion of social (class, familial, racial) origin.

c. *Commitments enforced by institutionalization.*—Because organizations are social systems, goals or procedures tend to achieve an established, value-impregnated status. We say that they become institutionalized. Commitment to established patterns is generated, thus again restricting choice and enforcing special lines of conduct. The attempt to commit an organization to some course of action utilizes this principle when it emphasizes the creation of an established policy, or other forms of precedent. Further, the tendency of established relations and procedures to persist and extend themselves, will create the unintended consequence of committing the organization to greater involvement than provided for in the initial decision to act.[18] Where policy becomes institutionalized as doctrine, unanalyzed elements will persist, and effective behavior will be framed in terms of immediate necessities. An official doctrine whose terms are not operationally relevant will be given content in action, but this content will be informed by the special interests and problems of those to whom delegation is made. Hence doctrinal formulations will tend to reinforce the inherent hazard of delegation.[19] A variation of this situation occurs when the role of participants comes to overshadow in importance the achievement of formal goals. Action then becomes irresponsible, with respect to the formal goals, as in the "fanatical" behavior of the TVA agriculturists.[20]

d. *Commitments enforced by the social and cultural environment.*—Any attempt to intervene in history will, if it is to do more than comment upon events, find it necessary to conform to some general restraints imposed from without. The organizers of this attempt are committed to using forms of intervention consistent with the going social structure and cultural patterns. Those who ascend to power must face a host of received problems; shifts in public opinion will demand the reformulation of doctrine; the rise of competing organizations will have to be faced; and so on. The institutional context of organizational decision, when not taken into account, will result in unanticipated consequences. Thus intervention in a situation charged with conflict will mean that contending forces will weigh the consequences of that intervention for their own battle lines. The intervening organization must therefore qualify decision in terms of an outside controversy into which it is drawn despite itself. More obviously, the existence of centers of power and interest in the social environment will set up resistances to, or accept and shape to some degree, the program of the organization.

e. *Commitments enforced by the centers of interest generated in the course of action.*—The organizational process continuously generates subordinate and allied groupings whose leaderships come to have a stake in the organizational status quo. This generation of centers of interest is inherent in the act of delegation. The latter derives its precarious quality from the necessity to permit discretion in the execution of function or command. But in the exercise of discretion there is a tendency for decisions to be qualified by the special goals and problems of those to whom delegation is made. Moreover, in the discretionary behavior of a section of the apparatus, action is taken in the name of the organization as a whole; the latter may then be committed to a policy or course of action which was not anticipated by its formal program. In other words, the lack of effective control over the tangential informal goals of individuals and subgroups within an organization tends to divert it from its initial path. This holds true whether delegation is to members and parts of a single organization, or to other organizations, as in the TVA's relation to the land-grant colleges.

These types of commitments create persistent tensions or dilemmas.[21] In a sense, they set the problems of decision and control, for we have identified here the key points at which organizational control breaks down. Operationally, a breakdown of control is evidenced in the generation of observable unanticipated consequences. This is the same as to say that significant possibilities inherent in the situation have not been taken into account. The extension of control, with concomitant minimization of unintended consequence, is achieved as and if the frame of reference for theory and action points the way to the significant forces at work.

The problems indicated here are perennial because they reflect the interplay of more or less irreconcilable commitments: to the goals and needs of the organization and at the same time to the special demands of the tools or means at hand. Commitment to the tools of action is indispensable; it is of the nature of these tools to be dynamic and self-activating; yet the pursuit of the goals which initiated action demands continuous effort to control the instruments it has generated. This is a general source of tension in all action mediated by human, and especially organizational, tools.

The systematized commitments of an organization define its character. Day-to-day decision, relevant to the actual problems met in the translation of policy into action, create precedents, alliances, effective symbols, and personal loyalties which transform the organization from a profane, manipulable instrument into something having a sacred status and thus resistant to treatment simply as a means to some external goal. That is why organizations are often cast aside when new goals are sought.

The analysis of commitment is thus an effective tool for making explicit the structural factors relevant to decision in organized action. Attention is directed to the concrete process of choice, selecting those factors in the environment of decision which limit alternatives and enforce uniformities of behavior. When we ask, "To what are we committed?" we are speaking of the logic of action, not of contractual obligations freely assumed. So long as goals are given, and the impulse to act persists, there will be a series of enforced lines of action demanded by the nature of the tools at hand. These commitments may lead to unanticipated consequences resulting in a deflection of original goals.[22]

THE COÖPTATIVE MECHANISM

The frame of reference stated above includes the directive that organizational behavior be analyzed in terms of organizational response to organizational need. One such need is specified as "the security of the organization as a whole in relation to social forces in its environment." Responses, moreover, are themselves repetitive—may be thought of as mechanisms, following the terminology of analytical psychology in its analysis of the ego and its mechanisms of defense. One such organizational mechanism is ideology; another, which has been the primary focus of this study, we have termed coöptation. In the Introduction we have defined this concept as "the process of absorbing new elements into the leadership or policy-determining structure of an organization as a means of averting threats to its stability or existence." Further, this general mechanism assumes two basic forms: Formal coöptation, when there is a need to establish the legitimacy of authority or the administrative accessibility of the relevant public; and informal coöptation, when there is a need of adjustment to the pressure of specific centers of power within the community.

Coöptation in administration is a process whereby either power or the burdens of power, or both, are shared. On the one hand, the actual center of authority and decision may be shifted or made more inclusive, with or without any public recognition of the change; on the other hand, public responsibility for and participation in the exercise of authority may be shared with new elements, with or without the actual redistribution of power itself. The organizational imperatives which define the need for coöptation arise out of a situation in which formal authority is actually or potentially in a state of imbalance with respect to its institutional environment. On the one hand, the formal authority may fail to reflect the true balance of power within the community; on the other hand, it may lack a sense of historical legitimacy, or be unable to mobilize the community for action. Failure to reflect the true balance of power will necessitate a realistic adjustment to those centers of institutional strength which are in a position to strike organized blows and thus to enforce concrete demands. This issue may be met by the kind of coöptation which results in an actual sharing of power. However, the need for a sense of legitimacy may require an adjustment to the people in their undifferentiated aspect, in order that a feeling of general acceptance may be developed. For this purpose, it may not be necessary actually to share power: the creation of a "front" or the open incorporation of accepted elements into the structure of the organization may suffice. In this way, an aura of respectability will be gradually transferred from the coöpted elements to the organization as a whole, and at the same time a vehicle of administrative accessibility may be established.

We may suggest the hypothesis: Coöptation which results in an actual sharing of power will tend to operate informally, and correlatively, coöptation oriented toward legitimization or accessibility will tend to be effected through formal devices. Thus, an opposition party may be formally coöpted into a political administration through such a device as the appointment of opposition leaders to ministerial posts. This device may be utilized when an actual sharing of power is envisioned, but it is especially useful when its object is the creation of public solidarity, the legitimization of the representativeness of the government. In such circumstances, the opposition leaders may become the prisoners of the government, exchanging the hope of future power (through achieving public credit for holding office in a time of crisis) for the present function of sharing responsibility for the acts of the administration. The formal, public character of the coöptation is to fulfill the function of an adjustment to organized centers of institutional power within the community, it may be necessary to maintain relationships which, however consequential, are informal and covert. If adjustment to specific nucleuses of power becomes public, then the legitimacy of the formal authority, as representative of a theoretically undifferentiated community (the "people as a whole"), may be undermined. It therefore becomes useful and often essential for such coöptation to remain in the shadowland of informal interaction.

The informal coöptation of existing nucleuses of power into the total (formal plus informal) policy-determining structure of an organization, symptomatic of an underlying stress, is a mechanism of adjustment to concrete forces. On this level, interaction occurs among those who are in a position to muster forces and make them count, which means that the stake is a substantive reallocation of authority, rather than any purely verbal readjustment. Formal coöptation, however, is rather more ambiguous in relation to de facto reallocations of power. The sense of insecurity which is interpreted by a leadership as indicating a need for an increased sense of legitimacy in the community is a response to something generalized and diffuse. There is no hard-headed demand for a sharing of power coming from self-conscious institutions which are in a position to challenge the formal authority itself. The way things seem becomes, in this context, more important than the way they are, with the result that verbal formulas (degenerating readily into propaganda), and formal organizational devices, appear to be adequate to fill the need. The problem becomes one of manipulating public opinion, something which is necessarily beside the point when dealing with an organized interest group having an established and self-conscious leadership.

Formal coöptation ostensibly shares authority, but in doing so is involved in a dilemma. The real point is the sharing of the public symbols or administrative burdens of authority, and consequently public responsibility, without the transfer of substantive power; it therefore becomes necessary to insure that the coöpted elements do not get out of hand, do not take advantage of their formal position to encroach upon the actual arena of decision. Consequently, formal coöptation requires informal control over the coöpted elements lest the unity of command and decision be imperiled. This paradox is one of the sources of persistent tension between theory and practice in organizational behavior. The leadership, by the very nature of its position, is committed to two conflicting goals: if it ignores the need for participation, the goal of coöperation may be jeopardized; if participation is allowed to go too far, the continuity of leadership and policy may be threatened.[23]

THE EMPIRICAL ARGUMENT RESTATED

Apart from the interest of analytical theory, the statement above explains the special focus of this inquiry and the basis for its obviously selective approach to the TVA experience. That frame of reference has guided the empirical analysis, of which the following is a brief recapitulation.

1. *The grass-roots theory became a protective ideology.*—In chapter ii, an attempt was made to explain the high self-consciousness of the TVA, as expressed in the grass-roots doctrine, on the basis of the function of that doctrine in facilitating acceptance of the Authority in its area of operation and in fulfilling the need for some general justification of its existence as a unique type of governmental agency. The TVA was revolutionary both to the attitudes of local people and institutions and to the federal governmental system. By adopting the grass-roots doctrine the Authority was able to stand as the champion of local institutions and at the same time to devise a point of view which could be utilized in general justification of its managerial autonomy within the federal system. However, allegiance to this doctrine, and translation of it into policy commitments, have created serious disaffection between TVA and other branches of the federal government, including the Department of Agriculture and the Department of the Interior. As a result, on the basis of the TVA experience, these departments have been moved to oppose the extension of the TVA form of organization to other areas, a fact which is consequential for the future of the Authority itself.

2. *The agricultural program was delegated*[24] *to an organized administrative constituency.*—In the major example within TVA of grass-roots procedure—the Authority's fertilizer distribution program—there was con-

structed a strong constituency-relation involving the land-grant college system on the one hand and the Agricultural Relations Department of TVA on the other. This constituency relation may be viewed as a case of informal coöptation, wherein strong centers of influence in the Valley were absorbed covertly into the policy-determining structure of the TVA. The TVA's Agricultural Relations Department assumed a definite character, including a set of sentiments valuing the land-grant college system as such and accepting the mission of defending that system within the Authority. In effecting this representations, the TVA agriculturists have been able to take advantage of the special prerogatives accruing to them from their formal status as an integral part of the Authority, including the exercise of discretion within their own assigned jurisdiction and the exertion of pressure upon the evolution of general policy within the Authority as a whole. The special role and character of the TVA agricultural group limited its outlook with respect to the participation of Negro institutions as grass-roots resources and created a special relation to the American Farm Bureau Federation. Yet the operation of this coöptative process probably did much to enhance the stability of the TVA within its area and especially to make possible the mobilization of support in an hour of need. In this sense, one cannot speak of the decisions which led to this situation as mistakes.

3. *In a context of controversy, the TVA's commitments to its agricultural constituency resulted in a factional alignment involving unanticipated consequences for its role on the national scene.*—In the exercise of discretion in agriculture, the TVA entered a situation charged with organizational and political conflict. The New Deal agricultural agencies, such as Farm Security Administration and Soil Conservation Service, came under attack of the powerful American Farm Bureau Federation, which thought of them as threats to its special avenue of access to the farm population, the extension services of the land-grant colleges. Under the pressure of its agriculturists, the Authority did not recognize Farm Security Administration and sought to exclude Soil Conservation Service from operation within the Valley area. This resulted in the politically paradoxical situation that the eminently New Deal TVA failed to support agencies with which it shared a political communion, and aligned itself with the enemies of those agencies.

4. *Under the pressure of its agriculturists, the TVA gradually altered a significant aspect of its character as a conservation agency.*—The TVA agricultural group, reflecting local attitudes and interests, fought against the policy of utilizing public ownership of land as a conservation measure and thus effectively contributed to the alteration of the initial policy of the Authority in this respect. The issue of public ownership is taken as character-defining in the sense that it is a focus of controversy and division, and it was such within the TVA for an extended period. The single-minded pursuit of its ideological and constituency interests led the agricultural group to involve the Authority in a controversy with the U.S. Department

of the Interior over the management of TVA-owned lands. In this matter, as in those mentioned above, the mechanics of pressure and representation are detailed in the body of the study.

5. *The grass-roots utilization of voluntary associations represents a sharing of the burdens of and responsibility for power, rather than of power itself.*—In chapter vii, the voluntary association device—especially, but not exclusively, in the agricultural program—is interpreted as a case of formal coöptation, primarily for promoting organized access to the public but also as a means of supporting the legitimacy of the TVA program. Typically, this has meant that actual authority, and to a large extent the organizational machinery, has been retained in the hands of the administering agency. After nine years of operation, the county soil associations handling TVA fertilizer were found to be still tools of the county agent system, to which the TVA test-demonstration program was delegated. In connection with this analysis, an operational test for locating control over coöpted citizens' groups is described, as suggested in the question: Is approach to the association by outside elements channeled through officials of the coöpting agency?

IMPLICATIONS FOR DEMOCRATIC PLANNING

In venturing this interpretation, we are pointing to some of the significant problems which must be faced when the attempt is made to combine democracy and planning.[25] For planning implies large-scale intervention and the extended use of organizational instruments. If such concepts as "democracy" are to be more than honorific symbols which mobilize opinion, it is essential to make explicit the forces which will operate to qualify and perhaps transform the democratic process.

There are three major considerations, three sources of paradox and tension, which emerge out of this study, so far as it has implications for democratic planning:

1. Ideologies must be seen in the context of the needs they serve; it is a reliable assumption that something more urgent than patterns of belief will lie behind the strong advocacy of doctrine by an organizational leadership. The unanalyzed terms must be closely examined, for it is also a reliable expectation that some covert adaptation in terms of immediate necessity will have provided content for emotion-laden but procedurally indefinite terms. It is perhaps a good rule to see whether the ambiguities, the inherent dilemmas, of the attempt to fulfill doctrinal demands are squarely faced; where these are denied out of hand, the ideological function of the doctrine is obliquely confirmed.

2. It is essential to recognize that power in a community is distributed among those who can mobilize resources—organizational, psychological, and economic—and these can effectively shape the character and role of governmental instrumentalities. This has a dual significance. It may result in the perversion of policy determined through representative institutions; and at the same time, this fact offers a tool for ensuring the responsibility

of public agencies to their client publics. Consequently, it is naïve to suppose that there is anything inherently bad in the situation wherein private organizations paralleling but independent of a governmental administrative structure have a decisive influence on its social policy. Again, however, the situation is inherently ambiguous. This ambiguity must be explicitly recognized, and its mechanics understood, if realistic controls are to be instituted.

3. The tendency of democratic participation to break down into administrative involvement requires continuous attention. This must be seen as part of the organizational problem of democracy and not as a matter of the morals or good will of administrative agents. A realistic examination of the factors which define formal coöptation also permits us to make explicit precisely those points at which changes in procedure will be effective in reinforcing meaningful democracy.

In general, therefore, we have been concerned to formulate some of the underlying tendencies which are likely to inhibit the democratic process. Like all conservative or pessimistic criticism, such a statement of inherent problems seems to cast doubt upon the possibility of complete democratic achievement. It does cast such a doubt. The alternative, however, is the transformation of democracy into a utopian notion which, unaware of its internal dangers, is unarmed to meet them.

The TVA has been a particularly good subject for the analysis of these problems. This is so precisely because it may be said that the Authority has, on the whole, very effectively achieved some of its major purposes, including the mobilization of a staff of very high quality. No one is surprised when a weak or corrupt governmental agency does not fulfill its doctrinal promise. When, however, a morally strong and fundamentally honest organization is subject to the kind of process we have described, then the pervasive significance of that process becomes materially enhanced. In a sense, it is just because TVA is a relatively good example of democratic administration that the evidences of weakness in this respect are so important. It is just because the TVA stands as something of a shining example of incorruptibility in such major matters as noncapitulation to local political interests in the hiring of personnel or to local utility interests in public policy that the evidence of covert coöptation in the agricultural program attains its general significance.

For the things which are important in the analysis of democracy are those which bind the hands of good men. We then learn that something more than virtue is necessary in the realm of circumstance and power.

NOTES

[1] John Dewey, *Problems of Men* (New York: Philosophical Library, 1946), p. 221.

[2] Although responsibility for the analysis rests solely with the author, it should be emphasized that this study was made possible by the willingness of TVA to make its records and personnel available. This is a happy precedent which we may hope will be followed by other organizations, public and private.

[3] Some of the materials quoted in the study are unofficial in the sense that they would be vigorously edited before receiving even the public status of a memorandum

sent to another department within TVA. This would be so with comparable documents in any large organization, public or private.

[4] The author spent most of his year's stay at TVA in daily contact with personnel of the agency. A number of weeks was spent in intensive contact with extension service personnel in the field.

[5] For a fuller statement than the summary which follows see Philip Selznick, "Foundations of the Theory of Organization," *American Sociological Review*, 13 (February, 1948).

[6] Thus, while approaching his materials within a guiding frame of reference, the author was not committed by this framework to any special hypothesis about the actual events. Indeed, he began his work with the hypothesis that informally the grass-roots policy would mean domination by TVA, because of its resources, energy, and program. After the first two months in the field, however, this hypothesis was abandoned as a major illuminating notion.

[7] For discussion of informal organization see F. J. Roethlisberger and W. J. Dickson, *Management and the Worker* (Cambridge, Mass.: Harvard University Press, 1941), p. 524ff; also Chester I. Barnard, *The Functions of the Executive* (Cambridge, Mass.: Harvard University Press, 1938), Chap. ix; Wilbert E. Moore, *Industrial Relations and the Social Order* (New York: Macmillan, 1946), Chap. xv.

[8] See Talcott Parsons, "The Present Position and Prospects of Systematic Theory in Sociology," in *Twentieth Century Sociology,* George Gurvitch and Wilbert E. Moore, eds. (New York: Philosophical Library, 1945).

[9] As Robert K. Merton has pointed out to the author, the concept of "basic needs" in organizational analysis may be open to objections similar to those against the concept of instinct. To be sure, the needs require independent demonstration; they should be theoretically grounded independently of imputations from observed responses. However, we may use the notion of "organizational need" if we understand that it refers to stable systems of variables which, with respect to many changes in organizational structure and behavior, are independent.

[10] In terms of origins, the TVA's policy—though not the grass-roots doctrine *qua* doctrine—of channeling its agricultural program through the land-grant colleges of the Valley states may be adequately referred to such factors as the nature of the formal agricultural program, the resources available for its implementation, and the administrative rationale which seemed conclusive to leading participants. Moreover, these factors may sustain the continued existence of the policy, and it may therefore seem superfluous when extraneous factors are brought in and somewhat tangential explanations are offered. But when we direct our attention to the meaning of the policy in terms of certain indirect but internally relevant consequences—as for the role of TVA in the agricultural controversy—we have begun to recast our observation of the policy (taken as a set of events) itself. We are then concerned not with the question, "how did the grass-roots policy come into being?" but with the question, "what are the implications of the grass-roots policy for the organizational position and character of TVA?"

[11] Consequences unanticipated from the viewpoint of the formal structure are not necessarily undesired. On the contrary, the result may be a satisfactory adjustment to internal and external circumstances, upon which the leadership may find it convenient to declare that the results were actually intended, though close analysis might show that this is actually a rationalization. In this type of unintended consequence, some need is fulfilled. The same unintended consequence may fulfill a need for a part of the organization and at the same time cause difficulties for the whole, and conversely. Many unintended consequences are, of course, sociologically irrelevant. For an early statement of this general problem, see Robert K. Merton, "The Unanticipated Consequences of Purposive Social Action," *American Sociological Review*, I (December, 1936).

[12] Where unintended consequences occur due to error, or to individual idiosyncrasy, they are sociologically irrelevant. However, there is often, though not always, a

systematically nonrational factor at work whose presence is manifested by mistakes and personality problems.

[13] This follows, of course, from the hypothetical, and therefore discriminating and ordering, status of the end-in-view. See John Dewey, *Logic: The Theory of Inquiry* (New York: Holt, 1938), pp. 496–497.

[14] The use of the terms "end-in-view" and "anticipated" may easily lead to the fallacy of formulating this problem as one of the subjective awareness of the participants. This is a serious error. What is really involved is that which is anticipated or unanticipated by the system of discrimination and judgment which is applied to the means at hand. This may, and very often does, involve subjective anticipation or its want, but need not do so. Moreover, the system may be adjusted so as to be able to take account of factors previously unpredicted and uncontrolled. This addition of systematically formulated criteria of relevance occurs continuously, as in the recognition of morale factors in industry. In the situation detailed above, the high self-consciousness of the American Farm Bureau Federation apparently led it to anticipate the possible rivalry from a new organization set up under the Agricultural Adjustment Administration, since it took steps to ward off this threat. See above, p. 588. This is no accidental perspicacity but a result of the systematic consideration of just such possible consequences from the implementation of new legislation. However, the tendency to ignore factors not considered by the formal system— not so much subjectively as in regard to the competence of the system to control them—is inherent in the necessities of action and can never be eliminated.

[15] As in the TVA's commitment to become a successful electric power business; this type of commitment was much milder in the distribution of fertilizer, permitting adaptation in this field which would contribute to the fulfillment of the prior commitment to electricity.

[16] Our use of the notion of unanticipated consequence assumes that the functional significance of such consequences is traceable within a specific field of influence and interaction. Thus price decisions made by a small enterprise affect the market (cumulatively with others), with ultimate unanticipated and uncontrolled consequence for future pricing decision. This is not an organizational process. When, however, the retailer builds up good will or makes decisions which will enforce his dependence upon some manufacturer, these are organizational acts within a theoretically controllable field, and are analyzable within the frame of reference set forth above.

[17] In the TVA, the agriculturists made vigorous efforts to extend their interpretation of the grass-roots policy to the Authority as a whole; in respect to the federal government, the TVA attempts to have its special interpretation of administrative decentralization become general public policy.

[18] See above, p. 70f.

[19] We have reviewed above, pp. 59–64, the unanalyzed abstractions in TVA's grass-roots doctrine, which are given content and meaning by the pressure of urgent organizational imperatives.

[20] See above, p. 205ff.

[21] In effect, we have restated here some of the basic points made in the discussion above of the inherent dilemmas of the TVA doctrine. See pp. 69–74.

[22] The British Labor Party, when it assumed power in 1945, had to accept a large number of commitments which followed simply from the effort to govern in those circumstances, independently of its special program. "Meeting a crisis," in a women's club as well as in a cabinet, is a precondition for the institution of special measures. To assume leadership is to accept these conditions.

[23] The analysis of unanticipated consequence and commitment is indispensable to the interpretation of behavior in terms of the coöptative mechanism. The commitments made in the course of action generate unanticipated consequences; in analyzing the function of these consequences we must construct a theory which will explain them as events consistent with the needs and potentialities of the system. At the same

time, it must be understood that to formulate such defensive mechanisms as coöptation is to state possible predicates. For the full understanding of organization it will be necessary to construct a system of such relevant responses which can serve to illuminate concrete cases.

24 Some TVA officials would question the use of "delegated" here. However, this seems to be the most significant summary word to use, in terms of its implications. Moreover, in his own summation of TVA policy upon the occasion of his leaving the TVA chairmanship, David E. Lilienthal said: "The TVA has by persistent effort delegated and thereby decentralized its functions. . . ." New York *Times*, November 13, 1946, p. 56.

25 We speak here only of the implications of this analysis. That the grass-roots approach has wider implications of importance for democratic planning is sufficiently obvious.

40 SHELDON L. MESSINGER

Organizational Transformation: A Case Study of a Declining Social Movement

It is generally recognized that the organized arms of value-oriented social movements[1] may remain intact long after the movements themselves have lost general impetus. While it is to be expected that these structures will adapt to their changed circumstances, little attention has as yet been given to either the process or product of this adaptation. This paper reports a study of certain organizational consequences of the decline of the Townsend Movement.

THE TOWNSEND MISSION AND THE
END OF RECRUITMENT

While the old age pension movement seems to be gaining impetus in the United States, the Townsend Movement has all but vanished. To understand this seeming paradox it is necessary to examine the Townsend mission. This has been, and continues to be, not simply national pensions for the aged, but national pensions for the aged *as a mechanism for alleviating or preventing economic dislocation*. The mission is a blending of issues born of the 1930s, and the continued identification of Townsendites with it aids in understanding the movement's decline and the nature of its remaining structure.

Two sorts of data support this characterization of the Townsend mission, as well as the continued identification of the Organization with it.

First, the Townsend Plan,[2] major subject of most Townsend pronouncements, has maintained features directly linking pensions to economic re

Reprinted from *American Sociological Review*, 20:1 (1955) pp. 3–20 by permission of the author and the publisher.

construction. Its provision requiring that the pension be spent within thirty days is intended to provide jobs by keeping money in circulation. Its stipulation that prospective recipients must cease work to become eligible is designed to combat "technological unemployment."[3] These are the key to Townsend claims that theirs is not "just another pension plan." Further, leaders justify changes in other features of the Plan as occasioned by the aim of economic reconstruction. For example, the famous "200 dollars a month," from the first a legislative impediment, was formally discarded in all forms in 1943. Informally it is still mentioned as "essential to the Plan" in the sense that at least this much is requisite to "keep the economy going." Other changeable features, justified in all their forms as necessary to economic reconstruction, include the means of financing and designation of those to receive the pension.

Second, the Organization aside from the Plan has continued to link the pension and depression issues. In 1936, a year after passage of national social security legislation, the Organization changed its name from "Old Age Revolving Pensions, Ltd." to "Townsend National Recovery Plan, Inc.," emphasizing that its mission was far from complete. Not until 1948 did the less anachronous "Townsend Plan, Inc." become the organizational style. The *Townsend National Weekly*, official newspaper of the Organization, has become since 1941 a veritable compendium of "signs" pointing to "impending" economic disaster. Throughout World War II and the post-war boom, Townsendites continued to circulate tracts stressing that their Organization aimed at "a program to bring about full industrial production for the Nation . . . [and] make jobs for the jobless."[4]

While such aims may again gain currency, it is suggested that under the changed conditions following the end of the depression the Townsend mission was deprived of relevance. Continued identification with this mission has constituted a serious block to Townsend membership maintenance and to the recruitment of new Townsendites. Combined with the short life-expectancies of old Townsendites, this has meant a rapid depletion of the Organization's ranks (see Table 1).[5] In this situation, other "single-

TABLE 1. NATIONAL AND CALIFORNIA TOWNSEND MEMBERSHIP DECLINE, 1936–1951

	National membership	Percent drop	California membership	Percent drop
1936	2,250,000		330,000	
1951 . . :	56,656	97.5	6,839	97.9

Sources: National and California membership figures for 1936 from U. S. House of Representatives, Select Committee Investigating Old Age Pension Organizations pursuant to H. Res. 443, *Hearings*, 74th Cong., 2nd Sess., Washington, D. C.: 1936 (hereafter: *Hearings: H. Res. 443*), pp. 41–42, 208. National membership for 1951 from Holtzman, *loc. cit.* California membership figure for 1951 compiled from records in the Townsend Archives.

minded" old age groups, working to modify existing state aid legislation, have developed to absorb the membership which might earlier have gone to the Townsendites. It is in this context that the Townsend Organization has been transformed.

ORGANIZATIONAL TRANSFORMATION

The Tendency to Deflection   Townsend leaders have attempted to cope with the challenge to their social base. In the process, they have been constrained to direct action in ways deflecting the Organization from its central mission.

The first indication of this tendency came in early 1940 when California Townsendites were urged to aid in qualifying an initiative readjusting state aid legislation.[6] While the campaign was brief and the initiative was not qualified, the event is noteworthy since before this time national leaders had actively campaigned against any proposal at the state level.[7] Further, they had always carefully disassociated themselves from state "aid" proposals. The "pension," on a national level and not involving indigence requirements, was the proper Townsend goal.

Leadership purposes in supporting this proposal are not far to seek. Urging his lieutenants to support the measure, the California leader said: "Even if we should fail [to qualify it], it is believed we can secure enough publicity and good will to justify the effort. We think we can enlist many to join our ranks as a result of this campaign."[8]

In 1943, California Townsendites entered a full-blown campaign for state old age pensions.[9] The nature of this measure permitted it to be presented by both national[10] and state leaders as a "first step" toward the national Townsend Plan. Thus, while only a state-wide proposal with a dollar demand geared to existing state aid legislation (60 dollars was asked), both the "compulsory spending" and "cease work" features of the national Plan were intact. Further, indigence requirements were absent, meaning effectively the end of a state "aid" program and the institution of "pensions" if the measure passed.[11]

The initiative was qualified and placed before the voters in November 1944. It was defeated by over a million votes.[12]

By 1947 membership was at a new low, recruitment at a dead halt, and George McLain's old age pressure-group successfully competing for the allegiance of the California aged. Aware of the challenge, the California leader proposed a new local effort to national headquarters by saying:

> [Even] Dr. Townsend [who is generally opposed to local efforts] has consistently said that "we *must* put on an initiative in California . . . even if we know we will fail before we start. . . ." [This] for the reason that GM [George McLain] has announced that he, too, is going to sponsor a constitutional amendment proposing practically the same objectives. . . . If we fail to present . . . [a local] program, it is only natural that a large number of our own members will be inclined to support him in his efforts. . . . Many people

have lost hope and interest in any national program becoming a reality in the near future.[13]

By no stretch of the imagination could the new measure proposed by state leaders be identified as a "little Townsend Plan."[14] First, unlike the 1943–1944 proposal, it was specifically drawn within the framework of existing state legislation for old age assistance and indigence requirements were present.[15] Second, both the all-important "compulsory spending" and "cease work" provisions of the Plan were absent. Townsend propaganda could no longer claim that their measure would effect any significant change in the economic structure.[16]

National leaders at first opposed making a new localized proposal on the grounds that another defeat would do the Movement's national position no good.[17] In August 1947, conceding to California's pressures, they suggested that campaign funds should be raised *outside* the Organization.[18] As late as October 1947, in the midst of efforts to raise money in California for the promotion of the initiative, national leaders carried out two mass meetings in the state to collect funds for national headquarters over the unanswered objections of the California leader.[19]

By June 1948 it was clear that Townsendites had not qualified their initiative, but that McLain had qualified his. State leaders remained as silent as possible in the face of this proposal with "practically the same objectives" and tried to refocus membership attention on national issues.[20]

The passage of McLain's constitutional amendment at the polls was quickly followed by a move for repeal. When the repeal initiative qualified, California Townsend leaders faced a serious dilemma. They could not support repeal, for the advantages brought to the aged by McLain's amendment were patent—e.g., a raise in monthly grant, the end of "relative's responsibility." Nor could they fight repeal, lest an issue now entirely identified with McLain absorb all their membership's attention and funds. To meet the situation, California leaders tried to straddle the fence by proposing measures to the legislature to supplant McLain's.[21] National leadership, on the other hand, insisted that the Townsend Organization stay clear of the battle, on the belated grounds that it was for national, not state, pensions. In July 1949, with a repeal measure on the ballot, the California leader wrote the following to national headquarters:

> We [California leaders] thought that [some anti-repeal statement] was necessary as many of our members are supporting McLain financially and attending his meetings, to do what they can to hold the gains they have received. . . . [Now, in view of your position] . . . it seems all we can do is drift; let McLain get the money and our members and let things take their course and keep trying to focus attention of the Washington, D. C. work.[22]

As late as 1953, the crisis continued. Too weak to promote state legislation directly, state leadership fluctuated between "preserving gains" made by others, "preventing setbacks," all within the framework of state aid legislation, and focusing attention on national issues. But now, for state leaders, the national issue, above all, is simply success. Late in 1952 the California leader wrote:

> I realize that we have always felt that it was necessary to stick to our "full program," but if the Republicans will not now accept it "in full," it seems to me that we should try to take the lead with a bill *they will accept* and get something during the next session. . . . I feel that if we don't do something along this line, we can expect McLain to capitalize on the situation and we will lose more and more of our few supporters.[23]

What we have seen here is a tendency to deflection from central aims on the part of Townsend leaders. At the national level, this tendency has been largely checked through a clearer appreciation of the "drift of things" by national leaders themselves. For this drift could only eventuate in the break-up of the national Organization. At the state level, leaders have tended to exchange identity for security in their search for a viable mission. But here, the pressure from national leadership, plus the successful capturing of vital issues by competing groups,[24] have served to hold state leaders within the Organization and to the Townsend mission.

The Tendency to Salesmanship   Loss of mass support has brought increasing financial difficulty to the Townsend Organization.[25] Adaptation to this circumstance has transformed Townsend leader-follower relations in such a way as to make recruit interest in the Townsend mission increasingly problematical.

Aside from advertising in the *Townsend National Weekly*,[26] early Townsend income came largely from the small contributions of individual members. Propaganda materials were sold in large quantities, and royalties accrued from such items as Townsend auto-stickers, buttons, and license-plate holders. It is to be noted that all of these devices *assume commitment on the part of contributors* to the Townsend Organization and its mission.

By 1939, however, members were being urged to purchase *consumable* items bearing the Townsend name. This year saw a Townsend candy bar, then "Townsend Old Fashioned Horehound Drops." In 1940, a Townsend coffee was announced. A little later a "Townsend Club Toilet Soap" and a "Townsend Club Granulated Soap" appeared. In all of these enterprises the Organization merely lent its name; funds, if received, accrued from royalties. The change from auto-stickers, etc., was small but significant because purchase of these new items did not assume commitment to the Organization or its Plan. Townsendites were urged to ask for these items at their usual shopping places, thus, to encourage store owners to stock them. The Organization had yet to become a distributor itself. This was to come.[27]

Beginning in 1943, a series of health foods was offered to members. Of these, "Dr. Townsend's Vitamins and Minerals" soon became the major item. At first distributed only from national headquarters, by 1951 state offices had become distribution points, and Club members were selling pills on commission. In this year, the pills provided one-fifth of the total national income. Intraorganizational communications of all kinds reveal in this period a striking shift from programmatic matters to concern with promoting this product. Perhaps even more significant for the long run, advertising of the pills has come to leave the Organization and its Plan unmentioned. The most elaborate piece yet prepared (1953) is simply titled "Vitamins and Minerals by Francis E. Townsend, M.D." Its message is entirely one of "health" and "price." Headquarters for the pills is identified as "Dr. Townsend's Vitamins and Minerals" rather than the earlier "Townsend Plan, Inc." Besides this, national radio advertising has been considered, and discussions of this matter have placed promotion of the Plan aside.

This type of money-raising activity is to be clearly differentiated from that of earlier days. Townsend leaders have come to purvey items whose purchase assumes no commitment to the Townsend mission. The pills, especially, are amenable for presentation to others, *once to be seen as potential Townsendites*, without invoking any discussion of the Organization and its aims.

The transformation of leadership activities from the presentation of a program to the purveying of products can be traced in the present approach to recruitment as well. In May 1952, discussing a proposal to offer a 50 percent commission to members who brought in new recruits, Dr. Townsend said:

> We have innumerable people in our clubs who can be taught to sell. Let's push them into learning by making it necessary to do so if they wish to remain members of a club. After they have learned *what* to do, I believe they will continue to do—with a 50 percent bait as inducement.[28]

In October of the same year, national headquarters distributed a "training manual" designed to "double the readership of *Townsend National Weekly* and the membership of each Townsend club."[29] The striking quality of this "manual" is that it makes clear that Townsend leaders *no longer even seek active support at large*. The issue has become simply support in itself. Members are told:

> Many big business organizations give their salesmen sales manuals written from long experience in the technique of winning friends to a product. We've done the same for you. . . . Whether you're building a model boat or being a BUSY BEE, tools and technique are the secret of success.[30]

How to extract the "cost" in manageable installments is outlined; little is said about the urgency or value of the mission at hand. The total impression received is that the best salesman is he who receives money with the least pain to the customer. And this is no doubt correct. For Townsend leaders no longer seek "converts" so much as "customers."

The Tendency to "Pure" Recreation   Membership activity at the level of the Clubs[31] provides a final example of the transformation of the Townsend Organization.

Townsend Club "business meetings" are remarkably similar in both form and content. Similarity of form has been encouraged by the various *Townsend Club Manuals,* each containing a procedural outline, plus local leadership unpracticed in organizational ways. Whatever variation is found in content is largely accounted for by the make-up of the Club membership. Clubs with a preponderance of highly religious members substitute "sings" for card playing. Aside from formalities, Club meetings are given to discussions of plans for social activities such as are discussed below. The usual meeting is attended by less than fifteen persons, lasts a half an hour, and is adjourned. But no one leaves. More likely than not, five or ten more people enter. Card tables are set up, and what seems to the writer to be the "real" business of the evening begins: recreation. This latter may last for several hours.[32]

This pattern may even be formalized. Examination of Club minutes often revealed that at some time in the past a motion had carried to limit the "business meeting" to an hour or less. Not all members agree that this is the proper order of things. Almost every Club has its "vocal Townsendite," a member always ready to take the floor and present the Organizational mission. Precisely toward these members such motions had been directed. The "vocal Townsendite," once perhaps a Club president, had become an outcast in his own Club. If in any executive role, he can ordinarily be found on the membership committee—a position nobody seemed to want, for obvious reasons. And even here he may remain under fire: many members feel that the membership committees misrepresent Club aims by "selling the Plan too hard," i.e., presenting its realization as imminent ("even now").

Not only are membership social activities built right into Club meetings, but some Clubs have additional "pot-luck nights" or "weekly dances" specifically designed to attract nonmembers. These activities would seem to furnish ideal occasions for recruitment and the distribution of Townsend propaganda. The evidence in hand suggests that once they did, but no more. Several Club leaders informed the writer that propagandizing would only lower participation, thus reduce sorely needed funds. As public interest in the Plan has flagged, there has been a related change in the nature of Townsend social activities. They have become from the viewpoint of Townsend Club leaders purely fund-raising devices. In turn these activities have become, from the viewpoint of nonmember participants, purely social.

The "vocal Townsendite" may object to this. In one Los Angeles Club a member insisted that the *Townsend National Weekly* be sold at social events and recruiting attempts made. This same member, then Club president, was the occasion of so much dissension in Club ranks that he was not reelected—which is unusual in Club histories. The next (and 1953) president, while mildly unhappy that many who attend Club social functions "don't know what we stand for," seems more distressed by any falling-off of attendance at these affairs. Further, he regards social groups (e.g., public park dance clubs) as his "most serious competition," not the McLain Organization.

This phenomenon is not far different from that of the Townsend pills. The object of these affairs, as with the pills, is to raise money. This is best done, now, on a "business" basis. The business at hand, in this instance is providing recreation. And to this business local Townsend leaders apply themselves.

SUMMARY AND CONCLUSIONS: THE PROCESS AND PRODUCT OF ADAPTATION TO DECLINE

In the ascendant phases, when social forces press for reconstruction and changes are still in the offing, the concern of leaders and members of social movements alike is with those things that must be done to translate discontent into effective and concerted action. An evident condition of this orientation is discontent itself. In turn, this discontent must be supplied or renewed by social forces which, it must be believed, can be ameliorated by banding together. These provide the dynamic of value-oriented social movements, as well as the characteristic missions with which their organized arms become identified.

When the movements themselves lose impetus through a shift in the constellation of social forces, their organized arms are deprived of conditions necessary to sustain them in their original form. But organizations are not necessarily dissolved by the abatement of the forces initially conjoining to produce them. They may gain a certain degree of autonomy from their bases and continue to exist. We will expect, however, that the abatement of the particular constellation of social forces giving rise to the movement will have important consequences for the remaining structure. The most general of these is, perhaps, increasing lack of public concern for the organizational mission. This is reflected in the ending of public discussion of the issues which the organization represents or, perhaps better put, with these issues in the frame of reference that they are placed by organizational representatives. Within the organization, the abatement of social forces spells dropping membership and, more serious in the long run, the end of effective recruitment. This latter may be reinforced by the development of alternative organizational structures competing for the same potential membership. The end of recruitment is quickly transformed into financial difficulty. Where the organization has been geared to financial support from its own adherents, this last consequence will be especially crucial.

The organized arms of declining social movements will tend to adapt to these changed conditions in characteristic ways. We can broadly describe this adaptation by asserting that the dominating orientation of leaders and members shifts *from the implementation of the values the organization is taken to represent* (by leaders, members, and public alike), *to maintaining the organizational structure as such*, even at the loss of the organization's central mission.[33] To this end, leaders will be constrained to direct action toward new issues or in new ways which will attenuate the organization's identification with the particular set of aims held to be central to it. In this process, the locus of issue-selection will tend to move outside the organization, to alternative leaderships who highlighted the growing irrelevance to most of the traditional central mission. Presumably, a new mission may be found.[34] Where this is not the case, leaders will be forced to search out new means of financing as the traditional mode of appeal and reap falls on fewer and deafer ears. In this process, members, and especially potential members, will cease to be regarded as "converts" and will come to be seen as "customers." Finally, membership activities, initiated in a context of declining public interest to support a faltering organization, will work to turn what were once the incidental rewards of participation into its only meaning. This last, by altering the basis for whatever recruitment may take place, would seem to insure that the organization, if it continues to exist, will be changed from a value-implementing agency to a recreation facility. In sum, the organizational character will stand transformed.

ACKNOWLEDGMENTS

Acknowledgment is gratefully made to the Institute of Industrial Relations, University of California, Berkeley, for financial assistance in carrying out the research during the early months of 1953; to Mr. P. Leonard Jacobs and Mr. Leonard Symes, for suggestions regarding the ordering and interpretation of the data; and to Mr. John C. Cuneo, California State Organizer, Townsend Plan, Inc., for the cooperation which he and his staff extended to the writer.

NOTES

[1] "Value-oriented social movements" is a phrasing suggested to the writer by Ralph H. Turner. It refers to social movements fundamentally oriented toward rendering some change in the social structure and of sufficient force to develop organization.

[2] That version which received the widest publicity may be found in the pamphlet *Old Age Revolving Pensions, A National Plan . . . Proposed by Dr. F. E. Townsend* (Long Beach, California: Old Age Revolving Pensions, Ltd., 1934). For a more recent version see *Townsend National Weekly*, August 1, 1953. (These and other pamphlets, letters, and newspapers cited here may be found in the Townsend Archives, Library, University of California, Los Angeles.)

[3] See, e.g., *Do You Really Know the Townsend Plan?* (Townsend Press, n.d.), a pamphlet published during World War II and still circulated.

[4] *Why I Am For the Townsend Plan* (Cleveland, Ohio: Townsend Press, n.d.).

[5] Since the age-sex composition of the Townsend membership is not available, it is not possible to guage with any accuracy the loss of membership due to death and that due to dropping out. However, the large yearly membership declines following

1939 (when yearly figures first became available) indicate that major losses came from dropouts. See Abraham Holtzman, "The Townsend Movement: A Study in Old Age Pressure Politics," dissertation, Harvard University, Cambridge, Mass., 1952, p. 267 (unpublished), for yearly Townsend membership figures 1939–1951.

The long-run personnel problem is, of course, effective recruitment. The considered opinion of Townsend leaders and members is that remaining Townsendites are all "old-timers." In personal contacts with over one hundred California Townsendites, the writer found no variation in this conjecture and met only one person who had joined the Organization since 1948. The growth of such structures as George McLain's California Institute of Social Welfare, since 1941 the major old age pressure-group on the California scene, is an additional indication of what has happened to Townsend recruitment. Of McLain's 60–70,000 members in 1953, less than one percent had ever belonged to the Townsend Organization. (According to a questionnaire administered by the Institute of Industrial Relations, University of California, Berkeley.)

[6] The text of the proposal is given in full in *Townsend National Weekly*, California Edition, April 13, 1940. Its major aim was to block state recovery measures directed at old age aid recipients. For evidence that the tendency to deflection, detailed here only for the California case, was general throughout the Organization, see Holtzman, *op. cit.*, p. 512ff.

[7] See Holtzman, *op. cit.*, p. 510ff.

[8] Letter from John C. Cuneo, National Representative [for California], Townsend National Recovery Plan, Inc. (hereafter: TNRP, Inc.), to Members of the [California] State Advisory Board, Modesto, Calif.: n.d. (mim.).

[9] The proposal may be found in State of California, Secretary of State, *Proposed Amendments to Constitution, General Election, 1944* (hereafter: *Proposed Amendments: 1944*), Sacramento, Calif.: State Printing Office, 1944, p. 11.

[10] Holtzman (*op. cit.*, p. 516) reports that national headquarters contributed over 69,000 dollars to the California campaign. Further, speakers were provided and the *Townsend National Weekly* covered the campaign in detail.

[11] In George McLain's opinion it also meant the end of grants-in-aid under Federal Social Security Legislation, as he took pains to point out in his "Argument Against Initiative Proposition No. 11," *Proposed Amendments: 1944*, p. 12. He added: "The proposed law would pension rich and poor alike, thereby lessening the value of the dollar in the hands of the needy—an unjust and vicious proposal." Compare this with later Townsendite handling of McLain issues, below.

[12] State of California, Secretary, *Statement of Vote, General Election, 1944*, Sacramento, California State Printing Office, 1944, p. 29.

[13] Letter from John C. Cuneo, California State Organizer, TNRP, Inc. to Robert C. Townsend (son of Dr. F. E. Townsend and *de facto* head of the Organization), Treasurer, TNRP, Inc., Modesto, Calif.: August 14, 1947.

[14] The initiative, which may be found in the Townsend Archives, proposed raising state aid to 75 dollars per month, reduction of recipients age to 60 years, and institution of a one percent "gross income tax" to finance the measure.

[15] It is clear from the *Minutes* of [the Townsend California] State Council Meeting at Los Angeles, Calif.: July 26 to 27, 1947, p. 2, that California strategists felt a lesson of the 1943–1944 campaign to have been that the closer to existing legislation, the more chance of success.

[16] About this time, Townsend state leaders began to talk about instituting the "fundamental principles" of the Plan. This euphemism has since spread to the national level. In the 1947–1948 campaign the "gross income tax" was offered as "the fundamental principle."

[17] Letter from Robert C. Townsend, Treasurer, TNRP, Inc. to John C. Cuneo, California State Organizer, TNRP, Inc., Cleveland, Ohio: July 17, 1947.

[18] Letter from Robert C. Townsend, Treasurer, TNRP, Inc. to John C. Cuneo, California State Organizer, TNRP, Inc., Cleveland, Ohio: August 14, 1947.

[19] It should be noted that during the October national call the California leader advised members to raise money for *it* outside the Organization! See *California Club Bulletin*, Modesto, Calif.: September 6, 1947.

[20] Of particular interest in this connection is the *California Club Bulletin*, Modesto, Calif.: June 10, 1948, immediately following notification of the failure of the initiative to qualify for the ballot. State leaders also indirectly recommended a "no" vote on the McLain initiative through an issue-endorsing group of which they were members. See *News Letter* of the California Legislative Conference, San Francisco, Calif.: n.d. Probably sent October 1948.

[21] At least this was their declared intent; it is not clear whether action was taken. The California leader was driven to state his intentions by "the continued statements by Geo. H. McLain . . . inferring that Townsend Plan leaders and I in particular, are uniting with 'reactionary groups' to try to repeal [the McLain amendment] . . . *THE TRUTH IS* your leaders are on the job doing everything possible to see that the major gains made . . . *ARE PRESERVED*." *Intra-organizational Bulletin*, Modesto, Calif.: January 22, 1949.

[22] Letter from John C. Cuneo, California State Organizer, Townsend Plan, Inc. (hereafter: TP, Inc.) to Robert C. Townsend, Treasurer, TP, Inc., Modesto, Calif.: July 28, 1949.

[23] Letter from John C. Cuneo, California State Organizer, TP, Inc. to Robert C. Townsend, Treasurer, TP, Inc., Modesto, Calif.: November 8, 1952.

[24] This should be taken to include the identification of the Townsend Organization with its traditional mission (*i.e.*, national pensions for economic reconstruction) by relevant publics. It is not a simple matter to escape an identity long and actively sought. Such escape is even more difficult when competing leaderships continually remind potential members of past failures.

[25] See Holtzman, *op. cit.*, pp. 313–18, 549–50, for 1934–1951 income figures.

[26] While income from this source was large in the early days of the Organization, it also seems that in those days this revenue went into the pockets of Dr. Townsend and the "co-founder" of the Organization, Robert E. Clements. See *Hearings: H. Res. 443, passim.*, on this point. Such revenues are, of course, dependent on mass circulation, and presently the newspaper carries little advertising.

[27] Mention of these early items may be found in *California Club Bulletins* for 1939–1940. Apparently none were successful; they are gone without a trace in 1953.

[28] Letter from Dr. F. E. Townsend, President, TP, Inc. to Mildred Atwood, Secretary to John C. Cuneo, Los Angeles, Calif.: May 19, 1952.

[29] *The Busy Bee Program*, n.p.: n.d. The "program" was part of a contest with prizes for those enlisting the most new members and readers.

[30] *Ibid.*

[31] The Clubs, established early in the history of the Organization, have always played an important role for Townsend leaders as nuclei for education, recruitment, and fund-raising. From 1100 Clubs in California in 1936, only 123 were left in 1952. They have shown a steady decrease in average membership, as well as numbers, since 1939 (the first year for which yearly records are available). E.g., in 1939 there were 91.3 members per California Club; in 1952, 45.0. (These figures are derived from records in the Townsend Archives.)

[32] At one large Los Angeles Club, far along in the transformation process described here, the meeting at 11 a.m. finds less than ten persons present. By 1 p.m., when card playing begins, there are ordinarily *over 50* persons present. A check indicated that less than one-third of these had ever been members of the Townsend Organization.

[33] We do not mean to indicate that leaders do not at all times perform maintenance functions. The crucial issues are what they must do, under changed conditions, to accomplish this and the explicitness with which the function is carried out.

[34] This seems unlikely. It would seem to involve, as a minimum, a shift in the organization's core membership, highly identified with the central mission; as well

as a shift in perspective that most leaderships seem unable to make. Further, the identification of the organization with its traditional mission by prospective members is almost assured by the actions of alternative leaders competing for this same social base.

41 Harry M. Scoble

Negro Politics: The Quest for Power

The basic theme of this chapter is that the American Negro seeks effective political power.[1] Negro leadership itself and Negro leadership in politics is a quest for power. However much the analyst focuses on specific Negro struggles for quality and desegregated public education, for fair employment and upgrading, for access to more and better housing, for better police protection and a simultaneous release from police brutality or harassment, or for other substantive policy goals; underlying all these struggles is a restless search for political power—for a say in the development of such policies. Only the self-determination of full adult manhood—or, in a political context, political power in a system that tends to be democratic—will resolve what social psychologists increasingly pinpoint as the collective identity crisis of American Negroes. Undoubtedly, one technique of response by those in power and being challenged for power will be an attempt to "restrict through partial incorporation"—the piecemeal granting of one or another minor substantive policy concession in the hope of undercutting a development of collective power that could be applied to the full range of problems facing the Negro. But such a response can only perpetuate the "benevolent paternalism" that has given rise to the crisis during the past century.

If Negro politics is a struggle to create power where none now exists, then a comprehensive analysis of such a quest must properly begin with an examination of constraints on power. This will provide a baseline for measuring how far the Negro has come and how far he has yet to go, and for assessing—as honestly and accurately as one can within the admitted limits of political science—how and when and under what conditions the Negro will wrest effective power from the political system.

In discussing constraints on power, one notes first that there are general limits, previously characteristic of powerless groups in other segments of American society as well as of the Negro, but there are also specific limits unique to the condition and experience of the Negro which make his struggle for power even more difficult.

Reprinted and abridged, with permission, from "Negro Politics in Los Angeles: The Quest for Power," by Harry M. Scoble, pp. 2–22, a paper prepared for the Los Angeles Riot Study, Institute for Government and Public Affairs, University of California, Los Angeles (1967).

Two of the general limitations are relevant here. First and foremost is the fact that Negroes are overwhelmingly of a lower socioeconomic status. In the population at large, according to the 1960 Census, only some 10 percent of the Negro population could be objectively classified as middle class or higher status. Lower-class status carries with it a host of revelant political implications.

In the language of social psychologists, motivational forces which lead to voting and other forms of political participation are weak or nonexistent among lower socioeconomic status categories: they particularly lack an internalized sense of the moral "oughtness" of civic duty, (characteristic of the League of Women Voters or the Citizen's Union types) as well as a sense of personal political efficacy (i.e., a politically specific manifestation of a generalized sense of competency and success in problem solving in all aspects of life). From the perspectives of decision theorists, information sources are weak, discontinuous, and simplistic—thus limiting rational political decisions. The political economist, in parallel fashion, would probably emphasize the lack of discretionary income within the lower orders—with all that this implies for "money in politics" in the lack of electoral contributions or of the dues-paying potential for political and interest group organization. Finally, the sociologist, with his special concern for structure and organization, would emphasize that those lowest in socioeconomic status lack the habit of organizational membership (other than in churches) and also the talents for organizational leadership. Leadership must come initially, if it comes at all, from the middle class, thus institutionalizing problems of internal cohesion in such organizations as are formally created. With his concern for social integration, the sociologist would also stress that successive censuses have revealed higher geographic/residential mobility among Negroes than whites. This mobility means that a larger proportion of Negroes cannot meet legal qualifications for voting at any one time. Since they lack formal education and its accompanying political sophistication, fewer Negroes than whites know how to avoid technical disenfranchisement in the North through use of absentee-ballot procedures.

However one might spell out the particular political implications of lower-class status in America (and I would hasten to stress that these implications are relative weaknesses rather than absolute lacks), the general political fact is that the collective resource base for politics is restricted and, from the viewpoint of potential leaders facing the individuals involved, exceedingly difficult to mobilize. For the primary resource base is sheer numbers, which may be modified and occasionally magnified by skillful leadership that instills singleness of purpose of interest-perception and/or intensity of ideological commitment. But this statement conceals a tactical implication which, in the case of the Negro, may also constitute a limitation. How can the unorganized be organized? How have excluded groups been brought into the American political system in the past? Political history indicates that those with power rarely if ever voluntarily relinquish that power; their capacity to withstand moral appeals to "self-evident" justice was great; they conceded and shared legitimate power only when their enlightened self interest revealed what the consequences of a refusal to yield power would be, i.e., when they faced counterforce or counterorganization. But how was such counterorganization created? From Daniel Shay in western Massachusetts in the 1780s through the suffragettes and the labor movement of the present century, two ingredients have been constant; demagogic leadership (as defined by the received opinion of the time, since there is no stable social science definition of demagoguery), and the resurrection or invention of disorderly—indeed, illegal—tactics. Shay was a demagogue; so were the labor organizers of the 1930s—that is, both leaders rubbed raw the sores of prevailing discontents because this proved the only efficient leadership technique for creating sufficient righteous anger to overcome the normal apathy of the unorganized and their fear. And, as identification and organization began to take place among the formerly unorganized, their leaders experimented with disorderly and illegal tactics—because these were more costly to those in power than the conventional tactics permitted by that day's "rules of the political game." Court procedures against debtors in western Massachusetts were abruptly terminated by the force implicit in a ring of muskets and pitchforks. Chaining oneself to the White House gates, insisting on going to jail rather than paying fines (and pleading guilty), demanding treatment as a political prisoner and attempting to enforce such demands through hunger strikes—these were some of the tactics employed by the suffragettes in the 1914–1920 period. In the 1930s, labor organizing committees took physical control of other people's property (the sit-in strike)—a tactic that was clearly illegal and that later was reaffirmed as illegal by the courts, *after* the Wagner Act victory, however.

This first general political limitation stemming from lower socioeconomic status may be applied to the Negro as follows. There are natural pressures on potential Negro leaders to employ demagoguery and to invent disorderly tactics. But because the Negro is a finite minority of roughly 11 percent of the nation's population, he cannot make it alone: he must have allies in his quest for power. To be maximally useful, such allies must come from the ranks of those already enjoying the luxury of relative power—labor unions and the vaguely-defined "white liberal community." But those with power (i.e., who can adequately defend their interests by conventional tactics) do not look with favor upon demagoguery and disorder—these are not "nice" techniques. Because of this, there is a special risk that Negro leaders will alienate their potential allies. Therefore, there are also natural pressures on potential Negro leaders to limit such techniques in practice, to deny their existence in public, and to quietly explain their necessity to potential allies. (One might add, from the point of view of the political system, that it would be desirable for the potential allies to understand and accept this historical necessity.)

A second, and lesser, general limitation (or constraint) on power should be noted. There is a price to be paid for power. As ethnic and other groups have gained effective political power, it has normally been indexed by a growing—absolute and relative—number of "members" in formal positions of governmental institutions. But, as a general rule, such appointees and elective officials have had to give up overt criticism of "the government" and the political system as the price of growing power. (The pressure on the appointee, judicial or executive, seems greater than that on the legislative official because the latter retains a restricted constituency of still-relevant "members.")

To become part of the power structure, yet to remain free of white (or WASP or "Anglo") control has generally been difficult if not impossible. This seems to apply particularly to the Negro, to judge from the contrasting careers of Congressmen Dawson and Powell. If this is a real limitation, then one should expect nongovernmental leaders increasingly to be and to remain the main source of Negro protest and criticism. That is, as Negro effective political power grows, we should also expect it to be accompanied by visible evidence of tension, division, and conflict among the growing Negro leadership aggregate.

The last paragraph has dealt with a special case of a general limitation on political power in America: constraints on the exercise of political power, once it is in the process of "becoming"—of being gained by a group. But this—which might be termed the "respectable-ization" of political leadership—has been common to all prior groups as they gained power and it has constituted a minor inefficiency in the process.

It is probably more important, therefore, to turn to specific limits on the development of *Negro* political power, arising out of factors unique in the situation and experience of American Negroes. For the Negro faces problems in developing political or perhaps any other type of leadership never previously faced by any other minority group in our society and polity. First, the Negro experienced slavery, with its calculated destruction of family structure, tribal identification, religion, language, and culture—until, sanctioned by physical violence, ego itself was destroyed. Human beings were systematically degraded to the status of depersonalized "things," of objects possessed and to be acted upon and dealt with at will. In short, no other minority group—probably not even the American Indian—has had to start from so low a point in the entire legal, moral, and intellectual structure of the dominant group in seeking to enter the system. This desperately low starting point has several important political consequences which, taken together, call into question the easy assumption of the "inevitability" of the Negro's politicization and assimilation following the "historical" pattern established by previous ethnic and religious minorities.

The low starting point for Negroes, compounded with other factors indicated below, may more generally mean—as Bayard Rustin has pointed out—that the doctrine of self help which previously proved efficient for other politicizing and assimilating minorities simply is not relevant in the case of the Negro. It seems more relevant to emphasize that demoralization and apathy, cynicism and violent rage are realistic responses of the Negro to the objective conditions of the situation; they are indeed "common sense" reactions. (Self help would seem to require a more positive emotional base upon which to build; and the visible gains derived from "lifting one-self by one's bootstraps" would then reciprocally reinforce such future orientations, hope, and faith in the system.) This may only be another way of saying that, for the Negroes, the problems of caste have been superimposed on those of class. The self-help practices proclaimed and followed by the Black Muslims may help an ex-convict, a prostitute, or simply a "lower-lower" *individual* to rise, but collectively such self-help doctrines tend toward the perpetuation of the ghetto with the insulation from power that the ghetto implies. Furthermore, with the possible exception of the late Malcolm X who—just prior to his murder—was apparently in the process of major realignment toward more conventional ideology, strategy, and tactics, the mainstream Black Muslims have been apolitical, if not anti-political, in their ideology and practices.

There is a further factor differentiating the Negro case: any apparent or pending gains by Negroes, individually or collectively, have been met by more intense emotional opposition, greater evasive inventiveness, and more violent physical force than was true of the other minorities.

There are two more manifestly political factors which also impel us to characterize the situation of the Negro as unique. Earlier ethnic and religious minorities, especially the "new immigrants" arriving in the nation between 1880 and 1915, came into the Northern and Western regions whose politico-economic dominance had been established by the Civil War. These migrant waves accompanied—indeed, were a contributing factor in—the political rise of Northern cities. (For example, the 1910 Census provided the first evidence that urban dwellers were increasing more than proportionately and that farmers were a *declining* minority.) That is to say, that historical trends and the ecology of politics were both favorable to the gaining of political power by these earlier minorities. By contrast, history and the ecology of politics have consistently combined to discount the potential resource of numbers of Negroes. First, the Negroes were inefficiently anchored in a regional concentration (and in a region which, after 1877, had the effective power to disfranchise them); and, beginning with World War I but accelerated by the Depression and World War II, they are now in the process of becoming inefficiently anchored in Northern metropolitan concentrations (i.e., at a time when central cities, as well as rural areas, are losing voting power in state and national legislatures).[2]

History has worked against the Negro's political rise in a second unique manner. In his quest for power, the Negro has arrived on the Northern scene too late to share an advantage enjoyed by the earlier minorities— and that was the urban boss and his political machine. It would be dangerously easy to evaluate the boss and his machine by romanticizing, to overestimate the efficiencies and to underestimate the social costs of urban machines—and yet such costs seem significant only if one shares and judges from the "nicer" middle-class perspectives of abhorrence of corruption or devotion to civil liberties. The boss and his machine valued the one raw political resource that the earlier minorities had; they constituted a visible, relatively cohesive, and powerful political leadership with which to deal or, alternatively, an organizational structure of control over "needed" and "desired" incentives and rewards. The machine was functional; it was a facilitative mechanism for the political, economic, and ultimately social integration of these earlier minorities; and, in a relatively peaceful manner, it encouraged enculturation into the wider political system at the same time that it tolerated subcultural diversity and even deviance. In a sense, the Northern Negro quest for power *began*—say, in the 1932 election—coincident with the decay of the machine; and, with the notable exception of Chicago, the Northern machine has already declined.[3] Nor is it readily apparent that functional equivalences of the machine are being or can be supplied elsewhere in the system. For example, the political struggle to control the machine-equivalent potentiality of the "war on poverty" program has now been resolved in favor of governors and mayors, not of Negroes and the poor. Lacking the structured politics of machines, Negroes today are faced with a far more fluid and difficult, if not dangerous, situation. "Party structures" are either fictitious, statutory entities or the discontinuous and decentralized personal followings of particular officeholders (so that a single bargain of electoral support for public policies can no longer be struck). Increasingly, access to money provides access to mass media and thus, access to electoral masses, rendering organizational talents less relevant (that is, "old style" organizational talents for voter mobilization are being displaced by fund-raising talents directed to different sources, among which Negroes are obviously not numbered). Where the Negro vote is mobilized or mobilizable, white politicians of both parties—for the present at least—seem increasingly to doubt that net gains are to be had by bidding for such support, since such electoral transactions now must occur in a more identifiable, public, and visible context and represent that risk of incurring a numerically larger backlash vote. Lastly, while one might expect traces of bossism and machines to persist *within* racial ghettos, and thus to remain important for intraracial politics, the fact remains that there are no stable larger structures of power outside the ghettos to link up to and from which to derive mutually rewarding bargains.

The final, and probably most important, unique characteristic of the contemporary situation lies in an extraordinary ambivalence toward and distrust of all Negro leadership: an *almost* paranoid fear of a "sellout."[4] Whether Negroes have in fact experienced greater leadership betrayal than earlier minorities must remain an open question. For the present, it is impossible to define "sellout" in a way that its frequencies can be measured and compared. Lacking operational definitions and quantifications, those who judge do so in terms of their perceptions of the "objective" needs of given groups—which perceptions ultimately derive from ideological perspectives. But, as in most politics, what is true is less important than what is believed to be true. The frequent charge of a sellout indexes an ambivalence toward, and distrust of, all kinds of leadership, including political, that is stronger and more devisive *and weakening* among Negroes in America than was true of any earlier minority as it was assimilated into economy, society, and polity.

There is no single explanation for this greater distrust and ambivalence. One major cause may be found in contrasting "Uncle Tomism" with leadership processes among what we here have termed "earlier" minorities. These earlier minorities accepted and expected that their group leaders would gain in affluence and influence, that their political leaders, for example, would gain in well-being also. This was "smart" for the individual, a gain for the group, and part of the new "system"—and it was rarely if ever interpreted as evidence of betrayal. But these other minorities, living in the Northern cities, were free to designate their own leadership (which presumably means, in the American context, that internal processes of self selection were not interfered with by the external community). The Negroes had no such experience and indeed had a contrary experience: whether under slavery or during the long redemptionist period, the Negroes were in the position of a colonial native population. Their only leaders were those the whites designated, chose to recognize, sent their messages through; all leaders were thus a constant and visible reminder of powerlessness and oppression. The experience left a strong and bitter residue.[5]

Moreover, certain practices exist today—even in Northern cities—which symbolically as well as functionally continue the tradition of external designation by whites of Negro leadership. As one illustration, the presidents of the Urban League and of the NAACP (National Association for the Advancement of Colored People) nationally and often locally, are white persons—a fact increasingly commented upon by younger Negro militants. More important is the Caucasian press of the Northern cities quite unwittingly continuing the tradition of designating "Negro leaders." In Los Angeles, for example, either of the two white daily newspapers regularly assigns a reporter—black or white—to cover the Negro communities, Negro leadership, or even Negro politics more narrowly conceived, as his newsbeat. On the other hand, practically any Negro who wants to can gain access to a room in one of the downtown hotels and stage a press conference. Reporters are assigned in rotation: they cover the event without prior knowledge or depth; they gratefully accept and use the mimeographed handouts; they unconsciously equate "spokesmanship" with "leadership"; they accept the *name* of an organization as evidence of the existence of a real membership; and they publicly identify the individual as a "Negro leader." Other whites—including the political leadership—tend only to read the white newspapers; they accept the identifications as real; they then try to deal with the Negro population through these individuals named; and they feel anger and frustration when they find that the latter "can't produce"—they also feel puzzled and confused by the bitter denials by *other* Negroes that "X" can or ever could lead or influence anybody. But bitterness toward both the interfering white community and the anointed spokesman would seem natural and may spill over into general doubt about all Negro leadership, raising the question as to how much such external interference has contributed in the past.[6]

If the Northern white communtiy unknowingly interferes in Negro politics by attempting to designate as leaders individuals with no demonstrated power or influence within the Negro community, it also interferes —this time more knowingly and much more in the tradition of the South— in a second important way. This interference lies in an official insistence on the right to discriminate within a *single* group of actual Negro leaders, anointing some as "legitimate" while rejecting, and refusing to deal with others who are labeled "unacceptable." A prime instance of this occurred in June, 1966 in Los Angeles when the City Police Commission acceded to demands for public hearings on police practices and police/Negro relations. On the first day of hearings, a delegation from the Temporary Alliance of Local Organizations (TALO)—which had been the main pressure for the hearings—appeared to testify and observe. TALO was the closest approximation, during the period of study, to a genuinely community-wide "organization of organizations" of Negroes in Los Angeles; it included representatives of organizations ranging from ministerial alliances and traditional civic and civil rights groups to black nationalists, youth gangs, and left-authoritarian "organizations." But the Police Commission refused to admit to the hearing anyone not on its "invitation" list— pointedly omitting at least one black nationalist and the leaders of two Negro area street gangs in the TALO delegation. While the effect of such official discrimination may well be strengthened support within the Negro community (or within segments of the community) for the *rejected* leaders, it is equally probable that this type of white interference adds further to general Negro distrust of their own leaders, at least those labeled as acceptable. If A is rejected while B is accepted, why is B so acceptable? Is B a "white" Negro? Has he sold out already? Is he about to sell out?

There may be a far more subtle and deep-seated explanation of the prevalent fear of sellout. The ambivalence and distrust of Negroes toward their leadership may also be born of an instinctive realization that most Negroes—if they are to gain at all—must gain as a *group*. (For most of them, it is not possible to rise individualistically, after a generation or two, through the final assimilative act of Americanizing their last name— or of "passing"; visible skin color remains, setting Negroes apart from earlier minorities.) But group gains require effective leadership: Negroes are thus more dependent on leadership than other minorities were—and dependence is rarely an ennobling human condition.

Negroes experienced the imposition of leadership over them to control them, and techniques remain today—even in the North—which constitute a continuing denial of their right to define their own leadership. Such experience is alien to that of any other group in America. (Even the Indians, when they were finally pushed onto the reservations, did not have their internal structures and processes of tribal government disturbed by the dominant whites.) Bitterness and suspicion remain the legacy. These negative emotions have real and disturbing consequences for the development of effective *political* leadership. If, today, a Negro gains real political influence over other Negroes, will not white political leaders inevitably accept him in a more passive sense than that described above, or actively seek him out and attempt to negotiate with him—simultaneously tending to destroy or undercut him? With the long-standing and increasing distrust of whites and with the highly emotional and moralistic nature of the appeals (e.g., by militant civil rights leaders within the Negro community) necessary to arouse the unorganized, the Negro political leader finds himself in an untenable situation in which acceptance and negotiation, or indeed, any identification with white leaders carries increasing costs. Negro followers fear, or are increasingly encouraged to fear, that such a Negro political leader will become locked into the "white power structure," a spokesman of and for the "Establishment." To the extent that such suspicions exist, a rising Negro political leader will generally gain less real power than he otherwise might; he will be less effective for achievement of Negro goals than he otherwise might; and he consequently is to be despised because he has obviously sold out. Despising him further weakens him. In short, Myrdal's principle of cumulative causation (or Merton's concept of the self-fulfilling prophecy) is at work. Alternatively, if the rising Negro leader realizes this inherent weakness in his own constituency and thus tries to transfer his base of power to the white liberal and labor communities, it is equal evidence of a sellout.

The problem of developing effective Negro political leadership is more particularly a problem of the dominant political culture. With the notable exception of the Civil War, the political system has functioned—and has therefore been acclaimed by many observers—by translating conflicts of principle into conflicts of interest, which interests are then "dealt" with, "bargained" over, "compromised." Furthermore, thus far the political system has functioned to provide only two alternative models for Negro political leaders in coming to terms with the dominant political culture: to accommodate oneself within it (i.e., to become a Dawson, quietly negotiating "non-negotiable principles" and risking identification as a "race-diplomat" if not as an "Uncle Tom" and consequent rejection by Negroes) or to stand as a critic outside the culture (i.e., to become a Powell, a militant "race-man," and to risk nonacceptance and ultimate outright rejection by the white political leadership). Neither model seems to provide effective political leadership for long-term Negro gains.

In summary, the purpose of this chapter is to stress that Negroes seek effective political power and to identify and explain both general and specific limitations affecting that quest.

The general limitations are two: the overwhelmingly lower socioeconomic status of Negroes (i.e., few resources that are difficult to mobilize politically, that require special leadership strategies which, in turn, entail special risks for the alliances and coalitions Negroes must form); and, more specifically, the norm for political/governmental leadership that "with power comes responsibility"—thus placing political leadership at a relative disadvantage compared with other types of leadership vis-à-vis the Negro community.

The special limitations ("the uniqueness of the Negro") on the Negro quest for power are both more numerous and more important: the experience of slavery has meant much lower starting points, rendering irrelevant earlier minorities' political experience, self-help doctrines, and so forth; the Negro has met and continues to meet much greater emotional— and political—resistance by whites; the late starting time of the Negro quest came after the decline of central cities and urban machines as power bases and facilitative mechanisms in the American political system; and, finally, the Negroes' greater fear of its leadership, arising out of both intragroup and external factors, occurs in the context of greater group need for leadership—weakening especially the development of effective political leadership.

While political science has not shared with economics the distinction of being termed "the dismal science," the charge is often made that political science—even with its newer tradition of political behavior approaches—is essentially conservative and status quoist: that it, especially through its reliance on functionalism, amounts—whatever the intent—to finding reasons for "what is" and, implicitly therefore, "what must be." Such is not the intent here; nor is it even to instill pessimism in the reader. Rather, the aim is realism—to provide as accurate a base as possible for understanding how tortuous the struggle has been and how difficult and how distant is the remainder of the Negro quest. Realism thus prevents us from making unwarranted assumptions that the Negro has already achieved effective political power, at least in the North, or that inevitably and shortly he must.

NOTES

[1] This is a *semi*final report on the study of Negro organizations, leadership, and politics in Los Angeles. Only three-quarters of the data requirements of the original research design have been accomplished. However, it is not anticipated that the major interpretive themes and conclusions presented here will be changed in any substantial degree by subsequent data. In this report, the conclusions are summarized under two broad themes: constraints on Negro power, and changes in Negro politics (broadly conceived) which preceded, accompanied, and/or were produced by the riots of 1965.

[2] It is not even safe to extrapolate confidently from population statistics and growth rates the assumption that Negroes necessarily and shortly will gain political and governmental power *within* central cities. American political history provides too many examples of the capacity of those declining in power to use their remaining power to further delay and dilute—if not prevent—the coming to power of new groups. (If one focuses only on legal extensions of franchise, it leads to the false conclusion that these complete and ratify the process of acquiring democratic po-

litical power. But the vote in non-Athenian society must be "translated" by processes and institutions—nomination processes; general election systems; scheme of representation; powers and relations of legislatures and executives and courts—which translation may be "true" or "false.")

At the municipal government level, as working-class ethnics threatened to and took electoral control of city council majorities, the "better elements" found it convenient to use their dwindling power to create a new layer of institutional authority over (and usually against) the City Council—in the form of a Board of Finance appointed by a mayor whom those latter elements still electorally controlled. While in the present century municipal reform—in the form of city managers, ceremonial mayors, and nonpartisan and/or at-large elections to city council—has had the demonstrated effect of depreciating the political potential of, among others, union members and Negroes.

At the state level, it is interesting that "the federal analogy" in state constitutions—providing for a legislative upper chamber in the image of the national Senate and thus based upon geography (farmers) rather than population (cities)—first made its appearance (about 1875) just as "undesirables" were beginning to crowd the cities.

At the national level, sociopolitical historians seem to have interpreted Prohibition as the *unsuccessful* reaction of Yankee Protestant rural America to the evidence of the censuses. But they have failed to note the parallel political success of Yankee Protestant rural *and white* America. For the words "compact, contiguous, and nearly equal" were omitted—presumably deliberately—from the 1929 Congressional Reapportionment and Redistricting Act, thus legally permitting systematic underrepresentation of urban populations in the House of Representatives. Change in this situation did not begin until 1962 (starting with the Supreme Court's decision in Baker vs. Carr). But by then, what rural America was to lose, suburban America would largely gain—for the 1960 Census revealed that central-city populations were essentially stagnant or absolutely declining and were uniformly declining relative to the other sectors.

One may also note the respectful attention accorded the American Bar Association's 1967 proposal to completely abolish the Electoral College and to provide for simple popular election of the president. This "reform" would have the effect—if it has not the intent—of diluting the primary electoral leverage Negroes now have in the political system (i.e., in the election of presidents, because of their strategic location in cities of large population, closely competitive two-party states which operate according to the "unit rule" in allocating all of the state's Electoral College vote to the plurality victor).

From this brief history of political/governmental reform, the analyst might well infer that city-county consolidation and other aspects of "metropolitan reform" will probably be employed, or at least attempted, to overcome the increasingly black statistics for central cities in future censuses.

Finally if this interpretive footnote looks dangerously like a "conspiracy theory," then perhaps we ought to face its implications rather than attempt to deny the facts leading to this conclusion.

[3] This may need clarification. The main argument is simply that the politicization and effective mobilization of Negro power would be easier, and the relevance of analogies to the historical experience of earlier minorities more convincing, if machines still existed. I do not wish to be understood as claiming that the quality of life of Chicago's Negroes is superior to that, say, of Los Angeles' or New York's *because* a machine exists in the former city. (We have neither the raw data nor the techniques of analysis that would sustain evaluations; at best we can only argue from—and about—particular examples drawn from limited time periods of observation, i.e., case-study materials.) Wilson's *Negro Politics*, surveying Chicago through 1959, seems to reach essentially a negative judgment—as to the dysfunctionality of Negro machine politics; yet one might note contrary and later

examples: in 1965, Los Angeles, and not Chicago, experienced the Watts riots and Mayor Yorty's response has been largely verbal and negative, coupled with demands for effective anti-rioting measures from a compliant state legislature; the 1966 riots that Chicago experienced were considerably less in magnitude than those in Watts and Mayor Daley has since attempted to negotiate "open occupancy" and a fairly wide range of other concessions to Negroes. In short, for the present, we must either suspend judgments or openly admit their time-bounded, particularistic, and qualitative nature.

[4] Evidence of this in Los Angeles was widely reported in the press at the time of the Watts riots; further evidence of this may be found in the criticisms by SLANT (Self Leadership Among All Nationalities Today) and other youthful black nationalists of John Buggs, Executive Director of the County Human Relations Commission, as a "house nigger" as contrasted with a "field nigger." This fear is also evident in the persistent comment in interviews for this study that "there *is* no Negro political leadership here"; in the dispute over seats for spectators; in black nationalists' and others' vehement criticisms of Negro ministerial leadership at the Deadwyler Inquest; and in the complaint printed in the *Los Angeles Sentinel* about "the National Association for the Advancement of SOME Colored People."

[5] One suspects, for example, that application of semantic-differential measurement techniques would reveal more negative connotations associated with the word "leader" for Negroes than for any other group. For example, there are a large number of derogatory synonyms for betraying leadership—"Uncle Tom," "handkerchief head," "house nigger," etc.

[6] There is a related factor, in that whites seem to expect and demand more of Negro leaders than they do of their own white leadership. (This is not, however, offered as a further explanation of Negro fear of sellout by Negro leaders; on the other hand, it may be interpreted as evidence of continued stereotyping by whites— and it is presumably galling to Negroes—in that it constitutes an additional denial of individual differences among Negroes.) This is the fact—perhaps born of Southern experience and Northern wish—that most whites act as if there is, or can and should be, an *all-purpose* leadership of Negroes by Negroes. It may be found, for example, in prevalent criticisms by white citizens and officials alike of Negro ministers—who did indeed influence female, aged, and/or middle-class parishioners—for not being able to get lower-class rioting teenagers to cease rioting. This exists despite all the sophistication that social scientists have contributed to our knowledge of the functional, specialized, restricted-arena, situationally-bound, and nontransferable nature of leadership in the white world.

PART IV

Significance of Values
in Sociological Analysis

COMMENTARY

It is not uncommon for student and instructor, in the introductory course, to confront one another over the questions of whether sociology is a science, and whether sociologists, by virtue of their particular knowledge, have a responsibility to assist in the shaping of public policy. In essence such questions derive from considerations of the significance of values in sociological analysis.

A fledgling discipline, sociology aspires to scientific status. Thus, in the erroneous belief that scientific knowledge is value free, sociologists have often eschewed a concern with values. And yet as a profession, if not as an academic discipline, sociology has been under constant pressure to confront policy problems. It is a matter of record, as John Madge points out in his discussion of *The Origins of Scientific Sociology*, that major theoretical and methodological advances in the field often have been made in research stimulated by the need for practical solutions to policy problems. This is evidenced in contributions made by Stouffer's study of *The American Soldier*, Myrdal's treatise *An American Dilemma*, Lazarsfeld's studies of presidential politics, *The Kinsey Report*, the Lynd's pioneer analyses of *Middletown*, and the Western Electric research carried out by Roethlisberger and Dickson, to mention but a few.

Values influence not only the formulation of sociological research, but they are themselves often the object of sociological investigation. As a result sociologists are unwittingly forced to confront the policy implications of the knowledge they have helped to discover and disseminate. Thus, it is not inappropriate in this final section to consider the significance of values in sociological analysis.

Alvin Gouldner, in "Anti-Minotaur: The Myth of a Value-Free Sociology," suggests that contrary to current interpretation Max Weber did not advocate a value-free sociology. According to Gouldner, although Weber was ambivalent regarding the question of values, he was quite explicit in cautioning that the sociologist could not escape from the difficult problems posed by the value relevance of their research and teaching.

In the next selection, "Traffic, Transportation, and Problems of the Metropolis," Scott Greer addresses himself to the question of how the sociologist might proceed with the analysis of events which are seen and evaluated differently from different vantage points in the social structure. Noting that "all investigation is oriented and limited by the questions that are asked, and [that] these, in turn, derive from the problems we face," Greer seeks to separate the analytical components of popularly defined problems. In an examination of problems of traffic and transportation in the metropolis he distinguishes the task of determining what is known and what is indeterminate from the tasks of defining what is desirable and assessing the utility of various means to the achievement of a desired end.

S. D. Vestermark's concern in "Social Science as Systematic Anxiety: A Case Study in the Civil Defense Dialogue" is with his responsibility to the public and to the scientific enterprise. The efficacy of the sociologist, as influencer of public policy, rests heavily upon the legitimacy of his inquiry. Thus, what is critical is an assessment of the assumptions of the thesis advanced by an advocate and the extent to which the thesis is subject to empirical evaluation. In his evaluation of Arthur I. Waskow's *The Shelter-Centered Society*, Vestermark provides an apt case study for an exploration of the problems involved.

42 ALVIN W. GOULDNER

Anti-Minotaur: The Myth of a Value-Free Sociology

This is an account of a myth created by and about a magnificent minotaur named Max—Max Weber, to be exact; his myth was that social science should and could be value-free. The lair of this minotaur, although reached only by a labyrinthine logic and visited only by a few who never return, is still regarded by many sociologists as a holy place. In particular, as sociologists grow older they seem impelled to make a pilgrimage to it and to pay their respects to the problem of the relations between values and social science.

Considering the perils of the visit, their motives are somewhat perplexing. Perhaps their quest is the first sign of professional senility; perhaps it is the last sigh of youthful yearnings. And perhaps a concern with the value problem is just a way of trying to take back something that was, in youthful enthusiasm, given too hastily.

In any event, the myth of a value-free sociology has been a conquering one. Today, all the powers of sociology, from Parsons to Lundberg, have entered into a tacit alliance to bind us to the dogma that "Thou shalt not

Reprinted from *Social Problems*, 9:3 (1962), pp. 199–213, by permission of the author and the publisher.

commit a value judgment," especially as sociologists. Where is the introductory textbook, where the lecture course on principles, that does not affirm or imply this rule?

In the end, of course, we cannot disprove the existence of minotaurs who, after all, are thought to be sacred precisely because, being half man and half bull, they are so unlikely. The thing to see is that a belief in them is not so much untrue as it is absurd. Like Berkeley's argument for solipsism, Weber's brief for a value-free sociology is a tight one and, some say, logically unassailable. Yet it is also absurd. For both arguments appeal to reason but ignore experience.

I do not here wish to enter into an examination of the *logical* arguments involved, not because I regard them as incontrovertible but because I find them less interesting to me as a sociologist. Instead what I will do is to view the belief in a value-free sociology in the same manner that sociologists examine any element in the ideology of any group. This means that we will look upon the sociologist just as we would any other occupation, be it the taxicab driver, the nurse, the coal miner, or the physician. In short, I will look at the belief in a value-free sociology as part of the ideology of a working group and from the standpoint of the sociology of occupations.

The image of a value-free sociology is more than a neat intellectual theorem demanded as a sacrifice to reason; it is, also, a felt conception of a role and a set of (more or less) shared sentiments as to how sociologists should live. We may be sure that it became this not simply because it is true or logically elegant but, also, because it is somehow useful to those who believe in it. Applauding the dancer for her grace is often the audience's way of concealing its lust.

That we are in the presence of a group myth, rather than a carefully formulated and well-validated belief appropriate to scientists, may be discerned if we ask, just what is it that is believed by those holding sociology to be a value-free discipline? Does the belief in a value-free sociology mean that, in point of fact, sociology is a discipline actually free of values and that it successfully excludes all nonscientific assumptions in selecting, studying, and reporting on a problem? Or does it mean that sociology *should* do so? Clearly, the first is untrue and I know of no one who even holds it possible for sociologists to exclude completely their nonscientific beliefs from their scientific work; and if this is so, on what grounds can this impossible task be held to be morally incumbent on sociologists?

Does the belief in a value-free sociology mean that sociologists cannot, do not, or should not make value judgments concerning things outside their sphere of technical competence? But what has technical competence to do with the making of value judgments? If technical competence does provide a warrant for making value judgments then there is nothing to prohibit sociologists from making them within the area of their *expertise*. If, on the contrary, technical competence provides no warrant for making value judgments then, at least sociologists are as *free* to do so as anyone else;

then their value judgments are at least as good as anyone else's, say, a twelve-year-old child's. And, by the way, if technical competence provides no warrant for making value judgments, then what does?

Does the belief in a value-free sociology mean that sociologists are or should be indifferent to the moral implications of their work? Does it mean that sociologists can and should make value judgments so long as they are careful to point out that these are different from "merely" factual statements? Does it mean that sociologists cannot logically deduce values from facts? Does it mean that sociologists do not or should not have or express *feelings* for or against some of the things they study? Does it mean that sociologists may and should inform laymen about techniques useful in realizing their own ends, if they are asked to do so, but that if they are not asked to do so they are to say nothing? Does it mean that sociologists should never take the initiative in asserting that some beliefs that laymen hold, such as the belief in the inherent inferiority of certain races, are false even when known to be contradicted by the facts of their discipline? Does it mean that social scientists should never speak out, or speak out only when invited, about the probable outcomes of a public course of action concerning which they are professionally knowledgeable? Does it mean that social scientists should never express values in their roles as teachers or in their roles as researchers, or in both? Does the belief in a value-free sociology mean that sociologists, either as teachers or researchers, have a right to covertly and unwittingly express their values but have no right to do so overtly and deliberately?

I fear that there are many sociologists today who, in conceiving social science to be value-free, mean widely different things, that many hold these beliefs dogmatically without having examined seriously the grounds upon which they are credible, and that some few affirm a value-free sociology ritualistically without having any clear idea what it might mean. Weber's own views on the relation between values and social science, and some current today are scarcely identical. While Weber saw grave hazards in the sociologist's expression of value judgments, he also held that these might be voiced if caution was exercised to distinguish them from statements of fact. If Weber insisted on the need to maintain scientific objectivity, he also warned that this was altogether different from moral indifference.

Not only was the cautious expression of value judgments deemed permissible by Weber but, he emphasized, these were positively mandatory under certain circumstances. Although Weber inveighed against the professorial "cult of personality," we might also remember that he was not against all value-imbued cults and that he himself worshiped at the shrine of individual responsibility. A familiarity with Weber's work on these points would only be embarrassing to many who today affirm a value-free sociology in his name. And should the disparity between Weber's own views and many now current come to be sensed, then the time is not far off when it will be asked, "Who now reads Max Weber?"

What to Weber was an agonizing expression of a highly personal faith, intensely felt and painstakingly argued, has today become a hollow catechism, a password, and a good excuse for no longer thinking seriously. It has become increasingly the trivial token of professional respectability, the caste mark of the decorous; it has become the gentleman's promise that boats will not be rocked. Rather than showing Weber's work the respect that it deserves, by carefully re-evaluating it in the light of our own generation's experience, we reflexively reiterate it even as we distort it to our own purposes. Ignorance of the gods is no excuse; but it can be convenient. For if the worshiper never visits the altar of his god, then he can never learn whether the first still burns there or whether the priests, grown fat, are simply sifting the ashes.

The needs which the value-free conception of social science serves are both personal and institutional. Briefly, my contention will be that, among the main institutional forces facilitating the survival and spread of the value-free myth, was its usefulness in maintaining both the cohesion and the autonomy of the modern university, in general, and the newer social science disciplines, in particular. There is little difficulty, at any rate, in demonstrating that these were among the motives originally inducing Max Weber to formulate the conception of a value-free sociology.

This issue might be opened at a seemingly peripheral and petty point, namely, when Weber abruptly mentions the problem of competition among professors for students. Weber notes that professors who do express a value stand are more likely to attract students than those who do not and are, therefore, likely to have undue career advantages. In effect, this is a complaint against a kind of unfair competition by professors who pander to student interests. Weber's hope seems to have been that the value-free principle would serve as a kind of "fair trades act" to restrain such competition. (At this point there is a curious rift in the dramatic mood of Weber's work; we had been listening to a full-throated Wagnerian aria when suddenly, the singer begins to hum snatches from Kurt Weill's "Mack the Knife.")

This suggests that one of the latent functions of the value-free doctrine is to bring peace to the academic house, by reducing competition for students and, in turn, it directs us to some of the institutional peculiarities of German universities in Weber's time. Unlike the situation in the American university, career advancement in the German was then felt to depend too largely on the professor's popularity as a teacher; indeed, at the lower ranks, the instructor's income was directly dependent on student enrollment. As a result, the competition for students was particularly keen and it was felt that the system penalized good scholars and researchers in favor of attractive teaching. In contrast, of course, the American system has been commonly accused of overstressing scholarly publication, and here the contrary complaint is typical, namely, that good teaching goes unrewarded and that you must "publish or perish." In the context of the German academic system, Weber was raising no trival point when he intimated that the value-free doctrine would reduce academic competition. He was linking the doctrine to guild problems and anchoring this lofty question to academicians' *earthy* interests.

Another relation of the value-free principle to distinctively German arrangements is also notable when Weber, opposing use of the lecture hall as an arena of value affirmation, argues that it subjects the student to a pressure which he is unable to evaluate or resist adequately. Given the comparatively exalted position of the professor in German society, and given the one-sided communication inherent in the lecture hall, Weber did have a point. His fears were, perhaps, all the more justified if we accept a view of the German "national character" as being authoritarian, that is, in Nietzsche's terms a combination of arrogance and servility. But these considerations do not hold with anything like equal cogency in more democratic cultures such as our own. For here, not only are professors held in, shall I say, more modest esteem, but the specific ideology of education itself often stresses the desirability of student initiative and participation, and there is more of a systematic solicitation of the student's "own" views in small "discussion" sections. There is little student servility to complement and encourage occasional professorial arrogance.

When Weber condemned the lecture hall as a forum for value affirmation he had in mind most particularly the expression of *political* values. The point of Weber's polemic is not directed against all values with equal sharpness. It was not the expression of aesthetic or even religious values that Weber sees as most objectionable in the University, but, primarily, those of politics. His promotion of the value-free doctrine may, then, be seen not so much as an effort to amoralize as to depoliticize the University and to remove it from the political struggle. The political conflicts then echoing in the German university did not entail comparatively trivial differences, such as those now between Democrats and Republicans in the United States. Weber's proposal of the value-free doctrine was, in part, an effort to establish a *modus vivendi* among academicians whose political commitments were often intensely felt and in violent opposition.

Under these historical conditions, the value-free doctrine was a proposal for an academic truce. It said, in effect, if we all keep quiet about our political views then we may all be able to get on with our work. But if the value-free principle was suitable in Weber's Germany because it served to restrain political passions, is it equally useful in America today where, not only is there pitiable little difference in politics but men often have no politics at all. Perhaps the need of the American university today, as of American society more generally, is for more commitment to politics and for more diversity of political views. It would seem that now the national need is to take the lid off, not to screw it on more tightly.

Given the historically unique conditions of nuclear warfare, where the issue would not be decided in a long-drawn-out war requiring the sustained cohesion of mass populations, national consensus is no longer, I believe, as important a condition of national survival as it once was. But if we no longer require the same degree of unanimity to *fight* a war, we do require a greater ferment of ideas and a radiating growth of political seriousness and variety within which alone we may find a way to *prevent* war. Important contributions to this have and may further be made by members of the academic community and, perhaps, especially, by its social science sector. The question arises, however, whether this group's political intelligence can ever be adequately mobilized for these purposes so long as it remains tranquilized by the value-free doctrine.

Throughout his work, Weber's strategy is to safeguard the integrity and freedom of action of both the state, as the instrument of German national policy, and of the university, as the embodiment of a larger Western tradition of rationalism. He feared that the expression of political value judgments in the University would provoke the state into censoring the University and would imperil its autonomy. Indeed, Weber argues that professors are not entitled to freedom from state control in matters of values, since these do not rest on their specialized qualifications.

This view will seem curious only to those regarding Weber as a liberal in the Anglo-American sense, that is, as one who wishes to delimit the state's powers on behalf of the individual's liberties. Actually, however, Weber aimed not at curtailing but at strengthening the powers of the German state, and at making it a more effective instrument of German nationalism. It would seem, however, that an argument contrary to the one he advances is at least as consistent; namely, that professors are, like all others, entitled and perhaps obligated to express their values. In other words, professors have a right to profess. Rather than being made the objects of special suspicion and special control by the state, they are no less (and no more) entitled than others to the trust and protection of the state.

In a *Realpolitik* vein, Weber acknowledges that the most basic national questions cannot ordinarily be discussed with full freedom in government universities. Since the discussion there cannot be completely free and all-sided, he apparently concludes that it is fitting there should be no discussion at all, rather than risk partisanship. But this is too pious by far. Even Socrates never insisted that all views must be at hand before the dialogue could begin. Here again one might as reasonably argue to the contrary, holding that one limitation of freedom is no excuse for another. Granting the reality of efforts to inhibit unpopular views in the University, it seems odd to prescribe self-suppression as a way of avoiding external suppression. Suicide does not seem a reasonable way to avoid being murdered. It appears, however, that Weber was so intent on safeguarding the autonomy of the University and the autonomy of politics, that he was willing to pay almost any price to do so, even if this led the University to detach itself from one of the basic intellectual traditions of the West—the dialectical exploration of the fundamental purposes of human life.

Insofar as the value-free doctrine is a mode of ensuring professional autonomy, note that it does not, as such, entail an interest peculiar to the social sciences. In this regard, as a substantial body of research in the sociology of occupations indicates, social scientists are kin to plumbers, house painters, or librarians. For most if not all occupations seek to elude control by outsiders and manifest a drive to maintain exclusive control over their practitioners.

Without doubt the value-free principle did enhance the autonomy of sociology; it was one way in which our discipline pried itself loose—in some modest measure—from the clutch of its society, in Europe freer from political party influence, in the United States freer of ministerial influence. In both places, the value-free doctrine gave sociology a larger area of autonomy in which it could steadily pursue basic problems rather than journalistically react to passing events, and allowed it more freedom to pursue questions uninteresting either to the respectable or to the rebellious. It made sociology freer—as Comte had wanted it to be—to pursue all its own theoretical implications. In other words, the value-free principle did, I think, contribute to the intellectual growth and emancipation of our enterprise.

There was another kind of freedom which the value-free doctrine also allowed; it enhanced a freedom from moral compulsiveness; it permitted a partial escape from the parochial prescriptions of the sociologist's local or native culture. Above all, effective internalization of the value-free principle has always encouraged at least a temporary suspension of the moralizing reflexes built into the sociologist by his own society. From one perspective, this of course has its dangers—a disorienting normlessness and moral indifference. From another standpoint, however, the value-free principle might also have provided a *moral* as well as an intellectual *opportunity*. For insofar as moral reactions are only suspended and not aborted, and insofar as this is done in the service of knowledge and intellectual discipline, then, in effect, the value-free principle strengthened Reason (or Ego) against the compulsive demands of a merely traditional morality. To this degree, the value-free discipline provided a foundation for the development of more reliable knowledge about men and, also established a breathing space within which moral reactions could be less mechanical and in which morality could be reinvigorated.

The value-free doctrine thus had a paradoxical potentiality: it might enable men to make *better* value judgments rather than *none*. It could encourage a habit of mind that might help men in discriminating between their punitive drives and their ethical sentiments. Moralistic reflexes suspended, it was now more possible to sift conscience with the rod of reason and to cultivate moral judgments that expressed a man's total character as an adult person; he need not now live quite so much by his past parental programing but in terms of his more mature present.

The value-free doctrine could have meant an opportunity for a more authentic morality. It could and sometimes did aid men in transcending the morality of their "tribe," to open themselves to the diverse moralities of unfamiliar groups, and to see themselves and others from the standpoint of a wider range of significant cultures. But the value-free doctrine also had other, less fortunate, results as well.

Doubtless there were some who did use the opportunity thus presented; but there were, also, many who used the value-free postulate as an excuse for pursuing their private impulses to the neglect of their public responsibilities and who, far from becoming more morally sensitive, became morally jaded. Insofar as the value-free doctrine failed to realize its potentialities it did so because its deepest impulses were—as we shall note later—dualistic; it invited men to stress the separation and not the mutual connectedness of facts and values: it had the vice of its virtues. In short, the conception of a value-free sociology has had *diverse* consequences, not all of them useful or flattering to the social sciences.

On the negative side, it may be noted that the value-free doctrine is useful both to those who want to escape *from* the world and to those who want to escape *into* it. It is useful to those young, or not so young men, who live off sociology rather than for it, and who think of sociology as a way of getting ahead in the world by providing them with neutral techniques that may be sold on the open market to any buyer. The belief that it is not the business of a sociologist to make value judgments is taken, by some, to mean that the market on which they can vend their skills is unlimited. From such a standpoint, there is no reason why one cannot sell his knowledge to spread a disease just as freely as he can to fight it. Indeed, some sociologists have had no hesitation about doing market research designed to sell more cigarettes, although well aware of the implications of recent cancer research. In brief, the value-free doctrine of social science was sometimes used to justify the sale of one's talents to the highest bidder and is, far from new, a contemposary version of the most ancient sophistry.

In still other cases, the image of a value-free sociology is the armor of the alienated sociologist's self. Although C. Wright Mills may be right in saying this is the Age of Sociology, not a few sociologists, and Mills included, feel estranged and isolated from their society. They feel impotent to contribute usefully to the solution of its deepening problems and, even when they can, they fear that the terms of such an involvement require them to submit to a commercial debasement of a narrow partisanship, rather than contributing to a truly public interest.

Many sociologists feel themselves cut off from the larger community of liberal intellectuals in whose pithy satire they see themselves as ridiculous caricatures. Estranged from the larger world, they cannot escape except in fantasies of posthumous medals and by living huddled behind self-barricaded intellectual ghettos. Self-doubt finds its anodyne in the image of a value-free sociology because this transforms their alienation into an intellectual principle; it evokes the soothing illusion, among some sociologists, that their exclusion from the larger society is a self-imposed duty rather than an externally imposed constraint.

Once committed to the premise of a value-free sociology, such sociologists are bound to a policy which can only alienate them further from the surrounding world. Social science can never be fully accepted in a society, or by a part of it, without paying its way; this means it must manifest both its relevance and concern for the contemporary human predicament. Unless the value relevances of sociological inquiry are made plainly evident, unless there are at least some bridges between it and larger human hopes and purposes, it must inevitably be scorned by laymen as pretentious word-mongering. But the manner in which some sociologists conceive the value-free doctrine disposes them to ignore current human problems and to huddle together like old men seeking mutual warmth. "This is not our job," they say, "and if it were we would not know enough to do it. Go away, come back when we're grown up," say these old men. The issue, however, is not whether we know enough; the real questions are whether we have the courage to say and use what we do know and whether anyone knows more.

There is one way in which those who desert the world and those who sell out to it have something in common. Neither group can adopt an openly critical stance toward society. Those who sell out are accomplices; they may feel no critical impulses. Those who run out, while they do feel such impulses, are either lacking in any talent for aggression, or have often turned it inward into noisy but essentially safe university politics or into professional polemics. In adopting a conception of themselves as "value-free" scientists, their critical impulses may no longer find a target in society. Since they no longer feel free to criticize society, which always requires a measure of courage, they now turn to the cannibalistic criticism of sociology itself and begin to eat themselves up with "methodological" criticisms.

One latent meaning, then, of the image of a value-free sociology is this: "Thou shalt not commit a critical or negative value judgment—especially of one's own society." Like a neurotic symptom this aspect of the value-free image is rooted in a conflict; it grows out of an effort to compromise between conflicting drives: On the one side, it reflects a conflict between the desire to criticize social institutions, which since Socrates has been the legacy of intellectuals, and the fear of reprisals if one does criticize—which is also a very old and human concern. On the other side, this aspect of the value-free image reflects a conflict between the fear of being critical and the fear of being regarded as unmanly or lacking in integrity, if uncritical.

The doctrine of a value-free sociology resolves these conflicts by making it seem that those who refrain from social criticism are acting solely on behalf of a higher professional good rather than their private interests. In refraining from social criticism, both the timorous and the venal may now claim the protection of a high professional principle and, in so doing, can continue to hold themselves in decent regard. Persuade all that no one must bell the cat, then none of the mice need feel like a rat.

Should social scientists affirm or critically explore values they would of necessity come up against powerful institutions who deem the statement or protection of public values as part of their special business. Should social scientists seem to compete in this business, they can run afoul of powerful forces and can, realistically, anticipate efforts at external curbs and controls. In saying this, however, we have to be careful lest we need-lessly exacerbate academic timorousness. Actually, my own firsthand im-pressions of many situations where sociologists serve as consultants indicate that, once their clients come to know them, they are often quite prepared to have sociologists suggest (not dictate) policy and to have them express their own values. Nor does this always derive from the expectation that sociologists will see things their way and share their values. Indeed, it is precisely the expected difference in perspectives that is occasionally desired in seeking consultation. I find it difficult not to sympathize with business-men who jeer at sociologists when they suddenly become more devoted to business values than the businessmen themselves.

Clearly all this does not mean that people will tolerate disagreement on basic values with social scientists more equably than they will with anyone else. Surely there is no reason why the principles governing social inter-action should be miraculously suspended just because one of the parties to a social relation is a social scientist. The dangers of public resentment are real but they are only normal. They are not inconsistent with the possi-bility that laymen may be perfectly ready to allow social scientists as much (or as little) freedom of value expression as they would anyone else. And what more could any social scientist want?

The value-free image of social science is not consciously held for ex-pedience' sake; it is not contrived deliberately as a hedge against public displeasure. It could not function as a face-saving device if it were. What seems more likely is that it entails something in the nature of a tacit bar-gain: in return for a measure of autonomy and social support, many social scientists have surrendered their critical impulses. This was not usually a callous "sell-out" but a slow process of mutual accommodation; both parties suddenly found themselves betrothed without a formal ceremony.

Nor am I saying that the critical posture is dead in American sociology; it is just badly sagging. Anyone who has followed the work of Seymour Lipset, Dennis Wrong, Leo Lowenthal, Bennett Berger, Bernard Rosen-berg, Lewis Coser, Maurice Stein, C. Wright Mills, Arthur Vidich, Philip Rieff, Anselm Strauss, David Riesman, Alfred McClung Lee, Van den Haag, and of others, would know better. These men still regard themselves as "intellectuals" no less than sociologists: their work is deeply linked to this larger tradition from which sociology itself has evolved. By no means have all sociologists rejected the legacy of the intellectual, namely, the right to be critical of tradition. This ancient heritage still remains embedded in the underground culture of sociology; and it comprises the enshadowed part of the occupational selves of many sociologists even if not publicly acknowledged.

In contrast with and partly in polemic against this older tradition, how-ever, the dominant drift of American sociology today is compulsively bent upon transforming it into a "profession." (Strangely enough, many of these same sociologists see nothing contradictory in insisting that their discipline is still young and immature.) This clash between the older heritage of the critical intellectual and the modern claims of the value-free professional finds many expressions. One of these occurred at the sociologists' national meetings in Chicago in 1958. At this time, the convention in a session of the whole was considering Talcott Parsons' paper on "Sociology as a Profession." After long and involved discussion, which prompted many members suddenly to remember overdue appointments elsewhere, Chicago's E. C. Hughes rose from the floor and brought a warm response by insisting that we were not a professional but, rather, a learned society. It was at this same meeting that the American Sociological Society rechristened itself as the American Sociological Association, lest its former initials evoke public reactions discrepant with the dignity of a profession.

Another indication of the continuing clash between the critical intellectual and the value-free professional is to be found in the Phoenix-like emergence of Young Turk movements, such as SPSSI, the Society for the Psychological Study of Social Issues, which arose in response to the depression of 1929. When it was felt by Alfred McClung Lee and others that these Turks were no longer so young, they founded the SSSP, the Society for the Study of Social Problems. Both these organizations remain on-going concerns, each characteristically interested in value-related work, and each something of a stitch in the side of its respective parent group, the American Psychological Association and the American Sociological Association.

The tension between the older conception of sociologists as intellectuals and the newer drive to professionalization is also expressed by the differences between the current Columbia or Harvard outlook and the so-called "Chicago tradition" which, with the change in that Department's character, is now either centered in Berkeley or is homelessly hovering. The difference between these two perspectives is most evident when they both embark on studies of the same institution.

A case in point can be found in the recent studies of medicine conducted by Columbia or Harvard and Chicago trained men. It is difficult to escape the feeling that the former are more respectful of the medical establishment than the Chicagoans, that they more readily regard it in terms of its own claims, and are more prone to view it as a noble profession. Chicagoans, however, tend to be uneasy about the very idea of a "profession" as a tool for study, believing instead that the notion of an "occupation" provides more basic guidelines for study, and arguing that occupations as diverse as the nun and the prostitute, or the plumber and the physician, reveal instructive sociological similarities. Chicagoans seem more likely to take a secular view of medicine, seeing it as an occupation much like any other and are somewhat more inclined toward debunking forays into the seamier side of medical practice. Epitomizing this difference are the very differences in the book titles that the two groups have chosen for their medical studies. Harvard and Columbia have soberly called two of their most important works, "The Student-Physician," and "Experiment Perilous," while the Chicagoans have irreverently labeled their own recent study of medical students, the "Boys in White."

One of the most interesting expressions of resistance to the newer, value-free style of "professional" sociology is the fascination with the *demimonde* of a talented group of these ex-Chicagoans. For them orientation to the underworld has become the equivalent of the proletarian identifications felt by some intellectuals during the 1930's. For not only do they study it, but in a way they speak on its behalf, affirming the authenticity of its style of life. Two of the leading exponents of this style are Howard S. Becker and Erving Goffman; the latter may become the William Blake of sociology.

As a case in point, Goffman's subtle study, "Cooling the Mark Out," takes its point of departure from an examination of the strategy of the confidence rackets. In the con game, Goffman points out, after the mark's loot has been taken, one of the con men remains behind "to cool the mark out," seeking to persuade him to accept his loss of face rather than squeal to the police. Goffman then uses this stratagem as a model to explode a great variety of legitimate groups and roles—the restaurant hostess who cools out the impatient customer, the psychoanalyst who cools out those who have lost in love. The point is insinuated that the whole world may be seen as one of marks and operators and that, in the final analysis, we are all marks to be cooled out by the clergy, the operator left behind for the job. This, it would seem, is a metaphysics of the underworld, in which conventional society is seen from the standpoint of a group outside of its own respectable social structures.

This group of Chicagoans finds itself at home in the world of hip, Norman Mailer, drug addicts, jazz musicians, cab drivers, prostitutes, night people, drifters, grifters, and skidders, the cool cats and their kicks. To be fully appreciated this stream of work cannot be seen solely in terms of the categories conventionally employed in sociological analysis. It has also to be seen from the viewpoint of the literary critic as a style or *genre* and in particular as a species of naturalistic romanticism, a term which I do not in the least intend opprobriously. That is, it prefers the offbeat to the familiar, the vivid ethnographic detail to the dull taxonomy, the sensuously expressive to dry analysis, naturalistic observation to formal questionnaires, the standpoint of the hip outsider to the square insider.

It may of course be asked, "Is it any the less sentimentally romantic to regard medical research on incurable patients as an 'Experiment Perilous'?" Possibly not. But it is at least much more *decorous* than seeing it as a process of "cooling the mark out." That, I suspect, is nearer the bone. The one thing that "classicists," whether sociological or literary, can never abide is a lack of decorum, even if the performance is in other respects brilliant. In sociology, objections to a lack of decorum as such are not made and, instead, often take the form of criticizing methodological deficiencies or moralistic proclivities. And, in truth, this Chicago group does betray persistent moral concerns, as evidenced, for example, by their readiness to focus on the degrading impact of the mental hospital on its inmates, or on the legal straitjacket in which the drug addict is confined.

The pathology characteristic of the *classicist* is too well known to require much comment: theirs is the danger of ritualism, in which conformity to the formal canons of the craft is pursued compulsively to the point where it warps work, emptying it of insight, significant truth, and intellectually viable substance. Of the classicist degenerating into neo-classicism we might say, with Roy Campbell, "They use the snaffle and the curb, all right, but where's the bloody horse?"

For its part, romantic social criticism is vulnerable from two directions. The usual occupational hazard of the romantic is, of course, excess, of the emotions or of the imagination. It may be guessed, however, that such excess stems not only from the personalities indigenous to those whom Romanticism attracts but, just as much, from the bitter attack upon them by the neo-classicist and from their resultant polemic. Again, and perhaps more importantly, this Romantic standpoint is vulnerable to the crasser temptations of its own talent-earned success. Indeed, they have now learned to mute their jive to the point where they can communicate profitably with their stockbrokers. Perhaps the time will come when they will no longer have to pretend to be respectable and when they will, instead, have to work at seeming cool. But that time is not yet. Whatever the outcome, they have shown us still another facet of the resistance to the emergence of a value-free professionalism in sociology, and they have given us still another evidence of the intellectual vitality of a critical stance.

Despite the vigor of this and other groups, however, I believe that they are primarily secondary currents whose very visibility is heightened because they are moving across the main ebb. The dominant drift in American sociology is toward professionalization, the growth of technical specialists, toward the diffusion of the value-free outlook to the point where it becomes less of an intellectual doctrine and more of a blanketing mood. American sociology is in the process of accommodating itself.

In its main outlines, such efforts at accommodation are far from new. For the doctrine of a value-free sociology is a modern extension of the medieval conflict between faith and reason. It grows out of, and still dwells in, the tendency prevalent since the thirteenth century to erect compartments between the two as a way of keeping the peace between them. One of the culminations of this tendency in the Middle ages is to be found in the work of the Arabian philosopher Ibn Rochd, better known as Averroës. Averroës had believed that absolute truth was to be found not in revelation but in philosophy, which for him meant Aristotle. He felt that revelation, faith, and the work of the theologians was a kind of footman's philosophy, necessary for those devoid of intellectual discipline and useful as a way of civilizing them.

Seeing theology as containing a measure of truth, albeit one inferior to that of philosophy and, being a prudent man, Averroës recommended that philosophers and theologians ought each to mind his own business and, in particular, that the philosophers, being intellectually superior, should show *noblesse oblige* to the theologians. He suggested that philosophers should keep their truth to themselves and write technical books which did not disturb or confuse simpler minds.

His disciples, the Latin or Christian Averroists, particularly at the University of Paris, accentuated this prudential side of their master's work; their strategy of safety was to define themselves as specialists, as technical philosophers. Their only job, said they, was to teach philosophy and to show the conclusions that flowed from it. These conclusions were "necessary" but, when at variance with the truths of revelation, it was not their job to reconcile them, said the philosophers. From this developed the so-called Doctrine of the Twofold Truth—the truths of philosophy which were logically necessary and the divine truths of revelation. If there were contradictions between the two, the philosophers merely reaffirmed their belief in revelation, and let it go at that. This sometimes took a cynical form as, for example, in John of Jaudan's comment, "I do believe that is true; but I cannot prove it. Good luck to those who can!" They thus built a watertight compartment between philosophy and faith, a separation which Saint Thomas continued and yet sought to transcend. To Saint Thomas, knowing and believing are distinct processes, each having its own separate and legitimate function and therefore not to be invaded by the other. In this view, there were two main classes of truths, both of which, however, derived from Divine Revelation. There were truths obtainable by natural reason alone, and there were truths of revelation, genuine articles of faith which elude the grasp of reason and which were susceptible neither to proof nor disproof by reason.

With the development of modern science varying efforts to accommodate it to religion continued, often taking the form of some kind of separatist doctrine in which each is assigned a different function and each is chastened to acknowledge the authority of the other in its own sphere. Weber's doctrine of a value-free sociology, which creates a gulf between science and values, is in this tradition; it may be regarded as a Protestant version of the Thomistic effort at harmonizing their relations.

The core of Weber's outlook rested on a dualism between, on the one hand, reason or rationality, especially as embodied in bureaucracy and science, and, on the other hand, more elemental emotional forces, partly encompassed in his notion of Charisma. He regards each of these forces as inimical to the other. He himself is ambivalent to each of them, viewing each as both dangerous and necessary.

On the one side, Weber is deeply concerned to protect the citadel of modern reason, the University, and fiercely opposes the professorial "cult of personality" which was the academic expression of the charismatic claim. This in turn disposes him to project an image of the University which is essentially bureaucratic, as a faceless group of specialists, each sovereign in his own cell and all sworn to forsake their individuality.

Nonetheless he also hates bureaucracy precisely because it submerges individuality and dehumanizes men and is thus led to deny that he intended to bureaucratize the University in pleading for the doctrine of a value-free social science. (Yet while this was doubtless not his *intention*, his two-pronged polemic against the cult of academic personality and in favor of the value-free doctrine does seem to drive him toward such a bureaucratic conception of the University.)

If Weber is concerned to protect even the bureaucratic dwelling places of rationality, he also seeks to confine bureaucracy and to circumscribe the area of its influence. In particular, he wishes to protect the highest reaches of statecraft from degenerating into a lifeless routine; he seeks to preserve politics as a realm in which there can be an expression of personal will, of serious moral commitment, a realm where greatness was possible to those who dared, preserved and suffered, a realm so powerful that it could overturn the institutional order or preserve it. He wants to safeguard high politics as an arena of human autonomy, of pure value choices, at its finest.

Yet Weber also fears for the safety of rationality in the modern world. He knows that there are powerful forces abroad which continue to threaten rationality, that there are still untamed things in men which he, more than most, had had to face. Not unlike Freud, Weber was both afraid of and drawn to these unbridled forces, the passionate Dionysian part of men. While he believed that they were being slowly subdued by an onmarching rationalization, he continued to fear that they could yet erupt and cleave modern institutional life. Although fearing these irrational forces, he also felt their disappearance from the modern world to be a "disenchantment," for he believed that they contained springs of vitality and power indispensable to human existence.

Weber is a man caught between two electrodes and torn by the current passing between them; he fears both but is unable to let go of either. He attempts to solve this dilemma by a strategy of segregation, seeking the exclusion of charismatic irrationality from certain modern *institutions*, such as the University, but admitting it into and, indeed, exalting its manifestations in the inward personal life of individuals. He wanted certain of the role structures of modern society to be rational; but he also wanted the role-players to be passionate and willful. He wanted the play to be written by a classicist and to be acted by romanticists. Unusual man, he wanted the best of both worlds. Yet whatever the judgment of his intellect, his sentiments are not poised midway between them, but tend toward one of the two sides.

This becomes clear when we ask, if science cannot be the basis of value judgments, what then, according to Weber, was to be their basis? To answer this, we must go beyond his formal doctrine of a value-free sociology, to Weber's own personal profession of belief. Weber certainly did not hold that personal values should derive from the existent culture, or from ancient traditions, nor again from formal ethical systems which he felt to be empty and lifeless. Unless men were to become inhuman robots, life, he insisted, must be guided by consciously made decisions. If men are to have dignity, they must choose their own fate.

To Weber as a man, only those values are authentic which stem from conscious decision, from a consultation of the inner conscience and a willful commitment to its dictates. From his *personal* standpoint, it is not really true that all values are equally worthy. Those consciously held by men are more worthy than those which are merely traditional and unthinkingly repeated. Those values that men feel deeply about and passionately long to realize are better than those which are merely intellectually appealing and do not engage their entire being.

In short, Weber, too, was seeking a solution to the competing claims of reason and faith. His solution takes the form of attempting to guard the autonomy of both spheres but, most especially I believe, the domain of conscience and faith. He wants a way in which reason and faith can cohabit platonically but not as full partners. The two orders are separate but unequal. For in Weber, reason only consults conscience and perhaps even cross-examines it. But conscience has the last word, and passion and will the last deed. Here Weber stands as half-Lutheran, half-Nietzschean.

If Weber thrusts powerfully at traditionalism, nonetheless his main campaign here is waged against science and reason and is aimed at confining their influence. To Weber, even reason must submit when conscience declares, Here I stand; I can do no other! Weber saw as authentic only those values that rest on the charismatic core of the self and on its claims to intuitive certainty. Weber, too, was a seeker after certainty, the certainty that is more apt to come from the arrogance of individual conscience. For while much may be truly said of the arrogance of reason, reason always seeks reasons and is ready to sit down and talk about them.

To Weber as a Protestant, the individual's conscience is akin to the voice of revelation. He would have been dismayed at the implications of considering it as the echo of parental remonstrations. To him, individual conscience was transcendental, while reason and science were only instrumental. Science is the servant of values and of personal conscience, which, like the heart, has reasons of its own. From Weber's standpoint, science and reason could only supply the means; the ends were to be dictated by values which, even if inscrutable, were to have the final voice.

I have therefore come to believe that the value-free doctrine is, from Weber's standpoint, basically an effort to compromise two of the deepest traditions of Western thought, reason and faith, but that his arbitration seeks above all to safeguard the romantic residue in modern man. I have personal reservations not because I doubt the worth of safeguarding this romantic component, but, rather, because I disagree with the strategy of segregation which Weber advances. *I believe that, in the end, this segregation warps reason by tinging it with sadism and leaves feeling smugly sure only of itself and bereft of a sense of common humanity.*

The problem of a value-free sociology has its most poignant implications for the social scientist in his role as educator. If sociologists ought not express their personal values in the academic setting, how then are students to be safeguarded against the unwitting influence of these values which shape the sociologist's selection of problems, his preferences for certain hypotheses or conceptual schemes, and his neglect of others. For these are unavoidable and, in this sense, there is and can be no value-free sociology. The only choice is between an expression of one's values, as open and honest as it can be, this side of the psychoanalytical couch, and a vain ritual of moral neutrality which, because it invites men to ignore the vulnerability of reason to bias, leaves it at the mercy of irrationality.

If truth is the vital thing, as Weber is reputed to have said on his deathbed, then it must be all the truth we have to give, as best we know it, being painfully aware and making our students aware, that even as we offer it we may be engaged in unwitting concealment rather than revelation. If we would teach students how science is made, really made rather than as publicly reported, we cannot fail to expose them to the whole scientist by whom it is made, with all his gifts and blindnesses, with all his methods and his *values* as well. To do otherwise is to usher in an era of spiritless technicans who will be no less lacking in understanding than they are in passion, and who will be useful only because they can be used.

In the end, even these dull tools will through patient persistence and cumulation build a technology of social science strong enough to cripple us. Far as we are from a sociological atomic bomb, we already live in a world of the systematic brainwashing of prisoners of war and of housewives with their advertising-exacerbated compulsions; and the social science technology of tomorrow can hardly fail to be more powerful than today's.

It would seem that social science's affinity for modeling itself after physical science might lead to instruction in matters other than research alone. Before Hiroshima, physicists also talked of a value-free science; they, too, vowed to make no value judgments. Today many of them are not so sure. If we today concern ourselves exclusively with the technical proficiency of our students and reject all responsibility for their moral sense, or lack of it, then we may someday be compelled to accept responsibility for having trained a generation willing to serve in a future Auschwitz. Granted that science always has inherent in it both constructive and destructive potentialities. It does not follow from this that we should encourage our students to be oblivious to the difference. Nor does this in any degree detract from the indispensable norms of scientific objectivity; it merely insists that these differ radically from moral indifference.

I have suggested that, at its deepest roots, the myth of a value-free sociology was Weber's way of trying to adjudicate the tensions between two vital Western traditions: between reason and faith, between knowledge and feeling, between classicism and romanticism, between the head and the heart. Like Freud, Weber never really believed in an enduring peace or in a final resolution of this conflict. What he did was to seek a truce through the segregation of the contenders, by allowing each to dominate in different spheres of life. Although Weber's efforts at a personal synthesis brings him nearer to St. Thomas, many of his would-be followers today tend to be nearer to the Latin Averroists with their doctrine of the twofold truth, with their conception of themselves as narrow technicians who reject responsibility for the cultural and moral consequences of their work. It is precisely because of the deeply dualistic implications of the current doctrine of a value-free sociology that I felt its most appropriate symbol to be the man-beast, the cleft creature, the Minotaur.

43 Scott Greer

Traffic, Transportation, and Problems of the Metropolis

No society in history has ever controlled space as well as the American society of mid-twentieth century. Never before has the average man had, at his command, instruments which are able to turn a coast-to-coast journey into a five-hour sojourn in a jet liner, while a machine in his garage places distant cities and diverse places within easy reach. If we remember the peasant of the past, who rarely traveled as far as 50 miles from home in a lifetime, the magnitude of the contemporary accomplishment is more striking. Americans have domesticated the great barrier of space, rendered the tool of its conquest into an individual weapon, and distributed it to the populace as a rightful consumer article.

Because the United States is the extreme example of modern, mobile, urban society (in 1957 Americans owned 64 percent of all motor vehicles on earth) we shall confine this discussion to our own society. As other nations approach our own intensive use of the automobile, they will face the identical problems. Large-scale society demands large-scale motion— and America is a nation in motion. In 1956 Americans traveled 628 billion miles, in 65 million vehicles, over 3,400,000 miles of public roads and streets.[1] In fact, automobile ownership and travel by Americans has been increasing much faster than the population in recent decades. Since 1920 the rate of increase for automobiles has been 10 times that for people and today there is a motor vehicle for every 3 Americans. The average American family spends one-eighth of its income for transportation, while the nation as a whole will spend a trillion dollars on transportation in the next 15 years. The entire economy is heavily dependent upon the automobile complex; our city layout and our new building assume mobility; we are committed because the very conditions of the society require such movement of people and goods to carry on the business of survival.

SOME COSTS OF TRANSPORTATION

It is estimated that the present American level of living requires the movement of 18 tons of material per year for each American. This movement of goods (or funded energy) is closely related to economic growth. "For every billion dollars of gross national product, we transport about three billion tons of goods and materials a distance of one mile."[2] In exchanging goods and services over a continental nation we increase our general access to the material wealth of the world, but, in doing so, we invest a great deal of energy in that exchange. In fact, America cannot exist at its present level of economic achievement without continuing to move and as it prospers it will require still more movement.

There are important costs, economic and otherwise. Wilfred Owen presents a graphic statement of the economic costs:

> In one year automotive transport consumes the wool from seventeen million sheep, the leather from half a million cattle, and enough cotton to outfit every American maid, young and old, with twenty dresses. An automobile eats up everything from ground walnut shells (for automatic transmissions) to corn, sugar cane, and beeswax. Every car uses seven miles of electric wiring, and one out of every three radios is on the road.[3]

Our notion of the economic cost becomes more precise when we reflect that 10,300,000 persons are employed full time in vehicular transport businesses—making, servicing, and driving vehicles powered by the internal combustion engine. One out of every 7 persons employed in the United States (from 21,000 in Vermont to nearly 1,000,000 in California) works full time as a servant or maker or adjunct to these machines.[4]

Furthermore, a substantial part of the tax bill is for highways, streets, and roads. Federal, state, and local governments spent over 2 billion in 1929, 7½ billion in 1956, and the total moves rapidly toward an annual bill of 10 billion dollars. Since 1925 we have, in fact, spent well over 100 billion dollars for a place to drive.[5]

This tally does not complete the sum of the financial costs, for the automobile itself is a destructive weapon of great efficacy. The cost of motor vehicle accidents since 1933 totals $70,000,000,000. In 1958 the estimated cost was $5,600,000,000.[6] And, beyond the possibility of cost accounting, what was the value of the million persons killed in accidents since the beginning of the automobile age? The 37,000 persons who were killed in 1958, and the 110,000 who were injured? There is no yardstick in our society for gauging such costs as these.

Nor can we easily evaluate other less tragic but still noxious effects. How can we put a price upon pure air to breathe, a lucid sky and sharp horizons? The air pollution in some of our great cities is such that visibility may be limited to a few blocks; millions of persons are willing to consider such smog a serious problem. What is the cost of congestion, snarled traffic, the daily parade of millions, bumper-to-bumper, from one end of the metropolitan area to the other? Automobiles carefully designed and powered for cruising speeds of 70 miles an hour have an average speed of 16 miles an hour in the rush traffic of Boston or St. Louis. The journey to work, the most time-absorbing journey the average man takes, is probably as long and perhaps more strenuous today than it was 100 years ago, when most of the work force were able to walk from their homes to their factories or shops.

These are some of the considerations which have led many to talk about the "traffic problem," the "transportation dilemma," or the "metropolitan transportation problem." The automobile driver is the central actor in the piece. Whether as the villain, the hero, or merely a perplexed protagonist, it is the automobile driver who has made possible the enormous, sprawling urban centers of today, and automobile traffic has, in turn, produced such spectacular inconveniences and tragic statistics as we have reviewed.

TRANSPORTATION AND THE CITY

Because the cities are particularly dependent upon the daily, reliable circulation of millions of persons in a small space, and because they experience congestion, traffic accidents, and air pollution, regularly and predictably, they are the focus for the general concern with traffic and transportation as social problems. Almost half of all American driving in 1958, 267 billion miles, took place upon a mere tenth of the road surface in the nation.[7] The most congested traffic in the nation is a direct consequence of the fact that two-thirds of us live and pass most of our days within a space which is only a little more than 1 percent of the United States. This relatively tiny space is, however, crucial, for the United States is an urban nation. A preponderance, not only of the people, but also of the governmental and economic centers, the cultural and economic values, of the nation is concentrated in the areas of urban development.

Thus metropolitan traffic and transportation problems have become a matter of widespread concern, for they affect the everyday life of the average citizen in our urban society. The traffic jams, noise, confusion and congestion of the peak rush hour are universal occurrences in our cities. And in each city the use of the automobile has allowed the suburbs to spread farther and farther from the center of the city—with a consequent increase in the traffic from periphery to center. Furthermore, in most cities the automobile has competed so successfully with other transport media that it has greatly weakened the financial and economic position of the rapid transit and the bus line, yet the disappearance of public transportation today would leave an impossible situation, in which most of the space within the center city would have to be used for roads and parking. Public transportation, once among the most lucrative investments in the society, is today a cripple looking to the government for a subsidy in order to survive. Much of the clientele of bus and subway use it only for peak rush hour travel to work and back; many abandon it completely as their incomes go up and they move to suburban areas far from the dependable bus service of the central city.

It is against this background that the alarm of political leaders and experts in the field of transportation makes sense. The American nation is growing at a rapid rate, and most of its growth is within metropolitan areas. Estimates of 50 million new residents by 1975 may be overexuberant, but certainly the population will continue to increase rapidly in the near future. And with the population, in fact ahead of the population, the automobile and truck population will also increase. Owen predicts that 100 million vehicles will be operating on American streets and highways by 1975. Most of them will be used in urban areas for the daily journey to work which moves the suburbanites to the center of the metropolitan area and back.

The continually increasing investment in giant, divided-lane expressways is one method of preparing for this increase of traffic, but such preparation may not be adequate, for the more roads are provided, the greater the automobile ownership becomes. In fact, the Hollywood Freeway in Los Angeles carried, within one year, almost twice the number of vehicles it was expected to carry in the remote future.[8] Thus the increase in expressways does not solve the problem; at least until now it has resulted in an increase in automobile traffic. This in turn has further weakened the public transportation system; since it provides worse service, more people use the automobile. There are vicious circles within vicious circles; as we will note throughout the article, such patterns are not odd accidents, but are characteristic of problems in metropolitan society. They interest the social scientist because they indicate structure and interdependence. To the layman, leader, and policymaker, however, they are more likely to seem indications of doom and despair.

WHAT IS THE PROBLEM?

After this chorus of problem definitions, the student may feel that the nature of the traffic and transportation problem is clear; he also may feel that it is extremely complicated and perhaps insoluble. However, if one stands aside and deliberately questions the common sense definitions of the issue, the nature of the problem becomes unclear. If we ask "What's the problem?" and, close behind, "Whose problem is it?" we can begin to unravel the "metropolitan transportation problem" like Penelope's web into a skein of assumptions, guesses, and wishes. Extreme skepticism may be a powerful tool for analyzing the slogans used in public discourse.

For we must remember that congested streets of suburban "villages," filled for hours each day by the brisk or turgid streams of traffic going and coming from work, do not spell a problem to everybody. To the proprietors of service stations, drugstores, markets, restaurants and bars along the route, congested streets spell patronage, prosperity, more of the good things of this world. Their concern for the school children facing an impenetrable barrier of automobiles, the drivers languishing in captivity, the housewives trying to use a major traffic artery as the street of a small country town, is considerably tempered by their knowledge that this street, this store frontage, is their major purchase upon economic life. It is a condition for their work, and upon their work depends the welfare of *their* children and wives.

Nor is it certain that slow traffic and congested streets are such dreadful problems to the driver. He is very likely listening to sports events, the newscasts, or music on his auto radio. While many persons seem to become anxious and constrained, others manifest an easy fatalism in the moving stream (and still others make a game of it—running with the hares and baying with the hounds). Finally, driving to and from work is ordinarily faster than movement by bus or streetcar and, as a matter of fact, the slow pace of rush hour traffic has a positive value—fatal accidents are less likely, even though bent fenders and crushed radiators are common.

The fumes of automobile exhausts and the pollution of the air may seem to be absolutely undesirable. Still, movement through this polluted atmosphere is, for most drivers and passengers, a short portion of their day. It is a transitory episode, one which lies between the place of work at one extreme and the suburban neighborhood of their choice at the other. In the suburban areas the air is cleaner, and the streets are quieter. However disgusted they are while *en route*, many drivers are evidently willing to pay the price of a brief struggle twice a day in order to reach these havens. In fact, should a device which would absorb automobile exhaust fumes be required, many drivers would resist using it—even though its cost were only 5 percent of the price of the automobile. (The civic authorities of Los Angeles, considering such an ordinance, were frankly skeptical of the public's willingness to accept the additional burden.)

Accidents and deaths also seem absolutely repugnant. Certainly they are not the kinds of experience that many persons desire (though accident analysts do describe one type of person as "an accident running around looking for a place to happen"). Still, most accidents are relatively minor: only six fatal accidents occur in each 100,000,000 miles of driving. A person may easily see them as simply the "chances of the game," somewhat more probable than being struck by lightning, a little less likely than death by cancer. (As far as that goes, three times as many persons are injured each year in accidents at home as in traffic, and almost as many, 27,000, were killed at home in 1957.) Besides, automobile insurance (compulsory in many states) financially protects the driver from himself and others, and others from himself.

Nor is the "problem" of the desirable shape of cities a simple one; it also breaks down into a multitude of problems, many of which when examined seem ambiguous or nonexistent, and others of which seem to be special pleading for special interests. The struggle to support public transportation in the metropolitan area is, in large part, an effort to retain the present division of activities between the core of the city, the industrial districts, and the outlying residential areas.[9] It is certain that the gradual decay of public transportation will result in greater automobile traffic into the central city, or less traffic of any kind, or both. This is not, on its face, evidence that a problem exists.

In short, from our temporary position of extreme skepticism, it seems that the various "problems" exist only if we assume that certain values are held by everybody, or at least by all right thinking men. This may be so, but it is a question which requires an empirical answer. One way to test the assumption is to ask: Who is concerned? For the same events are seen and evaluated very differently, from different vantage points in the social structure.

Most observers leap immediately to one conclusion—those who own business and properties in the central city are concerned with its accessibility as a marketplace. However, cheap and speedy transportation downtown is not considered such a general good by the suburban merchant. Those who have cast their economic lot in the outer areas, whether in corner groceries or giant shopping centers, have a real and personal interest in the decline of retail trade in the central city. It is money in their pockets.

As for those who would be called upon to subsidize improved mass transportation to and from the center city, most of them do not use it, and many will resent supporting a transit line in addition to their automobile. You may question their rationality in choosing the automobile over the bus or streetcar, but you must remember that the family car is evidently of great value to them. The American people spend more for automobile transportation than they do for doctors, religion, charities, telephones, radio, television, furniture, electricity, gas, books, magazines, and newspapers combined.[10]

This is the crux of the matter: the population is, by and large, choosing what it wants and getting what it chooses. To be sure it is getting many other things, which it does not want, in the package. Still, the steady increase in automobile ownership, until 75 percent of American families are now wheelborne, testifies to the value of the automobile. Its increasing daily use, reflected in the traffic congestion and expanding freeways of the cities, indicates that heavy driving, polluted air, accident and death, the decline of public transportation, blight of the central city, and other "problems" are not overriding arguments. They are the price we pay.

If, however, people are getting what they want, what precisely is meant by a "metropolitan transportation problem"? At this point we must consider the basic question, What do we mean by "a problem"?

TOWARD SOME DEFINITIONS OF THE PROBLEM

Nothing is more important than the way we define our problems; all investigation is oriented and limited by the questions that are asked, and these, in turn, derive from the problems we face.[11] The multitudinous questions asked by those concerned with "the traffic and transportation problem" lead us to suspect immediately that they have quite different problems in mind, and that the solution of one does not necessarily help with another. Thus a reduction in congestion might make little or no difference in traffic fatalities. Furthermore, it frequently happens that the solution of one problem really complicates another, as an improved traffic flow of automobiles results in deterioration of the public transportation system and decline in the central city. Finally, some types of problems do not appear readily soluble by the same methods as others we have mentioned: what the future transport system *will* be, and what it *should* be, are hardly the same kind of question.

One approach to a clearer notion is to consider all problems as having something in common. In doing this we are making an arbitrary decision, for when we define a term we limit its use and exclude other notions, which may be equally interesting, in favor of the ones pinned down by the definition. Clarification is impossible, however, without such exclusion. We shall define a problem as a *human definition* of an indeterminate situation. An indeterminate situation will be defined as one in which some elements are clear to the actor (or definer) while others are unclear or unknown.

Thus in everyday life most of us have had problems with extreme traffic congestion—traffic jams. We have had one kind of problem, what might be called the simple action problem, in which our only question is, How can I get out of this traffic jam? If we are given to a speculative kind of thinking, we may also have developed another problem—the intellectual one, What causes traffic jams, anyway? (Our answers may range from moral condemnation of other drivers and of their ancestors to accurate knowledge of traffic flow patterns: the answers do not define the problem— quite the reverse.) Finally, we may ask a very complicated question. What should be done about traffic jams? This question rests upon two problems, What *can* we do, in the light of knowledge about the nature of traffic congestion? And what *should* we do, in the light of our own values? (Both questions have as one possible answer, "Nothing.")

In the first kind of problem, the goal is given and the means are indeterminate: there are many ways to get out of a traffic jam, including having a fatal heart attack. In the second kind of problem, the goal again is clear: to explain the nature of traffic jams so well that you can state the necessary and sufficient conditions for their appearance and disappearance. The means are again indeterminate—much will depend upon your notion of what constitutes satisfactory causal explanation. (You may believe in astrology and use a horoscope, or you may lay it all to sunspots.) In the third kind of problem, however, you are not really certain of either your goal or your means. Here you are asking both what *ought* to be so, and what *can* be so, *under what conditions*. These two parts of your question are closely interrelated, but the answer to one part does not necessarily provide an answer to the other. One might solve part of the transportation problem by saying that men should be able to fly, like Peter Pan—but this ignores the limits imposed by the second question: what can be expected to occur. Conversely, one might concentrate upon what can be so under what conditions—saying in effect, "What is, is right." To do so, however, is to avoid the problem, for the question of values has been answered by suppression.

The last kind of problem is the kind usually meant when we speak of the "metropolitan transportation problem": in the individual case, it is a moral problem, and in the collective case, it is a policy problem.

Problem Definers, Representatives, and Experts This leads us to the question, Who cares about the problem? What kind of people, playing what social roles, are defining the nature of the "metropolitan transportation problem"—and hence defining its possible solutions? We have noted the great variation in perspective resulting from differences in social roles; what can we say about those who define problems? We may note at once that it is not a random selection of "average people" who are concerned. Instead, our attention is drawn to two kinds of people: representatives and experts.

Among the representatives there are two major categories—those who represent various interest groups in the significant community, and those who hold political office and are supposed to represent communities as political entities. Those who represent interest groups—the taxpayers' association, the homeowners' league, the downtown businessmen, the union members, and so forth, will speak of and to the interest of their constituents. However, they will also carefully point out the importance of their constituents' welfare to the total society, and will, in fact, try to identify the two.

The metropolitan transportation problem will be very differently defined by a broadly based labor movement, concerned for the transportation needs of its members (many of whom use the buses in the central city), and by the suburban merchants interested in business for their shopping centers and, therefore, in better circumferential roads *around* the city. Those who fear higher taxes will take still another position; indeed, small property owners are probably less interested in transportation improvement than in the profit margin of real estate rentals—in whose determination property taxes are very important. Representatives will differ widely among themselves—both in defining the nature of the problem, and its likely solution.

Those who hold political office and are supposed to represent the communities as wholes may rely upon these representatives as spokesmen for the total population. They too are representatives, however, and their base of power remains their ability to get elected. As representatives of people in their district or city, and as representatives of the organized interests who are important to their constituents, they are frequently seen as interest brokers—persons who arrange a compromise among the struggling interest groups. However, we must remember that the political official does not act on a simple summing up of special interests. He is also a person with a position of power, who has a share in the direct control of the tax rate and tax expenditure, the laws of the city and their administration, and, underlying these, the police. The political representative whose power derives from elections is sensitive to the problems that affect the voters. He has, furthermore, the ability to perform significant public acts upon a public platform where he is visible to all. He may easily become a symbol and leader of the community.

When he faces the metropolitan transportation problem what is his definition? First, as a "super representative" of a laundry list of special interests, he is forced to consider the costs and benefits of the present situation for his constituents and the costs and benefits of change. Because taxes are based in part upon income and property, direct costs will be differentially assessed whenever the public treasury becomes a resource for change. Use of other public powers (the right of eminent domain for expanding freeways and public parking lots, the use of the traffic ordinances and the police to change a parking pattern or a prevailing speed rate) also costs some people more than it does others. At the same time, the benefits of public action are often differentially distributed. We have noted that subsidy of public transportation benefits the poor at the expense of the more prosperous; enormous programs of freeway construction benefit the automobile driver at the expense of the total economy. Of course, some benefits are not differentially distributed (pure air as a result of smog abatement, for example). Even so, the ratio between costs and benefits will vary widely—for the cost will be differentially assessed. (Thus in our example, the manufacturers who must buy expensive equipment for smog control pay more than does the employee, who benefits equally.) Any question of evaluating the metropolitan transportation problem is, then, a political question to the politico.

However, the political process, that machine which translates special interests into a general interest (and incidentally keeps the politician in office), has long-run consequences for the nature of the city. After all, the public policy which emerges *is* a program for the total community. Differential distribution of costs and benefits, the use of scarce public moneys for this project rather than that one, may change the basic shape of the city, its political structure, and its very system of values.

The political officeholder, as he realizes this, frequently begins to speak in terms of an entity which is inclusive of the various special interests and *more than the sum of its parts*. The mayor of the central city (the typical spokesman for a metropolitan area) begins to conceive of the future of his metropolitan area as a collective destiny. He talks of an ideal city of the future, whose outlines may be discerned in the contemporary flux. Thus his definition of the metropolitan transportation problem may be closely tied into his definition of the problem of the central city or the problem of the metropolitan area as a whole.

For the representatives of special interests, the goal may be clear and the chief problem that of finding and using the available means—to lower taxes, increase the efficiency of public transportation, revive the down-town shopping area, increase industrial location in the area, loosen up traffic congestion (or increase it). For the political representative, how-ever, the problem is much more complicated, for the means to achieving some of these goals are purchased at the price of others, and each cost is in terms of an alternate goal. The economist has a term for this: all costs may be considered "opportunity costs," for they reduce our opportunities to pursue alternatives. For the mayor of a great city, the congeries of problems we have discussed becomes an interlinked set of opportunities and opportunity costs. From his vantage point, each goal is achieved only at the expense of other goals, which other citizens would like to see real-ized. Since to choose one goal is to reject others, and since he is sensitive to many interests, he cannot avoid a broad definition of the problem.

The second major category of spokesmen we have noted are the ex-perts. These are persons with specialized competence in understanding, predicting, and controlling the repeating situations which we encounter in everyday life. They usually approach the metropolitan transportation prob-lem as staff men for political officeholders. The traffic flow of a great city requires an elaborate set of observations, analyses, and plans: the traffic engineer is indispensable. Air pollution requires another contingent of ex-perts. Professionals in public administration and the personnel system, road and highway engineers, planners, analysts of police organization and ad-ministration, and so on—the list is a very long one—each becomes a corps of exports on phases of the problem.

Such persons help clarify the consequences of decisions, the costs and benefits. They say, in effect, "define the goal and we will see what means can be used to attain it, and what it will cost you." Thus their typical definition of the transportation and traffic problems will center upon the kinds of means that would prove effective. Such an approach, however, neglects the total costs and is frequently inadequate even to solve a limited problem: the engineers concerned with improving traffic flow decide that automobile traffic cannot be considered apart from the changing usage of public transportation, nor can it be controlled without use of publicly fixed parking rates. The traffic-transportation-parking expert then points out that certain problems, such as rush hour traffic congestion, are un-avoidable if everybody wants to go to the same place, over the same streets, at the same time. He begins to think about staggering the work hours of the population or arranging the home and the place of work closer together, to *avoid* transportation. At this point he has become a planner, layout architect, sociologist. The tendency for the experts to break out of their role as specialized tools, and to approach a more complex definition of the problems, is a consequence of the interrelatedness of the different human activities which they study.

We have spoken as if all experts were official staff men of government. Many, however, are staff employees of private industry, chambers of com-merce, citizens' committees and civic commissions of one sort or another.

With greater or lesser bias in favor of some interests, they attempt to speak for the community as a whole. In such a role, their perspective on the problem tends to approach that of the governmental official who represents the community as a whole. They attempt to make clear the costs and benefits of the *status quo*, to suggest courses of action in the light of these, and to measure both present and possible future against some ideal city.

Such staff men, members of Planning Associations, Civic Associations, Downtown Associations, and the like, are critics of the *status quo*. (They are also critics of the future, insofar as they forecast it from trends in the present.) Their criticism ordinarily leads to suggestions for controlled change. Plans and recommendations are the expected products of study commissions and citizens' committees. Their reports are written as though the entire community were the client. The frequent failure of their plans to materially affect events, however, leads us to ask, Who, then, is the client? The provisional answer is, "Anyone who is interested." The staff men for the community are, in effect, trying to create a clientele—and serve it simultaneously. They are agitators and organizers, who sometimes create "problems" by simply defining or discovering them.

The Social Scientist as a Problem Definer   The social scientist first entered American society in a role very similar to that of a community staff man. The sociologist, for example, was first concerned with such social problems as crime, race relations, "Americanizing the immigrant," city planning and the prevention of slums. The problems were implicitly defined in terms of deviations from culturally given norms. The indeterminate aspect was, simply, the means to their achievement.

Furthermore, the social scientist was usually called upon to help solve public problems when it became clear that conventional practice or technological analysis (such as engineering) was inadequate to achieve the desired goals. Thus, in the case of the metropolitan traffic and transportation problem, it is becoming clear that the patterned behavior of human populations (and patterns in process of change) is at once the substance of many problems and the likeliest lead to their solution.

However, the origins of an intellectual discipline do not tell us what it is likely to become. When people concentrate upon systematic thinking and investigation in an area, they may very well end up by changing their subject matter as well as their method. The alchemist, intending to turn lead into gold, may become a chemist interested in the structure of matter. So sociology, first concerned with an area of human behavior for practical reasons ("What can we do about the traffic problem?") may, as a dynamic intellectual enterprise, cause the very questions to change as the problem is redefined. Instead of viewing a social problem as self-evident, we consider it as one definition of some aspects of the ongoing society.

In the beginning, the problem is really defined by the popular thought of the day; it is usually an issue, something to worry about and differ on, something for which people suggest moral and practical remedies. A statement that "it's a problem" is usually based upon all sorts of assumptions, about what should be, about what is, and about the means of changing the existing state of things into the ideal state. When the sociologist approaches such a popularly defined problem his first job is a rigorous intellectual analysis. When he does this, he will divide the problem into two different but interconnected sets of problems, the problems of general intellectual analysis, and the problem of social analysis. For convenience, we will discuss them separately.

THE INTELLECTUAL PROBLEM   The intellectual problem is, first, to determine what is known and what is indeterminate. The analyst begins with only the knowledge that someone thinks something is a social problem; the nature of their reasoning, their assumptions and conclusions, are the first objects for his study. He will find that the desirable social end, or the desirable social means to achieve it, or both, are in dispute. The assumptions and interpretations of desirability he will call the *normative* problem; those concerned with the possibility of achieving a given state of affairs, and the utility of different means, he will call the *empirical* problem.

Thus the statement "metropolitan transportation is a serious problem" requires that we ask such questions as these:

1. What is the present state of the transportation system? How is it working, how is it evaluated with respect to what norm?

2. What is the desired state of the system? How would it work, with respect to what norm is it desirable?

3. How can the present state of the system be moved toward the desired state (with respect to whatever norms are implied)? What would this cost with respect to other norms in the society; that is, what would be the side effects of such change?

Such analysis will lead, then, to further questions for the sociologist; these are scientific questions, deriving from the definition of the situation as a scientific problem. This problem is to interpret the circulatory system of the metropolis in terms of patterned social behavior. Such interpretation will require investigation of the transportation system as a social system, interdependent with other systems of behavior in the society. It will require analysis of what this system will be under specified circumstances. It will also require testing, through prediction and control, in order to see if the analysis corresponds with the nature of things.

An important aspect of this analysis will be the study of the transportation system as *socially problematic*. He will ask: Why the outcry? Why has metropolitan transportation been defined as a social problem in the first place?

THE SOCIAL PROBLEM   The sociologist defines a social problem as a subject for sociological investigation; such examination may or may not help expedite its social resolution. For, to the sociologist, these problems are integral parts of the continued existence of a society, predictable responses to social change. Though he and the layman may both speak of a given situation as a social problem, they mean quite different things; the layman's problem can be solved only through action or a change in the state of affairs. The sociologist's problem is solved through increased knowledge, yielding an explanation which is tested by prediction and control.

In a sociological frame of reference, most social problems result from social change: shifts in the environment, the tools men use, the relations of men to each other or the normative structure of the society. Such change is continually vitiating the old assumptions of what is normal, right, and to be expected. The situations men face are not adequately handled by their socially inherited definitions, and stable parts of the social environment become indeterminate and problematical. Out of collective definitions and collective choice comes an unanticipated world of new regularities, some of which violate old expectations and are seen as problems. A classic example is the effect of introducing the automobile into American society; the widespread ownership of automobiles produced great freedom of mobility and made privacy portable. This, in turn, made possible a freedom in social relations which was hard to come by in the small town of horse-and-buggy days. As one result, American courtship patterns were changed, not because anyone decided to change them, but because of the increasing freedom of unmarried adults from supervision by the elders. Such rapid changes of behavior produce violent responses from the guardians of morals, and many a sermon was preached on the subject of the younger generation and its road to perdition. In sociological terms, these changes destroy the agreement on norms, or socially effective definitions of what should be done.[12]

Eventually, however, the situation becomes stabilized again, though in a new pattern. Thus contemporary patterns of courtship are no longer objects of horror, though they are probably even looser than those which were so exciting to the generation of the 1920's. They have proved their merit (Americans marry at an earlier age than ever) and have become normatively defined. There is, in other words, a new state of the system, one in which early and socially unsupervised courtship is "no problem."

Political problems are that subclass of social problems resolved through the political process. Officeholders must define them more specifically and use their position to act (or not) with the state's monopoly over force and the state's treasury. Both the socially indeterminate situation and the social response to it are defined by political action. Here are some political questions, arising from political problems: When shall a bus line be suspended? Who shall pay for the streets? What is the legal speed limit? Or even (what was once a political problem)—How shall automobiles be introduced into the city? What are the rights of an automobilist as compared with a driver of a one-hoss shay?

Such questions all arise from the problem: What is the "best way" to use the automobile in this society? And this is part of a larger problem still: How shall we manage the circulation of men, energy, and goods in this metropolitan world?

SOCIAL CITY AND POLITICAL CITY

The central city and its suburban ring are as much a unity economically and socially as was true in the days of the compact urban mass, even though the geographical division of labor and rewards within that unity is different. However, the populations moving outward from the center have not been included in the governmental boundaries of the central city; beginning in the first decade of this century, the "outside" populations have resisted annexation by the central city, and have incorporated themselves into small residential enclaves, called variously "villages," "towns," and "cities." And, despite considerable recognition that the growth of such governmentally autonomous suburbs may be related to various urban problems, the process continues.

> Between 1952 and 1957 alone, 170 new municipalities came into being in metropolitan areas and 519 new special districts were created. By 1957, there were over 3,000 governments that could be said to possess more or less general municipal powers, and there was, of course, that awesome figure of 15,658 legally distinguishable local units [in metropolitan areas].[13]

Despite the fact that a majority of those who live in the suburban rings work in the central city, including a disproportionate number of the wealthiest and most powerful, and despite the fact that social ties of many kinds cross the boundaries from city to suburbs, the suburbs and the central city have no local government in common. Political boundaries fractionate the metropolitan complex.

This disjunction between political and social boundaries has important consequences for the polity of the metropolitan area. It means that no local governmental decision applying to all of the residents of the metropolis is possible. Yet many of the conditions which the citizens expect their government to control ("problems," that is), can be controlled only by an areawide normative order. As the Air Pollution Control Officer of Los Angeles County says, "Air pollution does not recognize political boundaries,"[14] nor do crime, epidemics, and other conditions which require governmental action. The change in the space-time ratio which has permitted a close integration of many activities within today's metropolitan areas has not been accompanied by any increased governmental integration.

Nor is there a public treasury for the metropolis as a whole. This creates continual problems of assessing the costs of public improvements, which, in terms of American political norms, are supposed to be paid by those who benefit, or at least by their neighbors and fellow citizens. For a great deal of the use value of facilities in the central city is realized by those who live in the suburbs; when the daytime population of the central city is increased by a million people, the public utilities, police force, buses and streetcars, and other services of the urban center must provide for them. Yet much of the suburban population which works in the city is extremely resentful of the city's efforts to tax them—through taxes on earnings and city sales taxes.

The inability to pass and enforce laws for the metropolitan area, and the inability to tax and spend for the area, mean, in brief, that there is no single polity for the metropolis. Such problems as those we have discussed earlier, the provision of a better transportation system for the area, the lessening of the strain on the transportation system through planning the locations of activities differently, cannot be carried out except through negotiation among whatever share of the 15,658 governments are located within a given region. The magnitude of this task is clear when we reflect upon the 97 municipalities in St. Louis County, ranging in size from 53,000 people to 60 people—or the 1400 governmental units in the greater New York metropolitan area.

Integration of policy is further handicapped by the differentiation of interest among the various governmentally defined subareas of the metropolis. The central city faces a problem of renovating or rebuilding much of the structure of the eotechnic city which is no longer useful for the fluid metropolis of today. Antiquated business buildings, deteriorated housing pre-dating the Civil War, and deteriorating public monuments on narrow streets which are nearly impassable by modern automobiles, all require great expenditures of public funds. At the same time the city's share of the metropolitan population is disproportionately made up of newcomers to the area who are poor and disadvantaged and require more public aid. Thus the central city has very specific and pressing interests and a need for a larger treasury.

> But taxable resources steadily declined, and as residential areas deteriorated, the slums took up 20 percent of the nonbusiness area, siphoning off 45 percent of total municipal expenditures but contributing only 6 percent of the revenue. As a further complication, as the city became more and more the educational or civic center of the region, the amount of tax-exempt property increased steadily. With service demands at least as high as when most of the urban population lived within its limits, and with the tax base declining relatively or absolutely, most large American cities ran out of money.[15]

For those identified with the fortunes of the central city, the pressing metropolitan problems are: what should be done and what can be done for the central city? Should the central city, housing a large and necessary portion of the unskilled and semiskilled labor force which makes the industrial complex of the metropolis possible, alone be forced to pay the deficits associated with such a population, while those who profit most from the city's work retreat to the suburbs? Similarly, should the city alone pay taxes for universities which serve the entire metropolitan region? art museums? symphonies?

Meanwhile, those who identify with the suburbs see different problems. Living in the seas of subdivision, where new public facilities must be developed from scratch, their taxes move steadily upward. The major child-producing regions of the country are in the suburban municipalities, and the bill for public schools is ordinarily two-thirds of the local tax bill. It climbs each year with each new generation of school children. Local taxes fall almost entirely upon home-owners in many suburban districts, for the commercial and industrial plants (which yield massive tax payments) are highly concentrated. The very smallness of most suburban municipalities, together with their definition by their residents as cities of homes, tend to eliminate all but the home-owner as taxpayer. While a few suburbs are tax rich because of the industry located within their boundaries, most of the others consist of nothing but single-family dwelling units.[16] The suburbanite sees the problems of the central city as no more pressing than those of his suburb, and feels, at most, that payment of an earnings tax through his employer in the central city should allow him to call it even.

From these divisions of interest, complex and lurid ideologies arise. The spokesman for the central city, manifesting little sympathy for the suburbs, proposes that they solve their problems by abandoning their "toy government" and acknowledging their unity with the city. The suburbanite retorts that the central city is old and decaying, taken over by Negroes, labor unions, and crooked political machines. Each side says, in effect, "Why should I pay taxes for the benefit of those others?" And, at the same time, the tax bill rises in central city and in suburb, while people in each area complain about problems common to both.

The Metropolitan Point of View   In 1933 R. D. McKenzie, in a famous monograph on metropolitan growth, remarked: "The larger cities of the country are becoming what might be termed regionally conscious."[17] This consciousness, visible at that time in efforts to integrate the governments of central city and suburb in St. Louis, Cleveland, and Pittsburgh, has continued to the present. According to a recent report, nearly 100 Metropolitan Surveys have been conducted in the past 20 years.[18] They have had differing foci, but all of them have been provoked by governmental fragmentation, "the Chinese wall between central city and suburbs" and the "crazy quilt pattern of government in the suburbs." Most have recommended some kind of governmental integration.

Beginning with problems of inadequate public services, inequitable taxation, and unable government, analysts time and again come to the conclusion that certain of these problems' are metropolitan in scope, problems of the entire complex, central city and suburb. Analyses of problems of traffic, slum increase, air pollution, sewerage disposal, and many others, have a way of leading to the conclusion that governmental fragmentation, if it has not actually caused some of the conditions which the analyst considers deleterious, has effectively prevented any improvement. Our brief discussion of the changing space-time ratio and its effect upon the shape of the city would indicate some reasons for this. The metropolis is one labor force, one economic complex, one circulatory system, and action in one part affects action in another part. Movement to the suburbs of certain populations has a reciprocal effect upon the central city; fluidity, or the daily movement of population between the various parts, affects them all.

The production and continuation of those situations which are considered metropolitan problems reflects the interdependence of the population within the urban region. The nature of the problems also reflects the interdependence of different kinds of social behavior. The person who chooses to move to the suburb does not just swell the population of a suburban municipality; he also vacates a home in the city, increases the traffic on the arteries between city and suburbs, takes his property tax payment from the city to the suburb, increases the burden on the suburban school system, and so on. When this person is multiplied by 100,000, the resulting situation becomes a congeries of social problems. Returning to our definition of a problem: changes in the tools men use for circulation have resulted in changes in the relations of men to each other, and the resulting situation is not adequately handled by the socially inherited definitions. The world of new regularities produced, a world in which home and work are in two different cities 20 miles apart, is one which creates many ambiguities, uncertainties, indeterminacies—that is, problems.

Traffic and Transportation: A Metropolitan Problem   Metropolitan problems are, in brief, those problems which are common to a metropolitan area, which are produced by the metropolitan nature of the local community, and which can be solved only through metropolitan-wide action. As problems, they are indeterminate social norms to some part of the population; either the social order which should be produced, or the means that should be used to produce it, or both, are socially undetermined. In the case of traffic and transportation we can infer, from statements of the problem, that there is fair agreement *at least* on the desired social order in a negative sense: the problem-definers speak of less congestion, greater ease and speed of travel, less air pollution, fewer accidents, fewer deaths, and so forth. Though the means are problematic (constituting *the* problem), the ends seem fairly clear.

The traffic-transportation system is, in this sense, a problem to a great many people in the metropolitan areas today, and to people scattered all over the metropolis. As sample surveys in metropolitan St. Louis indicate clearly, when a sample of the citizens were asked what change or improvement they would most like to see in the area, improvement in the transportation system was the number one choice.[19] The single most frequently mentioned aspect of traffic was congestion, indicating the inadequacy of the arteries for their load. The most frequently mentioned aspect of public transportation was irregular service and poor scheduling, indicating the results of the vicious circle in public transit in which a declining number of customers results in declining service.

These results are consistent with those from other metropolitan studies; in fact, from the point of view of the ordinary citizen, traffic and transportation is *the* metropolitan problem. Certainly the organizational system producing these citizen reactions is a metropolitan system; the interdependence of the metropolitan area, indicated when we speak of it as a single labor force and economic complex, can be maintained only through a circulatory system which is metropolitan in scope. The transportation system allows for the integration of what could be, after all, a giant collection of villages, in a complex geographical division of labor and rewards.[20] At the same time, the changing distribution of labor and residence within the metropolitan region produces those strains upon the traffic and transportation grid which are seen as problems.

Nor is it possible, in view of many experts, to improve this system very much (with respect to speed, congestion, and the other negative attributes mentioned earlier) without some kind of integrated control over the entire metropolitan transportation grid. As the public report of the Metropolitan St. Louis Survey states:

> A segmented approach is harmful in three major ways. It prevents the over-all planning of an orderly road system—one community may widen a street to take care of more traffic only to find its efforts thwarted by traffic backups caused by a narrow road in the next town. It does not distribute the burden of traffic costs equitably—taxpayers of one community are frequently forced to spend large sums to maintain an arterial road that primarily benefits residents of other communities. It permits local considerations to prevail over the interests of the area as a whole—municipal officials are not in a good position to view traffic matters in an over-all and long-range perspective because of pressures from local interests.[21]

Thus the decrease in the space-time ratio, which has allowed for urban concentration and, within the city, metropolitan spread and sprawl, has as one by-product an increasing pressure upon the facilities for circulation. A better fit between traffic and thoroughfares requires an order common to the entire metropolitan system of transportation.

If traffic and transportation are metropolitan, in what sense are they problems? We have indicated a sociological theory which explains the current urban transportation system as a product of increase in scale, the geographical division of labor, and shifts in the space-time ratio. Present transportation grids are predictable results of these developments. These results may be defined, however, in many different ways; one can as easily point to the progress in mobility and access to green pastures, as point to congestion and smog as problems. How have metropolitan problems, and specifically, metropolitan transportation problems, been defined?

There have been three major views of the metropolitan problem. These may be called the "crisis" definition, the "management" definition, and the "market" definition. Each has been a dramatic framework within which the problem definer has justified his criticism of the present and probable future of the metropolitan area.

Three Views of Metropolitan Problems   Those who have adopted the crisis definition of metropolitan problems have generally focused upon structures, of behavior or of matter, which were highly valued in an older normative system, and seem to be in danger of collapsing altogether. Some speak of the "Crisis in Metropolitan Transit," and point to the declining use and revenues of the public transportation systems; others emphasize the "Crisis of the Downtown Area," and cite the statistics which indicate an increasing number of automobiles entering the central business district, and a declining number of customers; still others may speak of the "Crisis in Housing," when one-fourth of the city is slum. Such an approach has a venerable history in American urban reform; "Save our city!" is an ancient battlecry. Behind the approach lies the implicit assumption that this particular structure is basic to the continued existence of the city as we know and value it.

Others, however, with a doctrine less dramatic but equally faithful to tradition, see the metropolitan problems as problems of efficiency, economy, and order. They note the large number of governmental units, dividing jurisdictions and power, and consider coordination impossible on its face. Counting the costs of the "crazy quilt" system, they demonstrate the profits to be made through merger. In the great tradition of American business enterprise, they see the local government industry as backward, unorganized, out of step with the times, and their argument for the existence of a problem, and for its solution, relies upon the advantage of organizational unity, large-scale operations, and administrative efficiency. In a phrase, they believe that to rationalize the government is to improve it.

The third approach, which we have called the market approach, seems at first to have less purchase on the old grounds of American ideology. Those who take this approach assume that there is a boom in the market for governmental goods, that the American people are beginning to demand governmental services which are not only equal to those of the past, but are improvements upon them, comparable to the material improvement of most other aspects of life. This approach does rest upon one of the sacred tenets of American ideology, despite its rather rakish appearance: it implicitly assumes that the population at large will determine what kind of metropolis it wants, in the long run, by its economic and political behavior.

In assessing these views, we must look carefully at the implicit assumptions upon which they rest. With respect to the crisis view, we must note carefully what is in crisis, how important that structure is for the metropolitan area as a whole, and what the probabilities of complete breakdown seem to be. In general, complete functional breakdowns in the necessary integration of the activities scattered over the geography of the metropolis do not seem likely. While motorists may spend longer hours at the wheel, the factories and offices run on schedule with a regularity which we would regard as almost miraculous, were we not habituated to the clock. While Los Angeles exhaust fumes are translated regularly into smog, the crowded coastal plain between the mountains and the sea continues to attract population from all over the nation. And, though one cannot take a sanguine view of the thousands who, each year, meet their death on the highway, freeway, or street, the mortality rate per mile of driving has not increased in recent decades; it has, in fact, declined. Public transit systems continue to deteriorate, but they do so chiefly because their ex-riders have adopted other, and presumably, in their eyes, superior ways of getting about.

The management definition of a metropolitan problem assumes that government is simply a business, supplying goods to a captive clientele. Efficiency, economy, in general a lowering of price and increase in quality or quantity, are the guiding norms which orient this approach. But we must ask: Efficiency and economy in terms of what values? Monetary values only? To be certain, one can make a good case for "economic man" to use public transportation, at least in his journeys to the central city where the routes and equipment are usually most efficient. But economic man has evidently decided upon another product; for whatever reasons, he chooses to be an auto jockey, a participant, rather than a passive passenger. As he moves, in fits and starts, through the corporation boundaries of one suburban village after another, he may curse governmental fragmentation under his breath, but the man who drives these roads during the rush hour is also likely to be the man who lives in one of the villages. He is also likely to vote against any kind of merger, for he values the autonomy of the village. He may be simply unintelligent or uninformed— or he may value both speedy driving and local control over traffic, and value the latter more highly. The limits of the business management perspective on metropolitan problems are clear: many of the values involved are nonfinancial.

The market approach rests upon the assumption that there are norms which, socially evolved and diffused, define the quality of governmental goods which people believe they have a right to expect. These we have called "consumption norms." They are closely related to what has been technologically and economically possible; thus the consumption norms for safety, speed and comfort on the streets and highways of the 1920's were significantly different from those of today. At the same time, they are not identical with the existing goods available; the chances are they are always somewhat above the present article in certain values. Thus the socially defined goal is determinate enough (though it is open ended, as desires are infinitely extensible); the means to achieving it (and the best choice among alternatives) is indeterminate. Indeed, that is the problem from this point of view. For, to those who espouse the market approach, the survival or death of public transit and the central city cannot, by definition, be fatal to the society. Public transit and the central city have simply lost their comparative position in the changing consumer

market; by a process of trial and error, of natural selection, these structures have lost out in the struggle. Nor is the market theorist impressed
with the argument for administrative efficiency and economy. As Sergei
Grimm, one of the most candid exponents of the position, remarks:

> In dealing with factors and trends, one must keep in mind certain inherent
> characteristics of our industrial civilization and of our socioeconomic system.
> Efficiency and economy are not basic objectives. The Constitution certainly
> does not set them up as such, on a par with life, liberty and the pursuit of
> happiness. This country is the land of waste, which is the price we pay for
> liberty and progress.[22]

As we evaluate these arguments, it seems that the exponents of the market position have the strongest claim to a correct interpretation of the
metropolitan transportation problem. We are not required to define the
"ideal city" in this approach, and can therefore pay more attention to
the emergent trends which point toward the limits within which the city
of the future will probably emerge. Nor are we required to justify a concern with the unreal yardsticks of efficiency and economy which, ideal
norms though they may be for a bureaucracy, omit that element of free
choice and change which is common in the wealthy society of increasing
scale. We are, however, led to ask: How accurate is the market mechanism in reflecting the relative desires of the local population?

Returning for a moment to the focus of the problem-definers, we can
reinterpret their delineations of the metropolitan transportation problem.
It will be recalled that these are composed of two parts: (1), the present
quality of transportation within the metropolitan area, in speed, ease, and
cost, and (2), the consequences of the present and projected circulatory
system for the other aspects of metropolitan society. We shall consider
each in turn.

PROBLEMS OF THE MARKET AND
PROBLEMS OF THE POLITY

While there is no imminent danger of a complete transportation breakdown in the metropolitan areas, there is widespread dissatisfaction with
the present system in many of them.[23] The contemporary transport system
in most metropolitan areas certainly provides the minimal degree of order
necessary to sustain the integrated pattern of behavior in a giant city:
as we have noted, people do get to work, for the most part on time; the
city is supplied with its necessaries and luxuries each day. However, those
who make a business of projections take seriously Owen's remarks about
the increase to 100,000,000 motor vehicles in the United States by 1975,
and, viewing the continuing spread of the suburbs, see only an increased
volume of traffic from the peripheries toward the center and back. Even
to sustain the present quality of transportation will require very large
investments of the society's surplus in the road system. And, even if the
chief aim is to prevent increased crowding of the roads, it may be necessary
for the public treasury to subsidize the mass transportation lines.

To be sure, it is possible that the quality of transportation could decline without materially affecting the integration of the metropolis; the additional time and work necessary to get around could be absorbed by the nonfinancial sector of the economy—the leisure time of the population. However, if the problem is defined as the discrepancy between the conditions people now experience and those they feel they deserve, such a solution is no solution.

This discrepancy, it has been suggested earlier, is due to the general rise in aspirations in the metropolitan population, rather than a decline in transportation facilities. In a society where job level, educational level, and real income level have been increasing steadily for several decades, most of the rewards of most men have been increasing in quantity and quality. There is one exception. The goods and services produced by public enterprise have not kept pace with those produced by the private economy. This is not unrelated to our earlier point, that the management definition of metropolitan problems emphasizes the organizational backwardness of urban government, the anarchy resulting from many units of government in a single area.

The consumer problem, however, the problem of quality and quantity of public goods, arises less from inefficiency and diseconomy than from simple poverty. To quote an eminent scholar of public finance, "This is the root of the metropolitan financial problem: How to divert a larger share of resources to government use, or, more simply, how to get more funds than existing revenue systems will produce, without unduly impinging on private production."[24]

Lyle C. Fitch (who is First Deputy City Administrator of the City of New York), then goes on to point out that "Metropolitan financial problems arise primarily from the lack of adequate machinery rather than from any lack of capacity. Presumptively, today's large urban communities, being typically the focal points of wealth and income, have the resources to meet their urban needs." Thus the problem of the provision of more acceptable transportation systems is not economic; it is, rather, a *fiscal* problem. That is, it results from inability to collect from the public funds adequate for needed expenditures.

Many goods and services can be purchased by the contemporary American only as a citizen, through the government. As Justice Holmes remarked, "When I pay taxes, I buy civilization." No man, whatever his income and ability to pay, can purchase less congestion on main thoroughfares of the journey to work than any other man (just as he cannot purchase more personal safety on the city sidewalks at night, or less smog in his downtown place of work during the day). The market mechanism, which seems to work well enough in many cases, does not work at all in respect to some products which loom large in everyday life.

The equivalent mechanism is, of course, the government. Government is a supplier with a natural monopoly. But American local government is traditionally weak in this role; perhaps it is a heritage of the days when government was largely a matter of patronage and pelf—at any rate, 4 out of 10 people in metropolitan St. Louis felt that their taxes were too high for the benefits they derived from local government.[25] Yet the fiscal policy of local government is largely controlled by referenda; tax increases and bond issues are usually submitted to the voters.

The development of a planned improvement in the metropolitan traffic and transport grid is further handicapped by the lack of any one governmental agency to assess taxes, plan the system, and make and enforce the rules of the road. In the absence of such an agency, the constituent municipal governments may or may not happen to cooperate; nobody can force them to. But, to develop a *metropolitan agency* requires, in most states, a separate vote in at least the central city and the suburbs. And here again, the voter registers his suspicion of government by voting the agency down.[26]

Thus the metropolitan transportation problem, when viewed as a question of the discrepancy between the quality of transportation available and the consumption norms of the population, may be reduced to a conflict between the governmental norms of Americans, on one hand, and their consumption norms on the other. Since the governmental norms control the means mechanism for achieving the consumption norms, one or the other must change. Americans must either accept slower transportation as the price of governmental fragmentation and cheap taxes, or they must accept governmental integration and with it a more centralized control of street design and driving rules, together with higher taxes.

Most of the social costs of traffic can be reduced, if not eliminated, through more extensive and uniform control of streets, automobiles, and drivers. Properly designed express highways with limited access are substantially safer than conventional arterials and volume is related to accidents.[27] The mortality rate from accidents can be reduced by safety appliances, and exhaust fumes can be almost eliminated through attachments. In each case, effective use of the means requires a political decision—and the limits of the polity will be reflected in the costs of transportation.

The second part of what is defined as the metropolitan transportation problem arises out of changes in other aspects of metropolitan society which result from the shift in the space-time ratio and the circulatory system. Of these changes the most central is that in the function of the central city. Francis Bello puts it succinctly:

> Perhaps the central question is whether the city will continue to serve as a unifying core for its surrounding metropolitan region, or whether it will be utterly fragmented. The key to this problem is transportation. Planners fear that if urban transportation costs—not only in money but in time and wear and tear on the rider—rise much further, they will cancel out all the advantages of the city.[28]

This problem is immensely more complicated than that of improving the quality of transportation, though it is easy to see that they are related: the reason for its complication is simply that here the socially defined goal, the norm, is itself indeterminate.

The desirable city of the future cannot be authoritatively defined at present, in such a way that everyone must agree. Nobody knows if the city of the past, highly centralized, dominated by the concentration of tall buildings and great factories toward the hub of transportation, is a possible form for the city of the future. The growth in the population far away from the central city in the suburbs, the continual flow of population outward as income rises, and the appearance of factories and shopping centers in the outlying regions, suggest that the older pattern need not, and probably cannot, be maintained—given the way of life chosen today by most urban Americans.

Much of the congestion of downtown streets is a consequence of our commitments to the older geometry of the city, to older structures and streets designed for the Age of Steam, foot passengers, and the horse car. The older structures still represent, however, an immense proportion of the funded energy, the capital of the society. And, as the city is continually built and rebuilt, the new development also represents a commitment— the city of the future must take account of these social assets. Such building rests upon the possibilities of circulation, however, and to many people changes in transportation represent possible control over future development.

> Looking at the impact of alternative transportation schemes, there is no question, for example, that the construction *and full utilization* of a subway system for rail transportation converging on the center of Washington, D. C. would greatly intensify land uses in the downtown area, whereas a beltline expressway circling the area would promote the objective of greater dispersal.[29] [italics added]

The full utilization which Owen specifies, however, can be brought about only through maintaining the present division of labor between the center and the periphery; while this may be a foregone conclusion in some cities, it is less certain in others. "The key," as Owen adds, "is not an open-sesame for the planner, because its use depends on what is technologically feasible and publicly acceptable." And this, as noted, is by no means clear, for there is no "official line" on the city of the future. In the meantime it grows, by leaps and bounds, with a decrease in over-all density and an increasing automobile population. While public transportation may still be important in the journey to work, particularly in very large cities, an increasing share of all urban circulation is by automobile.

The shape of the city is being determined by the collective choices which millions of people are making and have made. Their options are the diffusely settled neighborhoods of suburbia and the automobile, or a commitment to the older structures of the city which is slowly dwindling as many facilities are decentralized. To change the net results of this drift would require a government which had the power to settle upon the land-use of the society, to build the transportation facilities as part of a long-term plan, and to use the power of the public treasury and the police to coerce and channel the growth of the future city. Such a government would necessarily control the entire metropolitan area, not just the central city.

There is a long history of spectacular failure in the creation of such governments in America. The American, when faced with a choice between changing his norms for enlarged local government and gaining greater control over his environment, on the one hand, and limiting local government on the other, has voted for the latter.

Most of the societal organization of space has been left to the free play of the market in land, with the transportation system a net product. Most of the societal organization of interaction on the road has been left to the free play of the market for automobiles, with the accident and death rate a net product. The society has allowed a maximum of individual choice within a minimal working order.

It seems likely, therefore, that the provision of improved transportation within the metropolitan area, if it takes place, will be the result of a consumer's interest expressed through voting for highway bonds, for special districts which are concerned only with transportation, and through programs which originate at the state or Federal level where no direct referendum is necessary. Such a development of the urban roadway system will violate all of the canons of planning, for the side consequences of new development for neighborhood, central city, or metropolis will not be evaluated by one agency which is concerned for them all—that is, one polity. However, roadways will be improved, and the chips will fall where they may.

The resulting conditions will violate many norms: the city of today does not approximate the "ideal city" of an earlier epoch, nor will the future city now coming into being. However, it is likely that the normative definition of the city is in process of change, approaching the diffuse metropolis looped together with freeways. Those who regret the concentrated glamour and activity of the central city in the days of the streetcars are probably cultural conservatives, rather than definers of problems for the total society. Although their voices are influential with the men who formulate and carry out the polity, they seem to be less influential than those of the suburban land developers and officials, the taxpayers and the automobile drivers, the plural interests of a pluralistic society.

NOTES

[1] *Automobile Facts and Figures* (Detroit: Automobile Manufacturer's Association, 1957). For the world comparison see *Statistical Abstract of the United States*, Commerce Dept., Bureau of the Census (Washington, D. C., 1959), Sec. 34.

[2] Wilfred Owen, "Automotive Transport in the United States," *Annals of the American Academy of Political and Social Science*, 320 (1958), p. 6.

[3] *Ibid.*, p. 2.

[4] *Automobile Facts and Figures*, p. 44.

[5] *Ibid.*, p. 56.

[6] *Accident Facts*, National Safety Council, Chicago, 1959, pp. 13, 59. The bill for 1958 may be broken down into: Property Damage, $1,900,000,000; Wage Loss, $1,500,000,000; Medical Expenses, $150,000,000; Overhead Cost of Insurance, $2,050,000,000.

[7] *Automobile Facts and Figures*, p. 63.

[8] Wilfred Owen, *The Metropolitan Transportation Problem* (Washington, D. C.: The Brookings Institution, 1958), p. 35.

[9] To be sure, it is sometimes justified as an effort to maintain adequate transportation for the "needs" of the portion of the population which cannot afford to own an automobile. However, such justification must be seen for what it is: a redistribution of income, with taxes upon the entire population paying for the movement of one part of the population.

[10] Owen, "Automotive Transport in the United States," *op. cit.*, p. 4.

[11] Robert K. Merton, "Notes on Problem-Finding in Sociology," in *Sociology Today*, R. K. Merton, L. Broom, and L. S. Cottrell, Jr., eds. (New York: Basic Books, 1959), pp. ix–xxxiv. See also John Dewey, *Logic, The Theory of Inquiry* (New York: Holt, 1938), Chaps. 24–25. Also F. S. C. Northrop, *The Logic of Science and the Humanities* (New York: Doubleday, 1959), esp. Chap. 1, "The Initiation of Inquiry."

[12] For a general discussion of the social effects some major inventions had on American society see William F. Ogburn, with the assistance of S. C. Gilfillan, "The Influence of Inventions and Discovery," in *Recent Social Trends in the United States*, Report of the President's Research Committee on Social Trends (New York: McGraw-Hill, 1933).

[13] R. C. Wood, *Suburbia: Its People and Their Politics* (Boston: Houghton Mifflin, 1959), p. 69. There are many other studies of these phenomena; a work oriented toward policy problems is John C. Bollens, *The States and the Metropolitan Problem* (Chicago: Council of State Governments, 1956).

[14] "Statement of S. Smith Griswold, Air Pollution Control Officer, Los Angeles County, Calif.," *Unburned Hydrocarbons*, Hearing Before a Subcommittee on Interstate and Foreign Commerce, House of Representatives, 85th Congress (Washington, D.C.: Government Printing Office, March 17, 1958), p. 108.

[15] Wood, *Suburbia, op. cit.*, pp. 71–72.

[16] This variation is illustrated in suburban St. Louis County, where the assessed valuation (that is, taxable property) *per capita* in the wealthiest school district is 18 times that in the poorest. See, *Background for Action*, First Public Report, The Metropolitan St. Louis Survey, Pt. 1, "The People" (University City, Mo., 1957).

[17] R. D. McKenzie, "The Rise of Metropolitan Communities," in *Recent Trends in the United States*, Report of the President's Research Committee on Social Trends (New York: McGraw-Hill, 1933), p. 451.

[18] Government Affairs Foundation, *Metropolitan Surveys: A Digest* (Chicago: Public Administration Service, 1958).

[19] Cf. *Path of Progress for Metropolitan St. Louis*, pp. 55–59.

[20] Cf. William Bascomb, "Urbanization Among the Yoruba," *American Journal of Sociology*, 60 (1955), pp. 446–54, for an example of African cities which are much closer to an agglomeration of villages than to a metropolitan area.

[21] *Path of Progress for Metropolitan St. Louis*, p. 59.

[22] S. N. Grimm, *Annals of the American Academy of Political and Social Science*, 320 (1958), p. 105.

[23] See section above, "Traffic and Transportation: A Metropolitan Problem."

[24] Lyle C. Fitch, "Metropolitan Financial Problems," *Annals of the American Academy of Political and Social Science*, 314 (1957), pp. 66 and 67.

[25] Research report of the Metropolitan St. Louis Survey (unpublished).

[26] Control of traffic and transportation was one of the chief aims of many plans defeated during the past few years, including the St. Louis City-County District Plan, the Cleveland Metropolitan County Plan and the Nashville and Davidson County Plan.

[27] *Accident Experience: Expressways vs. Arterials*, Chicago Area Transportation Study, prepared by Irving Hoch (Chicago, 1959). See also Grimm's suggestions for improved design as a method of decreasing accidents, *op. cit.*, pp. 106–109, and W. Owen, *The Metropolitan Transportation Problem, op. cit.*, pp. 43–45.

[28] Francis Bello, "The City and the Car" in *The Exploding Metropolis*, The Editors of Fortune (New York: Doubleday, 1958), pp. 32–33.

[29] Owen, *The Metropolitan Transportation Problem, op. cit.*, p. 223.

44 S. D. Vestermark, Jr.

Social Science as Systematic Anxiety: A Case Study in the Civil Defense Dialogue

Arthur I. Waskow, *The Shelter-Centered Society*

AN UNCERTAIN DIALOGUE ON PUBLIC POLICY

In a complex democracy, public policy frequently becomes the subject of a dialogue among the voices that speak for various alternatives. Sometimes this dialogue centers within the formal institutions for stating and legitimizing public policy: the institutions of government. When there are collisions of basic perceptions and values, however, the dialogue frequently broadens its scope. It then includes voices and interests outside government, and the crucial test for democracy is then not merely resolving the policy issue, but creating and understanding the institutional conditions for the dialogue through which policy emerges and gains acceptance.

As part of a larger, continuing civil defense program, the executive branch of the federal government has sought with varying degrees of intensity to define and enlist support for several shelter programs over the past five years. These shelter programs have become the subject of a broad dialogue on national security policy. Articulate groups of social scientists, quick to sense a relation between these programs and the whole range of the human condition in a democratic society, have been drawn into the dialogue. Their entrance has come at an especially strategic moment in the history of the social sciences, for social scientists have benefited from the rise in prestige and authority of science as a social institution; their views have become increasingly, sharply salient to other participants in a policy dialogue, including those who are government policy-makers. Within government, the policy-maker or policy analyst is increasingly responsive to those scientists he sees as relevant, as he gropes toward the development of rational standards for assessing the effects of alternative policies which are being considered in response to perceived or anticipated needs.

Reprinted from *The Journal of Conflict Resolution*, 9:2 (1965), pp. 264–287, by permission of the author and the publisher.

In this favorable climate, some social scientists have been quick to speak. For example, a social psychologist has written about shelters (Klineberg, 1962, p. 26):

> To burrow beneath the ground for weeks, or even longer, means for human beings a denial of most of the values which have been acquired slowly and painfully in the process of creating a democratic society. Instead of community there is a splintering into isolated individuals or tiny groups. Instead of cooperation there is violent competition for available space. Instead of mutual aid, there is a selfish struggle for individual survival.
>
> Psychiatrists speak of regression when adults behave in a manner appropriate to children. We may speak of social regression when a whole community behaves in a manner characteristic of primitive, archaic, even animal-like existence, almost to the point of recreating a Hobbesian war of all against all.

Indeed, the scope of the issues and the passions aroused by them in the shelter debate have constantly verged on bitter controversy. They have worked to erode and render uncertain the bases upon which social scientists have entered dialogue with policy-makers and other interested groups, and to raise the larger question of what the foundations of the dialogue should be.

This essay is a case study of one contribution from one sector of the social science community to the dialogue on shelters. This contribution raises compelling questions about the nature and conditions of the dialogue. Here, however, the emphasis will be on examining the content of this particular contribution and the ways in which its elements are related to each other within a larger structure. The particular elements and the larger structure form an identifiable way of making assertions about events in the uncertain future, shaped by a special view of contemporary society. Within this special view, questions about the desirability of shelters tend to receive predetermined answers. In the case in point, the predetermination tended strongly to be *against* the desirability of building shelters. For present purposes, however, a discussion of the particular policy judgment is relatively unimportant. More important is an examination of the ways in which the form and content of a scientific contribution can structure attitudes toward particular policies, beyond merely explicating and delineating more clearly the nature of the policy alternatives themselves.

The material for this case study comes from an analysis of *The Shelter-Centered Society*, by Arthur I. Waskow. In January 1962 the Peace Research Institute (PRI) of Washington, D.C., sponsored a "Conference on Potential Implications of a National Civil Defense Program." A number of prominent social scientists from several disciplines attended. Waskow, a member of the PRI staff, acted as final *rapporteur*, and *The Shelter-Centered Society* was his summary report (Waskow, 1962a, now out of print).[1]

This report has received a significant audience since its initial publication. It appeared in condensed form in *Scientific American* (Waskow, 1962b) and its arguments were incorporated in a book, *America in Hiding*, of which Waskow was co-author (Waskow and Newman, 1962). Waskow sought to point out, in a supplementary article (Waskow, 1962c), that the original PRI report was a series of *hypotheses*, perhaps alluding indirectly to the informal but lively controversy that had already begun over the meaning and tenor of the original report's phraseology and substantive propositions. Six months later Adam Yarmolinsky, then a special assistant to the Secretary of Defense, vigorously assailed *The Shelter-Centered Society* at the fortieth annual meeting of the American Orthopsychiatric Association. He spoke of it as "pseudo-science" (Greenberg, 1963, p. 1034). Nevertheless, the original report continued to be perceived by others as a body of persuasive materials on the possible acute dangers of shelter-building. For example, it was cited in testimony before the subcommittee of the U.S. House of Representatives, which was cognizant of the 1963 fallout shelter program authorization (Solomon, 1963, p. 4258). Clearly, *The Shelter-Centered Society* has become part of the dialogue on the shelter program.

This case study examines the central propositions of Waskow's report in the framework of the state of knowledge from which they derive and the more general orientation to American society which they seem to reflect. Because of the special place of a partially ideological view of American society in the report, a separate section of this essay is devoted to considering that view. These parts of the analysis suggest why *The Shelter-Centered Society* depicts a precarious world which is particularly threatened by a shelter program, and how this view of the world has been mobilized in the report to introduce constraints into the larger policy dialogue. These constraints may reflect the special institutional placement of certain social science orientations, in relation to the policy process and to the society at large. At the same time they also point to fundamental ambiguities in the relations between all social scientists and policy-makers in a policy dialogue.

EFFECTS OF A SHELTER PROGRAM:
ANALYSIS OF SOME PROPOSITIONS

The principal general conclusions presented in *The Shelter-Centered Society* are to be found in this summary statement (Waskow, 1962a, p. 1):

On the basis of available social-science knowledge and research data, the conferees came to three major conclusions:
That the existence of a shelter-centered civil defense system would be a wholly new departure in American history.
That once entered upon, a shelter program will prove extremely difficult to limit or to reverse.
That the program may act upon a number of well-known mechanisms of individual and social behavior in such ways as to create a series of specific dangers to the effectiveness of American foreign policy and to American democratic values.[2]

An important subsidiary point on the same page is that, "If these specific difficulties do develop, they will impose enormous burdens upon an already burdened government, especially on the Office of Civil Defense but also on other branches of the government."[3]

Underlying these major conclusions are many particular conclusions, assertions, or assumptions about the effects of a shelter program on American social processes, and about the particular institutional or interpersonal processes and mechanisms which will mediate these effects. These statements are sometimes supported with allusions to data in the social sciences or to general social-behavioral constructs or propositions which are thought to summarize well-established social facts. But though the grounds are varied, together these particular conclusions form a structure of argument. The conclusions resulting from this structure can be summarized in the form of several far-reaching, specific findings about the effects of shelter-building on American life.

For analytic purposes these summary findings can be considered to form four substantive propositions, upon which most of the admonitions of *The Shelter-Centered Society* depend. By assessing each proposition in turn, it may be possible to gain a clearer perspective on the themes and meanings of Waskow's report.

Proposition 1: Shelter-building will have high salience in the "public's" perceptions, and is related in the "public's" perceptions to increased likelihood of war.[4]

In looking at civil defense in "historical perspective," Waskow (1962a, p. 2) reports:

> The conferees found that announcement of the new civil defense program represented simultaneously a highly authoritative threat of personal death and social destruction on the one hand, and on the other hand a governmental promise that there is a way to meet this threat.

This reflects a conclusion about the dynamics of American public opinion in the face of civil defense and shelters—"An enemy military threat can be ignored, denied, suppressed in one's mind; but civil defense is immediately visible, tangible, and unavoidable" (Waskow, 1962a, p. 2).

The high visibility and salience of civil defense and shelter programs are recurrent themes in the shelter dialogue. Yet, in spite of the *a priori* reasons for thinking that shelters and civil defense are uniquely visible, it is instructive to consider other "domestic threats" which have also been throught at the time to be present and highly salient in "public opinion." At the height of the McCarthy episode in the early 1950s, when charges of Communist infiltration of the federal government were apparently having their first great impact on American thinking, Stouffer surveyed a national cross-section on attitudes toward civil liberties and Communism. He found (Stouffer, 1955, p. 59—italics in original):

The big overwhelming response to the question, *What kind of things do you worry about most?* was in terms of personal and family problems. Eighty percent of the men and women in the cross-section answered *solely* in these terms. And many of the remainder answered in the same terms but went on to express anxiety about other problems. Ten percent professed no worries about any problems.

The number of people who said that they were worried either about the threat of Communists in the United States or about civil liberties was, even by the most generous interpretation of occasionally ambiguous responses, *less than 1 percent!*

Even world problems, including the shadow of war, did not evoke a spontaneous answer from more than eight percent. It will be argued, of course, that some people tend to suppress or mask deep anxieties about which they can do little. Being unconscious, the anxieties cannot be reported. Even if we grant this possibility, it is still hard to argue that the American people, as of the summer of 1954, were consumed with anxieties about war, not to mention internal Communism or civil liberties. Otherwise we should have heard more frequent spontaneous comments, even if the respondent talked first of personal or domestic affairs.

Writing in *The Liberal Papers*, Riesman and Maccoby (1962, p. 24) acknowledge this persisting characteristic of American opinion and attitude, even as they argue its dangerous implications for the American posture in the world:

> It may be that people feel safer in this country because it is big and powerful and seemingly remote from the traditional areas of danger. This is an irrational feeling in the modern world of deterrence, since our fearful power and our weapons themselves become a lightning rod inviting attack; nevertheless, the feeling does seem to exist. A Gallup poll in January 1960 roughly mirrored the results of a poll taken by Samuel Stouffer a few years ago: when people in a national cross section are questioned about their worries a large proportion of them mention health and family troubles, and another fraction money troubles, but only one in fourteen allude to the international situation. Yet half the Gallup sample also thought that there would be another war before too long—a war that, as the general texture of their answers indicates, has very little reality for them.[5]

This persistent finding about American perceptions of salient problems might be explained by saying that it takes time for an issue or a problem to build. Possibly, in 1954 the public had not yet been fully sensitized to the Communist issue; possibly, in 1961 the public had not yet become fully aware of the international environment within which civil defense programs were being proposed. Perhaps only recently have anxieties about the state of the world become fully manifest in surveys of Americans' attitudes and perceptions. If attitudes toward the likelihood of war are taken as some measure of a generalized anxiety about contemporary world conditions which would stimulate perceptions of threats in their day-to-day lives, then an increase in public feelings that war is likely might give some ground for anticipating that civil defense programs will be highly threatening.

Among the data presented at the PRI conference which produced *The Shelter-Centered Society* were the interview results from a national probability sample of 1,474 adults in 48 states. The survey was conducted by the Survey Research Center, University of Michigan, under the direction of Dr. Stephen Withey, who was a participant in the PRI conference.[6] Waskow said, apparently referring to these data (1962a, pp. 4–5, italics in original), that they "have already shown that the President's call for civil defense, regardless of what he intended, was *seen* as a warning of intense and immediate danger of war ('Why else should he want us to do this?'), a warning that negotiations with the Soviet Union were not working."

There are two contentions here. One is that there was an increase in public opinion and a heightening of public anxiety that a big war was likely. The second is that an increase in activity and calls for civil defense measures is a signal to the public that a big war is likely. Withey's published data tend to contradict both contentions.

Regarding the question of public perceptions of the likelihood of war, Withey's published data offer comparisons of answers to a replicated question for four different years, and include two surveys for 1961. As shown here in Table 1, these data suggest a relative stability in public perceptions

TABLE 1. DISTRIBUTION OF ANSWERS TO THE QUESTION:
"How likely do you think it is that we're in for another big world war?"

	Apr. 1952	Mar. 1954	June 1956	Oct. 1961	Nov. 1961
Very likely	17%	23%	17%	11%	9%
Likely	36	24	21	23	24
Maybe, pro-con	9	9	10	21	15
Unlikely	21	25	21	23	20
Very unlikely	1	6	15	8	17
Don't know	12	9	12	13 ⎞	15
No answer	4	4	4	1 ⎠	
	100%	100%	100%	100%	100%

Source: Withey, 1962, p. 36.

of a big war threat, although there is the suggestion that perceptions of big war as "very likely" or "likely" have decreased, while perceptions of war as "unlikely" or "very unlikely" have either remained reasonably stable or increased. Thus, insofar as reported perceptions and opinions about war's likelihood are clues to anxiety about war, these data do not suggest a mounting overt anxiety among the American public. A significant group *does* regard war as "likely" in some degree, but it is far from being a majority.

According to the Michigan data, members of the American public varied widely in degrees of information about current world affairs. Table 2 details the answers to a solicitation of comment about world affairs, phrased as follows: "Here are some things you might have heard about in the news in recent months. Could you say a word or two or a sentence about: trouble in Berlin, the Congo, Polaris, the Peace Corps, the Missile Gap, Troika?"

Table 2. Distribution of Knowledge on Current World Affairs Topics (later 1961)

Knows none	23%	
Knows "Berlin"	15	
Knows "Congo" too	10	
Knows "Polaris" and previous two	10	
Knows "Peace Corps" and previous three	13	⎫
Knows "Missile Gap" and previous four	13	⎬ "Informed"
Knows "Troika" and previous five	15	⎭
No answer	1	
	100%	

Source: Withey, 1962, p. 47.

These findings are consistent with Stouffer's on the degree of awareness of public issues. Here, when *specific* attempts are made to elicit information on crucial public issues during a time of crisis, almost one-quarter of the respondents cannot comment on any of the issues, while 15 percent know "Berlin" only. Contrasting with this group, of course, is a relatively well-informed group constituting 41 percent of the sample. But the wide differential in information, coupled with the relative stability of the public's perceptions of the imminence of war, suggests that there was no uniformly spread, increasing tension about war. Concern did exist, but a more highly differentiated description and model of "the American public" are needed in order to locate this tension, specify its scope, and examine its effects.

In late 1961, when the Michigan surveys were conducted, the emphasis in the federal shelter program was beginning to shift from stimulating construction of private family fallout shelters toward locating, marking, or constructing community and large-group shelters under federal-local arrangements. It can be reasonably assumed, however, that this shift was not generally known to the public; thus, one indicator of the degree of overt individual support for the shelter program remained—whether individuals had taken concrete steps to build shelters. The Michigan surveys included questions about this. Table 3 from Withey's report shows that very few Americans had shelters or plans for shelters.

Motivations for shelter-building were also explored by the Michigan surveys. Respondents who had not built shelters were asked what might

TABLE 3.   DISTRIBUTION OF ANSWERS TO QUESTIONS:

"Do you have a place fixed up for a fallout shelter?" If Yes, "How do you happen to have one?" If No, "Do you have any plans to build or fix up a fallout shelter in the next few weeks?"

Has shelter	2%
No shelter, immediate plans	2
No shelter, distant plans	2
No shelter, no plans	94
	100%

Source: Withey, 1962, p. 39.

persuade them to do so. As shown in Table 4, the most frequently mentioned reason is that war is "unavoidable or very likely." But since perceptions of the likelihood of war had remained relatively stable (Table 1), the evidence from Table 4 helps at least in part to explain why so few shelters had been built. It might be possible to design studies to explore the hypothesis that failure to build a shelter represents an avoidance of world danger, an avoidance reinforced by the technical burdens of "do-it-yourself" shelter-building. But if, as Tables 1, 3, and 4 suggest, perceptions of the likelihood of war are stable, and if many individuals would not build a shelter until war seemed much more likely to them, then the large-scale lack of shelter-building is evidence of the widespread existence of a relatively low degree of perceived threat.[7]

If, then, shelters were a crucial component of the civil defense program in the latter part of 1961, there is some reason to think that that program was not widely or clearly present in American perceptions of tasks that were immediately salient to living in the world of that time. Given the limited presence of the shelter-building alternative in public perceptions

TABLE 4.   DISTRIBUTION OF ANSWERS TO THE QUESTION:

"You don't have a shelter to go to now. Say within the next year or two you have one! What do you think would have had to happen to make you have a shelter?"

War unavoidable or very likely	43%
More information on and more confidence in shelters	4
More money or financial aid	10
Government requirement	6
Social pressure, "everyone doing it"	3
Personal conditions	11
Don't know	14
Have one or plan to	4
Nothing could make me get a shelter	12
(More than one item could be mentioned, so total exceeds	100%)

Source: Withey, 1962, p. 39.

and actions, and the extent to which war was *not* perceived to be likely, it is difficult to see how "the new civil defense program" was a "highly authoritative threat," much less "a government promise."[8]

In summary, an examination of relevant data on American "public opinion," particularly of those which formed the basis for presentations at the PRI conference, does not support the fundamental, dual position advanced in *The Shelter-Centered Society*: that shelter-building was a demonstrable preoccupation of large numbers of the public and was thus highly salient in the public's perceptions of the world, and that shelter-building was related in the public's perceptions to increased likelihood of war. Where there *is* concern about shelters or the likelihood of war, the significance of this concern can be revealed only through a description of the structure of American public opinion which is more differentiated and complex than that provided in *The Shelter-Centered Society*.

Proposition 2: Shelter-building is "dissonant" with disarmament negotiations and other specific efforts toward the relaxation of international tensions, especially because "civil defense fits into a view of the world in which negotiation has failed and war is looming."

The basic claims about American public opinion which are advanced in the first proposition provide support for additional groups of propositions, about the ways in which shelter-building will (1) shape public behavior and attitudes toward particular measures for reducing dangerous conflict among nations, and (2) impel public behavior toward disrupting those crucial integrative processes which maintain the highly valued characteristics of American social life.

Regarding measures which might be taken by the American government to reduce dangers in the arena of international conflict, *The Shelter-Centered Society* reports that civil defense programs will undercut public support for the government's efforts to negotiate disarmament:

> It was the unanimous judgment of the scholars that a pro-disarmament reaction is extremely unlikely. They agreed that those people wholly committed to supporting disarmament before the call for civil defense might take the call as a signal for desperately intensifying their previous efforts. But for almost all of the people, the scholars agreed, civil defense and disarmament are what is known in social psychology as "dissonant"—that is, civil defense fits into a view of the world in which negotiation has failed and war is looming, while disarmament fits into a view of the world in which negotiation seems possible and war seems avoidable [Waskow, 1962a, p. 4].

Waskow and the PRI conferees seemed to rely especially upon formulations of the "cognitive dissonance" concept prominently associated with Festinger. In Festinger's words (1957, p. 260):

> . . . the human organism tries to establish internal harmony, consistency, or congruity among his opinions, attitudes, knowledge, and values. That is, there is a drive toward consonance among cognitions. In order to deal with

this notion in a somewhat more precise manner, I have imagined cognition to be decomposable into elements or, at least, clusters of elements.

Noting that cognitive elements "can exist in irrelevant, consonant, or dissonant relations," Festinger continues, "Two cognitive elements are in a dissonant relation if, considering these two alone, the obverse of one element follows from the other" (pp. 260–61). Two central hypotheses result from considering possible relations of dissonance among cognitive elements (p. 263):

(1) The presence of dissonance gives rise to pressures to reduce that dissonance.
(2) The strength of the pressure to reduce dissonance is a function of the magnitude of the existing dissonance.

It is not necessary to assume that relations of consonance or dissonance among cognitive elements are *logical* relations, following formal rules of logical consistency, even though Festinger puts the dissonance relation in quasi-logical terms. Indeed, there would appear to be a variety of dimensions within which cognitive elements such as opinions, attitudes, and perceptions of fact may be seen to be consonant or dissonant. Festinger's approach to dissonance highlights the tensions which may exist among elements as the individual interacts with environment and assimilates new elements or behaves with reference to one element, and it emphasizes that the processes of living require a constant adjustment of dissonance within the multidimensional personality processes of individuals. In reporting the potential attractions of civil defense for authoritarian personalities, *The Shelter-Centered Society* also recognizes potentialities for dissonance and ambiguity in the cognitive lives of contemporary Americans:

Several associated kinds of troublesome personalities might assert themselves if precautions are not taken. First, the people who "want to get it over with." . . . Others may be hoping not that the bombs will drop but that the threat of their dropping will create roles of special power as super-policemen for them. There are many people who have only a limited ability to tolerate modern American life with its shifting realities, its conflicts, its luxury, and its attachment to disorder and ambiguity [Waskow, 1962a, p. 12].

Given these approaches to dissonance and the uncertainties of the contemporary social world, what is it to say that "civil defense and disarmament are . . . 'dissonant'—that is, civil defense fits into a view of the world in which negotiation has failed and war is looming . . ."? One of the key interpretive problems lies in the words "fits into." Particularly if Festinger's phrase about the "obverse follows" were taken literally, the words "fits into" could imply that there is a *logical contradiction* between civil defense and disarmament. That is, because it is claimed that civil defense is associated with one view of the world and disarmament with another, it is therefore claimed that civil defense and disarmament must be mutually exclusive. In this interpretation, "views of the world," whether they be views where "negotiation has failed and war is looming" or where "negotiation seems possible and war seems avoidable," are internally consistent and cognitively coherent total sets of perceptions *and* conclusions about the world.

On another level of analysis, however, the conclusion that civil defense is dissonant with disarmament has a different meaning. On the level of *empirical evidence, The Shelter-Centered Society* implies that "almost all of the people" report or show in some reliably observable way that civil defense is "dissonant" with disarmament negotiations. It is implied that empirical evidence will show that the two are mutually exclusive because they exist as parts of mutually exclusive world views.

How could people give evidence that they feel civil defense is dissonant with disarmament? A beginning might be made by determining whether respondents see civil defense and shelters as reflecting an increase in war dangers. Analysis of the first substantive proposition of *The Shelter-Centered Society* has suggested both the low salience of shelters and the low incidence of opinions that general war was highly probable. Possibly, however, if the questions were put somewhat differently, respondents might see civil defense and the shelter program as not only *reflecting* but also *accelerating* trends toward a more dangerous world.

The 1961 Michigan survey asked individuals about the relationships they perceived between building shelters and the likelihood of war. Although it is somewhat unclear from the format, Michigan's Survey Research Center apparently asked two complementary questions: (1) "[Do you agree or disagree that] If we built shelters for everyone, war would be *less* likely to happen. Why do you say so?" (2) "[Do you agree or disagree that] If we built shelters for everyone, war would be *more* likely to happen. Why do you say so?" The distributions of answers are shown in Tables 5a and 5b. These data suggest that for a majority of Americans, shelter-building is irrelevant to the processes which enhance international tensions. Since the questions are in hypothetical form, they do not directly

Table 5a. Distribution of Answers to the Question:
"If we built shelters for everyone, war would be *less* likely to happen. Why do you say so?"

Agree		19%
Disagree	because shelters (CD) irrelevant, wouldn't make any difference	63
Disagree	because shelters (CD) provocative to Russia	1
Disagree	because shelters (CD) tempt us to run risks; brinkmanship; makes us war-minded or less afraid of war	1
Disagree	for other reason	2
Disagree,	unclear	2
	No opinion	12
		100%

TABLE 5b. DISTRIBUTION OF ANSWERS TO THE QUESTION:
"If we built shelters for everyone, war would be *more* likely to happen.
Why do you say so?"

Agree		5%
Disagree	because shelters (CD) irrelevant, wouldn't make any difference	65
Disagree	because shelters (CD) would *deter* Russia, show Russia we mean business	8
Disagree	because shelters (CD) would reduce likelihood of war, alert public to real dangers	2
Disagree	for other reason	3
Disagree,	unclear	4
	No opinion	13
		100%

Source for both tables: Withey, 1962, p. 42.

measure the extent to which the announcement of a shelter program is a highly threatening symbol or index of increasing tensions. Nevertheless, it seems clear that the majority of the sample made a separation between shelters and those processes which cause war or contribute to the stability or instability of international conditions.[9]

Withey concludes that "When people think of shelters, they predominantly think of 'survival,' and only a small minority regard shelter policies as provocative or as deterrent" (1962, p. 20). He does discern important differences between those who strongly support "shelter policy" and those who strongly support a number of specific disarmament steps (Withey, 1962, p. 19; italics in original):

"Shelter policy" (a rather vague term at the time of this study) is *most strongly supported by those who see nuclear attack as likely and very imminent and hitting other areas more severely than that in which the respondent lives.* The supporters tend to be women more than men, the less informed more than the well informed, those with lower incomes more than with higher incomes, and those with less than college education.

"Arms control, test bans, disarmament steps in one form or another, and similar measures" seem to be *most strongly advocated by those who see nuclear attack as unlikely and not very imminent, if it were to occur, but the severity of local hazards is not so relevant.* Many think such policies should be tried but hesitate to recommend them because of the hazards involved.

Note that while shelter policy receives strongest support from those who see attack as likely, and disarmament steps receive strongest support from those who see attack as unlikely, the findings do not show whether support of shelter policy is positively or negatively correlated with support of disarmament steps. They pertain only to the characteristics of those who tend to support each of these policy areas, when each one is considered as a separate area. Standing alone, these findings do not permit the conclusion that individuals who support shelter policies are necessarily unlikely to support disarmament steps, or vice versa.

Indeed, in discussing the general orientations of Americans toward the Cold War, Withey says (1962, p. 10, italics in original):

> The expansion or extension of Russian or Communist influence is regarded as the continuing threat that keeps the "cold war" going. There is no *majority* agreement on how to handle this threat except through "aid" programs, though compromise solutions might well be able to solicit majority support if they permitted certain combinations of policies that tended both to maintain security *and* show promise of reducing tensions. Interview answers hinted at this but no direct questions were raised on this matter.

In terms of the conceptual apparatus (e.g., "fits into," "view of the world") of *The Shelter-Centered Society* and the reported consensus of the PRI conference, would "compromise solutions" which "permitted certain combinations of policies that tended both to maintain security *and* show promise of reducing tensions" contain dissonant elements? The conclusion must be that they would. Yet the empirical evidence suggests that there may be substantial support for such "dissonant" solutions. When this evidence is noted in the light of the finding that the principal connotation of "shelter" is "survival" and not "provocation" or "deterrence," it seems that shelter policy was not felt to be "dissonant" with potential disarmament or tension reduction measures by the majority of the American public in late 1961. There is some evidence, at least, that many people viewed the two policies as unrelated in their consequences, or as parts of a *total* address to a complex world.

Used with only limited reference to the available empirical evidence, such concepts as "dissonance" and "view of the world" establish *a priori* pressures toward a limited, logically consistent view of the "public's" capacities to see and understand issues. "Dissonance" becomes a characteristic of a logically unified, internally consistent "view of the world" which can exclude just those complementary policy responses which men make to complex social reality.

If "dissonance" is meant to imply "perceived contradiction," however, then it should be noted that, as an empirical matter, the majority of Americans did not report some perceived or implied contradiction, incongruity, or conflict between civil defense or a shelter program and disarmament steps. Indeed, it is possible that many might perceive these programs as complementary parts of a total address to a complex world. It is possible to argue, on the evidence discussed here, that many Americans have achieved what they might feel to be adequate—indeed, highly adaptive—cognitive orientations toward a world of "disorder and ambiguity." Any potential dissonance between civil defense and disarmament steps may have been resolved, for some individuals, through the unifying conception that both are alternative forms of *insurance*. Regardless of the insurance concept, however, if the individual considers civil defense and disarmament steps to be alternative ways of coping with the state of current world tensions, his acceptance of a need to entertain these alternative views may imply that he has satisfactorily coped in some sense with a key ambiguity of contemporary American life.

Whether one cognitive element is dissonant with another depends upon the way it is held by the observer of a complex world. *The Shelter-Centered Society* concludes that dissonance between civil defense and disarmament steps is a necessary result of the *logically defined* state of the *world*, about which each policy must be taken as evidence, instead of being at least partially the result of the state of the *individual* who *perceives* the world. But "dissonance" is a result of the total frame of reference and experience of the perceiver, not merely of the constraints imposed upon him by the world. In part, civil defense and disarmament are both pieces of evidence about the world *to the observer*, who may experience them as dissonant with, consonant with, or irrelevant to each other.

Possibly the PRI conferees themselves felt the two policies could not represent logically compatible interpretations of evidence about the world's condition. At any rate, there is a tendency in the conceptual apparatus of the report to turn away from empirical evidence which would enable the independent analyst to refine the meaning of "dissonance" as well as, possibly, to conclude that civil defense and disarmament steps are not dissonant clusters of cognitive elements.[10]

Proposition 3: Shelter-building will be divisive and obsessive in American society, setting group against group and undermining a delicate balance among American social institutions.

Although some evidence suggests that the shelter program was neither especially prominent nor threatening in Americans' views of the world in 1961, *The Shelter-Centered Society* presents the conclusion that "announcement of the new civil defense program represented simultaneously a highly authoritative threat of personal death and social destruction . . . and . . . a governmental promise that there is a way to meet this threat" (Waskow, 1962a, p. 2). On this basis it is stated that

The probable effect of this powerful threat and promise is to bring about three distinct reactions in the population. First, the threat generates enormous anxiety in almost the entire population. Secondly, the promise of some protection provides a considerable amount of relief from the anxiety. The relief, however, can scarcely be as widespread or as permanent as the anxiety, since the relief depends upon continuous conviction that the shelter program is adequate, while the anxiety can disappear only if the threat disappears. Finally, among some people—an unknown proportion of the population— a civil defense program would create not only anxiety but a dark attraction to the world of which civil defense is a warning—the world wiped clean of complications, ambiguities, and dissensions. For them, oblivion for all or survival and great power for themselves would be preferable to anxiety, tension, and a perpetual state of threat. The coexistence in the population of deep anxiety, precarious hope, and an obsessive concern with violence and death would constitute a new situation for American society [Waskow, 1962a, pp. 2–3].

This passage not only presents a first set of conclusions about the effect of the civil defense "threat" and "promise" in the population; it also contains more fundamental approaches and conclusions about the workings of American society. These approaches and conclusions form a reasonably consistent framework within the whole report.

Here, "threat" activates "enormous anxiety." That this "enormous anxiety" arises "in almost the entire population" means that this "anxiety" is an essentially homogeneous phenomenon and force, acting essentially uniformly in a relatively undifferentiated social mass. It is consistent with this model of homogeneous forces acting in an undifferentiated population that "the promise of protection" provides "relief." The "promise" relieves the pressure, and "relief" comes, homogeneously acting and homogeneously felt. Inherent in this relief is a tragic, dialectical contradiction: the logic of the situation dictates that any hope must be at best "precarious," for it must depend upon belief in an inherently infirm shelter program, while the "anxiety" released and nurtured by the "threat" endures and haunts as long as the threat persists. This is not merely a rhetoric of metaphor; it is an implicit social theory.

In a later passage it is argued that, in confronting American society with a new situation, civil defense shelter-building will create specific vulnerabilities in American institutions:

One of the most important areas that civil defense may affect is the "web of community" on which the assumptions of national and democratic unity are based.

It has sometimes been hoped and argued that the shelter program might enhance a national sense of community, by making the common danger to survival obvious to all. But the conferees, on the basis of sociological evidence from the past, were unanimous in doubting that feelings of community could be thus enhanced. They pointed out that people actually working together to face danger perceived as equally threatening to all, in a civil defense program perceived as equally protective of all, might well have their community solidarity increased. But the danger of attack weighs differently on different Americans, the usefulness of shelters is vastly different in different situations, and the work of building and operating shelters would actually be done by distinct groups along different lines at different levels of expense and with different risks of benefit or loss accruing. In these conditions, the conferees said, the evidence suggests that strains in community will be exaggerated and certainly could not be smoothed over.

Already, the civil defense effort has strained some threads in the web of community. Some have concluded that shelters (private or public) would be useless to them unless they were prepared to limit the number of entrants to those whom the shelter could physiologically support. They have therefore announced their intention of excluding neighbors, or people from the next block, or strangers from the next county, or casual visitors to town, from the family or community shelter. Suburbia has been pitted against city, one state against another. These strains cannot be expected to disappear. It is indeed likely that they would worsen as cities realize how vulnerable they are to thermonuclear attack, as racial and ethnic groups compete for space in and access to community shelters, as farmers realize that suburban refugees will deplete their food stocks.

Might city-dwellers, considering their own situation hopeless while the rest of the nation seems protected by civil defense, react by leaving the cities, or—if they could not leave—by hating the rest of the nation? Might there be sizable emigrations from North America? [Waskow, 1962a, pp. 8–9.]

Comparing this passage to the immediately previous one, it can be seen that the emphasis has shifted from describing pressure exerted by a homogeneous force on a relatively undifferentiated population to describing how this pressure will break an unstable social structure into conflicting components. The threats raised by civil defense are now said to act differentially and to be differentially perceived, so that they will fractionate groups held together in a "web of community." Because the effects of civil defense efforts will exist and act in such different ways, however, there is an evident contradiction between describing threats raised by civil defense as, on the one hand, a homogeneously exerted and experienced force and, on the other hand, a differentially perceived and acting set of threats which will fractionate groups held together in a "web of community."

This problem in shifting from a set of "force" and "threat" metaphors to a set of concepts and metaphors which denote and connote social structure is one instance of a persisting tendency in *The Shelter-Centered Society* to blur the analytic levels to which concepts refer. In suggesting that the "web of community" will be broken by the shelter program, the discussion uses levels of concept which are suited to describing relatively small groups in active competition. Just as solidarity might be enhanced if "people" were "actually working together to face danger perceived as equally threatening to all," so will the actual effects of the shelter program be far different, since "the danger of attack weighs differently," "the usefulness of shelters is vastly different," and "the work of building and operating shelters would actually be done by distinct groups along different lines at different levels of expense and with different risks of benefit or loss accruing." Thus, community solidarity erodes not because the threats surrounding civil defense necessarily destroy senses of individual participation in "primary groups" or somewhat larger "interest groups," but rather because these threats set groups against each other.

Because of the failure to stabilize the referent of "group" in these passages, however, a rhetoric more suited to describing visible, interpersonal or intergroup relations of face-to-face contact becomes a rhetoric portraying society as a collection of vast, self-aware, potentially warring groups in a disintegrating social structure. The homogeneous entity "suburbia" struggles with "city," racial and ethnic "groups" compete for space, farmers watch suburban refugees who are after their food, city-dwellers flee the cities as a vast group—and collide, by inference, with the farmers. In the grand climax, "emigrations" may possibly leave North America. In this imagery of conflict and anxiety, social process is seen essentially as an extension of competitive intergroup relations, after the conditions for interpersonal cooperation have been dissolved. The "web of community" is seen as a set of relations constantly strained by inherent centrifugal forces. When it breaks—here, as a result of the group motivations aroused by civil defense—the social resultant is an aggregation of competing groups. But as the report moves from imagery descriptive of *forces acting* to imagery descriptive of *groups acting*, a constant theme remains. Conflicting groups, impelled by competing forces and motives, provide the dynamism behind social institutional change.

Paradoxically, even though this emerging model of American society rests explicitly on a notion of social conflict, it has no way of conceptualizing behavior which deviates from norms or the forms of institutionalized consensus *except* as this behavior constitutes a difficult-to-manage threat to the entire community, or a threat conceived in terms total to the community. Thus, those possibly pathological individuals who "have concluded that shelters (private or public) would be useless to them unless they were prepared to limit the number of entrants" come to represent dangerous, whole-group trends. The analytic scheme of the report does not contain the tools for discriminating normal from pathological behaviors and individual from group behaviors; without such tools there is no way to describe individual extremism or pathology without seeing it as a manifestation of group process. Nor is it possible to discriminate levels of institutional process in the whole social structure which might control or guide potential excesses, or show how possible excesses reflect particular conditions.

The image of social conflict presented in *The Shelter-Centered Society* emphasizes not only a large degree of potential intergroup conflict but also the delicate, precarious balance which exists among groups. Civil defense, says the report, will add new "vested interests" to a society whose social policies are already subject to the powerful demands of interest groups:

> The creation of civil defense will bring to life in every nook and cranny of the nation special institutions economically dependent on and deriving their power and prestige from a civil defense program—governmental agencies, private builders and suppliers, a cadre of trained shelter managers, etc. Once established, the vested interests of these groups and institutions might well become an obstacle to efforts to end the arms race, if that meant eliminating civil defense [Waskow, 1962a, p. 6].

Yet, though social policies and social change result from collisions among interest groups, this societal model involves no process of dynamic equilibrium or self-generating change and evolution. Rather, society is in static equilibrium, and change produces discord.

The domestic impact of civil defense may also have important effects upon American images of the Soviet Union. Civil defense may create new institutions and interests, *thereby subtracting funds, energy, and excitement from existing institutions and interests.* Where existing groups see civil defense threatening the goals they feel important (for example, where teachers see it as a drain on expenditures for education) might these groups respond with dismay, bewilderment, and anger? If so, psychological findings suggest that they would not direct their anger at the leaders who had called for civil defense, since doing so would stir unconscious fears that they might isolate themselves from their fellow countrymen. . . . Instead, the dismay and anger would probably be refocused into fury at the Communists who would be seen as the real cause of the disturbance and deprivation. Such fury, if it should develop, might make it extremely difficult for the American government to negotiate with the Communists, even on issues where negotiation would be in the American national interest [Waskow, 1962a, footnote to p. 5; italics added].

In this model of society, civil defense programs cannot stimulate expansion of the society's resources or institutional life. Rather, from essentially fixed capabilities and resources, something would have to be subtracted. This subtraction would lead to outward-turning, disruptive pressures on other societies as groups "displace" the aggressions resulting from these frustrations.[11]

If "new institutions and interests" subtract "funds, energy, and excitement from existing institutions and interests," then goals must be limited in this static society; since society can have only a certain number of institutions and goals, various groups are in competition for limited resources. Ultimately, this competition can become a conflict between two polarized groups—the "leaders" and the "people." A clever adversary could manipulate this basic tendency to polarize.

By waiting until we are well into a particular civil defense program and then clearly and publicly disposing forces so as to make that program useless (for example, by declaring all large cities prime targets or by waiting until we have fallout shelters and then announcing that most missiles will be exploded at high altitudes so as to cause great fires instead of fallout), the Soviet Union could nullify years of preparation of civil defense. *Thus it could suggest to the American people that the American government's promises of protection were illusory, and create a deep disillusion with those promises and with a government that had made them. Serious thought must be given to this possibility that civil defense will lay open to Soviet psychological warfare the American trust between people and government* [Waskow, 1962a, p. 13, italics added].

The conclusion that the American polity could polarize marks the further emergence of a theme from the imagery used in discussing the divisive consequences of shelter-building and civil defense. Within the idea that society is a set of pressures, conflicting groups, and strains in shifting, uncertain, precarious equilibrium is the implication that man is constantly in danger of losing control of the process. Institutions for integrating pressures and resolving conflicts do not effectively exist; the many levels at which individual behavior is articulated with the economy and the polity are dissolved. Large-scale social processes constantly threaten to subordinate individual or group behavior to primary, warring interests. The political process, in this view, does not permit the many bases for instituting, legitimizing, and carrying through public programs—bases which characterize a pluralistic, democratic polity. The individual citizen no longer experiences highly differentiated opportunities to express opinion or participate in the public, semi-public, or private organizational life of the society. As public policy and individual behavior are subjected to the simple determinism of conflict among groups in precarious equilibrium, the model of society in the report approaches a *reductio ad absurdum* of the sociologist's perspective. Ultimately, the inhabitants of the society described by the model are alienated from the social forces operating in the society. They are *victims* of social forces rather than *participants* in many levels of social process.[12]

Proposition 4: As a result of social processes stimulated or released by a comprehensive shelter program, America will become a "shelter-centered society."

The report's intermediate conclusions about American social process provide a framework for conclusions about the effects of civil defense programs, and these conclusions further specify the projections made about American society. Proposition 4, above, constitutes the central, summary conclusion. Since it appears as the title of the report and not as a formally stated conclusion, however, there are special problems in evaluating its meaning. "The shelter-centered society" may be a *characterological typing* of society, a *summary prediction* of likely effects, or a *summary description* of social reality based on empirical study. The evidence in the text suggests that the title is a prediction on two levels.

The first level of meaning is found in the foreword to the report. According to James J. Wadsworth, then president of the Peace Research Institute,

> An operating shelter-centered civil defense system might have important effects upon the psychology of individual Americans and upon our society in general that would affect American attitudes toward peace and war. The Peace Research Institute therefore brought together some eminent behavioral scientists who could examine these matters and lay out, for further study, important questions about the possible effects of living in a shelter-centered society [Waskow, 1962a, p. i].

At the least, living in such a society could structure the attitudes of the public toward issues going far beyond immediate questions of civil defense; thus, the shelter program could have a widely pervasive effect on the definition and resolution of issues of public policy. On this first level of meaning, *The Shelter-Centered Society* refers to the possibility that a civil defense shelter system will significantly determine the framework of discourse on public issues.

This interpretation of the title implies a second, more general meaning of "shelter-centeredness." Recurring throughout the report is the theme that "the possible effects of living in a shelter-centered society" will be to produce a society preoccupied and ruled by its shelters. Shelters could become the "center" of society and societal process, of cultural values, of individual living, and of the most intimate anxieties of individuals.

In this more general meaning, where does the *prediction* that society will be shelter-centered cease, and the *affirmation* begin that a shelter-building society *must* be shelter-centered? The metaphors and models of social process in the report imply the inevitability of shelter-centeredness. The title encourages acceptance of these metaphors and models and short-cuts constructing a full demonstration of how shelter-building could cause shelter-centeredness. The title contains the fundamental hypothesis of the essay. With repetition of the title, the reader feels a natural pressure toward the conviction that a shelter-building program will unleash a society-wide preoccupation with shelters and with far-reaching institutional processes to support, or control, or moderate the effects of this program.

AMERICAN SOCIAL PROCESS: IMAGERY AND IDEOLOGY

The Shelter-Centered Society is a vehicle for admonitions about the undesirable or dangerous consequences of a civil defense shelter program for American society or for the American international posture. In supporting these admonitions, the imagery and social theory in the report give principal emphasis to particular ways in which conflicts are caused and mediated through cultural values and institutional processes in the American nation.

The imagery, models, and implicit social theory form part of the logic for a number of specific conclusions about the probable effects of a shelter program on American social structure or public opinion. In the present analysis these conclusions have been summarized and reduced to the form of four substantive propositions. Under scrutiny, however, an important difference emerges between the kinds of test that can be applied to the first two propositions and the tests that can be applied to the last two. Propositions 1 and 2 can, in part, be treated as hypotheses subject to direct empirical confirmation or disconfirmation. To support the conclusions involved, the report invokes or alludes to data on American public opinion or mechanisms of opinion formation. On the other hand, Propositions 3 and 4 are projections of likely large-scale social processes which will result in important social institutional changes in America. Varieties of evidence are introduced to develop the arguments, but in the current state of the behavioral sciences a precise, direct empirical test of these propositions is not feasible. For this reason their plausibility depends especially on the adequacy of the imagery, social theory, and social models used to frame and support them. Short of complete empirical validation and test, a sense of this "adequacy" must begin in the extent to which the imagery and models appear to be analogous to, or to correspond with, their referents in contemporary American institutions and social processes.

Available data and empirical generalizations directly contradict the images and conclusions offered in *The Shelter-Centered Society* and all four of its fundamental propositions. This suggests that the view of American society in the report is inadequate, misleading, or not strictly relevant to the task of projecting the likely effects of a civil defense shelter program. Given the ambiguities inherent in contemporary efforts to make firm predictions about possible changes in American institutions, it is useful to ask how the imagery and social theory of *The Shelter-Centered Society* could lead to such debatable conclusions. Such an inquiry might suggest how images and models form a framework within which social problems are systematically perceived, and how such unified frameworks come to be attractive to analysts.

Of basic importance to this inquiry is that the framework which emerges in the report discussed here seems to involve a unified view not only of American society but, more generally, of the condition of man in complex society. Propositions 1 and 2 contain the beginnings of this view in that they rest on the conclusion that a shelter program is a highly visible threat which arouses both anxiety and rigidity of behavior; these responses are supposed to be easily discernible, relatively undifferentiated, and widely pervasive. The view receives more development in the imagery and models which frame Propositions 3 and 4. Here the effects of a shelter program are somewhat differentiated: the great fears and anxieties aroused by shelters and the civil defense program fractionate the social structure. The imagery and models become those of group conflict. There is no allusion either to integrative institutions which might mediate group conflict, or to the possibility that individual aberrations could be neurotic or psychotic deviant cases. Instead, emphasis is on clearly defined interest groups in potentially violent, unmediated conflict. The civil defense program supposedly disrupts the unstable equilibrium among these groups and, by threatening to subtract energy from commitments to existing forms of group life, it further reveals this equilibrium to be static, even though precarious. Ultimately the civil defense program creates conditions threatening the relation of "trust" which exists between citizens and government. In the environment of competing, conflicting groups, such a loss of "trust" could polarize society into two deeply distrustful strata: a stratum of leaders and a much larger stratum of disillusioned citizens, each of whom belongs to an interest group which (as a homogeneous entity trying to maximize its objective self-interest) must be in disruptive conflict with other interest groups.

Civil defense and the shelter program are thus seen as undermining the basis for democratic politics; in the "shelter-centered society" the individual can no longer meaningfully be said to be a participant in political processes. The complex ways in which the individual citizen gives political support and receives responsive government, through a hierarchy of formal and informal institutional processes, is dissolved. Instead, individuals participate in crucial social and political processes principally as members of threatened pressure groups. In such a political environment extremism is imminent, and pressures exist to polarize the political structure of the society into a leadership elite and a relatively undifferentiated mass of followers who may or may not try to resist the elite. Increasing desperation will further magnify the social cleavages already accentuated by the shelter program, and all rational political discussion is threatened.

> The differences in overall values and outlook between those who would tend to support and those who would tend to oppose shelters would be made more intense by the all-encompassing nature of the program and its potent appeal to the hope of survival if all would work together. Already the issue seems to have engendered a polarization of American politics, as increasing numbers of people become willing either to carry the shelter argument to its "logical" conclusion in "Minutemen" guerrilla preparedness or to use mass public demonstrations to press home their opposition to civil defense. This atmosphere of desperate expressive behavior suggests a serious and growing danger to calm and free political discussion [Waskow, 1962a, p. 10].

Taken together, the metaphors, images, rhetoric, and models of *The Shelter-Centered Society* formulate American social and political processes as either imminently or actually a form of what is frequently described today as "mass society" (Kornhauser, 1959; Gusfield, 1962).[13] Typically, mass societies are complex ones in which the horizontal and vertical differentiation of institutional and organizational life has decayed. This decay leads to a political and social situation in which individuals are available for totalitarian mobilization. Mass societies, it has been argued, are associated with the emergence of authoritarian extremist movements, one type case being the National Socialist movement in Germany in the 1930's (Kornhauser, 1959).

A clear theme of *The Shelter-Centered Society* is that contemporary America will, under the influence of a civil defense program, increasingly resemble a mass society, vulnerable to authoritarian, extremist, and totalitarian pressures which lead to a new political order. This could be a challenging hypothesis for further study, but the failure of the PRI report to deal with evidence which clearly contradicts this theme suggests that the theme is more than a hypothesis.

Indeed, the climactic themes of *The Shelter-Centered Society* exhibit many of the characteristics of ideology. An ideology may be defined as a unified, selective view of the social world which characterizes a group of adherents, and through which this group defines not only the present meaning and condition of society and its institutions but also desirable and undesirable future states of society. An ideology gives intellectual and perceptual order to the social world and assigns it meaning. In understanding not only the internal structure of the ideology but also the social mechanisms through which it gains development and support, it is frequently important to determine the ways in which the ideology gives selective emphasis to special features of the world (Mannheim, 1953; Sutton *et al.*, 1956, pp. 3–6; White, 1961), and how values—sometimes positive, sometimes negative—are assigned to these features.

The PRI report essentially calls on policy-makers and the public to pay attention to ways in which a shelter program could release social forces leading to social conditions which the conferees and the *rapporteur* find both vividly possible and intensely undesirable. Specifically, it suggests that the shelter program will accelerate trends toward a mass society and toward the alienation of individual citizens from their political institutions and their fellow citizens. In the report, the basic imagery and models of American society used to examine the possibility of a "shelter-centered society" define mass society and alienation as possible—indeed, probable— outcomes of a truly comprehensive shelter program. Of course, even if it could be shown to be an ideological statement, this would not necessarily invalidate the report as a contribution to the dialogue on shelters and civil defense. But a meaningful contribution must involve conclusions and assumptions which are relevant to the institutional processes it presumes to evaluate, and these conclusions and assumptions should be testable. Thus, it has been especially important to note the contradictions between the picture of American social processes in *The Shelter-Centered Society* and the data and theory available to evaluate this set of conclusions and assumptions. The degree of this contradiction in itself provides evidence that *The Shelter-Centered Society* expresses a sharply selective, ideological definition of American institutional processes.

Ideological themes can offer clues to the composition and motives of the groups supporting them; however, the meaning of the existential basis for a "correspondence" between ideological themes and the position in the social structure of their adherents remains a complex theoretical and empirical issue (Merton, 1957). Furthermore, if the previous analysis of Proposition 1 has a general meaning, it is that great care must be exercised in imputing distinctive cognitive-attitudinal orientations to any large sector of the public.

Given these cautions about inferences to be drawn from examining ideological statements, it is nevertheless possible to offer a fundamental hypothesis about the meaning of possible ideological themes in *The Shelter-Centered Society*. Its general view of American social institutions has much in common with what Lipset and White have identified as ideologies characteristic of the social position of certain American intellectuals (Lipset, 1960; White, 1961). The theme of alarm and protest derives not merely from the dehumanizing consequences of thermonuclear war and its countermeasures, but more generally from perceived trends in American society which these countermeasures will stimulate. Among these trends are the increasing instability in the precarious harmony and equilibrium of community life; the potential dissolution of political life into conflicting, self-interested groups within which the alienated individual must find his locus for action; the readiness of the population to resonate to widely pervasive, uncontrolled threats; and the pressures toward authoritarian conformity exerted by the social institutions of urban society. Just as a major sector of the "intellectuals' critique" of American society points to these and similar trends as pressures on individual freedom in American social life today, so does *The Shelter-Centered Society* define the dangers of civil defense in terms of images, metaphors, and models which assume these trends. Perhaps, borrowing the words of C. Wright Mills, both various intellectual critiques of industrial society and *The Shelter-Centered Society* share a common "professional ideology of social pathologists" (Mills, 1943).

If *The Shelter-Centered Society* were an ideological product of the strains on the social role of intellectuals speaking out against the dehumanization and dangers they perceive in contemporary American society, then there would be a shift in its status as a contribution from the social science community to the shelter dialogue. As a goad to thinking about the consequences of a shelter program, *The Shelter-Centered Society* could continue to act as a useful polemic. But before it could have the prestige accruing to a scientific assessment and projection of events, its images of the present as well as the future of American society would have to be not only exciting and compelling, but also empirically relevant and convincing.

(ED. NOTE: *A discussion by Arthur Waskow of the points raised in this article appears in a later issue of* The Journal of Conflict Resolution.)

ACKNOWLEDGMENTS

A number of the author's colleagues have contributed to this paper, but the author acknowledges with pleasure a special debt to the discussion and editorial comments of Peter G. Nordlie. He also acknowledges with appreciation several stimulating exchanges on the larger issues of this paper with Arthur I. Waskow. A draft of this paper under the same title was circulated among several groups of interested professionals, including the National Academy of Sciences—National Research Council Committee on Behavioral Research (Advisory to the Office of Emergency Planning).

NOTES

[1] *The Shelter-Centered Society* creates special difficulties for the independent reader, who does not have access to all the data and minutes of the conference. Clearly, Waskow had to draw together many professional orientations to the social sciences. While the conferees are represented as being in agreement with the substance of the report, the production of a compressed, unified statement covering broad issues of policy and far-reaching interpretations of data clearly required the interposition of editorial and interpretive functions by the *rapporteur*. The scope of these functions remains somewhat unclear, but it will be suggested later that at least some of the data presented at the conference support conclusions precisely the opposite from those drawn by Waskow.

The Peace Research Institute dissolved in 1963 and its principal professional members entered a new research organization, the Institute for Policy Studies, in Washington, D.C.

2 On the same page Waskow writes that "This report should be regarded as a series of questions to American publics and leadership, though the specifics of the problems are only occasionally posed in question form." This imposes a recurring demand on the reader that he try to determine the degree of probability attached by Waskow to a particular statement: is it imaginative speculation, a hypothesis, a generalization from ordered data and confirmed hypotheses, or a statement of widely accepted "fact," supported by replicated cases and a stable structure for formulating propositions? This is not mere stylistic quibbling, for on the same page Waskow says (italics added): "Applying the established *knowledge* of social scientists to the situation which *might* be created by the existence of a civil defense system *cannot*, of course, *produce iron-clad predictions* of what will happen. But it can point to the kinds of problems that *are likely to develop*—problems whose avoidance or solution *will tax* all the ingenuity of people and government, problems which therefore *demand* serious thought before action is taken that *could make* them and their consequences *impossible to cope with.*"

This last passage is representative of the whole report. Here, "iron-clad predictions" are denied, implying a tentative note to further statements, yet the sentence immediately following suggests much more certainty that specific events and situations will develop in the future. Variations in the degree of probability of projected events and situations are never considered systematically; the syntax and rhetoric of *The Shelter-Centered Society* slip back and forth from implications of tentativeness to assertions of near certainty. Thus, the form in which statements are put is one of the important preconditions for the emergence of an anxious, partially ideological, largely unverified view of large-scale social process under the influence of shelters.

3 There is an interesting implication of institutional rigidity and inflexibility here. Perhaps the latent theme could be stated, "When will the camel's-back of government break?"

4 This proposition contains two predicate elements and thus it might be considered to be two related propositions. Since "will have high salience in the 'public's' perceptions" and "is related in the 'public's' perceptions to increased likelihood of war" tend to be interlinked, mutually reinforcing findings in *The Shelter-Centered Society*, for convenience they will be treated here as elements of the same proposition.

Regarding all four propositions analyzed here, it should be noted that *disconfirmation* of a proposition does not necessarily imply that its opposite could be confirmed if it were subjected to empirical scrutiny.

5 The sociologist of knowledge would find the Riesman and Maccoby commentary on the Stouffer finding to present an interesting problem in the structure of communication processes within a professional subculture, particularly regarding the extent to which "well-known" pieces of information are shared within the subculture. The collection of essays led by the Riesman and Maccoby paper also included one by Waskow, and Riesman participated in the 1962 PRI conference which produced *The Shelter-Centered Society*.

The main writing of the present case study occurred before the availability of findings from research on public reactions to the assassination of President Kennedy in November 1963. On the basis of a National Opinion Research Center modified probability national sample, Sheatsley and Feldman (1964, p. 193) observe that "the fact that two-thirds of the public were reached [by the news] in one hour, 9 out of 10 in two hours, and almost everybody in less than four hours contrasts sharply with findings by Gallup and others that only rarely are more than 80 percent of the population *ever* aware of any given personality or event." While the vivid clarity and suddenness of the assassination lent it to rapid reporting by mass communication facilities centered at the scene, it is noteworthy that the reactions reported by the survey respondents were dominated by intensely personal feelings—most frequently that of being sorry for the wife and children. Of the five reactions which were, by far, the most frequently reported, only one—"shame that this could happen in our country"—contained any clear reference to the country or political system at large (p. 196). Sheatsley and Feldman also report (p. 203) that "there was no consensus concerning the ultimate responsibility for the assassination. When asked, 'In your own opinion, who or what should really be blamed for the assassination of President Kennedy—aside from the man who actually fired the gun?' 41 percent either had no opinion or blamed only the assassin. Only 1 person in 5 answered in ideological tems, 15 percent blaming Communists or leftists, and 5 percent assigning the blame to right-wingers or segregationists. A total of about 1 person in 4 placed the ultimate blame on the public generally or on the environment. . . . Fourteen percent specifically blamed the assassination on poor security measures."

[6] Withey says (1962, pp. 1–2) that the subjects of the survey were interviewed during September and October of 1961, "shortly after the death of Dag Hammarskjöld, when tensions were at their peak in the Berlin crisis of that fall, and at the time of UN crisis over the Secretariat and that agency's policy in the Congo. There is evidence from studies done in November 1961 and in early 1962 that tensions and apprehensions have somewhat diminished since the time of the survey reported here. It is possible, therefore, to regard these findings as expressing U.S. attitudes at a time of crisis, but interpretations should be tempered by the knowledge that the heat of public concern has cooled a little."

[7] On the characteristics of shelter-builders see, for example, Ekman et al. (1963). This study compared the characteristics of members of a peace action group with those of a shelter-building group. "The two groups differed not only in their beliefs about shelters but in their attitudes toward war, United States foreign policy, the motives of the Soviet Union, political affiliation and activity, risk-taking behavior, their own descriptions of themselves and of the opposite group, and a number of general social issues. Finally, each group had misperceptions about the other, one group [the peace action group] exaggerating, the other underrating, the differences" (p. 94). See also Berrien et al. (1963). Levine and Cole (1964) studied the social structural correlates of attitudes toward fallout shelters in nine communities of the northeastern U.S. Among other findings, they reported that while shelters were of relatively little importance to the public, they were clearly favored by the public, especially if financed by nonlocal government. See also Berlo et al. (1963) and Nehnevajsa (1964).

[8] In a conversation with the author, Withey suggested again that the subjective *probability of war* is but one index of threat. He would attach important weight to at least two other indicators of threat: *timing* (when in the next months or years war is seen as likely to come) and degree of expected *hazard* (anticipated type and severity of attack effects in relation to the location and situation of the respondent). He tends to feel that, on these two indices, respondents in his study showed a somewhat higher degree of threat perception than on the probability-of-war index. (See Withey, 1962, especially pp. 3–5, 13–19, 36–38.) But he also remarks (p. 4), "Neither likelihood nor estimates of timing are clear indexes of threat. Only a little more than half of those that think war could come within two years also regard the likelihood as more than even chances. Eighty percent of those who see war as more than ten years away also see the likelihood as even chances or more improbable. On the other hand, it is clear that likelihood and timing estimates are related quite strongly. The greater the guessed likelihood the more imminent the war is likely to be estimated. The lesser the likelihood the more distant the possibility." (Cf. Levine and Cole, 1964, pp. 30–64.)

Data gathered several months before the 1961 Michigan surveys and before the heat of the Berlin crisis give some further indication of the widespread low degree of awareness about civil defense matters in the American public. Erskine (1961) reports on an American Institute of Public Opinion sample of July 5, 1961. An unspecified number of respondents were asked: "What is your feeling about the way Civilian

Defense is being handled in this local area—do you think it is being handled well or poorly, or do you have little or no knowledge about this?" Answers were distributed as follows:

	Well	Poorly	Little or no knowledge
National total	22%	19%	59%
By geographic region:			
East	28	19	53
Midwest	19	17	64
South	17	14	69
Far West	22	32	46

[9] Note the implications of Table 5a and 5b for the previous proposition on the high salience of shelters and increased likelihood of war.

[10] For a summary and analysis of a number of possible relations between arms control and civil defense policies, see Wiener (1963).

[11] Note the ready translation of the "frustration–displacement–aggression" hypothesis to the level of intergroup and institutional conflict. Regarding "the Communists who would be seen as the real cause of the disturbance and deprivation," a case can be made that the Communists are, after all, the root cause of whatever disturbances and deprivations are entailed in meeting their threat. The problem is to control the deleterious consequences of these disturbances and deprivations and to remain aware, at the same time, of why such consequences arose in the first place.

[12] Thus the worry in *The Shelter-Centered Society* that the civil defense program might be "irreversible." "What in some senses is the most worrisome possibility arising from the civil defense program is that regardless of any particular difficulty created by the program, it might prove to be irreversible. The social, psychological, and political momentum generated by the particular operating system might make it impossible for us to change our minds once the program was under way. While this might seem a universal problem of established institutions, the problem would be accentuated by the nature of the civil defense program. . . ." (Waskow, 1962a, p. 14).

[13] It should be noted that, in the construction of models and theory in the social sciences, metaphorical language sometimes has special power. Thus, the critique in this paper of the metaphors and imagery in *The Shelter-Centered Society* should not be construed as a rejection of the usefulness of metaphor (see Back, 1963, and Nash, 1963).

REFERENCES

BACK, KURT W., "The Game and the Myth as Two Languages of Social Science," *Behavioral Science*, 8 (1963), pp. 66–71.

BERLE, DAVID, et al., *The Fallout Protection Booklet: (I) A Report of Public Attitudes toward and Information about Civil Defense* (East Lansing, Mich.: Michigan State University College of Communication Arts, Department of Communication, April 1963).

BERRIEN, F. K., SCHULMAN, CAROL, and AMAREL, MARIANNE, "The Fallout-Shelter Owners: A Study of Attitude Formation," *Public Opinion Quarterly*, 27 (1963), pp. 206–16.

EKMAN, PAUL, et al., "Divergent Reactions to the Threat of War," *Science*, 139 (1963), pp. 88–94.

ERSKINE, HAZEL GAUDET, ed., "The Quarter's Polls: 'Civil Defense,'" *Public Opinion Quarterly*, 25 (1961), p. 659.

FESTINGER, LEON, *A Theory of Cognitive Dissonance* (White Plains, N.Y.: Row, Peterson, 1957).

GREENBERG, D .S., "Civil Defense: Debate Flares Again as Two Partisans Share Platform on Behavioral Science Role," *Science,* 139 (1963), pp. 1034–35.

GUSFIELD, JOSEPH R., "Mass Society and Extremist Politics," *American Sociological Review,* 27 (1962), pp. 19–30.

KLINEBERG, OTTO, "Dangers of the Shelter Psychology," in *A National Shelter Program: Its Feasibility and Its Cost—A Report by a Group of Independent Specialists* (New York: privately printed by the authors, 1962), pp. 26–27.

KORNHAUSER, WILLIAM, *The Politics of Mass Society* (Glencoe, Ill.: The Free Press, 1959).

LEVINE, GENE, N., with COLE, JONATHAN, *The American Public and the Fallout-Shelter Issue: A Nine-Community Survey. Vol. III: Perspectives and Opinions on the Fallout-Shelter Issue* (New York: Columbia University Bureau of Applied Social Research, March 1964).

LIPSET, SEYMOUR MARTIN, "American Intellectuals: Their Politics and Status," in *Political Man: The Social Bases of Politics* (Garden City, N.Y.: Doubleday, 1960).

MANNHEIM, KARL, *Ideology and Utopia: An Introduction to the Sociology of Knowledge* (New York: Harcourt Brace, 1953).

MERTON, ROBERT K., "The Sociology of Knowledge," in *Social Theory and Social Structure,* rev. ed. (Glencoe, Ill.: The Free Press, 1957).

MILLS, C. WRIGHT, "The Professional Ideology of Social Pathologists," *American Journal of Sociology,* 49 (1943), pp. 165–80.

NASH, HARVEY, "The Role of Metaphor in Psychological Theory," *Behavioral Science,* 8 (1963), pp. 336–45.

NEHNEVAJSA, JIRI, *Civil Defense and Society* (Pittsburgh: University of Pittsburgh Department of Sociology, July 1964).

RIESMAN, DAVID, and MACCOBY, MICHAEL, "The American Crisis," in *The Liberal Papers,* JAMES ROOSEVELT, ed. (Garden City, N.Y.: Doubleday Anchor Books, 1962).

SHEATSLEY, PAUL B., and FELDMAN, JACOB J., "The Assassination of President Kennedy: A Preliminary Report on Public Reactions and Behavior," *Public Opinion Quarterly,* 28 (1964), pp. 189–215.

SOLOMON, LAWRENCE N., "Statement of Dr. Lawrence N. Solomon, American Psychological Association," in *Civil Defense—Fallout Shelter Program: Hearings before Subcommittee No. 3, Committee on Armed Services, US House of Representatives,* I (Part II), 1963, pp. 4255–63.

STOUFFER, SAMUEL A., *Communism, Conformity, and Civil Liberties: A Cross-Section of the Nation Speaks Its Mind* (Garden City, N.Y.: Doubleday, 1955).

SUTTON, FRANCIS X., HARRIS, SEYMOUR E., KAYSEN, CARL, and TOBIN, JAMES, *The American Business Creed* (Cambridge, Mass.: Harvard University Press, 1956).

WASKOW, ARTHUR I., *The Shelter-Centered Society: A Report of a Peace Research Institute Conference on Potential Implications of a National Civil Defense Program, January 13–14, 1962* (Washington, D.C.: Peace Research Institute, 1962a [out of print]).

WASKOW, ARTHUR I., "The Shelter-Centered Society," *Scientific American,* 206 (1962b), pp 46–51.

WASKOW, ARTHUR I., "Civil Defense, Democracy, and the Self-Destroying Prophecy," *American Behavioral Scientist,* 6 (1962c), pp. 3–6.

WASKOW, ARTHUR I., and NEWMAN, STANLEY L., *America in Hiding* (New York: Ballantine Books, 1962).

WHITE, WINSTON, *Beyond Conformity* (Glencoe, Ill.: The Free Press, 1961).

WIENER, ANTHONY J., *Arms Control and Civil Defense, Annex IV: The Domestic Political Interactions (HI-216-RR/IV)* (Harmon-on-Hudson, N.Y.: Hudson Institute, Aug. 20, 1963).

WITHEY, STEPHEN B., "The US and the USSR: A Report of the Public's Perspectives on United States-Russian Relations in Late 1961" (Ann Arbor, Mich.: University of Michigan Survey Research Center, March 1962 [mimeographed]).

SUGGESTED ADDITIONAL READING

Part I—Preliminaries

BERELSON, BERNARD, and STEINER, GARY A., *Human Behavior: An Inventory of Scientific Findings* (New York: Harcourt, Brace & World, 1964).

BERGER, PETER L., *Invitation to Sociology: A Humanistic Perspective* (Garden City: Doubleday, 1963).

FARIS, ROBERT E. L., ed., *Handbook of Modern Sociology* (Chicago: Rand McNally, 1964).

MILLS, C. WRIGHT, *The Sociological Imagination* (New York: Grove Press, Inc., 1961).

Part II—Theoretical Constructs and Research Strategies

Critical Concepts in Sociological Analysis

GOULD, JULIUS, and KOLB, WILLIAM L., *A Dictionary of the Social Sciences* (New York: The Free Press, 1964).

PARSONS, TALCOTT, *et al.*, eds., *Theories of Society: Foundations of Modern Sociological Theory* (New York: The Free Press, 1965).

Methods and Techniques of Sociological Analysis

CICOUREL, AARON V., *Method and Measurement in Sociology* (New York: The Free Press, 1964).

FESTINGER, LEON, and KATZ, DANIEL, eds., *Research Methods in the Behavioral Sciences* (New York: Dryden Press, 1953).

GARFINKEL, HAROLD, *Studies in Ethnomethodology* (Englewood Cliffs, N.J.: Prentice-Hall, 1967).

GLASER, BARNEY G., and STRAUSS, ANSELM L., *The Discovery of Grounded Theory: Strategies for Qualitative Research* (Chicago: Aldine Publishing Co., 1967).

RILEY, MATILDA WHITE, "Sources and Types of Sociological Data," *Handbook of Modern Sociology*, ROBERT E. L. FARIS, ed. (Chicago: Rand McNally, 1964).

WEEB, EUGENE J., *et al.*, *Unobtrusive Measures: Nonreactive Research in the Social Sciences* (Chicago: Rand McNally, 1966).

Part III—Aspects of Social Structure and Social Process

Dimensions of the Social Order

BENDIX, REINHARD, and LIPSET, SEYMOUR MARTIN, eds., *Class, Status, and Power: Social Stratification in Comparative Perspective*, 2nd ed. (New York: The Free Press, 1966).

BLAU, PETER M., and SCOTT, W. RICHARD, *Formal Organization* (San Francisco: Chandler Publishing Co., 1962).

DAVIS, JAMES A., "Compositional Effect, Role Systems, and the Survival of Small Discussion Groups," *Public Opinion Quarterly*, 25 (1961), pp. 575–84.

DAVIS, JAMES A., et al., "Analyzing Effects of Group Composition," *American Sociological Review*, 26 (1961), pp. 215–25.

ETZIONI, AMITAI, *A Comparative Analysis of Complex Organizations* (New York: The Free Press, 1961).

GREER, SCOTT, *Social Organization* (New York: Random House, 1955).

LENSKI, GERHARD E., *Power and Privilege: A Theory of Social Stratification* (New York: McGraw-Hill, 1966).

LIPSET, SEYMOUR MARTIN, and BENDIX, REINHARD, *Social Mobility in Industrial Society* (Berkeley: University of California Press, 1959).

SHIBUTANI, TAMOTSU, and KWAN, KIAN M., *Ethnic Stratification: A Comparative Approach* (New York: Macmillan, 1965).

STINCHCOMBE, ARTHUR L., "Social Structure and Organizations," in *Handbook of Organization*, JAMES G. MARCH, ed. (Chicago: Rand McNally, 1965).

Maintenance of the Social Order

BRIM, ORVILLE G., JR., and WHEELER, STANTON, *Socialization After Childhood* (New York: Wiley, 1966).

BLAKE, JUDITH, and DAVIS, KINGSLEY, "Norms, Values, and Sanctions," in *Handbook of Modern Sociology*, ROBERT E. L. FARIS, ed. (Chicago: Rand McNally, 1964).

DURKHEIM, EMILE, *Professional Ethics and Civil Morals* (Glencoe, Ill.: The Free Press, 1958).

EISENSTADT, S. N., *From Generation to Generation* (New York: The Free Press, 1964).

PIAGET, JEAN, *The Moral Judgment of the Child* (New York: The Free Press, 1965).

MACIVER, ROBERT M., *Society* (New York: Rinehart, 1937).

Tensions in the Social Order

BECKER, HOWARD S., ed., *The Other Side: Perspectives on Deviance* (New York: The Free Press, 1967).

CLOWARD, RICHARD A., and OHLIN, LLOYD E., *Delinquency and Opportunity: A Theory of Delinquent Gangs* (New York: The Free Press, 1966).

COLEMAN, JAMES S., *Community Conflict* (Glencoe, Ill.: The Free Press, 1957).

JOURNAL OF CONFLICT RESOLUTION, "Approaches to the Study of Social Conflict: A Colloquium," *Journal of Conflict Resolution*, 1:2 (June, 1957).

LEMERT, EDWIN M., *Social Pathology* (New York: McGraw-Hill, 1951).

SMELSER, NEIL J., *Theory of Collective Behavior* (New York: The Free Press, 1963).

TURNER, RALPH H., "Collective Behavior," in *Handbook of Modern Sociology*, ROBERT E. L. FARIS, ed. (Chicago: Rand McNally, 1964).

Changes in the Social Order

BARRINGER, HERBERT R., et al., eds., *Social Change in Developing Areas* (Cambridge: Schenkman Publishing Co., 1965).

MOORE, WILBERT E., and FELDMAN, ARNOLD S., eds., *Labor Commitment and Social Change in Developing Areas* (New York: Social Science Research Council, 1960).

WILSON, GODFREY, and WILSON, MONICA, *The Analysis of Social Change* (Cambridge, England: The Cambridge University Press, 1945).

SELZNICK, PHILIP, *TVA and the Grassroots* (New York: Harper & Row, 1966).

Part IV—Significance of Values in Sociological Analysis

MADGE, JOHN, *The Origins of Scientific Sociology* (New York: The Free Press, 1967).

MILLS, C. WRIGHT, "The Professional Ideology of Social Pathologists," *American Journal of Sociology*, 49 (1963), pp. 165–80.

SJOBERG, GIDEON, *Ethics, Politics, and Social Research* (Cambridge: Schenkman Publishing Co., 1967).

WEBER, MAX, "Science as a Vocation," in *From Max Weber: Essays in Sociology*, H. H. GERTH, and C. WRIGHT MILLS, eds. (New York: Oxford University Press, 1958).